November 5–8, 2013
Salvador, Brazil

I0027527

**Association for
Computing Machinery**

Advancing Computing as a Science & Profession

WebMedia'13

Proceedings of the 19th Brazilian Symposium on
Multimedia and the Web

Sponsored by:
SBC

In cooperation with:
ACM SIGWEB & ACM SIGMM

**Association for
Computing Machinery**

Advancing Computing as a Science & Profession

The Association for Computing Machinery
2 Penn Plaza, Suite 701
New York, New York 10121-0701

Notice to Past Authors of ACM-Published Articles
ACM intends to create a complete electronic archive of all articles and/or other material previously published by ACM. If you have written a work that has been previously published by ACM in any journal or conference proceedings prior to 1978, or any SIG Newsletter at any time, and you do NOT want this work to appear in the ACM Digital Library, please inform permissions@acm.org, stating the title of the work, the author(s), and where and when published.

ISBN: 978-1-4503-2559-2 (Digital)

ISBN: 978-1-4503-2653-4 (Print)

Additional copies may be ordered prepaid from:

ACM Order Department
PO Box 30777
New York, NY 10087-0777, USA

Phone: 1-800-342-6626 (USA and Canada)
+1-212-626-0500 (Global)
Fax: +1-212-944-1318
E-mail: acmhelp@acm.org
Hours of Operation: 8:30 am – 4:30 pm ET

Printed in the USA

WebMedia 2013 Chairs' Welcome

It is our great pleasure to welcome you to the *19th Brazilian Symposium on Multimedia and the Web – WebMedia 2013* is an annual symposium sponsored by the Brazilian Computer Society (SBC) and is the most important forum for researchers and professionals in the Multimedia, Hypermedia and Web areas in Brazil. This is WebMedia's 19th edition and it seeks to bring together researchers, undergraduate and post graduate students and practitioners, both from Brazil and from abroad, to present and discuss research problems related to any and all of the symposium's topics.

WebMedia 2013 is being held in Salvador, capital of the Brazilian state of Bahia, from November 5th to 8th. Salvador was the first colonial capital of Brazil and it is notable for its cuisine, music and architecture. It is also known as Brazil's capital of happiness due to its countless popular outdoor parties, especially its street Carnival.

This year, the WebMedia is mainly organized by the Federal University of Bahia and University of Salvador, having many other sponsors and supporters including academic institutions, industry, government and learned societies. The sponsors and supporters are listed elsewhere in these proceedings.

The Symposium's program is composed of 13 technical sessions, 4 mini-courses, panels, 3 inner workshops on Multimedia, Hypermedia and Web domains (Thesis and Dissertation Workshop, Tools and Applications Workshop and Undergraduate Research Workshop), as well as 3 international and invited talks.

The papers accepted for publication in the WebMedia 2013 proceedings include 29 full papers and 24 short papers. The call for papers attracted 87 full paper and 62 short paper submissions, from Brazil, Korea, Canada, Netherlands and Austria, for acceptance rates of 33% and 38%, respectively. The Symposium's Program Committee worked very hard to perform the selection of these papers that will be presented and published from among many submissions of excellent quality. We thank all the submitting authors for their research efforts and for their submissions and congratulate those who had their work accepted. Finally, we would like to thank the members of the Program and Organization committees, as well as the reviewers. Their volunteer work was essential to the success of the Symposium.

We hope that you will find this program interesting and thought-provoking and that the symposium will provide you with a valuable opportunity to share ideas with other researchers and practitioners from institutions around the world.

WebMedia 2013 Conference Co-Chairs

Cássio V. S. Prazeres
Federal University of Bahia

Paulo N. M. Sampaio
University of Salvador

WebMedia 2013 Program Co-Chairs

André Santanchè
University of Campinas

Celso A. S. Santos
Federal University of Espírito Santo

Rudinei Goularte
University of São Paulo

Table of Contents

Digital TV, Ubiquitous and Mobile Computing I: Ubiquitous and Context-Aware Computing

Digital TV, Ubiquitous and Mobile Computing II: Mobile Computing and Interaction

Web and Social Networks I: Analysis in the Social Web

Web and Social Networks II: Web, Models and Architectures

Multimedia II: Media Coding and Transmission, 3D Video and QoS

Digital TV, Ubiquitous and Mobile Computing III: Digital TV Languages and Models

Web and Social Networks III: Web Systems and Services

Multimedia III: Media Personalization and Recommendation Systems

Digital TV, Ubiquitous and Mobile Computing IV: Digital TV Applications and Interaction

Digital TV, Ubiquitous and Mobile Computing V: Digital TV Development and Systems

Web and Social Networks IV: Web Recommendation and Analysis

WebMedia 2013 Organization

General Chairs: Cássio V. S. Prazeres *(Federal University of Bahia)*
Paulo N. M. Sampaio *(Salvador University)*

Program Chairs: André Santanchè *(University of Campinas)*
Celso A. S. Santos *(Federal University of Espírito Santo)*
Rudinei Goularte *(University of São Paulo)*

Workshop of Undergraduate Research Chairs: Renan G. Cattelan *(Federal University of Uberlândia)*
Frederico A. Durão *(Federal University of Bahia)*

Workshop on Tools and Applications Chairs: Jorge A. P. Campos *(Salvador University)*
Rodrigo O. Spínola *(Salvador University)*

Workshop on Ongoing Thesis and Dissertations Chairs: Alessandra A. Macedo *(University of São Paulo)*
Manoel C. Marques Neto *(Federal Institute of Bahia)*

Short Courses Committee: Renato F. Bulcão Neto *(Federal University of Goiás)*
Iwens G. Sene Júnior *(Federal University of Goiás)*

Steering Committee Chairs: Fernando M. Trinta *(Federal University of Ceará)*
Mário M. Teixeira *(Federal University of Maranhão)*

Steering Committee: André Santanchè *(University of Campinas)*
Cássio V. S. Prazeres *(Federal University of Bahia)*
Celso A. S. Santos *(Federal University of Espírito Santo)*
Graça Bressan *(University of São Paulo)*
Guido L. Souza Filho *(Federal University of Paraíba)*
José Valdeni de Lima *(Federal University of Rio Grande do Sul)*
Luiz F. G. Soares *(Pontifical Catholic University of Rio de Janeiro)*
Maria G. C. Pimentel *(University of São Paulo)*
Paulo N. M. Sampaio *(Salvador University)*
Regina M. Silveira *(University of São Paulo)*
Valter Roesler *(Federal University of Rio Grande do Sul)*

Program Committee (continued):

Regina Araujo *(Federal University of São Carlos)*
Renan Cattelan *(Federal University of Uberlândia)*
Renata Fortes *(University of São Paulo)*
Renato F. Bulcão-Neto *(Federal University of Goiás)*
Renato Fileto *(Federal University of Santa Catarina)*
Roberto Willrich *(Federal University of Santa Catarina)*
Rodrigo Assad *(Federal University of Pernambuco)*
Ronaldo Husemann *(Federal University of Rio Grande do Sul)*
Rudinei Goularte *(University of São Paulo)*
Seiji Isotani *(University of São Paulo)*
Silvio Cazella *(University of Vale dos Sinos)*
Tatiana A. Tavares *(Federal University of Paraiba)*
Thais V. Batista *(Federal University of Rio Grande do Norte)*
Valter Roesler *(Federal University of Rio Grande do Sul)*
Vaninha Vieira *(Federal University of Bahia)*
Vinicius Garcia *(Federal University of Pernambuco)*
Windson Viana *(Federal University of Ceara)*

Additional reviewers:

Almerindo Rehem
Anelise Jantsch
Arthur Godoy
Bruno Y. L. Kimura
Caio Viel
Deller James Ferreira
Demostenes Zegarra Rodríguez
Denis Salvadeo
Diego Barboza
Diogo Martins
Diogo Pedrosa
Douglas Mattos
Eduardo Araújo
Eduardo Cruz Araújo
Erick Baptista Passos
Erick Lazaro Melo
Esdras Silva
Eveline R. Sacramento

Fernanda Lopes
Fernando Lemos
Glauco Amorim
Guilherme Lima
Inaldo Maia
Izaias Faria
Joel Santos
Kamila Rodrigues
Lincoln Rocha
Marcio Moreno
Paulo Rego
Paulo Roberto Reis Jansen
Rafael Boucinha
Raoni Ferreira
Roberto Gerson Azevedo
Tiago Pomponet
Tiago Ribeiro

WebMedia 2013 Sponsor & Supporters

Sponsor:

In cooperation with:

Supporters:

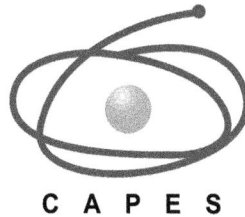

Institutional donor/supporters:

Universidade Federal da Bahia

Multimedia: from Information Source to Components of Transformational Games

Michael G. Christel
Carnegie Mellon University
Entertainment Technology Center
Pittsburgh, PA 15219
+1 412-268-7799
christel@cs.cmu.edu

ABSTRACT

This summary overviews a keynote talk that the author is giving at the WebMedia conference. Christel will discuss his journey with multimedia research over the past six years, taking him from Carnegie Mellon University's Computer Science Department into the Entertainment Technology Center (ETC). The story begins with the use of speech recognition, image processing, and language technologies to automatically process large video corpora. Such processing facilitates more efficient retrieval. As demonstrated by top scores in the international TRECVID benchmarking forum, Christel's CMU Informedia research group has experienced success in finding relevant video shots quickly from large masses of material. The emphasis is on leveraging the intelligence of a human user in the interactive retrieval loop, with lessons shared in visual analytics papers.

That work drew the attention of oral historians, who amassed large quantities of video stories that were not easily accessible. The value of synchronized metadata to open up these collections for the web audience illustrates the power of multimedia processing to help organize and present cultural repositories. As the user community appreciated the layers of meaning within these often riveting stories, Christel was drawn to the power of multimedia elements in entertainment technologies, including games.

Transformational games are designed to change the player in some way, such as improving health habits, changing attitudes, or providing education. The ETC provides multidisciplinary teams of graduate students with skills in visual arts, design, sound, programming, and production the opportunity to create such games in the course of a semester-long project. Christel will briefly overview this development process, and then demonstrate some of the ETC-produced games, highlighting the role of multimedia elements within them and the promise of the work to positively affect the game player.

Categories and Subject Descriptors

H5.1 [**Information Interfaces and Presentation**]: Multimedia Information Systems.

General Terms

Design, Human Factors.

WebMedia '13, Nov 05-08 2013, Salvador, Brazil
ACM 978-1-4503-2559-2/13/11.
http://dx.doi.org/10.1145/2526188.2528279

Keywords

Digital video libraries, oral histories, transformational games.

1. MULTIMEDIA PROCESSING TO OPEN UP INFORMATION SOURCES

The Informedia research group at Carnegie Mellon University formed in the 1990s to investigate the application of speech recognition, image processing, and language processing technologies for the automatic analysis of multimedia. Depending on the audio and/or video source material origins and quality, the automatic techniques produce accurate to very noisy and error-prone descriptors. However, integrating across multiple techniques and bringing in an intelligent human user to review and direct investigations can sidestep the noise and result in improved information precision. A series of experiments, including those conducted under the NIST TRECVID annual series, are surveyed in [1] and will be introduced to start off the multimedia keynote discussion. Video especially is a very rich information medium, but looking through thousands of hours of video to find specific examples is impractical; through automated techniques, that task becomes feasible.

2. SYNCHRONIZED METADATA FOR ORAL HISTORIES

The HistoryMakers is an African American oral history archive using speech alignment, image processing, and language understanding technologies to promote multiple levels of access to fuel the viewing of the actual video recordings in a large oral history corpus [2]. Tens of thousands of stories are accessible in oral histories processed through Informedia technologies at thehistorymakers.com and www.idvl.org. The stories are made much more efficient for navigation and exploration through the use of synchronized, i.e., time-aligned, multimedia descriptors, which provide access down to the spoken word level within stories. The value to the user is both informational, but also at times educational and entertaining, which leads into another consideration for multimedia on the web: as a component within transformational games.

3. TRANSFORMATIONAL GAMES

Jesse Schell, a fellow faculty member at the ETC along with Christel, encourages "tranformational games" rather than "serious games" as a phrase in which the focus remains on how the game is changing the user. Two examples are games that teach the user, and games promoting a healthy lifestyle. Schell presents ways in which a game can be better designed, including the use of "juicy" systems that reward the player in many ways at once [3]. One way to present such rewards is through visual effects, aural effects, and synchronized audiovisual effects, i.e., by folding multimedia elements into the game experience. Other game design "lenses" [3] include providing an optimal flow to keep the user engaged, and providing surprise to keep interest, both of which can be accomplished through multimedia integration in games.

3.1 Multimedia to Illustrate Teaching Points

The ETC-produced game *Invasion!!* done with the Chicago Field Museum makes use of video elements for illustration of an invasive species [4]. Specifically, Asian carp behavior are shown and U.S. Great Lakes experts' testimony presented regarding the potential effects of the Asian carp in the lakes. Elements of the game are reinforced through incorporation of the video footage.

3.2 Multimedia in Interactive Documentary

Another ETC student team, *Project Xense*, makes use of video to deliver a first-hand experience about cochlear implants [5]. A series of videos shows interactive memories of gradual hearing loss and the regaining of it through implants. The ETC project *Atomic Zone* pushes the integration of multimedia into a more immersive experience, an interactive documentary in which the user explores the extent of the Hiroshima damage in the aftermath of the historical 1945 bombing [6]. The Unity game engine is employed to present narrative aspects through visuals, sound, and animations, allowing users to witness the damage that a nuclear explosion can inflict. The user is not forced to sit through a number of animations and slide shows of photographs. Playing all of them would make *Atomic Zone* a more linear documentary with the same experience for all, and decrease the narrative setting of being "in" the city after the bombing and being able to explore on your own. Playtests with high school and college students confirmed the value of choice and control in the experience: Dickie [7] notes that players will invest more in and learn more from experiences if they retain choice and control.

3.3 Multimedia to Enhance Juiciness of Transformational Games

A game can be focused on implicit learning, such as *neuraltone* which provides an experience such as defeating space ships while implicitly learning about sound categories [8]. The extra overlay of more visual richness and music tracks appeal to players and keep them playing longer with learning benefits. Cognitive scientists can manipulate the game to determine if game reward systems as outlined in [3] also increase implicit sound learning.

A game for health is *CardioActive*, which brings in an array of devices (Kinect, Wii Balance Boards, heart rate monitors) to provide two cooperative players with an exergame experience [9]. Through the use of sounds and imagery, a subway tunnel and station world is textured to increase its appeal and encourage longer and more active game play. Playtests confirm that the players find the theme and soundtrack appealing, and view the experience more as a satisfying game than exercise.

A game may have multiple objectives, as does *Beanstalk*, which endeavors to teach balance and torque, scientific inquiry, and socio-emotional learning skills like asking for help and cooperation [10]. The site workingexamples.org shares lessons on *Beanstalk*, *Invasion!!*, and other digital media for learning.

Multimedia elements – sounds, music, animations, video clips – are building blocks that through good game design and programming can produce transformational games. Multimedia has always been a rich information source, capable of persuading and educating if the proper sources could be found, and through automated processing techniques the information seeking tasks could be streamlined. Multimedia can also be an instrument for change through its contribution to transformational games.

4. ACKNOWLEDGMENTS

Informedia successes stem from a wealth of talented researchers working under Alex Hauptmann and before him Howard Wactlar. Oral history work was spurred on by Julieanna Richardson of The HistoryMakers. ETC work benefits from various client sponsors, with the creative, multidisciplinary student teams producing works of merit as demonstrated during the keynote talk.

5. REFERENCES

[1] Christel, M. 2009. *Automated Metadata in Multimedia Information Systems: Creation, Refinement, Use in Surrogates, and Evaluation.* Morgan & Claypool, San Rafael, CA.

[2] Christel, M. Stevens, S., Maher, B., and Richardson, J. 2010. Enhanced Exploration of Oral History Archives through Processed Video and Synchronized Text Transcripts. In *Proceedings of the Int'l Conf. on Multimedia*, 1333-1342. DOI=http://doi.acm.org/10.1145/1873951.1874215.

[3] Schell, J. 2008. *The Art of Game Design: A Book of Lenses.* Morgan Kaufmann, Burlington, MA.

[4] ETC *Invasion!!* game, posted to BrainPOP in 2013, http://www.brainpop.com/games/invasion!!/.

[5] ETC *Project Xense*, 2012, Carnegie Mellon University, http://www.etc.cmu.edu/projects/tatrc/.

[6] Sciannameo, N., Cano, R., Durkin, N., Hamel, E., Hsu, J., Lee, A., Stevens, S., Harger, B., and Christel, M. 2013. Atomic Zone: An Immersive Interactive Web Documentary Built with the Unity3D Game Engine. In *Proc. 2013 18th International Conference on Computer Games* (Louisville, KY, July-Aug. 2013), 191-196.

[7] Dickey, M. 2006. Game Design and Learning: A Conjectural Analysis of How Massively Multiple Online Role-Playing Games (MMORPGs) Foster Intrinsic Motivation. *Educ. Tech. Research and Development* 55(3), 253-273.

[8] Kimball, G., Cano, R., Feng, J., Feng, L., Hampson, E., Li, E., Christel, M., Holt, L. L., Lim, S., Liu, R., and Lehet, M. 2013. Supporting Research into Sound and Speech Learning through a Configurable Computer Game. In *Proc. IEEE Games Innovation Conference* (Vancouver, Sept. 2013).

[9] Navarro, P., Johns, M. L., Lu, T.-H., Martin, H., Poduval, V., Robinson, M., Roxby, A., and Christel, M. 2013. Webz of War: A Cooperative Exergame Driven by the Heart. In *Proc. IEEE Games Innovation Conference* (Vancouver, Sept. 2013).

[10] Christel, M., Stevens, S., et al. 2013. Beanstalk: A Unity Game Addressing Balance Principles, Socio-Emotional Learning and Scientific Inquiry. In *Proc. IEEE Games Innovation Conference* (Vancouver, Sept. 2013).

Extracting Context from the Web to Help Visually Impaired Pedestrians Develop Cognitive Maps of Their Environments

Khai N. Truong
The University of North Carolina at Charlotte
9201 University City Blvd
Charlotte, NC, USA
ktruong8@uncc.edu

ABSTRACT

A rich cognitive map of an environment can enhance an individual's experience within the space. However, acquiring knowledge about an environment can be challenging for people with visual impairments. They often need support by sighted people to understand what is in the environment, associate meaning to these objects and places, identify where different objects and places are positioned, and their spatial relationship with each other. In this talk, I will present how the power of the Web can be leveraged in ubiquitous computing tools to help a user learn an environment. I will discuss what information is required by visually impaired pedestrians, when and where to provide this information, and also how to collect and present it. Finally, I will describe how this work can be extended to benefit the general population.

Categories and Subject Descriptors

H.5.2 [**Information Interfaces and presentation**]: User Interfaces

General Terms

Human Factors

Keywords

geographical information representation; users with visual impairments; assistive technology

Designing and Developing Interactive Multimedia Applications

Nuno Correia
CITI, Faculdade de Ciências e
Tecnologia, Universidade Nova de
Lisboa
2829 -516 Caparica, Portugal
nmc@fct.unl.pt

ABSTRACT

This talk presents the design and development process of interactive multimedia and multimodal systems used in diverse environments. The technologies, including new sensors, interaction surfaces and semantic information processing techniques will be described in the context where they were used. The systems result from collaborative projects in several fields, ranging from cultural heritage to contemporary art and dance. The dialogue with stakeholders from different areas and the impact on the resulting outcomes will be discussed, along with the process of setting up, specifying and developing interdisciplinary projects and the methodologies that are used. Recent work on motion annotation to help choreographic work, image analysis of paintings and digital art projects will be described. The academic and research environments and programs in which this work is done are also presented.

Categories and Subject Descriptors

H.5.1 [**Information Interfaces and Presentations**]: Multimedia Information Systems; H.5.2 [**Information Interfaces and Presentations**]: User Interfaces.

General Terms

Algorithms, Performance, Design, Human Factors.

Keywords

Interactive Multimedia, Mobile and Augmented Environments, Information Processing, Interaction.

1. INTRODUCTION

Rich interaction spaces, virtual environments, interactive narratives, and ubiquitous computing, suggest new contexts of use and new computational models and software solutions. There are many new and many unsolved research questions in the multimedia and hypermedia research areas, including the semantic problem, the integration of different modalities, the development of authoring tools, the massive amount of heterogeneous data that is being produced, and the need for appropriate interfaces with the users. Another important change relates to the contexts of use, specially the ones that result from

the availability of mobile and ubiquitous computing environments. All these changes enabled a wide use of new interfaces and processing techniques in new application domains. Among these are cultural heritage and arts, where interactive technology can play a role in the creation of the work of art itself or in supporting exploration activities or preservation of artifacts.

These interdisciplinary projects involve different stakeholders, including artists, curators, museum administrations and teams with multiple skills that need to work together. Art and science approaches and methods are sometimes used in the same project and the boundaries are not always easy to define, and have impact in the development process. For example, evaluation techniques commonly used in human computer interaction systems are difficult to apply and face some resistance in artistic contexts, even when the work of art is an interactive system in itself. However, there is no alternative to this diversity, integrating knowledge from multiple contexts, including arts, technology, and science to achieve meaningful results that have an impact on people daily lives. The projects that are described briefly in the next section share some of these characteristics and had the contributions of, among others, scientists, designers, artists, historians, or choreographers.

2. PROJECTS

The first projects to be presented support storytelling activities with increasing control from the user. The InStory project [20], enabled to receive narratives in a mobile device when navigating in the real world, using contextual information about the state or characteristics of the user. The InStory project defined a flexible computational architecture that integrates heterogeneous devices, different media formats and narrative modes. Interfaces were carefully designed in order to convey the spirit of the place where the project was tested, Quinta da Regaleira, Sintra, Portugal, and the desired mood for the user. This mobile project led to two other projects, mainly developed by Tiago Martins while doing is PhD at Kunstuniversität, Linz. Wolves and Sheep that takes an humorous view of mobile location games and a narrative, Noon, that uses a specially developed wearable device, the Gauntlet [6], that augments the interaction possibilities. This device has several sensors, including an RFID reader, a digital compass, accelerometers, and a Bluetooth interface to connect to mobile devices for display and interaction. This device supports interaction and narrative possibilities that going beyond what the smart phones used previously supported.

While developing these narrative projects in cultural heritage sites an additional concern was raised related with providing users with mechanisms to contribute and enrich storylines or media archives.

This concern was addressed in the Memoria project [5] mobile interface, an application to share and access personal memories when visiting historical sites, museums or other points of interest. With this interface people can navigate the memory space of the place they are visiting and, using their mobile devices, view what has interested them or other people in past occasions. The system consists of a retrieval engine and a mobile user interface that allows capture and automatic annotation of images. More recently, several other projects that use image processing in cultural heritage settings were also developed. These projects include an image based web system to visit past museum exhibitions and algorithms to analyze early twenty century paintings.

Museums are a natural laboratory for user interaction techniques and we conducted an extended experiment of using a multitouch surface to access a museum collection [4]. Besides providing navigation mechanisms regarding the collection tools for sharing information were also available to the users. Different types of user tests and observations were carried out regarding the provided features. As a follow up of this work, we have recently concluded a project for exploring illuminated manuscripts in educational settings. The project has three components that can be used together or separately. These components cover different aspects of the medieval illuminations experience and use several interaction techniques taking into account the affordances of each interface. The Virtual Scriptorium uses a calligraphic interface to enable the experience of producing digital illuminations and it provides some background information about the illuminations being produced. The Interactive Panel is a large interactive multitouch surface and provides information about medieval manuscripts from scientific, social, artistic and historical points of view. Finally, the Augmented Book combines the physicality of the book, the codex, with digital materials related to how it was made and the beauty of its content.

The performing arts can also benefit with computational tools to support creative processes. The TKB project developed a video annotator [1] that supports multimodal annotation and is applied to contemporary dance as a creation tool. It was conceived to assist the creative processes of choreographers, working as a digital notebook for personal annotations. The prototype, developed for Tablet PCs, is a real-time multimodal video annotator based on keyboard, pen and voice inputs. Two types of annotations were defined: annotation marks and regular annotations. The annotations marks correspond to pre-defined events in contrast to regular annotations that do not have a pre-defined structure. Motion tracking defines the dynamic behavior of the annotations and voice input complements the other modalities.

The last part of the talk will be devoted to exploratory projects where technology was an integral part of artistic projects, in particular the TimeMachine project [3], done in collaboration with the Lisbon-based art group CADA. One of the outcomes of the project is an application running on mobile devices that captures location data and uses this information to provide a subjective map of the user behavior using several visualizations. Time Machine has artistic goals related with the use of computing artifacts in everyday life. The system relies on a carefully designed data processing layer able to capture daily life behaviors. In the talk, the design process, the computational architecture and the results obtained with the system are described. Reflections regarding the challenges in the development and data capture processes are also provided, considering the rich experience of developing the project to a level where it can represent the everyday routine of its users.The diverse interactive projects that are presented share some common themes and concerns. The increasing mobility and availability of sensors, the interaction with other areas of knowledge and other practitioners such as artists, leads to requirements in terms of development tools and teams that go beyond the computer science laboratory. Reasoning about these projects and their development contexts helps in addressing the challenges for existing and future computational frameworks.

3. ACKNOWLEDGMENTS

The work reported here owns a lot to the people that inspired me and led me to explore these topics. I am especially grateful to all the colleagues and students from IMG (Interactive Multimedia Group) that participated in the projects and contributed with their enthusiasm and insights to the results. The research was partially funded by the Portuguese Foundation for Science and Technology and CITI/DI/FCT/UNL (PEst-OE/EEI/UI0527/2011).

4. REFERENCES

[1] Cabral, D., Valente, J., Silva, J. Aragão, U., Fernandes, C., Correia, N. 2011. A Creation Tool for Contemporary Dance using Multimodal Video Annotation. In *Proceedings of the 19th ACM international conference on Multimedia* (MM '11). ACM, New York, NY, USA, 905-908. DOI=10.1145/2072298.2071899 http://doi.acm.org/10.1145/2072298.2071899

[2] Correia, N., et al. 2005. InStory: A System for Mobile Information Access, Storytelling and Gaming Activities in Physical Spaces. In *Proceedings of ACE 2005 - ACM SIGCHI International Conference on Advances in Computer Entertainment Technology* (Valencia, Spain, June 2005). ACM, New York, NY, USA, 102-109. DOI=10.1145/1178477.1178491 http://doi.acm.org/10.1145/1178477.1178491

[3] Correia, N., Lopes, C., Hawkey, J., Oliveira, S., and Perriquet, O. 2012. Personal Routine Visualization Using Mobile Devices. In *Proceedings of the 11th International Conference on Mobile and Ubiquitous Multimedia* (MUM'12). ACM, New York, NY, USA. DOI=10.1145/2406367.2406437 http://doi.acm.org/10.1145/2406367.2406437

[4] Correia, N., Mota, T., Nóbrega, R., Silva, L., and Almeida, A. 2010. A Multi-Touch Tabletop for Robust Multimedia Interaction in Museums. In *ACM International Conference on Interactive Tabletops and Surfaces* (ITS '10). ACM, New York, NY, USA, 117-120. DOI=10.1145/1936652.1936674 http://doi.acm.org/10.1145/1936652.1936674

[5] Jesus, R., Abrantes, A., Correia, N., 2011. Methods for Automatic and Assisted Image Annotation. *Multimedia Tools Appl.* 55(1): 7-26 (2011)

[6] Martins,T., Sommerer, C., Mignonneau, L., Correia, N. Gauntlet: A Wearable Interface for Ubiquitous Gaming. In *Proceedings of the 10th international conference on Human computer interaction with mobile devices and services (MobileHCI '08)*. ACM, New York, NY, USA, 367-370. DOI=10.1145/1409240.1409290 http://doi.acm.org/10.1145/1409240.1409290

Accessibility of Web and Multimedia Content: Techniques and Examples from the Educational Context

André Pimenta Freire, Raphael Winckler de Bettio, Elaine das Graças Frade,
Fernanda Barbosa Ferrari, José Monserrat Neto e Helena Libardi
Federal University of Lavras
Campus Universitário, CX. Postal 3037
Lavras, MG, Brazil
+55 35 3829-1536
{apfreire, raphaelwb, monserrat}@dcc.ufla.br,
{elaine.frade, feferrari}@ded.ufla.br, hlibardi@dex.ufla.br

ABSTRACT

Developing accessible Websites is essential to enable disabled people to have access to content and day-to-day services. As stated by Tim Berners-Lee, the inventor of the Web, "access to the Web by everyone regardless of disability is an essential aspect". This paper presents a summary of a short course on techniques to help design more accessible Web and multimedia content for people with different types of disabilities, presented at the 19th Brazilian Symposium on Multimedia and The Web. The course included examples from educational contexts, including issues with text, images, audio, video, structural elements and navigation, discussing how different accessibility issues may affect users with different types of disabilities.

Categories and Subject Descriptors

H.5.4. [Hypertext/Hypermedia]: User issues
H.5.2. [User interfaces]: Evaluation/methodology

General Terms

Design, Human Factors.

Keywords

Web accessibility, Multimedia accessibility, Inclusive Design.

1. INTRODUCTION

Including people with disabilities and providing them with access to online education, work, entertainment and other services is an essential goal to be achieved by society. In order for Websites to be more inclusive, it is very important that developers be aware that their target public may include people who have some disability, be it visual, hearing, physical, cognitive or some specific learning difficulty such as dyslexia. The needs of all of those users need to be taken into consideration by developers.

In the particular case of the Brazilian legislation, the Decree/Law 5.296/2004, all federal governmental bodies are required to adhere to accessibility guidelines. Besides legal requirements, making Websites more accessible brings a number of benefits, with the possibility of broadening the number of costumers.

WebMedia'13, November 5–8, 2013, Salvador, Brazil.
ACM 978-1-4503-2559-2/13/11.
http://dx.doi.org/10.1145/2526188.2528538

In the short course summarised in this paper, basic concepts and techniques for making Web and multimedia content were presented. The course, presented at the 19th Brazilian Symposium on Multimedia and the Web, also included examples from the educational context.

2. ACCESSIBILITY OF WEB AND MULTIMEDIA CONTENT

The concept of accessibility for people with disabilities, as defined by ISO 9241-Part 141 brings it closer to the concept of usability, defining it as the "usability of a product to the people with the widest range of capabilities", which includes people with disabilities.. According to ISO 9241- *Standard on Ergonomics of Human System Interaction*- Part 11, the concept of usability is defined as "the extent to which a product can be used by specified users to achieve specified goals with effectiveness, efficiency and satisfaction in a specified context of use".

In order for accessibility to be effectively addressed in Websites, it is of utmost importance that people with disabilities be included in the design and evaluation of Websites [3, 4].

Conforming to Web accessibility guidelines can also be very helpful to provide a first step to making Websites more accessible. One of the most well-known sets of accessibility guidelines is the Web Content Accessibility Guidelines (WCAG) [1], defined by the Web Accessibility Initiative (WAI) of the World Wide Web Consortium (W3C), with its first version published in 1999 and the current version 2.0 published in 2008.

WCAG 2.0 is organised hierarchically around four principles, that Web content should be: perceivable, operable, understandable and robust. It is composed by a set of 61 success criteria grouped under each of the four principles. Each success criterion is assigned a conformance level, ranging between A, AA and AAA. In order for a Website to be level-A conformant, it has to conform to all success criteria at level A.

3. ASSISTIVE TECHNOLOGY AND THE USE OF THE WEB BY PEOPLE WITH DISABILITIES

Cook e Polgar [2] define Assistive Technology as "a wide range of equipments, services, strategies and practices conceived and applied to minor the problems encountered by people with disabilities". The use of Assistive Technology by people with disabilities has a significant influence on the way they use Websites. It is very important that Web developers know the main features of AT in order to develop Websites that work appropriately with them.

Some examples of Assistive Technology used by disabled users include screen reader software by blind users, which synthesises all textual content from Web pages into voice. This has a significant impact on how blind users use Websites, given they use primarily input via keyboard and are only able to have access to content that is described textually.

Other examples include screen magnification software used by partially-sighted users, alternative input devices used by physically-disabled users and enhancement with captions and sign-language interpretations used by deaf and hearing disabled users.

4. TECHNIQUES TO PRODUCE ACCESSIBLE WEB AND MULTIMEDIA CONTENT

Using appropriate techniques to make Web and multimedia content more accessible is essential to users with disabilities. In this course, some important techniques were presented to help developers make different types of content more accessible, including examples from the educational context.

4.1 Textual content

Textual content is one of the most usual means to make information available on Websites. Although it is simpler to make text more accessible to technologies such as screen readers, it is very important that care be taken to make sure text is accessible to people with different disabilities, especially in educational contexts.

Different users can have difficulties with the way text is presented, including issues with colour contrast, typography and layout. Dyslexic students could have difficulties with certain configurations of paragraphs, font types and contrast of colours, which could also affect users who are partially-sighted.

Besides providing appropriate presentation of text, it is also very important to consider the use of language that is understandable by the target-audience of a Website.

4.2 Images

When images are used in Websites, it is important to make sure they will be accessible to all users, especially when they carry important information in them. For example, in an educational Website, images with maps, graphs and other information need to have alternative textual descriptions that allow blind users with screen readers to have access to them.

It is also very important to make images with flexible presentation that can be adapted to users with low vision, such as in the case of images and illustrations in educational content that need to be viewed satisfactorily even in enlarged sizes and with different colour arrangements.

4.3 Audio and Video

Providing accessible multimedia content is also very important to users with disabilities. Users with visual disabilities need audio description of visual content in videos in order to understand the content. For example, blind students watching a video of historical sites need explanations of visual scenery and silent scenes.

Deaf and hearing disabled users also need captioning and sign-language interpretation of auditory content in videos and transcriptions of audio in content such as podcasts.

4.4 Headings and structural elements

The use of structural elements is very important to a number of users with disabilities. For screen-reader users, for example, the use of appropriate mark-up for headings, lists, tables and other structural elements enables them to use the resources from their Assistive Technologies to enhance their navigation and have access to different parts of content.

For example, on a Web page with different topics in a course class, blind users can have an overview and get the specific content they want by listing the headings on a page.

4.5 Links and navigation

The navigation structure of a Website has a significant impact on the way people with disabilities use Websites. It is very important that users can identify the destination of links and know quickly how to get to information they need. For example, if links are not properly labelled, blind users with screen readers can have problems identifying where to go when they use a list of links.

4.6 Forms and interactive elements

Forms and interactive elements have to be designed in order to enable users with different disabilities to use them. All elements have to have their functionality identifiable by assistive technologies, using labelling mark-up. They also need to be accessible to users who only use the keyboard as their means of data input.

5. CONCLUSION

This paper presented a summary of a short course on techniques to produce more accessible Web and multimedia content, including basic concepts of Web accessibility, Assistive Technology, and techniques for different types of content and media used in Websites, along with examples from the educational context.

6. ACKNOWLEDGMENTS

Thanks to the "Centro de Educação à Distância" (CEAD) from the Federal University of Lavras for the support to develop this work. We also thank the support from the Accessibility Nucleus (NAUFLA) of the Federal University of Lavras.

7. REFERENCES

[1] Caldwell, B., Cooper, M., Reid, L. G., Vanderheiden, G. 2008. *Web Content Accessibility Guidelines 2.0*, Web Accessibility Initiative (WAI), World Wide Web Consortium (W3C), Available online at http://www.w3.org/TR/WCAG20, last access in May 2013.

[2] Cook, A. M.; Polgar, J. M. 1995. Assistive Technologies: Principles and Practices". Mosby – Year Book, Inc.

[3] Disability Rights Commission. 2004. *The Web: access and inclusion for disabled people: A formal Investigation conducted by the Disability Rights Commission*, London: The Stationery Office.

[4] Power, C., Freire, A. P., Petrie, H., Swallow, D. 2012. Guidelines are only half of the story: accessibility problems encountered by blind users on the web. In *Proceedings of the SIGCHI Conference on Human Factors in Computing Systems* (CHI '12). ACM, New York, NY, USA, 433-442.

HTML5, CSS3 and JQuery Mobile
for Intelligent Home Control

José Antonio Camacho-Guerrero
Innolution Sistemas de Informática Ltda
Rua Magda Perona Frossard 770-2, Ribeirão Preto/SP
+55 16 34411404
jose.camacho@innolution.com.br

Alessandra Alaniz Macedo
Universidade de São Paulo
FFCLRP-Department of Computer Science and
Mathematics
Av. Bandeirantes 3900 Ribeirão Preto/São Paulo
+55 16 36024863,
ale.alaniz@usp.br

ABSTRACT

Web pattern technologies such as HTML5, CSS3, JQuery and JQueryMobile have been used to develop web applications in different scenarios. As a use case, these technologies are being exploited in order to develop domotics systems. In the past, automatic environments were limited to big industries. Nowadays this scenario is rapidly changing. Home Control System (HCS) are became frequent and part of modern home. HCS' users are looking for quality of life and sustainability. Our work present and discuss the following items: 1) Development of human computer interface to HCS using some web technologies: HTML5, CSS3, JQuery and JQueryMobile; and 2) Concepts and components of HCS; 3) Examples of HCS and Primary Health System (PHS); and 4) Use Cases.

Categories and Subject Descriptors

Primary Classification:

H.5.2 User Interfaces (D.2.2, H.1.2, I.3.6)

H.5.2 User Interfaces (D.2.2, H.1.2, I.3.6)

Additional Classification:

B.4.1 Data Communications Devices

B.4.1 Data Communications Devices

B.4.3 Interconnections (subsystems)

B.4.3 Interconnections (subsystems)

General Terms

Management, Measurement, Design, Experimentation, Security.

Keywords

Html5, CSS3, JQuery, JQueryMobile, Domotics, Home Control System, Health Care Systems

1. INTRODUCTION

Automation is intended to integrate system functions aiming to control a device. Nowadays the automation is more present in environments seeking to increase the quality of life and sustainability through the efficient use of equipment, energy and services. A few years ago, automation was limited to industries, but nowadays this technology has wide use in homes, malls and other types of institutions.

The Home Control Systems (Home Control System - HCS) are becoming more common and part of modern dwellings. The computerized alarms, indoor environmental comfort systems and other applications are technologies that can favor families and their homes with different socio-economic conditions Some technologies, such as systems for lighting control, are usually present in homes, apartments and offices of medium and high socio-economic conditions, big companies, theaters, hotels and hospitals.

The health system shows up in need of automation, since most services and administrative procedures are still done manually, toughening the control of data and information management. Researchers at the University of Hertfordshire in UK, developed a project to care for the elderly, through the identification of heartbeat and other medical signs. Sensors were installed to capture vital signs and, in case of severe changes, they sent warnings to relatives and/or medical centers. In Brazil, healthcare professionals, members of the program PHC (Primary Health Care), use an application PHCS (Primary Health Care System) on a mobile device in the network infrastructure to carry out monitoring and preventive actions in their patients [1].

The various branches of automation have in common the same principles of control, using software and hardware, logic controllers and programming languages, and various types of sensor devices and actuators. Regarding, the concept of automation should establish conditions for all involved subsystems: lighting controls, security, air conditioning, power control, fire, etc. Automation should also put these subsystems to work together in an optimal way. For this, it is necessary to know all potential uses in homes and classify all available technologies to implement automation. Nowadays, the fact that the web is present in different hardware environments made it becomes the target of professional related automation.

For a long time, the idea of web development was exclusively associated with building pages that offered users access to specific HTML content. Web development was commonly associated with the development of web sites, on the internet or intranet. Associated with the content, web development can also be used to refer to the visual design of the pages and the development of electronic commerce. However, with the popularization of the Internet, new users needs have emerged in several areas. As a result, the new requirements include communication tools, email, games, social networking, e-commerce, security, automation and telemetry.

Led by Tim Berners - Lee , the W3C (World Wide Web Consortium) was created aiming to define standards, protocols and guidelines for developing web applications[2]. In 2006, W3C and the Web Hypertext Application Technology Working Group (WHATWG)[3] joined efforts by adding new features and correcting problems of the HTML versions giving rise to the HTML5 version. The HTML5 specification also introduces markup and application programming interfaces (APIs) for complex web applications, designed to make it easy to include and manipulate graphics and multimedia content and to enrich the semantic content of web documents.

Here, we intend to mention the latest standards for web application development: HTML5, CSS3, JQuery and JQueryMobile; and rapidly illustrate their use in domotics systems. The technologies help the visualization and control of static and dynamic information. As a case study, we plan to discuss and apply technologies in building an app to control home automation.

2. TOPICS OF INTEREST
In our home control context, the topics of interest are:

- Development of User Interfaces for Control Hardware Web.
  - o HTML5 language
  - o CSS3
  - o JQuery and JQueryMobile
- Physical Concepts and Components for Automation.
  - o Study Case
  - o Architecture

3. STUDY CASE: A HOME CONTROL SYSTEM
As a study case we use the home automation system SIAM (Integrated Automation and Monitoring). SIAM is also a Brazilian industry that develops hardware and software for automation, telemetry, access control and remote surveillance.

SIAM products are aiming to increase the comfort, control and safety of their customers in their homes or workplaces. Using a data network, it is possible to automate functions and providing security for various applications, including automotive systems and telemetry controls.

SIAM products are supported by a distributed architecture, where each sensor and each actuator has a unique identifier and associated actions to monitor and control devices. Sensors and actuators are interconnected by a data network that enables the exchange of information with the central management. Figure 3.1 illustrates the system architecture that supports SIAM communication software and hardware.

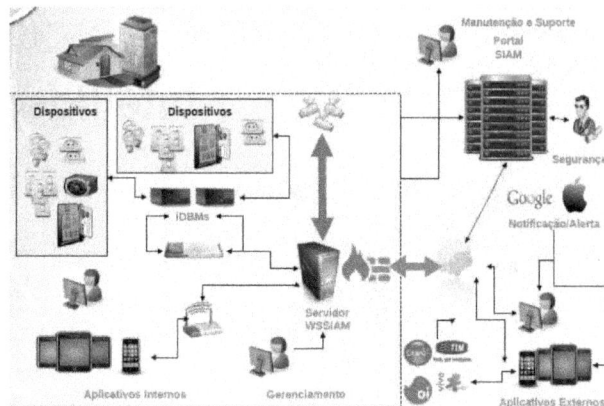

3.1 - Architecture of the home automation system SIAM

Figure 3.2 illustrates video elements and elements for lighting control and access to doors. When pressed a button, the event is triggered by touchstart browser. This event is being monitored by a method coded in a javascript file. When the event is triggered, the script triggers a service command which validates the permission and sends a request to the control hardware.

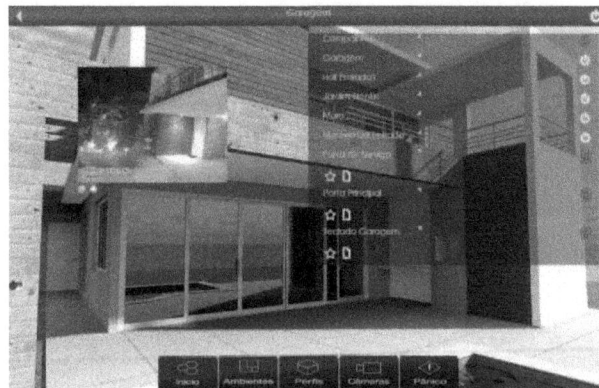

3.2 Home Control Web Interface

4. ACKNOWLEDGMENTS
Our thanks to FAPESP for supporting the presentation of the work and the company SIAM by the environment.

5. REFERENCES
[1] Barros, V. F. A. and Pinto JR, J and Borges, R. C. 2011. Aplicativo Móvel para Automação e Monitoração do Sistema de Atenção Primária a Saúde. Cadernos de Informática V.6. Universidade Federal de Goiás. Goiânia, Goiás, p 241-244.

[2] W3C. 2013. World Wide Web Consortium. Url: http://w3c.com/. Last access on 20/08/2013.

[3] WHATWG. 2013. Web Hypertext Application Technology Working Group. url: http://www.whatwg.org/. Last access on 20/08/2013.

Development of Interactive Virtual Environments using Java and Kinect Technologies

Almerindo N. Rehem Neto
Instituto Federal de Sergipe
Campus Lagarto
Lagarto – SE – CEP 49400-000
almerindo.rehem@gmail.com

Celso A. S. Santos
Federal University of Espirito Santo
Vitória - ES - CEP 29075-910
saibel@inf.ufes.br

Lucas A. de Carvalho,
Clebson Canuto
Instituto Federal de Sergipe
Campus Lagarto
{lucas.aragaoc,clebson.canuto}
@gmail.com

ABSTRACT
This short course presented in WebMedia 2013 has the mission to show new concepts of the framework OpenNI (Open Natural Interaction) version 2.2 and the development of applications using hardware capture depth, such as the Microsoft Kinect sensors and Carmine 1.08 PrimeSense's so adherent the standards of OpenNI.

Categories and Subject Descriptors
H.5.2 [Users Interfaces]: Evaluation/methodology, Interaction Styles.

H.1.2 [User/Machine Systems]: Human Factor, human information processing

General Terms
Human Factors, Languages, Experimentation

Keywords
Natural Interaction, Gesture recognition, *Framework*, Sensors, Kinect, Java.

1. INTRODUCTION
The evolution of technologies to capture users' interactions, oftentimes ubiquitously, created new paradigms to the interactive applications of interfaces conception. The Kinect [1] is one of the most important commercial icons that characterize this new way of thinking about interfaces, making the user-machine interaction more natural.

Despite the initial focus at the interactive game area, researchers and developers have used Kinect to build environments of natural interactions [2] [3]. Actually, it can be said that natural interaction seeks to create an environment where the user manipulate the machine and don't notice which are the artifacts used or don't have to learn a new vocabulary that corresponds to the instructions of this interface [4].

The mainly innovation of Kinect is the conception of a depth map which allows the device to deliver 3D information of the full scene, including player/actor and not only the control information. To obtain this result, the Kinect supports itself on the concept of

WebMedia '13, November 05-08 2013, Salvador, Brazil
ACM 978-1-4503-2559-2/13/11.
http://dx.doi.org/10.1145/2526188.2528540

structured light: a well-define standard projection light that permits the information calculation of the scene based on the combination between the standards of the projected object and the projection distortion according to the obstacles found by the light [5].

The Kinect has many resources (sound, image, depth, infra-red, motion drive) with a high level of precision and synchronism inside a single device. Those resources offer many possibilities of interaction between users and services e computer applications. However, there are many shapes and technologies to access those resources. In the attempt to solve this impasse, the PrimeSense turns available the OpenNI framework (Open Natural Interface) and the NiTE module (Natural Integration Middleware) [6] [2].

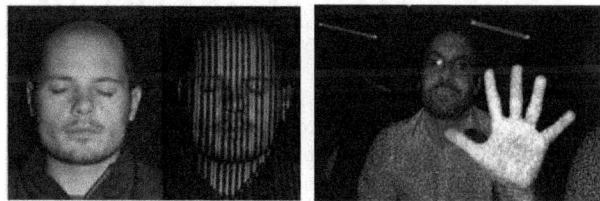

Figure 1. Structure light (a) used at the face mapping [7] and (b) cloud of light's points emitted from the IR sensor of Kinect.

The purpose of this short curse is to introduce a standardized way of developing modules of components which added could enable the virtual interactive environment construction based on gesture communication. Through the presented approach, the created components can be shared and reused in new applications, besides it permits the creation of an ecosystem library and applications to assist developers of this area. More details can be found in [8] and [11] references.

2. THE OPENNI FRAMEWORK
The framework conception is with a layer of abstraction that provides interfaces to the software components (middleware) and for the physical devices through an API. This API enables a multiple components records (modules) at the framework which are responsible for producing or processing data from physical sensors on a flexible way.

Nowadays, the components which are supported by OpenNI architecture are grouped in two types, the sensors modules (RGB camera, 3D sensor, IR camera, and microphone) and middleware (body and hand analysis, gesture detection, scene analysis). On the other hand, the frame work is now passing through an architecture redesign. The previous stable version of OpenNI (1.5 version) suffered criticism because of its using complexity, although it boosted the scientific community and the development of many applications when it became popular. The 1.5 version demanded the use of many code lines to the conception of simple tasks besides it has conceptions with a high level of complexity which hamper the understanding of the framework operation. After different suggestions of improvement and aiming attend to the scientific community of developers, the PrimeSense, main maintainer of OpenNI, started the conception of a new architecture (called 2.x OpenNI), in theory, simpler and easier to use [6].

The short course focuses in practical points of programming using the framework OpenNI, providing the basic and essential knowledge to any developer initiate your own applications related to natural interaction inside of the platform. The text includes (1) assembly and configuration of the development environment, (2) the integration between Java OpenNI wrapper [9] and NetBeansIDE [10], (3) the creation of a basic application with Java and OpenNI, (4) the creation of a application simulating a physical device, and (5) an application to track the movements of the hands (hand Tracking).

While OpenNI is responsible for the communication and obtainment data from compatible devices and connection to the system, the NiTE is responsible for processing and recognition of data. With this processing, it is possible to: (i) obtain which users present in the scene, (ii) identify the pixels belonging to each user and the background, (iii) create a mapping of the major joints of users and (iv) detecting the hand position in space (hand tracking).

3. A SIMPLE EXAMPLE: THE VIEW OF IMAGES OVER USER'S HANDS IN SCENE

The goal of the short course is to provide opportunities for interaction with a virtual environment based on the Kinect platform and provide basic concepts for building interfaces display and interaction with an icon or image. Through these concepts and with small changes in the sample code, the developer can build Java applications with natural user interfaces based on virtual objects, movements and gestures.

Figure 2. Screenshot of an application that recognizes a gesture and start tracking hand displaying an image on the position of the hand screened.

The goal of the short course is to make the participants able to build applications that use interactive visual sensor data RGB in conjunction with the tracking features of the hands of the users present in the scene and these overlapping hands with a certain image. The result of the implementation is shown in Figure 1.2. In it, the icon of the research group *Touching The Air* appears in the hands of users on the scene after they successfully perform a certain gesture monitored by the *middleware*.

4. CONCLUSION

This short course is about the development of applications focused on build natural interaction environments using the OpenNI framework and Java language. The intention here isn't exhausting this subject, but raises important issues and share some of the new technologies related with the natural interaction. It presents some concepts on natural interaction, devices involved and their evolution, as well as a more detailed explanation about the Kinect and all the motivation for the research related to this platform.

5. ACKNOWLEDGMENTS

The authors thank CAPES (Brazil) for their financial support to the first author through a scholarship, to Instituto Federal de Sergipe (IFS) and to PrimeSense Corporation for the equipments and support.

6. REFERENCES

1 Microsoft. *Kinect Web Site. http://www.xbox.com/pt-br/Kinect.* 2010.

2 PRIMESENSE CORP. *PrimeSense Natural Interaction. http://www.primesense.com/.* 2011.

3 MICROSOFT RESEARCH. *Kinect for Windows SDK. http://research.Microsoft.com/en-us/um/redmond/projects/Kinectsdk/default.aspx.* 2010.

4 Rehem Neto, A.N., Santos, C.A.S., and Carvalho, L. A. Touch The Air: Um Framework Orientado a Eventos para Ambientes Interativos. In *Webmedia* (2013).

5 Crawford. *How Microsoft Kinect Works. http://electronics.howstuffworks.com/microsoft-kinect.htm.* 2010.

6 OPENNI ORG. *OpenNI Corporation Web Site. http://www.openni.org.* 2011.

7 Quest, Shape. *Point Cloud Data from Structured Light Scanning. http://www.shapecapture.com/gallery3.htm.* 2010.

8 Rehem Neto, A.N., Santos, C.A.S., and Andrade, M. V. R. Interfaces para aplicações de Interação Natural baseadas na API OpenNI e na Plataforma Kinect. In *Webmedia* (2011).

9 Rehem Neto, A.N., Santos, C.A.S., and Andrade, M. V. R. DESENVOLVIMENTO DE AMBIENTES VIRTUAIS INTERATIVOS USANDO JAVA E KINECT. In *Webmedia* (2013).

10 NETBEANS. *NetBeans IDE - The Smarter and Faster Way to Code. https://netbeans.org.* 2013.

11 OPENNI ORG. *OpenNI User Guide. htp://www.openni.org/images/stories/pdf/OpenNI_UserGuide.pdf.* 2012.

12 OPENNI FOR JAVA. *Wrapper OpenNI. http://www.openni.org/projects/java-wrapper/.* 2013.

Mobile Development using Web Technologies Focusing on Games

André Santanchè
IC - Unicamp - University of
Campinas
Av. Albert Einstein, 1251
Campinas - SP, Brazil
santanche@ic.unicamp.br

Renoir Boulanger
W3C, WebPlatform.org project
W3C/MIT, 32 Vassar Street
Cambridge, MA, USA
renoir@w3.org

Gabriela Viana
École Polytechnique de
Montréal
2900, boul. Édouard-Montpetit
Montréal (Québec), Canada
gabriela.viana@polymtl.ca

Ricardo Panaggio
IC - Unicamp - University of
Campinas
Av. Albert Einstein, 1251
Campinas - SP, Brazil
panaggio@ic.unicamp.br

Bruno Melo
IC - Unicamp - University of
Campinas
Av. Albert Einstein, 1251
Campinas - SP, Brazil
brunoamelo@gmail.com

Hugo Aboud
IC - Unicamp - University of
Campinas
Av. Albert Einstein, 1251
Campinas - SP, Brazil
hugoaboud@gmail.com

ABSTRACT

Games are typically challenging applications to develop and they are omnipresent in the mobile platforms. Besides the hardware limitations and heterogeneity of mobiles, we are experiencing a "software platform epoch". Platforms like iOS, Android and Windows Phone offer to developers complete hermetic environments, which come with compatibility side effects, constraining applications to be reimplemented in order to address each platform. One of the most promising approaches to face this platform battle is based on the combination of Web technologies – HTML5, CSS3 and JavaScript – to produce platform-independent applications for mobiles. The question here is how to achieve the balance between independence and performance, required by games. This mini-course gives an overview of this scenario focusing in aspects addressed to game development.

Categories and Subject Descriptors

D.1 [**Programming Techniques**]: Miscellaneous; D.2.12 [**Software Engineering**]: Interoperability

General Terms

Languages

Keywords

mobile development, web-based development, games, html, css, javascript

1. INTRODUCTION

The Web-based development in the mobile context raises some suspicion. There are doubts concerning the performance of the applications and the flexibility to build "non-form" interfaces, as those required by games. This scenario has been changing. Several organizations and people are working to transform the Web in a universal platform to develop applications, including mobile devices. In the last years, Web technologies have evolved to enable the development of complete applications and have reached the performance to afford games development. This Web as platform to develop mobile applications is the central focus of this tutorial. Games is the case study, which pervades the topics.

We further present the main topics of the tutorial.

2. OVERVIEW OF HTML5 AND CSS3 FOR APPLICATIONS

This section presents an overview of some fundamental concepts of HTML5 and CSS3 technologies, which are important in the tutorial, as well as notions of responsive and adaptable design. It exploits innovations of HTML5 and CSS3 to produce responsive applications. The section is organized in the following topics:

- Presentation of HTML5 and CSS3
- Separation content-style
- Responsive and adaptable
- Semantics in Web documents

3. VECTOR GRAPHICS, SVG, CANVAS AND WEBGL

Web technologies are able to go beyond the classic document-oriented building model, to the vector space exploration. Vector graphics are not limited to images inserted inside documents, since they can be applied to model the entire interface. This is specially important in game development. For this reason, this section gives a special attention to this subject and is organized as follows:

- SVG
- Canvas
- SVG animation
- Tools for SVG

4. JAVASCRIPT FOR APPLICATIONS AND DOM

JavaScript is the main programming language in Web browsers. Even though it has been designed to develop small scripts inside Web pages, the language became the best option to develop platform independent applications over Web browsers. The HTML5 introduced new technologies and APIs, which empowers the JavaScript to produce complete applications even in local environments, as mobile devices. This section introduces key topics to develop JavaScript-based apps, exploiting the advances in HTML5. It is organized as follows:

- DOM - Document Object Model
- Selector
- Events

5. MARKUP AND STYLE ENGINEERING

The interaction between programs and markup in the Web development requires new techniques and design patterns. This section presents an overview of this scenario, as well as some recent initiatives to enhance a markup-driven development, interacting with JavaScript. The section is organized as follows:

- Markup patterns
- Creating markup modules
- CSS preprocessors
- JavaScript markup-driven development

6. WEB COMPONENTS

The challenge of producing a Web Component Model goes beyond a JavaScript software component model, since the kernel of the Web is built over a data-driven approach, i.e. documents are hosts and give structure to apps. On the other hand, components are fundamental for a Web app engineering. This section summarizes important topics of this model under construction, focusing in two main aspects:

- Templates
- Shadow DOM

7. EVOLUTION OF ARCHITECTURES FOR MOBILE DEVELOPMENT

There are several options to build mobile apps using Web technologies. The decision for an architecture depends on the target platform and the application requirements. This section gives an overview of these architectures and their main aspects. It is organized as follows:

- Apps using Web as secondary technology
- Apps using Web as primary technology
- Native Web apps

8. DESIGN OF INTERFACES AND USABILITY ISSUES

The design of Web-based interfaces for mobile devices requires planning and attention to usability issues. This section summarizes the main steps to plan, design and evaluate these interfaces. It is organized as follows:

- Plan the design process
- User context specification
- User needs specification
- Conceive solutions compatible with user needs
- Interface verification and validation
- Requirements evaluation
- Task analysis with users - Validation

9. CONCLUDING REMARKS

The Web is a platform that most of the mobile users are familiarized. Beyond supporting portable apps among hardware and OS platforms, the research in Web development have been looking for innovative techniques to produce responsive applications, which can be explored in the mobile domain. This tutorial gives an overview of this "under construction" scenario.

Acknowledgments

Work partially financed by FAPESP, o Microsoft Research FAPESP Virtual Institute (NavScales project), CNPq (Mu-ZOO project) and PRONEX-FAPESP, INCT in Web Science (CNPq 557.128/2009-9) and CAPES, as well as individual grants from CNPq.

Multimodal Late Fusion Bag of Features Applied to Scene Detection

Bruno Lorenço Lopes
Universidade de São Paulo (USP)
São Carlos - São Paulo - Brazil
blopes@icmc.usp.br

Rudinei Goularte
Universidade de São Paulo (USP)
São Carlos - São Paulo - Brazil
rudinei@icmc.usp.br

ABSTRACT

Recent advances in technology have increased the availability of video data, creating a strong requirement for efficient systems to manage those materials. To make efficient use of video information, first, the data has to be automatic segmented into smaller, manageable and understandable units, like scenes. This paper presents a new, multimodal video scene segmentation technique. The proposed approach is to combine Bag of Features based techniques (visual and aural) in order to explore the latent semantic obtained by them in complementary way, improving scene segmentation. The results achieved showed to be promising.

Categories and Subject Descriptors

H.3.1 [**Information Storage and Retrieval**]: Content Analysis and Indexing; H.3.3 [**Information Storage and Retrieval**]: Information Search and Retrieval

General Terms

Algorithms, Experimentation, Measurement

Keywords

Multimedia, Scene Detection, Visual Descriptors, Audio Descriptors, Bag of Features

1. INTRODUCTION

Sales of digital devices, like cams and smartphones, capable of capturing digital images have been expanding every year. This fact have led to a significant raise on digital content (photos, videos and audio) generation [37]. Websites, like Youtube[1] and Instagram [2], which provide services for people to share digital content, have become very popular nowadays mainly because people can choose when they want to access a specific content.

---

[1] http://www.youtube.com
[2] http://www.instagram.com

However, the large volume of content provided by sites such as these brings difficulties to the users to find the desired content. This problem, associated with the search for constant interactivity on multimedia's applications, have stimulated recent researches that aim to provide easy and transparent access to content, in special in the Personalization and Adaptation area [23, 30, 38].

Personalization investigates suitable means of customizing and/or filter content according to preferences, interests and needs of a particular user. It encompasses different services that can be categorized as [1, 26]: content selection, recommendation systems and summarization systems. Content selection involves multimedia items search by criteria defined by users. By contrast, in recommendation, interest items are automatically offered to user based on its preferences profile or its content access history. In turn, summarization aims to produce a reduced and semantically significant version of the content to user. Most of current efforts on Personalization services are addressed to video content [5, 21].

Personalization systems have a common requirement: content data knowledge. These data about the content are called metadata and they can be used as a means of acquiring semantic information. Semantic information may form a link between computional representation of a content and the user interpretation of data, reducing semantic gap, that is defined as the lack of this link [35]. In digital videos, one of first stages in order to acquire semantic information is segmentating the video in smaller units, computationaly easier to deal with: frames, shots and scenes [7].

There are many proposed methods in literature that segment a video in shots, exploring techniques ranging from histograms and transforms to multimodality. The shot concept is well defined, as a serie of consecutive frames acquired continually by a unique cam that represent a continuous action in time and space [11]. State-of-art in this area shows methods that ensure a high precision [34].

However, shot detection methods tends to generate a large number of segments, what may difficult content navigation. Moreover, a shot description level tends to be insignificant to event perception [28]. Another problem found in these methods is that generally they are specific area-oriented, and may not be applied to another areas. Because of these facts, video segmentation in semantically human comprehensible units is very interesting, and opens space to the scene segmentation.

On the other hand, scene segmentation is more challenging than shot segmentation because it depends on the scene concept which is semantically richer. Unlike shot definition, there isn't a unique scene definition. So, scene segmentation techniques face problems such as: dependency of scene definition adopted; lack of synchronization between audio and video; and the subjectivity of the scene concept definition [39].

An important problem found in the scene segmentation field is that the techniques available in the literature (see Section 2) focus on finding video segments containing singles objects (persons) or events. These techniques usually don't handle semantic complex segments. These segments are closer to the common user understanding of a scene, which should be characterized by the semantic relation between the shots that compose it - meanwhile neighbouring shots can be visually different, they do represent the same subject. For instance, in a TV news program, a part of the video between two anchorman (the presenter of the news program) appearances, composed by three visually different shots semantically related, the most apropriate segmentation would find only one scene. However, most of related work, using more narrow scene definitions, will find three scenes.

An interesting approach to face that problem, as far as we know not yet explored in the field, is to use the latent semantic provided by Bag of Features (BoF) techniques. BoF extracts features - local descriptors - from images, clustering together the similar ones and building dictionaries (code-books) of "visual words" [40], which can be used later for retrieval purposes. During the retrieval phase, the visual word from an input query image is compared with those on the dictionary. Due to the high discriminative power of the local descriptors, BoF is very efficient on discover of which group (cluster) each object belongs, although it is not able to classify the groups [40]. This latent semantic can be used to discover which video shots belong to the same scene (group).

In this paper we explore BoF in a multimodal fashion. First, we use only visual features to segment a video into scenes. Second, we use only audio features. Then, we combine their results in a process called late fusion, in expectancy to get better segmentation results whereas the different nature of used medias (visual and aural) may capture complementary intrinsic semantic present in the video allowing us to identify semantically complex segments. This paper is organized as follows. Section 2 presents a review on scene segmentation techniques, considering their advances and weakness. Section 3 details our scene detection techniques based on the BoF model. In Section 4, we report our experiments and their results. Section 5 sumarizes and provides conclusions about our work.

2. SCENE SEGMENTATION

Scene Segmentation is a very important step in content's indexing, retrieval and personalization since scene is a concept that is semantically meaningful for the user. In this section, some of the researches in this area are presented.

Chaisorn et al. [6] demonstrate that TV news structure can be divided as one opening, composed with the most important news summary, and the main part, in which the news are organized in accordance with the geographic interest, and categories such politics, entertainment, and sports. Moreover, usually a scene begins with the anchorman introducing the subject that will be presented. They propose a two level method. First level identifies and classifies shots in thirteen pre-defined categories, using a decision tree. The second identifies scenes, by means of Hidden Markov Models, a stochastic method. This method takes advantage of the news domain structure, making it not generic to other domains.

Liu et al. [23] developed a prototype system of content personalization and adaptation for three-screen services based on users profiles. All the acquired content is subjected to content analysis modules as shot and anchorperson detection, and multimodal story segmentation. Then, the content is indexed and can be rendered on many devices. This system has to find the anchorman in order to detect scene boundaries, what makes it dependant from the news domain.

Yeung et al. [41] proposed a graphic representation of a video using scene transition graphics. In this graph each shot is a node and the edges are the transition between scenes. This graph can be divided using a similarity restriction in order to represent scenes. Although the presented technique is based on low visual features, which are domain-independent, and is able to detect events and locales, the authors agree that using semantics could enhance their technique. Our work proposes exactly this, with BoF technique being the key to extract semantics.

Hanjalic and Lagendijk [16] use a similar technique for MPEG videos, identifying what they call logical story units, in movies domain. They defined LSU as being "the series of temporally contiguous shots, which is characterized by overlapping links that connect shots with similar visual content elements." This definition excludes semantically complex segments, since they are characterized by the same subject, independent of visual dissimilarities, but our scene detection technique could be used to improve its results.

Sakarya and Telatar [33] developed a graph partition based method to detect scenes transitions, allowing use of multiple features. In this regard, a unidimensional signal is constructed for each shot similarity characteristic. Subsequently, the signal is filtered, and any unnecessary information is eliminated. Then, K-Means algorithm is used to obtain scene transitions candidates. Finally, a false positive elimination phase is executed to improve precision. Movies and television series were used in the tests. The scene definition considers continuous actions or fixed setting. This definition is more flexible than others from related work considering only visual similarities, but doesn't consider segments semantically related, the main goal of this work.

For Zhai and Shah [42], scene detection can be handled as a point-change problem, therefore a scene transition always occurs when the central concept changes. The Markov Chain Monte Carlo (MCMC) was adapted to detect scene changes in films and home movies. Parameters such scenes number and scene transitions location are changed iteratively, and a set of independent Markov chains is used to avoid erroneous detections that occur when only one chain is used. The author uses "recovery" to compute the precision and recall. In our opinion, this is not the best way, because it does not consider the boundaries discover, but if a detected scene has 50% or more of overlap with a true scene.

Rasheed and Shah [31] proposed a method for coded MPEG-1 videos that initially segments the video in shots. One or more keyframes are extracted from each shot by the activity quantity, and moving content is identified. Backward Shot Coherence (BSC) is applied to identify shots that are candidate to be in the same scene. The last step consists in compare duration and content of each scene, and if they are similar, these scenes are clustered as a unique scene. The domains explored were Hollywood movies and talk shows. The drawbacks of this technique is that it only works with MPEG-1 compressed file, a problem that we don't face in our technique.

In a different line, Kläser et al. [17] proposed a method to action detection in videos using BoF, with person localization techniques. Person and upper body detectors are used to create boxes that limit the actors and their closest neighbouring areas. Only features contained by the limiting boxes are used. The code book is generated with 4000 features, sampled in a random way, what, according to the authors, is a faster way than using K-Means to generate the code book, with similar performance. Three databases where chosen: KHT, UCF and Hollywood, containing respectively normal daily actions, sport actions and common actions in movies. The results were superior to similar works. However, this work differs from our proposal, since it consist in determine previous established actions, not semantically related segments. But it demonstrates the power of BoF to recognize visual semantic present in the video.

Klaser et al. [18] proposed a human centered method to detect and localize human actions in videos. This localization is spacial and temporal (in each frame). Initially, a technique to detect human actor in each frame is applied. Then, these detections are relationed by a general purpose tracker called KLT, originating tracks. For each action, a search is done in these tracks in order to identify the frames that contain this action, and its location in each frame. Although there is an evident semantic relationship among the frames, this method only identifies semantic relationship among similar frames. Also, an action does not necessarily determines a scene. It can be only one part of a scene or shot, such a handshaking or a kiss, for instance.

Yang and Jiang [40] presented a scene classification technique based on BoF. In their work, features were extracted from keyframes and they applied techniques used in text categorization such as stop word removal, term weighting and feature selection. This work relates to our in the sense that BoF is used in videos, but their objective is to classify scenes, different from our that is to segment the video.

Chasanis et al. [8] proposed a method that uses locally weighted Bag of Visual Words to detect scenes and chapters in movies. Although the method presented good results, its definition of scene is related to a set of shots representing a continuous action or that take place in same location, but doesn't handle semantically related segments.

As can be seen, related work focus on finding video segments containing single objects (persons) or events and/or use very restrict scene definitions. This makes difficult to apply those techniques to detect semantically complex segments. In Section 3 we describe how to use BoF in order to capture latent semantics, segmenting videos into scenes - including scenes containing semantically complex segments.

3. SCENE SEGMENTATION USING BAG OF FEATURES

In this paper, we adopt the same scene definition presented in [43]: "A scene or a story is a group of semantically related shots, which are coherent to a certain subject or theme". This definition links scene with the subject, not

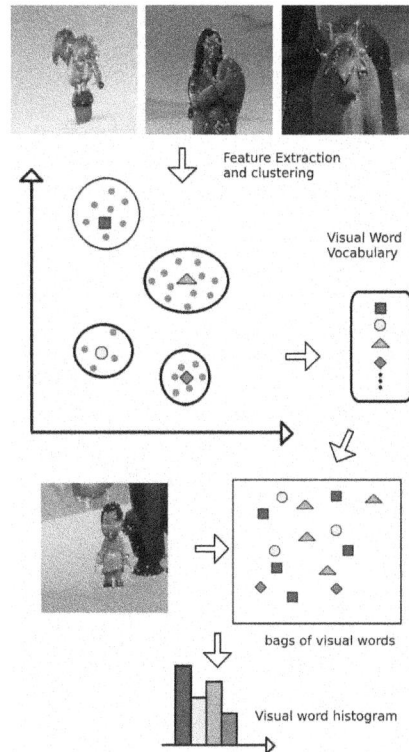

Figure 1: Bag of Features technique (image adapted from [40]).

with the place or the objects presented in each shot, and is independent from the video domain.

With this definition, our technique detect scenes combining two techniques based on BoF, that is is shown in Figure 1. A briefly explanation about BoF is found in Subsection 3.1. In Subsection 3.2, we detail the first technique, which uses visual descriptors in order to detect scenes. Subsection 3.3 presents the second technique, based on audio descriptors. Subsection 3.4 presents our scene segmentation technique, that combines the results from the first two techniques, in a late fusion way.

3.1 Bag of Features

Bag of Features is based on the succesful Bag of Words technique, widely used in document classification and text retrieval areas. The main idea behind Bag of Words is to compute a representation of a text that is the number of each word from a vocabulary that appears in the text. BoF generally depends on a image database, represented by the three images on the top of Figure 1. A visual feature extractor[3], like SIFT (Scale-Invariant Feature Transform) [24], is used to identify interest points in every image (keyframes from shots previously segmented) and to compute a multidimensional vector for each interest point. These vectors are called visual descriptors. The interest points are represented by the yellow points on the images and the descriptors are represented by the red points.

In a multidimensional space, those descriptors tend to be closer to some other vectors, and farther from others. So, closer vectors constitute a cluster. Theses clusters can be

---

[3]An algorithm to detect and describe visual features.

found with a cluster algorithm, like K-Means [25]. For each cluster, a centroid is calculated, and it represents the entire cluster. In the Figure 1 they are represented by the blue, yellow, green and purple polygons. These centroids are called visual words, and the set of visual words is called codebook.

The size K of the codebook is an important factor in the BoF performance. Smaller values reduce the computational resources, as memory and processing power, used to compute the results, but different descriptors may be represented with the same visual word, what reduces the technique discriminative power. On the other hand, big values increase computional resources, and very similar descriptors may be represented by different words. Therefore, it is important to determine a size K that fulfill the requirements in tems of precision and computational resources, which varies with the kind of application. Although there are methods to automatically determine this size [12], the most common approach used in many works is testing a range of K values to find the best results.

With the codebook, a new image can be represented by a histogram with the amount of descriptors that are part of every cluster found. That histogram is obtained finding, for each descriptor of the image, the most closer visual word to it present in the vocabulary, according to a distance function. The histograms computed in that way are a compact image representation and may be used to find (latent) semantically related images, as shown in many works, as [4, 10]. So, images with similar histograms tend to be semantically similar in visual terms.

3.2 Scene Segmentation Technique with Visual Descriptors

As stated before, BoF is a technique that can extract latent semantic from images. It is a desirable property in the context of scene segmentation, since shots that belong to the same scene tend to preserve some visual elements, like actors or objects [19]. Thereby, scene segmentation can be seen as the act of grouping semantic related shots. So, BoF technique could be used to represent every shot in the video, and then, similar shots could be clustered.

However, to apply BoF to all frames from one video shot, in order to create a representation of it, could be computationaly expensive, because a shot can be composed of a large number of frames. One possible solution to this problem is to select a reduced set of frames from each shot, that can properly represent it. In this technique, we employed the keyframe selection technique presented at Subsection 3.2.1. After the selection of representative frames from each shot, we extract SIFT visual descriptors from those frames and apply BoF to compute a histogram to each shot. Then, each histogram is smoothed and the scene cuts are detected. These two steps are detailed in subsection 3.2.2.

3.2.1 Keyframes Detection

The method described here was adapted from [9]. In this method, a 3D HSV normalized histogram is used to represent each frame from one shot. Each histogram has 8 bins for hue, 4 bins for saturation and 4 bins for value. The spectral clustering method [29] organize all the histograms from the shot in k groups. The k number of groups is determined automatically, and can be different accordingly to each shot. For each group identified, the medoid, which is the histogram with maximal average similarity to all the

Figure 2: Key frames from shots of Gone in 60 Seconds scene.

other, is selected, and the frame it represents is considered one of the shot key frames.

This method has a high precision in represent shots [9] and is able to define automatically the number of keyframes per shot, two desirable characteristic to our technique.

3.2.2 Scene Cut Detection

Although BoF histograms can preserve the semantic present in similar shots, there are situations in which consecutive shots are visually different, but are in the same scene. One example is in a phone dialogue scene between two characters. They may be in completely different places, so histograms from its scene shots can be very different, but they appear intercalated. In this case, one visual technique could segment its scene in many shots, although they are semantically related. It would be desirable a way to indicate that neighboring shots have an importance in a determined shot. Near shots have stronger influence than far shots.

This situation can be seen in Figure 2, that presents keyframes from a sequence of shots that are in the same scene. In this scene, the thiefs talk using radios. It is important to notice that many different characters are talking, and they are in different places. We can see that shots 4 and 7 (from left to right and from top to bottom) are visually very different from the other, although they are in same scene.

In text domain, the idea of neighboring elements influencing each element has been investigated using a local smoothing kernel [20]. This kernel determines how much one word will interfere in their neighboring words. It is possible to apply the same idea in video domain [8]. Words of a text, can be translated to shots of a video, and paragraphs to scenes, since each paragraph is a piece of the whole subject of the text, as each scene represents one of the subjects of the video. Shot normalized histograms can be smoothed with the use of a gaussian kernel. Considering a shot t, its smoothed histogram SH is computed from its normalized histogram, in the following equation:

$$SH_t = \sum_{n=1}^{N} H_{t-n}.K_\sigma(t-n), \qquad (1)$$

Where K is a gaussian kernel [13], with zero mean, and standard deviation σ and N is the number of shots. The number

Figure 3: Key frames from shots of A Beautiful Mind scene.

of neighbour shot histograms that will be used to compute the smoothed histogram depends of the σ value, therefore, adjusting this value makes possible to determine that number. Thus, the value determines the level of contextual information preservation. The higher its value, the higher the number of shot histograms used, and consequently, there will be a increased shot grouping in one scene. We have tried a range of integer numbers varying from 4 and 12, and the value 8 presented best results, so we choose to use it in our experiments. To determine the scene cuts, we compute the Euclidean Difference between consecutive histograms and find the local maximum.

3.3 Scene Segmentation Technique with Audio Descriptors

Audio descriptors have been used in many works that address problems like speaker recognition [27], spoken and unspoken audio clips [3] content-based audio and music retrieval [14], video copy detection [22], among other. Three of the more commonly known audio descriptors are MFCC (Mel-Frequency Cepstrum Coefficients) and LPCC (Linear Prediction Cepstral Coefficients) and Chroma [15].

These descriptors' capacity to describe the audio is very useful to many problems resolution, as the ones mentioned. Figure 3 demonstrate one scene cut that could be detected using this audio descriptors capacity. In that figure the first three shots, represented by one of their keyframes, are a scene where John and Alicia talk about John doing home tasks. In the next three shots, Alicia asks John because she thought the garbage men didn't work at night. Although the shots visual are very similar (same place and same actors), from an audio perspective, they are different, since Alicia began to do the dishes, making a caracteristic noise and changing the subject of the conversation.

Many works in audio and video segmentation area make use of these descriptors [36]. Meanwhile, in general, these works need to train a base in order to be able to detect some kind of events, or to determine rules to classify scenes. Furthermore, the precision and recall of such techniques tend to fall if it is used to segment videos or audios very distinct from the ones present in the base.

For this reason, it would be good to use a technique that does not depend on a previous trainning. So, we decided to adapt the technique presented in Subsection 3.2 to use audio descriptors. Some adaptations were needed in order to apply that technique with audio descriptors, because these descriptors have some differences in comparison to visual descriptors, which will be presented in Subsection 3.3.1.

3.3.1 *Audio Descriptor Adjustment*

Visual descriptors can be extracted from each video frame, or from each video key-frame. For a particular video frame, many points of interest are detected, and a respective visual descriptor is computed. So, each frame is represented by a set of visual descriptors. For the audio, it's a little different situation. One audio segment can be sampled such that the number of samples is equal to the number of video frames. But a frame represents one instant from the video, and the sample from the audio represents one period of it.

Despite this difference, one sample could be seen as an audio frame. However, each audio sample generates only one audio descriptor, while each video frame generates many visual descriptors. So, if we apply BoF, each audio sample will be represented by a histogram with only one audio word. This way, it would be very difficult to capture the level of similarity between segments, because or they would be considered equal, if they were represented by the same word, or completely different, if they were represented by different words.

One possible way to overcome this problem is to reduce the sample period, elevating the number of audio descriptors computed between two video frames. In this manner, one audio frame would be represented not only by one audio descriptor, but by a set of descriptors, what is equivalent to the visual descriptors. Details of how these adjustments were employed in our technique are in Subsection 3.3.2.

3.3.2 *Scene Detection Technique Adapted to Audio Descriptors*

We decided to evaluate this technique using largely known MFCCs descriptors. These descriptors have been sucessfully used in tasks like speaker recognition [27]. In order to use these descriptors, we first generated Wav audio files from the selected videos with FFMPEG [4], with sample rate of 44100 Hz. Then, we used MARSYAS [5] to compute audio descriptors using not overlapped windows with 256 samples.

So, 7 audio descriptors were extracted to represent each audio frame. We chose to use all the audio frames from each shot, instead of selecting key audio frames, like in the visual features technique. Doing this, the number of audio descriptors used to represent one shot rises, increasing the performance of the technique to represent each shot.

3.4 Late Fusion Scene Segmentation Technique

Essentially there are two possible ways to fusion features: early fusion and late fusion. In the first manner, the features are combined at an early stage, trying to explore the correlation between them. One difficult that arises is the features synchronization [2]. The second possible way is late fusion, which consists in combine local decisions, based on individual features, in order to produce a final decision [2]. We chose this approach to combine the results from visual and audio features techniques. Our final decision follow some rules: 1) If two detected scene cuts are less than 3 shots away, they are fusioned in only one, which is given by their mean; 2) Else, it cut is held.

With this approach, we ensure that near false positives from visual and audio techniques will be fusioned, what will reduce the total number of false positives. This can lead to

---

[4]https://www.ffmpeg.org/
[5]http://www.marsyasweb.appspot.com/

19

new true positives, since the average of them may be correct. On the other hand, distant true positives will be held, increasing the number of them, and consequently increasing the technique's recall. The drawback is that distant false positives will be kept, what could affect precision.

4. EXPERIMENTS AND RESULTS

All the three techniques were evaluated with three different measures: precision, recall and F-Measure. In order to explain these measures, it is important to define some concepts. First, a ground truth is a database formed by the set of manually identified scene cuts. These cuts are determined by a human observer and are admitted as the real scene cuts. A true positive (T_p) is the cut detected by the technique evaluated that correspond to one of the real cuts in the ground truth. On the other hand, a false positive (F_p) is defined as a cut detected by the technique that doesn't correspond to a real cut. A false negative (F_n) is a real cut that was not identified by the technique.

Precision evaluates the proportion of scene cuts identified by the technique that are real cuts according to ground truth [32]. A higher value in precision indicates that the technique is effective in determine real scene cuts. Precision is given by the following equation [32]:

$$P = \frac{T_p}{T_p + F_p} \qquad (2)$$

Recall assess the proportion of real cuts that are identified by the technique [32]. A higher value demonstrate that the technique covers the majority of real scene cuts. It is given by the following equation [32]:

$$R = \frac{T_p}{T_p + F_n} \qquad (3)$$

F-Measure (F_1) is a harmonic mean of precision and recall [32]. This measure is very interesting, since a technique only present a higher value in F-Measure if it has a higher value in precision, and recall. In other words, one technique must find the majority of real scenes cuts, and the majority of the identified scene cuts must be correct. This is very desirable to scene segmentation techniques. Other characteristic of this measure is that it being a harmonic mean, it avoids that, for example, a technique with low precision, and very high recall present a good result. F-Measure is given by the following equation [32]:

$$F_1 = \frac{2.P.R}{P + R}, \qquad (4)$$

As long we didn't find any groundtruth considering semantically complex segments, we decided to choose a collection of movies with a representative number of semantically complex segments. We chose 3 Hollywood movies: A Beautiful Mind, Gone in 60 Seconds and Ice Age. Those movies belong to different genres, and are evaluated in other scene segmentation works.

An human observer manually identified all shots and scenes in order to form the groundtruth. The lenght of each movie in minutes, as the number of shots and scenes is present in table 1. Tables 2, 3 and 4 present the results of the audio, video and multimodal techniques for, respectively, the movies: A Beautiful Mind, Gone in 60 Seconds and Ice Age. We used vocabularies with 500 words to the audio and video techniques. This value has proven to get the best

Table 1: Movies in groundtruth with lenght and number of shots and scenes

Video	Lenght	Shots	Scenes
A Beautiful Mind	135	1656	95
Gone in 60 Seconds	117	2737	148
Ice Age	81	1384	64

results from the range of 100 to 600 words. The analysis of the results permits us conclude that the visual technique shows a better performance, not only in precision, but also in recall, compared with the audio technique. Therefore is possible to infer that images tend to capture an important part of the video semantic. On the other way, the audio

Table 2: Results of the audio, video and multimodal techniques applied in the film "A Beautiful Mind".

A Beautiful Mind			
	Audio	Video	Multimodal
T_p	48	49	64
F_p	30	30	46
F_n	46	45	30
Precision	61,54	62,25	58,18
Recall	51,64	52,13	68,09
F-Measure	55,81	56,65	62,75

technique can present, in some cases, a similar performance to the visual one, with the benefit of having a considerably low computional cost. In addition, the audio technique is able to identify scene cuts not detected by the visual one. This fact explains better recall results obtained by the multimodal technique, which merges the true positives found by the two techniques. However, the multimodal technique suffers from a reduction in precision compared to the techniques individually, since the false positives from the two techniques are incorporated to the final result.

Table 3: Results of the audio, video and multimodal techniques applied in the film "Gone in 60 Seconds".

Gone in 60 Seconds			
	Audio	Video	Multimodal
T_p	65	94	118
F_p	60	44	84
F_n	82	53	29
Precision	52	68,12	58,42
Recall	44,22	63,95	80,27
F-Measure	47,79	65,96	67,62

Nevertheless, the increase in the recall obtained by the multimodal technique is superior to the precision decrease, so the F-Measure is higher than the individual techniques in all the movies evaluated. Also, the technique was able to handle semantically complex segments as the ones shown in Figures 2 and 3, different of others from related work. This fact proves that combining distinct nature techniques, as the visual and audio techniques, can be beneficial, because the latent semantic extracted by the BoF technique is different in each technique, and they can be succesfull combined, using, for example, late fusion.

Table 4: Results of the audio, video and multimodal techniques applied in the film "Ice Age".

Ice Age			
	Audio	Video	Multimodal
T_p	34	34	49
F_p	34	30	52
F_n	29	29	14
Precision	50	53,13	48,51
Recall	53,97	53,97	77,78
F-Measure	51,91	53,54	59,76

5. CONCLUSIONS

This work presented a multimodal technique to detect scenes in semantically complex segments. Since existent techniques doesn't handle this problem, it is not possible to compare our results with them. Although the results are not high, they are important because they showed that the technique can detect these semantically complex segments.

This objective is achieved with the use of BoF, that captures the latent semantic in each shot, generating a dictionary with representative words. Then, the technique cluster the shots in meaningful scenes, exploring different and complementary medias (audio and visual) existent in the video, combining audio and video descriptors in a flexible way.

Its limitation is that it finds many false positives, what decreases the precision. But future work may focus in apply the proposed technique in other domains, as the evaluation of audio and/or video descriptors. It is also important to investigate other ways to combine the results in order to increase the results, in special the precision, reducing the number of false positives.

6. ACKNOWLEDGMENTS

This work was supported by grants #2011/05238-0 and #2011/00422-7, São Paulo Research Foundation (FAPESP), and by National Council for Scientific and Technological Development (CNPq).

7. REFERENCES

[1] G. Adomavicius and A. Tuzhilin. Toward the next generation of recommender systems: A survey of the state-of-the-art and possible extensions. *IEEE Trans. on Knowl. and Data Eng.*, 17(6):734–749, June 2005.

[2] P. K. Atrey, M. A. Hossain, A. E. Saddik, and M. S. Kankanhalli. Multimodal fusion for multimedia analysis: a survey, 2010.

[3] R. G. Bachu and S. Kopparthi. Separation of voiced and unvoiced using zero crossing rate and energy of the speech signal. 2008.

[4] Y. Cai, W. Tong, L. Yang, and A. G. Hauptmann. Constrained keypoint quantization: towards better bag-of-words model for large-scale multimedia retrieval. In *Proceedings of the 2nd ACM International Conference on Multimedia Retrieval*, ICMR '12, pages 16:1–16:8, New York, NY, USA, 2012. ACM.

[5] C. Cao, S. Chen, W. Zhang, and X. Tang. Automatic motion-guided video stylization and personalization. In *Proceedings of the 19th ACM international conference on Multimedia*, MM '11, pages 1041–1044, New York, NY, USA, 2011. ACM.

[6] L. Chaisorn, T.-S. Chua, and C.-H. Lee. The segmentation of news video into story units. In *Multimedia and Expo, 2002. ICME '02. Proceedings. 2002 IEEE International Conference on*, volume 1, pages 73 – 76 vol.1, 2002.

[7] S.-F. Chang and H. Sundaram. Structural and semantic analysis of video. In *Multimedia and Expo, 2000. ICME 2000. 2000 IEEE International Conference on*, volume 2, pages 687 –690 vol.2, 2000.

[8] V. Chasanis, A. Kalogeratos, and A. Likas. Movie segmentation into scenes and chapters using locally weighted bag of visual words. In *Proceedings of the ACM International Conference on Image and Video Retrieval*, CIVR '09, pages 35:1–35:7, New York, NY, USA, 2009. ACM.

[9] V. Chasanis, A. Likas, and N. Galatsanos. Efficient video shot summarization using an enhanced spectral clustering approach. In *Proceedings of the 18th international conference on Artificial Neural Networks, Part I*, ICANN '08, pages 847–856, Berlin, Heidelberg, 2008. Springer-Verlag.

[10] C.-F. Chen and Y.-C. F. Wang. Exploring self-similarities of bag-of-features for image classification. In *Proceedings of the 19th ACM international conference on Multimedia*, MM '11, pages 1421–1424, New York, NY, USA, 2011. ACM.

[11] A. Chianese, V. Moscato, A. Penta, and A. Picariello. Scene detection using visual and audio attention. In *Proceedings of the 2008 Ambi-Sys workshop on Ambient media delivery and interactive television*, AMDIT '08, pages 4:1–4:7, ICST, Brussels, Belgium, Belgium, 2008. ICST (Institute for Computer Sciences, Social-Informatics and Telecommunications Engineering).

[12] M.-T. Chiang and B. Mirkin. Intelligent Choice of the Number of Clusters in K-Means Clustering: An Experimental Study with Different Cluster Spreads. *Journal of Classification*, 27(1):3–40, 2010.

[13] P. F. Evangelista, M. J. Embrechts, and B. K. Szymanski. Some properties of the gaussian kernel for one class learning. In *Proceedings of the 17th international conference on Artificial neural networks*, ICANN'07, pages 269–278, Berlin, Heidelberg, 2007. Springer-Verlag.

[14] J. T. Foote. Content-based retrieval of music and audio. In *MULTIMEDIA STORAGE AND ARCHIVING SYSTEMS II, PROC. OF SPIE*, pages 138–147, 1997.

[15] T. Giannakopoulos, A. Makris, D. Kosmopoulos, S. Perantonis, and S. Theodoridis. Audio-visual fusion for detecting violent scenes in videos. In S. Konstantopoulos, S. Perantonis, V. Karkaletsis, C. Spyropoulos, and G. Vouros, editors, *Artificial Intelligence: Theories, Models and Applications*, volume 6040 of *Lecture Notes in Computer Science*, pages 91–100. Springer Berlin Heidelberg, 2010.

[16] A. Hanjalic, R. Lagendijk, and J. Biemond. Automated high-level movie segmentation for advanced video-retrieval systems. *Circuits and Systems for Video Technology, IEEE Transactions on*, 9(4):580 –588, jun 1999.

[17] A. Kläser, M. Marszałek, I. Laptev, and C. Schmid. Will person detection help bag-of-features action recognition?, 2010.

[18] A. Kläser, M. Marszałek, C. Schmid, and A. Zisserman. Human focused action localization in video, 2010.

[19] N. Kumar, P. Rai, C. Pulla, and C. V. Jawahar. Video scene segmentation with a semantic similarity. In B. Prasad, P. Lingras, and R. Nevatia, editors, *IICAI*, pages 970–981. IICAI, 2011.

[20] G. Lebanon, Y. Mao, and J. Dillon. The locally weighted bag of words framework for document representation. *J. Mach. Learn. Res.*, 8:2405–2441, Dec. 2007.

[21] C. Liu. A unified user preference based framework for video content personalization. *SIGMultimedia Rec.*, 2(4):4–5, Dec. 2010.

[22] Y. Liu, W.-L. Zhao, C.-W. Ngo, C.-S. Xu, and H.-Q. Lu. Coherent bag-of audio words model for efficient large-scale video copy detection. In *Proceedings of the ACM International Conference on Image and Video Retrieval*, CIVR '10, pages 89–96, New York, NY, USA, 2010. ACM.

[23] Z. Liu, D. C. Gibbon, H. Drucker, and A. Basso. Content personalization and adaptation for three-screen services. In *Proceedings of the 2008 international conference on Content-based image and video retrieval*, CIVR '08, pages 635–644, New York, NY, USA, 2008. ACM.

[24] D. G. Lowe. Distinctive image features from scale-invariant keypoints. *Int. J. Comput. Vision*, 60(2):91–110, Nov. 2004.

[25] J. B. MacQueen. Some methods for classification and analysis of multivariate observations. In L. M. L. Cam and J. Neyman, editors, *Proc. of the fifth Berkeley Symposium on Mathematical Statistics and Probability*, volume 1, pages 281–297. University of California Press, 1967.

[26] J. Magalhães and F. Pereira. Using mpeg standards for multimedia customization. *Sig. Proc.: Image Comm.*, 19(5):437–456, 2004.

[27] M. J. Md. Rashidul Hasan. Speaker identification using mel frequency cepstral coefficients. In *3rd International Conference on Electrical & Computer Engineer*, number 2004, pages 565–568, Dhaka-Bangladesh, 2004. ICECE.

[28] P. Mohanta and S. Saha. Semantic grouping of shots in a video using modified k-means clustering. In *Advances in Pattern Recognition, 2009. ICAPR '09. Seventh International Conference on*, pages 125 –128, feb. 2009.

[29] A. Y. Ng, M. I. Jordan, and Y. Weiss. On spectral clustering: Analysis and an algorithm. In *ADVANCES IN NEURAL INFORMATION PROCESSING SYSTEMS*, pages 849–856. MIT Press, 2001.

[30] W. Park, S. Kang, and Y.-K. Kim. A personalized multimedia contents recommendation using a psychological model. *Comput. Sci. Inf. Syst.*, 9(1):1–21, 2012.

[31] Z. Rasheed and M. Shah. Scene detection in hollywood movies and tv shows. In *Computer Vision and Pattern Recognition, 2003. Proceedings. 2003 IEEE Computer Society Conference on*, volume 2, pages II – 343–8 vol.2, june 2003.

[32] C. J. V. Rijsbergen. *Information Retrieval*. Butterworth-Heinemann, Newton, MA, USA, 2nd edition, 1979.

[33] U. Sakarya and Z. Telatar. Graph partition based scene boundary detection. In *Image and Signal Processing and Analysis, 2007. ISPA 2007. 5th International Symposium on*, pages 544 –549, sept. 2007.

[34] A. F. Smeaton, P. Over, and A. R. Doherty. Video shot boundary detection: Seven years of trecvid activity. *Comput. Vis. Image Underst.*, 114(4):411–418, Apr. 2010.

[35] A. W. M. Smeulders, M. Worring, S. Santini, A. Gupta, and R. Jain. Content-based image retrieval at the end of the early years. *IEEE Trans. Pattern Anal. Mach. Intell.*, 22(12):1349–1380, Dec. 2000.

[36] H. Sundaram and S. F. Chang. Video Scene Segmentation using Video and Audio Features. *Proc. IEEE international Conference on Multimedia and Expo (ICME)*, 2000.

[37] S. M. M. Tahaghoghi, H. E. Williams, J. A. Thom, and T. Volkmer. Video cut detection using frame windows. In *Proceedings of the Twenty-eighth Australasian conference on Computer Science - Volume 38*, ACSC '05, pages 193–199, Darlinghurst, Australia, Australia, 2005. Australian Computer Society, Inc.

[38] B. Tseng, C.-Y. Lin, and J. Smith. Using mpeg-7 and mpeg-21 for personalizing video. *MultiMedia, IEEE*, 11(1):42 – 52, jan.-march 2004.

[39] J. Wang, L. Duan, H. Lu, J. Jin, and C. Xu. A mid-level scene change representation via audiovisual alignment. In *Acoustics, Speech and Signal Processing, 2006. ICASSP 2006 Proceedings. 2006 IEEE International Conference on*, volume 2, page II, may 2006.

[40] J. Yang, Y.-G. Jiang, A. G. Hauptmann, and C.-W. Ngo. Evaluating bag-of-visual-words representations in scene classification. In *Proceedings of the international workshop on Workshop on multimedia information retrieval*, MIR '07, pages 197–206, New York, NY, USA, 2007. ACM.

[41] M. Yeung, B.-L. Yeo, and B. Liu. Segmentation of video by clustering and graph analysis. *Computer Vision and Image Understanding*, 71(1):94 – 109, 1998.

[42] Y. Zhai and M. Shah. A general framework for temporal video scene segmentation. In *Computer Vision, 2005. ICCV 2005. Tenth IEEE International Conference on*, volume 2, pages 1111 –1116 Vol. 2, oct. 2005.

[43] Y. Zhai and M. Shah. Video scene segmentation using markov chain monte carlo. *Multimedia, IEEE Transactions on*, 8(4):686–697, 2006.

Video Scene Segmentation by Improved Visual Shot Coherence

Tiago H. Trojahn
Universidade de São Paulo (USP)
São Carlos - São Paulo - Brazil
ttrojahn@icmc.usp.br

Rudinei Goularte
Universidade de São Paulo (USP)
São Carlos - São Paulo - Brazil
rudinei@icmc.usp.br

ABSTRACT

Nowadays, there a increasing interest in video scene segmentation due huge amount of videos available through services like YouTube. Although there are some techniques which obtain relatively good precision and recall values when segmenting the video in scenes, they are somewhat limited because the high computational cost.

A well know technique to accomplish video scene segmentation is the shot coherence model, which presents lower precision and recall than state of art methods, like machine learning and multimodality, but stands out for being simple. The improvement of the techniques based on shot coherence models could be beneficial to these state of the art segmentation methods.

That way, this paper presents a new technique for scene segmentation using shot coherence and optical flow features. The technique is presented and evaluated through a series of precision, recall and F1 values, obtaining results close or even better of those obtained by related works.

Categories and Subject Descriptors

I.4.6 [**Image Processing and Computer Vision**]: Segmentation

General Terms

Algorithms

Keywords

Multimedia, Video Scene Segmentation, Video Summarization

1. INTRODUCTION

In recent years, there has been an increase in multimedia content authoring, mainly due to the proliferation of low-cost capture and encode devices. Technological advancements enabled people to access content using different types of devices, such as notebooks, mobile phones and tablets, anywhere, anytime. In addition, the interactive nature of the Web influenced the rise of new services in which users explore different navigation paths, consuming much available multimedia information, including video. Examples of these kind of service are Facebook[1] and YouTube[2]. It is also important to note that currently users not only access content but also actively produce them. This context leads to the overload information problem: how to find content of interest in the huge amount of available information [29]?

A research area looking to find solutions to overcome the aforementioned problem is Content Personalization and Adaptation (P&A) [19] by means of services like Content Selection, Recommendation and Summarization [1]. These services aim to help users to select specific content of interest over enormous databases, being well suited for video retrieval tasks.

Video personalization systems require metadata to be extracted in order to represent the content [9]. Thus, it is necessary to split videos in smaller units, reducing the data volume in order to facilitate processing. Such units can be frames, shots or scenes. Frame segmentation is a solved problem. Video shot segmentation has being explored in the last two decades [3]. However, digital video scenes segmentation is still a research area presenting many challenges. It is a more complex process than frame or shot segmentation, mainly due the subjectivity involved when working with semantics [27].

The related literature reports different video scene segmentation techniques. The state of the art ones can be grouped in two approaches: based on machine learning (ML) and based on multimodality (MM). Machine learning based techniques use methods like neural networks or genetic algorithms in order to model the video structure, identify, group and classify segments, making possible to identify scenes transitions. Some of those techniques reach good performance for shot segmentation (F1 measure next to 90%) [26, 4] and for scene segmentation (accuracy next to 80%) [31]. Unfortunately, ML methods require a previous training phase and/or complex fitness functions, making the segmentation process expensive.

Multimodal techniques process more than a single media type in order to perform the segmentation. For instance, techniques using visual and aural media present in a video process both source of information, run two separate segmentations and then make a fusion of the results. The di-

[1] www.facebook.com
[2] www.youtube.com

verse nature of the used media produce different results and, merging them, commonly produce an increase in the precision. However, there is also an increase in the processing costs [21, 8].

An alternative poorly explored in recent years are the visual coherence (VC) based techniques. They use only visual features which can be extracted from a single video stream in order to detect dissimilarities between consecutive shots, allowing scene transition detection. Usually, these techniques present lower precision results than ML or MM based techniques and are limited by the input video format [23, 7]. However, as positive points: they are simpler; they can be used together with those other techniques; they can be tunned to improve precision. This last point is an interesting one. In spite of its potential, as VC was explored first and, very close in time, ML and MM techniques arose with better results, VC was left in background by segmentation research community.

In this paper we present a new video scene segmentation technique based on VC. The proposed technique first extracts visual features from a video (histograms and movement), using histograms coherence in order to calculate possible scenes transitions. With that, a video can be analyzed by it's static features (histograms) and also it's motion dynamics, allowing to capture scene's latent semantics, improving segmentation results.

The results obtained shown that our technique performance is closer to the state of the art ones (higher in some cases) while the technique remains simpler than those based on ML and MM. In addition, our approach is not limited by video input format, like previous VC techniques.

This paper is organized as follows: the **Section 2** presents related work. **Section 3** presents our technique in details and **Section 4** presents our evaluation tests. **Section 5**, finally, presents our conclusions.

2. RELATED WORK

The huge amount of digital video available resulted in a high interest for video segmentation, specially scene detection [31, 34, 7].

This interest resulted in a number of different approaches to the problem, coming from different fields (computer vision, AI, CBVR, and so on). As a side effect, each field or application domain defined "scene" following some particularities. In this way, scene definition is not consensual.

Altheide, for example, define scene as "information units" [2]. That definition, however, is too generic, which results in problems to define scene transitions and to compare it to other techniques.

Graber, in other hand, presents a more restrict definition, considering scene as "visual scenes" [11]. Even so, the definition remains generic and needs fixed thresholds to determine scene transitions.

More recent works define scene as "one or more consecutive shots which are semantically correlated" [12]. That definition is less generic than the previous definitions because uses the well know concept of shots. The semantic correlation has been achieved by shot correlation [23, 7] or by latent semantics obtained through visual dictionaries [5].

In this paper, we use the last scene definition. That way, a scene:

- is composed by a set of one or more consecutive shots.

- transition coincides with a shot transition, this way, a scene cannot change during the same shot.

- contains semantic relationship, which is given by the visual coherence and/or the motions dynamics among shots.

Unlike related work, that definition is practical and takes into account situations where adjacent shots are visually dissimilar, but semantically related.

In terms of segmentation techniques, state of the art scene methods usually can be classified into machine learning, multimodality and, more recently, based on bag of features.

The machine learning techniques uses methods like neural networks and genetic algorithms in order to segment a video, achieving accuracy results up to 80% [31]. However, those techniques [28, 36] require a previously learning process, which is slow and has high computational cost.

The multimodal techniques try to segment a video using multiple data streams to achieve a better overall segmentation. These methods [12, 35, 22, 25], however, are dependent of others streams like audio and subtitles which does not are always present and, even if are present, impose a higher processing cost than processing only a single stream.

The bag of features techniques [18, 5],extracts some features of video segments, usually shots, in order to build a dictionary of "visual words" [30]. Features extracted from input images (key-frames) can then be used to search in the dictionary looking for similar segments, which can be clustered in order to form scenes. These methods achieve good results, above 90% of precision [5]. However, the building of the dictionary and the clustering procedures are known to demand high computational costs.

Another approach which can be used to achieve scene segmentation is the coherence models techniques. Although it is a well known technique, it is simple and has the potential to achieve good results. These techniques tries to merge a group of shots in scenes evaluating similarity, usually through histograms [16, 7]. Rasheed and Shah [23], one of the most impacting work on coherence models, used the shot coherence, calculated through histograms intersection and MPEG-1 motion vectors to estimate the motion dynamics, achieving at most 84% of F-measure [23] in the movies domain.

In this paper, we used the coherence models based on histograms similarity and motion dynamics to perform scene segmentation achieving better results than Rasheed and Shah [23] and close to the state of the art ones, like Chasanis et al. [5], which uses the locally weighted bag of words to achieve scene segmentation.

3. THE TECHNIQUE DESCRIPTION

The **Subsection 3.1** presents a description of the segmenting technique. The first phase of our algorithm is presented at **Subsection 3.2** and the second phase is presented at **Subsection 3.3**.

3.1 Method Description

The technique is divided in two phases: the features extraction and the scenes segmenting. The feature extraction phase is responsible to extract the visual features which is going to be used in the segmentation procedures. The scenes segmentation phase uses the results of the first phase to merge the shots in scenes. That division on phases was developed to be able to replace the first phase or even the scene segmentation for another technique with equivalent functionality. The technique developed is briefly described in the **Figure 1**.

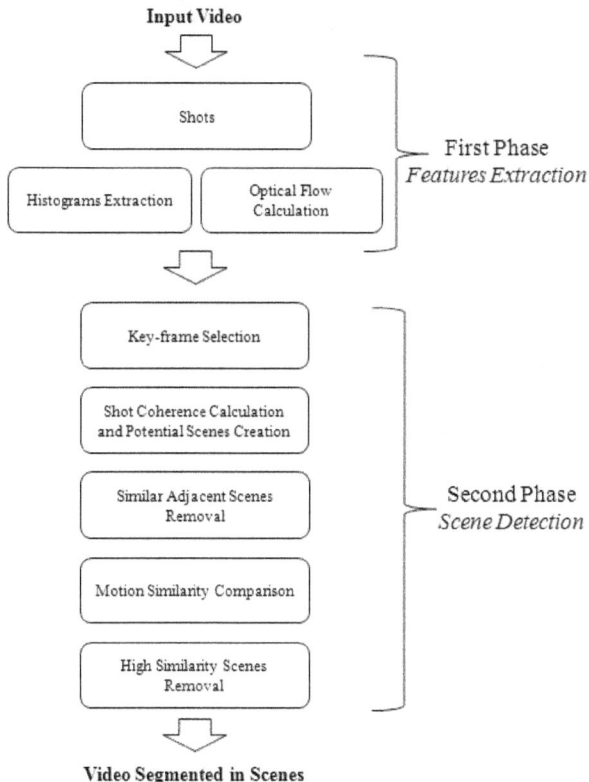

Input Video

Shots

Histograms Extraction | Optical Flow Calculation

First Phase
Features Extraction

Key-frame Selection

Shot Coherence Calculation and Potential Scenes Creation

Similar Adjacent Scenes Removal

Second Phase
Scene Detection

Motion Similarity Comparison

High Similarity Scenes Removal

Video Segmented in Scenes

Figure 1: The video scene segmentation technique divided in two phases.

The first phase of our technique, the features extraction, is presented at **Section 3.2** and the second phase of the technique, the scenes segmentation, is described in **Section 3.3**.

3.2 First phase: Features Extraction

The first phase comprises of the phase where the technique' features are extracted. Those extracted features are the histograms, a color feature, and the optical flow, a motion feature which will be used only in the second phase of the technique.

The histograms are extracted in the HSV color space, commonly used in related work [3, 23] as it presents higher precision values at the same recall when comparing with the RGB color space [14]. The histograms uses 8 bins for H, 4 for S and 4 for V [5, 6] and are normalized.

The optical flow feature is extracted comparing edge pixels of adjacent frames: If a particular pixel shifted from a frame to another, an optical flow vector is created containing the initial and final position of the pixel. More details of the optical flow extracted and it's utilization are described in **Subsection 3.3.4**.

With the features extracted, the shots can be determined using the histograms' absolute differences and the histograms'

intersection of two adjacent frames. These histogram comparison methods was selected because presented better results than other measures, like Manhattan distance [10]. With those values, using sliding windows with locally generated thresholds, the shots can be determined.

3.3 Second phase: Scene Segmentation

The second phase of our technique is the scene segmentation. In this phase, the shots are merged to form a scene which follows the scene definition discussed at **Section 2**. This phase comprises the procedures a) Key-frames selection; b) Shot coherence calculation and potential scenes creation; c) Similar adjacent scenes removal; d) Motion similarity comparison and; d) High-similar scenes removal.

Each procedure is described in the following subsections, being discussed in the processing order. It is to been noted that all values used in the procedures was carefully evaluated through extensive empirical tests.

3.3.1 Key-frames Selection

A shot, following the definition [17], can be seen as a set of consecutive frames. Processing all video frames is not practical, so, a common approach is to select a key-frame, which is going to represent the whole shot from there and on. The literature contains a number of key-frame selection techniques [32, 15, 13, 6], but the problem remains open. Traditionally, the first or the middle frame of the shot is selected as the key-frame. In our technique, we developed a new key-frame method which tries to better represent complex shots with motion and scenario changes.

First, we select the frame which with is most similar with all other frames in the shot. For that, we calculate the similarity using the histogram's intersection, considering two frames "similar" when they present at least 95% of histogram intersection. This frame is automatically selected as one of the key-frames of the shot. If two or more frames present the same similarity value, the first one to appear is selected. It is important to note that every shot has, at least, one key-frame.

After the first key-frame be selected, more key-frames are selected searching for the next frame which is most similar with all other frames of the shot. But, this time, the frame must not have similarity equal or above 95% with any other previously selected key-frame. In addition, the key-frame candidate must be similar with at least 10% of the total frame number of the shot.

With that procedure, is obtained a set of key-frames which are dissimilar among them and every key-frame of the set represent at least 10% of the total shot frame number. These key-frames are them used in the posterior procedures to achieve the scene segmentation.

3.3.2 Shot Coherence Calculation and Potential Scenes Creation

After the key-frames were chosen, our technique calculates the shot coherence of a shot with other N previous shots. In this paper, this coherence value is called as Backward Shot Coherence Weighted (BSCW). The coherence, in this paper, is a color similarity value of a particular shot obtained evaluating some previous shots. This similarity is measured using the histogram intersection of at least two frames and, in case of the BSCW calculation, are used the shots' key-frames selected as described at **Subsection 3.3.1**. The histogram intersection of two adjacent frames, H_1 and H_2, represented as $Inter(H_1, H_2)$, is defined at **Equation 1**.

$$Inter(H_1, H_2) = \sum_i^N min(H_1(i), H_2(i)) \qquad (1)$$

Where i is a color level, N is the total color levels of the histogram, $H_1(i)$ is the i-value of the histogram H_1 and $min(H_1(i), H_2(i))$ is the lowest value between $H_1(i)$ and $H_2(i)$.

The BSCW value calculating method is a improvement over the BSC technique [23], which consist on the progressive increase of the coherence towards the shot being analyzed. The BSC is a shot coherence value obtained comparing the key-frames in a window of N shots. The BSCW, however, is BSC value which was multiplied by a value called "Temporal Memory" (TM). The TM value increase the BSCW value near shots of those being analyzed, because older previous shots do have less impact to the current shot than a newer previous shots.

To obtain the BSCW value of each shot, first is calculated the Shot Coherence (SC) of an shot in a window of previous N shots. The **Equation 2** presents the SC value calculation between shots i and j where i and j contains n and m key-frames, respectively.

$$SC_j^i = \max_{f^x \in K_i, f^y \in K_j} \left(Inter\left(f^x, f^y \right) \right) \qquad (2)$$

Where $Inter\left(f^x, f^y \right)$ is the histogram intersection of the key-frames f^x and f^y of shots K_i and K_j, respectively.

The BSCW value, described in **Equation 3** is calculated taking the maximum SC value in a window of length N, considering the Temporal Memory (TM):

$$BSCW_i = \max_{0 \leq k \leq N-1} \left(SC_i^{i-k} \cdot TM_k \right) \qquad (3)$$

The SC_i^{i-k} results in a value in the range $[0, 1]$ and, so, the BSCW resulting value is greater than or equal to 0. However, all BSCW values above 1.0 are considered as 1.0 and so the BSCW is a numerical value in the range $[0, 1]$, where 0.0 means "no coherence" and 1.0 means "total coherence".

The **Equation 4** describes the Temporal Memory value calculation.

$$TM_x = 1.0 + (0.05 \cdot x) \qquad (4)$$

In other words, the BSCW value presents $TM = 1$ when $x = 0$ (the first of $N - 1$ shots being considered), and the higher TM when $x = N - 1$ (the last of $N - 1$ shots being considered). The number of shots which will be analyzed is an important value which may depends on video domain and other particularities like chronological similarity. In this paper, we followed the number of shots used by the BSC technique, which are 10 shots [23].

The BSCW value has some characteristics, explained below:

- The first shot of the video have BSCW value set to 0.

- The BSCW value increases as similar shots are seen.

- When a new and dissimilar shot is shown, the BSCW value drops.

- The shots "fade" from the memory and are totally "forgotten" over time, a direct analogy with the spectator who forget older shots.

The BSCW value in the beginning of a scene is lower because previous shots are significantly dissimilar to the current shot. Over time, the BSCW value increases due to greater similarity among the shots of the current scene. When the BSCW value drops, the scene probably ended: the shot is flagged as a Potential Scene Boundary (PSB).

In our technique, a PSB is detected when a) the BSCW value drops at least 15% from the previous shot to the current shot and/or; b) the BSCW value drops at least 5% from the previous shot to the current shot and the following BSCW value also drops at least 5%.

At this point, a scene segmentation can be returned to user using the PSBs. However, the precision at this point is low because of a significantly high number of false positives. To improve the technique, was developed a set of procedures to identify incorrect PSBs and erase them. These procedures are described in the following subsections.

3.3.3 Similar Adjacent Scenes Removal

After the initial PSB creation, we try to find those potential scenes, called scene for now on, which does have high similarity between them. For that, we developed three procedures to merge scenes which present high visual similarity.

The first procedure developed removes scenes which are too small to correctly represent a scene with high semantics embedded. In this procedure, we analyze scenes which are formed by only one shot and merge them with adjacent scenes if they are sufficiently similar. If two key-frames are at least 95% similar or all key-frames presents at least 10% of average similarity, the small scene is merged with the scene which presents higher similarity.

The second procedure is inspired by the BSC technique [23], which uses a parameter called T_{color} to evaluate two adjacent scenes and merge them if at least two key-frames presents similarity above that value. In our technique, the minimum value to merge two scenes in this procedure is 60% of histogram' similarity.

The third and last procedure is an improvement over the second procedure, which, in turn, merges more than one scene at the same time. In this procedure, three scenes are analyzed and, if a pair of these scene are considered similar enough, these two scenes are merged. However, if the first and last scene are considered similar, the three scenes are merged into one. In this procedure, we merge all scenes if the first and third scenes present at least 40% of minimum histogram similarity. In the other cases (merging the first and second or the second and third scenes), it is required a minimum similarity of at least 20%.

3.3.4 Motion Similarity Comparison

The Similar Adjacent Scenes Removal procedure merges scenes with high color similarity, adequate to most scenes without high motion, like dialogues. However, some scenes with weak color correlation causes a over-segmentation in the technique, thus, another feature needs to be analyzed.

Our goal is to create a technique which does not have the requirement of video stream input type, like similar works [23, 7]. In other words, every standard input video format must be accepted and correctly processed. To achieve that, we used the optical flow to calculate if adjacent scenes must be merged together, lowering the over-segmentation caused by scenes with weak color correlation.

In this paper we use the Lucas and Kanade algorithm with pyramids, described at [33], obtaining a single number for every frame which depict the number of pixels whose positions has varied from one frame to another. With that number, we first merge consecutive frames which present similar "motion" content, in other words, scenes with similar average optical flow value.

In this sense, in a window of three scenes, we merge them if the average optical flow value varies at most 20%. If the first and third scenes presents that propriety, the three scenes are merged into a single scene. After that, we can search for consecutive scenes which presented a high motion content to merge them. In our method, we use the video frame resolution to determine the threshold used to detect a "high motion" scene. The **Equation 5** describes the Th threshold.

$$Th = \frac{\frac{Video_{width}*Video_{heigth}}{(Block_{size})^2}}{1.75} \qquad (5)$$

That way, if two adjacent potential scenes presents optical flow value over of the Th threshold, both scenes are merged together.

3.3.5 *High Similarity Scenes Removal*

The last method developed to improve the precision of the technique is the High Similarity Scenes Removal. This procedure was developed because the previous procedures may result in adjacent scenes with high key-frames dissimilarity, but which may be similar to the following scene. An example of this error is presented in **Figure 2**.

Figure 2: Example of three consecutive shots' key-frames which may be considered as three separated scenes.

In this method, using a sliding window of size three, if the first and third scenes presents high similarity (95% or mote of maximum similarity between two key-frames and at least 50% of average similarity of the key-frames), the method merge them into a single scene. That is the case of adjacent shots which present low visual similarity but are semantically related, which can be detected by the technique.

In the end, the technique returns the potential scenes which was processed as a scene segmentation file and the algorithms end. The evaluation of the results obtained for scenes segmentation is presented in **Section 4**.

4. TECHNIQUE EVALUATION

In this section, we present a set evaluation tests of the technique when segmenting videos in scenes. The **Subsection 4.1** describes the video database used in our tests. The **Subsection 4.2** presents the metrics precision, recall and F-measure, used in this evaluation. The **Subsection 4.3** presents the results obtained by our technique and, finally,

in **Subsection 4.4**, our results are compared to other video scene segmentation techniques.

4.1 Video Database

To evaluate a video scene segmentation technique, is needed a ground-truth database composed of videos and the desirable scenes of those videos. That way, we selected a set of movies which can be easily obtained in stores, and manually created a ground-truth for each video segment. The details of the video database used in our evaluation are presented in **Table 1**. *Pirates* refers to the movie *Pirates of the Caribbean: The Curse of the Black Pearl*, released in 2003.

Table 1: Details of the video database used in evaluation.

Movie name	# frames	# shots	# scenes
A Beautiful Mind	53148	433	41
Back to the Future	46382	330	25
Gone in 60 Seconds	83095	1200	113
Ice Age	56436	686	72
Pirates	42187	609	37

4.2 Evaluation Metrics

In addition to a ground-truth video database, it is also necessary a common metric which can be used by both techniques. In this sense, we used the precision, recall and F-measure (also know as F1) [20].

The precision measures the proportion of detected scenes which are correct. The recall, in turn, measures the proportion of correct scenes which has detected. Good results are obtained when both, precision and recall, are high (in the 0-100 range, where 100 is the best), so, it is common to express results as a mean value between these two metrics. In this way, is preferable to use harmonic means (like F-measure) instead of arithmetic means. Those metrics are broadly adopted by video segmentation related work, providing a good baseline for comparisons.

Precision, recall and F1, as defined by [24] , are given, respectively, by **Equations 6, 7** and **8**.

$$Precision = \frac{tp}{tp + fp} \qquad (6)$$

$$Recall = \frac{tp}{tp + fn} \qquad (7)$$

$$F1 = 2 \cdot \frac{Precision \cdot Recall}{Precision + Recall} \qquad (8)$$

Where tp stands for "true positive", fp stands for "false positive" and fn stands for "false negative".

4.3 Evaluation Settings

The results of precision, recall and F1 values when segmenting the defined video database and comparing with a ground-truth with 120 frames tolerance are presented in **Table 2**.

To perform the tests, we implemented the technique using the OpenCV[3] library. The computer used in the evaluation tests has a Intel® Core™ i7 980 processor with 16GB of RAM memory. The videos was encoded in the H.264/AVC format at 24fps, in the 720p resolution. However, the compression details are not significant, since the information needed by the technique can be extracted from any input video format, compressed or not. The shots were provided by a ground-truth shot segmentation manually obtained. The results of the evaluation are presented in **Subsection 4.4**.

Table 2: Precision, recall and F1 score of our technique when segmenting the video database in scenes.

Movie name	Precision	Recall	F1
A Beautiful Mind	87.17%	82.92%	85.00%
Back to the Future	90.90%	80.00%	85.10%
Gone in Sixty Seconds	89.52%	83.18%	86.23%
Ice Age	87.50%	87.50%	87.50%
Pirates	80.95%	91.89%	86.07%

4.4 Evaluation Results Analysis

The obtained results shows a F1 score above 85% for all videos used in the evaluation, those results are superior of those obtained in similar works like [23] and [7], which also uses shot coherence towards video scenes segmentation.

The results obtained are close of those reported by state-of-art techniques, like those based in the bag of features. As comparison, we selected two approaches to scene segmentation, one based in the coherence models (BSC [23]) and the other using a bag visual words (BVW [5]). The first was selected because it also uses the shot coherence to achieve the scene segmentation, the second was selected because explores the latent semantics of the videos. In addition, both techniques presents good rates for precision and recall in the movie domain, being examples of state-of-the-art methods (based on visual coherence and latent semantics, respectively).

The precision comparison using the *A Beautiful Mind* and *Gone in Sixty Seconds* movies is presented in **Figure 3**.

The results shows that our technique obtained results above of those reported by BSC, another technique which uses the coherence models. In addition, our technique presented a higher precision than the other two techniques in the *Gone in Sixty Seconds* movie, even the BVW which uses a bag of visual words of histograms.

The recall comparison using both movies is presented in **Figure 4**.

In the recall analysis, our technique presented results near of those reported in BSC and BVW. However, due to the high number of scenes used in our definition (41 and 113 for the movie *A Beautiful Mind* and *Gone in Sixty Seconds*, respectively), the number of false negative influenced in the lower result when comparing with other techniques.

The F1 comparison using the using both movies is presented in **Figure 5**.

---

[3]OpenCV (Open Source Computer Vision) is a library of programming function for application development in Computer Vision area (www.opencv.org)

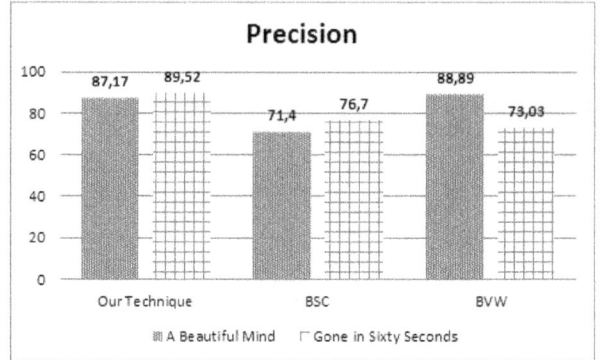

Figure 3: Comparisons between our technique with the BSC and BVW in terms of precision.

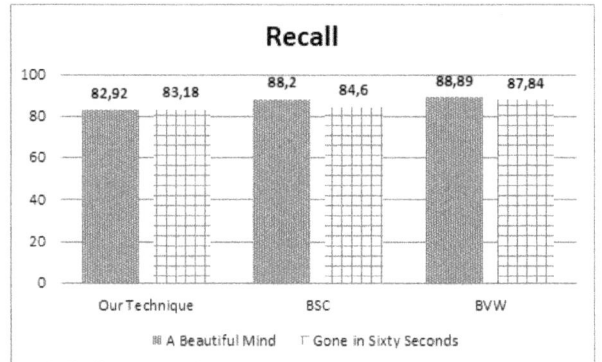

Figure 4: Comparisons between our technique with the BSC and BVW in terms of recall.

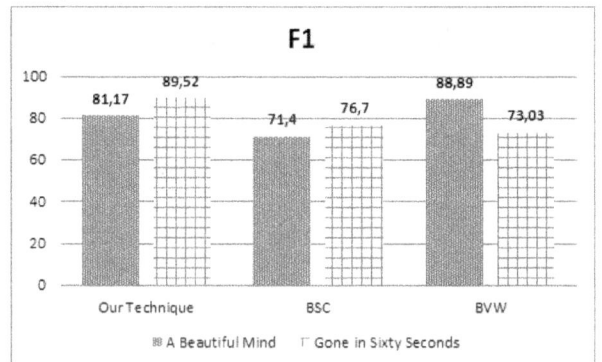

Figure 5: Comparisons between our technique with the BSC and BVW in terms of F1.

Finally, in terms of F1, the results show that our technique obtained better results than those reported by the BSC, a technique which also uses coherence models, and close results of those reported in the BVW, even surpassing the BVW technique in the *Gone in Sixty Seconds* movie.

5. CONCLUSIONS

In this paper, we presented a new video scene segmentation technique which can be performed using only video streams of any standard video format. The technique details was presented along a precision recall and F1 evaluation of a customized video database. The results was compared to two state of art video scene segmentation techniques, a technique based on shot coherence and a technique which represents the video latent semantic through bag of visual words.

The results show that we obtained better results of those reported by similar techniques [7, 23]. In addition, the technique achieved results close of those reported in scene segmentation method based on bag of visual words, even surpassing it in some cases.

The technique developed can also identify scenes which presents low visual similarity, but are semantically related. Those scenes are identified and merged at the end of the second phase of the technique through motion and visual neighbor similarity.

With that, our technique can be used by other techniques, like in multi-modal methods, to improve their visual segmentation reducing the computational cost and improving the precision and recall values obtained.

As future works, we intend to perform evaluation tests in other video domains, like sports and news, comparing its performance with state of the art video scene segmentation techniques in such domains.

6. ACKNOWLEDGMENTS

This work was supported by grants #2011/16796-3 and #2011/00422-7, São Paulo Research Foundation (FAPESP) and by CNPq.

7. REFERENCES

[1] G. Adomavicius and A. Tuzhilin. Toward the next generation of recommender systems: A survey of the state-of-the-art and possible extensions. *IEEE Trans. on Knowl. and Data Eng.*, 17:734–749, June 2005.

[2] D. L. Altheide. *Media power / David L. Altheide*. Sage Publications, Beverly Hills, 1985.

[3] L. Bai, S.-Y. Lao, H.-T. Liu, and J. Bu. Video shot boundary detection using petri-net. In *Machine Learning and Cybernetics, 2008 International Conference on*, volume 5, pages 3047 –3051, july 2008.

[4] X. Cao and P. N. Suganthan. Neural network based temporal video segmentation. *International Journal of Neural Systems*, 12(3):263–269, 2002.

[5] V. Chasanis, A. Kalogeratos, and A. Likas. Movie segmentation into scenes and chapters using locally weighted bag of visual words. In *CIVR '09*, pages 35:1–35:7. ACM, 2009.

[6] V. Chasanis, A. Likas, and N. Galatsanos. Efficient video shot summarization using an enhanced spectral clustering approach. In *Artificial Neural Networks - ICANN 2008*, volume 5163 of *Lecture Notes in Computer Science*, pages 847–856. Springer Berlin Heidelberg, 2008.

[7] H. Chen and C. Li. A practical method for video scene segmentation. In *Computer Science and Information Technology (ICCSIT), 2010 3rd IEEE International Conference on*, volume 9, pages 153–156, july 2010.

[8] D. B. Coimbra and R. Goularte. Digital video scenes identification using audiovisual features. In *Proceedings of the XV Brazilian Symposium on Multimedia and the Web*, WebMedia '09, pages 43:1–43:4. ACM, 2009.

[9] N. Dimitrova, J. Zimmerman, A. Janevski, L. Agnihotri, N. Haas, D. Li, R. Bolle, S. Velipasalar, T. Mcgeeand, and L. Nikolovska. Media augmentation and personalization through multimedia processing and information extraction. In *Personalized Digital Television*, volume 6 of *Human-Computer Interaction Series*, pages 203–233. Springer Netherlands, 2004.

[10] A. Doherty and A. Smeaton. Automatically segmenting lifelog data into events. In *WIAMIS '08*, pages 20–23, 2008.

[11] D. Graber. Seeing Is Remembering: How Visuals Contribute to Learning from Television News. *Journal of Communication*, 40(3):134–155, 1990.

[12] J. Huang, Z. Liu, and Y. Wang. Integration of audio and visual information for content-based video segmentation. In *Image Processing, 1998. ICIP 98. Proceedings. 1998 International Conference on*, pages 526–529 vol.3, 1998.

[13] C. Jang and S. Lee. Object motion based video key-frame extraction. In *ACM SIGGRAPH ASIA 2010 Posters*, SA '10, pages 22:1–22:1. ACM, 2010.

[14] S. Jeong. Histogram-based color image retrieval. Technical report psych221/ee362, Stanford university, Mar. 2001.

[15] J. Jun, S. Lee, Z. He, M. Lee, and E. S. Jang. Adaptive key frame selection for efficient video coding. In *PSIVT'07*, pages 853–866, Berlin, Heidelberg, 2007. Springer-Verlag.

[16] J. Kender and B.-L. Yeo. Video scene segmentation via continuous video coherence. In *Computer Vision and Pattern Recognition, 1998. Proceedings. 1998 IEEE Computer Society Conference on*, pages 367–373, 1998.

[17] I. Koprinska and S. Carrato. Temporal video segmentation: A survey. *Signal Processing: Image Communication*, 16(5):477–500, 2001.

[18] N. Kumar, P. Rai, C. Pulla, and C. V. Jawahar. Video scene segmentation with a semantic similarity. In *Proceedings of the 5th Indian International Conference on Artifcial Intelligence*, IICAI 2011, pages 970–981, 2011.

[19] Y. Lu, N. Sebe, R. Hytnen, and Q. Tian. Personalization in multimedia retrieval: A survey. *Multimedia Tools and Applications*, 51:247–277, 2011. 10.1007/s11042-010-0621-0.

[20] C. D. Manning, P. Raghavan, and H. Schütze. *Introduction to Information Retrieval*. Cambridge University Press, 2008.

[21] M. Manzato, D. Coimbra, and R. Goularte. An enhanced content selection mechanism for personalization of video news programmes. *Multimedia Systems*, 17:19–34, 2011.

[22] G. Poulisse and M. Moens. Unsupervised scene detection in olympic video using multi-modal chains. In *Content-Based Multimedia Indexing (CBMI), 2011 9th International Workshop on*, pages 103–108, june 2011.

[23] Z. Rasheed and M. Shah. Scene detection in hollywood movies and tv shows. In *Computer Vision and Pattern Recognition, 2003. Proceedings. 2003 IEEE Computer Society Conference on*, volume 2, pages II – 343–8 vol.2, june 2003.

[24] C. G. Rijsbergen. *Information Retrieval*. Butterworths, London, 2 edition, 1979.

[25] P. Sidiropoulos, V. Mezaris, I. Kompatsiaris, H. Meinedo, and I. Trancoso. Multi-modal scene segmentation using scene transition graphs. In *MM '09*, pages 665–668. ACM, 2009.

[26] A. F. Smeaton, P. Over, and A. R. Doherty. Video shot boundary detection: Seven years of trecvid activity. *Computer Vision and Image Understanding*, 114(4):411 – 418, 2010. Special issue on Image and Video Retrieval Evaluation.

[27] A. W. M. Smeulders, M. Worring, S. Santini, A. Gupta, and R. Jain. Content-based image retrieval at the end of the early years. *IEEE Trans. Pattern Anal. Mach. Intell.*, 22(12):1349–1380, Dec. 2000.

[28] Y. Song, T. Ogawa, and M. Haseyama. Mcmc-based scene segmentation method using structure of video. In *Communications and Information Technologies (ISCIT), 2010 International Symposium on*, pages 862 –866, oct. 2010.

[29] T. T. Souza and R. Goularte. Video shot representation based on histograms. In *Proceedings of the 28th Annual ACM Symposium on Applied Computing*, SAC '13, pages 961–966. ACM, 2013.

[30] E. Valle and M. Cord. Advanced techniques in cbir: Local descriptors, visual dictionaries and bags of features. In *2009 Tutorials of the XXII Brazilian Symposium on Computer Graphics and Image Processing*, pages 72–78, 2009.

[31] B. Wu, X. Jiang, T. Sun, S. Zhang, X. Chu, C. Shen, and J. Fan. A novel horror scene detection scheme on revised multiple instance learning model. In *Advances in Multimedia Modeling*, volume 6524 of *Lecture Notes in Computer Science*, pages 359–370. Springer Berlin Heidelberg, 2011.

[32] E. A. Yfantis. An algorithm for key-frame determination in digital video. In *Proceedings of the 2001 ACM Symposium on Applied Computing*, pages 312–314. ACM, 2001.

[33] J. yves Bouguet. Pyramidal implementation of the lucas kanade feature tracker. *Intel Corporation, Microprocessor Research Labs*, 2000.

[34] X. Zeng, X. Zhang, W. Hu, and W. Li. Video scene segmentation using time constraint dominant-set clustering. In *Advances in Multimedia Modeling*, volume 5916 of *Lecture Notes in Computer Science*, pages 637–643. Springer Berlin Heidelberg, 2010.

[35] S. Zhang, H. Li, and S. Zhang. A multi-modal video analysis system. In *Communication Software and Networks (ICCSN), 2011 IEEE 3rd International Conference on*, pages 176 –179, may 2011.

[36] Y. Zhu, Z. Ming, and J. Zhang. Video scene classification and segmentation based on support vector machine. In *IEEE International Joint Conference on Neural Networks, 2008. IJCNN 2008*, pages 3571 –3576, june 2008.

An Efficient Access Method for Multimodal Video Retrieval

Ricardo C. Sperandio, Zenilton K.G. Patrocínio Jr., Hugo B. de Paula, Silvio J.F. Guimarães
Departamento de Ciência da Computação
Pontifícia Universidade Católica de Minas Gerais – PUC Minas, Brazil
rcarlini@gmail.com, {zenilton, hugo, sjamil}@pucminas.br

ABSTRACT

Efficient and effective handling of video documents depends on the availability of indexes. Manual indexing is unfeasible for large video collections. Video combines different types of data from different modalities. Using information from multiple modalities may result in a more robust and accurate video retrieval. Therefore, effective indexing for video retrieval requires a multimodal approach in which either the most appropriate modality is selected or the different modalities are used in collaborative fashion. This paper presents a new metric access method – $Slim^2$-tree – which combines information from multiple modalities within a single index structure for video retrieval. Experimental studies on a large real dataset show the video similarity search performance of the proposed technique. Additionally, we present experiments comparing our method against state-of-the-art of multimodal solutions. Comparative test results demonstrate that our technique improves the performance of video similarity queries.

Categories and Subject Descriptors

H.2.4 [**Database Management**]: Systems—*Multimedia databases*; H.3.1 [**Information Storage and Retrieval**]: Content Analysis and Indexing—*Indexing methods*

General Terms

Algorithms, Experimentation, Performance

Keywords

Content-based video retrieval, metric access methods, multimodal video retrieval

1. INTRODUÇÃO

Em face da utilização crescente de sistemas para recuperação de vídeos, surge a necessidade de prover mecanismos para o armazenamento, indexação e recuperação eficientes deste tipo de mídia. Nesses sistemas, a indexação e consulta são feitas, trivialmente, por meio de anotações e/ou metadados cadastrados previamente para cada um dos vídeos da base de dados.

Contudo, segundo [15], esta abordagem é inadequada para grandes bases de dados de vídeos, pois envolve grande esforço humano na geração de anotações/metadados, além do fato de que descrições ambíguas e/ou incompletas podem impactar negativamente no resultado da busca. Sendo assim, a utilização do próprio conteúdo do vídeo para a indexação e recuperação poderia contribuir para melhoria deste cenário, dando origem aos sistemas de recuperação de vídeo baseados em conteúdo (*Content-Based Video Retrieval* – CBVR). A busca por similaridade é a base principal para o funcionamento dos sistemas de recuperação baseados em conteúdo, sendo alvo de vários estudos nas últimas duas décadas [1]. No caso de vídeos digitais, a busca por similaridade tem geralmente focado exclusivamente no uso das informações visuais, negligenciando uma importante fonte de informação suplementar: a trilha acústica do vídeo.

Neste trabalho será apresentado um novo método de acesso métrico, a $Slim^2$-tree, que permite a indexação e recuperação de vídeos por meio da utilização de informações de várias modalidades. Experimentos realizados demonstraram sua eficiência quando comparada com outras soluções multimodais. Além disso, ela também suporta consultas utilizando apenas uma modalidade com custo computacional similar a de uma solução monomodal "especializada".

O restante deste artigo se encontra organizado da seguinte forma. A Seção 2 aborda os principais conceitos e trabalhos relacionados à recuperação de vídeo baseada em conteúdo utilizando várias modalidades. Um novo método de acesso métrico – $Slim^2$-tree – é proposto e descrito em detalhes na Seção 3. A avaliação experimental do método proposto juntamente com a análise dos resultados obtidos é feita na Seção 4. Finalmente, a Seção 5 apresenta as conclusões deste trabalho e propostas de direções futuras de investigação.

2. TRABALHOS RELACIONADOS

O suporte a consultas multimodais – aquelas que envolvem dados de mais de uma natureza, como visual ou acústica – é de grande valia para se lidar com CBVR. Consultas como, por exemplo, "*encontre vídeos de telejornais com a presidenta Dilma Rousseff falando sobre a Copa em 2014*", exigem mais de uma modalidade para serem respondidas adequadamente.

Segundo [2, 18], a combinação de resultados de múltiplas modalidades pode melhorar consistentemente o tempo e a

WebMedia'13, November 5–8, 2013, Salvador, Brazil.
Copyright 2013 ACM 978-1-4503-2559-2/13/11 ...$15.00.
http://dx.doi.org/10.1145/2526188.2526204.

precisão da recuperação quando comparada à utilização isolada de cada modalidade. Entretanto, o uso de várias modalidades envolve a adoção de estratégias de fusão. Em [2], diferentes técnicas de fusão são descritas e analisadas, destacando-se principalmente as técnicas de *early fusion*, em que diversas características extraídas dos dados são combinadas antes de (e/ou durante) seu efetivo processamento; e as técnicas de *late fusion*, em que as características são processadas separadamente e os resultados de seu processamento combinados *a posteriori*. Por exemplo, em [8], apresenta-se o método de *late fusion* para a segmentação multimodal de telejornais cujos resultados são superiores aos obtidos quando utilizadas informações de apenas uma modalidade.

Por sua vez, a necessidade de se armazenar e recuperar informações mais complexas, como imagens, sons, vídeos, entre outros, desencadeou uma série de estudos, uma vez que estes tipos de dados não obedecem a uma "Relação de Ordem Total" – ROT [17]. Técnicas, como *R-tree* e *kd-tree*, entre outras, basearam-se no conceito de espaço vetorial [10] e representam as informações como pontos de forma a agrupá-los e organizá-los no espaço. Contudo, para certos domínios de dados, como CBVR, seria necessário um grande número de dimensões no espaço vetorial, ocasionando um problema conhecido como *"maldição da dimensionalidade"* [5]. Para esse cenário foram desenvolvidos métodos de acesso métricos que suportam consultas por similaridade, em que uma função de distância métrica representa a (dis)similaridade dos dados. Segundo [3], a escolha adequada desta função de distância melhora efetivamente os resultados das consultas por similaridade. Em [19], são descritas diversas estruturas para indexação em espaços métricos. Estas estruturas são baseadas na seguinte abordagem: determinar partições dos objetos usando uma função de distância métrica, sendo um dos elementos escolhido como representante (pivô) deste conjunto. Durante uma consulta, os pivôs são utilizados para diminuir o espaço de busca por meio de um critério de poda obtido pela aplicação da *desigualdade triangular* – que permite obter limites inferiores e/ou superiores para as distâncias entre a consulta e todos os elementos de um conjunto a partir da distância entre a consulta e o pivô do conjunto.

As primeiras estruturas métricas propostas, como a *VP-tree* e a *FQ-tree*, eram estáticas, não dando suporte a inserções nem remoções após sua criação [19]. Já a *M-tree* [7] procurou resolver essa deficiência. Ela é uma árvore balanceada dinâmica, na qual os dados são armazenados nas folhas, de forma análoga à *B⁺-tree*. Os nós internos têm apontadores que direcionam o acesso às folhas. Cada nó possui no máximo m objetos, sendo cada um deles chamado de representante (ou pivô), em torno do qual se estabelece o raio de cobertura do nó. Este paradigma se tornou muito popular, e muitos métodos de acesso estendendo a *M-tree* foram propostos. Em relação ao presente trabalho, duas extensões merecem destaque: a *Slim-tree* [16] e a *M²-tree* [6].

A *Slim-tree* objetiva a minimização das sobreposições entre regiões. Assim como na *M-tree*, o espaço é dividido em regiões (sub-árvores) não disjuntas, cada uma definida por um objeto representativo (O_r) – utilizado como referência para os demais objetos da sub-árvore, e por um raio de cobertura que deve ser grande o suficiente para abranger todos os elementos armazenados na sub-árvore. Isso permite aos algoritmos de busca podar ramos inteiros da árvore, comparando a distância entre o objeto de consulta O_q e O_r, com o raio de consulta $r(O_q)$ e o raio da sub-árvore $r(O_r)$, valendo-

se da desigualdade triangular. A diminuição da sobreposição é obtida pela utilização de uma heurística denominada *Slim-down* que realiza a movimentação de objetos entre as folhas da árvore de forma conveniente para diminuir o raio de cobertura dos nós. A *Slim-tree* também propôs uma heurística de inserção baseada na ocupação mínima (*MinOccup*) e o uso da *Minimum Spanning Tree* – MST durante a divisão de nó e escolha dos representantes.

Já a *M²-tree* foi desenvolvida para dar suporte a buscas "complexas" sobre objetos representados por vários descritores de características. Essa abordagem armazena em uma única estrutura os descritores relativos aos múltiplos espaços métricos, permitindo até a utilização de funções de distância distintas para cada característica. Nesta abordagem cada objeto (o_i) pode ser representado por várias características ($o_i[1], o_i[2], \ldots, o_i[n]$). O nó folha apresenta os valores das características ($o_i[j], \forall j = 1, \ldots, n$) e suas respectivas distâncias para o nó pai ($d_j(o_i[j], p_i[j])$), enquanto o nó interno é estruturado para conter, para cada O_r, o valor associado para cada característica ($p_r[j]$), seus respectivos raios de cobertura ($r_r^c[j]$) e distâncias ($d_j(p_r[j], p^p[j])$) para o objeto representativo associado a ele no nó pai (p^p). A Figura 1 exibe uma representação da estrutura dos nós da *M²-tree* considerando duas características distintas. Além disso, em [6], uma função de *score* monótona não-decrescente é utilizada para se realizar a fusão das distâncias de cada característica em um único valor usado na inserção e na busca.

Outras estruturas para múltiplas características foram propostas na literatura. Na *MOSAIC-tree* [12], múltiplas características são indexadas em camadas. Para cada camada (representando uma característica) é usada uma árvore multidimensional (*R-tree*), com os nós folha da camada superior apontando para a raiz da árvore seguinte na camada inferior. Contudo o uso de *R-trees* limita sua aplicação a descritores com poucas dimensões. A *MFI-tree* [13] se utiliza de um único valor de distância, obtido através da combinação linear das distâncias entre as várias características do objeto e seu respectivo pivô. Contudo determinar os pesos para tal combinação não é trivial. Já a *TEMPOM²-tree* [9] utiliza duas estruturas em paralelo, a primeira é uma *M²-tree*, usada para indexar o vídeo com base em suas características de conteúdo; enquanto que a segunda fornece uma representação da estrutura temporal do vídeo. Por fim, a *M³-tree* [4] suporta buscas por meio da combinação dinâmica (definida no momento da busca) de várias métricas, apesar de utilizar uma única combinação de distâncias durante a construção da estrutura.

3. SLIM²-TREE

A *Slim²-tree*, proposta neste trabalho, assim como a *M²-tree*, suporta a indexação de múltiplas características (de diferentes domínios) utilizando um único índice e uma função de *score* monótona não-decrescente para realização da fusão

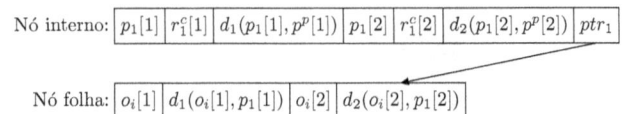

Nó interno: | $p_1[1]$ | $r_1^c[1]$ | $d_1(p_1[1], p^p[1])$ | $p_1[2]$ | $r_1^c[2]$ | $d_2(p_1[2], p^p[2])$ | ptr_1 |

Nó folha: | $o_i[1]$ | $d_1(o_i[1], p_1[1])$ | $o_i[2]$ | $d_2(o_i[2], p_1[2])$ |

Figura 1: Representação dos nós da *M²-tree* considerando duas características distintas.

(*early fusion*). Contudo, suas políticas de gerenciamento de nós são semelhantes às utilizadas pela *Slim-tree*.

As estruturas monomodais, como a *M-tree* e a *Slim-tree* são capazes de indexar objetos de um espaço métrico $\mathcal{M} = (\mathcal{D}, d)$ – onde $\mathcal{D}$ é o domínio de dados e d é uma função métrica de distância utilizada para determinar a (dis)similaridade. Já a M^2-*tree* e a $Slim^2$-*tree* proposta permitem a indexação de objetos representados por uma coleção de espaços métricos $\mathcal{M}^n = \{(\mathcal{D}_i, d_i), \forall i = 1, \ldots, n\}$, sendo cada par $(\mathcal{D}_i, d_i)$ associado a uma modalidade.

Como os nós da $Slim^2$-*tree* delimitam hiper-regiões no espaço métrico, torna-se possível utilizar a desigualdade triangular nas operações de inserção e busca. Por existirem n domínios $\mathcal{D}_i$, cada qual associado a uma modalidade com suas respectivas funções de distância d_i, a região do nó é definida com base nas informações de todas as n funções de distância. Portanto, as regiões associadas aos nós na $Slim^2$-*tree* não são simplesmente esferas como na *Slim-tree*, mas restringem o espaço de forma mais complexa. Sendo assim, cada nó da $Slim^2$-*tree* está associado a uma região definida por múltiplos domínios, onde cada domínio corresponde a um espaço métrico distinto.

Logo, ao serem consideradas n características $F_1, \ldots, F_n$ com suas respectivas métricas $d_1, \ldots, d_n$ e um objeto representativo $O_r = (O_r.F_1, \ldots, O_r.F_n) \in \mathcal{D}_1 \times \ldots \times \mathcal{D}_n$, a região de O_r sobre o espaço métrico multi-domínios $\mathcal{M}^n$ pode ser vista como um ortante positivo de um espaço de n-domínios.

Na estrutura dos nós folha, para cada objeto O_j são armazenados seu identificador $oid(O_j)$, suas n características $F_i \ \forall i = 1, \ldots, n$, bem como as n distâncias $d_i(O_j, P(O_j))$ de O_j para $P(O_j)$, pai de O_j, isto é, o objeto de roteamento O_r presente em um nó N^p de um nível imediatamente superior que faz referência ao nó N no qual O_j está armazenado. A Tabela 1 sumariza a estrutura de cada uma das entradas dos nós folha. Portanto, uma entrada em um nó folha pode ser caracterizada da seguinte forma:

$entry(O_j) = \langle oid(O_j),$

$array\_of \langle O_j.F_i, d_i(O_j, P(O_j)) \ \forall i = 1, \ldots, n \rangle \rangle.$

Já nos nós internos, para cada objeto de roteamento O_r são armazenados: o apontador $ptr(T(O_r))$ que faz referência para o nó raiz da sub-árvore $T(O_r)$ coberta por O_r; o número de entradas ne contidas nas folhas da sub-árvore $T(O_r)$; as n características F_i atribuídas a O_r durante a promoção, juntamente com seus n raios de cobertura $r_i(O_r) > 0$ e as n distâncias $d_i(O_r, P(O_r))$ de O_r para seu pai $P(O_r)$ presente no nível superior da árvore (caso o nó não seja a raiz). A Tabela 2 sumariza a estrutura de cada uma das entradas dos nós internos. Dessa forma, uma entrada em um nó interno pode ser caracterizada da seguinte forma:

$entry(O_r) = \langle ne, ptr(T(O_r)),$

$array\_of \langle O_r.F_i, d_i(O_r, P(O_r)), r_i(O_r) \ \forall i = 1, \ldots, n \rangle \rangle.$

A Figura 2 representa graficamente a relação entre os nós da $Slim^2$-*tree* no caso de $n = 2$ domínios.

Tabela 1: Estrutura da entrada de um nó folha.

Símbolo	Definição
$O_j.F_i$	Valor da característica do objeto O_j no domínio $\mathcal{D}_i$.
$oid(O_j)$	Identificador do objeto O_j.
$d_i(O_j, P(O_j))$	Distância, no domínio $\mathcal{D}_i$, de O_j para seu pai (obj. roteamento O_r).

Tabela 2: Estrutura da entrada de um nó interno.

Símbolo	Definição
$O_r.F_i$	Valor da característica do objeto O_r no domínio $\mathcal{D}_i$.
ne	Número de entradas contidas nas folhas da sub-árvore $T(O_r)$.
$ptr(T(O_r))$	Apontador para a raiz da sub-árvore $T(O_r)$.
$r_i(O_r)$	Raio de cobertura do objeto O_r no domínio $\mathcal{D}_i$.
$d_i(O_j, P(O_r))$	Distância, no domínio $\mathcal{D}_i$, de O_r para seu pai.

Algoritmo 1 Inserção na $Slim^2$-*tree*.

```
 1: procedure INSERT(N, entry(O_n))
 2:     Input: N nó da Slim²-tree; entry(O_n) nova entrada.
 3:     Output: A árvore com o novo elemento entry(O_n).

 4:     if N isROOT and N isEMPTY then
 5:         STORE(N, entry(O_n))                  ▷ Insere entry(O_n).
 6:     else
 7:         if N isLEAF then
 8:             if N isFULL then
 9:                 SPLIT(N, entry(O_n))          ▷ Transbordamento.
10:             else
11:                 STORE(N, entry(O_n))
12:             end if
13:         else
14:             ptr(T(O_r))←CHOSESUBTREE(N, entry(O_n))
15:             INSERT(ptr(T(O_r)), entry(O_n))
16:         end if
17:     end if
18: end procedure
```

3.1 Construção da Slim²-tree

Os algoritmos para a construção da $Slim^2$-*tree* especificam como os objetos são inseridos, bem como os transbordamentos são gerenciados.

Primeiramente, deve-se definir os parâmetros de construção da $Slim^2$-*tree*: o número de modalidades – n; os domínios das n modalidades e suas respectivas distâncias, isto é, $\mathcal{M}^i = (\mathcal{D}_i, d_i), \forall i = 1, \ldots, n$; a função de *score* S_f utilizada e o número máximo m de objetos por nó.

Para a **inserção** de novos objetos, o algoritmo (ver Alg. 1) percorre a $Slim^2$-*tree* recursivamente, tentando localizar o nó "mais adequado" para acomodar o novo objeto O_n. A inserção irá desencadear uma divisão, ao final, caso o nó folha selecionado esteja cheio.

O princípio utilizado para se determinar o nó "mais adequado" é localizar uma sub-árvore $T(O_r)$ para qual não há necessidade de aumento do raio de cobertura do elemento roteador O_r de $T(O_r)$, i.e. $d_i(O_r, O_n) \leq r_i(O_r), \forall i \in 1, \ldots, n$. Caso múltiplas sub-árvores sejam qualificadas por obedecerem essa propriedade, a escolha é feita com base em uma das seguintes heurísticas comuns à *Slim-tree*:

Random: escolhe aleatoriamente o nó entre os qualificados;

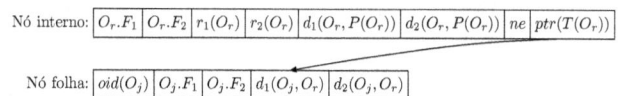

Figura 2: Representação dos nós da $Slim^2$-*tree* para a indexação usando $n = 2$ domínios.

`MinDist`: escolhe, dentre os nós qualificados, o que apresenta a menor *distância multimodal* entre seu centro e o novo objeto;

`MinOccup`: escolhe, dentre os nós qualificados, o que apresenta a menor ocupação.

Em [16], demonstra-se que a política `MinOccup` apresenta os melhores resultados e, portanto, neste trabalho fez-se a opção pela adoção dessa heurística.

A determinação do conjunto de objetos de roteamento qualificados que não necessitam de incremento em seus raios de cobertura é otimizada, por meio da desigualdade triangular. Caso não haja qualquer objeto de roteamento para o qual $d_i(O_r, O_n) \leq r_i(O_r), \forall i \in 1, \ldots, n$, a escolha será pela heurística que seleciona o objeto de roteamento que minimiza o incremento da função de *score* S_f, ou seja,

$$\min\{S_f(d_i(O_r, O_n) - r_i(O_r)), \forall i \in 1, \ldots, n\},$$

o que é possível em virtude da função de *score* ser monótona não-decrescente. A ideia é minimizar o volume médio de cobertura associado a cada objeto de roteamento.

Assim como ocorre em outras árvores métricas dinâmicas, a *Slim²-tree* segue um princípio de construção *bottom-up*. O transbordamento de um nó N é realizado por meio da alocação de um novo nó N' irmão de N (isto é, no mesmo nível), e pela divisão das entradas (objetos) entre os dois nós. Além disso, promove-se para o nó pai N^p cópias de dois objetos O_{r_1} e O_{r_2} que serão utilizados como pivôs das novas regiões formadas pelos nós N e N'. Quando a raiz for dividida, uma nova raiz é criada e a árvore cresce um nível.

A promoção escolhe, de acordo com algum critério, dois objetos de roteamento O_{r_1} e O_{r_2}, para serem inseridos no nó pai N^p. Por sua vez, o particionamento divide as entradas do nó transbordado (conjunto $\mathcal{N}$) em dois subconjuntos disjuntos $\mathcal{N}_1$ e $\mathcal{N}_2$ que são respectivamente armazenados em N e N'. Implementações específicas dos métodos de promoção e de particionamento definem a política de divisão. Independentemente da política específica de divisão, a semântica dos raios de cobertura é preservada. Sendo assim, se um nó folha é dividido os raios de cobertura do objeto promovido O_{r_x} de um subconjunto de entradas $\mathcal{N}_x$ são dados por:

$$r_i(O_{r_x}) = \max\{d_i(O_j, O_{r_x}) \mid \forall O_j \in \mathcal{N}_x\}, \forall i \in 1, \ldots, n$$

ao passo que se o transbordamento ocorrer em um nó interno os raios são definidos por:

$$r_i(O_{r_x}) = \max\{d_i(O_{r_x}, P(O_{r_x})) + r_i(O_{r_x}) \mid \\ \forall O_{r_x} \in \mathcal{N}_x\}, \forall i \in 1, \ldots, n$$

garantindo que $d_i(O_j, O_{r_x}) \leq r_i(O_{r_x}), \forall i \in 1, \ldots, n$ seja válido para quaisquer objetos em $T(O_{r_x})$.

Uma política "ideal" de promoção deveria promover os objetos O_{r_1} e O_{r_2} e redistribuir os elementos restantes em conjuntos $\mathcal{N}_1$ e $\mathcal{N}_2$, associados respectivamente a O_{r_1} e O_{r_2} de forma a se obter sobreposições e volumes mínimos.

A política de divisão da *Slim²-tree* segue a abordagem baseada na MST utilizada na *Slim-tree* [16]. Dada uma coleção $\mathcal{N}$ de entradas do nó N a ser dividido e considerando c a cardinalidade do conjunto $\mathcal{N}$, constrói-se um grafo completo G com c objetos e $c \times (c-1)/2$ arestas, em que o peso de cada aresta é dado pela distância entre os objetos conectados. Como a *Slim²-tree* associa mais de um valor de distância a cada par de entradas, utiliza-se para ponderar

Algoritmo 2 Particionamento e promoção.

1: **procedure** PROMOTEANDPARTITION($\mathcal{N}, O_{r_1}, O_{r_2}, \mathcal{N}_1, \mathcal{N}_2$)
2:     **Input:** $\mathcal{N}$ conj. de entrs do nó acrescido do novo elem.
3:     **Output:** Elems de rot. O_{r_1} e O_{r_2} e seus conjs $\mathcal{N}_1$ e $\mathcal{N}_2$.

4:     $M_V[x][y] \leftarrow S_f(d_i(O_x, O_y) \forall i = 1 : n)$ ▷ Dists entre O_x e O_y
5:     $G \leftarrow$ GRAPH(M_V)   ▷ Grafo das distâncias
6:     $MST \leftarrow$ KRUSKAL(G)   ▷ Obtém MST.
7:     REMOVELONGEST($MST, \mathcal{N}_1, \mathcal{N}_2$)   ▷ Remove aresta.
8:     $O_{r_1} \leftarrow$ PROMOTEHEURISTIC($\mathcal{N}_1, M_V$)   ▷ Promove central.
9:     $O_{r_2} \leftarrow$ PROMOTEHEURISTIC($\mathcal{N}_2, M_V$)
10: **end procedure**

Algoritmo 3 Consulta por abrangência multimodal (RS).

1: **procedure** RS($N, O_q, r(O_q)$)
2:     **Input:** N: Nó da árvore; O_q: obj. de consulta; $r(O_r)$: raio.
3:     **Return:** Conj. dos ids das objs O_j t.q. $S_f(d_i(O_j, O_q), \forall i = 1, \ldots, n) \leq r(O_q)$.

4:     $O_p \leftarrow$ PIVOT(N)   ▷ Pai do nó N.
5:     $ResultSet \leftarrow \emptyset$ ▷ Conjunto resposta.
6:     **if** $N \neg$ISLEAF **then**
7:         **for all** $entry(O_r) \in N$ **do**   ▷ ∀ objetos de roteamento.
        Verifica se o resultado da função de *score* atende os critérios da desigualdade triangular.
8:           **if** $|S_f(d_i(O_p, O_q) - d_i(O_r, O_p) \forall i = 1 : n)| \leq r(O_q) + S_f(r_i(O_r) \forall i = 1 : n)$ **then**
9:             **if** $S_f(d_i(O_r, O_q) \forall i = 1 : n) \leq r((O_q) + S_f(r_i(O_r) \forall i = 1 : n))$ **then**
10:               RS($ptr(T(O_r)), O_q, r(O_q)$)
11:             **end if**
12:           **end if**
13:         **end for**
14:     **else**
15:         **for all** $entry(O_j) \in N$ **do**
16:           **if** $|S_f(d_i(O_p, O_q) - d_i(O_j, O_p) \forall i = 1 : n)| \leq r(O_q)$ **then**
17:             $ResultSet \leftarrow ResultSet \cup \{oid(O_j)\}$
18:           **end if**
19:         **end for**
20:     **end if**
21:     **return** $ResultSet$
22: **end procedure**

a aresta de G entre os objetos O_x e O_y o valor dado por $S_f(d_i(O_x, O_y), \forall i \in 1, \ldots, n)$, isto é, o valor obtido pela função de *score* para as distâncias entre O_x e O_y em todos os domínios.

Gera-se, então, a MST a partir de G e o particionamento é obtido por meio da remoção da maior aresta que forme dois subconjuntos $\mathcal{N}_1$ e $\mathcal{N}_2$ cujas quantidades de elementos sejam equilibradas [16]. Para cada subconjunto, a promoção se dá pela escolha do elemento que apresente a menor soma das distâncias máximas para todos os demais elementos.

O Alg. 2 apresenta as políticas de promoção e particionamento da *Slim²-tree* baseadas na MST.

3.2   Consultas na Slim²-tree

A *Slim²-tree* suporta consultas por abrangência (em que se fixa um raio de busca) e pelos k-vizinhos mais próximos, além de suas respectivas variações baseadas em uma única modalidade ou em múltiplas modalidades.

As consultas por abrangência na *Slim²-tree* podem ocorrer tanto de forma "monomodal" – onde apenas uma das modalidades é considerada – ou multimodal, quando todas as modalidades são analisadas simultaneamente sob a óptica da função de *score* empregada.

Dada uma coleção de objetos indexados $\mathcal{C}$, um objeto de consulta O_q e um raio de consulta $r(O_q)$, a consulta por abrangência $\text{range}_i(O_q, r(O_q), \mathcal{C})$ para uma dada modali-

Tabela 3: Informações sobre a base de vídeos.

Categoria	Classe	Nº Vídeos	Nº Clipes	Duração
Musical	Adele	04	5.878	01:37:59
	RogerWaters	04	18.102	05:01:43
Documentário	Africa	03	2.701	00:45:01
	Oceano	01	2.699	00:44:59
Esporte	F1	05	4.844	01:20:47
	Futebol	16	9.954	02:46:01
Notícias	Telejornal	03	6.671	01:51:12
Cartoon	Simpsons	03	3.865	01:04:27
Variedades	Nigella	03	5.169	01:26:10
	TopGear	03	11.027	03:03:48
Séries de TV	BigBang	03	3.834	01:03:55
	Total	48	74.744	20:45:44

dade i consiste em retornar todos os objetos $O_j \in \mathcal{C}$ tais que $d_i(O_j, O_q) \leq r(O_q), \forall i = 1, \ldots, n$. Por sua vez, uma consulta por abrangência multimodal com uma função de *score* S_f monótona não decrescente em todos os seus argumentos, $\text{range}_{S_f}(O_q, r(O_q), \mathcal{C})$, consiste em localizar todos os objetos $O_j \in \mathcal{C}$ tais que $S_f(d_i(O_j, O_q), \forall i = 1, \ldots, n) \leq r(O_q)$. Outra possibilidade de pesquisa por abrangência na $Slim^2\text{-}tree$ é por meio da especificação do raio para cada modalidade em separado, $\text{range}_r(O_q, r_1(O_q), \ldots, r_n(O_q), \mathcal{C})$. Nesse caso, serão retornados todos os objetos O_j tais que $d_i(O_j, O_q) \leq r_i(O_q), \forall i = 1, \ldots, n$.

O Alg. 3 apresenta o algoritmo RS para a busca por abrangência multimodal $\text{range}_{S_f}(O_q, r(O_q), \mathcal{C})$ com uma função de *score* S_f. Devido a restrições de espaço, os outros algoritmos de busca serão omitidos. Em todos os algoritmos, a desigualdade triangular é utilizada para otimizar o desempenho das operações de consulta ao minimizar tanto o número de cálculos de distância quanto o de acessos a disco.

Já o algoritmo de busca kNN_Search recupera os k vizinhos mais próximos de um objeto de pergunta O_q – supõe-se que pelo menos k objetos são indexados pela $Slim^2\text{-}tree$. Os passos do algoritmo de busca kNN_Search são semelhantes aos do algoritmo RS (ver Alg. 3); entretanto, os critérios de poda são dinâmicos, uma vez que os raios de pesquisa são definidos pela distância entre O_q e O_k – o k-ésimo vizinho mais próximo localizado pela busca em um dado momento. A implementação da busca pelos k vizinhos mais próximos pode ser tanto monomodal quanto multimodal, bastando fazer uso da característica e da distância da modalidade selecionada, no caso monomodal, ou da função de *score* S_f, no caso multimodal.

4. RESULTADOS EXPERIMENTAIS

A metodologia proposta para a avaliação da $Slim^2\text{-}tree$ consiste em indexar uma base composta por clipes de vídeos obtidos em sítios públicos na Internet, utilizando características visuais e acústicas. Inicialmente, os vídeos foram segmentados em clipes de duração fixa (1 s). A Tabela 3 apresenta informações detalhadas sobre a base de clipes de vídeos.

Para cada clipe foi extraído um quadro-chave (o central) sendo este redimensionado para uma resolução de 32×32 *pixels*, e o conteúdo acústico é amostrado em 22,05 kHz, 16 bits, monaural. O descritor global visual *GIST* [14] foi extraído de cada quadro-chave, resultando em um vetor de características com 960 dimensões. Sobre os dados acústicos foram calculados os coeficientes para a representação da fala baseados na percepção auditiva humana, *MFCC* [11]

com janelas de aproximadamente 40 ms e sobreposição de 25%, gerando para cada janela um vetor de características com 13 dimensões. Em seguida, os vetores de cada janela foram concatenados em um único vetor de características de 377 dimensões. Em cada domínio, os dados foram normalizados de forma simples (*min-max normalization*) e, ao final, um total de 149.488 descritores (metade visuais e metade acústicos) foram armazenados na $Slim^2\text{-}tree$. Para ambas as modalidades, utilizou-se a distância euclidiana.

Para a análise de desempenho foram realizadas um total de 3.500 consultas selecionadas de forma aleatória ($\approx 5\%$ do número total de clipes da base). A Tabela 4 exibe de forma detalhada a distribuição dos clipes selecionados para cada classe. Além disso, na construção do *groundtruth* considerou-se como resposta correta (relevante) para uma dada consulta qualquer clipe de vídeo que pertença a mesma classe da consulta.

Como na literatura não foi encontrada nenhuma estrutura especificamente desenvolvida para indexação multimodal de vídeos com base nos conteúdos visual e acústico, os resultados da $Slim^2\text{-}tree$ foram comparados com os obtidos pela $M^2\text{-}tree$ e pela técnica de *late fusion* a partir da fusão dos resultados obtidos mediante a utilização de duas $Slim\text{-}trees$ – uma para cada modalidade. Uma vez que não foi possível o acesso à implementação original, desenvolveu-se uma versão da $M^2\text{-}tree$ baseada nas políticas padrão da $M\text{-}tree$ – em conformidade, com o descrito por seus autores em [6, 19]. A função de *score* utilizada tanto pela $Slim^2\text{-}tree$ como pela $M^2\text{-}tree$ foi $S_f = \max\{d_i, \forall i = 1, \ldots, n\}$.

O gráfico da Figura 3 mostra os valores de precisão média obtidos pela $Slim^2\text{-}tree$, pela $M^2\text{-}tree$ e pela técnica de *late fusion* considerando todas as 3.500 consultas. Nota-se facilmente que os resultados obtidos pela $Slim^2\text{-}tree$ e pela

Tabela 4: Distribuição das consultas realizadas.

Classe	Nº Consultas	% da Classe
Adele	284	4,83%
Africa	89	3,30%
BigBang	183	4,77%
F1	234	4,83%
Futebol	481	4,83%
Jornal	322	4,83%
Nigella	235	4,55%
Oceano	129	4,78%
RogerWaters	876	4,84%
Simpsons	129	3,33%
TopGear	538	4,88%
Total	3.500	100%

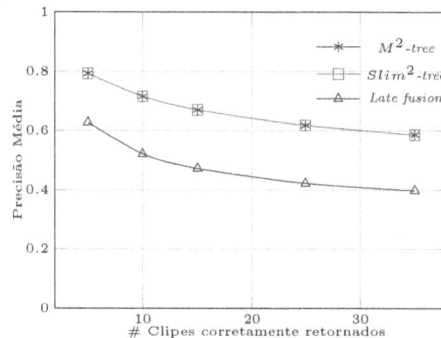

Figura 3: Precisão média (Global).

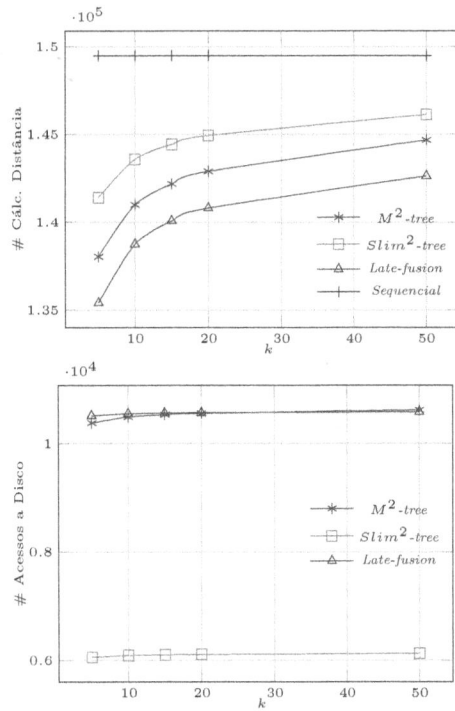

Figura 4: Número médio de acessos a disco e de cálculos de distância para busca k-NN multimodal (Global).

M^2-tree foram equivalentes entre si e muito superiores aos obtidos com a técnica de *late-fusion*. Além disso, os valores de *mean average precision* – MAP obtidos pela $Slim^2$-tree, pela M^2-tree e pela técnica de *late fusion* foram, respectivamente, 21,62%, 21,62% e 21,45% (que são estatisticamente equivalentes com um nível de confiança de 95%).

Contudo, apesar da equivalência dos resultados de MAP entre as três abordagens, elas apresentaram tempos computacionais distintos. A Figura 4 apresenta os números médios de acessos a disco e os números médios de cálculos de distância para buscas pelos k vizinhos mais próximos das 3.500 consultas. A $Slim^2$-tree apresentou reduções significativas em relação ao número médio de acessos a disco quando comparada a M^2-tree e a técnica de *late-fusion* ($\approx$ 40%), respectivamente. Já em relação ao número médio de cálculos de distância, a $Slim^2$-tree e a M^2-tree apresentaram resultados praticamente equivalentes (com uma diferença inferior a 1,3%). O gráfico da Figura 5 apresenta os valores de tempo médio por consulta para $Slim^2$-tree, para M^2-tree e para a técnica de *late fusion*.

A Figura 6 apresenta os números médios de acessos a disco e de cálculos de distância para buscas pelos k vizinhos mais próximos utilizando apenas a modalidade visual, enquanto que a Figura 7 apresenta as mesmas métricas para buscas pelos k vizinhos mais próximos utilizando apenas a modalidade acústica. Em relação ao número de cálculos de distância, tanto a $Slim^2$-tree quanto a modificação da M^2-tree obtiveram resultados próximos daqueles obtidos por uma *Slim-tree* "especializada". Contudo, em relação ao número de acessos a disco, a $Slim^2$-tree foi muito superior a modificação da M^2-tree, obtendo resultados novamente bem próximos daqueles obtidos por uma *Slim-tree* "especializada".

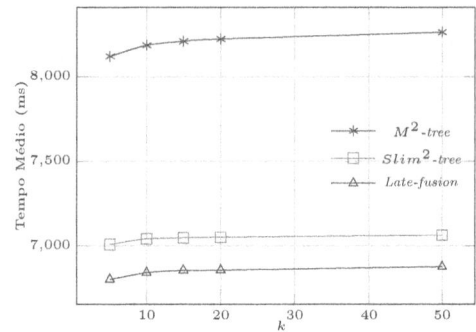

Figura 5: Tempo médio para busca k-NN multimodal (Global).

Na Figura 8 são apresentados os resultados de precisão média para algumas das classes de vídeos (pelo menos uma de cada categoria). Nota-se que os resultados obtidos tanto pela $Slim^2$-tree quanto pela M^2-tree são superiores aos obtidos pela técnica de *late fusion*. Em particular, a melhoria é maior para as categorias e classes em que existe maior correlação entre os conteúdos visuais e acústicos, bem como quando eles apresentam pouca variabilidade ao longo de todo o vídeo o que torna mais fácil o reconhecimento de um clipe de vídeo da mesma classe, como, por exemplo para os clipes das classes *Adele* e *F1*.

Na subseção 3.2, destacou-se que a $Slim^2$-tree também permite a busca por meio de apenas uma das modalidades armazenadas. De modo a se avaliar essa capacidade, os resultados da busca monomodal obtidos pela $Slim^2$-tree

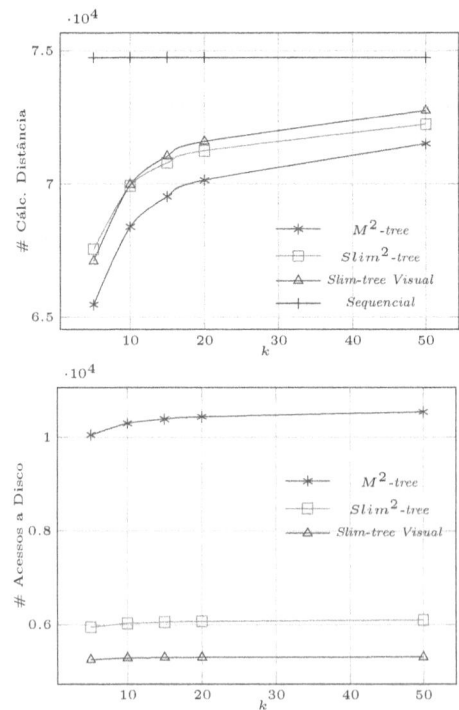

Figura 6: Número médio de acessos a disco e de cálculos de distância para busca k-NN monomodal – modalidade visual (Global).

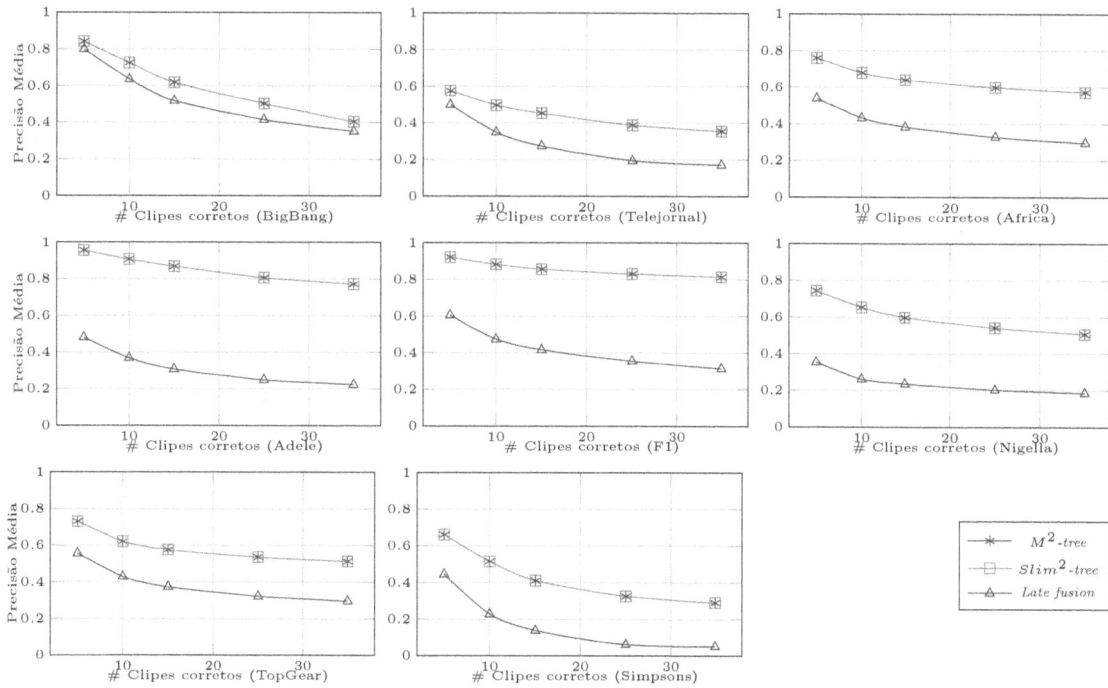

Figura 8: Precisão média por classe.

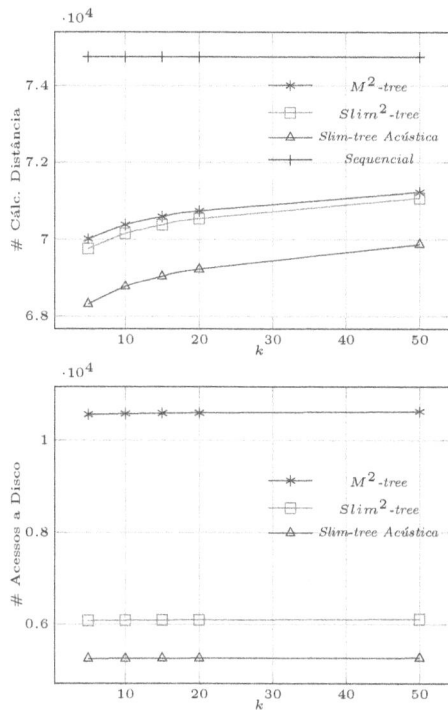

Figura 7: Número médio de acessos a disco e de cálculos de distância para busca k-NN monomodal – modalidade acústica (Global).

foram comparados com aqueles apresentados por uma *Slim-tree* "especializada" para a mesma modalidade e por uma adaptação da M^2-*tree* para essa finalidade (vale destacar que a proposta original da M^2-*tree* não possui essa capacidade). Uma vez que as estruturas são exatas, os resultados de precisão obtidos por essas três abordagens para uma busca monomodal pelos k vizinhos mais próximos das 3.500 consultas foram idênticos (o que já era esperado). Porém, o custo computacional da busca monomodal realizada pela *Slim*²-*tree* fica bem próximo do custo da busca monomodal realizada por uma *Slim-tree* "especializada".

A Figura 9 apresenta os valores de tempo médio por consulta monomodal para *Slim*²-*tree*, para M^2-*tree* e para uma *Slim-tree* "especializada". Apesar das diferenças entre a *Slim*²-*tree* e a M^2-*tree*, ambas apresentam resultados muito próximos para o tempo médio por consulta monomodal. Isto pode estar relacionado à plataforma de alto desempenho para operações de acesso a disco que foi utilizada nos testes. Além disso, os valores de tempo médio para *Slim*²-*tree* e para M^2-*tree* ficaram de 1,5 a 3 vezes maiores que os de uma *Slim-tree* "especializada" dependendo da modalidade, o que está relacionado com a maior quantidade de bytes por objeto ($1,4\times$ para modalidade visual e $3,5\times$ para modalidade acústica) que estas estruturas manipulam quando comparadas a uma *Slim-tree* "especializada".

Por fim, pode-se dizer que a *Slim*²-*tree* apresenta uma grande vantagem em relação as demais abordagens multimodais avaliadas, pois com apenas uma única estrutura (a *Slim*²-*tree*) é possível se realizar tanto buscas multimodais como buscas monomodais, sendo que estas últimas apresentam um custo computacional comparável ao da utilização de uma estrutura "especializada" em uma única modalidade.

5. CONCLUSÕES

Este trabalho apresenta um novo método de acesso métrico – *Slim*²-*tree*, que permite a indexação e recuperação

37

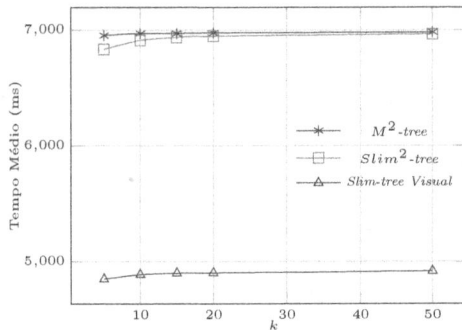

(a) Modalidade visual.

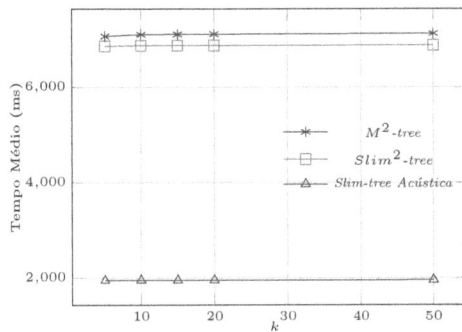

(b) Modalidade acústica.

Figura 9: Tempo médio para busca k-NN monomodal (Global).

eficiente de vídeos através do uso de informações de várias modalidades para a caracterização de seus conteúdos.

Experimentos realizados sobre uma grande base de clipes de vídeo demonstraram a eficácia e a eficiência da abordagem proposta quando comparada com outras soluções para busca multimodal. Além disso, a $Slim^2$-tree também possibilita a realização de consultas utilizando apenas uma das modalidades com custo computacional similar a solução monomodal "especializada".

Entre as possíveis linhas de investigação no futuro, destacam-se: a análise do impacto de diferentes funções de *score*, a avaliação de desempenho frente a um número crescente de modalidades e a avaliação de impacto do uso de múltiplas características de uma mesma modalidade.

6. ACKNOWLEDGMENTS

The authors are grateful to PUC Minas, CNPq, CAPES and FAPEMIG for the financial support of this work.

7. REFERENCES

[1] J. Almeida, E. Valle, R. S. Torres, and N. J. Leite. DAHC-tree: An effective index for approximate search in high-dimensional metric spaces. *JIDM*, 1(3):375–390, 2010.

[2] P. K. Atrey, M. A. Hossain, A. El Saddik, and M. S. Kankanhalli. Multimodal fusion for multimedia analysis: a survey. *Multimedia Systems*, 16(6):345–379, Apr. 2010.

[3] P. H. Bugatti. Análise da influência de funções de distância para o processamento de consultas por similaridade em recuperação de imagens por conteúdo. Master's thesis, Universidade de São Paulo, 2008.

[4] B. Bustos, S. Kreft, and T. Skopal. Adapting metric indexes for searching in multi-metric spaces. *Multimedia Tools Appl.*, 58(3):467–496, June 2012.

[5] E. Chávez, G. Navarro, R. Baeza-Yates, and J. L. Marroquín. Searching in metric spaces. *ACM Comput. Surv.*, 33(3):273–321, Sept. 2001.

[6] P. Ciaccia and M. Patella. The M2-tree: Processing complex multi-feature queries with just one index. In *1st DELOS Workshop: ISSQDL*, 2000.

[7] P. Ciaccia, M. Patella, and P. Zezula. M-tree: An efficient access method for similarity search in metric spaces. In *Proc. 23rd VLDB'97*, pages 426–435, 1997.

[8] D. B. Coimbra and R. Goularte. Segmentação multimodal de cenas em telejornais. In *XVII Webmedia*, pages 229–236, 2011.

[9] M. Döller, F. Stegmaier, S. Jans, and H. Kosch. TempoM2: A multi feature index structure for temporal video search. In *AMM*, volume 7131, pages 323–333. Springer, 2012.

[10] V. Gaede and O. Günther. Multidimensional access methods. *ACM Comput. Surv.*, 30(2):170–231, 1998.

[11] T. Ganchev, N. Fakotakis, and G. Kokkinakis. Comparative evaluation of various MFCC implementations on the speaker verification task. In *Proc. SPECOM*, pages 191–194, 2005.

[12] S.-T. Goh and K.-L. Tan. MOSAIC: A fast multi-feature image retrieval system. *Data & Knowledge Engineering*, 33(3):219 – 239, 2000.

[13] Y. He and J. Yu. MFI-tree: An effective multi-feature index structure for weighted query application. *Comput. Sci. Inf. Syst.*, 7(1):139–152, 2010.

[14] A. Oliva and A. Torralba. Modeling the shape of the scene: A holistic representation of the spatial envelope. *IJCV*, 42(3):145–175, 2001.

[15] J. Shao, H. T. Shen, and X. Zhou. Challenges and Techniques for Effective and Efficient Similarity Search in Large Video Databases. *PLDV*, 1(2):1598–1603, 2008.

[16] C. Traina, A. Traina, B. Seeger, and C. Faloutsos. Slim-trees: High performance metric trees minimizing overlap between nodes. In *7th EDBT*, pages 51–65, 2000.

[17] T. G. Vespa. Operação de carga-rápida (bulk-loading) em métodos de acesso métricos. Master's thesis, Universidade de São Paulo, São Carlos, 2007.

[18] R. Yan and A. G. Hauptmann. A review of text and image retrieval approaches for broadcast news video. *Inf. Retr.*, 10(4-5):445–484, Oct. 2007.

[19] P. Zezula, G. Amato, V. Dohnal, and M. Batko. *Similarity Search: The Metric Space Approach*. Advances in Database Systems. Springer, 2010.

LIG: An Interactive Video System for Tablets

Cleber Matos de Morais
Universidade Federal da Paraíba
João Pessoa, Paraíba, Brasil
cmorais@pq.cnpq.br

Guilherme Pontes Leitão
Universidade Federal da Paraíba
João Pessoa, Paraíba, Brasil
guipon@gmail.com

Amanda Carvalho Diniz
Universidade Federal da Paraíba
João Pessoa, Paraíba, Brasil
mandahcarvalho@gmail.com

Marianna Cruz Teixeira
Universidade Federal da Paraíba
João Pessoa, Paraíba, Brasil
mariannactx@gmail.com

Augusto Ygor Machado
Universidade Federal da Paraíba
João Pessoa, Paraíba, Brasil
ygor.midias@gmail.com

Misaki Tanaka
Universidade Federal de Pelotas
Pelotas, Rio Grande do Sul, Brasil
miisaki@pq.cnpq.br

ABSTRACT

The portable digital devices's market has grown in recent years. The devices' interaction possibilities have become more sophisticated with the multitouch capacitive screens. The touch used to control the narrative flow of those devices poses challenges to communicators, programmers, designers, and developers in general. Products and current concepts cannot meet all the possible and incessant demand that portable interactive media, especially tablets, cause. Thus, the main purpose of this paper is to present the development of the Interactive Language Gestures (LIG) and its playback system designed to be used in digital videos interaction in order to expand videographic hypertext narratives for tablets. The LIG system encompasses the application (AppLIG), the language for creating hypertext videos (XLIG), the audio stream transition language to keep videos uninterrupted (XSLIG), and finally, the production and assembly diagram (DLIG). The LIG system allows to store and display navigation between videos without the need for graphical interfaces.

Categories and Subject Descriptors

H.5.1 [**INFORMATION INTERFACES AND PRESENTATION**]: Multimedia Information Systems – *video*.

General Terms

Design, Languages.

Keywords

Video interativo, *tablet*, multimedia, LIG.

1. INTRODUÇÃO

O mercado de dispositivos portáteis digitais (como celular, *tablet* e *ipod*) tem crescido nos últimos anos ([2], [3] e [4]). Os meios de interação desses dispositivos vêm se sofisticando com as

alternativas multitoques das telas capacitivas. Por exemplo, a 11ª edição do Festival Internacional de Linguagem Eletrônica (FILE 2011) [1] promoveu o FILE Tablet 2011, que selecionou 22 aplicativos para *tablets*, dentre eles, o Antograph que permite desenhar com a ponta dos dedos e o resultado deste desenho é composto por elementos que se movem e criam uma cena. Sobre o resultado da cena vir a ser reconhecida como vídeo, neste caso em particular, constata-se que a cena vai ser criada sem possibilidade de edição; o máximo que se pode fazer é interferir com desenhos, sem criar narrativa, apenas criar uma cena.

Além disso, há um mercado emergente de consumo de mídias baseado nesse suporte pessoal. No entanto, as formas de narrativa ainda não se apropriaram dessas novas peculiaridades, especialmente da aplicação gestual do multitoque para o fluxo de narrativas hipermidiáticas. O modo primordial de interação com esses aplicativos é o toque, atuando como principal condutor de conteúdos, mas também pode funcionar como meio produtor/transformador de cenas audiovisuais. O uso do toque para controle do fluxo narrativo desses dispositivos impõe desafios a comunicadores, programadores, designers e desenvolvedores de modo geral.

Observando esse contexto, este artigo tem como objetivo apresentar o sistema **Linguagem Interativa de Gestos (LIG)** utilizado na interação de vídeos digitais voltados para *tablet*. Através do multitoque na tela capacitiva do *tablet*, o sistema LIG capta os gestos (padronizados para tela multitoque) para produzir respostas dentro do contexto de vídeo interativo nos moldes do LIG.

O artigo está organizado da seguinte forma: na Seção 2, são apresentados trabalhos relacionados sobre gestos e vídeos interativos em *tablets*; o sistema LIG e uma explanação sobre as suas definições e funcionamento, além das propriedades e princípios da aplicação LIG são apresentados na Seção 3; a Seção 4 descreve o protótipo desenvolvido e os principais resultados obtidos até o momento; e por fim, as conclusões e os trabalhos futuros são delineados na Seção 5.

2. TRABALHOS RELACIONADOS

Numa revisão sobre gestos, os estudos apresentados em [5] revelam que a omissão de controles visuais enriquece a experiência do usuário com a interface. O uso dos gestos contextualizados na informação promove uma maior orientação ao conteúdo, minimizando (deixando transparente) a interface. Autores em [6] reconhecem que os gestos podem ser usados em diversas aplicações para controle de ações multimídias. Existem entre os gestos alguns que são reversíveis e que agem de forma bem naturais para o utilizador. A este experimento analisado, a maioria dos participantes usou uma mão, às vezes duas, de acordo com a ação. Além desses, [7] realizou uma análise da metáfora dos gestos de Barman no contexto de troca de arquivos entre dispositivos móveis. Desta forma, as ações realizadas pelos usuários estão de acordo com modos de gestos executado no cotidiano, levando em consideração a relação metafórica da ação mediada pelos dispositivos. Numa aplicação mais próxima, em 2010 foi lançado o projeto *Touching Stories* para Ipad. O projeto criou uma sequência de vídeos que possuem interatividade, usando interfaces e metáforas já estabelecidas com os jogos "*click and play*" das gerações anteriores dos jogos de computador. As alternativas de interação e narrativa são previstas e fechadas na maioria dos vídeos.

Os produtos e conceitos percebidos nos trabalhos relacionados anteriormente não conseguem ainda atender à demanda possível e incessante que as mídias interativas portáteis, especialmente os *tablets*, provocam. As possibilidades narrativas são hipertextualmente complexas, tendendo a um infinito de possibilidades de interação, acesso e uso. Mas até o presente momento, nenhuma aplicação consegue lidar com a complexidade dos vídeos interativos de forma a apoiar a navegação e exploração de forma não linear para a narrativa videográfica. Assim, entende-se que ainda há um espaço para investigação na forma que se usa, produz e conta histórias para os dispositivos com essas características.

3. O SISTEMA LIG

O sistema de Linguagem Interativa Gestual (LIG) foi criado com a ideia de desenvolver um modelo abstrato que permita criações de obras audiovisuais por diferentes produtores. Esta linguagem constitui uma plataforma que possibilita montar conteúdos variados, seguindo os preceitos dessa linguagem, para produzir narrativas hipertextuais de forma simples, deixando o trabalho complexo apenas na parte de produção.

A principal preocupação na criação da LIG é a liberdade da linguagem para ser utilizada, viavelmente, em diversas aplicações. Desta forma, não há nenhum impedimento ao autor/editor no que ele pode fazer e como ele pode fazer. Não é limitada a somente uma aplicação (como educacional ou artística), pode-se aplicar a diversos contextos, com diversas formas e complexidades narrativas, das mais simples às mais complexas, a navegação é construída com o usuário através de intuição narrativa das oportunidades oferecidas pelo autor no contexto do filme.

3.1 Princípios da LIG

O vídeo interativo para *tablets*, segundo a LIG, tem parâmetros que devem ser obedecidos para uma maior fluidez e experiência para o usuário. Assim, as produções que pretendem atender à especificação do LIG devem seguir os princípios enunciados abaixo.

3.1.1 Gestos consistentes

Cada gesto da linguagem possui consistência. Isto quer dizer que ele sempre está disponível para o usuário, a qualquer momento, sobre qualquer objeto na tela e, sempre que o usuário realizar aquele gesto fará uma ação com semântica determinada pelo gesto. Os gestos são: (1) *Pinch out*: o gesto de "extensão", que serve para interagir com algum objeto em cena, sendo essa uma ação que pode ser revertida; (2) *Pinch in*: o gesto de "reversão" do

Pinch Out; (3) Duplo para baixo: o gesto de "escolha" é a interação que não tem reversão (volta) e (4) triplo para direita, com Ver histórico (estes gestos serão melhor explicados na seção 3.2). Esse repertório pode ser aumentado de acordo com o desenvolver da linguagem e durante o processo de validação no produto final.

3.1.2 Liberdade de uso

A linguagem permite, por definição, que o produtor possa criar diversos tipos de produtos a partir dos princípios básicos. O espaço de criação do LIG permite obras de vários gêneros ou formatos de interação, usando os mesmos gestos.

3.1.3 Interface zero

A proposição do sistema LIG é que não exista nenhum elemento adicional visual demarcando a área de interação, para que não haja interferência dos elementos visuais de entrada na composição da imagem e para que possa ser explorado de acordo com intuição do usuário. Antes do vídeo começar, o usuário será informado de todos os gestos que poderão ser feitos da obra e de que o seu uso pode ocorrer a qualquer momento do vídeo. Todas outras ações acontecerão com pontos de interação definidos na produção e montagem do filme, de acordo com a história.

3.1.4 Narração ininterrupta

Durante os vídeos que estiverem no formato do LIG, não deverá haver perguntas ou pausas para a escolha da célula seguinte. As interações só serão possíveis se o usuário tiver a intuição ou o interesse de saber mais, podendo as produções videográficas terem ou não interação. Caso o usuário não interaja, dependendo do roteiro, o vídeo passará para uma célula seguinte que dê continuidade ao fluxo do vídeo.

3.1.5 Produção de histórico

Mesmo que não seja usado em todos os momentos, todo filme com suporte ao LIG cria registro de histórico da navegação e dos saltos narrativos realizados. A principal intenção é realizar, se o autor da obra permitir, navegações sobre o histórico e as escolhas feitas durante a execução do filme. Alguns gêneros, como ficção científica, podem não necessitar desse recurso; mas para filmes educacionais, é possível promover uma compreensão sobre diversos fatores do aluno e interesse no produto, por exemplo.

3.2 Gestos LIG

Seguindo os princípios do sistema, cada gesto só realiza um tipo de ação. No entanto, isso não limita o que pode ser mostrado, mas somente como esse novo texto (no sentido *lato*) se relaciona com o outro. Cada ação possui uma representação gestual, baseada inicialmente nos gestos mais comuns nos *tablets* e que tem a execução semelhante com a ação a ser representada, conforme a Figura 1.

O dicionário inicial do LIG é composto por quatro ações: (1) extensão, (2) retração, (3) escolha e (4) ver histórico. A ação de (1) extensão tem o objetivo de aproximar um conteúdo narrativo adicional ao conteúdo principal sem necessariamente mudar o fluxo narrativo. Assim, o usuário pode entrar num conteúdo de extensão e, ao término, voltar ao exato ponto que havia interrompido na célula que o chamou. A (2) retração é uma ação de interrupção da célula estendida, voltado antecipadamente à célula anterior. Dentro da extensão também é permitido adicionar um filme além do que chamou como alvo da condição de finalização da extensão, inclusive com estruturas condicionais complexas. Desta forma, a extensão pode verter para outros caminhos narrativos, que podem ser desfeitos a cada momento, por uma retração. Outro gesto importante é a (3) escolha. Diferentemente da extensão, a escolha não permite uma reversão da ação de troca de célula. A razão disso é para assegurar uma mudança de trama que gerará implicações consistentes durante todo o filme. Deste modo, o usuário se torna um agente ativo para a construção e reconstrução da trama no filme em tempo de exibição. Por fim, existe o gesto de (4) ver histórico que permite mostrar o caminho percorrido pelo usuário dentre as suas opções hipertextuais. O propósito do histórico é mostrar ao usuário quanto ele explorou, quanto falta a ser explorado e quais caminhos que ele poderia explorar ainda. Nem todas as opções serão ativas durante todos os filmes, cabe ao direto/editor/autor especificar quais opções de histórico são permitidas para o filme. Por exemplo, num vídeo educativo, faria muito sentido mostrar ao aluno onde ele está e o que há de vir, mas numa trama de suspense, a opção do histórico estaria desabilitada.

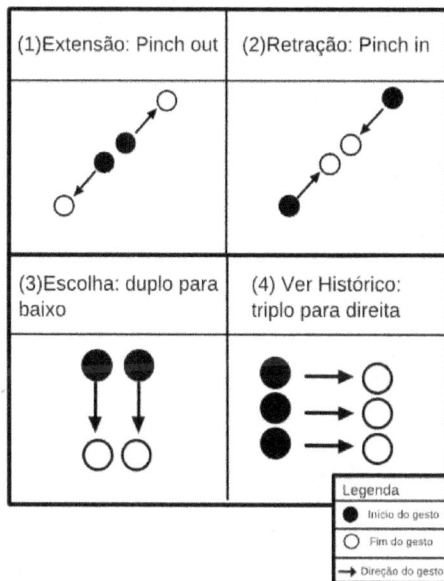

Figura 1. Gestos do sistema LIG

4. RESULTADOS PRELIMINARES

A partir da descrição do sistema LIG apresentado anteriormente, implementou-se um protótipo, com o objetivo principal de analisar a viabilidade e a interação do sistema proposto. Para tanto, foi necessário desenvolver diversos módulos, como a linguagem para criação de vídeos hipertextuais (XLIG, descrita na Seção), uma aplicação para reproduzir vídeos LIG em tablets, uma marcação de áudio para manter a não-interrupção do vídeo LIG (XSLIG), e por fim, o diagrama (DLIG).

4.1 A linguagem XLIG

A linguagem aberta e extensível, denominada como XLIG (XML para LIG), foi desenvolvida baseada em XML para dar suporte à criação de vídeos hipertextuais. A estrutura da linguagem permite que o produtor do vídeo defina, através de tags, todas as propriedades de cada vídeo, bem como as interações que podem ser utilizadas pelo usuário. O arquivo XLIG será carregado previamente à execução do vídeo, servindo para que o aplicativo prepare anteriormente todos os arquivos de vídeo a serem

carregados e pré-carregados - os quais são definidos como células - e que gestos devem ser feitos para se chegar a cada célula.

A Figura 2 mostra um exemplo da linguagem XLIG, onde as linhas de 4 a 13 representam as propriedades do vídeo e de 15 a 27, a definição do gesto de escolha dessa célula. Para demais gestos, utliza-se outra *tag*, por exemplo para o gesto de extensão, usa-se a *tag <extension>*.

4.2 A marcação de transição de som XSLIG

Na montagem dos vídeos, percebeu-se que, para manter a não-interrupção das cenas, a transição de áudio é mais impactante que a transição da imagem. Dentro da primeira especificação da LIG, as informações de áudio eram presumidas no próprio vídeo, mas durante a interação, os vídeos tinham sua trilha interrompida pelo usuário num momento qualquer, causando a sensação de quebra da continuidade. Foi constatado que o preenchimento do áudio auxilia na composição do efeito de transição das imagens. Para atender a essa necessidade, foi especificado uma linguagem (denominada XSLIG), também baseada em XML, que representa efeitos e ritmos de forma autônoma para as cenas e suas transições.

O XSLIG é um primeiro esboço para composição dinâmica entre áudio e vídeo de forma a permitir transições baseadas em hipertexto para engenheiros e *designers* de som adaptarem os elementos sonoros à dinâmica de mudança e fragmentação advinda dessa narrativa. A principal atuação do XSLIG é na trilha sonora e efeitos, deixando a voz na trilha principal dos arquivos de vídeo.

```
1  <?xml version="1.0" encoding="UTF-8"?>
2  <lig>
3  <video>
4    <properties>
5    <id>1</id>
6      <file>inicio.mpg</file>
7      <duration>00:08:59</duration>
8      <codec>flv</codec>
9      <resolution>
10       <x>1920</x>
11       <y>1080</y>
12     </resolution>
13   </properties>
14   <target>2</target>
15   <choice ord="1">
16     <time>
17       <begin>00:03:38</begin>
18       <end>00:04:59</end>
19     </time>
20     <area>
21       <xa>0</xa>
22       <ya>0</ya>
23       <xb>200</xb>
24       <yb>300</yb>
25     </area>
26     <target>3</target>
27   </choice>
28 </video>
```

Figura 2. Exemplo da linguagem XLIG

4.3 A aplicação reprodutora de vídeos LIG (AppLIG)

O principal componente de funcionamento do LIG é a aplicação reprodutora de vídeos LIG, denominada AppLIG. O reprodutor deve ser capaz de ler o arquivo XLIG, o arquivo XSLIG e, reproduzir vídeos LIG, de acordo com a interação do usuário. A principal preocupação do reprodutor é não causar sensação de troca de vídeos após a interação. A aplicação também deve processar as metainformações do vídeo, no arquivo XLIG e criar relacionamento entre as partes, inclusive com encadeamento e condicionamento complexos entre si.

A AppLIG foi desenvolvida em Adobe Air, uma vez que a mesma proporciona desenvolvimento multimídia rápido para protótipos e é facilmente portável para as principais plataformas de tablets, como Android e iOS.

4.4 O diagrama de produção DLIG

Durante a produção dos primeiros vídeos LIG, percebeu-se a necessidade de reorganizar também o processo de produção. As representações normais de produção de filmes (roteiro e *storyboard*) não contemplam toda a dinâmica da linguagem. Deste modo, foi necessário criar uma representação que comportasse a complexidade dos vídeos interativos. Para tal, foi criada uma notação de diagrama, chamada de DLIG, para atender essa demanda. O objetivo principal é unir, numa representação gráfica, dados de fluxos narrativos, relações temporais e espaciais para interação no âmbito da pré-produção videográfica. A complexidade de produção de um vídeo interativo hipertextual pode ser atenuada se o DLIG for utilizado durante o processo de concepção.

4.5 Discussão

A partir deste primeiro protótipo, percebeu-se a importância de concentrar esforços em duas áreas de desenvolvimento do LIG: a produção de vídeo interativo com suporte para *tablet* e o desenvolvimento de uma nova narrativa hipertextual para vídeo. Um dos primeiros resultados que a LIG pretende resolver é o hiato entre os produtores de vídeo e os editores de conteúdos multimídia, criando um espaço autônomo para os produtores de vídeo experimentarem novas criações sem ser limitado a um ambiente de produção multimídia fechado e difícil de ser atualizado e/ou reconfigurado. A narrativa hipertextual, que teve seu auge no final da década de 80 e esmaeceu no final dos 90, pode ser retomada com um novo suporte e com uma maior preparação cognitiva dos usuários, familiarizados agora com a web e sua estrutura narrativa. O grande desafio dessa produção é conseguir viabilizar a produção de um filme interativo, considerando a grande quantidade que possibilidades de escolhas que o usuário pode escolher.

O sistema LIG tem possibilidade infinita de montagem, mas os produtores não possuem recursos infinitos (tempo e dinheiro) para produção. A proposta dos diagramas LIG é uma forma de contornar essas dificuldades, mas a composição depende também da forma que a história será contada pelos roteiristas e a familiaridade da produção com a linguagem.

5. CONCLUSÕES E TRABALHOS FUTUROS

Este artigo apresentou uma proposta de linguagem para montagem e exibição de vídeos, denominada LIG, com a possibilidade de criação de narrativas hipertextuais, onde o usuário pode navegar através de intuição narrativa das oportunidades oferecidas pelo produtor do vídeo. Como resultados preliminares, construiu-se um protótipo de um sistema LIG, contemplando as linguagens XLIG e XSLIG, bem como a AppLIG, que possibilita a reprodução de vídeos LIG em tablets. Esses resultados se propõem a atender, segundo os princípios estabelecidos pela LIG, à oportunidade advinda do novo mercado de tablets e o consumo de conteúdo videográfico, que pode ser interativo.

Como trabalhos futuros, é fundamental realizar uma avaliação do desempenho do sistema e da construção da narrativa com a LIG. Num segundo momento, pretende-se integrar as marcações de ação com diversas captações automáticas de movimento existentes, facilitando a detecção de áreas de ação e a geração do arquivo XLIG. Também será prospectada a criação de um editor visual de XLIG, no qual o diretor pode marcar e criar as *tags* LIG diretamente sobre o vídeo, em tempo real. Por fim, uma possível integração da entrega de filmes e suas partes de forma distribuídas em rede, ao invés de um pacote já completo com todas as partes.

A AGRADECIMENTO

Este trabalho foi desenvolvido com recursos do Edital 007-2011 MCTI/CNPq/MEC/CAPES.

REFERÊNCIAS

[1] FILE 2001. Disponível em http://www.file.org.br. Acesso em julho de 2013.

[2] Floro, P. Crescimento dos tablets no Brasil foi de 164%. Venda de PCs segue caindo. Disponível em http://blogs.ne10.uol.com.br/mundobit/2013/06/13/crescimento-dos-tablets-no-brasil-foi-de-164-venda-de-pcs-segue-caindo/. Acesso em julho de 2013.

[3] Campi, M. Venda de tablets crescerá 68% e de PCs cairá 10%, diz Gatner. Disponível em http://info.abril.com.br/noticias/mercado/2013/06/venda-de-tablets-crescera-68-e-de-pcs-caira-10-diz-gartner.shtml. Acesso em julho 2013.

[4] Info Exame. Tablets passarão desktops no Brasil em 2013. Disponível em http://info.abril.com.br/noticias/extras/tablets-passarao-desktops-no-brasil-em-2013-10072013-0.shl. Acesso em julho de 2013.

[5] Schulze, F,. Woerndl, W. 2011. Using touch gestures to adjust context parameters in mobile recommender and search applications. In *IEEE International Conference on Collaboration Technologies and Systems* (CTS). 389-396.

[6] Varga, E., Verlinden, J., Klaas, O., Langenhoff, L., Steen, D. and Verhagen, J. 2008. A Study on Intuitive Gestures to Control Multimedia Applications. In *Proceedings of International Conference Interfaces and Human Computer Interaction*, 25-27.

[7] Yoo, J. W., Choi, W., Park, K. W., Park, K. H. 2009. An intuitive data transfer technique using bartender's gestures. In *Proceedings of the seventeen ACM international conference on Multimedia*. 991-992.

Towards a Distributed Architecture for Context-Aware Mobile Applications in UbiComp

João Lopes, Rodrigo Souza, Cláudio Geyer
Federal University of Rio Grande do Sul - Porto Alegre-RS, Brazil
{jlblopes,rssouza,geyer}@inf.ufrgs.br

Cristiano Costa, Jorge Barbosa
University of Vale do Rio dos Sinos - São Leopoldo-RS, Brazil
{cac,jbarbosa}@unisinos.br

Márcia Gusmão, Patricia Davet, Alexandre Souza, Ana Pernas, Adenauer Yamin
Federal University of Pelotas - Pelotas-RS, Brazil
{mzgusmao,pdavet,arrsouza,marilza,adenauer}@inf.ufpel.edu.br

ABSTRACT

The applications in Ubiquitous Computing (UbiComp) environments must be aware of their contexts of interest and adapt to changes in them. Thus, a major research challenge in the area of UbiComp is related to context awareness. Considering the high distribution, heterogeneity, dynamism, and mobility of ubiquitous environments, this paper presents an architectural model for context awareness, called EXEHDA-UC (Execution Environment for Highly Distributed Applications - Ubiquitous Context awareness). The proposal includes elements to support contextual data acquisition, actuation on the environment, and processing of contextual information. We consider that the main contribution of this work is an architecture that supports the managing of the acquisition, storage, and processing of context data, in a distributed way, independently of the application, in an autonomic and rule-based perspective. To assess the functionalities of the EXEHDA-UC, we present a case study, highlighting the prototypes developed, technologies employed, and tests realized.

Categories and Subject Descriptors

C.2.4 [**Computer Systems Organization**]: Computer-Communication Networks—*Distributed Systems*

Keywords

Ubiquitous Computing, Context Awareness, Distributed Architecture

1. INTRODUCTION

The Mark Weiser's classic article [11], considered the

precursor of Ubiquitous Computing, describes the basic assumptions of this computational paradigm: ubiquity and transparency. These assumptions generate several challenges related to user access to computing environment, anywhere, any time, with any device, non-intrusively, keeping user focus on their activities. In this perspective, the computational system must interact in autonomic way, no matter where the user is, constituting a highly distributed, heterogeneous, dynamic and mobile environment [3].

In this sense, one of the main research problems in the area of UbiComp is context awareness, which refers to the ability of applications to realize changes in the characteristics of the ubiquitous environment, which are of its interest, and respond to these changes through an adaptation process [10]. This class of computational systems, reactive to the context, opens perspectives for the development of richer, elaborate and complex applications, exploring the dynamism of modern computational infrastructures and user mobility [8].

The literature review indicates several challenges in the support of context awareness for ubiquitous applications, including: (i) context acquisition from distributed and heterogeneous sources, (ii) context processing and actuation on the environment, and (iii) context dissemination to interested users in a distributed and timely way [2].

The main objective of EXEHDA-UC[1] is to contribute to the Context Recognition and Adaptation Subsystem of EXEHDA middleware [9]. The proposal aims at designing a software architecture that offers to applications support for acquisition, storage, and processing of contextual information, as well as the procedures for actuation on the environment, in a distributed way, independently of applications, in a rule-based autonomic perspective, and with support to mobility.

The paper is organized as follows. Section 2 describes the design of the proposal. Section 3 presents a case study. Section 4 discusses related work. Finally, section 5 presents the concluding remarks.

2. DESIGN OF THE PROPOSAL

The applications of ubiquitous environment managed by

[1]Partially supported by FAPERGS CNPq PRONEX Green-Grid project

EXEHDA should be distributed, mobile, context-aware, and available from anywhere, any time. The EXEHDA includes in its structure a core and services loaded on demand. The main services provided are organized into subsystems related to ubiquitous access, communication, distributed execution, context recognition and adaptation.

In the proposed design we employed a rule-based and event-driven approach, both among modules of the software architecture, as well as with the applications. In this way, we enable the possibility of associating processing rules to the contexts of interest, which can be triggered automatically whenever an event occurs. The event, in our view, relates to changes in the context status.

The EXEHDA-UC encompasses two types of servers: Border Server, responsible for interaction with the environment through sensors and actuators, and Context Server, responsible for processing the contextual information. These servers are located in cells of the ubiquitous environment managed by EXEHDA, where each cell has one Context Server and can contain several Border Servers.

The proposed architecture enables communication: (i) among Border Servers and Context Servers; (ii) among Context Servers located in different cells of ubiquitous environment managed by EXEHDA; (iii) with other middleware services, or applications. An overview of this architecture is shown in Figure 1, in which the components are mapped over the ubiquitous environment.

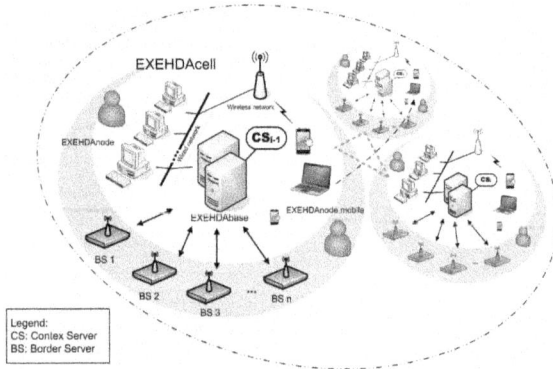

Figure 1: Ubiquitous Environment

The architecture can acquire contextual information in autonomic way, as well as allow remote actuation on the environment through electromechanical devices. In ubiquitous environment, different information is scattered, being necessary to be collected through sensors geographically distributed for the users have access to this information. This collected data should also be stored for further processing by both middleware as applications.

The description of EXEHDA-UC, presented in the next sections, is organized based on their servers and corresponding features, being carried out the necessary associations between them, and with the other services of the EXEHDA middleware.

2.1 Border Server

The proposed architecture for the Border Server includes three modules targeted to: (i) manage sensor networks,

(ii) make publications, and (iii) manage actuator networks. A detailed view of the architecture is shown in Figure 2.

Sensing Module provides handling of sensor networks, enabling the individualization of processing by sensor. It covers aspects from physical management (interfaces, reading frequency) until computational normalization (validation, translation) of the collected values. Also enables publication of the information collected by sensor networks in Context Server. This module consists of six components following described.

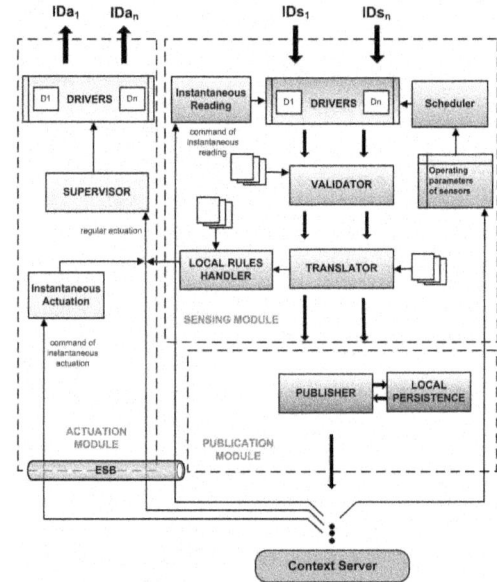

Figure 2: Border Server

Operating Parameters of Sensors Component specifies the driver to be used for reading different sensors, as well as the agenda to data acquisition. This agenda handles sensors individually, allowing the specification of periodic readings, linked to dates and/or specific times. This component is defined by the user in the Context Server, using a YAML file [2]. The specifications available in the Repository of Context are used and, once ready, the YAML file is transferred to the Border Server.

Based on the Operating Parameters of Sensors, the Scheduler Component triggers readings, considering the user's application interest. The Scheduler uses the clock of the Border Server to trigger its procedures, being possible to specify the frequency of occurrence. Each activation is triggered a YAML parser to interpret the sensor which should be read and activated the corresponding driver.

The sensor's driver is responsible for the acquisition of physical value measured by the sensor. It is usual that each type of sensor has a specific form of access to data acquisition. The strategy of encapsulating the driver operation aims to prevent that the operational differences of each driver may have an impact in the other layers of software architecture. Among other aspects this encapsulation improves the maintenance (replacement of sensors, updating drivers). The driver of each sensor is individualized by an identification code, allowing the

---

[2]http://www.yaml.org

addition of a new driver or the modification of an old driver, without further specification.

The Validator assesses whether a particular data collection should be published or not, using criteria specified by user-defined rules. These criteria are based on rules, for example, a rule may state that should only be published values whose variance is greater than 5% from the previous reading, or publish values that are in a certain range. The rule is identified in Operating Parameters of Sensors Component, considering the sensor ID (IDs).

Translator Component performs the adequacy of the collected data to the nature of the user application, also by a rule. For example, temperature ranges can be converted into descriptions such as "High", "Medium", "Low", through a procedural rule. This component helps to optimize the volume of data transferred between servers, also increasing the readability of the collected data.

Instantaneous Reading Component enables reading of a sensor, considering application's demand, at any time. The requests can come from user's applications or Context Servers, as a result of rules implementation. It employs an Enterprise Service Bus (ESB) for receiving asynchronous requests and, considering the sensor ID, triggers the corresponding driver.

The Local Rules Handler processes contingency rules intended to prevent the devices involved reach critical states. These rules act on the management mechanism of actuation, enabling or disabling actuators. This component is activated whenever occurs the reading of a particular sensor, acquiring high importance when the communication with the Context Server is interrupted by problems in the network infrastructure.

Publication Module is responsible for coordinating the main data flow between Border Servers and the Context Server, promoting the publication of all collected data and ensuring a Local Persistence in the periods that the publication be frustrated. This module is composed by Publisher Component, which interoperates with Collector Module of the Context Server, performing submissions of collected data. These submissions are made using the ESB of Acquisition Module, individualized by application. Depending on the nature of the application, for security, data are transferred in encrypted way.

Actuation Module is responsible for managing the actuators. This module is composed by Instantaneous Actuation Component, which receives asynchronous commands at any time, via an ESB. These commands are originated from the Context Server, as a result of the execution of a rule, as well as from a user application. The parameters used are the ID of the actuator and the corresponding operation patterns (duration, power activation, etc..), which are passed to the Supervisor Component for processing. The Supervisor component binds actuation commands from three different sources: the regular actuation, the instant actuation, and those from the Local Rules Handler. Once received the parameters to control the actuation the Supervisor can activate the required driver for the actuator that is being managed.

In order to identify anomalous behavior related to management of the actuators, the Supervisor has a specification for actuator (IDa) of how many times for a unit of time is expected to occur transitions in the state of the actuator. The objective is to identify potential

conflicts between rules in Context Server and rules of contingency in Local Rules Handler Component, as well as unconformities between instant actuation commands, triggered by the user, and active rules on the servers. Also, this component handles the parameters for activate the actuators, implementing through drivers the procedures of activation and deactivation, control of operational power, validity time of actuation, among others.

The actuator's drivers has a similar purpose to the sensor's drivers, i.e. they encapsulate the procedures specific to each actuator, most often employing libraries and/or software provided by the manufacturers. This approach preserves the spread of implementation aspects to the upper layers of the Border Server's architecture.

2.2 Context Server

The modules of Context Server, following described, interoperate in the provision of the functionalities for context awareness services. Each of these modules is responsible for one stage of context awareness, since its acquisition until the time that is stored and/or passed on to anyone who requested the contextual information. An overview of the Context Server architecture is illustrated in Figure 3, characterizing the relationship with Border Servers, other middleware services, other remote Context Servers, and user applications.

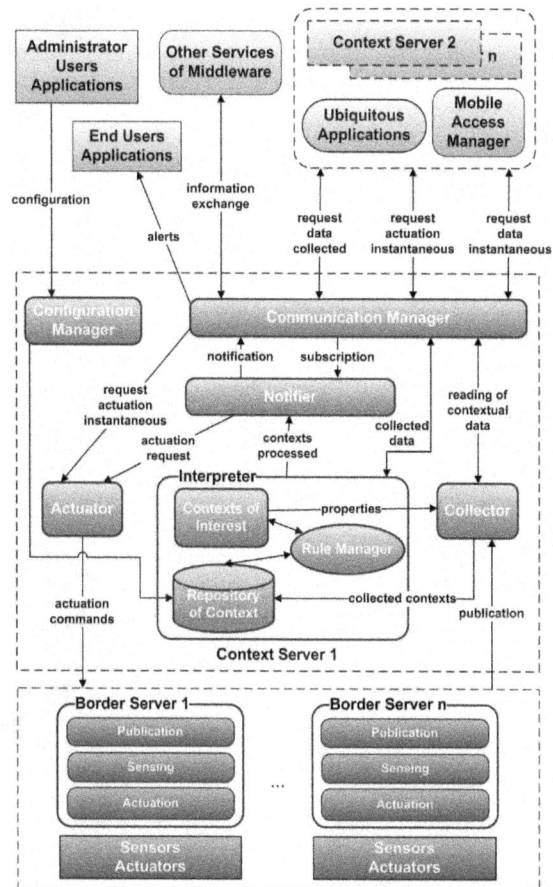

Figure 3: Context Server

Collector: provides support for the capture of contextual information, collected by Border Servers, considering logic (software interfaces) and/or hardware sensors. This module presents a server behavior whose functionality is implemented through an ESB, allowing Border Servers, whenever there are significant variations in contextual data, can publish these data.

Actuator: in charge of the actuators control (activation, deactivation, and configuration), after being notified by other Context Server modules. This module receives actuator's identifier and operational parameters to be used and interoperates with Border Servers for trigger the actuators. In general, the Actuator Module is responsible for triggers the ubiquitous environment actions that change the state of the environment, enabling the use of context awareness in applications for automation and control.

Interpreter: processes contextual information based on Contexts of Interest of applications. This module maintains a Repository of Context, which employs a relational model for the context representation. In this repository are stored the information obtained by the Collector, providing a historical view of contexts. The structure of Repository of Context reflects the organization of the EXEHDA middleware's architecture, contemplating the relationships between applications, components, sensors, environments, and contexts of interest. The repository also stores architecture's configuration data, and the publications from the existing sensors in ubiquitous environment. These data are used by the Rule Manager Component, which triggers the appropriate actions, depending on the context status. The nature of the rules (logical, numeric, temporal...) is a consequence of the application domain managed by EXEHDA-UC.

Notifier: deals with notifying the result of context processing performed by the Interpreter. This module receives, through the Communication Manager, subscriptions from all services and/or applications that requiring notifications about the context state. The Notifier also receives all decisions of actuation, resulting from the autonomic treatment of context rules.

Communication Manager: used by remote Context Servers and/or applications to request contextual data and/or to trigger actuators. This module provides the dissemination of context information to other middleware services, as well as it can send messages to users. It receives requests through an ESB, and interoperates with other architectural components using messages, as well as with users using public protocols for sending messages over the cellular network (SMS - Short Message Service), Google Talk, and emails. The module includes a repository responsible for storing information necessary for sending alerts.

Configuration Manager: allows the management of Context Server settings, including specifications of sensors and actuators, as well as information of equipment which the context is being collected.

2.2.1 Mobile Access Manager

This module provides mobile access to EXEHDA-UC. It is organized in two blocks (see Figure 4): (Block A) display contextual information, and (B block) proactive alerts.

Particularly, the provision of proactive alerts on a hardware platform that can follow the user, while he/she performs its activities in different places, maximizes the ubiquity of the proposed context awareness service.

Block A: Display of Contextual Information

This block provides graphical and textual reports for users, considering their contexts of interest. The communication with the Context Server happens employing a two-step protocol. In the first is made an inspection of the context information that is being treated. In the second, data are requested for a specific contextual information in a time interval. The features of this block are organized into three modules, following described.

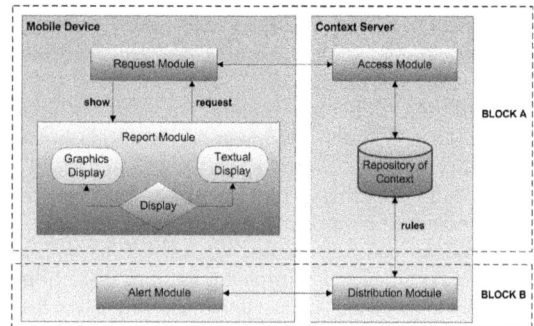

Figure 4: Mobile Access Manager

Report Module: this module displays contextual information on the mobile device. The main operations available through its interface are: (i) to request the list of contextual information which are handled by the Server Context, (ii) to select contextual information that is displayed in the report, (iii) to select the report type: graphical or textual, and (iv) to enable for user, once the report is displayed, alternatives to customization of the period of data shown.

Access Module: this module consists of a service that runs in the Context Server, having access to the Repository of Context. The features of this module are: (i) to return the list of contextual information managed by the Context Server, and (ii) to return the contextual information relevant to the user's context of interest, in a specific time interval.

Request Module: aims at requesting the contextual information to the Access Module, considering a demand of the Report Module. This module has three functions: (i) to request the list of all the contextual information handled by the Context Server, (ii) to request a specific contextual information desired by the user in the specified time interval, (iii) to send this request the Access Module through the ESB, and (iv) to receive and interpret contextual information from the Access Module, making them available to the Report Module.

Block B: Handling Proactive Alerts

This block is intended to notify the user when the occurrence of events of interest, through proactive notification. The functionalities of the block are organized into two modules, described as follows.

Alert Module: runs on the mobile device, providing alerts to users. For this, the native mechanism for notification of the mobile platform is used. This option provides to the user an integrated management of alerts on their mobile device. Its main functions are: (i) to recover, in the time interval specified by the user, alerts from the

Distribution Module, and (ii) to provide for the user these alerts in the notification area of the mobile device.

Distribution Module: runs on the same equipment of the Context Server, under uninterrupted operation. Its main functions are: (i) to receive alerts to mobile devices produced by Rule Manager Component of Context Server, and (ii) to provide alerts to mobile devices. This module operates keeping the alerts produced by different contextual rules, treated in the Interpreter Module of Context Server. This module is accessed by mobile devices through the Communication Manager of Context Server, which uses an ESB to provide access to different functionalities of the Context Server.

3. CASE STUDY

This section summarizes the main aspects of the case study, related to the AMPLUS project[3], used to evaluate the functionalities of EXEHDA-UC. The case study includes tasks related to sensing, collection, processing, and notification of context. In this case study was developed an application (see section 3.1) for Web interface and mobile devices, whose usability was evaluated by the users (see section 3.2).

AMPLUS project was designed to provide context-aware services, allowing storage of contextual states that meet the equipment of the Didactic Laboratory of Seed Analysis (LDAS)[4], throughout the time of implementation of various tests, and a proactive actuation when necessary.

The scalability and robustness were the criteria used to select the technologies used for prototyping of mechanisms for collecting, storing, and processing of context, as well as actuation on the environment. In this sense, the code of the Border and Context Servers is written in the Python language. The XML-RPC (Extensible Markup Language - Remote Procedure Call)[5] is employed to implementation of the ESB, used for interoperability. The Repository of Contexts uses PostgreSQL for deployment of databases. The sensors and actuators communicate at 1-Wire protocol[6].

3.1 Developed Application

The developed application uses two approaches, defined with users of the LDAS, one addressed to Web interface and other to mobile devices.

The Web interface allows the selection of the context of interest to be displayed, providing a textual report with relevant data collected last week. Along with this report is available a menu that lets the user to select a graphic visualization of data, as well as the creation of custom reporting.

The graphical report (see Figure 5) provided by the system allows simultaneous viewing of information from multiple sensors. The selection of sensors is made from a menu that supports multiple selection. Also is available a resource inspection which allows comparison of values at a given moment of time. The time window of the data being displayed can be set by the user via the same graphical interface that displays the sensing values.

A feature that performs the contextual data crossing,

---

[3]http://amplus.ufpel.edu.br/
[4]http://amplus.ufpel.edu.br/ldas
[5]http://www.xmlrpc.com
[6]http://ubiq.inf.ufpel.edu.br/1-wire/

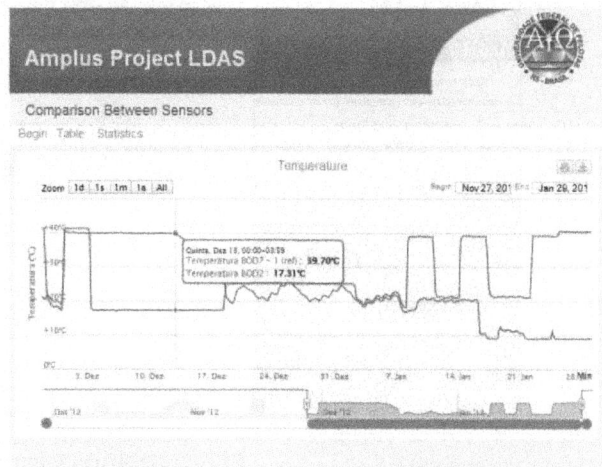

Figure 5: Graphical Report

involving multiple sensors from different rules, was designed to provide data for researches in LDAS. All manipulation is done through the Web interface with facilities for adding, removing, and editing rules and parameters, as shown in Figure 6.

Still, in order to promote the proactivity of AMPLUS Project with the user community, we developed interfaces for communication services: email and SMS to the cellular network. These messages are produced from the processing of contextual rules autonomously by the Context Server.

The routine of the laboratory workers implies mobility in different physical environments of the LDAS. To address this situation, an interface was developed for visual alert, which is activated whenever a device is in a state that requires attention. Considering this alert, details can be inferred through the computer interface of the AMPLUS Project.

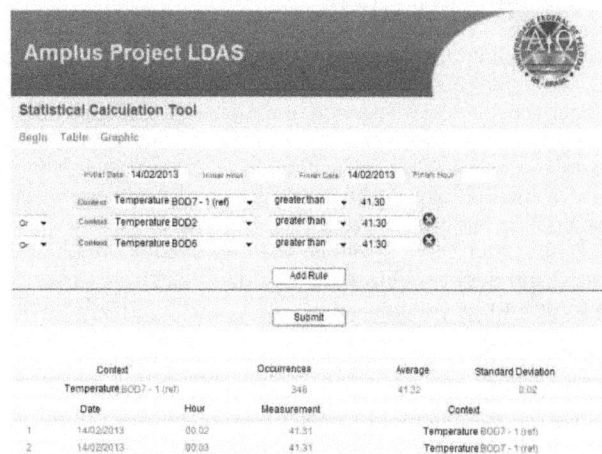

Figure 6: Contextual Data Crossing

The interface for mobile access was targeted to the Android platform (see Figure 7). Through the initial interface the user can select the sensor to be displayed, either through a textual or graphical report. These reports enable the user to specify display interval (hour, day, week), and the vertical axis adjustment is done automatically,

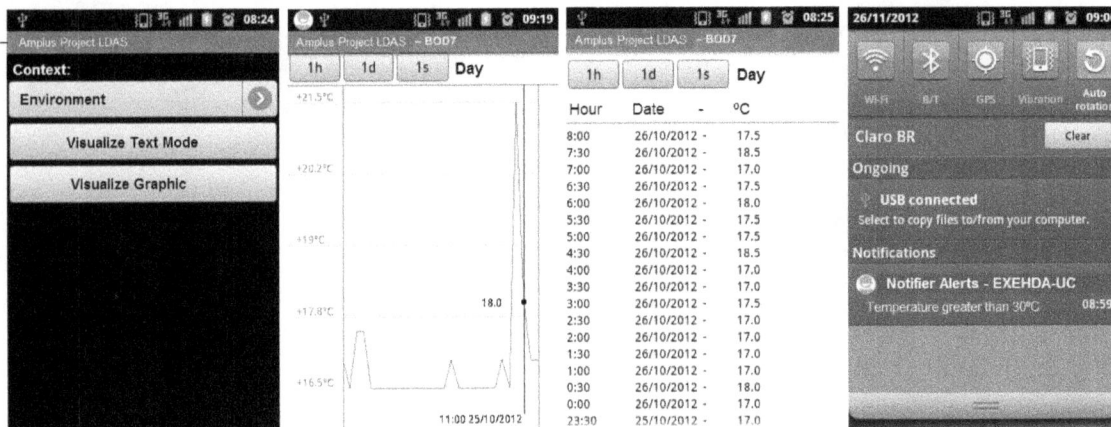

Figure 7: Interfaces of the Mobile Application

minimizing the use of scrolling. The display of alerts is done through the interface provided by the Android platform itself. This aspect enhances the integration between the alerts mechanism and the functionalities of the user's smart phone.

3.2 Acceptance Evaluation

This section presents the experiment details and the results obtained with the application's evaluation. The evaluation regards the application acceptance, which involved LDAS volunteer users. For the study we considered 4 teachers, 5 students, and 1 technician. Each participant used a mobile device and a desktop. We performed a basic training on the application operation beforehand. Participants were asked to use the application and respond to an evaluation questionnaire regarding the experience in the use of the system.

The answers should be within a range of five points, ranging from 1 point (totally disagree) to 5 points (totally agree). To evaluate the model acceptability, checking the system usability, the questionnaire were defined based on the Technology Acceptance Model (TAM) [12]. The TAM model considers the following main themes for application acceptance: (i) Ease of Use: means the degree in which users evaluating the application may reduce their effort; (ii) Usefulness: means the degree in which users evaluating the application may improve their performance.

Table 1 and Table 2 contain the questionnaire applied to users, and answers obtained. The questions were designed in order to be simple, short and direct. Both tables present the question at the first column and the percentage obtained with the number of users in brackets following from "Totally Disagree" to "Totally Agree". The last column shows the consolidation average percentage score obtained by the responses, which varied between zero and five.

Analyzing the results it can be seen that approval is high for both ease of use, as for the usefulness. However, there were results in the range "indifferent" in the last two issues of usefulness. This can be interpreted as a concern for the quality control of experiments developed in LDAS, which depends basically on the use of autonomic mechanisms, without the usual human intervention, for issuing alerts for contextual states that require immediate actuation. In this case, a strategy that can be adopted is to intensify

the testing and validation with users and start a gradual deployment of applications.

4. RELATED WORK

The study of related work (CARE [1], CoCA [6], HiCon [5], Solar [4], WComp [7]) has been done considering the main design assumptions of EXEHDA-UC: (i) distributed architecture, (ii) support for sensor and actuator networks, (iii) autonomic acquisition of context data, (iv) support for rule processing, and (v) support for distributed actuation.

The architectures studied did not maintain a decentralized approach for all stages of the context processing, which is not appropriate for the requirement of large scale distribution of ubiquitous environments. In turn, the architectural model of EXEHDA-UC is structured in a distributed way, at all stages of handling context information, from acquisition to the actuation.

The EXEHDA-UC can manage sensor and actuator networks, optimizing the management both of acquisition of context data from various types of sensors, usual in computational environments for providing ubiquitous applications, as the distributed actuation. Such feature is found in part in projects CoCA and HiCon, which have support to sensor networks. The project WComp allows actuation on the environment, however, does not support actuator networks.

With the exception of the CARE and Solar projects, the others allow the use of specific mechanisms for acquisition, adopting a strategy of separation between the acquisition and use of context. Besides contemplating this aspect, the EXEHDA-UC presents a differential that consists in the employment of an autonomic approach in the collection of contextual data, as these continue to be obtained by the mechanism, even if the applications involved in their use are not been in operation.

In most projects, the handling of rules is restricted to a few steps of the context processing. The EXEHDA-UC distinguished by its software architecture has been designed to support distributed processing of customizable rules, which can be linked to different treatment levels of contextual data, both in Border Servers as in Context Servers.

Table 1: Ease of Use Evaluation

Question	Totally Disagree	Partially Disagree	Neutral	Partially Agree	Totally Agree	Average
1. The application is easy to understand.	0,0%(0)	0,0%(0)	0,0%(0)	40,0%(4)	60,0%(6)	4,6
2. The application is easy to use.	0,0%(0)	0,0%(0)	0,0%(0)	30,0%(3)	70,0%(7)	4,7
3. The options are clear and objectives.	0,0%(0)	0,0%(0)	10,0%(1)	20,0%(2)	70,0%(7)	4,6
4. With little effort I can select a context of interest.	0,0%(0)	0,0%(0)	0,0%(0)	20,0%(2)	80,0%(8)	4,8
5. With little effort I can access the graphical reports.	0,0%(0)	0,0%(0)	0,0%(0)	30,0%(3)	70,0%(7)	4,7

Table 2: Usefulness Evaluation

Question	Totally Disagree	Partially Disagree	Neutral	Partially Agree	Totally Agree	Average
1. The options presented are relevant.	0,0%(0)	0,0%(0)	0,0%(0)	30,0%(3)	70,0%(7)	4,7
2. The application makes it easy to obtain contextual data from multiple sensors.	0,0%(0)	0,0%(0)	0,0%(0)	40,0%(4)	60,0%(6)	4,6
3. The application makes it easy my mobility.	0,0%(0)	0,0%(0)	0,0%(0)	40,0%(4)	60,0%(6)	4,6
4. The application makes it easy the immediate actuation, considering the sending of one alert or message.	0,0%(0)	0,0%(0)	30,0%(3)	30,0%(3)	40,0%(4)	4,1
5. I would use this application in my work at LDAS.	0,0%(0)	0,0%(0)	30,0%(3)	20,0%(2)	50,0%(5)	4,2

5. CONCLUDING REMARKS

Aiming at reducing the development effort of ubiquitous applications in EXEHDA, the context conditions are proactively monitored by EXEHDA-UC, causing the developer be discharged of managing aspects such as collection, processing, and storage of contextual data. In EXEHDA-UC we use a collaborative approach between application and middleware, which allows the developer to tailor rules to govern the behavior of the application's software components.

Another relevant characteristic of EXEHDA-UC, compared with the related work, is that it manages the acquisition of context data, its processing and storage independently of applications, in a rule-based and autonomic perspective. The use of rules in different parts of the distributed architecture of EXEHDA-UC is a significant differential.

Among others, the following aspects should be considered in future works: (i) to explore case studies in which processing rules employ higher level inference mechanisms; and (ii) to use EXEHDA-UC for providing situation awareness, in which are anticipated future situations of the different contexts in the ubiquitous environment.

6. REFERENCES

[1] A. Agostini, C. Bettini, and D. Riboni. Hybrid reasoning in the care middleware for context awareness. *Int. J. Web Eng. Technol.*, 5(1):3–23, May 2009.

[2] P. Bellavista, A. Corradi, M. Fanelli, and L. Foschini. A survey of context data distribution for mobile ubiquitous systems. *ACM Comput. Surv.*, 44(4):24:1–24:45, Sept. 2012.

[3] R. Caceres and A. Friday. Ubicomp systems at 20: Progress, opportunities, and challenges. *Pervasive Computing, IEEE*, 11(1):14–21, 2012.

[4] G. Chen, M. Li, and D. Kotz. Data-centric middleware for context-aware pervasive computing. *Pervasive Mob. Comput.*, 4(2):216–253, Apr. 2008.

[5] K. Cho, I. Hwang, S. Kang, B. Kim, J. Lee, S. Lee, S. Park, J. Song, and Y. Rhee. Hicon: a hierarchical context monitoring and composition framework for next-generation context-aware services. *Network, IEEE*, 22(4):34 –42, july-aug. 2008.

[6] D. Ejigu, M. Scuturici, and L. Brunie. Hybrid approch to collaborative context-aware service plataform for pervasive computing. *Journal of Computers*, 3:40–50, 2008.

[7] N. Ferry, V. Hourdin, S. Lavirotte, G. Rey, M. Riveill, and J.-Y. Tigli. Wcomp, a middleware for ubiquitous computing. In E. Babkin, editor, *Ubiquitous Computing*, volume 1, chapter 8, pages 171–176. InTech, 2011.

[8] M. Knappmeyer, S. Kiani, E. Reetz, N. Baker, and R. Tonjes. Survey of context provisioning middleware. *Communications Surveys Tutorials, IEEE*, 15(3):1492–1519, 2013.

[9] J. L. Lopes, R. S. Souza, M. Z. Gusmao, C. A. Costa, J. V. Barbosa, A. C. Yamin, and C. R. Geyer. A model for context awareness in ubicomp. In *Proceedings of the 18th Brazilian symposium on Multimedia and the web*, WebMedia '12, pages 161–168, New York, NY, USA, 2012. ACM.

[10] T. Silva, C. Celes, V. Mota, and A. Loureiro. Overview of ubicomp research based on scientic publications. in:. In *Simpósio Brasileiro de Computação Ubíqua e Pervasiva*, Curitiba, PR, 2012. SBC.

[11] M. Weiser. The computer for the 21st century. *Scientific American*, 3(265):94–104, Setembro 1991.

[12] C. Yoon and S. Kim. Convenience and tam in a ubiquitous computing environment: The case of wireless lan. *Electron. Commer. Rec. Appl.*, 6(1):102–112, Jan. 2007.

Multimedia Multi-device Educational Presentations Preserved as Interactive Multi-video Objects

Caio Cesar Viel[1], Erick Lazaro Melo[1], Maria da Graça Pimentel[2], Cesar A. C. Teixeira[1]
[1]Universidade Federal de São Carlos, Brazil – [2]Universidade de São Paulo, Brazil
{caio_viel|erick_melo|cesar}@dc.ufscar.br, mgp@icmc.usp.br

ABSTRACT

The capture of lectures or similar presentations is of interest for several reasons. From the attendee's perspective, students may use the recordings when working on homework assignments or preparing for exams, or to watch the contents of a missed class. From the instructor's perspective, a captured lecture may be evaluated, recaptured for improvements, or reused as complementary learning material. Moreover, captured lectures may be a valuable resource for e-learning and distance education courses. In this paper we detail the design rationale associated with the development of a prototype platform for the ubiquitous capture of live presentations and their transformation into a corresponding interactive multi-video object. Our approach includes capturing important context information which, when incorporated into the multimedia object, enables one to interact with the recorded lecture in novel dimensions. We tested our prototype by using case studies involving instructors and students, which allowed us to identify important features and novel uses for the platform.

Categories and Subject Descriptors: H.5.1[**Multimedia Information Systems:**] *Video.* H.7.2[**Document Preparation**]*Hypertext/hypermedia, Index generation, Markup languages.*

General Terms: Design, Documentation.

Keywords: Interactive Multi-video, E-learning, Ubiquitous Capture, Capture and Access, NCL.

1. INTRODUCTION

The literature reports several efforts that focus on the preservation of lecture presentations (e.g. [6], [8], [24], [14]). In our work, the term *educational presentation* has a broad meaning that includes not only traditional lectures but also related activities, such as problem solving sessions.

We are aware that there are strong divergences among educators as to the efficiency of the lecture format as a method of instruction. For instance, while Bauerlein [2] remarks that "one of the axioms of progressivism education is that the lecture format is an inefficient and, potentially, alienating method of instruction", Schwerdt and Wuppermann [27] remark that "contrary to contemporary pedagogical thinking, we find students score higher on standardized tests in the subject in which their teachers spent more time on lecture-style presentations than in the subject in which the teacher devoted more time to problem-solving activities". Although the model of interactive multi-video lectures such as the one described in this work may impact on the teaching or the learning experiences, such discussion is out of the scope of this paper. We present the rationale applied in the development of a prototype environment for the ubiquitous capture of live presentations and transformation of the presentations into equivalent interactive multi-video learning objects.

In our work, capturing a (multimedia) presentation means (using multiple devices toward) recording one or more video and audio streams of the speaker, images presented on the screen or projector, writings and drawings made on whiteboards, and also capturing contextual information that is relevant to the corresponding playback. The captured information is then transformed into synchronized video streams and static media that compose the resulting multimedia object. We refer to the result as an interactive multi-video object because it is mainly composed of multiple synchronized videos. Therefore, we call an *interactive multi-video object* the composition of several videos, audio and static media, properly synchronized and with facilities for flexible interaction and browsing.

The problem. Although recording lectures is a common practice (in universities), producing quality video lectures demands high operational costs (cameraman, video director, editors and other audiovisual professionals). To reduce the operational costs, in the past decades many tools for the automatic capture of lectures were developed (e.g, [6], [8] [11], [13], [15], and [22]). However, most capture tools for the educational domain record video only and slide streams and generate, as a result, a *single* video/audio stream as a lecture video or podcast. The value of multi-video has been recognized in scenarios that include newscasting and real-time videoconferencing.

Our proposal. We propose a capture and access-based model targeted at capturing much of the content presented in a classroom. The capture process, pervasive and without human mediation, triggers the automatic generation of an interactive multi-video object associated with the lecture. We built a prototype platform for the ubiquitous capture of live presentations and their transformation into a corresponding interactive multi-video object. Our approach includes capturing important context information which, when incorporated into the multi-video object, allows one to interact with the recorded lecture in novel dimensions. The student may be able, for example, to use a multi-window panel to review multiple synchronized audiovisual content that includes the slide presentation, the lecturer's web browsing, the whiteboard content, video streams with focus on the lecturer's face or the lecturer's full body, among others. The student has the option to select, at any time, which video object is more relevant to be exhibited in the main (larger) screen. The student is also able to execute semantic browsing operations using points of interest like slide transitions, spoken keywords, lecturer's interactions, etc. Moreover, facilities can be provided for users to annotate the captured lecture while watching it, as suggested by the watch-and-comment paradigm [10].

Case studies. We evaluated our proposal by means of case studies in which we invited instructors and students to use the system in different settings. We report data relative to multi-video objects generated automatically by the prototype, and also summarize data relative to the interactions students had with the interactive multimedia objects generated. For instance, the main operation performed by the students was the selection of which component of the multi-video object was to be presented in the main (larger) window. Also, an important feature of the prototype is the logging of all interactions performed by the users while watching the lecture: this allows a detailed analysis of which portions of the presentations students review the most, for instance, which is useful [5] for instructors to evaluate their own performance during the lecture [28].

This paper is organized as follows: in Section 2 we discuss related works; in Section 3 we describe our proposed model to preserve educational presentations, discussing decisions that guided our design; in Section 4 we present our current prototype and describe a multi-video object generated by a live presentation; in Section 5 we discuss case studies in which instructors used the prototype to capture lectures; and in Section 6 we present the conclusions and future works.

2. RELATED WORK

Most of the systems designed to record lectures use, instead of multi-video objects, a single video stream as the resulting product of a captured session (e.g. [3], [7], [11], [17], [22]).

In the work of Liu et al. [18], lectures are captured in a similar process to the aforementioned ones, resulting a single video stream. The difference is that the set of slides used in the presentation is added to the video stream. However, the slides are not synchronized with the video. Given that the result is single-video-stream, students do not have autonomy to choose the camera that gives them the best view of the lecture for each situation, or to focus on a particular point of interest .

ClassX is a tool designed for online lecture delivery [15] [23]. A live lecture is captured by means of a high definition camera (AVCHD) stream split into several virtual standard resolution cameras. By using tracking techniques, the most appropriated virtual camera for a given moment is chosen and streamed to the remote students. The students also have the opportunity to choose a different stream from another virtual camera or even watch the original AVCHD stream.

A synchronized slide presentation is also offered, but it does not offer navigation facilities.

Schulte et al. [26] propose the REPLAY system for producing, manipulating and sharing lecture videos, which is similar to the above-mentioned ones. Two differences must be pointed out: the use of computational vision to recognize written words, and of MPEG-7 to index the videos. REPLAY allows semantic navigation even though it does not produce a multi-video object.

Dickson et al. [13] [14], Brotherton and Abowd [6] and Cattelan et al. [9] present more advanced features for capturing context information based on image processing and audio transcription. In these works, hypermedia documents are generated with interfaces that provide several ways of indexing the recorded information.

The model for capturing and recovering lectures presented in this paper allows more flexibility than the ones above mentioned. The flexibility comes from the ability to specify which context information is captured, how the context information is combined to generate alternative navigation interactions in the resulting multi-video object, and to promote live interventions in the classroom during the capture process — for example, when there is a change in the illumination of the room.

3. CAPTURE & ACCESS MODEL

In order to produce quality lecture videos, the traditional lecture recording process usually requires the presence of audiovisual professionals, such as cameramen to operate the cameras, a video director to select the best frame or camera, and an editor to generate the final version of the lecture video. These professionals increase the operational cost of producing a lecture video and may prevent the wide adoption of lecture capturing. Furthermore, their influence in the lecture may add noise to the communication process between the instructor and the students, making the resulting learning object less effective. Our proposal works toward a self-service approach, allowing instructors to record lectures themselves.

Some existing solutions rely on computational vision, tracking techniques and sensors to perform camera orchestrations in a attempt to produce a single video or audio stream output. The model we propose goes a step further, as depicted in Figure 1. It aims at capturing the lecture in its entirety by recording much of the content presented in the classroom. The capture process is pervasive, does not rely on human mediation and automatically generates an interactive multi-video object designed to preserve as much of the lecture content and context as possible.

Our model demands an environment (usually a classroom) which is instrumented with physical devices (Figure 1(1)) such as video cameras, microphones, (interactive) whiteboards and projectors. The instrumented classroom may also contain sensors, such as temperature and luminosity sensors, and secondary screens, such as notebooks, TVs, tablets, etc. The video cameras should be positioned where it is possible to frame important views of the environment (instructor, students, whiteboard, slides, etc.).

Computer devices capture the content produced by the physical devices used in the classroom (e.g. whiteboards and slides) and represent them as video, audio and data streams (Figure 1(2)). Cameras produce video (and audio) streams, microphones produce audio streams, and sensors produce

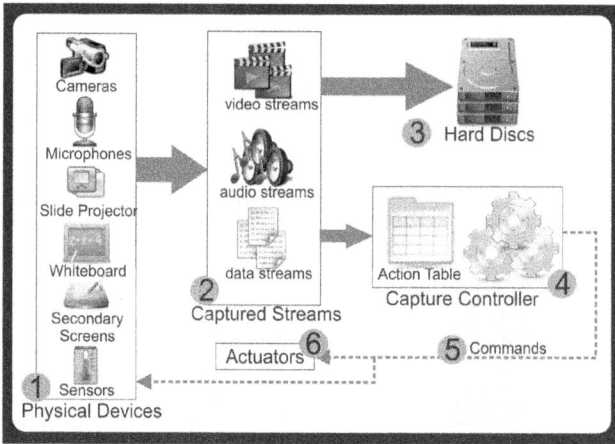

Figure 1: Capture Workflow

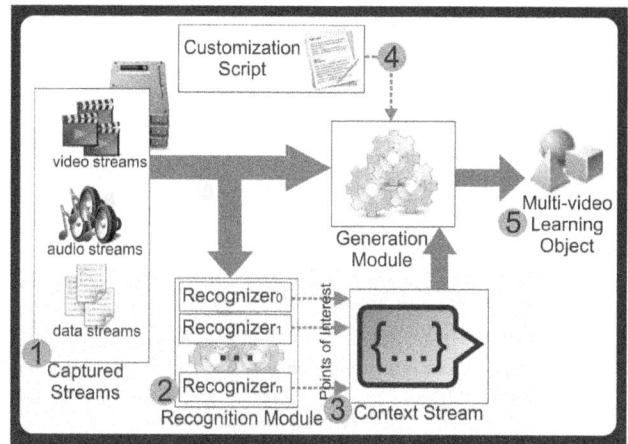

Figure 2: Multi-video object generation

data streams. By capturing the screen output from the secondary screens or by intercepting the signal sent to the slide projector, we can also produce video streams. The electronic whiteboard can produce both data and video streams: by capturing ink strokes, we can generate a data stream, and by intercepting the output signal sent to the projector, we can generate a video stream.

All captured streams are stored (Figure 1(3)) for further use in the multi-video object generation. The streams are also sent to the *capture controller* (Figure 1(4)), a component responsible for managing the capture process. The *capture controller* uses signal processing to analyze the captured streams and to send commands (Figure 1(5)) back to the physical devices and actuators (Figure 1(6)) located in the classroom.

The instructions in the *capture controller* are defined in a customizable action table. The action table is used to define actions for events that may occur during the capture process, such as zooming into the image of a specific camera, when the lecturer starts talking, or activating an actuator in order to reduce the light intensity, when the lecturer starts a slide presentation.

Our model allows the instructor to record a full lecture using several short-duration modules, which means that a multi-video presentation can be composed of one or more modules. This does not only allow the lecturer to take breaks during the recording process, but also to associate different modules to specific tasks. The lecturer may, for instance, prepare a problem solving presentation with one exercise per module. It is important to observe that students are able to navigate among the modules of the multi-video presentation (e.g., by skipping from one exercise to the other). Reusing modules to compose a new presentation is another advantage of splitting the recording process into modules — reuse is in fact one of the main aims of learning objects [19].

All the analysis and conversion process involved in the captured streams can demand a lot of computational power and time. Once the capture of the streams is concluded, all the corresponding information is transferred to a server. The video, audio and data streams (Figure 2(1)) are sent to the *Recognition Module* (Figure 2(2)). The *Recognition Module* is composed of several recognizer components and each of them uses one or more captured streams to detect

points of interest. Points of interest are moments in the lecture that, because they carry context information, may act as useful anchors for students and instructors. They may represent changes in the context of the lecture (e.g., the instructor moves from writing on the whiteboard to executing a video or program-based demonstration in his notebook), or moments of particular importance for the course (e.g., the instructor makes comments related to assignments, homework or exams). The points of interest can be used to provide semantic-based navigation on the multi-video object, allowing students to seek for the next slide transition, for instance.

Since many types of points of interest can be conceived by using different sensors, devices and other computer-based analysis techniques, the *Recognition Module* must publish an interface to allow developers to add new recognizer components as needed. By combining all the identified points of interest, the *Recognition Module* generates the *Context Stream* (Figure 2(3)). As a result, the *context stream* contains information about what and when something happened during the lecture.

The *Generation Module* in Figure 2 consumes all streams (context, audio, video, etc.) to generate a multi-video object. Content and format customizations of the multi-video object may be necessary in order to best suit (i) a course profile (e.g. a course which only uses a whiteboard does not need a slide presentation stream), (ii) the lecturer's style (e.g. if the instructor says "for instance" too often, it may not be a selective enough keyword), and (iii) the students' particular needs (e.g. some adaptation on the images for students with visual impairments may be necessary). The customization can be defined by a *Customization Script* (Figure 2(4)), which is used as input by the *Generation Module*. In the current version the customization is defined by an *ad hoc* set of rules, but in future versions they can be described in a declarative language similar to Business Modeling Language [12].

The multi-video object (Figure 2(5)) is composed of videos and other captured media — with the association of the appropriate metadata, they should become multi-video learning objects[1]. Although the multi-video object is not able to reproduce the live lecture experience in its totality (which

---

[1]http://www.ieeeltsc.org/

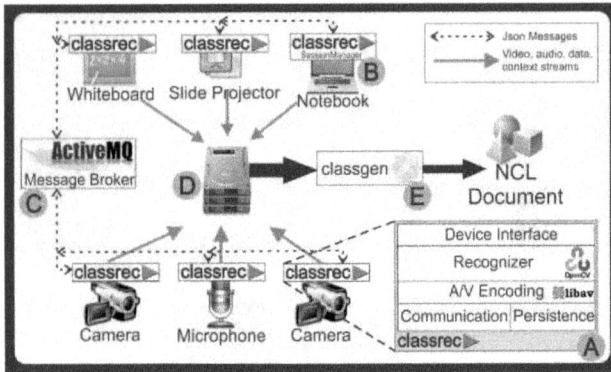

Figure 3: Prototype Overview

(a) Front   (b) Read

Figure 4: Instrumented Room

would involve live interactions, odors, temperature, etc.), it offers several interaction alternatives for the students while they are watching the lecture. These may diminish the loss of not having the students present in the classroom, when direct interaction between instructor and students usually bring benefits to the learning process.

4. PROTOTYPE

As a proof-of-concept of the model presented in the previous section, we developed a prototype tool for capturing lectures and generating multi-video learning objects. This prototype was mainly developed in Python.

Figure 3 depicts an overview of the prototype tools. The prototype is composed of three main parts: the *Capturing tool* used to capture streams; the *Processing tool* in charge of stream analysis and the generation of the multi-video object; and the *Presentation tool*, which allows the user to playback the multi-video object.

The capture tool prototype was deployed in an instrumented multi-purpose classroom (Figure 4). In the front of the classroom (Figure 4(a)) there is a conventional whiteboard, an electronic whiteboard and a notebook in which the presenter can browse the web or use any other software. The interactive whiteboard can be used to present slides (there is a Bluetooth presenter to control the presentation) and it allows drawing and writing over the screen. At the back side (Figure 4(b)) we placed two AVCHD, each one framing the interactive or the conventional whiteboard. We also placed a webcam as a wide-shot cam, framing the whole front of the room. As the room is a shared space in the university, the equipment is stored in lockers.

Capturing tool

The *Capturing tool*, named *Classrec* (Figure 3(A)), carries out the capturing process. Each computer used in the capturing process runs an instance of *Classrec*, and one of these instances is selected to be the session manager (Figure 3(B)). It corresponds to the *Capture Controller* of the workflow (Figure 1). The session manager is responsible for handling the lecturer's stimulus and for controlling the other *Classrec* instances, keeping them synchronized.

The capturing process is based on video streams. *Classrec* captures content (video and audio streams) produced by AVCHD and outputs produced by computers (such as computer screens, slide presentations, etc.).

We opted to capture the electronic whiteboard output as a video stream instead of its strokes. This was done because a video stream is more portable than strokes and, given modern video encodings, such as H.264/MPEG-4, and the static nature of whiteboard outputs, the bit rate of the video stream is low. We could record a stroke stream, but it would require a specialized engine to play it back (as it happens with other systems).

Some streams, such as slides, whiteboards, computer screens, can have segments with a lot of static content, but they are still captured as video streams. A possible improvement would be to replace the video for a combination of non-static content videos and a single image to represent a static segment (video with no changes during a period of time).

Classrec records audio/video streams using the *libav* library[2]. It also records metadata about the lecture, such as module structure, available streams and authoring information in an XML file named *XML lecture*.

The communication among the different applications is carried out using the Apache ActiveMQ message broker (Figure 3(C)).

In the instrumented classroom, all that lecturers who wish to record their educations presentations need to do is to press a button to start the capturing process and then they can deliver lectures as usual, whether to an audience of students or to no one. When they have finished delivering the lecture, all they need to do is to press another button. The *Classrec*'s instances carry out all the complex process of synchronously recording the different streams from the different devices and sent then to the Processing Tool.

Processing tool

The *Processing tool*, named *Classgen* (Figure 3(E)), performs the multi-video generation process. *Classgen* uses information relative to the video streams and other metadata recorded by *Capturing tool* as input that is registered into the *XML lecture* file. It also supports an XML configuration description language, which allows the specification of which recognizers (and its inputs) and which codecs should be used to encode audio and video.

We not only considered points of interest suggested in the literature (e.g. [6], [9], [14]), but also designed novel ones. Points of interest implemented are:

- Module transition: usually denotes a change in the explanation context.
- Slide transition: similarly to Module transition, it also usually denotes a change in context.

---

[2]Libav - http://libav.org/

- Whiteboard interaction: the starting instant of a sequence of annotations made on the whiteboard, which usually denotes an explanation.
- Lecturer close-up: the instructor may explicitly look at the camera placed in the front the the classroom, which allows capturing a face close-up, to create a corresponding point he wishes to emphasize.

It is important to observe that, in the current version of our tool, instructors and students are already offered options for highlighting their own points of interest in the form of comments and annotations, while watching the multi-video document.

We are working on to offer other points of interest, e.g.:

- Secondary device interaction: to mark points in which the instructor uses a secondary device (e.g. to show a video or to run a program-based demonstration).
- Spoken keywords: words that denote some context relative to the lecture. They may be generic as "important" or "exercise", or lesson-dependent as "Lake ecosystem" or "Shakespeare".
- Change in voice intonation and speech speed: can denote that some lessons are important or complicated.
- Students' intervention: can denote a meaningful question or addition to an explanation.
- Lecturer's gestures: can denote that something is important or indicate the connection between the different views of the contents (such as whiteboard and slide). The processing will focus on gestures made during the lecture.

Classgen uses the OpenCV library[4] to perform pattern recognitions in order to identify points of interest for composing the context stream. The media manipulation during the orchestration process and the audio/video conversion is handled by the libav library. We have implemented recognizers capable of detecting (i) the presence of a lecturer in a video stream; (ii) whether the lecturer is facing a camera; (iii) slide transitions; and (iv) interactions with electronic whiteboard or PC.

The detections (i) and (ii) are performed by using *Haar* training. We check 3 frames every second in order to look for objects such as a face or a full body. A frame that contains the object is a success, and a frame that does not contain the object is a fail. We consider the beginning of a point of interest when there are at least three successes in a row; the point of interest finishes when there are three fails in a roll. We also established a minimum duration and a time distance for the point of interest. For instance, for a close-up of the instructor to be considered a point of interest, it should last at least 5 seconds and be 5 seconds apart from another close. If two closes are detected in a period of time shorter than this time, they are combined as a single point of interest. These values are configurable so as to take into account false positive matches.

For points of interest of types (iii) and (iv), we compare subsequent frames in order to detected variations. For instance, when there is a significant difference between two subsequent frames from the video stream generated from the slide projection capture, we identify a slide transition point of interest. We also group near points of interest of the same type as a single point of interest.

It is also possible to specify an orchestration of video streams in order to produce a new video stream. This is useful in environments with multiple cameras recording different angles of the lecturer. Through the XML configuration description language, it is possible to select which stream will be used in the orchestration and how to orchestrate them. For instance, it is possible to specify that when a recognizer detects the lecturer's face in video segments, the camera orchestration stream should include that segment.

After performing the recognition, orchestration and video conversion, the information generated by these processes (the points of interest, the orchestration stream, the converted streams) are stored in the *XML lecture*. The XML is then passed to a component of the *Processing tool* responsible for generating the final multi-video object (Figure 3(5)). Our prototype generates NCL[3] [1] documents, but the *Classgen* can be extended to generate other types of multi-video objects, such as HTML5 pages or stand-alone desktop, tablet or smartphone applications.

The XML configuration description language can also describe the video streams (including the orchestration, if any) and points of interest will be used in the final multi-video object. It is also possible to generate different multi-video objects using the same recorded lecture (for instance, by using the orchestration stream or not).

Presentation tool

It is desirable to offer students a platform-independent way to access the captured lectures. We would like to avoid students having to install specific software to playback the lectures. To fulfill this requirement, two possibilities were considered: (i) generating an HTML5+JavaScript multi-video object and (ii) generating a multi-video object based on a synchronization language like NCL or SMIL.

The multi-video object generated from the capture imposed some challenges. In the scenario where we have considered the generation of the object directly in HTML5 + JavaScript, a large development effort to implement the synchronization capabilities was demanded. We also noticed that most obstacles identified in the HTML5-based implementation would be easily overcome with the use of a declarative language specialized in media synchronization. However, there were no solutions to support it that did not demand external plug-ins.

As a result of these needs, we were motivated to propose and develop a multimedia presentation engine based on standard Web technologies. We conducted an implementation based on HTML5 + JavaScript that enables the presentation of multi-video NCL documents, named Web-NCL [4] [20]. Thanks to WebNCL, any device that has an HTML5-compatible browser (PC, Smart TV, Tablet, Smart Phone, etc.) can present NCL documents natively.

The choice to implement support to the NCL language was made because it is a powerful language for media synchronization that has been adopted as the standards for iDTV [1] and IPTV [16, 21]. A good side effect of this choice was the possibility to reuse the content generated in different platforms. It is important to observe that the generation of the NCL documents demanded solving interesting document engineering problems, as detailed elsewhere [29].

Figure 5 illustrates the playback of three NCL learning objects generated by the prototype. The NCL document

---

[3] Nested Context Language - http://ncl.org.br/en

[4] WebNCL is an open-source software, available at http://webncl.org

(a) Multiple Videos   (b) Full-screen

(c) Timeline

Figure 5: Multi-video learning objects

offers some facilities for students. One of these facilities is the synchronization of the captured audio/video. The multi-video object synchronizes the multiple audio/video streams, so students can see what was written in the whiteboard when the lecturer points to the slide presentation. This synchronization is essential to recover the whole audiovisual context of the captured lecture at a given moment. It is also possible to insert non-synchronized complementary media to the multi-video object like, for instance, an image from a textbook.

The multi-video object offers a more semantic and easier way to navigate in the captured lecture than timeline navigation. For instance, a student can move forward to the next slide transition or backwards to the previous one. When the lecturer begins to write something in the whiteboard, the student can skip all the writing process and see the final result. In a future implementation, students will also be able to search for a keyword to command navigation (e.g., to go to be next point in which the lecturer sais "for instance"). It is important to observe that a timeline-based navigation is always available: even though timelines are traditionally not available in declarative documents (i.e., NCL and SMIL documents), they are such a usual tool for navigation in video that our users explicitly demanded them to be available.

Similar to in-classroom lecture, wherein the student can pay attention to different spots (the lecturer, whiteboard, slide presentation, the textbook, or another screen), the multi-video object allows the student to choose which video stream he wishes to see and he can even see more than one at the same time.

Finally, the student has the facility to make annotations in the multimedia object by means of the watch-and-comment paradigm. For instance, he can mark some part of the lec-

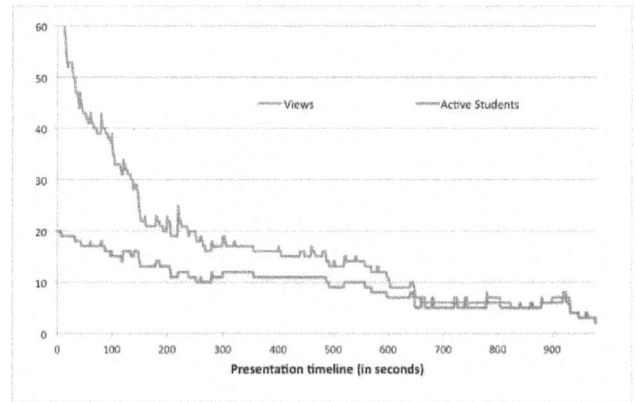

Figure 6: Students' Attendance

ture as important or irrelevant, or he can delimit a snippet of the lecture which he did not understand for further research or to ask the professor or tutor. He can also make comments on the lecture via audio or text when in-classroom students would make notes with paper and pencil.

5. CASE STUDIES

We invited seven professors to use the prototype and record their presentations. Four of them recorded a lecture simulation (without students), one professor a conventional lecture, with real students, one recorded a problem solving class and one professor recorded a lecture simulation and a problem solving class. Information about the generated multimedia learning objects are summarized in Table 1. The table shows that, while the duration of the sessions and type of resources used varied among the instructors, the size of the resulting interactive multi-video object was always of an order not feasibly achievable without the use of an automatic authoring approach.

The prototype was also used to record a term paper presentation, two M.Sc. qualification exams, one M.Sc. defense, and several demos for workshops.

After a short explanation of how to use the capture tool, all lecturers could perform the recording alone, meeting the proposed self-service approach. Since the room is a real classroom, the lecturers could perform their presentations naturally, despite the cameras. Some of them did not modularize the presentation and record a single long module. We also observed that most lecturers did not use all the resources available in the environment.

After interacting with the multimedia learning objects generated from the capture of their lectures, we asked to the professors to, anonymously, answer a survey. The survey was organized in five parts: the first had questions about the purpose of capture lectures, the second had questions about the instrumented classroom infrastructure, the third had questions about the experience of capturing a lecture using our system, the fourth had questions about the user interface available for controlling the capture process and the fifth had questions about the multimedia learning object interface.

We have also carried out three case studies in real scenarios with traditional modality students of Computer Science and Computer Engineering courses and with distance education students of Information Systems. In each case study we

Table 1: Multimedia Learning Objects Statistics

	Duration (seconds)	Modules	Resources Used	NCL Size (MB)	Lines of Code
Lecture (i)	2299	1	Cameras, Slide	1	17672
Lecture (ii)	2682	3	Cameras, Slide, Whiteboard	1.2	21238
Lecture (iii)	1894	4	Cameras, Slide	0.6	11257
Lecture (iv)	2002	1	Cameras, Slide	0.7	12881
Lecture (v)	3559	1	Cameras, Slide	1.3	23261
Lecture (vi)	2295	12	Cameras, Slide, PC	1.6	29933
Lecture (vii)	5879	12	Cameras, Slide, Whiteboard	1.4	25993
Lecture (viii)	4695	12	Cameras, Slide, Whiteboard, PC	1.8	33394

invited a professor to capture an educational presentation. One presentation was for a Computer Organization course, another for a Design and Analysis of Algorithms course, and the third was for a Database course.

The resulting multimedia learning objects were made available for students on the Web via WebNCL and, by using the WebNCL's log API, we logged the interactions performed by the students. We also asked the students to anonymously answer a survey. The survey was organized in three parts: the first had questions about the purpose of capture lectures, the second about their experience in interacting with the multimedia learning object, and the third about its interface.

When asked about the purpose of capture lectures in order to generated multimedia presentations, both students and professors agreed that it is relevant. In addition, among the adjectives available to classify the feeling of recording a lecture by themselves, most professors selected "satisfied", "independent" and "motivated". Among the adjectives available to classify the experience of interacting with the multimedia learning object, most students chose "satisfied" and "independent". Students also pointed out that the multimedia learning object has helped them to understand the subject.

Figure 7 summarizes the interactions performed by the students. Note that 60% of the interactions were performed in order to select the main video. When asked about the facilities offered by the multimedia object, most students pointed out that the possibility of choosing which videos to see and the browsing facilities offered by the multimedia presentations are useful. A student declared "I really liked the multimedia lecture, especially the fact that I was able to rewind and listen again to an explanation. The different videos are cool."

When asked about the division in modules, both professors and students pointed out that this feature was relevant. Professors also declared that it helped them to organize their presentations. We also observed that students tend to be more active when interacting with a multimedia presentation than when watching a video lecture, since they have more control in presentation reproduction, such as selecting the main video or semantic browsing.

Figure 6 summarizes the watching attendance of module 1 of one of the presentations . The horizontal axis is the number of seconds of the module 1 (which is 974 seconds). The blue line represents the number of times the instant was watched by students, and the red line the number of different students watched that instant.

Since a module always starts from 0 seconds, it is natural that the attendance of the first seconds is bigger. The points

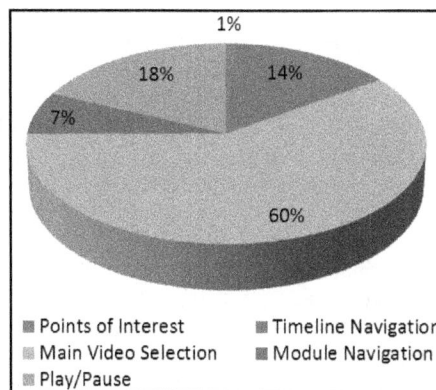

Figure 7: Interactions Categories

where the blue line is above the red line mean that the moment was watched more than once by the same students. This graphic can be useful for lecturers to find out which parts of a lecture are more useful or important for the students. For instance, around the second 213 there is a local maximum point, which is the same moment a slide transition occurs in the multi-video object. A more detailed analysis of interactions performed by the students is reported elsewhere [28].

6. FINAL REMARKS

In this paper we present a model and corresponding system for the preservation of multi-device educational presentations. Capturing both the content presented on multiple devices and important context information from different angles allow the generation of an interactive multi-video document that tries to preserve the level of reality of the presentation as much as possible. From the multi-video it is possible to reconstitute and explore the lecture in dimensions not achievable in the classroom.

The construction of an infrastructure to capture different views of an educational presentation in order to generate an equivalent multi-video object and to present it allowed testing concepts with instructor and students so as to identify improvements.

Our plans for future works include designing analysis tools to facilitate the extraction of useful information from the large amount of data generated by students navigating over the captured presentation, as demanded by specialists from the educational domain [25]. Moreover, we plan to offer alternative capture infrastructures using low end and mobile equipment such as smartphones, which is a growing demand [25].

Acknowledgments

We thank the Brazilian agencies CAPES, CNPq, FAPESP and FINEP for financial support to our research. We thank FAPESP for financial support for the presentation of this paper at Webmedia 2013.

7. REFERENCES

[1] ABNT. Associação Brasileira de Normas Técnicas. 2007. Digital Terrestrial Television Standard 06: Data Codification and Transmission Specifications for Digital Broadcasting. Technical report, Part 2–GINGA-NCL: XML Application Language for Application Coding (São Paulo, SP, Brazil), 2007.

[2] M. Bauerlein. The chronicle of higher education - lectures on the benefits, June 2011.

[3] M. Bianchi. Automatic video production of lectures using an intelligent and aware environment. In *Proc. Intl. Conference on Mobile and Ubiquitous Multimedia (MUM)*, pages 117–123, USA, 2004. ACM.

[4] G. Bradski. The opencv library. *Doctor Dobbs Journal*, 25(11):120–126, 2000.

[5] C. Brooks, C. Thompson, and J. Greer. Visualizing lecture capture usage: A learning analytics case study. In *Proc. Work. Analytics on Video-based Learning (WAVe)*, 2013.

[6] J. A. Brotherton and G. D. Abowd. Lessons learned from eclass: Assessing automated capture and access in the classroom. *ACM Trans. Comput.-Hum. Interact.*, 11(2):121–155, June 2004.

[7] E. Canessa, C. Fonda, L. Tenze, and M. Zennaro. Apps for synchronized photo-audio recordings to support students. In *Proc. WAVe'2013*, 2013.

[8] E. Canessa, C. Fonda, and M. Zennaro. One year of ictp diploma courses on-line using the automated eya recording system. *Comput. Educ.*, 53(1):183–188, 2009.

[9] R. G. Cattelan, L. A. Baldochi, and M. G. Pimentel. Experiences on building capture and access applications. In *Proc. Brazilian Symp. on Multimedia and Hypermedia Systems*, pages 112–127, 2003.

[10] R. G. Cattelan, C. Teixeira, R. Goularte, and M. D. G. C. Pimentel. Watch-and-comment as a paradigm toward ubiquitous interactive video editing. *ACM Trans. Multimedia Comput. Commun. Appl.*, 4(4):28:1–28:24, Nov. 2008.

[11] H.-P. Chou, J.-M. Wang, C.-S. Fuh, S.-C. Lin, and S.-W. Chen. Automated lecture recording system. In *Proc. Intl. Conf. on System Science and Engineering*, pages 167 –172, july 2010.

[12] A. Corallo, E. Caputo, and V. Cisternino. Business Modelling Language': a framework supporting interoperability in cluster of SMEs. In *Digital EcoSystems and Technologies Conference (DEST)*, pages 107 –112, 2007.

[13] P. E. Dickson, D. T. Arbour, W. R. Adrion, and A. Gentzel. Evaluation of automatic classroom capture for computer science education. In *Proc. Conference on Innovation and Technology in Computer Science Education (ITiCSE)*, pages 88–92. ACM, 2010.

[14] P. E. Dickson, D. I. Warshow, A. C. Goebel, C. C. Roache, and W. R. Adrion. Student reactions to classroom lecture capture. In *Proc. Innovation and technology in computer science education*, ITiCSE '12, pages 144–149, New York, NY, USA, 2012. ACM.

[15] S. Halawa, D. Pang, N.-M. Cheung, and B. Girod. Classx: an open source interactive lecture streamingsystem. In *Proc. ACM Intl. Conference on Multimedia (MM)*, pages 719–722. ACM, 2011.

[16] ITU-T. Nested Context Language (NCL) and Ginga-NCL for IPTV Services - Recommendation ITU-T H.761. Technical report, 2009.

[17] F. Lampi, S. Kopf, and W. Effelsberg. Automatic lecture recording. In *Proc. ACM Intl. Conf. Multimedia (MM)*, pages 1103–1104. ACM, 2008.

[18] T. Liu and J. Kender. Lecture videos for e-learning: current research and challenges. In *Proc. IEEE Conference on Multimedia Software Engineering*, pages 574 – 578, 2004.

[19] R. McGreal. Learning objects: A practical definition. *International Journal of Instructional Technology and Distance Learning*, 1(9):21–32, 2004.

[20] E. L. Melo, C. C. Viel, C. A. C. Teixeira, A. C. Rondon, D. d. P. Silva, D. G. Rodrigues, and E. C. Silva. WebNCL: a web-based presentation machine for multimedia documents. In *Proc. Brazilian Symp. Multimedia and the web (WebMedia)*, pages 403–410. ACM, 2012.

[21] M. Moreno, C. Batista, and L. Soares. Ncl and itu-t's standardization effort on multimedia application frameworks for iptv. *ACM, October*, 2010.

[22] T. Nagai. Automated lecture recording system with avchd camcorder and microserver. In *Proc. ACM SIGUCCS Fall Conference*, pages 47–54. ACM, 2009.

[23] D. Pang, S. Halawa, N.-M. Cheung, and B. Girod. Classx mobile: region-of-interest video streaming to mobile devices with multi-touch interaction. In *Proc. ACM Intl. Conf. on Multimedia (MM)*, pages 787–788. ACM, 2011.

[24] M. d. G. Pimentel, R. G. Cattelan, and L. Baldochi. Prototyping applications to document human experiences. *Pervasive Computing*, 6(2):93–100, 2007.

[25] M. Ronchetti. Videolectures ingredients that can make analytics effective. In *Proc. WAVe'2013*, 2013.

[26] O. A. Schulte, T. Wunden, and A. Brunner. Replay: an integrated and open solution to produce, handle, and distributeaudio-visual (lecture) recordings. In *Proc. ACM SIGUCCS fall conference: moving mountains, blazing trails*, SIGUCCS '08, pages 195–198, USA, 2008. ACM.

[27] G. Schwerdt and A. C. Wuppermann. Sage on the stage: Is lecturing really all that bad? *Education Next*, 11(3):62–67, 2011.

[28] C. C. Viel, E. L. Melo, M. d. G. Pimentel, and C. A. C. Teixeira. How are they watching me: learning from student interactions with multimedia objects captured from classroom presentations. In *Proc. Intl. Conf. Enterprise Information Systems (ICEIS)*, 2013.

[29] C. C. Viel, E. L. Melo, M. d. G. C. Pimentel, and C. A. C. Teixeira. Go beyond boundaries of itv applications. In *Proc. ACM Symposium on Document Engineering (DocEng)*, pages 263–272. ACM, 2013.

Developing a Ubiquitous Tourist Guide

Humberto Moura, Cristiano Costa,
Sandro Rigo, Eduardo Silva, Jorge Barbosa,
Luiz G. da Silveira Jr., Matheus Wichman
Universidade do Vale do Rio dos Sinos (Unisinos)
São Leopoldo, Brasil
humbertomoura@humbertomoura.com.br,
{cac, rigo, jbarbosa, lgonzaga} @unisinos.br,
{eduardofsilva182, matheus.wichman} @gmail.com

Underléa Bruscato
Universidade Federal do Rio Grande do Sul (UFRGS)
Porto Alegre, Brasil
underlea.brsucato@ufrgs.br

ABSTRACT

In the tourism area, the use of mobile devices brings significant benefits, considering the associated mobility, the instant access and the quality of the tourist information provided. One of the applications in this field is the electronic tourist guide, which provide information to tourists to better enjoy their trip. In this perspective, this work proposes a model that uses mobile and ubiquitous tourism concepts to improve tourist experience. We had developed a prototype for iOS focused on the Caminhos de Pedra tourist itinerary, in Bento Gonçalves / Rio Grande do Sul. Using this prototype, we carried on two evaluations, regarding the ontology proposed and usability. As a result, we could verify that the proposed model helps people to better experience their trips.

Categories and Subject Descriptors

H.4.3 [**Communications Applications**]: Information browsers, J.4 [**Social and Behavioral Sciences**], J.m [**Miscellanious**].

General Terms

Algorithms, Design, Experimentation, Human Factors.

Keywords

Mobile Computing; Ubiquitous Computing; Context Awareness; Web Semantic; Usability; Tourism.

1. INTRODUÇÃO

A indústria do turismo, é considerada como um dos maiores setores do mundo, gerando 11% do produto interno bruto (PIB) global, sendo que somente viagens representam 6% das exportações mundiais totais [1][2]. Considerando a popularização do acesso e o avanço tecnológico dos dispositivos móveis, como *tablets* e *smartphones*, espera-se o desenvolvimento de software que utilize os recursos de mobilidade e de acesso à informação turística a qualquer hora e de qualquer lugar.

No mercado, existem diversos Guias Eletrônico de Turismo, do inglês *Electronic Tourist Guide* (ETG), que exploram conceitos como os de Serviços Baseados em Localização (Location Based Services - LBS) [3], para a busca de Pontos de Interesse (POIs). O

turismo móvel, ou do inglês *mobile tourism* (m-tourism), caracteriza essa área que envolve o uso de aplicativos que fornecem serviços turísticos com conteúdo multimídia executados em dispositivos móveis [4]. Entretanto, poucos ETGs utilizam os demais conceitos associados à computação ubíqua, como os de sensibilidade ao contexto, o perfil do usuário e o ambiente em que ele se encontra [5]. Nesse âmbito, o turismo ubíquo, ou em inglês *ubiquitous tourism* (u-tourism) [6] é a expansão do conceito de turismo móvel, no qual os usuários acessam conteúdos de turismo através de dispositivos móveis, incorporando conceitos de computação ubíqua, tais como a sensibilidade ao contexto e a inteligência, através do uso da web semântica.

Nesse âmbito, o objetivo desse artigo é apresentar um modelo de ETG que considere as características da computação ubíqua. Esse modelo se insere no que vem sendo chamado de u-tourism e se caracteriza por ser aderente a questões de sensibilidade ao contexto, tanto no que tange a localização quanto demais contextos dos usuários, tais como preferências (alimentação, meios de locomoção, etc.), restrições (como de tempo e de dinheiro) e demais interesses (tipos de atrações preferidas, experiências anteriores, etc. De acordo com Dey [13], contexto é qualquer informação que possa ser usado para caracterizar a situação de entidades (pessoa, lugar ou objeto) que são considerados relevantes para a interação entre um usuário e uma aplicação, incluindo o usuário e a aplicação propriamente dita. São tipicamente informações de contexto a localização, identidade e estado de pessoas, grupos e objetos computacionais e físicos.

Além disso, é proposta uma ontologia de turismo que é utilizada para criar um sistema de recomendação, permitindo que atrações melhor avaliadas e relacionadas com os contextos do usuário possam ganhar maior visibilidade. Para avaliar o modelo proposto, foi desenvolvido um ETG para a região dos Caminhos de Pedra em Bento Gonçalves no Rio Grande do Sul. Esse protótipo foi avaliado quanto à qualidade e exatidão da ontologia proposta, bem como com o intuito de verificar a percepção de utilidade e a facilidade de uso pelos usuários.

O artigo está organizado em 6 seções. A próxima seção apresenta os principais conceitos envolvidos no trabalho, como os de turismo eletrônico, turismo móvel e turismo ubíquo. A Seção 3 descreve trabalhos relacionados, envolvendo computação móvel, ubíqua e aplicações em guias eletrônicos de turismo. Na Seção 4 é apresentado o modelo turismo ubíquo proposto, com especial ênfase na descrição da ontologia. A implementação e avaliação são descritas na seção 5. Por fim, a Seção 6 apresenta as conclusões e possíveis trabalhos futuros.

2. TURISMO ELETRÔNICO, MÓVEL E UBÍQUO

Onde ir e o que fazer, em um limitado período de tempo disponível, são problemas comuns encontrados por turistas quando visitam uma cidade pela primeira vez. Tendo em vista que cidades são grandes espaços de informação, para visitar estes espaços é necessário utilizar muitos guias, livros e mapas que provêm grande quantidade de dados.

E-*Tourism* ou *turismo eletrônico* consiste na digitalização de todos os processos e cadeias de valor da indústria do turismo, viagens, hotelaria e restauração que permitem às organizações maximizar sua eficiência e eficácia [7].

A atividade de turismo pode ser dividida em três fases das quais os turistas podem se beneficiar dos sistemas de informação [8]: planejamento, turismo e lembranças. A *fase de planejamento*, que é anterior à viagem do turista, corresponde ao conhecimento do destino da viagem, dos meios de transporte que serão utilizados, dos principais pontos turísticos que serão visitados, dentre outras informações. A *fase de turismo* propriamente dita, compreende a visita aos pontos de interesse, ou seja, locais que alguém considera útil ou interessante, e atrações. Já na *fase de lembranças*, o turista já finalizou a sua viagem e necessita recordar através de fotos, vídeos e outros elementos informações sobre sua viagem turística.

Guias Eletrônicos de Turismo (ou do inglês *Electronic Tourist Guide* – ETG) são aplicativos que utilizam os dispositivos móveis como plataforma chave para o usuário, oferecendo informações turísticas e uso de serviços de turismo de diversas formas [4]. *Guias Móveis de Turismo* são projetos que utilizam dispositivos móveis como o objeto central do turista [9].

Os aplicativos de guias de turismo móvel, bem como os guias tradicionais, são elementos úteis, porque a informação já está catalogada de forma clara e estruturada, permitindo que os turistas encontrem facilmente a informação necessária, por exemplo, a lista de guias turísticos sugeridos restaurantes destacando menus e horários, alojamento com números de telefone e endereços, e assim por diante [10].

O uso desses dispositivos portáteis leva ao conceito de computação móvel que pode ser resumida como *"informação nas pontas dos dedos a qualquer momento e de qualquer lugar"* [11]. Grandes inovações em áreas como tecnologias de rede sem fio, eficiência de energia e software cada vez mais adaptado aos dispositivos móveis têm tornado esse paradigma uma realidade [11].

O uso da computação móvel aplicada ao turismo, leva ao conceito de *turismo móvel*, em que os usuários acessam conteúdos de turismo através de dispositivos móveis [10]. Esse conceito representa uma tendência, relativamente nova, no campo de turismo e envolve o uso de dispositivos portáteis, tais como smartphones e tablets, como guias de turismo eletrônico [7]. Por outro lado, os turistas, atualmente, esperam ter acesso a informações de turismo personalizadas em qualquer lugar, a qualquer hora e de qualquer dispositivo [12].

Guias de turismo ubíquo (Ubiquitous Tourist Guide – UTG) são guias móveis de turismo que acrescentam, além das características de mobilidade, conceitos de turismo ubíquo [9]. Nesse âmbito, o *turismo ubíquo*, ou em inglês *ubiquitous tourism* (u-tourism) é a expansão do conceito de turismo móvel [9], no qual os usuários acessam conteúdos de turismo através de dispositivos móveis, como celulares, smartphones, tablets e *Personal Digital Assistants*

(PDAs) [6]. No turismo ubíquo, estão fortemente relacionados os conceitos de sensibilidade ao contexto [13] e web semântica [14].

3. TRABALHOS RELACIONADOS

Na literatura científica são encontrados diversos trabalhos relacionados ao turismo móvel. Para estudo de trabalhos relacionados, foram selecionadas aquelas propostas que já apresentam alguma característica no âmbito do turismo ubíquo.

O Mytilene [7] tem por objetivo adaptar conteúdos multimídia de turismo obtidos em *sites* Web para serem utilizados por um turista em um dispositivo móvel. A proposta fornece serviços de recomendação baseados no perfil do usuário, localização, avaliação e comentários dos pontos de interesse do turista. Uma das características importantes deste projeto é o suporte à multiplataforma, para que a aplicação se torne portável para vários dispositivos. Este trabalho não utiliza uma ontologia como forma de representação da informação.

O projeto IYOUIT [15] é uma aplicação para dispositivo móvel, sensível ao contexto, desenvolvida pelo laboratório DOCOMO Euro-Labs de Munique, juntamente com o Telematica Instituut da Holanda. O objetivo da aplicação é coletar dados de contexto utilizando o telefone celular, permitindo compartilhar as experiências do usuário através de e amigos e comunidades online. O IYOUIT utiliza tecnologia de Web Semântica para abstrair os dados sobre o turista e o ambiente. Desta forma, dados quantitativos são mapeados para ontologias de contexto para que com o uso de um domínio de conhecimento especializado, a aplicação possa derivar descrições conceituais complexas de situações e eventos do usuário, não fazendo uso de ontologias

A proposta do csxPOI [16], acrônimo para *collaborative semantic and context-aware Points-Of-Interest*, é a criação, colaboração e compartilhamento de pontos de interesse semânticos através de uma aplicação móvel. O csxPOI permite descrever lugares com propriedades semânticas colaborativas através do uso de ontologias, definição de um vocabulário e uma hierarquia de um conjunto de pontos de interesses que podem ser utilizados para que usuário final possa estender as classes dos POIs de forma colaborativa. O csxPOI utiliza dados externos obtidos pela DBPedia [17] para busca de informações sobre os pontos de interesses pesquisados. Utiliza, também, técnicas de Data Mining, para incrementar a qualidade de colaboração de POIs, como o tratamento de pontos de interesse repetidos. ;Estes POIs obtidos através da DBPedia são armazenados em uma ontologia otimizada, tendo sido preferido a não reutilização de ontologias já existentes por questões de otimização de desempenho.

O projeto Murshid [18] é uma aplicação móvel sensível ao contexto que orienta turista em viagens para os Emirados Árabes Unidos. O Murshid fornece um conjunto de serviços como notificação de eventos especiais, previsão do tempo, câmbio, tradução de idiomas, localização e compartilhamento. Cada serviço fornece orientação turística de acordo com o contexto do usuário, adaptando suas funcionalidades de acordo com o ambiente que está relacionado. Além de utilizar informações de contexto, o Murshid considera também o perfil dos usuários.

4. MODELO PROPOSTO DE GUIA DE TURÍSMO UBÍQUO

A arquitetura do modelo proposto parte de três premissas básicas sobre computação ubíqua [5], que são: (i) acesso à computação em qualquer momento e qualquer lugar; (ii) a computação se integra as necessidades das pessoas, se adaptando ao perfil do usuário; (iii) a computação se adapta ao contexto do ambiente.

Além dessas premissas básicas, este modelo possui alguns requisitos gerais: (i) ser um Guia de Turismo Ubíquo, possuindo funcionalidades para a sugestão de pontos de interesse baseados em contextos e restrições do turista e do ambiente onde ele se encontra; (ii) empregar uma ontologia de forma que possam ser inferidas informações importantes sobre o perfil do turista e o contexto; (iii) ser utilizado em qualquer lugar e a qualquer momento, não dependendo de acesso à Internet no uso do aplicativo; (iv) buscar dados de fontes externas para que as informações turísticas sejam as mais atualizadas e completas possíveis; (v) possibilitar a interação entre os usuários permitindo trocar sugestões entre turistas que tenham interesse em comum ou esteja visitando lugares próximos; (vi) ter integração com redes sociais, tais como Facebook e Twitter, para usuários divulgarem e compartilharem suas lembranças; (vii) permitir que a comunidade construa o guia através da criação e avaliação de pontos de interesse e rotas.

Na Figura 1, é possível observar a arquitetura do modelo proposto. Esta arquitetura é formada por um componente cliente e outro servidor. O servidor é constituído por componentes que se comunicam entre si, indicados por setas unidirecionais ou bidirecionais de acordo com o fluxo de informação. Os turistas através dos dispositivos móveis acessam os serviços da camada cliente. Estes por fim, se necessário, se comunicam com o servidor.

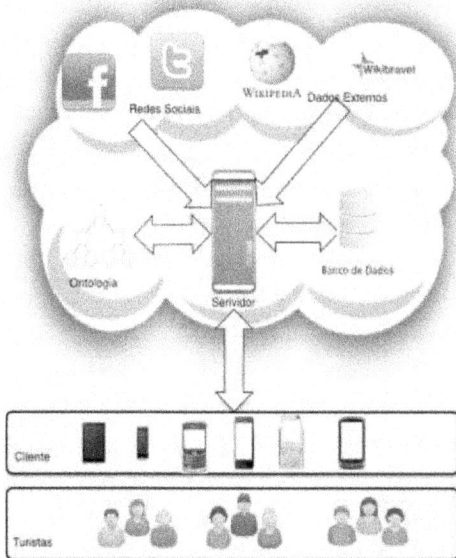

Figura 1. Arquitetura Proposta para o Turismo Ubíquo

As informações básicas, como configurações de autenticação ficam armazenadas em banco de dados e dados que necessitam armazenar informações semânticas, como o contexto do ambiente, ficam salvos na ontologia. O servidor obtém os dados referentes aos pontos de interesse de diversas fontes de dados externas como a Wikipedia e o WikiTravel, para que as informações sejam mais completas. O servidor também se comunica com as redes sociais, e permite que o turista possa compartilhar experiências com informações de contexto como local.

4.1 Servidor de Turismo

A camada servidor do modelo proposto, apresentada na Figura 2, é composta pelos seguintes componentes: Base de Conhecimento, Perfil do Usuário, Contexto do Ambiente, POI, Rota, RA (Realidade Aumentada), Mapa e Interação Social.

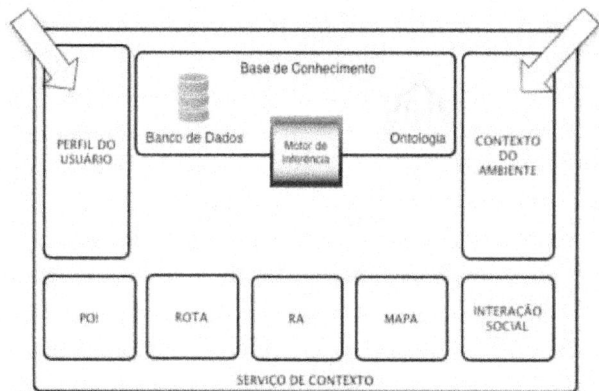

Figura 2. Componentes do Servidor de Turismo Ubíquo

A Base de Conhecimento é composta por um banco de dados, uma ontologia e um motor de inferência. O banco de dados é necessário para que possam ser armazenadas informações básicas, que não necessitam de inferência sobre o sistema, como exemplo, os dados de autenticação do cliente. Já na Ontologia, ficam armazenados os dados de contexto do ambiente e do perfil do turista. Esses dados são necessários para que sejam feitas inferências, como por exemplo para recomendar serviços como POIs ou rotas para o turista. A ontologia foi implementa utilizando no componente servidor o motor de inferência Jena, da Apache Foundation. No motor de inferência são realizadas todas as consultas necessárias para deduzir informações a partir dos componentes Contexto do Ambiente e Perfil do Usuário. Após estas consultas, as informações são mescladas, tornando os dados de um determinado Ponto de Interesse unificados.

No componente de Perfil do usuário são obtidos e atualizados os dados de contexto. Estes dados são obtidos automaticamente através da integração com a rede social Facebook, sendo totalmente transparente ao usuário. No Contexto do ambiente, os dados de contexto do local são obtidos através de dados externos como a Wikipedia e a Wikitravel para complementar as informações a serem exibidas ao turista.

No componente denominado POI, são prestados os serviços criação de novos pontos de interesse e também de sua recomendação e avaliação, de acordo com os dados passados pelo componente Base de Conhecimento. A Rota é responsável pela recomendação e criação de novas rotas definidas pelo usuário, sendo baseadas no contexto analisado pela Base de Conhecimento. No item RA, ou Realidade Aumentada, são prestados serviços de visualização em Realidade Aumentada, propondo uma alternativa a visualização tradicional por mapa geográfico. O Mapa é o componente responsável por exibir as informações sobre os POIs e rotas em um mapa da região. No componente Interação social, é feita a interação dos turistas, como a troca de mensagens entre eles, baseado em interesses em comum ou proximidade de localização.

4.2 Cliente de Turismo

Essa camada, como apresentada na Figura 3, é composta por cinco componentes. A Interface Gráfica é o componente responsável pela iteração entre o turista e a aplicação, servindo de suporte para todas as funcionalidades da aplicação.

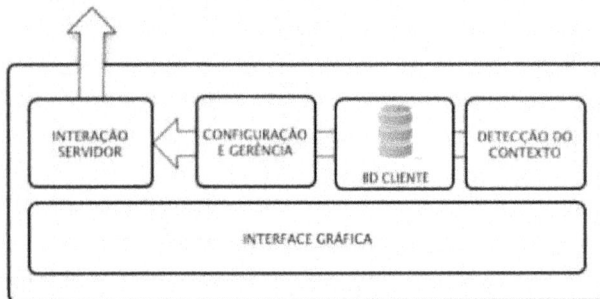

Figura 3. Componentes da Camada Cliente do Modelo de Turismo Ubíquo

No componente Detecção de Contexto, é possível detectar contextos como a localização atual do turista, através de sensores como GPS ou antena Wi-Fi. No BD Cliente são armazenadas todas as informações que necessitam ser persistidas no dispositivo móvel, como usuário e senha do turista, POIs e Rotas. O componente Configuração e Gerência é responsável por toda a configuração da aplicação, como método de autenticação, integração com redes sociais, entre outros. Finalmente, na Iteração Servidor, este componente gerencia o acesso do cliente ao servidor, incluindo a estratégia de criação de um cache para os dados de POIs e Rotas para serem utilizados off-line.

4.3 Ontologia para Turismo

Na definição da arquitetura de um sistema de turismo, provou-se a necessidade da utilização de um mecanismo para possibilitar a inferência de informações turísticas baseadas no perfil do usuário e suas preferências. Optou-se pela escolha do uso de ontologias, tendo em vista as necessidades de inferências do modelo. As principais classes da ontologia desenvolvida pode ser observada na Figura 4, onde foram denominadas *Tourist*, *AvaliableTime*, *Rating*, *Tour*, *Point of Interest*, *Context*, *Location*, *Restriction* e *Profile*.

Na Figura 4, podem ser observados dois tipos de linhas: tracejadas e não tracejadas. As linhas tracejadas representam o conceito de propriedades de objeto, formando assim o relacionamento do tipo "tem um". As linhas não tracejadas descrevem o conceito de herança, também conhecido como relacionamento do tipo "é um".

A classe *Tourist* representa um turista na ontologia proposta. Este turista possui um *Profile*, conforme descrito na Seção 3.1, e um *AvaliableTime*, que é a classe que representa a quantidade de tempo disponível, entre outras informações do turista para a viagem. A classe *Tour* representa um itinerário ou rota personalizado pelos turistas. Cada rota é composta de dois ou mais POIs, que são da classe *PointOfInterest*, representando os pontos de interesse disponíveis. Cada ponto de interesse, por sua vez, possui *Ratings*, que são as avaliações e comentários feitos sobre aquele ponto por outros turistas. A ontologia também possui as classes *Context*, *Location* e *Restriction* que representam respectivamente um contexto, uma localização e restrições que o turista possa ter como restrições de tempo ou financeiras.

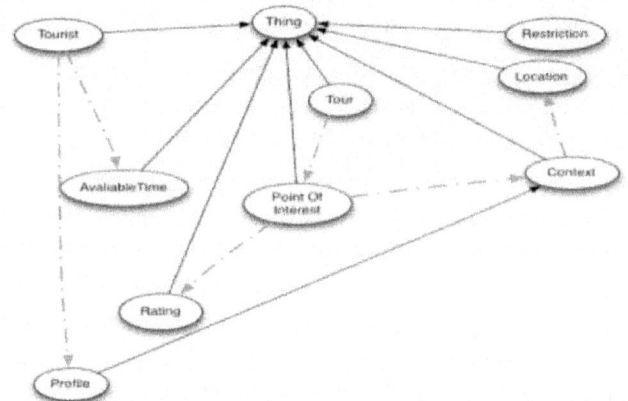

Figura 4. Principais Classes da Ontologia proposta para o Turismo Ubíquo

5. Implementação e Avaliação

Para avaliação do modelo proposto foi desenvolvido um protótipo para os Caminhos de Pedra em Bento Gonçalves no Rio Grande do Sul. Neste protótipo, foram acrescidas as principais funcionalidades propostas no modelo, tais como uso da ontologia, contextos e restrições, para avaliar o funcionamento do modelo em um cenário real.

O protótipo, conforme telas apresentadas na Figura 5, foi desenvolvido para a arquitetura iOS da Apple, sendo suportada por iPhones e iPads. Para a codificação foi utilizada a IDE *Xcode*, juntamente com a linguagem *Objective-C*, ferramentas consideradas padrão para o desenvolvimento nesta plataforma.

Para a definição e desenvolvimento da ontologia foi utilizada a ferramenta livre *Protégé*. No lado servidor foi utilizado o banco de dados *PostgreSQL*, por ser software livre e não possuir custos de licença, integrado ao framework Apache Jena, como motor de inferência para a ontologia, além da utilização da linguagem SPARQL para realizar as consultas necessárias à ontologia. A comunicação entre o servidor e o cliente foi deita através de chamadas HTTP via JSON (*JavaScript Object Notation*), objetivando máximo desempenho do servidor.

Para avaliação do modelo, foram realizadas duas experimentações. A primeira foi planejada com o objetivo de analisar a ontologia proposta em relação à qualidade e exatidão. A segunda experimentação, consiste em uma avaliação para verificar a percepção de utilidade e a facilidade de uso pelos usuários.

Figura 5. Algumas telas do protótipo desenvolvido para os Caminhos de Pedra

5.1 Avaliação da Ontologia

Para a avaliação da Ontologia foi utilizada uma técnica baseada em métricas, proposta na metodologia denominada FOEval, Full Ontology Evaluation [21]. A FOEval permite aos usuários selecionarem um conjunto de métricas que possam auxiliar no processo de avaliação das ontologias, atribuindo pesos a cada uma e possibilitando a avalição das ontologias armazenadas local ou remotamente. As ponderações usadas nas métricas são partes da própria metodologia de avaliação A metodologia possui um amplo conjunto de métricas, que são denominadas: cobertura, riqueza, nível de detalhe, abrangência, conectividade e eficiência computacional [21].

A utilização desta metodologia se baseou em três etapas. A primeira etapa, denominada *Preparação*, consistiu em decidir quais seriam as ontologias avaliadas e classificadas: locais ou remotas. A segunda etapa, que é denominada *Métricas*, consistiu em determinar a partir de um conjunto de métricas, quais seriam utilizadas no processo de avaliação, e, opcionalmente, atribuir pesos para cada uma usada de acordo com a percepção de impacto e importância dela no processo. Na terceira etapa, denominada *Avaliar,* as ontologias foram avaliadas para cada métrica utilizada, e então, atribuída uma pontuação numérica. A partir destes dados, uma pontuação global para a ontologia foi calculada como uma soma ponderada das suas pontuações obtidas nas métricas.

Na primeira etapa foi escolhida a abordagem de avaliação local. Na segunda etapa foram escolhidas as métricas de avaliação denominadas *riqueza, detalhamento global* e *eficiência computacional*. Estas métricas foram escolhidas por melhor se adaptarem as necessidades deste trabalho. A métrica *riqueza* permite verificar se uma determinada ontologia é rica em termos de relações e atributos, estes sendo importantes critérios para uma ontologia. A métrica de *detalhamento global* avalia como o conhecimento está agrupado em diferentes categorias e subcategorias na ontologia, permitindo conhecer se uma determinada ontologia tem predominância vertical ou horizontal.

Já a métrica *eficiência computacional* foi selecionada tendo em vista a importância de verificar o desempenho da ontologia.

Para calcular a riqueza, são realizados três cálculos. A *riqueza de relação* (RR) que mensura a diversidade das relações, assumindo que quanto maior quantidade de relações não hierárquicas, mais rica é a ontologia. Outro cálculo realizado é da *riqueza de atributo* (RA) que consiste no número médio de atributos que são definidos para cada classe que pode indicar a quantidade de informações relativas a dados de instância, quanto mais atributos são definidos maior conhecimento a ontologia transmite. Finalmente, é calculada a riqueza da ontologia (RO), a partir dos valores de RR e RA.

Os resultados obtidos para a ontologia proposta foram 0,72 pontos para RR; 2,61 pontos para RA; e, 3,33 pontos para RO. Esses resultados demonstram que a ontologia é mais rica em atributos do que em relações. Além disso há em média de 2,61 atributos por classe e de 0,72 relações por classe. O RO obtido pode ser empregado na comparação da riqueza da ontologia proposta com a riqueza de outras ontologias para a área de turismo.

O cálculo de *nível de detalhamento global, é* definido pela média do número de subclasses divididos pelo número de classes da ontologia. Ao efetuarmos esta fórmula na ontologia proposta, foi obtido o valor 39 para o total de subclasses, e 0,02 para o detalhamento global. Esses resultados demonstram que a ontologia proposta é bem dividida em termos de classes e subclasses, sendo muito próximo do meio termo entre tipos de taxonomia vertical e horizontal.

O cálculo da métrica de eficiência computacional considera o uso de uma ontologia de avaliação e uma ontologia candidata. No caso da ontologia candidata foi assumida a possibilidade da ontologia crescer 10 vezes, ou seja, os dados relativos a quantidade de classes, instâncias e outros elementos serem multiplicados por 10. Aplicando a fórmula proposta na

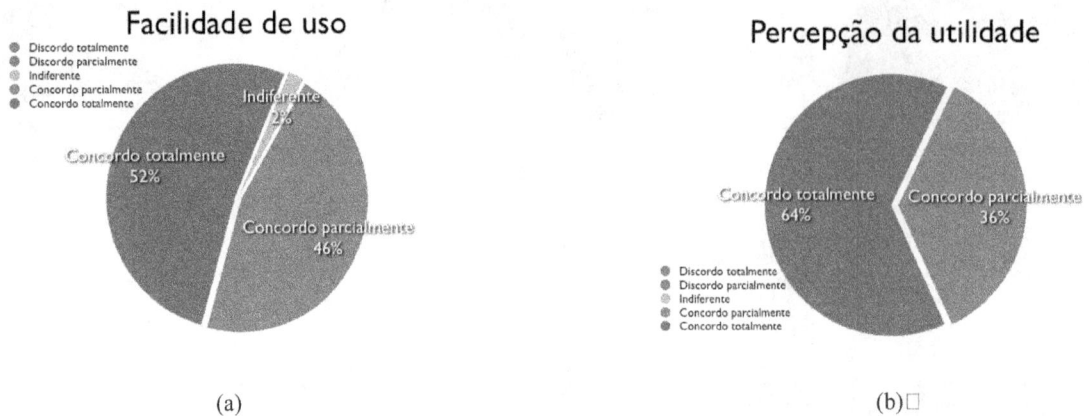

Figura 6. Resultados obtidos na avaliação de usabilidade

metodologia, obteve-se o valor 2,04. A eficiência computacional demonstrou ser facilmente processável, apesar do crescimento simulado, pois seu valor ficou relativamente próximo de zero.

Devemos considerar que os valores obtidos pela avaliação FOEval não considerar os eventuais pesos das métricas, assumindo que todas possuem a mesma importância, além de observar que os valores dos parâmetros utilizados nesta avaliação mudam constantemente, tendo em vista o crescimento natural da ontologia e o seu uso.

Avaliação da Usabilidade

Como segunda avaliação do modelo, foi realizada uma análise da usabilidade usando o modelo TAM, proposto por [22] e expandido por [23]. De acordo com [22] os estudos mostram que, entre os vários fatores que as pessoas consideram mais importante para aceitar ou rejeitar uma aplicação, a percepção de utilidade, ou seja, a medida em que o usuário avalia que a aplicação pode melhorar a sua experiência, é a variável mais importante a considerar. A segunda variável mais importante é chamada de facilidade de utilização, a qual é definida como o grau em que uma pessoa acredita que a utilização de um sistema está livre de estresse. Esta variável complementa a primeira, porque de acordo com pesquisas apenas a aplicação não é suficiente para ser útil, porque os benefícios da aplicação deve superar o seu esforço para usá-la [22].

A metodologia TAM foi empregada para mensurar a aceitação do modelo. Esta avaliação envolveu 20 (vinte) usuários voluntários da universidade, dentre colegas, alunos, funcionários e professores que avaliaram o protótipo de ETG (Figura 5), tendo como objetivo verificar a percepção de utilidade da aplicação e facilidade de uso percebida do modelo proposto.

Após uma breve demonstração do funcionamento do ETG, os voluntários foram convidados a tentar utiliza-lo simulando as seguintes tarefas que foram previamente demonstradas: (i) preenchimento de dados do usuário. (ii) busca de informações de pontos de interesse turísticos da região, (iii) criação de rotas personalizadas baseadas nestes pontos. (iv) visualização dos pontos de interesse utilizando o mapa da região e visualização por uma lista por categorias. Depois da experimentação do ETG, estes

voluntários responderam a um questionário de 10 (dez) perguntas, com o objetivo de avaliar a aceitação do modelo, verificando assim a usabilidade do sistema. Os resultados obtidos estão resumidos na Figura 6.

Apesar do alto índice de aceitação de facilidade de uso, resumido no gráfico (a) da Figura 6, há espaço para melhorias. Por exemplo podem ser otimizadas, em nível de facilidade de uso, as opções de criação de rotas e de busca de pontos turísticos. Uma das alternativas para tratar estes pontos é a criação visual de rotas no mapa e a exibição de linhas entre os pontos de interesse de uma rota para torna-la mais fácil de ser utilizada. Já a percepção de utilidade, conforme resumo apresentado no gráfico (b) da Figura 6, indica inexistência de discordância ou indiferença por parte dos usuários, indicando forte aceitação por parte dos mesmos.

6. Conclusão

O turismo ubíquo possui um grande potencial a ser desenvolvido, incluindo a exploração de características de sensibilidade ao contexto, onde este modelo está inserido. Obter informações turísticas a qualquer hora e em qualquer lugar torna-se relevante no mundo atual, onde o uso escasso de recursos, como o tempo do turista e suas restrições é facilitado pelo uso de tecnologias cada vez mais inteligentes e assertivas.

Neste trabalho procurou-se levar em consideração o perfil do turista e o contexto onde ele está inserido, criando-se uma ontologia para otimizar a sua experiência turística da região, fazendo uso da mobilidade característica de grande valor dos dispositivos móveis. Como resultado, além do conhecimento adquirido e entendimento das necessidades do turista, quanto à avaliação de aceitação do modelo, foi possível observar o interesse e a aprovação dos usuários em relação ao aplicativo.

O modelo proposto, considerando todos os trabalhos relacionados estudados, é o único que integra localização, perfil e histórico, com a detecção automática de perfil. Além disso, permite acesso a dados tanto offline como online. Outra característica importante é a junção de aspectos de UTG, como web semântica e ciência de contexto, aplicados a um modelo geral de turismo.

Como trabalhos futuros, pretende-se adicionar suporte a diferentes plataformas de desenvolvimento, como Android. Outro foco do trabalho será a criação de um módulo de realidade aumentada. Também pretende-se pesquisar a integração com outros software de turismo.

7. Agradecimentos

Os autores gostariam de agradecer a União Européia por financiar a pesquisa através do projeto Alfa-Gaviotas (Edital Alfa III). Também gostaríamos de agradecer a CAPES, FAPERGS e CNPQ que também apoiam essa pesquisa através da concessão de bolsas.

8. Referências

[1] Hannes Werthner and Francesco Ricci. 2004. E-commerce and tourism. *Commun. ACM* 47, 12 (December 2004), 101-105. DOI=10.1145/1035134.1035141.

[2] OMT. World Tourism Barometer. Madri, v. 7, n. 2, junho 2009. Available in http://www.unwto.org/facts/eng /barometer.htm

[3] A. Dey; J. Hightower; E. de Lara; N. Davies. Location-Based Services. *Pervasive Computing, IEEE* 9, 1 (March 2010), 11-12. DOI=10.1109/MPRV.2010.10.

[4] Kenteris, M. et al. 2010. Electronic mobile guides: a survey. *Personal and Ubiquitous Computing*. 15, 1 (Apr. 2010), 97–111.

[5] da Costa, C. et al. 2008. Toward a General Software Infrastructure for Ubiquitous Computing. *Pervasive Computing, IEEE*. 7, 1 (2008), 64–73.

[6] Michele Ruta, Floriano Scioscia, Eugenio Di Sciascio, and Giacomo Piscitelli. 2010. Location-Based Semantic Matchmaking in Ubiquitous Computing. In *Proceedings of the 2010 IEEE/WIC/ACM International Conference on Web Intelligence and Intelligent Agent Technology - Volume 03* (WI-IAT '10), Vol. 3. IEEE Computer Society, Washington, DC, USA, 124-127. DOI=10.1109/WI-IAT.2010.300.

[7] D. Buhalis. *Tourism*: Information technology for strategic tourism management. Prentice Hall, Harlow, 2003.

[8] R. Watson; S. Akselsen; E. Monod; L. Pitt. 2004. The Open Tourism Consortium: laying the foundations for the future of tourism. *European Management Journal*, 22, 3, (2004), 315-326.

[9] Gavalas, D. and Kenteris, M. 2011. A web-based pervasive recommendation system for mobile tourist guides. Personal and Ubiquitous Computing. 15, 7 (May. 2011), 759–770.

[10] B. Brown; M. Chalmers. 2003. Tourism and Mobile Technology, in *Proceedings of the 8th European Conference on Computer Supported Cooperative Work*, pp. 335-355, Helsinki, Finland, 2003.

[11] M. Satyanarayanan. 2011. Mobile computing: the next decade. *SIGMOBILE Mobile Computing and Communications Review*. 15, 2 (Aug. 2011).

[12] W. SCHWINGER et al. 2009. Context- Awareness in Mobile Tourism Guides. *Handbook of Research on Mobile Multimedia*, 2nd ed., Information Science Reference.

[13] A.K. Dey. 2001. Understanding and Using Context. *Personal and Ubiquitous Computing*. 5, 1 (Jan. 2001).

[14] M. d'Aquin; N.F. Noy. 2012. Where to publish and find ontologies? A survey of ontology libraries. *Web Semantics: Science, Services and Agents on the World Wide Web*. 11, (2012), 96–111.

[15] S. Boehm et al. Introducing IYOUIT, The Semantic Web-ISWC 2008. Springer Berlin Heidelberg, 2008. 804-817.

[16] Braun, M. et al. 2010. Collaborative Creation of Semantic Points of Interest as Linked Data on the Mobile Phone. Technical Report N. 1/2010, Universitat Koblenz.

[17] Becker, C. and Bizer, C. 2008. DBpedia mobile-a location-aware semantic web client. (2008). Proceedings of the Semantic Web.

[18] Ahmed Echtibi, Mohamed Jamal Zemerly, and Jawad Berri. 2009. Murshid: a mobile tourist companion. In Proceedings of the 1st International Workshop on Context-Aware Middleware and Services: affiliated with the 4th International Conference on Communication System Software *and Middleware (COMSWARE 2009)* (CAMS '09). ACM, New York, NY, USA, 6-11. DOI=10.1145/1554233.1554236

[19] M. d'Aquin; N.F. Noy. 2012. Where to publish and find ontologies? A survey of ontology libraries. *Web Semantics: Science, Services and Agents on the World Wide Web*. 11, (2012), 96–111.

[20] A.K. Dey. 2001. Understanding and Using Context. *Personal and Ubiquitous Computing*. 5, 1 (Jan. 2001).

[21] A. Bouiadjra; S. Benslimane, FOEval: Full ontology evaluation, *Proceedings of 7th International Conference on Natural Language Processing and Knowledge Engineering*, NLPKE 2011, Tokushima, Japan, 2012.

[22] F. Davis. 1989 Perceived usefulness, perceived ease of use, and user acceptance, MIS Quarterly, 13, 3, (1989), 318–34.

[23] C. Yoon; S. Kim. 2007. Convenience and TAM in a ubiquitous computing environment: the case of wireless LAN, *Electronic Commerce: Research and Applications*, 6, 1, (Jan. 2007), 102-112.

CSCoupons: Applying Context-Sensitivity to Increase Fast Food Advertising Usefulness

Rodrigo Falcão

Vaninha Vieira

Computer Science Department / Federal University of Bahia (UFBA)

Av. Adhemar de Barros, s/n, Campus de Ondina – 40.170-110 – Salvador – BA – Brazil

{rodrigompf,vaninha}@dcc.ufba.br

ABSTRACT

Companies spend too much money on advertising in order to improve their sales. However, the ratio between investment and effective sales is low. Increasing the usefulness of provided ads and discount coupons is an ongoing challenge in advertising, in order to enhance return on investments, reducing wastage and increasing revenue. Ubiquitous computing offers many features that are considered compliant to advertising needs. A key aspect in ubiquitous computing is the use of context to provide more relevant information to users, according to their current situation and environment. This paper introduces CSCoupons, a mobile context-sensitive system to deliver discount coupons. We conduct an experiment with a developed prototype of CSCoupons to assess the ideas about fast food coupons in shopping malls. To measure the usefulness of delivered discount coupons, we compared two versions of the prototype: with and without considering context information. The preliminary results show context-sensitivity highly increases advertising usefulness.

Categories and Subject Descriptors

H.3.4 [**Information Systems**]: Systems and Software – *User profiles and alert services.*

J.1 [**Computer Applications**]: Administrative Data Processing – *Marketing.*

General Terms

Measurement, Experimentation

Keywords

Context-aware computing, ubiquitous advertising, ubiquitous computing, mobile computing

1. INTRODUCTION

It is estimated that less than a half of resources applied in advertising effectively promotes sale of products and services [8]. John Wanamaker, a department store owner and pioneer in marketing [11], said that he knew that half of the invested money on advertising was wasted, but his problem was he didn't know which half. Therefore, increasing advertising usefulness is an ongoing challenge for researchers and professionals in the advertising industry.

A study conducted in the United States and presented in 2006 estimated that only 41% of what is spent on advertising generates sales [8]. It is necessary to spend continuous efforts in order to discover ways to increase the sales [7], knowing how useful ads can be, in other words, to know ads usefulness, i.e. capability to produce a sale.

Researchers [9] have employed efforts to promote alignment between ubiquitous computing (UC) and advertising, given the fact that the results produced by the first area reveal themselves useful to meet the challenges of the second.

In this work, we focused a specific class of advertisements - offers, in form of discount coupons - and how the use of context can make them more useful to customers.

Research in the area of discount coupons on mobile platforms are scarce [3], even more if we seek context sensitivity. In industry, in the other hand, there are many websites and mobile applications for discount coupons delivery, although contextual information is underexplored (as seen in collective buying systems).

We projected and introduce CSCoupons, a mobile application for context-sensitive discount coupons delivery. The domain for this experiment is discount coupons for fast food restaurants. We performed the context modelling and implemented a prototypical mobile application for coupons delivery simulation. In order to measure the gain obtained on using context in this field, a second prototypical application was implemented for discount coupons delivery, but without context-sensitivity. The usefulness of offers submitted in both cases are measurable and the results intend to demonstrate if the context-sensitive approach is more effective.

The paper is organized as follows: Section 2 presents some concepts; Section 3 reviews similar works; Section 4 introduces CSCoupons; Section 5 shows an experimental evaluation; and Section 6 presents our conclusions and further work.

2. CONCEPTS

The original vision of ubiquitous computing pointed to advances in hardware and software that would support an entire embedded systems universe, spread in connected devices, surrounding us by hundreds, so integrated into our day-to-day that technology will "disappear" [14]. A fundamental challenge in this scenario is to develop "calm technologies" (that inform and calm), where computers act both on focus and on peripheral of human attention, making information transit easily between these two areas [15].

Context-sensibility is a core aspect of ubiquitous computing [10] [1]. Context-sensitive systems are applications that use context to adapt its behavior in different situations or circumstances, promoting more relevant services to users or information to better support tasks performance [12].

Ubiquitous advertising, or pervasive advertising, is the given name for the use of ubiquitous computing technologies for advertising purposes [9]. Ubiquitous advertising is faced as the killer application for the 21st century [6]. Indeed, advertising and UC have approached on the perception that the former has challenges and goals broadly aligned with what has been researched in the second.

Among the main problems that advertising faces are targeting advertising and evaluating ads effectiveness. An interesting aspect of ubiquitous advertising is that a trigger for shopping should be, at the same time, calm and engaging: ubiquitous advertising is supposed do be calm when we don't need it, but engaging and inspiring when we want it [9].

Based on the relevance and usefulness degrees presented in [9], we consider there are three main ways to look at results of exposing a consumer to an ad: *Irrelevant*: the ad doesn't get customer's interest; *Relevant but useless*: the ad gets customer's interest, but it doesn't generate a sale; *Useful*: the ad gets customer's interest and it generates a sale.

About the buying behavior patterns of consumers, there are four categories [9]: *extensive decisions* (demand high cognitive and emotional involvement, take time to be taken, such as the purchase of a house); *habitualized purchase decisions* (almost automatic or routine decision process); *limited decisions* (taken when there is no choices); and *impulsive purchase decisions* (strongly driven by emotions). In the *impulsive purchase decisions* category, what happens is the realization of a stimulus to which the consumer responds with a purchase – a trivial example of stimulus is a promotional offer. A contemporary phenomenon that exploits this behavior is the collective shopping sites – most of them also available on smartphones and tablets.

3. RELATED WORK

As context-sensitive coupons delivery systems are not wide explored [3], we reviewed two similar studies on mobile advertisement area.

Tag Match Advertising [4] (TMA) is a proposal that mixes RFID readers and location services embedded in smartphones to enrich the information about products and services, offering georeferenced advertising. Its approach seeks to take one of Internet advertising model (where the user search for information and receives, in addition to content, advertising) to the mobile environment.

AdNext [5] is an ubiquitous advertising system based on discovery of visiting patterns in a shopping mall to identify which is the most probably "next place" that a customer will visit, in order to support delivery of more relevant ads to customers. Their strategy aims to increase the relevance of the ads by discarding those that will not probably be interesting (e.g. an advertisement for a restaurant delivered minutes after the user have had lunch). The mechanism for learning visiting patterns is collective, i.e. it is based on data provided by many users, obtained with techniques for identifying indoor location using Wi-Fi networks. This approach incorporates the use of a learning pattern technique to acknowledge user's sequential patterns.

Both TMA and AdNext use only users locations as contextual element (actually AdNext uses a learning machine approach to predict user location and try to infer user current needs).

Indeed, user location is relevant for ad's delivery. The use of location - and the consequent development of location-aware applications - is increasing and becoming more widespread among smartphone users. In United States, 50% of adults and 75% of all users use location based services in theirs mobile devices [16].

However, consumer context has much more to offer in order to make ads more useful (e.g., customer's habits, preferences, restrictions etc.).

4. CSCoupons: CONTEXT-SENSITIVE OFFERS DELIVERY

This work proposes CSCoupons (*Context-Sensitive Coupons*), an ubiquitous and context-sensitive offers delivery platform for mobile devices. We seek to investigate in which ways ubiquitous computing techniques can support the ad's usefulness problem. As a motivating scenario, for the current version of our proposal, we consider the domain of discount coupons delivered in fast food restaurants area in shopping malls. CSCoupons is a mobile application that presents daily discount coupons to users, according to variations observed in his/her context. We seek to assess whether context-sensibility increases the offers usefulness – and how much it does. Offers usefulness is measured by the coupons redemption's rate.

Next subsections discuss the proposed context model, the CSCoupons architecture and the aspects concerning the implementation of two versions of prototypical application: with and without context sensitivity.

4.1 Context Model

For modeling a context-sensitive system, it is important to identify what is considered "focus of attention" [2][13], which involves recognizing the *actor* performing a *task* that can be enriched through using context. In CSCoupons, the *actor* is the consumer (ad's target) whose task is to find a fast food restaurants to lunch in shopping malls. Table 1 shows the CSCoupons context model, according to this focus of attention.

Three entities were identified: Consumer, Restaurant and Coupon. For each entity we indicate the considered contextual elements raised during the problem analysis. Contextual elements can be static (doesn't change over time), dynamic (changes over time), explicit (informed by the user) and implicit (obtained without user intervention).

4.2 Architecture

CSCoupons architecture are divided in two parts: server side (general software infrastructure to support context-sensitive coupons delivery) and mobile client side (specific features for mobile deployments). We organized them as shown in Figure 1.

The very core of CSCoupons architecture is the server side *Context Manager* module. It implements a submodule called *acquiring context* to receive coupons data (local, date, features) generated by advertisers (for the purpose of gather customer data, there is another *acquiring module* in the mobile client side). The submodule *processing context* transforms raw data into meaningful context data, in order to get a context-sensitive coupon. This context-sensitive coupon is delivered to customers by the *notifier* submodule.

Table 1. CSCoupons context model

Entity	Contextual Element	Static	Dynamic	Explicit	Implicit
Consumer	Sex Gender	X		X	
Consumer	Birthday	X		X	
Consumer	Preferred kind of food	X		X	
Consumer	Preferred payment method	X		X	
Consumer	Location		X		X
Consumer	Time		X		X
Consumer	Have lunched?		X		X
Restaurant	Location	X		X	
Restaurant	Accepted Payment method	X		X	
Restaurant	Kind of food	X		X	
Restaurant	Evaluation		X	X	
Coupon	Price	X		X	
Coupon	Expiration	X		X	
Coupon	Kind of food	X		X	

4.3 Prototype Implementation

Two prototypical applications for fast food discount coupons were developed: CSCoupons and SimpleCoupons. The CSCoupons is context-sensitive, so it implements the context model and architecture presented in previous sections. The SimpleCoupons was developed to support the experimental studies (Section 5) and does not consider context changes. It shows at startup a discount coupon offer (identified randomly). Both applications produce only one coupon per day, so after accepting or refusing an offer, no more coupons will be available until the end of the day (when the coupon expires).

The developed prototypes are mobile applications built on the Android platform. We choose Android because it is an open platform, widely used on most mobile smartphone devices, easing application distribution for the experiment.

In its current version, CSCoupons considers a subset of the contextual elements presented in Table 1: user's preferred kind of food, user and restaurant's locations, current time and offer's kind of food.

CSCoupons checks, near lunchtime (between 11:00am and 2:00pm), if the smartphone holder is near a shopping mall (where several fast food options can be found). If so, it notifies the user with a discount coupon offering for a restaurant in that shopping whose available offer is compatible with user's food preferences. The coupon is valid only for the day it is delivered.

When the application starts, CSCoupons verifies if the device's location services are active – if they are not, it asks for activation.

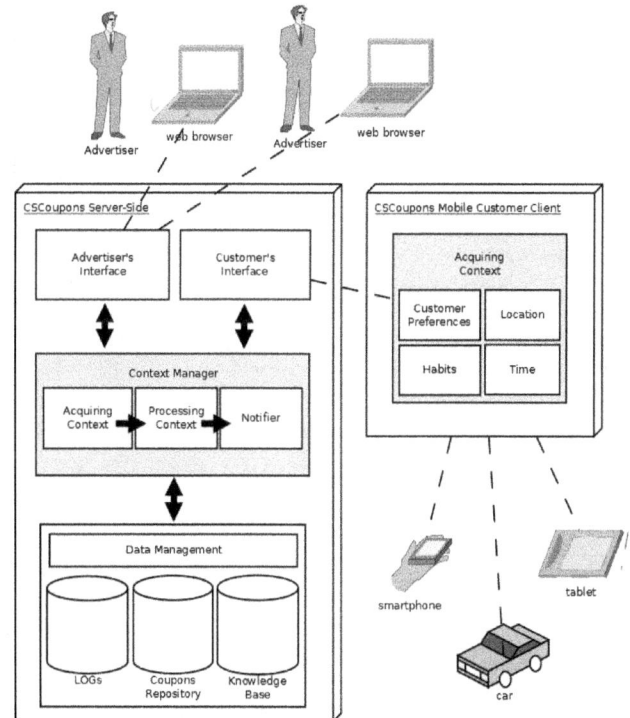

Figure 1. CSCoupons Architecture

Proximity between user and shopping malls is verified through location services embedded in customer's smartphone. These services use Wi-Fi networks, mobile networks and GPS satellites.

The first time the software is launched, it displays a screen for the user to configure his/her food preferences (pasta, meat, and so on). CSCoupons does not require any user interaction until the application identifies an offer and notifies the user about it. In Android OS, offer notifications are presented in the notification bar. When the user opens a notification, a new screen appears describing the coupon (restaurant, address, kind of food, discount value). The consumer has two options: to accept or to refuse the offer. Every time an user accepts (or refuses) an offer, a log record is inserted.

The second version of the prototype, without context-sensitivity (SimpleCoupons), does not generate automatic offers notification. When it is raised, a discount coupon offering is shown for a fast food restaurant and the application ends. As done in CSCoupons, acceptances and refusals are recorded in a log.

5. EXPERIMENTAL EVALUATIONS

To evaluate our proposal we performed with 5 (five) volunteers a preliminary experimental study in the city of Salvador/BA during a seven-day period. SimpleCoupons was given to 1 (one) volunteer while another 4 (four) volunteers used CSCoupons. In both cases, they received textual instructions about how to use the programs. All participants live in Salvador/BA, are male and have between 25 and 34 years old.

A list of 294 simulated discount coupons was manually generated. It was loaded and stored on the mobile devices during the applications' installation time. This number represents the number of mapped shopping malls (6) times the number of kinds of food we defined (7) times the number of days of the experiment (7), i.e., there was one coupon for each shopping mall, for each kind of food, for each day.

At the end of the seven-day period of the experiment, log files were collected from volunteers' devices. The log records date and time of coupons offering, and the consumer's decision (accept or refuse). The offer's usefulness for a volunteer i (U_i) is given by the ratio between the amount of coupons accepted (A_i) and the total generated offerings for that volunteer (O_i). Offers that do not have any record of acceptance or refusal are ignored. In these cases, the user probably was notified but ignored it.

$$U_i = A_i / O_i \qquad (1)$$

The offers's usefulness for each application (OU_i) is given by the sum of offers's usefulness for each participant i in the experiment with the application, divided by the total number n of volunteers using the application.

$$OU_i = \sum_{i=1}^{n} U_i / n \qquad (2)$$

Although we admit that sample is not yet sufficiently representative, parcial finds are pointing to our expectations. Preliminary results indicate less coupons offering but more acceptance of coupons in the context-sensitive featured application, what suggest a calmest and more useful user experience. While SimpleCoupons ensures one coupon daily, CSCoupons relies on time rules (lunchtime), space rules (proximity to shopping malls) and user preferences.

The usefulness of the coupons discount was higher in the context-sensitive featured prototype: 71% of CSCoupons discount coupons were accepted (therefore considered useful), while only 20% of the offers did not observe context were accepted.

6. CONCLUSIONS AND FURTHER WORK

This paper discusses the opportunity to increase the usefulness rate of advertisements through features of ubiquitous computing. For this, it was developed a study on offers for fast food restaurants and it was proposed CSCoupons, a context-sensitive mobile application for discount coupons delivery for fast food restaurants.

We presented CSCoupons' context model and architecture and discussed the implementation aspects of a preliminary prototype of the system as well as the preliminary results with an experimental study performed in the city of Salvador-BA.

In order to evaluate the gain promoted by the use of context in the distribution of fast food discount coupons, a prototype similar to CSCoupons was developed, however without use of any contextual element. We performed an experiment to compare the usefulness of offers in these two applications.

The preliminary results suggest the advantage on using context to deliver discount coupons for fast food restaurants.

As ongoing work we indicate the following (i) the execution of the planned experiment with more users during a longer period of time in closest to real conditions (restaurants, offers, consumers); (ii) the evolution and implementation of the modules described for the proposed architecture, including the overall distribution chain from the offer creation by the advertiser to the use of the coupon by the user; (iii) the incorporation of more contextual elements processing into the application and evaluating how the incorporation of each new contextual element can contribute to the growth in the offers' usefulness.

As opportunity for future work we indicate the use of machine learning techniques to provide more implicit than explicit entries of contextual elements. Providing personalized services involves discovering user's habits and preferences, which can change over time [1]. We do believe it leads to a calmest, pleasant and, therefore, useful user experience. For instance, not annoying consumers with things that do not matter to him/her, perceiving him/her in a non intrusive way and engaging him/her in opportunities only at the best time, location and for best reason.

7. REFERENCES

[1] Baldauf, F., Dustdar, S. e Rosenberg, F. "A survey on context-aware systems". Int. Journal of Ad Hoc and Ubiquitous Computing. 2007.

[2] Brézillon, J., & Brézillon, P. (2007). Context modeling: Context as a dressing of a focus. In Modeling and Using Context (pp. 136-149). Springer Berlin Heidelberg.

[3] Dickinger, A., e Kleijnen, M. "Coupons going wireless: Determinants of consumer intentions to redeem mobile coupons". Journal of Interactive Marketing, 22(3), 23-39. 2008.

[4] Jun, Jungho e Kyoung Jun Lee. "Design of Tag Match Advertising System and the Evaluation of the Business Model." Asia-Pacific Services Computing Conference, 2008. APSCC'08. IEEE. 2008.

[5] Kim, Byoungjip, et al. "Adnext: a visit-pattern-aware mobile advertising system for urban commercial complexes." Proceedings of the 12th Workshop on Mobile Computing Systems and Applications. ACM, 2011.

[6] Krumm, J. "Ubiquitous Advertising: The Killer Applications for the 21st Century", IEEE Pervasive. 2010.

[7] Lasinger, P., Bauer, C. "Situationalization, the New Road to Adaptive Digital-out-of-Home Advertising". Proceedings of IADIS International Conference e-Society, 162-169. 2013.

[8] Marsland, L. "How Much Advertising Actually Works?" http://www.bizcommunity.com/Article/196/119/9593.html. 2006.

[9] Müller, J., Alt, F. e Michelis, D. "Pervasive Advertising", Pervasive Advertising, Chapter 1. Spring. 2011.

[10] Strang, T. e Linnhoff-Popien, C. "A Context Modeling Survey", First International Workshop on Advanced Context Modelling, Reasoning and Management, UbiComp. 2004.

[11] Tucker, J. "What's a Job Good For?", Mises Institute http://mises.org/daily/5171/Whats-a-Job-Good-For. 2011.

[12] Vieira, V., Caldas, L. R. e Salgado, A. C. "Towards an Ubiquitous and Context Sensitive Public Transportation System". 4th International Conference on Ubi-media Computing. 2011.

[13] Vieira, V., Tedesco, P., & Salgado, A. C. (2011). Designing context-sensitive systems: An integrated approach. Expert Systems with Applications, 38(2), 1119-1138.

[14] Weiser, M., "The computer for the 21st century", Scientific American, vol. 265, no. 3. pp.66-75. 1991.

[15] Weiser, M. and Brown, J.S. "The Coming Age of Calm Technology". Xerox PARC. 1996.

[16] Zickuhr, K. "Three-quarters of smartphone owners use location-based services". Pew Research Center. 2012

Touch The Air: An Event-Driven Framework for Interactive Environments

Almerindo N. Rehem Neto
IFS-Instituto Federal de Sergipe
Campus Lagarto
Lagarto–SE – 49400-000
almerindo.rehem@gmail.com

Celso A. S. Santos
DI – UFES
Vitória–ES – 29075-910
saibel@inf.ufes.br

Lucas A. de Carvalho
IFS-Instituto Federal de Sergipe
Campus Lagarto
Lagarto–SE – 49400-000
lucas_aragaoc@hotmail.com

ABSTRACT

Since the advent of *Kinect*, there has been an outbreak of applications that go beyond mouse and keyboard interfaces. Applications developers aim to enrich and re-imagine these interfaces using gesture and voice commands recognition for controlling some virtual and real world objects using a natural interaction mechanism. Aligned to this, there are problems to set a standard for these interfaces, plus a huge effort in performing simple tasks such as connecting sensors, processing data, recognizing gestures and running actions in real or virtual world. This paper proposes an extendable event-driven *framework* that improves the life cycle of designing and building interactive environments, making it possible to interact with both real and virtual environments.

Categories and Subject Descriptors

H.5.2 [Users Interfaces]: Evaluation/methodology, Interaction Styles, Natural Language, Standardization
H.1.2 [User/Machine Systems]: Human Factor, human information processing

General Terms

Human Factors, Languages, Experimentation, Framework

Keywords

Natural Interaction, Gesture recognition, Framework, Sensors, *Kinect*

1. Introduction

Human Computer Interaction is a multidisciplinary subject that involves areas such as computing, psychology, linguistic, and others. In order to offer users an adequate way to interact with computational platforms, we should consider knowledge about human capacity limitations, technological restrictions and evolutions (in terms of devices and processing types/power), and context. The evolution of technologies for capturing user interactions (usually in ubiquitous ways) created new paradigms for the conception of interfaces for interactive applications.

WebMedia'13, November 5–8, 2013, Salvador, Brazil.
Copyright © 2013 ACM 978-1-4503-2559-2/13/11...$15.00.
http://dx.doi.org/10.1145/2526188.2526216

The invention of *Kinect*[1], and the development of the *OpenNI*[2] framework (an open source SDK), together with the dissemination of videos with experimental results on the Web (especially on *YouTube*), originated a huge movement on the direction of creating and developing application for such technological platform and for the paradigm of interaction based on gesture recognition.

Gesture based interfaces usually facilitate the communication between users and applications, however, they bring problems that are apparently unsolvable by developers, such as: How to standardize, create and reuse gesture based interfaces? How to simplify the development process for gesture recognition?

In this work, we understand the term 'natural interaction' as the use of gesture and/or voice as the mean of communication between users and computational applications, different from the conventional keyboard, icons and mouse interaction.

Here we present the first results related to greater agility on the development process of interactive applications based on *Kinect*; we also identify common tasks on the development of the solutions, and propose a framework for developers of applications with interfaces based on gesture recognition, making it possible to standardize and reuse code and tasks. Our proposal is based on the compilations of tasks, commonly executed by developers in this domain. The set of identified tasks are based on varied scientific and technological work produced since the invention of *Kinect* and other tools associated with it [6], [12]-[26].

2. Representation and recognition of user actions in virtual interactive environments

Pinhanez [6] proposes a pioneering way of representing and recognizing user actions in interactive environments. In that work, they studied many different important aspects on that domain: (i) ways of modelling user actions; (ii) formalization of actions; (iii) methods for representing actions; and (iv) action frames and the motivation using them inside interactive environments.

One of the main contributions from Pinhanez [6] is the formalism of the representation of actions, called *action frames*, which we used as the theoretical bases for the framework proposed in this paper (see section 3.5). Such formalism extends the conception of Schank et al. [7] with the inclusion of *IA-networks* [8] to represent a timely structure of sub-actions layers. That work not only provided important concepts in the area, but also used them in practice through the implementation of real interaction environments in a pioneering way.

Amongst those environments, we can mention the one from the Project "It/I", a theatrical play that aimed to check if the main

---

[1] http://www.microsoft.com/en-us/*Kinect*forwindows/

[2] htt //www o enni or /

73

character and the computer on the stage could keep an efficient interaction in a longer and more complex history. The leftmost part of Figure 1 shows the architecture used to compile the play "It/I" The computational view that is processed in runtime is presented on the top right of the figure; the bottom right part shows the gestures used for recognition and execution for a certain action.

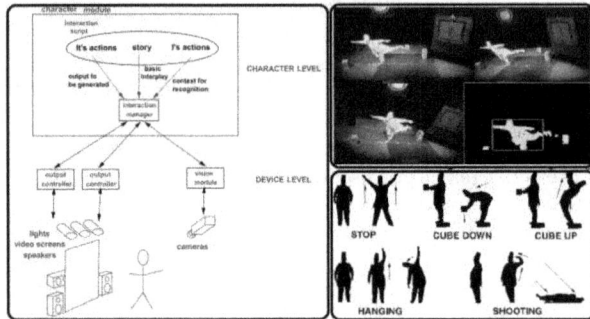

Figure 1. a) Architecture; b) Computational view; c) Five gestures used on Project "It/I" [6]

The works described from [12] to [26] represent varied research and results on the use of *Kinect* sensors as the data input in interactive environments. In general, each of them proposes some sort of processing on the data (usually images) obtained from the sensors. In most of the work we researched, some type of recognition (object, gesture, location, etc.) is performed after the processing stage, finishing with a representation of the recognition on interfaces available for the end user. The pieces of work that did not relate to recognition of some patterns were also related to the processing of data from the sensors [16][17][18][25]. However, they did it with the objective of trying to improve the performance and accuracy of the obtained information, or to provide ways of interactions between the end users and the virtual objects in the interactive environment.

The interactive environment project "It/I" presented in the beginning of this section reflects exactly the tasks mentioned above, i.e.: i) reception of data through varied sensors; ii) processing of data to recognize some sort of interaction; and iii) an action to be performed that, in those cases, aimed the virtual environment (the projection of objects in the scene) and the real environment (e.g. the selection of different light scheme for a certain action or scene).

From those pieces of work mentioned above, we could put together a set of activities commonly executed during the conception of software for interactive environment that are based on the recognition of user actions. This set of tasks is shown in Figure 2. The tasks were grouped into three generic categories, aggregating the most common tasks from developers of this type of interfaces: Data Access, Processing and Action. The figure also depicts the flow of common activities that must be executed by a developer to extract the data from the sensors (RGB, DEPTH, IR), do some processing, use some of some data already stored as a template, detect presence or recognize what is desired and, finally, execute some action in response to the processing performed.

Mapping the commonly executed tasks by developers in interactive environments, as well as the classification presented in Figure 2, will help in the definition of the architecture of the framework propose in this paper, which will be described in details in section 3.

The work from Pinhanez [6] already brought some of the important concepts that are similar to the ones discussed in previous paragraphs, such as recognition, management and representation of actions in interactive spaces. However, due to

technological restriction from their time, the authors presented a very complex architecture, which required many components and devices for simulations and testing of the concepts. Furthermore, there was enormous effort and development time to interact with all software components and information input devices (camera sensors, microphones, lights, etc.).

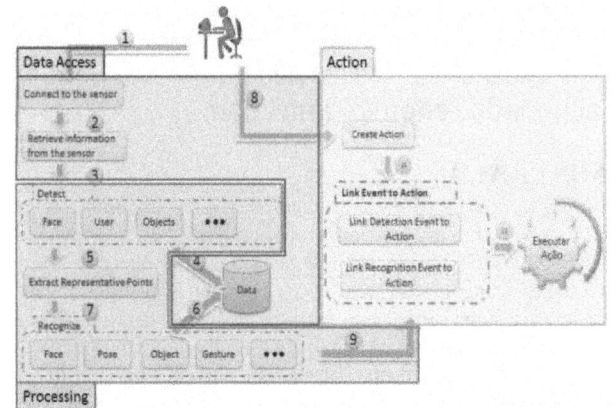

Figure 2. Diagram of the activity flow by category of similarity

We can consider that the main challenges for the standardization and improvement on the time to build interactive environments would be: i) identify which gestures are most natural for the interaction with the user interfaces; ii) finding out how to add new visual components without adding more programming complexity; iii) knowing how to recognize new interactions with the environment; iv) adding new actions to the system in a simple and fast manner. This paper focus on solving the issues above, by developing an extendable framework that: i) improves the life cycle of interactive environments and ii) makes it possible to integrate actions resulting from the interaction, both with the real environment (actions on the objects of real world) and with the virtual environment (actions on objects that compose the interface).

3. The *Touch The Air Framework*

A framework can be defined as an specification or an implementation (e.g., a collection of classes) that provides a general solution for some application domain [19]. This paper presents a framework called *Touch The Air* (*TTAir*, in short). *TTAir* should not be seen as a tool for IHC, but as a specification and implementation of a set of methods and functions to facilitate and standardize the development of interactive applications based on the *Kinect* platform.

The *TTAir* framework was built to fullfill the following specific requirements:

- Allow that users store information from different sensors in a standardized manner, creating a database of important information for future processing and inferences.

- Simplify the presentation of the pieces of information, creating models and hiding all complexity from the presentation on screen; In other words, users do not need to know or create ways of presenting information from their applications. They simply need to use pre-built functionalities of the models that are already available, or to extend them.

- Simplify the way the information obtained from sensors are processed by using a set of methods commonly used by the scientific community; that means that users do not need to know how to recognize a pose, for example. They would simply use a recognizer of such pose that would already be available in the framework.

- Help developers develop their own interfaces based on gestures, following the programming architecture standardized by the framework. This way, interactive applications developed from the environment could become more flexible, reusable and interoperable.

Besides these specific features, and according to what has been exposed before, applications for interactive environment should propose solutions for some problems, which were treated in the following way by the *TTAir* framework:

- The association of events captured by actions: the environment provides a module of abstraction of technologies for this objective. As an example of implementation (validating this abstraction provided by the environment), we used *OpenNI* for Java [9] to decode the information from sensors. Nevertheless, this does not mean that other similar technologies, such as *MS Kinect SDK* [10], *LibFreenect* [11], and others cannot be used.

- Mapping/Storage of multimodal information: the *TTAir* framework provides another module (which abstracts the location of the pieces of information) for storing captured media. These pieces of information may be located in an relational or object oriented (SGBD's) databases or in XML files.

- Synchronization of sensor's information with capture times (timestamps): the framework has a presentation module that abstracts the media exhibition in synch with the instant it was captured. This permits that varied types of information, such as voice, RGB images and depth images, widgets, visual effects or even actions to be executed, be presented synchronized in a timely manner.

- Navigation between the presentation layers: the framework, through its presentation module, makes available many layers to be exhibited. Each layer represents a piece of information obtained from a sensor or created by the developer herself. For example, if there were three layers, each representing a RGB image, a depth image and information about a user in the scene, it would be possible to give the user some navigation control over those layers. The framework provides a mechanism for interactive navigation that allows users to navigate through the layers, by going to the first, next, previous or last layer, deciding how long the layer should remain visible and displaying its content.

As we will show in the following section, *TTAir* makes the development of applications in interactive environments possible, without worrying with typical problems from this application domain (association, storage, processing, synchronization and presentation). Furthermore, the modular architecture of *TTAir* (which will be presented in the coming sections) simplifies the addition of new functionalities, promotes great code reuse and good interoperability between applications developed with the framework.

3.1 The proposed architecture

Figure 3 shows a general view of the architecture designed to su ort the varied develo er's needs (identified and mentioned earlier), in the *TTAir* framework. The loosely coupled modular architecture allows developers to use the modules in isolation or together with the other modules, depending on what is needed.

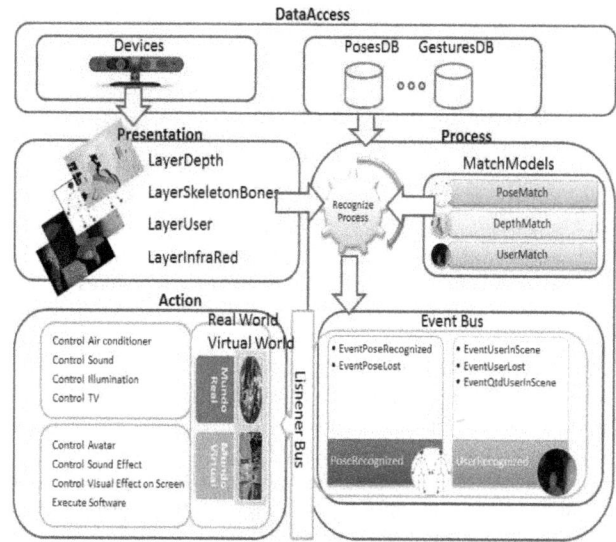

Figure 3.   General view of the *TTAir* framework's architecture.

In the next sections, we describe in details all the modules that compose *TTAir* (*DataAccess*, *Presentation*, *Process* and *Action*), including examples on how to use them.

3.2 Data Access Module
This module aims to make transparent the access to the data repositories, such as a DBMS (relational or object oriented), a Web Service, XML, or any other type. Besides, this module also encapsulates the access to data in physical devices, e.g. RGB sensors, Infrared and Depth from *Kinect* [1] or similar.

3.3 Presentation Module
This module is basically composed by two other modules: i) *Layer Module*, which is responsible for introducing the concept of layers, and ii) GUI module, which has a set of standard widgets for interaction with the end user. These two main sub-modules are described below.

3.3.1 Layer Module
This module is in charge of managing the base units of the *TTAir* framework known as *Layers*. To better understand this module, we need to comprehend the concept of layers adopted by the framework, which combines the Java concepts that refer to *GlassPanel* and to the *LayeredPanel* [4]. That is, the module provides a set of containers (similar to *Glasspanel*) that encapsulate the data structure of input sensors (e.g. *Kinect*) and offer superposition resources, similarly to those offered by the *LayeredPanel*.

Each *Layer* is an abstraction of the data structure captured by external sensors, with the possibility of graphically representing such structures, making them visible (or not) to the end user. In its current version, the framework implements the following *Layers*:

- **LayerDepth**: encapsulates the depth sensor, and add some methods commonly used by developers (e.g. the calculation of the distance from a spatial area of an image to the *Kinect*);

- **LayerRGB**: incorporates the RGB sensors, permitting the exhibition (or not) of RGB images to the end user;

- **LayerSkeletonBones**: uses other layers, such as *LayerDepth* and *LayerSkeleton*, to offer developers the representation of joints and bones through coordinates in R^3.

- **LayerUser**: uses the layers *LayerDepth* and *LayerRGB* and encapsulates the data that represents a person in the scene. This way, it permits the exhibition of only the pixels that represent the person in the captured scene. Furthermore, it contains methods that are commonly by developers, such as the calculation of the centre of mass of the user, the number of users in the scene, etc.

- **LayerInfraRed**: makes it possible to display an image captured using the *Kinect* in absence of illumination. This layer encapsulates all functions and data structures of the infrared sensor.

3.3.2 GUI Module
Following the same concept from Java Swing, this module provides a set of basic components of a GUI for applications that require interaction with the end user via a visual interface. This module facilitates the conception of the interfaces that allow the integration of actions in the real and virtual worlds. Such environments are referred in this work as "mixed interactive visual environment"

It is common sense that interfaces based in gestures simplify the communication between users and applications. However, due to the lack of standards on this area, developers become lost with many questions when creating their applications: **What gesture to choose to access certain functionalities or services? What objects best represent the navigability or the access to those functionalities or services?** The fact is that the answers to these questions are left for the imagination and creativity of developers and are not reused in a systematic way in other works. We can also observe new forms of control of interfaces (excessively varied and unexpected) in the new *hacks* [2] available in the Web nowadays.

The questions above are mitigated when we present the possibility of registering visual interfaces that already respond to certain gestures. This allows the framework to grow with the experiences of users. For example, in case developers study new interfaces and their ways of interaction with users, they will be able to register them (interfaces and ways of interactions) in this module, so that other developers can reuse them, avoiding the worry with this important phase of the conception of application for interactive environments.

To summarize the above, in order to fulfil the ever so growing demand for a simple and easy to use visual API, the GUI module was created as an extension of Java for mixed visual interactive environments. As an example, some components provided by the framework are depicted below.

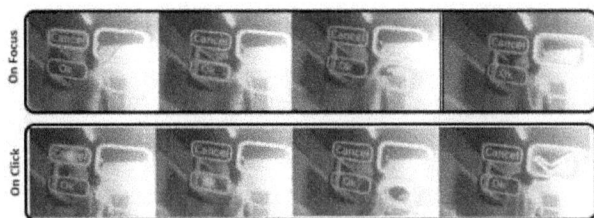

Figure 4. *Widgets* exhibited in mixed visual environment, illustrating the *OnFocus* and *OnClick* events in different buttons.

Figure 4 shows some widgets and their forms of interaction with the end user (already available in the framework). These widgets correspond to the interaction of manual gestures, with the *OnFocus* and *OnClick* events and can be easily implemented by developers using *TTAir* components.

Currently, the GUI Module provides only four buttons that extend the type *TTAir*Button (*TTAirOk, TTAirCancel,*

TTAirRadioButton e TTAirCheckButton - Figure 4), and a component of type *TTAir*Label, which allows loading images or texts inside the buttons. Note that this module allows developers to create and register new widgets to be used later by the whole framework.

3.4 Proccess Module
The Process Module is responsible for all the processing part of the framework. It follows a concept that is similar to the stimulus/response one studied in an area in Psychology known as Behaviourism [3]:

> *"Psychologists of this field defined the terms 'response' and 'stimulus' to refer to something that an organism does and to the environment variables that interact with the subject"*

The Process module can be considered the main part of the framework, being responsible for receiving input information (environment variables that interact with the organism – *Stimulus*) and providing the identification of the stimulus as the output (which we will refer in this work as *Events*). The happening of an event triggers the production of a response (the production of some action to be executed that causes a change in the state or behaviour in the real or in the virtual world).

The stimuli that can be generated by the framework are represented by a set of events previously registered, and the responses are represented by a set of actions to be executed. Both events and actions can easily be added to the modules of the framework, allowing each developer to register events and actions in a personalized way according to the requirements of the interactive virtual environment to be implemented.

3.4.1 Recognizer Process
The concept of the Recognizer Process is essentially the materialization of the stimulus/response idea discussed above. In other words, a recognizer can receive external stimuli, use processing models (*Process Match* models, described later in 3.4.2) and identify the reception of a stimulus from an event (see Figure 3). The latter will cause actions to change behaviour or state in the virtual and/or real worlds, in case there are actions associated with the identified event.

More than one recognizer can be registered in the processing layer. This feature makes it more flexible to create new stimuli identifiers (new recognizers). This means that users will be able to create recognizers for poses, gestures, users, distance, etc. Each of these recognizers has the same characteristics: (i) stimuli recognition; (ii) receiving a processing model; (iii) processing the stimuli based on the processing model; and (iv) stimulus identification through the creation of an event that represents the stimulus.

Another relevant feature of this module is the use of the concept of *Processing Model*, which is a mathematical form used by the processing layer (in general, by recognizers) to identify the stimuli and create the corresponding events. This means that, in a situation where developers need to recognize a pose, they will be able to use the model for stimuli comparison already registered in the module (e.g. *PoseMatch* model). Another option would be developers creating their own model if the accuracy of the models already registered is not satisfactory for the environment to be implemented. Therefore, this concept gives freedom to developers to come up with their own processing calculations (*Match Models*) and register them in the processing module to be used by Recognizers.

The following topic describes in detail how a *Recognizer* and a *Match Model* work. Both are implemented in the *TTAir* framework and were used in the examples of recognition of poses of distinct users presented in the coming sections.

3.4.2 Pose Recognize e Pose Match Models

The following diagram illustrates the main steps followed by the *PoseRecognizer* in order to store and compare similar poses. This recognizer is already implemented in the processing layer of the current version of *TTAir*.

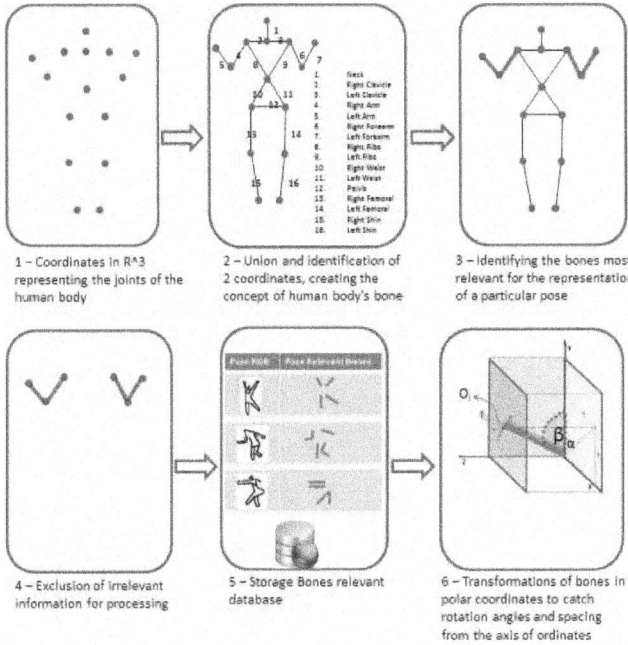

1 - Coordinates in R^3 representing the joints of the human body

2 - Union and identification of 2 coordinates, creating the concept of human body's bone

3 - Identifying the bones most relevant for the representation of a particular pose

4 - Exclusion of irrelevant information for processing

5 - Storage Bones relevant database

6 - Transformations of bones in polar coordinates to catch rotation angles and spacing from the axis of ordinates

Figure 5. Steps from the processing layer, used for the recognition of poses of the end user.

The **step 1** shows how the R^3 coordinates are obtained, where each coordinate represents a joint in the human body, detected by using *Kinect*.

The concept of bones (used as the smallest representative unit of a pose in this layer) is created in the **step 2**. Each bone is unique and carries an identifier which symbolizes its real representation. If we want to capture or compare the right forearm of a person, for example, we just need to capture the bone with the identifier "ri ht forearm"

A pose may contain bones that are irrelevant for its representation (e.g. in a situation where the user is being monitored only from the waist up, the bones representing the legs would not be unnecessary, and would just increase the demand for processing power and increase the response time). In Figure 5, the **steps 3 and 4** correspond exactly to the part to the processing in which the end user selects the most representative bones for the detection of a pose, and excludes those that are not representative.

The **step 5** illustrates the physical storage of the data structure that represents the pose and the corresponding representative bones, in a data base or in a file.

The **step 6** shows the representation of each bone through the polar coordinates. This way, it is possible to extract the rotation and inclination angles (α and β, respectively) of each bone, in relation to the coordinate axis (Figure 6). This way, we can then compare if a bone of a person in a position similar to any other bone, independently of their length. This means that it is possible to compare if the position of the left arm of a child is similar to the position of the left arm of an adult in R^3 or in R^2, by using the comparison of the angles α and β of each bone.

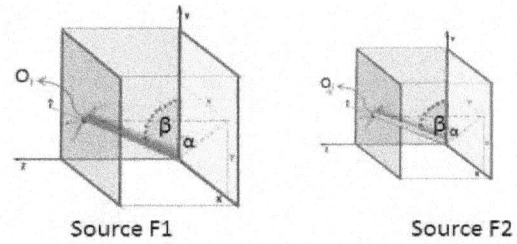

Source F1   Source F2

Figure 6. Representation of a segment obtained from a capture that represents a bone, using polar coordinates.

The comparison and the calculations of similarities are implemented following the concepts of the *Processing Models* described previously. In this work, this model is represented by *PoseMatch*, formalized in the following paragraphs.

The similarity calculations in R^3 used for testing in the framework (Figure 6) have the following formalization:

Given two bones of index *i* of distinct sources B_iO_1 and B_iO_2, where *B* represents the bone and *O* represents the source/origin, we can consider that in similar positions (P_i) in R^3, if P_i is satisfied, according to the following equations:

$$\text{Pi} = \sum_{i=1}^{n} \text{So}_i \geq c$$

where: *c* is the accuracy constant of the pose P_i and

$$So_i = \left[\left(\left| \alpha B_i O_1 - \alpha B_i O_2 \right| \leq k \right) \wedge \left(\left| \beta B_i O_1 - \beta B_i O_2 \right| \leq k \right) \right]$$

where: *S* represents the bone similarity; α and β, the angles of rotation and distancing in relation to the coordinates axis and *k*, the constant for the accuracy of bone similarity.

3.4.3 Other Comparison Models

Other comparison models could be used for recognition. Among them, we can mention those models based on distance vectors, colour histogram calculations, in Optic-flow or yet, models that use typical algorithms from the AI domain. Currently, the framework only uses the comparison method based on angles mention above. However, other modules that extend the functionalities of the processing layer are being developer at the moment. It is also possible to create a new comparison model and simply register it in the processing layer, associating it with the independent recognizing module. This way, the recognizing module will be able to use this method to estimate the similarity between the desired structures.

3.4.4 Event Controller Module

This module manipulates all the possible events that can be identified by the environment. It is possible to register new events, extend or reuse the existent ones. Each event is associated to the semantic identification of each stimulus received externally.

The module handles some eneric events like "Reco nized Pose" or "Lost Pose", commonly used in virtual interactive environments. Furthermore, more specific events such as "Person in Pain", "Person Fell", "Sad User", usually linked to "smart" interactive environments, could also be handled by this module.

Recognizers use this module in order to represent semantically stimuli that are being recognized. Besides, the module is also used to associate the stimuli with the actions to be performed.

3.5 Action Controller Module

Following the stimulus/response concept described in section 3.4, this module is exactly the part responsible for the change in behaviour or state in the virtual or real world. One of its main functions is to control the order and execution of actions that are associated to some event (identification of a stimulus). The way it works is based on the association of an event to one or more actions (using the *bind*() method), creating then a bus of actions per event, as illustrated in Figure 7.

This way, the bus of actions (*Action Bus*) makes it possible the registration of actions to be executed, concurrently or sequentially, accepting temporal precedence and synchronization. In other words, developers are free to come up with better ways to perform a set of actions that are linked to an event. The output generated by *TTAir* to represent the action bus is generated using Gantt graphs, as displayed in the Figure 7. The graphs illustrate how the actions are organized in terms of order of execution, in a sequential or concurrent way, with or without precedence.

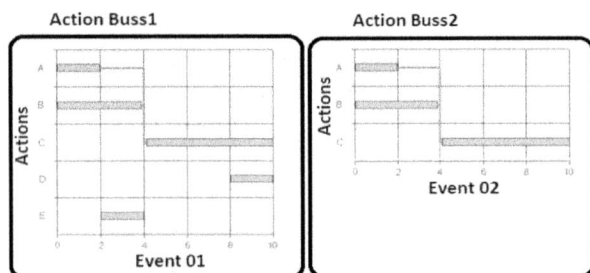

Figure 7.   Visual representation of the action bus.

4. A simple example of usage

This section presents a very simple example using the *TTAir* framework, to illustrate how simple and agile it is to develop applications that use devices like *Kinect* to display or process captured information.

Visualization of the skeleton tracking with RGB: In this example, we make an overlap of layers, showin the user's skeleton layer (skeleton tracking) over the RGB sensor layer. The tasks for detecting the user in the scene, calibration, tracking of the skeleton, connection with the RGB and DEPTH sensors are executed without the need for the user to know the details of the interaction with the sensors (Table 1).

Table 1.   Piece of code that extracts data from the *Kinect*'s RGB sensor using the TTAir framework.

```
/* Kinect connnection, RGB sensor data capture and
   encapsulation of this structure in a layer */

    ALayerShape rgb = new LayerRGB();

/* User detection on the scene, calibration, extraction the
   joints (Skeleton Tracking) and encapsulation of this
   structure in a layer */

    ALayerShape skeleton = new LayerSkeletonBone();

/* Sets which bones of the skeleton are visible on the
   screen captured */

    ((LayerSkeleton)skeleton).setVisibleBoneByID(EBone.ALL);

/* Creates the component layer manager and adds the skeleton
   layer overlying the layer of RGB */

    ScreenPanel scp = new ScreenPanel();
    scp.addLayerShape(rgb);
    scp.addLayerShape(skeleton);
```

Figure 8 illustrates all the code needed to execute the previous example and the result of the execution, using the *TTAir* proposed framework.

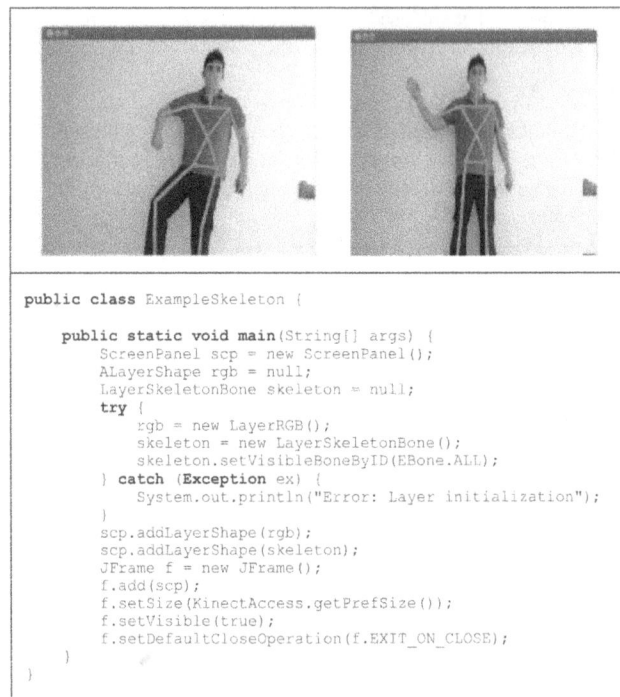

```
public class ExampleSkeleton {

    public static void main(String[] args) {
        ScreenPanel scp = new ScreenPanel();
        ALayerShape rgb = null;
        LayerSkeletonBone skeleton = null;
        try {
            rgb = new LayerRGB();
            skeleton = new LayerSkeletonBone();
            skeleton.setVisibleBoneByID(EBone.ALL);
        } catch (Exception ex) {
            System.out.println("Error: Layer initialization");
        }
        scp.addLayerShape(rgb);
        scp.addLayerShape(skeleton);
        JFrame f = new JFrame();
        f.add(scp);
        f.setSize(KinectAccess.getPrefSize());
        f.setVisible(true);
        f.setDefaultCloseOperation(f.EXIT_ON_CLOSE);
    }
}
```

Figure 8.   At the bottom, all fhe code needed for visualizing the skeleton tracking with the RGB sensor and, at the top, the result of its execution on the side.

5. Case Study

In order to evaluate the applicability of the *TTAir* framework, we realized an experiment with students from the integrated courses of informatics and automation at the Federal Institute of Sergipe (Lagarto-SE), with ages ranging from 15 to 17 years old. The experiment started with a general explanation of *TTAir*'s architecture and of some simple usage examples. After that, we requested the students to develop application with the resources offered by the framework.

Despite the fact that the experiment was not the main focus on this work, and that it did not follow a formal methodology, we would like to expose some interesting results: (i) the students were very motivated with the task and generated applications within 20 hours in the research lab (in 5 classes of 4 hours per day each); (ii) there are strong evidences that the resources offered by the framework reduce the workload of the students, making it simpler and more efficient the construction of virtual interactive environments simpler and more efficient. Two of the applications produced from the experiment are presented below:

1. *TTAirLAMP* – Virtual Switch: This application allows the end user to put two light bulb icons in the screen. These icons are resized according to the movements of the hands of the user, and fixed in a desired position after the recognition of a pre-defined gesture. Once the icons are in a fixed location, they trigger events whenever the user positions his/her hands over the area of the icon. Such events result in an action in the real world by turning a light bulb on.

Figure 9 shows the architecture used by the example *TTAirLAMP* and the gestures that can be recognized by the developed software. Gestures (a) and (b) are used to resize the bulb icon in the interaction window, whilst gesture (c) is used to turn the light on and off.

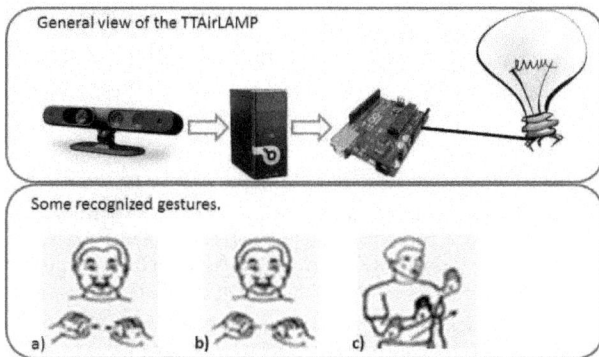

Figure 9. General view of the *TTAir*LAMP and some recognized gestures.

Figure 10 shows the final result of running the application. On the left side, the user positions and resizes the virtual interactive objects (light bulbs). The circuit that actions the real bulbs are presented on the right of the figure. It makes use of an Arduino UNO R3[3], which is responsible for establishing the connection with the computer through an USB port, receiving, interpreting commands and sending a 5V signal so that the relay associated with the received command closes the 127V circuit that feeds the bulb. Each real bulb is activated as soon as the user interacts with the virtual bul. When the user removes the hands from the icon that represents the virtual bulb, the corresponding real bulb is switched off.

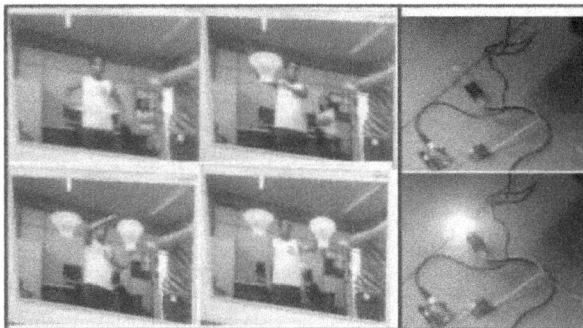

Figure 10. Final result of *TTAir*LAMP in execution.

2. *TTAirTVRemote* – Virtual TV Remote Control: This application has the same basic principles from *TTAirLAMP*, since it allows that users positioned in from the *Kinect*s's sensor perform movements that will be recognized by the software and that will trigger actions in the real and virtual environments. In this case, the action is an infrared command that controls a TV.

Figure 11 shows the architecture used and the recognized gestures. Gestures (a) and (b) are used to reduce and increase the TV volume. Gestures (c) and (d) are used to navigate through TV channels (back and forward). Figure 12 shows the circuit that emulates the TV control and the result of the user interacting with *TTAirTVRemote* to change to the next channel in the TV guide. The same Arduino UNO R3 was used here, with the same functions as exposed before, but triggering an *IRCod* signal to an infrared transmitter.

Both examples (***TTAirLAMP*** and ***TTAirTVRemote***) were developed together by students of the informatics and automation courses. The informatics students used *NetBeans* with Java and the *TTAir* framework for implementing the logical part of the applications. The automation students implemented the part of actions with the real world, used for receiving the commands through the USB port: (i) switching

---

[3] http://arduino.cc/en/Main/arduinoBoardUno

the flow of the current, allowing the bulb to be switched on, in the case of *TTAirLAMP* and (ii) sending infrared commands, in the same frequency of the remote control, to control the volume and zapping through TV channels, in the case of *TTAirTVRemote*.

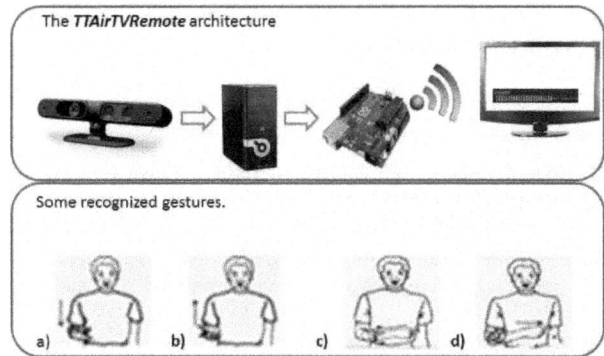

Figure 11. The ***TTAirTVRemote*** architecture and some recognized gestures.

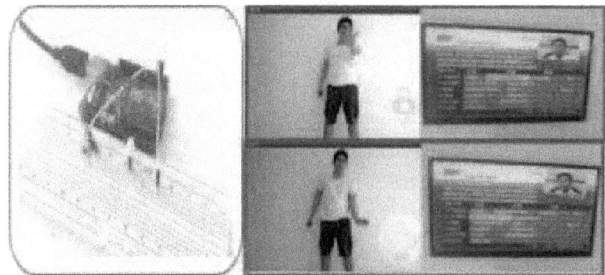

Figure 12. Circuit to send infrared commands to the TV (left) and the result of the interaction with *TTAirTVRemote* (right).

6. Conclusions

In this work, we contextualize the evolution of environments that involves natural interaction, in an attempt to bringing forward common problems faced when developing applications for this domain. Then, we make an explanation about the trends in standardization in the scientific and commercial environments with the *OpenNI* platform, and expose critical points related to the lack of coverage in the full application development process in the virtual interactive environment area.

This paper offers answers to some open questions to the varied difficulties, identified by researching articles from the academic community. The biggest contribution of this paper is to offer a modular framework, event-oriented, that permits the fast execution of tasks in the process of building applications in the area of natural interaction which is still lacking similar solutions. The proposed solution is sufficiently generic to be applied in many computing areas, such as hand-gesture recognition, human-activity recognition, body biometrics estimation, 3D surface reconstruction, immersive systems, among others.

The experimental evaluation (done through examples of usage) allows us to affirm that there are strong evidences that the *TTAir* framework simplifies the development of virtual interactive applications, as well as reducing the amount of lines of code to execute tasks that are common in the development of such applications. The experiment we performed as a proof of concept, which involved high school students, without a deep knowledge of programming or Java, offered, as result, two interactive applications based on the recognition of gestures and with certain level of complexity, which were prototyped very quickly, allowing the testing of components, and obtaining an initial evaluation on the simplicity of usage of the *TTAir* framework on the development of interactive environments.

As future work, we intend to use a more formal approach [27] to evaluate the framework, considering the point of view of its potential users, plus the definition of metrics that allow us to compare the proposed solution with others that already exist.

7. REFERENCES

[1] *Kinect* Web Site. *URL*: http://www.xbox.com/pt-br/*Kinect*

[2] *Kinect* hacks. Hacks para o *Kinect*. *URL*:http://*Kinect*hacks.net/.

[3] A.M.B. Bock; O. Furtado; M. L. T. Teixeira. Psicologias: Uma Introdução ao Estudo de Psicologia. Ed. Saraiva, 13º Ed, 3 triagem 1999-2001. ISBN 85-02-02900-2

[4] Oracle. RootPane LayeredPane.*URL*: http://docs.oracle.com/javase/tutorial/uiswing/components/rootpane.html. Acessado em 16/05/2013

[5] OpenNI Communtiny *URL*: http://community.openni.org/openni/topics/openni2_2. Acessado em 16/05/2013

[6] C. S. Pinhanez. Representation and recognition of action in interactive spaces. Phd Thesis, Massachusetts Institute of Technology, 1999.

[7] R. C. Schank; N. M. Goldman; C. J. Rieger III; C. K. Riesbeck. *Conceptual Information Processing*. North-Holland. 1975.

[8] J. F. Allen. Maintaining Knowledge about Temporal Intervals. *Communications of the ACM*, vol. 26 (11), pp. 832-843. 1983.

[9] OpenNI for Java. *URL*:http://www.openni.org/projects/java-wrapper/.

[10] *Kinect* SDK. *URL*: http://www.microsoft.com/en-us/*Kinect*forwindows/.

[11] Lib FreeNeck. *URL*: https://github.com/Open*Kinect*.

[12] Y. Zou; W. Chen; X. Wu; Z. Liu. Indoor localization and 3D scene reconstruction for mobile robots using the Microsoft *Kinect* sensor. *In*: 10th IEEE Int. Conf. on Ind. Informatics, Jul.2012. p.1182-87.

[13] G. Zhao; H. Liu; L. Yu; B. Wang; F. Sun. Depth-Assisted Face Detection and Association for People Counting. *Pattern Recognition*, 15, Apr 2013.

[14] M. Zollhoefer; M. Martinek; G. Greiner; M. Stamminger; J. Suessmuth. Automatic reconstruction of personalized avatars from 3D face scans. *Comp. Animation and Virtual Worlds*, 15, Apr. 2013.

[15] Computer Animation and Virtual Worlds. Publisher John Wiley and Sons Ltd. Chichester, UK. vol. 22 Issue 2-3, Apr. 2011. pp.195-202. ISSN: 1546-4261

[16] L. Gallo, A.P. Placitelli; G. De Pietro. A *Kinect* NUI for 3D Medical Visualization. Nat. Res. Council of Italy. *URL*: http://gesture. chalearn.org/dissemination/icpr2012/demonstration-competition

[17] L. Gallo; A.P. Placitelli; M. Ciampi. Controller-free exploration of medical image data: Experiencing the *Kinect*. *In*: 24th Int. Symp. on Computer-Based Medical Systems. Jun. 2011. pp.1-6.

[18] H. Zhang; Y. Song; Z. Chen; J. Cai; K. Lu. Chinese Shadow Puppetry with an Interactive Interface Using the *Kinect* Sensor. *Computer Vision – ECCV 2012. Workshops and Demonstrations. Lecture Notes in Computer Science*. vol. 7584, 2012.

[19] MDF Section 8 – Glossary. [on line]. *URL*: http://www.medinfo.rochester.edu/hl7/v3.0/mdf_08.htm. Arquivo capturado em 12/03/2005.

[20] L. Xia; C.-C. Chen; J.K. Aggarwal. Human detection using depth information by *Kinect*. *In*: IEEE Conf. on Computer Vision and Pattern Recognition Workshops. Jun. 2011. pp.15-22.

[21] T. Nakra; Y. Ivanov; P. Smaragdis; C. Ault. The USB Virtual Maestro: an Interactive Conducting System. *In*: NIME2009, pp.250-55. *URL*: www.cs.illinois.edu/~paris/pubs/nakra-nime09.pdf

[22] F.A. Kondori; S. Yousefi; L. Haibo; S. Sonning, S. Sonning. 3D head pose estimation using the *Kinect*. In: *Int. Conf. on Wireless Communications and Signal Processing*. Nov. 2011. pp.1-4. DOI: 10.1109/WCSP.2011.6096866

[23] K.A. Funes Mora,; J. Odobez. Gaze estimation from multimodal *Kinect* data. In: *IEEE Conf. Computer Vision and Pattern Recognition Workshops*. Jun. 2012. pp. 25-30.

[24] W. Susanto; M. Rohrbach; B. Schiele. Object Detection with Multiple *Kinect*s. *Computer Vision – ECCV 2012. Workshops and Demonstrations. Lecture Notes in Computer Science*. vol. 7584, 2012, pp 93-102 3D , DOI: 10.1007/978-3-642-33868-7_10

[25] I. Oikonomidis; N. Kyriazis; A. Argyros. Efficient model-based 3D tracking of hand articulations using *Kinect*. *In*: Proc. of the British Machine Vision Conf. BMVA Press, Sep. 2011. pp. 101.1-101.11.

[26] L. Gallo; A.P. Placitelli. View-independent Hand Posture Recognition from Single Depth Images Using PCA and Flusser Moments. *In:* 8th Int. Conf. on Signal Image Technology and Internet Based Systems. Nov. 2012. pp.898-904

[27] Wohlin C. et al. *Experimentation in Software Engineering: An Introduction*. Kluwer Academic Publishers, 2000.

Evaluation of the Influence of Contextual Factors on the Interactions with Applications for Smartphones

Artur Henrique Kronbauer
PPGCOMP – UNIFACS
Rua Vieira Lopes, 02, Rio Vermelho
Salvador – BA, Brasil
CEP 41.940-560
arturhk@gmail.com

Celso A. S. Santos
DI – CT - UFES
Av. Fernando Ferrari s/n sala 8
Vitória – ES, Brasil
CEP 29.075-910
saibel@inf.ufes.br

ABSTRACT

The development of methodologies and techniques to evaluate smartphones usability is an emerging topic in the scientific community and triggers discussions about which methodology is most appropriate. The lack of consensus is due to the inherent difficulty on capturing context data in the scenarios where the experiments take place and on relating them to the found results. This work aims to correlate potential usability problems in mobile applications with contextual factors that may occur during users interactions on different devices, such as: environment luminosity, device screen resolution, and the user's activity while interacting with the application. The following methodology was applied to carry out a field experiment: (1) identification of contextual factors that may influence users' interaction; (2) use of UXEProject Infrastructure to support the automatic capture of applications' context data, by monitoring and storing quantitative, subjective and contextual data from applications' use; (3) implementation of experiments with real users, which have different profiles, on using three different mobile applications over an one year period. In this paper, we present and discuss the results obtained during this study.

Categories and Subject Descriptors

H.5.1 [Multimedia Information Systems]: Evaluation/ methodology.

General Terms

Experimentation, Human Factors.

Keywords

Usability Evaluation, Usability Experiment, Logging, ESM, Context, UXEProject.

1. INTRODUÇÃO

Com o contínuo avanço das redes sem fio e a grande proliferação dos *smartphones*, diversas aplicações estão sendo lançadas no mercado a cada dia. Atualmente, os requisitos da Computação Ubíqua, os quais preveem que os softwares façam parte do cotidiano das pessoas e estejam disponíveis, de forma transparente, "a qualquer hora, em qualquer lugar e a partir de qualquer dispositivo" [1], vem sendo cada vez mais explorados na construção destes aplicativos. Essa ubiquidade dos aplicativos é alcançada a partir do monitoramento automático de informações de contexto relativas ao uso desses dispositivos. Um contexto pode ser definido como um conjunto de informações que afeta a execução de uma aplicação, relacionadas às pessoas, objetos, lugares, tempo e espaço em que a aplicação é utilizada [2].

Coletar dados das experiências dos usuários de *smartphones* e associá-los ao contexto no qual as interações ocorrem é um grande desafio para a área de Interação Humano-Computador (IHC). As situações mudam e os resultados dos testes são altamente dependentes do contexto. Por exemplo, uma pessoa interagindo com um aplicativo móvel, sentada no sofá de sua casa, terá diferentes interferências externas quando comparado à realização da mesma tarefa ao caminhar pela rua.

Na literatura, é possível encontrar diversos autores que defendem a necessidade de relacionar a influência do contexto nas interações dos usuários com esses aplicativos [3]. Para a realização de estudos com esta abrangência, são necessárias metodologias e técnicas que permitam realizar experimentos com a capacidade de coletar dados contextualizados aos cenários onde as interações ocorrem [4]. Esse fato desencadeia diversas discussões quanto ao local da realização dos experimentos (em campo ou em laboratório) [5], bem como as técnicas que podem ser utilizadas para a extração do melhor conjunto de dados que caracterizem os experimentos [6].

Este trabalho foi motivado por essas discussões, tendo como principais contribuições:

1. Identificar as principais abordagens de avaliação utilizadas nos dias atuais para a avaliação de aplicativos para *smartphones*.

2. Utilizar a infraestrutura UXEproject, uma nova abordagem criada com a potencialidade de extrair e relacionar dados quantitativos, contextuais e subjetivos.

3. Apresentar os resultados de um experimento realizado em campo, relacionando fatores contextuais com métricas de usabilidade para aplicações em *smartphones*.

O restante deste artigo está estruturado em seis seções. Na Seção 2, é apresentado o estado da arte em avaliações de usabilidade para *smartphones*, contemplando a investigação das abordagens utilizadas para a realização dos experimentos de usabilidade. A Seção 3 descreve a infraestrutura *UXEProject* que foi adotada para a realização do experimento apresentado neste trabalho. Na Seção 4, é descrita a metodologia adotada para a execução do experimento realizado. Na Seção 5, são apresentados e discutidos os resultados obtidos. Finalmente, na Seção 6, são apresentadas as conclusões e perspectivas futuras.

2. O ESTADO DA ARTE

A relação entre contexto e usabilidade é um assunto amplamente discutido pela comunidade científica que estuda a influência dos cenários com relação às interações com *smartphones*. Segundo Mallick [7], as experiências mostram que os seres humanos normalmente interagem com sistemas de formas inusitadas. Uma vez que a previsão de tais formas de interação não é uma tarefa trivial, a realização de testes constitui uma atividade crítica para a garantia da usabilidade do aplicativo associado ao contexto de uso considerado. Desta forma, a inclusão de usuários e cenários reais nos testes é imprescindível para o delineamento das preferências dos usuários e a consequente adequação dos produtos a eles destinados [5].

Kawalek et al [8] sugerem a utilização de métodos de avaliação que contemplem diferentes ângulos de observação nos experimentos realizados nesta área, tais como dados quantitativos (métricas de usabilidade), a avaliação subjetiva (sentimento dos usuários) e dados contextuais (por exemplo, condições ambientais e características dos dispositivos). O principal problema, atualmente, é que se observa uma carência na literatura por abordagens que suportem esses três requisitos combinados em um único experimento, geralmente, apenas um ou dois deles são relacionados.

Coursaris e Kim [9] realizaram um levantamento sistemático, no período de 2000 a 2010, que permitiu identificar que 47% dos trabalhos de avaliação de dispositivos móveis são realizados em laboratório, 21% em campo, 10% utilizam ambos os cenários e 22% são realizados sem a participação de usuários. Um ponto a ser observado é que inúmeros estudos não consideram o caráter móvel de tais dispositivos, aplicando métodos de avaliação tradicionais. Outro fato que chama atenção nos resultados apresentados é que 47% dos estudos avaliam tarefas individuais e descontextualizadas, 46% são voltados para a tecnologia empregada e apenas 14% levam em consideração variáveis contextuais e as características dos utilizadores.

Com o objetivo de identificar a atual realidade das investigações de usabilidade atreladas a *smartphones*, foi desenvolvido um estudo entre os anos de 2008 a 2012, contemplando trabalhos que descrevem experimentos empíricos e investigam pelo menos um dos seguintes atributos de usabilidade: eficiência, eficácia, satisfação, aprendizagem, operabilidade, acessibilidade, flexibilidade, utilidade e facilidade de uso. As bases investigadas contemplaram a ACM, IEEE, Springer e Google Acadêmico, sendo selecionados 21 trabalhos que estão listados na Tabela 1 juntamente com as técnicas de investigação utilizadas.

Os resultados deste estudo são detalhados a seguir:

• Com relação às técnicas utilizadas para a coleta de dados nos experimentos, pode ser observado que 71,4% utilizam questionários, 19% *logging*, 14,2% observações diretas dos avaliadores, 14,2% entrevistas com os usuários, 19% a técnica *Think Aloud* e 28,5% outras técnicas menos tradicionais. A soma dos percentuais ultrapassa 100% porque 66,3% dos experimentos contemplam mais de uma técnica, como mostra a Tabela 1.

Tabela 1. Trabalhos que investigam a usabilidade de aplicativos para *smartphones*

Autores	Técnicas utilizadas
Burigat et al (2008) [10]	*Logging* e questionário
Sodnik et al (2008) [11]	Observação direta, entrevistas e dados do dispositivo (*Logging*)
Fitchett e Cockburn (2009) [12]	Observação direta e entrevistas
Chin e Salomaa (2009) [13]	*Logging* em servidores Web e questionários
Lai et al (2009) [14]	Questionário *on-line* e entrevistas cognitivas
Ebner et al (2009) [15]	*Thinking Aloud* e Questionário
Hansen e Ghinea (2009) [16]	Questionário
Bødker et al (2009) [17]	Questionários, grupos focais e entrevistas individualizadas
Kim et al (2010) [18]	Questionário
Li e Yeh (2010) [19]	Questionário
Maly et al (2010) [20]	*Logging*, *Thinking Aloud* (gravadores de áudio) e observação direta (câmeras de vídeo e anotações)
Grønli et al (2010) [21]	Questionário
Kang et al (2011) [22]	Questionários e análises baseadas na *Technology Acceptance Model* (TAM) e *Structural Equation Model* (SEM)
Fetaji et al (2011) [23]	MLUAT, Testes Qualitativos (Questionários) e Avaliações Heurísticas
Hegarty e Wusteman (2011) [24]	Questionários e *Think Aloud*
Grønli et al (2011) [25]	Questionário
Sparkes et al (2012) [26]	Anotações, *Think Aloud* e entrevista
Bradley et al (2012) [27]	Questionários
Schaub et al (2012) [28]	*Logging* e observação direta
Kirwan et al (2012) [29]	*Logging* e Questionário *on-line*
Spyridonis et al (2012) [30]	Questionário e entrevista

• A Tabela 2 apresenta o número de vezes que cada atributo de usabilidade foi contemplado nas investigações. É possível constatar que a Facilidade de Uso (100%), Satisfação (90,4%) e Eficácia (76,1%) são os atributos mais investigados.

Tabela 2. Quantidade absoluta de vezes que cada atributo de usabilidade foi investigado

Atributos	Nº de vezes investigados
Facilidade de uso	21
Utilidade	8
Flexibilidade	5
Acessibilidade	3
Operabilidade	3
Aprendizagem	7
Satisfação	19
Eficácia	16
Eficiência	11

- O número de participantes foi dividido em três faixas distintas: 55% dos experimentos utilizaram entre 5 a 24 participantes, 20% utilizaram de 25 a 44 participantes e 25% foram realizadas com um número acima de 44 usuários.

- Com relação ao cenário de investigação, observou-se que 52,3% dos experimentos foram realizados em laboratório, 33,3% em campo, 9,5% em ambos os cenários e 4,7% com simuladores.

- Um dos principais aspectos a ser destacado é que apenas 3 experimentos investigaram dados contextuais, sendo estes conduzidos em laboratório, indo de encontro as expectativas e anseios de inúmeros pesquisadores.

- O último ponto a ser salientado é que nenhuma das abordagens captura a impressão dos usuários com relação à usabilidade do aplicativo durante as suas interações, o que poderia proporcionar a correlação de dados subjetivos nas avaliações.

A principal constatação do levantamento bibliográfico realizado foi que, na maioria dos experimentos, são utilizados questionários para a coleta dos dados, o que pode dificultar a correlação de diferentes tipos de informações para a descoberta de problemas de usabilidade [31]. Além disso, na maioria dos casos, não são investigados fatores contextuais, o que é defendido por inúmeros pesquisadores como sendo um fator primordial para os avanços na área de avaliações da usabilidade [3][4][9].

3. A INFRAESTRUTURA *UXEPROJECT*

A infraestrutura *UXEProject* foi construída para dar suporte à avaliação de usabilidade a partir da análise de dados capturados diretamente dos dispositivos. O modelo formal que deu origem a infraestrutura pode ser encontrado na sua íntegra em [32].

A infraestrutura *UXEProject* é dividida conceitualmente em três unidades. Estas unidades abrangem: (1) o mapeamento das tarefas que serão investigadas; (2) o acoplamento das métricas de rastreabilidade que possibilitam a captura dos dados contextuais, estatísticas de usabilidade e informações subjetivas referentes às experiências proporcionadas aos usuários; e (3) o armazenamento e avaliação dos dados capturados durante os experimentos.

Para possibilitar a captura automática de dados referentes à interação do usuário e à utilização dos sensores presentes nos *smartphones*, é utilizada uma Biblioteca de Métricas construída com Programação Orientada a Aspectos (POA).

Na infraestrutura, o mapeamento das tarefas é construído por meio da captura dos métodos executados na aplicação a ser avaliada. A Equipe de Avaliação é responsável pela escolha e mapeamento das tarefas, bem como pela criação das métricas de captura de dados. É importante destacar que não é necessário nenhum tipo de programação para realizar estas atividades.

Nas próximas subseções, serão descritas as ferramentas utilizadas para contemplar os componentes previstos nas três unidades da infraestrutura.

3.1 Unidade de Mapeamento

A primeira ferramenta desenvolvida na infraestrutura contempla a preparação do código fonte para possibilitar o mapeamento das tarefas disponibilizadas nos aplicativos. Esta ferramenta foi denominada *Mapping Aspect Generator* (MAG).

A ferramenta MAG importa o código fonte da aplicação que se deseja mapear e cria um Aspecto que insere o método

onUserInteraction[1] nas classes referentes a camada de interação. Este processo possibilita detectar as ações dos usuários. Para obter o aplicativo pronto para ser mapeado, é necessário compilar o código fonte da aplicação com o Aspecto gerado. Após, basta embarcar a aplicação em um *smartphone* para realizar as interações.

Para a Equipe de Avaliação realizar o mapeamento das tarefas, foi desenvolvida outra ferramenta denominada *Automatic Task Description* (ATD). A ATD deve ser embarcada em um dispositivo e ser executada simultaneamente com a aplicação a ser mapeada. Assim, à medida que a Equipe de Avaliação interage com a aplicação, os métodos executados são capturados de forma automática para serem utilizados como passos para a conclusão de uma tarefa.

A base da ATD consiste na utilização de um filtro que identifica quando ocorre uma interação do usuário. Além disso, o filtro identifica quais classes, métodos e parâmetros da aplicação foram utilizados. Estas informações são armazenadas em um arquivo XML que será enviado ao servidor para ser utilizado na criação das métricas.

3.2 Unidade de Rastreabilidade

A ferramenta projetada para permitir a instrumentação das aplicações e possibilitar a captura de dados foi denominada *UXE Metrics Generation*. Esta ferramenta contém uma biblioteca que possui a estrutura das métricas para realizar as medições.

Inicialmente, a ferramenta recebe como entrada o arquivo XML gerado na Unidade de Mapeamento. A seguir, os métodos existentes no arquivo XML são acoplados à Biblioteca de Métricas disponível na ferramenta, permitindo a criação dos Aspectos responsáveis pela captura, transmissão e persistência dos dados. Por fim, basta compilar o código fonte da aplicação juntamente com os Aspectos gerados e embarcar a aplicação em um dispositivo que será utilizado por um usuário.

Para contemplar a coleta dos dados foram definidos três tipos de métricas. As métricas de usabilidade e contexto utilizam a técnica de *Logging* [10][11], enquanto que as métricas subjetivas utilizam a técnica *Experience Sampling Method* [33].

Para que os dados referentes aos experimentos pudessem ser transmitidos e armazenados em um banco de dados, foi contratado junto à empresa Amazon uma micro instância do serviço conhecido como *Amazon EC2*[2].

3.3 Unidade de Avaliação

Para contemplar os componentes definidos na Unidade de Avaliação, foram realizados os seguintes processos: (i) criar e configurar um servidor de FTP, outro de Banco de Dados (BD) e disponibilizá-los na Internet; (ii) realizar a modelagem de um BD e de um *Data Warehouse* (DW) para armazenar e possibilitar as análises das informações capturadas durante os experimentos; (iii) criar ferramentas para detectar a presença de novos arquivos no servidor de FTP, popular o BD e fazer a carga do DW; e (iv) escolher uma ferramenta OLAP para apoiar as análises dos dados

O Sistema Gerenciador de Banco de Dados escolhido para armazenar os dados foi o *MySql Community Server*. Para

---

[1] Maiores detalhes em http://developer.android.com/reference/android/app/Activity.html#onUserInteraction()

[2] Disponível em http://aws.amazon.com/ec2/

contemplar a carga dos dados no BD, foi desenvolvida uma ferramenta denominada de *Data Load*. Os passos executados por esta ferramenta são: detectar a chegada de novos arquivos no servidor de FTP, extrair os dados e carregá-los no BD.

A última ferramenta projetada (*ETL Maker*) realiza a extração, transformação e carga dos dados, transferindo-os do BD para o DW. Para facilitar a análise dos dados, foi escolhida a ferramenta OLAP *Pentaho Analysis Services*.

4. EXPERIMENTO REALIZADO

O experimento relatado neste artigo foi dividido em seis fases distintas, tomando como base as diretrizes propostas no *framework* DECIDE [34], que norteou a especificação dos passos realizados durante todas as fases do experimento.

4.1 Determinar o objetivo da análise

O foco principal do experimento é obter informações relacionando diferentes tipos de dados, com principal interesse para os fatores contextuais que podem interferir na usabilidade dos aplicativos que serão analisados.

4.2 Explorar perguntas a serem respondidas

Tomando como base o objetivo a ser alcançado, foi elaborado um conjunto de perguntas que direcionam os experimentos, a geração e análise dos dados:

- Qual a interferência da luminosidade do cenário de interação no desempenho dos usuários de aplicativos para *smartphones*?

- Quais as tarefas que sofrem maior interferência devido à posição do *smartphone* no momento das interações?

- Qual a interferência da movimentação do usuário no seu desempenho para interagir com os aplicativos?

- Qual a diferença de desempenho dos usuários em função da configuração dos seus *smartphones*?

- Que tipo de informações o contexto pode oferecer para melhorar a análise da usabilidade?

4.3 EsColher o método de avaliação

A abordagem de avaliação a ser utilizado neste trabalho deve contemplar as seguintes condições:

- O experimento deve ser realizado em campo.

- Sem supervisão.

- Por longo período de tempo.

- Com os dados sendo coletados automaticamente.

- Sem restrições quanto ao número de usuários.

- Sem a necessidade de conhecer como as aplicações foram desenvolvidas.

- Com a potencialidade de ser aplicada a qualquer aplicativo para a plataforma *Android*.

- Sem a necessidade da Equipe de Avaliação escrever códigos de programação.

- Com a possibilidade de analisar diferentes tipos de dados.

- Com a possibilidade de definir as tarefas a serem analisadas.

Diante das condições listadas, foi escolhida a infraestrutura *UXEProject* que dá suporte à todos os requisitos exigidos.

4.4 Identificar e Administrar as questões práticas

Nesta fase, foram levantados inúmeros pré-requisitos, dentre os quais podem ser destacados: (i) a escolha das aplicações a serem avaliadas; (ii) a definição das tarefas investigadas; (iii) a definição do grupo de usuários a participar do experimento e; (iv) os dados a serem considerados.

A primeira ação nessa fase, foi realizar uma pesquisa exploratória a fim de encontrar aplicativos com funcionalidades atrativas e com possibilidade de serem inseridas no cotidiano das pessoas. A escolha dos aplicativos levou em conta os seguintes pré-requisitos:

- O aplicativo deve ter sido desenvolvido na linguagem Java e para a plataforma *Android*.

- O código fonte do aplicativo deve estar disponível e com os direitos de uso explícitos.

- O aplicativo deve ter sido construído usando boas técnicas de programação e exibindo uma boa modularização das suas funcionalidades de forma a permitir que o código fonte possa ser instrumentado com POA.

4.4.1 Descrição dos Aplicativos e Tarefas Avaliadas

O primeiro aplicativo, chamado de Mileage, tem a finalidade de auxiliar os usuários no controle do gasto com combustível e outros serviços de manutenção de um automóvel, como troca de óleo, troca de pastilhas de freio, entre outros. No lado esquerdo da Figura 1, é apresenta a interface do aplicativo e, no lado direito, as tarefas investigadas no experimento.

Interface do Mileage	Tarefas Instrumentadas
	1. Cadastrar um veículo.
	2. Entrar com os dados de um novo abastecimento.
	3. Configurar um novo formato de data.
	4. Alterar dados no histórico dos abastecimentos.
	5. Adicionar um novo controle de manutenção.
	6. Visualizar o gráfico referente à variação do preço do combustível.
	7. Visualizar o gráfico referente à distância percorrida.
	8. Importar dados armazenados.

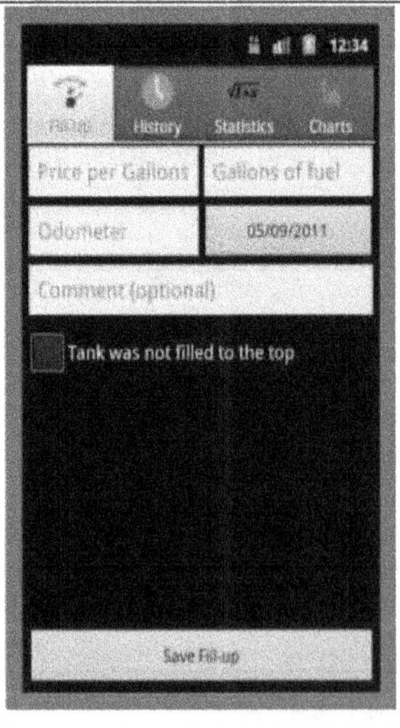

Figura 1 – Interface do Aplicativo Mileage e tarefas instrumentadas para sua avaliação.

O segundo aplicativo selecionado foi o ^3 (Cubed), um gerenciador de músicas e videoclipes. Seu menu principal possibilita escolher as músicas ou vídeos e executá-los. A interface do aplicativo, assim como as tarefas mapeadas, podem ser contempladas na Figura 2.

Interface do ^3 (Cubed)	Tarefas Instrumentadas
	1. Escolher uma música de uma lista de reprodução. 2. Criar uma nova lista de reprodução. 3. Inserir uma música a uma lista de reprodução. 4. Modificar a aparência da aplicação. 5. Escolher um novo tema de apresentação do aplicativo. 6. Acionar o equalizador.

Figura 2 – Interface do aplicativo ^3 (Cubed) e tarefas instrumentadas para sua avaliação.

O último aplicativo escolhido para o experimento foi o Shuffle, cuja interface é mostrada na Figura 3. Ele é um aplicativo de agenda de atividades que permite vincular tarefas a datas e horários, além de possibilitar o relacionamento a projetos e contextos (por exemplo, casa ou trabalho).

Interface do Shuffle	Tarefas Instrumentadas
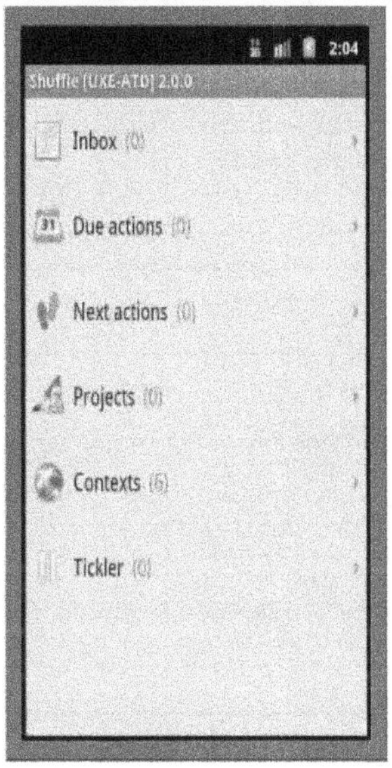	1. Inserir uma atividade. 2. Excluir atividades da caixa de entrada. 3. Modificar uma atividade. 4. Cadastrar um novo projeto com a escolha de um contexto disponível. 5. Cadastrar um novo contexto. 6. Excluir um contexto. 7. Modificar um projeto com a escolha de um contexto. 8. Realizar *backup* dos dados. 9. Acionar a opção de ajuda. 10. Criar uma atividade com agendamento.

Figura 3 – Interface do aplicativo Shuffle e tarefas instrumentadas para sua avaliação.

4.4.2 Recrutamento dos participantes

Outra ação realizada nesta fase foi definir o grupo de usuários que participariam dos experimentos. A escolha dos participantes foi em função dos perfis que estavam em análise e das características dos seus *smartphones*. Foram recrutados 21 participantes, levando em consideração à idade, nível de escolaridade, formação, ocupação e poder aquisitivo.

4.4.3 Dados Considerados no Experimento

A relação dos dados que são considerados no experimento foi definido em função das estratégias de captura providos pela infraestrutura *UXEProject*. Sendo assim, foram considerados os dados de usabilidade referentes às tarefas mapeadas, o perfil dos usuários, as características dos *smartphones* e os dados contextuais obtidos por meio dos sensores.

As características dos *smartphones* consideradas para compor o contexto das interações foram o tamanho e resolução da tela, cujas faixas de valores consideradas estão na Tabela 3.

Tabela 3. Características dos *Smartphones*

Características	Faixas de valores consideradas	
Resolução da Tela em Pixels	$\chi \leq 320 \times 240$	Baixo
	$320 \times 240 < \chi \leq 320 \times 480$	Média
	$\chi > 320 \times 480$	Alta
Tamanho da Tela em polegadas	$\chi \leq 2.4$	Pequeno
	$2.4 < \chi \leq 3.5$	Médio
	$\chi > 3.5$	Grande

Para contextualizar o ambiente no momento em que ocorrem as interações, são capturados dados referentes ao grau de luminosidade, à posição do aparelho durante as interações e à velocidade de deslocamento do usuário. Estes dados de contexto são capturados diretamente dos sensores dos aparelhos e seus valores de referência estão descritos na Tabela 4.

Tabela 4. Escala de valores para dados do ambiente

Fatores	Faixa de valores considerados	
Luminosidade	$\chi \leq 100$ lux	Baixo
	$100 < \chi \leq 10000$ lux	Média
	$\chi > 10000$ lux	Alta
Deslocamento	$\chi < 0,2$ m/s	Parado
	$0,2$ m/s $\leq \chi \leq 2,7$ m/s	Caminhando
	$\chi > 2,7$ m/s	Motorizado
Posição	Vertical	Horizontal	Mista

4.5 Decidir como lidar com as questões éticas

Para a realização do experimento, foi construído um *site* onde são disponibilizadas as explicações referentes à pesquisa e um termo de uso dos aplicativos. Para o usuário habilitar-se a realizar o *download* dos aplicativos, é necessário explicitar o seu consentimento em participar do experimento.

4.6 Estabelecer forma de avaliar, interpretar e apresentar os resultados

Na próxima seção serão apresentados os resultados das avaliações realizadas durante a condução do experimento. A coleta de dados ocorreu no período de 01/12/2011 a 30/11/2012.

5. RESULTADOS OBTIDOS

5.1 Análise da influência da luminosidade

Inicialmente, são observados os valores percentuais de tarefas completadas com erros em cada um dos aplicativos sob a ótica da variação da luminosidade. O objetivo é identificar a possível influência desta variável contextual nas interações. Para a realização da análise, a luminosidade foi isolada e relacionada com o percentual de tarefas completadas com erros em cada um dos aplicativos, como apresentado na Figura 4.

Como pode ser observado, foi detectado para todos os aplicativos que os maiores índices de tarefas completadas com erros ocorrem quando a luminosidade está muito alta ou muito baixa, ou seja, quando as condições do cenário de interação não estão nos parâmetros considerados normais, o que comprova a influência da luminosidade no desempenho dos usuários.

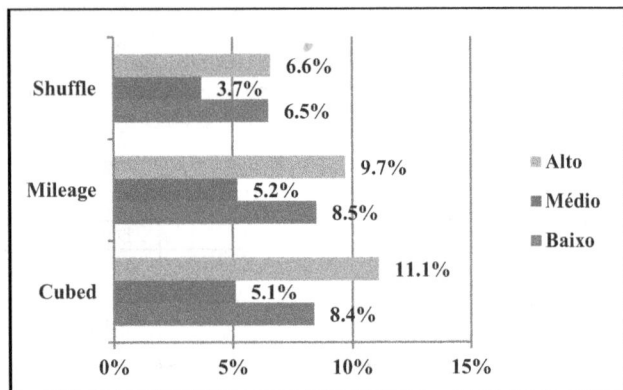

Figura 4 – Taxa de erros em função da luminosidade

5.2 Análise da posição de interação

A segunda análise está relacionada com a posição do *smartphone* durante as interações. O objetivo é encontrar problemas de usabilidade em determinadas tarefas referentes à posição de interação (vertical, horizontal ou mista). Na Tabela 5, é possível verificar as tarefas que tiveram uma taxa de erro acima de 10% relacionadas com a posição de interação. Informações desta natureza são úteis para os desenvolvedores da aplicação, já que em versões futuras do aplicativo podem ser inibidas as interações em posições com alta taxa de erros. A Tabela 5 mostra ainda que mais de 50% dos problemas ocorrem quando as tarefas são executadas na posição mista, ou seja, são iniciadas em uma posição e finalizadas em outra.

Tabela 5. Taxa de erro em função da posição de interação

Posição	Tarefas – Mileage	% Erros
Vertical	Cadastrar um veículo	16,7%
Misto	Cadastrar um veículo	14,3%
Vertical	Importar dados armazenados	21,1%
Horizontal	Importar dados armazenados	18,2%
Misto	Importar dados armazenados	20,0%
Posição	Tarefas – ^3 (Cubed)	% Erros
Misto	Escolher uma música de uma lista	11,2%
Misto	Inserir uma música a uma lista	16,7%
Vertical	Modificar a aparência da aplicação	10,6%
Horizontal	Escolher um novo tema	14,0%
Posição	Tarefas – Shuffle	% Erros
Misto	Inserção de uma nova atividade	12,9%
Misto	Excluir todas as atividades	14,3%
Vertical	Realizar um *backup* dos dados	14,3%
Misto	Acionar a opção de ajuda	20,0%

5.3 Análise da velocidade de deslocamento

A próxima avaliação refere-se à velocidade de deslocamento dos usuários no momento que realizam as suas interações. Normalmente, a velocidade varia em função de três possibilidades: usuário caminhando, usuário parado ou, ainda, utilizando algum meio de transporte.

Como pode ser observado na Figura 5, em todos os aplicativos é possível identificar que as ações realizadas sem deslocamento apresentam uma taxa de erro inferior às realizadas em movimento.

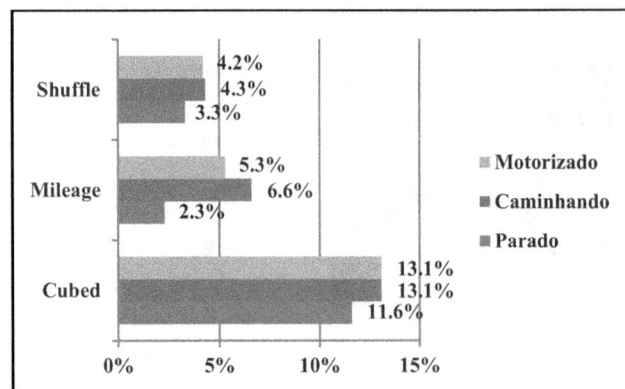

Figura 5 – Taxa de erro em função da velocidade de deslocamento

5.4 Análise das características físicas dos *smartphones*

As próximas análises verificam a existência de interferência das variáveis contextuais relacionadas às características dos *smartphones*, tais como, a resolução e o tamanho da tela. Para realizar esta avaliação, foi investigada a velocidade de execução das tarefas em função das características dos *smartphones*. Os dados apresentados no gráfico da Figura 6 possibilitam identificar que a resolução da tela influencia significativamente na velocidade de execução das tarefas, ou seja, quanto maior for a resolução, mais rapidamente as tarefas são concluídas. É possível verificar, no caso do aplicativo Cubed, que a resolução alta aumenta em média 26,03% a velocidade das tarefas quando comparado com a resolução baixa. No aplicativo Mileage, essa diferença é de 19,66% e, no Shuffle, é de 17,17%.

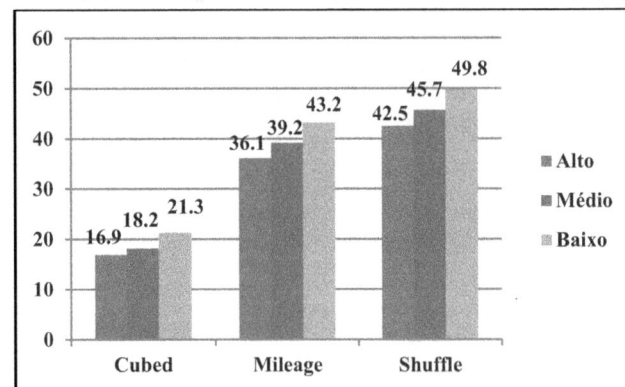

Figura 6 – Velocidade de Execução das tarefas em função da resolução da tela (em seg.).

A mesma análise realizada anteriormente foi concebida para a verificação da influência do tamanho da tela nas interações dos usuários. Analisando o gráfico apresentado na Figura 7, é possível verificar que o tamanho da tela é outra variável contextual que tem influência no desempenho dos usuários. No aplicativo Cubed, a velocidade média para a execução das tarefas diminui em torno de 4,1 segundos quando comparado com a utilização de *smartphones* com tela pequena. No caso do aplicativo Mileage, essa diferença é em torno de 6,9 segundos e, no caso do Shuffle, a diferença é de 10,9 segundos.

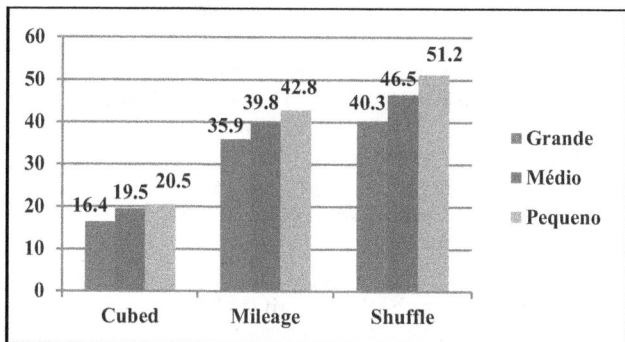

Figura 7 – Velocidade de Execução das tarefas em função do tamanho da tela (em seg.).

Um fato observado no mercado de *smartphones* é que, normalmente, os aparelhos com a tela menor também possuem baixa resolução. Desta forma, foi observado o desempenho dos usuários levando em conta as duas variáveis simultaneamente. A métrica utilizada para medir o desempenho foi o percentual de tarefas completadas com erro. No gráfico da Figura 8, é possível constatar que quanto menores o tamanho e a resolução da tela dos *smartphones* mais erros são encontrados nas tarefas executadas. A diferença entre os extremos, ou seja, telas grandes com resolução alta em relação a telas pequenas com resolução baixa são de 9,3% de tarefas executadas com erro.

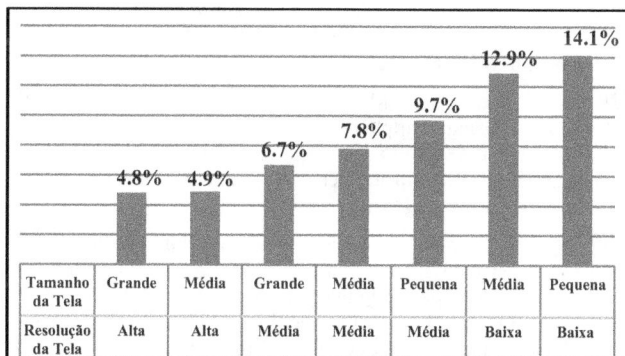

Figura 8 – Relação do tamanho e resolução da tela com o percentual de erros.

5.5 Análise do perfil dos participantes

Ao ser analisada a taxa de tarefas executadas com erros em conjunto com o perfil dos participantes, um fato intrigante foi observado. Ficou constatado que a incidência de erros na classe social de baixa renda é maior que nas demais classes. Para buscar uma explicação para este resultado, investigou-se o tipo de dispositivo utilizado por estes participantes no experimento. A constatação foi que a taxa de erros não estava relacionada ao poder aquisitivo dos usuários, mas à baixa resolução da tela dos dispositivos utilizados. Como a maioria das pessoas de baixa renda utilizaram *smartphones* com baixa resolução, analisando isoladamente a classe social, pode-se chegar a conclusões errôneas. Esta análise caracteriza uma das potencialidades da infraestrutura *UXEProject* já que permite associar diferentes fatores contextuais em uma única avaliação, diminuindo assim a possibilidade de conclusões erradas.

Na Figura 9, pode ser observado que, independente do poder aquisitivo, os erros são mais frequentes quando os usuários utilizam *smartphones* com baixa resolução.

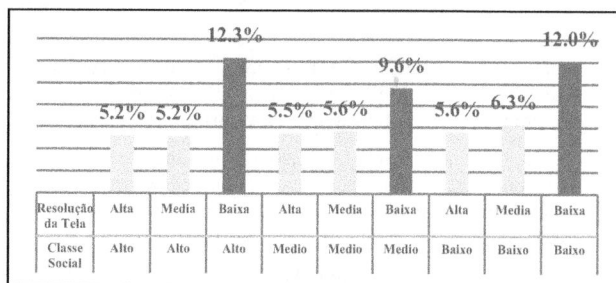

Figura 9 – Relação da taxa de erro em função do poder aquisitivo X resolução da tela.

6. CONCLUSÕES E PERSPECTIVAS

Em função dos dados apresentados na Seção 2 deste artigo, pode ser concluído que a maioria dos experimentos para avaliação de usabilidade de aplicativos para *smartphones* utiliza questionários para a coleta dos dados e não existe uma correlação entre as variáveis contextuais e os problemas de usabilidade observados. Este fato vai de encontro às expectativas de inúmeros pesquisadores da área.

Ficou constatado com os resultados obtidos no experimento que a infraestrutura *UXEProject* é uma boa solução para a investigação de problemas de usabilidade atrelados a diferentes tipos de dados, com destaque para a coleta de dados utilizando os sensores dos *smartphones*.

Com os resultados do experimento observa-se que cerca de 70% das interações ocorrem com os usuários parados, sem troca da posição de interação com o dispositivo e sob uma luminosidade do ambiente normal. Entretanto, quando estes fatores contextuais mudam, os usuários cometem mais erros e levam mais tempo para a execução das tarefas. Estas informações sugerem que os aplicativos deveriam, por exemplo: (i) inviabilizar a interação em posições onde se constata maior probabilidade de erros, forçando o usuário a interagir na posição apropriada; (ii) detectar a luminosidade externa e tentar equilibrar a luminosidade irradiada pelo dispositivo a fim de garantir uma boa visualização; e (iii) identificar a movimentação do usuário e disponibilizar apenas as funcionalidades mais usuais, diminuindo o número de objetos de interação com a aplicação.

Outra constatação importante é que a configuração dos *smartphones* interfere no desempenho dos usuários. Além disso, ficou comprovada a importância da correlação de diferentes tipos de informações para a conclusão dos resultados, como pode ser observado na relação da taxa de erros com pessoas de baixo poder aquisitivo.

Como perspectivas, pretende-se incorporar à infraestrutura *UXEProject* outros sensores, com a finalidade de realizar novas investigações considerando diferentes fatores contextuais.

REFERÊNCIAS

[1] Weiser, M. 1991. The computer for the 21st century. Scientific American, v. 265, n. 3, 66-75.

[2] Vieira, V., Tedesco, P. and Salgado, A. C. 2011. Designing context-sensitive systems: An integrated approach. In: Expert Systems with Applications, v. 38, n. 2, 1119-1138.

[3] Hansen, J. 2012. An Investigation of Smartphone Applications: Exploring usability aspects related to Wireless Personal Area Networks, Context-awareness, and Remote Information Access. Doctor' thesis, School of Information Systems, Computing and Mathematics – Brunel University.

[4] Balagatas-Fernandez, F. and Hussmann, H. 2009. Evaluation of User-Interfaces for Mobile Application Development Environments. In HCI. New Trends, v. 5610, Springer, 204-213.

[5] Jensen, K. L. and Larsen, L. B. 2007. Evaluating the Usefulness of Mobile Services Based on Captured Usage Data from Longitudinal Field Trials. In Proc. of 4th Int. Conf. on Mobile Technology, Application and Systems. ACM, 675-682.

[6] Zhang, D. and Adipat, B. 2005. Challenges, Methodologies, and Issues in the Usability Testing of Mobile Applications. International Journal of HCI, 18(3), 293-308.

[7] Mallick, M. 2003. Mobile and wireless design essentials. Wiley, New York.

[8] Kawalek, J., Stark, A. and Riebeck, M. 2008. A New Approach to Analyze Human-Mobile Computer Interaction. Journal of Usability Studies, 3(2), 90-98.

[9] Coursaris, C. K. and Kim, D. J. 2011. A Meta-Analytical Review of Empirical Mobile Usability Studies. Journal Usability Studies, 6(3), 117-171.

[10] Burigat, S., Chittaro, L. and Gabrielli, S. 2008. Navigation techniques for small-screen devices: An evaluation on maps and web pages. Int. Journal of HC Studies, 66(2), 78-97.

[11] Sodnik, J., Dicke, C., Tomazic, S. and Billinghurst, M. 2008. A user study of auditory versus visual interfaces for use while driving. Int. Journal of HC Studies, 66(5), 318-332.

[12] Fitchett, S. and Cockburn, A. 2009. Evaluating reading and analysis tasks on mobile devices: A case study of tilt and flick scrolling. In The 21st Ann. Conf. of the Australian CHI, 255-232.

[13] Chin, A. and Salomaa, J. P. 2009. A user study of mobile web services and applications from the 2008 Beijing Olympics. In 20th ACM conf. on Hypertext and Hypermedia, 343-344.

[14] Lai, J., Vanno, L., Link, M., Pearson, J., Makowska, H., Benezra, K. and Green, M. 2009. Life360: Usability of Mobile Devices for Time Use Surveys. In. American Association for Public Opinion Research annual conference, Hollywood, FL, 5582–5589.

[15] Ebner, M., Stickel, C., Scerbakov, N. and Holzinger, A. 2009. A Study on the Compatibility of Ubiquitous Learning (u-Learning) Systems at University Level. Universal Access in HCI. App. and Serv. Springer Lect. Notes in Comp. Science, v. 5616, 34-43.

[16] Hansen, J. and Ghinea, G. 2009. Multi-platform Bluetooth remote control. IEEE International Conference for Internet Technology and Secured Transactions, 1-2.

[17] Bødker, M., Gimpel, G. and Hedman, J. 2009. Smart Phones and their Substitutes: Task-Medium Fit and Business Models. In 8th Int. Conf. on Mobile Business, IEEE Comp. Soc., 24-29.

[18] Kim, S., Lee, I., Lee, K., Jung, S., Park, J., Kim, Y. B., Kim, S. R. and Kim, J. 2010. Mobile web 2.0 with multi-display buttons. Communications of the ACM, 53(1), 136-141.

[19] Li, Y. M., and Yeh, Y. S. 2010. Increasing trust in mobile commerce through design aesthetics. Computers in Human Behavior, 26(4), 673-684.

[20] Maly, I., Mikovec, Z. and Vystrcil, J. 2010. Interactive analytical tool for usability analysis of mobile indoor navigation application. In: The 3rd Int. Conf. on Human Syst. Int., IEEE, 259-266.

[21] Grønli, T., Hansen, J. and Ghinea, G. 2010. Android, Java ME and Windows Mobile interplay: The Case of a Context-Aware Meeting Room. 24th Int. Conf. on Advanced Inf. Net. and App. Work., IEEE Computer Society, 920-925.

[22] Kang, Y. M., Cho, C. and Lee, S. 2011. Analysis of factors affecting the adoption of smartphones. In ITMC, IEEE International, 919–925.

[23] Fetaji. B, Ebibi, M. and Fetaji, M. 2011. Assessing Effectiveness in Mobile Learning by Devising MLUAT Methodology. Int. Journal of Computers and Communications, 5(3), 178-187.

[24] Hegarty, R. and Wusteman, J. 2011. Evaluating EBSCOhost Mobile. Library Hi Tech, 29 (2), 320-333.

[25] Grønli, T., Hansen, J. and Ghinea, G. 2011. Integrated Context-aware and Cloud-based Adaptive Application Home Screens for Android Phones. 14th Int. Conf. on HCI. Springer, 427-435.

[26] Sparkes, J., Valaitis, R. and Mckibbon, A. 2012. A Usability Study of Patients Setting Up a Cardiac Event Loop Recorder and BlackBerry Gateway for Remote Monitoring at Home. Off. Jour. of the American Telemedicine Association, 18(6), 484-490.

[27] Bradley, P. R., et al. 2012. Smartphone Application for Transmission of ECG Images in Pre-Hospital STEMI Treatment. Proc. of the IEEE Syst. and Infor. Eng. Design Symp. 118-123.

[28] Schaub, F., Deyhle, R. and Weber, M. 2012. Password Entry Usability and Shoulder Surfing Susceptibility on Different Smartphone Platforms. Proc. of the 11th Int. Conf. on Mobile and Ubiquitous Multimedia, ACM.

[29] Kirwan, M., Duncan, M. J., Vandelanotte, C. and Mummery, W. K. 2012. Using smartphone technology to monitor physical activity in the 10,000 Steps program: a matched case-control trial. Journal of Medical Internet Research. Available at http://www.jmir.org/2012/2/e55/.

[30] Spyridonis, F. Grønli, T., Hansen, J. and Ghinea, G. 2012. Evaluating the Usability of a Virtual Reality-Based Android Application in Managing the Pain Experience of Wheelchair Users. 34th Ann. Int. Conf. of the IEEE EMBS - Engineering in Medicine and Biology Society, pp. 2460-2463.

[31] Courage, C. and Baxter, K. 2005. Understanding your user: a practical guide to user requirements, methods, tools, and techniques. São Francisco: Morgan Kaufmann Publishers.

[32] Kronbauer, A. H., Santos, C. A. S. and Vieira, V. 2012. Smartphone Applications Usability Evaluation: A Hybrid Model and Its Implementation. 4th International Conference on Human-Centred Software Engineering, Springer, 146-163.

[33] Ickin, S., Wac, K., Fiedler, M., Janowski, L., Hong, J. and Dey, A. K. 2012. Factors Influencing Quality of Experience of Commonly Used Mobile Applications. IEEE Communications Magazine, 48-56.

[34] Sharp, H., Rogers, Y., Preece, J. 2007. Interaction design: beyond human-computer interaction. 2nd New York: John Wiley & Sons.

A Heuristic Evaluation of a Mobile Annotation Tool

Bruna C. R. Cunha, Olibário J. Machado Neto, Maria da Graça Pimentel
Universidade de São Paulo
São Carlos, SP - Brazil
{brunaru, olibario, mgp}@icmc.usp.br

ABSTRACT

Modern mobile devices are natural multimedia devices that enable one to access, manage and transmit multiple types of media such as video, photo, audio and maps. Video playing on these devices is becoming part of everyday life for many users. Aiming to enhance the video playback activity, we built a tool that allows temporal video annotation on mobile devices: text, audio and digital ink annotations can be added to the video using Android-based tablets and smartphones. Annotations can be passed along users through the sharing options available on the devices. We conducted a heuristic evaluation with ten experts and the results are discussed in this paper. Two different sets of heuristics were used to find a wider collection of issues. One of them is proposed by us and was developed especially for mobile devices. With this work, we expect to contribute with the theme of authoring on mobile devices in terms of user interface and evaluation.

Categories and Subject Descriptors

H.5.2 [**Information Interfaces and Presentations**]: User Interfaces—*Graphical user interfaces (GUI)*

General Terms

Design, Human Factors

Keywords

video annotation; mobile devices; authoring; user interfaces

1. INTRODUCTION

The recent improvement of mobile devices, in terms of user interface and performance, made these devices very popular. People can use these devices to perform a series of tasks and watching videos became a common activity among many users. In video-sharing websites that allow online playback of the videos, making comments is a form of entertainment, discussion, exchange of ideas and questions. However, in

conventional systems, such as YouTube, comments are a secondary feature. Shareable annotations enrich several activities such as reviewing video lessons, in which colleagues can share knowledge and questions, or entertainment, in which relatives who live far away can share their emotions about long distance events. Given the wide potential of annotations, many works on this theme have been conducted (e.g. [5] [6] [8]), yet works that encompass video annotations using the current mobile devices are still few.

We have designed the MoVia mobile annotation tool [1], and in this paper we present a heuristic evaluation performed to improve its user interface. The tool aims to explore the creation and sharing of temporal annotations made by users while watching videos on their mobile devices. We seek alternatives that can enhance the user experience by considering features of mobile devices. Since expert users are not the focus of this study, usability evaluations are continually made to improve the ease of use. Therefore we performed an initial usability evaluation with users in an early version of the tool and a heuristic evaluation in a later version. The evaluation considered two sets of heuristics: the traditional one, proposed by Nielsen [9] and a modified one, proposed by us, with adaptations for mobile devices. We present the design and the features of the tool, the developed set of mobile heuristics and the results of the evaluation.

In this paper, Section 2 summarize results that show the importance of research on video-based annotations, Section 3 outlines the features of the MoViA tool, Section 4 details the evaluation and Section 5 presents our final remarks.

2. VIDEO ANNOTATION

Among the works on video annotation we outline some that allow the addition and synchronous playback of annotations. The SemTube [2] is a web system that enables users to make textual annotations on YouTube videos with temporal and spatial properties. It is possible to add free text, controlled vocabulary and tags suggested by ontologies. Annotations can be easily shared by a URL address. Authors state that the main limitation of the work is the lack of support for multiple tracks of annotations. The Coreographer's Notebook [12] is a web annotation tool for dancers and choreographers that allows annotating recorded dance rehearsals. The system enables synchronous and asynchronous annotations using text, digital ink and even video. Its layout occupies a lot of space on the screen, which can be a disadvantage. Aiming to integrate video annotations with social media, the work of Kopt et al. [4] presents a system integrated with Facebook that permits annotations on objects of the video.

By selecting an area of the video, automatic image tracking is executed to identify an object. Text, image, link and video annotations can be associated with the object. The works above do not discuss the implementation or the possibility of use of the tools on mobile devices. In terms of collaborative annotation on video using mobile devices, two contributions are as follows. The Documatic tool [11] allows users to annotate and edit a video while the recording is being performed with an Android device. Its goal is to ease the digital video creation process, especially in projects of small and independent teams for documentary production. It is possible to pass along a documentary project for other filmmakers to extend the work iteratively. However, the tool is targeted at expert users to assist the filmmaking process so that the document produced by the mobile tool can later be edited into a professional tool. Huang and Fox [3] present a collaborative annotation tool on Android-enabled devices with focus on real-time data streams. The tool allows synchronous annotations in the form of text or digital ink, and also supports communication with a desktop version of the tool. The focus of their work is on the performance of their annotation framework and studies with users or usability tests of the tool were not reported.

3. MOBILE VIDEO ANNOTATION TOOL

The MoViA tool was developed as an Android application due to the potential better user experience and performance achieved by the native application when compared with a web based system. An important aspect of this application is that it was designed to be executed with the same interface regardless of screen size. The tool was tested with three real devices with very distinct sizes of screen: 4 inches, 7 inches and 10'1 inches. The design of the interface tried to solve and minimize particular issues such as intuitive addition of annotations, control of digital ink and audio annotations, display in different screen sizes, variable screen orientation and multiple annotations displayed concurrently.

Annotations are made on recorded videos when the user is watching them and cannot be made during capture. We chose this approach because it requires less cognitive effort and allows pausing the video to include textual and ink annotations. Our approach considers time-dependent video annotations: when the user adds an annotation, it is linked to the respective instant of execution of the video. The system allows the addition of text, audio and digital ink. Figure 1 displays the playback interface of the system. The vertical layout displays the video on the top screen with ratios calculated according to the screen size of the device and the video resolution. The duration of display of a text annotation is at least three seconds and increases with the number of characters of the text. The control of audio and digital ink annotation is accomplished via buttons that activate and deactivate these features. In the horizontal layout, the application only shows the video in full screen with annotations, and does not allow the addition of new ones. The display behavior in the vertical (annotation) and horizontal (view) modes was based on the YouTube app for Android system in order to be familiar to users. It is possible to see annotations made by other authors concurrently during the playback: all annotations can be seen at the same time. Users can choose a main author whose annotations will be shown right below the video while annotations added by other users will appear in a reserved area at the bottom. In

Figure 1: Playback and annotation screen.

this way, annotations that occur at the same time or very closely can be shown concurrently. Audio and ink annotations are played according the main author.

Currently, the application permits the asynchronous sharing of textual annotations. When the sharing button is pushed, file sharing options become available according to the options available on the user's device (Bluetooth, Dropbox, etc.). Thus, the user is able to share the annotations by using the infrastructure from the applications he uses. The annotations are organized as XML files, which can be downloaded easily by other users and imported by the tool. Another feature of the tool is the possibility to navigate between points of interest, in this case, annotation points. The main challenges for video navigation identified in this work are related to screen size and sensitivity of touch screens. Having observed this, we designed a navigation screen that, for each available annotation, shows a thumbnail, the time when it was added and the annotation text. The navigation screen for audio and digital ink follows the same model, but the text is replaced by an indicator that informs what kind of annotation it is (ink or audio). When the thumbnail or text is touched, the video progress jumps to the corresponding annotation time, i.e. it jumps to the point of interest. On the navigation screen there are also options that allow the annotations to be edited or removed. The MoViA tool also captures context information during the annotation activity. In this work, we consider the context dimensions defined by

Truong et al. [13]: who (Google user name of the author), what (type of captured annotation and event from Google calendar), when (date of creation), where (address where the interaction took place), how (device's model and Android's version). The application captures context information in a ubiquitous way, so users do not have to provide any information to the system. Information is captured using the device features and personal stored data.

4. EVALUATION

Since our work focuses on interface and on user interaction, we performed evaluations to identify usability problems and to support an iterative development of the tool. On an early version of the tool, we performed a user-based usability evaluation with included questionnaires. The results of these initial assessments helped us to improve the interface and to identify requisites for future versions. In this paper we report the results of a second-stage evaluation. We conducted a heuristic evaluation, as detailed next. Usability heuristics are a useful tool for evaluating user interfaces because of their practical convenience, ease of use and low cost [9]. A heuristic evaluation involves a small set of specialist evaluators who explore the interface of an application and associate usability problems they identify with a set of usability guidelines, called heuristics. In our experiment, two sets of heuristics were used: the traditional ones proposed by Nielsen [9], because of its popularity among researchers, and an extended set of heuristics compiled by us to evaluate the usability of user interfaces of mobile devices. Since Nielsen and Molich [10] propose to use between three to five specialists to perform an heuristic evaluation, each of the evaluations was conducted with five evaluators. The ten evaluators had concluded a Human-Computer Interface course and they had already applied heuristic evaluations on other interactive systems.

4.1 Heuristics

The extended set of heuristics used in this work aims to find problems on mobile devices' interfaces that would not be found by using the traditional Nielsen's heuristics. As detailed elsewhere [7], we compiled this set based on the traditional Nielsen's heuristics, on the analysis of other literature results, on the identification of common usability problems found in popular Android applications, and on brainstorming session with specialists. The 11 heuristics, extended from Nielsen's, are:

1. **Use of screen space**: the interface must be designed in a way that the components get neither so close, nor so distant from one another. The more related the components are, the closer they must appear on the screen. Interfaces must not be overwhelmed with a large number of items.
2. **Consistency and standards**: the application must maintain the components at the same place and in the same configuration throughout the interaction. Related functionalities must have related interactions. The appearance of the components (e.g, size and color) must stay the same on every screen of the application.
3. **Visibility and easy access to all information**: all information on the screen must be visible and legible, both in portrait and landscape orientations. Media must be fully exhibited, unless the user opts to hide

them. The elements on the screen must be adequately aligned and contrasted.
4. **Mapping between components and functionalities**: the user must be able to interact with the components without any ambiguities.
5. **Adequacy between messages, functionalities and users**: the interface must speak the user's language in a natural and non-invasive manner. Instructions to perform functionalities must be clear and objective.
6. **Error prevention and recapture of the last stable state**: the system must be able to prevent errors. If this is not possible, the interface must notify users and go to the last stable state or give the control to users so that they decide what to do.
7. **Ease of data input**: the application must make clear to users which data they should enter.
8. **Ease of access to the functionalities**: the main functionalities of the application must be easily found by users, preferably with one interaction only. Furthermore, the most frequently used functionalities must be made in more than one way, by using shortcuts for example. No functionality should be difficult to find.
9. **Immediate and notable feedback**: feedbacks must be easy to identify and understand, users must be aware of the system state. Local refreshments of the screen must be preferred over global refreshments to maintain the current state. The interface must give users the choice to hide messages that appear repeatedly. When processing long tasks, users should be able to concurrently perform other tasks. Feedbacks should be polite and positive, but not redundant or obvious.
10. **Help and documentation**: systems must provide help options with useful information focused on the user's tasks and common problems. Help information should be easy to find.
11. **Reduction of users' memory load**: users must not have to remember information from a previous screen to complete a task. The information on the screen must be clear and sufficient for each task.

Evaluations using the two sets of heuristics follow the same procedure. Each problem identified has to be associated with a heuristic and a severity rating, which goes from 0 to 4 [9]: (**0**) I don't agree that this is a usability problem; (**1**) cosmetic problem: it does not need to be fixed unless extra time is available; (**2**) minor usability problem: fixing it should be given low priority; (**3**) Major usability problem: so should be given high priority; (**4**) usability catastrophe: it's imperative to fix before product release.

4.2 Results and discussion

An analysis was performed on the problems encountered to unify the results of distinct experts and to identify the problems with degree of severity from moderate to high. The use of two different sets of heuristics helped to find many issues that would be identified by only one of them. We emphasize that most of the problems reported have already been solved. The major usability problems and possible or implemented solution are as follows:

- **Additional authors' selection screen**: the screen responsible for the additional authors's choice was very similar to the user selection screen. The difference in role was not clear enough, which could lead users to think they are making the same choice again. This kind of situation should be avoided. We think that this is an important issue to discuss, since Android applications have standardized components and a uniformed layout and thus is not difficult to make similar mistakes when designing mobile applications in general. Messages to users in the form of dialogs and minor changes in the interface can correct the problem. A help option can also facilitate the understanding.

- **Audio and digital ink activation buttons**: the function of ink and audio annotation buttons was not obvious due to the lack of feedback and information. In the current version of the tool, we included alert messages and graphical icons with familiar pictures to improve the comprehension. When the user touches the activation button, an alert message pops on the screen informing that the functionality was turned on. Changing icons when performing an interaction is also a good feedback. In the current version, the icons change color from red to green when activated.

- **Position of the alert messages**: by default, the Android operating system positions the temporary alert messages near the bottom of the screen. In our application this was a negative behavior, since it was considered difficult to notice them. In the newest version of the tool, all alert messages are centralized.

- **User help**: the need for an option to help users was also identified. The tool was designed to be simple but it did not show to be simple enough. Upcoming versions will add documentation. Another alternative is to provide an interactive tutorial.

- **Grouping of the navigation functionality**: in the evaluated version of the tool there was a navigation button for each annotation type. Grouping the buttons together and implementing a unified screen are solutions that save space and facilitate the access to the annotations. The current version implements a centralized navigation screen for all types of annotations, which can be alternated through radio buttons.

- **Proximity of buttons with related functionalities**: the proximity of functionalities is not adequate. The evaluation identified that the button to view the context information of the video was not in an adequate position because of its proximity to the button used to share the annotations with others. The size of the screen is a limiting factor in our case, but the context button could be isolated at the bottom.

- **Automatic pause**: it was identified that it is desirable that the video pauses automatically when the user is adding an ink or audio annotation. The current version implements this behavior.

- **Annotations when in landscape layout**: the majority of the specialists considered that users should be able to add annotations in landscape layout. The application should provide a way to activate the annotation commands in this visualization layout.

5. CONCLUSIONS

This paper we present a heuristic evaluation of a video annotation tool for mobile devices [1]. The tool allows the realization of time-dependent text, audio and digital ink annotation. A navigation feature permits one to jump to points where annotations exist. Annotations can be shared by using applications and services of the system. Context information is also captured during the authoring process.

Our main contribution, besides the MoViA tool itself, is the result of the heuristic evaluation made by ten experts using two set of heuristics. This development approach should be useful for works that involve modern mobile devices in general: we consider that the results of the heuristic evaluation contributed not only to our developed tool, but with projects which involve mobile devices, touchscreens and annotations, serving as apprenticeship basis.

Future work is planned in terms of implementing features as the ones suggested in the previous section. The Movia tool is available at the Google Store at no cost: new features will be added in future versions.

Acknowledgments

We thank FAPESP (grant #2011/17040-0) and CNPq for financial support.

6. REFERENCES

[1] B. C. Cunha, O. J. Machado Neto, and M. G. Pimentel. Movia: a mobile video annotation tool. In *Proc. ACM Symposium on Document Engineering (DocEng)*, pages 219–222. ACM, 2013.

[2] M. Grassi, C. Morbidoni, and M. Nucci. A collaborative video annotation system based on semantic web technologies. *Cognitive Computation*, 4:497–514, 2012.

[3] T. Huang and G. Fox. Collaborative annotation of real time streams on Android-enabled devices. In *Intl. Conf. on Collaboration Technologies and Systems (CTS)*, pages 39–44, 2012.

[4] S. Kopf, S. Wilk, and W. Effelsberg. Bringing videos to social media. In *IEEE International Conference on Multimedia and Expo*, pages 681–686. IEEE, 2012.

[5] R. Laiola Guimarães, P. Cesar, and D. C. Bulterman. Creating and sharing personalized time-based annotations of videos on the web. In *Proc. ACM Symposium on Document Engineering (DocEng)*, pages 27–36. ACM, 2010.

[6] R. Laiola Guimarães, P. Cesar, and D. C. Bulterman. "let me comment on your video": supporting personalized end-user comments within third-party online videos. In *Proc. Brazilian Symposium on Multimedia and the web (WebMedia)*, pages 253–260. ACM, 2012.

[7] O. Machado Neto and M. G. Pimentel. Heuristics for the assessment of interfaces of mobile devices. In *Proc. Brazilian Symposium on Multimedia and the web (WebMedia)*. ACM, 2013.

[8] B. Meixner, J. Köstler, and H. Kosch. A mobile player for interactive non-linear video. In *Proc. ACM Intl. Conference on Multimedia (MM)*, pages 779–780. ACM, 2011.

[9] J. Nielsen. *Usability Engineering*. Morgan Kaufmann, 2 edition, 1994.

[10] J. Nielsen and R. Molich. Heuristic evaluation of user interfaces. In *Proc. ACM Conf. on Human Factors in Computing Systems*, pages 249–256. ACM, 1990.

[11] A. Quitmeyer and M. Nitsche. Documatic: participatory, mobile shooting assistant, pre-editor, and groundwork for semi-automatic filmmaking. In *Proc. European Conference on Interactive TV and Video*, pages 135–138, 2012.

[12] V. Singh, C. Latulipe, E. Carroll, and D. Lottridge. The Choreographer's Notebook: a video annotation system for dancers and choreographers. In *Proc. ACM Conf. on Creativity and Cognition*, pages 197–206, 2011.

[13] K. N. Truong, G. D. Abowd, and J. A. Brotherton. Who, what, when, where, how: Design issues of capture & access applications. In *Proc. Intl. Conference on Ubiquitous Computing*, pages 209–224, 2001.

Heuristics for the Assessment of Interfaces of Mobile Devices

Olibário Machado Neto
ICMC–University of Sao Paulo, Brazil
olibario@icmc.usp.br

Maria da Graça Pimentel
ICMC–University of Sao Paulo, Brazil
mgp@icmc.usp.br

ABSTRACT

Although usability heuristics are a useful tool for the evaluation of interactive user interfaces, the traditional Nielsen's heuristics were created without mobile computing in mind. Other heuristics proposed for mobile applications, usually derived solely from the traditional heuristics, consider aspects that are not directly related to the software's visualization layer to which user interfaces belong. In this study, we extended Nielsen's heuristics to derive other heuristics specifically for the usability evaluation of mobile user interfaces. Two separate sets of specialists evaluated an Android application using Nielsen's heuristics and the heuristics we derived: the latter allowed the identification of more usability problems.

Categories and Subject Descriptors

D.2.2 [**Design Tools and Techniques**]: [User interfaces]

General Terms

Design; Measurement.

Keywords

Human factors; usability evaluation; interface design; mobile computing.

1. INTRODUCTION

Although Nielsen's heuristics [9] are the most used to perform heuristic evaluations [8], they were not created having mobile applications in mind. In fact, researchers have been working on heuristics that are specific for the mobile context due to the peculiarities encountered when using such devices instead of traditional desktop applications. In this study, we compile a set of heuristics based on problems identified when evaluating some popular mobile devices applications which were difficult to associate with Nielsen's heuristics. We used Nielsen's work along with other research results related to user-centered design [6] [8] [13] to compile our heuristics.

We present both the design approach we used to compile the heuristics and the results of using them in the evaluation of an Android application, which was also evaluated using the traditional Nielsen's heuristics. The application was evaluated by ten different experts, five for each set of heuristics. The results show that the heuristics for mobile were able to find more usability problems and are promising towards being more effective to evaluate the usability of mobile device interfaces. However, it is important to observe that the fact that each of the heuristics for mobile devices extends one of Nielsen's original ones contributed to the success our results, since all experts were trained in using Nielsen's heuristics.

It is worth mentioning that studies in laboratories such as the ones we conducted are common in mobile human-computer interaction research [7].

The remainder of this paper is organized as follows: in Section 2 we review related work; in Section 3 we present the steps we used towards arriving at the heuristics we compiled; in Section 4 we describe how we compared both sets of heuristics. In Section 5 we present our final remarks.

2. RELATED WORK

Bertini et al. [2] have already proposed a set of 8 heuristics that are specific for the evaluation of mobile device' interfaces, and which were validated by experts by performing heuristic evaluations. Their study took into account Nielsen's 10 original heuristics and related work on the theme of evaluation of applications for mobile devices. Their report lacks detail about the application used for the evaluation of the heuristics. When compared with Nielsen's, their set of heuristics found about the same number of cosmetic and catastrophic problems, and a higher number of minor and major problems — it took the experts approximately 50% longer to use the proposed set, which contains 2 heuristics less than in Nielsen's proposal.

In their research, Moraveji et al. [8] propose heuristics based on human factors which combine knowledge from years of empirical studies about factors that stress the user when he interacts with mobile devices.

Williams [13] summarizes four basic principles from the area of typographical design, which are abbreviated as CARP (Contrast, Alignment, Repetition, Proximity). Dix et al. [6] offer 15 principles for the design of interactive systems organized in three categories: learnability, flexibility and robustness. Most of the principles were compiled originally for professionals of interactive applications built for Hyper-Card [1].

Along with Nielsen's 10 traditional heuristics, we considered the literature, such as the above, for the compilation of the heuristics for mobile devices we reporte in this paper.

3. HEURISTICS FOR MOBILE DEVICES

3.1 Inspection by Simulation

We analyzed four of the most popular Android-based applications for a period of fifteen days, in order to identify usability problems and verify whether each of these problems could easily be associated to at least one of Nielsen's heuristics. Since some problems could not be clearly categorized in any of Nielsen's heuristics and others were difficult to be associated with the heuristics, we concluded that a specialization of Nielsen's heuristics for the evaluation of mobile device interfaces would be useful. We then categorized these problems and, based on results reported in the literature, compiled a set of heuristics specifically for the evaluation of mobile device interfaces.

The Android applications were Facebook, Twitter, Gmail and Foursquare, because of their popularity and because they serve different purposes. We installed the applications on two Android-based devices in early August 2012. The devices were a Samsung Galaxy 5 I5500 smartphone with a 2.8" display and a Motorola XOOM tablet with a 10.1" screen, both possessing touch screen technology.

The usability assessment was carried out via "simulation of use". This is an inspection method in which experts simulate the behavior of novice users in order to anticipate the usability problems or to identify them as they appear [10]. After the inspection, we grouped the identified problems into categories to compile a set of heuristics specific for evaluating the usability of interfaces of mobile devices. Later, we discussed the heuristics for mobile devices in two brainstorming sessions held with five specialists, so as to improve the heuristics.

3.2 Compilation

The inspection identified 20 usability problems in Facebook, 8 in Foursquare, 15 in Gmail and 10 in Twitter. Some problems were only detected when using the smartphone. Similarly, there were problems that were only observed in the tablet.

The inspection by simulation of use found 19 different categories of problems, which were associated to Nielsen's heuristics. However, some of the categories could not be associated directly to any of Nielsen's heuristics. Others could be associated with some approximations. These associations are shown in Table 1.

At the end of the first brainstorming session, the specialists suggested analysing each category of problems and associated heuristic, and then adding instructions regarding the usability principles to each of them in order to enrich their content. This activity was carried out separately and the results were discussed in the second brainstorming session. The result was a set of heuristics compiled to assess the usability of mobile devices, which we then used to evaluate the MoViA annotation tool. Because these heuristics are a combination of several usability studies, we highlight in, Table 2, the studies which were associated with each of the heuristics.

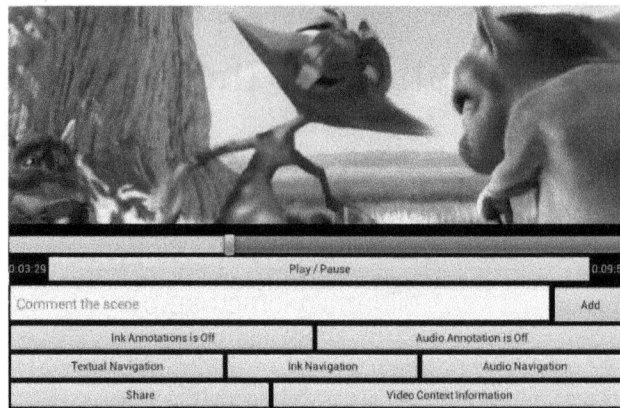

Figure 1: Main screen of the MoViA multimedia annotation tool.

4. VALIDATION OF THE HEURISTICS FOR MOBILE DEVICES

This stage was characterized by executing heuristic evaluations to assess another tool towards validating the appropriateness of the heuristics for mobile devices. The MoViA annotation tool [5], which was chosen because it was unknown to the evaluators, allows users to create and share time-based annotations while watching videos on mobile devices. The tool supports text, ink and audio annotations, which are associated to the content of the video while it is watched, and can be played back and shared afterwards. The main screen of the multimedia annotation tool is shown in Figure 1.

The heuristic evaluation of the multimedia annotation tool was held by ten usability specialists with knowledge of the Android operating system and experience with touch screen devices. The mobile device used by the specialists was the Motorola's XOOM tablet.

All of the five specialists who used the traditional Nielsen's heuristics owned a touch screen smartphone equipped with the Android operating system. In turn, among the five specialists who used the novel heuristics, only one did not own a smartphone with these features, despite having used these kinds of smartphones sporadically. Three specialists of each group have already programmed Android applications.

The experts were not pressured by time to perform the heuristic evaluations. Each evaluation was performed individually, so that no specialist knew the problems reported by others. All the screens of the applications were accessed by the specialists to detect the largest possible number of usability problems..

The five specialists who evaluated the usability of the annotation tool with the heuristics for mobile devices used the Table 2 to guide their evaluations. The other five specialists used Nielsen's heuristics also arranged in a similar table.

The five specialists who used the traditional heuristics detected 8, 13, 12, 11 and 11 usability errors, respectively, while the numbers of problems detected by the experts who used the heuristics for mobile devices were 16, 13, 18, 19 and 22. Naturally, some of these problems overlapped. After the elimination of repeated problems, we concluded that 75 distinct usability problems were found. Of these, 20 were only found by the evaluators who used Nielsen's heuristics

Table 1: Association between the categories and Nielsen's heuristics.

Category of problem	Nielsen's heuristic
Use of screen space, according to the orientation	6. Recognition rather than recall (approximated)
Consistency of the interface	4. Consistency and standards
Standardization of the interface.	4. Consistency and standards
Visibility of the information presented on the screen.	6. Recognition rather than recall (approximated)
Suitability of the component to the functionality	
Clarity of mapping between the component and information displayed	
Positioning of the interface components.	8. Aesthetic and minimalist design (approximated)
Objectivity and clarity of the message	2. Match between system and the real world
User language.	2. Match between system and the real world
Error prevention.	9. Help users recognize, diagnose, and recover from errors
Recovery of the previous state of the system	3. User control and freedom
	9. Help users recognize, diagnose, and recover from errors
Ease of data input	6. Recognition rather than recall (approximated).
Ease to access the functionality	6. Recognition rather than recall
Visibility of possible interactions	
Feedback easily interpreted and with local scope	1. Visibility of system status
Application must be self-restraint	
Help and documentation	10. Help and documentation
Minimization of the user's memory load.	5. Error prevention
	6. Recognition rather than recall
Personalization	7. Flexibility and efficiency of use

Table 2: Heuristics for evaluating the usability of mobile device interfaces: second version.

Heuristic	Description
1. Use of screen space	The interface should be designed so that the items are neither too distant, nor too stuck [9] [13]. Margin spaces may not be large in small screens to improve information visibility [11]. The more related the components are, the closer they must appear on the screen [13]. Interfaces must not be overwhelmed with a large number of items [9].
2. Consistency and standards	The application must maintain the components in the same place **and look** throughout the interaction, to facilitate learning and to stimulate the user's short-term memory [9][11]. Similar functionalities must be performed by similar interactions [11].The metaphor of each component or feature must be unique throughout the application, to avoid misunderstanding.
3. Visibility and easy access to all information	All information must be visible and legible, both in portrait and in landscape [2]. This also applies to media, which must be fully exhibited, unless the user opts to hide them. The elements on the screen must be adequately aligned and contrasted [13].
4. Adequacy of the component to its functionality	The user should know exactly which information to input in a component [2], without any ambiguities or doubts. Metaphors of features must be understood without difficulty [9].
5. Adequacy of the message to the functionality and to the user	The application must speak the user's language in a natural and non-invasive manner, so that the user does not feel under pressure [8]. Instructions for performing the functionalities must be clear and objective [9].
6. Error prevention and rapid recovery to the last stable state	The system must be able to anticipate a situation that leads to an error by the user [9] based on some activity already performed by the user [8]. When an error occurs, the application should quickly warn the user [9] and return to the last stable state of the application. In cases in which a return to the last stable state is difficult, the system must transfer the control to the user, so that he decides what to do or where to go [9] [6] [8].
7. Ease of input	The way the user provides the data can be based on assistive technologies, but the application should always display the input data with readability, so that the user has full control of the situation. The user should be able to provide the required data in a practical way [9] [2].
8. Ease of access to all functionalities	The main features of the application must be easily found by the user, preferably in a single interaction [11]. Most-frequently-used functionalities may be performed by using shortcuts or alternative interactions [9]. No functionality should be hard to find in the application interface. All input components should be easily assimilated.
9. Immediate and observable feedback	Feedback must be easily identified and understood, so that the user is aware of the system status [9]. Local refreshments on the screen must be preferred over global ones, because those ones maintain the status of the interaction. The interface must give the user the choice to hide messages that appear repeatedly. Long tasks must provide the user a way to do other tasks concurrently to the task being processed. The feedback must have good tone and be positive and may not be redundant or obvious [8].
10. Help and documentation	The application must have a help option where common problems and ways to solve them are specified. The issues considered in this option should be easy to find [9].
11. Reduction of the user's memory load	The user must not have to remember information from one screen to another to complete a task. The information of the interface must be clear and sufficient for the user to complete the current task [9].

Table 3: Number of usability problems identified

Severity	Nielsen's	Mobile
Cosmetic problem	7	22
Minor problem	21	31
Major problem	19	19
Catastrophic problem	7	16

(26.67% of the total), whereas 38 were only found by experts who used the heuristics for mobile devices (50.66% of the total).

Considering absolute figures, the results obtained by the heuristics for mobile devices were better than those obtained by the traditional ones because more problems were found in each category. A summary result of this comparison is shown in Table 3, which lists the total number of problems detected by all specialists (before removing repeated ones). We also observed that the heuristic "Consistency and Standards" was the one that encountered the larger number of problems.

It is important to observe that, because some usability problems were only found by the specialists who used the traditional heuristics, we considered revisiting the heuristics so that they would be able to identify these problems. However, we first analyzed the problems detected and concluded that, event though none of the specialists identified the problem using the heuristics for mobile devices, the problems could in fact be associated with at least one of the heuristics. As a result, no change was made to the set of heuristics for mobile devices.

Finally, it is interesting to point out that the heuristics for mobile devices were also used to evaluate the usability of a popular News application available in Google Play called "UOL Notícias". This application was evaluated in other mobile operating systems using devices with different screen sizes (2.7", 3.5" and 10.1") and all the problems found by the specialists could be associated with at least one of the heuristics for mobile devices.

5. FINAL REMARKS

Similarly to the results presented by Bertini et al. [2], our heuristics for mobile devices, extended from Nielsen's, were able to find a larger number of problems than the traditional ones did, with the difference that the profiles of our research assessors were clearly exposed so as to balance the two groups of evaluators.

Despite sharing similar results in terms of the amount of problems detected, in Bertini et al. [2] the heuristics were not able to identify many cosmetic problems, whereas in our study the number of problems detected with the heuristics for mobile devices was always higher than the number obtained with the use of the traditional heuristics.

It is important to observe that all specialists were trained in using Nielsen's heuristics, which certainly impacted the results – in particular because each of the heuristics for mobile devices extends one the original ones with aspects observed from contributions of other authors. These results suggest that the heuristics we compile seem more adequate to be used in the evaluation of mobile devices. Nevertheless, our work lacks more comprehensive experiments with other mobile applications, in different development phases and including aspects of accessibility [3] – which we plan to carry out in the near future.

As a future work, we also plan to consider new parameters related to the way users interact with mobile devices, which are constantly evolving through interdisciplinary researches results of Psychology and Sociology, among other areas. Moreover, we should also consider aspects that are related to collaboration [4] and to context information [12] (e.g. time and location) that usually affect the interfaces of applications built for mobile devices.

Acknowledgments

We thank Bruna C.R. da Cunha for the collaboration in the design of the MoViA annotation tool. We also thank all those who participated in the evaluations. We thank CNPq, FAPESP and CAPES for financial support.

6. REFERENCES

[1] Apple. *HyperCard Stack Design Guidelines (Apple Computer Inc.* Addison-Wesley, 1989.

[2] E. Bertini, S. Gabrielli, and S. Kimani. Appropriating and assessing heuristics for mobile computing. In *Proceedings of the Working Conference on Advanced Visual Interfaces*, AVI '06, pages 119–126. ACM, 2006.

[3] L. Burzagli, M. Billi, E. Palchetti, T. Catarci, G. Santucci, and E. Bertini. Accessibility and usability evaluation of MAIS designer: a new design tool for mobile services. In *Proc. Intl. Conf. on Universal access in human-computer interaction: ambient interaction (UAHCI)*, pages 275–284. Springer, 2007.

[4] K. M. Callum and Kinshuk. Mobile technology in collaboration: evaluation of a web-based discussion board. *Int. J. Mob. Learn. Organ.*, 2(4):318–328, 2008.

[5] B. C. Cunha, O. J. Machado Neto, and M. d. G. Pimentel. Movia: a mobile video annotation tool. In *Proc. ACM Symposium on Document Engineering (DocEng)*, pages 219–222. ACM, 2013.

[6] A. Dix, J. E. Finlay, G. D. Abowd, and R. Beale. *Human-Computer Interaction (3rd Edition)*. Prentice-Hall, Inc., 2004.

[7] J. Kjeldskov and C. Graham. A review of mobile hci research methods. In *Proc. of Mobile HCI 2003 (LNCS 2795)*, pages 317–335. Springer, 2003.

[8] N. Moraveji and C. Soesanto. Towards stress-less user interfaces: 10 design heuristics based on the psychophysiology of stress(chi'12 extended abstracts). pages 1643–1648. ACM, 2012.

[9] J. Nielsen. In J. Nielsen and R. L. Mack, editors, *Usability inspection methods*, chapter Heuristic evaluation, pages 25–62. John Wiley, 1994.

[10] J. Preece. *Human-computer interaction.* Addison-Wesley, 1994.

[11] B. Shneiderman and C. Plaisant. *Designing the user interface: strategies for effective human-computer interaction.* Addison-Wesley, 5th ed edition, 2009.

[12] J. Varsaluoma. Scenarios in the heuristic evaluation of mobile devices: Emphasizing the context of use. In *Proc. Intl. Conf. on Human Centered Design (Part of HCI International)*, pages 332–341. Springer, 2009.

[13] R. Williams. *The Non-designers Design Book: Design and Typographic Principles for the Visual Novice.* Non Designer's Design Book. Peachpit Press, 2005.

Measuring Sentiments in Online Social Networks

Matheus Araújo
UFMG
Belo Horizonte, Brasil
matheus.araujo@dcc.ufmg.br

Pollyanna Gonçalves
UFMG
Belo Horizonte, Brasil
pollyannaog@dcc.ufmg.br

Fabrício Benevenuto
UFMG
Belo Horizonte, Brasil
fabricio@dcc.ufmg.br

ABSTRACT

Sentiment analysis has being used in several applications including the analysis of the repercussion of events in online social networks (OSNs), as well as to summarize public perception about products and brands on discussions on those systems. There are multiple methods to measure sentiments, varying from lexical-based approaches to machine learning methods. Despite the wide use and popularity of some those methods, it is unclear which method is better for identifying the polarity (i.e. positive or negative) of a message, as the current literature does not provide a comparison among existing methods. This comparison is crucial to allow us to understand the potential limitations, advantages, and disadvantages of popular methods in the context of OSNs messages. This work aims at filling this gap by presenting a comparison between 8 popular sentiment analysis methods. Our analysis compares these methods in terms of coverage and in terms of correct sentiment identification. We also develop a new method that combines existing approaches in order to provide the best coverage results with competitive accuracy. Finally, we present iFeel, a Web service which provides an open API for accessing and comparing results across different sentiment methods for a given text.

Categories and Subject Descriptors

J.4. [**Computer Applications**]: Social and behavioral sciences Miscellaneous; H.3.5 [**Online Information Services**]: Web-based services

General Terms

Human Factors, Measurement.

Keywords

Twitter, emoticons, análise de sentimentos, redes sociais.

1. INTRODUÇÃO

Redes sociais online têm se tornado uma importante plataforma de comunicação que agrupa diversas informações, entre elas opiniões e sentimentos expressos por seus usuários em simples conversas

ou mensagens. A quantidade de usuários ativos e o volume de dados criados diariamente nessas redes é impressionante. Uma plataforma popular nos dias de hoje é o Twitter que, sozinho, possui mais de 200 milhões de usuários, que compartilham cerca de 400 milhões de tweets [1] por dia [25]. Nesse contexto, pesquisadores e empresas conseguem coletar esses dados para análises de conteúdo em grande escala [11].

Diversos estudos no contexto de redes sociais estão focados na identificação e monitoramento de polaridade em mensagens compartilhadas, partindo da hipótese que a quantidade expressiva de dados postados uma parcela significante estaria relacionada ao humor e a emoções expressas pelos usuários. Análise de polaridade em mensagens possui inúmeras aplicações, especialmente no desenvolvimento de sistemas capazes de capturar opiniões públicas relacionadas a eventos sociais [16] e até mesmo lançamentos de produtos em tempo real.

Entretanto, pouco se sabe sobre como os vários métodos propostos funcionam no contexto das redes sociais online. Métodos para análise de sentimentos vem sendo muito utilizados para desenvolver aplicações sem estudo prévio a respeito da aplicabilidade do método no contexto desejado, assim como suas vantagens, desvantagens e potenciais limitações quando comparados a outros métodos. De fato, muitos desses métodos foram propostos para análise de sentenças longas e não para análise de mensagens curtas em tempo real. Além do mais, poucos esforços foram feitos com o objetivo de comparar tais métodos.

Nesse trabalho, temos como objetivo preencher essa lacuna na comparação de métodos para análise de sentimento. Utilizamos 2 bases de dados diferentes provenientes de redes sociais online para comparar 8 métodos propostos na literatura: LIWC, Happiness Index, SentiWordNet, SASA, PANAS-t, Emoticons, SenticNet e SentiStrength. A primeira base consiste de cerca de 1,8 bilhões de mensagens coletadas do Twitter [11], representando um histórico completo da rede no período coletado. Dessa base de dados fomos capazes de filtrar tweets associados a 6 eventos sociais relacionados a tragédias, lançamento de produtos, política, saúde e esporte. A segunda base de dados consiste de uma coleção de textos rotulados por humanos para positivo e negativo [22]. A partir de bases de dados reais, comparamos os 8 métodos para análise de sentimentos em termos de abrangência (a fração de mensagens capturadas por cada método) e concordância (a fração de sentimentos corretamente identificados por cada método).

Entre os vários resultados encontrados, podemos sumarizar alguns deles:

---

[1] Mensagens com no máximo 140 caracteres compartilhados na rede social online Twitter.

1. Os métodos possuem diferentes graus de abrangência, variando entre 4% e 95% quando aplicados a dados associados a eventos reais. Isso sugere que, dependendo do método utilizado, apenas uma pequena fração de mensagens será analisada, podendo levar a resultados enviesados ou não representativos.

2. Nenhum método alcançou níveis altos de abrangência e concordância ao mesmo tempo. O método Emoticons atingiu a maior acurácia (acima de 85%), porém uma das menores abrangências (4–13%).

3. A concordância dos métodos, quando aplicados aos dados rotulados, variaram entre 33% e 80%, sugerindo que uma mesma amostra de dados pode ser interpretada de forma diferente dependendo do método escolhido.

4. Existe desacordo entre os métodos na predição de sentimentos para diferentes eventos considerados. Para o caso do evento da queda de um avião, metade dos métodos detectaram mais positividade do que negatividade. O mesmo é observado em outros eventos onde eram esperados uma maior quantidade de sentimentos negativos.

Baseados nessas observações, desenvolvemos um novo método para análise de sentimentos que consiste da combinação dos métodos estudados com objetivo de alcançar maior abrangências e acurácia competitivas com relação aos métodos existentes. O restante do artigo está organizado como se segue. A seguir, descrevemos os 8 métodos utilizados para comparações. Depois, apresentamos as métricas para comparações, assim como uma descrição sobre as bases de dados utilizadas. Na seção 4 apresentamos os resultados alcançados no processo de comparação, e então propomos um método para detecção de sentimentos. Por fim, concluímos e apresentamos direções para trabalhos futuros.

2. MÉTODOS

Esta seção apresenta uma breve descrição dos 8 métodos para análise de sentimentos que são discutidos neste trabalho.

2.1 Emoticons

Talvez o jeito mais simples de identificar polaridade de uma mensagem seja baseado na análise de emoticons [14]. Nos últimos anos, emoticons tem se tornado tão populares que alguns foram adicionados ao conhecido Dicionário de Oxford [2]. Emoticons são principalmente baseados em faces e podem expressar sentimentos de felicidade ou tristeza, embora uma grande quantidade deles não representam faces, por exemplo o emoticon <3 que representa um coração, que expressa amor ou afeição.

Para extrair polaridade de emoticons utilizamos um conjunto dos emoticons populares em sites como Yahoo e MSN [4, 1], descritos na Tabela 1. A tabela também inclui as variações mais comuns para emoticons que expressam polaridade positiva, negativa e neutra. Mensagens com mais de um emoticon foram associadas à polaridade do primeiro emoticon encontrado. No entanto esses casos ocorreram poucas vezes e foram irrelevantes na nossa base de dados.

Como podemos esperar, a taxa de mensagens em redes sociais online que contém pelo menos 1 emoticon é muito baixa se comparado ao total de mensagens que poderiam expressar algum sentimento. Trabalhos recentes verificaram que essa taxa é menor que

Tabela 1: Emoticons e suas variações

Emoticon	Polaridade	Símbolos
	Positivo	:) :] :} :o) :o] :o} :-) :-] :-} =) =] =} =^] =^) =^} :B :-D :-B :^D :^B :^D :^B =B =^B =^D :') :'] :') =') ='] ='} <3 ^.^ ^.^ ^_^ ^^ :* =* :-* ;) ;] ;} :-p :-P :-b :^p :^P :^b =P =p \o\ /o/ :P :p :b =b =^p =^P =^b \o/
	Negativo	D: D= D-: D^: D^= :(:[:{ :o(:o[:'(:^[:^{ =^(=^{ >=(>=[>=} >=(>:-{ >:-[>:-(>=^[>:-(:-[:-(=(=[=^{ :^[>:-=(>=[:'(:'[:'{ ='(='{ ='[:(:\ =/ :/ =$ o.o O_o Oo :$:-{ >:-{ >=^(>=^{ :o[
	Neutro	:| =| :-| >.< >< >_< :o :0 =O :@ =@ :^o :^@ -_- -_-' -_- -_-' :x =X =# :-x :-@ :-# :^x :^# :#

10% [18, 14]. Entretanto, emoticons vem sendo frequentemente utilizados em combinações com outros métodos para a construção de bases de treinamento para técnicas de aprendizado de máquina supervisionada [19].

2.2 LIWC

LIWC (Linguistic Inquiry and Word Count) [21] é uma ferramenta para análise de texto que estima componentes emocionais, cognitivos e estruturais de um dado texto baseada no uso de dicionários contendo palavras e suas respectivas categorias. A título de exemplo, no LIWC a palavra "agree" pertence a 5 categorias: *assent*, *affective*, *positive emotion*, *positive feeling*, e *cognitive process*. Portanto, além de detectar *positive* ou *negative feeling* em um texto, o LIWC também fornece outras categorias de palavras.

A ferramenta é unicamente comercial e fornece funções otimizadas, como a permissão para inclusão de dicionários personalizados. Para este trabalho, utilizamos a versão LIWC2007, a versão mais recente do sistema, e o dicionário padrão para o idioma Inglês, que consiste de 4.500 palavras e mais de 100 categorias. O software pode ser encontrado em http://www.liwc.net/. Com o objetivo de medir polaridade, examinamos a taxa de sentimentos positivos e negativos em termos das categorias de *emotion* e *affective*.

2.3 SentiStrength

Entre os métodos baseados em abordagens de aprendizado de máquina está o SentiStrength [22], que compara métodos de classificação supervisionadas e não-supervisionadas. O trabalho utilizou para classificação uma versão expandida do dicionário do LIWC [21], com a adição de novas características para o contexto de redes sociais. Essas características incluem conjuntos extras de palavras positivas e negativas, um conjunto de palavras que dão maior entonação para um sentimento (ex.: "very" ou "somewhat"), um conjunto de emoticons com polaridade associadas e percepções de pontuações repetidas (ex.: "Cool!!!!"). Para avaliar o método, autores utilizaram bases de dados rotuladas de 6 diferentes fontes Web 2.0: MySpace, Twitter, posts no Digg, comentários no fórum da BBC e Runners Word, e Youtube.

O SentiStrength consiste da combinação das técnicas que produziram melhor resultados entre as citadas acima. Neste trabalho utilizamos a versão 2.0 do método, que está disponível em [3].

2.4 SentiWordNet

SentiWordNet [13] é uma ferramenta muito utilizada em mineração de opinião, e é baseado no dicionário léxico WordNet [17]. Esse dicionário agrupa adjetivos, verbos e outras classes gramaticais em conjuntos chamados *synset*. O SentiWordNet associa a cada *synset* do WordNet três valores de pontuação que indicam o sentimento de um texto: positivo, negativo e objetivo (neutralidade). Cada pontuação é obtida utilizando um método de aprendizagem de máquina semi-supervisionada, e variam de 0 a 1, com soma igual a 1. Para melhor entender o funcionamento do método, suponha que para um dado $synset$ $s = [bad, wicked, terrible]$ tenha sido extraído de um tweet. O resultado obtido pelo método é 0,000 para positividade, 0,850 para negatividade e 0,150 para objetividade, respectivamente. A avaliação do SentiWordNet foi feita utilizando-se um dicionário léxico rotulado.

Nesse artigo utilizamos a versão 3.0 do SentiWordNet, disponível em http://sentiwordnet.isti.cnr.it/. Para associar polaridade baseados nesse método, consideramos a média da pontuação dos $synsets$ e diremos que um texto dado é positivo se o valor resultante para positivo for maior que o valor encontrado para negativo. Pontuações para objetividade não foram consideradas nesse trabalho para determinar polaridade.

2.5 SenticNet
SenticNet [10] é um método para mineração de opinião e análise de sentimentos que explora técnicas de Inteligência Artificial e Web Semântica. O objetivo do SenticNet é inferir polaridade de textos em nível semântico, e não sintático. O método utiliza técnicas de Processamento de Linguagem Natural (PLN) para criar significados semânticos ou polaridade para aproximadamente 14.000 conceitos, nome dado pelos autores. Por exemplo, para interpretar a mensagem "Boring, it's Monday morning", SenticNet primeiramente tenta identificar conceitos, que neste caso seriam "boring" e "Monday morning". E então calcula a polaridade para cada conceito, nesse caso -0,383 para "boring", e +0,228 para "Monday morning". O resultado final para sentimentos no dado exemplo seria de -0,077, que consiste na média dos valores encontrados para cada conceito.

O SenticNet foi testado pelos autores como uma ferramenta para medição de níveis de polaridade em opiniões de pacientes sobre o *National Health Service* na Inglaterra [9]. Autores também testaram o método em base de dados coletadas do LiveJournal, onde mensagens foram rotuladas em 130 estados de humor pelos próprios usuários, e que foram transformados em positivo e negativo [19, 20]. Nosso trabalho utiliza a versão 2.0 do SenticNet, disponível em http://sentic.net/.

2.6 SASA
Empregamos ao trabalho mais uma técnica baseada em aprendizado de máquina, o SailAil Sentiment Analyzer (SASA) [23]. O SASA foi originalmente proposto como um método para análise de 17.000 tweets rotulados associados as eleições norte-americanas de 2012. A ferramenta, de código aberto, foi avaliada no Amazon Mechanical Turk (AMT) [5], onde *turkers* rotularam tweets como positivos, negativos, neutros ou indefinidos. Esse método foi acrescentado a nossa análise por ser uma ferramenta aberta e ainda não ter sido comparado com nenhum outro método para análise de sentimentos da literatura. Utilizamos o pacote Python SASA na versão 0.1.3, disponível em https://pypi.python.org/pypi/sasa/0.1.3.

2.7 Happiness Index
Happiness Index [12] consiste de uma escala de sentimentos que utiliza o popular *Affective Norms for English Words* (ANEW) [8]. O ANEW é uma coleção de 1.034 palavras associadas a dimensões afetivas de valência, excitação e dominância. Happiness Index foi construído baseado no ANEW e calcula pontuações com valores entre 1 e 9 para um texto dado, indicando a "quantidade" de felicidade que existe naquele texto. Autores calcularam a frequência

em que cada palavra do ANEW aparece no texto e então computa o peso médio encontrado, levando em consideração apenas o sentimento de valência. Para validação, autores aplicaram o método em letras e títulos de músicas e mensagens de blogs. Como resultados, autores encontraram que níveis de felicidade em letras de músicas tiveram um decréscimo entre 1961 e 2007, mas aumentou nas amostras extraídas de blogs.

Com objetivo de adaptar o Happiness Index para detectar polaridade, consideramos que qualquer texto classificado pelo método no intervalo [1..5) como sendo negativo e [5..9] como sendo positivo.

2.8 PANAS-t
O PANAS-t [15] é uma escala psicométrica para detecção de humor que captura flutuações de humor no Twitter. O método consiste de uma versão adaptada do *Positive Affect Negative Affect Scale* (PANAS) [24], que é uma escala bastante conhecida na psicologia. O PANAS-t é baseado em um largo conjunto de palavras associadas a 11 sentimentos: jovialidade, autoconfiança, serenidade, surpresa, medo, tristeza, culpa, hostilidade, timidez, fadiga e atenção. O método foi desenvolvido para detectar qualquer acréscimo ou decréscimo de sentimentos ao longo de um período.

Para associar textos a sentimentos específicos, o PANAS-t primeiramente utiliza uma base de comparações para cada sentimento baseados em uma coleta completa do Twitter. Em seguida, o método calcula a pontuação $P(s)$ para cada sentimento s em um dado período, com valores resultantes entre $[-1, 0; 1, 0]$ para indicar a variação desse sentimento. Por exemplo, dado um conjunto de tweets que contêm $P("surpresa")$ igual a 0,250, isso significaria que o sentimento de surpresa teve um acréscimo de 25% quando comparado a um dia típico. De forma análoga, $P(s) = -0,015$ significa que houve um decréscimo de 1,5% do sentimento s. Para avaliação do método, os autores apresentaram evidências do seu bom funcionamento em eventos globais populares. Neste trabalho consideramos os sentimentos de jovialidade, autoconfiança, serenidade e surpresa como sentimentos positivos, e medo, tristeza, culpa, hostilidade, timidez e fadiga como sentimentos negativos. O sentimento de atenção foi considerado neutro, e foi desconsiderado das nossas análises.

Um método similar ao PANAS-t consiste de uma adaptação do *Profile of Mood States* (POMS) [7], uma escala psicológica que mede 6 escalas de humor: tensão, depressão, raiva, vigor, fadiga e confusão. Entretanto, esse método não foi incluído nas nossas análises pois este não está disponível mesmo sob requerimento.

3. METODOLOGIA
Após apresentar os 8 métodos para análise de sentimentos que iremos analisar, descrevermos nossa base de dados e as métricas utilizadas para as comparações entre eles.

3.1 Base de Dados
Neste trabalho utilizamos 2 bases de dados.

3.1.1 Histórico Completo do Twitter
A primeira base utilizada consiste de um histórico completo de tweets postados no período entre a criação da rede, em 2006 até Agosto de 2009 [11]. Essa base de dados contêm cerca 55 milhões de usuários com 1.9 bilhões de links entre eles e quase 1.8 bilhões de tweets postados nesse período. Essa base é apropriada para o nosso propósito pois engloba todos os usuários que configuraram seus tweets como públicos, não consistindo de uma simples amostra, aliviando viés. Mais importante, essa base nos permite analisar a repercussão de eventos populares passados e avaliar os métodos em cenários reais.

Tabela 2: Sumário de informações dos 6 eventos analisados

Evento	Período	Palavras-chave
Airfrance	01–06.06.2009	victims, passengers, A330, 447, crash, airplane, airfrance
Eleições-EUA2008	02—06.11.2008	voting, vote, candidate, campaign, mccain, democrat*, republican*, obama, bush
2008Olimpíadas	06—26.08.2008	olympics, medal*, china, beijing, sports, peking, sponsor
Susan Boyle	11—16.04.2009	susan boyle, I dreamed a dream, britain's got talent, les miserables
H1N1	09—26.06.2009	outbreak, virus, influenza, pandemi*, h1n1, swine, world health organization
Harry Potter	13—17.07.2009	harry potter, half-blood prince, rowling

Escolhemos 6 eventos que foram amplamente discutidos por usuários do Twitter[2]. Dentre esses, sumarizados na Tabela 2, há assuntos relacionados a tragédias, estreias, política, saúde e esporte. Para extrair apenas tweets associados a esses eventos identificamos o conjunto de palavras-chave em sites de notícias, blogs, Wikipédia e informações individuais. Dado nossa lista selecionada de palavras-chave, conseguimos filtrar tweets relacionados pela base de dados. Esse processo é similar ao que é aplicado em ferramentas de mineração na coleta de dados associados a tópicos específicos.

Limitamos a duração de cada evento pois palavras-chave populares são tipicamente alvo de *spammers* após certo tempo [6]. A primeira coluna apresenta o nome do evento a que iremos nos referir no restante do artigo. Como a tabela não apresenta um gabarito dos sentimentos associados a cada um dos 6 eventos, iremos utilizar esses dados para comparar sentimentos detectados por todos os métodos.

3.1.2 Base Rotulada da Web 2.0
A segunda base de dados contem 6 conjuntos de mensagens rotuladas por humanos como positivas ou negativas, disponibilizada em estudos dos desenvolvedores do método SentiStrength [22]. Essa base de dados inclui uma grande quantidade de textos do MySpace, Twitter, Digg, fórum do BBC e do Runners World, e comentários do Youtube. A Tabela 3 sumariza a quantidade de mensagens em cada base e a fração de sentimentos positivos e negativos rotuladas.

Tabela 3: Dados rotulados

Dados	# Mensagens	Pos / Neg
Twitter	4.242	58,58% / 41,42%
MySpace	1.041	84,17% / 15,83%
Youtube	3.407	68,44% / 31,56%
Fórum da BBC	1.000	13,16% / 86,84%
Runners world	1.046	68,65% / 31,35%
Digg	1.077	26,85% / 73,15%

Como essa base de dados rotulada, poderemos analisar a acurácia com que cada método identifica polaridade nesses dados. Em razão do SentiStrength ter sido treinado utilizando esses dados, ele será desconsiderado dessas análises.

3.2 Métricas para Comparações
Definimos as métricas utilizadas para avaliar os métodos que estamos analisando considerando os seguintes valores:

		Observação real	
		Positivo	Negativo
Predição	Positivo	a	b
esperada	Negativo	c	d

Sendo *a* o número de mensagens corretamente classificadas como positivas (*true positive*), *b* o número de mensagens negativas classificadas como positivas (*false positive*), *c* o número de mensagens

[2]Eventos Destaques do Twitter em http://tinyurl.com/yb4965e

positivas classificadas como negativas (*false negative*), e *d* o número de mensagens negativas classificadas como negativas (*true negative*). Para comparar e avaliar os métodos, consideraremos as seguintes métricas: taxa de *true positive* (*recall*): $R = a/(a + c)$, taxa de falso positivos: (*precision*) $P = a/(a + b)$, acurácia: $A = (a+d)/(a+b+c+d)$, e F-measure: $F = 2 \cdot (P \cdot R)/(P+R)$. Em muitos casos iremos utilizar apenas o F-measure para avaliação, já que essa medida testa acurácia e depende da precisão e *recall*.

Escolhemos utilizar as métricas acima já que elas possuem aplicações diretas. A taxa de *true positive* (*recall*) pode ser entendida como a taxa em que mensagens positivas foram corretamente identificadas (R), enquanto que a taxa de *true negative* é entendida como a taxa em que mensagens negativas foram preditas como negativas. A acurácia representa a taxa em que um método identificou sentimentos corretamente (A). A taxa de precisão calcula o quão próximo os valores medidos estão um do outro (P). Também utilizamos a F-measure para comparar resultados, já que ela relaciona precisão e *recall*. Idealmente, um método para identificação de polaridade alcança o máximo valor para F-measure, 1, significando que a classificação de polaridade foi perfeita.

4. RESULTADOS DAS COMPARAÇÕES
Com o objetivo de identificar vantagens, desvantagens e possíveis limitações dos métodos na detecção de polaridade, apresentamos os resultados das comparações feitas sobre eles.

4.1 Abrangência
Para cada evento descrito na Tabela 2, computamos a abrangência dos 8 métodos analisados. A Figura 1(a) apresenta o resultado para o evento Airfrance, que relata o trágico acidente de avião em 2009. Como podemos perceber na figura, os métodos SentiWordNet e SenticNet obtiveram a maior abrangência nesse período, com 90% e 91% respectivamente, seguido pelo SentiStrength, com 61%. Emoticons e o PANAS-t conseguiram capturar menos de 10% dos tweets relevantes do evento.

No caso das eleições norte-americanas de 2008, a Figura 1(d) mostra que SentiWordNet, SenticNet e SASA tiveram as maiores porcentagens de abrangência, com 90%, 88% e 67%, respectivamente. De fato, SentiWordNet e SenticNet foram ambos os métodos com a maior abrangência verificada em todos os eventos da Tabela 2, intercalando entre eles a primeira posição. Nos outros eventos, SentiStrength, LIWC e SASA ficaram na terceira e quarta posição.

Esses resultados também mostram que, apesar de poucos métodos alcançarem altas abrangências, a porcentagem de tweets não identificados é significante para a maioria deles. Essa porcentagem pode representar o erro do método na detecção de sentimentos. Uma segunda análise feita verifica a fração de tweets que podem ser identificados se combinarmos mais de 1 método. Para cada evento, combinamos todos os métodos 1 a 1, iniciando pelo que obteve a maior até o que obteve menor abrangência. Ao combinarmos 2 métodos, fomos capazes de aumentar a abrangência em mais de

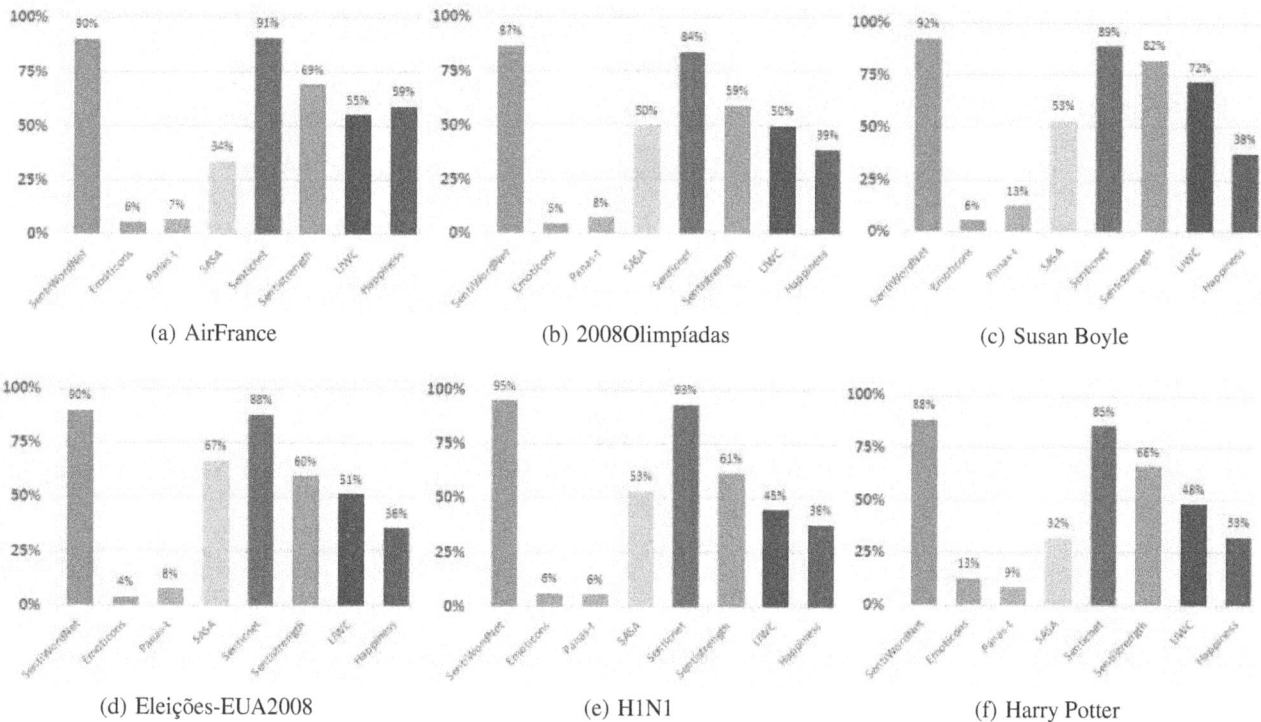

(a) AirFrance   (b) 2008Olimpíadas   (c) Susan Boyle

(d) Eleições-EUA2008   (e) H1N1   (f) Harry Potter

Figura 1: Abrangência dos 6 eventos.

Tabela 4: Porcentagem de concordância entre os métodos

Métrica	PANAS-t	Emoticons	SASA	Sentic-Net	Senti-WordNet	Happiness Index	Senti-Strength	LIWC	Média
PANAS-t	-	60,00	66,67	30,77	56,25	-	74,07	80,00	52,53
Emoticons	33,33	-	64,52	64,00	57,14	58,33	72,00	75,00	60,61
SASA	66,67	64,52	-	64,29	60,00	64,29	61,76	68,75	64,32
SenticNet	30,77	60,00	64,29	-	64,29	59,26	63,33	73,33	59,32
SentiWordNet	56,25	57,14	60,00	64,29	-	64,10	52,94	62,50	59,04
Happiness Index	-	58,33	64,29	62,50	70,27	-	65,52	71,43	56,04
SentiStrength	74,07	75,00	63,89	63,33	52,94	65,52	-	75,00	66,67
LIWC	80,00	75,00	68,97	73,33	58,82	83,33	75,00	-	73,49
Média	48,72	63,85	64,65	60,35	59,95	56,40	66,37	72,29	-

92,75% em todos os eventos. Também notamos que, utilizando essa estratégia, a porcentagem de tweets não identificados foi menor que 7,24% para todos os eventos. Esses resultados são importantes pois conseguimos mostrar que podemos atingir melhores abrangências quando combinamos vários métodos.

4.2 Concordância

A seguir, examinamos o grau com que diferentes métodos concordam na polaridade de um conteúdo. Por exemplo, quando 2 ou mais métodos detectam sentimentos em uma mesma mensagem, pode ser importante checar se esses sentimentos foram os mesmos, o que poderia aumentar a confiança da classificação.

A Tabela 4 apresenta a porcentagem da concordância de cada método com todos os outros. Para cada método na primeira coluna, calculamos a fração de mensagens que concordaram com cada método na primeira linha, aos pares. Nossos resultados sugerem que alguns métodos atingem alto grau de concordância quando combinados, como é o caso do LIWC e PANAS-t (80%), enquanto outros possuem pouca concordância, como é o caso do SenticNet e PANAS-t (30,77%). PANAS-t e Happiness Index não concorda-

ram em nenhuma detecção. A última linha da tabela apresenta a média da concordância de cada método com os outros 7. Podemos perceber que o método com maior concordância com outros foi o LIWC, sugerindo que este consiste de um método interessante para ser combinado com outros.

Esses resultados indicam que os métodos variam muito em termos de concordância em que predizem polaridade, variando entre 33% e 80% . Isso implica que, para uma mesma base de dados, a escolha de métodos para detecção de sentimentos pode resultar em diferentes observações. Em particular, para aqueles métodos em que a concordância foi menor que 50%, a polaridade sempre mudará (de positivo para negativo, ou vice versa).

4.3 Capacidade da Predição

A seguir, apresentamos uma análise da capacidade de predição de cada método em termos de predição correta de polaridade. Mostraremos resultados para precisão, *recall*, acurácia e F-measure. Para computar essas métricas, utilizamos a base rotulada do SentiStrength [22] para positivo e negativo descrita em §3.2.1.

Para comparar os resultados de performance de predição para cada

Tabela 5: Média da performance de predição dos métodos para a base rotulada

Metric	PANAS-t	Emoticons	SASA	Sentic-Net	Senti-WordNet	Happiness Index	Senti-Strength	LIWC
Recall	0,614	0,856	0,648	0,562	0,601	0,571	0,767	0,153
Precision	0,741	0,867	0,667	0,934	0,786	0,945	0,780	0,846
Accuracy	0,677	0,817	0,649	0,590	0,643	0,639	0,815	0,675
F-measure	0,632	0,846	0,627	0,658	0,646	0,665	0,765	0,689

Tabela 6: F-measures para os 8 métodos

Método	Twitter	MySpace	Youtube	BBC	Digg	Runners World
PANAS-t	0,643	0,958	0,737	0,296	0,476	0,689
Emoticons	0,929	0,952	0,948	0,359	0,939	0,947
SASA	0,750	0,710	0,754	0,346	0,502	0,744
SenticNet	0,757	0,884	0,810	0,251	0,424	0,826
SentiWordNet	0,721	0,837	0,789	0,284	0,456	0,789
SentiStrength	0,843	0,915	0,894	0,532	0,632	0,778
Happiness Index	0,774	0,925	0,821	0,246	0,393	0,832
LIWC	0,690	0,862	0,731	0,377	0,585	0,895

método, apresentamos a Tabela 5, com a média dos resultados obtidos para cada base rotulada. É importante lembrar que o F-measure alcança seu melhor valor em 1 e pior em 0. Podemos observar que o método com melhor F-measure foi o Emoticons (0,846), porém o de menor abrangência, como já verificado. O segundo melhor método em relação ao F-measure foi o SentiStrength, que obteve uma abrangência muito maior se comparado ao método Emoticons. É importante notar que a versão que estamos utilizando do SentiStrength foi treinada com os dados rotulados utilizados nessa análise a execução de experimentos deste método nessa essa base de dados poderia potencialmente apresentar viés. Ao invés disso, computamos as métricas de predição para o SentiStrength baseados em valores reportados em experimentos dos próprios autores [22].

A Tabela 6 apresenta o F-measure calculado para cada método para cada base rotulada. Podemos perceber que os 8 métodos apresentam variações nos seus resultados ao longo das diferentes bases de dados, resultando em diferentes performances quando expostos a bases informais (ex.: Twitter e MySpace) ou formais (ex.: BBC e Digg). Por exemplo, para mensagens da BBC, o método SentiStrength foi o com maior F-measure (53%). Por outro lado, para a base de dados do MySpace o maior F-measure foi obtido pelo PANAS-t, e a média dos F-measures de todos os métodos nessa base foi de 72%.

4.4 Análise de Polaridade

Até o momento, analisamos a abrangência e a performance de predição para os métodos. A seguir fornecemos uma análise mais profunda sobre como a polaridade varia em diferentes bases de dados e apresentamos potenciais "armadilhas" que precisamos ter cuidado ao monitorar e medir polaridade em redes sociais.

A Figura 2 apresenta a polaridade dos métodos quando expostos a diferentes bases de dados. Para cada base e método, calculamos a porcentagem de mensagens positivas e negativas identificadas. O eixo-Y mostra a porcentagem de mensagens positivas subtraídas das negativas. Apresentamos no mesmo gráfico uma curva que representa o gabarito para essa análise, possível em razão da base de dados rotulada utilizada nessa análise. Assim, quando mais próximo a essa curva, melhor foi a predição de polaridade do método. SentiStrength foi desconsiderado dessa análise já que o mesmo foi treinado utilizando a base de dados envolvida no processo de construção do gráfico.

A partir dos resultados obtidos, podemos realizar diversas observa-

ções interessantes. Primeiramente, podemos perceber que a maioria dos métodos tendem a apresentar mais sentimentos positivos que negativos, já que observamos poucas curvas abaixo daquela que representa o gabarito para a base. Segundo, podemos notar que muitos métodos obtiveram apenas valores positivos, independente da base de dados analisada. Uma observação interessante é o fato de o método SenticNet ter apresentado as maiores taxas de abrangência, porém identificou polaridades incorretas para conjuntos de dados predominantemente negativas.

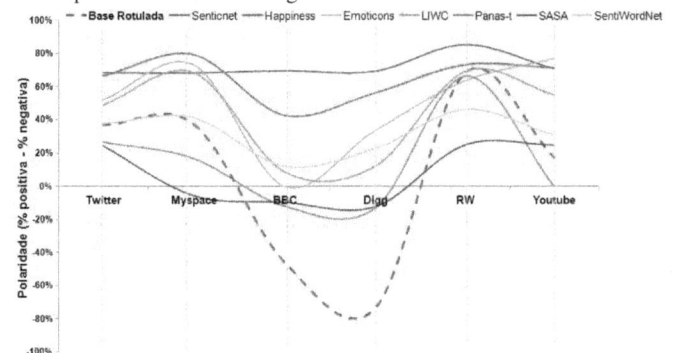

Figura 2: Polaridade dos 8 métodos

O viés na identificação de sentimentos positivos apresentado pela maioria dos métodos pode atrapalhar a detecção em tempo real de ferramentas desenvolvidas para esse contexto, já que essas simplesmente aplicam esses métodos em dados coletados e calculam a taxa de mensagens positivas e negativas nos textos. Os resultados poderiam potencialmente conter viés devido ao método utilizado. Com objetivo de verificar esse viés, realizamos o mesmo tipo de análise para cada evento filtrado do Twitter. A partir dessa análise, verificamos que a maioria dos métodos apresentam resultados positivos mesmo em eventos como H1N1, do qual esperávamos uma maior quantidade de tweets expressando sentimentos negativos. Da mesma forma, o evento Airfrance foi considerado positivo por 4 métodos, embora a polaridade tenha ficado próxima de zero para a maioria deles.

5. MÉTODO COMBINADO

Tendo em vista os diferentes graus de abrangência e acurácia dos 8 métodos para detecção de sentimentos analisados, apresentamos

(a) Comparação

(b) Combinação incremental

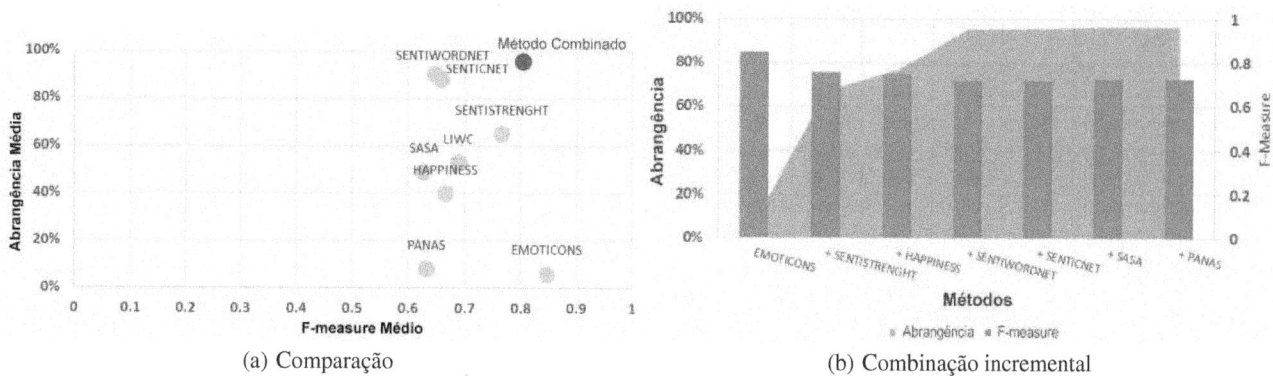

Figura 3: Abrangência *vs.* F-measure, para todos os métodos

um método que consiste da combinação destes métodos.

5.1 Método Combinado

Construímos um método que consiste na combinação de 7 dos 8 métodos analisados, ao qual damos o nome de **Método Combinado**. Esse novo método inclui os seguintes métodos: PANAS-t, Emoticons, SentiStrength, SentiWordNet, SenticNet, SASA e Happiness Index. O LIWC foi omitido do processo de construção do método por razões de restrições de cópia. O Método Combinado analisa a média harmônica (F-measure) da precisão e *recall* de cada método e distribui diferentes pesos para cada um deles.

Para avaliação, testamos nosso método sobre a base de dados do SentiStrength [22] que consiste de mensagens rotuladas por humanos do AMT (veja descrição na §3.1.2). Calculamos o F-measure e a média de abrangência em cima desses dados. Também computamos a abrangência baseada na base de dados que consiste em um histórico completo do Twitter, utilizando a média de abrangência através dos 6 eventos analisados (veja descrição na §3.1.1).

A Figura 3(a) compara a abrangência e F-measure dos 7 métodos utilizados nesta seção, assim como do Método Combinado. O resultado mostra a eficácia do Método Combinado, que conseguiu alcançar abrangência de 95%, como esperado. A acurácia e precisão do método também se manteve relativamente alta, com F-measure igual a 0,730, valor menor que o método com melhor performance, o Emoticons, porém maior que todos os outros métodos analisados.

Enquanto combinar todos os métodos de detecção de sentimentos pode melhorar a abrangência, há apenas um pequeno ganho marginal dessa quando começamos a aumentar o número de métodos na análise. A Figura 3(b) apresenta essa característica, onde adicionamos métodos na ordem Emoticons, SentiStrength, Happiness Index, etc (apresentada no eixo-X). Enquanto o método Emoticons nos dá a menor abrangência (menos de 10%), esta começa a aumentar (70%) quando adicionamos o método seguinte, nesse caso o SentiSrength (região alaranjada da figura). O F-measure, por outro lado, decresce levemente como podemos ver nas barras em azul na figura, e continua a cair na medida com que métodos novos são adicionados.

A medida que combinamos mais métodos, a abrangência aumenta pouco. De fato, combinando os primeiros 4 métodos atingimos uma abrangência de 95%, deixando pouco espaço para melhoras após esse ponto. Podemos também notar que, apesar da acurácia e precisão decrescer, assim que mais métodos são combinados, o F-measure ainda permanece acima dos 0,7. Isso pode indicar que combinar todos os métodos não necessariamente traz os melhores resultados. Ao invés disso, melhores resultados poderiam ser al-

cançados escolhendo o conjunto de métodos que melhor se ajusta ao que o usuário necessita. Dessa forma, poderíamos desenvolver aplicações reais envolvendo poucos métodos, porém com bons resultados.

5.2 iFeel

Este trabalho permitiu o desenvolvimento de um sistema Web que chamamos de iFeel. O iFeel consiste de uma ferramenta que permite a comparação do resultado de detecção de sentimentos para vários métodos facilmente. O sistema também dá acesso aos resultados do Método Combinado, que tipicamente dará melhor abrangência e acurácia. Acreditamos que esse sistema é muito útil, já que poderá auxiliar pesquisadores e empresas na análise de sentimentos em dados particulares. A Figura 4 apresenta uma *screenshot* do funcionamento do iFeel para a mensagem de teste "I'm feeling too sad today :(".

Figura 4: *Screenshot* da ferramenta iFeel

O iFeel está disponível para acesso em www.ifeel.dcc.ufmg.br.

6. CONCLUSÕES

Pesquisas recentes em redes sociais online vêm adotando vários métodos para análise de sentimentos em conteúdo postado na Web. Vários desses se tornaram populares e estão sendo utilizados em ferramentas para medir a polaridade em redes sociais online. Nesse artigo, apresentamos diversas comparações entre 8 métodos muito utilizados: SentiWordNet, SASA, PANAS-t, Emoticons, SentiStrength, LIWC, SenticNet, e Happiness Index.

Nossos estudos de comparações focaram na detecção da polaridade (positivo ou negativo) em conteúdo da Web, porém ainda não considerou outros tipos de sentimentos (ex.: afetos psicológicos como raiva, calma, etc). Adotamos várias métricas para medir a eficácia de um método: abrangência (medindo a fração de mensagens que foram capturados por um método), concordância (medindo a concordância entre a polaridade entre os métodos utilizando uma base de dados rotulada), taxa de *true positive* (taxa em que mensagens positivas foram corretamente identificadas), taxa de *true negative* (taxa em que mensagens negativas foram preditas como negativas), acurácia (taxa em que um método identificou sentimentos corretamente), precisão (calcula o quão próximo os valores medidos estão um do outro) e F-measure, que relaciona precisão e *recall*. Como resultados, percebemos que os 8 métodos possuem variados graus de abrangência e acurácia, e não existe um método com melhores resultados sempre. Esses resultados nos levou a construção de um novo método que consiste da combinação dos outros na tentativa de alcançar melhores abrangências e acurácia satisfatória. Esse método foi apresentado com nome Método Combinado.

Neste trabalho, apresentamos um cenário de comparação entre vários métodos para análise de sentimentos. Para realizar esta tarefa, cobrimos um amplo conjunto de pesquisas em análise de sentimentos e realizamos um esforço significativo em contatar seus respectivos autores para ter acesso aos métodos. Infelizmente, em muitos casos, ter acesso aos métodos não foi fácil e portanto realizamos estudos com base em apenas 8 métodos. Como trabalhos futuros pretendemos incorporar mais métodos existentes na literatura para comparação, como o *Profile of Mood States* (POMS) [7] e *OpinionFinder* [26]. Além disso, gostaríamos de expandir as categorias de sentimentos comparados para além de polaridade positivo e negativo.

7. AGRADECIMENTOS

Esse trabalho teve apoio do Conselho Nacional de Desenvolvimento Científico e Tecnológico (CNPq), da Fundação de Amparo à Pesquisa do estado de Minas Gerais (FAPEMIG), da da Coordenação de Aperfeiçoamento de Pessoal de Nível Superior (CAPES) e também do Instituto Nacional de Ciência e Tecnologia para a Web (InWeb).

8. REFERENCES

[1] Msn messenger emoticons. http://messenger.msn.com/Resource/Emoticons.aspx.

[2] Omg! oxford english dictionary grows a heart: Graphic symbol for love (and that exclamation) are added as words. tinyurl.com/klv36p.

[3] Sentistrength 2.0. http://sentistrength.wlv.ac.uk/Download.

[4] Yahoo messenger emoticons. http://messenger.yahoo.com/features/emoticons.

[5] Amazon. Amazon mechanical turk. https://www.mturk.com/. Accessed June 17, 2013.

[6] F. Benevenuto, G. Magno, T. Rodrigues, and V. Almeida. Detecting spammers on twitter. In *Collaboration, Electronic messaging, Anti-Abuse and Spam Conference (CEAS)*, 2010.

[7] J. Bollen, A. Pepe, and H. Mao. Modeling public mood and emotion: Twitter sentiment and socio-economic phenomena. *CoRR*, abs/0911.1583, 2009.

[8] M. M. Bradley and P. J. Lang. Affective norms for english words (ANEW): Stimuli, instruction manual, and affective ratings. Technical report, Center for Research in Psychophysiology, University of Florida, Gainesville, Florida, 1999.

[9] E. Cambria, A. Hussain, C. Havasi, C. Eckl, and J. Munro. Towards crowd validation of the uk national health service. In *ACM Web Science Conference (WebSci)*, 2010.

[10] E. Cambria, R. Speer, C. Havasi, and A. Hussain. Senticnet: A publicly available semantic resource for opinion mining. In *AAAI Fall Symposium Series*, 2010.

[11] M. Cha, H. Haddadi, F. Benevenuto, and K. P. Gummadi. Measuring User Influence in Twitter: The Million Follower Fallacy. In *Int'l AAAI Conference on Weblogs and Social Media (ICWSM)*, 2010.

[12] P. S. Dodds and C. M. Danforth. Measuring the happiness of large-scale written expression: songs, blogs, and presidents. *Journal of Happiness Studies*, 11(4):441–456, 2009.

[13] Esuli and Sebastiani. Sentwordnet: A publicly available lexical resource for opinion mining. In *In Conference on Language Resources and Evaluation*, 2006.

[14] P. Goncalves and F. Benevenuto. O que tweets contendo emoticons podem revelar sobre sentimentos coletivos? In *II Brazilian Workshop on Social Network Analysis and Mining (BraSNAM)*, 2013.

[15] P. Goncalves, W. Dores, and F. Benevenuto. Panas-t: Uma escala psicometrica para analise de sentimentos no twitter. In *I Brazilian Workshop on Social Network Analysis and Mining (BraSNAM)*, 2012.

[16] A. Hannak, E. Anderson, L. F. Barrett, S. Lehmann, A. Mislove, and M. Riedewald. Tweetin' in the rain: Exploring societal-scale effects of weather on mood. In *Int'l AAAI Conference on Weblogs and Social Media (ICWSM)*, 2012.

[17] G. A. Miller. Wordnet: a lexical database for english. *Communications of the ACM*, 38(11):39–41, 1995.

[18] J. Park, V. Barash, C. Fink, and M. Cha. Emoticon style: Interpreting differences in emoticons across cultures. In *Int'l AAAI Conference on Weblogs and Social Media (ICWSM)*, 2013.

[19] J. Read. Using emoticons to reduce dependency in machine learning techniques for sentiment classification. In *ACL Student Research Workshop*, pages 43–48, 2005.

[20] S. Somasundaran, J. Wiebe, and J. Ruppenhofer. Discourse level opinion interpretation. In *Int'l Conference on Computational Linguistics (COLING)*, pages 801–808, 2008.

[21] Y. R. Tausczik and J. W. Pennebaker. The psychological meaning of words: Liwc and computerized text analysis methods. *Journal of Language and Social Psychology*, 29(1):24–54, 2010.

[22] M. Thelwall. Heart and soul: Sentiment strength detection in the social web with sentistrength. http://migre.me/fHgj9.

[23] H. Wang, D. Can, A. Kazemzadeh, F. Bar, and S. Narayanan. A system for real-time twitter sentiment analysis of 2012 u.s. presidential election cycle. In *ACL System Demonstrations*, 2012.

[24] D. Watson and L. Clark. Development and validation of brief measures of positive and negative affect: the panas scales. *Journal of Personality and Social Psychology*, 54(1):1063–1070, 1985.

[25] K. Wickre. Celebrating twitter7. http://migre.me/fHgjA.

[26] T. Wilson, P. Hoffmann, S. Somasundaran, J. Kessler, J. Wiebe, Y. Choi, C. Cardie, E. Riloff, and S. Patwardhan. Opinionfinder: a system for subjectivity analysis. In *HLT/EMNLP on Interactive Demonstrations*, 2005.

How Do Metrics of Link Analysis Correlate to Quality, Relevance and Popularity in Wikipedia?

Raiza Tamae Sarkis Hanada,
Maria da Graça Campos Pimentel
ICMC – Universidade de São Paulo
{rhanada, mgp}@icmc.usp.br

Marco Cristo
Universidade Federal do Amazonas
Instituto de Computação
marco.cristo@icomp.ufam.edu.br

ABSTRACT

Many links between Web pages can be viewed as indicative of the quality and importance of the pages they pointed to. Accordingly, several studies have proposed metrics based on links to infer web page content quality. However, as far as we know, the only work that has examined the correlation between such metrics and content quality consisted of a limited study that left many open questions. Despite the fact that these metrics showed to be successful in the task of ranking pages provided as answers to queries submitted to search engines, it is not possible to determine the specific contribution that factors such as quality, popularity, and importance have on the results. This difficulty is partially due to the fact that such information about Web pages in general is hard to obtain. Unlike ordinary Web pages, the quality, importance and popularity of Wikipedia articles are evaluated by human experts or might be easily estimated. Thus, it is feasible to verify the relationship between link analysis metrics and the afore mentioned factors in Wikipedia articles. This is our goal in this work. In order to accomplish that, we implemented several link analysis algorithms and compared their resulting rankings with the ones created by human evaluators regarding factors such as quality, popularity and importance. We found that the metrics are more correlated to quality and popularity than to importance, and that the correlations are moderate.

Categories and Subject Descriptors:
H.3[INFORMATION STORAGE AND RETRIEVAL].
H.3.m[Miscellaneous]

General Terms: Measurement.

Keywords: Link Analysis, Wikipedia, Quality of Content.

1. INTRODUCTION

As result of a large and fast expansion, the Web became a huge collection of decentralized and disorganized documents. Nevertheless, many companies have successfully developed tools to find information on the Web. Such tools are the search engines that allow users to declare their information needs by means of queries and find relevant information. To accomplish this task, ranking algorithms sort pages according to their scores. These scores are estimated based on various pieces of evidence. Among them, those based on the Web link structure play an important role. To them, the Web is modeled as a directed graph where nodes represent pages and edges represent links. The study of the properties and relations that can be inferred from this graph is called Link Analysis.

According to a common intuition in Link Analysis, when the author of a page creates a link to another page, he endorses the content of the page he is pointing to, suggesting that it is of good quality and can be considered an authority on a particular subject [12]. In this work, we refer to this intuition as "quality hypothesis". According to this hypothesis, the content quality of page p can be inferred by which and how many pages cite p, or equivalently, the *reputation* of p. This assumption contributes to the idea that the more a page is pointed to by another page, the higher the probability that it is preferred by a user among several alternative pages on the same topic.

As far as ranking the results of a query is concerned, the literature reports the use of several metrics based on Link Analysis [2]. The results of these metrics are usually evaluated by human experts to check how relevant the pages returned are to the queries provided. Although the evaluation of these strategies confirms that Link Analysis is useful to rank pages according to their relevance, they do not confirm that the "Quality hypothesis" holds. The difficulty lies in the fact that the degree of quality of a web page is very hard to obtain. As a result, as far as we know, this hypothesis has not been fully verified.

Confirming that hypothesis is even harder when we observe that quality is not the only factor that contributes for a page to be cited. Other factors investigated in literature are the *importance* and the *popularity* of the page [6]. These factors, besides quality, compose central concepts to this work and deserve more careful discussion. Given a set of alternative options, the term quality refers to a level of excellence that, when assigned to a specific option, allows us to distinguish it from the others. However, quality perception is subjective, which implies that different users may assign different degrees of quality to a same page. In this sense, it would be more correct to say that, in addition to good quality, highly cited pages also have good reputation. Reputation refers to the opinion that people have about something. A concept related to reputation is popularity.

A popular page is one that attracts many users, such as the entry pages of major News portals and pages with large content appeal. Important pages, in turn, are those that people think that have great value or interest, such as pages of services provided by the government.

Unlike Web pages, Wikipedia[1] articles are explicitly evaluated by its community in terms of quality and importance. In addition, the community maintains detailed statistics of the number of visits articles receive over time, which can be used to estimate their popularity. Given the availability of information from Wikipedia, we investigated the correlation between link analysis metrics and factors such as content quality, popularity, and importance in Wikipedia articles.

In this work, we provide a large-scale study about how link analysis metrics and various factors correlate to each other. An important contribution is the better understanding of the nature of the link analysis metrics. As consequence of this study, new metrics can be suggested to automatically estimate content quality and rank pages, at least as far as the Wikipedia is concerned. These areas are promising, given the impact in various applications such as searching, recommendation and automatic quality assessment.

Among the results, we observed that the metrics we studied are more correlated to quality and popularity than to importance. All correlations were either weak or moderate.

This paper is organized as follows. In Section 2, we present related work. In Section 3, we describe the concepts and methods necessary to understand this work. In Section 4, we present the collections that we used in our study and compare their link structures. In Section 5, we present experiments and discuss the obtained results. Finally, in Section 6 we present our conclusions.

2. RELATED WORKS

As far as we know, the only study reported in the literature that directly verified the correlation between Link Analysis and content quality was performed by Amento et al. [1]. In their work, the authors found that there is a correlation between some traditional link analysis metrics and content quality. Many of their results, however, were not statistically significant due to the small number of human evaluators, pages and topics they used. Also, they verified a lack of consensus regarding the opinion of the evaluators. In general, the authors concluded that, among the studied metrics, simple metrics such as Indegree are as efficient as complex metrics such as HITS and PageRank. In addition, they noted that metrics are more related to popularity than to quality. Unlike the aforementioned work, the use of Wikipedia allowed us to verify their results in large scale since our database has much more articles reviewed by humans covering much more topics. Further, we also studied the impact of other factors such as popularity and importance, which can be obtained independently from the Wikipedia itself.

Since (the structure of) the Wikipedia and the web may be different, the results found for Wikipedia may not necessarily be valid for the web. Several papers have studied the differences between these two collections. For instance, in the study presented by Smith [15], the authors discussed the different roles played by web links and the similarities with bibliometrics citations. In particular, the authors concluded

[1] http://pt.wikipedia.org

that only 20% of the web links are similar to scientific citations. We believe that links in Wikipedia are more similar to scientific citations than other pages on the Web. Likewise, Gleich et al. [9] observed differences in rankings obtained using Pagerank when applied to Wikipedia and to the web. Upon applying PageRank to the Wikipedia graph, varying the values of the dampening factor the authors found rankings different from those expected. In another effort, Kamps and Koolen [10] conduct a study on Wikipedia and found that, compared to Web, Wikipedia has a denser link structure, outlinks are more useful than inlinks to infer article importance, and link analysis can be used to improve the performance of search engines.

Other research results related to ours are ones that attempt to automatically assess the quality of Wikipedia articles [7, 8, 14]. In these works, the authors study how to estimate the quality of articles based on different types of features, including those extracted from the link structure of Wikipedia. Unlike our work, only internal links to the Wikipedia graph were used in all these previous studies. In our experiments, we also include links from outside the `wikipedia.org` domain. Thus, we take into consideration non-encyclopedic links that do not follow Wikipedia standards and requirements and belong to a large neighborhood of pages. This was necessary since a large neighborhood was required for a comprehensive analysis of complex metrics such as PageRank.

3. RELATED CONTENT

3.1 Link Analysis

As previously discussed, ranking algorithms can use many strategies to infer the importance of Web pages. One of them, which we refer to as link analysis, consists in analyzing the Web graph to estimate the overall importance of each page. The intuition behind link analysis is that a link from page p_1 to p_2 can represent a vote for the reputation of p_2. This way, we infer that the content quality of p_2 is probably good. In the traditional link analysis, the Web is seen as a directed graph where nodes represent pages and vertices represent links between pages. Three traditional link-analysis metrics are Pagerank [13], Indegree, and Outdegree [5], which we describe in the following paragraphs.

PageRank computes the reputation of a page as the probability of a random surfer visiting that page. Given page p, the PageRank formula is:

$$PR(p) = \frac{c}{N} + (1 - c) \sum_{q \in I} \frac{PR(q)}{Out(q)} \quad (1)$$

where c is the damping factor, $Out(q)$ is the number of pages pointed to by q, I is the set of pages that point to page p, and N is the number of pages in the collection.

Indegree consists in counting, for each page p, the number of pages that point to p. Similarly, Outdegree consists in counting, for each page p, the number of pages that p points to. Although these methods are simple and very susceptible to noise and spam, they have been proven useful both for Web applications and Wikipedia.

Since links internal to hosts and domains commonly used for navigational purposes (e.g. menus), previous work in the literature have shown that they are biased and play a less important role for quality estimation. Therefore, some variants of traditional algorithms have been proposed to remove or unweight these links. In the following paragraphs, we describe a family of algorithms for link analysis that incorporate robust strategies to disposal links [3].

Methods proposed by Berlt et al. [3] treat the web as a hypergraph rather than as a graph. The directed hypergraph $\mathcal{H} = (\mathcal{V}, \mathcal{E})$, used by the authors, consists of a set of vertices $\mathcal{V}$ and a set of hyperarcs $\mathcal{E}$, where $\mathcal{E} \subseteq 2^{\mathcal{V}} \times \mathcal{V}$, $\epsilon = (G, v) \in \mathcal{E}$, $v \notin G$, and $G \subset \mathcal{V}$ is a set of vertices. Thus, a hyperarc of a group G always points to a single vertex that does not belong to G. Web pages are still viewed as vertices of the graph. However, the set of pages is partitioned into non-overlapping blocks, where pages are grouped according to an affinity criterium. A block partition $\mathcal{B}$ in the hypergraph points to v through a hyperarc $\epsilon = (\mathcal{B}, v)$ if and only if, there is at least one page $\mathcal{B}$ that has a link to webpage v and $v \notin \mathcal{B}$. Thus, in this model, hyperarcs represent a page within a block that points to a page outside the block. Berlt et al. [3] consider three partition criteria:

- Page-based partition: block consists of a single web page. The resulting graph corresponds precisely to the traditional web representation as a directed graph;

- Host-based partition: all pages of a block belong to the same web host [2];

- Domain-based partition: all pages of a block belong to the same web domain [3].

Representing a web as a hypergraph, Berlt et al. [3] proposed host-based and domain-based versions of PageRank (HyperPagerank) and Indegree (HyperIndegree). By using a sample of the Brazilian Web, Berlt et al. [3] showed that these methods outperformed traditional algorithms such as PageRank and Indegree, with the advantage of being less susceptible to spam. From these methods, we selected HyperIndegree to study in this paper since it presented the best overall performance. In particular, we will refer to domain-based HyperIndegree as *HInD* and to host-based HyperIndegree as *HInH*.

The authors also implemented PageRank, Indegree, and Outdegree versions that do not take into account links internal to hosts (host-based internal links) and domains (domain-based internal links). We will refer to those methods that discard host-based internal links as *PRH*, *InH*, and *OutH*, and to the ones that discard domain-based internal links as *PRD*, *OutD* and *InD*. Table 1 summarizes the link analysis

---

methods we implemented, where $\mathcal{H}_p$ is the page-based hypergraph, $\mathcal{HHiper}_h$ is the host-based hypergraph and $\mathcal{HHiper}_d$ is the domain-based hypergraph.

Table 1: Link Analysis Methods evaluated in this work. $h(p)$ **is the host of** p **and** $d(p)$ **is the domains of** p.

Method	Description
In(v)	# of links to v in $\mathcal{H}_p$
Out(v)	# of links from v in $\mathcal{H}_p$
PR(v)	Pagerank in $\mathcal{H}_p$
InH(v)	# of link from i to v in $\mathcal{H}_p$, $\forall_i$ $h(i) \neq h(v)$
OutH(v)	# of link from o to v in $\mathcal{H}_p$, $\forall_o$ $h(o) \neq h(v)$
PRH(v)	PR(v), where the link ℓ is visited if $h(\ell) \neq h(v)$
InD(v)	# of links from i to v in $\mathcal{H}_p$, $\forall_i$ $d(i) \neq d(v)$
OutD(v)	# of links from o to v in $\mathcal{H}_p$, $\forall_i$ $d(o) \neq d(v)$
PRD(v)	PR(v), where the link ℓ is visited if $d(\ell) \neq d(v)$
HInH(v)	# of links from v in $\mathcal{HHiper}_h$
HInD(v)	# of links to v in $\mathcal{HHiper}_d$

3.2 Quality, Importance and Popularity on Wikipedia

Wikipedia is a digital encyclopedia available on the internet in about 280 languages. The Portuguese version has more than 700,000 pages. This encyclopedia has an open edit control policy which, in general, enables any person to modify any content.

All articles must follow five principles: (a) the content should be consistent with what is expected of an encyclopedia, (b) articles should be written under a neutral point of view, (c) all content is free to be edited, modified and updated; (d) editors should interact in respectable and civilized manners, and (e) rules are not firm and can be modified at any time.

In Wikipedia, articles are constantly evaluated by the community according to its importance. To evaluate their importance, editors organize articles into projects according to specific topics such as Biology, Mathematics or Biography. Editors of a project are in charge of rating its articles according to their importance to the project topic. Since an item can be associated with many projects, it may have many importance ratings. Importance ratings range from 1 to 4 and are described in Table 2.

Table 2: Importance ratings established by Wikipedia

Imp	Descripption
1	Articles focused on a very specific knowledge domains.
2	Articles focused on specific knowledge domains, but that deal with fairly well known subjects. These articles cover usually subtopics of a major article.
3	Important articles that cover significant aspects of the project topic.
4	Most important articles about the project topic.

Unlike the importance evaluation process, all projects must agree with the quality assigned to an article. Therefore, the quality labeling is done by the community according to a general criterion, described in Table 3. The quality rates range from 1 to 6. Articles with quality rates 1 to 4 can be promoted or demoted by the editors. As for the remaining rates, 5 and 6, promotion and demotion is performed by the community, by means of an election, after a careful article review.

---

[2] For the host name, the URL is first pre-processed by removing the initial prefixes "http://" and "www.". After that, the host name is defined as a sequence of characters that starts at the beginning of the resulting string and ends at position immediately before the first bar. For example, in the URL `http://noticias.uol.com.br/politica`, the host name is `noticias.uol.com.br`.

[3] To find the domain name, the host name is split into tokens according to the positions of the dots ("."). Thus, for the URL `noticias.uol.com.br`, we obtain the tokens "news", "uol", "com" and "br". The last part contains the identifier of the country and the second to last part contains the type of service provided (in some cases, these parts may be empty). The third to last part part contains the name of the server. For the given example, all parts exist. The country identifier is "br", the service is identified as "com" and the server name is "UOL". The union of these three parts composes the domain `uol.com.br`.

Table 3: Quality ratings established by Wikipedia

Qua	Description
1	Minimum: very small articles, usually containing a few lines or just a phrase. However, they have useful information and should not be discarded.
2	Drafts: short articles that are not complete or have little information. Also long articles without references. Unlike the minimum articles, they are larger.
3	Articles with references and larger than drafts, but not yet well developed.
4	Articles with developed content, references, but not verified information.
5	Good: Articles clearly and correctly written, covering major topics without being unfocused, and whose quotes were verified. They have links to all related articles in Wikipedia and follow the style guidelines (covering topics such as the use of images, layout, etc.). Normally, such articles are waiting for promotion to the featured rating or were rejected for promotion and expect improvements.
6	Featured: articles chosen by the community, among the good ones, to appear on the entry page of Wikipedia.

Table 4: Joint distribution of quality (Qua) and importance (Imp) ratings.

		Imp					
		-	1	2	3	4	total
Qua	1	1344	107	203	321	22	1997
	2	199	84	357	201	157	998
	3	36	62	206	87	109	500
	4	28	10	17	69	141	265
	5	23	10	20	43	51	147
	6	2	1	4	8	15	30
	total	1633	276	810	733	495	3937

Table 5: Number of links in the extracted collections (Wbr10 and Wpt10).

	Wbr10	Wpt10	Total
Wbr10	4,471,078,526	48,629	4,471,127,155
Wpt10	49,184	22,108,902	22,158,086

To determine how popular an article is, the Wikipedia community records the number of daily visits a site receives over the period of two years. These statistics can be obtained through the service http://stats.grok.se/.

4. COLLECTIONS & LINK STRUCTURES

For gathering link analysis statistics, we used data from two collections: a sample of a general Web dataset, Wbr10, and a dump from the Portuguese Wikipedia.

The Wbr10 collection provided to us a large external link structure to Wikipedia. This structure is useful for evaluating metrics based on information from *host* and *domain*, especially Pagerank variants. Wbr10 was collected by the InWeb [4] project in September 2010 and contains most of the pages in domain br during the crawling period. This collection has about 124 million web pages, 73 million hosts, 62 million domains and 6.8 billion links. Since Wbr10 collection consists of pages in Portuguese collected in September 2010, we also chose to use a Portuguese Wikipedia dataset referring to September 2010. It is important to note that Wikipedia articles were not originally included in Wbr10 since they belong to the domain org and not br. Wikipedia has about 612,000 articles and 22 million links. From the articles, about 69,000 were manually labeled according to their quality.

To evaluate the correlation between link analysis metrics and quality, popularity and importance factors, a random sample was extracted from the 69,000 reviewed articles in the Wikipedia. In this work, this sample is called Wpt10. Wpt10 consists of 3,937 articles, covering 100 categories (eg Astronomy, Brazil, Geography, World War II, Rock, etc). A joint distribution of importance and quality is given in Table 4. Since 1,633 articles of Wpt10 had no importance evaluated by its corresponding projects, we create another sample, which we refer to as Wpt10i. Wpt10i contains only articles from Wpt10 which were evaluated according to importance.

Graph $\mathcal{H}_p$ consists of the linkage structure comprising all the pages in Wbr10 and Wpt10 datasets. Note that external links to both collections are not part of this graph.

---

[4] http://www.inWeb.org.br

Out from the 124,300,583 pages that compose $\mathcal{H}_p$, 99.5 % are Wbr10 documents, which corresponds to a rich amount of data available for metrics that take advantage from links external to Wikipedia (eg, PageRank). The 123,688,772 documents from Wbr10 that compose $\mathcal{H}_p$ are connected by 4,471,127,155 links in $\mathcal{H}_p$, but just 48,629 are links to pages in collection Wpt10. In turn, articles from Wpt10 have 22,158,086 links, from which 22,108,902 point to other Wpt10 articles. The linkage information of these datasets is summarized in Table 5.

Table 6 presents inlinks (indegree), outlinks (outdegree) and page size (in characters) statistics of both collections.

Wbr10 pages have an average size of about 4,270 characters (median 2.063), while articles of Wpt10 are longer (average size of 53,700 characters and median of 30.043). In large part, this is due to the rules of Wikipedia that require articles must provide complete information about their topics. As expected, the maximum values of Outdegree and Indegree are larger in Wbr10, since it is an order of magnitude larger than Wpt10. Both collections present similar figures for the mean of inlinks (links to documents) and outlinks (links from document) by document, that is, about 36. However, the Wpt10 median of inlinks (3) is three times greater than the meadian of Wbr10 (1), which suggests that Wpt10 is more close connected.

The high density of links on Wikipedia is confirmed by several other statistic studies reported in the literature. For example, in the work of Kamps and Koolen [10], the high density is associated with two main reasons. First, Wikipedia guidelines are clear in defining when and to where links must point and encourage authors to place links to the Wikipedia itself (which provides more information about the subject matter) or to external pages that confirm the information provided by the article (Encyclopedism). In addition, robots constantly check missing links, so they are inserted automatically at any time. As opposed to a common Web collection and as a result of the large link density, Wpt10 graph consists of a single component, in other words, a large set of linked pages.

Figure 1 shows the size distribution of Wbr10 pages and Wikipedia articles, in addition to their values of Indegree and Outdegree. In particular, Figures 1(c)- 1(f) show the number of Inlinks and Outlinks of the collections. More

Table 6: Link collections stats of Wbr10 and Wpt10.

		Min	Max	Mean	Median	Std deviation
Wbr10	Indegree	0	6,594,549	36.14	1	1,205.32
	Outdegree	0	11,973	36.14	19	81.73
	Length of pages	0	10,428,864	4,270.26	2,063	39,204.40
Wpt10	Indegree	0	113,330	36.23	3	503.29
	Outdegree	0	2,488	36.19	17	72.09
	Length of articles	0	5,760,990	53,699.80	30,043	98,484.50

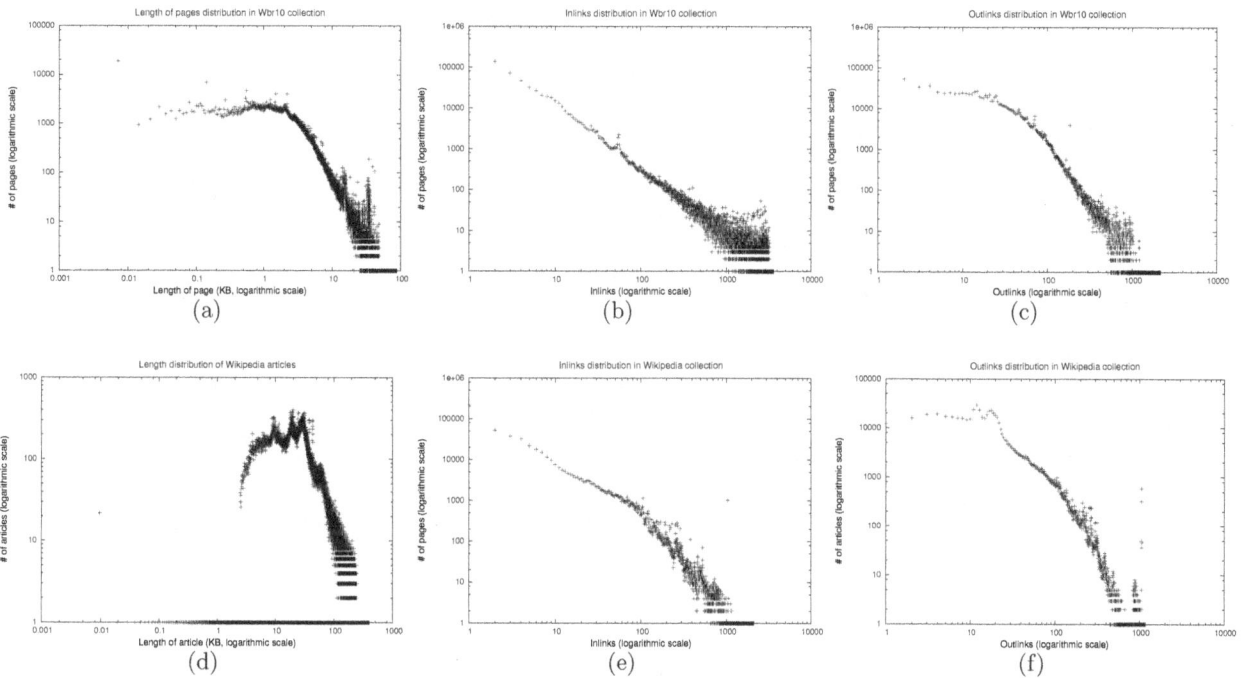

Figure 1: Pages length distribution to Wbr10 (a); Inlinks distribution to Wbr10 (b); Inlinks distribution to Wbr10 (c); Articles length distribution to Wpt10 (d); Inlinks distribution to Wpt10 (e); Inlinks distribution to Wpt10 (f).

precisely, we counted only the number of pages pointing to a certain page or pointed by that page.

In Figure 1-c-f we observe that all distributions follow a power law. In Wbr10, this is more clear to Indegree than to Outdegree. In Wpt10, distributions are more smooth. The difference between the distributions of inlinks and outlinks is smaller in Wpt10 than in Wbr10, suggesting that outlinks behave like inlinks on Wikipedia, something also highlighted by Kamps and Koolen [10]. This is probably due to the nature of semantic links in Wikipedia on which, if a link from p_1 to $p2$ means that $p2$ is relevant to p_1, it is expected that p_1 is also relevant to $p2$. Considering Figures 1a-b that present the size distributions of documents in these two collections, we can observe that, contrary to what occurs with inlinks and outlinks, none of the distributions seem to follow a power law.

Table 7: Correlations between values of indegree (IN), outdegree (OUT) and length (LEN) of pages/articles of Wbr10 and Wpt10 collections.

	IN × OUT	IN × LEN	OUT × LEN
Wbr10	0.310	-0.005	-0.004
Wpt10	0.468	0.2555	0.444

Table 7 shows correlations between three measures assessed in this analysis for collections Wbr10 and Wpt10. Correlations were obtained by applying the correlation metric Kendall τ in 20,000 documents, randomly selected from each collection. Table 7 confirms the similar behavior of Wpt10 inlinks and outlinks. Moreover, we can observe a clear relationship between the amount of outlinks in Wikipedia articles and the length of them, which does not occur in Wbr10. This correlation between outdegree and the size of Wikipedia articles can be explained by the Wikipedia guidelines which require the linking of other Wikipedia articles. These links are places along the article content. Thus, the higher the content, the greater is the need to link other articles.

5. EXPERIMENTS

5.1 Evaluations

To verify the correlation between metrics of link analysis and quality, popularity and importance, we used a correlation coefficient method. The main idea is to rank Wikipedia articles according to each metric described in Table 1 and to each factor, that is, quality, popularity and importance. We then used the Kendall τ Coefficient [11] to infer whether the rankings are correlated.

Kendall τ Coefficient is a statistical measure used to evaluate ranking correlation, that is, the similarity of two sorted datasets. Let $(x_1, y_1), (x_2, y_2), ..., (x_n, y_n)$ be a set of observations from two joint random variables, X and Y, respectively. Any pair of observations (x_i, y_i) and (x_j, y_j) is considered concordant if rows of both elements agree, that is, if both $x_i > x_j$ and $y_i > y_j$ or both $x_i < x_j$ and $y_i < y_j$. A couple of observations (x_i, y_i) and (x_j, y_j) is considered discordant if $x_i > x_j$ and $y_i < y_j$ or $x_i < x_j$ and $y_i > y_j$. If $x_i = x_j$ or $y_i = y_j$, the pair is not concordant neither discordant. The Kendall τ Coefficient is defined as $\tau = \frac{n_c - n_d}{\sqrt{(n_0 - n_1)(n_0 - n_2)}}$, where $n_0 = n(n-1)/2$,

$n_1 = \sum_i t_i(t_i - 1)/2$, $n_2 = \sum_j u_j(u_j - 1)/2$, n_c is the number of concordant pairs, n_d is the number of discordant pairs, t_i is the number of tied values in the i-th group of ties for X, and u_j is the number of tied values in the j-th group of ties for Y. The values of τ vary from -1 (perfect inversion) to +1 (perfect agreement). A value of zero indicates no correlation. We considered weak correlations Kendall τ values between -0.3 and 0.3; correlation is moderate when Kendall τ values range from -0.3 to -0.7 or 0.3 to 0.7. Finally, strong correlations correspond to values between -0.7 and -1.0, or 0.7 and 1.0.

5.2 Results

In this section, we present the correlation values we obtained. Table 8 shows the values of Kendall τ obtained by correlating link analysis metrics with quality, popularity and importance factors in the sample Wpt10i. Note that this sample contains only 2,307 articles from the Wpt10 sample that were labeled according to their importance. For each metric we highlighted in bold the most correlated factors.

According to Table 8, link analysis metrics are more correlated with popularity than quality and importance (direct correlation). The correlations are weak or moderate. These correlations were mostly weak for importance while for quality and popularity these correlations were mostly moderate. For graphs that eliminate links to the same hosts or domains, there was little difference between the correlations of Indegree, Outdegree and PageRank variants. These few changes have occurred due to the fact that almost the same links were eliminated in the graphs generated for hosts and domains.

In many cases, the PageRank variants were less correlated with quality than with simple metrics, such as Indegree (eg, host- and domain-based Indegree variants as compared with host- and domain-based PageRank variants) and Outdegree (eg, original PageRank when compared to the original Outdegree). In fact, Outdegree results were satisfactory for quality. As observed by Berlt et al.[3] for the Web, host- and domain-based Indegree variants were more correlated with the quality than traditional Indegree and PageRank metrics. Furthermore, the Hypergraph variants, proposed by Berlt et al. [3], obtained some of the highest correlations with the quality factor. These results reinforce the findings made for Web by the same authors.

The result obtained for Outdegree, regarding quality, is expected since Wikipedia recommends that articles cite external pages that confirm the information they provide and internal pages that provide additional information to the reader. This recommendation is also taken into account by judges evaluating the quality of Wikipedia articles. The high correlation value found for Outdegree when compared with other metrics may also occur because the Outdegree measure is correlated with the article size (Kendall τ 0.550) and the article size (number of characters) is correlated with the quality of the Wikipedia articles (Kendall τ 0.682). According to the literature, the size of the article is highly correlated with the quality [4]. This result is reinforced by other authors [10] which assert that outlinks behave like inlinks on Wikipedia. Thus, unlike the observed in the Web, where inlink-based metrics are dominant, in Wikipedia, outlinks-based metrics may also be useful.

Regarding popularity, the metrics more correlated are Indegree variants (mainly HInH and HInD). When consider-

Table 8: Kendall τ values for the sample Wpt10i (only pages with importance).

	In	Out	PR	InH	OutH	PRH	InD	OutD	PRD	HInH	HInD
Quality	0.277	**0.403**	0.353	0.364	0.363	0.363	0.364	0.363	0.364	0.373	0.376
Popularity	**0.376**	0.347	**0.529**	**0.603**	**0.379**	**0.589**	**0.603**	**0.379**	**0.589**	**0.616**	**0.615**
Importance	0.309	0.238	0.339	0,233	0.105	0.226	0.234	0.105	0.226	0.230	0.228

Table 9: Kendall τ values for the sample Wpt10 (pages with and without importance).

	In	Out	PR	InH	OutH	PRH	InD	OutD	PRD	HInH	HInD
Quality	0.444	**0.516**	0.468	0.451	**0.396**	0.450	0.452	**0.396**	0.451	0.461	0.463
Popularity	**0.467**	0.406	**0.558**	**0.561**	0.356	**0.553**	**0.561**	0.356	**0.553**	**0.574**	**0.573**

ing the complete page graph without discarding links, the PageRank metric has the highest correlation to popularity, but still, their correlation is lower than those observed for Indegree and variants, including PageRank variants. The similarity found between the computed values for Indegree and PageRank metrics (In, InH, InD, PR, PRH, and PRD) is also observed for quality and importance.

While Indegree variants were the most correlated with popularity, the metrics most correlated with importance were the traditional ones (In, Out, PR) applied directly on the original page graph. The best result was obtained by PageRank, followed by Indegree.

Unlike we found reagrding the quality factor, for both popularity and importance factors, Outdegree and its variations (OutH and OutD) presented correlation lower than the ones observed for other metrics.

As described above, most of the articles that have no importance score are evaluated with quality score 1 (in particular, from 1,633 articles eliminated, more than 65 % have quality score 1). As can be seen in Table 4, about 70 % of the articles have no importance assessment. To better understand the impact of missing articles, we verified the relations in our larger sample, Wpt10. Table 9 shows the Kendall τ values obtained when correlating links analysis metrics with quality and popularity factors in Wpt10. As a result of using a large sample with several poor-quality articles, all correlations became stronger. The increase of the correlation values can be observed, in particular, for quality. The sudden change observed in the correlations may indicate that these articles have very specific characteristics when compared to the others, because its growth has affected the overall results.

Outdegree metric and quality factor are correlated with the size of the article (Kendall τ 0.444 and 0.682, respectively), which explains the good correlation between Outdegree and quality factor. Outdegree metric and variations of Indegree using hypergraph (HInD and HInH) are still well correlated with quality, as well as PageRank. We can observe very similar performance between PageRank and Indegree metrics. This result is justified by the strong correlation observed between these metrics (values Kendall τ between 0.795 and 0.965). This is an important result, since Indegree is a metric that requires a smaller amount of resources to be calculated. This result also confirms earlier observations made for the Web [1, 3].

Although the highest correlation with quality was observed for Outdegree, its variants presented the lowest correlations with quality. This result can be explained by the fact that most of the links in Wikipedia point to Wikipedia itself, so there is little difference between host and domain parti-

tioning. In this work, this problem is even greater since the Wikipedia sample we used has few external links in Wbr10. This happens because many Portuguese Wikipedia articles are translations of their English versions. Thus, many external links were not part of our calculations. As a result most of the existing Outlinks were discarded when using host- and domain-based graphs.

Regarding the popularity factor, it is possible to observe that Outdegree variants also have lower correlations, still reflecting the small amount of external links found in our collections. As observed for the quality factor, the results for Indegree metrics approached results of PageRank metrics. However, variations of Indegree are more correlated to popularity than variations of PageRank. As observed for quality, Indegree variants using the concept of hypergraph (HInH, HInD) performed well, being the most correlated to the popularity factor.

Considering the impact observed after discarding a quality category in previous experiments, we now examine how the correlations are affected when different quality taxonomies are used.

In Table 10 we present the results obtained considering samples with three different quality taxonomies. These samples are Wpt10, Wpt1234x56 and Wpt1x23456. The first taxonomy corresponds to the original taxonomy Wpt10 with the quality classes 1 to 6. In the second taxonomy, we used only two classes: rigorously evaluated articles versus superficially evaluated articles. In the third taxonomy, we also used two classes: minimal/sketch articles versus larger articles.

As we can see in Table 10, there is little impact on the correlation values when the quality class 1 is separated from each of the others (Wpt10) and from all of them taken together (Wpt1x23456). This suggests that much of the correlation observed is in the separation between the low-quality class and other classes, which reinforces the observation made in Table 9. Also in this table, we can note that the separation between the less rigorously evaluated articles from the more rigorously evaluated articles (Wpt1234x56) caused a large drop in the correlation observed when all classes are separated (Wpt10). Thus, the studied metrics were not good to distinguish articles evaluated as high quality from the others. These results show that link information was not useful to discern quality in Wikipedia, except in the case of class 1.

6. CONCLUSIONS

We studied the correlation of eleven link analysis metrics with quality, relevance and popularity factors in samples of Wikipedia. In the experiments, we observed that link analysis metrics are more correlated to popularity than to qual-

Table 10: Kendall τ values for sample Wpt10 (original quality classes, 1-6), Wpt1234x56 (two classes: superficially evaluated articles versus strictly evaluated articles) and Wpt1x23456 (two classes: sketches/minimum articles versus larger articles).

	In	Out	PR	InH	OutH	PRH	InD	OutD	PRD	HInH	HInD
Wpt10	**0.444**	**0.516**	0.468	**0.451**	**0.396**	**0.450**	**0.452**	**0.396**	**0.451**	**0.461**	**0.463**
Wpt1x23456	**0.444**	0.476	**0.472**	0.441	0.350	0.440	0.441	0.350	0.439	0.452	0.451
Wpt1234x56	0.147	0.232	0.168	0.199	0.187	0.198	0.199	0.187	0.199	0.203	0.202

ity and importance. The correlations observed range from weak to moderate. Host- and domain-based metrics presented similar performance, excepted by of Indegree. Simple metrics such as those based on Indegree and Outdegree are "competitive" with PageRank and low quality articles are decisive for the correlations. We also presented a brief comparison of the structures of Wikipedia links and Brazilian Web samples.

In future work we intend to verify how the metrics studied correlate with quality, relevance and popularity when combined. We also plan to explore new metrics for predicting data factors using machine learning techniques. We also intend to study the impact of categories on correlations and methods based on topics, such as HITS [12]. In such a study, we aim at verifying if our current findings are equally valid regardless the topics of pages. We also intend to study how factors correlate to methods that treat reputation and quality as moving concepts according to their topics. HITS, for example, considers that an authority on a topic is not necessarily an authority on another topic – so, the reputation of the article changes according to the article topic.

Acknowledgment

The authors would like to thank CNPq (grants 307.861/2010-4 and 484.816/2011-0) and FAPEAM by financial support for this research. M.G. Pimentel would like to thank FAPESP, CAPES and CNPq by financial support, and FAPESP by financial support to present this work.

7. REFERENCES

[1] B. Amento, L. Terveen, and W. Hill. Does authority mean quality? predicting expert quality ratings of web documents. In *Proceedings of the 23rd Annual International ACM SIGIR Conference on Research and Development in Information Retrieval*, SIGIR '00, pages 296–303, New York, NY, USA, 2000. ACM.

[2] R. Baeza-Yates, P. Boldi, and C. Castillo. Generalizing pagerank: damping functions for link-based ranking algorithms. In *Proceedings of the 29th Annual International ACM SIGIR Conference on Research and Development in Information Retrieval*, SIGIR '06, pages 308–315, New York, NY, USA, 2006. ACM.

[3] K. Berlt, E. S. de Moura, A. Carvalho, M. Cristo, N. Ziviani, and T. Couto. Modeling the web as a hypergraph to compute page reputation. *Information Systems Frontiers*, 35(5):530–543, July 2010.

[4] J. E. Blumenstock. Size matters: word count as a measure of quality on wikipedia. In *Proceedings of the 17th International Conference on World Wide Web*, WWW '08, pages 1095–1096, New York, NY, USA, 2008. ACM.

[5] T. Bray. Measuring the web. *Proceedings of the 5th International World Wide Web Conference on Computer Networks and ISDN Systems*, 28(7-11):993–1005, 1996.

[6] J. Cho and S. Roy. Impact of search engines on page popularity. In *Proceedings of the 13th International Conference on World Wide Web*, WWW '04, pages 20–29, New York, NY, USA, 2004. ACM.

[7] D. H. Dalip, M. A. Gonçalves, M. Cristo, and P. Calado. Automatic assessment of document quality in web collaborative digital libraries. *Journal of Data and Information Quality*, 2(3):14:1–14:30, Dec. 2011.

[8] P. Dondio and S. Barrett. Computational Trust in Web Content Quality: A Comparative Evalutation on the Wikipedia Project. *Informatica*, 31(2):151–160, 2007.

[9] D. F. Gleich, P. G. Constantine, A. D. Flaxman, and A. Gunawardana. Tracking the random surfer: empirically measured teleportation parameters in pagerank. In *Proceedings of the 19th International Conference on World Wide Web*, WWW '10, pages 381–390, New York, NY, USA, 2010. ACM.

[10] J. Kamps and M. Koolen. Is wikipedia link structure different? In *Proceedings of the Second ACM International Conference on Web Search and Data Mining*, WSDM '09, pages 232–241, New York, NY, USA, 2009. ACM.

[11] M. Kendall. *Rank correlation methods*. Griffin, London, 1948.

[12] J. M. Kleinberg. Authoritative sources in a hyperlinked environment. *Journal of ACM*, 46(5):604–632, Sept. 1999.

[13] L. Page, S. Brin, R. Motwani, and T. Winograd. The pagerank citation ranking: Bringing order to the web. Technical Report 1999-66, Stanford InfoLab, November 1999. Previous number = SIDL-WP-1999-0120.

[14] L. Rassbach, T. Pincock, and B. Mingus. Exploring the feasibility of automatically rating online article quality, 2008.

[15] A. G. Smith. Web links as research indicators: analogues of citations? *Information Research*, 9(4), July 2004.

Polarity Analysis of Micro Reviews in Foursquare

Felipe Moraes, Marisa Vasconcelos, Patrick Prado
Jussara Almeida e Marcos Gonçalves
{felipemoraes,marisav,patrickprado,jussara,mgolcalves}@dcc.ufmg.br
Universidade Federal de Minas Gerais, Belo Horizonte, Brasil

ABSTRACT

On Foursquare, one of the currently most popular location-based social networks, users can not only share which places (venues) they visit but also leave short comments (tips) about their previous experiences at specific venues. Tips may provide a valuable feedback for business owners as well as for potential new customers. Sentiment or polarity classification provides useful tools for opinion summarization, which can help both parties to quickly obtain a predominant view of the opinions posted by users at a specific venue. We here present what, to our knowledge, is the first study of polarity of Foursquare tips. We start by characterizing two datasets of collected tips with respect to their textual content. Some inherent characteristics of tips, such as short sizes as well as informal and often noisy content, pose great challenges to polarity detection. We then investigate the effectiveness of four alternative polarity classification strategies on subsets of our dataset. Three of the considered strategies are based on supervised machine learning techniques and the fourth one is an unsupervised lexicon-based approach. Our evaluation indicates that effective polarity classification can be achieved even if the simpler lexicon-based approach, which does not require costly manual tip labeling, is adopted.

Categories and Subject Descriptors

H.3.5 [**Online Information Services**]: Web-based services; J.4 [**Computer Applications**]: Social and Behavioral Sciences

Keywords

Web 2.0 applications, Sentiment Analysis, Micro-reviews

1. INTRODUÇÃO

A popularização do acesso aos *smartphones*, a disponibilidade de tecnologias de geolocalização como GPS (*Global Positioning System*) e o crescente interesse nas redes sociais possibilitaram o surgimento de redes sociais baseadas em geolocalização (LBSN do inglês *Location-Based Social Network*), como o Foursquare e redes que se utilizam de serviços de geolocalização como o Google Plus

e o Instagram[1] dentre outras. Com mais de 30 milhões de usuários, o Foursquare é a LBSN mais popular atualmente. Nessa rede social, os usuários podem, além de compartilhar a sua localização em uma variedade de locais (*venues*), compartilhar suas experiências e opiniões através de micro-revisões ou *tips*.

As *tips* são textos curtos e informais adicionados por usuários do Foursquare a respeito de algum local (*venue*) já frequentado por eles. Geralmente, elas provêem algum tipo de recomendação sobre o local ou serviço oferecido, mas podem também conter críticas ou reclamações. Além disso, os usuários também podem curtir (*like*) uma *tip*, demonstrando assim seu interesse e fazendo com que essa *tip* fique mais visível para o resto da comunidade. Além de úteis para os próprios usuários da rede, as *tips* também são essenciais para os proprietários desses locais, já que esse *feedback* pode ajudá-los a aperfeiçoar o funcionamento do próprio negócio.

Este trabalho analisa métodos para detecção da polaridade ou sentimento em micro-revisões em duas bases de *tips* coletadas do Foursquare. A análise de polaridade tem o objetivo de identificar automaticamente a atitude do autor a respeito de um determinado tópico ou o tom utilizado no texto inteiro, classificando esse conteúdo em positivo ou negativo. Métodos propostos para detecção de polaridade possuem diversas aplicações que vão desde sumarização de opiniões, por exemplo, em revisões online [19] até aplicações que monitoram a opinião das pessoas em tempo real [6]. No contexto do Foursquare, a identificação ou detecção da polaridade de uma *tip* pode ser usada para sumarizar o sentimento de diversos usuários sobre um local e fornecer ao proprietário uma visão geral sobre o que estão falando sobre o seu empreendimento. Além disso, os próprios usuários podem se beneficiar desse tipo de informação para os auxiliar na escolha de um local para visitar. Contudo, o Foursquare traz desafios próprios no que concerne a detecção de polaridade das micro-revisões. Em particular, *tips* são geralmente curtas (limitadas a 200 caracteres) e bastante informais, o que significa que a informação coletada pode não ser suficiente para detecção da polaridade do texto. Além disso, gírias e expressões (por exemplo, "legalll!!!") comumente encontradas em redes sociais, dificultam muito a análise.

As técnicas de detecção de polaridade existentes podem ser agrupadas em *supervisionadas* e *não supervisionadas*. Nas técnicas supervisionadas, classificadores automáticos são treinados a partir de exemplos que podem ser manualmente rotulados ou obtidos de alguma outra base rotulada disponível [1, 3, 5, 16, 17, 19]. Dentre as técnicas não supervisionadas, as mais utilizadas são aquelas baseadas em listas de palavras positivas e negativas (léxico), em que a classificação é feita considerando a polaridade de cada termo do texto [3, 5, 16, 17]. Cada uma dessas abordagens possui vanta-

---

[1] http://foursquare.com/, http://plus.google.com/ e https://instagram.com/

gens e desvantagens. A abordagem supervisionada apesar de eficaz para classificação de polaridade em ambientes "tradicionais" [18], é muito dependente do conjunto de dados rotulados para o treinamento dos modelos. Como esses dados são rotulados por pessoas, esses rótulos também podem estar sujeitos a erros de classificação devido à interpretação do texto. Além disso, o número de instâncias de treino afeta o desempenho da classificação em termos da acurácia, que está diretamente relacionada à cobertura do maior número de cenários possíveis [12], o que implica em custos altos para geração de grandes bases de treinamento. Esses problemas são minimizados com a utilização de abordagens que fazem uso de léxicos que não requerem nenhum treinamento para classificação da polaridade dos dados e podem ser aplicados em uma variedade de contextos ou aplicações. Contudo, não há léxicos disponíveis que sejam totalmente adequados para todos os domínios de aplicação (e.g., gírias comuns nas redes sociais estão ausentes na maioria dos léxicos [9]). Isso se deve a fato que os usuários podem utilizar palavras cujos sentimentos são sensíveis ao tópico do domínio [12]. Mais ainda, para textos curtos como as micro-revisões, não há um consenso sobre a melhor abordagem [5, 3, 17]. Essa falta de consenso é um dos principais motivadores de nosso estudo.

Neste contexto, este artigo avalia a eficácia de quatro técnicas diferentes para detecção automática da polaridade de *tips* no Foursquare. São consideradas tanto técnicas supervisionadas quanto não supervisionadas. As abordagens supervisionadas analisadas são três classificadores comumente utilizados no contexto de análise de sentimento: Naïve Bayes, Máxima Entropia e SVM (*Support Vector Machine*) [11, 15, 24]. Como abordagem não supervisionada foi proposta e analisada uma técnica baseada no léxico SentiWordNet [4].

Para avaliação dessas abordagens, foram utilizadas duas bases de *tips* coletadas do Foursquare: uma base rotulada manualmente por voluntários e outra base com *tips* contendo pelo menos um emoticon[2]. As duas bases foram caracterizadas em relação ao conteúdo textual de suas *tips* e a localização geográfica do local onde as *tips* foram postadas. Os resultados da avaliação apontam que a abordagem não supervisionada (léxico) produz resultados comparáveis aos dos métodos supervisionados, sem os custos de rotulação. Foi observado também que em ambas as bases, a abordagem não supervisionada (léxico) é a melhor para se detectar *tips positivas*, enquanto que para detecção de *tips negativas*, o melhor método é o classificador Naïve Bayes, que, dentre os métodos supervisionados, foi o que apresentou melhor eficácia.

O restante deste artigo está organizado como segue. A Seção 2 discute trabalhos relacionados, e a Seção 3 descreve as bases de dados usadas. A Seção 4 apresenta uma breve análise das principais características das *tips* e sua distribuição geográfica. As técnicas de detecção de polaridade analisadas são apresentadas na Seção 5, enquanto os resultados desta avaliação são discutidos na Seção 6. Finalmente, a Seção 7 apresenta as conclusões e trabalhos futuros.

2. TRABALHOS RELACIONADOS

Na literatura existem vários trabalhos sobre análise de sentimento, principalmente de textos longos, mais especificamente revisões longas [16, 19]. Porém, trabalhos que analisam textos curtos como as *tips* do Foursquare ainda compõem uma área recente de investigação. Todos esses trabalhos podem ser agrupados em duas principais abordagens: métodos supervisionados [1, 3, 5, 17] e métodos não supervisionados baseados em léxicos [3, 5, 17].

---

[2]Emoticons são sequências de caracteres tais como :) que representam expressões faciais.

No contexto de revisões online, os principais trabalhos de análise de polaridade ou sentimento focam em revisões longas. Por exemplo, Pang *et al.* [19] comparam vários algoritmos de classificação supervisionados (Naïve Bayes, Máxima Entropia e SVM) para detecção de sentimento em revisões de filmes. Cada revisão foi representada como um *bag-of-words* baseada em unigramas e bigramas, e a melhor acurácia foi obtida pelo método SVM utilizando unigramas. Ohana *et al.* utilizam o léxico SentiWordNet também para a classificação automática da polaridade em revisões de filme. Os autores propõem duas abordagens para a realização dessa tarefa. Na primeira abordagem, o léxico foi utilizado para contabilizar a pontuação das palavras positivas e negativas do texto. A polaridade da revisão era determinada pela polaridade com maior pontuação. Na segunda abordagem, os autores utilizaram as pontuações positivas e negativas para o treinamento de um modelo supervisionado baseado no SVM. Para o presente estudo, cujo foco é em textos curtos, nós utilizamos um método não supervisionado semelhante à primeira abordagem proposta por Ohana *et al.* [16] para detecção da polaridade de *tips* no Foursquare. A representação dos termos de uma *tip* também foi modelada como uma *bag-of-words*. No entanto, nossos resultados foram melhores com a utilização de TF-IDF (i.e., produto do *Term Frequency* pelo *Inverse Document Frequency* [2]), ao invés do uso de unigramas ou bigramas.

Os trabalhos que analisam a polaridade de textos curtos focam majoritariamente em redes de micro-blogs como o Twitter [1, 5, 17]. Em Aisopos *et al.* [1], os autores propõem um método para classificação de *tweets* em positivos e negativos baseado em evidências textuais e evidências relacionadas ao contexto social do autor do *tweet* (tamanho da rede social e polaridade das mensagens dos seguidores). Assim, os atributos foram modelados pelo TF-IDF e o rótulo de um *tweet* foi determinado pela presença de emoticons positivos ou negativos, tal qual a abordagem adotada aqui para rotulagem de uma das bases analisadas.

Alguns poucos trabalhos realizaram comparações entre as abordagens supervisionadas e não supervisionada para classificação da polaridade em textos curtos [5, 3, 17]. Em Go *et al.* [5], os autores demonstram que os mesmos métodos supervisionados propostos por Pang *et al.* [19] para revisões longas podem ser aplicados a textos curtos como *tweets* ao comparar a acurácia desses métodos com um método não supervisionado baseado em um léxico extraído do site *Twittratr*[3]. Em Bermingham *et al.* [3], os autores concluíram que os métodos supervisionados (SVM e Multinominal Naïve Bayes) apresentaram melhor desempenho, em termos de acurácia, que um método não supervisionado baseado no SentiWordnet no contexto de *tweets* e microrevisões do site Blippr. Já em Paltoglou *et al.* [17] os autores propõem um método não supervisionado baseado no léxico LIWC [21] para classificação de sentimento de *tweets* e comentários no MySpace e no Digg, e mostram que o método proposto supera, em termos de acurácia, três métodos supervisionados (Naïve Bayes, Máxima Entropia e SVM).

Portanto, pode-se observar que não há um consenso entre os trabalhos [5, 3, 17] sobre o melhor tipo de abordagem a ser aplicada em textos curtos. Nosso trabalho pretende contribuir com essa discussão, focando na análise de polaridade de *tips* no Foursquare, um ambiente "ruidoso" mas rico de informação. Até onde sabemos, este é o primeiro trabalho que investiga polaridade de sentimento neste contexto.

3. BASES DE DADOS

O Foursquare é a maior e a mais popular rede social baseada em geolocalização (LBSN), atualmente com mais de 30 milhões

---

[3]http://twittratr.com/.

de usuários pelo mundo[4]. As aplicações desenvolvidas para serviços de LBSN são baseadas na tecnologia GPS (Global Positioning System) que permite aos usuários interagir, compartilhar e recomendar locais (*venues*) baseados em sua localização atual. Os *venues* são representações virtuais de locais do mundo real, como escolas, lojas, restaurantes ou aeroportos, entre outros. O Foursquare classifica os *venues* em 9 categorias pré-definidas: "Food", "Travel & Transport", "Great Outdoors", "Nightlife Spots","Professional& Other Places", "Residences", "Shops& Services", "Colleges & Universities"e "Arts & Entertainment". Para indicar o local onde o usuário se encontra ele deve realizar um *check in*, informando seus amigos da rede social onde ele se encontra naquele momento.

Além de compartilhar locais, os usuários podem realizar recomendações, adicionando comentários sobre esses locais através de *tips*. *Tips* são como resenhas, porém mais concisas e limitadas a 200 caracteres, que podem ter um caráter informativo, recomendativo ou descritivo, relatando experiências dos usuários. As *tips* podem ser avaliadas por outros usuários, que podem curtí-las (*like*) tornando-as mais visíveis à comunidade do Foursquare.

A avaliação das abordagens de detecção de polaridade de uma *tip* foi feita utilizando duas bases de *tips* coletadas do Foursquare: uma rotulada manualmente por voluntários e outra composta por *tips* com pelo menos 1 emoticon. As duas bases são subconjuntos de uma base de aproximadamente 10 milhões de *tips* postadas por 13 milhões de usuários coletada de Agosto a Outubro de 2011 usando a API do Foursquare. Além disso, na construção das duas bases (manual e emoticon) foram consideradas somente *tips* postadas em *venues* onde a língua oficial[5] é a língua inglesa[6].

A **base manualmente rotulada** (ou simplesmente base manual) foi construída da seguinte maneira. Foram selecionadas aleatoriamente 1.250 *tips* para serem rotuladas por 15 voluntários. Cada *tip* foi analisada por um grupo de três voluntários evitando assim a ocorrência de empates. Para cada avaliador voluntário, foi apresentado uma amostra de 250 *tips* e algumas informações, como o nome e a categoria do *venue* onde foi postada a *tip*. Foi pedido aos voluntários que rotulassem o conteúdo de cada uma das *tips* como positiva, negativa ou neutra. Foi observado que os voluntários concordaram em 94% das *tips* selecionadas[7], resultando na seguinte classificação: 57,78% das *tips* foram classificadas como positivas, 15,64% como negativa enquanto que 26,58% foram consideradas como sendo neutras. Como em [1, 19], este trabalho foca na classificação entre as polaridades positiva e negativa. Desta forma, as *tips* neutras foram desconsideradas para nossas análises. Finalmente, para essa base foram consideradas apenas *tips* com pelo menos 1 palavra no SentiWordNet. Após esta filtragem, foram mantidas 851 *tips* para constituir a base manualmente rotulada.

Já para a **base com emoticons**, foram selecionadas 3.512 *tips* com pelo menos 1 emoticon dentre todas as *tips* em inglês. Emoticons podem servir com rótulos ruidosos (*noisy labels*), em que o símbolo :) em uma *tip* pode indicar que a *tip* contenha uma polaridade positiva, enquanto que :(pode indicar uma polaridade negativa [20]. São chamados de ruidosos porque certos textos não são facilmente classificáveis como, por exemplo, aqueles que expressam sarcasmo. Como em [1, 5], foi assumido que emoticons

positivos (:)', '(:', ':-)', '(-:', ':)', ':D', '=D' indicam *tips* positivas enquanto que emoticons negativos ':(', '):', ':-(', ')-:', ': (', ') :'. indicam *tips* negativas. Para que as tips pudessem ser consideradas pelo método não supervisionado, foram consideradas, em ambas as bases, somente tips com pelo menos uma palavra no SentiWordNet. Com a aplicação desse filtro, foi removida apenas uma pequena fração de tips (até 1,6%) de ambas as bases.

A Tabela 1 sumariza as principais características das duas bases de *tips* utilizadas em nossos experimentos na Seção 6.

Table 1: Sumário das bases de tips utilizadas nos experimentos

	Número de Tips		
	Positivas	**Negativas**	**Total**
Tips manualmente rotuladas	669	182	851
Tips com emoticons	3014	440	3.454

4. ANÁLISE DAS BASES DE TIPS

Nesta seção, são caracterizadas as duas bases de dados utilizadas na avaliação dos métodos de detecção da polaridade de *tips* no Foursquare. Três tipos de atributos foram considerados: textual, tópico discutidos pelas *tips* e a distribuição geográfica dos *venues* aos quais as *tips* foram associadas.

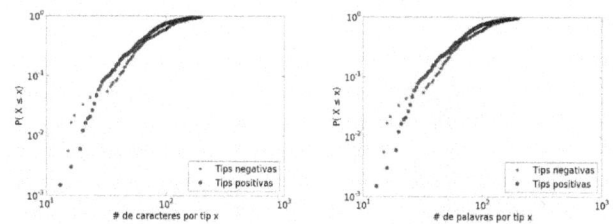

(a) Número de caracteres por tip   (b) Número de palavras por tip

Figure 1: Tamanho das tips da base manualmente rotulada

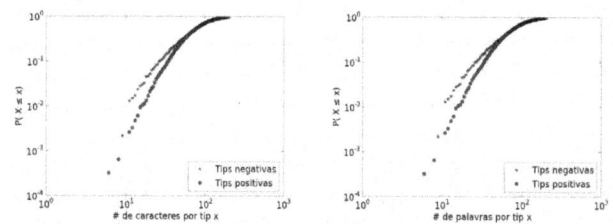

(a) Número de caracteres por tip   (b) Número de palavras por tip

Figure 2: Tamanho das tips da base de emoticons

As Figuras 1 e 2 mostram as funções de distribuição de probabilidade acumulada (CDF) do número de caracteres e do número de palavras por *tip* positiva e por *tip negativa* para as bases manual e de emoticons, respectivamente. Ambos os eixos estão em escala logarítmica. Os dois grupos de gráficos mostram pouca diferença entre *tips* positivas e negativas. Entretanto, na base manual, há uma maior tendência para *tips* negativas serem mais longas. De fato, as *tips* negativas nesta base têm em média 93 caracteres e 17 palavras,

[4]http://foursquare.com/about
[5]http://en.wikipedia.org/wiki/List_of_official_languages
[6]Essa restrição foi feita já que as ferramentas utilizadas pelo método não supervisionado para computação da polaridade são restritas à língua inglesa.
[7]Pelo menos dois voluntários concordaram com a mesma polaridade. 6% da tips avaliadas foram descartadas, porque não houve consenso entre os avaliadores.

enquanto que as *tips* positivas têm em média 82 caracteres e 15 palavras. Isto sugere que os usuários do Foursquare tendem a ser mais detalhistas ao expressar algum tipo de experiência negativa. Essa característica das *tips* negativas por ser útil para o dono do estabelecimento, que pode ter um *feedback* mais detalhado sobre pontos negativos do seu negócio. Já para a base de emoticons, as diferenças são menores, com tamanhos intermediários (entre 10 e 100 caracteres) sendo ligeiramente mais frequentes entre as *tips* positivas. Em média, as *tips* negativas têm 81 caracteres e 16 palavras enquanto as positivas têm em torno de 83 caracteres e 16 palavras. Esta pequena diferença entre as duas bases pode ser consequência do maior ruído na rotulação da base de emoticon.

Além do tamanho das *tips*, foi também analisada a frequência de diferentes palavras nas *tips* positivas e negativas das duas bases. A Figura 3 mostra as nuvens de palavras para *tips* positivas nas duas bases. A Figura 4 mostra nuvens equivalentes para *tips* negativas. Para as *tips* positivas, podemos notar que os adjetivos *great*, *best* e *good* são os mais frequentes em ambas as bases. Já para as *tips* negativas, os termos mais frequentes são substantivos como *place*, *food* e *service*. Note a presença de palavras positivas como *good* e *best* nas *tips* negativas, que mostram a importância de outros termos negativo como *not* para determinação do sentimento da *tip*. Este aspecto foi tratado na determinação da polaridade da *tip* pela abordagem não supervisionada baseada em léxico. Comparando as duas bases, podemos observar que palavras relacionadas a bares e restaurantes como *food*, *chicken* e *sandwich* também aparecem com frequência em *tips* positivas das duas bases, o que demonstra a preferência dos usuários por esses locais.

(a) Base manualmente rotulada   (b) Base com emoticons.

Figure 3: Palavras mais utilizadas em *tips* positivas

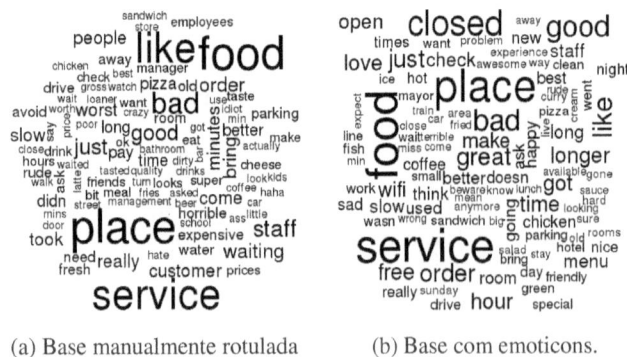

(a) Base manualmente rotulada   (b) Base com emoticons.

Figure 4: Palavras mais utilizadas em *tips* negativas

Foram analisados também os principais assuntos ou tópicos discutidos pelas *tips* de cada uma das bases, considerando também a categoria do *venue* ao qual a *tip* foi associada[8]. Para isso, foi utilizado o léxico LIWC - *Linguistic Inquiry and Word Count* [21]. O LIWC é uma ferramenta para análise de texto que avalia componentes emocionais, cognitivos e estruturais de um texto através do uso de um dicionário de mais de 2.300 palavras classificadas em 80 tópicos ou categorias. Esse léxico vem sendo muito explorado em vários contextos principalmente para análise de sentimento em redes sociais [17, 23]. Para essa análise foram considerados 12 desses tópicos que descrevem aspectos psicológicos (emotivos, perceptivos e processos biológicos) e de interesse pessoal (trabalho, lazer, casa e família), por estarem relacionados ao objetivo de classificar as *tips* em positivas e negativas. Foram geradas as distribuições de tópicos para cada uma das 4 categorias de *venues* mais frequentes, utilizando as frequências relativas de cada tópico do LIWC nas palavras das *tips*. As Figuras 5 e 6 mostram essas distribuições separadas por polaridade de *tips* nas duas bases. Para cada curva representando uma categoria de *venue*, um valor mais alto (mais externo) em um dos eixos implica em maior frequência do tópico correspondente nas *tips* associadas a *venues* daquela categoria.

Os resultados indicam que dinheiro (*money*) e trabalho (*work*) são assuntos muito frequentes tanto em *tips* positivas quanto em negativas, nas duas bases. Em particular, dinheiro é muito proeminente na categoria associada a lojas e serviços (*Shops & Services*) enquanto assuntos ligados a trabalho são mais discutidos dentro da categoria relacionada a escritórios (*Professional & Other Places*), com exceção das *tips* negativas da base manual, onde trabalho é mais discutido dentro de locais relacionados a restaurantes (*Food*) e lojas (*Shops & Services*). Pode-se observar uma diferença significativa entre a distribuição dos assuntos discutidos nas *tips* negativas em cada uma das bases. Na base manual, termos relacionados a raiva (*anger*) e a saúde (*health*) são muito utilizados em *tips* das categorias relacionadas a restaurantes e aos escritórios, respectivamente. Já para a base de emoticons, termos ligados a casa (*home*), raiva e tristeza são muito usados em *tips* das categorias que englobam bares e boates (*Nightlife Spots*) enquanto raiva e tristeza são tópicos também frequentes em *tips* negativas ligadas a restaurantes.

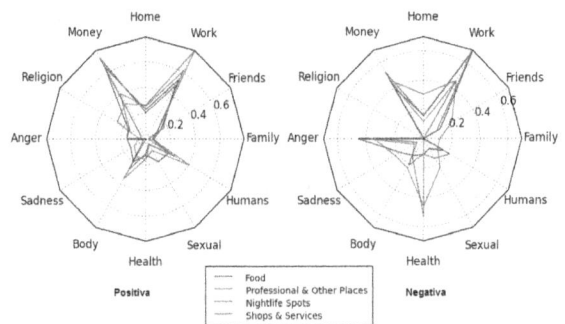

Figure 5: Principais tópicos discutidos nas *tips* positivas (à esquerda) e negativas (à direita) da base manual

Considerando que o foco das duas bases é em *tips* da língua inglesa, foi analisada também a distribuição das polaridades das *tips* do país de língua inglesa com o maior número de tips coletadas (Estados Unidos). As Figuras 7 e 8 mostram as distribuições das *tips* positivas e negativas, respectivamente, por estado americano para a base manualmente rotulada. Os números dentro de cada estado

---

[8]Para esta análise, foram selecionadas as categorias de *venues* com mais *tips*.

116

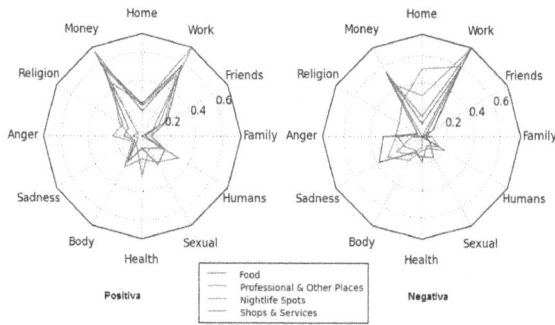

Figure 6: Principais tópicos discutidos nas *tips* positivas (à esquerda) e negativas (à direita) da base de emoticons

no mapa, indicam o número de *tips* postadas em *venues* naquele estado. Califórnia e o de Nova Iorque são os estados com maior concentração de *tips* (positivas e negativas). Dentre os estados com mais *tips* coletadas, Nova Iorque e a Pensilvânia aparecem com a maior proporção de *tips* positivas para negativas (4 positivas para 1 negativa). A conclusão principal destas figuras é que, no geral, há uma tendência muito maior das pessoas adicionarem *tips* positivas, e isto é generalizado por todos os estados do país.

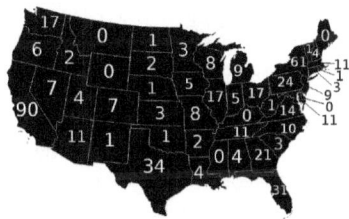

Figure 7: Distribuição de *tips* positivas da base manualmente rotulada por estado americano.

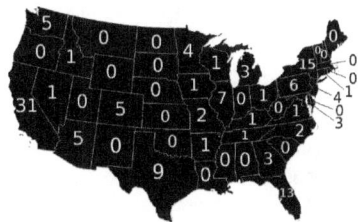

Figure 8: Distribuição de *tips* negativas da base manualmente rotulada por estado americano.

5. DETECÇÃO DE POLARIDADE

Nesta seção são discutidas as técnicas usadas para detecção automática da polaridade (positiva ou negativa) de uma *tip*. Primeiramente, são apresentadas as técnicas de aprendizagem supervisionada. Em seguida, é descrita a técnica não supervisionada baseada em léxico adotada neste trabalho.

5.1 Técnicas Supervisionadas

No geral, as técnicas supervisionadas têm o mesmo funcionamento. Dado um conjunto de treino formado por instâncias (*tips*) que são representadas por vários atributos e previamente rotuladas nas classes de interesse (polaridades), o algoritmo *aprende* um modelo de classificação que pode ser posteriormente aplicado a dados não rotulados (conjunto de teste). Foram analisados 3 algoritmos de classificação automática supervisionada: Naïve Bayes (NB), Máxima Entropia (ME) e Máquina de Vetores Suporte (SVM) [11, 15, 24]. Os três algoritmos são considerados o estado-da-arte em classificação textual.

Para os três algoritmos, cada *tip* foi modelada como uma *bag-of-words*, como em [19]. Entretanto, ao invés de considerar os unigramas da *tip* como atributos, foi utilizada a mesma representação proposta em [1]: cada *tip* t é modelada como um vetor $p_1, ...p_n$, onde p_i é a frequência ponderada da palavra i na *tip* t normalizada pela frequência da palavra i na base de treino (TF-IDF). Experimentos preliminares demonstraram que esta representação leva a resultados superiores aos obtidos usando unigramas ou bigramas. Note que foram removidas as *stopwords* de cada *tip* antes da representação. Os valores de p_i são os atributos explorados pelos algoritmos de classificação.

O Naïve Bayes (NB) é um classificador probabilístico, baseado na aplicação do teorema de Bayes, que tenta inferir as probabilidades de um novo documento (ou *tip*) pertencer a cada uma das classes (polaridades) definidas [24]. Ele é utilizado em diversas aplicações como, por exemplo, filtragem de spam, diagnósticos de doenças e para classificação da polaridade de textos [3, 19]. Para este trabalho, foi utilizada a versão multinomial (MBN) desse classificador, que é mais adequada para a classificação de textos [13]. Nessa versão, a probabilidade de uma classe é parametrizada por uma distribuição Multinomial.

A principal desvantagem do Naïve Bayes é a premissa de independência entre os atributos explorados pelo classificador, que é dificilmente observada na prática. O método Máxima Entropia [15] não assume independência entre os atributos e estima as probabilidades fazendo o mínimo de restrições possíveis. As restrições expressam algum tipo de relacionamento entre os atributos e as classes e são derivadas do conjunto de treino. A distribuição de probabilidade que melhor satisfaz as restrições é aquela com a maior entropia.

Finalmente, o modelos baseados em Máquina de Vetores Suporte (SVM) [11], que também são muito utilizados para classificação em textos, tentam encontrar o melhor hiperplano, definido no espaço dos atributos, que separa as instâncias do treino e que tem a maior distância (margem) entre essas instâncias. O SVM permite a utilização de várias funções de *kernel*, que auxiliam a resolução de vários tipos de problemas. Nós utilizamos aqui o *kernel* linear, já que o número de instâncias é menor que o número de atributos.

Foram utilizados nos experimentos as versões do Naïve Bayes e Máxima Entropia implementadas pela ferramenta *scikit-learn*[9] e a versão do SVM disponível no pacote LIBSVM[10].

5.2 Técnica Não Supervisionada

Os métodos supervisionados precisam de instâncias pré-rotuladas (treino) para o desenvolvimento dos classificadores. Os modelos não supervisionados minimizam essa necessidade, pois exploram o conteúdo do texto para realizar a classificação. Nessa seção é descrita a abordagem não supervisionada baseada em léxico que foi utilizada em nossos experimentos.

---

[9]http://scikit-learn.org/
[10]http://www.csie.ntu.edu.tw/~cjlin/libsvm/

Léxicos de opiniões são listas de palavras que expressam algum tipo de opinião positiva ou negativa (e.g., "amazing" ou "bad"). Essas listas são muito utilizadas por métodos de detecção de polaridade [16], que tipicamente definem a polaridade pelo número de palavras positivas ou negativas. Os léxicos são construídos manualmente para cada contexto de aplicação. Porém, diferentemente dos conjuntos de treino explorados por técnicas supervisionadas, que são tipicamente específicos da aplicação alvo, léxicos podem ser genéricos o bastante para serem úteis para estudos de aplicações e contextos diferentes. Logo, o custo de construção do léxico pode ser amortizado em um número muito maior de aplicações e investigações. Um aspecto a se considerar na escolha de um léxico é o número de termos incluídos nele ou sua cobertura. Este número pode impactar a eficácia dos métodos que fazem uso do léxico [16]. Assim, vários trabalhos [3, 7, 16, 23] que utilizam métodos não supervisionados para detecção de polaridade fazem uso de léxicos já conhecidos como o SentiWordNet [4] e o LIWC [22]. Para o nosso trabalho, foi escolhido o SentiWordNet como base da técnica não supervisionada avaliada pois sua cobertura é maior que a do LIWC.

O SentiWordNet é um recurso léxico para mineração de opinião baseado em outra ferramenta léxica, o WordNet [14]. WordNet é um dicionário léxico em inglês que agrupa nomes, verbos, adjetivos e advérbios em conjuntos de sinônimos, ou *synsets*, cada qual expressando um conceito distinto[11]. O SentiWordNet associa três pontuações - positivo, negativo e neutro - para cada *synset* do WordNet, representando a força de um sentimento positivo, negativo ou neutro associado àquela palavra. Essas pontuações estão normalizados entre 0 e 1, de tal forma que a soma seja 1.

A abordagem não supervisionada consiste dos seguintes passos para classificar uma dada *tip* em positiva ou negativa:

1. Classificação Gramatical e Lematização[12].: cada palavra de uma *tip* é associada a uma única classe gramatical, tal como adjetivo, advérbio, verbo e pronome através da utilização de *parser part-of-speech*. Em seguida, cada palavra da *tip* é convertida à sua forma canônica, por exemplo, verbos no passado vão para sua forma infinitiva.
2. Tratamento de negação:[12] a polaridade de uma palavra pode ser influenciada caso um termo de negação (por exemplo, *not*) a anteceda. Para lidar com esse cenário, é construída uma árvore de dependência que modela as relações gramaticais de cada palavra ou frase da *tip*. Assim é possível identificar quais palavras da *tip* são influenciadas pelo termo de negação. Essas palavras têm as pontuações positiva e negativa, fornecidas pelo SentiWordNet, invertidas.
3. Sentido da palavra: uma palavra no *SentiWordNet* pode possuir múltiplos *synsets* associadas à mesma classe gramatical. Para contornar esse problema, foi considerada a média das pontuações de todos os *synsets* associados àquela palavra.
4. Polaridade da *tip*: atribui-se pontuações positiva, negativa e neutra à *tip*, cada uma calculada como a média das pontuações correspondentes dos *synsets* de todas as palavras da *tip* que foram encontradas no SentiWordNet. Uma *tip* é considerada com polaridade positiva se a sua pontuação final positiva é maior que pontuação negativa, caso contrário ela é considerada negativa e vice-versa. Se os valores das médias da pontuação positiva e negativa empatarem ou se houver apenas pontuação neutra, a polaridade da *tip* é considerada indefinida e essas *tips* são descartadas.

---

[11]Cada possível significado de uma mesma palavra está em *synsets* diferentes
[12] Esta fase foi implementada usando a ferramenta disponível em `http://www-nlp.stanford.edu/software/corenlp.shtml`.

6. AVALIAÇÃO

Esta seção descreve a metodologia de avaliação adotada na análise dos métodos de detecção de polaridade de *tips* (Seção 6.1) e discute os principais resultados obtidos (Seção 6.2).

6.1 Metodologia de Avaliação

A avaliação dos métodos apresentados na Seção 5 foi feita utilizando validação cruzada de 5 partes em cada uma das bases de *tips* descritas na Seção 3. Em outras palavras, cada base foi dividida em 5 partes, das quais 4 foram usadas como conjunto de treino e a parte restante foi usada como teste. O processo foi repetido 5 vezes, utilizando cada uma das partes como teste e produzindo assim 5 resultados. O conjunto de treino foi utilizado apenas para as abordagens supervisionadas, para "aprender"os modelos de classificação. Todos os métodos foram avaliados sobre os conjuntos de testes. Para evitar o desbalanceamento entre as classes (positiva e negativa), que afeta a acurácia da predição, foi utilizado a técnica de *undersampling* [8], em que a menor classe determina o número de instâncias de cada classe usadas para o treino. Assim, para cada rodada da validação cruzada foi efetuada 5 amostragens de cada uma das classes do treino. Desse modo foram produzidos 25 resultados diferentes para cada base de *tips*. A próxima seção apresenta resultados para cada abordagem que são valores médios desses 25 experimentos juntamente com intervalos de confiança de 95%.

A acurácia de cada método foi avaliada utilizando três métricas: precisão, revocação e F1 [2]. A precisão p de uma classe c é o número de *tips* corretamente classificadas na classe c sobre o total de *tips* preditas como sendo da classe c. A revocação r de uma classe c é o número de *tips* corretamente classificadas na classe c sobre o número de *tips* na classe c. A métrica F1 é a média harmônica, $2pr/(p+r)$, entre a precisão p e revocação r, sintetizando o valor das duas métricas. Foram computados valores de precisão, revocação e F1 para cada classe (polaridade) separadamente, assim como valores médios para as duas classes.

6.2 Resultados

As Tabelas 2 e 3 mostram os resultados de cada uma das abordagens supervisionadas, Naïve Bayes (NB), Máxima Entropia (ME) e SVM, e não supervisionada (Léxico) para as bases de *tips* manualmente rotuladas e com emoticons, respectivamente. Os melhores resultados (incluindo empates estatísticos) são mostrados em negrito. A significância desses valores foi testada utilizando um teste-t pareado [10] considerando uma confiança de 95%.

Considerando a precisão por classe de polaridade, pode-se observar que para ambas as bases, os melhores valores são aqueles obtidos pelos métodos supervisionados Naïve Bayes e SVM. Em particular, o método Naïve Bayes apresenta ganhos de até 3,51% e 2,78% sobre os demais métodos em *tips* da base manual e na base de emoticons, respectivamente, e não apresenta diferença estatisticamente significativa com o método SVM em ambas as bases. Para a classe negativa, os melhores valores de precisão na base manual ocorrem quando a abordagem não supervisionada baseada em léxico é utilizada (ganhos de até 22,68% sobre os demais métodos), enquanto que para a base de emoticons, o léxico se apresenta empatado com o SVM e o Naïve Bayes. Note que, no geral, os valores de precisão para a classe negativa são menores que os da classe positiva. Isto ocorre devido ao desbalanceamento entre as classes (Tabela 1), principalmente na base de emoticons. Este desbalanceamento leva a uma dominância da maior classe (positiva) sobre os resultados da classificação. Finalmente, considerando a precisão média não foi observada diferença estatisticamente significativa entre o Naïve Bayes (supervisionado) e o método baseado no léxico (não supervisionado) para a base manualmente rotulada. Já para

Table 2: Resultados da base de *tips* manualmente rotuladas

	Método	Classe Positiva	Classe Negativa	Média
Precisão	Naïve Bayes	**0,9173±0,0067**	0,4333±0,0180	**0,6753±0,0103**
	Máxima Entropia	0,9017±0,0092	0,3950±0,0206	0,6484±0,0120
	SVM	**0,9097±0,0096**	0,4169±0,0221	0,6633±0,0127
	Léxico (SentiWordNet)	0,8861±0,0121	**0,4846±0,0390**	**0,6853±0,0189**
Revocação	Naïve Bayes	0,7311±0,0126	**0,7547±0,0241**	**0,7429±0,0119**
	Máxima Entropia	0,7015±0,0201	0,7124±0,0364	0,7070±0,0146
	SVM	0,7176±0,0270	**0,7302±0,0387**	0,7239±0,0157
	Léxico (SentiWordNet)	**0,8183±0,0180**	0,6159±0,0276	0,7171±0,0154
F1	Naïve Bayes	0,8133±0,0083	**0,5496±0,0190**	**0,6814±0,0116**
	Máxima Entropia	0,7879±0,0116	0,5058±0,0222	0,6469±0,0135
	SVM	0,8003±0,0166	**0,5278±0,0226**	0,6640±0,0157
	Léxico (SentiWordNet)	**0,8502±0,0118**	**0,5369±0,0313**	**0,6935±0,0187**

a base de emoticons, os métodos supervisionados SVM e Naïve Bayes são os que produzem os melhores resultados com ganhos (estatisticamente significativos) de até 3,38%.

Em termos de revocação para a classe positiva, o método baseado em léxico supera os métodos supervisionados em até 16,65% para a base manual e em até 14,71% para a base de emoticons. No entanto, para a classe negativa, a melhor revocação ocorre com os métodos supervisionados Naïve Bayes e SVM (empate estatístico) em ambas as bases, com ganhos de até 37,78%. Os grandes ganhos na classe negativa levam a uma superioridade dos métodos supervisionados considerando a revocação média nas duas classes: os melhores resultados na base manual foram obtidos com o Naïve Bayes, enquanto que, na base de emoticons, Naïve Bayes e SVM aparecem empatados como os melhores métodos.

Considerando a métrica F1, que combina revocação e precisão, o método baseado em léxico produz os melhores resultados para *tips* da classe positiva em ambas as bases. Para a classe negativa, foi observado um empate entre Naïve Bayes, SVM e o método baseado em léxico na base manual, enquanto que na base de emoticons esse empate é somente entre Naïve Bayes e SVM. No geral, Naïve Bayes e o método baseado em léxico aparecem empatados como os melhores métodos em termos de F1 médio nas duas bases, enquanto que na base de emoticons este empate também inclui o SVM.

Os resultados obtidos podem ser sumarizados como segue:

- O método não supervisionado baseado em léxico apresenta resultados estatisticamente superiores ou empatados, em termos do F1 médio, com os melhores métodos supervisionados (Naïve Bayes e SVM) nas duas bases de *tips*. Assim, se o objetivo da aplicação é recuperar tanto *tips* positivas quanto *tips* negativas, a um custo baixo (sem rotulação manual), o método baseado em léxico é preferível.

- O método baseado em léxico melhora o F1 da classe positiva em até 7,91%. Logo, esse método deve ser utilizado para aplicações cujo foco é recuperação de *tips positivas*.

- Se o foco é a detecção de *tips negativas*, os melhores métodos são os supervisionados, em especial, os métodos Naïve Bayes e SVM. Para a base com emoticons, esses métodos supervisionados apresentam um ganho de até 11,11% na detecção de *tips* negativas.

- Todos os métodos produzem bons resultados para as três métricas na base rotulada manualmente (diferença de até 19,5%), o que pode refletir um maior ruído (p.ex: sarcasmo) e uma maior incerteza na rotulação automática via emoticons que afeta a eficácia dos métodos.

Em suma, neste trabalho foi mostrado que no contexto de micro-revisões, mais especificamente *tips* no Foursquare, o método não supervisionado obteve, no geral, uma acurácia comparável à dos melhores métodos supervisionados (Naïve Bayes e SVM), sem os custos associados a esses últimos. Entretanto, é preciso ressaltar que a escolha do melhor método deve levar em consideração os custos e restrições de cada tipo de abordagem. Um método supervisionado geralmente requer que um conjunto de treino manualmente rotulado seja construído. A rotulação automática, explorando por exemplo emoticons, pode ser feita, mas sua eficácia está limitada à presença de emoticons na *tip*[13] assim como sujeita a ruído e maior incerteza. Já o método não supervisionado analisado requer a disponibilidade de um léxico para o idioma alvo. Além disso, para este método, existe a restrição do tamanho do vocabulário que é coberto pelo léxico, o que pode fazer com que certas *tips* não possam ser classificadas. Em particular, o método de detecção de polaridade baseado no léxico SentiWordNet, publicamente disponível [16] e amplamente usado na literatura, não pode ser aplicado em 1,4% e 1,6% das *tips* originalmente obtidas nas bases manual e de emoticons respectivamente, já que nenhuma das palavras usadas nestas *tips* estavam presentes no léxico[14].

7. CONCLUSÃO

Neste trabalho foram analisados métodos para detecção de polaridade ou sentimento de *tips* do Foursquare. Na literatura sobre análise de sentimento não existe um consenso sobre qual é a melhor abordagem para textos curtos, como as *tips* no Foursquare. Logo, foram avaliados tanto métodos supervisionados - os algoritmos Naïve Bayes, Máxima Entropia e SVM - quanto um método não supervisionado baseado no léxico SentiWordNet.

Estes métodos foram avaliados em duas bases de *tips*: uma rotulada manualmente e outra rotulada automaticamente explorando a presença de emoticons. Os resultados da avaliação mostraram que, no geral, o método não supervisionado baseado em léxico obteve resultados comparáveis aos produzidos pelos melhores métodos supervisionados (Naïve Bayes e SVM) sem os custos e limitações de construção do conjunto de treino associados a esses últimos. No entanto, a escolha do método deve levar em consideração objetivos específicos: se o objetivo é detectar principalmente *tips* positivas, o método não supervisionado é o mais indicado, enquanto os métodos supervisionados (Naïve Bayes e SVM) são os mais indicados para a detecção de *tips* negativas. Esta escolha deve levar em conta

---

[13]Somente 3,39% das *tips* de língua inglesa na nossa base de 10 milhões de *tips* contêm emoticons.

[14]Estas *tips* foram filtradas das duas bases (vide Seção 3).

Table 3: Resultados da base de *tips* rotuladas com emoticons

	Método	Classe Positiva	Classe Negativa	Média
Precisão	Naïve Bayes	**0,9393±0,0033**	**0,2457±0,0110**	**0,5925±0,0056**
	Máxima Entropia	0,9270±0,0040	0,2193±0,0098	0,5731±0,0050
	SVM	**0,9399±0,0040**	**0,2394±0,0133**	**0,5896±0,0065**
	Léxico (SentiWordNet)	0,9139±0,0054	**0,2416±0,0127**	0,5778±0,0070
Revocação	Naïve Bayes	0,6888±0,0078	**0,6936±0,0181**	**0,6912±0,0087**
	Máxima Entropia	0,6670±0,0078	0,6400±0,0156	0,6535±0,0085
	SVM	0,6698±0,0227	**0,7028±0,0266**	**0,6863±0,0096**
	Léxico (SentiWordNet)	**0,7651±0,0055**	0,5101±0,0247	0,6376±0,0122
F1	Naïve Bayes	0,7946±0,0051	**0,3623±0,0133**	**0,5785±0,0078**
	Máxima Entropia	0,7756±0,0055	0,3261±0,0118	0,5508±0,0075
	SVM	0,7807±0,0153	**0,3554±0,0150**	**0,5681±0,0128**
	Léxico (SentiWordNet)	**0,8328±0,0040**	0,3271±0,0156	**0,5800±0,0086**

também a disponibilidade de recursos para o uso de cada método. Em particular os custos de construção manual ou as limitações da construção automatizada (p.ex: explorando emoticons) de um conjunto de treino precisam ser considerados para a adoção de um método supervisionado, enquanto a disponibilidade e a cobertura de um léxico para a língua alvo têm que ser avaliadas para a escolha do método não supervisionado.

Como trabalhos futuros, pretendemos avaliar os métodos em outras bases de micro-revisões para validação dos resultados e desenvolver uma solução híbrida que combine as abordagens supervisionada e não supervisionada.

8. AGRADECIMENTOS

Esta pesquisa é parcialmente financiada pelo Instituto Nacional de Ciência e Tecnologia para a Web - INCTWeb (MCT/CNPq 573871/2008-6), CNPq, CAPES e FAPEMIG.

9. REFERENCES

[1] F. Aisopos, G. Papadakis, K. Tserpes, and T. Varvarigou. Content vs. Context for Sentiment Analysis: a Comparative Analysis over Microblogs. In *Proc. ACM HT*, 2012.

[2] R. Baeza-Yates and B. Ribeiro-Neto. *Modern Information Retrieval - The Concepts and Technology Behind Search.* Pearson Education Ltd., 2011.

[3] A. Bermingham and A. Smeaton. Classifying Sentiment in Microblogs: is Brevity an Advantage? In *Proc. CIKM*, 2010.

[4] A. Esuli and F. Sebastiani. SENTIWORDNET: A Publicly Available Lexical Resource for Opinion Mining. In *Proc. LREC*, 2006.

[5] A. Go, R. Bhayani, and L. Huang. Twitter Sentiment Classification using Distant Supervision. Technical report, Department of Computer Science, Stanford University, 2009.

[6] P. Guerra, A. Veloso, W. Meira, Jr, and V. Almeida. From Bias to Opinion: a Transfer-Learning Approach to Real-Time Sentiment Analysis. In *Proc. SIGKDD*, 2011.

[7] A. Hamouda and M. Rohaim. Reviews Classification Using SentiWordNet Lexicon. *The Online Journal on Computer Science and Information Technology*, 2(4):120–123, 2011.

[8] H. He and E. A. Garcia. Learning From Imbalanced Data. *IEEE Trans. on Knowledge and Data Engin.*, 21(9):1263–1284, 2009.

[9] X. Hu, J. Tang, H. Gao, and H. Liu. Unsupervised Sentiment Analysis with Emotional Signals. In *Proc. WWW*, 2013.

[10] R. Jain. *The Art of Computer Systems Performance Analysis: Techniques for Experimental Design, Measurement, Simulation, and Modeling.* Wiley, 1991.

[11] T. Joachims. Text Categorization with Support Vector Machines: Learning with Many Relevant Features Machine Learning. In *Proc. ECML*, 1998.

[12] Y. Lu, M. Castellanos, U. Dayal, and C. Zhai. Automatic Construction of a Context-Aware Sentiment Lexicon: an Optimization Approach. In *Proc. WWW*, 2011.

[13] A. McCallum and K. Nigam. A Comparison of Event Models for Naive Bayes Text Classification. In *Proc. AAAI/ICML Workshop Learning for Text Categorization*, 1998.

[14] G. A. Miller. WordNet: a Lexical Database for English. *Communications of ACM*, 38(11):39–41, 1995.

[15] K. Nigam, J. Lafferty, and A. Mccallum. Using maximum entropy for text classification. In *Proc. IJCAI*, 1999.

[16] B. Ohana and B. Tierney. Sentiment Classification of Reviews using SentiWordNet. In *Proc. IT & T*, 2009.

[17] G. Paltoglou and M. Thelwall. Twitter, MySpace, Digg: Unsupervised Sentiment Analysis in Social Media. *ACM Trans. on Intelligent Systems and Technology*, 3(4):66:1–66:19, 2012.

[18] B. Pang and L. Lee. Opinion Mining and Sentiment Analysis. *Foundations and Trends in Information Retrieval*, 2(1-2):1–135, 2008.

[19] B. Pang, L. Lee, and S. Vaithyanathan. Thumbs up? Sentiment Classification using Machine Learning Techniques. In *Proc. EMNLP*, 2002.

[20] J. Read. Using Emoticons to Reduce Dependency in Machine Learning Techniques for Sentiment Classification. In *Proc. ACL Student Research Workshop*, 2005.

[21] Y. Tausczik and J. Pennebaker. The Psychological Meaning of Words: LIWC and Computerized Text Analysis Methods. *Journal of Language and Social Psychology*, 29(1):24–54, 2010.

[22] Y. R. Tausczik and J. W. Pennebaker. The Psychological Meaning of Words: LIWC and Computerized Text Analysis Methods. *Journal of Language and Social Psychology*, 29(1), 2010.

[23] A. Tumasjan, T. Sprenger, P. Sandner, and I. Welpe. Predicting Elections with Twitter: What 140 characters Reveal about Political Sentiment. In *Proc. ICWSM*, 2010.

[24] H. Zhang. Exploring Conditions For The Optimality Of Naïve Bayes. *International Journal of Pattern Recognition and Artificial Intelligence*, 19(2):183–198, 2005.

Extracting Knowledge from the Web and Social Media for Progress Monitoring in Public Outreach and Science Communication

Arno Scharl
MODUL University Vienna
Department of New Media Technology
Am Kahlenberg 1, 1190 Vienna, Austria
+43 (1) 3203555 500
scharl@modul.ac.at

David D. Herring
National Oceanic and Atmospheric Administration
NOAA Climate Program Office, 1315 East-West
Highway, Silver Spring, MD 20910-3282, USA
+1 (301) 7341207
david.herring@noaa.gov

ABSTRACT

Given the intense attention that environmental topics such as climate change attract in news and social media coverage, key questions for large science agencies such as the *National Oceanic and Atmospheric Administration* (NOAA) are how different stakeholders perceive the observable threats and policy options, how public media react to new scientific insights, and how journalists present climate science knowledge to the public. This paper investigates the potential of semantic technologies to address these questions. It introduces the NOAA Media Watch and presents a detailed case study of how the metrics and visualizations of the webLyzard Web intelligence platform are used to track information flows across online media channels. Building upon this platform, we present a novel framework to measure the impact of science communication and public outreach campaigns – through a combination of quantitative and visual methods that go beyond sentiment analysis and related opinion mining approaches.

Categories and Subject Descriptors

H.3.1 [**Content Analysis and Indexing**]: Linguistic processing; H.3.3 [**Information Search and Retrieval**]: Information Filtering; I.7.5 [**Document Capture**]: Document analysis.

General Terms

Measurement, Documentation, Performance, Human Factors.

Keywords

Web intelligence, visual analytics, semantic technologies, online media monitoring, science communication.

1. INTRODUCTION

People's health, security and economic well-being are closely linked to weather and climate. Every day communities around the world grapple with environmental challenges due to extreme weather and changing climate conditions. Policy leaders, businesses, resource managers, and citizens are asking for information to help them address climate-related risks and opportunities.

Web-based communication and engagement channels such as online news and social media play important roles in the information-gathering process. Leading science organizations such as the *National Oceanic and Atmospheric Administration* (NOAA) benefit from a thorough understanding of who uses these media channels, and how. NOAA is mandated by the United States Congress to advance scientific understanding of how the Earth's climate system works, and to share the resulting knowledge with the public. NOAA concentrates on climate-related challenges facing society today in the following areas: (i) reducing vulnerability and improving resilience to extreme weather and climate events; (ii) preparing for drought and water resource challenges; (iii) protecting coastal communities and coastal infrastructure from inundation due to sea level rise and storm surges; (iv) identifying and managing threats to marine ecosystems; and (v) developing strategies for mitigating and adapting to climate-related changes.

The NOAA Climate.gov Web portal provides climate-related information in a way that is easy to access and use, helping people to understand the state of the climate system and its impacts on their lives and livelihoods – both now and in the future so that they can make more informed decisions. To engage with stakeholders and disseminate scientific results, the NOAA Climate Program Office employs a three-pronged strategy:

- Publishing data and information via www.Climate.gov, an interactive Web portal that is designed to reach large numbers of people across four public segments: policy leaders and decision makers, scientists and data users, educators, and the climate-interested public.

- Directly engaging with small numbers of our target groups in interactive events designed to build relationships and to foster deeper, richer exchanges of information.

- Encouraging our partners and news media to syndicate, host, and republish our content in their websites and broadcasts.

Like all U.S. federal agencies, NOAA must demonstrate measurable progress toward its goals. Because there is no one-size-fits-all approach, the Climate Program Office uses a combination of evaluation approaches: (i) track visitors to Climate.gov and review how these visitors rate our online content; (ii) conduct focus groups and surveys designed to measure our Quality of Relationship with each target public; and (iii) use the NOAA Media Watch, a Web intelligence tool to monitor how others host, report on, and discuss published climate science information.

Today, Web-based media channels and semantic technologies add an important dimension to science communicators' ability to assess and evaluate online communications. For exploring this dimension, the webLyzard platform (www.weblyzard.com) has become an essential part of NOAA's evaluation strategy. Several years ago we began using the system to track online communications efforts that otherwise could not be measured – e.g., learning about sudden spikes or dips in news or social media coverage on NOAA's climate research and data products, or climate-related topics and relevant societal challenge areas. The NOAA Climate Program Office also wants to know how the number of articles in a given period compares to the long-term average for a given topic, especially during spike events [5; 8], and whether overall sentiment in online articles is positive or negative [11].

2. WEB INTELLIGENCE

The NOAA Media Watch allows us to determine trends and semantic associations with just a few clicks. Its interactive information exploration and retrieval interface sheds light on stakeholder perceptions, reveals flows of relevant information between these stakeholders, and provides success metrics for assessing the effectiveness of awareness and public outreach campaigns.

Figure 1 shows an analysis of online media coverage related to the term "coast" and a range of associated topics, including: coastline, coastal inundation, coastal flooding, coastal communities, coastal infrastructure, and coast erosion. The trend chart depicts the weekly frequency of news reports on the topic "coast" from May 1 to Nov 7, 2012 (the Atlantic hurricane season).

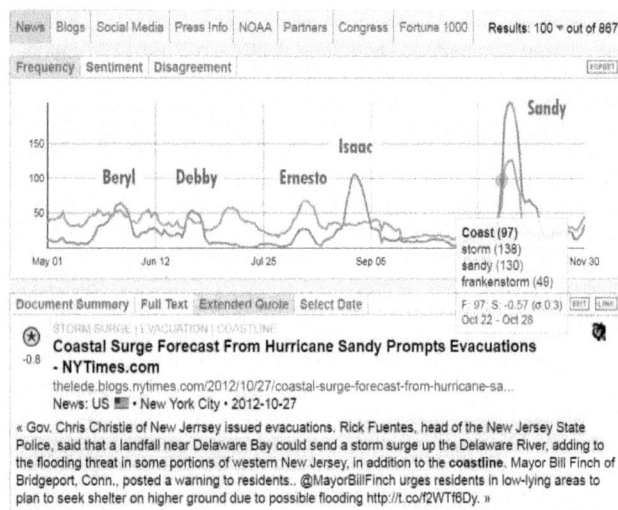

Figure 1. Media monitoring of the Atlantic hurricane season 2012 using the NOAA Media Watch (search term: "coast")

On average, between 50 and 75 news articles per week referred to coast-related terms. We saw six spikes during that period in which the number of reports climbed significantly higher than average due to tropical storms or hurricanes approaching the U.S. coast – Tropical Storm Beryl received media attention in late May (207 articles), TS Debby in late June (221 articles), TS Ernesto in early August (148), TS Isaac in late August (376), Hurricane Leslie in mid-September (145), and Hurricane Sandy in late October (659).

Figure 2 presents the complete dashboard [7] of the NOAA Media Watch. It provides rapid synchronization of multiple coordinated views [6] including tag clouds, geographic maps, keyword and ontology graphs, as well as document clusters in two- and three-dimensional information landscapes [9]. These visualizations help users to understand the context of the extracted knowledge while navigating the knowledge repository. The shown query on "cli-

mate science" for the first quarter of 2013, for example, reveals that discussions about extreme weather events including droughts in North America and the unprecedented heat wave in Australia remain dominant topics in Anglo-American news media coverage.

When extreme events like Hurricane Sandy happen, people often turn to NOAA and ask: "Was this due to global climate change?" Such questions often cannot be answered by a simple yes or no. Extreme events happen with or without climate change. Yet today, such events happen in the context of a warming world. We know that a warmer atmosphere has a greater capacity to hold water vapor, which means heavy rain events are likely to grow more extreme. We also know that sea level along New York's coast is about 30 cm (1 foot) higher today than it was a century ago, which means hurricane Sandy's surge of seawater was made more severe. But these points are nuances, and nuances like these often get overlooked in today's fast-paced lifestyles in which we demand instant answers packaged into easily digestible sound bites. Climate science almost never lends itself to sound bites, which increases the challenge to science agencies like NOAA when communicating with non-scientist publics [2].

Being able to monitor the number and nature of news reports and public dialogs in the blogosphere is very important to assess whether authors and their readers understand the nuances of climate science, such as the differences between natural climate variability and human-induced climate change. In case of misleading or wrong conclusions, a real-time analysis of online media can help agencies like NOAA to diagnose the problem and take corrective action – e.g. using semantic technologies to improve our understanding of when and how people are "spinning" information about climate science in ways that are not accurate.

To embed the collected knowledge into existing workflows, the NOAA Media Watch supports a range of export formats, including RSS, HTML, and PDF for textual data, and CSV for time series date. This is in line with calls for a *Semantic Social Web*, in which data isn't locked away within data silos but can be easily integrated and exchanged between applications [3].

A public showcase of the semantic technologies presented in this paper in the form of a Web content aggregator about climate change and related environmental issues [7] is available at www.ecoresearch.net/climate; its dashboard resembles the NOAA Media Watch, but provides fewer analytical functions and uses different Web media sources and input filter criteria.

3. ONLINE SUCCESS MEASURES

The potential of semantic technologies for progress monitoring in science communication is not only reflected in the interactive visualizations of the webLyzard dashboard, but also in its analytical services and success metrics. The emphasis in communication assessments needs to shift from measures of output to measures of *outcome*. The majority of Web intelligence and social media monitoring tools provide frequency statistics and language characteristics such as positive and negative sentiment [10; 11]. While sentiment is an important and insightful indicator, even if measured accurately it fails to address some of the most fundamental questions of decision makers. The ongoing research presented in this paper will provide implicit observations (as compared to explicit data collection methods such as questionnaires) and tailored success measures (as compared to generic metrics from natural language processing such a sentiment) to measure the attitudes and preferences of social media users.

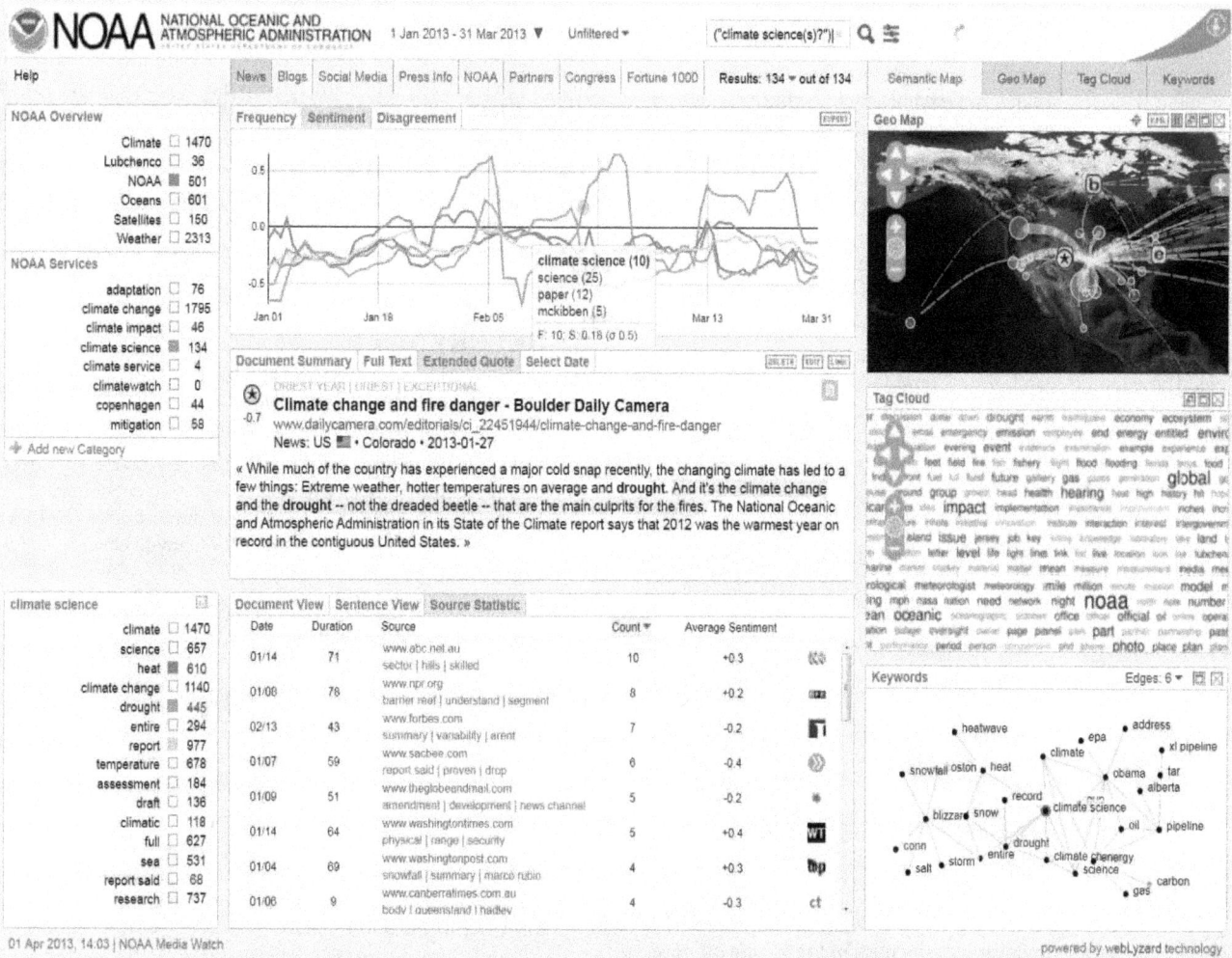

Figure 2. Visual analytics dashboard of the NOAA Media Watch (search term: "climate science")

3.1 Quantitative Analysis

From a commercial and exploitation perspective, such a dynamic assessment beyond sentiment allows real-time insights into the success of marketing and public outreach activities. Measuring attention and sentiment is descriptive in nature.

What we intend to measure, by contrast, is whether communication targets have been reached – i.e., whether the chosen communication strategy has an impact on observable patterns in online coverage, and how consistently a message is being conveyed.

The new metric shows whether an organization or its products and services were associated with desired topics considered important, whether they were in line with corporate communication goals, and whether undesired topics and media coverage were avoided successfully. This analysis goes far beyond language characteristics such as positive and negative sentiment.

In the case of the NOAA Climate Program Office, for example, a desired association with "climate change" contributes positively to the success metric, although the term typically carries a negative sentiment. The new metric is adaptive and part of an iterative feedback cycle, customized to an organization's evolving communications and dissemination goals. To specify these goals, analysts have the opportunity to create lists of desired and undesired topics, and update them in line with changing priorities.

3.2 Visual Analysis

This section describes how measures of online success can be represented in visual form, including an interactive stacked bar chart to be implemented using the *Data-Driven Documents* (D3) JavaScript library [1], as well as information landscapes computed through a combination of hierarchical cluster analysis [4] and force-directed placement algorithms [9].

The stacked bar representing the metric will consider the number of desired vs. undesired associations, as well as the number of positive vs. negative references (measuring the popularity of a brand, organization, person, or topic). While the algorithmic part and work on the computation of the metric has been completed at the time of writing, the authors expect the visual chart representation to be completed in the third quarter of 2013. The representation will be synchronized with the dashboard shown in Figure 2. Tooltips will display additional metadata; e.g., topics and opinion leaders responsible for observable changes. The adaptive calculation enables analysts to assign weights to the individual components of the success metric and thereby configure the computation according to their perceived importance for progress monitoring.

Dynamic topography information landscapes [9] are a powerful way to show the positioning of an organization vis-à-vis desired and undesired terms. NOAA Media Watch visualizes longitudinal changes in large document repositories in near real time. Based on a dynamic clustering of news and social media documents, the resulting landscape resembles a geographic map. Hills represent document clusters around a common topic, while valleys or oceans indicate low document density in sparsely populated areas of the information space. The height of a hill indicates the size of the corresponding topical cluster, while its compactness corresponds to the cluster's cohesion – i.e., the similarity of articles based on a vector space representation. Hills (clusters) are labeled with dominant terms and phrases from the underlying documents to provide a high-level navigational aid for the users.

Figure 3 exemplifies this type of representation based on rendering approximately 5,000 documents taken from environmental blogs. By mapping search results onto the information landscape, communication analysts can track which terms are closely related with an organization, and whether a campaign had an impact on the relative position.

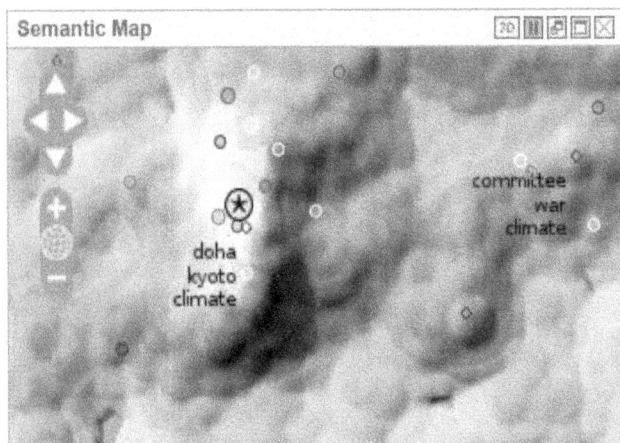

Figure 3. Dynamic topography information landscape on news media coverage about "climate change"

4. CONCLUSION AND OUTLOOK

While Web-based media channels have provided us with quick access to exponentially greater amounts of information, the public's ability to discern credible from non-credible sources appears to be declining. We need to better understand human perceptions and biases, and challenges associated with clear and effective communication. This is particularly true for science agencies like NOAA that are mandated to share scientific data with the public in ways that benefit society and enhance decision making. This requires the effective use of new media to listen to our audiences, directly engage with stakeholders, create shared meaning, and identify and address myths and misconceptions. If we are to succeed in making in-roads into the myriad societal challenges presented by climate change then it is clear that semantic technologies and media monitoring platforms such as the NOAA Media Watch have a vitally important role to play.

Future research will incorporate additional features into the computation of the hybrid success metric, and transform the bitmap-based information landscape component to a dynamic Scalable Vector Graphics (SVG) representation, supporting on-the-fly computations instead of weekly updates. This will enable us to extend the synchronization mechanism and highlight areas and peaks in the landscape that are related to the current search and the content of the displayed subset of Web documents.

Acknowledgement

Key components of the presented system were developed within the DIVINE (www.weblyzard.com/divine) research project, funded by *FIT-IT Semantic Systems* of the Austrian Research Promotion Agency (www.ffg.at) and the Austrian Federal Ministry for Transport, Innovation and Technology (www.bmvit.gv.at). The data acquisition component has recently been extended within the uComp research project (www.ucomp.eu), funded by the Austrian Science Fund (www.fwf.ac.at) through the European CHIST-ERA program (www.chistera.eu).

5. REFERENCES

[1] Bostock, M., Ogievetsky, V. and Heer, J. (2011). "D3: Data-Driven Documents", *IEEE Transactions on Visualization and Computer Graphics,* 17(12): 2301-2309.

[2] Bowman, T. (2008). Summary Report: A Meeting to Assess Public Attitudes about Climate Change. Silver Springs: National Oceanic and Atmospheric Administration (NOAA), George Mason University Center for Climate Change Communications.

[3] Breslin, J.G. and Decker, S. (2007). "The Future of Social Networks on the Internet: The Need for Semantics", *IEEE Internet Computing,* 11(6): 86-90.

[4] Farahat, A.K. and Kamel, M.S. (2009). Document Clustering Using Semantic Kernels Based on Term-Term Correlations. *IEEE International Conference on Data Mining (ICDM-2009), Second International Workshop on Semantic Aspects in Data Mining*. Miami, United States: 459-464.

[5] Gruhl, D., Guha, R., Liben-Nowell, D. and Tomkins, A. (2004). "Information Diffusion Through Blogspace", *13th International World Wide Web Conference*. New York, USA: ACM Press. 491-501.

[6] Hubmann-Haidvogel, A., Scharl, A. and Weichselbraun, A. (2009). "Multiple Coordinated Views for Searching and Navigating Web Content Repositories", *Information Sciences,* 179(12): 1813-1821.

[7] Scharl, A., Hubmann-Haidvogel, A., et al. (2013). Media Watch on Climate Change – Visual Analytics for Aggregating and Managing Environmental Knowledge from Online Sources. *46th Hawaii International Conference on Systems Sciences (HICSS-46)*. R.H. Sprague. Maui, USA: IEEE Press: 955-964.

[8] Scharl, A., Weichselbraun, A. and Liu, W. (2007). "Tracking and Modelling Information Diffusion across Interactive Online Media", *International Journal of Metadata, Semantics and Ontologies,* 2(2): 136-145.

[9] Syed, K.A.A., Kröll, M., et al. (2012). "Incremental and Scalable Computation of Dynamic Topography Information Landscapes", *Journal of Multimedia Processing and Technologies* 3(1): 49-65.

[10] Weichselbraun, A., Gindl, S. and Scharl, A. (2010). "A Context-Dependent Supervised Learning Approach to Sentiment Detection in Large Textual Databases", *Journal of Information and Data Management,* 1(3): 329-342.

[11] Weichselbraun, A., Gindl, S. and Scharl, A. (2013). "Extracting and Grounding Contextualized Sentiment Lexicons", *IEEE Intelligent Systems,* 28(2): 39-46.

A Formal Approach for the Specification of Digital Complex Objects

Ticiana O. Toffoli[1], Nádia P. Kozievitch[2],
Marcos A. Gonçalves[3], and Ricardo da S. Torres[1]
[1]Institute of Computing, University of Campinas, Campinas, SP, Brazil
[2]Department of Computer Science, Federal University of Technology, Curitiba, PR, Brazil
[3]Department of Computer Science, Federal University of Minas Gerais, Belo Horizonte, Brazil
ticiana.toffoli@gmail.com, nadiap@utfpr.edu.br, mgoncalv@dcc.ufmg.edu,
rtorres@ic.unicamp.br

ABSTRACT

Complex objects (COs) have surged as a way to integrate different digital resources under a same logical unit in order to facilitate aggregation and reuse. However, there is still a lack of consensus on precise theoretical foundations for COs, especially regarding design and specification, which compromise their utility and integration with existing software tools. Moreover, there has been little investigation on aspects related to the modeling of COs by the end user, much due to the lack of appropriate tools for this goal. In this work, we present a new Digital Library (DL) metamodel specially designed for the CO modeling which is grounded in formal theoretical specification for COs. More specifically, our goal is two-fold: (i) to indirectly validate our CO formalization by instantiating it within a DL modeling tool – 5SGraph; and (ii) to investigate the difficulties of CO modeling and specification by real users using the specified metamodel. Experiments with real users indicate that the use of the metamodel and the graphical tool facilitates the understanding of the COs structure and the modeling process.

Categories and Subject Descriptors

H. Information Systems [**H.m. Miscellaneous**]: Databases

General Terms

Theory

Keywords

Digital Libraries, Complex Object, 5S Framework, Content-Based Image Retrieval

1. INTRODUCTION

With the advance and use of new technologies, huge collections of heterogeneous digital information resources have been created by many communities and even by individuals.

Digital Libraries (DLs) are a type of complex information system that has been developed throughout the years with the goal of managing such heterogeneous collections in a community-oriented way, trying to promote information integration, reuse, and interoperability. Particularly, in order to better integrate, unify, manage, and support these heterogeneous information resources, as well as their interconnections, the notion of complex objects (COs) has emerged [15].

COs allow the integration and aggregation of different digital objects within a single logical unit, facilitating management and mainly *reuse*. These ideas have been exploited, for instance, in solutions for integration and interoperability among DLs [19]. However, few existing repository software tools (like Fedora [18]) allow the specification of COs. Furthermore, these tools still have to be better integrated with different CO technologies and services (such as annotations [6]). In fact, the proliferation of different technologies and implementations for COs without a common ground and understanding about the underlying issues behind this type of concept goes exactly on the opposite direction for which COs were designed: reuse and integration. Moreover, it is not clear what is the difficulty for content creators to understand and model their own COs so they can in fact take full advantage of them in their collections and repositories. To tackle some of these issues, there has been effort towards formal definitions and descriptions for COs [24]. The benefits of adopting a formal model include the abstraction of general characteristics and common features, and the definition of structures for organizing components (e.g., aggregations, relationships). A precise specification of requirements also strengthens the correctness of an implementation [12].

In this article, we propose solutions for the specification of DLs instances that manage COs. For that, based on a formal definition of COs we propose a new metamodel for specifying DLs of COs through a domain-specific visual modeling tool: 5SGraph [35]. More specifically, our goal is two-fold: (i) to indirectly validate our CO formalization by instantiating it within a DL modeling tool; and (ii) to investigate the difficulties of CO modeling and specification by real users using the specified metamodel. Specifically for the second goal, we run a pilot usability experiment in which users had to model several types of COs using the extended 5SGraph, including a complex case of legal documents modeling. Experimental results demonstrate that in fact the use of the tool facilitates the understanding of COs structure and the modeling process, thus confirming the usefulness of the extended 5SGraph for modeling DLs of COs.

In sum, the main contributions of this article are: (i) the definition of a DL metamodel based on a formal characterization of COs to be used in the specification of DLs that manage COs; (ii) the extension of 5SL (a domain-specific language [11]) and 5SGraph to handle COs; (iii) the presentation and the validation of the new metamodel in the 5SGraph with real users; and (iv) the characterization of legal documents as COs.

This article is organized as follows. Section 2 contains an overview of fundamental concepts necessary to understand this work. The proposed metamodel for COs is described in Section 3. The experimental usability validation is discussed in Section 4. Finally, conclusions and future work are presented in Section 5.

2. FOUNDATIONS
This section presents some fundamental concepts for the understanding of our work, including aspects related to COs, formal models for DLs, and the 5S framework tools.

2.1 Complex Objects
Multiple definitions have been used [15] in the literature to name the integration of resources into a single digital object such as *Aggregations* [34], *Component-Based Objects* [30,31], *Complex Objects* [16,18,27], or *Compound Objects* [2]. In this work we adopt the same definition of structuring digital objects present in [2] (DOI is an acronym that stands for Digital Object Identifier):

- **atomistic** (Figure 1a): encompass the situation when the user has a single file in a preferred format (made up from a single or multiple data/files). An electronic thesis and dissertation (ETD) in PDF format is an example.

- **compound** (Figure 1b): made up from multiple content files, which may have different formats. Together, these multiple files represent a digital object. As an example, consider an ETD that has texts files and images files or other data in non-textual format.

- **complex** (Figure 1c): made up from a network of digital objects within a repository, having at least one of these data as a digital object. An ETD which is composed by a software tool developed during the research, along with the respective pdf file, is an example.

According to Krafft et al. [17], COs are single entities that are composed of multiple digital objects, each of which is an entity in and of itself. Cheung et al. [6] defined a CO as the encapsulation of various datasets and resources generated or utilized during a scientific experiment or discovery process, within a single unit, for publishing and exchange. In other words, a complex object is an aggregation of objects, that can be grouped together and manipulated as a single object.

COs have also been defined as aggregations of distinct information units that, when combined, form a logical whole [19].

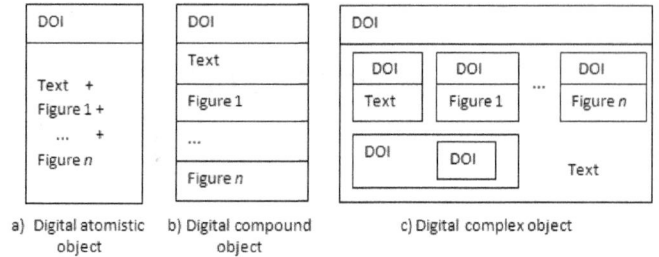

Figure 1: Digital objects: (a) atomistic, (b) compound, and (c) complex

Several CO formats arise from different communities [26,27]. From scientific computing, standards such as the Network Common Data Form (NetCDF)[1], Hierarchical Data Format (HDF)[2], and Extensible File System (ELFS) [13] can be cited. HDF and NetCDF, for example, are used in multidimensional storage and retrieval, while ELFS is an approach to address the issue of high performance I/O by treating files as typed objects.

From the persistent data storage perspective, there are representations like the Metadata Encoding and Transmission Standard (METS) [7]. Other technologies have been proposed, like the multimedia framework MPEG-21 [4], and the Moving Picture Experts Group - 21 Digital Item Declaration Language (MPEG-21 DIDL) [3]. Additional new standards have emerged, like SQL Multimedia and Application Packages (SQL/MM) [21], or web-based learning content specifications, such as SCORM [1]. These new standards and representations arose new research questions regarding usability and evaluation problems with the COs [15,24].

Among applications/tools for COs, we can mention LORE [10] and Escape[3].

2.2 Digital Libraries and Formal Models
Due to the their complexity and intersections with several knowledge areas and different types of information systems, formal theories and frameworks have been created and used to model, define, and describe DLs. Among the several approaches available for formalizing digital libraries and COs, we can mention the DELOS Reference Model [5], the Open Provenance Model (OPM) [22], the Europeana Data Model (EDM) [8] and the 5S Framework [12]. Earlier work related to COs goes back decades, such as [9,33].

In the Digital Library community, the DELOS Reference Model [5] provides an ontology for digital libraries, defining concepts in a language. The model is grouped under six main categories: content, user, functionality, quality, policy, and architecture. In particular, in the context of COs, the DELOS Reference Model manages resources which can be composed of smaller resources (with the relation

---

[1]http://www.unidata.ucar.edu/software/netcdf/. Accessed 04 June 2011.
[2]http://www.hdfgroup.org/. Accessed 04 June 2011.
[3]http://code.google.com/p/surf-escape/. Accessed 01 May 2012.

<*hasPart*>) and linked to other resources (with the relation <*associatedWith*>), to form compound artifacts. DELOS was also the major inspiration for models such as [20], where features like representation, content, and description are used as a first-order language to describe a DL.

The Europeana Data Model (EDM) [8] builds upon established standards like RDF(S), OAI-ORE, SKOS, and Dublin Core. In essence, EDM provides an integration medium for collecting, connecting and enriching the descriptions provided by content providers. Regarding COs, Europeana offers semantic contextualization for the object representations in such a way as to enable complex semantic operations on these resources.

Still in the Digital Library community, we also can mention the Open Provenance Model (OPM) [22]. In essence, OPM allows the provenance information to be exchanged between systems, and can be used to define models, or to support a digital representation of provenance. Regarding COs, we can mention that OPM supports composability, using dependencies, objects (nodes), rules (such as "generated by", "controlled by") and a graph notation to specify provenance information.

However, these models are not general enough to cover other topics (such as description of societies and scenarios) and extensions available in digital libraries, such as the use of mathematical formalisms for services (e.g., annotation, CBIR, and recommendation). The 5S Framework (Streams, Structures, Spaces, Scenarios, and Societies) [12] differs from these models within the levels of abstraction, comprising other additional concepts such as scenarios and societies, as an underlying foundation for DLs. The 5S abstractions are useful to better understand and relate many DL concepts. These key concepts were further extended to consider several common DL components, services, and different contexts related to DLs. As an example, consider the CO definition [15], validated through the use of SuperIDR [23], a tool that manages images, metadata, marks, and annotations in the Ichthyology and Parasitology domain [25].

The formal CO definition [15] which extends the original definition of a digital object in the 5S framework comprises a tuple $cdo = (h, SCDO = DO \cup SM, S)$ where:

1. $h \in H$, where H is a set of universally unique handles (labels);

2. $DO = \{do_1, do_2, \ldots, do_n\}$, where do_i is a digital object or another CO;

3. $SM = \{sm_1, sm_2, \ldots, sm_n\}$ is a set of streams;

4. S is a structure that composes the CO cdo into its parts in $SCDO$.

Note that the mentioned definitions consider the metadata of an object in a separate catalog [12]. The structural component S, which can be instantiated in many forms, serves to represent any structure that provides internal organization and interconnections among the components of a CO.

In this article in particular, we instantiate the above definition into a metamodel used in a software tool to specify, model and maintain semantic constraints over COs.

2.3 5S Framework Tools
Tools based on the 5S framework have been built to facilitate DL development, mainly in the tasks of requirements gathering, conceptual modeling, and DL building [14], as shown in Figure 2. The main objective is to tailor DL services, exploring the metamodel and respective applications.

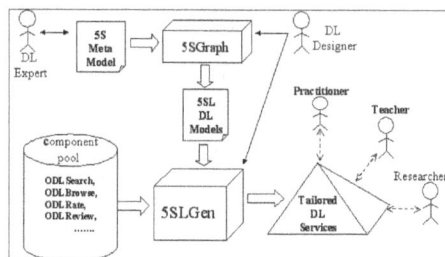

Figure 2: Overview of the architecture for DL modeling and generation [11].

5SL [11] is a domain-specific language providing a precise DL specification tool. It can facilitate prototyping, aid validation of implementations, and serves as a generic digital library (metamodel) whose instantiation produces models of specific DL systems. A metamodel provides the building blocks, and sets up the relationships among these building blocks. An XML syntax is used in 5SL and consists of five modeling perspectives based on the 5S main concepts.

With the goal of helping developers to understand and produce DL models, the 5SGraph tool [35] was build based on 5S and 5SL. It works like a requirements gathering tool which helps in the DL development. Initially its interface loads a DL metamodel, so users can create DL models adapted to a specific domain following the metamodel structure. The models are build in a bottom-up fashion, specifying and detailing each model perspective. These are then stored in 5SL using XML files.

3. A METAMODEL FOR COMPLEX OBJECTS
This section presents the defined CO models and their specification in 5SL. Later these specifications are used in the 5SGraph tool to model COs in specific DL instances.

3.1 Extending 5SL
To create a new metamodel for the specification of COs, the following questions need to be answered: *How to formally define a new metamodel that represents a generic DL of COs? Which extensions of the current 5S framework instantiated in 5SL would be needed for this?* The current metamodel specifies only digital simple objects [12]. *How could we extend it to also define COs?*

The types of streams currently defined in 5SL are restricted to those most commonly used to define the basic content of digital information (i.e, text, image, video, audio, and software). A compound object on its turn may have more than one stream when compared to an atomistic object. Both of these objects are identified in the extended metamodel by the *SimpleObject* component (referred as the *Document* component in the original metamodel). COs on their turn are represented by a new component: the *ComplexObject*.

A CO must be compounded by another digital object (a simple object or another CO). The new *Object* component was created to represent a digital object that compounds a CO. Figure 3 shows the relationships between *Object*, *SimpleObject*, *ComplexObject*, and *Stream* components.

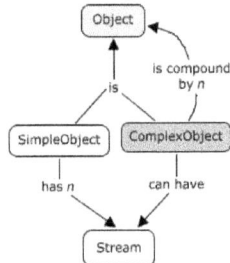

Figure 3: Components of the new metamodel of DLs

In summary, the new components created in the metamodel to define COs include:

ComplexObject: represents a CO; it aggregates at least another digital object and others streams.

Object: represents an object (of the DL) that compounds a CO. It can be atomistic, compound, or complex.

With these new components, the DL collection can also support COs, in addition to the management of simple objects. Note that for the CO extension, only the Structural model was updated. The Streams, Spaces, and Societies models have not been changed in the new metamodel with the inclusion of COs. On the other hand, the Scenarios model could be extended with new services, such as the *view in context* service [23] (providing intra-objects browsing).

3.2 Extending 5SGraph

Considering the CO formal definition [15] and the new 5SL components presented in the previous section, this section shows how the CO extension in 5SL can be used to specify DLs of COs using the 5SGraph tool.

The following extensions were included in the new 5SGraph metamodel:

- The original component *Document* was renamed to *SimpleObject*.

- The new 5SL extension *Object* was added.

- The new 5SL extension *ComplexObject* was added. The *ComplexObject* concept was shortened to *ComplexObj* so the *ComplexObj* word can be viewed in its entirety in the 5SGraph interface.

In summary, only the Structural model was updated in 5SGraph. Figure 4 highlights the extensions, within the *Structural* model of the 5SGraph tool. Note that the *Collection* component was extended to specify COs. For that, *ComplexObj* tag was added as subnode of the *Collection* tag, having its *constraint* attribute value equals "*" (asterisk), meaning that *Collection* may have any number of *ComplexObj* instances. In particular, services such as navigation could explore not only the aggregation, but also individual objects. Figure 5 shows the metamodel extensions loaded in 5SGraph tool interface. The new components *ComplexObj* and *Object* are highlighted in bold rectangles. Examples of specific DL models are presented in the next Section.

```
<Collection type="DataType">
    <SubNodes>
        <SimpleObject constraint="*"/>
        <ComplexObj constraint="*"/>
    </SubNodes>
    <Icon name="coll.gif" />
    <Property>
        <TextField name="Description" />
        <TextField name="Creator" />
        <TextField name="Maintainer" />
    </Property>
</Collection>
<SimpleObject type="DataType">
    <SubNodes>
        <Stream constraint="*" />
    </SubNodes>
    <Icon name="doc.gif" />
    <Property>
        <TextField name="Structed_Stream" load="true"/>
    </Property>
</SimpleObject>
<ComplexObj type="DataType">
    <SubNodes>
        <Object constraint="*"/>
        <Stream constraint="*" />
    </SubNodes>
    <Icon name="co.gif" />
    <Property>
        <TextField name="Structed_Stream" load="true"/>
    </Property>
</ComplexObj>
<Object type="DataType">
    <SubNodes />
    <Icon name="object.gif" />
    <Property>
        <ComboBox name="Object" src="Collection" />
    </Property>
</Object>
```

Figure 4: *ComplexObj* and *Object*: new components in the metamodel of the 5SGraph tool

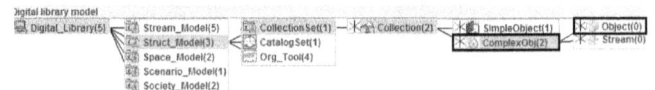

Figure 5: *ComplexObj* and *Object*: new components in the interface of the 5SGraph tool

3.3 Case Study

This section presents examples of the specification and reuse of COs for modeling DLs using the 5SGraph tool. Only the *Stream* and *Structural* models are described in this section, since both are the only ones which are considered in order to handle aggregations.

The complexity of the information included in a legal resource, and the difficulty to interconnect all the layers in appropriate manner has brought the attention from the scientific community [28,29]. Our study demonstrates the specification of legal documents as COs. Examples of legal documents include Laws, Deliberations, and Regulations. These documents are created to organize a respectful set of rules and guidelines that are enforced by political and social institutions to regulate the relations among people. In our case study, we focus on Brazilian laws, although our metamodel can be used to represent legal documents of other countries. The structure of Brazilian laws follows the organization defined in Complementary Laws published in 1998[4] and 2001[5]. These documents define that a legal text has three parts: a preliminary part, which indicates the context of the legal document; a normative part, where the legal text is shown; and a final part, where functions and signatures, regulation effective dates, and transitory arguments, as examples, are specified.

The normative part structure of Brazilian legal documents is shown in Figure 6 (adapted from Projeto LexML[6]). Article is the basic unity and can be aggregated by Subsections, Sections, Chapters, Titles, Books, and Parts. The objective is to organize the logic and the hierarchy of the legal text. Also, Articles can be complemented by Paragraphs or Lines, expressing aspects like exceptions. Paragraphs can be discriminated in Lines; lines can be an aggregation of Letters and Letters of Items.

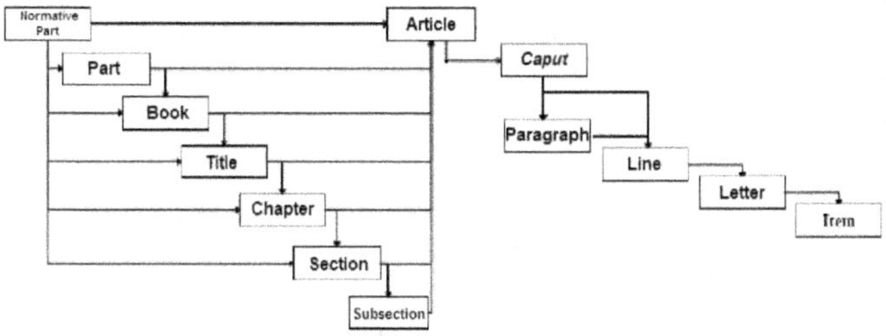

Figure 6: Structure of normative part in legal documents (adapted)

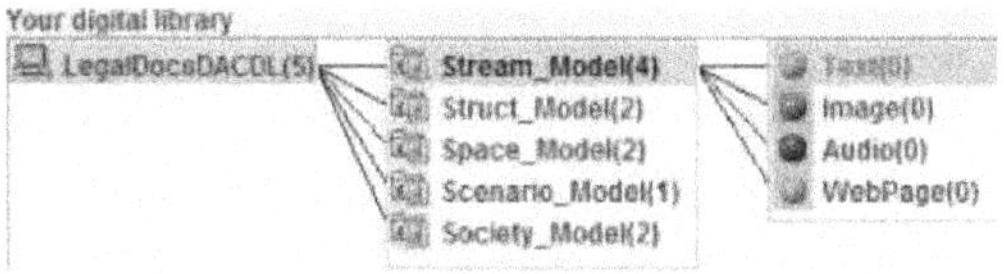

Figure 7: Streams of legal documents specified in the 5SGraph tool

[4]http://www.planalto.gov.br/ccivil_03/Leis/LCP/Lcp95.htm. Accessed 20 February 2012.

[5]http://www.planalto.gov.br/ccivil_03/Leis/LCP/Lcp107.htm. Accessed 20 February 2012.

[6]http://projeto.lexml.gov.br/. Accessed 20 February 2012.

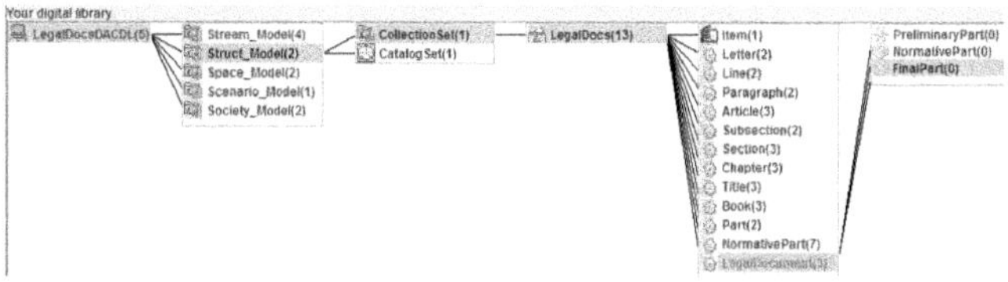

Figure 8: Legal document specification in 5SGraph tool interface

The normative part elements (e.g., chapters, articles, paragraphs, *etc.*) are considered COs because they usually have an identification number (handle), subelements (see Figure 6), text (streams), and they are organized through the structure of legal documents. Consequently, a legal document is a CO since it has a handle (usually the document name); normative part elements (digital objects); text (streams), and the legal structure. Consider the following example: a legal document A includes a legal text T containing several articles; later, a legal document B is published, defining changes in one of the articles of T, (for example, article X of T), defining a new article X'. In that scenario, after B is published, the new legal text created (say T') is composed by the new article X' and the remaining articles of T. Whenever a legal document (CO B in our example) is published to alter, include, or remove legal text elements of other legal document (CO A), new versions of these elements are created. A legal text may have therefore different versions over time.

Turning back our attention to the 5SGraph modeling of legal documents with the extended metamodel, to represent the normative structural part, initially the stream types are defined (Figure 7): (i) *Text* according to characters of normative texts; (ii) *textitImage* referencing possible images used in the legal text; (iii) *Audio*, allowing the publication of documents in audio; and (iv) *WebPage*, to visualize the documents. Figure 8 shows an Item element from the normative part as a simple object, defined as *Text* stream type. Note that Article and other elements are created as COs since they can aggregate other subelements. Figure 9 lists the Article element created by the 5SGraph tool, in XML. The NormativePart element is created in accordance with the legal documents structure. The legal document is then composed by PreliminaryPart, NormativePart, and FinalPart elements. Preliminary and final parts are composed by text, while the normative part is composed by articles, grouped by other elements. Figure 10 shows the XML file created by the 5SGraph tool for the normative part and legal document specifications.

The 5SGraph tool also allows the reuse of COs defined through its interface. The user only needs to save the requested node in a XML file, and then, loads this file/node in another model. In the legal context, we could reuse some elements of Brazilian legal structure into another country legal model, if the elements can be matched.

Therefore, the specification of these cases show that it is possible to use the 5SGraph tool, with the proposed metamodel, to specify and reuse types of COs. Moreover, the interface

```
<ComplexObj name="Article">
    <Structed_Stream></Structed_Stream>
    <Object name="Paragraph">
        <Object>"Paragraph"</Object>
    </Object>
    <Object name="Line">
        <Object>"Line"</Object>
    </Object>
    <Stream name="ArticleCaput">
        <Stream>"Text"</Stream>
    </Stream>
</ComplexObj>
```

Figure 9: Article element in 5SL file generated by 5SGraph

```
<ComplexObj name="NormativePart">
    <Structed_Stream></Structed_Stream>
    <Object name="Part">
        <Object>"Part"</Object>
    </Object>
    <Object name="Book">
        <Object>"Book"</Object>
    </Object>
    <Object name="Title">
        <Object>"Title"</Object>
    </Object>
    <Object name="Chapter">
        <Object>"Chapter"</Object>
    </Object>
    <Object name="Section">
        <Object>"Section"</Object>
    </Object>
    <Object name="Subsection">
        <Object>"Subsection"</Object>
    </Object>
    <Object name="Article">
        <Object>"Article"</Object>
    </Object>
</ComplexObj>
<ComplexObj name="LegalDocument">
    <Structed_Stream></Structed_Stream>
    <Object name="NormativePart">
        <Object>"NormativePart"</Object>
    </Object>
    <Stream name="PreliminaryPart">
        <Stream>"Text"</Stream>
    </Stream>
    <Stream name="FinalPart">
        <Stream>"Text"</Stream>
    </Stream>
</ComplexObj>
```

Figure 10: Legal document elements in 5SL file generated by 5SGraph tool

visually shows the COs structure defined, facilitating the understanding of the objects. The next section demonstrate the validation of the new metamodel by DL students.

4. VALIDATION

This section describes a pilot experiment in which users had to model several types of COs using the extended 5SGraph. Six students of the University of Campinas (Unicamp) with basic knowledge about DLs were volunteers. The students analyzed if the new metamodel was helpful in building DL models of COs, considering the following measures:

Effectiveness

Completion rate: percentage of participants who complete each task correctly.

Goal achievement: percentage of tasks achieved completely and correctly.

Efficiency

Task time: time to complete each task.

Closeness to expertise: minimum task time of the faster participant divided by task time of each participant.

Satisfaction

Satisfaction was measured using the final questionnaire where participants rated the overall effectiveness and satisfaction based on his/her observation.

The experiment also analyzed participants suggestions and difficulties.

4.1 Setup

The interaction among tutors and students used questionnaires and the 5SGraph application.

The evaluation process adopted the following steps:

- Choosing participants with some knowledge about DLs.

- Filling in a form with details on participants' previous knowledge.

- Running three tasks in 5SGraph tool concerning CO specification, with increasing levels of difficulty.

- Filling in a form about the 5SGraph tool, concerning its usability, learnability, and effectiveness.

- Analyzing the resulting files created after each CO modeling task.

- Analyzing results for effectiveness, efficiency, and user satisfaction.

Table 1: Number of participants versus knowledge before experiment

How much/Knowledge of	English	Dig Lib	5S	COs	5SGraph
None	0	0	1	0	2
Little	0	1	2	3	2
Reasonable	1	3	2	2	2
Much	4	1	0	0	0
Expert	1	1	1	1	0

All the participants were graduated students in Computer Courses (one Master student, three PhD students, and one has PhD degree). Table 1 shows the participants' English skills, and their previous knowledge about DLs, the 5S framework, COs, and the 5SGraph tool. The participants were also questioned about their experience in DL construction. Four of them had already built DLs of technical reports, ETDs, for fish species, historical documents, and digital documents of Unicamp. But none of the participants had used a software tool for specification.

The participants were asked to perform three tasks related to the specification of the following digital objects (using the *Stream* and *Structural* models in 5SGraph):

- Task 1: specify a simple object. In this task, the participant, using 5SGraph, should specify the structure of a thesis with image (related to the figures of the thesis) and text streams.

- Task 2: specify a CO. In this second task, it was expected that the participant specified the structure of a thesis and its developed software where it could be possible to access the software independent of the thesis access. To achieve this, the participant should specify text streams and a digital software object both compounding a thesis.

- Task 3: specify COs aggregating others COs. For this task, the participant should specify a legal document, using 5SGraph. A legal document structure is made of preliminary part (text streams), normative part (articles that can be detailed in paragraphs, lines, letters, and items where all these elements have text streams and can be accessed individually), and final part (text streams).

4.2 Results and Discussion

In general, a better understanding about COs and their structuring was observed from the participants after the experiment. Measure results are shown in Table 2. The relative high completion rates and the high goal achievement rates prove the effectiveness of 5SGraph for specifying COs. Task 3 shows a lower completion rate and longer duration due to the high level of difficulty of this task and because instructions were missed by some of the participants in the task specification (as reported by them). Regarding closeness to expertise, the measures for Task 2 were lower than for Task 1 because this task included the specification of a new CO. However, even with the higher level of difficulty, Task 3 demonstrates that users could achieve a much closer performance when compared to the expert (participant with the best performance) after Task 2. This result is similar to the one reported in a previous study of 5SGraph [35] which means that the tool is easy to learn.

Table 2: Summary of results: measures average

	Task 1	Task 2	Task 3
Completion Rate (%)	100.00	80.00	50.00
Mean Goal Achievement (%)	100.00	98.33	89.17
Mean Task Time (min)	4.33	8.17	10.5
Mean Closeness to Expertise	0.72	0.55	0.61

Comments and suggestions included the possibility of a top-down specification of COs where a CO is first specified and later its components are defined and the structural validation of a CO specification regarding its conformance to a predefined XML Schema. All participants mentioned that they would be comfortable in specifying other COs with 5SGraph and that they found 5SGraph satisfactory and useful for the task of specifying COs. Later these 5SL-based specifications

could be integrated with other application tools (such as code generators like 5SGen [32]) to allow customized modeling and implementation of CO-based DLs. Note that anyone interested in digital libraries and complex objects (or even multimedia integration) would benefit from our approach, mainly extending the CO concepts already mentioned, or using the theoretical 5S framework, or even exploring the 5S applications.

5. CONCLUSION

In this article we present a new metamodel specially designed for the specification of DLs of COs. The proposed extensions to the original metamodel are based on a formalization of COs which allows a clearer understanding of their properties.

We validated our proposals by instantiating the CO formalization within a domain-specific visual modeling tool – 5SGraph (through a complex case study on legal documents), as well as with experiments with real users. Experimental results confirmed the usefulness of the extended tool to specify models of DLs that manage COs, helping users to understand the COs structure, and allowing COs reuse in others applications.

As future work, we want to further explore issues related to CO reuse and the automatic generation of DLs, given 5SL-based specifications, for instance, for CO-aware repositories like Fedora.

6. ACKNOWLEDGMENTS

We would like to thank CAPES, FAPESP, Fundação Araucária, FAPEMIG, and CNPq.

7. REFERENCES

[1] Advanced Distributed Learning (ADS). Sharable Content Object Reference Model (SCORM), available at `http://www.adlnet.org/index.cfm?fuseaction=SCORDown`, 2004.

[2] C. Awre. Managing compound objects within Fedora, Knowledge Exchange Group - Enhanced E-theses Project Deliverable 9. 2009.

[3] J. Bekaert, P. Hochstenbach, and H. V. de Sompel. Using mpeg-21 didl to represent complex digital objects in the los alamos national laboratory digital library, available at `http://www.dlib.org/dlib/november03/bekaert/11bekaert.html`. *D-Lib Magazine*, 9(11), November 2003.

[4] I. S. Burnett, F. Pereira, R. V. de Walle, and R. Koenen. *The MPEG-21 Book*. John Wiley & Sons, 2006.

[5] L. Candela, D. Castelli, N. Ferro, Y. Ioannidis, G. Koutrika, C. Meghini, P. Pagano, S. Ross, D. Soergel, M. Agosti, M. andDobreva, V. Katifori, and H. Schuldt. The DELOS Digital Library Reference Model - Foundations for Digital Libraries. Version 0.98, DELOS Digital Library, 02 2008.

[6] K. Cheung, A. Lashtabeg, and J. Drennan. SCOPE: A scientific compound object publishing and editing system. *IJDC*, 2(2):4–18, 2008.

[7] M. V. Cundiff. An introduction to the Metadata Encoding and Transmission Standard (METS). *Library Hi Tech.*, 22(1):52–64, 2004.

[8] M. Doerr, S. Gradmann, S. Hennicke, A. Isaac, C. Meghini, and H. V. de Sompel. The Europeana Data Model (EDM). In *IFLA 2011: World Library and Information Congress: 76th IFLA General Conference and Assembly, Gothenburg, Sweden*, 2010.

[9] E. A. Fox and R. K. France. Architecture of an expert system for composite document analysis, representation, and retrieval. *International Journal of Approximate Reasoning*, 1(2):151 – 175, 1987.

[10] A. Gerber and J. Hunter. Authoring, editing and visualizing compound objects for literary scholarship. *Journal of Digital Information (JoDI)*, 11(1), 2010.

[11] M. A. Gonçalves. *Streams, Structures, Spaces, Scenarios, and Societies (5S): a formal digital library framework and its applications*. PhD thesis, Virginia Tech, 2004.

[12] M. A. Gonçalves, E. A. Fox, L. T. Watson, and N. A. Kipp. Streams, Structures, Spaces, Scenarios, Societies (5S): a formal model for digital libraries. *ACM Transactions on Information Systems (TOIS)*, 22(2):1–43, 2004.

[13] J. F. Karpovich, A. S. Grimshaw, and J. C. French. Extensible file system (ELFS): an object-oriented approach to high performance file I/O. *ACM SIGPLAN Notices*, 29(10):191–204, 1994.

[14] R. Kelapure, M. A. Gonçalves, and E. A. Fox. Scenario-based generation of digital library services. In *ECDL'03*, pages 263–275, 2003.

[15] N. P. Kozievitch, J. Almeida, R. S. Torres, N. A. Leite, M. A. Gonçalves, U. Murthy, and E. A. Fox. Towards a Formal Theory for Complex Objects and Content-Based Image Retrieval. *Journal of Information and Data Management (JIDM)*, 2(3):321–336, 2011.

[16] N. P. Kozievitch, R. S. Torres, A. Santanchè, D. C. G. Pedronette, R. T. Calumby, and E. A. Fox. An infrastructure for searching and harvesting complex image objects. *The Information - Interaction - Intelligence (I3) Journal*, 11(2):39–68, 2011.

[17] D. B. Krafft, A. Birkland, and E. J. Cramer. Ncore: architecture and implementation of a flexible, collaborative digital library. In *JCDL*, pages 313–322. ACM, 2008.

[18] C. Lagoze, S. Payette, E. Shin, and C. Wilper. Fedora: an architecture for complex objects and their relationships. *IJDL*, 6(2):124–138, 2006.

[19] C. Lagoze and H. V. Sompel. Compound information objects: the OAI-ORE perspective. *Open Archives Initiative Object Reuse and Exchange, White Paper*, 2007.

[20] C. Meghini, N. Spyratos, and J. Yang. A data model for digital libraries. *International Journal on Digital Libraries (IJDL)*, 11(1):41–56, 2010.

[21] J. Melton and A. Eisenberg. SQL multimedia and application packages (SQL/MM). *SIGMOD Rec.*, 30(4):97–102, 2001.

[22] L. Moreau, B. Clifford, J. Freire, Y. Gil, P. Groth, J. Futrelle, N. Kwasnikowska, S. Miles, P. Missier, J. Myers, Y. Simmhan, E. Stephan, and J. V. den Bussche. The open provenance model — core specification (v1.1). *Future Generation Computer Systems*, December 2009.

[23] U. Murthy. *Digital libraries with superimposed information: supporting scholarly tasks that involve fine grain information*. PhD thesis, Virginia Tech, 2011.

[24] U. Murthy, N. P. Kozievitch, J. Leidig, R. S. Torres, S. Yang, M. A. Gonçalves, L. M. Delcambre, D. Archer, and E. A. Fox. Extending the 5S framework of digital libraries to support complex objects, superimposed information, and content-based image retrieval services. Technical Report TR-10-05, Virginia Tech, April 2010.

[25] U. Murthy, L. T. Li, E. Hallerman, E. A. Fox, M. A. Pérez-Quiñones, L. M. Delcambre, and R. S. Torres. Use of subimages in fish species identification: a qualitative study. In *JCDL*, pages 185–194, 2011.

[26] L. Nelson and H. V. de Sompel. IJDL special issue on complex digital objects: Guest editors' introduction. *International Journal of Digital Libraries (IJDL)*, 6(2):113–114, 2006.

[27] M. L. Nelson, B. Argue, M. Efron, S. Denn, and M. C. Pattuelli. A survey of complex object technologies for digital libraries. Technical report, NASA/TM-2001-211426, 2001.

[28] M. Palmirani, L. Cervone, and F. Vitali. A legal document ontology: The missing layer in legal document modelling. In G. Sartor, P. Casanovas, M. A. Biasiotti, M. Fernndez-Barrera, P. Casanovas, and G. Sartor, editors, *Approaches to Legal Ontologies*, volume 1 of *Law, Governance and Technology Series*, pages 167–178. Springer Netherlands, 2011.

[29] H. Sahilu and S. Atnafu. Change-aware legal document retrieval model. In *Proceedings of the International Conference on Management of Emergent Digital EcoSystems*, MEDES '10, pages 174–181, New York, NY, USA, 2010. ACM.

[30] A. Santanchè and C. B. Medeiros. A Component Model and Infrastructure for a Fluid Web. *IEEE Transactions on Knowledge and Data Engineering*, 19(2):324–341, February 2007.

[31] A. Santanchè, C. B. Medeiros, and G. Z. Pastorello Jr. User-author centered multimedia building blocks. *Multimedia Systems*, 12(4):403–421, March 2007.

[32] R. Shen, N. S. Vemuri, W. Fan, and E. A. Fox. Integration of complex archeology digital libraries: An etana-dl experience. *Inf. Syst.*, 33(7-8):699–723, Nov. 2008.

[33] G. Vossen. On formal models for object-oriented databases. *SIGPLAN OOPS Mess.*, 6(3):1–19, July 1995.

[34] K. Williams and H. Suleman. A survey of digital library aggregation services. In *Scholarship at Penn Libraries, available at http://works.bepress.com/martha_brogan/10*, 2003.

[35] Q. Zhu. 5SGraph: a modeling tool for digital libraries. Master's thesis, Virginia Tech, 2002.

Comparing the Multimodal Interaction Technique Design of MINT with NiMMiT

Sebastian Feuerstack
OFFIS – Institute for Information
Technology, Escherweg 2
26121 Oldenburg, Germany
feuerstack@offis.de

Ednaldo Brigante Pizzolato
Universidade Federal de São Carlos
Rodovia Washington Luís, km 235
São Carlos - São Paulo – Brasil
ednaldo@dc.ufscar.br

ABSTRACT

With new sensors that can capture hand and body movements in 3D, novel interaction techniques gain importance. But development of new forms of interaction is highly iterative, depends on extensive user testing and therefore is expensive. We propose a model-based notation using statecharts and mappings to ease multimodal interaction technique design. This model-based specification can be used to communicate designs, for evaluation and to enable re-use. Our contribution continues previous research on model-based interaction technique design considers multimodal interaction and addresses problems like the state explosion, error management and consideration of output modalities mentioned by earlier research. We evaluate our notation by comparing it with NiMMiT referring to the same use case to identify similarities, strength and problems.

Categories and Subject Descriptors

H.5.2 [**Information Interfaces and Presentation**]: User Interfaces - Input devices and strategies, Interaction styles, Prototyping; D.2.2 [**Software Engineering**]: Design Tools and Techniques – User Interfaces.

General Terms

Design, Human Factors, Languages.

Keywords

Interaction Techniques, Interaction Metaphors, Multimodal Interaction, Model-Based Design.

1. INTRODUCTION

The great variety of different devices to access and control services in smart environments can be used to improve human-computer interaction to be more natural by considering and combining several modes of access in one interaction. Decades of research have been performed to figure out suitable interaction techniques for certain control modes. After the desktop and WIMP interaction metaphor have been introduced, the emerging variety of devices continuously substitutes classic interaction techniques

that were optimized for the desktop PC. The Post-WIMP term sums up the trend to design interaction techniques specifically to a certain combination of an application and one or more interaction devices and their control modes.

Non-traditional interfaces that consider modes like speech or gestures and media such as augmented and hyper-reality offer a high degree of freedom in interaction design but make the design process cumbersome since extensive user testing is usually required to figure out an efficient and accessible way of interaction.

High-level description languages have been developed to ease the design of multimodal interaction techniques by providing means to design, prototype, communicate and store interaction techniques to be re-usable. Model-based user interface design is a widely adopted practice to shorten development-cycles [12]. The Cameleon Reference Framework [4] revealed several shared models between different proposals. Most of them start with a task model, and then follow an incremental abstract-to-concrete transformational process through several transitional models, such as an abstract one, a modality independent one and several concrete ones to consider specific platform capabilities.

Recent research proposes to execute models instead of transforming them into executable code [11]. This has the advantage that models can be still edited while already in execution, facilitates experimental prototyping and model observation at runtime to analyze user behavior.

In this paper we present our approach to design multimodal interaction techniques that we present and discuss in line with preceding research about interaction techniques descriptions, such as in InTml [9] and ICO [14] but focus on a comparison with NiMMiT [1], which is to the best of our knowledge the most recent proposal.

Like NiMMiT, our approach combines a data flow with a state-chart description with the overall goals to allow designers communicate about the functionality of an interaction technique and to offer a platform that can directly execute the design models to enable rapid prototyping and comparison of different interaction technique variants for user testing.

The intention of our model-based MINT design notation [8] is to consider the problems and drawbacks that have been identified by the authors of NiMMiT in [16]:

1. The state explosion for complex interaction technique designs that we tackle by separating the design into two types of models: statecharts for mode and media interactor design and mappings to define the data flow.

2. The missing consideration of undo steps. These are required to recover from failed action that the interaction technique

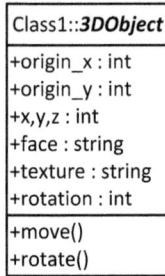

Fig. 1. Static model of the 3DObject.

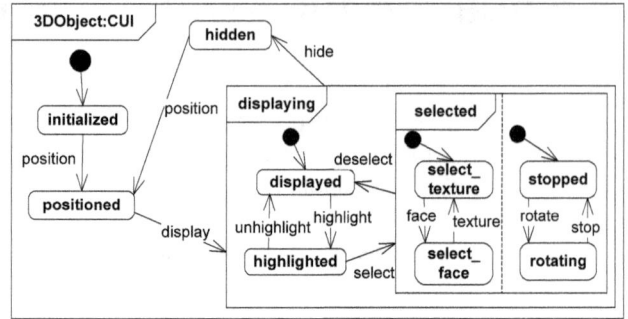

Fig. 2. Statechart of a 3D object to describe the behavior of its graphical presentation.

depends on while it is applied; we include the specification of undo steps as a notation feature in the data flow-based multimodal mappings.

3. The missing incorporation of output modalities as part of the model abstraction. In NiMMiT output modalities are added by custom tasks, which need to be coded or scripted. We separate the modality design from the interaction technique design and therefore make both, output media formats as well as the control modes characteristics re-usable and referable for the interaction technique design.

The paper is structured as follows: In the next section we present the basic idea of our approach: First, the interactor-based modeling of interfaces and interaction resources followed by an introduction about the multimodal mapping concept. They are used to synchronize models and combine interactors. We use the same interaction technique use case as it was presented for describing and evaluating NiMMiT: the Object-in-Hand metaphor to explain our approach and to ease the comparison between NiMMiT and MINT. Further notations are only discussed briefly, since they have been already compared to NiMMiT in [3]. Then, in the next section we compare both approaches in detail and list downsides and problems of both proposals. The comparison considers: the design models, the capabilities to model multimodal interactions, the capability to reuse existing models, error handling and iterative prototyping features. Finally, in the last section we conclude our approach.

2. MODELING INTERACTION TECHNIQUES

In [1] two different approaches for interaction modeling have been identified: State-driven notations based on formal mechanisms of finite state machines, such as the Harel State Tables [10] and data-driven approaches that define activities and their connections using data input and output ports. Following [1] in the interaction design domain state-driven notations have been used in ICO [14] and the Interact Objects Graph [5], whereas data flows have been applied in inTml [8], and Icon [6]. A data flow notation is also used in iStuff [17] to interconnect devices and in the Open Interface Framework [18] to compose multimodal interactions by combining device drivers, with filters and fusion algorithms. In data flow notations the control flow is managed by the data and therefore the major part of the control is defined inside the interconnected components. State-driven notations explicitly define the control by transitions and conditions. In [1] the authors mention a study that revealed that the lack of data handling is a restricting aspect for interaction technique modeling. Further on,

they state that with data flow notations the enabling and disabling of parts of an interaction technique can only be designed by complex structures. These motivated them to propose NiMMiT that merges both types of notations into "easy-to-learn and easy-to-read diagrams" [1].

3. MINT MULTIMODAL INTERACTION MODELING

Our approach on modeling multimodal interaction in based on three types of diagrams: UML class diagrams, SCXML-based statechart models, and a custom flow chart-based mapping notation that interconnects statecharts and is based on the multimodal relationships defined by the CARE properties [15].

As a running example to explain our approach we refer to the same interaction technique that has been used as a case study in NiMMiT, the Object-In-Hand metaphor that we briefly present in the next section. A detailed description and evaluation of this metaphor can be found in [2].

3.1 The Object-In-Hand-Metaphor

The Object-In-Hand metaphor is a two-handed interaction technique that is utilized in 3D worlds where common tasks are navigation, object selection and object manipulation.

The technique eases object manipulation and implements a sequential process: First the user points to an object, which then gets highlighted. The user confirms the selection by a click using the pointing device button and then uses the non-dominant hand to move the object to the center of the 3D scene by a grab gesture (a closed hand) towards the dominant hand. As long as the closed

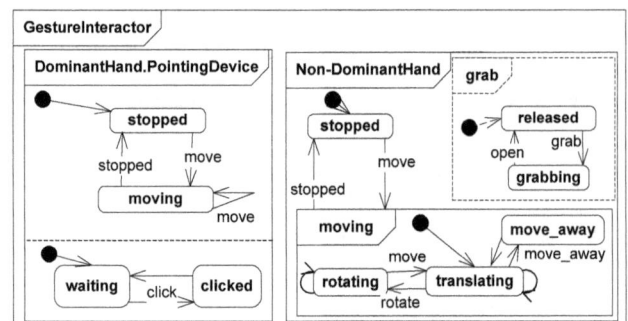

Fig. 3. Statechart of the control modality.

hand remains near the dominant hand holding the pointer, the object can be manipulated. In the NiMMiT case study changes of object faces and textures can be manipulated with the dominant pointing hand and object rotation is supported by rotating the non-dominant while it remains closed. Finally, with a throw away gesture the centralized object can be moved back to its original position in the 3D scene.

3.2 Interactor Modeling

With the MINT framework, multimodal user interfaces are assembled by interactors. An interactor mediates information between a user and an interactive system. It can receive input from the user to the system and send output from the system to the user. Each interactor is specified by a statechart that describes the interactor's behavior and uses a data structure to store and manipulate data that it receives from or sends to other interactors. We use UML class diagrams to specify the data structure. Figure 1 depicts the class definition of the 3DObject that contains the attributes and member functions that can be accessed by the mappings.

Figure 2 presents a concrete interactor that specifies the behavior of a 3D object representation that can be manipulated using the Object-in-Hand metaphor. During the application and before its presentation in the 3D scene it is positioned based on the pre-set object coordinates. While it is displayed as part of the scene, it can be highlighted and then be selected for manipulation. During object selection either the face or the texture can be set and the object can be rotated simultaneously to its manipulation.

A control mode, like the two-handed gesture interactor for performing the Object-In-Hand metaphor, depicted in figure 3, is specified by a statechart as well: It distinguishes between a dominant and a non-dominant hand that it processes in parallel. It assumes that the user interacts with a pointing device in the dominant hand that additionally offers a button. For the implementation of the interactors, the statecharts get instantiated as state machines and implement the API to the device driver to access a modality or to the final interface representation of the 3D object. Different to data flow-based implementations that black-box their components [18], [17] the statechart represents a model to the driver to reflect the component's relevant behavior. It can be used for the interaction by querying for active states or by subscribing to get notified about state changes. Further on, the data flow can be controlled, which we describe in the following section.

3.3 Multimodal Mappings

Multimodal mappings connect interactors. They are defined at three different levels of abstraction:

- *Application level*: A multimodal mapping that connects specific interactor instances; e.g. "If the 'confirm reservation' button is pressed then close the window."

- *Interactor level*: A mapping that is pre-defined together with the interactor designs ("the meta level") to be used later on for concrete application development. E.g. "Each time a button is pressed play a 'click' sound".

- *Metaphor level*: A mapping that specifies an interaction paradigm, such as e.g. a "drag-and-drop" or a "double-click" that was prepared to work with the designed interactor set.

Figure 4 depicts the relevant mappings to specify the Object-In-Hand interaction technique to manipulate the 3D object interactors using the gesture interactor. We use a custom notation: Boxes with rounded edges stand for "observations" of state changes. Boxes with sharp edges define "actions", which are backend function calls (FC), event triggers or the activation of another mapping. Observations and actions are connected by an operator that specifies a relation between the observations. The default relation is a sequential one „S", which defines a top-down sequential processing of the observations. Actions are always processed sequentially. Further operators are based on the CARE properties [17]: A complementary "C" relation set observations that complement each other and need to be retrieved in a temporal window Tw. An assignment "A" requires a set of observations of a specific mode, redundant "R" relations require at least two observations from different modes, to execute the actions, and equivalent "E" relations define alternative observations.

The Object-In-Hand interaction technique is composed by five multimodal mappings: Two interactor level mappings ("Highlighting", "Selection") and three mappings at the metaphor level.

Both interactor level mappings define the way that the pointing device is used to control the concrete media representation of the interface. Interface highlighting happens if the pointing device is directed to a 3D object. Thus, if the pointing device remains for a certain amount of time in the same position, it is assumed to be "stopped", which evaluates the first observation of the highlighting mapping to true and sets the coordinates of the pointer. Since the mapping specifies a sequential relation, only

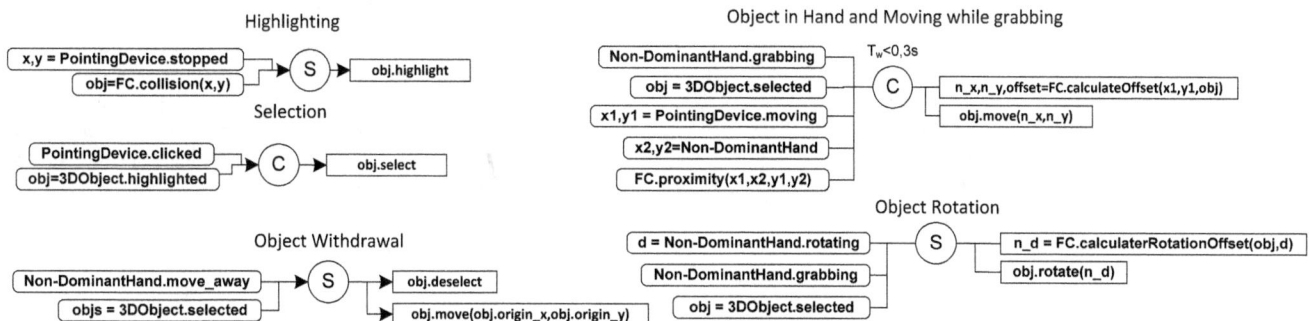

Fig. 4. The multimodal mappings used to model the Object-in-Hand interaction technique.

after the coordinates of the stopped pointer are known the mapping checks for a collision of the pointer with a 3D object. In case there is a collision, the object is saved in the "obj" variable and the mapping triggers its action to send a highlight event to this object.

In the same manner the selection mapping is processed and runs in parallel to the other mappings. But since it requires an object to be highlighted while the pointing device button is "clicked" (the complementary "C" relation), it is connected to the "highlighting" mapping.

The Object-In-Hand interaction technique is specified by three mappings. For the sake of brevity we will just describe the Object-In-Hand mapping, which is the most complex one. Since it specifies a complementary relation, all observations are processed at the same time, in a temporal window of Tw = 300ms. The arrowless lines define this mapping as a binding: As long as the observations remain true, updated variables of the observations are directly fed into sequential processing of the actions. The actions calculate the object offset to the center of the scene and then moves the selected object.

4. COMPARISON with NiMMiT

In this section, we compare MINT with NiMMiT [1], which was to the best of our knowledge the first notation for modeling multimodal interaction techniques that combined a state-driven with a data flow-driven modeling. Other, data flow-driven notations have been already evaluated by the authors of NiMMiT in [3].

This section is structured into several subsections. First we briefly describe the NiMMiT notation using the Object-In-hand use case, then we compare both notations in detail by analyzing their design models, the capacity to consider multimodal interaction, identify mechanism to support reuse and error management, and finally discuss their processes to support iterative prototyping.

4.1 NiMMiT

Figure 5 depicts the NiMMiT diagram of the Object-In-Hand interaction technique as presented by the authors in [2]. NiMMiT diagrams can be read like state transition diagrams. Thus, an interaction has a start and end state, depicted as cycles and several intermediary states connected by transitions and task chains. Events, generated by user inputs trigger a task chain that is depicted as a shaded rectangle. Task chains describe a sequential process of interconnected tasks. Each task (e.g. "Calculate Offset") can exchange data using input and output ports (e.g. "offset", "origin") with other tasks of the same chain. The geometry of the black symbol defines the data type. Using labels, data can be shared over the entire diagram and between task chains. Labels are depicted beside a task chain (e.g. "selected") and are connected to input or output ports. After a task chain has been processed a transition to the next state is performed. NiMMiT models can be-reused in a hierarchical structure. For instance the "Select Object" task is specified in a different model.

4.2 Design Models

The NiMMiT notation implements the requirements to be event-driven, state-driven, data flow-driven, and the support for hierarchical reuse. The inclusion of all four aspects in one single diagram is an advantage of the notation.

MINT requires three different types of models: class diagrams, statecharts, and multimodal mappings, but captures the interaction technique specification by the multimodal mapping notation. Both approaches use a proprietary notation that needs to be learned.

The distribution into a set of multimodal mappings to compose an interaction technique specification of MINT solves the state explosion problems from NiMMiT with complex interaction techniques. Since all MINT mappings are processed in parallel by default, no explicit transitions need to be added. An example is the handling of the "gesture_moveaway" event that is used to finish the interaction technique use and moves the manipulated 3D object back to its original position. With MINT the "Object Withdrawel" mapping is always active by default (figure 4).

With NiMMiT (figure 5), explicit transitions have to be defined for each new state in that the "gesture_moveaway" event should be supported. MINT also supports sequential composition of mappings, to specify that one successful mapping can activate another mapping and therefore reflect the default behavior of NiMMiT. But in our experience this behavior is rarely needed. A strict prevention of a certain behavior that was available in a previous context irritates users. Often certain behavior also does not need to be restricted explicitly: For instance, it is not a problem that the "gesture_moveaway" gesture is also active in the case that no object has been selected. Much more frequently, we have experienced commands that have been predefined to control a certain interface, in that a specific interaction technique is embedded and therefore needs to consider predefined commands. An example are the interactor-level mappings that are common interface commands and are reused in the interaction technique and need to be considered to be used in all subsequent steps of the interaction technique. Using NiMMiT a command that always can be processed can only be modeled by adding transitions to all states of the interaction technique specification.

4.3 Multimodal Interaction

Both notations consider multimodal interaction. In NiMMiT sequential, parallel and equivalent relations are implemented by event-based conditions with the transitions (and, or). With MINT, the operators that connect observations with actions are used to specify: sequential, complementary, assignment, equivalent and redundant relations. Additional, with MINT, a temporal window can be set to specify temporally related events.

Different to MINT, NiMMiT does not explicitly design the capabilities of modalities. Instead, it requires modalities to trigger events to that an interaction technique can react. Events can be grouped into "families" according to their originating modality or device. Whereas it preserves simplicity, which was one of the design goals of NiMMiT, this approach has two limitations:

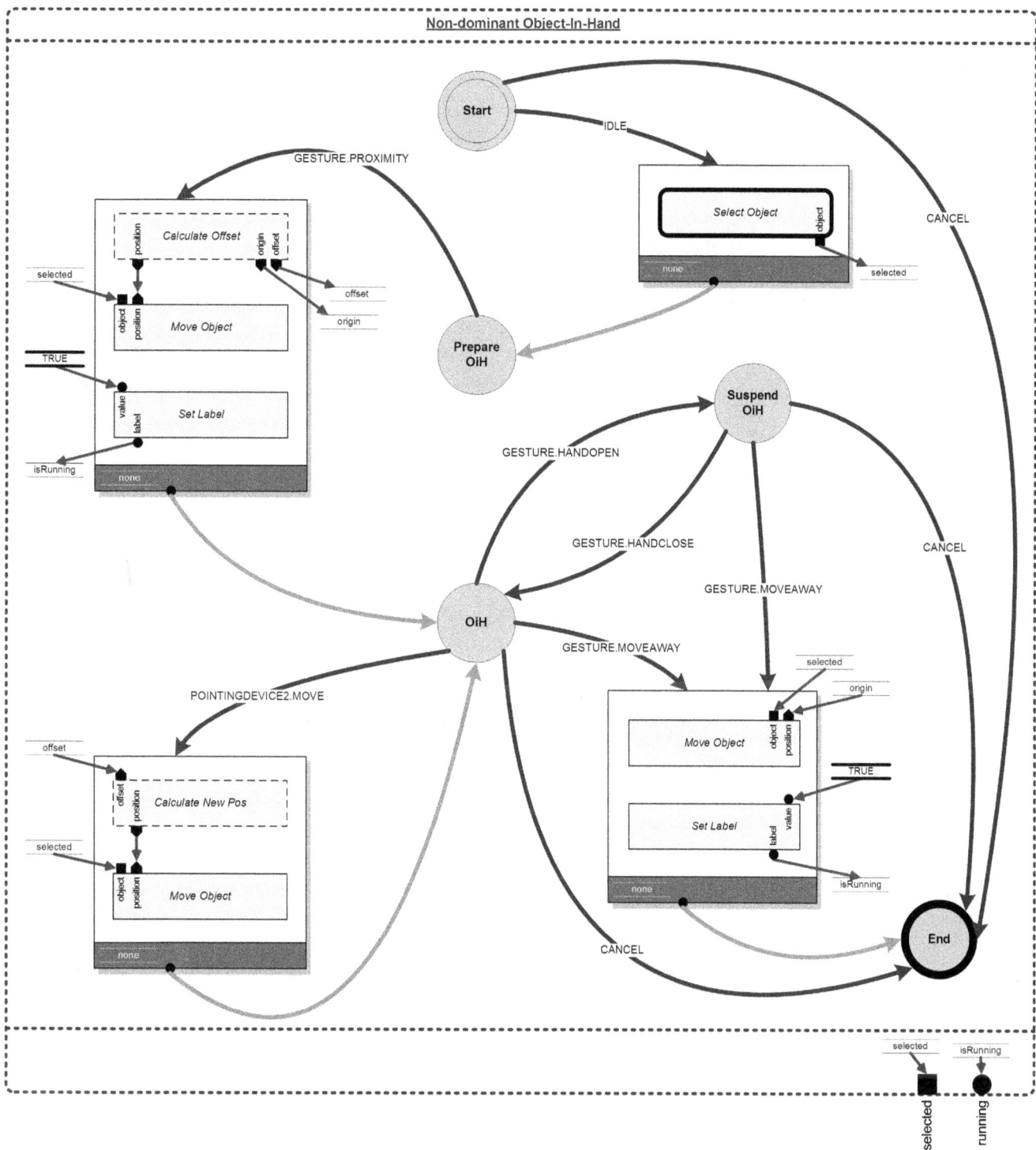

Fig. 5. The NiMMIT model for the dominant hand part of the Object-in-Hand interaction technique. Taken from [[1]]

First, output modalities need to be controlled by custom scripted tasks, as the authors mentioned in [1]. With MINT there is no difference in the design and usage of input (that we call mode) and output modalities (which we call media). Figure 6 illustrates an example that adds a second modality to an existing mapping that specifies object highlighting: a confirming "clicking" sound that is played each time an object gets highlighted. There are two ways to design this behavior with MINT. One option is to model the redundant output (visual highlighting and sound output) as an application level mapping like shown in figure 6a using the redundant operator. The other option is a more abstract interactor level mapping definition that defines that always, if an object is highlighted (independently if it was triggered by the pointing device), a sound should be played.

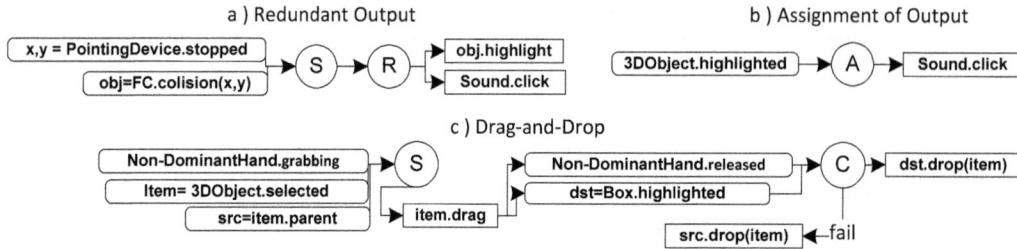

a) Redundant Output

x,y = PointingDevice.stopped
obj=FC.colision(x,y)
S → R
obj.highlight
Sound.click

b) Assignment of Output

3DObject.highlighted → A → Sound.click

c) Drag-and-Drop

Non-DominantHand.grabbing
Item= 3DObject.selected
src=item.parent
→ S
item.drag
Non-DominantHand.released
dst=Box.highlighted
→ C → dst.drop(item)
src.drop(item) ← fail

Fig. 6. Mappings with redundant output (a+b) and error handling (c).

Second, to our knowledge, with NiMMiT, a data flow can be specified only between tasks. Tasks of different task sets can exchange data using variables that are called labels. But data input or output from modalities is not considered explicitly in the design notation. An example is depicted in figure 5 by the "PointingDevice2.Move" event triggering the transition originating from the "OiH" state. The task set that is activated by this transition consumes data from the "offset" label that has been calculated by a preceding task set. But which modality is used to produce the output position data is hidden within the "Calculate New Pos" task. In MINT the data flow between a modality and the interaction technique is specified explicitly. Thus, for instance in the "Object In Hand" mapping of figure 4, the data flow of the moving pointing device is set to move the 3D object (as long as it remains in proximity to the non-dominant hand).

4.4 Reuse

An interaction technique frequently includes reoccurring elements, such as tasks to select, remove or confirm. Thus, supporting reuse when modeling new interaction techniques prevents re-designs of already existing techniques.

NiMMiT supports encapsulation of tasks for a hierarchical reuse. Such a task encapsulation is used in the Object-in-Hand NiMMiT model depicted in figure 5. The "Select Object" task has been separately designed, since object selection can be considered a very common task, and therefore has been reused for the Object-in-Hand model.

Different to the explicit reference in NiMMiT, in MINT a set of mappings without the need for direct references defines an interaction technique. This has the advantage that if an interaction

technique depends on several reusable tasks that should be available in all of the states of the new interaction technique there is no need to explicitly reference the included component.

From the ease-of-use perspective the implicit reference (by existence) is rather hard to use as it requires the designer to know about all active mappings. But often most of the mappings are defined at the interactor-level and are connected to a specific modality or device. Thus, like in our example in figure 4, mappings define actions or events for a specific device, like the pointing device, which should be always used for selecting and highlighting objects. In practice interactor level mappings are easy to memorize since they usually define the default actions for a specific modality or device.

4.5 Error Handling

NiMMiT does not include error handling to recover from a failure that happens when an interaction technique is used [16].

In MINT, multimodal mappings can consider error cases. Figure 6c illustrates how an error handling can be defined to undo an action that has been partly done using an interaction technique. The mapping defines a drag and drop interaction technique between 3D objects that are stored in two different boxes. By defining a fail-case for the second operator (the complementary relation) the mapping ensures that after a user has started to drag a 3D object, it is returned to its origin box if the user has failed to drop it to another box.

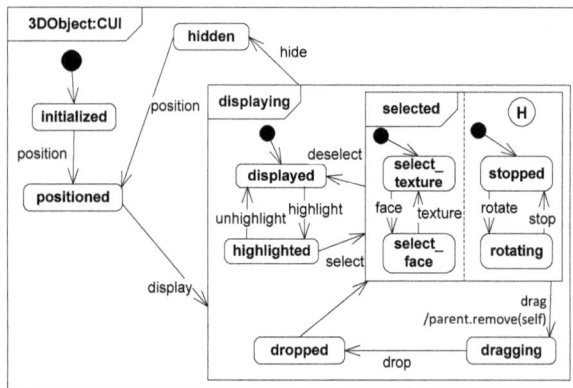

Fig. 7. Redesign of the 3DObject Statechart to consider drag-and-dropping.

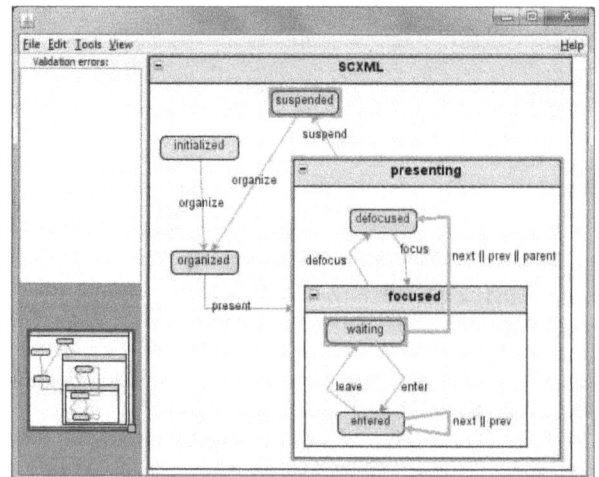

Fig. 8. The adopted scxmlgui editor to design SCXML-based statesharts.

4.6 Iterative Prototyping

Both, MiMMiT and MINT offer an application framework to interpret the diagrams at runtime to quickly test and compare design alternatives without much coding effort. To further support the designer creating new interaction techniques both notations are tool supported and save their models in XML. According to [1] the NiMMiT process is a sequential one: After a NiMMiT model has been designed with a tool, it is saved in XML, and the loaded and executed in the application framework.

In MINT the initial deployment of the interaction technique to the platform follows the same process like NiMMiT, but requires two design tools: One, an adopted version of the scxmlgui editor [13], is used to specify the statechart for describing the behavior of the widgets and the interaction resources, and a second one to design the multimodal mappings. Figure 8 shows a screenshot of the former one.

After the platform has been started with the initial deployment of a prototype, both design tools can be connected to the platform to observe the mappings and states of the statecharts being activated while the interaction technique is used. In MINT the iterative prototyping cycle length has been further reduced: statecharts can be manipulated when the application is running with the restriction that a state cannot be removed while it is active. An animation of the active states in the design tool supports the designer to identify these states. Manipulations at runtime ease to correct usability problems and to fix errors when they occur.

Figure 6c) depicts a further interaction technique, a drag-and-drop like technique that enables a user to grab 3D objects out of a box into another one. This mapping can be added as a new mapping at system runtime without the need to restart running applications. But for the mapping to function with the 3D object, the object's behavior needs to be adjusted by adding two new states: "dragging" and "dropped" to the statechart like depicted in figure 7.

We have evaluated the MINT framework against the requirements of the W3C multimodal initiative, which requires a multimodal toolkit to implement a structural mechanism for user interface composition, an explicit control structure, an extensible event definition mechanism, consider data modeling, and offer reusable components in [8]. Further on, the MINT framework has been classified by using the characteristics for multimodal frameworks proposed by Dumas et.al. [7]. An initial performance analysis has been performed [8].

5. CONCLUSION

This paper presents MINT, a model-based approach to design multimodal interaction techniques. The graphical notation combines statecharts to design modalities and media features, uses data flow based mapping, and is targeted to allow the explorative design of multimodal interactions to compare different variants without much coding effort.

Previous approaches can be classified in either statechart-driven or data flow-driven proposals. NiMMiT was the first graphical notation to combine both, but suffers from a set of limitations: State explosion for complex models, no explicit design support for output modalities, and missing error handling.

MINT addresses each of these aspects by separating statechart and data flow into two different complementary models and a notation for defining recovery steps inside the definition of the interaction

techniques. We illustrate our approach by using the same use case that has been used for describing NiMMiT: The Object-In-Hand interaction technique. We demonstrate further advances of MINT that reduce the iterative prototyping cycles by supporting model manipulation at runtime to improve usability and inconsistencies.

6. ACKNOWLEDGMENTS

Sebastian Feuerstack is grateful to the Deutsche Forschungsgemeinschaft (DFG) for the financial support of this work.

7. REFERENCES

[1] Boeck, J. D.; Vanacken, D.; Raymaekers, C. & Coninx, K. (2007), 'High-Level Modeling of Multimodal Interaction Techniques Using NiMMiT', *Journal of Virtual Reality and Broadcasting* **4**(2).

[2] Boeck, J. D. ; Cuppens, E.; De Weyer, T.; Raymaekers, C. & Coninx, K. (2004), Multisensory interaction metaphors with haptics and proprioception in virtual environments, *in* 'Proceedings of the third Nordic conference on Human-computer interaction', ACM, New York, NY, USA, pp. 189--197.

[3] Boeck, J. D.; Raymaekers, C. & Coninx, K. (2007), Comparing NiMMiT and data-driven notations for describing multimodal interaction, in 'Proceedings of the 5th international conference on Task models and diagrams for users interface design', Springer-Verlag, Berlin, Heidelberg, pp. 217--229.

[4] Calvary, G.; Coutaz, J.; Thevenin, D.; Limbourg, Q.; Bouillon, L. & Vanderdonckt, J. (2003), 'A Unifying Reference Framework for Multi-Target User Interfaces', *Interacting with Computers* **15**(3), 289--308.

[5] Carr, D. A. (1997), 'Interaction Object Graphs: An Executable Graphical Notation for Specifying User Interfaces', *Formal Methods in Human-Computer Interaction*, Springer, pp. 141--155.

[6] Dragicevic, P. & Fekete, J.-D. (2004), Support for input adaptability in the ICON toolkit, *in* 'Proceedings of the 6th international conference on Multimodal interfaces', ACM, New York, NY, USA, pp. 212--219.

[7] Dumas, B.; Lalanne, D. and Oviatt, S. (2009), 'Multimodal interfaces: A survey of principles, models and frameworks', Human Machine Interaction, pp. 3--26.

[8] Feuerstack, S. and Pizzolato, E. (2012 Engineering Device-spanning, Multimodal Web Applications using a Model-based Design Approach, WebMedia 2012, the 18th Brazilian Symposium on Multimedia and the Web, October 15-18, 2012, São Paulo/SP, Brazil

[9] Figueroa, P.; Green, M. & Hoover, H. J. (2002), InTml: a description language for VR applications, *in* 'Proceedings of the seventh international conference on 3D Web technology', ACM, New York, NY, USA, pp. 53--58.

[10] Harel, D. (1987), 'Statecharts: A visual formalism for complex systems', *Sci. Comput. Program.* **8**(3), pp. 231-274.

[11] Lehmann, G.; Blumendorf, M.; Feuerstack, S. & Albayrak, S. (2008), Utilizing Dynamic Executable Models for User Interface Development, *in* T. C. Nicholas Graham &

Philippe Palanque, ed., 'Interactive Systems - Design, Specification, and Verification', Springer-Verlag Gmbh.

[12] Meixner, G.; Paterno, F. & Vanderdonckt, J. (2011), 'Past, Present, and Future of Model-Based User Interface Development', *i-com* **10**(3), pp. 2-11.

[13] Morbini, F. (2011), 'Scxmlgui', http://code.google.com/p/scxmlgui/, last accessed 08/01/13

[14] Navarre, D.; Palanque, P.; Bastide, R.; Schyn, A.; Winckler, M.; Nedel, L. & Freitas, C. (2005), A Formal Description of Multimodal Interaction Techniques for Immersive Virtual Reality Applications, *in* Maria Francesca Costabile & Fabio Paternò, ed., 'Human-Computer Interaction - INTERACT 2005: IFIP TC13 International Conference, Rome, Italy', Springer-Verlag GmbH, , pp. 170.

[15] Nigay, L. & Coutaz, J. (1997), Multifeature Systems: The CARE Properties and Their Impact on Software

Design'Intelligence and Multimodality in Multimedia Interfaces'.

[16] Raymaekers, C.; Vanacken, L.; Boeck, J. D. & Coninx, K. (2008), High-Level Descriptions for Multimodal Interaction in Virtual Environments, *in* 'Proceedings of CHI 2008'.

[17] Ringel, M.; Tyler, J.; Stone, M.; Ballagas, R. & Borchers, J. (2002), iStuff: A Scalable Architecture for Lightweight, Wireless Devices for Ubicomp User Interfaces, *in* 'Proceedings of UBICOMP 2002'.

[18] Serrano, M.; Nigay, L.; Lawson, J.-Y. L.; Ramsay, A.; Murray-Smith, R. & Denef, S. (2008), The openinterface framework: a tool for multimodal interaction., *in* 'CHI '08 Extended Abstracts on Human Factors in Computing Systems', ACM, New York, NY, USA, pp. 3501--3506

jRDFa: Browsing and Visualization of Linked Data on the Web

André Carlomagno Rocha, Tito Gardel P. Filho, Marilton Cerqueira, Cássio V. S. Prazeres
Universidade Federal da Bahia – Departamento de Ciência da Computação
MultiViUW: Laboratório de Pesquisa e Experimentação em
Multimídia, Computação Visual, Computação Ubíqua e Web
Av. Adhemar de Barros, Ondina, Salvador-BA, Brasil
{andreluiz, titogardel, mmcerqueira, prazeres}@dcc.ufba.br

ABSTRACT

Several efforts in research and development of technologies have been spent to publish data in open standard formats. The main project in this regard is the Linked Open Data, which goal is to create an open and semantic Web of Data, enabling processing and understanding the data by software agents. However, not only the machines can take advantage of the explicit semantics of data. People can take advantage from the semantic of the data to explore unknown concepts, new relationships and to obtain personalized access to relevant resources and services. However, it is not trivial for a user without experience with Web of Data, to satisfactorily explore and use these data. This paper presents the jRDFa, an approach to support the web developer interested in presenting to non-technical users, semantic data embedded in HTML pages in RDFa format. This paper also presents two ways of presenting data in RDFa that were created using the jRDFa: tooltips visualization and facets navigation. To evaluate the proposed approach, this paper presents results of experiments on HTML pages with embedded jRDFa.

Categories and Subject Descriptors

H.5.4 [**INFORMATION INTERFACES AND PRESENTATION**]: Hypertext/Hypermedia – *Navigation, User issues.*

Keywords

Linked Data, jRDFa, Visualização, Navegação, Tooltips, Facetas.

1. INTRODUÇÃO

A representação da informação na Web tem evoluído de um espaço global de documentos interligados, a Web de Documentos, para um espaço global em que tanto documentos quanto dados podem estar conectados. No intuito dessa evolução está um conjunto de melhores práticas para publicar, conectar, reutilizar e consumir dados estruturados na Web conhecido como *Linked Data* [3]. A adoção dessas melhores práticas está possibilitando o desenvolvimento de um ambiente global de dados, chamado de Web de Dados [5]. Segundo Bizer [4], a Web de Dados e a Web de Documentos podem conviver, no mesmo espaço e ao mesmo tempo.

Nesse sentido, esforços para aproximar essas duas abordagens (documentos e dados) têm sido realizados, como é o caso da recomendação W3C RDFa [1]. O RDFa é uma das formas de serializar dados estruturados no formato RDF [13]. Especificamente, RDFa permite embutir triplas RDF em documentos HTML usando os próprios atributos da linguagem de marcação. Ao incorporar essas estruturas de metadados em páginas HTML, autores são capazes de indicar aos agentes de software o significado de dados que são exibidos para usuários humanos (informações legíveis por humanos), transformando-os em dados legíveis por máquinas [15].

Na prática, RDFa refere-se a dados semânticos – obedecendo aos princípios de *Linked Data* – embutidos na Web de Documentos, de tal forma que possam ser lidos e entendidos por máquinas [2]. Entretanto, não apenas as máquinas podem se beneficiar da semântica explícita e da estruturação dos dados que seguem os princípios de *Linked Data* [17]. Pessoas podem se beneficiar da semântica dos dados para explorar conceitos desconhecidos, novos relacionamentos e obter acesso personalizado a recursos e serviços relevantes. Contudo, não é trivial, para um usuário sem experiência com a Web de Dados, explorar e usar esses dados de maneira satisfatória [6].

Para Camarda et al. [7], apesar das centenas de milhares de triplas RDF já existentes na Web de Dados, é difícil encontrar ferramentas de apresentação fáceis de usar, que sejam realmente baseadas em padrões RDF e capazes de demonstrar a eficácia do modelo *Linked Data*. Davies et al. [9] argumentam que: se a finalidade é a de que os usuários finais possam contribuir para a Web de Dados da mesma forma que eles contribuem para a Web de Documentos, então eles precisam de ferramentas, adequadas à sua condição de usuários não técnicos, que lhes permitam fazê-lo. Além disso, para Cheng et al. [8], comparado com hipertexto da Web, *Linked Data* pode satisfazer mais precisamente as necessidades de informação, no entanto, ainda faltam ferramentas direcionadas para usuários não técnicos.

Considerando os benefícios que podem ser obtidos por usuários finais diante da semântica dos dados, a falta de habilidade desses usuários no trato com tais dados e a carência de ferramentas com foco na apresentação de dados semânticos, baseadas nos princípios *Linked Data*, este trabalho apresenta a jRDFa (*Javasript for RDFa*).

A jRDFa é uma abordagem para apoiar o desenvolvedor Web que deseja apresentar, para seus usuários, dados semânticos embutidos em páginas HTML no formato RDFa. A abordagem proposta está implementada como uma biblioteca *Javascript*, que fornece recursos para lidar, de forma simples e fácil, com as informações semânticas contidas nessas páginas. A biblioteca abstrai as tarefas de recuperação e tratamento de tais informações, deixando o desenvolvedor livre para se ater apenas na criação de suas formas de apresentação. Para demonstrar a utilização da biblioteca, duas formas de apresentação de conhecimento semântico foram desenvolvidas: uma usando visualização por *tooltips* e outra usando navegação por facetas.

O restante deste artigo está estruturado da seguinte forma: a Seção 2 apresenta e descreve jRDFa, que é a abordagem proposta neste trabalho; na Seção 3 são descritas duas formas de apresentação de informações semânticas geradas pela jRDFa; a Seção 4 apresenta experimentos realizados para avaliação de desempenho da biblioteca; na Seção 5 são apresentados trabalhos relacionados à abordagem proposta neste artigo; e na Seção 6 são apresentadas algumas considerações finais e direções para trabalhos futuros.

2. jRDFa: *JavaScript for RDFa*

A abordagem jRDFa (*JavaScript for RDFa*) é uma proposta que foi desenvolvida com objetivo de possibilitar que usuários humanos também possam tirar proveito da semântica explícita da Web de Dados. A proposta possibilita a recuperação de dados semânticos contidos em páginas Web, mais precisamente em documentos HTML, e fornece informações previamente tratadas que podem ser utilizadas para melhorar a experiência das pessoas com a Web de Dados, por meio de formas dinâmicas de apresentação.

Neste trabalho, a jRDFa foi implementada como uma extensão à biblioteca jQuery, que é uma biblioteca *JavaScript*, independente de navegador (*browser*), criada com o intuito de simplificar o desenvolvimento de scripts em documentos HTML. Dessa forma, a implementação da jRDFa também é uma biblioteca *JavaScript*, para documentos HTML e independente de navegador.

Na prática, o objetivo da biblioteca é extrair conteúdo semântico, representado por RDFa, de páginas HTML e prover visualização e navegação desse conteúdo para usuários humanos.

Esta seção apresenta os detalhes da arquitetura da biblioteca jRDFa, seu funcionamento e forma de utilização. A seção também descreve os dois algoritmos propostos neste trabalho para resolver dois problemas encontrados durante o desenvolvimento da proposta: o problema do *blank node* e o problema da ancoragem.

2.1 Arquitetura da jRDFa

A biblioteca jRDFa é composta por quatro módulos principais: Módulo de Apresentação (MAP), Módulo de Resolução Blank Node (MRB), Módulo de Resolução Ancoragem (MRA) e Módulo de Aquisição (MAQ). Esses módulos estão distribuídos em três camadas, como pode ser visto na Figura 1: Camada de Interface e Apresentação (CIA), Camada de Processamento Semântico (CPS) e Camada de Aquisição RDFa (CAR).

Na Camada de Aquisição RDFa (CAR) os dados semânticos contidos na página Web, descritos por meio de RDFa, são recuperados e adicionados a um grafo RDF, criado no momento do carregamento da biblioteca. Em seguida, esses dados são enviados para a Camada de Processamento Semântico (CPS), com o objetivo de serem tratados adequadamente. O resultado desse tratamento são informações semânticas mais amigáveis, próprias ao consumo de usuários não técnicos. Em outras palavras, o tratamento diz respeito à renomeação de recursos RDF de forma conveniente, abstraindo os URIs, para oferecer uma melhor compreensão ao usuário.

Depois do processamento dos dados na CPS, as informações tratadas são encaminhadas para a Camada de Interface e

Apresentação (CIA). Essa camada pode ser estendida, por meio do Módulo de Apresentação (MAP), com novas formas de apresentação (navegação e visualização, por exemplo), usando as informações amigáveis fornecidas pela biblioteca. Neste artigo, duas formas de apresentação foram desenvolvidas, como extensão do módulo MAP, e são descritas e discutidas na Seção 3.

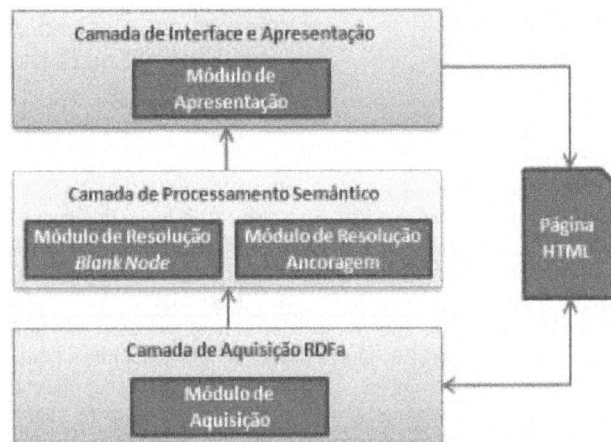

Figura 1. Arquitetura jRDFa.

Explicando o fluxo mais detalhadamente, após o término do carregamento da página Web, o MAQ (Módulo de Aquisição) recupera todas as entradas RDFa contidas no documento, por meio de um *parser* semântico (Green Turtle [11]) e monta o grafo correspondente. Ou seja, nesse momento todas as informações semânticas (triplas RDF) contidas na página Web são recuperadas e adicionadas a um grafo RDF. Em seguida, esse modelo é enviado para a CPS, onde é tratado pelos MRB (Módulo de Resolução Blank Node) e MRA (Módulo de Resolução Ancoragem) para resolver os respectivos problemas (seções 2.2 e 2.3).

Depois de processado e atualizado, o modelo é encaminhado, sob a forma de informações amigáveis, para a CIA que, por meio do MAP (Módulo de Apresentação), será responsável por apresentar as informações semânticas ao usuário. O MAP possui interfaces bem definidas que o desenvolvedor deve obedecer, para criar novas formas de apresentação, que vão recuperar as informações amigáveis a serem utilizadas na apresentação exibida para o usuário. Por exemplo, o desenvolvedor pode criar uma visualização de dados semânticos na forma de *tooltips*. Quando o usuário passar o ponteiro do mouse sobre um recurso RDF, um *tooltip* será exibido contendo as informações amigáveis relacionadas a tal recurso. Da mesma maneira, o desenvolvedor pode criar uma navegação facetada usando as informações tratadas pela biblioteca. Assim, o usuário terá à sua disposição a opção de navegar por meio de facetas em dados relacionados aos recursos presentes na página Web que ele está visitando.

2.2 Resolução do problema do *blank node*

Durante o processo de aperfeiçoamento da proposta, alguns problemas peculiares à natureza estruturada dos dados foram encontrados e tratados. O primeiro deles é o problema do *blank node*. Em um grafo RDF, um *blank node* é um nó que representa um recurso para o qual não foi definido um URI ou um literal. Um *blank node* só pode ser usado como sujeito ou objeto de uma tripla e um recurso representado por um *blank node* é chamado de recurso anônimo.

Como o objetivo da jRDFa é apresentar dados semânticos para usuários não técnicos, a exibição de um recurso anônimo (não nomeado por um URI ou literal), identificado apenas por um *ID*, torna-se um problema para a compreensão das informações. Para resolver essa questão, todos os *blank nodes* são resolvidos utilizando o algoritmo apresentado na Figura 2. Com esse algoritmo todos os *blank nodes* são nomeados antes da disponibilização das informações amigáveis para a camada de apresentação (CIA).

```
1. triplesArray = getTriplesBySubject(BlankNode)
2. forEach(triplesArray)
3.     objectsArray.add(triplesArray.getObject())
4. endForEach
5. return = getRepresentObj(objectsArray)
```

Figura 2. Algoritmo de resolução de blank nodes.

O algoritmo funciona da seguinte forma, primeiro, *triplesArray* (linha 1 da Figura 2) armazena todas as triplas que possuem um determinado *blank node* como sujeito. Para cada uma dessas triplas, *objectsArray* (linha 3 da Figura 2) armazena o objeto da tripla. Ao final do processo, o algoritmo retorna o objeto que melhor representa o *blank node*. Essa tarefa é realizada pela função *getRepresentObj* (linha 5 da Figura 2), que determina o objeto mais representativo, considerando o predicado de cada objeto em *objectsArray*. Por exemplo, o dado que melhor representa uma pessoa é seu nome. Portando, se o *blank node* se refere a uma pessoa, o objeto que melhor representa esse recurso é o que possui o predicado *name*.

A Figura 3 exibe parte da lista de predicados considerados como mais representativos. A lista está ordenada por prioridade, onde *name* é o predicado de maior representatividade.

Para definir a lista, primeiro foram consideradas as características comuns encontradas na variedade de tipos de recursos presentes na Web de Dados (pessoa, organização, evento, produto, lugar, entre outros). Para muitos desses tipos, a informação que melhor os representa é seu nome (João, SBC, WebMedia2013, Notebook 123abc, Salvador, etc.). No entanto, no caso de um recurso não possuir nome (ou o nome não ter sido definido), a informação mais amigável, a ser apresentada para um usuário final, é o email seguido do título. Por exemplo, considerando um artigo acadêmico, talvez não seja comum definir um nome para tal recurso nem, tão pouco, um email, mas, muito provavelmente, seja definido um título. Recursos como páginas Web ou arquivos mantidos na Internet são certamente melhor representados por seus endereços eletrônicos (por exemplo, uma URL). Essa lógica foi seguida para todos os tipos de recursos. Nos casos em que o recurso não possui nome, email, título ou URL, pode possuir um endereço (addressLocality), no caso de um lugar, ou pode possuir um preço (lowPrice), no caso de um produto, e assim por diante conforme Figura 3.

O segundo ponto considerado foi a heterogeneidade dos termos utilizados pelos diversos vocabulários contidos na Web de Dados. Muitos vocabulários definem as mesmas informações utilizando termos distintos. Por exemplo, o vocabulário FOAF define um nome como *name* ou *givenName* e uma imagem como *img*, *image* ou *depiction*. Dessa forma, neste trabalho todas as variações fazem parte da lista. A quantidade de vocabulários existentes hoje na Web de Dados deve continuar crescendo. A lista de predicados foi baseada apenas nos vocabulários mais conhecidos e frequentemente utilizados (foaf, schema, dc, skos, dentre outros). A lista também pode ser incrementada com a análise de novos vocabulários.

1.	name	9.	addressLocality
2.	givenName	10.	lowPrice
3.	familyName	11.	mbox
4.	email	12.	...
5.	title	13.	...
6.	homepage	14.	...
7.	Organization	15.	...
8.	type	16.	...

Figura 3. Parte da lista de predicados mais representativos.

De modo geral, um determinado *blank node* pode ser sujeito de mais de uma tripla. Por exemplo, podem existir três triplas contendo o mesmo *blank node* como sujeito: a primeira com predicado *givenName*; a segunda com predicado *homepage*; e a terceira com predicado *email*. Com base na lista de predicados, o algoritmo vai resolver da seguinte forma: o objeto que melhor representa esse *blank node* é aquele que possui o predicado *givenName*, pois esse predicado tem prioridade sobre *email* e *homepage*. A partir daí, esse recurso (inicialmente tratado por um *ID*) passa a ser conhecido pelo valor contido no objeto da tripla que possui o predicado *givenName*. O valor desse objeto pode ser João ou Maria, que visualmente tem mais significado para o usuário que, por exemplo, um *email* como joao@dcc.ufba.br, ou uma *homepage* como http://www.maria.com.

2.3 Resolução do problema da ancoragem

O problema da ancoragem diz respeito a mapear um recurso (com todos os dados aos quais ele está ligado diretamente) para um elemento HTML, contendo a informação que melhor representa tal recurso (<*span*>infoMaisRep</*span*>). Esse mapeamento é importante porque facilita a exibição de recursos para os usuários finais, organizando as informações em pontos estratégicos da página.

Para encontrar a informação mais representativa de um determinado recurso na página HTML, foi criado neste trabalho o algoritmo de resolução de ancoragem apresentado na Figura 4. Esse algoritmo recupera tal informação por meio do algoritmo de resolução de *blank nodes*. Com essa informação, o conjunto de dados, que representa o recurso, pode ser ancorado na página Web por meio de um elemento DOM HTML.

```
1. representInfo = resolvesBlankNode(subject)
2. element = representInfo.getDOMElement()
3. If (element.isNotSpan())
4.     span = createsNewSpan(); span.content = element.content
5.     element.content = empty; element.appendAsChild(span)
6.     element = span
7. endIf
8. anchorsInfoSet(element)
```

Figura 4. Algoritmo de resolução de ancoragem.

O tipo de elemento escolhido para essa tarefa foi o elemento *span*, por não alterar o layout da apresentação. Nos casos em que o elemento retornado pelo algoritmo de resolução de *blank nodes* já for do tipo *span*, a ancoragem (mapeamento) é efetivada. Nos outros casos, um novo elemento do tipo *span* é criado e adicionado ao DOM como filho do elemento retornado, e, em seguida, a ancoragem é efetivada no novo elemento *span*. O conteúdo do elemento retornado (informação mais representativa) é transferido para o novo elemento *span*.

Por exemplo, considerando que o recurso "pedro" é sujeito de três triplas: *pedro-temNome-Pedro*; *pedro-temEmail-pedro@ufba.br;* e *pedro-temTipo-Pessoa*. Essas informações dizem respeito à pessoa nomeada Pedro e formam um conjunto único de informações. Esse conjunto será atrelado a um elemento HTML da página para melhor apresentar informações sobre Pedro, quando necessário. Esse elemento deve conter como valor o dado mais representativo do recurso "pedro", por exemplo, seu nome. Dessa forma, o elemento que envolve a string "Pedro" será escolhido.

Portanto, o algoritmo de resolução de ancoragem começa utilizando o algoritmo de resolução de *blank nodes* (ver linha 1 da Figura 4), descrito anteriormente, para descobrir o dado mais representativo de um recurso.

Após definir qual o dado mais representativo do recurso, o algoritmo de resolução de ancoragem vai ancorar o conjunto de informações referentes a tal recurso no elemento HTML, que tem como valor exatamente o dado mais representativo do recurso. Para isso, o algoritmo recupera o elemento usando *getDOMElement* em *representInfo* (linha 2 da Figura 4). Se o elemento recebido for um *span*, já é possível ancorar o conjunto de informações nesse elemento (linhas 3 e 8 da Figura 4). Caso contrário, o algoritmo cria um novo elemento *span* e atribui a ele o conteúdo do elemento recebido (linha 4 da Figura 4). Após isso, o conteúdo do elemento recebido é apagado (linha 5 da Figura 4), pois o conteúdo agora está no elemento *span* recentemente criado. Por fim, o novo elemento *span* é inserido na árvore DOM HTML (linha 5 da Figura 4), como filho do elemento recebido e o conjunto de informações é ancorado nesse *span* (linha 6 da Figura 4). O motivo para usarmos *span* é que esse elemento não altera os aspectos de exibição das páginas Web (i.e. não modifica o *layout* criado pelo desenvolvedor da página).

Outros trabalhos, que também tratem da apresentação de conteúdo semântico RDFa, podem se deparar com os problemas de resolução de *blank nodes* e de resolução de ancoragem. Os algoritmos com as soluções para esses problemas, apresentados neste trabalho, foram implementados, na biblioteca jRDFa, e avaliados (Seção 4). Dessa forma, esses algoritmos podem ser indiretamente utilizados em outros cenários bem como podem ser diretamente reutilizados a partir da biblioteca desenvolvida neste trabalho.

2.4 Funcionamento e Utilização

O conhecimento semântico amigável fornecido pela biblioteca jRDFa é disponibilizado por meio de uma interface, que oferece um objeto Javascript contendo um *map* {infoset : x, HTMLelement : y}. O *infoset* é um conjunto único de informações de um determinado recurso e *HTMLelement* é o elemento HTML onde esse conjunto de informações deve ser ancorado. De forma simplificada, essa interface pode ser imaginada como uma função Javascript, *getSemanticInfo()*, que retorna o referido objeto. De posse desse objeto Javascript, as apresentações podem ser construídas utilizando as informações que ele fornece.

A biblioteca jRDFa foi desenvolvida completamente em Javascript e pode ser adicionada a qualquer aplicação Web. Para usar a biblioteca, é necessário incluir o arquivo *jRDFa.js* (linha 7 da Figura 5) e suas dependências (*Green Turtle* e *JQuery*, linhas 9 e 11, respectivamente, da Figura 5) no diretório da aplicação, fazendo referência aos arquivos nas páginas Web em que se deseja mostrar as apresentações semânticas. Além disso, para dar início ao processo, é necessário incluir um pequeno *script* nas páginas, tal como exibido nas linhas 13 a 19 da Figura 5.

Figura 5. Referências e script de carga jRDFa.

Dessa forma, a ferramenta já está apta a fornecer informações semânticas tratadas e amigáveis dinamicamente, sem intervenção do desenvolvedor. Ou seja, depois do correto carregamento da página e posteriormente da biblioteca, o objeto *map* (fornecido pela interface da biblioteca pela função *getSemanticInfo()*) já está disponível para uso pelo desenvolvedor. A implementação da biblioteca assume que as páginas Web, contendo marcações RDFa, são válidas e bem formadas, obedecendo a recomendação W3C RDFa 1.1[1].

3. jRDFa: VISUALIZAÇÃO E NAVEGAÇÃO

Esta seção descreve duas formas de apresentação desenvolvidas para demonstrar a viabilidade da proposta. A primeira foi criada para apresentar dados semânticos por meio de *tooltips* dinâmicos. A segunda utiliza facetas para permitir a navegação, de forma simples e prática, nesses dados. As formas de apresentação, aqui chamadas de *tooltips* e facetas, foram criadas tomando em consideração apenas a apresentação, visualização e/ou navegação dos dados. As questões relacionadas com a recuperação e tratamento dos dados semânticos presentes nas páginas foram deixadas a cargo da biblioteca jRDFa.

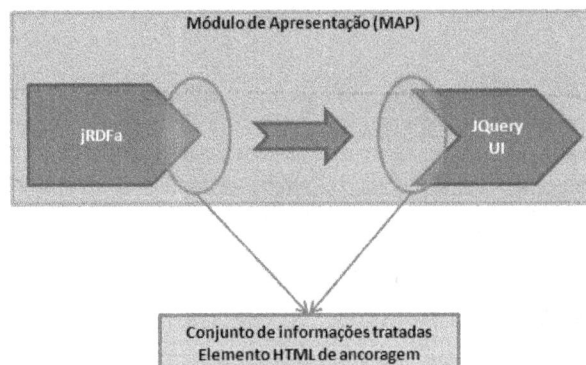

Figura 6. Comunicação entre jRDFa e JQueryUI.

Para criar novas formas de apresentação, foi utilizada a biblioteca de interface de usuário *Javascript JQueryUI*. Essa biblioteca facilita a criação das apresentações, por exemplo, *tooltips* ou facetas, fornecendo toda a parte de interface gráfica com o usuário, de forma que é necessário se ater apenas as informações que serão apresentadas. Para que os *tooltips* ou as facetas funcionem corretamente, a biblioteca *JQueryUI* exige, como parâmetros, os textos que serão adicionados como informação e exibidos no corpo do tipo de apresentação escolhido, bem como, o elemento HTML onde o *tooltip* ou a faceta será ancorado.

A Figura 6 mostra o esquema do processo de comunicação entre as bibliotecas dentro do módulo MAP. Conforme descrito

---

[1] http://www.w3.org/TR/rdfa-syntax/

anteriormente, a biblioteca jRDFa fornece um objeto *Javascript* contendo exatamente as informações solicitadas pela biblioteca *JQueryUI*. Portanto, a criação das formas de apresentação foi facilitada pela utilização da proposta jRDFa. A saída da biblioteca jRDFa foi usada como entrada da biblioteca *JQueryUI*. Esse processo foi realizado, de forma simples, utilizando o Módulo de Apresentação (MAP) da biblioteca jRDFa em sua Camada de Interface e Apresentação (CIA).

3.1 Visualização por Tooltip

Neste trabalho, a visualização por *tooltips* (caixas de informações ocultas, acionadas por uma determinada ação do usuário) consiste na exibição de *tooltips* dinâmicos contendo conhecimento semântico oriundo das marcações RDFa presentes na página Web. Esse conhecimento, muitas vezes, não está disponível para o usuário humano, pois o objetivo principal de tais dados é servir de informação útil para agentes de software.

A biblioteca *JQueryUI*, descrita anteriormente e ilustrada na Figura 6, facilita a criação de *tooltips* fornecendo toda a parte de interface gráfica com o usuário. Para que os *tooltips* funcionem corretamente a biblioteca *JQueryUI* recebe como parâmetro, por meio da biblioteca jRDFa, os textos que serão adicionados como informação e exibidos no corpo dos *tooltips*, bem como, o elemento HTML onde o *tooltip* deve ser ancorado.

Figura 7. Página Web com RDFa embutido.

Por conseguinte, os *tooltips* são criados contendo esses conjuntos de informações amigáveis e ancorados nos elementos HTML, ambos fornecidos pela biblioteca jRDFa. Assim que o usuário passa o ponteiro sobre um elemento que ancora um *tooltip*, informações, sobre aquele recurso RDF, são exibidas. Por exemplo, considerando que na página exibida para o usuário, existe um texto que contem a string "Paulo" e essa string foi definida como informação mais representativa do recurso "paulo". Dessa maneira, quando o usuário passar o ponteiro sobre essa string, um *tooltip* é imediatamente exibido. Esse *tooltip* contém um conjunto de informações amigáveis sobre Paulo. Esse conjunto pode exibir o telefone, *email*, *homepage*, endereço, organização, foto, amigos e várias outras informações sobre o recurso RDF Paulo, que não são exibidas na página Web. A Figura 7 apresenta uma página Web comum, que possui marcações RDFa com o objetivo de disponibilizar dados estruturados para agentes de software.

Pode-se observar que a página da Figura 7, mesmo contendo dados estruturados *Linked Data*, por meio de marcações RDFa, mostra poucas informações para o usuário final. É possível perceber apenas que a página possui informações sobre uma pessoa chamada "Alice Birpemswick", com seu *email*, telefone, além do nome de outras pessoas, "Bob", "Eve" e "Manu", que, aparentemente, não possuem associação com Alice.

As Figuras 8 e 9 exibem a mesma página Web da Figura 7, contudo, dessa vez utilizando a biblioteca jRDFa e a visualização por *tooltips* para exibir o conhecimento semântico existente na página através de informações amigáveis direcionadas para o usuário comum.

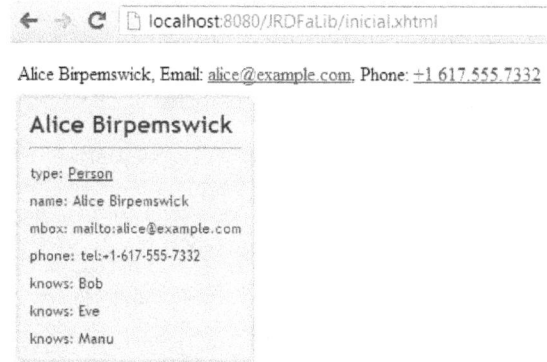

Figura 8. Tooltip mostrando informações de Alice.

Na Figura 8, pode-se ver o conjunto de informações de "Alice Birpemswick", mostrando que, além de suas informações básicas como *email* e telefone, ela conhece "Bob", "Eve" e "Manu". Essas últimas informações de relacionamento entre "Alice" e seus amigos não são visíveis na página Web exibida para os usuários sem a utilização da biblioteca jRDFa.

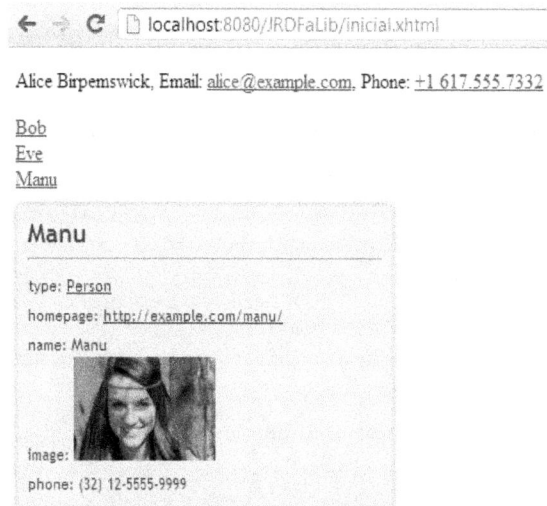

Figura 9. Tooltip mostrando informações de Manu.

Na Figura 9, é possível ver as informações que as marcações RDFa guardam acerca da pessoa "Manu". Na página Web apenas o nome "Manu" está disponível para visualização dos usuários. Entretanto, passando o ponteiro sobre essa string o *tooltip* exibe todo um conjunto de informações sobre "Manu" (*homepage*, imagem e telefone). Essas informações estariam inicialmente disponíveis apenas para agentes de software não fosse a utilização da biblioteca jRDFa em conjunto com a visualização por *tooltips*.

3.2 Navegação Facetada

A classificação em facetas busca ser um meio flexível para catalogar itens de informação. As facetas vêm sendo utilizadas em diversos cenários, como uma alternativa às classificações hierárquicas e enumeradas, inerentemente mais rígidas e de difícil manutenção. A origem do conceito de facetas é antiga, Taulbee [18] cita o trabalho de Ranganathan [19], que sugeriu a utilização do esquema em facetas na classificação de livros em um trabalho que começou em 1924.

Neste trabalho, o modelo de navegação facetada aproveita campos de metadados e valores para fornecer aos usuários uma lista de opções visíveis, com o objetivo de aperfeiçoar suas consultas e tornar o conteúdo das páginas Web, visualmente, mais fácil de ser encontrado. A forma de apresentação em navegação facetada, criada com base nas informações produzidas pela biblioteca jRDFa, consiste em fornecer uma aba oculta (preferencialmente no canto esquerdo da página), em forma de menu vertical, disponibilizando facetas semânticas para navegação nos dados estruturados, definidos por meio de RDFa, na página Web. No modo oculto, o usuário pode ver apenas uma faixa vertical translucida no canto da página (não prejudica o *layout* da página), indicando a presença da aba de navegação facetada. Assim que o ponteiro é posicionado sobre essa faixa, ela se estende, em direção ao centro, para apresentar o menu vertical de facetas semânticas.

Assim como na visualização por *tooltips*, a biblioteca *JQueryUI*, descrita anteriormente e ilustrada na Figura 6, facilita a criação das facetas fornecendo toda a parte de interface gráfica com o usuário. Para que as facetas funcionem corretamente a biblioteca *JQueryUI* recebe como parâmetro, por meio da biblioteca jRDFa, um objeto *Javascript*, contendo um conjunto único de informações, relacionado a um determinado recurso e o elemento HTML que possui o valor que melhor representa esse mesmo recurso (elemento de ancoragem). No caso das facetas, a biblioteca *JQueryUI* precisa receber como entrada básica o valor do item de menu origem e as informações que serão associadas a esse item de menu (além de outras informações de controle, como nível de taxonomia, por exemplo).

Portanto, considerando o exemplo do recurso "alice", pode-se passar, como valor do item de menu origem, o valor do objeto mais representativo desse recurso, o nome "Alice". Como informações que serão associadas ao item de menu "Alice", pode-se passar o conjunto único de informações relacionadas ao recurso "alice". Desse modo, as informações semânticas amigáveis produzidas pela biblioteca jRDFa podem ser facilmente utilizadas como entrada da biblioteca *JQueryUI*, para criação de navegação facetada. Isso proporciona uma navegação facilitada nos recursos *Linked Data*, possibilitando a descoberta de novos conhecimentos, antes disponíveis apenas para as máquinas. A Figura 10 apresenta como essa estrutura é exibida para o usuário.

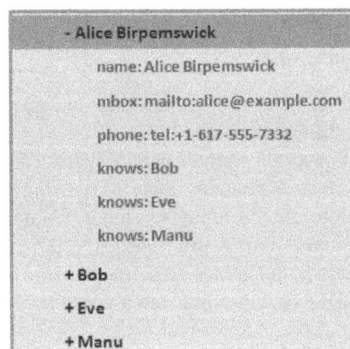

Figura 10. Aba de navegação facetada simples.

Outra forma interessante de usar a essência do modelo de navegação facetada, é passar como item de menu origem o valor do elemento *type*, contido em todo conjunto único de informações de um recurso. O elemento *type* indica o tipo do recurso (pessoa, organização, produto, evento, entre outros). Dessa forma, pode-se passar como informações associadas a esse item de menu uma lista contendo os recursos do tipo determinado. Por exemplo, passando o valor "Pessoa" como item de menu origem para a biblioteca *JQueryUI*, e como informações associadas a esse item de menu os recursos "bob", "eve", "manu" e "alice", a biblioteca automaticamente apresentará na aba de navegação facetada a opção "Pessoa (4)". Isso facilita a navegação entre os recursos

RDF, definidos por meio de RDFa, dando uma visão clara ao usuário final do conteúdo presente na página e abstraindo as questões técnicas que envolvem o padrão *Linked Data*.

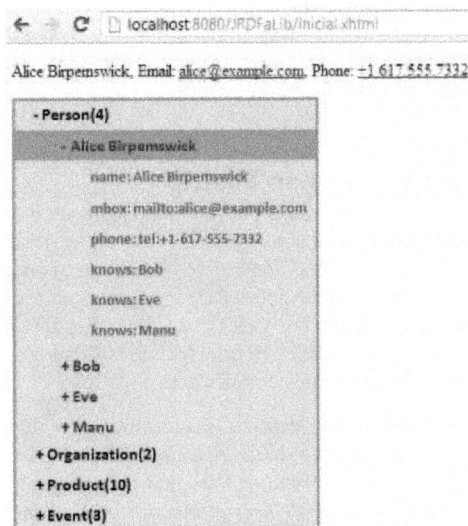

Figura 11. Aba de navegação facetada completa.

Unindo os dois exemplos citados de utilização da navegação facetada, com a utilização da biblioteca jRDFa, tem-se uma poderosa e, por outro lado, amigável forma de navegação em dados semânticos *Linked Data*. A Figura 11 mostra a aba de navegação facetada explorando o conhecimento semântico presente da página Web.

4. AVALIAÇÃO DA BIBLIOTECA jRDFa

Devido ao fato da biblioteca jRDFa realizar um *parser* no DOM HTML em busca de marcações RDFa durante o carregamento da página Web, o desempenho na exibição das páginas pode ser afetado pelo uso da biblioteca. Além disso, a biblioteca precisa montar um grafo RDF contendo todas as triplas contidas na página e gerar a forma de visualização/navegação. Todo esse processo é realizado em tempo de carregamento da página HTML. Com o objetivo de analisar o impacto de desempenho no carregamento das páginas Web processadas pela biblioteca jRDFa, foram realizados alguns experimentos levando em conta a quantidade de triplas RDFa contidas na página e o respectivo tempo de carregamento da mesma. A Tabela 1 exibe os resultados de medições de desempenho (tempo de carregamento da página) dos experimentos realizados.

Tabela 1. Tempo de carregamento (ms = milisegundos)

Quant. de Triplas	Com jRDFa	Sem jRDFa
20	100ms	100ms
200	150ms	120ms
2.000	520ms	320ms
20.000	6.950ms	2.350ms
100.000	96.200ms	19.200ms

É possível notar na Tabela 1 e na Figura 12 que páginas contendo até 200 triplas RDFa apresentam diferença de desempenho quase nula em relação à utilização ou não da biblioteca jRDFa. De fato, observando a Figura 12, os experimentos mostraram que em páginas contendo até 2.000 triplas RDFa a diferença de desempenho é pouco alterada. A métrica tempo de carregamento utilizada na Tabela 1 para avaliar o comportamento da biblioteca jRDFa é diretamente dependente do ambiente (CPU, memória, etc.) de execução dos experimentos. Dessa forma, para melhor avaliar o comportamento da biblioteca, foi utilizado o cálculo da escalabilidade, apresentado na Figura 13, que avalia o comportamento da biblioteca em várias iterações à medida que se aumenta o número de triplas RDFa na página.

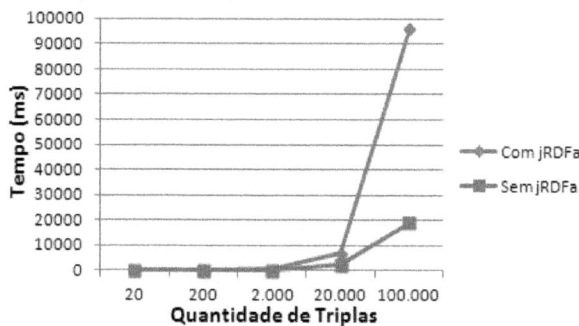

Figura 12. Tempo de carregamento da página.

A escalabilidade foi medida calculando a variação do tempo de carregamento da página dividida pela variação da quantidade de triplas na página a cada iteração, ou seja, à medida que se aumenta a quantidade de triplas RDFa. Dessa forma, a escalabilidade (ECB) foi calculada utilizando a seguinte equação:

$$ECB = \frac{TCarregamento(i) - TCarregamento(i-1)}{QuantTriplas(i) - QuantTriplas(i-1)}$$

Conforme pode ser observado na Figura 13, cada ponto no gráfico corresponde a uma medida de escalabilidade correspondente a cada momento em que a página tinha 200, 2.000. 20.000 ou 100.000 triplas RDFa. É importante notar na Figura 13 que o comportamento do carregamento da página, com ou sem a biblioteca jRDFa, é semelhante até a quantidade de 20.000 triplas.

Os experimentos realizados tiveram o objetivo de avaliar os limites de desempenho (computabilidade) da biblioteca, chegando ao ponto de se colocar 100.000 triplas RDFa em uma única página HTML. Considerando a avaliação realizada, concluiu-se que a utilização da biblioteca jRDFa não impacta o carregamento da página quando a mesma possui até 2.000 triplas RDFa. Segundo Bizer et al. [21], existem na Web atual cerca de 168 milhões de páginas HTML com RDFa embutido e com uma média de apenas 6,4 triplas RDFa por página HTML. Pode-se notar na Tabela 1 e na Figura 12 que a utilização da biblioteca jRDFa, com até 20 triplas por página HTML, não impacta no tempo de carregamento da página que se mantém em 100ms (com ou sem a jRDFa).

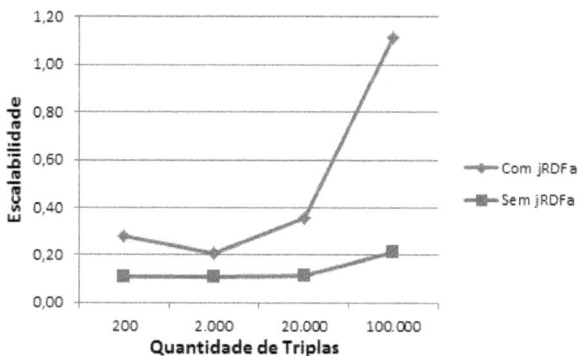

Figura 13. Escalabilidade.

Do ponto de vista de avaliação de usabilidade, a jRDFa utiliza recursos de navegação e visualização já bastante utilizados em aplicações Web: *tooltips* e *facetas*. Dessa forma, a usabilidade

desses recursos já foi avaliada em outros trabalhos na literatura, como, por exemplo, por Oren et al. [22].

5. TRABALHOS RELACIONADOS

Nesta seção são discutidos alguns trabalhos que tratam de apresentação de dados na Web de dados. A pesquisa foi concentrada, principalmente, nas áreas de navegação e visualização de formatos Linked Data, além de trabalhos que visam extração de informações em páginas Web.

Lin e Hu [14] apresentam o HTMLParser, que é um método para analisar páginas HTML e efetivamente extrair conteúdos de forma linear ou aninhada. O *parser* possui filtros e *tags* personalizadas, oferecendo uma interface de utilização simples. As aplicações que utilizam HTMLParser têm como principais aspectos a extração e transformação de informações. O trabalho dos autores é similar ao Módulo de Aquisição (MAQ) proposto neste trabalho. Entretanto, o MAQ tem funcionalidades específicas para extração de RDFa de páginas HTML, que não é o objetivo da proposta de Lin e Hu.

Hepp et al. [12] propuseram o RDF2RDFa, que parte do princípio de que muitos potenciais usuários da Web Semântica têm dificuldades técnicas para publicar conteúdo no formato estruturado (e.g usuários de Sistema de Gerenciamento de Conteúdo ou Wikis). Dessa forma, RDF2RDFa permite o uso de RDFa para embutir triplas RDF não triviais no formato de elementos invisíveis *div/span* em documentos HTML preexistentes, simplificando a publicação de conteúdo em formato RDF em conformidade com *Linked Data*. Ao inserir RDFa utilizando elementos invisíveis nas páginas HTML, Hepp et al. deixam claro que o foco deles é disponibilizar essas informações para agentes de software. Dessa forma, é possível utilizar a biblioteca jRDFa, proposta neste artigo, para expor as informações também para pessoas.

Camarda et al. [7] apresentam a ferramenta *LodLive*, que tem como objetivo principal navegar em recursos RDF usando uma visualização em grafo dinâmico. A diferença principal para a proposta apresentada neste artigo é que a jRDFa pode ser estendida com diversas formas de apresentação, enquanto que o foco do *LodLive* é a navegação utilizando grafos RDF.

Cheng et al. [8] propõem um navegador *Linked Data* chamado MyView, que permite aos usuários consultarem *Linked Data* por navegação, de uma coleção de entidades para outra. O navegador permite que usuários façam consultas na Web de Dados e utilizem essas consultas para navegar sobre os dados. Claramente, os objetivos de Cheng et al. são diferentes da proposta apresentada neste artigo. O objetivo do jRDFa é permitir ao usuário visualizar/navegar em informações RDFa embutidas nas páginas HTML que ele está visitando.

Batista e Schwabe [20] apresentam o *LinkedTube*, que é um serviço para criar relações, semânticas ou não, entre vídeos disponíveis na Web. Para as relações semânticas, os autores realizam consultas, em bases de vídeos e em bases *Linked Data,* para gerar as relações entre os vídeos no formato RDF. Os resultados das relações criadas podem ser visualizados diretamente em RDF ou em uma interface HTML criada especificamente para o *LinkedTube.* A biblioteca jRDFa, proposta neste trabalho, poderia ser utilizada no *LinkedTube,* assim como em outras ferramentas HTML, para apresentar dados RDF serializados como RDFa.

A análise dos trabalhos relacionados evidenciou que a apresentação (visualização e navegação) para usuários não técnicos na Web de Dados ainda é um problema em aberto e que muita coisa ainda pode ser proposta. Este trabalho identificou a relevância de construir uma biblioteca *Javascript* para apoiar o desenvolvedor Web, interessado em apresentar, de forma simples e eficiente, dados estruturados no formato RDFa para tais usuários.

6. CONSIDERAÇÕES FINAIS

A semântica explícita na Web de Dados pode trazer benefícios para uma grande diversidade e tipos de usuários. Em especial, usuários sem experiência com esse espaço global de dados precisam de ferramentas que os apoiem na descoberta de informações interessantes e novos relacionamentos, na exploração de conceitos desconhecidos e na apresentação do conhecimento estruturado.

A proposta apresentada neste artigo está fundamentada e inserida nesses aspectos, dado que permite a usuários comuns terem acesso a informações semânticas, muitas vezes ocultas em marcações RDFa de páginas Web. Os *tooltips* e as facetas, exibidos pela biblioteca jRDFA proposta neste trabalho, visam facilitar a apresentação dessas informações simplificando-as e, consequentemente, ajudando as pessoas a entender melhor tais informações, que, na maioria das vezes, têm como usuários alvo os agentes de software.

Os experimentos realizados demonstraram a viabilidade da proposta da jRDFa do ponto de vista de desempenho. Avaliações com grupos de usuários podem ser realizadas com o objetivo de descobrir tendências no comportamento das pessoas ao se depararem com essas informações semânticas e estruturadas da Web de Dados. Isso pode possibilitar a descoberta: i) de limitações da proposta não observadas até então; ii) de aspectos relativos à apresentação das informações, tais como, forma, posicionamento, tamanho, cor, dentre outros. O estudo de usuário ainda pode revelar novas ideias e abordagens a serem seguidas no decorrer do desenvolvimento da biblioteca.

Como trabalhos futuros, pretende-se adicionar à biblioteca um módulo de consulta a Web de Dados, para permitir que a partir de um recurso obtido na página, execute-se uma consulta em um *endpoint* Linked Data, através de SPARQL e obtenham-se dados relacionados. Isso enriquece o conjunto de informações exibidas em um *tooltip* ou nas facetas e permite que as pessoas de fato vivenciem a Web de Dados.

AGRADECIMENTOS: Os autores agradecem a CAPES, CNPq, FAPESB e RNP, pelo apoio financeiro às pesquisas.

7. REFERÊNCIAS

[1] Adida, B., Herman, I., Sporny, M. and Birbeck, M. 2012. RDFa Primer, http://www.w3.org/TR/xhtml-rdfa-primer/ (visitado em 28/04/2013).

[2] Adida, B., McCarron, S., Herman, I. and Birbeck, M. 2012. RDFa Core 1.1: Syntax and processing rules for embedding RDF through attributes, http://www.w3.org/TR/rdfa-syntax/ (visitado em 28/04/2013).

[3] Berners-Lee, T. 2006. Design Issues: Linked Data. *http://www.w3.org/DesignIssues/LinkedData.html* (visitado em 28/04/2013).

[4] Bizer, C. 2011. Evolving the web into a global data space. In *Proceedings of the 28th British national conference on Advances in databases* (BNCOD'11), Alvaro A. A. Fernandes, Alasdair J. G. Gray, and Khalid Belhajjame (Eds.). Springer-Verlag, Berlin, Heidelberg, 1-1.

[5] Bizer, C., Heath, T., and Berners-Lee, T. 2009. Linked Data---The Story So Far. *International Journal on Semantic Web and Information Systems (IJSWIS)*.

[6] Brunetti, J., Auer, S., and García, R. 2012. The Linked Data Visualization Model.

[7] Camarda, D. V., Mazzini, S., and Antonuccio, A. 2012. LodLive, exploring the web of data. In *Proceedings of the 8th International Conference on Semantic Systems* (I-SEMANTICS '12), Harald Sack and Tassilo Pellegrini http://doi.acm.org/10.1145/2362499.2362532.

[8] Cheng, G., Wu, H., Gong, S., Zhang, H. and Qu, Y. (2011). Browsing Linked Data with MyView. *In Proceedings of The 10th International Semantic Web Conference (ISWC2011)*.

[9] Davies, S., Hatfield, J., Donaher, C., and Zeitz, J. 2010. User Interface Design Considerations for Linked Data Authoring Environments. *In Proceedings of LDOW*.

[10] Dietzold, S., Hellmann, S., and Peklo, M. 2008. Using Javascript RDFa Widgets for Model/View Separation inside Read/Write Websites. *4th Workshop on Scripting for the Semantic Web (SFSW)*.

[11] Green Turtle https://code.google.com/p/green-turtle/ (last viewed April 28, 2013).

[12] Hepp, M., García, R. and Radinger, A. 2009. RDF2RDFa: Turning RDF into Snippets for Copy-and-Paste. *8th International Semantic Web Conference (ISWC)*.

[13] Klyne, G., and Carroll, J. 2004. Resource Description Framework (RDF): Concepts and Abstract Syntax. *W3C Recommendation 10 February 2004*. Series editor: Brian McBride, http://www.w3.org/TR/rdf-concepts/ (last viewed April 28, 2013).

[14] Lin, S., and Hu, Y. 2010 An Approach of Extracting Web Information Based on HTMLParser. *Information Technology and Computer Science (ITCS), 2010 Second International Conference on*, vol., no., pp.284-287, 24-25.

[15] Pereira, M., and Martins, J.A. 2012. aRDF: a plugin to expose RDFa semantic information using Grails. In *Proceedings of the 6th Euro American Conference on Telematics and Information Systems* (EATIS '12), Rogerio Patricio Chagas do Nascimento http://doi.acm.org/10.1145/2261605.2261622.

[16] Talis http://docs.api.talis.com/platform-api/output-types/rdf-json (last viewed April 28, 2013).

[17] Ziegler, J. 2011. Semantic web meets UI: context-adaptive interaction with semantic data. In Proceedings of the 29th Annual European Conference on Cognitive Ergonomics (ECCE '11). http://doi.acm.org/10.1145/2074712.2074716

[18] Taulbee , O. E. Classification in information storage and retrieval, in 20th National Conference. Cleveland, Ohio, United States: ACM Press, 1965, pp. 119–137.

[19] Ranganathan, S. Prolegomena to Library Classification, 2nd ed. London: Library Association, 1957.

[20] Batista , C. E. C. F. e Schwabe, D. 2009. LinkedTube: semantic information on web media objects. In Proceedings of the XV Brazilian Symposium on Multimedia and the Web (WebMedia '09). ACM, New York, NY, USA , 7 pages.

[21] Bizer, C., Mühleisen, H., Harth, A., Stadtmüller, S., Meusel, R., Schuhmacher, M., Völker, J. and Eckert, K. 2012. Web Data Commons Extraction Report, http://webdatacommons.org/2012-08/stats/stats.html (visitado em 15/07/2013).

[22] Oren, E., Delbru, R. and Decker, S. 2006. Extending Faceted Navigation for RDF Data. In Proceedings of The Semantic Web - ISWC 2006. Lecture Notes in Computer Science Volume 4273, 2006, pp 559-572.

Enhancing Collaborative Sketching Activities with Context-aware Adaptation Guidelines

Vivian Genaro Motti, Ugo Sangiorgi, Jean Vanderdonckt
Louvain Interaction Laboratory - Universite catholique de Louvain
Place des Doyens 1 - 1348 - Louvain la Neuve - Belgium
vivian.genaromotti,ugo.sangiorgi,jean.vanderdonckt@uclouvain.be

ABSTRACT

Designing interactive systems for multiple contexts of use becomes a burden when the end user interaction takes place in distinct scenarios whose specific characteristics and constraints vary and must be carefully considered. Stakeholders face then two main challenges: they are not aware of *what* among several context information is significantly relevant to consider, or *how* to appropriately adapt the user interfaces according to the information considered. Furthermore, stakeholders cannot simply rely on existing UI editors once they usually do not provide enough support for adaptation. Thus, adaptation is often ignored, resulting in user interfaces that are only suitable for static and conventional contexts of use. To support the design of user interfaces that are properly adapted to their target context, this paper proposes a novel methodology to enhance sketching activities by proposing to the end user context-aware adaptation guidelines. This work aims at raising awareness about context-aware adaptation since the early stages of the UI design.

Keywords

Collaborative sketching; Context-aware adaptation; Collaborative design; UI Prototyping.

Categories and Subject Descriptors

H.5.2 [**User Interfaces**]: Prototyping

1. INTRODUCTION

Users currently interact from contexts that vary concerning the user's profiles (e.g. their preferences and impairments), their platforms (e.g. devices and connections) and environments (e.g. the brightness and the noise level). Due to such variety, for stakeholders it is a challenge to carefully consider the characteristics and constraints of these contexts during all phases of the user interface development. Thus, adaptation is often ignored, either because stakeholders are not aware of relevant characteristics and constraints of the context, or because they are aware but unable to correctly address related issues to implement and to provide efficient adapta-

tion. Consequently, stakeholders tend to adopt a "one-size-fits-all" approach, providing UIs that are suitable for a conventional and static context of use. By doing so, accessibility issues may raise, hindering or even preventing the end user to accomplish her goals.

Due to the inherent challenges in properly considering many different contexts of use and in efficiently providing adaptation since the early phases of the development process, in this work we propose a novel approach that support adaptation within user interface editors, aiding stakeholders to consider context-awareness during all the development phases, starting from low fidelity prototypes. Such approach not only raises awareness for contextual differences but also facilitates the adoption of adaptation guidelines. The approach proposed consists in enhancing the electronic sketching and prototyping activities according to the envisaged context(s) of use.

Multi-platform sketching is defined as the activity of drawing with an electronic stylus in different devices while still having the same system running on those different devices [15]. GAMBIT has been developed as a multi-platform collaborative tool for user interface design that enables users to sketch and to prototype UI's on different devices. To augment the sketching activities by guiding stakeholders through the development of adapted UI's according to the target context, three main dimensions of context have been considered:

- *Multi-platform*: ensures more suitable results by enabling the sketching, prototyping and testing of the UI's to be performed on the target device. GAMBIT has been built with HTML5 and JavaScript being capable of running on any device with browsing capabilities, through a browser or embedded into a native application;
- *Multi-user*: since the user profiles vary in many aspects, e.g. preferences, expertise levels (novice, intermediate, advanced) or impairments (visual, cognitive, motor), also distinct requirements and needs must be considered for the UI;
- *Multi-environment*: for varied constraints and characteristics, different adaptation techniques are applicable. For instance taking into account the brightness and the stability levels in order to provide users appropriate UI elements.

This paper is organized as follows: the next section motivates this work, presents and discusses related works; then Gambit is described, followed by the novel proposed approach to support context-aware adaptation guidelines for sketching.

2. MOTIVATION AND RELATED WORK

User Interface design is inherently a complex interdisciplinary activity, often involving designers, programmers, users and stakeholders. UI designers often use sketched prototypes since not all the UI specifications are known at design time, but rather evolve significantly over time when design sessions are organized. De-

Tool	Feature	Fidelity	Portability	Collaboration	Export	License	Guidance
Balsamiq [1]	Sketching	Low	Web or client version for Mac, Windows, Linux	Sharing in almost real time via DropBox	As PNG or XML	Payed	
JustInMind [3]	Prototyping		Runs on Windows, and Mac	Publish and Share with UserNote	As HTML, to Microsoft Word or Open Office	Payed	Emulators to adapt to mobile web apps.
Maqetta [4]	Sketching	Low & high	Web version run across browsers (except IE), (no support for tablets)	Asynchronous	As a zip file	Open Source	Widgets libraries for mobile apps. (Dojo)
SketchFlow [5]	Prototyping	Low & high	Web or client version for Windows		As XAML, or to Microsoft Work	Payed	

Table 1: Analysis of existing UI editors concerning their: features, fidelity levels, portability, collaboration, export formats, license and guidance.

signers and usability professionals can find usability problems at an early stage of design, before substantial resources are invested in flawed designs.

Several tools that support the UI design, sketching and prototyping are available. MAQETTA, for example, is a visual authoring tool for designing HTML5-based UI's, it adopts a WYSIWYG approach. Because MAQETTA is also a web-based application, no plugins or downloads are required. Although it permits the design of UI mockups, context-aware adaptation is not integrated as a feature [4]. Besides MAQETTA, there are also other graphical editors to support activities of sketching and prototyping UI's in varied fidelity levels. Four popular tools that support UI sketching and prototyping have been analyzed for reference (Table 1):

- BALSAMIQ [1] to quickly sketch interfaces and to communicate design ideas (balsamiq.com);
- JUSTINMIND [3] a platform for defining prototypes for web and mobile applications (www.justinmind.com);
- MAQETTA [4] a web-based visual authoring of HTML5 user interfaces, WYSIWYG (maqetta.org);
- SKETCHFLOW [6] an editor to create interactive prototypes (www.microsoft.com/silverlight/sketchflow).

Such tools effectively support UI prototyping and sketching, however they do not focus on context-aware adaptation. By using those, designers tend either to ignore context or to manually implement various different UI versions.

For stakeholders considering the significant differences in current contexts of use is challenging to implement interactive systems. *User profiles* vary according to their age, expertise levels, preferences and needs. The *platforms* have different screen dimensions, interaction modalities, and capabilities. The *environments* have different brightness, noise and stability levels. These differences impact the requirements for GUI's, and if certain characteristics are not properly considered the interaction may be hindered or even prevented. However, for designers, it is not scalable to take each context detail into account so that many different versions of the same system are implemented. Currently, to generate context-aware UIs, designers must be aware of the target context, and also properly know how to apply adaptation, for instance by following standard guidelines [7] or well-known patterns [9], [5]. There exist tools to support the UI design and electronic sketching, however they do not provide support to consider context-awareness and design guidelines. Thus, the resulting UI's are not always suitable to their actual contexts, unless several versions of the same UI have been implemented, which among other problems, considerably de-

lay in their time to market. The main shortcomings of such tools regarding context-aware adaptation of UI's are:

Firstly, such tools are already not adapted, being implemented to run in a conventional context of use of an able-bodied user in a Desktop PC in a stable environment (i.e. office). Although practitioners may be more familiar working in their traditional workspace, because the design occurs outside the target context, the results may be inaccurate. For instance, by designing mobile applications in a smartphone, a more realistic result can be achieved, specially concerning screen dimensions and performance constraints.

Second, contextual information is not supported, or it is but limited e.g. to screen sizes. Stakeholders are not aware of *which* information to consider and *how* to consider. No support is provided concerning usability guidelines and patterns.

Third, by being inflexible such tools force users to sketch and to prototype one version of the same application dedicated to each context. When various contexts must be covered it becomes not scalable to properly ensure adaptation.

Finally, although users with different profiles work often in large teams, such tools not always support collaboration, thus either all stakeholders must be co-located or they cannot simultaneously access and edit the project, thus pipelining their tasks. By matching different skills and expertise in a synchronous project collaboration, better results can be obtained.

Besides this, when the context is considered just during late development phases, if the resulting UI's are not satisfactory, significant re-work may be needed. When usability tests and experiments are conducted during later stages, results may be incorrect once a high fidelity prototype is already available, discouraging users to negatively evaluate the resulting UI's.

3. ENHANCING SKETCHING WITH ADAPTATION

Sketching is a powerful tool for the UI design. For [11], the presence of ambiguity in early stages of design broads the spectrum of considered solutions and tends to result in a higher quality design. Fostering creativity is important since design is essentially a problem of *wicked nature*, i.e. the process of solving it is identical with the process of understanding it [14]. In wicked problems, in initial phases the designer does not have a clear understanding of what to produce and has only a vague goal in mind, thus to support the design with an interactive system, it is important that the system does not get "in the way" between the designer and the solution.

GAMBIT offers a flexible setup where users can choose their preferred devices for interacting – i.e. devices that are more suitable for sketching input can be used for pen interaction, while large displays can be used for visualization (Figure 1 middle). By observing UI design sessions on IT companies in Belgium, a cycle of 3 main activities has been identified:

- **Sketching:** one or more participants produce sketches to express the ideas.
- **Sharing:** the participants often share the drawings using a big sheet of paper and post-its. The sheets are arranged as a storyboard on a wall for discussion.
- **Discussing:** the participants refine the sketches based on what their discussion results.

GAMBIT provides a large (infinite) workspace where users can add images and sketch. Parts of the workspace can be shared among different platforms, composing a virtual meeting room. The tool is an essential part of a research on sketching user interfaces, its usage in current design practices also considers the diversity of contexts of use. To do so, users can test the interfaces on the same device in which it is intended to be used. GAMBIT's requirements are presented in [15].

3.1 Methodology

By informing the designer about possible design flaws related to the context of use at the sketching and the prototyping phases could aid to anticipate design flaws and potential usability issues before the interface is ready.

To enhance the sketching activity as it is currently supported towards the effective consideration of context-awareness, we propose to augment it by integrating adaptation guidelines. This methodology involves three main steps (Figure 1):

1) **Describing the Context.** by means of an XML description of the target context, users provide the characteristics the user, the platform and the environment (Figure 1 top).
2) **Sketching the UI's.** the UI's are sketched in the user preferred device(s) (Figure 1 middle). Since not all the devices have the same resolution or performance, each device is suitable for each basic activity (sketching, sharing and discussing) [15, 16]. The UI elements are recognized according to a standard library.
3) **Adapting the UI Sketches.** based on the GUI elements recognized, and in the target context that has been parsed, relevant guidelines are searched, retrieved and and suggested to the end user (Figure 1 bottom).

3.2 Design Decisions

The contexts can be expressed by means of a descriptive XML document, however if the user sketch in the target device, its specification can be automatically verified and retrieved. Other information, as the user profile and the target environment, must be either explicitly expressed by the user, or a conventional scenario of interaction can be adopted.

Algorithms can automatically recognize the UI elements involved in the sketch. Previous works, as UsiSketch [10], for instance, discuss and present algorithms that automatically recognize sketch elements for GUI's. An alternative solution consists in enabling the end user to tag the sketched elements. This approach may reach more accurate results, however it delays the original task. An hybrid approach is also suitable, e.g. enabling the user to associate gestures to the sketch to indicate whether a rectangle represents an image or a button.

Based on the elements recognized in the UI, and the context provided, the system can then automatically search for and present

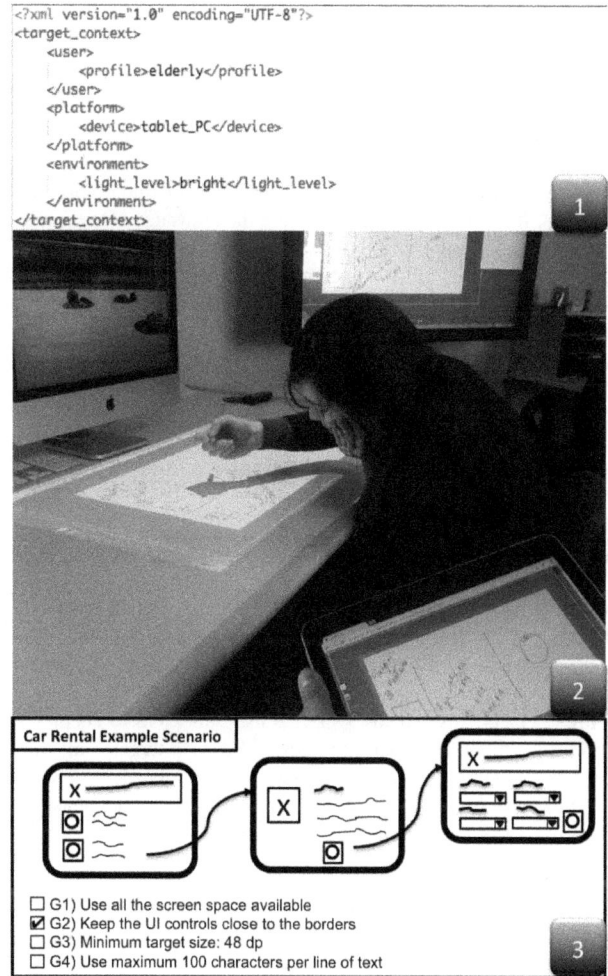

Figure 1: The 3 main interaction steps for the enhanced sketching tool: first the end user provides a description of the target context, then while sketching, the tool automatically recognizes the interface layout and its UI elements, proposing relevant adaptation techniques (as guidelines).

relevant guidelines for the end user. The UI guidelines and patterns can be retrieved from (i) a pre-defined catalog as reports [13], (ii) an online repository (e.g. the W3C accessibility guidelines [7]), (iii) a local repository integrating many sources, or (iv) third-party cloud-based web services.

The UI guidelines cover up to 3 GUI's dimensions: contents, presentation and navigation. The *contents* include the different formats, as images, texts, videos and elements that support the user tasks. Based on the context, such contents can be removed, resized, replaced, etc. The *presentation* concerns the layout of GUI's, i.e. the contents distribution can follow a certain alignment, balance, or specific re-arrangements. And the *navigation* in an interactive system is structured by a task tree (e.g. with CTT [2] or HTA). Although a unique task tree enables the same goals to be achieved in different contexts of use, many groupings and hierarchies are possible to better suit tasks in different scenarios; e.g. concerning the screen dimensions, if the user interacts from a small screen (smart phone), few tasks must be presented at a time.

These dimensions cover 3 abstraction levels (the properties of the UI elements, their layout in the UI and the arrangement among

UI's). Because Gambit also captures the navigation, all 3 levels can be supported (semantic annotations may be needed to aid the selection of relevant guidelines though).

A semi-automatic approach can be applied to suggest changes for the sketches, i.e. once the guidelines' list is presented, the user is in charge of analyzing it, judging whether it is indeed appropriate, modifying the UI, and changing the guideline's status (as checked). It is also important to capture the relevance of the guideline, aiming at improving the methodology performance. Given that design sessions often concern a specific application domain, the suggested guidelines must cover a generic purpose, following specific constraints of context of use and UI elements, but still being domain-independent.

3.3 Case Study

Our case study scenario consists in designing graphical user interfaces for a car rental system, targeting a tablet platform, an elderly user, and an environment with bright light level.

Table 2: The UI guidelines matching context and UI sketch elements.

Context	Content	Presentation	Navigation
User	G1: prefer drag and pinch gestures	G2: provide visual feedback	G3: keep distance between targets
Plat.	G4: use maximum 100 characters per line of text	G5: use all screen space available	G6: keep UI targets at the borders with 8mm at least
Env.	G7: prefer dark tones	G8: ensure contrast	

In our study 3 GUI's are needed to accomplish a user task: first the user accesses a list of cars, then one car is selected and further information about it is presented, finally the dates and location for pickup and delivery are selected. Each car is described by an image and a text. To complete the rental, the user has a confirm button after the car description. By scrolling the UI, the user navigates through the list of cars. Figure 1 bottom shows the UI's and a set of 4 guidelines presented to the user, concerning the tablet platform, and the characteristics of the sketches. Table 2 complements this set, based on the context (user, platform and environment) and on the UI's (content, presentation and navigation) [12], [8].

4. FINAL REMARKS

Although many tools support UI design, they do not integrate UI guidelines. In the current technological landscape the contexts of use can vary significantly. However designers are unaware of *which* and context information to consider and *how* to do it. By integrating UI guidelines in UI sketching tools, stakeholders can be aware of relevant guidelines, generating enhanced UI's. This paper proposes enhanced sketching by means of a novel approach, illustrated with a case study.

5. ACKNOWLEGDEMENTS

Projects: Serenoa (E.C. FP7 (FP7-ICT-2009-5)) and QualIHM (Region Wallonne, Dir. generale operationnelle de l'Economie, de l'Emploi et de la Recherche DGO6).

6. REFERENCES

[1] Balsamiq Mockups: Rapid Wireframing Tool, 2012. `www.balsamiq.com`.

[2] Concur Task Trees (CTT), 2012. `http://www.w3.org/2012/02/ctt/`.

[3] JustInMind: a platform to define web and mobile apps., 2012. `http://www.justinmind.com/`.

[4] Maqetta: Visual Authoring of HTML5 User Interfaces in the browser., 2012. `http://dojofoundation.org/projects/maqetta`.

[5] My UI Pattern Browser, 2012. `myuipatterns.clevercherry.com`.

[6] SketchFlow: Expression Studio Ultimate, 2012. `http://www.microsoft.com/silverlight/sketchflow/`.

[7] Web Content Accessibility Guidelines (WCAG) 2.0, 2012. `http://www.w3.org/TR/WCAG/`.

[8] Android Tablet Guidelines, 2013. `http://developer.android.com/distribute/googleplay/quality/tablet.html`.

[9] Yahoo! Design Pattern Library, 2013. `http://developer.yahoo.com/ypatterns/`.

[10] Coyette, A., Schimke, S., Vanderdonckt, J., and Vielhauer, C. Trainable sketch recognizer for graphical user interface design. In *INTERACT (1)* (2007), 124–135.

[11] Goel, V. "Ill-Structured Representations" for Ill-Structured Problems. In *Proceedings of the Fourteenth Annual Conference of the Cognitive Science Society*, vol. 14, Lawrence Erlbaum (1992), 130–135.

[12] Kobayashi, M., Hiyama, A., Miura, T., Asakawa, C., Hirose, M., and Ifukube, T. Elderly user evaluation of mobile touchscreen interactions. In *Human-Computer Interaction–INTERACT 2011*. Springer, 2011, 83–99.

[13] Motti, V. G., and Vanderdonckt, J. A Computational Framework for Context-aware Adaptation of User Interfaces. In *Proc. of the Research Challenges in Information Sciences Conference - RCIS '13* (2013), 12.

[14] Rittel, H. Dilemmas in a general theory of planning. *Policy sciences 4*, 2 (1973), 155–169.

[15] Sangiorgi, U. B., Beuvens, F., and Vanderdonckt, J. User Interface Design by Collaborative Sketching. In *Proc. of the Designing Interactive Systems, DIS '12*, ACM Press (Newcastle, U.K., 2012), 378.

[16] Sangiorgi, U. B., Motti, V. G., Beuvens, F., and Vanderdonckt, J. Assessing Lag Perception in Electronic Sketching. In *Nordic Conference on Human-Computer Interaction* (Copenhagen, DK, 2012).

Similarity Evaluation in XML Schema and XLink

Marta Mota
Universidade Salvador - UNIFACS
mrtmota@gmail.com

Paulo Caetano da Silva
Universidade Salvador - UNIFACS
paulo.caetano@pro.unifacs.br

Sidney Viana
Centro Universitário Dinâmica das
Cataratas - UDC
sidney.viana@gmail.com

ABSTRACT

XML SCHEMA is a standard defined by W3C widely used in the specification of XML elements. Another standard by W3C is XML Linking Language (XLink), a language that specifies how elements should be declared in XML documents in order to define links between two or more resources. XLink and XML Schema are emerging Internet standards applied in varying contexts such as XBRL Language. Similarity evaluation is an important process in data management and serves as support for one of its core activity: duplicate detection. Thus, the classification of XML elements according to the similarity between them is becoming increasingly useful in the area of XML data management. This paper presents a process for similarity evaluation between XML elements defined with the use of XML Schema and XLink and an experiment. The experiment applies the proposed process to the context of the XBRL concepts, an example of XML elements created with extensive use of XML Schema and XLink.

Categories and Subject Descriptors

I.5.3 [Clustering]: Similarity measures.
I.7.2 [Document Preparation]: Markup languages.

General Terms

Standardization, Languages, Theory, Experimentation.

Keywords

Data Management, Similarity Evaluation, Duplicate Detection, XLink, XBRL.

1. INTRODUCTION

XML schemas emerged from the need to restrict the content of an XML document to enable automatic processing. The use of a schema enables the creation of subsets of XML for specific domains, facilitating and regulating information exchange. Thus, the XML Schema Definition (XSD) was created, a specification recommended by W3C, also called XML Schema. XML Schema allows you to specify elements and attributes that can appear in an XML document, as well as the order of presentation of the elements, cardinality, hierarchy, data types, and default values for these elements [9].

The representation of relationships is a key aspect in databases, enriching the semantics of the information. In order to enhance the representation of relationships, complementing XML, the W3C defined the XML Linking Language (XLink) that specifies how elements should be declared in XML documents in order to define links between two or more resources [5].

With XML Schema and XLink, the use of XML as a language for data representation and their relationships have evolved and become increasingly frequent. An example is XBRL (eXtensible Business Reporting Language) [6], a language based on XML, XML Schema and XLink for dissemination and exchange of financial information. XBRL has been adopted by many institutions and companies around the world, supported by a global consortium with over 650 members.

The extensive use of XML Schema and XLink increases the occurrence of quality problems and leads to the need for greater control over XML documents created using these standards. The discipline of Data Quality Management has the feature of managing the various aspects related to the collection, maintenance, enhancement and sharing of data. In Data Quality Management, duplicate detection is one of its core activities.

Let $E = (e_1, e_2, ..., e_n)$ be a set and $sim(e_1, e_2)$ a similarity function expressed as a number n ranging from 0 to 1. A value closer to 1 reflects a greater similarity between the fields. The task of duplicate detection is to find all sets of (e_i, e_j) pairs such that $sim(e_i, e_j) > \theta$, where θ is a threshold that indicates the pairs are duplicates. Duplicate detection benefits many applications, such as data cleaning and data integration.

Similarity evaluation is an important support to the activity of duplicate detection since it determines the degree of similarity between the data. The similarity evaluation process has received considerable attention in the academic world. Initially, studies focused on the classification of similarity between atomic data, essentially strings. Then emerged studies to evaluate similarity of data in the presence of relationships which can be represented in a structured model (relational) or semi-structured model (data in XML format).

Similarity evaluation in XML introduces some challenges due to its particular characteristics. In XML databases, there may be differences in the structure of elements that represent the same entity. Even documents that follow the definitions of a single XML schema can represent elements in different ways due to the properties of optionality and cardinality of their attributes. The use of XML Schema and XLink to create XML documents introduces new challenges to the process of similarity evaluation in this context, since it adds semantic information relevant for the classification of similarity.

The focus of this study is to evaluate the similarity between XML elements created with the use of XML Schema and XLink. The objective of this paper is to present a process and an experiment to do such evaluation. The experiment applies similarity classification techniques identified through a literature review and adapt them to the context of concepts represented by the XBRL language, an example of XML elements created with extensive use of XML Schema and XLink.

This paper is structured as follows: Section 2 addresses related works. Section 3 presents the proposed process. Section 4 presents the experiment conducted in the context of the XBRL Language. Finally, conclusions and future work are summarized in Section 5.

2. RELATED WORK

In similarity classification, evaluated data can be of various types. [8] presents a survey classifying data as simple (atomic data without relationships) or complex (data related to each other). In literature, similarity measures for simple data can be found based on the concept of edit distance, tokens or using phonemes. Each measure is best suited to a particular type of application or context.

Distance based measures [12]; [14]; [17]; [21] work effectively for typographical errors. However, in cases where the fields may suffer rearrangement, these measures do not work well since they tightly consider the position of the character to classify the similarity. Token based measures compare fields after dividing them into smaller pieces that are subsets of the original field (tokens). The idea is that if the fields are similar, they will have common tokens. The advantage of using tokens is that they are insensitive to changes in position. Belonging to this set are measures [15]; WHIRL [4] and QGrams [20]. Phonetic measures are useful to detect fields that are phonetically similar, but spelled differently. The most commonly used measures are Soundex and New York State Identification and Intelligence System - NYSIIS [18].

One of the first approaches for complex data was presented in [1]: a top-down approach for the detection of duplicate elements in data warehouses with hierarchical relationships, based on the concept that the similarity between two elements depends on the similarity between its child elements. Since then, several methods were proposed for classification of similarity on complex data, always relying on joining measures for both the content and the structure (relationships) of the data.

Methods for evaluation of structure similarity can be classified according to the representation of the elements [19]. Some approaches represent documents as trees; others represent elements in a Vector Space Model or as graphs. In XML documents, some methods are based on the similarity between the paths of elements to evaluate the similarity of structure between the documents [13].

In XML document similarity evaluation context, Dogmatix [22] outlines a three step process for XML documents similarity evaluation based on the first model proposed in the area [10]. The first step is to define the elements of the XML document to be represented in tuples. The second step is the creation of tuples with the data elements defined in first step. The third step is the application of a similarity measure proposed on tuples, based on string simple similarity measures.

Involving XML Schema, [16] presents a survey on schema matching techniques. Since the study presented here considers a single element level, schema matching is not relevant, although automatic schema matching is an important area of study of similarity evaluation in the presence of relationships.

XLink relationships are hierarchical structures [5], created through parent-child relationships. They may or may not be structured. Few studies on similarity with XLink can be found. [3] introduces a graph-based distance measure over structure obtained from XLink.

In the context of XBRL language, studies on Data Quality Management can be found, such as [2] and [23]. [23] evaluated the similarity between concepts represented by XBRL, comparing only their names, not their structures.

3. PROCESS

The process proposed for similarity evaluation of XML Elements defined in XML Schemas and using XLink, is showed at Figure 1.

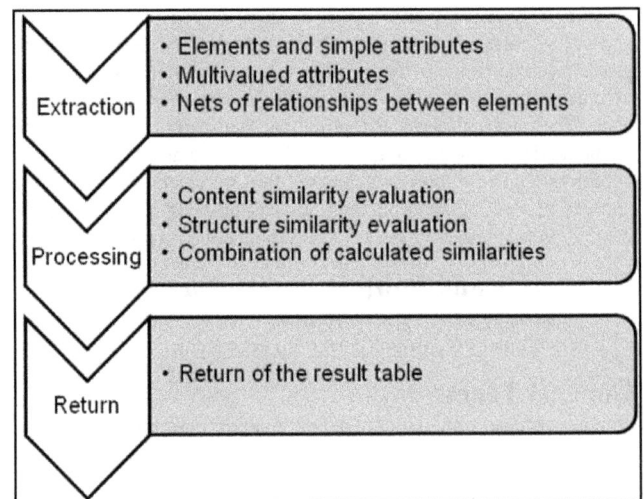

Figure 1 – Process for similarity evaluation

The first step is the extraction of relevant information. Elements and its simple attributes (content information) are extracted from the XML schema document where they are defined; semantic information is extracted from the XLinks. All XLinks involving the extracted elements are navigated and its other resources extracted. Resources that are not of the element type are stored as multivalued attributes (content information). Resources of the same element type are relationships between them and considered as structure information. Structure information extracted from XLink differentiates this work from process proposed in [22].

The extracted information is stored in a database. Then, elements are compared for content and structure similarity and these calculated values are combined into a single similarity value. The result is a table of pairs of elements and their calculated similarities. The result can be used as input to more specialized activities such as: cleaning duplicate elements, grouping elements according to their similarity, element information retrieval and others.

The proposed process uses the most basic approach for elements comparison, in other words it compares each element with all other elements of the dataset, evaluating similarity between them.

Thus, each element is compared to $(n-1)$ elements, leading to $n \times (n-1)$ comparisons and complexity of $O(n^2)$.

4. EXPERIMENT

This section presents an experiment made for similarity evaluation, applying the proposed process on XBRL concepts. XBRL concepts define the terms that will be reported through the facts in the XBRL reports (called XBRL instances). XBRL concepts are declared in a XML document through XSD Schema <element> tag and have attributes which define its content. Semantic information about concepts indicating relationships, restrictions and details are expressed through linkbases, which may be within the XML Schema or in separate XML documents (called linkbases).

XBRL uses five types of links: Calculation, Presentation, Definition, Label and Reference. The first three form nets of relationships between concepts, the other two between concepts and strings. A collection of documents (XML Schema and Linkbases) with the definition of concepts is given the name of "XBRL taxonomy" [6].

In this work, the *name* attribute is considered as a relevant simple content for similarity evaluation of XBRL Concepts, since the XBRL recommendation suggests that its value should be indicative of the financial concept it represents. XBRL Concepts labels, defined in label linkbases, are considered as a relevant multivalued attribute. QGrams [20] was the measure chosen for similarity evaluation of XBRL Concepts attributes since it accepts transpositions and abbreviations and does not need a delimiter to obtain tokens.

Structure can be obtained through the relationships between concepts defined in the Calculation, Definition and Presentation linkbases. From the Calculation and Presentation linkbases, one can obtain a well defined network of hierarchical relationship without cycles. The Definition linkbases are diverse, allow all types of cycle and represent various networks (e.g. specialization, domain dependency and dimensional). The experiment presented here uses existing techniques for hierarchical approaches and applies them only in the information present in the calculation and presentation linkbases, through a hierarchical path-based measure, based on [13].

Information was extracted using Arelle tool (www.arelle.org), v 1.0.0. The experiment was conducted on 4 taxonomies of companies in the same market segment and same state (Massachusetts), applied to reports submitted to the United States - Securities and Exchange Commission (US-SEC). The US-SEC allows companies that report their financial data to extend the original taxonomy provided by the US-SEC (US-GAAP) and to incorporate concepts that they feel are relevant and necessary to be informed.

The purpose of this evaluation was to identify similarities between new concepts created by these taxonomies that extend the US-GAAP standard taxonomy. The selection of companies in the same market segment aimed to restrict the taxonomies to a context that facilitates the identification of recurrence in creating new concepts as they are companies whose operation is similar and probably have the same need to use concepts for representation of its financial facts.

The identification of similar concepts between the extended taxonomies can help detection of duplicate concepts which may be useful, for instance, in integrating the taxonomies in case of merging companies.

The selected market segment was "Services - Computer Programming Services" whose Standard Industrial Classification code (SIC) is 7371. On June 2013, the latest taxonomies of all active Massachusetts companies in the segment SIC-7371 were downloaded from US-SECs public site. The list of companies with their respective quantities of new concepts is presented in Figure 2.

Preffix	Company	Qty.
azpn	ASPEN TECHONOLOGY INC	55
dwre	Demandware Inc	25
type	Monotype Image Holdings Inc.	28
wrtu	VIRTUSA CORP.	73
	Total New Concepts	181

Figure 2 – Companies of the experiment

First, the defined relevant information was extracted: concepts, names, labels and relationships. Then, similarity between all concepts was evaluated using the basic approach; therefore 16,290 evaluations of pairs of concepts (181 * 180 / 2) were performed. On average, the each pair evaluation took 0.79s and the whole experiment took 3.6 hours.

Of the 16,290 total pairs, 75 pairs were found with total mean similarity (content and structure) greater than 0.5 (0.46%). If we consider only pairs with concepts belonging to different companies, the total of 75 pairs with mean similarity greater than 0.5 falls down to 5 (0.03%). The 5 pairs are shown if Figure 3.

ConceptA		ConceptB		Similarities		
Tax.	Name	Tax.	Name	Cont.	Strct.	Mean
type	NumberOfSubsidiariesForeign	dwre	NumberOfSubsidiaries	0.70	0.66	0.68
type	NumberOfSubsidiariesDomestic	dwre	NumberOfSubsidiaries	0.68	0.63	0.65
vrtu	ShareBasedCompensationArrangementByShareBasedPaymentAwardEquityInstrumentsOtherThanOptionsGrantDateFairValue	azpn	ShareBasedCompensationArrangementByShareBasedPaymentAwardEquityInstrumentsOtherThanOptionsExpectedToVestWeightedAverageGrantDateFairValue	0.40	0.66	0.58
vrtu	ShareBasedCompensationArrangementByShareBasedPaymentAwardNonOptionEquityInstrumentsOutstandingIntrinsicValue	azpn	ShareBasedCompensationArrangementByShareBasedPaymentAwardEquityInstrumentsOtherThanOptionsExpectedToVestOutstandingNumber	0.57	0.55	0.56
vrtu	ShareBasedCompensationArrangementsByShareBasedPaymentAwardOptionsExpirationTerm	azpn	ShareBasedCompensationArrangementByShareBasedPaymentAwardContractualTerm	0.34	0.57	0.50

Figure 3 – Pairs with more similarity

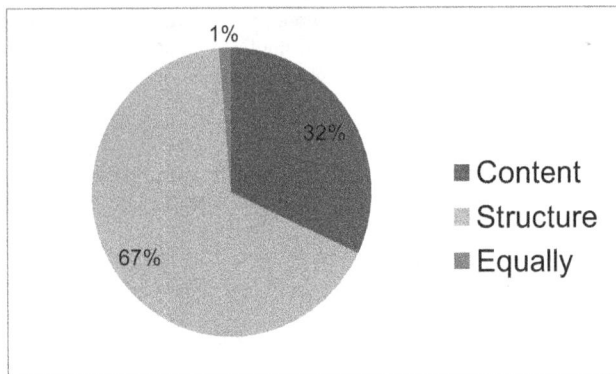

Figure 4 – Contribution to Mean Similarity

A comparison of importance between structure and content similarity can be evaluated analyzing the graph shown if Figure 4. 67% of the pairs with similarity greater than 0.5 (50 pairs out of 75) had structure similarity as the major contributor (Structure similarity > Mean). This demonstrates the importance of structure similarity to the process.

5. CONCLUSION AND FUTURE WORK

The utility of a similarity evaluation process in XML elements declared using XML Schema and XLink becomes undeniable in front of the growing use of these standards. This work proposes a process and demonstrates its feasibility through an experiment conducted on XBRL concepts, since XBRL is based on XML, XML Schema and XLink.

As future work, we intend to apply different techniques of similarity evaluation in order to compare them and detect which one best fits the context of XML Schema and XLink, especially in the structure similarity evaluation.

In addition, analyzing the performance of the similarity evaluation process is an important future work, since the experiment presented does not address this issue. So is the analysis of methods for combining individual similarity measures into a unique value.

In the context of XBRL experiment, the use of other techniques will allow inclusion of new information relevant to the process, such as Definition linkbase relationships, XBRL Dimensions [11] and XBRL Formula [7] extensions. We intend to explore the results of similarity evaluations on several XBRL taxonomies, subjecting them to the analysis of experts to evaluate the efficiency of the process. Also, develop an interface for execution by lay users, in order to facilitate the engagement of experts.

6. REFERENCES

[1] Ananthakrishna, R.; Chauduri, S. and Ganti, V., 1999. Eliminating fuzzy duplicates in data warehouses. *In Proceedings of the International Conference on Very Large Data Bases*, p.586-597

[2] Bartley, J.; Chen, A. Y. S. and Taylor, E. Z., 2011 A comparison of XBRL filings to corporate 10-ks-evidence from the voluntary filing program. *Accounting Horizons*, v. 25, n. 2, p. 227-245.

[3] Catania, B., & Maddalena, A., 2002. A clustering approach for XML linked documents. *In Database and Expert Systems Applications, 2002. Proceedings. 13th International Workshop on. IEEE.*, pp. 121-125

[4] Cohen W. W., 1998. Integration of Heterogeneous Databases Without Common Domains Using Queries Based on Textual Similarity. *In Proceedings of ACM International Conference on Management of Data (SIGMOD)*, p.201-212.

[5] Derose, S.; Maler, E.; Orchard, D., 2001 XML Linking Language (XLINK) 1.0, W3C Recommendation, Available at: http://www.w3.org/TR/xlink

[6] Engel, P.; Hamscher, W.; Shuetrim, G.; Vunkannon, D. e Wallis, H., 2003. Extensible Business Reporting Language (XBRL) 2.1. Available at: http://www.xbrl.org/ Specification/XBRL-RECOMMENDATION-2003-12-31.pdf

[7] Engel, P.; Herm, F.; Morilla, V.; Richards, J.; Shuetrim, G.; Vunkannon, D. e Wallis, H., 2009. Formula 1.0. Available at: http://www.xbrl.org/Specification/formula/REC-2009-06-22/formula-REC-2009-06-22.html

[8] Elmagarmid, A.K.; Iperioris, P.G. and Verykios, V.S., 2007. Duplicate record detection: A survey. *In IEEE Transactions on Knowledge and Data Engineering*, Vol.19, No.1, p.95-99.

[9] Fallside, D. C.and Walmsey, P., 2004 XML SCHEMA Part 0: Primer W3C Recommendation. Available at: http://www.w3.org/TR/2004/REC-xmlschema-0-20041028/

[10] Fellegi, I. P., Sunter, A. B., 1969. A Theory for record linkage. Journal of the American Statistical Association. v.64, n.328, p.1183-1210.

[11] Hernández-Ros, I. and Wallis, H., 2012, XBRL Dimensions 1.0. Available at: http://www.xbrl.org/ specification/ dimensions/ rec-2012-01-25/ dimensions-rec-2006-09-18+corrected-errata-2012-01-25-clean.html

[12] Jaro, M. A., 1976. *UNIMATCH: A Record Linkage System, User's Manual.* U.S. Bureau of the Census, Washington, DC.

[13] Kade A. M. and Heuser, C. A., 2008. Matching XML Documents in Highly Dynamic Applications. *In Proceedings of the ACM Symposium on Document Engineering*, p.191-198.

[14] Levenshtein, V. I., 1966. Binary codes capable of correcting deletions, insertions and reversals. *In Soviet physics doklady*, Vol. 10, p. 707.

[15] Monge, A. E.; Elkan, C. P., 1996. The Field Matching Problem: Algorithms and Application. *In Proceedings of International Conference on Knowledge Discovery and Data Mining (KDD)*, p.267-270.

[16] Rahm, E. and Bernstein, P.A, 2001. A survey of approaches to automatic schema matching. VLDB Journal 10, v.4. p.334-350

[17] Smith, T. F. and Waterman, M. S., 1982. Identification of Common Molecular Subsequences. *In Journal Molecular Biology*, Vol.147, p.195-197.

[18] Taft, R. L., 1970. *Name Search Techniques*. New York State Identification and Intelligence System, Albany.

[19] Tekli, J.; Chbeir, R.; Yetongnon, K., 2009. An overview on XML similarity: background, current trends and future directions. *In Computer Science Review*, Vol.3, No.3, p.151-173.

[20] Ukkonen, E., 1992. Approximate String Matching with q-Grams and Maximal Matches. *In Theoretical Computer Science*, Vol.92, No.1, pp.191-211.

[21] Waterman, M. S.; Smith, T. F.; Beyer, W. A., 1976. Some biological sequence metrics. In Advances in Math, Vol.20, No.4, p.367-387.

[22] Weiss, M. e Naumann, F., 2005. DogmatiX Tracks down Duplicates in XML. In Proceedings of the ACM SIGMOD International Conference on Management of Data. p.96-110.

[23] Zhu, H.; Wu, H., 2011 Quality of data standards: framework and illustration using XBRL taxonomy and instances. *Electronic Markets*, v. 21, n. 2, p. 129-139.

Delay-aware DWT-based Image Transmission in Wireless Visual Sensor Networks

Daniel G. Costa
DTEC – UEFS
State University of Feira
de Santana
Brazil
danielgcosta@uefs.br

Luiz Affonso Guedes
DCA – UFRN
Federal University of Rio
Grande do Norte
Brazil
affonso@dca.ufrn.br

Francisco Vasques
IDMEC – UP
University of Porto
Portugal
vasques@fe.up.pt

Paulo Portugal
INESC TEC – UP
University of Porto
Portugal
pportugal@fe.up.pt

ABSTRACT

Wireless sensor networks have been employed as an effective tool for a large set of monitoring applications, directly supporting applications not addressed by conventional Internet-based technologies. Camera-enabled sensors enhance the applicability of those networks allowing innovative visual monitoring functions. Sometimes, source nodes will perform real-time monitoring of an area of interest, where visual data packets will need to be transmitted with minimum delay. However, energy depletion of the nodes that compose the transmission paths may hamper the network capability to deliver packets with time constraints. In such context, we propose a delay-aware image transmission mechanism where the relevancies of DWT subbands are considered when forwarding packets to the next hop toward the sink. In fact, parts of DWT-based encoded visual data may have different relevancies for the reconstruction of the original visual information and those relevancies may be exploited when forwarding packets. In the proposed approach, high-relevant packets are forwarded through paths with lower average end-to-end delay, while the remaining packets flow through paths high higher delay, allowing that low-quality versions of the transmitted images reach the sink as soon as possible. Moreover, the best paths will need to relay fewer packets, potentially reducing energy consumption and enlarging their lifetime. We present simulation results to attest the benefits of the proposed mechanism.

Categories and Subject Descriptors

C.3 [**Special-Purpose and Application-Based Systems**]: Real-time and embedded systems.

Keywords

Delay-aware transmission; DWT coding; Real-time image transmission; Wireless visual sensor networks.

1. INTRODUCTION

The development of wireless sensor networks (WSN) has changed the way a large variety of information types are gathered from the environment. Information as humidity, pressure, temperature,

luminosity, among others, can be retrieved from wide and hard-access areas, or even from small indoor regions, providing a wealth resource for many applications not addressed by Internet-based networks [2][26]. Great efforts in the last decades have turned wireless sensor networks into a feasible and affordable technology for monitoring applications for different purposes.

Sensor nodes can be equipped with a low-power camera, allowing visual monitoring of an area of interest. Visual sensing significantly enhances the perception of the monitored field and there are a wide range of potential applications in both civilian and military areas that benefit from the use of camera-enabled sensor nodes [4][8]. In short, wireless visual sensor networks (WVSN) consist of a number of battery-operated self-organizing nodes where some or all of them are endowed with a low-power camera. Particularly, the limited energy supply is a critical factor that turns energy preservation into a major optimization issue, especially when visual information is retrieved from the monitored field. Energy is required for processing and communication procedures, but the communication costs are usually much higher than the computational costs [17][21].

In general words, we can expect that the energy consumption rate will be a direct function of the amount of information to be transmitted over the network, although other issues related with the operation of physical and MAC protocols will also play an important role in the overall energy consumption. In such way, a reasonable approach to preserve energy is to reduce the amount of information to be transmitted over the network.

Wireless visual sensor networks may be deployed for online real-time monitoring, where visual data collected by source nodes will need to be delivered as soon as possible to the sink, for instant visualization, storage or processing [1]. In many cases, sensors will be massively deployed, resulting in nodes scattered over the monitored field. In such context, there may be many active transmission paths from the sources to the sink, each one with particular characteristics in terms of residual energy and average end-to-end delay. When real-time transmission is required, the paths with lower delay will be excessively used to meet the latency requirements, potentially reducing their expected lifetime. In other words, the network capability to deliver data packets with time constraints will be shortened when every single packet is forwarded through the best (lower delay) paths.

Visual source nodes can encode still images using Discrete Wavelet Transform (DWT), a transform that decomposes original images in different subbands. Each DWT subband will have a particular relevance for the reconstruction of the original images and those relevancies may be exploited for network optimizations.

In fact, one subband is the most relevant and presents a low-quality version of the original image, while the remaining subbands contain vertical, horizontal and diagonal details for the decoding process.

We propose a delay-aware DWT-based image transmission mechanism to save energy over paths with lower end-to-end delay, potentially enlarging their lifetime and assuring real-time delivery for longer. The relevancies of DWT subbands are considered when deciding the appropriate transmission path. Such decision will be performed in source nodes and in intermediate nodes that receive traffic from more than one source. Doing so, energy is preserved over paths with lower average end-to-end delay, since they will receive less traffic along the time.

When employing the proposed approach, low-quality versions of the transmitted images will sooner reach the sink. The complementary details of the images will still be transmitted, but will flow over paths with average higher end-to-end delay. Applications will typically use that information to increase the quality of the previously received images. This coarse-to-clear image reconstruction allows quick processing of low-quality images, but still assures that high quality images will be very soon available for processing or storage.

The remainder of this paper is organized as follows. Section 2 presents the related works. Some fundamental concepts related with the presented work are discussed in Section 3. Section 4 brings the proposed transmission approach. Some simulation results are presented in Section 5, followed by conclusions and references.

2. RELATED WORKS

Optimizations of image transmission in wireless visual sensor networks have been largely investigated in last years, where different aspects as energy preservation, error recovery, congestion control and timeliness have been frequently addressed [10]. We are mainly concerned with works that investigate packet forwarding in wireless sensor networks and that exploit image coding for prioritization purposes.

The work in [18] proposes a full-reliable transmission mechanism for high-priority DWT subbands, while the remaining DWT subbands are transmitted in a semi-reliable mode. The idea is that intermediate nodes may silently drop low relevant packets according to the current energy level of the node and the relevance of the packets' payloads, saving energy with some quality loss of the received images. In [19], authors exploit DWT coding to reduce the total amount of information to be transmitted by source nodes when transmission paths face congestion. The relevancies of DWT subbands are considered by intermediate nodes when deciding if packets must be silently dropped, where low relevant packets are the first to be dropped. A similar prioritization approach is adopted in [9], where DWT-based data packets are transmitted under different reliability services according to the relevancies of the packets' payloads. In that work, only high-relevant packets are always retransmitted if corrupted.

Besides exploitation of DWT coding for prioritization purposes, some works have investigated packet forwarding and routing, also influencing our work. In [20], authors propose a routing mechanism where higher relevant packets are routed through more reliable paths. Doing so, those packets will be transmitted over paths with a lower average error rate and node failures. A multipath routing scheme is proposed in [27], where the relevance

of the encoded data is exploited for path selection. The relevance is based on the splitting of the original data in audio and video substreams, each one with a particular priority level. That proposed approach routes the most relevant packets through paths with lower end-to-end delay for multimedia streaming, considering a set of available node-disjoint paths.

The way images are transmitted and reconstructed may also be optimized. The work in [7] proposes a transport protocol that allows synchronization of image transmission from multiple sources, assuring the same level of quality for the received images. For that, images are encoded by a progressive coding algorithm, where the source images are compressed through multiple scans with progressively increasing details. The idea is that a low-quality version of the transmitted images can be exhibited very quickly at the destination, with gradual refinements when more data packets arrive. In fact, that work aims at a better use of the available transmission bandwidth, with low or absent concern to the average end-to-end transmission delay.

We propose an innovative image transmission mechanism for real-time monitoring that exploits the relevancies of DWT subbands to reduce energy consumption over the paths with lower average end-to-end delay, in a different way of [7][20][27]. As in [9][18][19], the characteristics of DWT coding are considered when prioritizing packets, achieving a quick coarse-to-clear reconstruction of images, as in [7]. And although we are proposing a mechanism that may provide images with progressively increasing quality, we are proposing herein a selective routing approach that brings additional results for coding-level progressive image transmission mechanisms, as presented in [7][13].

3. FUNDAMENTAL CONCEPTS

Wireless visual sensor networks may be deployed for real-time monitoring of an area of interest. We propose a delay-aware image transmission mechanism that exploits DWT coding to reduce energy consumption over the paths with lower average end-to-end delay, in order to prolong the network capability to deliver real-time packets.

In this section we present the fundamental concepts related with our work, focusing on transmission delay, energy consumption and DWT image coding.

3.1 Average end-to-end delay

Wireless sensor networks will be typically composed of many ad hoc multihop transmission paths from source nodes to the sink. In those paths, packets will be relayed by a number of intermediate nodes. In fact, the transmission delay may be originated from different aspects of wireless communications, as the radio operation, the MAC protocol, the congestion control approach, the error recovery mechanism and the transmission rate.

Usually, radio hardware will be composed of a single wireless antenna, and thus the radio must be active to receive packets from neighbor nodes. Energy is consumed when the radio is turned on, but no packet may be received during some periods of activation. Such periods of idle listening may rapidly deplete the energy resources of the nodes, requiring the adoption of MAC protocols that insert sleeping periods into the radio operation [12]. During sleeping time the node is unable to process or relay packets, increasing the end-to-end communication delay.

The operation characteristics of some medium access control protocols may also affect the communication delay, especially when packets collide, according to the adopted mechanism to discipline the use of the communication link. End-to-end congestion and error control mechanisms will also affect the perceived delay of the communication. At last, interferences are usually unpredictable. Such complex scenario is hard to formulate, pushing us to adopt some level of simplification or to employ computational discrete event simulators, as presented in Section 5.

We assume that each link between node h and node $(h + 1)$, in path p, will have an average end-to-end delay of $d_{(p,h)}$. The average end-to-end delay of a path p is formulated in (1), where each path p is composed of $H(p)$ intermediate nodes.

$$L(p) = \sum_{h=0}^{H(p)} \left(d_{(p,h)} \right) \quad (1)$$

In such way, for a network composed of n routing paths $P = \{p_1, ..., p_n\}$, we can expect that each path p_i has an end-to-end transmission delay of $L(p_i)$. Based on (1), we can roughly state that the end-to-end delay increases when packets have to cross more hops, and if $H(p_i) > H(p_j)$, we can expect that $L(p_i) > L(p_j)$. Therefore, we will compare the end-to-end delay of different paths through the number of intermediate nodes, in the same way of [11][27].

Besides the number of hops, the transmission rate may also impact the communication delay, directing affecting the sleeping time and MAC layer collisions and retransmissions. However, if we define t_i as the transmission rate in path p_i and t_j as the transmission rate in path p_j, and if $t_i > t_j$ for $H(p_i) = H(p_j)$, we cannot expect that $L(p_i) > L(p_j)$ since different periods of node sleeping may compensate the additional number of packets to be transmitted. In such cases, the average end-to-end delay will depend on many factors, turning imprecise the definition of mathematical models.

This basic theoretical analysis of end-to-end delay is based on average measures of transmission latency and thus they are inaccurate to estimate the communication delay of particular packets. However, it gives us a reasonable approach to identify the best paths in terms of transmission delay. We will rely on simulation results instead of theoretical analyses when assessing the performance of the proposed transmission mechanism.

3.2 Energy consumption

The actual energy consumption in each node due to communication depends on many factors, as the employed radio hardware, the transmission power and the physical and MAC protocols, resulting in a complex scenario. In fact, transmission paths may be disabled when intermediate nodes run out of energy. Many works have tried to formulate analytical models for energy consumption, which always incorporate some level of simplification [6][14]. We defined a simplified energy consumption model in order to support our theoretical assumptions, although the assessment of the proposed optimization approach will be performed by computational simulations.

Images are expected to be transmitted in small data packets (reducing the error probability [16]) and with the same size, and typically many packets will be necessary to transmit even small pieces of visual data. The transmission of packets with the same size is a reasonable approach for most wireless visual sensor

networks and packets will be transmitted with maximum size for lower overhead. We consider that every data packet has the same size in bits, k, corresponding to the entire packet (data payload plus protocol headers). The size in bits of all protocol headers in each packet is defined as z, resulting in an effective payload area of $(k - z)$ in each data packet.

For a network composed of S source nodes, we assume that each source node s, $s = 1,...,S$, will transmit $D_{(s)}$ data packets. Considering either lossless or fully-reliable wireless links, each intermediate node in the path from the source s to the sink will have to relay at least $T.f_{(s)}.D_{(s)}$ data packets, for T seconds and a transmission frequency of $f_{(s)}$.

The consumed energy to send and receive bits in each intermediate node h depends on its transmission power, $Pwt_{(p,h)}$, and the power for bits reception, $Pwr_{(p,h)}$. The time for transmission of 1 bit is $tx_{(p,h)}$, according to the transmission rate. The formulation in (2) roughly defines the energy consumption in hop h of path p, $Et_{(p,h,s)}$, for transmission from source s. The same is valid for the energy consumed due to packet reception, $Er_{(p,h,s)}$, and the sum of both energy values in all hops results in the energy consumption over the entire path, $E_{(p,s)}$.

$$Et_{(p,h,s)} = T.f_{(s)}.D_{(s)}.k.Pwt_{(p,h)}.tx_{(p,h)}$$
$$Er_{(p,h,s)} = T.f_{(s)}.D_{(s)}.k.Pwr_{(p,h)}.tx_{(p,h)}$$
$$E_{(p,s)} = \sum_{h=0}^{H(p)+1} \left(Et_{(p,h,s)} + Er_{(p,h,s)} \right) \quad (2)$$

The basic formulation in (2) could be still considerably extended to incorporate new elements, as packet retransmissions, transmission of ACK messages and radio hardware switching among transmitting, receiving and sleeping modes. However, we are mainly concerned herein with estimation of the energy consumption during transmission over the paths, and the amount of information to be transmitted ($D_{(s)}.k$) seems to play an important role even with addition of new variables. Moreover, more energy is expected to be consumed when packets have to be transmitted through more intermediate nodes (higher $H(p)$). In such way, energy saving should be achieved when fewer packets have to be transmitted over the paths.

Our basic assumption that supports our proposed transmission approach is that shorter paths provide lower average end-to-end delay. In addition, we expect that energy saving will be achieved when fewer packets have to cross the transmission paths.

3.3 DWT image coding

Still images are snapshots of the monitored target or scene. Before transmission, every image have to be properly encoded following some coding technique, where the final quality vary according to the application requirements: grayscale low-resolution images may be suitable for some types of monitoring, while colored high-resolution images are expected for high definition applications or when resource-rich sensors are deployed.

Wavelet transform has been employed in wireless visual sensor networks as an effective mechanism for image coding. While in the progressive technique the source image is compressed through multiple scans with progressively increasing details, wavelet-based techniques like Discrete Wavelet Transform (DWT) involves two-dimensional wavelet decomposition of the original image, giving low and high frequency subbands. Wavelet coefficients are quantized, coded and transmitted as a bit stream. DWT has been considered as a flexible option for image coding, allowing a series of cross-layer optimizations for energy preservation with low impact on the application overall quality [5][10][25].

DWT decomposes a signal by passing it through two filters: a lowpass filter L and a highpass filter H. The lowpass subband represents a down-sampled low resolution version of the original signal, while the highpass subband contains residual information. All information from lowpass and highpass filters is necessary for the perfect reconstruction of the original signal at the receiver side [5], and digital images will be processed as two-dimensional signals. A 2D DWT processes images considering the rows and columns, generating four subbands: LL, LH, HL and HH. The LL subband represents the lowest resolution and a half-sized version of the original image, while the remaining subbands contains vertical, horizontal and diagonal details for the decoding process. Such processing produces two groups of relevance, but the LL subband could be transformed again to generate more levels of resolution. In general, to achieve t levels of resolution, the 2D DWT have to be applied $(t-1)$ times.

We assumed that original images are encoded by the Le Gall 5-tap/3-tap wavelet [23], a DWT that is based on binary shifter and integer additions. This option has been considered as a feasible approach for resource-constrained wireless visual sensor networks and there are a few works that employ the same wavelet for image coding in WVSN [10] [18].

Figure 1 presents an original image that is processed by a DWT applied once and twice, resulting in two and three levels of resolution, respectively from left to right.

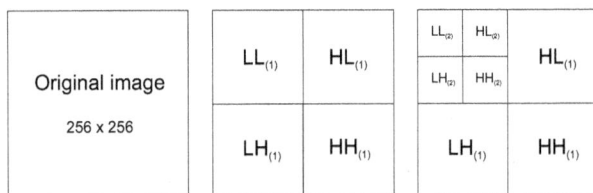

Figure 1. DWT decomposition of an original image.

Typically, each packet will carry data of only one DWT subband, since packets are expected to be small. An original image i will size $B_{(i)}$ bits, and $k << B_{(i)}$. As DWT subbands have different relevancies for the reconstruction of the original images, packets may be transmitted under different transmission services.

4. PROPOSED APPROACH

Camera-enabled source nodes are deployed to transmit visual data packets to the sink of the network and typically those packets will have the same priority in standard WVSN. In fact, wireless visual sensor networks are likely to be composed of several source nodes, which may be connected to the sink through more than one transmission path. Moreover, a single intermediate node may belong to more than one transmission path, depending on the nodes positions after deployment and the available paths discovered by the employed routing protocol. In such way, visual active sensors and some intermediate nodes may be connected to more than one path and packets that need to be transmitted to the next hop may be relayed to one among many destinations.

When real-time monitoring is required, every incoming packet will be relayed to the path with lowest average end-to-end delay,

meeting the transmission requirements of the application. However, such behavior may rapidly deplete the energy resources of the best path, early increasing the overall delay of packets transmitted over the network. If only high-relevant packets were forwarded to the path with lowest delay, energy could be saved, prolonging the network capability to deliver real-time data.

We propose a packet forwarding mechanism that exploits the relevancies of DWT image coding to reduce energy consumption over the paths with lower end-to-end delay. Each packet will be assigned to a QoS (Quality of Service) level according to the relevance of the packet's payload. We assume that every original image will be processed by a 2-level 2D DWT, resulting in seven different subbands: $LL_{(2)}$, $LH_{(2)}$, $HL_{(2)}$, $HH_{(2)}$, $LH_{(1)}$, $HL_{(1)}$ and $HH_{(1)}$. Each subband will be mapped to a value of Data Relevance (DR), a 2-bit number to be inserted into every transmitted packet, just after the fragmentation header z. Table 1 presents the mapping between the DWT subbands and DR. We decided to assign higher values of DR to subbands with higher relevance. The Data Relevance information also embraces the transmission of complementary scalar data, which is established to the lowest priority level (but could be associated to another level of relevance depending on the application monitoring requirements). Additionally, the header of the entire image, $o_{(i)}$, is necessary for the reconstruction of the image as a whole and thus will be transmitted with the highest relevance.

We can roughly state that 6.25% (plus $o_{(i)}$) of the original image will have DR=3, 18.75% will have DR=2 and 75% of the original image will be transmitted with DR=1, when DWT is configured to not alter the number of bits of the original images.

Table 1. Values for DR.

DWT subband	DR
$LL_{(2)}$ and $o_{(i)}$	3
$LH_{(2)}$, $HL_{(2)}$ and $HH_{(2)}$	2
$LH_{(1)}$, $HL_{(1)}$ and $HH_{(1)}$	1
Scalar data	0

If we define $W_{(i,DR)}$ as the number of packets to be transmitted for an image i according to the value of DR, we achieve the formulations in (3). We are assuming packets with the same size for simplicity, but the last packet after fragmentation may be smaller, as discussed in [11].

Active source nodes will include the value of DR in each transmitted data packet, according to the packets' payloads. Although such requirement may incur in additional energy consumption, the actual impact depends on the adopted MAC technology and wireless radio, and the inclusion of optimization information into data packets is a common approach largely adopted by the academic community [10].

When visual sensors collect image snapshots from the monitored field, each original image will be coded by a 2-level 2D DWT. The proposed approach determines that source nodes will transmit packets in sequence, but packets with higher DR must be transmitted earlier since they have higher priority. Moreover, during packet transmission, source and intermediate nodes will check the value of DR in order to verify the expected level of priority, where packets with higher DR will be processed and forwarded prior to low relevant packets. If source or intermediate nodes are connected to more than one transmission path, the value of DR will be considered when deciding the best destination, according to the definitions in Table 2. Note that the values for DR will be processed according to the number of available paths.

$$W_{(i,3)} = \left\lfloor \frac{\left\lceil \frac{B_{(i)}}{16} \right\rceil + o_{(i)}}{(k-z)} \right\rfloor$$

$$W_{(i,2)} = \left\lfloor \frac{\left\lceil \frac{3B_{(i)}}{16} \right\rceil}{(k-z)} \right\rfloor \quad (3)$$

$$W_{(i,1)} = \left\lfloor \frac{\left\lceil \frac{3B_{(i)}}{4} \right\rceil}{(k-z)} \right\rfloor$$

Table 2. DR-based packet relaying.

Path	DR of packets that must be forwarded through the path
2 available paths ($H(p1) < H(p2)$)	
p_1	3
p_2	0, 1 or 2
3 available paths ($H(p1) < H(p2) < H(p3)$)	
p_1	3
p_2	2
p_3	0 or 1
4 available paths ($H(p1) < H(p2) < H(p3) < H(p4)$)	
p_1	3
p_2	2
p_3	1
p_4	0
More than 4 paths ($H(p1) < H(p2) < H(p3) < H(p4) < H(p(4+i))$)	
p_1	3
p_2	2
p_3	1
p_4	0
$p_{(4+i)}$	Backup paths

Each source and intermediate node will have its own packet forwarding policy, with no interference of neighbor nodes, according only to the number of available transmission paths toward the sink. The backup paths are to be used when the main paths run out of energy, but their usages as redundant paths or for load balancing are out of the scope of this paper.

We assume that transmission paths are established using some routing protocol and that the available paths are already known by source and intermediate nodes. Some routing protocols as [3][22] can provide information of the number of hops of the paths, and we consider this information to estimate the average end-to-end delay, as defined in (1).

As a final comment, images can be reconstructed with low quality as long as packets are received at the sink side. For that, missing information (low-relevant packets will be delayed) will be replaced by zeros, but the sink may constantly update the reconstructed images when new packets arrive.

5. SIMULATION RESULTS

We conducted a series of computational simulations in order to validate the proposed DR-aware DWT-based transmission mechanism, aiming at the estimation of the average end-to-end delay and the energy consumption in experimental WVSN. The simulations were performed employing the framework Castalia [24], a C++ discrete event simulator based on the OMNeT++ platform. For this framework, we established that all nodes will be communicating employing a duty-cycle protocol [12].

The first simulation was concerned with the average end-to-end delay of a particular transmission path, since we have to validate our assumption that paths composed of more intermediate nodes will impose higher average end-to-end delay. Figure 2 presents the average end-to-end delay according to the number of hops of the path from a unique source node, for $T = 21600s$. We assume in this experiment that the visual source node is connected to the sink through a single multihop path, and that the source is transmitting uncompressed 64 x 64 8-bit grayscale still images, with $k = 133$ and $z = 30$. A 2-level 2D DWT is applied over the original images and 7 subbands are generated. Since subbands with different relevancies for the reconstruction of the original images are generated, we are not concerned with the content of each subband. Thus, the same results are expected for different images. We also consider three different transmission frequencies: $f_{(s)} = 0.1$, $f_{(s)} = 0.2$ and $f_{(s)} = 0.5$. At last, the distance between neighbor nodes is settled in 10m and they have a transmission power of 0dBm.

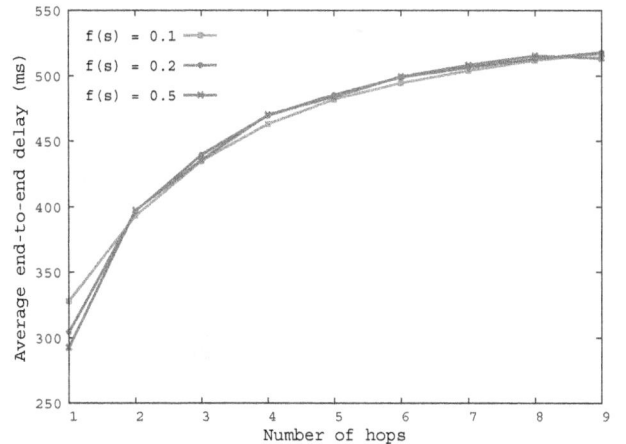

Figure 2. Average end-to-end delay.

The average-delay in Figure 2 was a function of the number of intermediate nodes of the path, as defined in (1). However, depending on the characteristics of the employed protocols, the transmission frequency may have very low impact on the communication delay, although the energy consumption will be affected when more packets have to be transmitted along the time, as expressed in (2). Although we cannot affirm that the transmission frequency has no impact in the average delay, since we considered a small scope of tests, we can expect that the number of hops of the path will have significant impact in the

161

end-to-end delay, but additional investigations are still required to assess the transmission latency in very large networks.

Figure 3 presents the results for energy consumption considering the same experiment, for the entire transmission path.

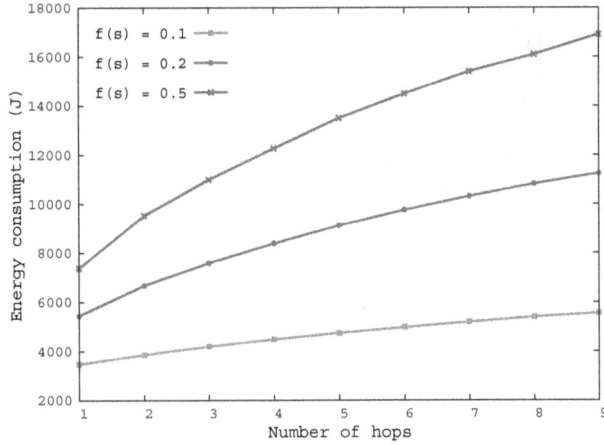

Figure 3. Energy consumption for different transmission frequencies.

A reasonable way to reduce energy consumption over a transmission path is to decrease the amount of information that have to cross it. Following the proposed transmission approach, only high-relevant packets will be transmitted over the paths with lower average end-to-end delay. In fact, the expected delay of each path will be measured according to the number of hops that compose the path. We can then estimate the energy savings when only those packets are transmitted through the best paths, potentially prolonging their transmission lifetime.

As stated before, every source node will transmit images processed by a 2-level 2D DWT. Figure 4 presents a communication scenario where one source node (s1) is connected to the sink through 3 node-disjoint paths.

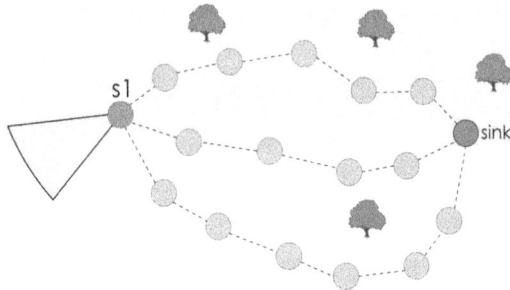

Figure 4. Communication scenario 1.

For that communication scenario, the best transmission path (lowest average end-to-end delay) is composed of 4 intermediate nodes (light blue circles). The average energy consumption over that path is presented in Figure 5, for $f_{(s)} = 0.1$ and considering a traditional transmission mechanism (without packet prioritization) and the proposed approach. Note that $W_{(i,3)} = 3$, $W_{(i,2)} = 8$ e $W_{(i,1)} = 30$, for an original image i sizing 64 x 64 bytes and $o_{(i)} = 40$ bytes, and that the traditional mechanism transmits whole images (40 packets each) through the best path in order to completely fulfill the application requirements for real-time transmission.

In the presented results, the average energy saving over the network is higher than 10% when employing the proposed approach, which is significant for general-purpose wireless image sensor networks.

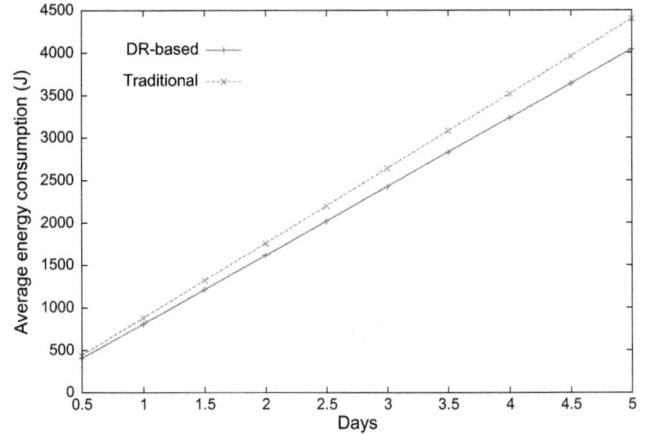

Figure 5. Average energy consumption over the path with lowest end-to-end delay, for the communication scenario 1.

In a different way, Figure 6 presents a small wireless visual sensor networks composed of 3 source nodes: s1, s2 and s3. In that scenario, one intermediate node belongs to more than one path and thus receives packets from more than one source node.

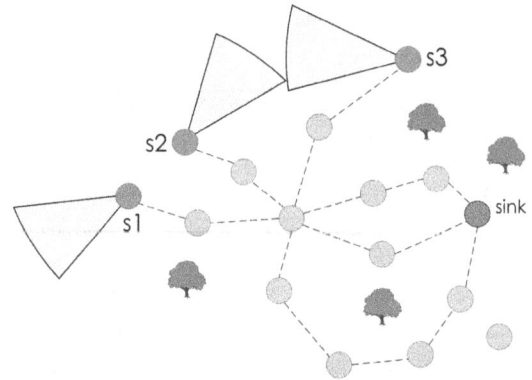

Figure 6. Communication scenario 2.

For the three source nodes in Figure 6, the best path (lowest average end-to-end delay) is composed of 3 intermediate nodes. The energy consumption over that path is presented in Figure 7, for $f_{(s)} = 0.1$.

As fewer packets were forwarded through the best path when applying the proposed approach, the energy saving was even higher, reaching 20%. In fact, the actual energy saving depends on many factors, as the network topology and configurations, the employed protocols operation, the transmission frequency and the original images sizes. When applying the proposed transmission approach, energy will be saved over the best paths, turning this solution into a valuable resource for wireless visual sensor networks. Although low-relevant packets will be delayed when routed through slow/large paths, they carry only complementary information to enhance the quality of the reconstructed images at the destination.

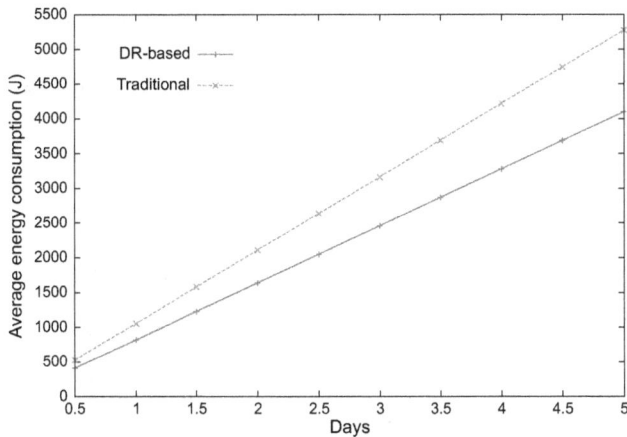

Figure 7. Average energy consumption over the path with lowest end-to-end delay, for the communication scenario 2.

For transmissions through node-disjoint paths, energy saving over paths with lowest end-to-end delay is significant and can prolong the network capability to deliver real-time data. However, in some cases there may be nodes that will behave like a "bottleneck" and the expected lifetime of the network as a whole may vary slightly for both assessed transmission approaches, in these cases. For homogeneous sensor networks where the energy resources of all intermediate nodes are the same, the expected network lifetime may be not significantly influenced by the proposed solution. Nevertheless, wireless visual sensor networks may be dynamic, with mobile nodes frequently adjusting the network topology. Moreover, new nodes may be deployed along the time and redundant nodes may be activated to compensate nodes with depleted energy. In all these cases, the outcome when employing the proposed transmission approach may be highly beneficial for WVSN.

Sometimes, two or more paths may have the same size, potentially providing the same average end-to-end delay. In such cases, any path could be used when forwarding high-relevant packets or all these paths could be reserved for packets with higher priority. In fact, source or intermediate nodes may take any decision, depending on the application requirements.

DWT image coding requires energy of the active source nodes. Although this energy was not accounted in the performed experiments, it is unlike the transmission of raw images, leading us to expect that even traditional transmission mechanisms would have energy costs for image coding.

As DWT subbands may reach the sink within different average latency, images may be reconstructed with different qualities along the time. Figure 8 presents an example of a reconstructed image in three different configurations: a) with only $LL_{(2)}$ (DR=3), b) with only $LL_{(2)}$, $LH_{(2)}$, $HL_{(2)}$ and $HH_{(2)}$ (DR=3 + DR=2) and c) with all subbands (DR=3 + DR=2 + DR=1). If packets are received in this sequence, we achieve a coarse-to-clear reconstruction of the transmitted images.

As wireless visual sensor networks may be deployed for a large variety of monitoring applications, with different sensing requirements, we expect that a coarse-to-clear reconstruction of the received images may be acceptable in many cases, with very low impact to the performed sensing functions.

a) Reconstructed with DR=3 visual data.

b) Reconstructed with DR=3 and DR=2 visual data.

c) Reconstructed with DR=3, DR=2 and DR=1 visual data.

Figure 8. Coarse-to-clear reconstruction of an image.

6. CONCLUSIONS

We have proposed a delay-aware DWT-based image transmission mechanism where high-relevant packets are transmitted through the shortest paths in order to reduce energy consumption over these paths, enlarging their lifetime. The packets priorities are assigned according to the relevance of DWT subbands for the reconstruction of the original images. This innovative idea can prolong the lifetime of paths with lower delay, potentially extending the network capability to deliver packets with time constraints and better addressing time-critical monitoring applications.

This work is not concluded yet and new investigations will be done to further outline the benefits of the proposed transmission approach. Particularly, we aim to perform additional verifications in simulated environments in order to bring more conclusive results concerning energy consumption and transmission delay. In such context, more complex sensor network scenarios will be considered when assessing the performance of the proposed transmission approach. As transmission paths may run out of energy and new nodes may be deployed along the time, the network configuration may acquire some level of dynamism, requiring automatic adaptation of the forwarding policies in source and intermediate nodes. Transmission of RGB images will be also verified. At last, future works will also consider the assessment of the application monitoring quality concerning the monitoring delay, considering Quality of Experience [15] metrics.

7. REFERENCES

[1] Akyildiz, I., Melodia, T., and Chowdhury, K. 2007. A survey on wireless multimedia sensor networks. *Computer Networks*, 51, 921-960.

[2] Akyildiz, I., Su, W., Sankarasubramaniam, Y., and Cayirci, E. 2002. Wireless sensor networks: a survey. *Computer Networks*, 38, 4, 393-422.

[3] Al-Karaki, J., and Kamal, A. 2004. Routing techniques in wireless sensor networks: a survey. *IEEE Wireless Communications*, 11, 6-28.

[4] Almalkawi, I., Zapata, M., Al-Karaki, J., and Morillo-Pozo, J. 2010. Wireless multimedia sensor networks: current trends and future directions. *Sensors*, 10, 7, 6662-6717.

[5] Antonini, M., Barlaud, M., Mathieu, P., and Daubechies, I. 1992. Image coding using wavelet transform. *IEEE Transactions of Image Processing*. 1, 2, 205-220.

[6] Bajaber, F., and Awan, I. 2011. Adaptive decentralized re-clustering protocol for wireless sensor networks. *Journal of Computer and System Sciences*. 77, 282-292.

[7] Boukerche, A., Du, Y., Feng, J., and Pazzi, R. 2008. A reliable synchronous transport protocol for wireless image sensor networks. In *Proceedings of IEEE ISCC*, Marrakech, Morocco, 1083-1089.

[8] Charfi, Y., Canada, B., Wakamiya, N., and Murata, M. 2009. Challenging issues in visual sensor networks. *IEEE Wireless Communications*, 16, pp. 16, 44-49.

[9] Costa, D., and Guedes, L. 2012. A discrete wavelet transform (DWT)-based energy-efficient selective retransmission mechanism for wireless image sensor networks. *Journal of Sensor and Actuator Networks*. 1, 1, 3-35, 2012.

[10] Costa, D., and Guedes, L. 2011. A survey on multimedia-based cross-layer optimization in visual sensor networks. *Sensors*, 11, 5439-5468.

[11] Costa, D., Guedes, L., Vasques, F., and Portugal, P. 2012. A routing mechanism based on the sensing relevancies of source nodes for time-critical applications in visual sensor networks. In *Proceedings of IEEE Wireless Days*. Dublin, Ireland.

[12] Dam, T. van., and Langendoe, K. 2003. An adaptive energy-efficient MAC protocol for wireless sensor networks. In *Proceedings of* SenSys, Los Angeles, USA, 1-10.

[13] Ferriere, P. Progressive image transmission using discrete wavelet transforms. 2006. US Patent US7092118 B2.

[14] Heinzelman, W., Chandrakasan, A., and Balakrishnan, H. 2002. An application-specific protocol architecture for wireless microsensor networks. *IEEE Transaction on Wireless Communications*, 1, 4, 660-670.

[15] Klima, M., Fliegel, K., Kekrt, D., Dostal, P., and Podgorny, R. 2009. Image quality and QoE in multimedia systems. In *Proceedings of the International Conference Radioelektronika*, Bratislava, Slovak Republic, pp. 3-10.

[16] Korhonen, J., and Wang, Y. 2005. Effect of packet size on loss rate and delay in wireless links. In *Proceedings of IEEE WCNC*, New Orleans, USA, 1608-1613..

[17] Lecuire, V., Duran-Faundez, C., and Krommenacker, N. 2008. Energy-efficient image transmission in sensor networks. *International Journal of Sensor Networks*, 4, 1, 37-47.

[18] Lecuire, V., Duran-Faundez, C., and Krommenacker, N. 2007. Energy-efficient transmission of wavelet-based Images in wireless sensor networks. *EURASIP Journal of Image Video Processing*. 1-11.

[19] Lee, J-H., Jun, I-B. 2010. Adaptive-compression based congestion control technique for wireless sensor networks. *Sensors*, 10, 4, 2919-2945.

[20] Leelapornchai, P., and Stockhammer, T. 2002. Progressive image transmission applying multipath routing in mobile ad hoc networks. In *Proceedings of the International Conference on Image Processing*, Rochester, USA, 553-556.

[21] Qaisar, S., and Radha, H. 2009. Multipath multi-stream distributed reliable video delivery in wireless sensor networks. In *Proceedings of the Conference on Information Sciences and Systems*. Baltimore, USA, 207-212.

[22] Shu, L., Zhou, Z.B., Hauswirth, M., Phuoc, D.L., Yu, P., and Zhang, L. 2007. Transmitting streaming data in wireless multimedia sensor networks with holes. In *Proceedings of the International Conference on Mobile and Ubiquitous Multimedia*, Oulu, Finland.

[23] Sidhu, N., Uppal, R., Kaur, K., Kaler, R. 2009. Analysis of wavelet Le Gall 5/3 transform in image watermarking. *International Journal of Recent Trends in Engineering*, 2, 4, 224-227.

[24] Tselishchev, Y., Boulis, A., and Libman, L. 2010. Experiences and lessons from implementing a wireless sensor network MAC protocol in the Castalia simulator. In *Proceedings of IEEE WCNC*, Sydney, Australia.

[25] Wang, W., Peng, D., Wang, H., Sharif, H., Chen, H-H. 2008. Energy-constrained distortion reduction optimization for wavelet-based coded image transmission in wireless sensor networks. *IEEE Transactions on Multimedia*. 10, 6, 1169-1180.

[26] Yick, J., Mukherjee, B., and Ghosal, D. 2008. Wireless sensor network survey. *Computer Networks*, 52, 12, 2292-2330.

[27] Zhang, L., Hauswirth, M., Shu, L., Zhou, Z., Reynolds, V., and Han, G. 2008. Multi-priority multi-path selection for video streaming in wireless multimedia sensor networks. *Lecture Notes in Computer Science*, 5061, 439-452.

An Architecture for QoS-enabled Video Telephony in a 3GPP 4G Evolved Packet Core environment

Fatna Belqasmi
Zayed University
Abu Dhabi
United Arab Emirates

Hanieh Alipour
Concordia University
Montreal
Canada

Malek El Ferjani
Higher School of
Communication of Tunis
(Sup'Com), Tunisia

Roch Glitho
Concordia University
Montreal
Canada

ABSTRACT

Video telephony is the real time exchange of voice and video between end-users, and is the basis of a wide range of applications. Quality of service (QoS) enables a level of network performance control which makes it possible to meet specific applications and/or end-user requirements. This paper proposes an architecture for QoS-enabled video telephony in a 3GPP 4G Evolved Packet Core (EPC) environment. The architecture uses EPC as enabler to provide a refined differentiated QoS scheme that does not exist in the state of the art. The scheme allows prioritization between different sessions of the same video telephony application running in the same network. End-users can therefore use one application for different purposes (e.g. for business video calls and for private video calls) by assigning the appropriate priorities. We have built a proof of concept prototype using the Fraunhofer Fokus OpenEPC as the 3GPP 4G EPC infrastructure and have made some preliminary performance measurements. The architecture and the operational procedures are presented, along with the prototype and the performance measurements. Related work is also reviewed.

Keywords

EPC; video telephony; differentiated QoS

1. INTRODUCTION

Video telephony is the conversational exchange of voice and video between end-users. It is the basis of a wide range of applications (e.g. business conference calls, multiparty games). Quality of Service (QoS) is a key ingredient of video telephony. It refers to the ability to control network performance in order to meet applications' and/or end-users' requirements [1]. The control is done via parameters such as latency, jitter, availability and data transfer rate.

End-users may have different requirements on the same application, depending on the circumstances in which they use it (i.e. the actual session). For instance, they may put more stringent requirements on a video telephony session at initiation depending

on its purpose (e.g. business negotiations vs. a private chat). They may even wish to upgrade the requirements on a video telephony session after its initiation, depending once again on the circumstances (e.g. an informal discussion about an open position that turns into a formal job interview).

More stringent requirements on a given video telephony session at initiation time (or upgrading the requirements during the session) might result in downgrading or even terminating other video telephony sessions running in the same network, when network resources are limited. There is indeed a need for a refined differentiated QoS that allows for prioritization between the different sessions of the same video telephony application.

It is not possible to support QoS (guaranteed and differentiated) over the Internet because the Internet provides Best-Effort service. 3G telecommunication networks do offer guaranteed QoS to some extent, but they does not provide the refined differentiated QoS we envision in this paper. End-users should be able to choose the specific QoS profile (e.g. Gold, Silver or Bronze) that meets their requirements at any given time (i.e. both before and after session initiation). For instance, an end-user can choose the Gold profile for business usage and the Silver profile for personal use, but should have the possibility to upgrade the silver profile to gold on the fly, depending on the importance of the specific personal session.

Our proposed scheme builds on the 3GPP 4G Evolved Packet Core (EPC). EPC [2] is the new IP-based core network of 4th generation mobile networks. It comes with the long term evolution (LTE) access network. However, it is access technology agnostic and it can be used with legacy 3GPP access networks (e.g. GPRS and UTRAN) and non-3GPP access networks (e.g. Wifi and Wimax). It has a flat and simplified architecture, with a clear separation between the control and the data plans. Figure 1 depicts its main entities.

The main entities of the EPC are: the serving gateway (SGw), the packet data network gateway (PDNGw), the mobility management entity (MME) and the policy and charging rules function (PCRF). The SGw is the access gateway for LTE technology. It acts as a local mobility anchor point for inter-eNodeB handover. The PDNGw is the termination point of the packet data interface connecting EPC to external packet data networks. It also performs various functionalities such as per-user-based packet filtering, policy enforcement and charging support. The MME manages tracking area list, supervises handovers between different base stations and is responsible for paging subscribers in the IDLE state. The PCRF is the entity which provides policy control (e.g.

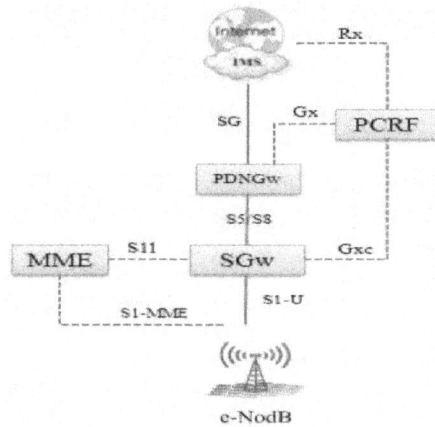

Figure 1: EPC main entities

QoS control) and charging control decisions. It is the key enabler of our architecture.

The rest of the paper is organized as follows. Section II presents usage scenarios; derives requirements and reviews related work. The proposed architecture is presented in section III followed by its implementation in section IV, including the performance measurements. We conclude in the last section.

2. USAGE SCENARIOS , REQUIREMENTS AND RELATED WORK

2.1 Usage scenarios
We assume in the scenarios that the end-users can select between the following classes of QoS profiles: Bronze, Silver, and Gold. This selection can be made prior to session initiation, at session initiation and even during sessions.

We start with a scenario where there is an ongoing video session between two Silver end-users. During the session, a Gold end-user initiates a voice session. However, the network does not have sufficient resources to support the two sessions. The system will downgrade the video communication between the two Silver end-users to audio in order to enable the voice session initiated by the Gold end-user.

 In the second scenario, there is a video session between two Gold end-users. Next,a Silver end-user initiates a voice session. Let us assume the network does not have enough resources to support the two communications simultaneously. The system will reject the demand of the Silver user and continue serving the two Gold users.

In the third scenario we assume a voice session between two Gold end-users, and then a Silver user initiates a video session. However, the network resources are limited. Therefore, the system will only allow voice for the session initiated by the Silver user to preserve the continuity of the existing voice session between the Gold end-users. Requirements

2.2 Requirements
The first requirement is that the architecture should support standard video telephony protocols, since a plethora of video telephony protocols already exists. Second, it should permit session creation, modification and deletion.

Furthermore, the architecture should support differentiated QoS of the video telephony service by giving end-users the opportunity to subscribe to given classes of service (e.g. Gold, Silver and Bronze) and have their sessions served with the corresponding parameters. End-users should also be able to change their subscription class, even during sessions.

Yet another requirement is that sessions of end-users with lower priorities should preferably be downgraded instead of being terminated when there is a resource problem in the network.

A last requirement is that the architecture should re-use the subjacent network (e.g. Internet or telecommunications network) with as little change as possible. Imposing changes to the underlying network can only slow down deployment and should be avoided.

2.3 Related work
The most well-known differentiated QoS scheme is certainly the IETF differentiated QoS architecture [3]. Packets are prioritized and forwarded at each router depending on their priority level. This architecture, however, is coarse grained. Packets are prioritized depending on the traffic type (e.g. voice vs. video). While it enables the prioritization of voice vs. video in the same session, it is not refined enough to enable prioritization between sessions.

Several differentiation schemes have been proposed for 3G networks. However, as shown in reference [4], none of them enables session level differentiation. The solution proposed in that reference allows session level differentiation but proposes heavy extensions to the IP Multimedia System (IMS) portion of a 3G network, and so it does not meet our last requirement.

A few references discuss the QoS aspects of video telephony in 4G. However, none of them tackles prioritization between video telephony sessions. Reference [5], for instance considers video telephony over downlink LTE links. It focuses on performance evaluation and shows that it is beneficial to provide QoS.

Reference [6] provides a differentiated QoS scheme for mobile video surveillance applications. Video surveillance applications are streaming applications and are fundamentally different from telephony applications which are real-time bilateral media exchange applications..

There are studies of the QoS aspects of video telephony in wireless environments in general. Reference [7] proposes a scheduler to provide QoS for video IP telephony in wireless environments. It is a round robin scheduler with minimal overhead, but differentiating between different sessions is not considered.

3. PROPOSED ARCHITECTURE
This section presents our overall architecture, discusses the main interfaces and procedures, and presents an illustrative scenario that describes how the architecture can be used.

3.1 Overall Architecture

We build on EPC as it is and assume that several video telephony application providers re-use the same EPC. The proposed architecture is depicted by figure 2. It has three layers: an application, an application-enabler, and an EPC layer.

The application layer includes five entities: the end-users, the video telephony application, the users' profiles, the application policy rules and the session information repository. The video telephony application creates and manages QoS-enabled video sessions between end-users. The users' profiles entity acts as a repository for two types of data: temporary and permanent. Temporary data relates to the user information that is stored by the application during registration (e.g. IP address and port number). Permanent data includes the user subscription information, such as the QoS profile and the media type the user has subscribed to (e.g. audio only, audio/video). The information about created sessions is stored in the session information repository (e.g. the session ID). The application policy rules entity includes the policies and rules that allow the application to choose the proper session to downgrade or to terminate in order to free up resources when needed. For choosing suitable sessions, the application policy rules entity needs to communicate with the session information repository and the users' profiles entity to get the list of ongoing sessions and the associated users' profiles.

The application-enabler layer includes two entities; the QoS enabler and the network policy rules. The QoS enabler ensures the communication between the application and the EPC network for QoS management. It communicates with the PCRF to establish/update sessions with the desired QoS profiles and reserve network resources. If not enough resources are available, the QoS enabler uses the network policy rules to identify the service provider whose sessions could be downgraded/terminated to liberate the needed resources. The selected service provider should satisfy a number of criteria (i.e. it should have a lower priority and a lower QoS profile).The EPC layer consists of the EPC network.

3.2 Interfaces

We assume that the session initiation protocol (SIP) [8] is used as the signaling protocol for session establishment. The end-users will therefore communicate with the video telephony application using SIP. The interfaces between the application and the users' profiles entity (i.e. RFa), the application policy rules (i.e.RFb), and the QoS enabler (i.e. RFd) are REpresentational State Transfer (REST)-based, as are the interfaces between the users' profiles entity and the application policy rules (i.e. RFc) and between the QoS enabler and the network policy rules (i.e. RF). We selected REST because it is standard-based, lightweight and can support multiple data representations (e.g. plain text, JSON and XML).

REST is a client-server architectural style for loosely coupled distributed systems. It models the information to act on as resources, and identifies each resource using a uniform resource identifier (URI). The resources are then accessed via a uniform interface. REST is not bound to a specific communication protocol, but it is mostly used with HTTP. The uniform interface is mainly composed of the following HTTP methods: GET, POST, PUT, and DELETE, which are used to read, create, update

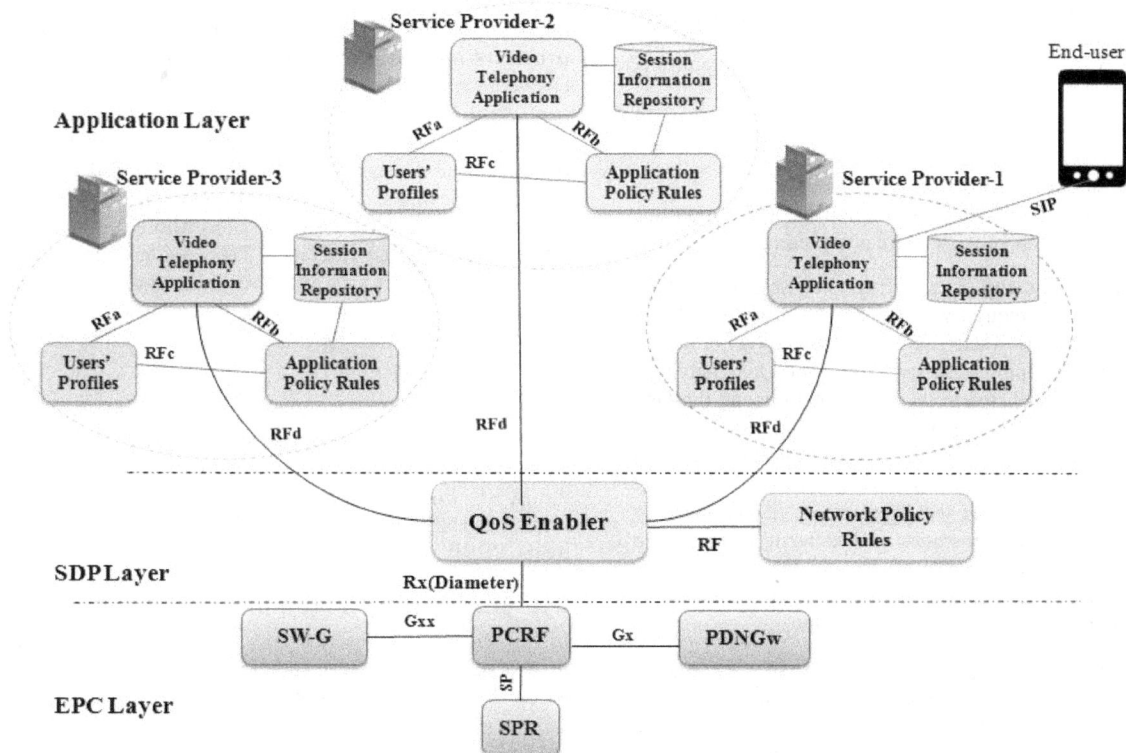

Figure 2: Proposed Architecture

and delete a resource respectively, even though there is no one-to-one mapping between the methods and the operations. More tutorial information on REST can be found in [9]. Table 1 summarizes the main resources we defined for the QoS enabler (i.e. the RFd interface).

Table 1 Main QoS Enabler Resources

Resources	Operation	HTTP Method: resource URI
List of sessions	Create: establish a new session	POST:/services/sessions
A specific session	Read: get information (e.g. QoS profile, download bandwidth) about a specific session	GET: /Services/Session/{SessionID}
	Update: modify a specific session (e.g. QoS profile, download bandwidth)	PUT: /Services/Session/{SessionID}
	Delete: end a specific session	DELETE: /services/sessions/{SessionID}

The communication between the QoS enabler and the EPC network (i.e. the PCRF) is ensured via a diameter interface. Diameter protocol is an Authentication, Authorization, and Accounting (AAA) protocol used in new generation networks and intended for applications such as network access and mobility in IP networks [10].

3.3 Procedures

This section discusses two main procedures: new session establishment and an ongoing session update. The supporting procedures (i.e. for resource release) are also presented.

New session establishment: To establish a new session, the end-user sends an INVITE request with the ID of the target end-user (i.e. the callee) to the video telephony application server of his/her service provider. The application server asks the QoS enabler to establish a new session between the two users, utilizing the QoS profile registered in the caller's profile. The QoS enabler communicates with the PCRF in order to execute the request. If not enough network resources are available, the PCRF will reject the request. The QoS enabler will then release (if possible) the resources needed for the new session and re-iterate its request to the PCRF. If not enough resources can be released, the new session request is rejected. Resource release is performed using the "resource release" procedure described below.

Session update: To update (downgrade or upgrade) an ongoing session, the end-user sends an update request to his/her service provider, which transfers the request to the QoS enabler. The update request should include the new QoS profile that the end-user is willing to use. The update procedure continues along the same path as for the new session establishment procedure. Indeed,

the QoS enabler issues a request for the session update with the new profile. If the request is rejected, the QoS enabler tries to release the necessary resources to support the update and then re-iterates the request. If no resources can be released, the update request is rejected.

Resource release: Resource release is an action based on the end-user and his/her service provider priority, and is performed in three steps. First, the QoS enabler identifies the service provider(s) whose sessions should be modified (i.e. downgraded or terminated). Second, it sends a resource release request to the selected providers, with the amount of resources to be freed up. Third, the target service providers identify and modify the appropriate sessions and report back to the QoS enabler. These three steps are detailed below.

Selection of the service provider(s) whose sessions should be downgraded/terminated: When a session establishment request is rejected by the PCRF, the QoS enabler asks the network policy rules to choose the proper service provider whose sessions should be downgraded (or eventually terminated). Let EUi be the end-user whose request was rejected and SPi be the EUi's service provider. The network policy rules entity chooses the service provider SPj that satisfies the following four conditions: 1) SPj has one or more ongoing sessions; 2) SPj has a lower priority than SPi; 3) downgrading (or eventually terminating) 'n' sessions belonging to SPj will free the amount of resources needed to establish the EUi session; and 4) SPj has the lowest priority among the other service providers that satisfy the first three conditions. If SPj is found, the network policy rules entity sends the SPj ID to the QoS enabler. If no SPj is found, the SPi ID is sent back to the QoS enabler.

Send a resource release request to the selected service providers and identify the sessions to be modified: The QoS enabler sends a resource release request to the chosen SPj application server (APj) with the amount of resources to be released. The ASj uses the application policy rules to identify the sessions to be downgraded (or terminated) as well as the number of these sessions. The session termination alternative is considered only if there are no sessions whose downgrading could release the requested resources. The sessions selected are those with the lowest priorities. If SPj=SPi, the chosen sessions should also have a lower priority than the session to be established. The information about the ongoing sessions is retrieved from the session information repository.

When the sessions to be modified have been identified, the ASj sends the appropriate modification request (i.e. session update or release) to the QoS enabler, which realizes the request via a call to the PCRF. Figure 3 summarizes the remaining steps for a new session establishment procedure after a request has been rejected by the PCRF.

3.4 Illustrative scenario

In this section, we describe how the first scenario presented in section II.A can be implemented using the proposed architecture. Figure 4 shows the associated sequence diagram.

During the audio/video session between the Silver end-users EU1 and EU2, a Gold end-user (EU3) sends an INVITE message to the video telephony application to have an audio session with another Gold end-user (EU4) (step 1). The application gets the profiles of users' profiles repository (steps 2 and 3), and extracts the necessary information for the establishment of the new session (e.g. the end-users' QoS profiles, IP addresses and port numbers). It then uses this information to construct a POST request that it sends to the QoS Enabler (steps 4). The QoS enabler issues an Authentication-Authorization-Request (AAR) diameter message to the PCRF, in order to reserve the network resources required for the new session (step 5). The PCRF replies with an Authentication-Authorization-Answer (AAA) to reject the QoS enabler's demand (step 6). We assume that this rejection is because there are not enough resources available to allow the establishment of the new session.

The QoS enabler then sends a request to the network policy rules entity to get the list of service providers whose ongoing sessions it can modify (steps 7 and 8). In this scenario, only one service provider ID is returned. The QoS enabler sends a POST request to the video telephony application (V.T Application) server of the selected service provider to request session modification (step 9). The application server consults the application policy rules entity (step 10), which checks the session information repository for the session to modify (steps 11 and 12).

The application policy rules entity replies with the ID of the session between the two Silver end-users (step 13), and the information that this session should be downgraded from audio/video to audio only. The application server then sends a re-

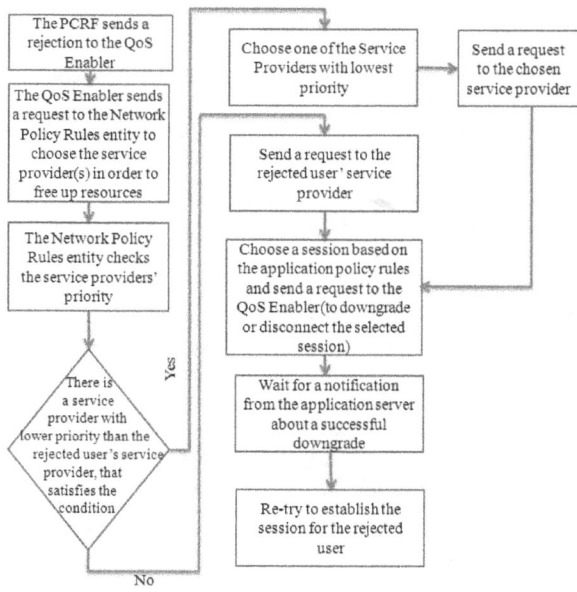

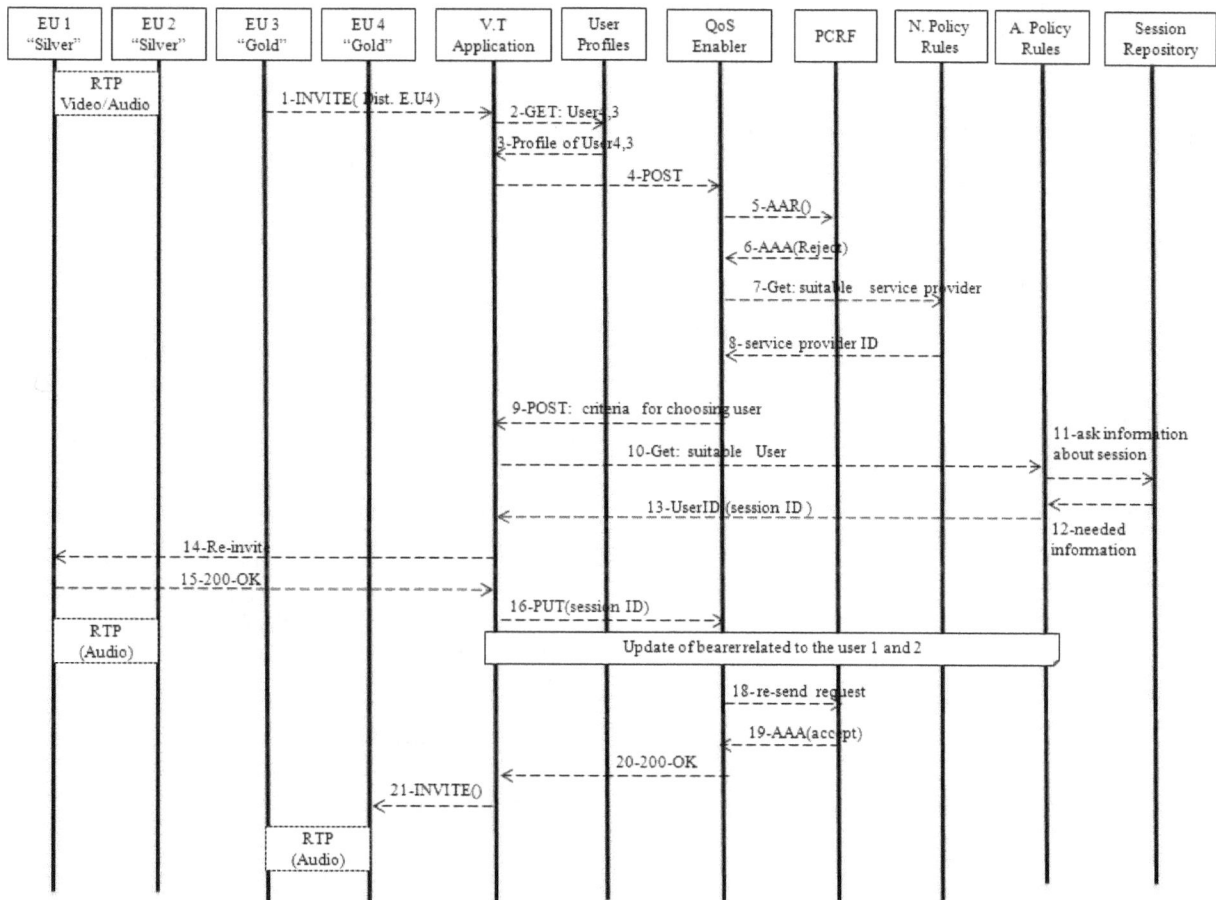

Figure 3: Session establishment procedure when not enough resources are available.

the users involved in the new session (EU3 and EU4) from the

Figure 4: Scenario

INVITE request to both users with the new parameters (i.e. audio only). For the sake of clarity, only the communication with EU1 is shown in the figure (steps 14 and 15).

Next, the application server sends a PUT request to the QoS enabler to ask for bearer updates for both EU1 and EU2 (step 16), which results in the release of the required resources. The QoS enabler then proceeds with the re-establishment of the God session between EU3 and EU4 (steps 18 to 21).

4. IMPLEMENTATION

In this section, we first present the implementation architecture and then we describe the implemented prototype, followed by the performance measurement.

4.1 Implementation architecture

Figure 5 depicts the implementation architecture, with a focus on the video telephony application, the application policy rules and the user profiles entities. As a SIP-based application, the video telephony application consists of a SIP Servlet [11], which is responsible for handling the received SIP messages (e.g. SIP INVITE) and for creating and sending the appropriate responses. The SIP Servlet uses a REST client to communicate with the REST-based entities of the overall architecture (e.g. the user profiles). A session manager constitutes the core component of the application. It executes the entire logic of the application related to session management. This includes session establishment and update, the selection of the ongoing sessions to be modified, and the management of the data stored in the session information repository.

The application policy rules entity is composed of a RESTful API module that exposes the entity functionalities via a RESTful interface, and a policy manager that is responsible for applying the service provider policies for selecting the sessions to be downgraded/terminated.

The users profiles entity includes a RESTful API module that implements the entity interface, a database that stores the users' profiles, and a profile manager that acts on the database and responds to the application's (and other entities') requests.

4.2 Prototype

As a prototype, we implemented a slightly modified version of the scenario described in section III.D. The session between the Silver end-users is terminated to allow the establishment of the Gold session, whereas in the scenario of section III.D the Silver session

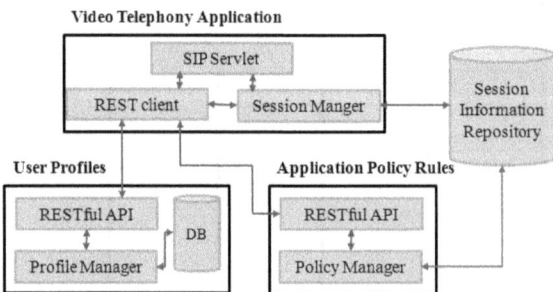

Figure 5: Implementation architecture

is downgraded. In addition, we assume that the four users have the same service provider and that this service provider is the one with the lowest priority. This simplifies the prototype implementation since it eliminates the need to implement the network policy rules entity. Indeed, the output of the network policy rules' execution is known, since it will return the ID of the service provider of the end-users involved.

Figure 6 illustrates the prototype components. We used OpenEPC release 2 prototype from Fraunhofer Fokus [12] as the underlying EPC network. The REST interfaces of the different components are implemented using the Restlet framework [13]. The Rx diameter interface of the QoS enabler is implemented using JavaDiameterPeer library [14].

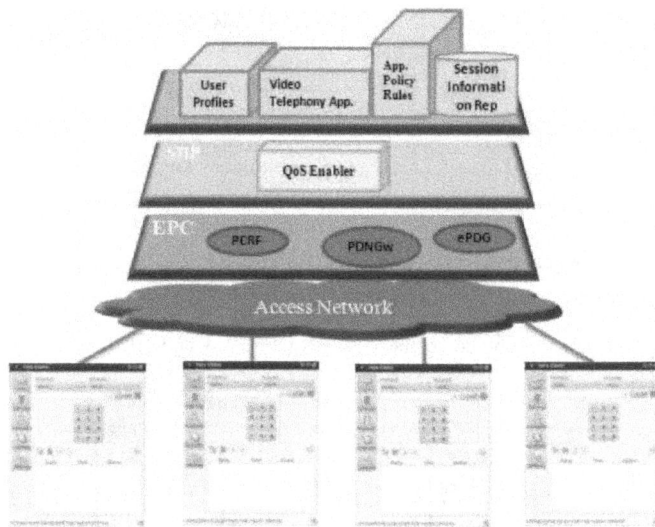

Figure 6: Prototype components

As end-users, we used YATA [15], an open source SIP client application. The end-users are connected to EPC via an enhanced packet data gateway (ePDG), using a WiFi access network.

The prototype setup consists of seven virtual machines, running on a VMware workstation 8 which is installed on an Intel Xeon(R) E5646 2.40 GH Desktop with 8 GB of RAM and Windows 7.

The first virtual machine runs the application layer entities (i.e. the video telephony application, users' profiles entity, application policy rules entity, and session information repository) along with the QoS enabler. The ePDG, the PDNGw and the four end-users are each running on a separate virtual machine. The first virtual machine is equipped with 2GB of RAM, whereas the other six virtual machines have 512MB of RAM. All of the virtual machines use Ubuntu Release 10.10 as their operating system.

4.3 Performance measurement

The performance of the prototype is assessed in terms of session establishment. The session establishment delay is the end-to-end time delay needed to establish a new session with a specific QoS profile, and so is the difference between the time when an end-user sends a SIP INVITE to the video telephony application and the time when the session is established with the callee. This includes the communication with the PCRF, the selection of the appropriate sessions to be modified, and the modification of such sessions. We also compare the session establishment delays between the cases where the resources are available and when resource release is needed.

The performance results are shown in Figure 7. The results are measured in milliseconds and each result is calculated as an average of 10 measurements. The delays for the session establishment when the resources are available are measured for the establishment of the first session between the Silver end-users. These delays have an average of 300 ms and are barely observable by the end-users.

As shown in the figure, the session establishment delays when resource release is needed (i.e. for the second session between the Gold end-users) are higher than when the resources are available. These longer delays are because of the extra delay for session modification (i.e. session termination in the context of the prototype). However, the end-to-end delays remain acceptable from the end-user point of view, with an average of 500 ms.

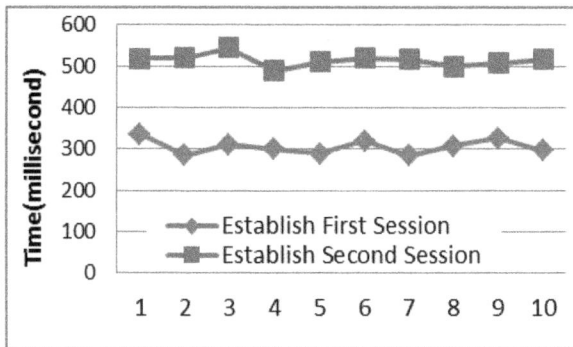

Figure 7: Performance results

5. CONCLUSION

We propose a novel architecture for QoS-enabled video telephony applications. The architecture uses EPC as an enabler to provide both guaranteed and differentiated QoS, two main QoS schemes that are critical for video telephony applications but which are not fully supported in the state of the art. It builds on EPC as it is and assumes that several video telephony application providers re-use the same EPC. A proof of concept prototype was successfully implemented using the Fraunhofer Fokus OpenEPC as a 3GPP 4G EPC infrastructure. The preliminary performance measurements show that the end-to-end delays for session establishment using the new architecture remain barely observable by end-users.

6. ACKNOWLEDGMENT

This work was partially supported by the Natural Sciences and Engineering Research Council (NSERC) of Canada through a Canada Research Chair grant.

7. REFERENCES

[1] A. Meddeb, Internet QoS: Pieces of the Puzzle, IEEE Communications Magazine, January 2010

[2] M. Olsson et al., SAE and the Evolved Packet Core: Driving the Mobile Broadband Revolution, Elsevier, Second Edition 2012

[3] S Blake et al., An Architecture for Differentiated Services, IETF, RFC 2475

[4] M. El Barachi, R. Glitho, R. Dssouli, Control Level Call Differentiation in IMS-Based 3G Core Networks, IEEE Network, January/February 2011, Vol. 25, No1

[5] D. Wang et al,, Video Telephony over Downlink LTE with/without QoS provisioning, Sarnoff Symposium 2011

[6] M Abu-Lebdeh, F Belqasmi, R Glitho, A 3GPP 4G Evolved Packet Core Based – Architecture for QoS Enabled Mobile Video Surveillance Application, Third International Conference on the Network of the Future, November 2012, November 2012, Tunis, Tunisia

[7] S. Dutt et al., A Novel Optimized Scheduler to Provide QoS for Video IP Telephony over Wireless Networks, High Performance Computing and Communications (HPCC) 2011

[8] J. Rosenberg et al., The Session Initiation Protocol, IETF RFC 3261, 2002

[9] F. Belqasmi, R. Glitho, C. Fu, "RESTful web services for service provisioning in next-generation networks: a survey", Communications Magazine, IEEE, vol. 49, no. 12, pp. 66–73, 2011.

[10] IETF, "RFC 3588 – Diameter Base Protocol", www.ietf.org, September 2003

[11] M. Kulkarni et al., SIP Servlet Specification, version 1.1, JSR 289 Expert Group, Aug. 2008.

[12] Fraunhofer Fokus OpenEPC; available on web at: http://www.openepc.net/index.html

[13] Restlet framework; DOI=http://www.restlet.org/

[14] Java Diameter Peer library;DOI= http://www.openimscore.org/project/jdp

[15] YATA ; DOI=http://yate.null.ro/pmwiki/

A Solution for Transmitting and Displaying UHD 3D Raw Videos Using Lossless Compression

Ruan D. Gomes
Federal Institute of Paraíba
Guarabira, Paraíba, Brasil
ruan.gomes@ifpb.edu.br

Yuri G. G. da Costa
LAViD/UFPB
João Pessoa, Paraíba, Brasil
yuriggc@lavid.ufpb.br

Lucenildo L. A. Júnior
LAViD/UFPB
João Pessoa, Paraíba, Brasil
lucenildo@lavid.ufpb.br

Manoel G. da Silva Neto
LAViD/UFPB
João Pessoa, Paraíba, Brasil
manoelgs@lavid.ufpb.br

Alexandre N. Duarte
LAViD/UFPB
João Pessoa, Paraíba, Brasil
alexandre@ci.ufpb.br

Guido L. de Souza Filho
LAViD/UFPB
João Pessoa, Paraíba, Brasil
guido@lavid.ufpb.br

ABSTRACT

This paper describes a software-based approach for transmitting, and displaying ultra high definition (UHD) videos (ex: 4K) in raw format (2D or 3D).The viability of using lossless compression algorithms for transmission, and exhibition of UHD raw videos was investigated. This approach allows the transmission of raw videos for supporting the development of distributed edition tools for UHD videos, and high quality visualization using a lower bandwidth. We conducted performance studies of eight lossless compression algorithms, aiming at analyze the compression ratio for 4K videos, and the latency in video encoding and decoding. Finally, a multi-thread version of the LZ4HC was integrated with the Fogo Player, which is a software-based 4K player developed in a previous work. We obtained a reduction of about 38% in bandwidth requirements, and a decoding latency that allowed the exhibition in real time of 4K videos.

Categories and Subject Descriptors

I.4 [**Computing Methodologies**]: Image Processing and Computer Vision—*Compression (Coding)*

General Terms

Algorithms, Performance

Keywords

UHD videos, 4K, 4K-3D, Lossless video compression

1. INTRODUCTION

With the advent of the 4K technology, the development of new applications for advanced visualization became possible, offering an image quality comparable to that offered by 35mm film and presenting the inherent advantages of the digitization, as the easier

storage and higher immunity to deterioration. These new applications may have a direct impact in different scenarios such as the Digital Cinema and the transmission and display of artistic performances and sports events in Ultra-High Definition (UHD). Besides applications focused on media consumers, new content production applications may emerge, such as tools and technologies to support collaborative editing and visualization of UHD content.

Nevertheless, the development of solutions to deal with UHD content presents many challenging aspects, mainly due to the large amount of data that must be processed. These new applications must deal with limitations related to storage, transmission and computational complexity of the algorithms for encoding and decoding the UHD content.

For example, 4K videos usually have a resolution of 4096 x 2160 pixels. Considering raw videos with 24 bits per pixel and 24 frames per second the resulting stream will have a bitrate of approximately 5 *Gbit*/s. For 3D videos it is necessary to transfer two streams, one for each eye. Thus, it would require a link of about 10 *Gbit*/s for real time transmission. All this without considering the overhead introduced by the transmission protocols. Using more quantization levels and higher frame rates would make this situation even worse.

This bandwidth problem could be mitigated with the use of lossy codecs, but there are some applications that requires the transmission of the raw data, such as distributed collaborative editing tools for 4K contents. Besides, some applications may require extreme image quality, such as telemedicine applications. For these applications, lossless compression could be used to help diminish the presented bandwidth requirements, while all the video information is preserved.

In this work we investigate the performance of a set of lossless compression algorithms, aiming at analyzing the compression ratio obtained for 4K videos and the speed of the encoding and decoding processes. Finally, we performed the integration of a multi-threaded version of the LZ4HC algorithm with the Fogo Player, a software-based 4K player described in our previous work [1]. We obtained a compression ratio of about 38% and decoding time that are compatible with real-time displaying of 4K videos by software.

2. RELATED WORK

There are several initiatives aiming to develop solutions for transmitting and displaying UHD videos [2, 3, 4, 5, 6]. Most of these works are based on the JPEG-2000 standard, which is the standard recommended by the Digital Cinema Initiative (DCI). However, due to the computational complexity of the algorithms defined by the JPEG-2000 standard, the solutions based on this standard relied on dedicated hardware to perform the encoding and decoding processes. These approaches, when compared to software-based approaches, have as common drawbacks the relatively higher cost and limited flexibility.

In a previous paper [1] we developed a software-based solution, called Fogo Player, for distributing, transmitting and displaying UHD videos. In this solution, all processing is performed using an architecture of parallel and distributed software components. This software-based solution is flexible in terms of resolution and coding algorithms. In the experiments presented in [1] we used the H.264 standard, however it is possible to integrate different coding standards to the solution.

In 2009, researchers at NTT (Network Innovation Laboratories) conducted the first experimental transmission of 4K raw videos using a 10 *Gbit*/s link. This experiment, conducted by Shiraia *et al.* [5], required a bitrate of about 6 *Gbit*/s since it used no method for data compression. The described solution is simple and presents a very small delay since it is not necessary to decode the video before displaying it. However, the solution requires a very high bandwidth and make it impossible to transmit a 4K-3D raw video using a 10 *Gbit*/s link.

On the other hand, using the approach presented in this paper, it would be possible to stream 4K-3D raw videos using about 7.5 *Gbit*/s, considering the flow generated by the video used by NTT and an average compression ratio of about 38%. Furthermore, with the reduction achieved by using lossless compression, it is possible to use four 1 *Gbit*/s interfaces instead of one 10 *Gbit*/s interface to transmit 4K raw videos. This represents a huge cost reduction in the network hardware. Fogo Player was designed to allow the use of multiple machines to display different parts of a 4K video synchronously.

2.1 Fogo Player

Fogo Player [1] enables the distribution, transmission, and displaying of 4K videos, with or without stereoscopy. It is based on a distributed architecture of software components. Different of other players found in our review, Fogo Player does not use dedicated hardware for decoding and displaying the videos. The Fogo Player's architecture allows easy integration of different technologies for video coding, which admits the use of the system also for the transmission of raw video using lossless compression algorithms. However, the algorithms used need to be quick enough to enable the transmission and display of UHD videos in real-time.

To handle 4K videos, Fogo Player slices the videos into quadrants in order to process them in parallel. To display the videos, the Fogo Player decodes in parallel each of the quadrants and displays them in a synchronized way on a wall of screens or using a projector. Parallel processing may be performed using multiple processors in a single machine or using multiple machines.

The Fogo Player's architecture allows the replacement of the modules responsible for decoding without affecting the operation of the rest of the player. In this work we performed the integration of a decoding module based on the LZ4HC algorithm.

3. A COMPARISON BETWEEN LOSSLESS COMPRESSION ALGORITHMS

The compression speed is not a critical requirement for on demand video streaming. However, decompression must be performed in real time as the video is received and displayed. On the other hand, real-time compression is also required for live video transmissions and this usually requires dedicated encoding hardware. In the case of collaborative editing applications, the videos can be compressed in parallel as professionals perform modifications in individual frames since the compression is applied only intra-frame.

We evaluated eight lossless compression algorithms in order to attest the feasibility of using this kind of compression for streaming 4K raw videos. The software libraries used are all open source and the algorithms and their license types are shown in Table 1.

All eight tested algorithms are based on the Lempel-Ziv algorithm, which makes use of a dictionary. These algorithms are optimized to achieve high speed of compression or decompression but have a relatively low compression ratio, especially when compared with the lossy algorithms used specifically to compress images and videos. However, these lossless algorithms have the advantage of allowing the complete reconstruction of the original video on the target, which is critical for some applications.

The LZ4 is a dictionary based algorithm which was developed for high speed compression and decompression of text files [8]. In general, dictionary-based algorithms convert variable-length symbol sets into fixed-size codes. Accordingly, symbol sequences that appear more constantly can be mapped into smaller codes. [9].

The LZ4HC algorithm is a variation of LZ4 with a higher compression ratio and a higher decompression speed. The disadvantage of LZ4HC over LZ4 is the compression time, which is substantially higher. However, for applications that are restricted on bandwidth for data transport and that perform more decompressions than compressions, the LZ4HC may be a good alternative.

Oliveira *et al.* [10] performed a comparison between the LZ4, the LZ4HC, and some versions of ZLIB algorithm to compress data from the LHC particle accelerator. In the experiment, the LZ4HC had a compression ratio of about 57%, against 50% of LZ4 and the decompression speed was about 20% higher compared to the LZ4. However, the LZ4 compression speed was 15 times higher compared to the LZ4HC.

Although the work of Oliveira *et al.* [10] have carried out a comparison between the LZ4 and LZ4HC algorithms, it is important to conduct studies of the performance of these algorithms considering image files, in order to verify the feasibility of using these algorithms in systems for video transmission and displaying.

This study also includes an analysis on the effects on performance and compression ratio of the usage of multiple threads for encoding and decoding video frames. In this case, before being encoded, the frames are divided into smaller blocks and the blocks are encoded in parallel using multiple threads

Since the vast majority of current processors have multiple cores, one can exploit this feature to get real parallelism in the encoding and decoding processes. However, subdividing the image into smaller blocks may result in a lower compression ratio.

4. RESULTS

The experiments were conducted on a IBM x3650 with 2 Xeon E5620 processors (eight 2.40 GHz physical cores) and 32 GB of RAM. The workload consisted in a set of 3000 frames with 4096 x 2160 resolution extracted from the 4K movie EstereoEnsaios [12], the first stereoscopic 4K film produced in Brazil.

Figure 1 shows the average compression speed of the 3000 frames using the eight selected algorithms. LZO presented the highest compression speed, processing 1353 *MByte*/s in the best case. This compression speed would make it possible to encode 4K-3D videos in software in real-time using a single machine. The LZ4 algorithm achieved the second highest compression speed, about 518*MByte*/s in the best case. The LZ4HC, as expected, had a very low compression speed in comparison with the other algorithms, being able to process about 44 *MByte*/s in the best case.

Table 1: Selected lossless compression algorithms.

Algorithm	Site	License Type
LZF	http://oldhome.schmorp.de/marc/liblzf.html	BSD-type
Snappy	http://code.google.com/p/snappy/	New BSD
LZ4	http://code.google.com/p/lz4/	New BSD
LZ4HC	http://code.google.com/p/lz4hc/	GNU Lesser
FastLZ	http://code.google.com/p/fastlz/	GPL
LZMAT	http://www.matcode.com/lzmat.htm	MIT
LZO	http://www.oberhumer.com/opensource/lzo/	GPL v2+
QuickLZ	http://www.quicklz.com/	GPL 1,2 e 3

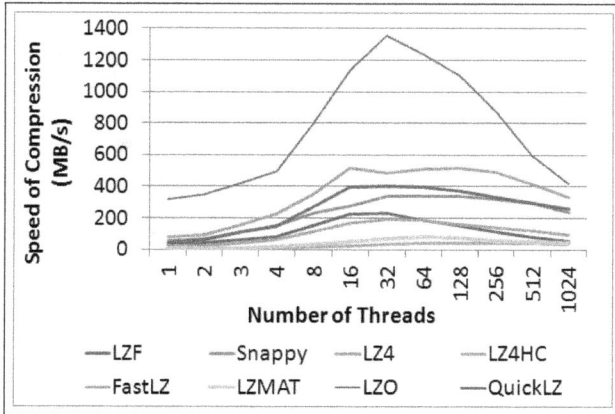

Figure 1: Compression speed of the selected algorithms.

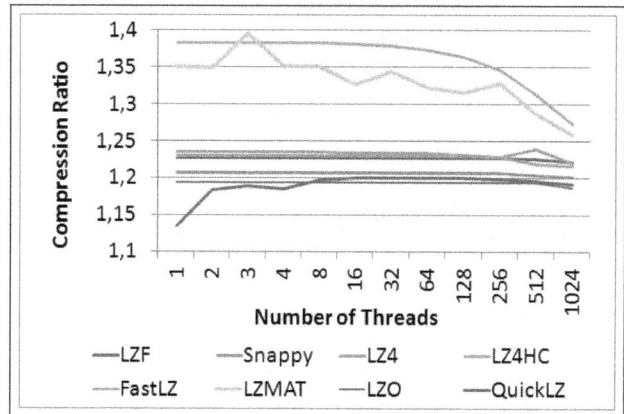

Figure 2: Decompression speed of the selected algorithms.

Figure 2 shows the average decoding speed of the eight algorithms. The LZO algorithm achieved again the best results, with a speed of about 1584 *MByte*/s in the best case. Following the LZO, the best performances were achieved by the LZ4, Snappy, and LZ4HC algorithms, respectively.

Surprisingly, in our experiments LZ4HC had a slower decompression speed than LZ4, what differs from the results obtained by Oliveira *et al.* [10] for the files generated by the LHC.

Once decompressed, a 4K video generates a bitstream of about 5 *Gbit*/s. Any of the four algorithms with the higher decoding speeds would be able to decode a 4K video in real time. With these algorithms is would also be possible to decode 4K-3D videos in real time, since the decoding and displaying of 4K-3D videos may be done in a distributed way using the Fogo Player.

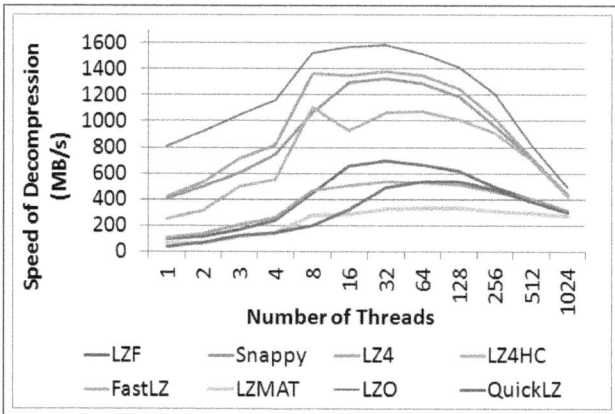

Figure 3: Compression ratio of the selected algorithms.

Figure 3 shows the compression ratio of the eight algorithms. The LZ4HC algorithm presented the highest average compression ratio (1.38 in the best case). The second best compression ratio was obtained with the LZMAT algorithm, but the speeds of compression and decompression of this algorithm were very low. The LZO algorithm presented a compression ratio of about 1.19 and the LZ4 presented a compression ratio of 1.23. Thus, although LZO and LZ4 have shown higher compression and decompression speeds, they showed a significantly lower compression ratio when compared to the LZ4HC.

As we see in the Figures, the number of threads have a direct influence in the three evaluated parameters. As the computer used in the experiments had 8 physical cores (16 virtual cores), we obtained a significant increase in speed of compression and decompression by using multiple threads. However, there is a limit to the number of threads used, due to the limitation on the number of cores and the scheduling overhead. For example, the LZ4HC algorithm presented the best results using eight cores.

Furthermore, we observed a worsening in the compression ratio in some algorithms when the number of threads was increased. This is due to the fact that smaller picture blocks have a lower level of redundancy compared to the full image. However, the compression ratio for the frames used does not vary significantly even considering 16 threads.

Although having achieved a low compression speed, the LZ4HC algorithm showed the best performance in our evaluation, since it presented a compression ratio significantly higher compared to the other algorithms and a fast enough decompression speed to decode 4K or 4K-3D videos in real time. This algorithm can be used to support distributed 4K editing applications since the coding process do not need to be performed in real time. This algorithm also works satisfactorily for the transmission of 4K raw videos on demand, since the compression is done off-line. In the latter scenario the encoding process can be done in a distributed way, as defined in the Fogo Player's architecture.

5. CONCLUSIONS AND FUTURE WORKS

The general goal of this work is to evaluate the feasibility of using lossless compression to reduce the bandwidth requirements of a software-based solution for transmitting and displaying UHD raw videos, with or without stereoscopy.

We performed a comparative study of 8 lossless compression algorithms in order to observe their compression and decompression speeds and the compression ratio achieved by each of the algorithms. We performed also a study to assess the impact of using multiple threads in these three parameters.

The results showed that LZ4HC algorithm is best suited for the application, since it presents a good compression ratio in comparison to the other algorithms, reaching 38% on average for the frames used in the experiments. In addition, the LZ4HC presented a decompression speed fast enough to allow the decoding of 4K videos (2D or 3D) in real time. We observed that the use of multiple threads can cause a significant increase in the compression and decompression speeds without significantly worsening the compression ratio.

As future work we intend to conduct performance studies of the Fogo Player using the LZ4HC algorithm for transmission and display in real-time of 4K raw videos over long distance networks, in order to verify the overall performance of the player and analyze network metrics, such as delay and bandwidth usage. We also intend to perform the world's first demonstration of a real time transmission of a 4K-3D raw video.

6. ACKNOWLEDGMENTS

The authors would like to thank the National Education and Research Network (RNP), CNPq and CAPES for their financial support.

7. REFERENCES

[1] Aquino Júnior, L. L., Gomes, R. D., Silva Neto, M. G., Duarte, A. N., Costa, R. E. O., Souza Filho, G. L. *A Software-Based Solution for Distributing and Displaying 3D UHD Films*, IEEE Multimedia, vol. 20, pp 60-68, 2013.

[2] T. Shimizua, D. Shiraia, et al.*International real-time streaming of 4k digital cinema*, Future Generation Computer Systems, vol. 22 , pp 929-939, 2006.

[3] T. Fujii, K. Shirakawa, D. Shirai, et al. *Digital cinema over optical network - status of super hd development*, in Optical Fiber Communication Conference and Exposition (OFC/NFOEC), pp 1-3, 2011.

[4] M. Kitamura, D. Shirai, K. Kaneko, et al. *Beyond 4k: 8k 60p live video streaming to multiple sites.*, Future Generation Computer Systems, pp 952-959, 2011.

[5] D. Shiraia, T. Kawano, T. Fujii, et al.*Real time switching and streaming transmission of uncompressed 4k motion pictures*, Future Generation Computer Systems, vol.25, pp 192-197, 2009.

[6] intoPIX. (2013, Maio) [Online]. Available: http://www.intopix.com

[7] B. Shi, L. Liu, and C. Xu. *Comparison between jpeg2000 and h.264 for digital cinema*, IEEE International Conference on Multimedia and Expo, pp 725-728, 2008.

[8] LZ4 Explained. (2013, Maio) [Online]. Available: http://fastcompression.blogspot.com.br/2011/05/lz4-explained.html

[9] Welch, T. A. *Technique for High-Performance Data Compression.*, IEEE Computer, 17, pp. 8-19, 1984.

[10] V. Oliveira, A. Pina, N. Castro, F. Veloso, A. Onofre. *Even Bigger Data: Preparing for the LHC/ATLAS Upgrade*. 6th Iberian Grid Infrastructure Conference, pp. 1-12, 2012.

[11] Chi, C. C., Alvarez-Mesa, M., et. al.*Parallel Scalability and Efficiency of HEVC Parallelization Approaches*, IEEE Trans. on Circuits and Systems for Video Technology, vol. 22, pp. 1827-1838, 2012.

[12] Group of Work in Advanced Applications for Remote Visualization from RNP. (2013, Maio). Available: http://4k3d.wordpress.com/tag/estereoscopia/

Evaluation of CUDA GPU Architecture as H.264 Intra Coding Acceleration Engine

Ronaldo Husemann
UNIVATES / UFRGS
Av. Osvaldo Aranha, 103
Porto Alegre – RS – Brasil
rhusemann@inf.ufrgs.br

Marco Gobbi
UNIVATES
Av. Alberto Tallini, 171
Lajeado – RS – Brasil
marcogobbi@universo.univates.br

Valter Roesler, José Valdeni Lima
II – UFRGS
Av. Bento Gonçalves, 9500 B. IV Porto
Alegre – RS – Brasil
{roesler, valdeni}@inf.ufrgs.br

ABSTRACT

Currently the high computational complexity makes it very difficult to produce a whole high definition real-time H.264 encoder solution, for conventional personal computer platform, based only on single-threaded software implementation. Considering that, the current paper analyses the potential of using modern general purpose graphical processing technologies, such as NVIDIA CUDA ® platform, as acceleration engines to improve the overall performance of a computer based H.264 intra video encoder. Performed experiments allowed discriminating the real gains when replacing a CPU based only solution by a GPU solution identifying some practical bottlenecks related with that technology. The most efficient proposal was finally compared with the original H.264/AVC reference code and the optimized x264 open source library codec, registering significant performance gains (in same cases higher than 7.6x).

Categories and Subject Descriptors

D.1.3 [**Concurrent Programming**]: Parallel programming

General Terms

Algorithms, Performance, Design.

Keywords

H.264 encoding, GPGPU, CUDA, parallel programming.

1. INTRODUCTION

A evolução recente das aplicações de multimídia foi sustentada principalmente pelo avanço das tecnologias de processamento de dados digitais. Neste contexto, os codificadores de vídeo digital foram especialmente projetados para comprimir os dados de vídeo, a fim permitir transferência de vídeos pessoais sobre canais de comunicação com largura de banda limitada [1].

Particularmente, o padrão de ITU-T H.264 é um dos mais recentes e aprimorados codificadores de vídeo, que vêm sendo

usados em diversas aplicações de multimídia, incluindo o sistema brasileiro de TV Digital (SBTVD). Infelizmente a eficiência de compressão melhorada do padrão H.264 foi alcançada somente ao custo de uma complexidade computacional bastante superior quando comparada com seus antecessores [2]

A fim de suportar este elevado custo computacional diferentes soluções de hardware dedicado têm sido buscadas. Nos últimos anos, pode-se notar a tendência crescente de uso de modernas GPUs (*Graphical Processing Units*), como alternativa para acelerar aplicações com alto potencial de paralelismo, considerando que estes processadores podem incorporar centenas de núcleos de alto desempenho em um mesmo encapsulamento [3].

De fato, este tipo de tecnologia parece particularmente apropriado para processamento H.264 Intra, onde o vídeo é dividido em distintos macroblocos de 16x16 pixels, que podem ser processados independentemente.

Diversos artigos relacionados relatam o ganho percebido ao se adotar execuções paralelas usando processadores gráficos. Para uma solução definitiva, entretanto é importante notar que o desempenho global do codificador não depende somente do nível do paralelismo, mas também de características internas como a hierarquia de memória, comunicações entre o processador central (CPU) e a plataforma com GPU, mecanismos de sincronização, entre outras.

Considerando isso, este artigo apresenta diversos dados práticos, focalizando na arquitetura da empresa NVIDIA, a fim ilustrar o real potencial do uso desta tecnologia como um motor de aceleração para um codificador de vídeo H.264 intra.

Como estratégia de validação esta proposta foi comparada com o software oficial da referência H.264, distribuído pela entidade de JVT (*Joint Video Team*), assim como a biblioteca de código livre x264 [4].

O artigo é organizado como segue: a seção 2 apresenta detalhes da arquitetura de GPU CUDA® e dos algoritmos internos de um codificador H.264 intra, a seção 3 descreve uma solução proposta para aceleração de processamento orientada à tecnologia de GPU CUDA®, a seção 4 traz os resultados obtidos que comparam a solução proposta com arquiteturas tradicionais baseadas em um processador central e finalmente, a seção 5 apresenta conclusões finais do artigo.

2. VISÃO GERAL

2.1 Tecnologia NVIDIA CUDA ®

Em anos recentes, as demandas de crescimento para processamento gráfico tridimensional, influenciadas principalmente pelo mercado de jogos de computador, conduziram a uma evolução muito rápida de arquiteturas dedicadas de processadores gráficos [5].

Neste cenário, os processadores gráficos compatíveis com tecnologia de CUDA® (*Compute Unified Device Architecture*) são compostos por multiprocessadores escalares, chamados *streaming multiprocessors* (SMs). Cada SM é composto de um número diferente de processadores independentes (*Stream Processors* - SP), que são capazes de operar com instruções em paralelo sobre uma memória compartilhada. Os blocos computacionais criados pelo algoritmo no nível do projeto são escalados automaticamente dentro de *grids* dos SMs, sempre buscando reduzir sua capacidade ociosa. Dentro da arquitetura CUDA® estes blocos são executados simultaneamente por diferentes *threads*, uma vez que cada *thread* é interpretada e processada em um SP próprio [6]. Uma representação simplificada desta arquitetura é mostrada na figura 1.

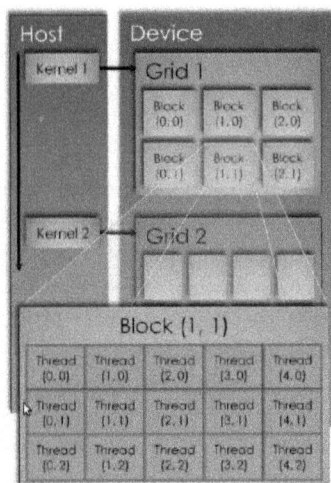

Figura 1. Estrutura interna da tecnologia CUDA®

A comunicação com o mundo externo ocorre com as memórias globais. Dentro da arquitetura CUDA®, podem ser usados quatro tipos de memórias: (i) memória interna dos registradores para cada SP, (ii) memória compartilhada entre o SPs da mesma unidade (mesmo SM), (iii) memória de constantes (somente leitura) e (iv) memória da textura (somente leitura também). Os acessos às memórias de constantes e de texturas são mais rápidos, pois ambas incorporaram memórias *cache* dedicadas para instruções e dados que simplificam os acessos a valores consecutivos ou adjacentes.

2.2 Codificação H.264 Intra

No padrão H.264 as seqüências de vídeo codificado são divididas em três tipos do quadro: I (*Intra*), P (*Predicted*) e B (*Bidirectional*). Os quadros I são comprimidos basicamente por algoritmos de transformada, quantização e entropia e podem ser usados como referência para outros frames. Os quadros P dependem temporalmente de quadros I, reusando dados deles a fim de reduzir o tamanho do fluxo final, enquanto que os quadros B dependerem de quadros I e P. O conjunto dos algoritmos, particularmente responsáveis para processar quadros I pode ser chamado como codificador H.264 Intra, representando uma parte essencial de todo o codificador H.264. Basicamente seis módulos são necessários para implementar um codificador H.264 Intra, onde três são usados para codificação direta (DCT, Hadamard e

quantização), e os outros três são responsáveis pela operação inversa (iDCT, iHadamard e dequantização). A seguir estes algoritmos são melhor explicados.

2.2.1 Algoritmos de transformadas

São dois os algoritmos de transformada, adotados pelo padrão H.264: DCT (*Discrete Cosine Transform*) e Hadamard [7]

O algoritmo para transformada DCT, ao operar com blocos de luminância, deve ser aplicado, cada vez sobre macroblocos de dados (blocos de 16x16 pixels). Para reduzir sua complexidade, cada macrobloco é dividido em 16 blocos dos 4x4 elementos, que são processados sequencialmente.

Já a transformada Hadamard opera somente sobre os coeficientes DC (primeiro elemento de cada bloco de 4x4) , resultantes da transformada DCT. Depois que todos os blocos 4x4 de um macrobloco foram processados pela DCT, o algoritmo de Hadamard arranja todos os valores DC em uma matriz reduzida de 4x4 elementos. O algoritmo interno (ao computar este bloco de 4x4 elementos DC) é muito similar ao da transformada DCT. Basicamente, a execução de um algoritmo de transformada, dentro de um codificador H.264 pode genericamente ser realizado em dois estágios como indicado abaixo:

$$\text{Estágio 1: } Y_1 = AX \quad\quad (1)$$
$$\text{Estágio 2: } Y = Y_1 . A^T \quad\quad (2)$$

Onde:

X representa o bloco de entrada;
A representa a matriz de transformada;
Y_1. representa o resultado do primeiro estágio;
A^T é a matriz de transformada transposta.

Todas as matrizes de transformada H.264 (DCT e Hadamard) podem ser implementadas com aritmética inteira [1].

2.2.2 Algoritmo de quantização.

O algoritmo da quantização do codificador H.264 é usado reduzir a definição dos valores de saída de acordo com o parâmetro QP (*Quantizer Parameter*) adotado, que pode variar 0 a 51, assim permitindo uma grande flexibilidade no controle da compressão final de dados.

No geral, o procedimento para executar isso requer recursos do ponto flutuante, mas o padrão H.264 adota um método alternativo, que permite o uso da aritmética inteira. O algoritmo da quantização H.264 é definido basicamente como [3]:

$$Q (i, j) = (|Y (i, j)| . MF + f) >> \text{qbits} \quad (3)$$
$$\text{sign} (Q (i, j)) = \text{sign} (Y (i, j)) \quad\quad (4)$$

Onde:

Y (i, j) representa o elemento da posição (i, j);
MF é o fator de multiplicação;
f é o valor de arredondamento selecionado;
qbits representa uma divisão por deslocamento de bit.

Os valores de MF, f e qbits são fixos de acordo com a norma H.264 e podem ser obtidos por tabelas predefinidas indexadas internamente dentro de bloco de 4x4 elementos pelos valores de QP e sua respectiva localização (i, j).

2.3 Trabalhos relacionados

Nos últimos anos, diversos autores propuseram o uso da tecnologia GPU como uma alternativa de melhorar o desempenho de codificadores de vídeo [4, 5, 9]. O trabalho [4], por exemplo, propõe uma execução paralela otimizada de IDCT utilizando arquitetura CUDA. A solução proposta introduz uma simplificação particular ao algoritmo original, quando os coeficientes avaliados zero são detectados, a fim reduzir o tempo de processamento. Os resultados experimentais apresentam ganhos variáveis, de acordo com o número de ocorrências de zero, oscilando de 1,7 a 7,7 vezes.

O trabalho [5] propõe uma solução paralela do codificador H.264, baseada na arquitetura CUDA. Nesta solução os dados de vídeo são alocados dinamicamente, por um mecanismo robusto da sincronização de *threads*. Diferentes modelos de placas padrão CUDA são usados, alcançando, no melhor caso, 7,6 vezes de ganho ao comparar esta proposta com uma solução tradicional.

Adicionalmente [9] propõe um algoritmo de estimativa do movimento para um codificador H.264/AVC adotando CUDA. Na solução inicialmente os pixels do bloco atual e do frame da referência são transferidos do processador central à memória de GPU. As *threads* executadas na GPU processam e acumulam seus resultados na memória compartilhada. Testes práticos foram feitos no software de referência JM9.0 (modelo aberto do codificador H.264), que foi estendido na solução proposta, com o uso de DirectX 9 API. Os resultados de melhoria do desempenho obtidos pela proposta apontaram para ganhos entre 1,5 e 3 vezes.

3. SOLUÇÃO PROPOSTA

Como comentado anteriormente, ao se usar a tecnologia CUDA, o algoritmo deve ser traduzido em threads paralelas, que executarão simultaneamente em unidades de processamento distintas. Particularmente, a solução proposta foi estruturada para trabalhar com um *grid* de tamanho 16x16, permitindo, desta forma, processar em paralelo um macrobloco H.264 inteiro.

Cada macrobloco de 16x16 pixels é implementado então por 16x16 threads, levando a um conjunto de 256 *threads*. Na solução proposta, o processamento das informações de cada pixel é feita uma *thread* individual, permitindo um elevado nível de paralelismo no processo de codificação. O algoritmo proposto executa a codificação intra de um macrobloco pela seqüência:

DCT;
Transformada Hadamard;
Quantização;
Dequantização;
Transformada Hadamard Inversa;
DCT Inversa;
Soma dos componentes | DC | e | AC |.

O último estágio apresentado (soma de valores | DC | e | AC|) representa uma preparação do algoritmo de entropia. O algoritmo de entropia do padrão H.264 é orientado a contexto, o significa que cada valor depende do último valor calculado, impedindo assim o paralelismo. Apenas sua preparação, por trabalhar com matrizes, pode ser realizada em paralelo e por isso foi incluída na solução.

No total, sete matrizes constantes foram usadas: (i) Matriz de DCT, (ii) DCTT, (iii) DCT-1, (iv) (DCT-1) T, (v) Hadamard, (vi) MF e (vii) PF (quantização inversa).

Três matrizes provisórias de tamanho 16x16 (tmp1 e tmp2, tmpAbs) são armazenadas na memória compartilhada, permitindo o acesso simultâneo por *threads* diferentes.

As matrizes tmp1 e tmp2 são reusadas nos cálculos de transformadas e quantização, ou seja, enquanto tmp1 armazena os resultados, a matriz tmp2 executa os cálculos e vice versa. A matriz tmpAbs armazena os valores quantizados absolutos que serão necessários no último estágio (somas de | DC | e | AC|).

Todos os procedimentos de transformada foram executados em dois estágios como indicado na equação (1), usando chamadas da sincronização entre processos, a fim assegurar a consistência dos dados. Os valores originais do macroblock são copiados inicialmente à matriz tmp2 (memória compartilhada), pois esta é mais rápida do que a memória global onde o frame original foi recebido. Basicamente, pode-se observar na seguinte expressão:

```
tmp1 = DCT * tmp2; Cada bloco de 4x4
tmp2 = tmp1 * DCTᵀ; Cada bloco de 4x4
```

A transformada Hadamard é implementada somente para componentes DC, o que demanda um conjunto de 16 *threads*. Sua implementação é ilustrada a seguir.

```
tmp1[dc] = Hadamard * tmp2[dc];
tmp2[dc] = tmp1[dc] * Hadamard;
tmp2[dc] = tmp2[dc] / 2;
```

A quantização é realizada da seguinte maneira:

```
tmp1 = sign (tmp2) * ((| tmp2 | * MF + f) >> b);
tmp1 = sign(tmp2) * ((|tmp2|*MF + f) >> b);
```

onde
```
f = 2*QP.Add, para DC;
f = 1*QP.Add, para AC;
b = QP.Bits + 1 para DC;
b = QP.Bits para AC;
```

A mesma abordagem foi adotada para executar as versões inversas de transformada e algoritmos da quantização. Após concluir estes cálculos, uma função adicional de saturação foi usada para proteger a definição dos valores do inteiro. Isso foi executado usando funções de mínimo e máximo (escala 0 a 255).

Finalmente pode ser calculada a soma dos componentes absolutos DC e AC. Para isto foi usado o método da redução. Na primeira etapa, somente 128 threads são usadas no somatório. Então, o número de threads ativas é reduzido a 64, 32 e assim até chegar ao valor final. Este mecanismo é mostrado na Figura 2.

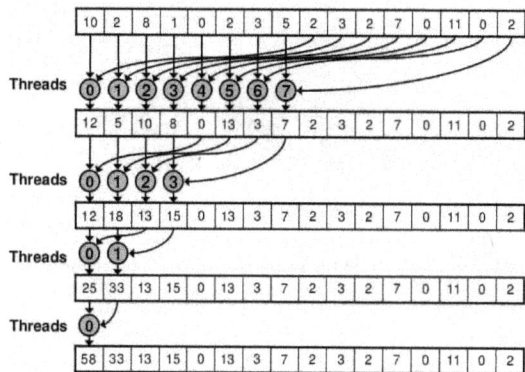

Figura 2. Processo de redução usado no cálculo da soma |AC| e |DC|

4. RESULTADOS EXPERIMENTAIS

A fim de possibilitar a comparação justa em um ambiente real de execução, a presente proposta foi implementada em ANSI C, e a seguir incorporada na versão 12.1 do software de referência. [9]. O cenário para testes foi baseado na seguinte configuração:

- Core i7-3770K 3.5GHz, 4C HT, 8MB cache
- Memória RAM 16GB DDR3 1600MHz
- Geforce PNY GTX 680 2GB GDDR5 6GHz
- CUDA Cores   1536

Avaliações iniciais apontaram para um atraso relativo muito significativo relacionado ao processo de comunicação entre CPU e GPU, chegando a ser maior que o tempo de codificação da placa CUDA. A fim de reduzir este atraso optou-se por reduzir a resolução dos pixels antes de cada transferência. Isso significa que os dados originais no PC tiveram a resolução reduzida de 16 bits a 8 bits. Dentro da arquitetura de GPU os dados são transformados e processados em 16 bits. Quando os cálculos encerram na GPU, os dados resultantes são reduzidos de 16 bits a 8 bits para retornar ao processador central. Este procedimento não afetou a qualidade do vídeo, pois o padrão H.264 é projetado se operar com valores de 8 bits. Uma representação gráfica disso é mostrada a seguir na forma de porcentagem. Pode-se observar que inicialmente o tempo de codificação representava apenas 19% do tempo total. Após a otimização das transferências, sua representação passou a 56%.

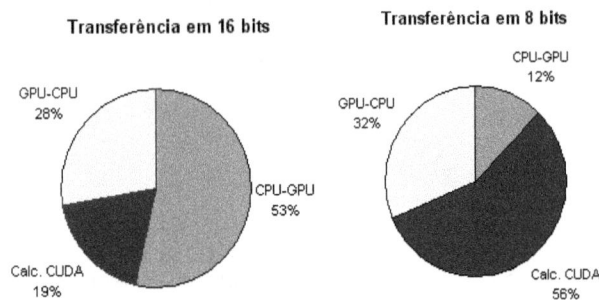

Figura 3. Comparação entre soluções de 16 e 8 bits

Outra característica importante que afeta o desempenho global desta solução é a largura de banda de comunicação.

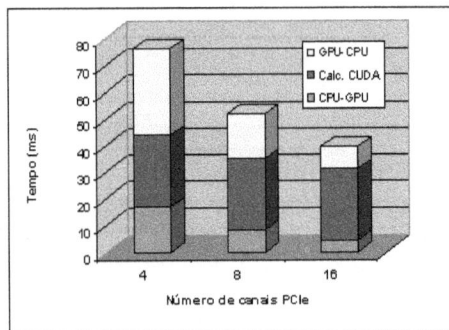

Figura 4. Influência do num. de canais no tempo total

Para ilustrar esta questão de forma prática o mesmo experimento foi realizado considerando diferentes ocupações de canais de comunicação PCIe. Percebe-se ao se observar a Figura 4 como o aumento da taxa efetiva de dados trafegados afeta o desempenho da solução, porém não de forma linear, pois o tempo de codificação não muda com o aumento da taxa de dados. Considerando-se estes aspectos a seguir são apresentados os

resultados finais obtidos da solução (transferência em 8 bits com 16x PCIe). A solução proposta foi executada e validada em dois ambientes: código de referência de JVT H.264 e biblioteca multi-*thread* x264, considerando distintas resoluções de video.

Tabela 1. Resultados finais de ganho obtido

Resolução	Código de referência	x264
CIF	5,46	2,29
4CIF	7,16	2,46
Full HD	7,67	2,59

5. CONCLUSÕES

O artigo atual propôs uma solução baseada em GPU para aceleração de um codificador H.264 intra. Diferentes características relacionadas como atrasos nos acessos de memória e canais de comunicação foram considerados para aumentar o desempenho da solução. Experiências práticas confirmam que estas características se não tratadas adequadamente podem afetar significativamente o desempenho global. Os resultados práticos indicam uma velocidade final acima de 7,6 vezes sobre o código de referência e 2,5 vezes sobre a biblioteca otimizada x264, confirmando-a assim apropriada para uma aplicação que busque características de tempo real.

6. REFERÊNCIAS

[1] Richardson I. E. G., H.264 and MPEG-4 Video Compression. England, Ed Wiley . Sons, v2 2003, 281p.

[2] Chen, and H.-Y Chen, "Physical Design for System-On-a Chip" in Essential Issues in SOC Design, Springer, 2009.

[3] Huang Y.-L., Shen Y.-C., Wu J.-L., Scalable computation for spatially scalable video coding using NVIDIA CUDA and multi-core CPU MM.09, October, 2009, China pp.361-370.

[4] W -N Chen, H -M Hang, .H.264/AVC motion estimation implementation on Compute Unified Device Architecture (CUDA), IEEE Int. Conf. Mult. Expo pp 697-700, 2008.

[5] Han T. D. and Abdelrahman T. S., Reducing Branch Divergence in GPU programs. Proceedings of the Fourth Workshop on GPGPU [S.l.]: 2011.

[6] NVIDIA. NVIDIA's Next Generation CUDA Compute Architecture: Fermi . 2009. 22 p.

[7] Song, T. et al. Parallel Implementation Algorithm of Motion Estimation for GPU Applications 6 p.

[8] Cheng, R. Yang, E. and Liu, T. Speeding up motion estimation algorithms on CUDA technology Asia Pacific Conference in Multimedia and Electronics 2010. pp. 93-96.

[9] Massanes F., Cadennes M. and Brankov J. G., CUDA implementation of a block-matching algorithm for Multiple GPU cards Journal of Electron Imaging. 2011 20(3) pp.1-21.

[10] Crow T. S. Evolution of the GPU. 2004. 59 p.

[11] Harris M. Optimizing Parallel Reduction in CUDA 2010, 38p.

[12] ITU – International Telecommunication Unit, H.264/SVC Reference Software for H.264, 2010.

Blurring Image Quality Assessment Method based on Histogram of Gradient

Sangwoo Ahn
The Department of Nanoscale
Semiconductor, Hanyang University
Seoul, Rep. of Korea
ahnsangwoo@hanyang.ac.kr

Jongjoo Park
The Department of Nanoscale
Semiconductor, Hanyang University
Seoul, Rep. of Korea
jongjoo@hanyang.ac.kr

Jongwha Chong
The Department of Nanoscale
Semiconductor, Hanyang University
Seoul, Rep. of Korea
jchong@hanyang.ac.kr

ABSTRACT

In this paper we propose a blurring image quality assessment (IQA) based on histogram of oriented gradients (HOG). The image quality can be determined by the slope value of the HOG of the target image. The representative line of HOG is approximated by a random sample consensus set (RANSAC). Simulation results performed on the LIVE image quality assessment database show that the proposed method aligns better with how the human visual system perceives image quality than several state-of-the-art IQAs.

Keywords: Image Quality Assessment, Human Visual System, Histogram of Gradient, Random Sample Consensus Set.

1. INTRODUCTION

With the rapid proliferation of digital imaging, IQA has become an important issue in image processing systems, including image acquisition, transmission, compression and restoration. IQA also is used to monitor image systems, adjust image quality, optimize algorithms and set parameters for image processing systems [1]. Subjective IQA is most reliable, but cannot be used for real-time systems and automated systems. Therefore IQA using computational models to evaluate image quality consistent with subjective evaluations is proposed.

Based on the availability of a reference image, IQA can be classified as full reference (FR) IQA, no reference (NR) IQA and reduced reference (RR) IQA [2]. The FR-IQAs are provided with the original undistorted image along with the distorted image whose quality is to be estimated. The RR-IQAs are provided with the distorted image and additional information about the original undistorted image from an additional channel or by incorporating some information from the distorted image. The NR-IQAs refer to algorithms that seek to estimate the quality of the distorted image without any knowledge of reference images [3]. The NR-IQA has difficulty constructing algorithms for estimating image quality. Recently, NR-IQA has become of great interest to researchers. Here, we propose a new method that we believe will be effective for NR-IQA.

The process of NR-IQA is very complex since there is no information about the original, undistorted image. Therefore, NR-IQAs are measurements of features and properties in the distorted images that are consistent with human-perceived quality. Among the various features and properties of distorted images, a gradient distribution, which can be shown in the HOG, is used in the proposed NR-IQA.

The shape of the HOG describes image quality in detail. However, generating numerical values from the shape of the HOG is a problem. Other approaches generally make use of heavy-tailed distributions [4]. In contrast, the proposed approach introduces a line estimation algorithm, RANSAC, for estimating the shape of the HOG. After performing RANSAC, the line representing the shape of HOG is obtained, and the slope of this line corresponds to the representative values of image quality.

In this paper, we propose a novel approach with no reference/blind image quality assessment. This approach makes computational complexity low with maintaining reliability and suggests new approximate method of the HOG.

Simulation results show that the proposed NR-IQA is consistent with subjective evaluations. Moreover the method is competitive with full-reference image quality assessment algorithms.

2. PROPOSED ALGORITHM

2.1 Histogram of Gradient

HOG is feature descriptor used in computer vision and image processing for the purpose of IQA, de-blurring, image segmentation and the others. The technique counts occurrences of gradient in localized portions of an image. Navneet Dalal and Bill Triggs, researchers for the French National Institute for Research in Computer Science and Control, described HOG in there paper [5]. In this work, they focused their algorithm on the problem of pedestrian detection in static images, although since then they expanded their tests to include human detection in film and video.

An image gradient is a directional change in the intensity or color of an image. Gradients have distorted images with a large proportion of their values on small values and un-distorted images have the opposite. This is because each pixel in a distorted image has an effect on the surrounding pixels. The combined influence of all pixels makes the gradients small. The histogram of gradient is written as follows (1) and it describes such a property concretely as shown in Figure 1.

$$H = \log(\sum (G_x[g] + G_y[g]))$$
$$G_x = I \otimes s_x, G_y = I \otimes s_y \tag{1}$$

where H is the HOG, I is the input image, G_x is the x-direction gradient image, G_y is the y-direction gradient image, s_x is the x-direction filter kernel which is set to [-1 0 1;-2 0 2;-1 0 1], s_y is the y-direction filter kernel which is set to [-1 -2 -1;0 0 0;1 2 1] and g is the gradient value. And range of $\sum$ is from -255 to 255.

(a)   (b)

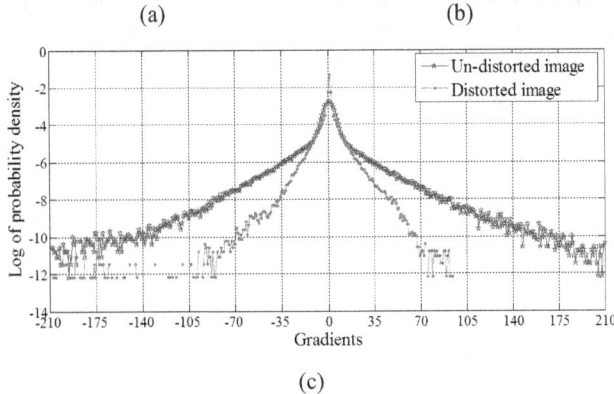

(c)

Figure 1. (a) is un-distorted, (b) is distorted image and (c) shows that the HOG can classify un-distorted and distorted image with certainty.

2.2 Random Sample Consensus Set and Slope Estimation

The RANSAC algorithm introduced by Fishler and Bolles in 1981 [6] is the most widely used robust estimator in the field of image processing. RANSAC is popular since it is simple and it works well in practice. However, its area usage is limited to 3D image processing, image warping and geometry estimation.

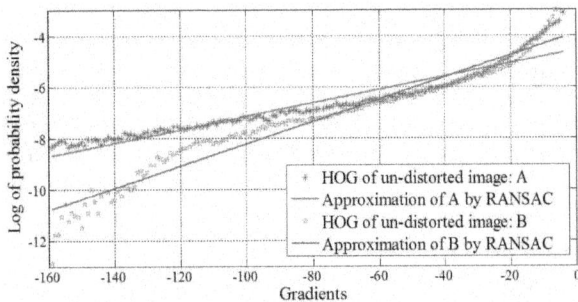

Figure 2. Approximation of the HOG by RANSAC

Therefore, in the proposed NR-IQA, a RANSAC-based IQA approach is first introduced for approximating the shape of the HOG. Unlike state-of-the-art approaches, the RANSAC-based approach uses straight line rather than complex functions like heavy tails distribution [7]. By only using straight lines, the shape of the HOG can be obtained. The assumption used in this paper is that the shape of the HOG is almost symmetric with respect to the y-axis. From this assumption, we apply RANSAC just to half of the HOG. Therefore, the amount of computation amount is

reduced by half. Figure 2 shows an example of RANSAC on the HOGs of distorted image and un-distorted image. Figure 2 describes that the different between distorted and un-distorted makes IQA possible.

We mention the slope estimation step for describing the flow of the proposed algorithm. However, when the line is obtained, slope estimation is a simple problem. The slope estimation step is only for calculating a numerical value representing image quality.

For further explanation, we verify the characteristic of the images. As image qualities decline, the slope values tend to have steeper slopes as shown in Figure 3. And it confirms that the characteristic assumed is valuable. Therefore we make use of the above characteristics to assess image quality.

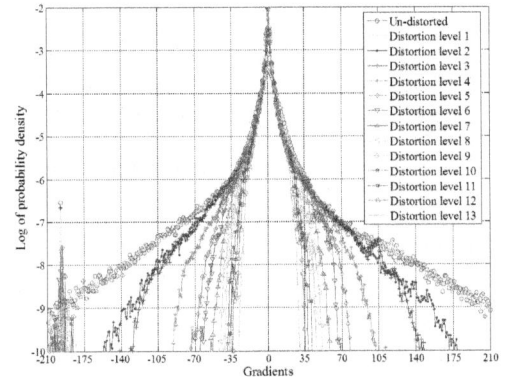

Figure 3. The Histogram of Gradient. This figure describes distorted images with a steeper slope, as expected.

2.3 Proposed Algorithm

After the HOG is obtained, we apply RANSAC for estimating the shape of the HOG. The line approximated by RANSAC is representative of the HOG. We assess image quality based on the approximated line. The slope of the line denotes the image quality in the proposed algorithm. Consequently, the main contribution of the proposed NR-IQA is its novel approach to applying RANSAC to the HOG.

Figure 4 is the pseudo code of the proposed algorithm. Where m is set to 2, t is set to 3 and d is set to 72. The number of iteration, N, is calculated by the equation (2).

$$N = \frac{\log(1-p)}{\log(1-u^m)} \qquad (2)$$

where p set to 0.99 is the probability that we obtain an outlier free subset. u set to 0.6 is the probability for an inlier. Therefore, in the proposed algorithm, N is set to 13.

Error function of the proposed algorithm has a significant effect on the accuracy. Error function for measuring how well estimated line fits the HOG is computed by distances between points and estimated line as follows (3).

$$Errorfunction = \sum_i \frac{|am_i + bn_i + c|}{sqrt(a^2 + b^2)} \qquad (3)$$

where the scope of i is from 0 to 255 according to the x-scale of the HOG. mi and ni are coordinate of each point on the HOG. a, b and c are parameter of the estimated line.

Algorithm 1. Proposed algorithm

Input:

I – Input image for IQA.

Output:

Q – Image Quality

Step 1. Histogram of Gradient

0. Given s_x = [-1 0 1;-2 0 2;-1 0 1];
   s_y = [-1 -2 -1;0 0 0;1 2 1];

1. $G_x = I * s_x$; $G_y = I * s_y$;
   where * here denotes the 2-dimensional convolution op.

2. Given size(I) = [m, n];
   for i = 1:m
       for j = 1:n
     for p = -255:0
         if ($I_{Gradient\ x}(m,n) == p\ |\ I_{Gradient\ y}(m,n)==p$)
         $H(p) = H(p)$ +1;
       end end
           end end

3. **return** H

Step 2. Slope Estimation via RANSAC

0. **Given** H- data from the histogram of gradient
m- the minimum number of data required to fit the line
N- the maximum number of iterations allowed in the algorithm
t- a threshold for determining when a data point fits a line
d- the number of close data requires to assert that a line fits well to data
return: fitline- line slope which best fit the data

1. **initial** *iteration* = 0; *fitline* = **null**; *besterr* = ∞;
2. **while** *iterations* < N
   maybeinliers = m randomly selected values from H;
   maybeline = line slope fitted to *maybeinliers*;
   alsoinliers = **null**;
   for every points in H not in *maybeinliers*
   if error function(point firs maybe model) < t
     alsoinliers = {*alsoinliers*, point};
   end
   if the number of elements in *alsoinliers* > d
   % this implies that we may have found a fitted line
   betterline = line slope fitted to all points in
     maybeinliers and *alsoinliers*;
   thiserr = error function(these points)
   if *thiserr* < *besterr*
     fitline = *betterline*;
     besterr = *thiserr*;
   end
       end
   iterations = *iterations* + 1;
   end
3. **return** *fitline*

Figure 4. Pseudo description code for the proposed algorithm with HOG and RANSAC.

Explanation of pseudo code of the proposed algorithm is described in here. Pseudo code of Figure 4 consists of two part mentioned before, one is HOG and the other is RANSAC algorithm. Firstly, we extract the HOG (Figure 4, Step 1). In this point, the values from HOG are varied from -255 to 0, like mentioned before, the symmetry characteristic of HOG for

minimizing computational complexity. Second, we estimate the optimized straight line most similar with calculated HOG (Figure 4, Step 2). The estimated straight line represents the calculated HOG before and its slope value represents the image quality of target image. Consequently, the main contributions of the proposed algorithm are two things: one is introducing new method for IQA with HOG and RANSAC, and the other is the evaluating method with error function.

3. SIMULATION RESULTS

We use the LIVE image quality assessment database [8] for improving the performance of the proposed NR-IQA algorithm. The LIVE IQA database consists of 29 reference images and five distortion types-JPEG, JPEG2000, Blur, Noise and FastFading (FF). With the LIVE IQA database, we can use a total of 808 distorted images along with the associated differential mean opinion score (DMOS), which represents the perceived quality of the image and was computed from subjective scores. Various IQA systems use LIVE database for simulation, therefore we can compare the performance with distributed DMOS scores.

We measure the Spearman's rank ordered correlation coefficient (SROCC), Pearson's linear correlation coefficient (PLCC), root mean square error (RMSE) and Kendall's rank correlation coefficient (KRCC) between the proposed NR-IQA and DMOS. The SROCC, PLCC, RMS and KRCC are non-parametric measures of statistical dependence between above two variables. This means that the methods compare the relative scores not the absolute scores. Therefore, we can evaluate the accuracy of various IQA systems with more considerations.

In first simulation, we compare the performance with various correlation methods. First simulation results are shown in Table 1.

Table 1. The proposed algorithm performance comparisons

Model	SROCC	PLCC	RMSE	KRCC
PSNR	0.8521	0.8845	13.364	0.6865
SSIM	0.9476	0.9449	8.946	0.7963
VSNR [9]	0.9271	0.9229	10.521	0.7610
MAD	0.9438	0.9394	9.368	0.7920
VIF [10]	0.9632	0.9598	7.667	0.8270
BIQI [11]	0.8357	0.8205	16.692	-
Proposed	0.8773	0.9237	13.126	0.7514

The items in Table 1 can be categorized into two groups. One group is the full-reference IQA: PSNR, SSIM, VSNR, MAD and VIF. The other group is the non-reference IQA: BIQI and the proposed algorithm. As shown in Table 1, full-reference IQA algorithms generally perform better than non-reference IQA algorithms. The primary objective of the proposed algorithm is improved performance compared with BIQI and PSNR and comparable performance with items of full-reference IQA. Table 1 show that the primary objective is achieved. However, the proposed NR-IQA has room for improvements. Therefore our future work is to improve the accuracy comparing to reference IQA algorithms.

Figure 5. Test images distorted by (a) Additive Gaussian noise, (b) Spatially correlative noise, (c) Impulsive noise, (d) Gaussian blur, (e) JPEG 2000 compression and (f) Luminance.

Second simulation show how well appropriates for subjective evaluation. The simulation results are shown in below Table 2.

In Table 2, we can know that the SSIM and VSNR, which have high score in first simulation, have also high accuracy. MAD and VIF have disadvantages on Impulsive noise and JPEG 2000 compression respectively. Sadly, the proposed algorithm has disadvantage on Gaussian noise also. However, the all of methods have similar ranking order with subjective evaluation. Therefore we can know that the proposed algorithm can be used for wide IQA for various image processing systems.

From the simulations, we can know that the proposed algorithm with HOG has quite good performance comparing to other methods. However, the proposed algorithm gains the upper hand to the NR-IQAs but, the lower hand to FR-IQAs. Therefore, in further researches, we will focus on the accuracy similar with FR-IQAs.

Table 2. The proposed algorithm performance comparisons

Model	(a)	(b)	(c)	(d)	(e)	(f)
Subjective	2	6	3	4	5	1
SSIM	2	6	3	4	5	1
VSNR	2	6	3	4	5	1
MAD	2	6	4	3	5	1
VIF	2	5	3	4	6	1
Proposed	3	6	2	4	5	1

4. CONCLUSIN

Researches about NR-IQA have become important topic. This is because that the NR-IQA can be used widely for various image processing systems. With diverse researches, HOS with RANSAC based method is not existed until now. Therefore this paper proposes new approach for NR-IQA system and improves the accuracy. In the future work, we research more in this topic for improving the accuracy of NR-IQA similar to FR-IQA methods.

5. REFERENCES

[1] Z. Wang and A. C. Bovik, Modern Image Quality Assessment, New York Morgan and Claypool Publishing Company, 2006.

[2] Z. Wang, A. C. Bovik, H. R. Sheikh and E. P. Simonecelli, "Image quality assessment: From error visibility to structural similarity," IEEE Transactions on Image Processing, vol.13, no.4, pp.600–612, Apr. 2004.

[3] A. K. Moorthy and A. C. Bovik, "Blind Image Quality Assessment: From NaturalScene Statistics to Perceptual Quality," IEEE Transactions on Image Processing, vol.20, no.12, pp.3350–3364, Dec. 2011.

[4]] R. Fergus, B. Singh, A. Hertzmann, S. T. Roweis and W. T. Freeman, "Removing camera shake from a single photograph," ACM Transaction on Graphics, vol.25, no.3, pp.787–794, Jul. 2006. DOI = http://dl.acm.org/citation.cfm?doid=1179352.1141956

[5] N. Dalal and B. Triggs, "Histograms of oriented gradients for human detection," IEEE Conference on Computer Vision and Pattern Recognition, vol. 1, pp. 886-893, June. 2005.

[6] M. Fischler and R. Bolles, "Random sample consensus: A paradigm for model fitting with applications to image analysis and automated cartography," Communications of the ACM, vol.24, no.6, pp.381–395, Jun. 1981. DOI = http://dl.acm.org/citation.cfm?doid=358669.358692

[7] K. Seshadrinathan, R. Soundararajan, A. C. Bovik and L. K. Cormack, "Study of Subjective and Objective Quality Assessment of Video," IEEE Transactions on Image Processing, vol.19, no.6, pp.1427–1441, Jun. 2010.

[8] H. R. Sheikh, Z. Wang, L. Cormack and A. C. Bovik, "LIVE Image Quality Assessment Database Release 2", http://live.ece.utexas.edu/research/quality.

[9] D. M. Chandler and S. S. Hemami, "VSNR: A Wavelet-Based Visual Signal-to-Noise Ratio for Natural Images," IEEE Transactions on Image Processing, vol.16, no.9, pp.2284–2298, Sep. 2007.

[10] H. R. Sheikh and A. C. Bovik, "Image information and visual quality," IEEE Transactions on Image Processing, vol.15, no.2, pp.430–444, Jan. 2006.

[11] A. K. Moorthy and A. C. Bovik, "A Two-Step Framework for Constructing Blind Image Quality Indices," IEEE Signal Processing Letters, vol.17, no.5, pp.513–516, May. 2010.

NCL+Depth: Extending NCL for Stereo/Autostereoscopic 3D Displays

Roberto Gerson de A. Azevedo   Luiz Fernando Gomes Soares

Departamento de Informática – PUC-Rio
Rua Marquês de São Vicente, 225
Rio de Janeiro – 22453-900 - Brasil
0055-21-3527-1500 Ext: 4330
{razevedo, lfgs}@inf.puc-rio.br

ABSTRACT

The availability of 3D-enabled displays, both stereoscopic and autostereoscopic ones, is growing in the market. However, most of the current multimedia digital TV standard for describing interactive applications does not take advantage of these technologies. A useful and flexible way to codify 3D-video to work with both stereoscopic and autoestereoscopic displays is using video plus depth-per-pixel information. In order to improve authoring of interactive digital TV applications written in NCL (Nested Context Language), the Latin-American standard for digital TV, this paper proposes some extensions to this language to allow multimedia authors to be aware of depth information. Among the new features provided it is the control and animation of depth information for synthetic and non-synthetic media objects. As it is based on 2D+depth information, the proposed extensions will enable multimedia authors to take advantage of stereo and autostereoscopic displays, and also are compatible with previous versions of NCL players.

Categories and Subject Descriptors

I.7.2 [**Document and Text Processing**]: Document Preparation – *Hypertext/hypermedia;* I.3.1 [**Computer Graphics**]: Hardware Architecture – Three-dimensional displays;

Keywords

Nested Context Language, 3DTV, Video-plus-depth, multimedia

1. INTRODUÇÃO

Nos últimos anos, vários dispositivos equipados com *displays* 3D, tanto estereoscópicos quanto autoestereoscópicos, já estão no mercado, à disposição de usuários finais [1]. Com esses novos *displays* disponíveis, o número de pessoas aptas a receber conteúdo 3D só tende a aumentar. Contudo, a quantidade de conteúdo que tira proveito das funcionalidades providas por esses dispositivos ainda é pequena e é um dos gargalos para a popularização dos serviços multimídia 3D.

Displays estereoscópicos produzem a ilusão de profundidade ao apresentar um par imagens que são vistas pelos dois olhos com um ângulo paralaxe. O ângulo paralaxe[1] é o ângulo entre as linhas de vista dos dois olhos que levam à disparidade entre as duas imagens projetadas nas retinas [2]. Esses dispositivos já estão disponível no mercado e são usados em TVs 3Ds, cinema 3D e aplicações móveis. Geralmente, eles requerem a codificação de pares de imagens que, ao serem apresentadas, devem ser filtradas (usualmente por meio de óculos) para que cada olho receba a "sua imagem" correspondente. Sistemas estereoscópicos têm a vantagem de serem uma solução simples e robusta [2], não necessitando de processamento complexo, como provisão e estimação da geometria da cena ou síntese adicional de cada *view*, e requerendo apenas a codificação de um par de vídeo estéreo. Existem vários métodos de codificação simples, como *side-by-side* ou *bottom-up*, e alguns outros que tiram proveito das dependências temporais entre cada *view*, bem como da interdependência entre cada uma dessas *views*.

Por outro lado, *displays* autoestereoscópicos apresentam uma imagem com ilusão de profundidade sem a necessidade da utilização de óculos [3]. Atualmente, as tecnologias mais utilizadas para esses displays são a *lenticular sheets* e a *parallax barriers*. Para permitir a visualização do efeito de paralaxe em mais de um ponto de vista, tais *displays* necessitam de uma quantidade de *views* bem maior do que apenas o par requerido pelos *displays* estéreo. Várias pesquisas têm sido realizadas nos últimos anos com relação à compressão de vídeo 3Dpara displays que permitem a visualização de mais de um ponto de vista [2] [4]. Codificação *multiview* (*e.g.* MPEG H.264 MVC [5]) e codificação usando mapas de profundidade (*e.g.* MPEG-C Part 3 [6]) estão entre as soluções mais comumente encontradas. Em alguns casos, também é proposta uma mistura dos dois [2]. Em especial, codificações que levam em consideração a geometria da cena, como é o caso dos mapas de profundidade, têm a vantagem de serem mais flexíveis – na medida em que permitem que vários pontos de vistas diferentes possam ser gerados no cliente – e permitirem uma compressão mais eficiente. O processo de renderizar os pares estéreo a partir das informações de profundidade – denominado *depth-image-based rendering* (DIBR) – é um problema por si só e tem sido tratado em vários trabalhos na literatura [2] [7] [8].

Além dos formatos de codificação de vídeo em si, outro problema que surge é a falta de recursos nas linguagens multimídia para tirar proveito desses dispositivos 3D. Com foco nesse último

---

[1] Quando o ângulo de paralaxe é zero, a imagem é percebida no plano do *display* 3D; um ângulo paralaxe positivo faz com que a imagem seja percebida atrás do plano do *display*; quando o ângulo é negativo a imagem é percebida na frente do *display*.

problema, neste artigo, são propostas extensões à linguagem NCL (Nested Context Language) [9] – linguagem declarativa padrão do Sistema Brasileiro de TV Digital e Recomendação ITU-T para serviços IPTV – que possibilitam a autores de aplicações multimídia NCL tirarem proveito dos recursos de displays 3D (tanto estéreo quanto autoestereoscópicos). As extensões propostas permitem: adicionar dados de profundidades a quaisquer objetos de mídia que fazem parte de uma aplicação; mixar o efeito de profundidade desses objetos; e animar os dados de profundidade dos objetos de mídia.

As extensões aqui apresentadas podem ser úteis em futuros padrões de 3DTV interativa, tanto para ambientes de TV Digital Terrestre como para IPTV. Além disso, as extensões e discussões apresentadas neste artigo também podem ser úteis para outras linguagens multimídia (declarativas e de *script*) 2D que queiram tirar proveito das funcionalidades de *displays* estereo/autoestereoscópicos. É importante salientar que as extensões propostas são compatíveis com versões anteriores da NCL, no sentido que dispositivos legados podem simplesmente ignorá-las (a Seção 6.1 discute esse problema de compatibilidade).

Com o objetivo de descrever as extensões propostas, este artigo está dividido como segue. A Seção 2 descreve a linguagem NCL de uma forma geral, evidenciando os principais pontos de interesse neste trabalho. A Seção 3 apresenta os principais requisitos para uma linguagem multímidia 2D ciente de dados de profundidade. A Seção 4 apresenta as principais extensões aqui propostas para cumprir os requisitos definido na Seção 3. A Seção 5 traz uma breve discussão de como é possível animar os dados de profundidade. Alguns aspectos de implementação e alguns experimentos são descritos na Seção 6. A Seção 7 compara as propostas deste artigo com os principais trabalhos relacionados. Por fim, a Seção 8 apresenta as conclusões e trabalhos futuros.

2. NCL: VISÃO GERAL

NCL é uma linguagem de cola de domínio específico para o sincronismo de mídias. Nesse sentido, NCL não busca definir o conteúdo das mídias em si, mas sim como elas se relacionam no tempo e no espaço. Objetos de mídia são definidos como elementos <media>. Cada elemento <media> pode conter um conjunto de propriedades (elemento <property>) – por exemplo, *top*, *left*, *width*, *height*, *transparency* etc.

Em especial, o *zIndex* é uma propriedade do objeto de mídia que define a sua ordem de renderização em relação aos outros objetos. Objetos de mídia com propriedade *zIndex* maior são renderizados sobre objetos com a propriedade *zIndex* menor. A Seção 2.1 detalha o funcionamento do algoritmo de renderização baseado em zIndex.

Todas as propriedades de um objeto de mídia podem ser especificadas, ou como elementos <property> dentro do próprio objeto de mídia, ou por meio de descritores (elemento <descriptor>). Os descritores permitem que um conjunto de propriedades seja definido apenas uma vez e reutilizado por outros objetos de mídia.

Adicionalmente, as propriedades de posicionamento (*left*, *top*, *width*, *height*, *right*, *bottom* e *zIndex*) também podem ser definidas por elementos <region>. Os elementos <region> permitem uma abstração "mais amigável" para definir onde os objetos de mídia serão apresentados, pois com elas é possível agrupar regiões e especificar seus dados de posicionamento relativos à sua posição na hierarquia.

Seguindo a mesma lógica das propriedades de posicionamento definidas em NCL, as extensões propostas neste artigo podem ser utilizadas nas regiões, descritores ou propriedades dos objetos de mídia. Independentemente de onde são definidas, essas informações podem ser posteriormente modificadas durante a execução da aplicação.

2.1 zIndex

As descrições de cena 2D, tais como as definidas em HTML, SVG ou NCL, usualmente trabalham com uma especificação de *zIndex* que informa a ordem de renderização dos objetos [10]. Essas linguagens seguem o algoritmo de desenho no qual os objetos são desenhados na ordem de *zIndex* associado a eles, permitindo o efeito de sobreposição dos objetos 2D. A Figura 1 demonstra o funcionamento desse algoritmo.

Como é possível observar na Figura 1, ao compor duas superfícies, gerando uma superfície final, os *pixels* das superfícies com *zIndex* menor serão sobreposto pelos *pixels* da superfícies com *zIndex* maior[2].

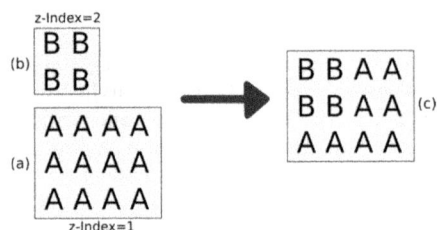

Figura 1: Exemplo do modelo de renderização baseado em zIndex.

Esse modelo funciona bem para aplicações puramente 2D, mas ele não é apropriado para o desenvolvimento de aplicações interativas para *displays* 3D, onde a profundidade (*depth* ou *z*) é uma dimensão inerente do serviço, assim como o são as posições horizontais e verticais [10].

Uma forma de tratar esses dados de profundidade é definindo um contexto de renderização completo em 3D. Contudo, essa definição, se apenas com o propósito de apresentar um botão ou menu com efeito de profundidade, parece um grande *overhead* para o autor. Nesse sentido, faz sentido incluir extensões em linguagens multimídia 2D para permitir o controle dos dados de profundidade – como é a proposta deste artigo para NCL.

3. REQUISITOS

Além das informações de profundidade que devem ser informadas por meio do documento NCL, os diversos objetos de mídia também podem trazer as informações de profundidade em seu próprio conteúdo (como é o caso de vídeos com codificações *vídeo-plus-depth*). Independente do caso, é responsabilidade do player NCL compor a apresentação multimídia de forma coerente.

Com as extensões propostas neste artigo, deve-se cumprir os seguintes requisitos e restrições:

- Suporte a displays estereoscópicos e autoestereoscópicos;

- Suporte a objetos de mídia com informação de profundidade definidas em seu próprio conteúdo;

---

[2] Em algumas linguagens, dependendo da orientação escolhida, é possível que o *zIndex* seja invertido, *i.e.*, objetos com *zIndex* menor sobrepõem objetos com z–Index maior.

186

- Suporte à inclusão, sobreposição e escala de informações de profundidade pelo autor do documento NCL;

- Suporte a alteração dinâmica dos dados de profundidade em tempo de execução (possibilitando, por exemplo, animação);

- Restrição: NCL deve continuar como uma linguagem de cola (tratando todos os objetos de mídia embutidos com a mesma API), sem se preocupar com o tipo do conteúdo desses objetos;

- Restrição: A compatibilidade com versões anteriores deve ser mantida (*i.e.,* o documento desenvolvido com as extensões aqui propostas deve poder ser exibido mesmo em players que não tratam as informações de profundidade, os quais poderão ignorar essas informações);

A seção a seguir detalha a proposta deste artigo para cumprir os requisitos acima.

4. EXTENSÕES NCL+DEPTH

De acordo com [11], os objetos em uma cena multimídia 2D com ciência de profundidade podem ser separados em duas categorias:

- aqueles com *profundidade uniforme* (*i.e.* todos os *pixels* possuem o mesmo dado de profundidade); e

- aqueles com *profundidade não-uniforme* (cada *pixel* pode ter um dado de profundidade diferente);

nesses últimos objetos, pode-se incluir aqueles com:

- *profundidade dinâmica* (*i.e.* objetos com profundidade não-uniforme que variam com o tempo).

4.1 Profundidade Uniforme

Para definir as informações de profundidade para objetos com profundidade uniforme é suficiente a utilização de um único parâmetro. Aqui iremos informá-lo como um *double* entre -1.0 e 1.0. Valores negativos informam que o objeto deve aparecer atrás do plano da tela, enquanto valores positivos informam que os objetos aparecerão na frente da tela. Objetos com valores 0.0 devem ser exibidos no plano da tela.

Seguindo a mesma lógica que os atributos associados a onde o objeto de mídia deve ser exibido na linguagem NCL, esse novo parâmetro pode ser associado a um objeto de mídia tanto por meio de regiões (um novo atributo *depthOffset*), a descritores (por meio do elemento <descriptorParam> com valor de atributo *name* igual a *depthOffset*) ou diretamente como propriedades dos elementos de mídia (elemento <property> com atributo *name* igual a *depthOffset*).

O código a seguir exemplifica como isso pode ser feito em NCL:

```
...
<regionBase>
  <region id="rg1" depthOffset="0.5"
          width="50px" height="50px"/>
  <region id="rg2" depthOffset="0.4"
          width="100px" height="100px"/>
</regionBase>
...
<descriptorBase>
  <descriptor id="desc1">
    <descriptorParam name="depthOffset"
                     value="0.5"/>
  </descriptor>
</descriptorBase>
...
<body id="nclBody">
  <media id="m1" descriptor="desc1">
```

```
    <property name="depthOffset"
              value="0.5"/>
  </media>
</body>
...
```

4.2 Mapas de profundidade estáticos

Mapas de profundidade podem ser especificados para objetos de mídia com profundidade não-uniforme por meio da propriedade *depthMap*. O valor da propriedade *depthMap* deve ser uma URI para uma imagem em escala de cinza que informa, para cada *pixel*, o valor da profundidade associada aquele *pixel*.

O código a seguir exemplifica como é possível associar uma imagem informando o mapa de profundidade a uma região, descritor ou objeto de mídia:

```
...
<regionBase>
  <region id="rg1"
          depthMap="maps/depth-map-image.bmp"
          width="50px" height="50px"/>
  <region id="rg2"
          depthMap="maps/depth-map-image.bmp"
          width="100px" height="100px"/>
</regionBase>
...
<descriptorBase>
  <descriptor id="desc1">
    <descriptorParam name="depthMap"
          value="maps/image-depth-map.bmp"/>
  </descriptor>
</descriptorBase>
...
<body id="nclBody">
  <media id="m1" descriptor="desc1">
    <property name="depthMap"
          value="maps/image-depth-map.bmp"/>
  </media>
</body>
...
```

Embora o ideal seja que o autor especifique as dimensões do mapa de profundidade iguais às dimensões dos objetos de mídia associados a eles, muitas vezes isso não é possível. Em alguns casos porque as dimensões dos objetos de mídia são definidas por meio de porcentagem (resultando em *pixels* absolutos diferentes dependendo do tamanho da tela), ou em outros, porque a própria dimensão do objeto de mídia é alterada durante a apresentação. A Figura 2 apresenta dois casos: um em que o dimensão do mapa de profundidade é menor do que a dimensão do objeto de mídia associado a ele (a); e outro em que a dimensão dos dados de profundidade é maior do que a dimensão do objeto de mídia (b).

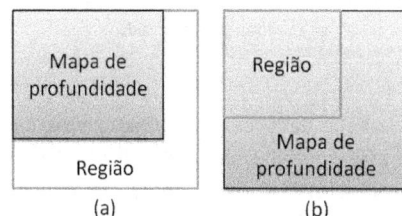

Figura 2: Exemplos de incompatibilidades entre a dimensão do mapa de profundidade e da dimensão do objeto de mídia.

Nesses casos, existem duas soluções possíveis: ou leva-se em consideração apenas os dados realmente especificados e, por exemplo, em (a) considera-se os dados de profundidade do objeto de mídia que estão fora do mapa de profundidade como 0; ou os dados de profundidade são redimensionados para o tamanho dos seus respectivos objetos de mídia – por exemplo, usando uma interpolação cúbica [12]. Nenhuma das soluções anteriores é ideal, mas a última parece ser uma solução um pouco melhor e por isso é utilizada na implementação atual. Outra possibilidade é utilizar uma solução similar à propriedade *fit* de NCL, permitindo ao autor da NCL definir qual o comportamento desejado.

4.2.1 Objetos de mídia com mapa de profundidade estático embutido

Dependendo da codificação utilizada, objetos de mídia também podem conter informações de profundidade embutida. Por exemplo, [11] define dois formatos: PNGD e PNGDS, onde o canal de transparência atua como um canal de profundidade. Outra possibilidade, que foi utilizada nos testes aqui apresentados principalmente por sua simplicidade, é a codificação lado a lado dos dados de cor e profundidade de imagens.

4.3 Mapas de profundidade dinâmicos

Além dos objetos de mídia com mapa de profundidade estático, também é possível definir objetos de mídia no qual os dados de profundidade variam com tempo. Assim como no caso anterior, os dados de profundidade podem ser definidos externamente ou a própria codificação da mídia já pode incluir esses dados.

4.3.1 Vídeo como profundidade dinâmica

A URL dos mapas de profundidade acima (propriedade *depthMap*) pode referenciar tanto para imagens (estáticas) em escala de cinza (e.g. BMP, JPG etc), como para vídeos, também codificados em escala de cinza. Ao especificar a URL de um vídeo como *depthMap* de um objeto de mídia, o autor define que a informação de profundidade daquele objeto varia com o tempo. Nesse caso, os dados de profundidade devem ser sincronizados com o objeto de mídia associado, durante a sua apresentação.

Além das já mencionadas incompatibilidades com relação à dimensão do objeto de mídia, no caso de mapas de profundidade dinâmicos também é possível que ocorram incompatibilidades temporais. A Figura 3 demonstra os casos em que: (a) a duração do mapa de profundidade é menor do que a duração do objeto de mídia; e (b) a duração do mapa de profundidade é maior do que a duração do objeto de mídia.

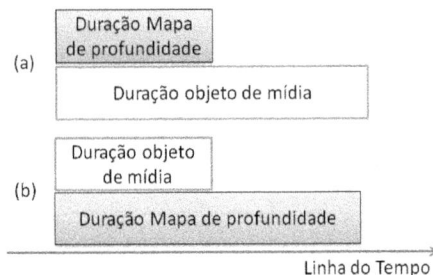

Figura 3: Exemplos de incompatibilidades entre a duração de um mapa de profundidade e a duração de um objeto de mídia.

Em (a) é possível tanto que o mapa de profundidade seja "executado" em *loop* durante toda a execução do objeto de mídia, como que os dados de profundidade sejam considerados 0 a partir do momento em que acabou a "execução" do vídeo que define o mapa de profundidade. Ambos os casos podem ser problemáticos e isso é dependente da aplicação. Sendo assim, o autor do documento NCL pode controlar o comportamento em tais casos por meio da propriedade *depthMapLoop* nos objetos de mídia. O valor dessa propriedade é um *booleano* que, quando *true* informa que o mapa de profundidade deve se "executado" em *loop*,

enquanto o objeto de mídia associado a esse mapa estiver sendo executado. O valor *default* dessa propriedade é *false*.

(b) não é um problema do ponto de vista de apresentação, uma vez que os dados de profundidade depois do objeto de mídia acabar sua execução serão simplesmente ignorados.

4.3.2 Objetos de mídia com mapa de profundidade dinâmicos embutido

Outro exemplo de objeto de mídia com mapa de profundidade dinâmica são os objetos de mídia que possuem codificação de profundidade embutida, como por exemplo, vídeo codificado em MPEG-C parte 3. Nesse caso, os problemas descrito nas Figuras 2 e 3 não existem.

Objetos de mídia 3D (*e.g.*, VRML, X3D, OBJ etc.) também possuem informações de profundidade embutida. Conforme discutido em [13], é possível embutir objetos de mídia 3D em NCL. Nesse caso, a informação de profundidade gerada pelo player do objeto de mídia deve ser repassada para o player NCL, para que sejam compostos com os dos outros objetos de mídia.

4.4 Escala de profundidade

Independente se um objeto de mídia tem profundidade embutida ou se essa profundidade é associada pelo documento NCL por meio de regiões, descritores ou propriedades, é possível escalar essa profundidade por meio da propriedade *depthScale*.

Assim como no caso anterior, também é possível definir essa propriedade por meio de regiões, descritores ou propriedades de objetos de mídia. O código a seguir exemplifica isso:

```
...
<regionBase>
  <region id="rg1" depthScale="0.5"
              width="50px" height="50px"/>
  <region id="rg2" depthScale="0.4"
              width="100px" height="100px"/>
</regionBase>
...
<descriptorBase>
  <descriptor id="desc1">
    <descriptorParam name="depthScale"
                value="0.5"/>
  </descriptor>
</descriptorBase>
...
<body id="nclBody">
  <media id="m1" descriptor="desc1">
    <property name="depthScale"
              value="0.5"/>
  </media>
</body>
...
```

A escala de profundidade afeta os dados de profundidade definidos tanto para objetos com profundidade uniforme, como para aquele com profundidade não-uniforme.

4.5 API NCLua para o controle de profundidade

Objetos de mídia imperativos também podem ser embutidos em documentos NCL. Entre eles estão os objetos NCLua [14]. Objetos NCLua são objetos de mídia imperativos que utilizam a linguagem Lua[3], linguagem padrão de script de NCL. Além das APIs padrões da linguagem Lua, autores de objetos NCLua

---

[3] http://www.lua.org

também têm à sua disposição alguns módulos adicionais, tais como *event*, *canvas*, *tcp* etc. Dentre esses, o módulo *canvas* oferece uma API para desenhar primitivas gráficas e imagens e é o mais relacionado com os dados de profundidade aqui apresentados. As seguintes funções estendem o módulo *canvas* de NCLua para possibilitar a criação de aplicações NCLua ciente de profundidade:

canvas:depthOffset() -> depthOffset: number

retorna o *depthOffset* associado ao canvas. *depthOffset* é um *double* entre -1.0 e 1.0.

canvas:depthOffset(depthOffset: number)

altera o *depthOffset* do canvas. O valor de *depthOffset* passado como parâmetro deve ser um *double* entre -1.0 e 1.0.

canvas:depthScale()->depthScale: number

usada para a leitura do valor corrente do *depthScale* associado ao canvas.

canvas:depthScale(depth-scale: number)

altera o valor do *depthScale*, onde o valor passado como parâmetro é um *double* entre 0.0 e 1.0.

canvas:depthMap(depth_map:string)

altera o valor dos *pixels* do *depthMap* associado ao *canvas*, baseado em uma imagem escala de cinza. Caso o tamanho da imagem seja diferente do tamanho do canvas, ela pode ser redimensionada. *depth_map* deve ser a URL de uma imagem em escala de cinza.

canvas:depthPixel(x, y: number)->depth: number

retorna a informação de profundidade (*depth*) do *pixel* na posição (x, y).

canvas:depthPixel(x, y, depth: number)

altera a informação de profundidade do pixel (x, y) para *depth*.

A função *canvas:flush()* é responsável por atualizar o *canvas* na tela (seguindo a técnica de *double buffering*), após uma sequência de operações de desenho ou composição. Com as informações de profundidade associadas ao *canvas*, agora é natural que o método *canvas:flush()* também atualize as informações de profundidade na tela.

O método *canvas:compose(x, y, canvas, src_x, src_y, src_width, src_height)* permite a composição de um canvas sobre outro. Nesse caso, os dados de profundidade também devem ser compostos, sendo que os dados do *canvas* de profundidade do *canvas* de origem sobrepõem os dados de profundidade do *canvas* de destino.

5. ANIMANDO OS DADOS DE PROFUNDIDADE

Independente de como são definidos, é possível controlar os dados de profundidade dos objetos de mídia dinamicamente, durante a execução da aplicação, por meio dos elementos <link> em NCL. O exemplo a seguir demonstra como é possível alterar o *depthOffset* de um elemento *button*, animando seu valor atual para 0.8, durante 5s.

```
...
<link ...>
  ...
  <bind role="set" component="button"
            interface="depthOffset">
    <bindParam name="var" value="1.0"/>
```

```
    <bindParam name="dur" value="5s"/>
  </bind>
</link>
...
```

O controle dinâmico dos dados de profundidade permite efeitos como, por exemplo, de um elemento gráfico entrando ou saindo da tela. Ao aplicar tal efeito, pode ser interessante combiná-lo com o efeito de escala, para que, ao sair da tela, o objeto de mídia também "cresça" de tamanho. O código a seguir exemplifica esse tipo de animação:

```
...
<link ...>
  ...
  <bind role="set" component="button"
              interface="bounds">
    <bindParam name="var"
            value="30%,30%,80%,80%"/>
    <bindParam name="dur" value="5s"/>
  </bind>
  <bind role="set" component="button"
            interface="depthOffset">
    <bindParam name="var" value="0.8"/>
    <bindParam name="dur" value="5s"/>
  </bind>
</link>
...
```

Para objetos NCLua, o controle dinâmico de profundidade, pode ser realizado por meio das funções descritas na Seção 4.5, em conjunto com temporizadores (função *event.timer(...)*) ou através de eventos da classe "user" [14].

6. EXPERIMENTOS

Para validar a proposta deste artigo, a integração dos novos atributos e propriedades de mídia à Implementação de Referência do Ginga-NCL[4] está em desenvolvimento. Essa integração foi favorecida por um trabalho anterior [15] que realizou o porte do Ginga-NCL para OpenGL[5]. Atualmente, a implementação dá suporte à definição de profundidade uniforme, escala de profundidade e mapas de profundidade estáticos e dinâmicos quando associados por meio de documentos NCL.

Até o momento da escrita deste texto, os únicos objetos de mídia com codificação de profundidade embutida são aqueles que são codificados com a informação de cor e de profundidade *side-by-side*. Como esses objetos de mídia são objetos de vídeo ou imagem codificados em *codecs* comuns (H.264, AVI, JPG, PNG etc.), para que o *player* NCL reconheça e extraia as informações de profundidade, nos testes executados foi necessário endereçar a exibição desses objetos aos novos *players* (que reconhecem os dados de profundidade). Para isso, a propriedade "player" no objeto de mídia foi utilizada da seguinte forma:

```
<media ...>
  <property name="player"
        value="VDP-Side-by-Side"/>
</media>
```

Na versão anterior do player NCL, cada player de objeto de mídia estava associado a uma superfície 2D, onde seu conteúdo era renderizado. Para o funcionamento com dados de profundidade, além da superfície 2D, também é necessário manter o mapa de profundidade para cada um dos players. Os quadros de mapas de profundidade podem ser atualizados pelos *players* de mídia, no caso de objetos de mídia com informações de profundidade

---

[4] Disponível em: http://www.softwarepublico.gov.br

[5] http://www.opengl.org

embutida, mas também podem ser modificados pelo player NCL (principalmente para aplicar as operações de *depthOffset* e *depthScale*). Por *default*, se um objeto de mídia não tem informação de profundidade associada, ele é renderizado no *depthOffset*=0.

A cada passo de renderização da cena NCL, primeiro, cada *player* atualiza sua superfície de cor e também de profundidade (caso o objeto de mídia tenha profundidade embutida). Depois disso, o player NCL pode aplicar as transformações necessárias nessas superfícies. Para o mapa de profundidade, são aplicados o *depthOffset* e o *depthScale*. Com as superfícies atualizadas, os pontos do mapa de profundidade são reprojetados no mundo 3D (contexto OpenGL) com suas respectivas informações de cor. Para evitar artefatos (principalmente "buracos vazios") nas imagens geradas, os pontos do mapa de profundidade foram triangularizados.

Se usarmos um *hardware* com suporte a DIBR, o próprio hardware se encarrega da geração das diversas *views* necessárias para o efeito de paralaxe. Contudo, os testes realizados até o momento não utilizaram esse tipo de hardware, se concentrando em PCs com monitores 2D tradicionais (no qual as *views* foram codificadas em anaglifo) e TVs 3D estereoscópicas (no qual as *views* foram codificadas *side-by-side* ou *top-bottom*). Por isso, um passo adicional de geração do par estéreo ainda se fez necessário.

Para gerar as duas *views* requeridas nos testes, os pontos no espaço 3D são projetados no plano da imagem de duas câmeras "virtuais", que estão localizadas nos dois pontos de vista do usuário. A concatenação da reprojeção (2D-3D) e da subsequente projeção (3D-to-2D) é usualmente denominada *image warping* [8].

A Figura 4 apresenta esquematicamente o posicionamento das câmeras utilizado para a geração do par de imagens estéreo, enquanto a Figura 5 sumariza o *pipeline* de renderização (para cada passo de renderização da cena NCL+depth) implementado atualmente.

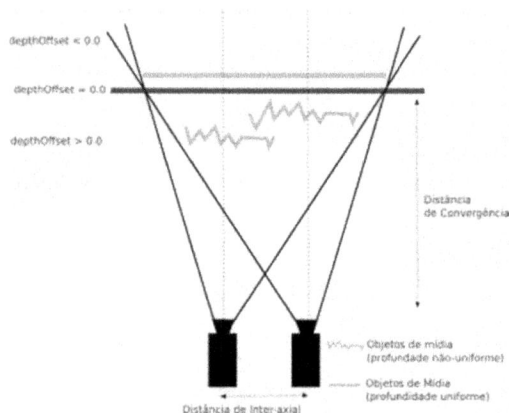

Figura 4: Geração do par estéreo a partir de uma cena NCL+Depth.

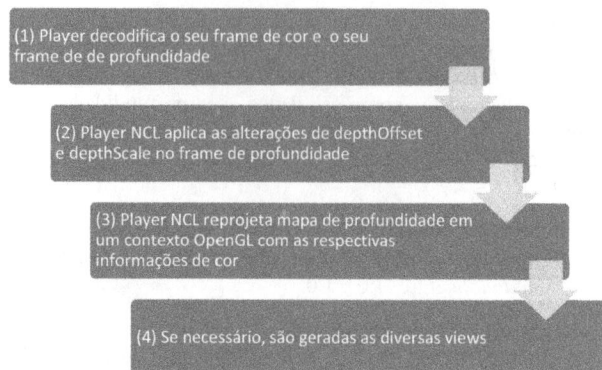

Figura 5: Pipeline de renderização com NCL+Depth.

6.1 zIndex X Profundidade

Visando compatibilizar o modelo de renderização baseado puramente em *zIndex* (discutido na Seção 2.1) com o modelo baseado em mapa de profundidade apresentado nesta seção, duas possibilidades foram investigadas:

(1) Os dados de profundidade têm prioridade, sendo que os dados de *zIndex* só serão levados em consideração quando mais de um *pixel* for renderizado na mesma posição do espaço 3D;

(2) O *zIndex* tem prioridade, sendo que ao projetar dois pixels em uma *view*, mesmo que o *depthOffset* de um *pixel* em particular seja maior, o valor de zIndex é o que prevalece;

A opção (1) parece ser a mais natural, e é implementada em OpenGL simplesmente renderizando todos os objetos no ambiente 3D na sua ordem de *zIndex* global e com teste de DEPTH habilitado em OpenGL. Contudo, ela traz o inconveniente de que, dependendo da combinação de *zIndex* e do mapa de profundidade, é possível que a aplicação seja apresentada de forma diferente em um ambiente que não leve em consideração os dados de profundidade (veja Figura 6). A opção (2) traz a vantagem de produzir sempre o mesmo resultado, independente se estamos em um ambiente NCL puramente 2D ou NCL+depth, mas pode parecer "contra-intuitivo" para ambientes puramente NCL+depth. Ela pode ser implementada em OpenGL da mesma forma que a anterior, mas desabilitando o teste de DEPTH.

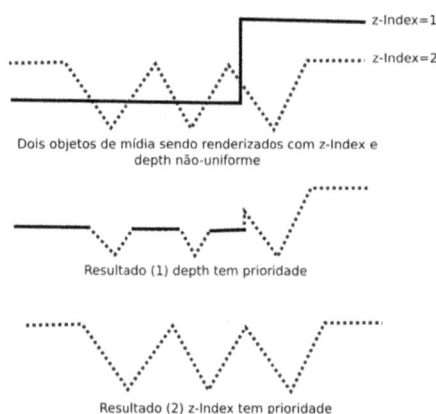

Figura 6: Incompatibilidades entre o modelo de zIndex e dados de profundidade.

Atualmente, a implementação dá suporte às duas formas. Até o momento, durante os testes, a opção (1) tem sido preferida, por ser mais natural no ambiente puramente NCL+depth. Para uma decisão final sobre esse tema (por exemplo, para ser definido em uma nova versão do padrão da linguagem) acredita-se que seja necessário uma pesquisa mais profunda com autores e usuários de NCL. Nesse caso, é possível que a opção (2) seja a mais vantajosa, por questões de compatibilidade. Se esse for o caso, é importante alertar autores NCL, talvez por um guia de boas práticas, para tentar evitar tais inconsistências em suas aplicações.

6.2 Aplicações Desenvolvidas
A versão atual da implementação já possibilita algumas aplicações NCL+depth interessantes. A Figura 7 demonstra duas dessas aplicações em execução.

Em (a), tem-se um exemplo que uma legenda e um menu (que permite alterar a cor e língua da legenda sendo exibida). Tanto o menu como a legenda tem informações de profundidade associadas por meio da propriedade *depthOffset*. O vídeo possui *depthOffset*=0, enquanto o menu e a legenda possuem *depthOffset*=0.5.

O exemplo (b) apresenta um menu de imagens. Ao navegar no menu, além de alterar a posição dos objetos e modificar o objeto com foco, também alteramos as informações de profundidade dos objetos. O objeto que tem o foco sempre terá *depthOffset*=1.0 (mais perto do usuário), enquanto os outros objetos mais distantes tem depthOffset menores (0.0 para o primeiro nível e -1.0 para o segundo nível).

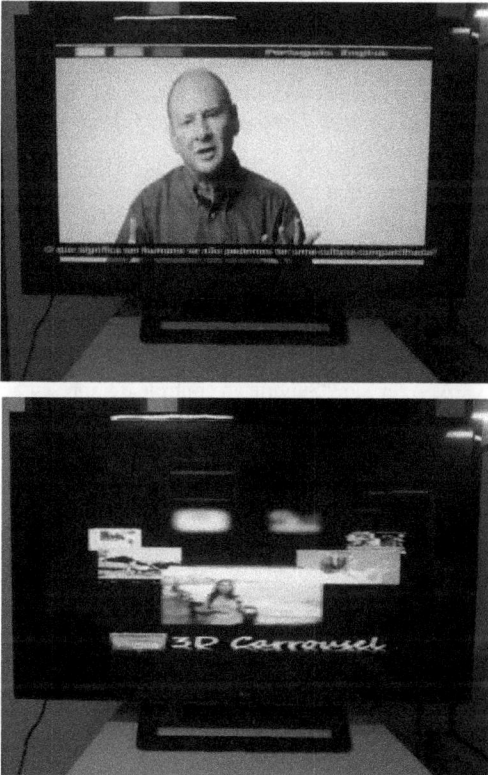

Figura 7: Exemplos de aplicações NCL+depth: (a) vídeo com legenda; (b) menu de imagens 3D.

7. TRABALHOS RELACIONADOS
Em [10] são levantados alguns dos principais requisitos para uma integração de ambientes 3D declarativos na Web. Um dos requisitos levantados é justamente a integração com *displays* estereo/autoestereoscópicos. Isso soa mais natural ainda em ambientes de 3DTV interativa, onde o conteúdo audiovisual transmitido já está codificado em 3D (*multiview* ou 2D +

profundidade). Tal integração já pode ser em parte promovida por linguagens que definem um ambiente 3D completo, como XMT [16] e X3D [17]. Nesse caso, quando a cena sintética 3D é renderizada, naturalmente tem-se as informações de profundidade. Mesmo assim, pode ser necessário algum ajuste para compatibilizar as informações de profundidade da cena com o vídeo 3D. Usar tais linguagens para a definição de aplicações simples como menus e legendas, entretanto, traz um *overhead* grande para a autoria – já que será necessária, também, a definição de posicionamento de câmeras, entre outras. Nesse sentido, as propostas deste artigo têm o potencial de simplificar a autoria de aplicações multimídia 2D que incluem efeitos de profundidade.

Contudo, este trabalho não é o primeiro cujo objetivo é a extensão de uma linguagem multimídia 2D que possibilite ao autor utilizar e controlar as informações de profundidade em suas apresentações. Em [11], por exemplo, Feuvre discute tais extensões para a linguagem SVG. O presente trabalho foi inspirado pelo trabalho de Feuvre, adaptando-o à NCL, estendendo-o para também tratar objetos com dados de profundidade dinâmicos, e adicionando APIs para a linguagem de script da linguagem multimídia (por meio do módulo *canvas* de NCLua).

Outros trabalhos também integram a geração de imagens estereoscópicas em linguagens multimídia. Em [18] Tsai apresenta um exibidor Flash[6] com suporte a uma ferramenta de configuração de mapas de profundidade para converter imagens 2D para 3D baseadas em algoritmo de DIBR (*Depth-Image-Based Rendering*). Nesse caso, os dados de profundidade são manipulados de uma forma única para toda a tela da apresentação, e não individualmente para cada objeto que faz parte da apresentação, como proposto neste artigo (e também em [11]). A proposta deste artigo reflete a própria arquitetura de NCL como linguagem de cola, que agora além de sincronizar objetos de mídia no tempo e relacioná-los nas dimensões vertical e horizontal, também o faz na dimensão da profundidade.

Um exemplo de integração de páginas Web com *displays* autoestereoscópicos é discutido por Nocent *et. al* em [19]. Nocent, entretanto, não integra nenhuma funcionalidade de profundidade à linguagem multimídia declarativa original (HTML), utilizando-se basicamente da API imperativa WebGL[7] para a geração das duas ou mais *views* necessárias. Dessa forma, o efeito de profundidade só é percebido dentro do canvas WebGL e não é suportado nos outros elementos da página Web. Na proposta deste artigo, o autor de NCL pode especificar e controlar dinamicamente os dados de profundidade de qualquer objeto de mídia que faça parte da aplicação, mantendo a característica de cola da linguagem. Note também que páginas HTML podem ser embutido em apresentações NCL e, logo, também terem seus dados de profundidade controlados.

8. CONCLUSÕES
Ao propor extensões à linguagem multimídia NCL e à sua linguagem de script NCLua para que os autores de aplicações multimídia possam controlar as informações de profundidade dos objetos de mídia, este artigo possibilita que uma nova gama de aplicações multimídia para *displays* 3D (em especial 3DTV) sejam desenvolvidas. Conforme discutido durante o artigo, incorporar esses dados em linguagens multimídia 2D tem a

---

[6] http://www.adobe.com/products/flash.html
[7] http://www.khronos.org/webgl/

vantagem de permitir aos autores, com um *overhead* pequeno, tirar proveito desses *displays* 3D. Por outro lado, ao integrar tais dados de profundidade, também é importante observar alguns problemas de compatibilidade com versões anteriores (em especial, se a linguagem utiliza um modelo de composição gráfica similar ao *zIndex* de NCL).

Os experimentos desenvolvidos até o momento se mostraram satisfatórios, mas ainda não são exaustivos. Em especial, dependendo da combinação dos dados de profundidade e *zIndex* pode-se facilmente encontrar os problemas de incompatibilidade descritos na Seção 6. Além disso, vários trabalhos futuros ainda se fazem necessário, entre os quais estão:

(1) Testes de outros algoritmos de DIBR para displays estereoscópicos;

(2) Testes com displays autoestereoscópicos;

(3) Pesquisas subjetivas com usuários finais sobre a qualidade das apresentações 3D gerada;

(4) Pesquisas subjetivas com autores de aplicações multimídia NCL sobre a facilidade de uso das extensões propostas (em especial, comparando com linguagens como X3D e XMT);

(5) Com base nas duas pesquisas acima, definição de *guidelines* de boas práticas para a autoria de aplicações multimídia 2D+depth;

(6) Definição de mapas de profundidade por meio de funções matemáticas (mais próximo de filtros SVG);

(7) Relação com objetos de mídia renderizados em regiões 3D [15] e transformações 3D CSS3.

(8) Integração com objetos de mídia 3D (que por *default* já possuem informações de profundidade) embutidos em NCL;

(9) Permitir que scripts NCLua alterem as informações de profundidade dos outros objetos de mídia;

(10) Suporte a objetos de mídia codificados em MPEG-C Part C e H.264 MVC (em especial, esse último possui relação com a integração de objetos estereoscópicos com a cena NCL+depth);

9. AGRADECIMENTOS

Os autores agradecem aos colegas do TeleMídia pelas discussões que resultaram neste trabalho e à Fundação de Amparo à Pesquisa do Estado do Rio de Janeiro (FAPERJ), pelo auxílio financeiro.

10. REFERÊNCIAS

[1] P. Benzie, J. Watson, P. Surman, I. Rakkolainen, K. Hopf, H. Urey e V. a. V. K. C. Sainov, "A Survey of 3dtv Displays: Techniques and Technologies.," *IEEE Transactions on Circuits and Systems for Video Technology,* vol. 17, nº 11, pp. 1647-1658, 2007.

[2] K. Muller, P. Merkle e T. Wiegand, "3-D Video Representation Using Depth Maps," *Proceedings of the IEEE,* vol. 99, nº 4, pp. 643-656, 2011.

[3] M. Halle, "Autostereoscopic Displays and Computer Graphics," em *ACM SIGGRAPH 2005 Courses*, Los Angeles, Californi, 2005.

[4] S.-Y. Kim e Y.-S. Ho, "Mesh-Based Depth Coding for 3D Video using Hierarchical Decomposition of Depth Maps," em *IEEE International Conference on Image Processing, 2007 (ICIP 2007)*, 2007.

[5] A. Vetro, T. Wiegand e G. J. and Sullivan, "Overview of the stereo and multiview video coding extensions of the H.264/AVC standard," *Proc. IEEE, Special Issue on 3D Media and Displays,* 2011.

[6] A. Bourge, J. Gobert e F. Bruls, "MPEG-C PART 3: Enabling the Introduction of Video plus Depth Contents," 2006.

[7] H. a. K. S. Shum, "A Review of Image-based Rendering Techniques," em *IEEE/SPIE Visual Communications and Image Processing (VCIP) 2000*, 2000.

[8] C. Fehn, "A 3D-TV Approach Using Depth-Image-Based Rendering (DIBR)," em *Proceedings of Visualization, Imaging, and Image Processing*, 2003.

[9] L. F. G. Soares, R. F. Rodrigues e M. F. Moreno, "Ginga-NCL: the Declarative Environment of the Brazilian Digital TV System," *Journal of the Brazilian Computer Society,* vol. 12, nº 4, pp. 37-46, Mar 2007.

[10] J. L. Feuvre, "Towards Declarative 3D in Web Architecture," em *Workshop Proceedings of CEURS (DEC3D)*, 2012.

[11] J. L. Feuvre, 2010. [Online]. Available: http://www.svgopen.org/2010/papers/54-SVG_Extensions_for_3D_displays.

[12] H. S. Prashanth, H. L. Shashidhara e K. N. Balasubramanya Murthy, "Image Scaling Comparison Using Universal Image Quality Index," em *International Conference on Advances in Computing, Control, Telecommunication Technologies, 2009 (ACT '09)*, 2009.

[13] R. G. A. Azevedo e L. F. G. Soares, "Embedding 3D Objects into NCL Multimedia Presentations," em *17th International Conference on 3D Web Technology*, 2012.

[14] F. Sant'Anna, R. Cerqueira e L. F. G. Soares, "NCLua: Objetos Imperativos Lua na Linguagem NCL," em *14th Brazilian Symposium on Multimedia and the Web*, 2008.

[15] R. G. A. Azevedo, "Suporte ao controle e à apresentação de objetos de mídia tridimensionais em NCL," Rio de Janeiro, 2010.

[16] M. Kim, S. Wood e L. Cheok, "Extensible MPEG-4 textual format (XMT)," em *ACM workshops on Multimedia (MULTIMEDIA'00).*, New York, NY, 2000.

[17] Web3D, *"Extensible 3D (X3D)", ISO/IEC 19776-1.2:2009.*, 2009.

[18] Y.-F. Tsai, C.-P. Young e C.-C. Ku, "Design and implementation of a flash player supporting stereoscopic image," em *Eighth Int. Conf. on Intelligent Information Hiding and Multimedia Signal Processing (IIH-MSP)*, 2012.

[19] O. Nocent, S. Piotin, A. Benassarou, M. Jaisson, Lucas e L., "Toward an immersion platform for the World Wide Web using autostereoscopic displays and tracking devices," em *17th International Conference on 3D Web Technology (WEB3D'12)*, 2012.

Automating the Analysis of NCL Documents with a Model-Driven Approach

Joel A. F. dos Santos
Laboratório MídiaCom
Departamento de Ciência da
Computação
Universidade Federal
Fluminense
joel@midiacom.uff.br

Christiano Braga
Language-oriented software
engineering research group
Departamento de Ciência da
Computação
Universidade Federal
Fluminense
cbraga@ic.uff.br

Débora C. Muchaluat-Saade
Laboratório MídiaCom
Departamento de Ciência da
Computação
Universidade Federal
Fluminense
debora@midiacom.uff.br

ABSTRACT

This paper presents a model-driven approach for the analysis of NCL documents. Structural and behavioral properties of NCL documents are verified guaranteeing its well-formedness and conformance with respect to the NCL language semantics. Document structural properties are verified using invariant validation and document behavioral properties are verified through model checking. The model-driven approach proposed is based on a formal and simplified model for representing the NCL document presentation behavior called Simple Hypermedia Model (SHM), used for the verification of document properties. In addition, this paper presents a prototype implementation of the proposed approach.

Categories and Subject Descriptors

D.2.4 [**Software Engineering**]: Software/Program Verification—*Validation*
; F.3.2 [**LOGICS AND MEANINGS OF PROGRAMS**]: Semantics of Programming Languages—*Program analysis*

General Terms

Verification

Keywords

Multimedia Analysis, SHM, Consistency verification, Multimedia Document Formal Modeling, NCL

1. INTRODUÇÃO

Documentos NCL (*Nested Context Language*) [1] são especificados como um conjunto de componentes, representando os objetos de mídia, e relacionamentos entre eles, definindo uma ordem para a apresentação dos objetos de mídia. Por ser uma linguagem declarativa, NCL enfatiza a descrição do comportamento de uma aplicação, ao invés dos passos necessários para sua implementação. Ainda assim, documentos com muitos componentes, e possivelmente organizados em uma estrutura complexa, podem apresentar problemas de especificação e/ou comportamentos indesejáveis. Problemas sintáticos surgem quando um documento NCL não segue a gramática da linguagem, podendo fazer com que formatadores NCL não consigam abri-lo. Problemas estruturais ocorrem quando um documento não segue a semântica estática de NCL, como, por exemplo, quando nós NCL não são propriamente declarados ou referenciados. Comportamentos indesejáveis na apresentação de um documento NCL surgem quando a computação induzida pelo documento NCL produz uma apresentação inesperada. Exemplos de comportamentos indesejáveis podem ser a não terminação e não alcance de partes do documento e uso concorrente de recursos, como um canal de áudio ou espaço na tela. Note que um documento bem definido (com respeito a gramática e sintaxe de NCL) pode apresentar comportamentos indesejáveis.

Uma aplicação NCL deve ser executada sem qualquer problema com respeito às expectativas do autor. Portanto, é importante que autores sejam capazes de identificar problemas na declaração de um documento NCL e prováveis comportamentos indesejáveis, antes de sua distribuição aos usuários finais.

Problemas de especificação (isto é, sintáticos, estruturais e comportamentais) podem ser identificados com o uso de ferramentas de autoria com suporte à análise de documentos, quando disponível, ou por inspeção do código. Uma tentativa comum de identificar comportamentos potencialmente indesejáveis é a simulação da apresentação de um documento. Esse processo, entretanto, usualmente não é *efetivo*, uma vez que diversas execuções seriam necessárias para a verificação de possíveis comportamentos indesejáveis, e pode ser *incompleto*, de uma perspectiva de corretude, uma vez que as computações representando a apresentação de um documento podem ser infinitas.

A natureza declarativa de NCL aponta para a possibilidade de a análise de tais documentos, isto é, uma verificação compreensiva de que um documento NCL satisfaz um conjunto de propriedades, pode se beneficiar de abordagens dirigidas a modelos.

Desenvolvimento dirigido a modelos (MDD) [18] é uma abordagem de desenvolvimento de software onde modelos são os principais artefatos do processo de desenvolvimento. Modelos são representados como instâncias de metamodelos, que são essencialmente gramáticas descrevendo a sintaxe de uma linguagem de modelagem, e podem ser usados para derivar diferentes artefatos de software, como código em uma linguagem de programação ou ainda outros modelos em diferentes níveis de abstração. Esse processo de derivação é chamado transformação de modelos, que relaciona linguagens de modelagem através de seus metamodelos. Sob essa perspectiva, MDD pode ser vista como uma transformação entre linguagens de modelagem aplicada a modelos em particular. A abordagem proposta neste artigo usa técnicas dirigidas a modelos para relacionar a linguagem NCL com uma notação formal, que permite a validação rigorosa de documentos NCL.

Neste trabalho, a análise é feita em duas etapas principais: a primeira é a análise da definição estrutural de um documento NCL, validando-o de acordo com as regras sintáticas e invariantes estruturais definidos pela semântica estática de NCL, isto é, suas regras de escrita; a segunda consiste da análise do comportamento da apresentação de um documento NCL, verificando se o documento apresenta algum comportamento indesejável. Diferentes técnicas de validação e verificação são aplicadas: (i) validação de invariantes OCL (*Object Constraint Language*) [28], isto é, a aplicação de invariantes OCL a um dado modelo de objetos, é usada para a análise estrutural; e (ii) verificação de modelos com LTL (*Linear Temporal Logic*) [7] é usada para a análise comportamental.

A análise estrutural é alcançada pelo uso de soluções existentes. A análise comportamental, por outro lado, representa a principal contribuição deste trabalho. Ela compreende a definição de um modelo formal chamado *Simple Hypermedia Model* (SHM) para a representação do comportamento de documentos NCL e a transformação da linguagem NCL para SHM. O uso de MDD para análise de documentos multimídia foi inicialmente proposto em [11]. Este artigo descreve as propriedades analisadas, o modelo SHM e a ferramenta aNaa, que implementa a abordagem proposta para análise de documentos NCL.

O restante deste artigo está organizado como segue. A Seção 2 apresenta trabalhos relacionados considerando a análise de documentos multimídia. A Seção 3 define algumas propriedades importantes de documentos NCL identificadas em trabalhos relacionados. A Seção 4 discute nossa abordagem de análise juntamente com o modelo SHM. A Seção 5 apresenta o uso da implementação da abordagem proposta para a análise de um documento NCL. A Seção 6 conclui o artigo ressaltando suas contribuições e apresentando trabalhos futuros.

2. TRABALHOS RELACIONADOS

A literatura é rica em discussão sobre a análise de documentos multimídia. Em geral, focando na análise comportamental *ou* na análise estrutural. Portanto, esta seção apresenta os trabalhos relacionados separando-os de acordo com seu foco.

2.1 Análise Estrutural

Honorato e Barbosa em [14] apresentam a ferramenta NCL-Inspector. Essa ferramenta apoia a autoria de aplicações NCL, dando suporte ao autor da aplicação em termos de qualidade de código. Com essa ferramenta, além de o autor poder analisar um código NCL em busca de erros de especificação, é possível apontar sugestões com respeito a boas práticas de programação. A análise, ou inspeção, do código NCL é feita com base em um conjunto de regras, formando um repositório de regras. Cada regra apresenta um padrão de código NCL e uma ação a ser tomada quando o padrão definido for encontrado. Ainda, cada regra nesse sistema é implementada como um plugin, dessa forma, o sistema como um todo pode ser estendido com a adição de novas regras. Para a inspeção de um documento, NCL-Inspector realiza o *parsing* do documento. Após essa etapa, a ferramenta cria uma árvore sintática abstrata que representa o documento NCL sendo inspecionado. A ferramenta caminha por essa árvore procurando por violações das regras existentes. As violações encontradas são apresentadas para o usuário para que ele possa corrigir o código da aplicação. A ferramenta pode agir diretamente sobre o texto do código da aplicação, permitindo a investigação de detalhes textuais, como o uso do caractere de tabulação (\t) para indentação do código.

Neto et al. em [20] discutem uma abordagem para análise estrutural e incremental de um documento NCL. O artigo define uma metalinguagem utilizada na representação dos elementos de NCL através de um conjunto de primitivas. As primitivas definem regras que devem ser satisfeitas pelos elementos da linguagem. A análise estrutural é feita verificando se cada elemento satisfaz as regras definidas pela sua primitiva. Para a análise incremental, somente os elementos modificados após a última análise, assim como os elementos que os referenciam, são analisados. Uma estrutura adicional é utilizada para identificar os elementos que devem ser analisados.

Troncy et al. em [23] apresentam VAMP, uma abordagem para analisar estruturalmente descrições MPEG-7 [15] criadas com diferentes ferramentas de anotação. VAMP tem por finalidade permitir a interoperabilidade de ferramentas de anotação, reduzindo a variação no uso de descrições MPEG-7. Além disso, também é utilizada para analisar descrições de acordo com restrições definidas pelo padrão MPEG-7 e o perfil [16] utilizado. Apesar de tanto MPEG-7 quanto perfis MPEG-7 definirem um XML Schema [25], ele não é suficiente para checar a consistência de descrições MPEG-7. Em [23] os autores apresentam um conjunto de, assim chamadas, violações em descrições, que resultam em documentos válidos com respeito ao XML Schema do MPEG-7. Portanto, para analisar estruturalmente essas descrições, VAMP usa uma ontologia (OWL-DL [24]) para representar os conceitos descritos no perfil MPEG-7 e regras lógicas (cláusulas de Horn [2]) para representar as restrições no uso de elementos de descrição.

Uma abordagem comum para a análise estrutural de documentos XML (uma forma de representação comum para documentos multimídia) é usar validadores baseados em XML Schema [25]. Tal abordagem verifica se restrições definidas no Schema são satisfeitas pela linguagem baseada em XML. Restrições são definidas sobre tipos de elementos e não sobre instâncias de elementos. Portanto, não podem ser usadas, por exemplo, para verificar se duas instâncias distintas de elementos fazem referência a uma mesma instância. Este tipo de verificação é importante para nosso trabalho e outros como [20].

2.2 Análise Comportamental

Santos et al. em [21] discutem uma abordagem para a análise comportamental da apresentação de documentos multimídia através de sua tradução para RT-LOTOS, um *framework* de álgebra de processos em tempo real. A modularidade e hierarquia de RT-LOTOS permitem a combinação de processos especificando a apresentação do documento com outros modelando a plataforma disponível. A análise em si consiste na interpretação do grafo de alcance mínimo construído a partir da especificação formal para provar se o evento correspondente ao fim da apresentação do documento é alcançado a partir do seu estado inicial. Cada nó no grafo representa um estado alcançável e cada aresta a ocorrência de um evento ou uma progressão temporal. A ferramenta apresentada em [21] pode analisar documentos NCM (*Nested Context Model*) [22] e SMIL (*Synchronized Multimedia Integration Language*) [27].

Oliveira et al. em [9] introduzem o HMBS (*Hypermedia Model Based on Statecharts*). Uma aplicação multimídia HMBS é descrita por um diagrama de estados que representa sua estrutura hierárquica, de acordo com seus nós, elos e seus componentes *human-consumable*. Esses componentes são expressos como unidades de informação, chamadas páginas e âncoras. Um estado no diagrama de estados é mapeado em páginas, transições e eventos representam as possíveis ativações de elos. Para a análise comportamental, o grafo de alcance do diagrama de estados para uma configuração específica é usado para verificar se alguma página não é alcançável. De maneira similar, é possível determinar se um certo grupo de páginas é apresentado simultaneamente, buscando configurações de estado contendo os estados associados a estas páginas. O grafo de alcance também permite a detecção de configurações a partir das quais nenhuma outra página pode ser alcançada ou que apresentam caminhos cíclicos.

Na e Furuta em [19] apresentam o sistema caT (*context aware Trellis*), onde um autor constrói a estrutura de um documento multimídia usando redes de Petri e associa objetos de mídia a lugares na rede. O trabalho apresenta redes de Petri como boas candidatas para modelar documentos multimídia, uma vez que sua sincronização é fácil de modelar e permite a análise de propriedades do documento. Para reduzir a complexidade na autoria gráfica e aumentar o reúso na rede, caT incorpora redes de Petri hierárquicas. caT possui uma ferramenta de análise que constrói a árvore de alcance do documento a ser analisado e investiga a existência de um estado terminal, isto é, se existe um estado onde nenhuma transição é disparada. caT também investiga se algum lugar da rede tem um número ilimitado de *tokens* e se todos os lugares possuem algum *token*. Tal análise é importante uma vez que *tokens* podem representar recursos escassos do sistema.

Felix em [13] apresenta uma abordagem para a análise de propriedades temporais de documentos multimídia através da aplicação de técnicas de verificação de modelos. O trabalho apresenta uma notação utilizada para a descrição de características relevantes da linguagem NCL, como suas características temporais. Tal descrição é transformada em uma rede de autômatos temporizados que indica o comportamento temporal do documento. A transformação cria uma máquina de estados para cada mídia no documento e uma máquina de sincronização para cada elo do documento. Uma máquina de sincronização é usada para reunir ocorrências de eventos nas máquinas de estados das mídias. O trabalho ainda apresenta uma ferramenta onde o autor pode definir fórmulas em lógica temporal para análise de propriedades temporais do documento. A análise é feita com um *model-checker*.

Bertino et al. em [3] propõem um modelo de autoria baseado em restrições. Uma aplicação multimídia nesse modelo consiste de diversas subapresentações, cada uma representando um tópico composto de objetos multimídia semanticamente relacionados. Todas as relações, temporal, de leiaute e estrutural, são especificadas em um único passo. O autor define um conjunto de restrições de alto nível que são usadas pelo sistema para agrupar automaticamente objetos em tópicos. O processo de geração da aplicação é responsável por três principais tarefas: checagem de consistência, geração da estrutura da apresentação e geração de tópicos. A consistência da apresentação é checada através da aplicação de regras de compatibilidade em cada par de restrições, detectando inconsistências. Antes da checagem, diversas regras de inferência são aplicadas a declaração inicial para determinar restrições, que mesmo não tendo sido definidas, são consequência das restrições definidas. Se uma inconsistência surge, o sistema aplica técnicas de relaxamento, reduzindo o conjunto de restrições até que a apresentação se torne consistente ou, quando não é possível, o autor deve rever a declaração. O processo de geração da estrutura da apresentação cria uma estrutura que reflete a declaração de uma dada aplicação. A estrutura é representada por um grafo dirigido onde cada vértice representa um tópico e arestas, conexões entre eles. Este processo sempre retorna um grafo consistente, caso contrário, o autor deve rever a declaração. Após essa etapa, o sistema relaciona objetos de mídia a tópicos. De acordo com as restrições, são criadas as conexões entre os tópicos e a consistência é checada antes de retornar o grafo final gerado. Se alguma falha ocorrer, o autor é avisado da inconsistência encontrada.

Elias et al. em [12] apresentam um algoritmo para a checagem dinâmica de relações espaço-temporais. No artigo, dinâmico significa que a checagem é feita durante a declaração da apresentação. Inconsistências temporais ocorrem quando o conjunto de restrições não pode ser satisfeito ao mesmo tempo. Incompletude de um conjunto de restrições ocorre quando há uma descontinuidade na apresentação, isto é, existe um conjunto de objetos de mídia que não são alcançados durante a apresentação. Caso ocorra alguma inconsistência em um conjunto de restrições, uma das restrições deve ser removida de forma a se obter um conjunto consistente. A remoção é feita relacionando um valor de prioridade a cada restrição. No caso de duas restrições inconsistentes possuírem a mesma prioridade, técnicas de relaxamento são aplicadas para determinar a restrição a ser removida. O artigo apresenta dois operadores *TEMPORAL* e *SPATIAL*, para modelar relações temporais e espaciais, respectivamente. A checagem de consistência é feita achando-se a árvore geradora mínima T para o grafo definido pelos objetos de mídia (vértices) e os relacionamentos entre eles (arestas). Para manter a consistência da apresentação e a natureza acíclica de T, relacionamentos que criam ciclos são removidos. A escolha é feita levando em consideração a prioridade de cada relacionamento. Para a checagem de completude, todos os vértices devem ser encontrados no conjunto que contém o primeiro objeto de mídia. Se essa busca retornar o conjunto de vértices de T, então todos os objetos de mídia da apresentação são alcançados direta ou indiretamente do objeto inicial. Caso contrário, o algoritmo apresenta uma mensagem de erro para que o autor defina restrições que façam o conjunto de restrições completo. Com o uso do operador *SPATIAL*, é possível determinar se A sobrepõe B e vice versa. A consistência espacial é checada da mesma forma que a temporal.

Bossi e Gaggi em [4, 5] propõem um sistema de autoria que inclui um módulo de análise do comportamento temporal de um documento multimídia. A análise é obtida através da definição de uma semântica formal para a linguagem SMIL [27]. A semântica proposta é definida através de um conjunto de regras de inferência inspiradas em lógica de Hoare. A principal característica da lógica de Hoare é que ela descreve como um comando, ou parte do código, muda o estado da computação. Desta forma a estrutura da linguagem SMIL pode ser enriquecida com assertivas expressando propriedades temporais que podem ser utilizadas durante a fase de autoria. Outra aplicação resultante da definição de uma semântica formal é o conceito de equivalência, que garante que um conjunto de *tags* SMIL pode ser substituído por outro sem modificar o comportamento da aplicação. A análise apresentada no artigo é feita durante a autoria do documento, sempre que o autor desejar ou quando salvar o código. Isto é feito para diminuir a ocorrência de mensagens de erro durante a criação da aplicação. As assertivas definidas pela semântica proposta no artigo especificam o estado temporal do sistema antes e depois da execução de uma *tag* SMIL ou conjunto de *tags*. Para a verificação de corretude do sistema, a ferramenta aplica axiomas, também definidos pela semântica proposta, para verificar se a *tag* ou conjunto de *tags* mudou corretamente o estado do sistema. Caso contrário, a ferramenta retorna ao autor o problema encontrado.

Júnior et al. em [17] usam uma abordagem dirigida a modelos para analisar o comportamento de um documento NCL. A análise é obtida através da transformação de um documento NCL em uma rede de Petri. Essa transformação é feita em duas etapas. Na primeira etapa, o documento é representado em uma linguagem chamada FIACRE como um conjunto de componentes (representando nós) e processos (representando o comportamento de um componente). A segunda etapa transforma a representação FIACRE em uma rede de Petri. A análise usa uma ferramenta de *model-checking* e fórmulas em lógica temporal representando as propriedades a serem verificadas.

2.3 Comparação dos Trabalhos Relacionados

As Seções 2.1 e 2.2 apresentaram o estado-da-arte na análise de documentos multimídia. O estudo da literatura citada nessas seções ajudou na especificação da abordagem de análise apresentada na Seção 4. As principais influências são: (i) o uso de uma abordagem formal, uma vez que esta traz a corretude, verificada com suporte ferramental, da análise pelo uso de descrições precisas da linguagem NCL; (ii) a definição de um conjunto de propriedades comuns para documentos NCL apresentadas na Seção 3.

Esta seção compara este trabalho com os apresentados nas Seções 2.1 e 2.2. A comparação apresentada é funcional, uma vez que a maioria das ferramentas não estão disponíveis atualmente para testes práticos.

Cada trabalho relacionado foca ou na análise estrutural *ou* na comportamental de documentos multimídia. É impor-

tante garantir que um documento multimídia tenha tido sua estrutura analisada antes de analisar seu comportamento, uma vez que uma falha na primeira pode tornar a segunda impossível de ser feita. Entretanto, não é possível identificar se os trabalhos apresentados na Seção 2.2 fazem alguma forma de análise estrutural antes da análise comportamental. Neste artigo, por outro lado, propomos uma ferramenta capaz de realizar tanto a análise estrutural quando a comportamental de documentos NCL.

Em [20, 17], os autores indicam serem capazes de analisar um documento multimídia de forma incremental. Tal forma de análise não é suportada neste trabalho, onde o documento completo é analisado.

3. PROPRIEDADES DE ANÁLISE

Com base no estudo dos trabalhos relacionados [21, 9, 20], foi definido um conjunto de propriedades para a análise de documentos NCL. Tais propriedades, aqui listadas, são classificadas como estruturais e comportamentais.

Propriedades estruturais são aquelas usadas para representar as regras sintáticas da linguagem NCL, definidas pela sua gramática e invariantes estruturais induzidos por sua semântica estática. Cada propriedade estrutural origina um conjunto de invariantes OCL, um para cada elemento da linguagem NCL onde um dado invariante pode ser aplicado.

A propriedade **sintática** especifica que a estrutura léxica e sintática de um documento deve estar bem formada com respeito a especificação da linguagem NCL. Por exemplo, as *tags* XML [26] usadas devem ser fechadas corretamente e pertencer ao *namespace* da linguagem. A propriedade **hierárquica** especifica que todos os elementos da linguagem devem conter elementos filhos válidos e com a cardinalidade correta. A propriedade de **atributo** especifica que todos os elementos da linguagem devem conter atributos válidos e que atributos obrigatórios devem estar especificados. Esta propriedade também especifica que cada identificador deve ser único e que atributos cujos valores são relacionados devem seguir as restrições definidas pela linguagem de autoria (suponha, por exemplo, um elemento com os atributos "type" e "subtype").

É importante ressaltar, que os conceitos XML de documentos válidos e bem formados são garantidos pelas propriedades até então apresentadas.

A propriedade de **referência** especifica restrições nas referências entre elementos. Em NCL, um elemento *port* pode referenciar um nó, através seu atributo *component*, e um ponto de interface desse nó através de seu atributo *interface*. A propriedade de referência, para o elemento *port*, especifica que o elemento referenciado pelo atributo *interface* deve ser um filho do elemento referenciado pelo atributo *component*. A propriedade de **composicionalidade** especifica que elementos internos a uma composição não devem referenciar outros externos a esta composição. A propriedade de **aninhamento de composições** especifica que uma composição não pode criar um loop de aninhamento. NCM permite o reúso de composições (contextos e switches). Estes elementos não podem aninhar a si mesmos, caso contrário o documento NCL se tornaria inconsistente. A propriedade de **reúso** especifica que um elemento não pode criar um *loop* de reúso.

Propriedades comportamentais são aquelas usadas para representar possíveis comportamentos indesejados na apresentação do documento. Cada propriedade comportamental origina um conjunto de fórmulas em lógica temporal [7], uma para cada âncora definida no documento. Âncoras são a menor unidade de informação representada em um documento NCL e serão apresentadas na Seção 4.1.

A propriedade de **alcance** especifica que todo elemento do documento deve ser alcançado durante sua execução. A propriedade de **terminação de âncora** especifica que um elemento do documento (âncora), uma vez executado (apresentado), deve terminar. A propriedade de **terminação de documento** especifica que a execução do documento multimídia como um todo deve terminar. A execução do documento termina se toda âncora do documento termina e não existem *loops* de execução no documento (por exemplo uma âncora reiniciando sua apresentação sempre que termina). A propriedade de **recurso** especifica que duas âncoras distintas não devem utilizar um mesmo recurso ao mesmo tempo, evitando sua sobreposição. Exemplos de recursos são um canal de áudio ou um espaço na tela.

O conjunto de propriedades definidas neste artigo representa propriedades comuns encontradas em trabalhos relacionados [21, 9, 20] sobre análise de documentos multimídia. Adicionalmente, outras propriedades específicas do documento podem ser definidas. Portanto, o conjunto de propriedades pode ser complementado com propriedades definidas pelo usuário. A verificação de tais propriedades é discutida na Seção 4, juntamente com uma explicação detalhada da abordagem dirigida a modelos proposta para análise de documentos NCL.

4. ANÁLISE DIRIGIDA A MODELOS

A análise dirigida a modelos é feita em duas etapas. Primeiramente, o documento NCL é representado como um modelo de objetos, instância de um metamodelo representando a sintaxe abstrata de NCL. Sobre esse modelo, invariantes OCL, representando as propriedades estruturais, são usados para verificar se o modelo satisfaz as regras sintáticas definidas pela gramática de NCL e seus invariantes estruturais. Então, uma representação do comportamento da apresentação do documento, utilizando um modelo formal, é gerada. Esta representação induz um sistema de transição onde fórmulas em lógica temporal (formalizando as propriedades comportamentais) são automaticamente checadas para verificar se um dado documento possui algum comportamento potencialmente indesejado. A Seção 4.1 apresenta o modelo SHM proposto para representar o comportamento da apresentação de um documento. A Seção 4.2 detalha a abordagem dirigida a modelos da análise proposta neste artigo.

4.1 Simple Hypermedia Model

A ideia por trás do modelo SHM é representar o comportamento de um documento NCL de maneira mais simples possível, mas que seja passível de uma verificação automática. Esta seção discute o modelo proposto SHM (*Simple Hypermedia Model*) junto com suas decisões de projeto.

O modelo SHM é uma simplificação do modelo NCM [22]. Uma vez que SHM foi projetado para ser o mais simples possível, diversas entidades do modelo NCM não estão presentes em SHM, como as que definem o leiaute espacial da apresentação. Adicionalmente, SHM não define nós de *composição* para aprimorar a estrutura lógica do documento. SHM também não define nós de *conteúdo*, representando, portanto, o conteúdo de um documento pelas suas menores unidades

de informação: *âncoras de conteúdo* e *âncoras de atributo*. Âncoras de conteúdo representam uma parte do conteúdo do nó, possivelmente todo o conteúdo, enquanto âncoras de atributo representam um atributo do nó e seu valor. Similar ao NCM, o comportamento de um documento SHM é definido por elos. A Equação 1 apresenta a forma geral de um documento SHM, onde A representa o conjunto de âncoras do documento, L, o conjunto de elos, e I, um conjunto de ações iniciais.

$$
\begin{aligned}
doc &= (A_{doc}, L_{doc}, I_{doc}), \quad onde \\
A_{doc} &= a_1, \ldots, a_m, \\
L_{doc} &= l_1, \ldots, l_n, \\
I_{doc} &= i_1, \ldots, i_k.
\end{aligned} \tag{1}
$$

Cada âncora em SHM está associada aos seus eventos de apresentação, seleção ou atribuição, onde cada evento está em um dos seguintes estados: *occurring*, *sleeping* e *paused*. Cada evento multimídia segue a máquina de estados NCM [22].

Assim como em NCM, um elo tem condições e ações. Condições devem ser satisfeitas de forma a ativar o elo e ações são executadas quando o elo é ativado, modificando o estado do documento. A condição de um elo pode ser satisfeita quando ocorrem transições em eventos multimídia relacionados às âncoras fonte e podem definir testes sobre o estado ou valor de uma âncora. Uma ação de um elo define uma transição que será induzida sobre o estado do evento multimídia relacionado à âncora alvo. Uma ação de um elo pode definir um atraso para sua aplicação.

Um documento multimídia é representado em SHM pelo seu ambiente e seu estado ($\rho \vdash d$). O ambiente do documento ρ representa a definição do documento, isto é, a definição de suas âncoras, elos e sua ações iniciais (ações aplicadas quando a execução do documento inicia). O estado do documento d é dado pelo estado de cada âncora no documento e, possivelmente, ações aguardando para serem aplicadas.

Tal representação do documento é obtida através da transformação de modelos discutida na Seção 4.2. De forma a poder derivar um documento de seu ambiente, SHM conta com uma teoria geral responsável pela execução do documento. Para isso, ela define a relação *SHM*, que possui a função *elapse* e as relações *natural* e *applyLinks* como premissas, e é executada repetidamente até que a execução do documento termine. A Equação 2 ilustra a relação *SHM*.

$$
\frac{elapse(d_1) = d_2 \quad d_2 \to_{natural} \langle as_3, ps_3, es \rangle}{\langle as_3, ps_3, es \rangle \to_{applyLinks} \langle as_4, ps_4, es' \rangle} \tag{2}
$$
$$
\overline{d_1 = \langle as_1, ps_1 \rangle \to_{SHM} \langle as_4, ps_4 \rangle}
$$

Um estado de um documento SHM (d_i) é dado pelo estado de suas âncoras (as_i) e ações de elos com atraso (ps_i). Cada âncora e ação com atraso possui um relógio em contagem regressiva, representando a duração de sua apresentação e seu atraso restante, respectivamente. A função *elapse* usa o valor desses relógios (em d_1) para calcular o máximo salto no tempo que pode ser efetuado, isto é, o tamanho do intervalo entre o tempo atual e o tempo onde a próxima ocorrência de evento irá ocorrer. Após calcular o valor do salto, a função *elapse* decrementa esse valor dos relógios das âncoras e ações (resultando em d_2).

A relação *natural* procura por ocorrências de eventos em âncoras (em d_2). Uma ocorrência pode ser o fim da apresentação de uma âncora (quando sua duração alcança zero) ou a seleção de uma âncora. Uma vez que cada âncora sendo apresentada pode ser selecionada, estados do documento concorrentes serão criados, representando a permutação das âncoras selecionadas. Além disso, a relação *natural* aplica as ações cujo atraso chegou ao fim, modificando o estado de âncoras do documento (resultando em d_3 e ps_3).

Ocorrências de eventos (es) que resultam de *natural*, podem disparar elos no documento SHM. A relação *applyLinks* avalia os elos que foram habilitados por estas ocorrências de eventos. Um elo é considerado habilitado quando suas condições casam com o (ou parte do) estado do documento. A aplicação de um elo consiste na mudança do estado do evento de apresentação, seleção ou atribuição (resultando em as_4, ps_4 e es'). Todos os elos habilitados são aplicados em todas as ordens possíveis, de forma que diferentes estados do documento podem ser alcançados após a aplicação dos elos.

4.2 Abordagem de Análise

A abordagem de análise (dirigida a modelos) apresentada neste artigo segue uma abordagem de contratos de transformação [6], como apresentado na Figura 1.

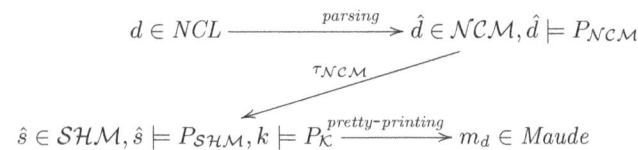

$$d \in NCL \xrightarrow{\quad parsing \quad} \hat{d} \in \mathcal{NCM}, \hat{d} \models P_{\mathcal{NCM}}$$

$$\tau_{\mathcal{NCM}}$$

$$\hat{s} \in \mathcal{SHM}, \hat{s} \models P_{\mathcal{SHM}}, k \models P_{\mathcal{K}} \xrightarrow{\quad pretty\text{-}printing \quad} m_d \in Maude$$

Figura 1: Uma abordagem de contratos de transformação para teorias em Maude de documentos NCL

onde NCL e $\mathcal{NCM}$ representam a sintaxe concreta e abstrata, respectivamente, da linguagem NCL, *Maude* e $\mathcal{SHM}$ são usadas para formalizar o comportamento de documentos NCL. $\tau_{\mathcal{NCM}}$ representa a transformação entre $\mathcal{NCM}$ e $\mathcal{SHM}$. A operação *parsing* representa um mapeamento onde um modelo d produz uma instância $\hat{d}$ de $\mathcal{NCM}$ e *pretty-printing* representa o mapeamento inverso de *parsing*. A notação $m \in M$ denota que um modelo m é (sintaticamente) *bem formado* com respeito a um metamodelo M.

Um contrato de transformação é uma especificação de uma transformação de modelos como um modelo $\mathcal{K}$ que relaciona os metamodelos das duas linguagens de modelagem. Portanto, a associação entre elementos da linguagem no modelo $\mathcal{K}$ pode ser restringido por diferentes tipos de propriedades (estruturais ou comportamentais). A ideia é que toda vez que uma transformação $\tau_{\mathcal{NCM}}$ é aplicada, primeiro o conjunto de propriedades $P_{\mathcal{NCM}}$ é verificado em $\hat{d}$, então as propriedades $P_{\mathcal{SHM}}$ são verificadas em $\hat{s}$. As propriedades $P_{\mathcal{K}}$ representando o contrato de transformação devem ser satisfeitas no modelo k, instância de $\mathcal{K}$, representando as associações entre os elementos em $\hat{d}$ e $\hat{s}$.

A Figura 1 ilustra a abordagem de contratos de transformação com a linguagem NCL como a linguagem de autoria e Maude [8] como a linguagem para formalizar documentos multimídia. Informalmente, módulos Maude são produzidos a partir de documentos NCL e propriedades comportamentais são representadas como fórmulas LTL (um tipo particular de lógica temporal), que são verificadas usando um verificador de modelos em Maude. A notação $m \models P_M$ significa que as propriedades P_M são satisfeitas no modelo m. As

propriedades $P_{\mathcal{K}}$, representando o contrato de transformação, podem ser tanto estruturais quando comportamentais.

Um exemplo de propriedade estrutural de um contrato de transformação entre NCL e Maude é que o número de âncoras e elos em NCL devem ser preservados pela transformação. Por preservação, queremos dizer que toda informação sobre âncoras e elos no documento NCL são representadas em sua contraparte em SHM. Um exemplo de propriedade estrutural de um contrato de transformação entre NCL e Maude é que o sistema de transição associado a um dado documento NCL e sua representação em Maude são bissimilares, isto é, essencialmente, toda computação em um sistema de transição deve ter uma contraparte no outro sistema de transição. Portanto, nós alcançáveis no documento NCL de origem deve também ser alcançáveis na representação em Maude e nós não alcançáveis devem ser mantidos assim. Bissimulação não é verificável automaticamente na versão atual da nossa implementação pois requer uma capacidade interativa de prova de teorema e aqui o foco é o processo completamente automático de verificação.

Na Figura 1, um documento NCL é transformado em um modelo NCM. Assim, dado um documento NCL d, se ($\hat{d} = parse(d)$) $\models P_{\mathcal{NCM}}$, isto é, se as propriedades estruturais de NCM são satisfeitas em $\hat{d}$, então a transformação de modelos $\tau_{\mathcal{NCM}}$ é aplicada a $\hat{d}$. A transformação de modelos $\tau_{\mathcal{NCM}}$ produz um modelo SHM representando o comportamento da apresentação de um documento multimídia.

Dado que um modelo SHM correto $\hat{s}$ é produzido pela aplicação da transformação $\tau_{\mathcal{NCM}}$ (isto é $k \models P_{\mathcal{K}}$, onde k associa elementos em $\hat{d}$ e $\hat{s}$), uma representação concreta m_d of $\hat{s}$ pode ser produzida na linguagem de especificação do verificador de modelos, no nosso caso, Maude. É importante ressaltar que o contrato de transformação expresso em $P_{\mathcal{K}}$ garante que a representação em SHM é devidamente construída a partir de um documento NCL. Portanto, dado m_d, é possível verificar com um *model-checker* as fórmulas em lógica temporal que representam as propriedades comportamentais. Contraexemplos produzidos pelo verificador de modelos, que representam caminhos onde uma dada fórmula não é satisfeita, são apresentados para o autor como sequências de elos indicando uma possível execução do documento para o comportamento indesejado encontrado.

A seção a seguir apresenta o uso da implementação da nossa abordagem para a análise de um documento NCL.

5. ANAA

A abordagem de análise de documentos NCL apresentada neste artigo foi implementada em uma biblioteca chamada aNaa (API NCL de Autoria e Análise) [10], que implementa tanto a análise estrutural quando a comportamental de documentos NCL. A API foi testada com documentos desenvolvidos pela comunidade de TV digital e disponibilizados no Clube NCL[1]. Adicionalmente, uma ferramenta foi construída com o uso da API aNaa e disponibilizada online[2] para um teste massivo de aNaa com respeito a aceitação dos usuários. Nesta seção é apresentado um documento muito simples cujo intuito é exemplificar como aNaa é capaz de identificar problemas em documentos NCL. Neste documento as propriedades estruturais (referência, composicionalidade e reúso) e comportamentais (alcance, terminação de âncora

---

[1] http://clube.ncl.org.br

[2] http://www.midiacom.uff.br/~joel/anaa4web

e de documento) não são satisfeitas. A Figura 2 apresenta parte do código NCL desse documento.

```
1  <ncl id='cenario' ...>
2    <head>...</head>
3    <body>
4      <port id='p_body' component='fig'
             interface='p_inner'/>
5      <media id='video' src='video.mp4'
             descriptor='desc'/>
6      <context id='inner' refer='inner'>
7        <port id='p_inner' component='fig'/>
8        <media id='fig' src='fig1.png'
               descriptor='desc'/>
9      </context>
10   </body>
11 </ncl>
```

Figura 2: Documento de exemplo

Análise estrutural. A propriedade de referência não é satisfeita porque a porta *p_body* faz referência ao nó *fig* e interface *p_inner*, que não é filha do nó *fig*. A propriedade de composicionalidade não é satisfeita pois a porta *p_body* faz referência ao nó *fig*, que não está na mesma composição que *p_body*. A propriedade de reúso não é satisfeita pois o contexto *inner* reúsa a si mesmo através de seu atributo *refer*. Cada problema é identificado pela aNaa com os invariantes apresentados na Figura 3, instâncias das propriedades de referência, composicionalidade e reúso.

```
1  -- Invariante instancia da propriedade de referencia
2  context NCLPort inv:
3    if self.interface->notEmpty() then
4      if self.component.oclIsKindOf(NCLMedia) then
5        self.component->forAll(c |
                c.oclAsType(NCLMedia).areas->exists(a |
                a = self.interface))
6      or
7        self.component->forAll(c |
                c.oclAsType(NCLMedia).properties
                ->exists(a | a = self.interface))
8    ...
9  -- Invariante instancia propriedade
        composicionalidade
10 context NCLPort inv:
11   if self.parentBody->notEmpty() then
12     self.parentBody.nodes->exists(a | a =
                self.component)
13   ...
14 -- Invariante instancia da propriedade de reuso
15 context NCLContext inv:
16   self.refer->forAll(c:NCLContext | c.referLoops())
```

Figura 3: Invariantes representando propriedades estruturais

Para corrigir os problemas identificados, o autor deve modificar o atributo *component* da porta *p_body* para *inner*. Dessa forma a porta continua mapeando o nó *fig* mas agora respeita a propriedade de composicionalidade, uma vez que o contexto *inner* é um de seus irmãos. A porta também respeita a propriedade de referência, uma vez que o atributo *interface* agora faz referência para uma interface do nó referenciado no atributo *component*. Por fim, o autor deve remover o atributo *refer* do contexto *inner*, para que este não reúse mais a si mesmo.

Uma vez tendo corrigido o documento da Figura 2, aNaa pode criar a sua representação no modelo SHM pela aplica-

ção da transformação $\tau_{\mathcal{NCM}}$. A Figura 4 apresenta a representação do documento em SHM.

$$doc = (A_{doc}, L_{doc}, I)$$
$$A_{doc} = \{a_{fig}, a_{video}\}$$
$$L_{doc} = \emptyset$$
$$I_{doc} = \{(a_{fig}, presentation, start)\}$$

Figura 4: Representação SHm do documento de exemplo

Note que os nós *fig* e *video* são representados por âncoras modelando o conteúdo total do nó (a_{fig} e a_{video}). Como o documento não especifica nenhum elo, L_{doc} é vazio. O mapeamento feito pela porta *p_body* é representado por uma ação inicial que inicia a âncora a_{fig} quando a execução do documento inicia.

Análise comportamental. A propriedade de alcance não é satisfeita pois a mídia *video* nunca é apresentada durante a execução do documento. Ambas as propriedades de terminação de âncora e de documento não são satisfeitas, pois a mídia *fig* uma vez apresentada (no início da execução do documento) nunca termina sua apresentação (ela não tem uma duração explícita). Cada problema é identificado pela aNaa com as fórmulas LTL apresentadas na Figura 5, instâncias das propriedades de alcance, terminação de âncora e terminação de documento.

```
1  -- Formula instancia da propriedade de alcance
2  -- F pre-occurring(video)
3  -- Formula instancia da propriedade de terminacao de
        ancora
4  GF pre-occurring(fig1) implies GF
        pre-sleeping(fig1)
5  -- Formula instancia da propriedade de terminacao de
        documento
6  GF doc-end
```

Figura 5: Fórmulas LTL representando propriedades comportamentais

Para corrigir o problema de alcance, o autor pode tanto criar uma porta mapeando para a mídia *video* quanto criar um elo que inicie a apresentação da mídia *video* quando a apresentação da mídia *fig* inicia. Para resolver os demais problemas, o autor pode tanto criar um elo que termine a apresentação da mídia *fig* quando a apresentação da mídia *video* terminar ou definir uma duração explícita para a mídia *fig* em seu descritor.

6. CONCLUSÃO

Este artigo apresentou uma abordagem dirigida a modelos para a análise de documentos NCL. A abordagem apresentada pode ser usada para a validação de documentos multimídia de acordo com as regras sintáticas e invariantes estruturais definidos pela semântica de NCL; e para a verificar se o documento apresenta um comportamento possivelmente indesejado. O processo de análise usa validação de invariantes OCL para as propriedades estruturais e verificação de fórmulas LTL por um *model-checker* para as propriedades comportamentais.

Este artigo também propôs uma representação formal do comportamento de documentos NCL, chamada SHM. O modelo SHM é uma simplificação do modelo NCM, também sendo baseado em eventos. SHM representa um documento como um conjunto de âncoras e elos. A abordagem proposta foi implementada na ferramenta aNaa, para a análise de documentos NCL.

A implementação atual considerou propriedades comuns derivadas de trabalhos relacionados. Um trabalho futuro é a incorporação de propriedades definidas pelo autor, permitindo a definição de propriedades de análise em alguma linguagem natural (inglês, por exemplo), que possa ser traduzida para invariantes OCL ou fórmulas LTL.

Documentos NCL são executados em plataformas com recursos limitados, como memória e largura de banda. Tais limitações podem interferir na execução do documento. Um outro trabalho futuro é considerar características da plataforma durante a verificação do comportamento do documento.

Outro trabalho futuro é considerar a análise espacial de um documento NCL, avaliando, por exemplo, relacionamentos espaciais que podem tornar a execução do documento inconsistente.

7. REFERÊNCIAS

[1] ABNT. Digital Terrestrial Television — Data Coding and Transmission Specification for Digital Broadcasting — Part 2: Ginga-NCL for Fixed and Mobile Receivers — XML Application Language for Application Coding, 2011. ABNT 15606-2:2011.

[2] Baral, C. and Gelfond, M. Logic programming and knowledge representation. *The Journal of Logic Programming*, 19:73–148, 1994.

[3] E. Bertino, E. Ferrari, A. Perego, and D. Santi. A Constraint-Based Approach for the Authoring of Multi-Topic Multimedia Presentations. In *ICME*, pages 578–581, 2005.

[4] A. Bossi and O. Gaggi. Enriching SMIL with assertions for temporal validation. In *ACM Multimedia*, pages 107–116, 2007.

[5] A. Bossi and O. Gaggi. Analysis and verification of SMIL documents. *Multimedia Systems*, 17(6):487–506, 2011.

[6] C. Braga, R. Menezes, T. Comicio, C. Santos, and E. Landim. Transformation contracts in practice. *IET Software*, 6(1):16–32, 2012.

[7] E. M. Clarke, O. Grumberg, and D. A. Peled. *Model Checking*. The MIT Press, 2000.

[8] M. Clavel, S. Eker, F. Durán, P. Lincoln, N. Martí-Oliet, and J. Meseguer. *All about Maude - A High-performance Logical Framework: how to Specify, Program, and Verify Systems in Rewriting Logic*. Springer-Verlag, 2007.

[9] M. de Oliveira, M. Turine, and P. Masiero. A statechart-based model for hypermedia applications. *ACM TOIS*, pages 28–52, 2001.

[10] J. A. F. dos Santos. Multimedia and hypermedia document validation and verification using a model-driven approach. Master's thesis, UFF, 2012.

[11] J. A. F. dos Santos, C. Braga, and D. C. Muchaluat-Saade. A Model-driven Approach for the Analysis of Multimedia Documents. In *SLE Doctoral Symposium*, pages 37–44, 2012.

[12] S. Elias, K. Easwarakumar, and R. Chbeir. Dynamic consistency checking for temporal and spatial relations in multimedia presentations. In *ACM SAC*, pages 1380–1384, 2006.

[13] M. F. Felix. *Formal Analysis of Software Models Oriented by Architectural Abstractions*. PhD thesis, PUC-Rio, 2004. in Portuguese.

[14] G. S. C. Honorato and S. D. J. Barbosa. NCL-Inspector: Towards Improving NCL Code. In *ACM SAC*, pages 1946–1947, 2010.

[15] ISO/IEC 15938. Multimedia content description interface, 2001.

[16] ISO/IEC 15938-9. Multimedia content description interface - Part 9: profiles and levels, 2005.

[17] D. P. Júnior, J. Farines, and C. Koliver. An Approach to Verify Live NCL Applications. In *WebMedia*, pages 223–232, 2012.

[18] S. J. Mellor, T. Clark, and T. Futagami. Model-driven development: guest editors' introduction. *IEEE software*, 20(5):14–18, 2003.

[19] J. Na and R. Furuta. Dynamic documents: authoring, browsing, and analysis using a high-level petri net-based hypermedia system. In *ACM DocEng*, pages 38–47, 2001.

[20] J. R. C. Neto, R. C. M. Santos, C. S. S. Neto, and M. M. Teixeira. Método de Validação Estrutural e Contextual de Documentos NCL. In *WebMedia*, pages 1–8, 2011. in Portuguese.

[21] C. Santos, L. Soares, G. de Souza, and J. Courtiat. Design methodology and formal validation of hypermedia documents. In *ACM Multimedia*, pages 39–48, 1998.

[22] L. F. G. Soares, R. F. Rodrigues, and D. C. Muchaluat-Saade. Modeling, authoring and formatting hypermedia documents in the HyperProp system. *Multimedia Systems*, pages 118–134, 2000.

[23] R. Troncy, W. Bailer, M. Höffernig, and M. Hausenblas. VAMP: a service for validating MPEG-7 descriptions w.r.t. to formal profile definitions. *Multimedia Tools and Applications*, 46(2):307–329, 2010.

[24] W3C Recommendation. OWL Web ontology language: reference, 2004.

[25] W3C Recommendation. XML Schema Part 0: Primer Second Edition, 2004.

[26] W3C Recommendation. Extensible Markup Language (XML) 1.0 (Fifth Edition), 2008.

[27] W3C Recommendation. Synchronized Multimedia Integration Language - SMIL 3.0 Specification, 2008.

[28] J. Warmer and A. Kleppe. *The Object Constraint Language*. Addison–Wesley, 1999.

Two Normal Forms for Link-Connector Pairs in NCL 3.0

Guilherme Augusto Ferreira Lima
Department of Informatics
PUC-Rio, Rio de Janeiro, Brazil
glima@inf.puc-rio.br

Luiz Fernando Gomes Soares
Department of Informatics
PUC-Rio, Rio de Janeiro, Brazil
lfgs@inf.puc-rio.br

ABSTRACT

In this paper, we investigate the problem of normal forms for links and connectors in NCL 3.0. We identify two such forms, called the First and Second Normal Forms (NF1 and NF2), in which links and connectors appear in simple terms. We also present normalization procedures (proofs), which show that for every NCL 3.0 program, there is an equivalent program in each of the forms. The mere existence of NF1 and NF2 makes the semantic analysis of programs simpler. Moreover, the symmetry exhibited by these forms suggests that the same principle of arbitrarily ordered evaluation underlies both the evaluation of link conditions and the execution of non-sequential compound actions.

Categories and Subject Descriptors: I.7.2 [Document Preparation]: Languages and systems

General Terms: Languages, Theory

Keywords: Connectors; links; NCL; Nested Context Language; normal form; semantics

1. INTRODUCTION

Links and connectors are the primary constructs for media synchronization in NCL 3.0 [1, 5]. Links define causal relationships between events in a presentation; connectors define reusable templates for links. Every link-connector pair[1] has two parts: condition and action. The condition specifies the events to be waited together with a predicate, or "assessment statement" in NCL terminology, to be evaluated at each occurrence of the former. The action specifies the events to be generated whenever the condition is satisfied, i.e., whenever the awaited events occur and, simultaneously, the associated predicate evaluates to true.

---

[1]We shall use the term "link-connector pair" to refer to the causal relationship denoted by a link together with its connector. This terminology is justified because, in terms of program behavior, these constructs are virtually indissociable, with the connector being an integral part of the link definition.

There are several ways in which one can restrict the form of links and connectors without affecting the expressiveness of NCL 3.0.[2] In this paper, we present two such restricted, or *normal*, forms with some interesting properties. More specifically, we show that for every NCL program X there is an equivalent program X' such that, for each link-connector pair ℓ in X', the following properties hold.

1. The condition of ℓ consists of an atomic condition together with a predicate.
2. The action of ℓ is either atomic or is the sequential composition of two atomic actions.

Properties (1) and (2) correspond to what we call the *First Normal Form* (NF1) for NCL programs. We also define a *Second Normal Form* (NF2), which consists of property (1) together with the following properties.

3. The action of ℓ is either of the same format as that of (2) or is the arbitrarily ordered, viz., parallel, composition of $n \geq 2$ actions of the same format as that of (2).
4. For every ℓ' in X' with $\ell' \neq \ell$, the condition of ℓ' is different from that of ℓ.

The implication of property (1) to works like [2, 3, 4, 6, 7, 8], which analyze the behavior of links and connectors in NCL, is immediate: one is freed from the intricate cases of link-connector pairs containing multiple conditions. Similar arguments apply to properties (2)–(4). However, properties (2)–(4) also have a subtler, more profound implication. The manifest symmetry between (2) and (3)–(4) suggests that the principle of arbitrarily ordered evaluation involved in the evaluation of conditions of distinct links is equivalent to that involved in the execution of non-sequential, or *parallel*[3], actions; an observation that might prove relevant for future semantic investigations.

We can convert any NCL program into an equivalent program in NF1 or NF2. The conversion, or *normalization*, procedure consists of several stages, or *reductions*, wherein link-connector pairs that violate the properties of the particular normal form are replaced by equivalent pairs that are satisfactory, or that are closer to be satisfactory than the original ones. The reductions are applied repeatedly until all link-connector pairs become satisfactory.

Although we try to be rigorous in justifying correctness of each reduction, our approach to language semantics is essentially informal. We consider two NCL programs X and X' *equivalent* iff (if, and only if) both define the same set of possible presentations. In particular, if X and X' are deterministic programs, then each defines a single presentation. These are considered equivalent iff, for every

---

[2]From now on, we shall simply speak of NCL with the suffix "3.0" being tacitly understood.

[3]We shall use the term "parallel" in the particular sense defined by the NCL specification [1, p. 61][5, p. 40], viz., that of evaluation in an arbitrary order, and not in the sense of concurrent evaluation, which is its usual meaning.

input event e, at any given time, the result of applying e to each presentation is exactly the same. By "result," we mean what users see on screen and hear from speakers. We extend this definition to nondeterministic programs X and X' by requiring that the set of results induced by e on X, at any given time, be equal to the set induced by e on X' at that same time, and vice versa.

To simplify the definition of the reductions we introduce, in Section 2, the abstract syntax ABS for the unified representation of link-connector pairs in NCL programs. ABS hides away some idiosyncrasies of the concrete syntax of NCL, e.g., the distinction between links and connectors, n-ary compositions, etc., that would complicate the definitions and proofs presented in Sections 3 and 4. Nevertheless, the mapping of ABS programs into equivalent NCL programs is straightforward. The same applies to the normalization procedures, which we define only for ABS programs. The mapping of these procedures into equivalent procedures that operate on NCL programs follows directly from the previous mapping.

The rest of the paper is organized as follows. Section 2 presents the syntax and semantics of ABS, and discusses the mapping of its programs into equivalent NCL programs. Sections 3 and 4 present, respectively, the First and Second Normal Form theorems for ABS programs, with their proofs corresponding to what we termed the "normalization procedures." Finally, Section 5 concludes the paper.

2. THE ABSTRACT SYNTAX

In this section, we introduce ABS, a simple language for the unified representation of link-connector pairs in NCL programs. First, we define the syntax of ABS, i.e., the structure of the expressions which we regard as well-formed programs. Then, we present the intended interpretation for these programs. Finally, we discuss the mapping of NCL programs into equivalent ABS programs.

ABS has five main syntactic sets: programs **S**, links **L**, conditions **C**, predicates **P**, and actions **A**. The structure of the members of these sets is given by the following BNF-like grammar, where '::=' read as "can be," '|' read as "or," ε stands for the empty string, and the metavariables S, L, C, P, and A, with or without super or subscripts, are assumed to range over the sets **S**, **L**, **C**, **P**, and **A**, respectively.

$$
\begin{aligned}
S &::= LS_0 \mid \varepsilon \\
L &::= C \to A \\
C &::= (C_0 \wedge C_1 \,?\, P) \mid (C_0 \vee C_1 \,?\, P) \mid (c \,?\, P) \\
P &::= (P_0 \wedge P_1) \mid (P_0 \vee P_1) \mid (\neg P_0) \mid p \\
A &::= (A_0, A_1) \mid (A_0 \,\|\, A_1) \mid a
\end{aligned}
$$

The definition of conditions (C), predicates (P), and actions (A) contain the metavariables c, p, and a. These are assumed to range over the primitive syntactic sets **c** of atomic conditions, **p** of atomic predicates, and **a** of atomic actions, respectively. The partial structure of the members of these primitive sets is given below.

$$
\begin{aligned}
c &::= u.v \mid \cdots \\
p &::= u.v_0 = v_1 \mid \cdots \\
a &::= u.v_0 := v_1 \mid \cdots
\end{aligned}
$$

Here '$\cdots$' stands for the omitted forms, i.e., those whose structure is of no particular interest to us, and the metavariables u and v, with or without subscripts, are assumed to range over the sets **u** of component (i.e., media, context, or switch) identifiers and **v** of arbitrary strings, respectively. We assume that the structure of the members of **u** and **v** is given.

By the above definition, an ABS program S is simply a finite list of links $L_1, L_2, \ldots, L_n$ with $n \geq 0$. Each link L_i, for $1 \leq i \leq n$, is of the form $C \to A$ and establishes that whenever condition C is satisfied, action A is executed. Condition C is either the conjunction ($\wedge$) or disjunction ($\vee$) of two other conditions C_0 and C_1 associated with a predicate P, viz., the expression at the right-hand side of symbol '?', or is an atomic condition c also associated with a predicate P. Predicate P, in turn, is either the conjunction ($\wedge$) or disjunction ($\vee$) of two other predicates P_0 and P_1, the negation ($\neg$) of another predicate P_0, or is an atomic predicate p. Finally, action A is either the sequential (,) or parallel ($\|$) composition of two other actions A_0 and A_1, or is an atomic action a.

Moreover, the atomic condition c specifies a single event to be waited (e.g., the pressing of a button), the atomic predicate p specifies a Boolean test involving the equality or inequality of properties (i.e., NCL <property> elements) and values (i.e., arbitrary strings), and the atomic action a specifies an event to be generated (e.g., the starting of the presentation of some media object). The particular forms of c, p, and a that were singled out are to be interpreted as follows: The atomic condition $u.v$ is satisfied whenever some value is stored in property v of component u, the atomic predicate $u.v_0 = v_1$ evaluates to true if the content of property v_0 of component u is equal to the string v_1, and the atomic action $u.v_0 := v_1$, if executed, stores the string v_1 into property v_0 of component u.

The mapping of an arbitrary NCL program X into an equivalent ABS program is direct if X satisfies the following restrictions.

1. Each connector of X is referenced by exactly one link.
2. The connectors and links of X contain no link, bind, or connector parameters, i.e., no <linkParam>, <bindParam>, or <connectorParam> elements.
3. The compound conditions and compound actions of all connectors of X have no *delay* attribute.
4. The simple conditions and simple actions of all connectors of X are referenced by exactly one bind (i.e., <bind> element) in the associated links.
5. The compound actions and compound statements of all connectors of X are binary and its compound conditions are either binary or ternary, and have exactly one child (assessment or compound) statement.

If X satisfies the above restrictions, we can build an equivalent ABS program by mapping each link-connector pair ℓ of X into an equivalent element of **L**. The mapping is defined by recursion as follows: For each ℓ, we map each of its <compoundCondition>, <compoundStatement>, and <compoundAction> elements into equivalent members of **C**, **P**, and **A**, respectively, and, at the basis of the recursion, we map each of its <simpleCondition>, <assessmentStatement>, and <simpleAction> elements, together with the associated <role> elements, into equivalent members of **c**, **p**, and **a**, respectively.

If, however, X does not satisfy restrictions (1)–(5), we first need to convert it into an equivalent satisfactory NCL program, which is then mapped into ABS. Since this extra conversion, or *prenormalization*, stage is not particularly enlightening we shall only discuss it briefly.[4] The prenormalization procedure consists, basically, of the consecutive application of steps (1)–(5) below.[5]

1. Make a copy of each connector that is referenced by more than one link and update the links to point to different copies.

---

[4] This stage is implemented by prenormalization module of the DietNCL conversion tool, cf. http://www.telemidia.puc-rio.br/~gflima.

[5] More precisely, for each step $1 \leq i \leq 5$ and each program X, if we apply the prenormalization steps (1)–(i) to X we get an equivalent program X' that satisfies restriction (i).

2. Replace, in each connector, the value of the parameters defined in the associated link.

3. Add the *delay* attribute of each compound condition (or action) to the *delay* of its components. Then remove the *delay* attribute from the parent composition. Repeat this procedure until all compositions have no *delay* attribute.

4. Replace each simple condition (or action) that is referenced by more than one bind by an equivalent compound condition (or action) and update the *role* of the referring binds to point to the new simple conditions (or actions). Repeat this procedure until every simple condition (or action) is referenced by exactly one bind.

5. Replace all simple conditions by a binary compound condition containing the original simple condition together with a tautological assessment statement. Then break all *n*-ary compound conditions, with $n \geq 3$, into an equivalent chain of binary ones, adding vacuous, tautological statements whenever necessary. Finally, repeat the breakage procedure for compound actions and compound statements.

3. FIRST NORMAL FORM

We now undertake the task of stating and proving the first normal form theorem for ABS programs. First, however, we need to introduce some notation.

Let e_0 and e_1 be elements of the same syntactic set. Then we write $e_0 \equiv e_1$ iff e_0 is identical to e_1, i.e., iff they have the same parse tree.

The *condition degree d* of a link $L \equiv C \to A$ is defined inductively by the following clauses.

1. If $C \equiv (c \, ? \, P)$ then $d = 0$.
2. If $C \equiv (C_0 \wedge C_1 \, ? \, P)$ or $C \equiv (C_0 \vee C_1 \, ? \, P)$, and the condition degrees of C_0 and C_1 are, respectively, d_0 and d_1, then $d = d_0 + d_1 + 1$.

Similarly, the *action degree d* of a link $L \equiv C \to A$ is defined by:

1. If $A \equiv a$ or $A \equiv (a_0, a_1)$ then $d = 0$.
2. If $A \equiv (A_0, A_1)$, with $A_i \not\equiv a$ for some $i = 0$ or $i = 1$, or $A \equiv (A_0 \parallel A_1)$, and the action degrees of A_0 and A_1 are, respectively, d_0 and d_1, then $d = d_0 + d_1 + 1$.

We shall use the letter 'F', with or without subscripts, to represent *flags*: specially crafted properties (i.e., `<property>` elements) that function as private variables. We use flags to simulate the behavior of the particular construction we are trying to eliminate. Flags may appear in conditions, predicates, and actions. E.g., link $(F \, ? \, P) \to A$ establishes that whenever some value is stored in flag F and, simultaneously, predicate P holds (i.e., evaluates to true), then action A is executed; link $(C \, ? \, F = 1) \to A$ establishes that whenever C is satisfied and, simultaneously, the content of flag F is equal to 1, then A is executed; and link $C \to F := 1$ establishes that whenever C is satisfied, then 1 is stored in flag F. Initially, every flag is assumed to contain 0.

We now prove a basic lemma about the elimination of non-atomic conditions.

LEMMA 1. *For any ABS program S there is an equivalent program S' such that each link L of S' has condition degree zero, i.e.,*

$$L \equiv (c \, ? \, P) \to A,$$

for some atomic condition c, predicate P, and action A.

PROOF. Let S be an arbitrary ABS program, and let L be some link of S with condition degree $d_c > 0$. Then either

$$L \equiv ((C_0 \, ? \, P) \vee (C_1 \, ? \, Q) \, ? \, R) \to A \qquad (1)$$

or

$$L \equiv ((C_0 \, ? \, P) \wedge (C_1 \, ? \, Q) \, ? \, R) \to A, \qquad (2)$$

for some conditions C_0 and C_1, predicates P, Q, and R, and action A.

In case (1), action A is executed if any of the conditions ($C_0 \, ? \, P$) or ($C_1 \, ? \, Q$) are satisfied and if, simultaneously, predicate R holds. We remove link L from S by transforming it into the links

$$(C_0 \, ? \, P \wedge R) \to A$$
$$(C_1 \, ? \, Q \wedge R) \to A,$$

which execute A if C_0 is satisfied and $P \wedge R$ holds, or C_1 is satisfied and $Q \wedge R$ holds, or both. Thus the transformation maintains the original behavior.

In case (2), action A is executed immediately after conditions ($C_0 \, ? \, P$) and ($C_1 \, ? \, Q$) are satisfied (in fact, just after the last one of them is satisfied) and only if, at that moment, predicate R holds. In this case, we remove link L from S by transforming it into the links

$$(C_0 \, ? \, P \wedge R) \to F_{C_0} := 1$$
$$(C_1 \, ? \, Q \wedge R) \to F_{C_1} := 1$$
$$(F_{C_0} \, ? \, F_{C_1} = 1) \to (F_{(C_0 \wedge C_1)} := v, A)$$
$$(F_{C_1} \, ? \, F_{C_0} = 1) \to (F_{(C_0 \wedge C_1)} := v, A)$$
$$(F_{(C_0 \wedge C_1)} \, ? \, \top) \to (F_{C_0} := 0, F_{C_1} := 0),$$

where $\top$ denotes some tautological predicate, e.g., ($p \vee \neg p$), and v denotes some arbitrary string. These links execute A immediately after condition ($C_0 \, ? \, P \wedge R$) is satisfied if ($C_1 \, ? \, Q \wedge R$) was satisfied earlier, or after ($C_1 \, ? \, Q \wedge R$) if ($C_0 \, ? \, P \wedge R$) was satisfied earlier. Thus the transformation maintains the original behavior.

In either case, the links replaced for L have condition degree less than d_c. Therefore, by successively repeating the transformations, we obtain an equivalent program S' in which all links have condition degree zero. $\square$

We proceed to prove the main result of this section.

THEOREM 1 (FIRST NORMAL FORM, OR NF1). *For any ABS program S there is an equivalent program S' such that each link L of S' has condition and action degrees zero, i.e.,*

$$L \equiv (c \, ? \, P) \to a_0 \qquad or \qquad L \equiv (c \, ? \, P) \to (a_0, a_1),$$

for some atomic condition c, predicate P, and atomic actions a, a_0, and a_1.

PROOF. Let S'' be the result of applying Lemma 1 to S, and let L be some link of S'' with an action degree $d_a > 0$. Then either

$$L \equiv C \to (A_0 \parallel A_1) \qquad or \qquad L \equiv C \to (A_0, A_1),$$

for some condition $C \equiv (c \, ? \, P)$ and actions A_0 and A_1.

In the first case, if condition C is satisfied then actions A_0 and A_1 are executed in "parallel," i.e., in an arbitrary order. We remove link L from S'' by transforming it into the links

$$C \to A_0$$
$$C \to A_1,$$

which clearly maintain the original behavior, since, in NCL, the order of evaluation of links is also arbitrary.

In the second case, if condition C is satisfied then actions A_0 and A_1 are executed in sequence, i.e., A_0 is executed before A_1. There are the following three possibilities. (Note that all of them guarantee that the links replaced for L execute A_0 before A_1 whenever C is satisfied.)

1. If $A_1 \not\equiv a$, for any atomic action a, we replace L by

$$C \to (A_0, F_{A_0} := v)$$
$$(F_{A_0} \ ? \ \top) \to A_1.$$

2. If $A_0 \equiv (A_0', A_0'')$, for some A_0' and A_0'', we replace L by

$$C \to (A_0', F_{A_0'} := v)$$
$$(F_{A_0'} \ ? \ \top) \to (A_0'', A_1).$$

3. If $A_0 \equiv (A_0' \ \| \ A_0'')$, for some A_0' and A_0'', we replace L by

$$C \to (A_0', F_{A_0'} := 1)$$
$$C \to (A_0'', F_{A_0''} := 1)$$
$$(F_{A_0'} \ ? \ F_{A_0''} = 1) \to (F_{(A_0'\|A_0'')} := v, A_1)$$
$$(F_{A_0''} \ ? \ F_{A_0'} = 1) \to (F_{(A_0'\|A_0'')} := v, A_1)$$
$$(F_{(A_0'\|A_0'')} \ ? \ \top) \to (F_{A_0'} := 0, F_{A_0''} := 0).$$

In any case, the links replaced for L have condition degree zero and have action degree less than d_a. Therefore, by successively repeating the transformations, we obtain an equivalent program S' in which all links have condition and action degrees zero. □

4. SECOND NORMAL FORM

We now turn to the statement and proof of the second normal form theorem for ABS programs. To characterize the structure of actions in this normal form, we introduce the concept of sequential degree.

The *sequential degree d* of a link $L \equiv C \to A$ is defined by:

1. If $A \equiv a$ or $A \equiv (a_0, a_1)$ then $d = 0$.
2. If $A \equiv (A_0 \ \| \ A_1)$ and the sequential degrees of A_0 and A_1 are, respectively, d_0 and d_1, then $d = d_0 + d_1$.
3. If $A \equiv (A_0, A_1)$, with $A_i \not\equiv a$ for some $i = 0$ or $i = 1$, and the sequential degrees of A_0 and A_1 are, respectively, d_0 and d_1, then $d = d_0 + d_1 + 1$.

The following corollary is a direct consequence of Theorem 1.

COROLLARY 1. *If S is an ABS program in NF1, then all its links have sequential degree zero.*

PROOF. By Theorem 1, every link of S has action degree zero. Thus, by the first clause of the definitions of action and sequential degrees, every link of S has sequential degree zero. □

We proceed to establish the main result of this section.

THEOREM 2 (SECOND NORMAL FORM, OR NF2). *For any ABS program S there is an equivalent program S' such that each link L of S' has condition and sequential degrees zero, i.e.,*

$$L \equiv (c \ ? \ P) \to A_0 \quad or \quad L \equiv (c \ ? \ P) \to (A_1 \ \| \ A_2 \ \| \ \cdots \ \| \ A_n),$$

for some atomic condition c, predicate P, and actions A_0, A_1, ..., A_n such that $A_i \equiv a$ or $A_i \equiv (a_0, a_1)$, for $0 \leq i \leq n$. Moreover, for each pair of distinct links $L' \equiv C' \to A'$ and $L'' \equiv C'' \to A''$ of S',

$$C' \not\equiv C'',$$

i.e., no two links of S' have the same condition.

PROOF. Let S'' be the result of applying Theorem 1 to S, and let $L' \equiv C' \to A'$ and $L'' \equiv C'' \to A''$ be links of S'' such that $C' \equiv C''$. Then, by Theorem 1, L' and L'' have condition degree zero, and by Corollary 1, they have sequential degree zero. We remove L' and L'' by transforming them into a single link of the form

$$C' \to (A' \ \| \ A''), \tag{3}$$

which clearly maintains the original behavior. Moreover, (3) has condition and sequential degrees zero—its condition degree is equal to that of C', which is zero, and its sequential degree is equal to the sum of the degrees of A' and A'', which are also zero. Therefore, by successively repeating the transformations we obtain an equivalent program S' in which all links have condition and sequential degrees zero and such that no two links have the same condition. □

5. CONCLUSION

In this paper, we investigated the problem of normal forms for links and connectors in NCL 3.0. Two such forms, termed the First and Second Normal Forms, were identified and precisely defined. Moreover, we showed that for every NCL 3.0 program there is an equivalent program in each of the forms. We also discussed the apparent duality between these forms, which suggests that the same principle of arbitrarily ordered evaluation underlies both the evaluation of conditions and the execution of non-sequential, "parallel" actions. We hope this result prove useful for future investigations.

A related problem, not addressed in this paper, is the question whether NF1 and NF2 are irreducible. We believe that to be the case, but we still do not have a proof, which might require the formalization of program semantics.

REFERENCES

[1] ABNT NBR 15606-2. Digital Terrestrial TV – Data coding and transmission specification for digital broadcasting – Part 2: Ginga-NCL for fixed and mobile receivers: XML application language for application coding. ABNT, São Paulo, SP, Brazil, November 2007.

[2] COSTA, R. M. R., MORENO, M. F., AND SOARES, L. F. G. Intermedia synchronization management in DTV systems. In *Proceedings of the 8th ACM Symposium on Document Engineering - DocEng'08* (São Paulo, SP, Brazil, September 2008), ACM, New York, NY, USA, pp. 289–297.

[3] DOS SANTOS, J., BRAGA, C., AND SAADE, D. C. M. A model-driven approach for the analysis of multimedia documents. In *Proceedings of the Doctoral Symposium of the 5th International Conference on Software Language Engineering - SLE 2012* (Dresden, Germany, September 2012).

[4] FELIX, M. F., HAEUSLER, E. H., AND SOARES, L. F. G. Validating hypermedia documents: A timed automata approach. Monografias em Ciência da Computação, PUC-Rio, Rio de Janeiro, RJ, Brazil, 2002.

[5] ITU-T RECOMMENDATION H.761. Nested Context Language (NCL) and Ginga-NCL for IPTV Services. ITU-T, Geneva, Switzerland, April 2009.

[6] LIMA, G. A. F., SOARES, L. F. G., NETO, C. S. S., MORENO, M. F., COSTA, R. R., AND MORENO, M. F. Towards the NCL Raw Profile. In *II Workshop de TV Digital Interativa (WTVDI) - Colocated with ACM WebMedia'10* (Belo Horizonte, MG, Brazil, October 2010).

[7] PICININ, JR., D., FARINES, J.-M., AND KOLIVER, C. An approach to verify live NCL applications. In *Proceedings of the 18th Brazilian Symposium on Multimedia and the Web - WebMedia'12* (São Paulo, SP, Brazil, October 2012), ACM, New York, NY, USA, pp. 223–232.

[8] YOVINE, S., OLIVERO, A., MONTEVERDE, D., CORDOBA, G., AND REITER, L. An approach for the verification of the temporal consistency of NCL applications. In *II Workshop de TV Digital Interativa (WTVDI) - Colocated with ACM WebMedia'10* (Belo Horizonte, MG, Brazil, October 2010).

Adaptive Layouts for Authoring NCL Programs

Glauco F. Amorim* §   Joel A. F. dos Santos§   Débora C. Muchaluat-Saade§
* Grupo de Pesquisa em Computação Aplicada
Escola de Informática - CEFET-RJ
§ Laboratório MídiaCom
Departamento de Ciência da Computação - Universidade Federal Fluminense
(gamorim, joel, debora)@midiacom.uff.br

ABSTRACT

This paper presents a layout module that incorporates the facility of specifying adaptive spatial layouts, providing automatic creation of regions and descriptors for NCL documents. Two types of adaptive spatial layouts are provided: *flowLayout* and *gridLayout*. Adaptive layouts are very useful for defining generic templates for hypermedia documents, where the number of components will be specified by the final NCL application. Therefore this proposal facilitates the authoring of hypermedia documents used for interactive content creation in the Brazilian Digital TV System.

Categories and Subject Descriptors

D.2.11 [**Software Engineering**]: Software Architectures

General Terms

Languages

Keywords

Leiautes, Templates, Autoria de Documentos, NCL, Aplicação Interativa, Ginga.

1. INTRODUÇÃO

Em aplicações hipermídia, é possível encontrar estruturas recorrentes que poderiam caracterizar uma família de documentos [9]. Essa família de documentos pode ser representada por especificações genéricas de programas, denominadas *templates* de composição [8]. Uma das vantagens de se utilizar *templates* pode ser percebida quando as aplicações ficam mais elaboradas. A quantidade de objetos e a necessidade de se definir relacionamentos entre eles aumentam consideravelmente, introduzindo mais complexidade na autoria de aplicações, além de possíveis erros. O uso de *templates* pode reduzir a quantidade e a complexidade do código de uma aplicação e diminuir a probabilidade de erros na confecção do código.

Normalmente, essas aplicações hipermídia envolvem a apresentação de vários tipos de mídia em exibidores que vão desde *smartphones* até aparelhos digitais de TV. Um exemplo destes tipos de aplicações seriam aquelas desenvolvidas na linguagem *Nested Context Language* (NCL) [12] para TV Digital. Para os tipos de mídia que são exibidos visualmente, é preciso definir as regiões na tela do exibidor para que as mídias possam ser apresentadas. Essa definição é feita manualmente informando as coordenadas iniciais (x, y), a largura e a altura de cada região.

Quando as aplicações possuem muitos objetos de mídia, a quantidade de regiões que devem ser determinadas é grande, o que torna o processo de definição de regiões trabalhoso e sujeito a erros. Linguagens para definição de *templates* de composição para documentos NCL [6, 9, 1], não oferecem modelos genéricos de leiautes espaciais, não permitindo definir conceitualmente um leiaute adaptativo, que inclua a criação de regiões onde as mídias serão apresentadas e descritores que definem parâmetros de exibição. Como (em geral) essas linguagens permitem a definição de um conjunto genérico de objetos (de mídia ou composições) que deve ser instanciado por quem utiliza um *template*, seria bastante útil poder definir um conjunto genérico de leiautes, que permitisse criar automaticamente definições específicas de apresentação visual de um documento. O objetivo deste trabalho, portanto, é propor um modelo que fornece a facilidade de definição de leiautes espaciais adaptativos na especificação de um *template*. O termo adaptativo se refere a possibilidade de adaptação da definição do leiaute de um *template* conforme a quantidade de componentes da composição que utilizará o *template*.

O restante do artigo está estruturado da seguinte forma. A Seção 2 comenta os trabalhos relacionados. Na Seção 3 o elemento genérico *Layout* é apresentado. Na Seção 4 é mostrado um exemplo de utilização do elemento e a Seção 5 finaliza o artigo com as conclusões e trabalhos futuros.

2. TRABALHOS RELACIONADOS

Pesquisas realizadas em [6] e [3] avaliaram alguns trabalhos que abordam a criação de documentos baseados em *templates* como LimSee3 [5], Lamp [7] e STAMP [2]. Mais recentemente, dois outros trabalhos apontam metodologias diferentes para a utilização de *templates* na linguagem NCL. A primeira é a linguagem TAL [9] e a segunda é a linguagem LUAR [1].

Outros trabalhos definem modelos de leiautes dinâmicos, mas fora do escopo de linguagens de autoria para TV Digital. Em [10], os autores propõem um sistema para criação e apresentação baseada em grade de documentos que se adaptam a várias condições de visualização e seleção de conteúdo. O sistema pode exibir conteúdos estáticos ou montar documentos dinâmicos utilizando diversas fontes diferentes. Ainda é proposto um conjunto de *templates* de leiautes que foram inspirados nos modelos dos jornais tradicionais. Cada *template* organiza uma coleção de conteúdos na região determinada pelo modelo. Já em [11], os autores apresentam uma solução para publicação de documentos digitais interativos que é baseada na autoria do documento e não em programação. A solução é genérica e descreve como definições de *templates* e de conteúdo de variáveis de elementos podem ser utilizadas para reduzir redundâncias e aumentar a flexibilidade dessas aplicações. As ideias propostas nesses trabalhos para definição de leiautes adaptativos serviram como referência para a proposta do modelo a ser apresentado a seguir.

Outras ideias surgiram de alguns gerenciadores de leiaute oferecidos pela linguagem de programação Java [4], que são usados para organizar os componentes de uma interface gráfica. Dentre os mais utilizados estão: *FlowLayout*, *GridLayout* e *BorderLayout*.

O *FlowLayout* é o gerenciador de leiaute mais simples. Nele, os componentes são dispostos da esquerda para a direita na ordem em que aparecem, isto é, na ordem em que são adicionados à janela. Quando não existe mais espaço em uma linha, é criada outra linha abaixo dela para apresentar o componente da interface gráfica.

O *GridLayout* é um gerenciador que divide a janela em um conjunto de células em uma grade retangular, de maneira que todas as células possuam a mesma dimensão. Uma janela pode ser dividida em linhas e colunas de acordo com os parâmetros passados.

O gerenciador *BorderLayout* divide uma janela em cinco regiões distintas: NORTH (região superior), SOUTH (região inferior), WEST (região à esquerda), EAST (região à direita) e CENTER (região central), onde os componentes serão inseridos. Diferentemente do *FlowLayout* e do *GridLayout*, a ordem de inserção é irrelevante, uma vez que a janela é separada em regiões fixas e a quantidade de objetos é pré-determinada, pois cada região aceita somente um componente.

Esses componentes, apesar de serem propostos para um contexto diferente de aplicações multimídia, representam bem a ideia de gerenciamento dinâmico de leiaute e, por isso, foram utilizados como base para o modelo de leiaute dinâmico proposto neste artigo.

3. ELEMENTO LAYOUT

Este artigo propõe um modelo para definir um elemento chamado *layout*, que permita a criação e o gerenciamento de leiautes bem conhecidos. Assim, o autor de um documento que usa um *template* deve especificar somente os objetos com conteúdo específico, instanciando os componentes genéricos do *template*. A definição das regiões e das características de exibição é feita durante o processamento do *template*, com base no elemento *layout*.

O elemento *layout* tem como função designar as regiões onde serão adicionadas as mídias e suas características de exibição. Ele possui como atributos obrigatórios: um identificador único (atributo *id*) usado para distinguir as diferentes ocorrências dos elementos no documento, um tipo (atributo *type*) usado para definir os diferentes tipos de leiautes que podem ser utilizados e um índice de sobreposição

(atributo *zIndex*) que define a ordem de sobreposição dos leiautes. Ele determina ainda os elementos filhos *format*, *cell* e *focus*, que definem o comportamento do leiaute.

O elemento filho *format* define informações de formatação da região que englobará todas as regiões menores (filhas) utilizadas para apresentar as mídias. As informações de formatação são: largura (atributo *width*), altura (atributo *height*) e coordenadas de início da região (atributos *top*, *left*, *right* e *bottom*). Essa região, denominada de região pai, pode ser visualizada na Figura 1 como a parte em branco que abrange todas as regiões das mídias. São ainda atributos desse elemento: alinhamento (atributo *align*), que estabelece o alinhamento das regiões filhas, aqui tratadas como células; espaçamento (atributos *hspace* e *vspace*), que definem o espaçamento horizontal e vertical entre as células; colunas e linhas (atributos *colums* e *rows*), que estabelecem o número de colunas e linhas que um leiaute pode ter, se for o caso.

O elemento filho *cell* define informações específicas de cada célula. Os atributos possíveis para esse elemento são: um identificador (atributo *id*) que é definido unicamente para cada célula; *width* e *height*, que determinam a largura e altura da célula. Com esses atributos, é possível que células do mesmo leiaute tenham tamanhos diferentes, desde que seja uma propriedade possível do leiaute indicado. As regiões que representam células podem ser visualizadas na Figura 1 como as áreas em amarelo.

Já o elemento filho *focus* descreve o comportamento de navegação interna de cada leiaute e entre os leiautes. Este elemento tem como atributos: *focusIndex* que determina um índice único de navegação para o *layout*. Este atributo, se existir, estabelece a possibilidade de navegação interna entre as células do leiaute. Para isso, os descritores correspondentes a cada célula são criados automaticamente com os atributos de navegação pertinentes à cada elemento do *layout*.

Para que exista navegação entre os leiautes, é necessário declarar pelo menos um dos seguintes atributos: *moveUp*, *moveDown*, *moveLeft*, *moveRight*. Estes atributos devem identificar o índice (*id*) do leiaute que deve receber o foco caso seja pressionada a respectiva seta enquanto o leiaute associado a esse identificador estiver em foco.

Por questão de simplicidade, somente a primeira e última células do leiaute terão seus índices de navegação alterados para permitir a navegação entre os leiautes. A navegação se dará sempre em direção à primeira ou última célula do leiaute definido no atributo, como demonstrado na Figura 1.

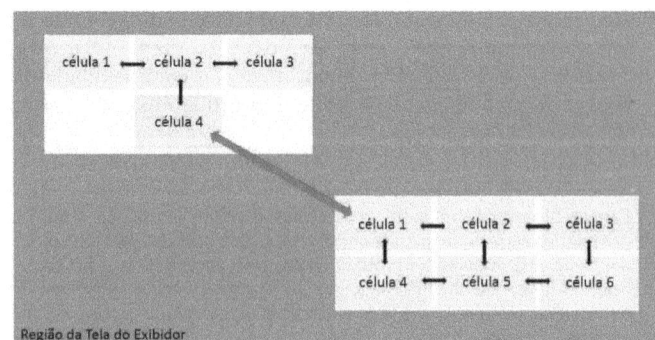

Figura 1: Exemplo de navegação dentro do leiaute e entre os leiautes.

Como mencionado anteriormente, assim como as regiões que são criadas automaticamente pelo elemento de leiaute, elementos chamados descritores, cuja função é definir os parâmetros de exibição de uma mídia em uma dada região, também o serão. O tipo mais simples de descritor a ser criado faz apenas uma associação com uma região. Contudo, em NCL, um descritor pode definir parâmetros adicionais de exibição de mídia, através de elementos filhos <descriptor-Param>. Isso poderá ser realizado através da inserção de parâmetros no elemento *layout*. Por exemplo, suponha que o desenvolvedor queira definir um parâmetro, denominado *fit*, para indicar como a mídia correspondente preencherá a região definida para ela. Então, seria necessário incluir o elemento filho *layoutParam*. Esse parâmetro é uma tupla $< name, value, cell >$. Cada *layout* pode conter diversos elementos *layoutParam*, definidos no formato mostrado na Figura 2.

```
<layout id="L2" type="gridLayout">
  ...
  <layoutParam name="fit" value="fill" cell="2"/>
  ...
</layout>
```

Figura 2: Exemplo de Parâmetros de Layout.

É possível definir um parâmetro para todas as células do elemento *layout*. Para isso, basta não declarar o atributo *cell*.

É importante estabelecer como os objetos de mídia de um documento que usa um *template* com leiaute adaptativo serão relacionadas às regiões construídas de acordo com cada leiaute. Um componente de um *template*, fica responsável por indicar qual leiaute irá utilizar. Ainda, cada objeto de mídia em um documento NCL que usa um *template* indica a qual componente do *template* se refere. Os objetos de mídia (referentes a um determinado componente) serão inseridas nas regiões do leiaute (usado pelo componente) na ordem em que estão declaradas no documento NCL, isto é, a primeira mídia declarada no documento NCL ocupará a primeira região (definida pelo leiaute) e assim sucessivamente. Quando mais nenhuma região puder ser criada dentro da região pai definida pelo leiaute, os objetos de mídia passam a ser inseridos nas regiões já existentes, começando da região inicial.

Para determinar quais gerenciadores de leiaute seriam oferecidos, foi feita uma análise das aplicações NCL interativas disponíveis no Clube NCL[1]. Após a pesquisa, foram identificados leiautes que se assemelhavam às características descritas pelos gerenciadores *FlowLayout* e *GridLayout* da linguagem Java, relatados na Seção 2. Outros leiautes encontrados não apresentavam uma estrutura bem definida ou podiam ser representados por composições do *FlowLayout* e *GridLayout*. Sendo assim, são fornecidos dois tipos de elementos *layout* identificados pelo atributo *type*: *flowLayout* e *gridLayout*, que serão expostos adiante.

f owLayout.

O leiaute definido pelo tipo *flowLayout* cria regiões da esquerda para a direita. Quando não existe mais espaço em uma linha, é criada outra linha abaixo dela e o mesmo critério é usado novamente. Como descrito anteriormente, cada elemento do tipo *flowLayout* pode ainda definir elementos filhos para compor todo o comportamento do leiaute. Os atributos possíveis para o elemento *format* são:

[1]http://clube.ncl.org.br

width, height, top, left, right, bottom, align, hspace e *vspace*. Para *cell* são: *id, width* e *height*. Já para *focus* os atributos possíveis são: *focusIndex, moveUp, moveDown, moveLeft* e *moveRight*. Um exemplo de utilização desse leiaute pode ser visualizado pelo código apresentado na Figura 3.

```
<layout id="L1" type="flowLayout" >
  <format align="center" hspace="10" vspace="10"
    top="0" left="0" width="80%" height="220" />
  <cell id="c1"   width="100" height="50"/>
  <cell id="c2"   width="50"  height="60"/>
  <cell id="c3"   width="100" height="30"/>
  <cell id="c4"   width="70"  height="50"/>
  <focus   focusIndex="1"/>
</layout>
```

Figura 3: Exemplo do código para o flowLayout.

gridLayout.

O leiaute definido pelo tipo *gridLayout* cria regiões em formato de grade. Para isso, são definidas as quantidades de linhas e colunas da grade. O preenchimento da grade é feito da esquerda para a direita e de cima para baixo. Ainda que a quantidade de objetos de mídia seja inferior à quantidade de regiões definidas, as regiões são criadas. A grade será sempre construída no centro da região-pai e, portanto, não terá o atributo *align* como no elemento *flowLayout*. Cada elemento *gridLayout* pode ainda definir elementos filhos para estabelecer o comportamento do leiaute. O elemento filho **cell** não é necessário nesse leiaute, pois as características de cada célula são derivadas da própria grade. Os atributos possíveis para o elemento *format* são: *width, height, top, left, right, bottom, hspace, vspace, columns* e *rows*. Já para o elemento *focus* os atributos possíveis são: *focusIndex, moveUp, moveDown, moveLeft* e *moveRight*. Um exemplo de utilização desse leiaute pode ser visualizado pelo código apresentado na Figura 4.

```
<layout id="L2" type="gridLayout">
  <format top="5" left="0" width="80%"
    height="220" columns="3" rows="2"
    hspace="10" vspace="10" />
  <focus focusIndex="1" />
</layout>
```

Figura 4: Exemplo do código para o gridLayout.

É importante ressaltar que os leiautes apresentados nessa seção também podem ser usados em conjunto para formar um padrão de regiões mais elaborado. A Seção 4 apresenta um exemplo de utilização conjunto de leiautes.

4. EXEMPLOS DE UTILIZAÇÃO DO ELEMENTO LAYOUT

Com o intuito de prototipar a utilização do elemento *layout*, a linguagem XTemplate 3.0 [6], em conjunto com seu processador foi alterado para possibilitar a definição deste elemento, bem como seu uso por componentes do *template*. As Figuras 5 e 6 mostram o leiaute e seu respectivo código.

No exemplo[2] (Figuras 5 e 6), a tela exibida utiliza a definição de dois *layouts* diferentes para compor sua estrutura. Um elemento *flowLayout* com três células ocupa a parte superior da tela de exibição, enquanto que um elemento *gridLayout* é utilizado na parte inferior. Ainda é possível perce-

[2]Aplicação álbum de fotos turísticas do Maranhão. Autoria: laboratório LAWS http://www.laws.deinf.ufma.br

ber uma imagem ao fundo que pode ser inserida utilizando-se qualquer um dos *layouts* ou descrevendo diretamente a região NCL no *template*.

Figura 5: Exemplo de aplicação que usa vários *Layouts*

```
...
<layout id="F1" type="flowLayout" >
  <format align="center" hspace="10" vspace="10"
    top="20" left="10" width="780"
    height="440"/>
  <cell id="c1" width="50" height="20"/>
  <cell id="c2" width="650" height="420"/>
  <cell id="c3" width="50" height="20"/>
    <focus focusIndex="1" moveDown="2" moveUp="2"/>
</layout>
<layout id="G2" type="gridLayout" >
  <format top="450" left="80" width="670"
    height="130" columns="5" rows="1"
    hspace="10" vspace="0" />
    <focus focusIndex="2" moveDown="1" moveUp="1"/>
</layout>

<region id="rgfundo" top="0" left="0" width="100%"
  height="100%">
...
```

Figura 6: Exemplo de código usado para gerar a tela da Figura 5

É possível perceber que a utilização dos elementos de *layout* facilita a definição do *template* e diminui a probabilidade de erros decorrentes de identificação incorreta das regiões ou emprego inapropriado de atributos. No exemplo, mesmo utilizando mais de um leiaute para construir a tela, o código fica mais simples e menor do que comparado à definição de regiões e descritores diretamente em NCL.

5. CONCLUSÕES

A definição de modelos de leiaute adaptativos é bastante útil, pois permite a definição de conjuntos de regiões e parâmetros de exibição que facilitam a autoria do *template*. Este artigo apresentou um elemento *layout*, que tem como objetivo fornecer a facilidade de definição de leiautes espaciais adaptativos. É importante ressaltar que esta facilidade não é apresentada por nenhuma linguagem para autoria de *templates* para documentos hipermídia.

Neste artigo foram apresentados dois tipos de leiautes: *flowLayout* e *gridLayout*, que têm comportamento similar aos componentes de leiaute oferecidos pela linguagem Java. Através da comparação dos códigos XML utilizados para representar *templates* com e sem a utilização dos elementos de leiaute, pode-se verificar a facilidade promovida pelo uso de leiautes adaptativos, principalmente em aplicações com uma grande quantidade de mídias visuais.

Como trabalhos futuros, pode-se citar a implementação de leiautes aninhados. Além disso, algumas facilidades podem ser acrescentadas ao elemento *layout*, como por exemplo a possibilidade de definição de qual célula deve ser utilizada para realizar a navegação entre elementos de leiaute distintos. Paralelamente uma avaliação massiva de usabilidade do elemento *layout* deverá ser feita, possibilitando detectar pontos que possam ser aperfeiçoados, bem como novos tipos de leiaute que possam ser oferecidos.

6. REFERÊNCIAS

[1] D. H. D. Bezerra, D. M. T. Sousa, G. L. S. Filho, A. M. F. Burlamaqui, and I. R. M. Silva. LUAR: A Language for Agile Development of NCL Templates and Documents. In *Webmedia*, 2012.

[2] I. M. Bilasco, J. Gensel, and M. Villanova-Oliver. STAMP: a model for generating adaptable multimedia presentations. *Journal of Multimedia Tools and Applications*, 25(3), Março 2005.

[3] J. R. Damasceno, J. A. F. dos Santos, and D. C. Muchaluat-Saade. EDITEC: Editor Gráfico de Templates de Composição para Facilitar a Autoria de Programas para TV Digital Interativas. In *WebMedia*, 2010.

[4] P. Deitel and H. Deitel. *How to Program: Early Objects, 9ª Edition*. Pearson Education, 2012.

[5] R. Deltour and C. Roisin. The limsee3 Multimedia Authoring Model. In *DocEng*, 2006.

[6] J. A. F. dos Santos and D. C. Muchaluat-Saade. XTemplate 3.0: spatio-temporal semantics and structure reuse for hypermedia compositions. *Journal of Multimedia Tools and Applications*, 61(3), Dezembro 2012.

[7] O. Gaggi and A. Celentano. A Laboratory for Prototyping and Testing Multimedia Presentations. *International Journal of Software Engineering and Knowledge Engineering*, 16(4):615–642, 2006.

[8] D. C. Muchaluat-Saade and L. F. G. Soares. XConnector & XTemplate: Improving the Expressiveness and Reuse in Web Authoring Languages. *The New Review of Hypermedia and Multimedia Journal, Taylor Graham Publisher*, 8, 2002.

[9] C. S. Neto, H. F. Pinto, and L. F. G. Soares. TAL Processor of Hypermedia Applications. In *DocEng*, 2012.

[10] E. Schrier, M. Dontcheva, C. Jacobs, G. Wade, and D. Salesin. Adaptive layout for dynamically aggregated documents. In *International conference on Intelligent user interfaces*, 2008.

[11] B. Signer, M. C. Norrie, N. Weibel, and A. Ispas. Advanced authoring of paper-digital systems. *Journal of Multimedia Tools and Applications*, Agosto 2012.

[12] L. F. G. Soares and S. D. J. Barbosa. *Programando em NCL 3.0: Desenvolvimento de Aplicações para Middleware Ginga, TV digital e Web*. Elsevier, 2009.

A Traffic Shaping Optimization Methodology for Web Systems

Caio Mesquita
Ulisses Cavalca
CEFET-MG
Computer Department
Belo Horizonte, MG, Brazil
caioboninho@gmail.com,
ulisses@ccc.cefetmg.br

Adriano C. M. Pereira
Federal University of
Minas Gerais (UFMG)
Dept. of Computer Science
Belo Horizonte, MG, Brazil
adrianoc@dcc.ufmg.br

Eduardo Carrano
Federal University of
Minas Gerais (UFMG)
Dept. of Electric Engineering
Belo Horizonte, MG, Brazil
egcarrano@ufmg.br

ABSTRACT

In recent years, computer networks have been characterized by heterogeneous traffic and dynamic management of different kinds of services. The web and network requirements have increased within time and, since bandwidth is limited, it becomes necessary to employ optimization procedures in order to make the network able to operate in its full capacity. Traffic shaping mechanisms implement Quality of Service (QoS) concepts to ensure acceptable service levels. This paper describes an approach for traffic shaping optimization. It is proposed a methodology based on throughput and packet loss optimization using genetic algorithms. This method was validated using actual data from a network infrastructure of a Public Educational Institution.

Categories and Subject Descriptors

C.2.3 [**Network Operations**]: Network management

Keywords

QoS, traffic shaping, optimization, World Wide Web, Internet Services

1. INTRODUÇÃO

Qualidade de Serviço (Qos) é um princípio para garantir robustez, escalabilidade, confiança e disponibilidade nos recursos das redes de computadores e web. Largura de banda é um recurso finito, apesar de alguns usuários de corporações terem uma visão contrária. Contratos de largura de banda podem ser expressivamente grandes em relação com a real carga de trabalho, o que implica em um elevado custo financeiro. Apesar do número de usuários e da demanda de serviços crescerem de acordo com o desenvolvimento de novas tecnologias, a largura de banda e outros recursos de rede precisam ser otimizados, de forma a minimizar o custo e maximizar a qualidade da rede.

Numericamente, redes que não atingem 100% de uso não requerem mecanismos de QoS [22, 15], nem *traffic shaping* (modelagem de tráfego). Teoricamente, a largura de banda disponível atende toda a demanda de tráfego no ambiente da rede. Entretanto, soluções de *traffic shaping* precisam ser robustas o bastante para lidar com qualquer comportamento desconhecido e demandas imprevistas. Esta visão propõe um equilíbrio entre a carga de tráfego real e largura de banda que seja suficiente viável. Em outras palavras, o ambiente da rede tem que ser configurado com uma taxa de valor máximo em que não ocorra congestionamento, e a modelagem de tráfego possa otimizar a demanda e perda de pacotes para os serviços.

Na mesma visão, redes congestionadas representam um desafio no gerenciamento de rede e no desempenho de *traffic shaping*. Soluções de Qualidade de Serviço não resolvem, em alguns casos, redes congestionadas, transmissões com atraso, e perda de pacotes. Embora esforços e ações sejam tomados no contexto de gerenciamento de redes, há cenários em que aumento de largura de banda é necessário. Isso ocorre quando a demanda da rede é muito superior do que os seus recursos podem oferecer.

Métodos de otimização, seja em abordagem mono ou multiobjetivo, têm sido amplamente utilizados na alocação eficiente de recursos e tomada de decisão. Técnicas de inteligência artificial [12, 10], tais como por exemplo Redes Neurais, Lógica Fuzzy, e Computação Evolucionária, representam métodos para maximar o desempenho e minimizar os custos. Naturalmente, a combinação desses métodos pode ser aplicada no contexto de gerenciamento do desempenho dos recursos da rede.

Esse trabalho aborda a necessidade de gerenciar e otimizar o desempenho de recursos Web, como por exemplo streaming de vídeo e áudio, P2P e aplicações Web 2.0. Propomos uma metodologia para modelagem de tráfego usando otimização multiobjetivo. O mecanismo de modelagem de tráfego implementa os conceitos de Qualidade de Serviço e usa a demanda oferecida (to_i) e perda de pacotes (d_i) como variáveis de decisão, sob demanda de tráfego td_i. A principal contribuição desse trabalho inclui uma metodologia para caracterizar, identificar e otimizar os parâmetros da modelagem de tráfego, como por exemplo taxa garantida (ar_i), limite de taxa (c_i), e prioridade (p_i) para cada classe i diferenciada de tráfego. Além disso, o trabalho propõe uma metodologia que pode ser aplicada em todos os mecanismos de modelagem de tráfego, que considera taxa garantida, limite de taxa, e prioridade como parâmetros de operação. Foi criado um conjunto de ferramentas (QoS-Tools) [1] para a emulação dos experimentos. Realizamos um estudo de caso utilizando o ambiente do CEFET-MG. Os resultados obtidos mostraram uma melhora no desempenho da rede utilizando as técnicas para otimização.

O restante deste artigo está organizado da seguinte forma. A Seção 2 apresenta os trabalhos relacionados. A seção 3 apresenta a metodologia proposta, com foco nas etapas de otimização. A seção 4 ilustra resultados obtidos no desenvolvimento dessa pesquisa, usando dados reais de um parque computacional institucional. Por fim, a Seção 5 apresenta a conclusão e trabalhos futuros.

2. TRABALHOS RELACIONADOS

Next Generation Network (NGN) inclui o conceito de *triple play*, em que considera vídeo, áudio e dados no mesmo ambiente de transmissão. Transferência baseada em pacotes, serviços convergentes, e capacidades de Qualidade de Serviço caracterizam NGNs no contexto de novas demandas em redes IP [13]. Além disso, futuras práticas no cenário de gerenciamento de rede sugerem equipamentos auto gerenciáveis, desempenho dinâmico e soluções baseadas em sistemas bioinspirados [7].

Soluções de QoS são classificadas como implementação de modelos IntServ (*Integrated Services*) and DiffServ (*Differentiated Services*). Os mecanismos de QoS IntServ, descritos pelo RFC 1633 [3], tem como principal característica a reserva antecipada de recursos para requisições individuais no ambiente de rede. Sua principal aplicação está concentrada em aplicações ou serviços de tempo real, que requerem um nível aceitável de serviço. O *IntServ* é uma arquitetura de QoS, implementada em grande parte dos roteadores, que garante a qualidade de serviço para conexões fim-a-fim. . DiffServ (RFC 2475 [2]) é definida pela solução de QoS em que os fluxos de conexão de rede podem ser agrupados em classes de tráfego. Em relação ao *IntServ*, o *DiffServ* se destaca como solução de QoS por ser uma arquitetura escalável e flexível. Qualquer mudança no ambiente e nos requisitos de qualidade de serviço, a partir da consideração de novos serviços, pode ser aplicada a partir de uma nova redefinição das regras do *DiffServ*. Por outro lado, em relação ao *IntServ*, o *DiffServ* não prevê, explicitamente, como os recursos de rede devem ser garantidos. A RFC 2475 [2] provê, basicamente, uma regulamentação na marcação e classificação dos pacotes relativos à serviços de rede que possuem maior prioridade.. Adicionalmente, as recomendações ITU-T Y.1291[1] discutem um *framework* para suporte de QoS em redes baseadas em pacotes. RFC 2212 [19] discute sobre a especificação da garantida de qualidade de serviço. Esse documento descreve uma abordagem para assegurar a larguda de banda e atraso nas conexões fim a fim e define os requisitos dos elementos da rede.

Canfora [4] introduz uma otimização de atributo de QoS aplicável em um grande número de cenários de rede. A função objetivo proposta combina os seguintes atributos de QoS: custo, tempo de resposta, disponibilidade e confiança. Programação inteira e algoritmos genéticos são aplicados para otimizar o problema, que é um problema NP-Difícil. Os algoritmos genéticos têm demonstrado bons resultados quand comparados com a programação inteira.

Yao and Chen[21] discutem o problema de otimização de QoS, em que consideram preço, tempo de resposta, disponibilidade , rendimento e reputação como atributos. O modelo de avaliação do QoS, em uma abordagem multiobjetiva, é representado por um vetor em uma função de serviço único. A principal contribuição é a aplicação do algoritmo *Nondominated Sorting Genetic Algorithm-II*(NSGA-II) na avaliação de soluções candidatas.

Rosemberg[18]reintroduz os atributos de QoS como um problema NP-difícil. Esse artigo define uma otimização meta-heurística para ser aplicada no problema de QoS, que pode ser implementado com Algoritmos Genéticos (GA), busca tabu (TS), e *Simulated Annealing* (SA). Além disso, os parâmetros de QoS desse trabalho são distribuídos em duas categorias, como atributos operacionais e negócios relacionados. Esta classificação aumenta em grande escala em serviço composição, como proposto pelos autores.

Pop[16] otimiza os atributos de QoS como, por exemplo, tempo de resposta, confiança, disponibilidade e custo. A principal contribuição é a implementação do *Differential Evolution* (DE), um algoritmo para esse tipo de problema. Suciu [20]compara SPEA e NSGA-II em uma abordagem de otimização multiobjetiva para QoS. Esse trabalho inclui tempo de resposta, classificação, disponibilidade e custo como atributos de QoS.

Chu and Lea [5] propõe um algoritmo de busca heurístico para resolver o problema de congestionamento mínimo, no contexto de encaminhamento entre os roteadores. O trabalho se concentra na otimização do QoS DiffServ e foca-se em achar as configuraçõs ótimas nos pesos dos *links*. O algoritmo usa uma busca interativa de duas fases: na primeira fase, os pesos dos *links* são dados para achar a pior matriz de tráfego; na segunda fase a matriz de tráfego é usada para achar as configurações dos novos pesos.

Uma implementação de computação evolutiva é proposta por Qaraawy [17] utilizando o método otimização de colônia de partículas (PSO). Nesse artigo é proposto um modelo de controlador PI c um algoritmo AQM para evitar congestionamento em redes de computadores. O controlador PI baseado em PSO fornece desempenho em diferentes cenários de redes congestionadas.

Os trabalhos relacionados aqui citados foram úteis no auxílio a uma definição mais clara da proposta de metodologia para modelagem de tráfego e QoS em redes de computadores. Além disso, outros trabalhos foram importantes para nos auxiliar em nossa proposta de otimização, inclusive determinando outras oportunidades futuras de extensão da abordagem aqui proposta e validada. Até onde temos conhecimento não existe um trabalho similar na literatura ao aqui proposto, o que caracteriza um aspecto inovador de nossa metodologia e técnica adotados, bem como impossibilita uma comparação direta com outras abordagens.

3. METODOLOGIA

Esta seção discute a classificação das classes de tráfego, modelo de carga de trabalho em redes de computadores, e limitações de *traffic shaping*. Além disso, apresenta o problema da modelagem de tráfego e os passos da metodologia proposta.

3.1 Discussão

A metodologia requer a classificação da demanda do tráfego de entrada e saída td_i, ordenada por serviço ou locali-

---

[1]disponível em http://sourceforge.net/projects/qostools/files/

zação, tais como serviços Web, DNS, SMTP, IP de origem e destino, dentre outros. Cada classificação corresponde uma classe de tráfego ct_i, ao qual possui atributos associados, tais como taxa de transmissão garantida ar_i, taxa máxima de transmissão ct_i e prioridade p_i.

Gerenciadores de filas ativas (AQM - Active Queue Managements), especialmente a implementação *Random Early Detection* (RED), fundamentam diversos estudos sobre análise do TCP. [9] propõem, em uma abordagem teórica, um modelo dinâmico não linear do comportamento do protocolo TCP para múltiplos fluxos. Esse trabalho considera os parâmetros da rede como por exemplo capacidade do link, tempo de carga de ida e volta, além de cenários congestionados. Adicionalmente, [11] linearizam o modelo dinâmico de Hollot, incluindo suporte de tráfego UDP. Mesmo com o RED como algoritmo de AQM, os autores realizaram simulações e avaliações através do Network Simulator 2 [14].

Embora estes trabalhos sugiram um modelo dinâmico para fluxos TCP e UDP, a metodologia proposta aborda a otimização da modelagem de tráfego em um intervalo de tempo estático δ_i. Pedidos feitos em δ_{i-1} refletem no desempenho da rede em δ_i, similarmente, pedidos feitos em δ_i refletem no intervalo δ_{i+1}. A otimização da modelagem de táfego X_i^* considera configurações ótimas somente no intervalo de tempo δ_i, e soluções ótimas X_j^* para δ_j precisam ser determinadas separadamente. Após uma análise estatística, como teste de variância (ANOVA), consideraremos $X_i^* = X_j^*$ se, e somente se, as características de tráfego nos instantes δ_i e δ_j forem idênticas.

O volume de tráfego do protocolo TCP é expressivo na maioria dos ambientes de rede, e consequentemente, o seu mecanismo de funcionamento representa um modelo dinâmico. A metodologia proposta otimiza os parâmetros de *traffic shaping* em um intervalo de tempo estático δ_i. Portanto, nessa metodologia proposta, não há a necessidade de diferencição do tráfego para protocolos de transmissão, tais como TCP, UDP e ICMP, para cada instante de tempo δ_i. A metodologia requer um volume de tráfego para cada classe de tráfego c_i, garantido pelo modelo CBR (Constant Bit Rate) de geração de carga.

Esse trabalho aborda a otimização dos parâmetros de QoS como um problema empírico, e considera o mecanismo de *traffic shaping* como modelo caixa preta. Para qualquer tipo de controle de tráfego que tem associado taxa de transmissão garantida (ar_i), taxa de transmissão máxima (c_i) e prioridade (p_i) como parâmetros de QoS, essa metodologia é robusta o bastante para ser aplicada. Vale ressaltar que esse trabalho adota o HTB como solução de *traffic shaping* em ambientes GNU/Linux.

3.2 Modelagem do problema

Seja um volume de tráfego T em um ambiente com a largura de banda L, classificado em diferentes classes de tráfego $ct_1, ct_2, \ldots, ct_i, \ldots, ct_n$. A taxa garantida ar_i, limite de taxa c_i e prioridade p_i caracterizam cada classe ct_i. Em cada intervalo de tempos δ_i considerado *throughput* td_i como carga na demanda de rede para cada classe ct_i, em que $\sum td_i = T$ representa o total da carga de trabalho. O mecanismo de *traffic shaping* fornece um *throughput* to_i, e em cenários congestionados, observa-se a perda de pacote assumidas por d_i. A Figura 1 ilustra o modelo proposto para otimização de *traffic shaping*.

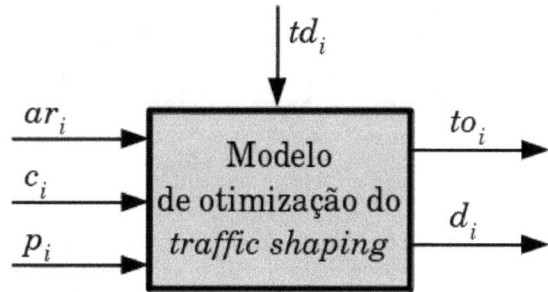

Figure 1: Modelo proposto para otimização de modelagem de tráfego

Como garantia de melhor esforço no ambiente de rede, a otimização de *traffic shaping* requer as seguintes restrições:

$$c_i = L \tag{1}$$

$$0 < ar_i \leq L \tag{2}$$

$$\sum_{i=1}^{n} ar_i = L \tag{3}$$

A taxa de transferência máxima c_i para todas as classes de tráfego possui o mesmo valor de largura de banda L (Equação 1). Todas as taxas garantidas devem ser contidas no intervalo $(0, L]$ (Equação 2) e a soma corresponde com a largura de banda L (Equação 3).

3.3 Etapas

Essa subseção representa as 5 etapas para a metodologia proposta, resumida na Figura 2.

3.3.1 *Caracterização do tráfego*

A etapa de caracterização da metodologia proposta tem como meta colher informações suficientemente representativas para a emulação do tráfego, etapa subsequente do método proposto. Essa coleta de dados permite, em um primeiro momento, um melhor entendimento e domínio do ambiente de rede avaliado. As variáveis de interesse no contexto da otimização de *traffic shaping* são: *throughput*, pacotes enviados, pacotes com erros/descartados e latência. As implementações dessa etapa foram feitas através de ferramentas como Cacti1, Zabbix2 ou até mesmo pelo protocolo SNMP, para obter informações descritivas do ambiente de rede. Essas ferramentas obtêm métricas de redes, tais como *throughput*, pacotes enviados, utilização do processador e consumo de memória. A metodologia proposta requer somente o *throughput* demandado td_i para cada classe de tráfego ct_i, em um intervalo de tempo predeterminado δ_i.

3.3.2 *Emulação de tráfego*

Esta etapa consiste na emulação do tráfego, com o objetivo de reproduzir as mesmas características do ambiente de rede em produção, para uma determinada carga de trabalho. A etapa prevê que dados de experimentação do tráfego, que caracterizam *throughput* e percentual de perda de pacotes, sejam capturados e utilizados posteriormente como conjunto de dados de treinamento na Identificação do Modelo. A Figura 3 ilustra o ambiente de teste com máquinas

Etapa A		Etapa B		Etapa C		Etapa D		Etapa E
Caracterização de tráfego	⇒	Emulação de tráfego	⇒	Identificação do modelo	⇒	Otimização	⇒	Análise

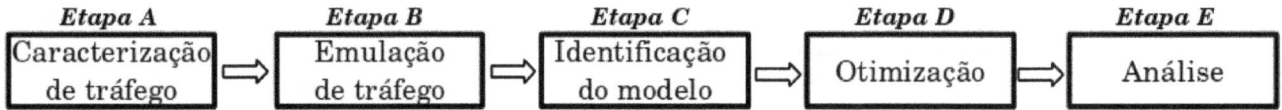

Figure 2: Etapas da metodologia proposta

virtuais (VM) implementado nessa proposta, ao qual será obtido um conjunto de dados relativo ao tráfego emulado, para que possa ser aplicado na etapa de identificação de modelo. $VM - 1$ e $VM - 3$ representam respectivamente a demanda da rede local e a Web. $VM - 2$ implementa o mecanismo de *traffic shaping* (HTB), através da ferramenta *traffic control*[2].

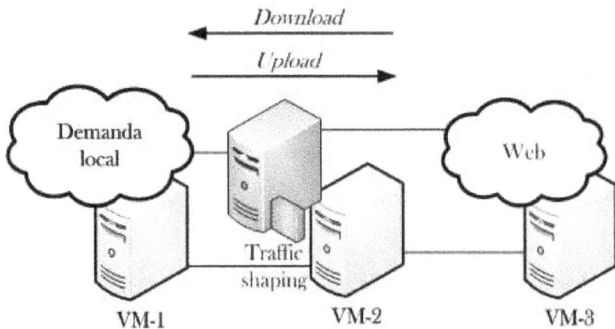

Figure 3: Ambiente de teste

No ambiente de teste, $VM - 1$ e $VM - 3$ geram respectivamente tráfego de entrada e de saída através do iperf [3]. O volume de tráfego demandado (td_i) será implementado pelo modelo CBR (Constant Bit Rate), através de transmissão com o protocolo UDP. Na $VM - 1$ as ferramentas de QoS desenvolvidas nesse trabalho geram, por meio de simulação de Monte Carlo, valores de taxa garantida (ar_i) e prioridade (p_i). Cada execução leva aproximadamente 2 minutos, em que 1 minuto é dedicado para configuração de cada iteração. Um cenário a ser avaliado espera, no mínimo, 2000 amostras para a etapa de identificação do modelo.

3.3.3 Identificação do modelo

A etapa de identificação do modelo matemático contempla a obtenção de função de aproximação que descreve o comportamento e funcionamento do mecanismo de *traffic shaping*. No contexto desse trabalho, o *Hierarchical Token Bucket* (HTB) será o mecanismo de *traffic shaping* a ser modelado. Sob o ponto de vista analítico, o HTB contém uma função de alocação de recurso de banda entre as classes de tráfego, o que, a princípio, elimina a necessidade dessa etapa. Entretanto, o *traffic control* não oferece métricas suficientes para a reconstrução do funcionamento analítico do HTB. Dessa forma, o seu comportamento será visto como um modelo caixa preta, podendo ser aplicado a qualquer mecanismo de *traffic shaping* que necessite de uma taxa de transmissão garantida (ar_i), taxa de transmissão máxima

[2]traffic control: http://tldp.org/HOWTO/ Traffic-Control-HOWTO/, acessado em 20 de Agosto de 2012

[3]iperf: http://sourceforge.net/projects/iperf/, acessado em 20 de Agosto de 2012

(c_i) e prioridade(p_i), submetidos à uma demanda de *throughput* (td_i). Como extrapolação da aplicação de toda a metodologia, essa etapa de identificação de modelo permite que qualquer mecanismos de QoS do tipo *DiffServ*, em conexões ponto a ponto, seja identificado. Dado um caso de uso com n classes de tráfego, a arquitetura das redes adaptativas empregadas nesta etapa terão n entradas, compostas por $ar_1, \ldots, ar_n$, e uma única saída descrita pelo *throughput* ofertado e percentual de perda de pacote. Consequentemente, a metodologia empregará n modelos para *throughput* ofertado e outros n modelos para percentual de perda de pacotes. A modelagem com n entradas e 1 saída tem como objetivo minimizar o erro de treinamento e validação dos modelos. Foi obtido então um modelo empírico e representativo do funcionamento de *traffic shaping* (HTB), por meio de uma função aproximada por uma Rede Neural Artificial *Multilayer Perceptron* (MLP) [8]. Para implementações com MLP, foram avaliados modelos com 3, 5, 10, 12, 15, 20, 25 e 30 neurônios na camada escondida, utilizando o algoritmo *Levenberg-Marquardt*, com taxa de aprendizado de 0,3, durante 1000 épocas. Vale ressaltar que esses parâmetros foram adotados com base nas configurações usualmente aplicadas em problemas que empregam redes adaptativas. Após uma bateria de experimentos, decidimos que para cada variável de saída, um modelo de rede neural com 5 neurônios na camada oculta será treinado 30 vezes. Os critérios de parada do processo de treinamento são 10^{-8} para erro de treinamento e gradiente, e 2000 épocas. A escolha da melhor rede neural de aproximação será feita em função do menor erro de validação. Esse modelo obtido é essencial para o processo de otimização, considerando que a avaliação de soluções candidatas requer um tempo de simulação praticamente inaceitável.

3.3.4 Otimização

Nessa etapa são implementadas variações de algoritmo genético para otimização mono objetivo de *throughput* e perda de pacotes, conforme apresentados na Tabela 1. O algoritmo genético implementa como método de seleção o *Stochastic Universal Sampling* (SUS) e o torneio binário, o cruzamento será através de interpolação real e *Simulated Binary Crossover* (SBX), e a mutação gaussiana e polinomial. A recombinação da população tem caráter elitista, onde apenas n indivíduos da população combinada entre pais e filhos irão compor a próxima geração. Essas variações visam avaliar o melhor desempenho do algoritmo para o problema de otimização de dados no contexto deste trabalho.

A otimização mono objetivo do *throughput* ofertado possui a função de avaliação descrita na Equação 4. A relação TO_i/TD_i indica o desempenho do *throughput* ofertado pelo *throughput* demandado para a classe de tráfego i. Valores de TO_i/TD_i próximos de 1 implicam no atendimento da classe de tráfego i, assim como TO_i/TD_i menores que 1 representam ambientes super demandados. Cada relação possui sua relevância associada aos pesos ω_i, que representa os valo-

Table 1: Variações dos algoritmos genéticos propostos

Variação	Seleção	Cruzamento	Mutação
AG-1	*Stochastic Universal Sampling* (SUS)	Interpolação real	Gaussiana
AG-2	*Stochastic Universal Sampling* (SUS)	Interpolação real	Polinomial
AG-3	*Stochastic Universal Sampling* (SUS)	*Simulated Binary Crossover* (SBX)	Gaussiana
AG-4	*Stochastic Universal Sampling* (SUS)	*Simulated Binary Crossover* (SBX)	Polinomial
AG-5	Torneio binário	Interpolação real	Gaussiana
AG-6	Torneio binário	Interpolação real	Polinomial
AG-7	Torneio binário	*Simulated Binary Crossover* (SBX)	Gaussiana
AG-8	Torneio binário	*Simulated Binary Crossover* (SBX)	Polinomial

res de prioridades $[1, n]$ normalizados entre $[1, 0]$. Como a otimização dessa variável contempla a maximização do *throughput* ofertado F^{TO}, na implementação dos algoritmos genéticos otimizar *throughput* ofertado equivale minimizar $-F^{TO}$.

$$F^{TO} = \sum_{i=1}^{n} \omega_i \frac{TO_i}{TD_i} \qquad (4)$$

Analogamente a Equação 5 apresenta a função de avaliação F^{PP} para minimização do percentual de perda de pacote PP_i. Cada PP_i de cada classe de tráfego i possui relevância associada aos pesos ω_i, compostos pelos valores de prioridades $[1, n]$ normalizados entre $[1, 0]$.

$$F^{PP} = \sum_{i=1}^{n} \omega_i PP_i \qquad (5)$$

A execução dos algoritmos genéticos prevê uma população de 100 indivíduos, avaliados ao longo de 200 gerações. Cada variação de algoritmos será executada 33 vezes, para que seja analisado a média das melhores soluções. A probabilidade de cruzamento será de 80% e a probabilidade de mutação 0,01% por variável. Ao final de cada execução será realizada uma busca local a partir da melhor solução encontrada. Essa busca local é definida por 1000 execuções da mutação polinomial sobre o melhor indivíduo, sendo substituído caso uma melhor solução seja encontrada. Cabe ressaltar que os parâmetros de execução dos algoritmos genéticos foram selecionados de acordo com as melhores práticas empregadas em computação evolucionária.

3.3.5 Análise

Esta etapa consiste na análise das variações de algoritmos genéticos implementadas na etapa de otimização. Adicionalmente é desejável a consideração de diferentes valores de largura de banda L, onde torna-se possível avaliar os parâmetros de configuração otimizados sob os diversos cenários de operação, em termos de capacidade de transmissão. Para uma infraestrutura de *traffic shaping* já existente, a análise também contempla a verificação entre os parâmetros operacionais definidos manualmente e as configurações ótimas encontradas na etapa de otimização. O conjunto de soluções obtido na etapa de otimização, analisados nessa etapa, permite a tomada de decisão para aplicação do melhor conjunto de configuração de *traffic shaping*.

4. ESTUDO DE CASO

A metodologia proposta foi aplicada em um estudo de caso real, observado na rede local do CEFET-MG. A infraestrutura dessa rede inclui serviços Web, DNS e de banco de dados, além de fornecer conexão à Internet para aproximadamente 1200 clientes. A ferramenta Cacti é usada para executar o gerenciamento da rede, além do *tc* na garantia do *traffic shaping* através do *HTB*.

Atualmente o CEFET-MG possui uma largura de banda de 1Gbps. Entretanto, o ambiente já operou com largura de banda de 6Mbps até fevereiro de 2012, para a mesma demanda de tráfego. Obviamente, esse cenário resultava em um ambiente bem congestionado. A solução de *traffic shaping* não era suficiente para assegurar níveis aceitáveis de serviço, o que motivou o desenvolvimento deste trabalho.

A demanda total de rede de dados do CEFET-MG foi dividida em 6 classes de tráfego, conforme apresentado na Tabela 2, que mostra os valores de *throughput* demandado na rede de dados para o dia 20 de setembro de 2012, de 12h às 13h, que serão utilizados como referência na aplicação da metodologia de otimização neste trabalho.

Neste trabalho, a implementação da metodologia para otimização dos parâmetros de *traffic shaping* considera 6 instâncias de testes, diferenciadas na largura de banda da infraestrutura de rede: INST-B1 - 36Mbps; INST-B2 - 30Mbps; INST-B3 - 24Mbps; INST-B4 - 18Mbps; INST-B5 - 12Mbps; INST-B6 - 6Mbps. A proposição dessas 6 instâncias de testes visa avaliar a alocação de recursos de transmissão de dados, de maneira que seja possível obter níveis de serviço aceitáveis com a implantação ótima de *traffic shaping*. Como a carga de tráfego de entrada e de saída é respectivamente 29,640 Mbps e 2,756 Mbps, o volume de tráfego de entrada torna-se objeto de otimização desta metodologia por representar um cenário congestionado e passível de aplicação de Qualidade de Serviço. A instância INST-B6 com largura de banda de 6Mbps será analisada mais detalhadamente, por representar o cenário de rede do CEFET-MG até fevereiro de 2012.

4.1 Otimização

Nesta seção são apresentados os resultados da identificação do modelo e otimização, conforme apresentados nas seções 3.3.3 e 3.3.4. Como a implementação da otimização de *traffic shaping* considera 6 classes de tráfego serão necessários 12 modelos de redes neurais para aproximação de função de *throughput* ofertado (to_i) e perda de pacotes (pp_i). A partir da Tabela 2 verifica-se que as classes de tráfego 20 e 30 possuem demanda muito maior que a largura de banda disponível (L= 6Mbps). Dessa forma, para o tráfego de entrada

Table 2: Tráfego em 20.set - 12h às 13h (granularidade 1 hora)

Classes de tráfego	Prioridade	Download [Kbps]		Upload [Kbps]	
10: Servidores locais	3	114	0,38%	199	7,22%
20: Web: Tráfego HTTP	4	15.160	51,15%	1.897	68,83%
30: Web: Redes sociais	6	13.357	45,06%	543	19,70%
40: CEFET-MG Web	1	159	0,54%	36	1,31%
50: CEFET-MG sistemas	2	801	2,70%	71	2,58%
60: Tráfego não classificado	5	49	0,17%	10	0,36%
Total		29.640	100,00%	2.756	100,00%

Table 3: Erro de treinamento e validação das redes neurais (INST-B6, *download*)

Variável	Erro		Variável	Erro	
	Treinamento	Validação		Treinamento	Validação
td_{10}	0,0075	0,0092	pl_{10}	0,0000	0,0000
td_{20}	0,0240	0,0259	pl_{20}	0,0172	0,0192
td_{30}	0,0246	0,0253	pl_{30}	0,0220	0,0238
td_{40}	0,0056	0,0075	pl_{40}	0,0000	0,0000
td_{50}	0,0003	0,0005	pl_{50}	0,0004	0,0000
td_{60}	0,0009	0,0072	pl_{60}	0,0000	0,0000

do ambiente, as redes neurais provenientes dessas classes de tráfego (td_{20}, td_{30}, pl_{20} e pl_{30}) possuem maior erro de treinamento e validação, conforme Tabela 3.

Após a obtenção dos modelos de aproximação de função, a partir da rede neural com menor erro de validação, as variações de algoritmos genéticos são aplicados para busca dos parâmetros ótimos de configuração. Conforme a função de avaliação do *throughput* ofertado (Equação 4), dado que todas as relações TO_i/TD_i sejam atendidas, o valor ótimo de cada solução será $-\sum \omega_i$. Como ω é o valor normalizado das prioridades das classes de tráfego, $\omega =$ [0,66 0,50 0,16 1 0,83 0,33], logo o valor de avaliação ótimo será $-3,5$. A Tabela 4 apresenta as melhores soluções encontradas para cada variação de algoritmo genético, além dos valores de referência da configuração manual de *traffic shaping* aplicado no CEFET-MG. Nessa implementação, a variação com seleção por SUS, cruzamento por SBX e mutação polinomial (AG-4) obteve o melhor desempenho.

Analogamente, as variações de algoritmos genéticos foram implementadas para otimização da perda de pacote. A função de avaliação da perda de pacotes (Equação 5) possui valor ótimo igual a 0. A Tabela 5 apresenta os resultados obtidos na otimização dessa variável e os valores de configuração manual do CEFET-MG, onde o algoritmo genético 4 (AG-4) novamente obteve melhor desempenho.

O efeito produzido pela otimização de *traffic shaping* reside no pronto atendimento das classes de tráfego com maior prioridade. Embora o HTB possua implicitamente esse comportamento na alocação de banda, o processo de otimização dos parâmetros de configuração forçou a oferta de *throughput* para as classes mais relevantes. A Figura 4 ilustra a alocação acumulada de largura de banda, a medida que cada classe de tráfego é atendida em função da sua prioridade. Pode-se observar que o *throughput* ofertado foi praticamente alocado para a classe de tráfego com prioridade 4. Analogamente, a perda de pacote foi diminuída a partir da classe de tráfego com prioridade 4. A metodologia foi realizada adotando

procedimentos estatísticos necessários para garantir sua validade em termos de validação e consistência do modelo. Os ganhos se mostraram significativos, lembrando que em configurações de ambiente com menos classes de tráfego fica mais simples identificar as melhores soluções, porém isso fica mais complexo em ambientes mais diversificados e também com carga de trabalho sob condições que requerem melhor otimização do tráfego.

Cabe ressaltar que quanto maior a complexidade da rede, em termos de controle de tráfego e convergência de serviços, maior o valor do trabalho aqui proposto. A aplicação da metodologia concentra-se na garantia de recursos de conectividade para locais que atuam como provedores de acesso à Internet, serviços Web e *cloud computing*. Além disso, a caracterização do tráfego em função de janelas de tempo e heterogeneidade das requisições é um importante aliado na otimização de QoS.

5. CONCLUSÃO

Esse trabalho propõe uma nova metodologia para a otimização multiobjetivo de modelagem de tráfego. Em um cenário de Redes da Próxima Geração (NGN), incluindo serviços Web, a garantia de parâmetros de QoS é essencial para fornecer níveis aceitáveis de serviço.

A metodologia proposta inclui estimação de carga de tráfego, caracterização e emulação, otimização de parâmetros QoS e futuramente análise de soluções. Essa abordagem aumenta a aplicabilidade em ambientes com grandes demandas de tráfego, até mesmo em redes congestionadas, caracterizadas por tráfego híbrido. O modelo de identificação do mecanismo de *traffic shaping*, implementado por uma rede MLP, permite que se otimize qualquer ferramenta de modelagem de tráfego baseada em taxa de transmissão garantida, taxa de transmissão limite, e prioridade. A metodologia foi construída pensando em ser aplicada de forma dinâmica, mas a modelagem do problema e formas de aplicação real mostraram que esse dinamismo para ser viável precisa ser contem-

Table 4: *Assured rate* ótimo: INST-B6 *throughput* ofertado (*download*)

AG	Fitness	ar_{10}	ar_{20}	ar_{30}	ar_{40}	ar_{50}	ar_{60}	$\sum ar_i$
AG-1	-2,94089	1210,2	35,5	37,1	2369,6	1511,6	836	6.000
AG-2	-2,94411	1340,8	91,5	1200,7	2778,9	216,8	371,3	6.000
AG-3	-2,94508	3362	185,7	237	74,8	1806,6	333,9	6.000
AG-4	**-2,94586**	**3346,2**	**56,4**	**30**	**30,3**	**1820,3**	**716,7**	**6.000**
AG-5	-2,94008	1710,5	238,2	2010,3	886,7	92,6	1061,8	6.000
AG-6	-2,94426	1313,3	29,8	1184,4	2853,9	571,4	47,3	6.000
AG-7	-2,94420	1362,3	115,5	1236,8	2871,8	201,7	211,8	6.000
AG-8	-2,94554	3535,3	211,1	30	30,1	1772,8	420,6	6.000
CEFET-MG	-2,9193	500	3400	1000	500	500	100	6.000

Table 5: *Assured rate* ótimo: INST-B6 perda de pacote (*download*)

AG	Fitness	ar_{10}	ar_{20}	ar_{30}	ar_{40}	ar_{50}	ar_{60}	$\sum ar_i$
AG-1	0,46400	1195,4	84,6	2735,6	1425,1	541,4	17,9	6.000
AG-2	0,46189	30,9	30	2595,8	30	3092,5	220,9	6.000
AG-3	0,46152	1357	30	2190,2	2362,8	30	30	6.000
AG-4	**0,46119**	**1416,8**	**30**	**2960,6**	**1375,3**	**30**	**187,3**	**6.000**
AG-5	0,47106	920,1	1224,3	2377,1	1288,5	167,1	22,9	6.000
AG-6	0,46174	55,5	30	2617,6	30	3063,6	203,3	6.000
AG-7	0,46134	1403	30	2903	1439,5	49,8	174,7	6.000
AG-8	0,46170	64,5	30	2627,3	30	3071,3	176,9	6.000
CEFET-MG	0,5242	500	3400	1000	500	500	100	6.000

plado como uma aplicação em janelas, de forma contínua, da metodologia proposta. Isso se justifica para ter uma modelagem mais precisa e também para viabilizar a execução do método em termos de complexidade. Isso requer que a monitoração das cargas de trabalho sejam sempre realizadas (como já costuma ser feito por times de administração de infraestrutura de rede) e que a forma de uso da proposta deste trabalho seja contínua. A metodologia foi empregada em um estudo de caso real, oriundo do CEFET-MG.

O presente trabalho traz uma forte contribuição na combinação de duas técnicas de inteligência artificial para otimização de problemas. Além disso, a abordagem empírica e a modelagem matemática caixa preta fortalecem a aplicabilidade deste trabalho em ambientes reais. Os resultados apresentados na Seção 4 ilustram ganho no *throughput* ofertado e perda de pacote para classes de tráfego mais relevantes, em função da carga de tráfego no intervalo de tempo considerado.

Como trabalhos em andamento, o presente trabalho abre perspectivas para a otimização multiobjetivo de *throughput* ofertado e perda de pacote, além da consideração da métrica latência na otimização dos parâmetros de QoS. Essa abordagem permite ao administrador da rede a tomada de decisão mais fundamentada sobre qual configuração de *traffic shaping* utilizar. A otimização multiobjetivo que estamos adotando é baseada no algoritmo *Nondominated Sorting Genetic Algorithm-II* (NSGA-II) [6].

6. AGRADECIMENTOS

Esta pesquisa é parcialmente apoiada pelo Instituto Nacional de Ciência e Tecnologia para a Web (INWEB - CNPq no. 573871/2008-6), CAPES, CNPq, Finep e Fapemig.

7. REFERENCES

[1] Y.1291: An architectural framework for support of quality of service in packet networks, 05 2004.

[2] BLAKE, S., BLACK, D., CARLSON, M., DAVIES, E., WANG, Z., AND WEISS, W. An Architecture for Differentiated Services. RFC 2475 (Informational), Dec. 1998. Updated by RFC 3260.

[3] BRADEN, R., CLARK, D., AND SHENKER, S. Integrated Services in the Internet Architecture: an Overview. RFC 1633 (Informational), June 1994.

[4] CANFORA, G., DI PENTA, M., ESPOSITO, R., AND VILLANI, M. L. An approach for qos-aware service composition based on genetic algorithms. In *Proceedings of the 2005 conference on Genetic and evolutionary computation*, GECCO '05. ACM, New York, NY, USA, 2005, pp. 1069–1075.

[5] CHU, J., AND LEA, C.-T. Optimal link weights for maximizing qos traffic. In *Communications, 2007. ICC '07. IEEE International Conference on* (june 2007), pp. 610 –615.

[6] DEB, K., PRATAP, A., AGARWAL, S., AND MEYARIVAN, T. A fast and elitist multiobjective genetic algorithm: Nsga-ii. *Evolutionary Computation, IEEE Transactions on 6*, 2 (apr 2002), 182 –197.

[7] GUPTA, A. Network management: Current trends and future perspectives. *Journal of Network and Systems*

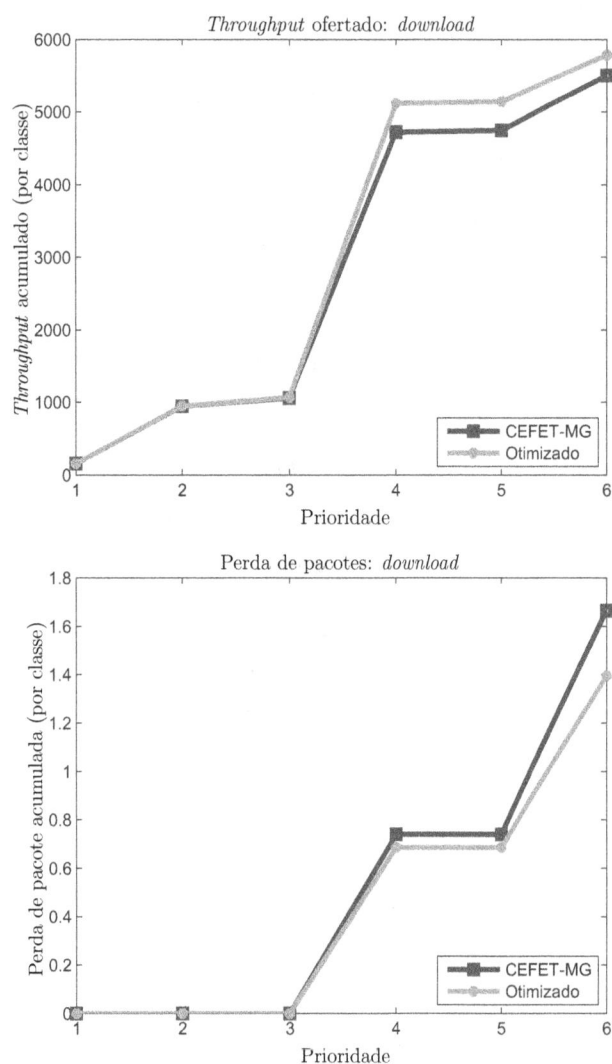

Figure 4: **Avaliação de cenários com diferentes larguras de banda (*download*)**

Management 14 (2006), 483–491. 10.1007/s10922-006-9044-7.

[8] HAYKIN, S. *Neural Networks: A Comprehensive Foundation*, 2nd ed. Prentice Hall PTR, Upper Saddle River, NJ, USA, 1998.

[9] HOLLOT, C., MISRA, V., TOWSLEY, D., AND GONG, W.-B. A control theoretic analysis of red. In *INFOCOM 2001. Twentieth Annual Joint Conference of the IEEE Computer and Communications Societies. Proceedings. IEEE* (2001), vol. 3, pp. 1510–1519.

[10] JÚNIOR, J. F., PEREIRA, A., MEIRA JÚNIOR, W., AND VELOSO, A. Methodology for fraud detection in electronic transactions. In *Proceedings of the 18th Brazilian symposium on Multimedia and the web* (New York, NY, USA, 2012), WebMedia '12, ACM, pp. 289–292.

[11] LI, W., ZENG-ZHI, L., AND YAN-PING, C. A control theoretic analysis of mixed tcp and udp traffic under red based on nonlinear dynamic model. In *Information Technology and Applications, 2005. ICITA 2005. Third International Conference on* (july 2005), vol. 2, pp. 747–750.

[12] LIMA, R. A. F., AND PEREIRA, A. C. M. Fraud detection in web transactions. In *Proceedings of the 18th Brazilian symposium on Multimedia and the web* (New York, NY, USA, 2012), WebMedia '12, ACM, pp. 273–280.

[13] LIU, Y., AND LIANG, X. New regulations to the next generation network. In *Communications and Mobile Computing, 2009. CMC '09. WRI International Conference on*, vol. 2. jan. 2009, pp. 172 –174.

[14] The Network Simulator ns-2 (v2.1b8a). http://www.isi.edu/nsnam/ns/, Oct. 2001.

[15] OLARIU, C., FITZPATRICK, J., PERRY, P., AND MURPHY, L. A qos based call admission control and resource allocation mechanism for lte femtocell deployment. In *Consumer Communications and Networking Conference (CCNC), 2012 IEEE* (2012), pp. 884–888.

[16] POP, F.-C., PALLEZ, D., CREMENE, M., TETTAMANZI, A., SUCIU, M., AND VAIDA, M. Qos-based service optimization using differential evolution. In *Proceedings of the 13th annual conference on Genetic and evolutionary computation* (New York, NY, USA, 2011), GECCO '11, ACM, pp. 1891–1898.

[17] QARAAWY, S., ALI, H., AND MAHMOOD, A. Particle swarm optimization based robust controller for congestion avoidance in computer networks. In *Future Communication Networks (ICFCN), 2012 International Conference on* (april 2012), pp. 18 –22.

[18] ROSENBERG, F., MÜLLER, M. B., LEITNER, P., MICHLMAYR, A., BOUGUETTAYA, A., AND DUSTDAR, S. Metaheuristic optimization of large-scale qos-aware service compositions. 97–104.

[19] SHENKER, S., PARTRIDGE, C., AND GUERIN, R. Specification of Guaranteed Quality of Service. RFC 2212 (Proposed Standard), Sept. 1997.

[20] SUCIU, M., CREMENE, M., POP, F., AND DUMITRESCU, D. Equitable solutions in qos-aware service optimization. In *Proceedings of the fourteenth international conference on Genetic and evolutionary computation conference companion* (New York, NY, USA, 2012), GECCO Companion '12, ACM, pp. 1537–1538.

[21] YAO, Y., AND CHEN, H. Qos-aware service composition using nsga-ii. In *Proceedings of the 2nd International Conference on Interaction Sciences: Information Technology, Culture and Human*, ICIS '09. ACM, New York, NY, USA, 2009, pp. 358–363.

[22] YU, B., AND XU, C. Efficient qos scheme in network congestion. In *Informatics and Management Science VI*, W. Du, Ed., vol. 209 of *Lecture Notes in Electrical Engineering*. Springer London, 2013, pp. 111–119.

A Comparative Analysis of Algorithms for Dynamic Web Services Composition with Quality of Service

Luis H. V. Nakamura
Institute of Mathematics and
Computer Science (ICMC)
University of São Paulo (USP)
São Carlos - SP, Brazil
nakamura@icmc.usp.br

Andre L. V. da Cunha
Institute of Mathematics and
Computer Science (ICMC)
University of São Paulo (USP)
São Carlos - SP, Brazil
andrelvc@icmc.usp.br

Júlio C. Estrella
Institute of Mathematics and
Computer Science (ICMC)
University of São Paulo (USP)
São Carlos - SP, Brazil
jcezar@icmc.usp.br

Marcos J. Santana
Institute of Mathematics and
Computer Science (ICMC)
University of São Paulo (USP)
São Carlos - SP, Brazil
mjs@icmc.usp.br

Regina H. C. Santana
Institute of Mathematics and
Computer Science (ICMC)
University of São Paulo (USP)
São Carlos - SP, Brazil
rcs@icmc.usp.br

ABSTRACT

In this paper three optimization algorithms were used in order to solve the problem of dynamic composition of Web services with Quality of Service (QoS). This combinatorial optimization problem arises when multiple services, which provide subfunctions for a complete function, are aggregated in an execution flow and presented to the user as a single service. This problem has been modeled in the context of two deterministic and one stochastic algorithms, aiming to determine the best flow in terms of QoS. Besides, a performance evaluation was executed considering the composition algorithms in some scenarios and comparing them in terms of response time and quality of the obtained solution. The stochastic algorithm proved to be more advantageous for these scenarios due the deadline exploitation on the search for an optimal solution, although it does not provide guarantees of optimality.

Categories and Subject Descriptors

H.3.5 [**Information Systems**]: Online Information Services – Web based service

General Terms

Algorithms, Languages, Measurement, Performance

Keywords

Web Service, Quality of Service, Dynamic Web Services Composition, Ant Colony Optimization

1. INTRODUCTION

Service-Oriented Architecture (SOA) consists of an architectural model for software systems that has a set of services available in a network as its basis [9]. In a large network, such as the Internet, the adoption of this architecture can facilitate interoperability and service reuse.

Interoperability is essential for creating integrated systems running on the inherently heterogeneous Web structure, making SOA a suitable approach in structuring these systems. Web services are the application of SOA to Web application development focused on programmatic interaction between its components. Such advantages have provided a great proliferation of Web services and many of them are available on the Web.

The use of Web Services can be better explored considering the use of two approaches that are targets of ongoing research: (1) Web Services Discovery and (2) Web Services Composition. In the former, the user seeks for a suitable Web Service to perform a certain task; additionally, it may require the task to be performed in a given time with a particular reliability, or impose restrictions over other QoS attributes. The latter consists of combining services in order to achieve greater functionality and the composer(s) (whether human or a system) must create the composition flow by selecting the appropriate Web Services. In other words, they may choose those that have compatible functionality, parameters, inputs and outputs, and additionally consider the QoS of each candidate service. However, when a large number of Web Services is considered, many of them may have the same functionality. In this case, for each service with a particular functionality required in the composition (*Abstract Web Service*) it will be available several candidate services (*Concrete Web Services*), as represented in Figure 1 [13].

In this context, the composition task can be classified into two types or stages: (1) "*Manual or Automatic*" Composition and (2) "*Static or Dynamic*" Composition [4]. The "*Manual or Automatic*" composition is the classification in which the execution flow of services must be defined. This flow (graph) can be set manually (for example, using tools and languages used in business processes (Business Process

217

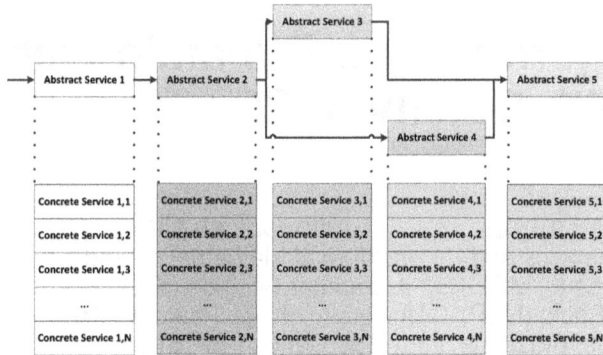

Figure 1: Relation between Abstract and Concrete Web Services. Adapted from [13].

Execution Language (BPEL)), or automatically, by applying Artificial Intelligence and Semantic Web techniques, so that the composition flow is performed without human intervention. The "*Static or Dynamic*" composition is related to the choice of a concrete Web service for each abstract Web service defined into the flow. In the static approach that association is made at design time, i.e. defined by the developer. In the dynamic composition, this association is made at runtime and the algorithm will consider the QoS values of the concrete Web services to choose the best composition.

The focus of this paper is related to Dynamic Composition considering QoS (QoS-aware Web Service Composition (QWSC)). A sequential composition flow was created manually and adopted in the experiments of this study, since the aim of this paper is to analyze and compare algorithms for dynamic composition, and thus direct the user to choose the suitable algorithm by showing the advantages and disadvantages of each proposal.

This paper is composed of five sections. In Section 2, related works are discussed. In Section 3, the implementation and the characteristics of the algorithms are presented. Section 4 presents the performance evaluations and result analysis. Finally, Section 5 contains the conclusions and suggestions for future work.

2. RELATED WORK

The dynamic composition of Web Services considering QoS is a *NP-hard* problem [5], and is treated as an optimization problem. An exhaustive search method (brute force) for Web services composition tests all the possible combinations of execution flows, and consequently can require a lot of processing, surpassing time limits (*deadlines*) that are generally used in Web systems, like e-commerce applications. According to [15], some methods for QWSC employ QoS models based on multi-dimensional and/or multi-objective optimization.

In [15] is presented a review about Web services composition based on bio-inspired algorithms, such as Ant Colony Optimization (ACO), Genetic Algorithm (GA), Evolutionary Algorithm (EA) and Particle Swarm Optimization (PSO). In that paper, several works and approaches are analyzed and investigated in order to present an overview of current research and point out future directions. The authors note that some researches are conducted in their own simulated

environments and emphasize the absence of a reference tool (benchmark) for Web services composition based on bio-inspired algorithms. This lack of standard or qualitative comparison raises questions of how the bio-inspired algorithms can solve the Web services composition problem with an increased performance, or how to configure the parameters of bio-inspired algorithms. The authors also classify these questions as yet unanswered, and underline the need for more research on bio-inspired algorithms in Web services composition.

In [10], it was proposed an ACO-based optimization algorithm for QWSC called DACO (Dynamic Ant Colony Optimization Algorithm Based on Multi-pheromones). The DACO's execution, which is done by simulation, is based on different QoS attributes that are set by various pheromones. In the experiments of that work, the authors did not compare the results of their algorithm with other ones.

In [11], it was developed an algorithm based on multiobjective ACO called MOACO (Multi-objective Ant Colony Optimization). In that paper, the authors define a service composition model and use MOACO to try to solve the Pareto optimization problem on the selection of services at the composition. They also affirm that the performance results of MOACO are superior to MOGA (QoS Global Optimization Based on Multi-objective Genetic Algorithm) [8]. Another similar work [18] also compares more thoroughly two approaches to multi-objective algorithms (MO); MO_ACO and MO_GA.

Other studies [12], [16], [17] also address the use of ACO-based algorithms in conjunction with Semantic Web resources. Some of these works create ontologies with semantic web resources to compose automatic execution flows, as well as ACO-based algorithms for dynamic composition.

In this paper, a study is made to identify the best settings, according to performance informations, for the proposed ACO algorithm. Once the optimal configuration is identified (number of ants, amount of pheromone, etc.), this ACO algorithm is compared with two other deterministic algorithms (Section 4). In addition to the performance evaluation and comparison of algorithms for the problem of dynamic service composition in sequential flows, this paper also contributes to the consideration of a deadline, which is a very important factor for various types of existing web applications (for example, soft real-time and e-commerce applications).

3. ALGORITHMS

We adapted three algorithms, two deterministic and one non-deterministic, for the QWSC problem. Initially, it will be discussed the importance of managing the QoS in composition flows and the attributes used to select the best service to become part of the composite flow.

Each Concrete Web Service has its own QoS attributes and, in order to calculate the QoS of the entire composition, it is necessary to use aggregation functions [2][7]. In Table 1, based from [2] [7], there are examples of five QoS attributes and aggregation functions that were used in this paper. The *Cost* and *Response Time* of a composition are simply the sum of the individual values of each service. Besides, the *Availability* attribute is calculated as the product of all participating services. Finally, the *Reputation* and *Confidentiality* attributes are the average value of the services present in the composition.

Table 1: Quality of Service Attributes [2] [7].

QoS Attributes	
Availability	$\prod_{i=1}^{i=n} Availability(\text{WSi})$
Cost	$\sum_{i=1}^{i=n} Cost(\text{WSi})$
Response Time	$\sum_{i=1}^{i=n} ResponseTime(\text{WSi})$
Reputation	$\sum_{i=1}^{i=n} Reputation(\text{WSi})*1/n$
Confidentiality	$\sum_{i=1}^{i=n} Confidentiality(\text{WSi})*1/n$

3.1 ACO - Ant Colony Optimization

Swarm Intelligence is a bio-inspired problem-solving paradigm that mimics the joint work of insect colonies [3]. In this case, a problem is modeled in a similar way to the natural habitat of a colony, and a computer is used to simulate various individuals performing some activities - like searching for food - on that habitat. At the end, the information left behind by the insects composes a solution to the problem.

Particularly, ant colonies uses a substance called pheromone to search for food: each ant deposits pheromone trails while rummaging the environment; when an ant sees a trail left by another ant, it tends to follow it, reinforcing the trail by depositing more pheromone on it. Alternatively, the ant can follow another direction, but with a lower probability. Furthermore, the pheromone is a volatile substance, which makes non-reinforced tracks to evaporate over time. This combination of reinforcement and evaporation leads to an almost minimum - if not minimum - path between the nest and the food source after some time. Applying this idea to solve mathematical problems is called Ant Colony Optimization (ACO) and the main application of it consists of solving NP-hard problems, which include some combinatorial optimization problems.

The ants create candidate solutions for the problem from the solution components by walking through a pathway in a *construction graph* $G_C(\mathbf{V}, \mathbf{E})$, where $\mathbf{V}$ denotes the set of vertices and $\mathbf{E}$ the edges of the graph. This graph is constructed by the designer based on the model, in basically two ways: associating each solution component $c_{ij} \in \mathbf{C}$ to a vertex or an edge of the graph. Then, as each ant walks on the graph, it deposits pheromone on each component that it decides to use in its solution. At the end, the solution found by the colony is given by the path in the graph that has the highest amount of pheromone. While walking through the construction graph creating its solution, each ant decides the next solution component it will adopt based on a stochastic process. In the Ant System, the probability that the solution component c_{ij} will be used as the next step of the k-th ant, assuming that this ant has already created a partial solution s^p at the present moment, it is given by Equation (1):

$$p_{ij}^k = \begin{cases} \dfrac{\tau_{ij}^{\alpha} \cdot \eta_{ij}^{\beta}}{\sum_{c_{il} \in \mathbf{N}(s^p)} \tau_{il}^{\alpha} \cdot \eta_{il}^{\beta}} & if \ c_{ij} \in \mathbf{N}(s^p) \\ \\ 0 & otherwise \end{cases} \quad (1)$$

In Equation (1), $\mathbf{N}(s^p)$ is the collection of feasible solution components; in other words, the collection of components that can be added to the partial solution s^p, forming a new partial solution $s^{p'}$ that is also feasible. In this same equation, τ_{ij} is the amount of pheromone left by other ants over the component c_{ij}, and η_{ij} is a problem-specific heuristic information that measures the *attractiveness* of the component. The coefficients α and β quantify the relative importance of the amount of pheromone and the heuristic information.

3.2 Dynamic Programming

One of the major challenges in designing exact algorithms for optimization problems is to ensure the optimality of the solution without check the whole search space. The reason for that is that exhaustive search is often impractical for the size of problems that arise in real world, motivating the creation of algorithms that are able to eliminate regions of the search space that certainly does not contain an optimal solution. One way to accomplish such "pruning" during search is to divide the initial problem into sub-problems that share other sub-problems, and then solve the sub-problems from the smallest up, until we find a solution to the original problem.

Despite of also finding the solution of a problem by combining solutions of sub-problems, Dynamic Programming (DP) differs from methods such as Divide and Conquer. This latter approach divides the problem into independent sub-problems, which do not share sub-solutions and hence can be solved in any order, whereas DP divides the problem into nested sub-problems that need to be addressed in a specific order. Dynamic Programming is based on the principle of optimality, which states that all sub-solution of an optimal solution are also optimal. Thus, for the development of the algorithms in this paper, it was used the four steps discussed in [1]:

- Characterize the structure of an optimal solution;

- Recursively define the value of an optimal solution;

- Calculate the value of an optimal solution in an ascending (bottom-up) way;

- Construct an optimal solution from the calculated information.

3.3 Branch and Bound

Many problems can be formulated as the minimization or maximization of an objective, given limited resources and concurrent constraints. By expressing the objective as a linear function of a set of variables and the constraints as linear equalities or inequalities involving these same variables, we have a linear programming problem [1]. Branch-and-Bound (BB) is an algorithm used to solve mixed integer programming problems, which are derived from linear programming problems.

There are several ways to develop a Branch-and-Bound algorithm. One of them is to use a relaxation of the original problem in order to apply the algorithm. A condition of relaxation means disregarding some of the restrictions of the original problem, so that it accepts solutions that would not be possible in the original problem.

The basic concept of the BB algorithm is to start from an initial problem and perform branchings, thus creating new problems with new restrictions. This makes the algorithm create a decision tree as new problems are generated. Then, when one of these problems offers a feasible solution that respects the previously relaxed condition, it is possible to prune this tree. Consequently, this makes the search space to be reduced, making the algorithm faster and more efficient.

A **linear constraint** is a linear equality or a linear inequality. A **linear equality** is an equation of the form:

$$f(x_1, x_2, \ldots, x_n) = b \qquad (2)$$

Where f is a linear function and b is a real number. Analogously, a **linear inequality** is an equation of the form:

$$f(x_1, x_2, \ldots, x_n) \leq b \qquad (3)$$

Or:

$$f(x_1, x_2, \ldots, x_n) \geq b \qquad (4)$$

Strict inequalities $(<, >)$ are disallowed in Linear Programming. A Linear Programming problem, or linear optimization problem, is formally defined as to minimize or maximize a linear objective function while respecting a finite set of linear constraints [1].

As the variables $x_1, x_2, \ldots, x_n$ are all numerical, each assignment of values to them can be seen as a point in $\mathbb{R}^n$. Therefore, the objective function is a $f : \mathbb{R}^n \to \mathbb{R}$ function, and each one of the linear constraints form a semi-space of $\mathbb{R}^n$.

An assignment of values that satisfies all constraints is called a **feasible solution**, and an assignment that violates at least one of the constraints is called an **infeasible solution**. The set of all feasible solutions is called the **feasible region**, and it is the intersection of the semi-spaces defined by the constraints. This region is also called a **simplex** and it will always be a **convex region**, since it is the intersection of semi-spaces defined by linear equations.

Each point in the feasible region has an associated objective function value, called **objective value**. Therefore, solving the optimization problem consists in finding which point(s) of the feasible region has (have) the highest objective value. Conceptually, it is possible to evaluate the objective value of each point of the simplex, and then determine which point maximizes this value, but this is clearly impossible to be realized in practice. For small problems, it is possible to employ a graphical method to find these points. However, it is important to note that the attributes and aggregation functions were considered in the algorithms discussed above.

3.4 Proposal

The goal of this paper is to present and discuss solutions for the Dynamic Web Services Composition problem using the algorithms described above. In this section some initial considerations are made about the problem, presenting some formal aspects that will be used in all the analyzed algorithms.

The first aspect to be discussed here is the definition of **abstract flow** and **concrete flow**. For this analysis, an abstract flow is defined as an ordered set of virtual services (also called tasks), and must be executed in a strictly sequential order. We will call each one of the n tasks of a problem t_i, and the set of tasks $\mathbf{T} = \{t_i, i = 1, 2, \ldots, n\}$. For each task t_i, it is defined a set of k_i real services (or simply services) $s_{ij}, j = 1, \ldots, k_i$, which perform the task t_i. The set of all the services of a problem is called $\mathbf{S_r} = \{s_{ij}, i = 1, 2, \ldots, n, j = 1, 2, \ldots, k_i\}$. A concrete flow is de-

fined as a choice of n services, one for each task, and it is denoted by $s = \{s_{1j_1}, s_{2j_2}, \ldots, s_{nj_n}\}$.

Each s_{ij} service is associated to one or more QoS attributes defined below. Prior to the formal definition of a QoS attribute, it is necessary to treat a problem related to the nature of attributes. Some of them are **increasing**, i.e., higher values indicate higher quality, while others are **decreasing**, meaning that larger values indicate lower quality. An example of an increasing attribute is *Availability*, and an example of a decreasing one is *Response Time*.

In addition, the attributes can be in different units of measure, and they can be valid at different intervals. For example, availability is dimensionless, and it assumes values between 0 and 1, whereas the response time is measured in units of time, with positive and unlimited values. If these differences are not treated properly, they can lead optimization algorithms to make wrong decisions. For example: depending on the metric used for comparison, a service with a response time of 1200ms and availability of 0.2 can be considered better than another that has a response time of 800ms and availability 1.0. Consequently a **normalization** process is required for the attributes, so as to make them comparable.

A possible normalization [14] represents all the attributes in the $[0, 1]$ interval in **increasing** order. In the case of an increasing attribute, this can be achieved by replacing the value Q of the attribute by a value Q', which is the difference between Q and the minimum value taken by the attribute among the considered services divided by the difference between the maximum and the minimum values assumed by the attribute (also in the considered services); for a decreasing attribute, its value is replaced by the difference between the maximum value assumed by it and the current value, also divided by the difference between the maximum and minimum values. This is summarized in equations [14] below:

$$Q' = \begin{cases} \dfrac{Q - Q_{min}}{Q_{max} - Q_{min}} & , \text{ if increasing} \qquad (5a) \\[3mm] \dfrac{Q_{max} - Q}{Q_{max} - Q_{min}} & , \text{ if decreasing} \qquad (5b) \end{cases}$$

Thus, a normalization of the data was considered in this paper to perform the QoS calculation on the three algorithms.

Although the algorithms use this same normalization process, some of their features are specific. For example, ACO is a stochastic algorithm based on the use of multiple independent computational agents that communicate during the search process. DP is a deterministic technique that reduces the extent of the search space, taking advantage of smaller solutions in the composition of bigger ones. BB is also a deterministic algorithm, which solves linear optimization problems with one or more integrality constraints.

4. PERFORMANCE EVALUATION

4.1 Environment Configuration

For the experiments, two computers were used, which were connected by a Gigabit Ethernet network. The characteristics of these computers are listed in Table 2.

Table 3: Virtual Machines 1, 2 and 3.

Characteristic	VM 1	VM 2	VM 3
Real Computer	Computer 1	Computer 2	Computer 2
Hypervisor	KVM	KVM	KVM
Number of Cores	4 @ 2.80GHz	1 @ 3.10GHz	1 @ 3.10GHz
RAM Memory	8 GiB	1GiB	1GiB
HD	20 GiB	8 GiB	6 GiB
OS	Linux 3.2.0-29-generic	Linux 3.2.0-29-generic	Linux 3.2.0-29-generic
Purpose	Apache-tomcat Server and Axis2	MySQL Server	Client

Table 2: Computers of the Experiments.

Item	Computer 1	Computer 2
CPU	Xeon X5660 @ 2.80GHz	Core i3-2100 @ 3.10GHz
RAM	12GiB	4GiB
HD	500 GiB	1 TiB
OS	Devian-kvm 2.6.32-5-amd64	Linux 3.0.0-26-generic

Table 4: Factors and Levels for Experiment 1.

Factor	Symbol	Level 1	Level 2
Relative importance of amount of pheromone	α	1	10
Relative importance of heuristic information	β	1	10
Number of ants	**A**	10	100
Pheromone evaporation coefficient	ρ	0.2	0.8

In order to perform the experiments, three virtual machines were created: a server with Apache-tomcat 6.0.26 and Axis2, another server with a MySQL 5.1 database, and another one with a client application. The configurations of these virtual machines are described in Table 3. The virtual machines interact as follows:

- The client, running on virtual machine 3 on real computer 2, requests a service composition to the server running in virtual machine 1 on real computer 1. The parameters the client sends are: the composition algorithm to be used, the number of tasks in the flow, the number of services per task, the table in the database that stores the QoS data of the services and an execution deadline for the composition algorithm.

- The server receives that request and performs a query on the database in order to load the QoS values that will be used in the composition. This is performed on virtual machine 2 on real computer 2.

- The server normalizes the QoS attributes based on Equations 5a and 5b, and invokes the composition algorithm over these data.

- The algorithm returns the best composition found, which is sent as a response to the client.

Five QoS attributes were used: Cost, Response Time, Availability, Confidentiality and Reputation. The first experiment aimed to determine the best configuration for ACO, once it is a metaheuristic that has several parameters.

4.2 Configuration for ACO

The first experiment, denominated Experiment 1, has four factors with two levels each, as shown in Table 4. For this experiment, the *full factorial design* [6] was adopted; that is, all possibilities were considered. However, an execution did not need to be performed, as the cases $\alpha = \beta = 10$ and $\alpha = \beta = 1$ are equivalent (Equation 1).

In all executions (repetitions) a deadline of 1000 ms was used to ACO. This means that it will execute for approximately this amount of time, and then it will use the composition with the greatest amount of pheromone as the final solution. This deadline is only for the execution of the composition algorithm, not for the complete client request. In each execution, the total Execution Time (ET) perceived by the client was measured, that is, the time span from the client request to the arrival of the response.

For each combination of factors, 30 consecutive requests from the client to the server were executed. It was also considered the use of any caching mechanism pertaining to the environment configuration and/or tools involved which might possibly influence the system performance. Even though the deadline is fixed, there are variations in ACO's total execution time between one request and another. Therefore, in each execution, the algorithm's execution time, the aggregate QoS of the best solution obtained and, thus, the ACO **effectiveness** for the corresponding configuration were calculated. The effectiveness of an ACO configuration, measured in **Hz**, is defined as follows:

$$\textbf{Effectiveness} = \frac{\textbf{Aggregate QoS}}{\textbf{Time (s)}} \quad [\text{Hz}] \qquad (6)$$

The average and standard deviation of the effectiveness of each ACO configuration are presented in Table 5. From the table, it can be concluded that the best configuration tested was the one in which $\alpha = 1, \beta = 10, \textbf{A} = 100$ and $\rho = 0.8$, as it had the highest average and lowest variance. In this configuration, there is a higher influence of the heuristic information about the amount of pheromone, a large numbers of ants and a more volatile pheromone.

This means that the assumptions made in choosing the heuristic information, i.e. that nodes with high total QoS are more likely to be in the optimal solution, are true. This is the case because the highest performance was obtained when $\beta > \alpha$.

In other words, when the heuristic information has higher influence than the amount of pheromone. Furthermore, the number of ants $\textbf{A} = 100$ is high, which combined with the larger value of β makes ants choose the nodes with the highest total QoS. The high value of ρ means that other paths are ignored quickly, concentrating the search around paths composed of nodes with high total QoS.

Moreover, it was noticed that the cases where $\beta > \alpha$ obtained higher average in general, followed by cases in which $\alpha = \beta = 1$, then by $\alpha > \beta$, which were cases that had worse average and higher standard deviation. The worst perfor-

Table 5: Average (in Hz) and standard deviation of ACO's effectiveness for various configurations.

Factors				Effectiveness	
α	β	$\mathbf{A}$	ρ	Average	Standard Deviation
1	1	10	0.2	0.60	0.0524
1	1	10	0.8	0.56	0.0518
1	1	100	0.2	0.68	0.0292
1	1	100	0.8	0.64	0.0322
1	10	10	0.2	0.69	0.0231
1	10	10	0.8	0.68	0.0297
1	10	100	0.2	0.69	0.0233
1	10	100	0.8	0.70	0.0199
10	1	10	0.2	0.53	0.0660
10	1	10	0.8	0.53	0.0687
10	1	100	0.2	0.51	0.0825
10	1	100	0.8	0.55	0.0657

Table 6: Factors Influence, in percent, on ACO's average effectiveness.

Factor(s)	Influence (%)
α	37.32
β	37.32
$\mathbf{A}$	10.53
ρ	1.31
α , β	0.58
α , $\mathbf{A}$	0.04
α , ρ	0.15
β , $\mathbf{A}$	0.04
β , ρ	0.15
$\mathbf{A}$, ρ	0.33
α , β , $\mathbf{A}$	8.20
α , β , ρ	3.64
α , $\mathbf{A}$, ρ	0.04
β , $\mathbf{A}$, ρ	0.04
α , β , $\mathbf{A}$, ρ	0.33

mance was obtained when $\alpha = 10, \beta = 1, \mathbf{A} = 100$ and $\rho = 0.2$, which got the worst average and highest standard deviation among the experiments.

This worse result is due to the fact that the little influence of the heuristic information, associated with the high number of ants and a very slow pheromone evaporation, makes ACO degenerate into a random search. Actually, in this case, ACO may perform worse than a random search: in the latter, the best solution found so far is kept; in ACO, this information is stored in the pheromone associated to the nodes, but the little evaporation makes nearly all the paths homogeneous in terms of pheromone concentration, when associated with a high number of ants and a little influence of the heuristic information in the decision of each ant. All of this degrades the obtained average and increases the standard deviation, the latter being typical of a random search.

Table 6 shows the factors influence, in percent, on the average ACO effectiveness. "f_1, f_2" indicates the influence of the combination of factor f_1 and factor f_2.

Also in the Table 6, it is noticed that the highest influence is exerted by the factors α and β, which shows that the heuristic information has significant influence on ACO performance. This configuration, in this experiment, will be used for the next experiments in this paper.

4.3 Evaluation and Analysis

For the evaluation and analysis, three different search spaces are used to evaluate the performance of each algorithm individually. Each search space is composed of flows containing 2, 6 and 12 tasks (Abstract Web Services) and each of these tasks can be performed by 200 services (Concrete Web Services).

The experiments were replicated 30 times consecutively and cache mechanisms were again considered. The Average and Confidence Intervals (CIs) (95%) were calculated. Furthermore, the experiments compare the performance (in terms of execution time) and the ability to compose a service composition flow with the best possible QoS levels in a given deadline. The algorithms Ant Colony Optimization (ACO), Branch and Bound (BB) and Dynamic Programming (DP) proposed in this paper were compared and the results were divided into three tables. It is important to note that ACO continues to execute until the end of the deadline due to

it characteristics, even if it has found the appropriate QoS. For this reason, to make a fairer comparison, ACO was also tested in the experiments using a minimum QoS as stopping criterion. This minimum QoS has the same value of that achieved by deterministic algorithms. Therefore, this variation in ACO algorithm, called here ACO-QoS, will execute until it find a QoS greater than or equal to the minimum QoS, or until the end of the deadline.

Table 7 contains the Execution Time (ET) and the QoS results for the service composition with a flow with two tasks (200^2 possibilities), considering an 1000ms deadline.

Table 7: Algorithms Execution Time (ET) with CIs and average QoS for the Flow with 2 Services.

	Algorithm	ET (ms)	CI. Min.	CI. Max.	QoS
1	ACO	1186.10	1179.66	1192.53	0.844634
2	ACO-QoS	292.90	217.26	368.53	0.846629
3	BB	210.76	202.47	219.05	0.846629
4	DP	173.80	168.79	178.80	0.846629

In these first results it is possible to note that, for this scenario (200^2), ACO (which considers only the deadline - ACO Deadline) is the worst algorithm. It has the worst execution time because it uses all the allowed time (deadline) and there is no guarantee that it can find the best solution. DP algorithm has better performance and ensures an appropriate QoS in the deadline. BB algorithm also ensures an appropriate QoS in the established deadline, but it has an execution time slightly longer than the one of DP. During the experiments, ACO-QoS obtained an adequate QoS before the deadline, but with execution time longer than the ones of DP and BB.

In Tables 8 and 9 are presented the Execution Time (ET) and QoS results collected to form the service composition with flows from six and twelve tasks (200^6 and 200^{12} possibilities) respectively, considering a deadline of 1000ms.

In the second experiment (200^6) it is possible to note that ACO has the largest execution time, and that BB, DP and ACO-QoS found the proper composition before the deadline (1000ms) again. Still in this second experiment, ACO did not reach a superior QoS than the others algorithms. DP

Table 8: Algorithms Execution Time (ET) with CIs and average QoS for the Flow with 6 Services.

	Algorithm	ET (ms)	CI. Min.	CI. Max.	QoS
1	ACO	1186.20	1180.29	1192.10	0.845857
2	ACO-QoS	462.43	329.66	595.19	0.849207
3	BB	763.76	732.13	795.40	0.847341
4	DP	172.50	168.68	176.31	0.847341

Table 9: Algorithms Execution Time (ET) with CIs and average QoS for the Flow with 12 Services.

	Algorithm	ET (ms)	CI. Min.	CI. Max.	QoS
1	ACO	1180.63	1176.51	1184.75	0.407374
2	ACO-QoS	294.00	261.91	326.08	0.412465
3	BB	2276.00	2195.54	2356.45	0.404224
4	DP	174.33	169.59	179.06	0.404224

algorithm had the same performance as in the previous scenario, which indicates that the number of combinations was not sufficient to affect its performance yet. Furthermore, BB algorithm was affected by that change, increasing its execution time, but it was still able to give a solution in the deadline. In this case, ACO-QoS's execution time get the second place, behind that of DP only, but it was able to reach a slightly higher QoS.

The behavior of the results of the third experiment (200^{12}) is similar to the second experiment, differing because BB algorithm sensed substantially the change in the search space, in such a way that it could not give a solution in the established deadline and got the last place, after ACO. Thus, in terms of performance, ACO-QoS was behind DP only, but could achieve a much superior QoS.

Based on these results, it is possible to conclude that as the size of the abstract flow increases, some algorithms are more sensitive in terms of performance than others. BB algorithm is influenced the most by this increase and it did not respect the deadline. The reason for that is the way the problem was modeled: many variables are created in the model that is passed on to the algorithm. For example, a flow with tasks 12 and 200 services results in a problem with $12 \times 200 = 2400$ variables, which may require many branches in the tree that BB opens, affecting its performance. However, PD algorithm was practically not affected by this increase in the search space, being the best option in this experiment in terms of execution time. ACO and its variation ACO-QoS are stochastic algorithms and not much can be affirmed about their results; it is only possible to note that a deadline of 1000ms is enough for the algorithm to find a good solution for the composition.

In terms of quality, the QoS level was affected when the search space changed from 6 to 12 abstract services. In the experiments, ACO and ACO-QoS achieved superior QoS levels than the others algorithms in the established deadline. However, they are non-deterministic, so there is no guarantee that this result will always be the same every time the algorithm is run; it may achieve from inferior results to the global optimum. There was also an attempt to compare the results with an algorithm that implements an exhaustive search called Brute Force (BF). The result was obtained only for the flow with 2 tasks, because BF did not give a solution for a composition with 6 task in the time defined

for the experiment (15 minutes), which made it impractical to continue the execution. Figure 2 presents the Execution Time (ET) results of the algorithms: Brute Force (BF), Dynamic Programming (DP), Branch and Bound (BB) and ACO (ACO Deadline). Figure 3 replicates earlier results replacing the results of ACO by those of ACO-QoS.

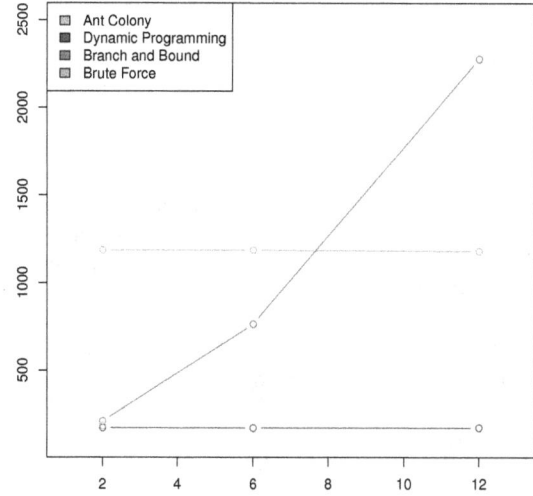

Figure 2: Average Execution Time of the Algorithms (ACO Deadline).

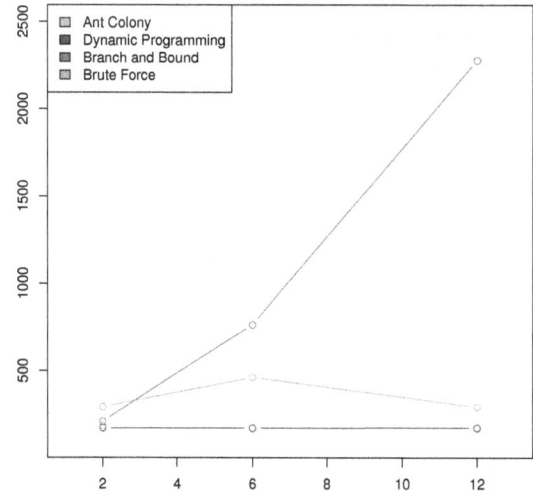

Figure 3: Average Execution Time of the Algorithms (ACO-QoS).

In terms of learning, we noticed that the use of stochastic algorithms can provide good solutions to such problems when we do not know a deterministic algorithm that solves them in acceptable time and with guarantees of optimality.

5. CONCLUSIONS AND FUTURE WORK

This paper presented the modeling, coding, and testing of three algorithms for Dynamic Web Services Composition. From the test results, it was possible to conclude that Dynamic Programming and ACO stand out as the most advantageous in terms of Execution Time and obtained QoS, respectively. In some cases, Branch and Bound algorithm can be considered, but should be avoided in large composition flows with deadline constraints. It was also observed that Dynamic Programming algorithm has an almost constant Execution Time, but due to modeling limitations, it may not be able to find the globally optimal combination. ACO has an Execution Time commensurate to that of DP; however, even though it may find the globally optimal solution, there is no guarantee for that.

The performance evaluation and the factor influence calculation were done to determine the best ACO configuration; this potentially contributed to the results obtained during the algorithm comparisons, reaffirming the importance of this step, which was proposed by [15]. This step must be done before using bio-inspired algorithms to achieve better performance on the service composition problem.

In this paper, only strictly sequential composition flows were treated. However, in future works, several other structural elements of parallelism and decision can be incorporated into the flow, making it richer and more powerful in terms of representing others real service composition situations. Further studies may be conducted to validate the use of the QoS attributes suggested in [2] [7] and used in this paper. For example, Confidentiality has an aggregation function that considers the average value of the services in the composition, which raises a question: if the worst case among the services used in the composition should be considered, because if a service is unreliable, then the entire composition may be compromised.

Other questions about performance and efficiency in obtaining QoS may be considered in future work, comparing the algorithms proposed in this paper to other types of algorithms, such as genetic algorithms, following examples of other studies [11][18] but adopting other criteria, such as time constraints (deadlines).

Acknowledgments
The authors thank FAPESP (Processes: 2011/09524-7 and 2011/12670-5) for the support given to the development of this work.

6. REFERENCES
[1] T. H. Cormen, C. Stein, R. L. Rivest, and C. E. Leiserson. *Introduction to Algorithms*. McGraw-Hill Higher Education, 2nd edition, 2001.

[2] P. do Prado, L. Nakamura, J. Estrella, M. Santana, and R. H. C. Santana. Different approaches for qos-aware web services composition focused on e-commerce systems. In *Computer Systems (WSCAD-SSC), 2012 13th Symposium on*, pages 179–186, 2012.

[3] M. Dorigo, M. Birattari, and T. Stutzle. Ant colony optimization. *Computational Intelligence Magazine, IEEE*, 1(4):28–39, nov. 2006.

[4] S. Dustdar and W. Schreiner. A survey on web services composition. *Int. J. Web Grid Serv.*, 1(1):1–30, Aug. 2005.

[5] M. D. P. G. Canfora and e. R. Esposito. A lightweight approach for qosaware service composition. *Proc. 2nd International Conference on Service Oriented Computing (ICSOC'04)*, pages 36 – 47, 2005. New York, USA.

[6] R. Jain. *The Art of Computer Systems Performance Analysis: techniques for experimental design, measurement, simulation, and modeling*. Wiley, 1991.

[7] J. M. Ko, C. O. Kim, and I.-H. Kwon. Quality-of-service oriented web service composition algorithm and planning architecture. *Journal of Systems and Software*, 81(11):2079 – 2090, 2008.

[8] S. Liu, Y. Liu, N. Jing, G. Tang, and Y. Tang. A dynamic web services selection strategy with qos global optimization based on multi-objective genetic algorithm. In *Grid and Cooperative Computing (GCC 2005)*, volume 1, pages 84–89, 2005. Springer Berlin, Heidelberg.

[9] Q. H. Mahmoud. *Oracle Tecnology Network*, April.

[10] Y. mei Xia, J.-L. Chen, and X. wu Meng. On the dynamic ant colony algorithm optimization based on multi-pheromones. In *Computer and Information Science, 2008. ICIS 08. Seventh IEEE/ACIS International Conference on*, pages 630–635, 2008.

[11] F. Qiqing, P. Xiaoming, L. Qinghua, and H. Yahui. A global qos optimizing web services selection algorithm based on moaco for dynamic web service composition. In *Information Technology and Applications, 2009. IFITA '09. International Forum on*, volume 1, pages 37–42, 2009.

[12] J. Shen, G. Beydoun, S. Yuan, and G. Low. Comparison of bio-inspired algorithms for peer selection in services composition. In *Services Computing (SCC), 2011 IEEE International Conference on*, pages 250–257, 2011.

[13] Y. sheng Luo, Y. Qi, D. Hou, L. feng Shen, Y. Chen, and X. Zhong. A novel heuristic algorithm for qos-aware end-to-end service composition. *Computer Communications*, 34(9):1137 – 1144, 2011. Special Issue: Next Generation Networks Service Management.

[14] S. Su, C. Zhang, and J. Chen. An improved genetic algorithm for web services selection. In *Proceedings of the 7th IFIP WG 6.1 international conference on Distributed applications and interoperable systems*, DAIS'07, pages 284–295, Berlin, Heidelberg, 2007. Springer-Verlag.

[15] L. Wang, J. Shen, and J. Yong. A survey on bio-inspired algorithms for web service composition. In *Computer Supported Cooperative Work in Design (CSCWD), 2012 IEEE 16th International Conference on*, pages 569–574, 2012.

[16] Y. Xia, C. Liu, Z. Yang, and J. Xiu. The ant colony optimization algorithm for web services composition on preference ontology. In *Advanced Intelligence and Awareness Internet (AIAI 2011), 2011 International Conference on*, pages 193–198, 2011.

[17] K. Yan, G. Xue, and S. wen Yao. An optimization ant colony algorithm for composition of semantic web services. In *Computational Intelligence and Industrial Applications, 2009. PACIIA 2009. Asia-Pacific Conference on*, volume 2, pages 262–265, 2009.

[18] W. Zhang, C. Chang, T. Feng, and H. yi Jiang. Qos-based dynamic web service composition with ant colony optimization. In *Computer Software and Applications Conference (COMPSAC), 2010 IEEE 34th Annual*, pages 493–502, 2010.

Automated Architectural Evaluation
of Web Information Systems

Felipe Pinto[1][2], Uirá Kulesza[1], Eduardo Guerra[3], João Maria Júnior[1], Leo Silva[2]

[1]Universidade Federal do Rio Grande do Norte, Natal, Brasil
[2]Instituto Federal de Educação, Ciência e Tecnologia do Rio Grande do Norte, Natal, Brasil
[3]Instituto Nacional de Pesquisa Espacial, São José dos Campos, Brasil

felipe.pinto@ifrn.edu.br, uira@dimap.ufrn.br, guerraem@gmail.com,
joao.mgcruz@gmail.com, leopontosilva@gmail.com

ABSTRACT

Traditional scenario-based architectural analysis methods rely on manual review-based evaluation that requires advanced skills from architects and developers. They are usually applied when the architecture is under development, but before its implementation has begun. The system implementation is one additional and fundamental element that should be used and considered during the software architecture evaluation. In this paper, we propose an approach to add information, which ideally should come from traditional evaluation methods, about scenarios and quality attributes to the source code of web-based systems using metadata. The main aim is to enable the automatic architecture analysis by producing a report with information about scenarios, quality attributes and source code assets, such as: (i) the potential tradeoff points among quality attributes, (ii) the execution time for scenarios and if it has failed or not. Up to now, the approach has been applied mainly to web-based systems, but it can be adapted to other software domains. The paper also presents the tool used to perform static and dynamic analysis, and the results of its application to an e-commerce web system and an enterprise information web system.

Categories and Subject Descriptors

D.2.11 [**Software Architectures**]: Data abstraction, Languages and Evaluation.

General Terms

Management, Documentation, Performance, Reliability, Security.

Keywords

Scenario-based methods, architecture, automatic evaluation, quality attributes, scenario, web systems.

1. INTRODUÇÃO

Nas últimas décadas vários métodos para avaliação de arquiteturas de software baseados em cenários e atributos de qualidade foram propostos [1] [2]. Tais métodos de avaliação usam cenários com o objetivo de analisar e exercitar determinados pontos da arquitetura. Esta metodologia permite obter

Permission to make digital or hard copies of all or part of this work for personal or classroom use is granted without fee provided that copies are not made or distributed for profit or commercial advantage and that copies bear this notice and the full citation on the first page. Copyrights for components of this work owned by others than ACM must be honored. Abstracting with credit is permitted. To copy otherwise, or republish, to post on servers or to redistribute to lists, requires prior specific permission and/or a fee. Request permissions from Permissions@acm.org.

WebMedia '13, November 05 - 08 2013, Salvador, Brazil
Copyright 2013 ACM 978-1-4503-2559-2/13/11...$15.00.
http://dx.doi.org/10.1145/2526188.2526193

entendimento em nível arquitetural para se alcançar os atributos de qualidade desejados [3].

Esses métodos tradicionalmente produzem relatórios como saída do processo. Em geral, as informações contidas nesses relatórios são relacionadas à análise de riscos das decisões arquiteturais. Alguns métodos, como o ATAM (*Architecture Tradeoff Analysis Method*) [1], produzem informações sobre pontos de sensibilidade e pontos de conflito (*tradeoffs*). Pontos de sensibilidade representam uma decisão arquitetural envolvendo um ou mais elementos arquiteturais críticos para satisfazer um atributo de qualidade particular. Por exemplo, o nível de confidencialidade em uma rede privada virtual (VPN – *Virtual Private Network*) pode ser sensível ao número de bits usados para encriptação. Por outro lado, os pontos de conflito representam decisões arquiteturais que afetam mais de um atributo de qualidade, sendo um ponto de sensibilidade para mais de um atributo. Por exemplo, alterar o nível de encriptação poderia ter um impacto tanto na segurança quanto no desempenho do sistema.

Métodos tradicionais de avaliação arquitetural são realizados manualmente através de reuniões e baseiam-se nas habilidades e conhecimentos dos arquitetos e avaliadores. Tais métodos são aplicados quando a arquitetura já foi especificada, mas a implementação ainda não foi iniciada. Porém, a implementação do sistema é um elemento adicional que pode ser usado na avaliação arquitetural quando disponível, pois fornece informações úteis se adequadamente analisado.

Em determinadas situações, quando um software evolui sofrendo erosões arquiteturais críticas [4], surge a necessidade de executar o processo de avaliação novamente porque a arquitetura projetada tem muitas diferenças em relação à arquitetura implementada [5]. O uso da implementação neste contexto possibilita a automação do processo, promovendo o reuso de informações críticas relacionadas à arquitetura durante sua implementação, teste e evolução. No contexto de evolução, uma proposta específica para o domínio web [6] guia os desenvolvedores durante a evolução da arquitetura gerenciando a adição de novos atributos de qualidade e conflitos entre eles. Porém, esta abordagem não pode ser caracterizada como um método de avaliação, nem tampouco lida ou utiliza informações provenientes do código fonte.

Este trabalho propõe uma abordagem de avaliação arquitetural semi-automatizada considerando informações obtidas através da análise do código fonte. Para isso devem ser providas informações relacionadas aos métodos de avaliação arquitetural em determinados artefatos da implementação através do uso de metadados (anotações, XML, etc). A abordagem provê uma ferramenta que executa análises estáticas e dinâmicas produzindo relatórios com informações relevantes sobre cenários, atributos de qualidade e artefatos de código. Algumas análises oferecidas são: (i) indicação dos cenários afetados por um atributo de qualidade particular; (ii) indicação de cenários potenciais para pontos de conflitos entre os atributos de qualidade e que deveriam requerer mais atenção da equipe de arquitetos; (iii) tempo de execução de um determinado cenário; e (iv) se ele foi executado com sucesso ou falhou. Nessa abordagem, quando a implementação do sistema evolui, pode-se manter os metadados, ou ajustá-los, e automaticamente gerar um novo relatório de avaliação com as informações atualizadas.

Atualmente, a abordagem tem focado e sido aplicada no contexto de sistemas de informação web. Em particular, ela já foi aplicada no contexto de um sistema web de e-commerce de caráter acadêmico e em um sistema web de gestão de informações acadêmicas. É importante notar que nossa abordagem não objetiva substituir métodos tradicionais de avaliação, pelo contrário, a ideia é que ela venha complementar tais métodos promovendo a avaliação contínua da arquitetura durante a implementação e evolução do sistema.

O restante desde trabalho está organizado como segue: a Seção 2 apresenta uma visão geral dos passos necessários para aplicar a abordagem; a Seção 3 apresenta a ferramenta de suporte fornecida; a Seção 4 ilustra a aplicação da abordagem em dois sistemas web; a Seção 5 apresenta alguns trabalhos relacionados; finalmente, a Seção 6 conclui o trabalho.

2. ABORDAGEM PROPOSTA

O principal objetivo da abordagem proposta é aumentar a automação da avaliação arquitetural através da condução de análises estática e dinâmicas que fazem uso de informações arquiteturais extras (metadados) adicionadas ao código fonte da aplicação.

É importante notar que a abordagem apresentada aqui é independente de linguagens de programação ou plataformas. Posteriormente, apresentaremos uma ferramenta que concretiza a mesma para sistemas implementados em Java e usa anotações como fonte de metadados. Para uma linguagem sem suporte a anotações poderíamos definir os metadados externamente ao código usando XML.

A abordagem é dividida em cinco passos, sendo eles: (i) escolher os cenários de avaliação para a arquitetura alvo; (ii) identificar o método de início de execução de cada cenário de avaliação escolhido; (iii) identificar atributos de qualidade no código fonte do sistema; (iv) adicionar informação arquitetural extra ao código fonte do sistema; e (v) executar as análises estáticas e dinâmicas com a ferramenta de suporte para avaliação arquitetural.

A Figura 1 apresenta uma visão geral da abordagem mostrando os artefatos de entrada e saída para cada etapa. As subseções a seguir detalham cada uma das atividades da abordagem.

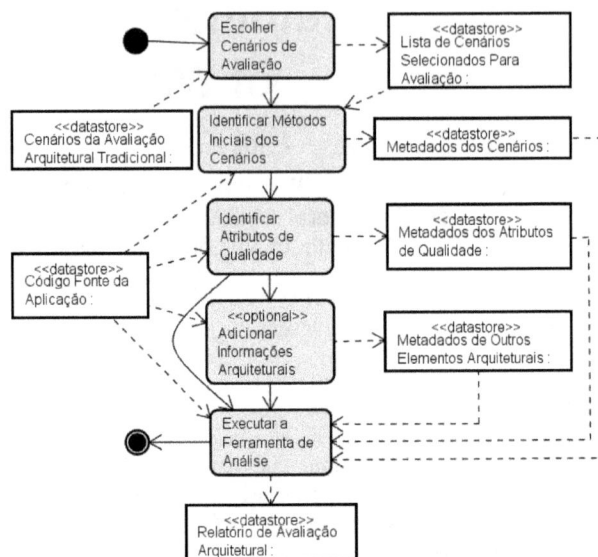

Figura 1. Diagrama de atividades UML ilustrando as etapas.

A abordagem proposta não se restringe a atributos de qualidade particulares, embora, atualmente, o foco principal da ferramenta desenvolvida seja os atributos de qualidade de desempenho e robustez. É importante perceber que a análise dinâmica é viável principalmente para aqueles atributos que podem ser quantificados durante a execução do sistema, enquanto a análise estática pode ser aplicada com o objetivo de prover rastreabilidade para quaisquer atributos que tenham código específico para sua implementação.

2.1 Escolher Cenários de Avaliação

A primeira etapa da abordagem consiste em escolher os cenários da arquitetura alvo da avaliação. Idealmente, nesta etapa, deve-se reusar informações que foram geradas em avaliações conduzidas durante a elaboração da arquitetura. Em particular, os cenários levantados durante a aplicação das técnicas tradicionais de avaliação arquitetural, como o ATAM ou outros [7], podem ser reusados neste momento.

2.2 Identificar Métodos Iniciais dos Cenários

Nesta etapa, é preciso identificar os pontos iniciais do código fonte onde é iniciada a execução de cada cenário escolhido na etapa anterior. Quando identificamos um ponto de início de execução para um cenário, podemos considerar que ele define caminhos de execução que podem ser abstraídos para grafos de chamadas [8], onde cada nó no grafo representa um método e cada vértice representa uma possível invocação.

Uma solução simples para associar os cenários ao código fonte é identificar o método que inicia a execução do cenário, considerando ele como o nó raiz do grafo. No caso de sistemas web, por exemplo, os métodos de início para execução dos cenários serão aqueles responsáveis pelo tratamento das requisições web (*front-end*). Baseado nas invocações destes métodos a outros métodos é possível montar o grafo de chamadas completo. A abordagem especifíca que o metadado para cenários (Scenario) define um nome (*name*) que o identifica e representa o método inicial de execução.

2.3 Identificar Atributos de Qualidade

Atualmente, a abordagem prevê a identificação de atributos de qualidade na granularidade de métodos. Em outras palavras, devemos associar metadados que representem os atributos de qualidade com métodos específicos. Por exemplo, quando um método particular deve ser monitorado considerando o atributo de qualidade de desempenho, ele deveria ser associado aos metadados específicos para tal atributo.

Como dito anteriormente, a abordagem não é restrita a um conjunto de atributos de qualidade particulares. Atualmente, são especificados metadados para dar suporte aos seguintes atributos de qualidade: desempenho, segurança, confiabilidade e robustez. A Figura 2 apresenta tais atributos.

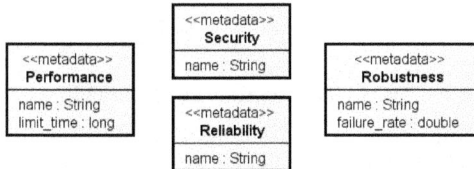

Figura 2. Metadados atualmente previstos pela abordagem.

Para o atributo de qualidade desempenho (`Performance`) deve-se fornecer o nome (*name*) e o tempo limite de execução (*limit_time*). O nome identifica de forma única ocorrências do atributo no código fonte da aplicação. O tempo limite é um inteiro em milissegundos que indica o tempo máximo esperado para que o método execute. O método associado com `Performance` deveria completar sua execução em um tempo menor ou igual ao indicado pelo valor de tempo limite. Como consequência, uma das possibilidades é monitorar a execução dos métodos e verificar se eles executam dentro do tempo esperado, fornecendo algum tipo de alerta caso isso não ocorra. Outra estratégia é comparar se o desempenho de determinados métodos têm melhorado ou degradado após uma evolução do cenário, indicando para os desenvolvedores os métodos em questão.

No caso do atributo de qualidade robustez (`Robustness`) é definido um nome único (*name*) e uma taxa máxima de falha (*failure_rate*). A ideia é monitorar a execução do sistema, detectando se a execução de determinados métodos associados com esse metadado falharam ou não durante sua execução. Um valor zero indica que o método nunca falhou, enquanto um valor um indica que o método falhou para todas as execuções. Quando a taxa de falhas de um método para um determinado número de execuções é superior ao valor especificado em *failure_rate*, um alerta é lançado aos desenvolvedores. Semelhante ao caso anterior, é possível analisar se os métodos associados apresentam taxas de falha menores ou maiores após uma evolução do sistema.

Os atributos de segurança (`Security`) e confiabilidade (`Reliability`) são tratados atualmente de forma mais simples. Ambos definem um nome (*name*) que deve ser único. O principal objetivo nestes dois casos é indicar quais partes do sistema estariam associadas de forma crítica com esses atributos. Dessa forma, é possível fazer o rastreamento deles no código fonte da aplicação permitindo, estaticamente, determinar para cada cenário quais atributos de qualidade o afetam, ou ainda, se o cenário tem potencial para conter pontos de conflito. Por exemplo, quando desempenho e segurança são requisitos dentro do mesmo cenário, é comum haver um acoplamento forte entre eles de forma que ambos se influenciem negativamente [6], ou seja, melhorar um

implica em degradar o outro. No contexto de um sistema web, adicionar um componente de criptografia aumenta o nível de segurança, mas certamente fará o desempenho ser reduzido.

2.4 Adicionar Informações Arquiteturais

A abordagem é voltada para avaliação arquitetural, assim ela encoraja a introdução de metadados que associem informações sobre elementos arquiteturais ao código fonte, como, por exemplo, os componentes. Atualmente, a abordagem define informações para o metadado `Component` que é identificado pelo seu nome e que permite indicar quais classes do sistema são consideradas componentes, possibilitando que o resultado da análise dos atributos de qualidade e cenários possa ser feita no nível de componentes, o que talvez seja mais interessante do ponto de vista arquitetural do que classes, dado as suas respectivas granularidades. É importante perceber, como indicado na Figura 1, que esta etapa não precisa ser executada, ou seja, é um passo opcional da abordagem.

2.5 Executar a Ferramenta de Análise

A última etapa da abordagem consiste em executar a ferramenta de análise arquitetural. A ferramenta faz um *parser* do código fonte e dos metadados definidos realizando automaticamente as análises que podem ser estáticas ou dinâmicas com base nas configurações fornecidas de cenários e atributos de qualidade.

Durante a análise estática a ferramenta constrói o grafo de chamadas usando como nós raízes os métodos indicados como pontos iniciais de cenários. Em seguida, usando essas informações a ferramenta é capaz de indicar: (i) os atributos de qualidade associados com um determinado cenário; (ii) quais cenários são potenciais para conter conflitos entre atributos de qualidade; (iii) quais métodos, componentes ou cenários poderiam ser afetados devido um atributo de qualidade particular; e (iv) realizar a rastreabilidade do código, mostrando onde estão os cenários, os atributos de qualidade e os componentes. Como o próprio nome sugere a análise estática não necessita que o sistema seja executado.

A análise dinâmica também tira proveito dos metadados adicionados, o que permite monitorar os atributos de qualidade, como desempenho e robustez, quantificando valores que possam indicar melhoria ou degradação deles. Além disso, invocações usando reflexão (*reflective calls*) ou realizadas através de uma referência do tipo *interface* são capturadas com total precisão apenas pela análise dinâmica. Dessa forma, a ferramenta possibilita: (i) calcular valores para o tempo de execução e taxa de falhas de métodos individuais e cenários completos; (ii) verificar se as restrições definidas pelos atributos de qualidade são respeitadas; (iii) salvar várias informações do contexto da execução; e (iv) adicionar mais informação útil à análise estática, aumentando a precisão dela, por exemplo, na detecção de pontos de conflitos entre atributos de qualidade.

3. FERRAMENTA DE SUPORTE

Nesta seção apresentamos a ferramenta implementada para dar suporte à abordagem definida na seção anterior no contexto de sistemas web. Ela foi dividida em dois componentes principais: (i) a análise estática é implementada como um *plug-in* do Eclipse; e (ii) a análise dinâmica é implementada com aspectos usando a linguagem AspectJ e disponibilizada através de um JAR.

3.1 Análise Estática

O componente de análise estática realiza um *parser* de projetos Java lendo o código fonte do sistema e os metadados definidos. Atualmente, a ferramenta analisa apenas os arquivos Java do projeto alvo, ignorando outros tipos, por exemplo, aspectos (AspectJ). Para representar os metadados especificados pela abordagem, a ferramenta adota anotações. As principais classes responsáveis pelo processamento são mostradas na Figura 3.

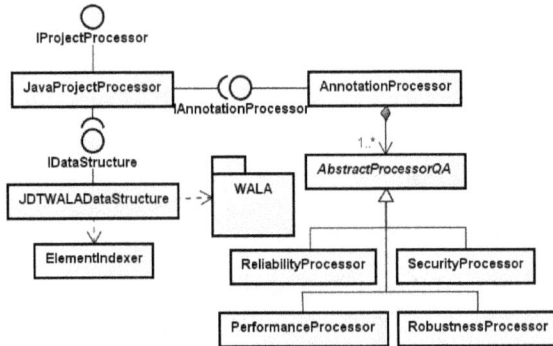

Figura 3. Diagrama de classes UML (análise estática).

A classe `JavaProjectProcessor` coordena o processo de criação do grafo de chamadas. O componente de análise estática usa o CAST (*Common Abstract Syntax Tree*) um *front-end* para análise de código fonte Java do WALA (*Watson Libraries for Analysis*) [9] que auxilia na construção do grafo dos cenários escolhidos. A classe `AnnotationProcessor` agrega um conjunto de classes concretas que definem estratégias capazes de processar diferentes anotações para atributos de qualidade. Cada uma dessas classes que especializam `AbstractProcessorQA` são responsáveis por processar a anotação de um tipo particular de atributo. Durante a leitura das anotações, a classe `AnnotationProcessor` também constrói uma lista contendo todos os cenários anotados.

A classe `JDTWALADataStructure` é usada para construir o grafo. Ela acessa as bibliotecas do WALA para realizar essa tarefa e permite acessar e manipular o grafo após ele ter sido construído. Esta classe também usa a classe `ElementIndexer` para construir índices de métodos, classes e anotações tornando o acesso ao grafo mais eficiente. Para isso `ElementIndexer` coleta informações navegando no grafo de chamadas e realizando um *parser* de algumas informações do código fonte.

O processo resumido de construção das estruturas de dados usadas na análise estática é mostrado na Figura 4. Inicialmente, `JavaProjectProcessor` usa `JDTWALADataStructure` para construir o grafo de chamadas e os índices. É importante lembrar que para montar o grafo serão usadas as bibliotecas do WALA (não representadas na Figura 4). `ElementIndexer` é usado para dar início ao processo de construção dos índices para acessar métodos e anotações. Após isso, uma instância de `AnnotationProcessor` processa a anotação de cenário (`@Scenario`), construindo a lista de cenários escolhidos. Em seguida, processa as anotações arquiteturais para componentes (`@Component`). Finalmente, processa cada anotação de atributo de qualidade (`@Performance`, `@Security`, `@Reliability`, `@Robusteness`) invocando todas as especializações de `AbstractProcessorQA`.

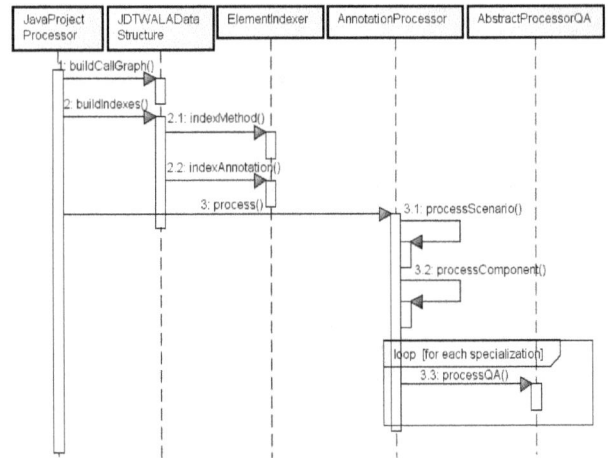

Figura 4. Diagrama de sequência UML (análise estática).

O componente de análise estática mantém um modelo de classes que associa todos os elementos e informações coletadas durante a análise do código fonte e das anotações. A Figura 5 mostra um diagrama parcial desse modelo. A classe `ScenarioData` agrega um método de início. `MethodData` referencia a classe onde o método foi declarado (`ClassData`) que pode ter sido definida no contexto de um componente (`ComponentData`). Um método (`MethodData`) pode possuir atributos de qualidade (`AbstractQAData`) que definem atributos específicos de acordo com seu tipo (`PerformanceData`, `SecurityData`, `ReliabilityData`, `RobustnessData`).

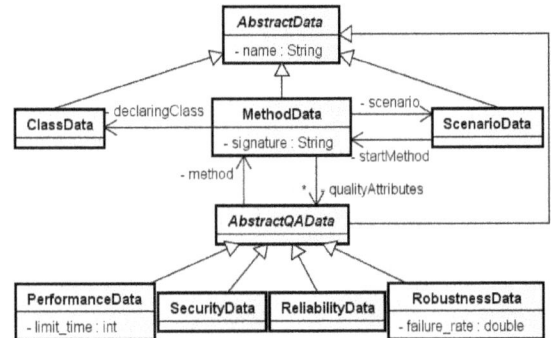

Figura 5. Modelo de classes para análise estática.

3.2 Análise Dinâmica

Na análise dinâmica aspectos monitoram a execução do sistema web, considerando os artefatos anotados. Idealmente, a ferramenta deve ser usada durante a execução dos testes do sistema, permitindo coletar dados da execução. A qualidade dos dados coletados pela análise estão diretamente relacionados aos testes executados para que o sistema seja monitorado, pois se eles não forçam situações problemáticas de erros, por exemplo, estes nunca ocorrerão e nunca serão detectados pelos aspectos.

A ferramenta, através dos aspectos implementados, intercepta e monitora a execução dos cenários, ou seja, métodos anotados com `@Scenario`. O fluxo de execução destes métodos é seguido, construindo-se um grafo de chamadas dinâmico que reflete o caminho exato de invocações realizadas para uma determinada execução do cenário em foco. Neste grafo, cada nó representa um método ou um construtor que foi invocado durante a execução do cenário. Em cada nó, são guardadas informações referentes aos seus atributos de qualidade de interesse, como o tempo de execução e se o mesmo executou com sucesso ou não.

Atualmente, o componente que implementa a análise dinâmica trabalha com quatro atributos de qualidade (segurança, desempenho, robustez e confiabilidade), sendo capaz de quantificar valores para dois deles (desempenho e robustez). Para o desempenho (*performance*) é calculado o tempo de execução para um método individualmente ou para um cenário completo, de acordo com o interesse. Para robustez (*robustness*) determina-se se o método ou o cenário completo foi executado com sucesso. Neste caso, a ferramenta considera que um método falhou se ele lançou alguma exceção para a entrada testada e, seguindo raciocínio semelhante, o cenário falhou se um ou mais de seus métodos falharam. Atualmente, não é feita uma quantificação semelhante para segurança (*security*) e confiabilidade (*reliability*), eles são usados para rastreabilidade de pontos importantes no código fonte e para auxílio na detecção de pontos de conflito entre os atributos.

É fornecido um aspecto para cada anotação de atributo de qualidade. Tais aspectos têm como objetivo monitorar a execução de métodos individuais que possuem uma anotação específica presente (@Performance, @Security, @Robustness ou @Reliability). Estes aspectos usam uma interface comum (IQAStrategy), o que possibilita desenvolvedores definirem suas próprias estratégias como ações extras que o aspecto pode realizar, além do seu comportamento padrão. Isso é útil, pois, em geral, essas estratégias variam até mesmo entre aplicações do mesmo domínio. A Figura 6 mostra cada aspecto implementado e a *interface* IQAStrategy que define o método execute(). Essencialmente para cada anotação de atributo de qualidade existe um aspecto e uma estratégia concreta.

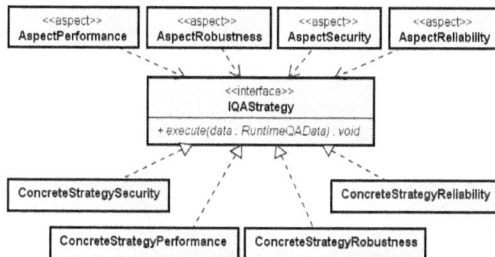

Figura 6. Aspectos e estratégias para atributos de qualidade.

A ferramenta fornece implementações padrões de estratégias, nas quais os aspectos capturam informações do contexto de execução relacionadas aos atributos de qualidade e as repassam para sua respectiva estratégia concreta que realiza o *log* dessas informações. Cabe ao desenvolvedor, que conhece as especificidades de sua aplicação, fornecer estratégias mais sofisticadas de acordo com a necessidade.

O método execute() da *interface* IQAStrategy recebe como parâmetro um objeto do tipo RuntimeQAData que contém informações sobre a anotação interceptada pelo aspecto. A Figura 7 mostra as implementações fornecidas para essa classe abstrata. São armazenados no modelo o método e a anotação correspondente do atributo de qualidade. Para desempenho (*performance*) é armazenado o tempo (*time*) que o método anotado levou para executar. Para robustez (*robustness*) é armazenada a exceção levantada (*exception*) caso o método tenha falhado. Atualmente, a ferramenta não armazena informações

extras, além da anotação e do método, para segurança (*security*) e confiabilidade (*reliability*).

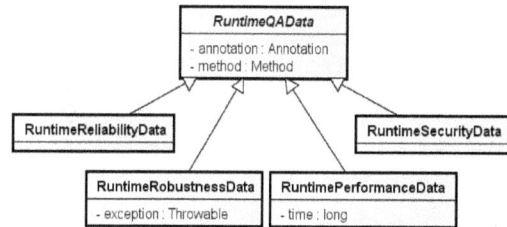

Figura 7. Modelo de classes para análise dinâmica.

Além dos aspectos individuais para atributos de qualidade, existe outro aspecto que monitora a execução dos cenários interceptando as invocações a partir de um ponto inicial determinado pelo método anotado com @Scenario. Assim, AspectScenario intercepta a execução de métodos com essa anotação que representam os pontos de início dos cenários e segue o fluxo de execução das invocações originadas a partir do ponto inicial. Dessa forma, o aspecto constrói um grafo de chamadas dinâmico (em tempo de execução) que representa uma execução particular de um cenário específico.

A estrutura de classes para suporte ao grafo dinâmico é mostrada na Figura 8. Para cada nova execução de cenário, um novo grafo é gerado (RuntimeCallGraph) e armazenado em uma lista de caminhos de execução (ExecutionPaths). Cada RuntimeCallGraph é referente a um cenário e possui o nome dele (*scenario_name*), além do nó raiz do grafo (RuntimeNode). Cada nó representa um membro (*member*) que, atualmente, pode ser um método ou um construtor e possui vários filhos representando suas invocações para outros membros. Cada nó possui os atributos *time* e *exception* que são, respectivamente, o tempo que ele levou para executar e a exceção caso ele tenha levantado alguma. Neste contexto, o tempo para execução do cenário é igual ao tempo de execução do seu nó (método) raiz.

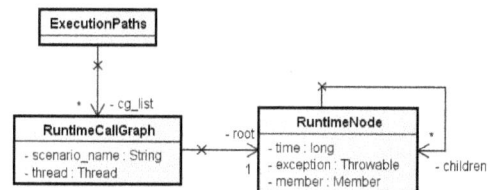

Figura 8. Modelo para grafo de chamadas dinâmico.

Ainda na Figura 8, além do nome do cenário, cada execução é identificada também usando informações da *thread* que executou o cenário. Em sistemas web, um mesmo cenário pode ter execuções paralelas originadas por requisições geradas por clientes diferentes. Imagine, por exemplo, dois clientes tentando se autenticar em um sistema web ao mesmo tempo, cada um deles terá sua própria execução do cenário de autenticação.

A análise dinâmica pode ser executada de duas formas. Desabilitar o aspecto de cenário e monitorar apenas os atributos de qualidade anotados nos métodos de forma individual. Ou desabilitar os aspectos individuais e focar apenas os cenários e atributos de qualidade capturados dentro de sua execução. Ambas as formas podem ser usadas em conjunto.

229

4. AVALIAÇÃO PRELIMINAR

A abordagem foi aplicada em dois sistemas. O primeiro foi um sistema de comércio eletrônico, no qual foi aplicada tanto a análise estática quanto a dinâmica. O segundo foi um sistema web de larga escala para gestão de atividades acadêmicas, no qual executamos a análise estática. Nosso principal objetivo foi conduzir uma avaliação inicial da abordagem verificando sua viabilidade na prática. Durante essa avaliação preliminar, não foi executado o quarto passo (que é opcional) da abordagem, que consiste na adição de informações arquiteturais extras.

4.1 Sistema Web de Comércio Eletrônico

O primeiro estudo foi realizado em um sistema de comércio eletrônico [10] [11] desenvolvido dentro da academia por estudantes de graduação e pós-graduação da UFRN (Universidade Federal do Rio Grande do Norte). Esse sistema implementa um produto de uma linha de produto de software para *e-commerce* descrita em [12].

Este estudo visou dois principais pontos da análise: (i) descobrir se existem potenciais cenários que mantenham conflitos entre seus atributos de qualidade, por exemplo, segurança e desempenho; e (ii) entender como os atributos de qualidade afetam cada cenário, por exemplo, verificando o tempo de execução do mesmo ou se ocorreram falhas na execução. Para o primeiro ponto, foi utilizada a análise estática, enquanto que para o segundo foi necessário executar a análise dinâmica. Os parágrafos a seguir reproduzem o passo-a-passo apresentado na Seção 2 necessários para aplicar a abordagem.

Como primeira etapa é preciso escolher os cenários que serão avaliados. Foram escolhidos um total de cinco cenários: (i) registro de informações de *login* – registra informações sobre *login* do usuário, como nome de usuário e senha; (ii) registro de informações pessoais – registra informações pessoais do usuário, como nome, endereço, data de nascimento, documento de identificação, etc; (iii) registro de cartão de crédito – registra informações sobre o cartão de crédito do usuário, como número e data de vencimento; (iv) pesquisa de produtos – permite pesquisar por produtos pelo seu nome, tipo ou característica; (v) incluir item para carrinho – permite ao usuário adicionar um item de produto ao seu carrinho de compras virtual.

No segundo passo foi adicionada a anotação `@Scenario` para cada um dos métodos iniciais de cada cenário a fim de identificá-los. Os métodos anotados foram, na mesma ordem de apresentação dos cenários: (i) `registerLogin()`; (ii) `registerUser()`; (iii) `registerCreditCard()`; (iv) `searchProducts()`; (v) `includeItemToCart()`. É interessante notar que como são métodos de início para execução dos cenários todos eles estão declarados dentro de classes *Managed Beans* do *framework Java Server Faces* (JSF).

Para executar o terceiro passo, foram escolhidos alguns métodos principais do sistema que estão associados com algum tipo de atributo de qualidade, sendo eles: (i) anotação `@Performance`, `@Reliability` e `@Robustness` para o método `save()` – usado para persistir em banco de dados os objetos do sistema, ele deveria executar o mais rápido possível, de forma confiável e sem falhar para entradas inesperadas; (ii) `@Security` para os métodos `registerLogin()`, `registerUser()` e `registerCreditCard()` – estes métodos manipulam informações confidenciais dos usuários tendo segurança como um de seus requisitos.

Finalmente, a última etapa é executar a ferramenta para realizar a análise automatizada. Primeiramente, foi executada a análise estática. A Tabela 1 apresenta uma visão parcial do relatório gerado. É possível observar que a ferramenta detectou para cada cenário quais atributos de qualidade são atuantes. Para os cenários de registro de informações foi detectado o atributo segurança, pois o método inicial desses cenários foi anotado com `@Security`. Para o cenário registro de cartão de crédito, especificamente, foram detectados os atributos de qualidade confiabilidade, desempenho e robustez. Isso aconteceu porque algum dos métodos presentes em um dos caminhos de execução desse cenário está relacionado com tais atributos, sendo o responsável neste caso, o método `save()` anotado com `@Reliability`, `@Performance` e `@Robustness`. Os outros cenários não tiveram atributos de qualidade associados.

Tabela 1. Atributos de qualidade que afetam cenários.

Cenário	Atributo de Qualidade
Registro de informações de login	Segurança
Registro de informações pessoais	Segurança
Registro de cartão de crédito	Confiabilidade Segurança Desempenho Robustez
Pesquisa de produtos	-
Incluir item para carrinho	-

Finalmente, analisando o contexto da Tabela 1, a ferramenta é capaz de responder o primeiro ponto levantado para o estudo, indicando que o cenário para registro de cartão de crédito, potencialmente, contém conflitos entre atributos de qualidade, pois existe mais de um deles atuando no mesmo, em particular, segurança e desempenho que são classicamente conflitantes.

Para verificar o segundo ponto do estudo é necessário calcular os valores dos atributos de qualidade. Para isso precisamos executar a análise dinâmica a fim de exercitar os cenários escolhidos executando o sistema com seu código fonte anotado e o conjunto de aspectos habilitados.

A Tabela 2 mostra algumas informações coletadas para os cenários de registro durante a análise. É possível ver que a ferramenta foi usada para rastrear os pontos dentro do cenário onde encontram-se métodos anotados e associados com atributos de qualidade. Por exemplo, o cenário registro de informações pessoais é afetado pelo atributo de segurança devido ao método `registerUser()`. Também foi calculado o tempo médio de execução e a taxa de falha para cada cenário.

Tabela 2. Amostra de dados coletados pela análise dinâmica.

Registro de informações de login	
Tempo de execução (ms):	4
Taxa de falha:	0%
@Performance:	-
@Security:	registerLogin()
@Reliability:	-
@Robustness:	-
Registro de informações pessoais	
Tempo de execução (ms)	3
Taxa de falha:	0%
@Performance:	-
@Security:	registerUser()
@Reliability:	-
@Robustness:	-
Registro de cartão de crédito	
Tempo de execução (ms):	152

Taxa de falha:	0%
@Performance:	save()
@Security:	registerCreditCard()
@Reliability:	save()
@Robustness:	save()

A ferramenta de suporte para a abordagem foi capaz, no contexto de um sistema web, de fornecer informações úteis relacionadas aos cenários e atributos de qualidade para execução da avaliação arquitetural automatizada, mais especificamente, ela é capaz de indicar pontos críticos do sistema que requerem mais atenção dos arquitetos e avaliadores, como pontos de conflito ou cenários que possuem tempo de execução ou taxas de falha muito altas. Neste contexto, consideramos que tanto a abordagem apresentada, quanto a ferramenta implementada são viáveis e úteis para esse tipo de aplicação prática.

4.2 Sistema de Gestão Acadêmica

O segundo estudo aplicou a análise estática definida pela abordagem para o projeto que implementa a arquitetura dos sistemas integrados acadêmicos desenvolvidos pela SINFO (Superintendência de Informática) na UFRN, em particular, o SIGAA (Sistema Integrado de Gestão de Atividades Acadêmicas). A SINFO desenvolve sistemas de informação de larga escala [13] para automação de atividades administrativas e acadêmicas em universidades. Os sistemas desenvolvidos possuem abrangência nacional e vêm sendo usados em várias instituições de ensino.

O principal objetivo deste estudo, ainda que de forma preliminar, é verificar como a abordagem, através da ferramenta implementada, se comporta quando aplicada a um sistema de larga escala. Devido à complexidade do sistema, até o momento foi conduzida apenas a análise estática de alguns cenários selecionados. Por enquanto, estamos interessados em: (i) determinar quais atributos de qualidade afetam determinados cenários; e (ii) quais cenários, potencialmente, podem conter pontos de conflito entre atributos.

Reproduzindo os passos da abordagem foram escolhidos como cenários para avaliação: (i) envio de mensagem (envio de e-mails); (ii) geração de documento autenticado (geração de documentos assinados com código digital); (iii) autenticação de usuário (através de página web convencional); e (iv) autenticação de usuário móvel (através de dispositivos móveis).

Para cada cenário foram identificados como métodos de início, respectivamente: (i) sendMessage(); (ii) execute(); (iii) userAuthentication(); (iv) mobileUserAuthentication(). Já os métodos anotados com atributos de qualidade foram: (i) getJdbcTemplate() com @Performance – usado para várias operações no banco de dados; (ii) enqueue() com @Security – usado para enfileirar mensagem que serão enviadas pela rede; (iii) createRegistry() com @Security – usado para criar registros de autenticação para documentos; (iv) toMD5() com @Security – usado para gerar *hashes* MD5 de textos, como senhas; (v) initDataSourceJndi() com @Robustness – usado para inicializar parâmetros do banco de dados.

A Tabela 3 apresenta uma visão parcial dos resultados gerados pela análise estática. Podemos ver quais atributos de qualidade afetam os cenários e quais cenários podem conter algum tipo de conflito, respondendo os pontos levantados no início do estudo. Seguindo o raciocínio que qualquer cenário afetado por mais de um atributo de qualidade tem potencial para conter algum tipo de conflito, apenas o cenário para envio de mensagens foi considerado livre de conflito.

Tabela 3. Cenários e atributos de qualidade.

Cenário:	Autenticação de Usuário
@Performance:	getJdbcTemplate()
@Security:	toMD5()
@Robustness:	initDataSourceJndi()
Conflito:	*Potencial*
Cenário:	Autenticação de Usuário Móvel
@Performance:	getJdbcTemplate()
@Security:	toMD5()
@Robustness:	initDataSourceJndi()
Conflito:	*Potencial*
Cenário:	Geração de Documentos Autenticados
@Performance:	-
@Security:	createRegistry()
@Robustness:	initDataSourceJndi()
Conflito:	*Potencial*
Cenário:	Envio de Mensagens
@Performance:	-
@Security:	enqueue()
@Robustness:	-
Conflito:	*Não*

5. TRABALHOS RELACIONADOS

Apesar de alguns trabalhos tratarem do tema relacionado à automação da avaliação arquitetural, não foram encontrados trabalhos relacionados que conduzam avaliações arquiteturais usando análises estáticas e dinâmicas através de metadados em código fonte. Esta seção discute trabalhos de avaliação arquitetural ou que propõem estratégias de análise similares as que foram usadas nesta abordagem.

Ao longo dos últimos anos, muitos métodos de avaliação arquitetural foram propostos, como ATAM, SAAM, ARID [1] e ALMA [2]. Estes métodos confiam em atividades de revisão manual e experiência dos avaliadores. A abordagem proposta neste artigo é complementar, provendo suporte semi-automatizado para avaliação com análise do código fonte. A ideia é possibilitar a avaliação arquitetural contínua durante a implementação e evolução do sistema.

Com estratégias similares, pesquisas recentes, também propõem adicionar informações extras ao código fonte visando algum tipo de análise automatizada ou apenas a documentação da arquitetura. Christensen & Hansen [14] usam anotações para adicionar informações sobre componentes e padrões de projeto ao código com o propósito de documentar a arquitetura. Mirakhorli et al [15] apresentam uma abordagem para rastrear interesses arquiteturais significantes no código, especialmente relacionados com táticas que seriam soluções para uma faixa de atributos de qualidade. Esses trabalhos, entretanto, não exploram o uso de informações combinadas de cenários e atributos de qualidade, ambos fundamentais para avaliação arquitetural.

Tibermacine & Zernadji [6] propõem uma abordagem para supervisionar a evolução de serviços de orquestração web considerando atributos de qualidade. A proposta é baseada na análise de documentação, sendo mostrado como decisões de projeto que afetam atributos de qualidade podem ser formalmente documentadas e como essa documentação pode ser usada para supervisionar alterações arquiteturais. O esquema contém informações sobre quais atributos de qualidade são conflitantes, permitindo saber se uma alteração na arquitetura que afeta algum atributo pode conflitar com outro. A principal diferença entre esse trabalho e a abordagem apresentada é que o primeiro não tira proveito da análise do código fonte, sendo a análise feita com base no esquema de documentação definido. A presente abordagem focaliza a análise no código fonte, permitindo executar a avaliação quando a implementação evolui. As duas abordagens podem ser combinadas. Inicialmente, quando apenas o projeto da arquitetura está disponível, pode-se aplicar a proposta de Tibermacine & Zernadji. Posteriormente, com a implementação do sistema disponível, é possível aplicar a presente abordagem visando supervisionar a adição de novos conflitos nos cenários quando o código fonte é alterado.

6. CONCLUSÃO

Este trabalho apresentou uma abordagem para automação da avaliação de arquiteturas de software através da análise do código fonte com metadados. Tais metadados provêem informações sobre cenários e atributos de qualidade, permitindo análises estáticas e dinâmicas do sistema. Uma ferramenta de suporte foi apresentada e a aplicação da abordagem foi realizada em dois sistemas web, um de caráter acadêmico e um sistema de larga escala. Os resultados preliminares sugerem que a ferramenta de suporte à abordagem é capaz de prover informações úteis ligadas aos cenários de avaliação e aos atributos de qualidade.

A abordagem apresentada está em evolução. Novas etapas estão sendo incluídas na mesma para permitir aplicá-la à análise e caracterização da evolução de arquiteturas de software considerando cenários e atributos de qualidade. Essencialmente, a abordagem está sendo expandida e aplicada no contexto de evoluções de sistemas web, objetivando determinar se houve degradação arquitetural, em termos de atendimentos de determinados atributos de qualidade, quando considerando uma evolução específica do sistema. A ferramenta de suporte à abordagem realiza as análises automaticamente após a anotação do código fonte, porém tais anotações ainda precisam ser adicionadas manualmente, o que confere um caráter semi-automático para o estágio atual da abordagem.

Agradecimentos. Este trabalho foi parcialmente financiado pelo National Institute of Science and Technology for Software Engineering (INES), financiado pelo CNPq, processos 573964/2008-4 e PDI – Grandes Desafios 560256/2010-8, e por SINFO/UFRN.

7. REFERÊNCIAS

[1] Clements, P., Kazman, R., Klein, M. 2002. Evaluating Software Architectures: Methods and Case Studies, Addison-Wesley.

[2] Bengtsson, P., Lassing, N., Bosch, J., Vliet, H. (2004). Architecture-level modifiability analysis (ALMA). Journal of Systems and Software. 69, 1-2 (January 2004).

[3] Kazman, R., Abowd, G., Bass, L., Clements, P. 1996. Scenario-Based Analysis of Software Architecture. IEEE Softw. 13, 6 (November 1996), 47-55.

[4] Silva, L., Balasubramaniam, D. 2012. Controlling software architecture erosion: A survey. J. Syst. Softw. 85, 1 (January 2012), 132-151.

[5] Abi-Antoun, M., Aldrich, J. 2009. Static extraction and conformance analysis of hierarchical runtime architectural structure using annotations. SIGPLAN Not. 44, 10 (October 2009), 321-340.

[6] Tibermacine, C. and Zernadji, T. (2011). Supervising the evolution of web service orchestrations using quality requirements. In Proceedings of the 5th European conference on Software architecture (ECSA'11).

[7] Muhammad and Gorton, I. (2004). Comparison of Scenario-Based Software Architecture Evaluation Methods. In Proceedings of the 11th Asia-Pacific Software Engineering Conference (APSEC '04).

[8] Holmes, R., Notkin, D. 2011. Identifying program, test, and environmental changes that affect behaviour. In Proceedings of the 33rd International Conference on Software Engineering (ICSE '11).

[9] WALA, T. J. Watson Libraries for Analysis: http://wala.sourceforge.net, May 2013.

[10] Torres, M. 2011. Avaliação Sistemática de Abordagens de Derivação de Produtos. Dissertação (Mestrado), Universidade Federal do Rio Grande do Norte (UFRN), Natal, Brasil, 2011.

[11] Aquino, H. M. (2011). Uma Abordagem Sistemática para o Teste de Linhas de Produto de Software. 2011. Dissertação (Mestrado), Universidade Federal do Rio Grande do Norte (UFRN), Natal, Brasil, 2011.

[12] Lau, S. Q. 2006. Domain Analysis of E-Commerce Systems Using Feature-Based Model Templates, MSc Thesys, University of Waterloo.

[13] SINFO. (2012). Superintendência de Informática, UFRN: http://www.info.ufrn.br/wikisistemas, May 2013.

[14] Christensen, H. B., Hansen, K, M. (2011). Towards architectural information in implementation (NIER track). In Proceedings of the 33rd International Conference on Software Engineering (ICSE '11).

[15] Mirakhorli, M., Shin, Y., Cleland-Huang, J., Cinar, M. 2012. A tactic-centric approach for automating traceability of quality concerns. In Proceedings of the 2012 International Conference on Software Engineering (ICSE 2012).

An Ad-Hoc Web of Things Service Bus

Sérgio Gramacho, Cássio Prazeres, Gustavo Bittencourt
Departamento de Ciência da Computação - Instituto de Matemática
Universidade Federal da Bahia (UFBA)
Caixa Postal 15.064 – 91.501-970 – Salvador – BA – Brazil
{sergioluis, prazeres, gustavo}@dcc.ufba.br

ABSTRACT

The Web of Things (WoT) is a new trend related to the Internet that have yet to scale to mass usage. Consumer and in-vehicle contexts can promote WoT to mass usage. For these contexts, ad-hoc operation and complexity abstraction is very important. This paper suggests the creation of an ad-hoc service bus for the WoT. The solution uses Bonjour and Link-Local technologies to provide the main needed functions for a WoT RESTFul service bus operation. A proof of concept was executed to demonstrate this proposition's viability in a ah-hoc network without any infrastructure.

Categories and Subject Descriptors

H.5.4 [**INFORMATION INTERFACES AND PRESENTATION**]: Hypertext/Hypermedia

General Terms

Design

Keywords

Web of Things, Service Bus, Ad Hoc, Network Multicast

1. INTRODUCTION

The Internet is now 40 years old. It started as a government research project called ARPANET in 1969 [10], which, when finished, was continued by involved organizations. From its initial goal of connecting isolated networks in a "network of networks" for information sharing, it had a major improvement in broad usage and visibility by the idea of standardized document sharing using a hypertext model proposed by Sir Tim Bernes-Lee in late 1980s. This proposal was called the World Wide Web (WWW) [1](The Internet of Documents). Later on we saw another big trend in the Internet related to people collaboration (The Internet of People).

A new trend in the Internet is now forecasted and perceived in which computers or devices with computational and

communication capabilities (Smart Things - ST) will be connected to the Internet to autonomously interact (Smart IP Things - SipT). A simple service provided by one device when combined with other services from other devices have the potential to execute complex and complete functions to people or to other devices. This is known as the "Internet of Things" (IoT) [4].

Despite having a standardized set of communication protocols (IP, TCP, UDP) that simplifies communications, on the applications perspective each SipT should provide its functions to people or other SipT through its APIs. Many efforts are still being made to standardize APIs for Smart Things and some have emerged as broadly adopted standards in specific application domains (UPNP/DLNA for the consumer media devices domain, SODA for enterprise service buses context etc.) [12] [2].

The Web of Things (WoT) is a proposition to make STs not only IP enabled but also Web enabled. The idea is to go beyond standardized communication using IP and leverage programmability capability to Smart Things by adopting the Web architecture, protocols and languages [5].

Complexity abstraction is very important to make STs viable in non specialized contexts, such as consumer market. It is important to provide automation, transparency and ad-hoc availability to STs, let it be Smart IP Thing or Web enabled Things (WeT). One way to do so is to make Smart Things interaction with each other and with people the least dependent on installed infrastructural components and on any Internet connection path, though considering an Intranet approach. This internal approach also simplifies security, as things in a local network context are less exposed to security issues.

This work has two main objectives: define a simple yet functional locally and ad-hoc available integration point for Smart Things (service bus) and provide high level of abstration to its operation in the Web of Things consumer market applications context.

2. BACKGROUND AND RELATED WORK

In their article introducing the Internet of Things (IoT), Gershenfeld, Krikorian and Cohen propose that devices interaction could be managed by software instead of the common approach of strict hard wired interaction pre defined by engineers in their installation [4]. To accomplish this and deal with the plethora of different networking technologies that these devices could minimally support, they propose an IP only (Internet Protocol) communication over the many possible physical layers, let it be a IP packet printed in a label, electrical impulses in the local electric network, electromagnetic waves carrying an IP Packet or light pulses. This is such a revolutionary proposition, somehow similar to the proposition of a packet network back in the time of the ARPANET, contrasting with circuit switching network used worldwide for telephony in that time.

Other proposition builds on the success of the Web and suggests each device as a Web Server. Through its web server functionality the device can offer its functions as web resources, accessed by other devices and by coordination frameworks using the Web architecture and its set of protocols, languages, etc. A great advantage of this proposition is to simplify the programmability for Smart Things. Instead of dealing with specific APIs for each domain or even each STs' manufacturer, one could use Web architectures, standards and protocols such as HTTP, HTML, RESTFul, XML, JSON to provide and to consume Web Things' services [5].

The referred coordination framework is a piece of the needed infrastructure for WoT. It is a software component which provides functions to the devices such as addressing, device and service registration, service discovery, composition and coordination (to represent a complex process execution dependent of many services). This kind of framework is also called "Service Bus".

Device interaction can be held in other way then using a service bus and web services. Some standards for device interaction rely on specific network APIs (Application Program Interfaces), such as UPnP.

Device communication network APIs are small and lightweight components embedded in devices that do not depend on any centralized component. They use peer-to-peer communication and are, therefore, very suitable in ad-hoc scenarios. However, this approach lacks some advanced functions such as service combination and coordination, semantic service discovery and service matching, as depicted in the model proposed by Yang [12].

A service bus relies on a specialized software component that centralizes information about available services and provides advanced functions. Such set of functions is least likely to be available in a distributed architecture and so are not commonly provided in Ad-Hoc scenarios such as consumer market. The details of a conceptual semantic service bus (explaining the functions of a semantic service bus) can be obtained in [12].

In Guinard's reference architecture for WoT, it is proposed that discovery functions should be held the same way as they are provided in the Web: by search engines such as Google. Embedded microformats are a way to provide semantics to these search engines. However, he recognizes the importance of having local discovery capabilities and therefore proposes an infrastructural component called LLDU (Local Lookup and Discovery Units): "... software components allow smart things to announce themselves and clients to search for specific (local) services offered by connected smart things." [5]. This component is conceptually the same as what we are calling a service bus. As an infrastructural component in the WoT reference architecture, it is expected that LLDU's operation to be a result of planning, installation and maintenance efforts of a specialist.

Trifa et al. [11] explain how the LLDU discover module can detect new WeTs using information existent in a network infrastructure element. They suggest an example of a network router using an open source firmware and a web management interface package. Despite being open and available for some router brands, the process of installing this firmware is limited to some router models and brands and is extremely difficult, only being viable if executed by highly specialized network professionals. Assuming the existence of such kind of equipment and person in a consumer market context is, again, unlikely.

The existence of the IP network and its essential services, such as IP address configuration (DHCP, BOOTP) and name resolution (DNS) are taken as granted, which is a good assumption when it comes to the Internet or an Enterprise context, but not quite true considering local contexts and ad-hoc usage situations (such as in consumer market or in vehicle usage - cars, trains, ships). This is recognized in [6]: "... real-world services are found in highly dynamic environments where devices and their underlying services constantly degrade, vanish, and possibly reappear. As such, this infrastructure cannot be considered as static and long-lived as traditional enterprise services."

When it comes to a consumer market, the success of an initiative is strictly related to its simplicity to users, and therefore it is very important to abstract any complexities by providing fully automated functions. An ad-hoc service bus is our first contribution to this objective.

A service bus can be considered a component in the application layer of the OSI network layers model and so it relies on the other layers to operate. In a consumer market context it is a risk to assume the network and its complimentary functions such as auto configuration (DHCP, BOOTP), name resolution (DNS), network service discovery (Zeroconf, Bonjour) as granted functionalities.

There is an opportunity to provide an adequate (in size and functions) service bus as an ad-hoc component, automatically available and self configured to consumer market applications. This Ad-Hoc Semantic Service Bus should be light enough to be self-provided by the devices, however functional enough to be an upgrade over simple device communications network APIs.

3. PROPOSED SOLUTION

In this paper it is proposed a set of components to provide the benefits of a service bus, however in an ad-hoc context. The basis for this proposition is the existence of any kind of link layer communication that can carry an IP network over it, such as cabled Ethernet, wireless Ethernet, bluetooth or other. Some main functions will be provided: IP address distribution, device name to IP address resolution, service bus instantiation, service bus identification, WoT identification and registration in the service bus.

For the IP address provisioning function, it is proposed the use of the "Link Local" standard [7]. Link local IP addresses is a mechanism in which a host can select an IP address using the reserved "169.254/16" prefix based on a random function. These addresses are for local network use only and cannot be routed to other networks. This function is currently being provided by many operating systems such as Linux, Windows, Mac OS X, iOS and Android.

The name to IP address resolution and network service identification functions will be provided by Bonjour. Bonjour is Apple's Multicast DNS implementation that became an IETF standard recently [8]. Bonjour (also known as Zeroconf) is available in many platforms, such as Mac OS X, iOS, Windows and POSIX OSes (Linux, UNIX, etc.) [3]. Bonjour uses multicast to allow network devices inform each other what names they have and what network services (TCP, UDP, port numbers) they provide.

A Bonjour service has three main informations: instance name, service type and domain [9]. The instance name identifies one specific service. The service type is any IP application protocol name, as recognized by IANA (such as tftp, http etc.), followed by an IP transport protocol name (UDP, TCP). When creating a new IP application protocol, one should register it on IANA for avoiding erroneous operations. This proposition is an example of IP application that is specific and should have its own IANA registered application name. Domain is a standard DNS domain or ".local" if not specified.

A WeT that is capable of working in this proposition's (AHSB) service bus should have a specific Bonjour service type (assuming `_ahsbus._tcp`). For now on this WeT will be referred as AhWeT. An AhWeT can be a web service only device (AHSB aware) or can be a web service device capable of AHSB instantiation. Using the same Bonjour service type, all AHSB's WeTs can be easily identified in the local network and, therefore, be registered in the AHSB when one becomes available.

An AhWeT that only provides service and cannot instantiate an AHSB (due to limited resources or security reasons, for example) will have a instance name following this pattern: `SVO::<BUS-NAME>`. The token `SVO` identifies this AhWeT as a service only device. Its computer name and tcp service port, informed in the Bonjour service publication process, will be used to form an URL for this device, such as: `http://computer-name:port-number/`. The `BUS-NAME` token, by default, is `AHSB`, however can be modified to a different name if separate buses were needed at the same time in the same local network. When a `SVO` AhWeT starts, it publishes its service using Bonjour and waits for HTTP requests.

An AhWeT which is capable of bus instantiation (AhWeT-bi) will differ from a service only (`SVO`) AhWeT in its Bonjour instance name and behavior. An AhWeT-bi can have three different instance names based on its current instantiation state: `SRV::<BUS-NAME>::<BackOffTime>`, `BKP::<BUS-NAME>::<BackOffTime>`, `SVC::<BUS-NAME>::<BackOffTime>`.

A `SRV` (AhWeT-bi in `SRV` state) is the AhWeT device who is currently providing the AHSB. It also provides its web service, as all other AhWeTs. This means that the `SRV` is running the piece of software which implements the AHSB functions. Only one `SRV` is allowed at a time. In the event of a `SRV` outage, a `BKP` AhWeT should immediately transform itself in a `SRV` and instantiate the AHSB. The `SVC` state is the one that all other AhWeT-bis will be. In the event of a `BKP` outage, `SVCs` will negotiate and only one of them will transform itself in `BKP`. The `BackOffTime` token is a randomly generated real number with 5 decimal digits precision and in the range of 1 to 5 seconds which is used in the states negotiation processes (later discussed).

The state negotiation process for `BKP` consists of waiting a randomly generated amount of time (back off time) then checking if still there is not any `BKP` on the network and checking if it (the AhWeT-bi instance) has the smallest back off time of all known AhWeT-bis. If the conditions are true, the AhWeT-bi instance with the smallest back off time assumes the `BKP` state. For the `SRV` state negotiation, only a `BKP` instance can assume it. The `BKP`, once detecting the absence of

a `SRV`, checks if there is no `BKP` collision and then assumes the `SRV` state immediately.

Collisions may occur in the `SRV` and `BKP` states' negotiation processes, so a collision resolution process was defined to solve these situations. All AhWeT-bis are capable of identifying a collision and falling-back to a `SVC` state, restarting the negotiation process.

When an AHSB is instantiated, the `SRV` AhWeT-bi has the role of registering in the AHSB all AhWeTs available in the local network, that conform to its `BUS-NAME`. After instantiated and having all AhWeTs registered in it, an AHSB may execute HTTP requests on registered AhWeTs to identify syntactic (for example using WADL) and semantic (using microformats or OWL) information about these AhWeTs. This last process is out of the scope of this work.

4. PROOF OF CONCEPT

To prove the viability of the proposed solution, two software components were developed and two experiments were executed. The first component is an application that implements an AhWeT behavior (Instant Bus - IB). The IB was developed using Objective-C language and used an Objective-C Mac OS X Bonjour API called NSNetService. IB has a graphical user interface that helps identifying its current state, Bonjour instance name and its random back off time in use. It also provides a function (button "Access Service Bus") to help accessing the currently available AHSB instance in the local network. When a click occurs, a web browser session is initiated using the URL of the current SRV.

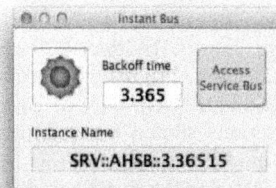

Figure 1: Instant Bus Application User Interface

The second component is an application developed using the MuleESB framework to represent the AHSB. This simple AHSB example (M-AHSB) can have AhWeTs registered in it and can list them as its main functions (a service bus registry function). M-AHSB uses RESTFul architectural approach for providing all its functions.

The first experiment (EXP1) consisted of starting 30 IB instances in the same computer at the same time and verifying if this set of IBs converged to a coherent state. A coherent state is defined as one in which only one SRV exists, only one BKP exists and many SVCs or SVOs can exist.

The started IBs registered as Bonjour services in the local network. Once a coherent state is reached, the current SRV IB was repeatedly closed in each step, allowing the BKP to assume as SRV and a new BKP to appear after the negotiation process (30 steps in each round). This process was repeated 10 times (10 rounds). The total number of collisions was 3 for the 10 rounds (300 steps). EXP1 has converged to a coherent state in each step of each round, after any automatic collision solution, if existent.

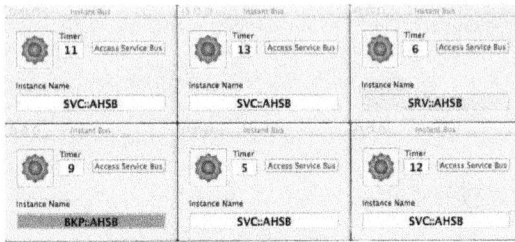

Figure 2: Coherent State Example

The second experiment (EXP2) was a simple verification that an IB could start and stop the M-AHSB depending on the IB state: when in SRV state, IB should maintain M-AHSB started. For all other states IB should maintain M-AHSB stopped. EXP2 also included the click of "Access Service Bus" button to open a web browser session accessing the SRV URL. EXP2 was successful in all 10 times it was executed.

5. CONCLUSION

The Web Of Things (WoT) and Internet of Things (IoT) are trends in the Internet that allow device to device interaction. WoT relies on the web set of protocols and standards to provide interaction, therefore it is of easier interaction comparing to accessing specific IP based APIs.

This work introduces a proposition to abstract the existence of a WoT Service Bus by making it an Ad-Hoc function of the WoT's WeTs themselves. IP Link-Local and Bonjour technologies were used to provide IP Addressing, Name to IP resolution, IP Service discovery, Bus Instantiation, WeTs registration in the Bus, Bus URL identification. Two software components were developed to test this proposition: Instant Bus (IB) and a RESTFul WoT Service Bus (M-AHSB). IB and M-AHSB functions should be embedded in any WeT that is to be capable of instantiating this proposition's service bus (AHSB - Ad-Hoc Service Bus).

IB has algorithms that use Bonjour functions to make only one M-AHSB instance (the SRV IB instance) available at a time, but also make one WeT readily available to assume (the BKP instance) and be aware of another WeT instances that can instantiate the AHSB (the SVC instances). Collision resolution algorithms are also provided. Proof of concept experiments were executed to demonstrate AHSB viability, showing how simple can be a WoT service bus instantiation in a "just created" network (Ad-Hoc) that had no infrastructure.

As future work, SRV and BKP selection algorithm can be reviewed and also an extended experimentation should be executed, using different operating system platforms and different Zeroconf stacks.

6. REFERENCES

[1] T. Bernes-Lee. Information Management: A Proposal. http://www.w3.org/History/1989/proposal.html, 1989. Access: 01/02/2013.

[2] N. Bui. Internet of Things Architecture Project Deliverable D1.1 - SOTA report on existing integration frameworks/architectures for WSN, RFID and other emerging IoT related Technologies. Technical Report 257521, Consorzio Ferrara Ricerche, 2011.

[3] M. O. Forge. New Bonjour Releases. http://www.macosforge.org, 2011. Access: 04/15/2013.

[4] N. Gershenfeld, R. Krikorian, and D. Cohen. The Internet of things. *Scientific American, volume 291 number 4*, pages 49–54, 2004.

[5] D. Guinard. *A Web of Things Application Architecture - Integrating the Real-World into the Web*. Doctor of science thesis, ETH Zurich, 2011.

[6] D. Guinard, V. Trifa, S. Karnouskos, P. Spiess, and D. Savio. Interacting with the soa-based internet of things: Discovery, query, selection, and on-demand provisioning of web services. *IEEE Transactions on Services Computing*, 3(3):223–235, 2010.

[7] IETF. Dynamic Configuration of IPv4 Link-Local Addresses. http://tools.ietf.org/html/rfc3927, 2005. Access: 04/15/2013.

[8] IETF. Multicast DNS. http://tools.ietf.org/html/rfc6762, 2013. Access: 04/15/2013.

[9] A. Inc. Bonjour Operations. https://developer.apple.com/library/mac/\# documentation/Cocoa/Conceptual/NetServices/ Articles/NetServicesArchitecture.html, 2013. Access: 04/15/2013.

[10] Silicon Valley Historical Association. History of Internet - Internet Timeline. http://www.siliconvalleyhistorical.org/home/ internet_timeline, 2013. Access: 01/24/2013.

[11] V. Trifa, D. Guinard, and S. Mayer. Leveraging the Web for a Distributed Location-aware Infrastructure for the Real World. In E. Wilde and C. Pautasso, editors, *REST: From Research to Practice*, chapter 3, pages 1–19. www.springerlink.com, 2011.

[12] K. Yang, S. Li, L. Zhang, and G. Pan. Semantic Device Bus for Internet of Things. *2010 IEEE/IFIP International Conference on Embedded and Ubiquitous Computing*, pages 341–346, Dec. 2010.

ProcessSearch: A Framework to Search for Business Processes on the Web

Rodrigo Costa dos Santos
COPPE/UFRJ - Brazil
+55 21 2514-5196
rcosta@cos.ufrj.br

Geraldo Bonorino Xexéo
COPPE/UFRJ - Brazil
+55 21 2562-8697
xexeo@cos.ufrj.br

Fellipe Duarte
COPPE/UFRJ - Brazil
+55 21 2562-8697
duartefellipe@cos.ufrj.br

Paula Nascimento
COPPE/UFRJ - Brazil
+55 21 2562-8697
pnascimento@cos.ufrj.br

Rodrigo Águas
COPPE/UFRJ - Brazil
+55 21 2562-8697
raguas@cos.ufrj.br

ABSTRACT

This paper presents a framework system, called ProcessSearch, which is used to search and identify business process descriptions stored on the web. Some metrics were proposed in order to identify the web documents describing a business process. Identifying descriptions of business processes is a difficult task because the web stores "bag-of-words" documents. Hence, the ProcessSearch framework has been constructed and implemented, using known technologies in information retrieval and computational linguistics. The result was a satisfactory list of web documents ranked (top-k) by relevance for some given keywords. For validation, a "precision at k" analysis was used to confirm the accuracy of the proposed metrics.

Categories and Subject Descriptors

H.3.1 [**Content Analysis and Indexing**]: *Linguistic processing*; H.3.3 [**Information Search and Retrieval**]: *Search process, Selection process*.

Keywords

Search Process; Information Retrieval; Content Analysis; Business Process Search.

1. INTRODUCTION

This article presents a solution, called ProcessSearch, which is capable of finding textual descriptions in web documents describing business processes, by basically analyzing bag-of-words (BoW) texts; or in other words, represented as vectors in the n-dimensional space. For this, a three-step approach was created to identify pages that describe business processes. Firstly, the tool collects pages to form the repository by using a predefined crawling strategy. Then, the pages are classified as describing or not describing business processes, based on content

filters. Finally, the specific business processes are retrieved based on keywords provided by the user.

According to Davenport [1], a business process is a set of structured activities and measures for producing a specific output and targeting a defined objective, which may be a single client or an entire market. There are several ways to represent these business processes and many of these processes are today simply described in documents on the web.

In the context of Business Process Management (BPM), the task of identifying a company's process models can be cumbersome and complex. Sometimes, a process model may be derived from existing models and an effort to find and adapt these models may be more effective than developing a new one — this concept was started by [2] and [3].

Accordingly, finding similar processes, process models, benchmarking, and best practices for an area or specific topic, can improve the productivity and quality of a mapping project. However, this is not an easy task, since most search engines only work with keywords and do not provide any means to identify if a page describes a process or another type of data structure or context.

Recent research has shown the difficulty of automatic model extraction for documents such as manuals, policies, acts and procedures, and other internal documents in an organization [4] and [5]. Various other models have been developed to search for process information. In [6], a process query language (PQL) was developed. In [7], a Business Process Model and Notation Query language (BPMN-Q) was developed. In [8], a new solution based on semi-structured data allows textual research of the business process. All of these studies use a database of business processes.

Thus, the present work has the challenge of proposing a framework for implementing the search of business processes related to unstructured data on the web.

Besides this introduction, this paper has three other sections. Section two defines the solution architecture and the metrics used for comparison; section three covers the validation of the experiment; and finally, the conclusion is in section four.

2. ARCHITECTURE OF THE SOLUTION

In this section, the architecture for the identification, search, and retrieval of business processes on the Web is presented. ProcessSearch is a framework for identifying content related to the business process and it is based on web pages.

The architecture of the framework proposed in this work is shown in Figure 1 and it consists of three layers: the Business Process Query layer which is responsible for interacting with the user, displaying the search screen, and doing the whole workflow of the consultation with the lower layers; the Business Process Data and Knowledge layer which is composed of the most important components of the search, such as the search engine and the document indexes, in addition to the repository for the classification of the documents; and the Data Gathering layer which is composed of an intelligent crawling engine for querying documents on the Internet. It is in this layer that process experts define the pertinence of the documents; that is, whether or not they describe business processes.

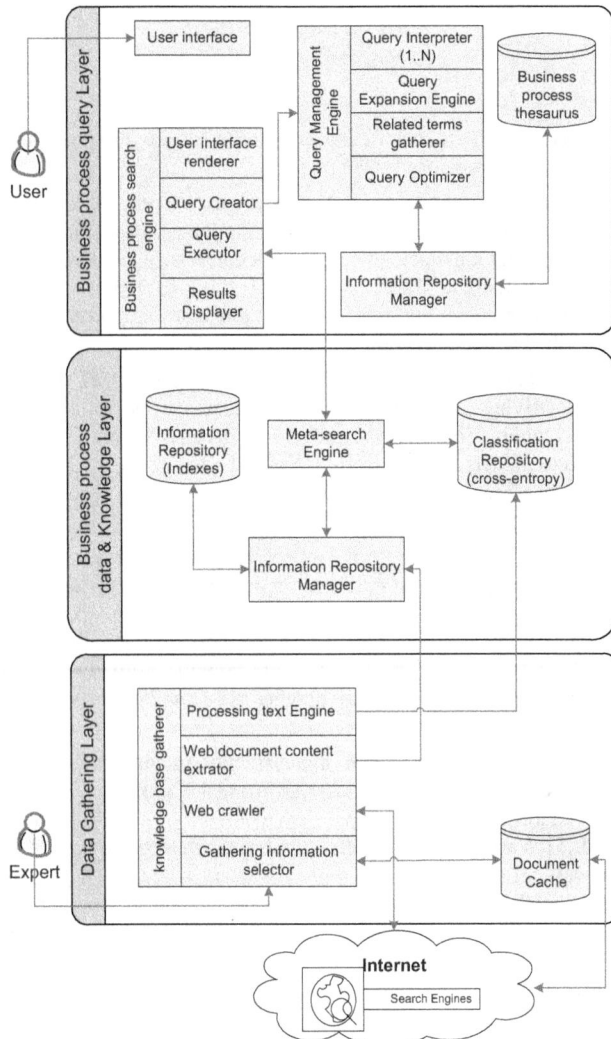

Figure 1. Architecture of the ProcessSearch framework.

2.1 Analysis for Identification of Business Processes

The approach for identifying business processes aims to perform an analysis that identifies similarities between a web document and a description of the business process. Such analyses are divided into three groups: Semantic, Contextual, and Clustering. Each analysis returns a value between 0 and 1 that represents the relevance of the document for describing a business process, in which 0 means that it is not relevant, and 1 means total relevance. Finally, the three values are consolidated into a single consolidated metric.

2.2 Semantic Analysis

The semantic analysis evaluates the terms of the web document, working with the part-of-speech (POS) elements such as nouns, verbs, adjectives, and adverbs [9]. Then, using computational linguistics one may infer the similarity to the writing of a business process, taking into account that there are fundamental terms which are commonly used in this type of description.

For the semantic analysis, we generated a list of "process verbs" that contained more than 350 typical verbs used for the description of business process activities. This list was obtained by extraction from the database of the SAP Solution Composer [10] which is a free offline tool containing all the maps of business processes from the integrated management system (SAP ERP).

All standard ERP processes and their descriptions were extracted from this database, covering financial analysis, human capital management, purchases and logistics, manufacturing, sales, and corporate services, among other scenarios. After this, we extracted the verbs used.

All word processing of the web documents was done in the TreeTagger program using the GATE platform [11]. GATE is a graphical development environment which enables users to develop and implement various natural language processing tasks. The TreeTagger plugin of the GATE platform consists of two programs: the training program that creates a complete parameter file from a lexicon, and another for creating the corpus.

All the web documents were labeled by GATE and the verbs were compared with a list of "process verbs"; that is, the verbs commonly used to describe business processes.

An innovation of this study was to use the concept of "stop verbs", which is similar to the concept known as "stop words" derived from the Search and Information Retrieval theme [12] and [13]. Generally, they are filtered and eliminated words, because they are not significant for the research.

For this experiment "stop verbs" were considered to be the modal verbs "can", "could", "dare", "may", "might", "must", "ought", "shall", "should", "will", and "would", as well as the verbs "to be" and "to have".

Additionally, with the help of an expert in business processes we extracted the words typically used to describe the SAP process. This word list was called "process words".

After this, the metric for evaluating semantic similarity of a web document became very simple, as shown in (1).

$$Sem(d_i) = Semantic\ metric\ of\ the\ i-th\ document$$
$$Sem(d_i) = \frac{N_{Pv} + N_{Pw}}{N_{Total} - (N_{Sv} + N_{Sw})} \ (1)$$

$$Where:$$
$$N_{Pv} = Number\ of\ process\ verbs$$
$$N_{Pw} = Number\ of\ process\ words$$
$$N_{Total} = Total\ number\ of\ terms$$
$$N_{Sv} = Number\ of\ stop\ verbs$$
$$N_{Sw} = Number\ of\ stop\ words$$

2.3 Contextual Analysis

The contextual analysis examines the relevance of the retrieved document based on the keywords provided by the user. Unlike other types of analysis, this is specific for each research; that is, it cannot be pre-processed, and it depends on each user interaction.

The contextual analysis uses the concept of semantic analysis and makes use of keywords used in the search, in order to extend the evaluation of the document, thus enriching its meaning and improving its ranking.

For contextual analysis, the evaluation of synonyms was done with WordNet which is an electronic lexical database in English [14]. For each keyword used in the search argument, a search of synonyms in WordNet was done and it was verified whether or not this set of words exists (synset).

The metric to search for the contextual similarity reuses some information retrieval techniques [12] for the document found. For each significant word entered by the user, a list of synonyms is obtained in WordNet. For each synonym, a new search is done in the document and a term frequency-inverse document frequency (tf-idf) weight is calculated. Finally, the sum of all the tf-idf is divided by the total number of synonyms found to determine the average tf-idf, as can be seen in (2).

$$Con(d) = \sum_{i=1}^{N_{t(d)}} \left(\frac{tf-idf\left(t_{i(d)}, d\right) + \sum_{k=1}^{N_{Syn}(t_{i(d)})} tf-idf\left(Syn_{k(t_{i(d)})}, d\right)}{N_{Syn}(t_{i(d)})} \right) \quad (2)$$

$$Where:$$
$$Con(d_i) = Contextual\ metric\ of\ the\ i-th\ document$$
$$t_{i(d)} = i-th\ term\ of\ document\ d$$
$$Syn_{k(t)} = k-th\ synonyms\ of\ term\ t$$
$$N_{Syn(t)} = Number\ of\ synonyms\ of\ term\ t$$
$$N_{t(d)} = Number\ of\ terms\ of\ document\ d$$

2.4 Clustering Analysis

In order to further enrich the search, clustering analysis was used to identify which documents describe business processes. For this a Naive Bayes classifier was used.

A Naive Bayes classifier is a simple probabilistic type, based on the application of Bayes' theorem with strong assumptions of independence (naive). For the training phase, we used thirty documents that describe business processes and twenty documents that do not. After this, the entire index was classified and, for each existing item in the index, the probability of being a business process or not was calculated based on the cross-entropy value. Then, to normalize this value; that is, to transform it into a value between 0 and 1, the probabilities were divided by the highest value, as can be seen in (3).

$$Clu(d_i) = norm(cross\_entropy(d_i)) \quad (3)$$

$$Where:$$
$$Clu(d_i) = Clustering\ metric\ of\ the\ i-th\ document$$
$$norm(\ ) = normalization function$$
$$cross\_entropy(d_i) = naiveBayes\ classification$$

2.5 Consolidated Metric

Finally, we proposed a similarity metric for consolidated business processes, as presented in (4), by taking into account a weighted average of the others. This was an attempt to verify whether the combination of the three metrics may be useful for improving the accuracy of the search results.

$$\frac{\left(w_{Sem} \times Sem(d_i)\right) + \left(w_{Con} \times Con(d_i)\right) + \left(w_{Clu} \times Clu(d_i)\right)}{w_{Sem} + w_{Con} + w_{Clu}} \quad (4)$$

$$Where:$$
$$w_{Sem} = weight\ for\ semantic\ analysis$$
$$w_{Con} = weight\ for\ contextual\ analysis$$
$$w_{Clu} = weight\ for\ clustering\ analysis$$

3. EXPERIMENT

To implement the framework described in Figure 1 of this paper, an experiment was conducted using the Java language.

For the collection of web documents on the Internet, the Apache Nutch web-search crawler software was used. To extract the content of the web documents returned, we used the Apache Solr enterprise search, which is the platform of the Apache Lucene project. Apache Lucene is used to provide Java-based indexing and to implement search and retrieval.

The crawler searched more than seventy-five thousand documents on the web and generated an index in Lucene. After this, the clustering and training were done. This generated the indexes and the cross-entropy value.

To run a Naive Bayes text classifier, LingPipe [15] was used. It is a word processing tool based on computational linguistics. To return the synonyms and their 'synsets', the WordNet software was used. WordNet is a large lexical database of the English language that groups words with their meanings, and morphological and syntactic classes (also known as a thesaurus).

The first step was to run the crawler to populate the index and build the experiment. It was introduced as a seed of Nutch to capture two large blocks of sites from the web pages — the first one on themes related to company business; for example, sales, accounting, payment, billing, contracting, purchasing, etc.; and another block with sites on topics not related to business; for example, news, sports, food, animals, and travel. The parameters used for the capture were: TopN = 10,000, which indicates that the crawler could sweep up to 10,000 links found on each new page; and Depth = 5, which indicates that the crawler should scan up to 5 different sites using the root of each link. With this configuration, it was possible to retrieve a collection of about 75,000 documents; however, even in this phase of the experiment it was not yet possible to know whether or not they described business processes.

The next step was to construct the classification of all the documents based on the Naive Bayes algorithm. For this, the training was done with about thirty documents describing business processes and twenty other documents that did not. These documents were evaluated by four experts in business processes and they were properly labeled. The training was done with the LingPipe tool which generated the cross entropy measure based on this training over the entire index. The values had to be normalized to generate a score between 0 and 1, where the document closest to 1 represents the highest entropy value, and 0 its opposite. These values were stored in the repository and the classification was available for use in the Business Processes Query layer.

For user interaction, a presentation layer was constructed with a screen similar to any search engine. Here the user places the keywords to be searched and ProcessSearch finds the documents that most closely resemble the description of the business process for that subject, based on semantic, contextual, and document clustering analysis.

To validate the experiment, a search was done using four keywords: "invoice payment", "recruitment", "purchasing", and "accounting". Four classification lists were generated for each keyword. The first twenty results were classified (top-k list, where k = 20). Each list was classified using the three proposed values: semantic, contextual, and clustering analysis (cross-entropy). The value of the consolidated analysis is in equation (4), with weights equal to one; that is, *WSem=1, WCon=1 e WClu=1*.

Finally, using the four lists of retrieved documents, the "K precision" was calculated — it measures the precision of the first K documents from a list of results. The judgement of the relevance in describing business processes was done by two experts. The results for the precision in K for each keyword are shown in Figures 2 to 5.

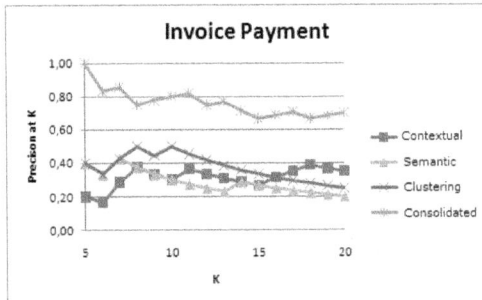

Figure 2. Precision in K for the keyword "Invoice Payment".

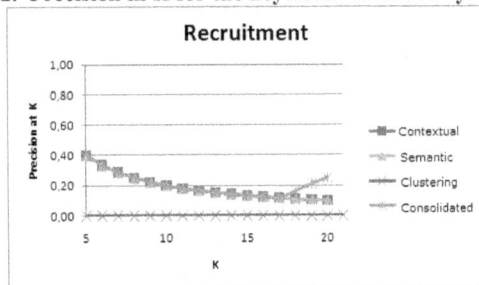

Figure 3. Precision in K for the keyword "Recruitment".

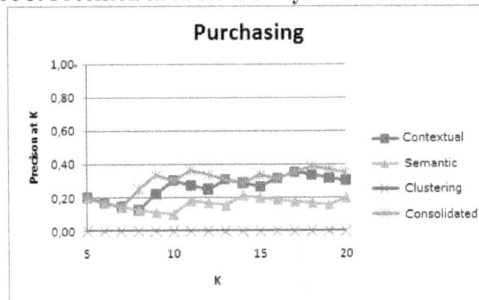

Figure 4. Precision in K for the keyword "Purchasing".

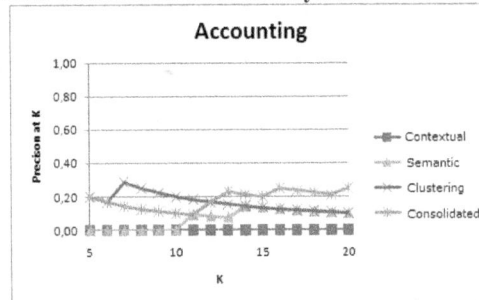

Figure 5. Precision in K for the keyword "Accounting".

4. CONCLUSION

The objective of the study was to introduce a system, known as ProcessSearch, to search for and identify business processes stored on the web. Some metrics were proposed in order to identify web documents that describe business processes divided into three groups: semantic, contextual, and clustering.

The framework was built and implemented in Java using the Lucene platform. The experiment was done by searching for documents on the web, using the keywords "invoice payment", "recruitment", "purchasing", and "accounting". For each word, an analysis of the precision in K was generated using the values found for each proposed metric. The consolidated metric had the best precision.

The number of relevant documents retrieved was high, and the result of the experience was satisfactory considering that it is difficult to identify the description of business processes in a bag-of-words model.

For future works, it is recommended to use a higher number of documents in the experiment and to study the behavior of different weights of 1 for the consolidated metric, in order to better investigate precision results. New metrics may also be proposed to enrich this theory.

5. REFERENCES

[1]   T. H. Davenport, *Process innovation: reengineering work through information technology*. Harvard Business Press, 1993.

[2]   T. Jin, J. Wang, N. Wu, M. La Rosa, and A. H. M. Ter Hofstede. *Efficient and accurate retrieval of business process models through indexing*. In Proceedings of the OTM-2010 – Vol. I, Berlin, Heidelberg, 2010, pp. 402–409.

[3]   M. Hammer, *Reengineering Work: Don't Automate, Obliterate*. Harvard Business Review, vol. 68, no. 4, pp. 104-112, 1990.

[4]   Li, J., Wang, H.J., Zhang, Z., J. Leon Zhao, *A policy-based process mining framework: mining business policy texts for discovering process models*. Information Systems and e-Business Management, Vol. 8, N.2 / March, 2010, Pages 169-188.

[5]   A. Ghose, G. Koliadis, A. Chueng, *Rapid business process discovery (R-BPD)*, Conceptual Modeling-ER 2007, p. 391–406, 2007.

[6]   M. Klein and A. Bernstein, *Towards high-precision service retrieval*. IEEE Internet Computing, vol. 8, no. 1, pp. 30–36, 2004.

[7]   A. Awad. *BPMN-Q: A Language to Query Business Processes*. In EMISA, pages 115–128, 2007

[8]   Carvalho, F.R.M., Valverde, R.F., and Jorge, E.M.F. *A solution for textual search using business processes management*. In Proceedings of EATIS. 2008.

[9]   Manning, Christopher D. *Foundations of Statistical Natural Language Processing*. MIT Press, 1999.

[10] SAP Solution Composer. (2011, May 10). [Online]. Available: http://www.sap.com/solutions/businessmaps/composer/index.epx

[11] H. Cunningham, K. Humphreys, R.J. Gaizauskas, and Y. Wilks, *GATE - a General Architecture for Text Engineering*. in Proc. ANLP, 1997, pp.29-30.

[12] G. Salton and M. McGill, *Introduction to Modern Information Retrieval*, 1984.

[13] R.A. Baeza-Yates and B.A. Ribeiro-Neto. *Modern Information Retrieval*, 1999.

[14] FELLBAUM, C. *WordNet: An electronic lexical database*, MIT Press, 1998.

[15] LingPipe. http://alias-i.com/lingpipe/index.html Acess 2011-10-27.

Enhancing the Accuracy of Ratings Predictions of Video Recommender System by Segments of Interest

Alessandro da Silveira Dias, Leandro Krug Wives, Valter Roesler

PPGC - Instituto de Informática - Universidade Federal do Rio Grande do Sul

Av. Bento Gonçalves, 9500, Porto Alegre, Brazil

{asdias,wives,roesler}@inf.ufrgs.br

ABSTRACT

The amount of video content that is available on the web grows at each instant. This fact implicates in an important issue – video content overload. One way to treat such problem consists on the use of recommender systems. In this sense, this paper proposes a method to enhance the accuracy of the predictions given by video recommender systems by the use of Segments of Interest (SOI). Based on the premise that users tend to like particular segments of a video more than the entire video, and that they are able to mark these segments, these can be used to identify similar people, i.e. the ones who have similar interests about videos. This similarity can be used to enhance the accuracy of the ratings predictions of traditional collaborative video recommender systems. To evaluate this approach, an experimental evaluation was performed. The results showed that the accuracy improvement is directly related with the level of participation of people marking SOI. Thus, as more people collaborate and interact, better will be the recommendation result.

Categories and Subject Descriptors

H.3.3 [**Information Search and Retrieval**]: Information Filtering; H.1.2 [**User/Machine Systems**]: Human information processing

General Terms

Experimentation, Human Factors, Measurement

Keywords

Video Recommender System; User preferences; Segments of Interest; Personalization; Interactivity

1. INTRODUCTION

With the evolution of information technology and telecommunications, along with digital convergence, the amount of video content available in the world grows at each instant. We can see many video websites, VOD services, and PVR (Personal Video Recorder) devices, which automatically record videos to people daily. For instance, over 72 hours of video content are

WebMedia '13, November 5-8, 2013, Salvador, Brazil
Copyright 2013 ACM 978-1-4503-2559-2/13/11...$15.00.
http://dx.doi.org/10.1145/2526188.2526201

uploaded to YouTube.com every minute [16]. This fact creates an important issue for the user: the overload of video content. One way to treat such an overload consists on the use of recommender systems, which filter content in order to deliver what is most interesting to the user.

Recommender systems are usually classified into the following categories (or methods), based on how recommendations are made [2]: Content-based (in which items similar to the ones the user preferred in the past will be recommended) and Collaborative (in which items that people with similar tastes and preferences liked in the past will be recommended). There is also the Hybrid approach, which combine collaborative and content-based methods in order to handle their inherent problems.

Such typical recommendation methods have performed well in several applications, including the ones for recommending books, CDs, news articles, and others since the mid 1990s. Furthermore, according to [1], in order to provide better recommendations and to be able to use recommender systems in arguably more complex types of applications, such as recommending vacations or certain types of financial services, most of the typical approaches need significant extensions.

In the video recommendation domain, several extensions for the typical approaches had been presented, for instance, [1], [7] and [13], which extensions are based on information about context, social networks and personality respectively. Besides these, some works are based on the annotation of interest points or segments on video. Through this kind of annotation, users can mark in the video stream points/segments that are more interesting for them. After performing a review in the literature of the field, we found that such an approach has not been widely explored: only two works were found. One suggest that annotations of interest points on the video stream could be used to improve recommender systems [12]. The other uses interest segments to generate content visibility in video recommender systems [3], and states that recommender systems do not exploit the fact that users tend to like particular segments of the video more than the rest.

In this context, this work presents an approach to enhance the accuracy of ratings predictions of video recommender systems using segments of interest. This approach takes into account that users tend to like more of particular segments of the video than the rest. These segments, called Segments of Interest (SOI), are used to find users with similar interests, or common taste, about video. Besides, in such an approach, when a pair of users has a number of intersections of segments of interest over a certain threshold in one video, and this pattern is repeated in a number of videos, it is considered that these users are similar, i.e. the pair has similar interests, or common taste, about video. The degree of this similarity is calculated through a utility function that is based on intersections of segments of interest. This function is used to enhance the accuracy of ratings predictions of video recommender systems with user based nearest neighbor collaborative recommendation; and can be used both in new systems as existing systems, and in different video environments, such as video websites, PVR devices and VOD services.

To evaluate the proposed approach, an experimental evaluation was performed considering the prediction accuracy in terms of accuracy of ratings predictions, in which the improvement was achieved with the use of SOI on videos. This improvement is directly related with the level of participation of people marking the segments, i.e., the ones who participate more actively and more interactive.

This work is divided in the following sections: Section 2 presents related works. Section 3 brings concepts of collaborative recommender systems. Section 4 presents the proposed approach. Section 5 details the implementation. Section 6 describes the experiments performed, discuss the results found, showing advantages and limitations of our approach. And Section 7 brings the conclusions and future work.

2. RELATED WORKS

In the domain of video recommendation regarding user's interest, we have found some works. For instance, a new way of viewing TV was proposed in [17]; they also present a system to retrieve and recommend video content related to what the viewer is currently watching. The content chosen by the viewer and the current segment on the video stream is assumed to reflect the viewer's interests at that point in time. Other works are [12] and [3].

CollaboraTV is presented in [12]. It is a system made to study new ways to watch TV and new interaction approaches among viewers. In such system, the user can put temporal linked annotations on videos or TV programs. One kind of annotation is the Interest Point. While users are watching a video, they can put positive or negative interest points in the current position of the video stream. These points are used to build interest profiles for users and communities of users. The authors suggest that the most popular positive interest points of different TV programs can be used to produce a new TV program. The system offers recommendations of the most popular TV programs and encourages the exchange of recommendations between users. They also suggest that these user annotations could be used to improve recommender systems.

In [3] the authors exploit the fact that users tend to like particular segments of the viewed content more than the rest. The extraction of these segments and their information is used to enrich the user experience, improving the quality of video recommender systems. After watching a video, users can mark segments by pointing their beginning and ending in the video stream. Additionally, users can rate each segment. With this information, a user profile of scene interest is built. The focus of the work is on the development of a method to extract scene segments from viewed content and on the presentation of a framework capable of presenting recommended content visibility. Our work differs from the previous ones in the sense that it focus on the classic item-based recommendation, more precisely, our work aims to enhance the accuracy of ratings predictions of video recommender systems by the use of segments of interest.

3. COLLABORATIVE RECOMMENDER SYSTEMS

Collaborative filtering is considered to be the most popular and widely implemented technique in recommender systems [15]. Moreover, it is the prominent technique in the video/movie domain [12].

The main idea of collaborative recommender systems is to exploit information about the past behavior or the opinions of an existing user community. Pure collaborative approaches take a matrix of given users-item ratings as the input and typically produce a numerical rating prediction or a list of recommended items as output, indicating to what degree the current user will like or dislike of a certain item [8].

One of the most researched approaches to produce predictions is the user based nearest neighbor collaborative recommendation. It receives the user-items ratings matrix and the active user as input. Then, it identifies other users (called "nearest neighbors") that had similar preferences to those of the active user (target of the recommendation) in the past. Then for every available item that the active user has not yet seem, a prediction is computed based on the ratings of its nearest neighbors. This kind of recommendation approach can be presented in a three-step algorithm (Figure 1): (a) computation of similarities between the active user and the remaining users, (b) neighborhood development, and (c) computation of prediction based on the weighted average of the neighbors' ratings on the target item. The possible rating values can be defined, for instance, in a numerical scale, for instance, in a one-to-five scale (from 1 - strongly liked, to 5 - strongly disliked).

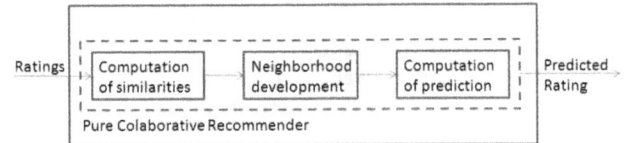

Figure 1: User based nearest neighbor collaborative recommendation in a three-step algorithm

For the first step, the Pearson correlation coefficient (Equation 1) is typically used.

$$sim(a, b) = \frac{\sum_{p \in P}(r_{a,p} - \overline{r_a})(r_{b,p} - \overline{r_b})}{\sqrt{\sum_{p \in P}(r_{a,p} - \overline{r_a})^2} \sqrt{\sum_{p \in P}(r_{b,p} - \overline{r_b})^2}} \quad (1)$$

where $sim(a,b)$ is the similarity of users a and b, and it is a Real value which ranges from -1 to +1; P is the set of available items and p is an item of this set; $r_{i,j}$ is the rating of user i to item j; and $\overline{r_i}$ is the average rating of user i.

At the neighborhood development step, the neighbors with positive correlation in relation to the active user are selected. Finally, if there is a minimum neighborhood size, an arithmetic prediction for an item is computed. The weighted average of all neighbors' ratings is computed using Equation 2.

$$pred(a, p) = \overline{r_a} + \frac{\sum_{b \in N} sim(a,b)*(r_{b,p} - \overline{r_b})}{\sum_{b \in N} sim(a,b)} \quad (2)$$

where $pred(a,p)$ is the rating prediction from item p to the active user a; b is a user from neighborhood N; $r_{b,p}$ is the rating given by user b to item p, and $\overline{r_i}$ is the average rating of user i; and $sim(a,b)$ is the similarity between user a and b.

4. THE PROPOSED APPROACH

Based on the fact that users can mark segments in the video stream that are more interesting for them, and that users tend to like of particular segments of the video more than the rest, this work presents an approach that uses these segments, called Segments of Interest (SOI), to enhance the accuracy of ratings predictions of video recommender systems.

4.1 Introductory Example

Figure 2 illustrates SOIs marked by a user in a video. The first one was marked from t_1 to t_2 seconds related to the video timeline, the second one from t_3 to t_4 seconds, and the third one from t_5 to t_6 seconds.

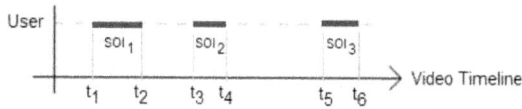

Figure 2: SOIs marked by a user in a video.

One SOI of a user in one video can have intersection with one SOI of another user, or with SOIs of other users. Figure 3 shows how SOIs of different users can be disposed along a video timeline. In this example, four users, u_1, u_2, u_3 and u_4, and their respective SOIs are presented. SOIs of users may have intersection with SOIs of other users. If the users are analyzed in pairs, when the number of intersections of SOIs of a pair of users is above a certain threshold, it is suspected that these users have similar interests, or common taste, about videos. However, this type of analysis should not be performed considering only one video, but a considerable number of videos. Therefore, the minimum quantity of videos where there is a minimum number of intersections of SOIs should be above a certain threshold too.

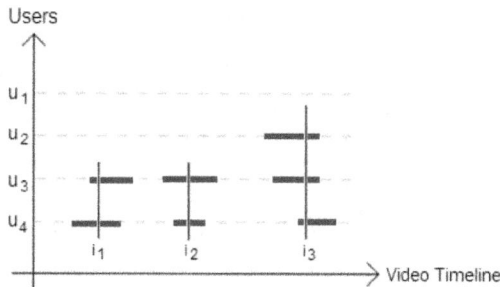

Figure 3: SOIs of users and its intersections showing possible common interests.

Figure 4 shows this analysis extended to a set of videos. In this figure, based on the intersection of the presented SOIs, there is a chance that users u_2 and u_4 have similar interests if we consider that there should be at least 2 intersections of SOIs on at least 3 videos.

The intersection size also must be regarded as a threshold in such analysis. It is considered that the intersection size of SOIs of a pair of user below a certain threshold is not interesting to find users with similar interests, or common taste, about video.

Such facts and thresholds can be described as follows: when a pair of users has at least N intersections of SOI, with a minimum acceptable size T, in one video and this pattern occurs in a set of at least M videos, we can suspect that these users have similar interests, or common taste, about videos. Faced with this possibility, we launched the following hypothesis: "interest segments can be used to find similar people, i.e., who have similar interests, or common taste, about video, and this similarity can be used to enhance the accuracy of ratings predictions of a video recommender system". Based on this proposition, in this example, if the threshold values are: to have at least 3 videos with at least 2 intersections of SOI in each video of minimum 10 seconds, users u_2 and u_4 are similar.

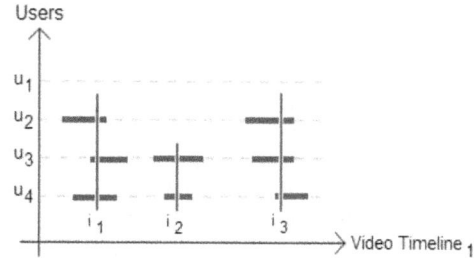

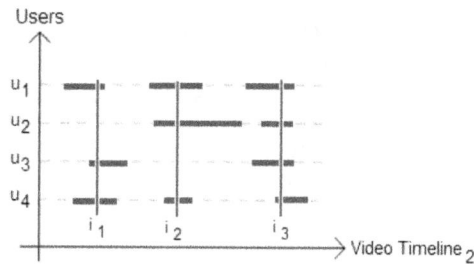

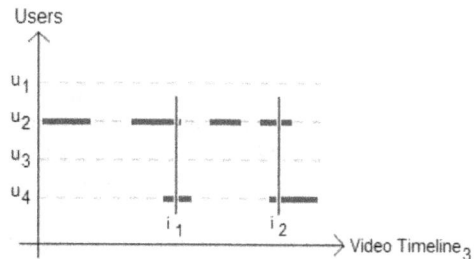

Figure 4: Intersections of SOIs in a set of videos.

It is also possible that users do not have marked any SOI in the video or have not ever seen the video. It is also possible that, when watching a video again, users can mark new SOIs or delete previous ones. It is important to allow such changes, allowing the evolution of user profiles over time, as these are actually dynamic.

Formally, the computation of the similarity between users based on segments of interest and the domain definition that describes the environment of a video recommender system with prediction accuracy of ratings predictions enhanced by segments of interest are presented in the following sections.

4.2 Formal Domain Definition

The environment of a video recommender system in which the accuracy of ratings predictions is enhanced by SOI is composed by:

- a set $U = \{u_1, u_2, u_3, \ldots, u_n\}$ of individuals (users);

- a set $V = \{v_1, v_2, v_3, \ldots, v_n\}$ of items (videos);

- a set of *SOIs*; where each segment of interest of a user u on video v (SOI_{uv_i}) corresponds to a segment marked by the user u on video v, with reference to the video timeline, and it is delimited by the beginning (x) and by the end (y) of the segment of interest, both in seconds, which can be denoted as follows:

$$SOI_{uv_i} = [x, y] \mid x, y \in \mathbb{N} \ and \ x < y$$

- a utility function $sim^{SOI}(u_b, u_o)$, which computes the degree of similarity s between a pair of users based on their segments of interest, and it is formally defined in Section 4.3. (The user u_b is the active user, target of the recommendation).

A user profile (P) in a recommender system can be modeled in different ways. For instance, in a pure collaborative filtering, users are modeled as a simple list containing the ratings provided by the user for some items. Now, through our approach, the user profile can be extended (P') from the set of their SOIs:

$$P' = P \cup \{SOI_{uv_1}, SOI_{uv_2}, ..., SOI_{uv_n}\}$$

4.3 Similarity between Users Based on Segments of Interest

To calculate the similarity between users based on their segments of interest, we proposed a utility function. In this work, this function uses intersections of SOIs on video of a pair of users $(u_b, u_o) \in U$ to compute a value s which ranges from 0 to +1, and which corresponds to the degree of similarity between the pair of users, as defined below.

$$u: U \ x \ U \to s \mid s \in \mathbb{R} \ and \ s \in [0,1]$$

When s is 0, the pair of user are not similar, i.e. they don't have similar interests, or common taste, about video; when s is 1, the users have the highest possible degree of similarity. In the remaining of this work, the utility function will be denoted as $sim^{SOI}(u_b, u_o)$, where u_b is the *base* user of the comparison and u_o is the *other* user, to be compared with the *base* user.

Table 1: Thresholds proposed for the utility function and rules for the definition of its values

Identifier	Description	Rules for Acceptable Values
T	minimum size of SOI intersection (acceptable size of intersection)	$T \in \mathbb{N} \wedge T > 0$
N	minimum quantity of SOI intersections with acceptable size T for video	$N \in \mathbb{N} \wedge N \geq 1$
M	minimum quantity of videos where there are N SOI intersections at least with acceptable size T	$M \in \mathbb{N} \wedge M \geq 2$

Furthermore, the utility function must take into account the proposed threshold values $(N, M \ and \ T)$ to compute the s to be returned. Different approaches can be employed for this computation. In this work, we proposed that s is the rate between the "total number of intersections of segments of interest on

videos have watched by the pair of users" and the "total number of segments of interest in watched videos by the base user", in which the result ranges from 0 to +1. Other approaches for estimating s are presented in Section 7. We also propose that the thresholds should receive the identifiers and rules for acceptable values presented in Table 1. These rules ensure that it has a set of videos where occurs at least one intersection with minimum acceptable size. The higher values of thresholds, the more rigid is the search for similar users and, therefore, more accurate is the similarity between the pair of users.

4.4 Enhancing the Accuracy of Ratings Predictions of Video Recommender Systems by Segments of Interest

Our approach extends the traditional pure collaborative recommendation approach in order to take into account more information that, in this case, are segments of interest. To enhance the accuracy of ratings predictions of a recommender system we propose the use of a utility function in a user based nearest neighbor collaborative recommender, as shown in Figure 5.

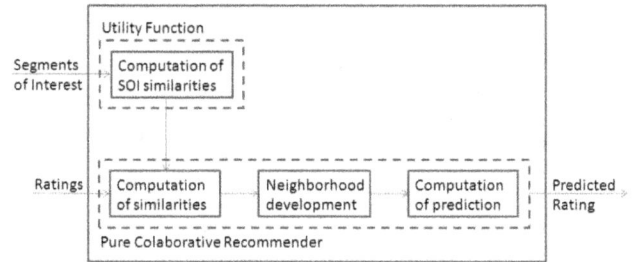

Figure 5: A user based nearest neighbor collaborative recommender under the action of the utility function based on segments of interest.

In this approach, the utility function acts increasing the degree of similarity between users, which is calculated by a user based nearest neighbor collaborative recommender in the step named "computation of similarities between the active and the remaining of the users", according to the following equation (3).

$$sim^{CFe}(a,b) = sim^{CF}(a,b) * (1 + sim^{SOI}(a,b)) \ (3)$$

where a is the active user (target of the recommendation), b is the other user with whom the similarity is calculated, sim^{CFe} is the enhanced similarity of the user based nearest neighbor collaborative recommender (collaborative filtering - CF, for short); sim^{CF} is the similarity of the user based nearest neighbor collaborative recommender based on Pearson correlation coefficient, and sim^{SOI} is the utility function. If the value computed by the utility function is 0, the collaborative filtering similarity does not change; if this value is greater than 0, it increases sim^{CF} proportionally.

In its turn, sim^{CFe} acts in the "computation of prediction" step (Equation 4) of the user based nearest neighbor collaborative recommender. Thus, users who have common interests about video with the active user have increased their weight when calculating the weighted average of all user ratings from the users in the neighborhood. That is, these users contribute more to compute the prediction, which is given by Equation 4.

$$pred(a,p) = \bar{r}_a + \frac{\sum_{b \in N} sim^{CFe}(a,b) * (r_{b,p} - \bar{r}_b)}{\sum_{b \in N} sim^{CFa}(a,b)} \ (4)$$

where $pred(a,p)$ is the rating prediction from item p to the active user a; b is a user from neighborhood N; $r_{b,p}$ is the rating given by user b to item p; $\bar{r}_i$ is the average rating of user i; and $sim^{CFe}(a,b)$ is the enhanced similarity between user a and b.

5. THE DEVELOPED SYSTEM

When dealing with the accuracy of ratings predictions on video recommender systems, historical datasets are often used in offline experiments. In many works such datasets are enriched with data collected, for instance, using crawlers on the Web. Depending on research type, artificial historical datasets can also be generated. However, there are not historical video datasets enriched with SOI; in our approach, the user participates more actively and more interactively; and this research works over similar interests, or common tastes, about video of users. Therefore, it was necessary to create a system. In such system, users can browse, choose, watch and rate videos, they can also mark their segments of interest. With the aid of this system, we have built a historical dataset with segments of interest.

Figure 6 shows a reference architecture for the developed system during this research. It was implemented as a web application. The server hosts the application, which user interface is similar to many video websites of nowadays, i.e., it has a screen containing a video gallery and where the user can browse videos, and a screen to watch videos. The client can be any device that contains a web browser, such as a desktop computer, a notebook, a smartphone, a tablet or a smart TV. This system only stores data from the video catalog and data generated during the use of the system. Videos are loaded directly from clients on demand from a video content provider, which in this case was YouTube.

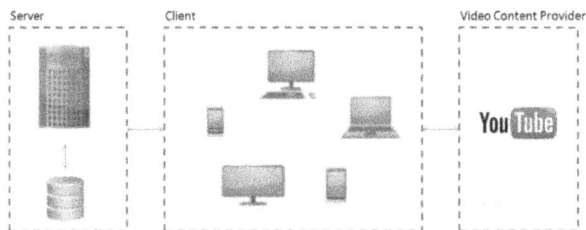

Figure 6: A reference architecture of the developed system

For the experimental evaluation, we used videos from a specific context: educational videos of a given subject. However, the experiment could have been done with videos from several domains, such as news, sports and movies. For this purpose, a video catalog containing 50 educational videos up 20 minutes duration from YouTube was built, using a crawler.

Figure 7 shows part of the screen of the system where the user watches videos. Through it, users can also rate videos by attributing one of the following options: "Very bad", "Bad", "Ok", "Good" and "Very good", which correspond respectively to the numerical ratings 1, 2, 3, 4 and 5 in the dataset. Users can also mark their segments of interest. This is performed through a double slider below the progress bar of the video player. Users can thus drag and drop the sliders to mark the beginning and end of each segment of interest. Additionally, the screen presents the sorted list of SOI already marked on the video and the user can delete one, if necessary. This approach is suitable for educational environments where users tend to be near the system screen, and can move forward and rewind the video several times during learning.

If the context was different, for instance, movies being watched in a smart TV, the segments could be marked differently, using specific buttons on the remote control or on a smartphone application, for example, while the user is watching the video.

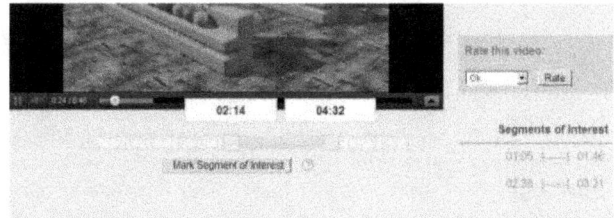

Figure 7: Part of the screen to present videos of the developed system.

5.1 Additional Components

In addition to the system developed, it was necessary to implement two components: a pure collaborative recommender component (user based nearest neighbor collaborative recommender), as presented in Section 3, and the sim^{SOI} component (the utility function), which calculates the similarity between pairs of users based on segments of interest, as presented in Section 4.3. These two components are used together, as specified in Section 4.4, in the video recommender system to enhance the accuracy of ratings predictions.

In this implementation, internally, the sim^{SOI} component uses an algorithm that computes the similarity degree of a pair of users in three steps: (a) load all SOIs of the *base* user and all SOIs of the *other* user in all videos watched by the *base* user; (b) verify whether the pair of users have a set of at least M videos where at least N intersections of SOIs per video occurs with a minimum acceptable intersection size of T seconds; and (c) compute the similarity value to be returned. If the verification on the step (b) is negative, the return value is 0. Otherwise, if it is positive, the return value is the rate between the "total number of intersections of SOIs on the videos watched by the pair of users" and the "total number of SOIs in watched videos by the *base* user". For example, in step (c), if a pair of users that have "total number of intersections of SOIs on the videos watched by the pair of users" equals to 25 and the "total number of SOIs in watched videos by the *base* user" equals to 50, then the rate is 25/50, i.e., the degree of similarity of this pair of user is 0.5 (which corresponds to an increase of 50% in sim^{CF}).

6. EXPERIMENTAL EVALUATION

The prototype was used by three different groups of students of the undergraduate course of Computer Science at UFRGS. A historical dataset was built, which contains 88 user profiles (40 from group one, 29 from group two and 19 from group three), 764 ratings of video and 269 segments of interest.

The experimental evaluation focused in the accuracy of ratings predictions on video recommendation. In order to do that, we used only the pure collaborative recommender component and the sim^{SOI} component, which is the utility function based on segments of interest. The objective was to compare the accuracy of ratings predictions of the pure collaborative recommender (baseline) against the same recommender, but under the action of the utility function based on segments of interest.

We performed the comparison through an offline experimental evaluation. According to [8], when we do not have hundreds of user profiles in the historical dataset at our disposal, the leave-one-out strategy (which is a variation of the *n*-fold cross validation technique) can make sense to be used as much data as possible for learning a model of prediction. However, before performing the rating prediction evaluation, some parameters needed to be set: the "minimum neighborhood size", for the collaborative recommender component, and the parameters N, M and T for the utility function. Therefore, the historical dataset was divided in 2 parts.

The first part, for setting parameters, was composed of 1/3 of the user profiles (28 user profiles), which were randomly selected comprising 1/3 of each group of users. With this data at hand, following the approach used in previous works such as [9] and [10], the leave-one-out approach was performed using the pure collaborative recommender component with different minimum neighborhood sizes starting at 2. For each minimum neighborhood size, all ratings predictions and all user ratings were used to calculate the prediction error of the system. For this, we used the Root Mean Square Error (RMSE). We found that the minimum prediction error occurs (i.e., the biggest accuracy occurs) when the minimum neighborhood size is 3, with the corresponding RMSE = 0.0205. This is the optimal value for this parameter in our dataset. Then this parameter was set in the pure collaborative recommender component, and, following the approach presented by [5] and [6], the leave-one-out was performed for different combinations of values of parameters M, N and T, from the utility function. For each combination, the prediction error of the system was computed by the RMSE, as previously. Then, the optimal values for these parameters were found, and they were $N = 2$, $M = 2$ and $T = 5$ with a corresponding RMSE = 0.0230, i.e., a pair of user is similar if it has 2 or more intersections of SOIs in one video with at least 5 seconds, and this pattern occurs in a set of 2 or more videos.

In the second part, with 2/3 of user profiles (60 user profiles), after setting the optimal values for the parameters in the system, the rating prediction evaluation was performed. Figure 8 shows the result of this evaluation.

The pure collaborative recommender component made 553 video rating predictions. When this component was tested again, but under the action of the utility function based on segments of interest, there was a decrease in the error of ratings predictions of 16.72% (i.e., the accuracy of ratings predictions increased). From the 553 predictions, 58 suffered the utility function action.

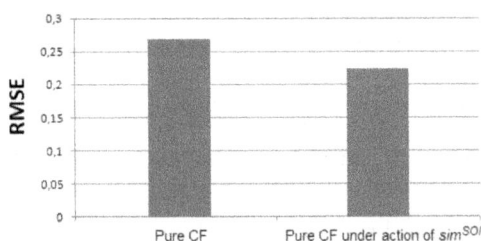

Figure 8: Error on the rating prediction evaluation with and without the use of the utility function based in segments of interest.

After this verification, to ensure that the result was reliable, i.e., to show that the result was not due to luck, the statistical significance Wilcoxon signed rank test was applied. This test was applied as proposed by [15], i.e., comparing the performance of the system for user profile (by RMSE) of both approaches. In this case, that means the "pure collaborative recommender" against the same "pure collaborative recommender, but under the action of the utility function based on segments of interest". In such test, the *p*-value found was 0.5566 (with 95% confidence), which showed that the result was not statistically significant. Statistical significant results must have a *p*-value $\leq$ 0.0005, with 95% confidence.

Faced with this fact, a verification was made on the historical dataset, which found that there were, according to the utility function, few users in the group with similar interests, or common taste, about video (only 12 from 60 users). Therefore, there weren't many user profiles to whom recommendations suffered the action of the utility function. As consequence, the result had no statistical significance. Furthermore, such verification found that there were many participants who didn't mark any SOI. From 60 user profiles used in the test prediction, only 29 have marked SOIs on video, less than 50%. This result shows that the benefit provided by our approach depends on the level of participation of people in the marking of segments of interest. It can be compared to one inherent problem on collaborative recommendation, named "data sparsity": which refers to the problem occurs when available data is insufficient for identifying similar users (neighbors) and it is a major issue that limits the quality of recommendations and the applicability of collaborative filtering in general. In addition, the proposed approach can be considered intrusive in the sense that it requires explicit feedback from the user and often at a significant level of user involvement. Not everyone likes to participate more actively and more interactively. Therefore, other ways to stimulate users to mark SOI must be investigated and used.

With our approach, the accuracy of ratings predictions of video recommender system was enhanced with use of SOI, on the other hand, the result was not statistically significant. Then additional tests were made.

In the first additional test, the same rating prediction evaluation was repeated, but using the historical dataset of each group of students separately. Figure 9 shows the rating prediction error of the recommender system on each of the 3 groups of students separately. In groups 1 and 3, there weren't users with similar interests, or common taste, about video according to the utility function, and then the recommender didn't suffer the utility function action. In group 2, on the other hand, there were users with similar interests, or common taste, about video, and so the utility function acted on the recommender. There was a decrease in the rating prediction error of 11.36%.

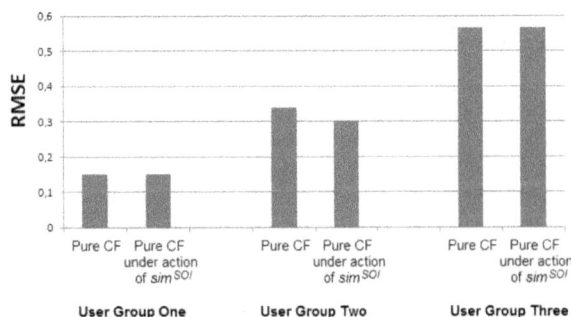

Figure 9: Error on the rating prediction evaluation with and without the utility function using the historical dataset of each group of students separately.

In addition to these tests, the same rating prediction evaluation was repeated, but simulating the evolution of the historical dataset, i.e., while the historical dataset grow up. For this, the rating prediction evaluation was performed using three historical datasets: the first one was composed of the historical dataset of the first group of students. The second one was composed of the historical dataset of the groups 1 and 2 of students. The third one was composed of the historical dataset of groups 1, 2 and 3 of students, i.e., all users. Figure 10 shows the error on the rating prediction evaluation with and without the utility function while the historical dataset grow up. In the first historical dataset (group 1 of students), there weren't users with similar interests according to the utility function, and then the recommender didn't suffer the utility function action, as presented earlier. In the second historical dataset (groups 1 and 2), there were users with similar interests, and so the utility function acted on the recommender. There was a decrease in the rating prediction error of 35.59%. In the third historical dataset (groups 1, 2 and 3), there were users with similar interests about video too, and thus the utility function acted on the recommender. Again, there was a decrease in the rating prediction error, of 16.72%, as presented earlier.

Such results show that in all cases where the utility function acted on the system there was a decreased on the prediction error, i.e. there was an increase on the accuracy of ratings predictions.

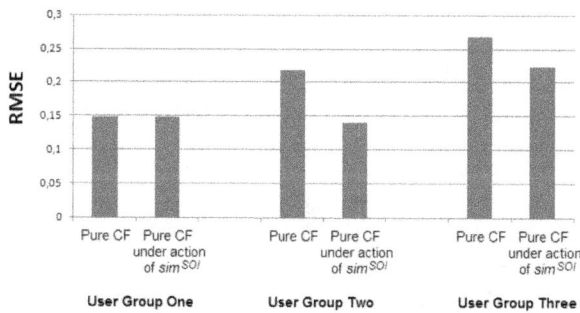

Figure 10: The rating prediction error of the recommender system with and without the utility function while the historical dataset grow up.

7. CONCLUSIONS

Users tend to like particular segments of the viewed content more than the rest. This paper showed an approach where users can mark specific segments of interest on videos, and these segments are used to create profiles of user's interest. These profiles, therefore, can be used to enhance the accuracy of ratings predictions of video recommender systems for users with similar profiles.

SOIs marked by users on video can have intersection with SOIs of other users. When the number of intersections of SOIs for a pair of users in one video is above a certain threshold, and this pattern occurs in a set of videos, above a certain threshold of quantity of videos, it is suspected that these users have similar video interests, or common taste. Faced with this possibility we launched the following hypothesis: "segments of interest can be used to find similar people, i.e. who have similar interests, or common taste, about video, and this similarity can be used to enhance the accuracy of ratings predictions of a video recommender system." Therefore, the objectives of this work were to verify if it would be possible to use segments of interest to enhance the accuracy of

ratings predictions of video recommender systems, and to validate the hypothesis launched.

Subsequently, an approach that uses SOI with collaborative recommender systems, which is the prominent technique of recommendation in the video/movie domain, was developed. Such approach extends the traditional collaborative recommendation approach, in order to take into account more information, which in this case are segments of interest. The user profile is extended and our approach aims to enhance the accuracy of ratings predictions of video recommender systems with a user based nearest neighbor collaborative recommender component. It can be used with a content-based recommender component in a hybrid approach. Moreover, such approach uses a utility function based on segments of interest, which acts over the step "computation of similarities between the active and the remaining of the users" of a user based nearest neighbor collaborative recommender.

To validate the proposed approach, firstly, it was necessary to develop a system in which users could browse, choose, watch and rate videos, and could mark their segments of interest. We created a set of videos and experimented a group of 88 users, building a historical dataset, where rating prediction evaluation through offline experiments was performed. The experimental evaluation of our proposal was performed about prediction accuracy in terms of accuracy of ratings predictions. The objective was to compare the accuracy of ratings predictions on pure collaborative recommender (baseline) against the same recommender, but under the action of the utility function based on segments of interest. The results showed that with the proposed approach there was a 16.72% decrease in the error of ratings predictions, i.e. the proposed approach increased the accuracy of ratings predictions on recommender systems. After this verification, a statistical significance test was performed, which showed that the result was not statistically significant. Faced with this fact a verification was made on the historical dataset, which found that there were, according to the utility function, few users in the group with similar interests, or common taste. Furthermore, it was found that the benefit provided by our approach depends on the level of participation of people in the marking of segments of interest. It can be compared to "data sparsity" problem on collaborative recommendation. In addition, the proposed approach can be considered intrusive in the sense that they require explicit feedback from the user and often at a significant level of user involvement. Not everyone likes to participate more actively and more interactively. Therefore, some way to stimulate people to mark segments of interest must be used.

With our approach, the accuracy of ratings predictions of the video recommender system was enhanced by segments of interest, on the other hand, the result was not statistically significant. So, additional tests were performed. These results showed that in all cases where the utility function acted on the system the prediction error decreased, i.e. there was an increase in the accuracy of ratings prediction. The accuracy improvement is directly related with the level of participation of people marking SOI, so, as the more people collaborate and interact, the better will the recommendation result.

Finally, the formal definition of the utility function and the formal domain definition that describes the environment of a recommender system with accuracy of ratings prediction enhanced by segments of interest allow such an approach to be applied to both new systems and existing systems in operation, and to be applied to different types of video systems (video websites, PVR devices and VOD services).

It is important to state that the historical dataset used in this research is available on-line for the community (see http://www.inf.ufrgs.br/~asdias).

As future work, one import task consists on study how to stimulate people to mark SOI. Nowadays, it is common the online video sharing on social networks. Therefore, one possibility could be the sharing of segment of interest among users in social networks.

In relation to the similarity calculation between users, other approaches could be used. For instance, similarity metrics used in interval data clustering can be used for this calculation, such as the Hausdorff distance [4] or the Minkowski interval distance [14].

In relation to the experimental evaluation, more work is needed in the sense of accuracy of usage predictions, robustness and privacy.

Another future task is to extend the proposition presented in this work to other media types (audio, text, image, and TV content). For example, text interest segments could be marked with a highlight text tool on e-books.

8. ACKNOWLEDGMENTS

This work is partially supported by CNPq (Brazilian Council for Scientific and Technological Development), and CAPES.

9. REFERENCES

[1] Adomavicius G., Tuzhilin, A. 2005. Toward The Next Generation of Recommender Systems: A Survey of the State-of-The-Art and Possible Extensions. In *IEEE Transactions On Knowledge And Data Engineering*, 17, 6 (2005), 734–749.

[2] Balabanovic, M., Shoham, Y. 1997. Fab: Content-Based, Collaborative Recommendation, In *Communications of the ACM*, 40, 3 (1997), 66-72.

[3] Chakoo, N., Gupta, R., Hiremath, J. 2008. Towards better Content Visibility in Video Recommender Systems, In *Frontier of Computer Science and Technology*, FCST'2008.

[4] Chavent, M., Lechevallier, Y. 2002. Dynamical Clustering of Interval Data: Optimization of an Adequacy Criterion based on Hausdorff distance. In *Classification, Clustering and Data Analysis*, 2002.

[5] Ghazanfar, M.; Prügel-bennett, 2010. A. An Improved Switching Hybrid Recommender System Using Naive Bayes Classifier and Collaborative Filtering, In *International Multi Conference of Engineers and Computer Scientists*, IMECS'2010.

[6] Ghazanfar, M., Prügel-bennett, 2010. A. A Scalable, Accurate Hybrid Recommender System, In *Knowledge Discovery and Data Mining*, WKDD'2010.

[7] He, J.; 2010. A Social Network-Based Recommender System. Ph.D. Dissertation. University of California at Los Angeles, Los Angeles, CA, USA.

[8] Jannach, D., Zanker, M., Felfernig, A., Friedrich, G. 2011. Recommender Systems: An Introduction. New York: Cambridge University Press, 2011.

[9] Koren, Y., Bell, R., Volinsky, C. Matrix Factorization Techniques for Recommender Systems. In *Computer*, 42, 8, (2009).

[10] 15 Lakiotaki, K., Matsatsinis, N., Tsoukias, A. Multicriteria User Modeling in Recommender Systems. In *IEEE Intelligent Systems*, 26 (2011).

[11] Lekakos, G., Caravelas, P. 2006. MoRe: a Recommendation Systems combining Content-based and Collaborative filtering. In *EUROITV Conference*, EUROITV '2006.

[12] Nathan, M., Harrison, C., Yarosh, S., Terveen, L., Stead, L., Amento, B. 2008. CollaboraTV: making television viewing social again. In *1st International Conference on Designing Interactive User Experiences for TV and Video*, UXTV'2008.

[13] Nunes, M. A. S. N.. Hu, R. 2012. Personality-based recommender systems: an overview. In *Sixth ACM Conference on Recommender Systems* (RecSys '2012). ACM, New York, NY, USA, 5-6.

[14] Peng, W., Li, T. 2006. Interval Data Clustering with Applications, In *Tools with Artificial Intelligence*, ICTAI'2006.

[15] Ricci, F., Rokach, L., Shapira, B., Kantor, P. B. 2011 Recommender Systems Handbook. New York: Springer.

[16] YouTube Statistics. URL "http://www.youtube.com/yt/press/statistics.html". Accessed in March, 2013.

[17] Sumiyoshi, H., Sano, M., Goto, J., Mochizuki, T., Miyazaki. 2010. CurioView: TV Recommendations Related to Content Being Viewed, In *Broadband Multimedia Systems and Broadcasting*, BMSB'2010

MapReduce Performance Evaluation for Knowledge-based Recommendation of Context-tagged Photos

Paulo A. L. Rego
Mestrado e Doutorado em
Ciência da Computação
(MDCC)
Universidade Federal do
Ceará
Fortaleza, Brasil
pauloalr@ufc.br

Fabrício D. A. Lemos
Grupo de Redes de
Computadores, Engenharia de
Software e Sistemas
Universidade Federal do
Ceará
Fortaleza, Brasil
fabriciolemos@great.ufc.br

Windson Viana
Instituto UFC Virtual
Universidade Federal do
Ceará
Fortaleza, Brasil
windson@virtual.ufc.br

Fernando Trinta
Grupo de Redes de
Computadores, Engenharia de
Software e Sistemas
Universidade Federal do
Ceará
Fortaleza, Brasil
fernando.trinta@lia.ufc.br

José N. de Souza
Grupo de Redes de
Computadores, Engenharia de
Software e Sistemas
Universidade Federal do
Ceará
Fortaleza, Brasil
neuman@ufc.br

ABSTRACT

Recommendation systems are a subclass of information filtering systems that aims at helping users in retrieving information. Recently, contextual information proved to be effective in improving the quality of results of Recommender Systems. However, Context-aware Recommender Systems still suffer performance issues for real-time recommendation, mainly due to the amount of items that should be considered for recommendation. In this paper, we present an evaluation of using MapReduce and its integration with a mobile system for implementing a knowledge-based algorithm for context-aware recommendation. To be effective, this photo recommendation algorithm should work with a large set of images annotated with contextual information. The MapReduce algorithm parallelizes the processing required to generate the recommendation results and so improved the system performance. The results of performance analysis showed, for instance, that cloud-based version of the reccomendation reaches a speedup of 7x with a image base with more than 41 million photos.

Categories and Subject Descriptors

D.1.3 [**Concurrent Programming**]: Distributed programming, Parallel programming; H.3.3 [**Information Search and Retrieval**]: Information filtering

General Terms

Algorithms, Performance

Keywords

Multimedia Systems, Recommender Systems, Mobile Cloud Computing

1. INTRODUÇÃO

Um dos desafios mais importantes em Sistemas de Informação é a sobrecarga de informações. Sistemas de Recomendação tentam resolver este desafio, auxiliando aos usuários na recuperação de itens (e.g., dados sobre restaurantes, imagens, produtos) através da proposição de uma lista reduzida de itens que atende às suas preferências, intenções e histórico de uso do sistema [1, 8]. O desenvolvimento de Sistemas de Recomendação Sensíveis ao Contexto (SRSC) foi motivado a partir de pesquisas que reconhecem uma dependência das necessidades de longo prazo do usuário em relação ao tempo, a localização e outras informações sobre o ambiente físico em torno dele [1]. A sensibilidade ao contexto introduziu, assim, um nível adicional de personalização, uma vez que leva em conta a influência da situação do usuário em sua avaliação dos produtos ou itens sugeridos pelo sistema de recomendação [1, 10].

Um SRSC pode envolver também a captura de informações contextuais em um dispositivo móvel (e.g., *smartphones, tablets*) que envia as informações adquiridas para que o Sistema de Recomendação calcule a lista de itens mais adequada à situação corrente do usuário. O desenvolvimento de um SRSC envolve, entretanto, uma grande quantidade de dados a serem manipulados para produzir boas recomendações, pois além das *features* tradicionais existentes em um sistema de recomendação clássico (e.g., características dos itens, dos usuários, avaliações dos itens), informações dinâmicas sobre o contexto do item (e.g., o restaurante está lotado) e a situação do usuário (e.g., localização) devem ser considerados durante os cálculos dos algoritmos de recomendação que, muitas vezes, são obrigados a realizar os cálculos em tempo real.

Devido à rápida ascensão de tecnologias de Computação em Nuvem, seus recursos estão sendo bastante utilizados em diferentes abordagens [12, 13, 9]. A Computação em Nuvem foi concebida para fornecer capacidade de computação elástica para o usuário final seguindo o princípio de pagamento baseado no uso [2]. A exploração bem sucedida de recursos de nuvem por máquinas estacionárias motivou o uso de recursos elásticos por dispositivos móveis, criando novo campo de pesquisa, chamado de *Mobile Cloud Computing* (MCC). Este novo paradigma de computação surgiu para suprir a crescente demanda da sociedade por agilidade na realização de suas atividades diárias, sejam elas para fins comerciais, acadêmicos ou domésticos. Além disso, MCC tem possibilitado o desenvolvimento de aplicações cada vez mais complexas para dispositivos móveis, fazendo da Nuvem o ambiente ideal para execução de tarefas computacionalmente intensas [6].

Diante de tamanha facilidade de acesso a recursos computacionais na Nuvem, novas soluções surgiram para explorar e alcançar um alto grau de paralelismo. MapReduce é um modelo computacional que se originou do paradigma de programação funcional, para o processamento de grandes conjuntos de dados em paralelo. Ele foi popularizado e, recentemente, patenteado pelo Google [5].

Dentro desse cenário, este trabalho pretende avaliar o impacto do uso do paradigma de MapReduce e Computação em Nuvem em um SRSC cujo alvo da recomendação é um usuário que utiliza um dispositivo móvel. Os objetivos da pesquisa são: (i) identificar estratégias que permitam a paralelização de um algoritmo de recomendação sensível ao contexto e (ii) quantificar em que situações essa abordagem é vantajosa. O Sistema de Recomendação Multimídia escolhido é MMedia2U [11], um sistema sensível ao contexto que utiliza um algoritmo baseado em conhecimento para realizar a recomendação de fotos a partir de uma base de fotos georeferenciadas do Picasa. O algoritmo de recomendação é baseado em cálculo de similaridade, que compara informações contextuais do usuário com informações contextuais associadas às fotos. O algoritmo foi, então, re-projetado para funcionar em uma arquitetura do tipo MapReduce. Os resultados da avaliação mostram que o algoritmo paralelizado é linearmente escalável, e foi alcançado um *speedup* de 7x para uma das configurações do ambiente de execução.

O restante deste artigo é organizado da seguinte forma: a Seção 2 apresenta uma fundamentação teórica sobre MapReduce e discorre sobre alguns trabalhos relacionados a essa proposta; a Seção 3 apresenta o MMedia2U e sua arquitetura baseada em Web Services; a Seção 4 trata da proposta do artigo e discorre sobre como o algoritmo de recomendação foi paralelizado; a Seção 5 apresenta os experimentos realizados; e, por fim; a Seção 6 conclui este artigo apresentando também perspectivas futuras desta pesquisa.

2. FUNDAMENTAÇÃO TEÓRICA

2.1 MapReduce com Hadoop

MapReduce tem se tornado um paradigma popular para processamento intensivo de dados. Ele é inspirado nas funções *Map()* e *Reduce()*, comumente usadas na programação funcional.

O *framework* Apache Hadoop[1] oferece uma biblioteca para a utilização do MapReduce. Os dados a serem processados são divididos e armazenados em blocos de tamanho fixo (padrão de 64 MB) em um sistema de arquivos distribuídos, chamado *Hadoop Distributed File System* (HDFS). Para a computação paralela ser eficiente e tolerante a falhas, os dados são replicados entre todas as máquinas participantes da computação (chamadas de nós), geralmente usando uma taxa de replicação de 3 (para que uma réplica de cada dado esteja presente em 3 nós). Nesse paradigma, um *Job* é dividido em diversas tarefas (*Tasks*) de computação e estas são movidas até os nós em que os dados se encontram, por isso, o sistema de execução atribui tarefas para que os nós, que mantêm as réplicas, possam processar os blocos de dados.

Usando Hadoop, os usuários escrevem duas funções: *Map* e *Reduce*. A fase *Map* toma como entrada os arquivos do HDFS, e as tarefas *Map* são criadas em paralelo e atribuídas a todos os nós participantes do *cluster*, para que todos os blocos possam ser consumidos e os resultados intermediários sejam gerados. As tarefas *Reduce* têm como entrada os resultados intermediários e são responsáveis por juntar esses dados e, após realizar seu processamento, gerar o resultado final que é escrito no HDFS. Esse resultado, gerado na fase de *Reduce*, pode servir como dado intermediário para outras funções *Map* e *Reduce*. A Figura 1 ilustra o fluxo de execução de uma aplicação MapReduce.

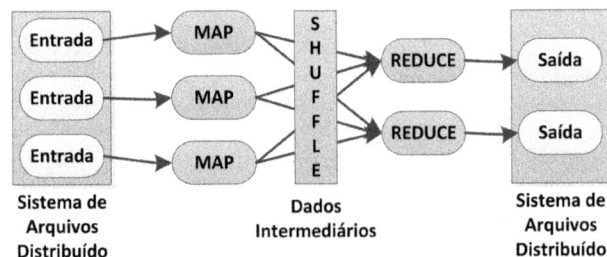

Figure 1: Fluxo de execução do MapReduce [5]

Com o Hadoop, cada máquina é configurada para executar um número de tarefas *Map* e *Reduce* ao mesmo tempo. Esse número de tarefas simultâneas depende da quantidade de recursos disponíveis (e.g. número de núcleos da CPU e quantidade de memória), assim como do tipo de *Job* a ser executado (CPU ou IO-*bound*). O nó *master* do Hadoop executa o processo *JobTracker* que distribui as tarefas para os nós *slaves* disponíveis. Os nós *slaves* executam o *TaskTracker*, que recebe as tarefas enviadas pelo *JobTracker*. Graças ao uso de replicação no HDFS, o Hadoop é tolerante a falhas de um nó *slave*. Caso ocorra erro no processamento de algum bloco, uma nova tarefa é designada a um outro nó *slave* que contenha a réplica daquele bloco.

2.2 Sistemas de Recomendação e a Computação em Nuvem

Em geral, um sistema de recomendação objetiva prever quais os itens que melhor satisfazem às preferências e necessidades dos usuários. Os algoritmos ou técnicas de sistemas de recomendação podem ser divididos em três paradigmas: Recomendação Colaborativa, Baseada em Conteúdo e Recomendação Baseada em Conhecimento [8]. Nas duas primeiras técnicas, um conceito importante é a pontuação ou

---

[1]http://hadoop.apache.org

avaliação que o usuário dá a um item. A recomendação baseada em conteúdo, por exemplo, parte do princípio de que um determinado usuário terá maior interesse em itens que tenham similaridade a itens avaliados anteriormente, por ele mesmo, como positivos. A recomendação colaborativa ou filtragem colaborativa parte do princípio de que usuários que demonstraram interesses similares no passado irão apresentar interesses também similares no futuro, assim, o sistema calcula avaliações baseadas nas avaliações de outros usuários. Um terceiro tipo de técnica é a recomendação baseada em conhecimento, que realiza a recomendação a partir das preferências informadas pelo usuário. Os itens passíveis de recomendação necessitam ser anotados com características objetivas para serem avaliados quanto a sua adequação às preferências. Modelos híbridos destas técnicas também existem objetivando sobrepujar inconvenientes de cada uma dessas técnicas (e.g., início frio, ausência de avaliações dos itens, matriz esparsa).

Sistemas Web, como Netflix, Amazon, Google News e Youtube, usam Sistemas de Recomendação para personalizar seu conteúdo para os usuários e devem lidar com uma grande quantidade de dados (itens, avaliações e usuários)[3, 4]. Esses sistemas utilizam soluções distribuídas como o MapReduce para realizar essas tarefas.

Em [3], por exemplo, o sistema de recomendação do Google News usa uma implementação de *MinHash clustering* e PLSI (*Probabilistic Latent Semantic Indexing*) baseada em MapReduce. O trabalho aborda questões de escalabilidade quando o número de usuários e itens, em um sistema de recomendação, cresce a muitos milhões e ambos passam por mudanças rápidas, e mostra que o ganho de escalabilidade do algoritmo não incorreu em perda de qualidade na recomendação. Em [4], os autores apresentam uma implementação distribuída, de uma abordagem de recomendação baseada em conteúdo, e que é usada pelo sistema de recomendação do Youtube, onde as recomendações são geradas através de uma série de computações com MapReduce, que percorrem um grafo com dados de usuários e vídeos.

O MapReduce já mostrou-se efetivo em outros trabalhos que utilizam sistemas de recomendação [9, 12, 13]. Em [12], um algoritmo MapReduce para o problema de recomendação de músicas foi desenvolvido. O algoritmo apresentado é capaz de trabalhar com dados particionados, e os autores mostraram a escalabilidade linear obtida com a reformulação do método de filtragem colaborativa baseado em similaridade de vizinhança. Os autores em [9] também apresentam um algoritmo escalável de filtragem colaborativa, baseada em itens, em que os três cálculos mais caros do algoritmo proposto foram divididos em quatro fases MapReduce.

Em [13], os autores utilizaram uma solução com múltiplos estágios MapReduce para operar no processador experimental *many-core* da Intel (chamado *Single Chip Cloud Computer*). Os autores avaliaram a solução proposta com uma aplicação de sistema de recomendação que utiliza filtragem colaborativa. Um *framework* foi desenvolvido para realizar filtragem colaborativa baseada em vizinhança. Esta foi a primeira proposta de uso de arquitetura *many-core* para sistemas de recomendação.

Como pode ser visto, o MapReduce já foi utilizado com sucesso em outro tipos de algoritmos de recomendação. Neste trabalho, em particular, foi avaliado como um algoritmo, baseado em conhecimento de um SRSC, pode ser adaptado para essa abordagem distribuída.

3. MMEDIA2U

O *Mobile Media to You* (MMedia2U) é um sistema multimídia de recomendação de fotos que se encaixa na categoria de sistemas de recomendação baseada em conhecimento. O MMedia2U recomenda fotos anotadas com informações contextuais e permite que um usuário acesse os itens recomendados a partir de seu dispositivo móvel [11]. Neste sistema, os usuários recebem recomendações de fotos geradas em um contexto similar ao seu, sendo essa similaridade uma função de três dimensões contextuais (espacial, social e temporal).

A abordagem de recomendação, proposta em nosso trabalho anterior [11], foca no uso de sistemas de recomendação por usuários em situação de mobilidade. Neste caso, a recomendação foi projetada seguindo uma arquitetura orientada a serviços cliente-servidor para computação móvel, baseada em *RESTFul Web Services*. Na arquitetura proposta, há dois participantes principais:

Dispositivo móvel: responsável pela aquisição de contexto, com dados brutos e não trabalhados, e pela interface de interação com o usuário;

Serviço de Recomendação: responsável pelo processamento dos dados e onde é executado o algoritmo de recomendação e a busca de itens.

Figure 2: Fluxo de Execução do MMedia2U

A Figura 2 apresenta uma visão geral do fluxo de execução do sistema. No passo 1, a aplicação de recomendação executada no dispositivo móvel é responsável por recuperar o contexto do usuário. Alguns tipos de informações, como localização, podem ser adquiridos a partir de sensores, como o GPS. Outros tipos dependem de informações passadas pelo usuário (e.g., o usuário informa à aplicação qual a atividade sendo desempenhada). No passo 2, a aplicação móvel acessa, a partir de uma chamada HTTP, o *Web Service* disponibilizado pelo serviço de recomendação, informando o contexto atual do usuário. O serviço de recomendação, hospedado inicialmente em um servidor Web, ao receber a requisição, realiza o enriquecimento de contexto do usuário (passo 3), incorporando novas informações a partir dos dados enviados. Os metadados das fotos, armazenados no repositório, são pesquisados e são comparados com o contexto passado (passo 4). No passo 5, é elaborado um *ranking* de acordo com os cálculos de similaridade implementados e as fotos, geradas em um contexto com maior similaridade ao do usuário, são enviadas ao dispositivo móvel. O cálculo de similaridade global do MMedia2U, entre um usuário e as fotos da base, é uma forma simples de média ponderada entre os cálculos de similaridade de todos os atributos contextuais do usuário considerados relevantes naquele instante (atividade, localização, data, período do dia, etc.) e as anotações contextuais das fotos. A determinação dos pesos pode ser feita manualmente (sem treinamento) ou usando uma base de treinamento (histórico de avaliações).

Uma vez calculadas as similaridades, as Top-N fotos com maior similaridade são escolhidas e o *ranking* é retornado ao dispositivo móvel (passo 6). Ele possui a URL das fotos e os seus metadados para que, além do conteúdo, o usuário possa também ter acesso às mesmas informações de contexto utilizadas pelo sistema.

4. PROPOSTA

Esta seção apresenta o MMedia2UE (*Mobile Media to You Extended*), uma extensão do MMedia2U, em que o poder de paralelização do algoritmo de recomendação proposto em [11] é explorado.

O presente trabalho fez alterações nos dois componentes, mas a maioria dos aperfeiçoamentos foi realizada no servidor de aplicação (Serviço de Recomendação). Utilizando-se dos conceitos de Computação em Nuvem e do modelo de programação *MapReduce*, o servidor foi reimplementado com o *framework* Apache Hadoop, para permitir o processamento distribuído de uma grande massa de dados. Diferente do trabalho anterior, o objetivo desse trabalho não é avaliar a qualidade da recomendação, mas sim mostrar o ganho de desempenho obtido ao utilizar o *framework* Hadoop para paralelizar os processos de Enriquecimento de Contexto e o Cálculo de Similaridade, realizados pelo Serviço de Recomendação. Essa informação é relevante, pois o tamanho da base de dados é um fator que impacta diretamente no tempo de resposta da aplicação e, por isso, deve ser considerado. A Figura 3 apresenta a visão geral da arquitetura e principais componentes da MMedia2UE.

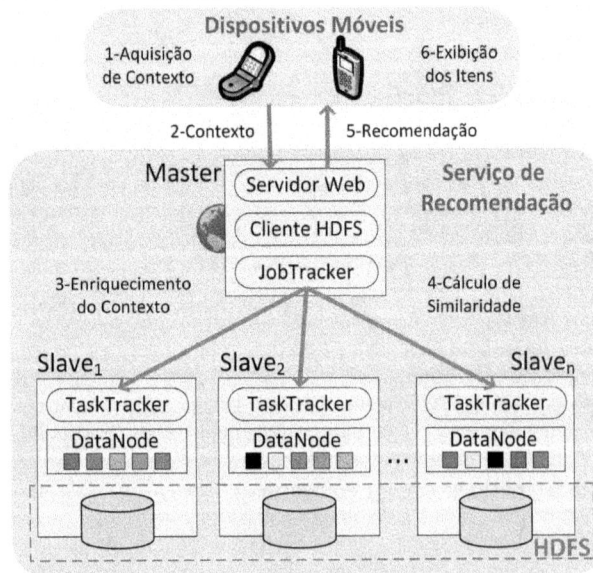

Figure 3: Visão geral do MMedia2UE

O dispositivo móvel, que é o responsável pela aquisição de contexto, comunica-se diretamente com o serviço de re-comendação, enviando as informações de contexto e aguardando a resposta com a lista das fotos mais similares. No serviço de recomendação, implementado no MMedia2UE com uma arquitetura distribuída, o servidor Web recebe a requisição e inicia um *Job*, que é distribuído entre diferentes nós de computação, utilizando o paradigma MapReduce.

Como o serviço de recomendação foi desenvolvido utilizando o *framework* Apache Hadoop, a base de dados com os metadados das fotos foi armazenada no HDFS em formato de texto. Além disso, um *Mapper* e um *Reducer* foram desenvolvidos para fazer o cálculo de similaridade, baseado nas anotações das fotos. A Figura 4 apresenta o fluxo de execução da aplicação implementada com Hadoop. Primeiro, várias tarefas *Map* são iniciadas para processar blocos de fotos. Em cada tarefa, o cálculo de similaridade é realizado para cada foto, os resultados são ordenados e as fotos com maior *ranking* (de cada bloco) são repassadas para a próxima fase do algoritmo (*Reduce*). A fase de *Reduce* inicia quando as primeiras tarefas *Map* são finalizadas. Durante essa fase, apenas uma tarefa *Reduce* é iniciada, e os resultados intermediários (Top-N) são combinados e ordenados para gerar o conjunto de fotos mais similares ao contexto de entrada (Top-N resultado). Assim que todas as tarefas (*Maps* e *Reduce*) forem finalizadas, a tarefa *Reduce* escreve o resultado final no HDFS.

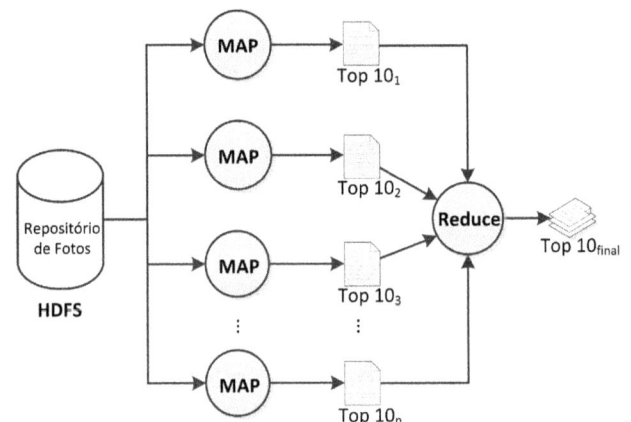

Figure 4: Fluxo de execução da implementação com Hadoop

Dependendo do tipo de requisição, o resultado final pode ser enviado pelo servidor Web para o dispositivo móvel imediatamente (requisição com resposta direta), ou apenas quando for solicitado (requisição com resposta indireta), como é ilustrado na Figura 5. É importante destacar que a versão paralela do algoritmo retorna exatamente o mesmo resultado da versão não paralela, pois a lista Top-N de imagens escolhidas é a mesma computada na versão original do algoritmo do Sistema de Recomendação MMedia2U (versão com único nó servidor).

A conectividade móvel é altamente variável em desempenho e confiabilidade. As redes sem fio variam em velocidade e confiabilidade e os seus usuários estão em constante processo de mobilidade, o que pode acarretar ausência ou queda de conexões [7]. Pensando nessas questões, duas formas de responder às requisições são propostas para o serviço de recomendação (Figura 5):

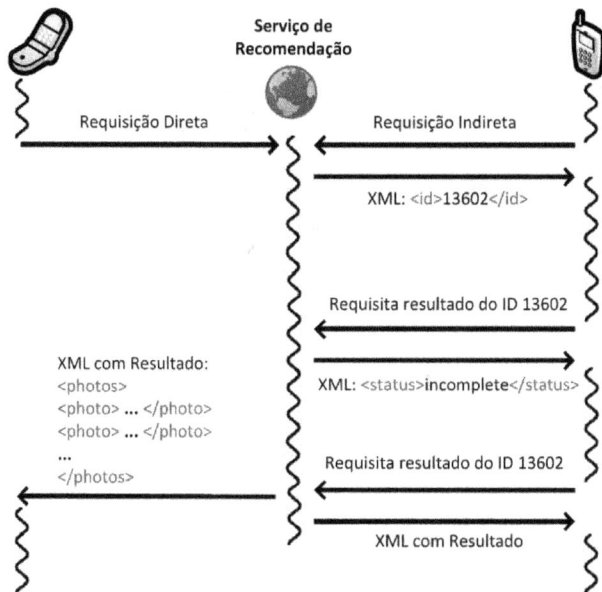

Figure 5: Exemplo de execução com os dois tipos de requisição disponíveis

Requisição com resposta direta: nesse caso, o servidor Web recebe a requisição e espera todo o tempo de processamento antes de enviar a resposta para o cliente;

Requisição com resposta indireta: nesse caso, ao receber a requisição, o servidor Web cria um *Job* de processamento e retorna o identificador desse *Job* para o cliente. Uma vez com o identificador, é possível fazer uma requisição pelo resultado do *Job*. Caso a resposta ainda não esteja pronta, uma mensagem é enviada para notificar que o *Job* está incompleto.

Essas duas maneiras de fazer requisição são importantes para aplicações móveis, uma vez que oferecem maior flexibilidade para o desenvolvedor. Apesar de ter que enviar mais mensagens, a requisição com resposta indireta é mais adequada para aplicações móveis nos casos em que o tempo de resposta é alto, pois evita possíveis erros causados pela perda de conectividade com o servidor. Este ponto é salutar para sistemas de recomendação, pois dependendo do tamanho da base de dados, o processamento pode levar vários minutos (como pode ser visto na seção de experimentos). Enquanto a aplicação que faz o cálculo de similaridades foi desenvolvida em Java, a aplicação Web foi desenvolvida em Ruby[2], usando a biblioteca Sinatra[3]. A aplicação Web é responsável por receber as requisições, chamar o módulo de processamento e enviar a resposta para o cliente.

4.1 Base de dados

Em [11], a base de dados era composta de menos de 600 fotos importadas do Picasa Web[4], utilizando seus Web *services* para consulta de fotos georreferenciadas disponibilizadas publicamente. Alguns atributos precisaram ser inseridos ou corrigidos nas imagens do Picasa Web, pois as fotos não

---

[2]http://www.ruby-lang.org
[3]http://www.sinatrarb.com
[4]http://picasa.google.com

continham todas as informações necessárias para o preenchimento do modelo de contexto.

O repositório mantinha as fotos e os metadados em formato XML (formato de exportação do Picasa Web). Para este trabalho, essa base de dados precisou ser organizada em uma estrutura diferente para trabalhar com Hadoop. Um *script*, escrito em Ruby, foi criado para acessar todos os arquivos e compilar as informações em um mesmo arquivo, com os dados de cada foto separados por linha.

Além da base inicial do Picasa Web, diversos *scripts* foram desenvolvidos para criar uma base maior, ao coletar fotos e metadados utilizando os *Web Services* do Panoramio[5]. Os *scripts* de coleta foram executados em máquinas virtuais da nossa nuvem privada e em máquinas virtuais na Amazon EC2. Mais de cem mil fotos foram coletadas, mas como nem todas elas continham informações de contexto, algumas fotos foram descartadas. Como o objetivo desse trabalho é avaliar o ganho de desempenho com a paralelização do algoritmo desenvolvido em [11], é importante testar diferentes tamanhos de base de dados. Por isso, foi necessário gerar metadados de fotos sinteticamente, uma vez que os metadados das fotos coletadas eram insuficientes para um teste de grande magnitude, pois totalizavam apenas 22 MB.

Fazer um levantamento acerca do tempo de processamento para diferentes tamanhos de base de dados é uma das contribuições desse trabalho, por isso foram criadas bases de dados com diferentes quantidades de fotos. A Tabela 1 apresenta a relação entre o tamanho do repositório de metadados de fotos e a quantidade de fotos.

Table 1: Relação entre o tamanho da base de dados e quantidade de fotos na base

Tamanho	Quantidade de Fotos
1 MB	4.101
5 MB	20.498
10 MB	40.996
50 MB	204.980
100 MB	409.960
250 MB	1.029.001
500 MB	2.062.103
1000 MB	4.124.206
5 GB	20.735.400
10 GB	41.234.562

5. EXPERIMENTOS

Diversos experimentos foram realizados para avaliar a implementação paralelizada do algoritmo de recomendação. Diferentes configurações de *cluster* Hadoop e quantidades variadas de fotos foram utilizadas para identificar o impacto do tamanho da base de dados no tempo de execução do algoritmo, e o nível de escalabilidade alcançado. O resto dessa seção apresenta detalhes dos experimentos realizados.

5.1 Ambiente de Experimentação

O ambiente de experimentação foi configurado na nuvem privada do nosso laboratório. Essa nuvem computacional é gerenciada com o software OpenNebula[6] e, para esse trabalho, foram utilizadas cinco máquinas físicas com dois processadores Intel Xeon CPU E5645 @ 2.40 GHz, 16 GB de

---

[5]http://www.panoramio.com
[6]http://www.opennebula.org

Comparação 1 x 5 x 10 x 50 MB

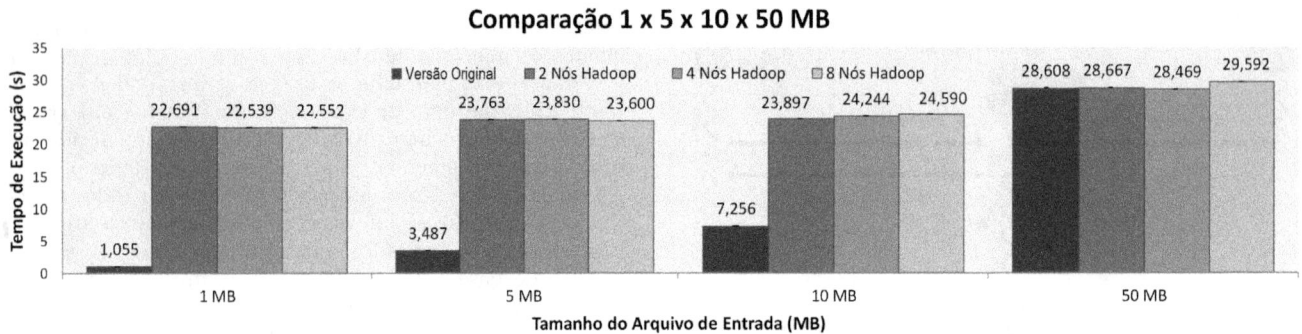

Figure 6: Resultado da execução para base de dados de 1, 5, 10 e 50 MB

Table 2: Configurações do serviço de recomendação

Configuração	Quantidade de MVs	Replicação no HDFS
Versão Original	1	-
2 Nós Hadoop	3	2
4 Nós Hadoop	5	3
8 Nós Hadoop	9	3

memória RAM, sistema operacional Ubuntu Server 12.04 (64 bit) e hipervisor KVM. Todas as máquinas físicas estavam interligadas através de uma rede Gigabit Ethernet.

O serviço de recomendação foi todo implantado em máquinas virtuais com o sistema operacional Ubuntu Server 12.10 (64 bit), processador com 1 núcleo, 4 GB de memória RAM e 30 GB de espaço em disco. O Apache Hadoop, versão 1.2.0, foi instalado em todas as máquinas virtuais, bem como o ambiente de execução do Java 1.6 (64 bit).

5.2 Procedimento do Experimento

Foram realizados experimentos com diferentes configurações para o serviço de recomendação. A Tabela 2 sumariza os quatro ambientes de execução criados. Na configuração *Versão Original*, apenas uma máquina virtual foi utilizada para executar o serviço de recomendação com o algoritmo original [11]. Para as demais configurações, *clusters* Hadoop foram configurados com 2, 4 e 8 nós Hadoop. Para esses casos, uma outra máquina virtual executava o nó *master* do Hadoop. Com isso, essas configurações eram formadas, respectivamente, por 3, 5 e 9 máquinas virtuais. O nó *master* foi configurado para não executar tarefas de *Map* ou *Reduce*, apenas o servidor Web e os serviços do Hadoop (*Namenode*, *Job Tracker*). As máquinas virtuais foram alocadas às máquinas físicas de tal forma que o nó *master* ficasse sempre sozinho em uma máquina física. Os nós *slaves* foram alocados um por máquina, nos *clusters* com 2 e 4 nós Hadoop, enquanto foram alocadas 2 nós por máquina física no *cluster* com 8 nós Hadoop.

Para o ambiente com 2 nós Hadoop, a taxa de replicação de dados no HDFS foi de 2. Já para os ambientes com 4 e 8 nós, a taxa de replicação foi de 3. Em todos os casos, o tamanho de bloco padrão do HDFS foi utilizado (64 MB).

Para avaliar as diferentes configurações do serviço de recomendação, uma requisição com resposta direta era enviada para o servidor Web, que respondia com os metadados das fotos recomendadas, após enriquecer o contexto e fazer o cálculo de similaridade. O tempo de resposta para a requisição era anotado para posterior análise e comparação. Para cada

par de configuração (tamanho da base X ambiente de execução), 10 experimentos (requisições) foram realizados (enviadas), os resultados (tempo de resposta) foram agrupados para calcular as médias e limites inferiores e superiores, com confiabilidade de 95%.

5.3 Resultados

A Figura 6 apresenta o resultado dos experimentos para bases de dados pequenas (1 a 50 MB), contendo entre 4.000 e 200.000 fotos (Tabela 1). Pode-se observar que o tempo de execução com a versão original é melhor nos três primeiros casos (1, 5 e 10 MB), embora ele aumente rapidamente (de 1 para 28 segundos, aproximadamente) com o crescimento da base de dados. Por outro lado, com a solução que usa Hadoop, observa-se que o tempo de execução aumenta pouco independente da quantidade de nós. Esse resultado é causado pelo fato das bases de dados serem muito pequenas (entre 1 e 50 MB) e não ocuparem nem um bloco HDFS inteiro (64 MB), o que faz com que apenas uma tarefa do tipo *Map* seja criada, independente de ter até 8 nós Hadoop no maior *cluster*. A diferença, entre os tempos de execução com a versão original e usando Hadoop, é de aproximadamente 20 segundos para a base de dados menor, e é causado pelo tempo que o ambiente de execução do Hadoop demora para preparar e alocar o *Job*. No pior caso da versão original, com a base de 50 MB, o tempo de execução foi aproximadamente o mesmo para todas as configurações do serviço de recomendação, variando de 28,608 a 29,592 segundos. Pode-se afirmar que enquanto a quantidade de dados a ser analisada for pequena (menor do que 64 MB), não existe vantagem em ter um ambiente de execução com mais de 1 nó Hadoop.

A Figura 7 apresenta o resultado dos experimentos para as bases de dados com 100, 250, 500 e 1000 MB (com a quantidade de fotos variando de 400.000 a 4.000.000, aproximadamente). Para a base de dados com 100 MB, observa-se que utilizar o servidor dedicado é a pior das opções, pois a requisição levou em média 39 segundos para ser respondida. Além disso, percebe-se que o tempo de execução foi aproximadamente o mesmo para as configurações com Hadoop (variando de 26,871 a 27,543 segundos). Esses tempos de execução parecidos para os *clusters* Hadoop eram esperados, uma vez que duas tarefas do tipo *Map* foram criadas, já que a base de dados foi dividida em dois blocos no HDFS, pois o limite de 64 MB de um bloco foi excedido. Conclui-se que não há vantagem em ter um *cluster* com 4 ou 8 nós Hadoop para esse tamanho de base de dados, uma vez que apenas dois deles são utilizados.

254

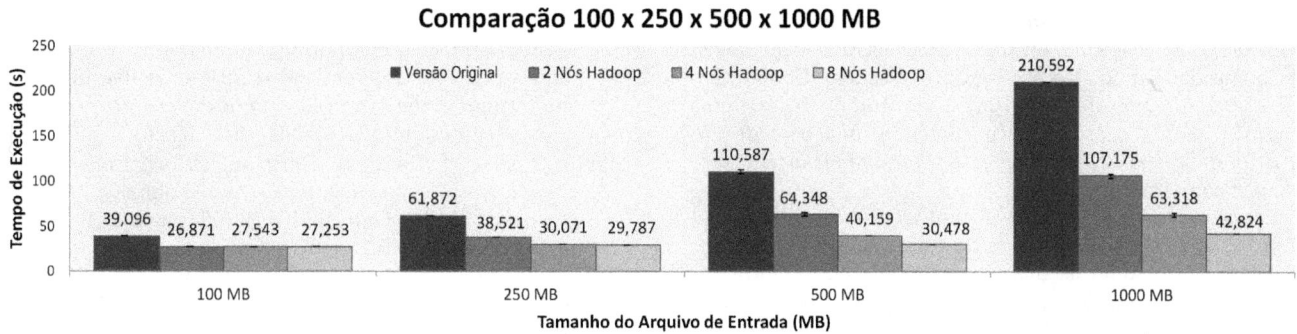

Comparação 100 x 250 x 500 x 1000 MB

Figure 7: Resultado da execução para base de dados de 100, 250, 500 e 1000 MB

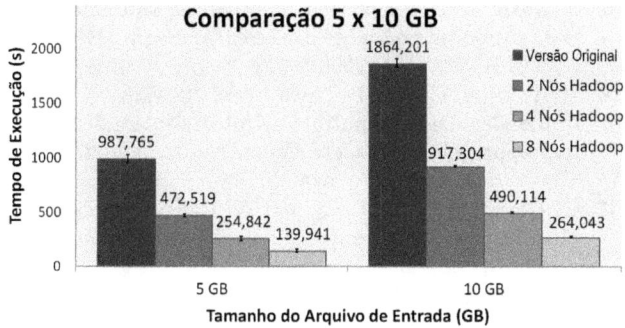

Figure 8: Resultado da execução para base de dados de 5 e 10 GB

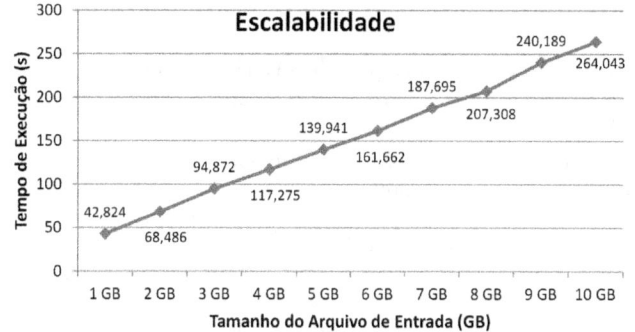

Figure 9: Escalabilidade linear alcançada para o *cluster* de 8 nós Hadoop

Para a base de dados com 250 MB, observa-se que utilizar *clusters* Hadoop com 4 ou 8 nós apresenta menores tempos de execução (cerca de 30 segundos). Quatro tarefas *Map* são exigidas com 250 MB de dados, o que faz com que o desempenho do *cluster* Hadoop com 2 nós torne-se pior do que o dos *clusters* com mais de 2 nós. Nesse ponto, a versão original já apresenta um tempo de execução mais de 2 vezes maior do que o melhor caso, uma vez que demorou em média 61,872 segundos para responder à requisição.

Para a base de dados com 500 MB, nota-se que o tempo de execução é diferente para todas as configurações. O *cluster* com 4 nós não consegue manter o desempenho do *cluster* com 8 nós, uma vez que é preciso executar oito tarefas *Map* (teto da divisão de 500 por 64). Para esse tamanho de base de dados, a vantagem de se utilizar o maior *cluster* é evidente. Já a versão original demora mais de 3 vezes o tempo do melhor caso. O comportamento se confirma ao analisar o resultado para a base de dados com 1000 MB, em que o tempo de execução no melhor caso é quase 5 vezes menor do que o tempo de execução no pior caso.

A Figura 8 apresenta o resultado dos experimentos para bases de dados grandes, de 5 e 10 GB, com aproximadamente 20 e 41 milhões de fotos, respectivamente. Assim como aconteceu para as bases de 500 MB e 1000 MB, nota-se que o tempo de execução com o *cluster* de 8 nós é bem menor se comparado aos tempos para as demais configurações. Para a base de dados de 10 GB, o ganho de desempenho foi considerável, alcançando um *speedup* de 7.

Por fim, um experimento foi realizado para avaliar a escalabilidade alcançada pelo algoritmo com a variação do tamanho da base de dados. A Figura 9 apresenta o tempo de resposta para bases de dados de 1 a 10 GB, variando de 1 em 1 GB, no *cluster* de 8 nós Hadoop. O resultado mostra que o algoritmo escala linearmente com relação ao crescimento da base de dados.

5.4 Discussão

Observou-se que o uso da solução paralelizada reduziu o tempo de resposta para as requisições no serviço de recomendação. A Tabela 3 apresenta o *speedup* alcançado para cada configuração. Com base nos resultados obtidos, pode-se afirmar que o algoritmo de recomendação paralelizado é escalável e pode ser utilizado em um ambiente distribuído para atender as requisições mais rapidamente. Além disso, pode-se afirmar que o algoritmo escala linearmente com relação à quantidade de fotos na base. Analisando os tempos de resposta para mesmo tamanho de base e diferentes tamanhos de *cluster*, constata-se que a solução também escala linearmente com relação à variação da quantidade de nós Hadoop, com um fator de 0,54. Ou seja, ao dobrar a quantidade de nós do *cluster*, o tempo de execução diminui aproximadamente 46% (e.g., com a base de 10 GB, ao aumentar de 4 para 8 o número de nós do *cluster*, o tempo de resposta diminuiu de 490 para 264 segundos, $490 * 0,54 = 264$).

Table 3: *Speedup* alcançado para diferentes configurações e tamanho de base

	250 MB	500 MB	1 GB	5 GB	10 GB
2 Nós Hadoop	1,60	1,71	1,96	2,09	2,03
4 Nós Hadoop	2,05	2,75	3,32	3,87	3,80
8 Nós Hadoop	2,07	3,62	4,91	7,05	7,06

Pode-se concluir que a implementação desenvolvida com o *framework* Apache Hadoop traz vantagens, mas dependente da quantidade de dados a serem processados. Enquanto o *cluster* com 8 nós Hadoop atingiu *speedup* de 7 para uma base de 10 GB, o *speedup* atingido para uma base de 250 MB foi de apenas 2, praticamente o mesmo alcançado pelo *cluster* com 4 nós.

Pode-se observar que não há vantagem em utilizar a solução com Hadoop para bases de dados de até 50 MB (se utilizado o tamanho de bloco padrão do HDFS). Para bases pequenas, a versão original mostrou-se até 20 vezes mais rápida (base de 1 MB). Tamanha diferença entre os tempos de execução está relacionada ao tempo que o ambiente de execução do Hadoop demora para preparar a execução do *Job*, que pode ser uma limitação para aplicações de tempo real.

6. CONCLUSÃO E TRABALHOS FUTUROS

Este trabalho apresentou uma avaliação de desempenho do uso do MapReduce para implementar um Serviço de Recomendação baseada em conhecimento de fotos anotadas contextualmente. A proposta segue os princípios de MCC, ao mover as tarefas computacionalmente intensivas do dispositivo móvel para a Nuvem [6].

Através de experimentos de avaliação de desempenho, para uma variedade de configurações e diferentes tamanhos de base de dados, foi observado que a solução apresentada diminui o tempo de execução, ao paralelizar o Enriquecimento de Contexto e o Cálculo de Similaridade do sistema MMedia2UE para bases de metadados maiores que 50 MB (200 mil fotos). Observou-se que o algoritmo escala linearmente com relação ao tamanho da base e à quantidade de nós no *cluster* Hadoop. Os resultados também mostraram que o ganho de desempenho depende da quantidade de dados a serem processados, e um *speedup* de 7x foi alcançado com o *cluster* de 8 nós. Entretanto, concluímos que é melhor usar a versão original do algoritmo em caso de bases inferiores ao tamanho do bloco do HDFS.

É importante destacar que a análise da qualidade da recomendação já foi comprovada em trabalho anterior [11], e que a versão paralelizada não altera a lista de resultados produzida pelo algoritmo de recomendação do MMedia2U e pode ser reutilizada em outras abordagens de recomendação baseada em conhecimento que utilizam cálculos de similaridade.

Como trabalho futuro, pretende-se estudar o comportamento da implementação com tamanho de bases e *clusters* Hadoop ainda maiores. Outro ponto interessante seria a adição de funções para processamento digital de imagens e das *tags* de conteúdo, afim de inferir outras informações relevantes para melhoria da qualidade da recomendação.

Agradecimentos

Este trabalho é parcialmente financiado pelo projeto INCT-MACC (processo CNPq 573710/2008-2) e pela FUNCAP (projeto número PJP-0072-00091.01.00/12).

7. REFERENCIAS

[1] G. Adomavicius, B. Mobasher, F. Ricci, and A. Tuzhilin. Context-aware recommender systems. *AI Magazine*, 32(3):67–80, 2011.

[2] R. Buyya, C. S. Yeo, S. Venugopal, J. Broberg, and I. Brandic. Cloud computing and emerging it platforms: Vision, hype, and reality for delivering computing as the 5th utility. *Future Generation Computer Systems*, 25(6):599 – 616, 2009.

[3] A. S. Das, M. Datar, A. Garg, and S. Rajaram. Google news personalization: scalable online collaborative filtering. In *WWW '07*, pages 271–280, New York, NY, USA, 2007. ACM.

[4] J. Davidson, B. Liebald, J. Liu, P. Nandy, T. Van Vleet, U. Gargi, S. Gupta, Y. He, M. Lambert, B. Livingston, and D. Sampath. The youtube video recommendation system. In *Proceedings of the fourth ACM conference on Recommender systems*, RecSys '10, pages 293–296, New York, NY, USA, 2010. ACM.

[5] J. Dean and S. Ghemawat. Mapreduce: simplified data processing on large clusters. *Commun. ACM*, 51(1):107–113, Jan. 2008.

[6] H. T. Dinh, C. Lee, D. Niyato, and P. Wang. A survey of mobile cloud computing: architecture, applications, and approaches. *Wireless Communications and Mobile Computing*, pages n/a–n/a, 2011.

[7] N. Fernando, S. W. Loke, and W. Rahayu. Mobile cloud computing: A survey. *Future Gener. Comput. Syst.*, 29(1):84–106, Jan. 2013.

[8] D. Jannach, M. Zanker, A. Felfernig, and G. Friedrich. *Recommender Systems: An Introduction*. Cambridge University Press, 1 edition, Sept. 2010.

[9] J. Jiang, J. Lu, G. Zhang, and G. Long. Scaling-up item-based collaborative filtering recommendation algorithm based on hadoop. In *Services (SERVICES), 2011 IEEE World Congress on*, pages 490–497, 2011.

[10] J. S. Lee and J. C. Lee. Context awareness by case-based reasoning in a music recommendation system. In *Proceedings of the 4th international conference on Ubiquitous computing systems*, 2007.

[11] F. D. Lemos, R. A. Carmo, W. Viana, and R. M. Andrade. Improving photo recommendation with context awareness. In *WebMedia '12*, pages 321–330, New York, NY, USA, 2012. ACM.

[12] S. Schelter, C. Boden, and V. Markl. Scalable similarity-based neighborhood methods with mapreduce. In *RecSys '12*, pages 163–170, New York, NY, USA, 2012. ACM.

[13] A. Tripathy, A. Patra, S. Mohan, and R. Mahapatra. Designing a collaborative filtering recommender on the single chip cloud computer. In *High Performance Computing, Networking, Storage and Analysis (SCC), 2012 SC Companion:*, pages 838–847, 2012.

Personalized Presentations from Community Assets

Rodrigo Laiola Guimarães[1,2], Pablo Cesar[2] and Dick Bulterman[1,2]

[1] VU: Vrije Universiteit Amsterdam	[2] CWI: Centrum Wiskunde & Informatica
De Boelelaan 1081	Science Park 123
1081 HV Amsterdam, The Netherlands	1098 XG Amsterdam, The Netherlands
+31 20 598 2988	+31 20 592 93 33

rodrigo@laiola.com.br, p.s.cesar@cwi.nl, dick.bulterman@cwi.nl

ABSTRACT

Creating compelling multimedia productions is a non-trivial problem. The problem is compounded when authors want to integrate community media assets: media fragments contributed by a potentially wide and anonymous recording community. In this paper, we report on a hybrid authoring approach that provides mixed support for automated creation and manual enhancement of personalized multimedia presentations. We target small-scale events (such as a high school music concert), where lightly annotated media assets are provided. Our assumption is that enthusiastic, but less experienced, editors (e.g., parents and family members) will want to highlight personal aspects of each event: a particular child, a particular instrument or a particular solo. This places a requirement on a system that helps users to select appropriate content of personal interest, and that helps building compelling presentations with minimum user effort. Based on a 4-years user-centered evaluation process, this paper provides useful insights into how a multimedia authoring system should be designed and architected for helping users in creating personalized video stories they care about.

Categories and Subject Descriptors

H.1.2 [**Models and Principles**]: User/Machine Systems – *Human factors*. H.5.1 [**Information Interfaces and Presentation**]: Multimedia Information Systems – *Audio, Video*.

General Terms

Design, Experimentation, Human Factors.

Keywords

Community-based authoring, Hybrid multimedia authoring, Automatic and manual processes, User-generated content, SMIL.

1. INTRODUCTION

Much of the media landscape has been, and continues to be, dominated by commercially produced content. Whether image, video, audio or (to a lessor extent) text, users today have become accustomed to experience highly polished media messages. In spite of the dramatic impact of user contributed content sites (such as *YouTube* and *Facebook*), the amount of personal videos being shared with family and friends (to say nothing of wide anonymous audiences) is still minimal [16]. A conservative estimate of media

WebMedia'13, November 5–8, 2013, Salvador, Brazil.
Copyright © 2013 ACM 978-1-4503-2559-2/13/11…$15.00.
http://dx.doi.org/10.1145/2526188.2526208

use indicates that average owners of smartphones and portable cameras capture hours of videos yearly, but that only minutes (or seconds) of content are being shared [12]. Does this mean that user-generated content is unimportant? No. Personal archives have a high degree of personal value: photos of family and friends, videos of small children, audio fragments that capture the sounds of people who have played an important role in one's life. Although there may always be exceptions, it is clear, that a short video showing a child's first violin solo will not attract the same audience as, say, a slickly produced commercial music video. This does not make the violin fragment less valuable.

This paper reflects on the traditional multimedia authoring workflow and argues that a fresh new look is required. We focus on community-based authoring, where content is contributed from many amateur sources and distributed within a relatively closed circle of viewers who have varying degrees of affinity with the produced content. We concentrate on the particular authoring task in which the relationships between casual authors and viewers can be exploited to create highly personal multimedia experiences.

We have developed a first version of an authoring system, subjected it to an extensive long-term evaluation process, and then developed an improved version that meets a set of refined user requirements. Our initial work enabled users to create video stories reusing collective content for individual needs. Our implementation made use of a narrative engine to automatically compile personalized stories. Our initial results showed a general enthusiasm from participants [8]. However, while the video compilations produced by the initial system were considered visually compelling, users missed the capability of personalizing those by adding their own 'imprint'. The complexity of authoring *personalized* video stories from community assets have led to the consideration of the following research question:

Where is the balance between automatic and manual processes when authoring personalized stories users care about?

We have approached this research question from three concrete and strongly interlinked perspectives. In particular, this paper investigates:

1. The degree to which multimedia authoring can be simplified by the use of a narrative engine to produce a 'rough cut' (an initial video story) automatically;

2. The degree to which this rough cut can be automatically tailored based on the relationships within an end-user's social network; and

3. The degree to which automatically generated stories can be easily refined and further personalized using intuitive manual extensions with minimal extra effort.

The primary contribution of this paper is the user-centered evaluation of a hybrid authoring system that allows amateur users to create personalized video stories for their close circle. This paper is structured as follows. Section 2 overviews our user-centered methodology and the technologies used in the prototype implementations. Then, Section 3 presents the evaluation we have carried out during the first phase. Section 4 describes the design of a new hybrid (or semi-automatic) authoring system that meets the functional user requirements elicited in phase 1. Next, Section 5 reports on the results from the user-centered evaluation of our second prototype, demonstrating the benefits of our hybrid authoring approach. In Section 6 we overview the related work. Finally, Section 7 concludes the paper offering a discussion about the lessons learned and future work.

2. METHODOLOGY

This paper is part of an extended study to better understand the role that multimedia authoring tools can play in improving social communications between friends and families living apart. In particular, we are interested in understanding how individual users can use community assets in a personalized manner to make unique video stories that can be shared within a social circle.

We have been actively investigating this problem for several years. The methodology reported in this paper integrates aspects of human-computer interaction (e.g., requirements gathering, iterative prototyping and user evaluation), multimedia, and document engineering. Potential users have been involved in the design and evaluation process since the beginning, starting with interviews and focus groups, leading up to the evaluation of a two-phased prototype system.

A set of parents from local high schools has actively collaborated with this research. Starting in December 2009, the parents were invited to a focus group that took place in Amsterdam; in April 2010 they recorded (together with some researchers) a concert of their children. From Jul-Sep 2010, these parents used our prototype application with the video material recorded in that concert. Based on the feedback and results, the software was re-designed in a second phase. This second time, we involved a high school in Woodbridge (UK), where a concert was recorded in November 2011. Subsequently, the parents that participated in that concert evaluated our second prototype implementation. During these years, we have systematically investigated mechanisms for helping users explore assets from a community collection of videos and to automatically generate 'stories' from these assets based on a narrative model.

Our authoring system, which is called *MyVideos*, has been implemented as a Web-based application, targeting users who operate computer software with minimal technical expertise or previous training. From the user viewpoint this means that they only need access to the public Internet and everything runs within a JavaScript-enabled Web browser on their device. The server components are hosted on a dedicated testbed with a high bandwidth symmetrical Internet connection and virtualized processor clusters dedicated to hosting Web applications and serving video. In our architecture, each school would rent space and functionality on the testbed, in order to make systems like ours available to their community.

The server-side of our system includes a Mongrel Web application server (implemented in Ruby and Rails), a narrative engine (implemented in Java) that creates personalized narratives (or stories), a MySQL database that stores all the relational data concerning the media assets, and a media server that stores the recorded video clips and delivers them through HTTP (*Hypertext Transfer Protocol*) video streaming. The communication between the Web application and the narrative engine uses JavaScript Object Notation (JSON)[1]. Only the application server and the video server are directly accessible through the Internet, while the remaining components are hidden to the outside world.

The client side only requires a Web browser and the *Ambulant Player*[2], for playing the video compilations in SMIL (*Synchronized Multimedia Integration Language*) [3]. The application on the client's devices was implemented using JavaScript and AJAX (*Asynchronous JavaScript and XML*). Additional JavaScript libraries have been used for simplifying the development of the client-side software. In particular, *YUI 2* and *jQuery* have been useful for event handling and AJAX interactions. For playback of individual video clips, two different solutions have been used. When supported by the browser, HTML5 video elements have been used (e.g., for the *iPad* implementation). Otherwise, we used an embedded *Flash* player.

3. COMMUNITY-BASED AUTHORING

Video, as a time-based medium, necessarily requires processing after capture. Editing, for instance, can be performed on a handheld smartphone to trim out poor and redundant content that is always captured alongside quality material. Editing is also required to create attractive artifacts for what we believe could later become valuable memories we want to watch and share with friends and family members. A simple juxtaposition of recorded fragments does not necessarily result in attractive mementos. But editing is not a simple process and people often do not want to engage with it. This is true for personal content from one source, but it is especially true when considering mixing content recorded at a single event from many sources: the community video problem. The purpose of this section is to describe our initial efforts to facilitate the creation of personalized stories from community assets.

The initial version of our system provided users two independent authoring threads: one completely manual and another one completely automatic (called *Editor* and *Composer*, respectively). The intention was to compare the quality of easy-to-create fully automated compilations with the amount of effort required to manually creating personalized video stories.

Figure 1 shows Composer, the thread for automatically assembling video compilations in our initial prototype system. Users only had to explicitly select the subject matter (i.e., people, songs, instruments) and two other parameters (style and duration). Then, by pressing the 'GO' button, a narrative engine would be triggered, and in less than three minutes a video using the assets captured by different cameras at the concert would be created. The narrative engine would select the most appropriate fragments of videos from the repository, based on the declared user parameters, and assemble them following narrative constructs.

The automatic authoring capabilities of the system were assessed using expert input. Three video professionals with between 5 and 20 years experience were interviewed. All three agreed with the basic footage preparation and narrative structures that were used to build the video compilations. They were especially keen with

---

[1] The services and technologies mentioned in this paper, if unknown, could very easily be identified via a simple online search; therefore they will not be Web-referenced.

[2] http://www.ambulantplayer.org

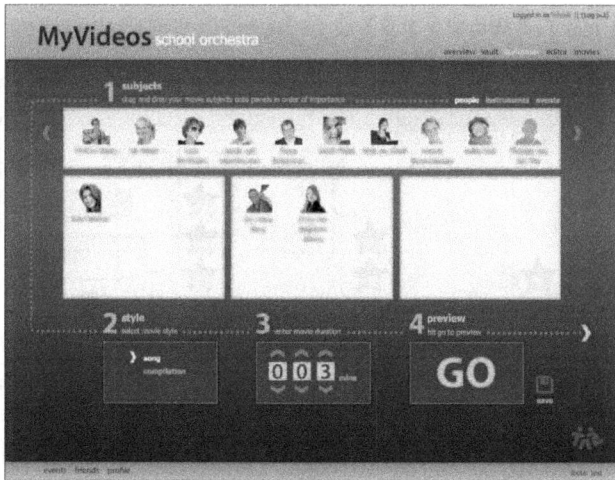

Figure 1. Initial prototype for automatic video editing.

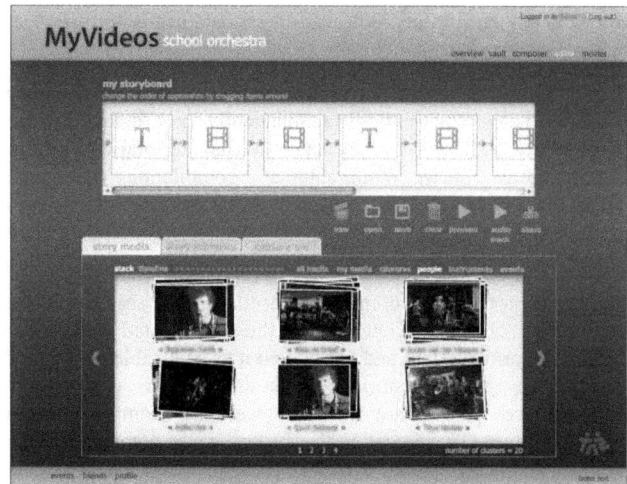

Figure 2. Initial prototype for manually editing videos.

the approach of using an audio track as a master timeline to drive the story development. They also concurred with our approach of automatically selecting alternative shots from cameras in parallel tracks and using rules that selected clips based on shot types.

Our initial prototype system also provided an interface for manually creating video compilations (Editor). Using the Editor, users could drag and drop recommended video clips from the shared repository to the storyboard (see Figure 2). For example, a parent could add more clips in which his daughter was featured for sharing with grandma, or instead add a particularly 'funny' moment from the event when creating a version for his brother.

Apart from allowing fine-tuning of productions, the Editor enabled users to perform enrichments. It provided mechanisms for including personal audio, video, and textual commentaries. For example, these could be subtitles aligned with the video clips commenting the event for others. Users could as well record an introductory audio or video, leading to more personalized stories.

The evaluation of the initial system was preceded by 3 social events. While the first two recording experiments mainly focused on the evaluation of the annotation processes and narrative structures, the third one, a school concert in Amsterdam, allowed us to engage a group of parents, relatives and friends of performers for evaluating the initial version of our system. In total around 197 media objects were captured by a core group of family members and friends. Twelve (12) cameras were used in a concert lasting 1 hour and 35 minutes. In the remaining of this section we discuss the lessons learned about the authoring threads during the evaluation of the first phase.

3.1 Phase 1 Evaluation

Seven (7) people, among relatives and friends of the performers that attended the school concert in Amsterdam, were recruited. All participants were Dutch. The average age of the participants was 37.1 years (SD = 20.6 years); 3 participants (42.8%) were female. Among the participants, 3 had children (ranging from 14 to 17 years old). All of them were currently living in the Netherlands, but the uncle of a performer that lived in the US. He was recruited to serve as an external participant (the only one that was not present in the concert). The prototype evaluation was conducted over a two-month span in the summer of 2010 (Jul-Sep).

In general, participants appreciated both approaches to create personalized video compilations and considered the functionalities

useful. Using our authoring tool they felt they could create more stories faster and easier (if compared to traditional systems – Q1.1-Q1.3 in Figure 3 from the evaluation of the first phase). Overall, the automatic assembled videos were considered visually compelling. Although participants also indicated that they would like to have more manual processes available to further personalize and fine-tune the video compilations (Q1.4-Q1.6).

"I want more portraits of my daughter (in this automatic generated compilation)... is it possible to edit an existing movie (in the Editor)?" (Father of a performer)

In the manual authoring thread participants could find and select their favorite video clips. However, a common complain was that they had to choose each and every clip for the compilation. Regarding optional processes, for most of our participants the possibility to include personal assets in a video compilation was seen as a way to personalize videos for a target audience. As shown in the results (Q1.5), such functionality was mostly

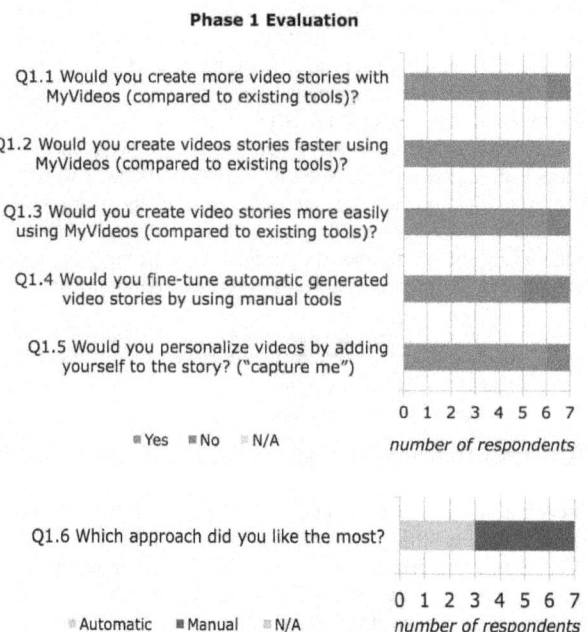

Figure 3. Results of the questionnaires in phase 1 evaluation.

appreciated. Participants indicated they would use it, for instance, when creating a birthday present video.

In the initial version of our prototype system users could either generate video compilations automatically (not being able to change these later on) or edit manually (having total control but starting from scratch). While automatic compilations were quite appreciated because of shot selection and camera diversity, users provided important evidences that manual processes were indispensable to reflect intimacy and effort.

Based on participants' comments, reactions, and answers to the questionnaires, we can conclude that they appreciated the benefits of our authoring system and considered it as a valuable vehicle for creating enjoyable memories. While these results were highly relevant, we were aware that they were not complete. More importantly was the indication that instead of the automatic or the manual authoring thread, a hybrid solution would better fit the participants' needs (Q1.4). In the next section, we discuss the functional requirements that motivated the design of a new version of our multimedia authoring system.

3.2 Requirements Gathering

Regarding manual authoring, participants identified a number of issues that could improve the creation process. Even though some participants were familiar with end-user video editing tools, for most of them this process was time consuming and complicated. Even though they appreciated the filtering functionalities included in the Editor, they indicated that they would not like to start authoring stories from scratch. Given the difficulties inherent in video editing, they would rather first use an automatic system that provided them with an already compiled story. Based on this feedback we introduce our first functional requirement:

i. *Not start from scratch:* users indicated their preference for an authoring paradigm, in which an initial narrative compilation would be created on their behalf. Such approach would simplify the authoring/editing task and increase their productivity;

Regarding automatic authoring, participants generally appreciated the easiness of use. The interface for automatically generating stories only required users to select a number of parameters such as duration, people, instruments, and songs to be shown in the compilation (see Figure 1). After a few minutes, users could watch a static narrative story based on their preferences. Even though they generally enjoyed the final results, they would have preferred that the system selected some of the parameters. In particular, they requested for automatic methods capable of identifying the interpersonal relationships with the performers of the concert. This discussion leads to our next requirement:

ii. *Consider implicit interpersonal relationships:* participants assumed that the system could automatically identify and process their interpersonal relationships with performers when creating video stories;

A common frustration with automatically generated videos in the initial prototype was that the automated process created a video story that could not be modified. Participants indicated that they would like to fine-tune (or personalize) automatic generated stories by using manual tools. They felt that the final result could potentially be more personal by adding assets and personal comments that more closely reflected their view of the event. This was of particular importance in video sharing situations, in which some participants wanted to send stories of the event to particular

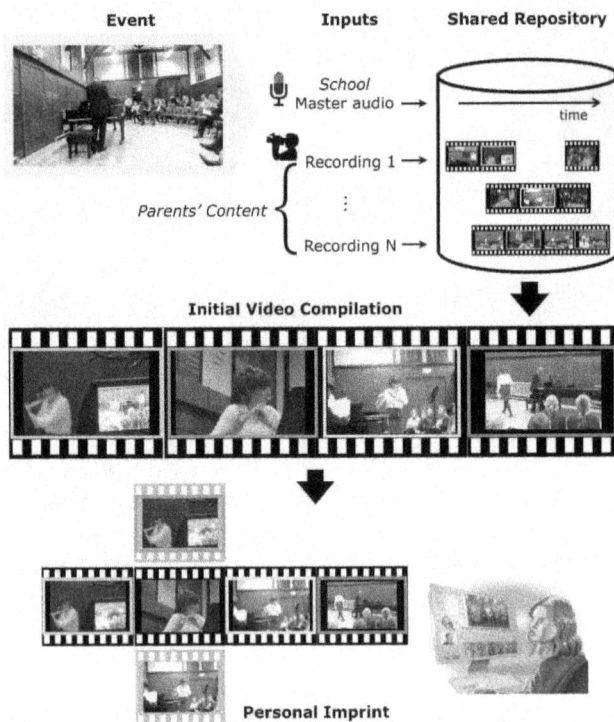

Figure 4. High-level workflow of our hybrid authoring tool.

people within their social circle, such as an uncle or the grandmother of a performer. Geared by this discussion on personal effort we present our last requirement:

iii. *Allow for personal imprint:* participants suggested that automatically generated compilations could be modified. They wanted to remain in control over the final production, being able to make small changes. This approach would allow them to make of that story their own.

Based on these requirements, we concluded that a new version of the authoring system was needed. The new approach would allow users to request a first compilation based on their implicit preferences and interpersonal relationships with performers. The system would then present an initial video narrative, which could be edited and personalized. This hybrid authoring system ambitiously brings together both automatic and manual processes, so that narrative segments can be compiled, adjusted and edited successively. In the next section we discuss our efforts in designing and implementing such new authoring paradigm.

4. HYBRID MULTIMEDIA AUTHORING

The high-level workflow of our new authoring tool is detailed in Figure 4. Since we intend to improve the creation of video compilations based on multi-camera recordings, the input material includes the school master track and the actual video clips that users agreed to upload. All video clips are stored in a shared video repository that also serves as a media clip browser in which parents, students, and authorized family members can explore (and selectively annotate) the videos.

In the new design, the event exploration is the starting point for the authoring process. With the goal of creating a personalized video compilation based on a song, the user simply clicks on one of the songs in the concert program interface for triggering the narrative engine (Figure 5). The engine is in charge of creating a

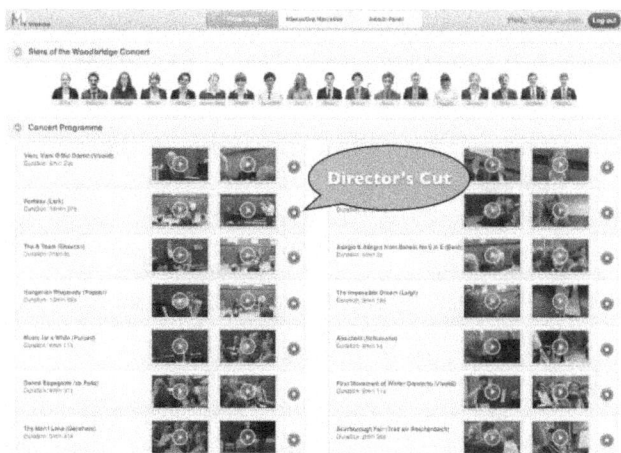

Figure 5. Triggering the Director's Cut compilation.

Figure 6. Director's Cut: an initial video compilation is created automatically by the system.

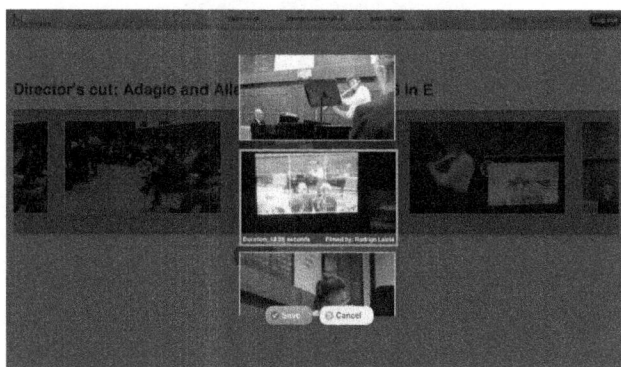

Figure 7. Director's Cut: visualizing alternative clips.

first montage from the video assets (and from video fragments) based on narrative structures and on interpersonal relationships (dependent on the identity of the user that is logged in). Such compilation, from now referred as the *Director's Cut*, can be later modified by the end-user for making it more personal.

Next, we discuss how the three requirements identified over our initial prototype have been considered in the design and implementation of the new authoring system.

4.1 Profiling Users

User profiling can facilitate the automatic creation of personalized video compilations. Traditional ways of user profiling include implicit activity monitoring (log) and explicit insertion of personal data. While these approaches provide relevant results for a

statistically significant group of people interacting during a considerable time span, they are not sufficient for our highly personalized environment. For this reason, we have implemented a mechanism to automatically compute the relationships between users and performers.

Our approach works as follows. First, we look at the songs each performer participated in. This is done by inspecting the annotations regarding performers in video clips, and searching for intersections with the songs in the event timeline. A key part of this procedure is that a ranking is associated to each song-performer match. Such ranking is calculated based on some parameters: the number of annotations each performer has in that particular song, the duration of these annotations (how long a musician is featured within a video clip), the quality of the annotated videos (e.g., high-definition or low-quality), and the shot type annotation (e.g., close-up or wide-shot). Note that this ranking can be tweaked by giving different weights to the parameters. Once all rankings have been calculated, they are normalized per song basis. This means that the performer with the highest ranking in a particular song gets 1; while another that is not featured in that same song (or has the lowest ranking) gets 0 (zero). All the other song-performer rankings will then fall in the [0, 1] range. Our assumption is that the song-performer rankings suggest the importance of a particular performer in a given song.

Second, we look at the capturing behavior of each recorder towards the musicians. In other words, a new set of song-performer rankings is calculated, but now on a recorder basis. By computing a normalized ranking for each recorder towards each of the performers in each of the songs, – and comparing with the general ranking calculated in the previous step – we derive their affection level. Previous results indicate that the affection level greatly influences the overall time a recorder spends capturing a specific musician [9]. Therefore, the recording habits can provide an important cue about the social relationships between recorders and performers. This information is stored globally in the database. Based on the normalized rankings, the narrative engine can create automatic compilations that not only take into account narrative constructs, but also the *interpersonal relationships* between the users of the system and the people featured in the video clips. This approach is aligned with our second requirement.

4.2 Automatic Generation of Stories

The first requirement identified in Section 3.2 was to provide automated authoring functionality, so the author does not have to *start from scratch*. Our system includes a reimplementation of the narrative engine used in the first phase. The new engine provides an initial video story, as a playlist of video fragments. By itself, this functionality addresses our first functional requirement.

The narrative server wraps a narrative engine as a Web application, so that, engine instances can be launched on the server. The Web application runs inside a generic Java Application Server (Tomcat) and it can handle request from other applications. These requests include the command dispatcher for starting/stopping the engine and the playlist dispatcher for requesting playlists. Further information about the narrative engine can be consulted elsewhere [7]. Figure 6 shows a video compilation created out of a song performance.

As we will discuss below, the implementation of the narrative engine was modified to provide a set of alternatives (video clips) that can replace specific parts of the initial Director's Cut, while still maintaining the narrative structure and storyline.

4.3 End-User Personalization of Stories

The third requirement we identified was the need for fine-tuning and further personalizing the automatically generated productions. To support manual personalization, the narrative engine does not only create a Director's Cut, but it also provides a set of alternative clips that can potentially replace parts of the compilation (see Figure 7).

Once an initial compilation is ready, the user can modify it, allowing for *personal imprint* (third requirement). In order to enable such functionality we use a structured playlist format. In our work, we selected W3C's SMIL playlist profile [3]. The benefit of SMIL is that it aims at integrating a set of independent multimedia objects (in our case video fragments) into a synchronized multimedia presentation. It contains references to the media items, not the media content itself, and instructions on how those media items should be combined spatially and temporally. Other approaches on video mashups [18] typically provide a final encoded video item, in which it is not possible to modify or enrich individual sequences. In our case, the richness of the SMIL language permits the user to perform dynamic operations on the initial video stories by simply modifying a text document (the SMIL file). The actual process of manipulating the document is hidden from the author, who simply sees an interactive user interface in the browser's Web page.

The video compilation generated by the narrative engine contains a set of references to video fragments (using `clipBegin` and `clipEnd` parameters). In addition, it provides a number of switch containers (`<switch>`) that contain the alternative clips (or set of clips), which can be selected for personalizing the initial story. Such alternative video clips have been selected by the narrative engine, so the narrative intent is not lost. For example, it will offer the option of selecting a different camera angle or of selecting a different point/person of interest. In addition to these features offered by the narrative engine, the end-user can decide to perform more radical modifications by adding other assets from the database or by enriching the video compilation (e.g., adding comments). All these modifications will be incorporated into the original SMIL file. For viewing purposes we use the Ambulant Player. The benefit of using SMIL is that the recipient of the video can easily further enrich and modify the video compilation, and send it to others or maybe return it to the original author, enabling reciprocity.

The combination of a profiling infrastructure based on interpersonal relationships, a narrative engine capable of creating attractive video compilations, and the use of manual mechanisms for tweaking and personalizing such compilations results in a unique authoring tool. The validation of our authoring tool for creating compelling personalized productions represents the major contribution of this paper, as reported in the next section.

5. EVALUATION

For the evaluation of the second prototype implementation, new recordings took place in the Woodbridge high school (UK) in November 2011. The concert lasted around 1 hour and 20 minutes. A total of 12 cameras were used to capture the concert, 8 of which were distributed among parents, relatives, and friends of performers. In total about 331 raw video clips were captured.

Thirteen (13) people (from 6 families) participated in the evaluation of our second prototype implementation. Participants consisted of performers, parents and other relatives of the teenagers that performed in the Woodbridge school concert. All

participants were English speakers and were currently living in the UK. Seven of them (~54%) were 40+ years old; the other 6 people were in the 11-20-age range, 4 of which performed in the concert. Six (6) participants were female. Participants kindly volunteered themselves for their participation, and the experiments were conducted over a two-month span in 2012.

Nine (9) participants filled in the questionnaires about the Director's Cut functionality. Based on our observations, responses to the questionnaires, and analysis of the collected audio/video material from the interviews, in this section we present the results and discuss the findings from the evaluation process.

5.1 Results and Findings

Figure 8 shows the answers given by the participants after making use of the Director's Cut functionality. In general, all participants appreciated the new prototype (Q2.1). Six participants said that the Director's Cut offers a better way to edit videos if compared to existing video editing software they know (Q2.2). The other 3 users claimed they were unfamiliar with such tools, and therefore, they were unable to judge.

Again, similarly to the results obtained with the initial system (Q1.1-Q1.3), almost all participants argued that they would create more video stories (Q2.3) and quicker (Q2.4) because the tool was easy to use (Q2.5).

"It was very easy to use and it selected which videos I wanted well." (Brother of a performer about the automatic generation component)

"Very easy to use (editing based on alternative clips). I wouldn't want to spend hours looking at a help menu. This was simple enough for me." (Mother of a performer)

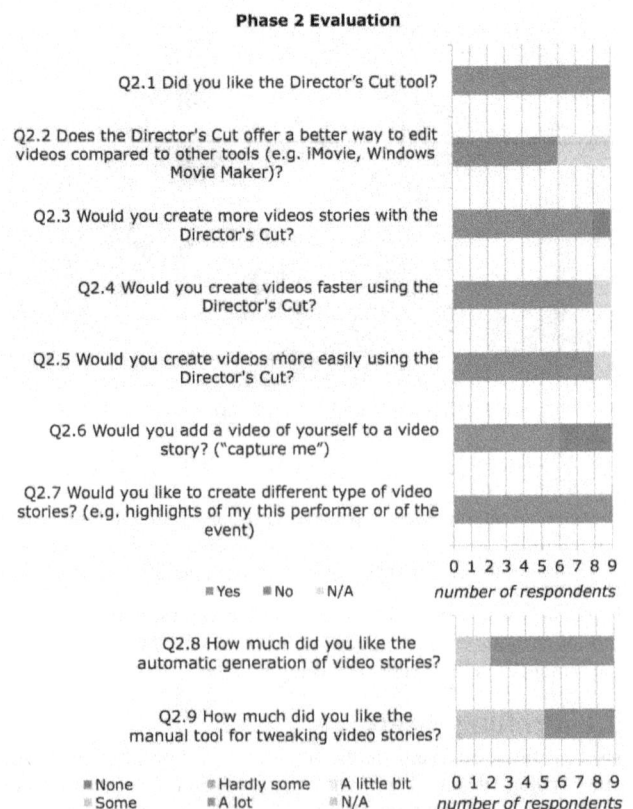

Phase 2 Evaluation

Q2.1 Did you like the Director's Cut tool?

Q2.2 Does the Director's Cut offer a better way to edit videos compared to other tools (e.g. iMovie, Windows Movie Maker)?

Q2.3 Would you create more videos stories with the Director's Cut?

Q2.4 Would you create videos faster using the Director's Cut?

Q2.5 Would you create videos more easily using the Director's Cut?

Q2.6 Would you add a video of yourself to a video story? ("capture me")

Q2.7 Would you like to create different type of video stories? (e.g. highlights of my this performer or of the event)

0 1 2 3 4 5 6 7 8 9
■ Yes ■ No ■ N/A   *number of respondents*

Q2.8 How much did you like the automatic generation of video stories?

Q2.9 How much did you like the manual tool for tweaking video stories?

■ None ■ Hardly some ■ A little bit
■ Some ■ A lot ■ N/A
0 1 2 3 4 5 6 7 8 9
number of respondents

Figure 8. Results of the questionnaires in Woodbridge (UK).

When asked whether they would add themselves to personalize a story (Q2.6), 6 users, mainly youngsters, mentioned this would be a good functionality. However, our senior participants claimed they would not do so. A similar feedback was obtained in the first evaluation process (Q1.6).

"It would be interesting to have a functionality to add other videos (that not only the ones suggested)." (Father of a performer)

All participants indicated they would like to create different types of productions (Q2.7). When questioned about the types of video stories they envisaged, the 'song-based' video came up as first choice among most of them. Some argued that depending on the social situation they would create and share different versions with different audiences.

"If my family misses my performance I would send the full performance to them... but if I want to send it to my singing teacher I would share a more focused version." (Performer)

Figure 9 shows some participants during the evaluation process. A one-to-one comparison between the first and the second phases is not reasonable (e.g., different users, events, tools). What we can say is that in the second evaluation both the automatic generation of initial video stories and the manual tools for tweaking had extremely good scores (Q2.8 and Q2.9 respectively). These results provide strong evidences that a hybrid framework builds on the best of each approach: assisting on complex tasks (*start from scratch*) but still making sure the user plays an active role in the process whenever desired (*personal imprint*).

5.2 Discussion

In this paper we provide useful insights into how a multimedia authoring system should be designed and architected, for helping users in recalling personal memories and in nurturing their close circle relationships. The main contribution of our work does not lay in the use of a specific technology (e.g., SMIL or Web standards) but in further understanding the fundamental trade-offs that enable better sharing of 'personal' media. Results from our evaluation process show that our end-user multimedia authoring tool provides a more fruitful approach than earlier work.

Although our research has reached its aims, there are some unavoidable limitations. First, the total amount of time spent to classify annotate the footage indicates that this is still a very challenging problem, especially when we consider dimly lit user-generated content with different quality, encoding etc. Although these annotations are essential in our authoring framework, this problem falls outside the scope of this paper.

As to the number of subjects participating in the evaluation, it is important to keep in mind that each subject needed to agree to many hours per evaluation. We found it difficult to find high school parents who would commit to this load. We are pleased that our parents – about 25% of the concert participants! – were motivated to contribute this block of time. The goals of the study make it impossible to do crowdsource testing, given the focus on highly personal media. Moreover, we are not aware of other studies that provide the same breadth.

Another limitation could be that we focused on a particular use case scenario. We reiterate that our participants represent a realistic sample of users: actual family members from 2 countries (NL and UK) that have been involved in the concert recordings and prototype evaluation. We agree that generalization to other events is an important problem, but before getting there we need to start somewhere. We see this as a topic for future work.

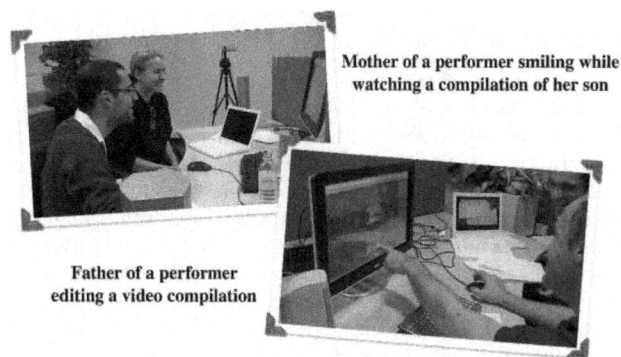

Figure 9. Participants interacting with the Director's Cut.

Finally, we acknowledge there are some limitations regarding the amount of automated personalization that a system can provide. Abstractly, given unlimited personalized annotations and unlimited information on all members of a potential target user community, we suspect that great strides could be made in automated personalization. The reality is, however, that for community assets, personalized annotations are limited, and the target user group is lightly profiled. This requires an interface that allows direct user intervention in creating content.

6. RELATED WORK

Since the early-mid 90's, multimedia authoring has been a prominent area of the WebMedia community's research agenda. A large body of research has been dedicated to multimedia synchronization languages [10] and systems [1][14]. In spite of all the advances, from the end-user's point of view multimedia authoring remains a complex task that demands considerable expertise. This limits the options open to authors and to viewers of rich multimedia content in creating and receiving focused, highly personal multimedia presentations.

Our work builds on previous findings in event detection [6], content recommendation [13] and synchronization/organization of user-generated content from popular music events [11]. Not to forget studies on the aggregated behavior of people and social media for better understanding users and the media itself [2]. However, we go a step further by integrating knowledge of the social relationships to better understand how community media can serve individual needs.

A number of research efforts have addressed content creation by focusing on video abstraction/summarization [20], automatic generation of video mashups from YouTube content [18] and configurable and interactive storytelling [5]. The main difference of our work lays on the fact that we do not aim at providing a complete description of an event based on the characteristics of individual media fragments, but personalized video stories (narratives) based on the social bonds between people. Convenience and personal effort are also important factors to consider when generating such narratives.

Other interesting works propose community video remixing tools [17], video repurposing tools [15] and video enrichment systems [4]. When compared with these approaches, our work intends to help casual users to generate stories in which social bonds between people play a major role. Similar to us, recent work has proposed a media sharing application that takes into account the interpersonal ties. This tool is capable of producing audio-visual media shows based on events, people, locations, and time [19]. In comparison to our work, this application does not allow for the creation of a narrative-based story based on multi-camera community recordings.

7. FINAL REMARKS

Creating compelling multimedia presentations remains a complex task. This is true for both professional and personal content. For professional content, extensive production support is typically available during creation. Content assets are well structured, content fragments are professionally produced with high quality, and production assets are often highly annotated (within the scope of the production model). For personal content, nearly none of these conditions exist: content is a collection of assets that are generally structured only by linear recording time, of mediocre technical quality (on an absolute scale), and with only basic automatic annotations.

The problem is made worse when authors use community assets of an event. In events such as high school concerts, a single concert can generate hundreds of video clips, taken from multiple vantage points, using tens of cameras. With our initial prototype we could generate syntactically correct automated video stories that served generic needs (much like a conventional video mashup). Our users found these compilations compelling but not their own: they missed a personal touch.

Providing direct user intervention has tremendous benefits: the user best knows his/her target audience. The differences between uncle Henry's interest and those of Grandma are often clear in the head of the human author, but largely inaccessible to an automated system. At the same time, end-users have only a limited amount of time and energy to create personalized stories (many are busy recording new content, rather than editing old content!). This requires a balance of complexity and functionality. We feel that our approach provides this balance. Based on user feedback as part of our 4-year study, we believe that it is possible to satisfy casual content creators while still allowing extensive personalization to take place if needed. These results directly answer our research question. We feel that our combination of automatic and manual processes is unique and powerful.

8. ACKNOWLEDGMENTS

The research leading to these results has received funding from the European Community's Seventh Framework Programme (FP7/2007-2013) under grant agreement no. ICT-2007-214793. Special thanks to all the partners and users involved in the *MyVideos* demonstrator.

9. REFERENCES

[1] Azevedo, R.G.A., Lima, B.S., Soares Neto, C.S. and Teixeira, M.M. 2009. An approach for textual authoring of hypermedia documents based on the use of programmatic visualization and hypertextual navigation. In *Proceedings of WebMedia '09*.

[2] Benevenuto, F., Rodrigues, T., Almeida, V., Almeida, J. and Gonçalves, M. 2008. Detectando usuários maliciosos em interações via vídeos no YouTube. In *Proceedings of WebMedia '08*, 138-145.

[3] Bulterman, D.C.A and Rutledge, L.W. *SMIL3.0 - Interactive Multimedia for Web, Mobile Devices and DAISY Talking Books*. Springer-Verlag, 2009. ISBN: 978-3-540-78546-0

[4] Cattelan, R.G., Teixeira, C., Goularte, R. and Pimentel, M.G.C. 2008. Watch-and-comment as a paradigm toward ubiquitous interactive video editing. *ACM TOMCCAP* 4, 4, Article 28 (Nov 2008), 24 pages.

[5] Cavazza, M., Champagnat, R. and Leonardi, R. 2009. The IRIS Network of Excellence: Future Directions in Interactive Storytelling. In *Proceedings of ICIDS '09*, 8-13.

[6] Figueirêdo, H.F., Silva, J.P.R., Leite, D.F.B. and Baptista, C.S. 2012. Detection of photos from the same event captured by distinct cameras. In *Proceedings of WebMedia '12*, 51-58.

[7] Frantzis, M., Zsombori, V., Ursu, M., Guimarães, R.L., Kegel, I. and Craigie, R. 2012. Interactive Video Stories from User Generated Content: a School Concert Use Case. In *Proceedings of ICIDS '12*, 183-195.

[8] Guimarães, R.L., Cesar, P., Bulterman, D.C.A., Zsombori, V. and Kegel, I. 2011. Creating personalized memories from social events: community-based support for multi-camera recordings of school concerts. In *Proceedings of ACM MM '11*, 303-312.

[9] Guimarães, R.L., Cesar, P., Bulterman, D.C.A., Kegel, I., and Ljungstrand, P. 2011. Social Practices around Personal Videos using the Web. In *Proceedings of the ACM WebScience '11*.

[10] ITU-T Rec. H.761, *Nested Context Language (NCL) and Ginga-NCL for IPTV Services*, Geneva, Apr. 2009. Available at http://www.itu.int/rec/T-REC-H.761.

[11] Kennedy, L. and Naaman, M. 2009. Less talk, more rock: automated organization of community-contributed collections of concert videos. In *Proceedings of WWW '09*, 311-320.

[12] Kirk, D., Sellen, A., Harper, R. and Wood, K. 2007. Understanding videowork. In *Proceedings of CHI '07*, 61-70.

[13] Manzato, M.G. and Goularte, R. 2009. Supporting multimedia recommender systems with peer-level annotations. In *Proceedings of WebMedia '09*.

[14] Marques Neto, M.C. and Santos, C.A.S. 2009. StoryToCode: a model based on components for specifying interactive digital TV convergent applications. In *Proceedings of WebMedia '09*.

[15] Pea, R., Mills, M., Rosen, J., Dauber, K., Effelsberg, W. and Hoffert, E. 2004. The Diver Project: Interactive Digital Video Repurposing. *IEEE MultiMedia* 11,1(Jan 2004), 54-61.

[16] Rainie, L., Brenner, J. and Purcell, K. 2012. *Photos and Videos as Social Currency Online*, The Pew Research Center's Internet & American Life Project, Sep 2012.

[17] Shamma, D.A., Shaw, R., Shafton, P.L. and Liu, Y. 2007. Watch what I watch: using community activity to understand content. In *Proceedings of ACM SIGMM MIR '07*, 275-284.

[18] Shrestha, P., de With, P.H.N., Weda, H., Barbieri, M. and Aarts, E.H.L. 2010. Automatic mashup generation from multiple-camera concert recordings. In *Proceedings of ACM MM '10*, 541-550.

[19] Singh, V.K., Luo, J., Joshi, D., Lei, P., Das, M. and Stubler, P. 2011. Reliving on demand: a total viewer experience. In *Proceedings of the ACM MM '11*, 333-342.

[20] Truong, B.T. and Venkatesh, S. 2007. Video abstraction: A systematic review and classification. *ACM TOMCCAP* 3, 1, Article 3 (Feb 2007).

Modeling, Characterizing and Recommendation in Multimedia Web Content Services

Diego Duarte, Adriano C. M. Pereira, Clodoveu Davis
Departamento de Ciência da Computação
Universidade Federal de Minas Gerais (UFMG)
Caixa Postal 486 – 31.270-901 – Belo Horizonte – MG – Brasil
{diegomd, adrianoc, clodoveu}@dcc.ufmg.br

ABSTRACT

Web content has gained much importance lately. One of the most important content types is online video, as demonstrated by the success of platforms such as YouTube. The growth in the volume of available online video is also observed in corporate scenarios, such as TV networks. This paper evaluates a set of corporate online videos hosted by Sambatech, a company that holds the largest platform for online multimedia content distribution in Latin America. We propose a novel analytical approach for video recommendation, focusing on video objects being consumed, and not on consumer profile data. After modeling this service, we characterize the contents from multiple sources, and propose techniques for video recommendation. Experimental results indicate that the proposed method obtains a gain of about 42% in precision for a set of five recommendations, as compared to a baseline that is based only on video metadata.

Keywords

Online Videos, Multimedia, Recommendation, Characterization

1. INTRODUÇÃO

Com o advindo da *Web 2.0*, conceito criado para explicar o momento atual da Web, onde o usuário não apenas consome informações, mas passa também a prover novas informações, a quantidade de conteúdo disponível cresce a cada dia. Nesse cenário, um dos conteúdos de maior crescimento é o de multimídia, impulsionado também pelo grande número de *gadgets* e outros aparelhos eletrônicos (como celulares, câmeras e tocadores de música) vendidos atualmente. Esse crescimento também é observado em redes corporativas. Grandes emissoras de TV, nacionais e internacionais, estão notando uma mudança de comportamento dos usuários, e muitas já disponibilizam parte de seu conteúdo online. Um exemplo é a Globo, maior rede de televisão nacional, que exibe em seu site praticamente toda sua programação.

Focamos nossa pesquisa nos cenários de vídeos online no ambiente corporativo. Para isso, contamos com uma base de dados da Sambatech[1], empresa que possui a maior plataforma de vídeos online da América Latina. Dentre seus clientes, temos SBT, Abril, e Anhanguera.

Nosso objetivo é conhecer melhor o funcionamento de serviços de conteúdo Web multimídia, e principalmente o comportamento de consumo de tal conteúdo. Para isso, propomos uma pesquisa com foco no objeto (no nosso caso, representado pelo vídeo) que está sendo consumido. A partir dessa investigação, também propomos um modelo de recomendação de vídeos para melhoria do serviço. Tais resultados possuem grande importância para os provedores de conteúdo e seus consumidores, uma vez que oferecem melhorias para o serviço, como, por exemplo, a personalização e recomendação de vídeos online. Podemos destacar como principais contribuições deste trabalho o modelo de caracterização e recomendação, com foco no consumo do objeto, usando diferentes dimensões (p. ex., horário de consumo e tipo de dispositivo de acesso).

2. TRABALHOS CORRELATOS

Cheng *et al.* [3] realizam um trabalho de análise dos vídeos do YouTube, obtidos de um *crawler* e chegando a um número de mais de 2,5 milhões de vídeos. Seus autores avaliam algumas características como popularidade das categorias e número de visualizações. Além disso, eles investigam a rede social dos vídeos do YouTube, criada pelos vídeos relacionados e conteúdo gerado pelo usuário. Tal rede possui características de "small-world" e de coeficiente elevado de agrupamento (*clustering*).

Os trabalhos Acharya *et al.* [1] e Chesire *et al.* [4] tiveram como foco a popularidade. O primeiro realizou suas análises com base em acessos de usuários a vídeos na Web, e identificou que a popularidade do conteúdo não segue uma distribuição Zipf. Já o segundo analisou a carga de trabalho de um servidor de fluxo de mídias de uma grande empresa, e observou que a sua popularidade segue uma distribuição de Zipf. Ambos os trabalhos chegam a resultados opostos, o que pode ser explicado pela diferença entre os conteúdos avaliados, ressaltando o impacto do ambiente de estudo.

O trabalho de Su e Khoshgoftaar [8] apresenta inúmeras técnicas de *Collaborative Filtering* (CF), uma das abordagens mais bem sucedidas para construção de sistemas de recomendação. A partir da descrição de suas principais vantagens e desvantagens, são descritas as principais técnicas de CF: *memory-based*, *model-based* e híbridas.

---

[1]Sambatech: http://www.sambatech.com/

Muitos trabalhos de recomendação utilizam dados do *Youtube*. Shumeet Baluja *et al.* [2] apresentam uma técnica com base em grafos gerados a partir das visualizações do usuário. James Davidson *et al.* [5] descreveram o sistema de recomendação do Youtube com foco em técnicas do tipo *Top-N*, levando em consideração o conteúdo do vídeo e as interações do usuário para a criação dos *rankings*. Sua classificação possui como base sinais (características dos vídeos, histórico do usuário, etc.), que são combinados linearmente para a geração de *rankings*, o que resulta em uma recomendação de 4 a 60 objetos. Nossa pesquisa, além de utilizar dados corporativos, apresenta maior foco nos aspectos de consumo do objeto, sem levar em conta o perfil do usuário que o acessa.

Em 2011, Ferreira [6] propôs uma metodologia de caracterização hierárquica do conteúdo multimídia. Podemos aplicar essa metodologia em nosso trabalho, segmentando nossas análises de acordo com os perfis de acesso identificados. Sendo assim, podemos explorar a camada de conhecimento definida nessa metodologia a partir de nossas análises e base de dados, o que contribui para a identificação dos padrões de acessos a conteúdos multimídia.

Todos os trabalhos correlatos contribuem para auxiliar na modelagem do problema endereçado neste trabalho. Nossa abordagem, ao propor o uso de modelos já consolidados na literatura com uma visão focada no consumo do objeto, vem trazer um novo potencial de ganho e aplicação a diferentes cenários da *Web*, que demandam mecanismos cada vez mais robustos e personalizados para recomendação.

3. MODELAGEM DO SERVIÇO

Assim como o *YouTube*, a Plataforma de Conteúdo Multimídia da Sambatech oferece meios de envio, armazenamento e gerenciamento não apenas de vídeos, mas de qualquer conteúdo multimídia. Dessa forma, um dos principais recursos dessa plataforma é o *Player*, que é responsável por servir tais conteúdos.

Embora todas as informações envolvendo essa plataforma sejam relevantes, nosso trabalho possui como foco uma determinada ferramenta desenvolvida recentemente: o SambaTech Track Module (STTM), que é um modelo para rastreamento de métricas na *Web*.

O objetivo do STTM é coletar todas as interações realizadas no *Player* da plataforma Sambatech. Dentre essas interações, temos, como exemplo, o número de visualizações de um determinado vídeo. Nossa pesquisa se desenvolverá com base nos dados coletados pelo STTM.

Existem diversas maneiras de se modelar o cenário de uma plataforma de conteúdo multimídia online, muitas dependendo inclusive do seu objetivo. Uma dessas opções tradicionalmente possui como principal entidade o usuário, e como ele interage com o conteúdo.

Propomos neste trabalho uma visão diferente, focada no objeto sendo consumido pelo usuário. Esse objeto corresponde ao conteúdo multimídia em questão, e pode ser um vídeo, imagem, áudio, etc. Tal objeto pode ser consumido de diversas maneiras, de acordo com o período de tempo, lugar ou tipo de usuário. Sendo assim, temos as seguintes definições.

- **Objeto**: conteúdo (vídeo, imagem, áudio, etc.) ofertado para o usuário. Possui diversos metadados, como título, descrição e gênero, além de especificações de

acordo com o que representa (tempo de duração para vídeos, dimensões para imagens, etc.);

- **Consumo**: situação onde um determinado objeto está sendo consumido. Tal cenário pode ser dividido em:
  - **Como/Quando/Onde?**: representa o cenário do consumo, e engloba informações de como (ex.: qual porcentagem de um vídeo foi vista), quando (ex.: a que horas uma imagem foi visualizada) e onde (ex.: de que cidade está sendo realizada o consumo) está sendo gerado o consumo;
  - **Quem?**: representa o usuário que está consumindo, assim como toda a gama de informações sobre ele, como sexo, idade, interesses, etc.

Esse modelo nos permite ter diferentes focos para a análise.

- **Foco 1:** isolando o objeto (sem nenhuma forma de consumo), levando em conta apenas os seus metadados e especificações.

- **Foco 2:** isola-se o objeto sendo consumido. Essa análise nos permite avaliar como, quando e de onde um objeto está sendo acessado.

- **Foco 3:** isola-se o objeto sendo consumido por um determinado usuário. Isso nos permite analisar os diferentes perfis de usuários que consomem um determinado objeto.

- **Foco 4:** por fim, unem-se todas as análises anteriores, formando o fluxo completo da forma com que um determinado objeto é consumido por um usuário.

Com esta segmentação, podemos propor diversas formas de recomendação de objetos, dependendo do foco com que estivermos trabalhando. Neste trabalho aplicamos esse modelo, com base nos dados reais obtidos, contemplando os focos 1, 2 e 4, este último combinando os dois primeiros. Cabe ressaltar que não dispomos de dados do foco 3, que permitiriam também levar em conta o perfil de cada usuário.

4. ESTUDO DE CASO

A seguir, apresentamos a descrição dos dados de nosso estudo, assim como a sua caracterização e aplicação da técnica de recomendação proposta.

4.1 Descrição dos Dados

Os dados obtidos para este estudo são fornecidos pelo SambaTech Track Module. Seus dados são coletados a partir do *Player* fornecido pela plataform da Sambatech, e possui informações de todas as visualizações de usuários.

Dessa forma, coletamos dados sobre todas as visualizações ocorridas entre **01 de Julho de 2012** e **31 de Julho de 2012**, que totalizam aproximadamente 60 milhões.

A seguir, segue a caraterização básica realizada para estes dados. Ressaltamos que, devido à característica da plataforma SambaTech, todos os estudos a seguir são realizados considerando-se apenas vídeos como objetos, já que representam quase a totalidade da base de dados fornecida.

4.2 Caracterização

A seguir, seguem algumas caracterizações realizadas, com a comparação entre os objetos do STTM (contendo apenas objetos da base de dados visualizados) e os objetos da Base de Dados (contendo todo o conjunto de objetos).

4.2.1 Duração

A cCDF (*Complementary Cumulative Distribution Function*) da duração para as mídias do STTM e da base de dados é exibida na Figura 1.

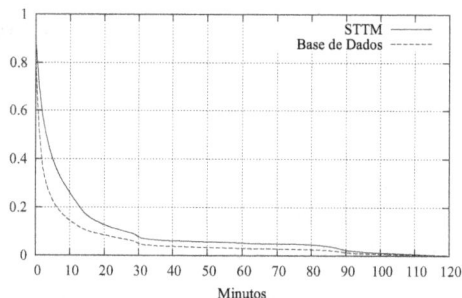

Figura 1: cCDF de Duração

Através da Figura 1, percebe-se que não existe muita distinção entre os grupos STTM e a base de dados. Também pode-se dizer que a grande maioria dos vídeos (quase 80% dos dados) possuem duração abaixo de 10 minutos.

4.2.2 Gênero

Exibimos nesta seção os histogramas por gênero para as mídias do STTM e da Base de Dados (Figura 2).

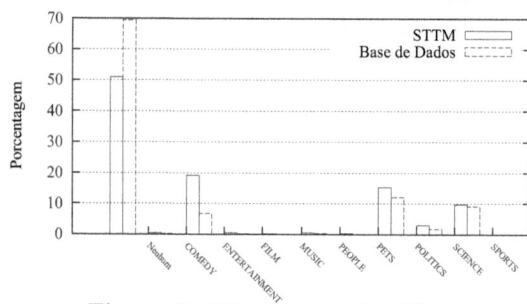

Figura 2: Histograma de Gênero

Na Figura 2, vemos a grande quantidade de mídias que não possuem gênero da Base de Dados (cerca de 70%). Esta mesma superioridade se mantém para as mídias visualizadas, embora em uma proporção menor (cerca de 50%). Porém, em ambos os grupos, os gêneros que aparecem com a maior quantidade de mídias são entretenimento, política e esportes.

4.3 Recomendação

A partir da modelagem definida na Seção 3, desenvolvemos uma recomendação com base no objeto (vídeo) sendo consumido. Dois dos problemas mais importantes da área de sistemas de recomendação estão associados à recomendação de *Melhor Item*, baseado nas classificações (*ratings*) de cada item, e de *Top-N* [7], baseado na recomendação de N potenciais itens interessantes para o usuário.

Considerando o nosso cenário de vídeos online, possuímos apenas a visualização de cada usuário. Dessa forma, a idéia principal de nossa aplicação se baseia na recomendação de uma lista de potenciais vídeos (*Top-N*).

Nossa proposta é a geração dessa lista de potenciais itens a partir da combinação de diversas dimensões do objeto. Seguindo a metodologia da Seção 3, tais dimensões podem ser a partir do: **Objeto**, agrupando apenas metadados como título, descrição, gênero e duração; **Como/Quando/Onde** *o objeto é consumido*, agrupando informações como popularidade, localização e horário do consumo; e **Quem** *está consumindo o objeto*, agrupando informações do usuário.

Dessa maneira, cada item i de nossa base de dados é comparada com todos os outros itens, utilizando um conjunto dessas dimensões. O resultado é um *ranking* de itens que mais se assemelham com i. Dessa forma, nossa lista de potenciais itens recomendados é definida a partir dos N itens que mais se assemelham a i.

Definido este processo, nossa hipótese é: *Quanto mais dimensões do consumo do item utilizarmos para a comparação entre itens, mais refinada será a geração de nossos rankings, e consequentemente, faremos uma recomendação melhor.*

4.3.1 Aplicação

Para a aplicação de nossa técnica de recomendação, definimos dois conjuntos de experimentos contendo as dimensões utilizadas para geração de *rankings*:

- **Baseline**: este primeiro conjunto utiliza apenas dimensões do objeto (metadados). As dimensões escolhidas foram gênero, duração, projeto[2] e tags.

- **Modelo Proposto (MP)**: este conjunto apresenta as mesmas dimensões do Baseline, além de dimensões de Como/Quando/Onde o objeto é consumido. Seu objetivo é demonstrar que, considerando-se mais informações do consumo do objeto, podemos melhorar nossa recomendação. As dimensões adicionadas foram popularidade, hora do acesso, dispositivo de acesso (se é *mobile* ou não) e *referrer* (referência do website que levou o usuário a acessar o vídeo).

Uma vez definidas as dimensões de cada conjunto, precisamos escolher o algoritmo utilizado para a comparação entre itens. Inúmeras técnicas são conhecidas para a realização de similaridade entre objetos. Para os propósitos desta pesquisa, utilizamos a Similaridade de Cosseno [9] como principal técnica de comparação entre os objetos.

4.3.2 Validação

Um ponto crucial para a definição de nossa técnica é o método de treinamento. Para isso, utilizamos como base de treino o conjunto de visualizações de cada usuário. Suponhamos que cada usuário possua um conjunto V de vídeos visualizados. Para cada $v \subset V$, geramos um lista de tamanho N contendo os itens mais semelhantes a v com base na similaridade entres esses objetos. Por fim, teremos um conjunto R contendo todos os vídeos recomendados para o usuário u de acordo com o seu conjunto de visualizações.

Feito isso, nossa base de teste contém as visualizações futuras do mesmo conjunto de usuários. Nossa validação utiliza uma variação da métrica de Precisão: caso o usuário tenha visto pelo menos um vídeo v do conjunto de itens recomendados R, a precisão de nossa recomendação foi 100%, caso contrário, nossa recomendação obteve 0% de precisão.

Esta variação é utilizada pelo seguinte motivo: como nossa base de dados possui a visualização de todos os vídeos da plataforma Sambatech, nossa recomendação de vídeos não é apresentada de fato para os usuários. Dessa forma, precisamos inferir se o usuário visualizou ou não um dos vídeos que teríamos recomendado utilizando a técnica proposta.

---

[2]Ex.: Projeto *Jornal da SBT* do cliente SBT

Porém, a não visualização de um vídeo recomendado não representa que a técnica foi falha, pois os vídeos não foram de fato apresentados como opção ao usuário.

4.3.3 Resultados

Com uma vasta base de dados, precisamos inicialmente definir o particionamento dos dados para treinamento e testes. Dessa forma, nossa base de treino possui dados de 01/07/2012, e a base de testes abrange o período de 02/07/2012 a 07/07/2012. Tal amostra representa boa parcela de nossa base de dados, o que consiste de um método consistente de validação experimental para sistemas de recomendação.

Demonstramos a seguir uma tabela com os resultados do experimento, comparando-se o Baseline e o Modelo Proposto (MP) apresentados na Seção 4.3.1, de acordo com quantidade de N itens recomendados a partir de cada *ranking*.

N	Baseline	MP	Comparação
1	8.91%	18.56%	+107.18%
3	16.84%	24.55%	+45.78%
5	19.31%	27.47%	+42.26%
10	23.48%	31.38%	+33.65%
30	31.26%	45.96%	+47.02%
50	34.12%	49.77%	+45.87%

Tabela 1: Resultados da Recomendação - Precisão

A partir dos resultados da Tabela 1, é possível perceber que a agregação de mais informação sobre o consumo do objeto para a geração dos *rankings* melhora a precisão da recomendação. A utilização do Modelo Proposto em comparação com o Baseline obteve melhorias maiores do que 40% na maioria dos experimentos.

Além disso, também é possível perceber que, com o aumento dos itens recomendados, a precisão dos resultados aumenta. Este resultado é explicado pela maneira como calculamos a precisão, uma vez que basta o usuário visualizar um vídeo do conjunto de recomendados para a precisão ser igual a 100%.

Por fim, podemos concluir que a recomendação de 5 itens seria a melhor opção para o recomendador, um vez que este valor trouxe ganhos significativos com relação ao baseline. Além disso, obteve um valor de precisão superior em relação ao N=1, e ainda sugerindo um conjunto de itens que é razoável no que diz respeito à recomendação de objetos.

5. CONCLUSÃO E TRABALHOS FUTUROS

Neste trabalho, realizamos a análise de um Serviço de Conteúdo Multimídia focado no ambiente corporativo. Nosso alvo foram os vídeos online hospedados pela empresa SambaTech, empresa que possui a maior plataforma de vídeos online da América Latina.

Apresentamos uma metodologia para a modelagem desse serviço com foco no objeto. Nesta abordagem, temos como centro o vídeo sendo consumido, onde encontramos três tipos de informação: do objeto; de como, onde e quando o objeto é consumido; e do usuário que consome. Realizamos também uma caracterização desse serviço, onde conseguimos compreender melhor o conteúdo que está sendo avaliado.

Propusemos uma técnica de recomendação apoiada no foco do objeto que está sendo consumido. O método tem como objetivo a geração de *rankings* de similaridade entre os vídeos de nossa base. Com os experimentos realizados,

fomos capazes de demonstrar que, quanto mais informações de consumo do objeto forem utilizadas para a geração dos *rankings* citados, melhores os resultados da recomendação.

Como trabalhos futuros, esperamos estudar mais profundamente diferentes dimensões dos objetos para o cálculo de similaridades. Além disso, pretendemos abordar mais a informação de quem consome o objeto (usuário). Por fim, vamos estudar a aplicação de diferentes métricas para a validação de nossa recomendação, além de, em parceria com a Sambatech, aplicar essas técnicas em um cenário real.

6. AGRADECIMENTOS

Esta pesquisa é parcialmente patrocinada pela Sambatech (www.sambatech.com.br) e parcialmente apoiada pelo Instituto Nacional de Ciência e Tecnologia para a Web (CNPq no. 573871/2008-6), CAPES, CNPq, Finep e Fapemig.

7. REFERENCES

[1] S. Acharya, B. Smith, and P. Parnes. Characterizing User Access To Videos On The World Wide Web. In *Proc. SPIE*, 2000.

[2] S. Baluja, R. Seth, D. Sivakumar, Y. Jing, J. Yagnik, S. Kumar, D. Ravichandran, and M. Aly. Video suggestion and discovery for youtube: taking random walks through the view graph. In *Proceedings of the 17th international conference on World Wide Web*, WWW '08, pages 895–904, NY, USA, 2008. ACM.

[3] X. Cheng, S. Member, J. Liu, S. Member, and C. Dale. Understanding the characteristics of internet short video sharing : A youtube-based measurement study. In *IEEE Transactions on Multimedia*, pages 1–10, 2009.

[4] M. Chesire, A. Wolman, G. M. Voelker, and H. M. Levy. Measurement and analysis of a streaming-media workload. In *Proc. of the 3rd conference on USENIX Symposium on Internet Technologies and Systems*, USITS'01, CA, USA, 2001. USENIX Association.

[5] J. Davidson, B. Liebald, J. Liu, P. Nandy, T. Van Vleet, U. Gargi, S. Gupta, Y. He, M. Lambert, B. Livingston, and D. Sampath. The youtube video recommendation system. In *Proceedings of the fourth ACM conference on Recommender systems*, RecSys '10, pages 293–296, New York, NY, USA, 2010. ACM.

[6] C. Gonçalves, L. Totti, D. Duarte, W. M. Jr., and A. Pereira. Rock: Uma metodologia para a caracterização de serviços web multimídia baseada em hierarquia da informação. In *XVII Simpósio Brasileiro de Sistemas Multimídia e Web (WebMedia), 2011*, pages 174 – 181, Florianópolis, SC, 2011.

[7] F. Ricci, L. Rokach, B. Shapira, and P. B. Kantor, editors. *Recommender Systems Handbook*. Springer, 2011.

[8] X. Su and T. M. Khoshgoftaar. A survey of collaborative filtering techniques. *Adv. in Artif. Intell.*, 2009:4:2–4:2, Jan. 2009.

[9] P.-N. Tan, M. Steinbach, and V. Kumar. *Introduction to Data Mining, (First Edition)*. Addison-Wesley Longman Publishing Co., Inc., Boston, MA, USA, 2005.

Using Video Embedding Markings for Supporting Content Sensitive Interaction in Multiple Contexts

Rostand Edson Oliveira Costa[1]
rostand@lavid.ufpb.br

Tiago Maritan U. de Araújo[1]
maritan@lavid.ufpb.br

Gutenberg P. Botelho Neto[1]
gutenberg@lavid.ufpb.br

Danilo Assis N. S. Silva[1]
danilo@lavid.ufpb.br

Raoni Kulesza[1]
raoni@lavid.ufpb.br

Guido Lemos Souza Filho[1]
guido@lavid.ufpb.br

[1]Universidade Federal da Paraíba - UFPB
Laboratório de Aplicações de Vídeo Digital – LAVID
João Pessoa – Paraíba

Abstract

Despite the numerous advances provided by Digital TV and Connected TV platforms, they have not provided significant gains to the television viewing experience. In the Connected TV platform, for instance, one relevant limitation is that the audiovisual content normally does not converse with the resources of these environments. In this work we propose a complementary approach to promote content-sensitive interactivity. This approach uses markup on video to promote content-sensitive interactivity based on self-contained hypermedia anchors. The anchors are self-contained metadata inserted synchronously with the narrative and contain necessary information to allow that a specific agent can lead the users to different contexts according to their interaction with the content. Our experiments show that is possible to create rich interactive narratives even with a limited set of anchor's classes, including support for pull, push and distributed modes.

Resumo

Apesar de inúmeros avanços, as iniciativas pioneiras de interatividade na TV Digital e nas plataformas de TV Conectada ainda não trouxeram ganhos significativos para o usuário na sua experiência de assistir televisão. Nas plataformas de TV Conectada, por exemplo, uma limitação relevante é que o conteúdo audiovisual normalmente não dialoga com os recursos de tais plataformas. Neste trabalho nós propomos como abordagem complementar, o uso de técnicas de marcação em vídeo para promover interatividade de forma sensível ao conteúdo baseada na criação de âncoras hipermídia autocontidas. As âncoras autocontidas são metadados inseridos de forma sincronizada com a narrativa contendo as informações necessárias que permitam que um agente específico possa conduzir o usuário para contextos diferentes de acordo com a sua interação particular com o conteúdo apresentado. Os experimentos realizados permitiram verificar que mesmo com um conjunto limitado de classes de âncoras é possível criar narrativas interativas ricas, com suporte aos modos *pull, push* e *distributed*.

WebMedia'13, November 5–8, 2013, Salvador, Brazil.
Copyright © 2013 ACM 978-1-4503-2559-2/13/11...$15.00.
http://dx.doi.org/10.1145/2526188.2526210

Categories and Subject Descriptors

H.5.4 [**Information Interfaces and Presentation**]: Hypertext/Hypermedia - *architectures, navigation, user issues.*

Keywords

Vídeo Digital, Sensível ao Conteúdo, Narrativa, Interatividade, Marcações Autocontidas, Hipermídia, Âncoras, Convergência.

1. Introdução

A sociedade atravessa uma fase de transformação que apresenta proporções sem precedentes na sua história recente. Como reflexo de uma maciça digitalização, as pessoas passaram a se relacionar através de formas e frequências inéditas, que extrapolam ou minimizam as tradicionais barreiras sociais, culturais e geográficas. Atualmente, interagir com os outros de forma ubíqua e transparente não é apenas possível, mas imperativamente necessário, independentemente da finalidade da interação.

A ampla e global disseminação do uso da Internet e a contínua oferta de novas e atrativas categorias de serviços potencializam o fenômeno, criando um círculo virtuoso que permanentemente atrai novos usuários e amplia as possibilidades de uso do ambiente.

A importância dessas mudanças pode ser observada no trabalho de Gesler [11], que aponta que 38% do tempo gasto para realizar uma tarefa no trabalho, está atualmente relacionado com a colaboração do trabalhador com sua equipe e atores externos. Tal colaboração é realizada através desses novos serviços, ferramentas e modos de interação social.

A convivência com tais facilidades está ajudando a criar um aculturamento coletivo no uso de recursos tecnológicos e moldando um novo perfil de comportamento, mais participativo e atuante. Entretanto, tal aculturamento leva a cobrança, por parte dos usuários, de poder contar sempre com funcionalidades equivalentes àquelas com as quais está acostumado, independentemente do contexto onde está consumindo o serviço.

Esta pressão dos consumidores tem levado a uma convergência entre contextos, serviços e tecnologias, principalmente nos cenários onde a interação em pauta é possível. As novas possibilidades de interação que se abrem através da soma de experiências anteriormente isoladas já começam a tomar forma em uma nova corrente que é definida neste artigo como *Interatividade 3.0*, que consiste na extensão da definição de Marc Benioff [3] de Web 3.0 para o domínio de aplicações multimídia interativas, ou seja, a construção da interação do usuário com base em uma infraestrutura pré-existente de hardware, serviços e plataformas programáveis.

Capitaneando este movimento estão os dispositivos móveis que evoluem continuamente, tanto em capacidade quanto em recursos, e se posicionam como símbolos do poder de conectividade e interação disponível atualmente.

A TV Digital, que também representa um importante cenário de digitalização pela relevância do seu alcance e impacto, já começa a receber a influência deste movimento incorporando funcionalidades da Internet e Web 2.0[1] e convergindo tecnologicamente com outros dispositivos (computadores pessoais e dispositivos móveis). Tal cenário permite que os serviços de TV agora se foquem em consumo de mídias sob demanda e sejam integrados com conteúdo e serviços Web. Como exemplos podemos citar as aplicações de TV Conectada [1] (do inglês, *Broadband TV*), que consiste na transmissão de conteúdo televisivo através da Internet, e de TV Social [12] (do inglês, *Social TV*), que integram os elementos da TVDI (conteúdo audiovisual principal e aplicação interativa) para mostrar o estado e contexto de outros usuários do sistema.

Atualmente, no entanto, a implantação em larga escala da interatividade nativa da TV Digital enfrenta algumas dificuldades, como, por exemplo, a pequena oferta de serviços interativos pelas emissoras de TV e a aposta de diversos fabricantes em plataformas próprias de interatividade, que incluem recursos de acesso à Internet, integração com redes sociais, serviços de vídeo sob demanda e outros aplicativos personalizados.

Em consequência disso, essas iniciativas ainda não trouxeram avanços significativos para o usuário na sua experiência de assistir televisão. Nas plataformas de TV Conectada, por exemplo, uma das limitações é que a interatividade oferecida não dialoga com o conteúdo audiovisual, oscilando entre TV com recursos de Internet e Internet com recursos de TV. Tal ênfase em recursos interativos sem conceito, propósito ou elaboração forma uma visão deturpada tanto dos telespectadores quanto de muitos profissionais do que é realmente TV e vídeo interativo e qual o seu potencial de enriquecimento da imersão do expectador na visualização e interação com o conteúdo apresentado [2].

Neste trabalho, é proposto o uso de técnicas de marcação visível ou invisível em vídeo para promover interatividade de forma sensível ao conteúdo baseada em ligações, ou âncoras[2], autocontidas. As ligações autocontidas são metadados inseridos no vídeo de forma sincronizada com a narrativa contendo as informações necessárias que permitam que um agente específico possa conduzir o usuário para contextos diferentes de acordo com a sua interação particular com o conteúdo.

É importante ressaltar que a proposta deste trabalho não é substituir as atuais abordagens de interatividade na TV, mas complementá-las. O objetivo é fortalecer a relação entre as mídias e o contexto de interação em algumas plataformas, como, por exemplo, nas plataformas de TV Conectada e TV Social, inserindo marcações com metadados embutidos no vídeo. Com isso é possível criar âncoras contendo pontos de ligação (elos ou *links*) para conteúdos interativos, e desenvolver agentes que podem interpretar essa narrativa interativa em múltiplos contextos. Por exemplo, marcações QR-code contendo elos embutidos para uma aplicação ou serviço sensível ao conteúdo podem ser inseridas no conteúdo da TV, e um dispositivo móvel (agente desacoplado) pode interpretar os metadados contidos

nessa marcação e executar a aplicação ou serviço correspondente, enriquecendo o contexto de interação.

Outra alternativa seria inserir marcações contendo documentos hipermídias inteiros (por exemplo, documentos NCL, SMIL ou HTML-5), que descrevem e direcionam a narrativa interativa, e desenvolver um agente acoplado na TV para interpretar essa marcação e executar os documentos hipermídia. Nesse último caso, a marcação poderia ser vista como uma alternativa para distribuição de aplicações hipermídia, similar ao carrossel de dados [29] utilizado na TV Digital.

Alguns testes realizados permitiram verificar que, utilizando a abordagem proposta, é possível criar narrativas interativas ricas utilizando, com suporte aos modos *pull*, *push* e *distributed*, mesmo com um conjunto limitado de classes de âncoras.

O restante do documento está organizado da seguinte forma. A Seção 2 faz uma revisão dos aspectos de interatividade e interação e apresenta algumas tecnologias correntes que podem ser usadas para incluir marcações em vídeo. Na Seção 3 é apresentado em mais detalhes o sistema proposto, relacionando as premissas básicas a serem atendidas, os componentes mínimos necessários e um conjunto elementar de classes de âncoras com os seus respectivos metadados. Na Seção 4 são apresentados os experimentos e métricas que foram definidos para validar a viabilidade do conceito e também uma análise dos resultados obtidos. A Seção 5 contém trabalhos relacionados e, finalmente, na Seção 6 são apresentadas as nossas considerações finais e indicação de trabalhos futuros.

2. Fundamentação Teórica

2.1 Interação e interatividade

Além da melhoria significa da qualidade de som e imagem, um sistema de TV digital interativo permite também a evolução na forma das pessoas acessarem o conteúdo através da possibilidade de integrar softwares e dados aos fluxos audiovisuais transmitidos pelas emissoras. Esta inovação cria oportunidades para a produção e desenvolvimento de novos serviços dos mais diversos tipos, por exemplo, acesso personalizado aos conteúdos, busca e navegação em guias eletrônicos de programação (EPGs), informações e programações adicionais, serviços comerciais, dentre outros [23].

Para melhor contextualizar o uso de marcações em vídeo, este trabalho se baseia em Bachmayer, Lugmayr e Kotsis [2] para organizar as características das aplicações de acordo com 3 (três) categorias: *pull*, *push* e *distributed*. O objetivo é contemplar os principais cenários de utilização dos serviços de TVDI de acordo com a estrutura da sua narrativa. As descrições de cada categoria são descritas a seguir:

Modo Push - agrupa os programas pertinentes à perspectiva tradicional da TV analógica. Apesar de acessar uma aplicação, o usuário é quase passivo diante do conteúdo produzido e transmitido pela emissora. São consideradas apenas as narrativas lineares e aquelas com possibilidades limitadas de opções. A ramificação do desenvolvimento do fluxo da narração é obtida com a adição de estórias paralelas dentro de um mesmo vídeo ou utilizando mais de um fluxo na transmissão. No primeiro a mudança da narração é realizada pela emissora e no segundo o telespectador toma a decisão de mudança ao mudar de fluxo para acompanhar outro ponto de vista da estória atual. Nesses cenários, é importante observar que o usuário tem influencia limitada para alterar o desenvolvimento da estória assim que ele a recebe. A resposta da interação com a emissora é sempre indireta, utilizando telefone, SMS, fax, e-mail, entre outros. O conteúdo e os dados da aplicação se limitam ao que foi pré-definido pela TV e que foi

---

[1] Termo criado por Tim O'Reilly para definir a Internet como plataforma, onde os usuários finais criam, modificam e distribuem seu próprio conteúdo.

[2] No escopo deste documento, os termos marcação, ligação e âncora serão usados de forma intercambiável para representar metadados inseridos no conteúdo audiovisual.

transmitido através de um canal unidirecional (difusão) controlado pela emissora, daí o nome *push*. Exemplos desses tipos de aplicações são: (1) "*Cul-del-sac*": aplicações sem relação temporal com o conteúdo principal[3]; (2) "*TV Voting*": aplicações com interatividade através de canal indireto com a emissora (telefone, SMS, email, site *Web* e etc.); (3) "*Add-On*": aplicações que complementam e são sincronizadas (dependência temporal) e enviadas paralelamente com o conteúdo principal, também conhecidas como "*Enhanced TV*"; (4) "*Y*'": aplicações que alteram a sequência ou o fluxo de exibição do conteúdo principal.

Modo pull: consiste em aplicações com suporte a comunicação direta e bidirecional com a emissora. Tal conexão, também conhecida com canal de retorno, pode ser realizada através de várias tecnologias: linha discada, ASDL, Wi-Fi, Wi-Max, 3G e etc. Como consequência, é possível a entrega de conteúdo individual, diferentemente do modo *push,* onde o conteúdo interativo é coletivo e todos os usuários recebem as mesmas possibilidades de interação. Tal aspecto tem fundamental importância nas possibilidades das narrativas das aplicações, pois agora é possível criar ramificações bem mais elaboradas. Por exemplo, é possível incluir na execução do programa interativo um desafio, condição de acesso ou obstáculo que deve(m) ser resolvido(s) por ou um ou vários usuários antes que o fluxo previsto na narrativa continue. Outra alternativa é a capacidade de guiar o usuário para caminhos específicos da narrativa limitando o número de opções a seguir de acordo com o resultado da interação com o usuário. Nesse contexto, três possibilidades são possíveis: (i) "labirinto com decisões obrigatórias"; (ii) "labirinto com gargalos" e; (iii) "labirinto com decisões opcionais" (Figura 1). Todos estes novos caminhos podem ser enviados individualmente pela emissora através do canal de retorno (por exemplo, novas fases de um jogo), economizando recursos do receptor e não limitando a quantidade de opções permitidas. Exemplo deste tipo de aplicação são jogos mais elaborados, aplicações de comércio eletrônico, acesso a serviços governamentais e educacionais, enquetes com resultados parciais divulgados no mesmo momento da interação e etc.

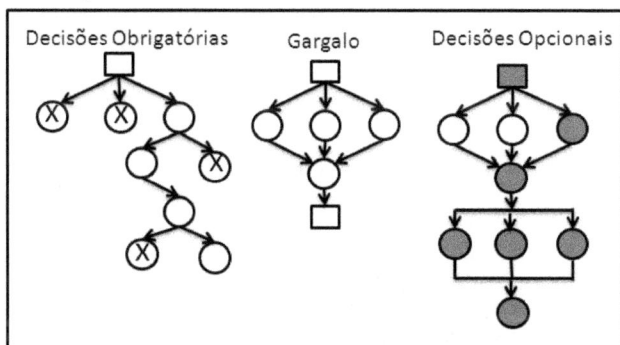

Figura 1 - Narrativas Não-Lineares (Labirintos)

Modo distributed: nesta categoria se encaixam aplicações mais recentes que exploram duas peculiaridades encontradas também nas aplicações Web 2.0: (i) localização e processamento distribuído pela Internet ou em outros dispositivos dos elementos que podem compor a aplicação interativa, por exemplo, um serviço Web (ii) colaboração dos usuários na construção da narrativa. No primeiro caso o benefício mais importante é agregar conteúdo, funcionalidades ou plataformas completas já disponíveis na rede. Um exemplo deste tipo de aplicação é a

integração de uma rede social com a transmissão de algum evento ao vivo para compartilhar suas opiniões com os outros usuários enquanto assistem a TV [6]. Para o caso de conteúdo produzido com a participação do consumidor, a colaboração pode ser explícita ou implícita. A primeira lida com sistemas que reagem a ações do consumidor através da manipulação do conteúdo transmitido ou criando elementos adicionais para o canal a partir dessas ações. A segunda suporta sistemas que observam o consumidor e realizam ações em *background*. Um exemplo do primeiro caso é um sistema que auxilia uma emissora na escolha de um conjunto de saídas a partir de vários de fluxos ao vivo, cobrindo um evento em tempo real onde o usuário pode atribuir notas ao conteúdo enviado e, dependendo da avaliação, a emissora pode modificar o conteúdo transmitido [17]. Já para o segundo caso, em Lee *et al.* [15] é descrito o *Emotional TV*, que busca a interação do usuário com a interpretação de emoções do telespectador através de uma bola sensitiva como dispositivo de entrada. Segundo Bachmayer, Lugmayr e Kotsis [2], esta categoria de aplicação é caracterizada como aplicações de narrativas evolucionárias, uma vez que o estado final da execução deste tipo de aplicação é não-determinístico, já que em nenhum momento do tempo é possível determiná-lo.

2.2 Marcação Digital em Vídeo

As marcações digitais em vídeo podem ser definidas como um conjunto de técnicas usadas para inserir dados em vídeo de forma transparente. Esses dados podem ser utilizados com diferentes propósitos, como, por exemplo, inserir mensagens escondidas de direitos autorais ou códigos seriais (impressão digital ou *fingerprint*) no vídeo [19], inserir URLs (*Uniform Resource Locator*) para *marketing* ou *e-commerce*[4], dentre outros.

Nas próximas Subseções apresentaremos exemplos de técnicas de marcação digital visível e invisível.

2.2.1 Marcações Digitais Visíveis

O exemplo mais comum de marcação digital visível são os códigos de barra bidimensionais, especialmente os QR-codes (*Quick Responde codes*) [13]. O QR-code é uma matriz ou código de barras bidimensional padronizado pela ISO (*International Organization for Standardization*) e IEC (*International Electrotechnical Commission*). Eles podem armazenar até 7089 caracteres numéricos, 4296 caracteres alfa-numérico, e possuem uma alta velocidade de leitura e de correção de erro [13]. Além disso, podem representar dados de diferentes tipos, como, por exemplo, dados numéricos, caracteres alfanuméricos, caracteres Kanji, códigos binários, códigos de controle etc.

Dentre os exemplos mais comuns de uso do QR-code pode-se destacar a representação de códigos de produtos comerciais, mensagens de texto, *e-mails*, URLs de páginas Web ou de vídeos *online*, etc.

2.2.2 Marcações Digitais Invisíveis

O exemplo mais comum de técnica de marcação digital invisível são as técnicas de esteganografia [19]. Essas técnicas procuram ocultar mensagens dentro de uma mídia. Em vídeos, por exemplo, as mensagens (dados) podem ser ocultadas nos pixels dos quadros de uma imagem. Diferentemente da criptografia que oculta o significado da mensagem, a esteganografia procura ocultar a existência da mensagem.

A técnica de esteganografia LSB (*Least Significant Bit*) [8], por exemplo, insere os dados da mensagem no bit menos significativo

---

[3] Normalmente representado pelo áudio e vídeo principal do programa ao vivo ou gravado da emissora.

[4] Disponível em www.shoppingcartsforwebsites.com/general/using-qr-codes-for-ecommerce

de cada pixel de uma imagem colorida. Essa técnica, embora tenha limitações, altera pouco o vídeo original.

Considerando imagens em alta definição (i.e., 1920x1080 pixels), é possível codificar cerca de 759 KB (1920 x 1080 pixels x 3 bytes por pixel / 8 bits = 759 KB) de dados por imagem.

Uma dificuldade encontrada no uso da técnica LSB é que os métodos de compressão de vídeo geralmente distorcem levemente os pixels dos quadros e podem consequentemente modificar a informação escondida. Existem algumas técnicas na literatura [16][5][18] que solucionam esses problemas, mas reduzem a capacidade de armazenamento de dados.

3. Usando Marcações em Vídeo para a Criação de Âncoras Autocontidas

O potencial do uso de hipermídia [21] para o desenvolvimento de narrativas não lineares e interativas tem sido amplamente discutido na literatura [4] [9].

Uma das razões para isso é que o uso de hipermídia permite apresentar conteúdo de forma personalizada. Cada apresentação do conteúdo pode ser uma experiência única que reflete o interesse específico que cada usuário constrói ao ter contato com as informações apresentadas e que depende da forma como ele reage aos pontos de ligação ofertados.

Na nossa abordagem, as marcações em vídeo são usadas para a inclusão de informações hipermídia contendo referências para outros contextos no próprio conteúdo audiovisual de origem. Diferentemente de anotações em vídeo [20] e hipermídia, normalmente baseadas em representações externas ao conteúdo, na nossa proposta as âncoras são autocontidas, ou seja, são criadas diretamente sobre o conteúdo transmitido ou distribuído. É importante observar que isso não implica em uma alteração irreversível na mídia original nem prejuízo na separação da lógica da aplicação dos conteúdos. Ela simplesmente consiste na aplicação das marcações ao conteúdo no momento da sua transmissão. Eventuais alterações na lógica da aplicação seriam refletidas nas respectivas marcações em eventuais futuras transmissões, de forma similar ao que ocorre com outras tecnologias.. Esta característica permite que o ponto de partida para a navegação entre os conteúdos possa ser o próprio conteúdo audiovisual, tornando o vídeo marcado um hipervídeo, uma particularização do conceito de hipermídia [22].

Dentre as vantagens no uso de técnicas de marcações diretamente sobre o conteúdo imediatamente antes do mesmo ser transmitido ou distribuído para a construção de narrativas com interatividade, pode-se destacar a independência com relação ao contexto ou tecnologia onde o conteúdo vai ser consumido, as quais podem ser feitas com um foco maior na construção das estruturas hipermídia não lineares propriamente ditas. Isto permite que tanto as narrativas lineares quanto as possíveis narrativas não lineares possam ser definidas nas fases de produção e pós-produção do conteúdo e finalizadas, com eventuais adaptações para o formato ou tecnologias alvo, no momento da transmissão/distribuição. Entretanto, existem desafios específicos para a implementação de hipervídeo que estão relacionados, principalmente, com a natureza fortemente linear dos vídeos (quadro a quadro), com as relações espaço-temporal entre cenas e com a inserção das âncoras [10]. Além de tais obstáculos, algumas premissas também precisam ser observadas:

- *compatibilidade*: a narrativa linear deve continuar a ser obtida em qualquer dispositivo capaz de reproduzir o formato original do vídeo;

- *consistência*: uma mesma mídia com marcações deve ser interpretada consistentemente por agentes diferentes em cenários distintos: *middlewares* de TV Digital, *widgets* de TV Conectada, BD/DVD *players*, s*tream video players* etc;

- *adaptabilidade*: as marcações devem oferecer níveis diferentes de aderência por parte dos agentes, permitindo que a interação possa ocorrer de acordo com os recursos de cada contexto;

- *escopo*: as marcações devem permitir referências tanto a um quadro, a um conjunto de quadros e também a elementos contidos em um quadro;

- *simplicidade*: as marcações devem representar ações atômicas e simples, que possam ser implementadas mesmo em contextos com recursos escassos.

O sistema de marcação autocontida em vídeo proposto é composto dos seguintes elementos básicos[5]:

- Conjunto de metadados representativo das classes atômicas de âncoras que permitam a criação das narrativas interativas desejadas;

- Técnica de marcação de vídeo que atenda as premissas anteriores e suporte a representação plena do conjunto de metadados descrito;

- Um módulo aplicador das marcações no conteúdo audiovisual;

- Agentes especiais para diferentes contextos que atuem na captura das marcações e interpretação das âncoras, sendo responsáveis pelo processamento local, quando houver. Tais agentes podem ser de duas categorias relacionadas ao seu grau de ligação com o reprodutor da mídia: acoplados ou desacoplados. O acoplamento do agente significa que o mesmo pode ter acesso direto aos quadros do vídeo;

- Mecanismos de tratamento local ou remoto das interações que permitam respostas adequadas e personalizadas para cada âncora, de acordo com o ponto da narrativa e do contexto do usuário.

O formato geral de uma marcação autocontida é representado pela tupla *m*:

$$m = < c, a_e, a_d >$$

onde:

- *c*: é a classe da marcação autocontida, que indica para o agente qual o tipo de ação que deve ser realizada para a âncora selecionada;

- a_e: são os atributos estáticos da âncora – foram inseridos no momento de criação da marcação e detalham como a ação deve ser executada pelo agente. A semântica de interpretação dos parâmetros estáticos depende tanto da classe da ação quanto do tipo do agente. Uma ação típica de escopo local para agentes acoplados pode ser transformada em uma ação remota por um agente desacoplado;

- a_d: são os atributos dinâmicos da âncora – devem ser coletados pelo agente no momento de ativação da âncora para complementar a forma de execução da ação. Representando um conceito similar às informações de

---

[5] As classes de âncoras descritas podem ser mapeadas ou adaptadas para os recursos das principais linguagens de marcação existentes. O objetivo de trabalhar com um conjunto reduzido próprio foi de facilitar a implementação dos protótipos e facilitar o entendimento dos conceitos envolvidos sem vinculação com nenhuma tecnologia em particular.

contexto presentes em hipertextos, a coleta de tais atributos está sujeita aos mesmos mecanismos de privacidade e segurança vigentes em cada agente.

Para efeito de validação dos conceitos apresentados neste artigo, foi definido um conjunto mínimo de marcações que podem ser combinadas para endereçar os principais modos de narrativa e distribuição de conteúdo apresentados na Seção 2. As classes básicas de marcação são as seguintes, considerando um ambiente de execução conectado:

Classe Flow - *Alteração do fluxo da narrativa*: As âncoras desta classe permitem que o fluxo corrente da narrativa seja alterado, através de transferência incondicional para um novo fluxo. No caso de narrativas distribuídas no modo *pull*, a alteração do fluxo pode ser feita localmente pelo agente através da sintonia de um novo canal. Nos modos *push* ou *distributed*, o tratamento da alteração do fluxo tanto pode ser feita localmente, pelo agente, quanto remotamente pelo transmissor do fluxo.

Classe Link – *Acesso a Contexto Complementar*: Esta classe permite que o usuário tenha acesso a um contexto complementar ao conteúdo apresentado de forma paralela com a narrativa. O comportamento do agente em resposta a âncoras desta classe é similar, independentemente do modo de distribuição adotado, e consiste em abrir uma nova janela para o contexto indicado nos atributos estáticos da âncora. Eventualmente, atributos dinâmicos podem ser solicitados ao usuário pelo agente para complementar a personalização do contexto complementar. Esta é uma das classes mais flexíveis, pois permite que a semântica de tratamento da âncora possa ser totalmente delegada para um processamento remoto. Por tal característica, a premissa da adaptabilidade será implementada com a inclusão de uma âncora alternativa da classe **Link** dentro dos atributos estáticos de outras âncoras, permitindo que o agente delegue o tratamento da âncora original para a URL indicada quando não dispuser dos recursos necessários para isso.

Classe Action – *Ação Local Específica*: Os atributos desta classe de âncora contêm referências para a execução pelo agente de um aplicativo específico para tratar a interação. Tais referências podem indicar uma URL para *download* do aplicativo ou se o mesmo está contido dentro da própria marcação[6]. O tratamento de âncoras desta classe independe do modo de distribuição adotado, mas apenas agentes acoplados suportam a recuperação do aplicativo direto da marcação. Atributos dinâmicos podem ser obtidos pelo agente e passados, juntamente com os atributos estáticos, como parâmetros para o aplicativo. Eventualmente, o aplicativo pode solicitar os seus próprios parâmetros.

Classe Load – *Pré-carga de Aplicativos*: Os atributos desta classe de âncora contêm referências para o pré-carregamento de aplicativos que serão posteriormente referenciados e executados através de âncoras da classe **Action**. Os aplicativos são recuperados a partir de URLs ou da própria marcação. Novamente, o comportamento do agente em resposta a âncoras desta classe não depende do modo de distribuição adotado, mas apenas agentes acoplados suportam a recuperação do aplicativo direto da marcação.

Classe Fork – *Seleção entre Âncoras Alternativas*: As marcações desta classe permitem que o usuário faça uma seleção entre duas âncoras possíveis em um determinado ponto da narrativa. A âncora selecionada, que pode ser de qualquer tipo, inclusive outra âncora **Fork**, é então interpretada e tratada adequadamente pelo agente. Um exemplo de aplicação de **Fork** é em narrativas do tipo

---

[6] Considerando o uso de técnicas de marcação de alta capacidade, como a esteganografia.

Y, onde cada opção é representada por duas âncoras do tipo **Flow**, permitindo que o usuário selecione o andamento desejado do fluxo dentre as duas opções apresentadas.

Usando o formato geral descrito anteriormente, uma representação dos metadados para as classes descritas pode ser a seguinte:

$anchor = < flow_m \mid link_m \mid action_m \mid load_m \mid fork_m >$

$file = < id, source=[url \mid frame] >$

$flow_m = < fl, \{type=[url \mid service], destination\}, \{\} >$

$link_m = < ln, \{url, params\}, \{\} >$

$action_m = < ac, \{<file>, params, <link_{alt}>\}, \{\} >$

$load_m = < ld, \{<file_1>, <file_2>, ..., <file_N>\}, \{\} >$

$fork_m = < fk, \{ label_1, <anchor_1>, label_2, <anchor_2>, <link_{alt}>\}>$

Na próxima Seção, descreveremos como foi conduzida uma prova de conceito do sistema proposto, apresentando os protótipos desenvolvidos, os experimentos realizados e os resultados obtidos.

4. Prova de Conceito

Nesta Seção descrevemos um conjunto de experimentos desenvolvidos para construir uma prova de conceito do sistema proposto. Esses experimentos procuram validar as classes de marcação apresentadas na Seção 3 para diferentes narrativas e cenários de distribuição de conteúdo.

Inicialmente, na Subseção 4.1, apresentamos os protótipos desenvolvidos para validar a proposta. Em seguida, na Subseção 4.2, apresentamos os experimentos realizados e os resultados obtidos da aplicação das classes de marcação nesses protótipos.

4.1 Implementação

4.1.1 TV Analógica - Agente desacoplado (celular)

Como uma TV analógica não possui capacidade de processar dados e, consequentemente, capturar as marcações e interpretar as âncoras, a interatividade usando marcações com âncoras autocontidas na TV analógica só pode ser concretizada com o auxílio de agentes desacoplados.

Para este cenário, utilizamos o celular como o agente desacoplado responsável por capturar as marcações e interpretar as âncoras, interagindo com o conteúdo (ou com os provedores de conteúdo) através de processamento remoto da interação. As âncoras são representadas por marcações feitas através de QR-codes (ver Seção 2.2). A estrutura desse protótipo é apresentada na Figura 2.

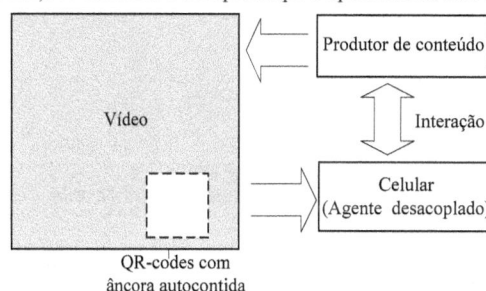

Figura 2. Protótipo do sistema para TV analógica com agente acoplado para celular

Conforme pode ser observado na Figura 2, inicialmente, o provedor de conteúdo insere marcações QR-codes com âncoras autocontidas que são capturadas e interpretadas pelo celular (agente desacoplado). Neste protótipo foram implementadas e validadas as âncoras da classe **Link**, via URLs (ver Seção 3).

Uma característica importante desse protótipo é que foi possível criar um cenário interativo para TV analógica apenas utilizando

marcações QR-code com âncoras no vídeo e celulares com capacidade de capturar e interpretar essas marcações.

4.1.2 TV Digital – Agente acoplado para OpenGinga

Devido a sua capacidade de processar informações multimídia/hipermídia e interagir de diferentes formas com esses conteúdos, a TV digital pode explorar as diferentes classes de marcação, narrativas, metadados e estratégias de distribuição de conteúdo apresentadas nas Seções 2 e 3.

No desenvolvimento do protótipo do sistema proposto para TV digital, um conjunto de ferramentas para leitura das âncoras e um navegador (*browser*) foram integrados ao Openginga [14] uma implementação de código aberto do *middleware* Ginga[7] do Sistema Brasileiro de TV Digital (SBTVD). A estrutura desse protótipo é apresentada na Figura 3.

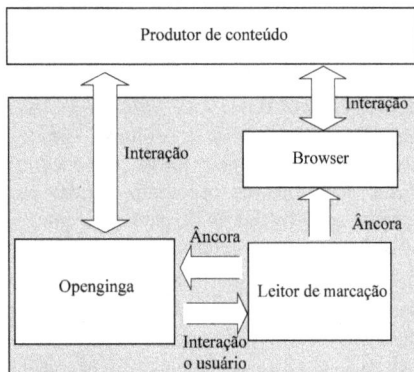

Figura 3. Protótipo do sistema para TV digital

Conforme pode ser observado na Figura 3, inicialmente, um agente Openginga monitora as interações do usuário. Quando o usuário interage com o vídeo marcado, por exemplo, acionando uma tecla do controle remoto, uma ferramenta "Leitor de marcação" captura essa marcação e a âncora autocontida nela. Ele então encaminha a âncora para ser interpretada por um *browser* ou pelo Openginga. O Openginga ou o *browser* interpretam essas âncoras e interagem com os conteúdos.

O protótipo foi desenvolvido para ler marcações do tipo QR-code e a técnica de esteganografia LSB. O "leitor de marcação" para QR-code utilizado foi o ZXing[8], uma biblioteca de código aberto para processamento de códigos de barra uni/bidimensionais. O "leitor de marcação" para esteganografia foi implementado em linguagem Java e o *browser* utilizado foi o *Mozilla Firefox*.

4.2 Resultados e Análise

Os experimentos com os protótipos apresentados na Seção 4.1 foram realizados utilizando vídeos da série de programas Geração Saúde 2 da TV Escola[9]. A série também possui um portal Web com jogos, blogs, vídeos e outras informações relacionadas à série.

Para validar marcações da classe **Link** (ver Seção 3), nos dois protótipos foi utilizada uma marcação QR-code no vídeo quando uma das personagens da série, Rita, posta informações em seu *blog*. Essa marcação QR-code contém uma URL endereçada para o *blog* da Rita[10] dentro do portal Web. Quando o usuário interage pelo agente Openginga ou pelo agente celular, a URL (âncora) é

extraída do QR-code e o *browser* é invocado para acessar o *blog* da Rita (um contexto complementar ao conteúdo) dentro do portal. Na Figura 4 são ilustradas duas capturas de tela desse cenário de interação para o agente Openginga. Na Figura 4 (a) é apresentado o vídeo com a marcação QR-code contendo URL para acesso ao novo contexto. Na Figura 4 (b) é apresentado o novo contexto sendo apresentado por um *browser* acoplado.

(a)   (b)

Figura 4. Experimento da classe Link.

Como na TV analógica só é possível interagir através de marcações da classe **Link**, na validação dos outras classes de marcação apenas o protótipo para TV digital foi utilizado.

Para validar as marcações da classe **Flow**, um vídeo alternativo e uma marcação QR-code contendo um *locator*[11] (localizador) para esse vídeo foram inseridos em um trecho do vídeo do programa. Nesse trecho, quando o usuário interage com o sistema acionando uma tecla do controle, o "leitor de marcação" extrai o *locator* (âncora) do QR-code. Usando esse *locator*, o Openginga então altera o fluxo da narrativa, apresentando o fluxo de vídeo alternativo. Na Figura 5, são ilustradas duas capturas de tela desta classe de marcação. Na Figura 5 (a), é apresentada uma captura de tela do trecho do vídeo do programa com o QR-code contendo o *locator* para o vídeo alternativo. Na Figura 5 (b), o vídeo alternativo é apresentado após a interação do usuário, alterando o fluxo da narrativa.

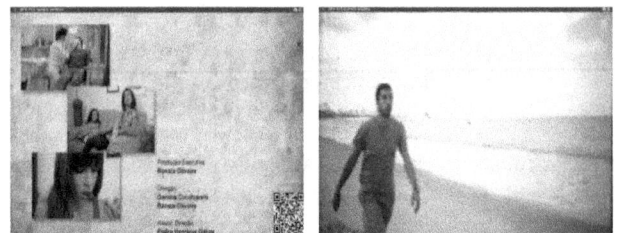

(a)   (b)

Figura 5. Experimento da classe Flow.

Para validar as marcações da classe **Action**, uma marcação QR-code contendo uma URL para *download* de uma aplicação Ginga foi inserida num vídeo da série sobre tratamento dentário. A aplicação Ginga desenvolvida para validar esse cenário apresenta informações adicionais sobre as doenças dentárias comentadas no programa. Quando o usuário interage acionando uma tecla do controle, a URL é extraída do QR-code e o *download* da aplicação é efetuado e a aplicação é executada no Openginga. Na Figura 6 são ilustradas duas capturas de tela desse cenário. Na Figura 6 (a) é apresentada uma captura de tela do vídeo com QR-code contendo URL para *download* da aplicação Ginga. Na Figura 6 (b) é ilustrada a aplicação sendo executada após interação e *download*.

---

[7] Disponível em www.ginga.org.br

[8] Disponível em code.google.com/p/zxing

[9] Disponível em www.geracaosaude.fm.usp.br

[10] Disponível em www.geracaosaude.fm.usp.br/?code=blog

[11] No Ginga, um *locator* é uma referência que associa um objeto de mídia ao conteúdo desse objeto.

Para validar as marcações da classe *Fork*, uma âncora do tipo *Action* e uma âncora do tipo *Link* foram inseridas nos metadados da âncora *Fork*. Essa âncora foi encapsulada em um QR-code inserido no mesmo trecho do vídeo usado para validar a classe *Link* (vídeo da Rita). Na Figura 7 são ilustradas algumas capturas de tela desse cenário. Na Figura 7 (a) é apresentada o QR-code com uma marcação *Fork*. Quando o usuário interage pela primeira vez, as duas opções de âncoras são apresentados para o usuário (Figura 7 (b)). Quando o usuário escolhe a âncora *Action*, a aplicação é recuperada (via *download*) e executada (Figura 7 (c)). Quando o usuário escolhe a âncora *Link*, o *browser* é invocado para acessar o *blog* da Rita (Figura 7 (d)).

(a)   (b)

Figura 6. Experimento da classe Action.

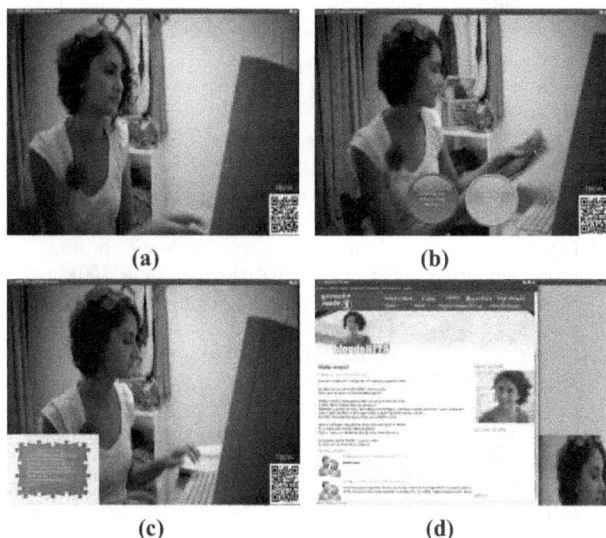

(a)   (b)

(c)   (d)

Figura 7. Experimento da classe Fork.

Por fim, para validar as marcações da classe *Load*, dois experimentos foram aplicados. O primeiro encapsulava uma aplicação interativa Ginga (a mesma usada para validar a classe *Action*) em quadros de um vídeo usando a esteganografia LSB. O segundo teste apontava na marcação para uma URL para *download* da aplicação.

Para reduzir o espaço de armazenamento ocupado pela aplicação e para evitar a codificação do seu sistema de arquivos, a aplicação interativa foi comprimida antes de ser encapsulada nos quadros do vídeo. Em consequência disso, um vídeo sem compressão foi utilizado para testar esses dois cenários. Embora vídeos sem compressão não sejam utilizados, em geral, nos sistemas de TV Digital, eles foram utilizados nesse teste apenas para validar o conceito. Para realizar essa tarefa, o *player* de vídeo do Openinga foi adaptado para permitir a apresentação de vídeos não-comprimidos.

Para confrontar os dois experimentos (armazenar a aplicação direto na imagem ou armazenar a URL para a aplicação), o tempo médio de *download* da aplicação a partir da imagem foi confrontado com o tempo de extração da aplicação a partir da imagem esteganografada.

Usando um modem 3G com uma conexão de 500 Kbps, o tempo médio de *download* da aplicação, em 10 repetições, foi de 1,913s. O tempo médio de extração da mesma aplicação a partir de uma imagem esteganografada, em 10 repetições, foi de 1,007s. Para os dois experimentos foi utilizado um computador com processador Intel Core I3 e 4GB de memória RAM DDR-3 e sistema operacional Ubuntu Linux 10.0.4.

Embora não seja possível concluir estatisticamente que o encapsulamento de aplicações por esteganografia apresente um desempenho melhor com relação ao tempo de carregamento, a utilização de aplicações encapsuladas por esteganografia permite que o usuário possa interagir de forma local com os conteúdos mesmo quando não possui canal de interatividade (ou canal de retorno).

Por fim, um conjunto de experimentos também foi realizado para avaliar a resolução mínima da marcação QR-code capturada pelos leitores de marcação.Para isso, foi aplicado um conjunto de testes usando diferentes resoluções de QR-code em dois diferentes vídeos. Nestes experimentos, foram testados QR-codes com as seguintes resoluções: 50x50 pixels, 100x100 pixels, 120x120 pixels, 140x140 pixels, 150x150 pixels, 175x175 pixels, 200x200 pixels.

Esses QR-codes foram inseridos nos vídeos e processados nos dois protótipos (agente celular e agente Openinga), que tentaram capturar e interpretar essas marcações. Após os testes, verificou-se que os QR-codes com resoluções iguais ou superiores a 150x150 pixels foram sempre reconhecidos, capturados e interpretados corretamente pelos dois agentes. Por outro lado, os QR-codes com resoluções inferiores a 150x150 pixels não foram reconhecidos ou detectados em nenhum dos casos testados.

5. Trabalhos Relacionados

O trabalho de Gradvohl et al [10] também propõe um modelo para a inserção de informações hipermídia em vídeo mas restrito ao padrão MPEG e sem a possibilidade de uso de agentes desconectados.

O uso da esteganografia para inclusão de informações em vídeos digitais foi abordado por Carvalho et al [5]. Embora com foco em aplicações relacionadas com segurança, os seus resultados ratificam a viabilidade da técnica para a nossa proposta e ajudam a entender os obstáculos que a compressão de vídeo impõe no uso da esteganografia.

Crowell [7] faz uma breve análise da recente, mas crescente tendência do uso de QR-code em comerciais de TV nos Estados Unidos. Similarmente à nossa abordagem, os celulares são os alvos principais de tais iniciativas que visam complementar as informações sobre os produtos anunciados levando os usuários a sítios com vídeos e outros dados.

Manzato e Goularte [24][25] desenvolveram vários trabalhos relacionados à adaptação de conteúdos de vídeo. No primeiro trabalho [24], os autores focaram no uso de técnicas de transcodificação para adaptar a apresentação de vídeo ao vivo para múltiplos dispositivos, modificando algumas características do vídeo, como, por exemplo, o tamanho do quadros do vídeo e a sua taxa de bits. Neste trabalho, no entanto, não é suportado o uso de múltiplos contextos e as adaptações são realizadas apenas no conteúdo do vídeo, não permitindo que os usuários acessem conteúdos interativos.

O segundo trabalho [25] descreve uma técnica para produzir conteúdos interativos a partir de múltiplas fontes, como por exemplo, a partir da Web, permitindo que os usuários tenham acesso a conteúdos dinâmicos gerados em tempo real durante a compilação do vídeo. Para isso, vários documentos estruturados baseados na especificação MPEG-J foram propostos. Uma limitação deste trabalho é que o uso desses padrões (MPEG-4 e MPEG-J) não são compatíveis com os atuais sistemas de TV Digital.

Rigo *et al.* [26], Cunha *et al.* [27] e Rodriguez *et al.* [28] apresentam propostas para anotação de vídeos em plataformas multimídia como, por exemplo, plataformas Web e dispositivos móveis. Rigo et al. [26], por exemplo, propõem o uso de interfaces Web baseadas em conhecimento para descrever conteúdos multimídia em repositórios Web e facilitar a recuperação. Cunha *et al.* [27] propõem uma ferramenta de autoria e navegação para vídeos em dispositivos móveis. Essa ferramenta permite adicionar anotações textuais em vídeos e produz uma tela de navegação que apresenta as anotações textuais em uma linha do tempo junto com miniaturas de quadros do vídeo associadas ao trecho do vídeo anotado.

6. Conclusões

Este trabalho propõe o uso de âncoras autocontidas, baseadas em marcações em vídeo, como uma abordagem complementar e multicontexto, para a promoção de interatividade sensível ao conteúdo audiovisual, dotando-o de características de hipervídeo.

Para validar o conceito, foram desenvolvidos protótipos de agentes acoplados e desacoplados que interpretaram as classes de âncoras propostas com marcações autocontidas baseadas nas técnicas de QR-code e esteganografia. Os tempos médios para recuperação, carregamento de aplicativos e URLs e resposta às âncoras também foram mensurados nos testes.

Os resultados obtidos nos testes permitiram verificar que mesmo com um conjunto limitado de âncoras, é possível criar narrativas interativas ricas com suporte a diferentes categorias de interação *pull, push* e *distributed*.

Os próximos passos da pesquisa serão direcionados a modelagem e validação formal de um conjunto mais elaborado de âncoras com os seus respectivos metadados, a investigação mais aprofundada das técnicas de marcação aplicáveis e também a construção de protótipos e cenários de interação mais complexos e sintonizados com a corrente da Interatividade 3.0.

7. Referências

[1]   B. Alfonsi. I Want My IPTV: Internet Protocol Television Predicted a Winner, *IEEE Distributed Systems Online*, 6(2):1-4, 2005.

[2]   S. Bachmayer, A. Lugmayr and G. Kotsis. Convergence of collaborative web approaches and interactive tv program formats. *International Journal of Web Information Systems*, 6(1):74-94, 2010.

[3]   M. Benioff. Welcome to Web 3.0: Now Your Other Computer is a Data Center. TechCrunchIT, 2008.

[4]   M. C. G. Braga, et al. Hipermídia: Uma jornada entre narrativas e roteiros. In *CONAHPA 2006*, pages 1-7, Florianópolis, 2006.

[5]   D. F. Carvalho, et al. Video steganography for confidential documents: integrity, privacy and version control, In *Proceedings of SIGDOC 2008*, pages 199-206, 2008.

[6]   K. Chorianopoulos. Content-Enriched Communication - Supporting the Social Uses of TV. *The Journal of The Communications Network*, 6:23-30, 2007.

[7]   G. Crowell. How to use QR Codes in Video Marketing and E-Commerce Video Marketing. Disponível em: http://www.reelseo.com/video-qr-codes/. Acesso: 20 Abril 2011

[8]   J. Fridrich, et al. Reliable detection of LSB steganography in color and grayscale images, In *Proceedings of International Multimedia Conference*, pages 27-30, 2001.

[9]   V. Gosciola. Roteiro para as novas mídias: Do Cinema às Mídias Interativas. São Paulo. Ed. Senac, 2008.

[10] A. L. S. Gradvohl, Y. Iano. An approach for interactive televison based on insertion of hypermedia information on MPEG standard video. In *Proceedings of IEEE International Symposium on Consumer Electronics*. Reading, United Kingdom, pages 25-30, 2004.

[11] Gesler. Knowledge Work Equals Four Work Modes. US Workplace Survey, White Paper, 2008.

[12] G. Harboe, N. Massey, et al. The uses of social television. *ACM Computers in Entertainment*, 6(1):1–15, 2008.

[13] ISO/IEC 18004:6 Information technology - Automatic identification and data capture techniques - Bar code symbology - QR Code. 2000

[14] R. Kulesza, J. Lima, S. Miranda Filho, et al. Ginga-J: Implementação de Referência do Ambiente Imperativo do Middleware Ginga. In: *Proceedings of the 16th. Brazillian Symposium on Multimedia and the Web (Webmedia 2010)*, Belo Horizonte, pages 35-42, 2010.

[15] C. J. Lee, C. Chang, H. Chung, C. Dickie and T. Selker. Emotionally reactive television, In *Proceedings of the Twelfth International Conference on Intelligent User Interfaces*, pages 1-4, 2007.

[16] B. Liu, et al. Secure Steganography in Compressed Video Bitstreams, In: *Proceedings of ARES 2008*, pages 1382-1387, 2008.

[17] C. M Williams, R. Wages. Video conducting the Olympic Games 2008: the iTV field trial of the EU-IST project live. In *Proceedings of the Third International Conference on Digital Interactive Media in Entertainment and Arts*, pages 436-440, 2008.

[18] K. Matsui, K. Tanaka,. Video-steganography: How to secretly embed a signature in a picture. *Journal of the Interactive Multimedia*.1(1):184-206, 1994.

[19] F. A. P. Petitcolas, et al. Information Hiding: A Survey. In *Proceedings of the IEEE*, 87(7):1062-1078, 1999

[20] A. N. Rehem. Um Framework para Anotação de Vídeos Digitais. Dissertação de Mestrado. Universidade de Salvador., Bahia, 2005.

[21] L. Santaella. Matrizes da linguagem e pensamento sonoro, visual, verbal: aplicações na hipermídia São Paulo: Iluminuras. 2001.

[22] N. Sawhney, D. Balcom and I. Smith, I. Authoring and navigating video in space and time. In *IEEE Multimedia*, 4(4)30-39, 1997.

[23] E. M. Schwalb. iTV Handbook Technologies and Standards. New Jersey: Prentice Hall, 724p., 2004.

[24] M. G. Manzato and R. Goularte. Live video adaptation: A context-aware approach. In *Proceedings of the 11th. Brazillian Symposium on Multimedia and the Web (Webmedia 2005)*, Poços de Caldas, pages 1-8, 2005.

[25] M. G. Manzato, D. C. Junqueira, D. C. and R. Goularte. Interactive News Documents for Digital Television. In *Proceedings of the XIV Brazilian Symposium on Multimedia and the Web (WebMedia 2008)*, Vila Velha, pages 1–6, 2008.

[26] W. Rigo, et al. Anotação de Conteúdo Multimídia em Repositórios com Interfaces Web baseadas em Conhecimento de Domínio. In *Proceedings of the XVII Brazilian Symposium on Multimedia and the Web (WebMedia 2011)*, Florianópolis, pages 1–8, 2011.

[27] B. C. R. Cunha, D. Pedrosa, R. Goularte, M. G. Pimentel. Video Annotation and Navigation on Mobile Devices. In *Proceedings of the XVIII Brazilian Symposium on Multimedia and the Web (WebMedia 2012)*, São Paulo, pages 261–264, 2012.

[28] K. R. H. Rodrigues, M. G. Pimentel, S. S. Pereira, C. A. C. Teixeira, FIND: Facilitating the Identification of Intervals and Moments for Incorporation of Additional Content in Continuous Media. In *Proceedings of the XVIII Brazilian Symposium on Multimedia and the Web (WebMedia 2012)*, São Paulo, pages 265–268, 2012.

[29] ISO/IEC 13818-6, *Generic coding of moving pictures and associated audio information – part 6: Extension for digital storage media command and control (DSM-CC)*, 1997.

MoveRC: Attention-aware Remote Control

Daniel Chagas
Universidade de Fortaleza
Av. Washington Soares, 1321, M11
Fortaleza, Brazil - 60811-905
+55 85 34773079

prof.daniel.chagas@gmail.com

Elizabeth Furtado
Universidade de Fortaleza
Av. Washington Soares, 1321, M11
Fortaleza, Brazil - 60811-905
+55 85 34773079

elizabethsfur@gmail.com

ABSTRACT

The progress of information technology has made objects continuously acquire new resources and communication skills, therefore we have to change the way we interact with them. As the mainstream media of the twentieth century, television has also followed this trend. TV is changing from a passive medium, from which the viewer only receives information, into an active media, with which there is interaction facilitated by the option of choice, participation and even creating new content. However, the experience of interactive television is often barred by the problems inherent to dealing with the remote control. Especially, when it comes to a task, that is too complex to be done with a standard remote control: the task of putting data in text format into the TV. This paper presents an ongoing research that addresses the input of text data in digital television proposing an attention-aware system.

Categories and Subject Descriptors

H.5.2 [**Information interfaces and presentation**]: User Interface-Input devices and strategies.

General Terms

Design, Experimentation, Human Factors.

Keywords

Alternative Remote Control, TV, Input, Attention-aware System, Arduino, Gyroscope.

1. INTRODUCTION

The evolution of digital television and its connectivity capabilities are creating new possibilities for viewers to interact with television content. Bachmeyer [2] affirms that there are two trends in interactive digital television (iDTV): the social iDTV, where the viewer uses his/her iDTV and its programs to socially interact through text; and the collaborative iDTV, where the viewer uses his/her iDTV for creating new content. However, both of the iDTV views underlie the problem of data input. Researches with the standard remote control (RC) show that its inefficiency in texting large amounts [4, 11] open precedent for developing new ways so one can interact with this device. In [4] researchers show that usability and accessibility issues in iDTV are derived from standard remote controls.

Figure 1. ©Daniel Chagas -User uses different perceptual modalities to type a letter (kinetic to move, visual to choose).

In the UK, in a survey reporting experiences with iDTV, Cooper [5] shows that the most common solutions for typing texts are the virtual keyboard, multi-tap keyboard, and the word prediction systems. Solutions engaging for full keyboards embedded in remote controls are mentioned in researches [10], however its high cost hinders economic viability. Several other studies, using voice [11, 14], gestures [12], mobile devices [16], or a combination of these modes of interaction [10] proved to be either inefficient for large text input, or too costly for mass market.

We believe in the combination of different ways of interaction, but what we see is that during the development of the physical devices and/or the development of the command language used by the user to interact, human cognitive factors are not considered. An important example is regarded to the human attention. Attention is seen as the set of mechanisms that allows the allocation of cognitive resources, which are assumed to be limited [15] (*attention as selection* paradigm).

Furthermore, existing solutions require that the viewer's attention switches between the input device (remote control), the iDTV and the content (television programs). All this alternating attention flowing between the viewer and iDTV impairs any attempt of natural interaction, and also pave the way for the need of researches that focus on the attention allocation of the iDTV users. Systems that take into account the attention allocation are called attention-aware systems [15].

By maintaining the well-established (but insufficient) paradigm of infrared RC and iDTV, iDTV application developers and iDTV device designers have forgotten to work the allocation of user attention.

This article describes the development of a new RC, which we named MoveRC, based on the principles of allocation of human attention. In fact, the requirements of the RC were set so the user interaction tasks with iDTV (such as reconnaissance, selection, feedback, etc.) are allocated in different cognitive areas. The RC we've proposed uses a combination of ways of interaction, including language commands by movements in order to maximize the automaticity of the input process data in iDTV (Figure 1).

In this article, we present a review of related work (Section 2), followed by the presentation of the main theories of divided attention (Section 3), and we conclude with a section where the RC prototyped solution is presented.

2. RELATED WORKS

Academic and commercial researches address the innovation in the interaction with iDTV. In [13] the authors used a Wiimote, the Wii videogame control to compare the efficiency of pointing tasks at the screen. The LG company has also created a simplified control that uses movements. However, neither of the solutions is focused on data input, but on the point-and-click interaction.

Solutions that use voice recognition also emerge in the gadgets. Samsung launched an iDTV that accepts voice commands for iDTV ordinary actions, such as swapping channels and volume control. However, in analyzes of specialized magazines these features proved to be impractical, as they are slow and exhausting.

Scholar researches on gestures and iDTV are quite common in academia. Many of them try to replace the RC, as PalmRC [6] which uses the palm as a way to replace the RC. The adoption of the Microsoft Kinect as an ideal platform for gestures produced several works that used it, as it is shown in [8] and [10].

The use of advanced devices (celular phones and tablets) replacing RC is also studied. Several papers analyze these interactions as it is shown in [7, 9]. All these solutions seek to work only the simple forms of interaction with iDTV: control of iDTV basic functions, selecting and sharing iDTV material. However, none of these proposals is directly addressed to the input of data in text format.

Exclusive solutions for iDTV data input in text format were found in the sources of this research. [10] presents the solution called SpeeG, interface that combines users voice commands with a gesture based real-time correction, allowing users to correct errors in speech recognition with hand gestures, using a special screen to point at the spoken letters/words. However, due to the slow speed input, similar to using a virtual keyboard, this solution also proved to be ineffective.

Since none of the studies we have reviewed showed an affordable solution for data input, the present research is justified. This accessibility refers to factors such as market cost, feasibility and simplicity of use. In the next section, we present the context that motivated us to study theories focused on the attention allocation in iDTV regarding using the RC.

3. REASONING AND CONTEXT

Analyzing sessions of users experiencing iDTV (similar in [9]), we have seen that each user divides his/her attention between the RC and the interactive application on the screen. This acknowledgement led us to realize that the problem of allocation of human cognitive resources should be elucidated by the iDTV design of interaction. Then, we proceeded studying theories of attention, tasks performed by the user when he/she is handling a data input RC, and the cognitive processes and factors that are involved in the routine of these tasks.

As results of this study are described as it follows, we've spotted three theories of divided attention that deserve special attention [15]:

- **Capacitive Theory:** Argue that a llimited pool of cognitive resources is available. Predicts that an individual who suffers an increase in the number of attention targets, necessarily reduces his/her cognitive resources available for each of the targets. Attention targets shall be construed as actual or imaginary-symbolic elements that require active or passive attention;

- **Cross-talk Theory:** which attribute errors and delays in multitasking to interferences between the contents of the information being processed. I.e.: A viewer tries to follow a iDTV program while talking about a different subject, will either suffer losses of program content, or will have trouble following the conversation;

- **Automaticity:** which refers to either innate or learned activities, that show to be automatic in the perception on action, automatic goal pursuit and a continual automatic evaluation of one's experience. Automaticity has as behavioral parameters: fast response tims; obligatory execution, have no interaction with other concurrent processes, the performance level remains constant no matter what other processes run in parallel, and is less sensitive to distractions. The importance of this theory to the interaction takes place through the natural little effort needed to accomplish the interactive task.

In the context of the RC manipulation for iDTV data input, using the virtual keyboard (most common modality in iDTV), the user is in a situation of attention shared between the tasks of thinking about on what to type, in manipulating the RC (for look at the keys and press them), and checking the result on iDTV screen. Roda [15] notes that it is often that the divided attention induces errors and delays in responses, and that most attention researches aims at the multitasking performance and to identify factors that influence multitasking.

The Table 1 shows the number of 'targets' to divide the resources of cognition and the number of tasks that the user performs. Switching between tasks, and the number of targets of attention make typing a tedious task, and it can hardly reach a state of automaticity (as in typing on a QWERTY keyboard).

Table 1. Switching tasks while typing on the iDTV

Cognitive Target	Task
-	1 - Think about what you want to text
Control Keys	2 - See and understand which RC key does what
Screen Cursor	3 - look at the iDTV screen and see on which letter the cursor is
Desired Letter(s).	4 - Finding in the iDTV screen, the desired letter and see how far from the cursor the desired letter is
TV Screen	5 - Pointing the RC to the iDTV correctly and type the letter
Text Box	6 - Check if the letter was typed correctly

To avoid multitasking loss of performance, [15] identifies four cognitive resources (dimensions) that can be shared without interference between cognitive tasks.

- **Perceptual Modalities:** The study of Wickens [15] predicts that different perceptual modalities (visual, auditory, somatic, kinesthetic, etc.) uses different non-conflicting resources.
- **Processing stages:** the authors of the study predict that during a cognitive process, the activities of perception and cognition (who share the same resources) use different set of resources than selection and execution.
- **Processing codes:** In the case of the study on the processing of human codes, the authors predicted that analog and spatial processes use a different set of resources than categorical and symbolic (linguistic) processes.
- **Visual Channels:** The authors predict that the focal vision uses different set of resources than ambient vision.

When there is the understanding of human cognitive resources, and this understanding is used to better allocate tasks in a given interaction, we have an attention-aware systems [14]. These systems reduce the information overload, limit the negative effects of interruptions, increase the situations of human knowledge on the environment (awareness), and support the user in multitasking situations [15].

It is important to note that there is a consensus that the user experience with technology directly influences the performance of the tasks (as the amount of times that the attention switch occurs, the time spent to make a text input etc.).

4. SOLUTION

The purpose of this research is initially presented by the description of the terms of the requirements of MoveRC, followed by the presentation of the RC's physic prototyping in development.

4.1 Requirements

The requirements described in this paper refer to the division attention between tasks of Table 1 investigating ways to optimize user interaction in manipulating the RC, i.e.: trying to find a RC that will establish an attention-aware system for iDTV. These requirements are: i) Human Performance: including the situations in which the division of attention does not cause loss of human performance, and ii) Usability: including the requirements in which the interaction should be as natural as possible. These requirements are based on four types of cognitive resources that have the minimal influence on multitasking, seek a state of use of automaticity.

Requirement 1: Separating tasks in different sensory modalities. In this proposal, data entry is accomplished through the use of movements. The user moves his wrist to select letters and receives a haptic feedback (vibratory) motion between letters, leaving the sense of sight free to remain fixed to the screen of iDTV. The separation of activities in different sensory modalities can be a determining factor to reduce the time of typing a text and attain a state of automaticity.

Requirement 2: Separating the viewer's perception of the selection and execution activities. Separating the viewer's perception of the activities of selection and execution can be a determining factor to mitigate the sight alternations. To do so, the MoveRC prototype uses the gyroscope to identify the choice of letter by motion. The user does not need to lay his/her sight on the RC, now that he/she will handle a single key, the one of letter selection. The single selection button also have a tactile feedback, so the user can easily identify if the button was pressed and if the command was sent to the iDTV.

Requirement 3: Make use of the notion of human movement of an object in space by defining the RC command language. To handle the control is a spatial process, while processing the codes on the screen of iDTV is a symbolic process. We assume that this separation will be a determining factor to reduce the cognitive load of the task of iDTV typing.

Requirement 4: To keep the main visual focus of the spectator on the iDTV screen, letting his/her peripheral vision encompasses the RC. And finally, we have the studies on the human visual channels. In the proposed solution, we have designed a RC use so that the viewer's visual focus is on the iDTV screen's virtual keyboard, and his/her peripheral vision encompassing the RC that is on his/her hands, helping him/her with the spatial perception. We assume that this is a determining factor for improved performance because it avoids the visual alternation between RC and TVD. The use of a second screen on the RC can help people with impaired vision to know which letter they are targeting..

4.2 Physical Prototyping

The high-fidelity physical prototyping is necessary given the nuances of interaction with physical objects through movement as the need to measure the user's cognitive (attention) load. For high-fidelity prototyping, one must use elements of physical computing, which involves the design of interactive objects that communicate with humans through sensors and actuators controlled by embedded software [3]. After study on the best way to accomplish this prototyping, the Arduino platform [3] was chosen because it proved to be ideal for low cost prototyping and manufacturing end, ensuring that solutions can actually researched the market to follow.

The prototyped MoveRC uses an Arduino Nano board connected to the gyroscope chip via breadboard, which records the movements in all axes. The X and Y axes move the cursor between the letters on the virtual keyboard. As the interaction of infrared RC with the iDTV is unidirectional (RC to iDTV), the RC is the one which controls selected letters, sending an infrared command to the iDTV to select the chosen letter. The RC has simplified keys, dedicated to the basic functions on television. Its built-in screen of 2" is intended to facilitate people with impaired vision to use it. In it the spectator will see witch keyboard letter is selected on the iDTV screen. Also there is an analogic joystick type button, for users who cannot or don't want to use the movement recognition from the MoveRC. Figure 2 shows the prototype implemented in its early stages. The idea behind the prototype is to give support to all four requirements described, by the movement sensors, the feedback actuators, and the additional visual output (LCD display).

The prototype is designed to be used in parallel with commercial equipment, replacing the native RC. To do so, the original RC infrared commands were captured and recorded by the prototype to be replicated. As application in iDTV, we used a simple text box software that displays the virtual keyboard and displays the cursor position according to the gyroscopic sensor control. The software, designed using NCL + Lua [1], also allows input of data via standard virtual keyboard and multi-tap, for the purpose of performance comparison.

Figure 2. © Daniel Chagas - MoveRC Prototype using Arduino Nano

The recommendations of costs were also taken into account, and a final prototype to mass production has a cost of just over US$ 25, given the simplicity of its circuit and the low number of sensors.

5. CONCLUSION AND FUTURE WORK

In this paper, requirements were defined requirements and presented an Arduino designed solution for a new RC. The requirements focused on solutions to improve the performance of the users about factors that influence the human attention allocation. Although the requirements have been based on theories and studies, the specificity of the authors included assumptions that need to be tested.

In a near future, the achievement of usability testing with the physical prototype developed will evaluate such assumptions in the event of data input via text, and use of the functions of the standard TV control (volume, channel change and mute key). We will verify, for example the speed performance rates and the users satisfaction, attempting to identify whether the use of wrist movements, being a natural process, will enable a data input with little cognitive effort.

If we had chosen an alternative system of low-fidelity prototyping, such as the Wizard of Oz, a paper prototype, the analysis in experiments of interaction of user behavior (his/her sense of interaction and attention charge) could have been affected. Moreover, we could not have seen the economic viability of the solution.

Despite being only the beginning of a research, we hope that the proposed interaction standard and development can inspire professionals to design new ways of interaction for iDTV, as in mobile devices and computers, respecting the different features of the division of user attention.

6. REFERENCES

1. Antonacci, M. NCL: Uma Linguagem Declarativa para Especificação de Documentos Hipermídia com Sincronização Temporal e Espacial. Dissertação (Doutorado) – PUC-RJ, (2000). Available at: http://goo.gl/F2RzZ.

2. Bachmayer, S., Lugmayr, A., and Kotsis, G. New social & collaborative interactive TV program formats. *Proceedings of MoMM'09*, (2009), 121.

3. Banzi, M. *Getting Started with Arduino (Make: Projects)*. Make Books, 2008.

4. Carmichael, A., Rice, M., Sloan, D., and Gregor, P. Digital switchover or digital divide: a prognosis for usable and accessible interactive digital television in the UK. *Univers. Access Inf. Soc.*, (2006), 400–416.

5. Cooper, W. The interactive television user experience so far. *Proceedings of the 1st international conference on Designing interactive user experiences for TV and video*, (2008), 133.

6. Dezfuli, N., Müller, F.B., Khalilbeigi, M., Huber, J., and Mühlhäuser, M. PalmRC: imaginary palm-based remote control for eyes-free television interaction. *Proceedings of the 10th EuroiTV'12*, ACM (2012), 27–34.

7. D'heer, E., Courtois, C., and Paulussen, S. Everyday life in (front of) the screen: the consumption of multiple screen technologies in the living room context. *Proceedings of the 10th EuroiTV'12*, (2012), 195–198.

8. Hannah, D., Halvey, M., Wilson, G., and Brewster, S. Using multimodal interactions for 3D television and multimedia browsing. *Procceddings of the 9th EuroiTV '11*, (2011), 181.

9. Hess, J., Ley, B., and Ogonowski, C. Jumping between devices and services: towards an integrated concept for social tv. *Procceddings of the 9th EuroiTV '11*, (2011), 11–20.

10. Hoste, L., Dumas, B., and Signer, B. SpeeG: A Multimodal Speech- and Gesture-based Text Input Solution. *Proceedings of the International Working Conference on Advanced Visual Interfaces*, (2012), 156–163.

11. Huang, E.E.M., Harboe, G., Tullio, J., et al. Of social television comes home: a field study of communication choices and practices in tv-based text and voice chat. *Proceedings of CHI'09*, (2009), 585–594.

12. Kray, C., Nesbitt, D., Dawson, J., Rohs, M., and Laboratories, D.T. User-Defined Gestures for Connecting Mobile Phones , Public Displays , and Tabletops. *Proceedings of the 12th MobileHCI 10*, , 239–248.

13. McArthur, V., Castellucci, S.J., and MacKenzie, I.S. An empirical comparison of "wiimote" gun attachments for pointing tasks. *Proceedings of the 1st EICS'09*, (2009), 203.

14. Rice, M. and Alm, N. Sociable TV: exploring user-led interaction design for older adults. *Proceedings of the 5th EuroiTV'07*, Springer-Verlag (2007), 126–135.

15. Roda, C. Human attention and its implications for human-computer interaction. In *Human Attention in Digital Environments*. Cambridge University Press, Cambridge, 2011, 322.

16. Vignaroli, L., Pero, R. Del, and Negro, F. Personalized newscasts and social networks: a prototype built over a flexible integration model. *Proceedings of the 21st WWW'12 Companion*, (2012), 433–436.

MARKER: A Tool for Building Interactive Applications for T-Learning

Sttiwe Washington F. de Sousa
Programa de Pós-graduação em Informática
Universidade Federal da Paraíba (UFPB)
João Pessoa, Brasil
sttiwew@gmail.com

Ed Porto Bezerra
Departamento de Informática
Universidade Federal da Paraíba (UFPB)
João Pessoa, Brasil
edporto@di.ufpb.br

Ismênia Mangueira Soares
Programa de Pós-graduação em Educação
Universidade Federal da Paraíba (UFPB)
João Pessoa, Brasil
ismamangueira@gmail.com

Edna Gusmão de Góes Brennand
Centro de Educação
Universidade Federal da Paraíba (UFPB)
João Pessoa, Brasil
ebrenna2@uol.com.br

ABSTRACT

The growth of distance education has been enhanced by Massive Open Online Course and by the production of content broadcasted on television. The type of learning undertaken by Interactive Digital Television (iDTV) is also called Television-Learning (T-learning). Due to the possibilities of interactivity emerged with the creation of middleware Ginga, the T-Learning can cover a large number of learners. The marking video is a set of techniques used to insert additional interactive content in a video. As the development of applications for iDTV is still a costly process, because it requires a multidisciplinary team of developers to create tools for producing interactive applications for iDTV is a promising solution. The need for specific knowledge of technology or programming language should not be a prerequisite for this team. This paper presents a tool, called MARKER, for building interactive applications for iDTV whose main actors are the teacher (content creator) and student (interactive video user).

Categories and Subject Descriptors

D.2.1 [**Programming Languages**]: Tool;

General Terms

Experimentation;

Keywords

T-learning, marking video, iDTV, distance education.

1. INTRODUCTION

The TV, over time, is undergoing a constant evolution, not only in the TV set itself, but also the various technologies that surrounds and makes possible further its viability in the propagation and dissemination of information.

These developments turned the TV on a medium that can carry a plethora of information. Thus, we can transmit data with greater complexity and take analog TV as a reference for data transmission. The infrastructure of the Digital TV (DTV) has brought itself a new model of television, changing the paradigm of "watching TV" [3]. This new model is essential for the implementation of technological change TVD [3With it, we can send any type of information such as text, audio, video or software. This can expand the market for television stations. Another paradigm shift has been caused by Social TV [14].

The development of applications for Interactive Digital TV (iDTV) is not a trivial process, since it requires multidisciplinary teams consisting of project managers, systems analysts, programmers, designers, and other professionals in the field to which you want to direct an application. For example, the area of education require the accompaniment of a teaching team [11]. However, the costs to keep this team can be high. Therefore, the adoption of tools for creating applications for iDTV can be a solution economically and technologically feasible.

2. MARKING ON VIDEO FOR INTERACTION

The marking on video consists of a set of techniques used to enter information into video seamlessly. Furthermore, the marking techniques can provide the video content increased, as is the case of entering a URL into a video for subsequent access to a site or other types of information [15].

Among the advantages of using video techniques markings on building interactive narratives, we highlight the lack of dependency between context and technology, and greater autonomy in the creative process and copyright [15].

Marking video provides a simple and efficient interactivity because it offers the user greater control over the media viewed, no longer limited to copy them or pause them [10].

According to its application, we classify the markings on video in visible and invisible. Each relates to the permissible access type for that content can be viewed [13].

The **visible markings** are displayed to showcase and raise the existence of complementary content. A marking visible on television context can be represented by any content (text, symbols, geometric shapes and any type of image or representation). Dimensional barcodes known as QR-code [9] are also visible markings digital because they can store a variety of data such as numeric digits, alphanumeric, byte Kanji characters and other symbols.

The **invisible markings** involve the study of techniques used in information hiding in digital media. One of the most widely used techniques for data hiding is steganography [1]. The steganography is widely used in the field of security to hide information, as in the case of the watermark that tries to prevent forgery, concealing copyright information. The use of steganography as a way of marking the digital video TVDI navigational can improve the user experience. The Ginga middleware supports this type of marking: through the tags <meta> and <metadata> it is possible include information or content [6].

The association of an object with the content accessed by it, can be expressed through the use of icons representative of multiple intelligences (MI) [18]. Figure 1 shows icons of spatial intelligence.

Spatial intelligence				
Name	Compass rose	Geometric figure	Globe	Astronaut	Hourglass
Symbol					
Percentage	100%	85,7%	100%	100%	71,4%

Figure 1 Icons representing the multiple intelligences

The representative icons are classified as: musical, bodily kinesthetic, logical mathematical, spatial, interpersonal and linguistic. For each symbol a study observing the percentage that best represents intelligence. For example, spatial intelligence can be well represented (100%) by the symbols of the compass, globe and astronaut.

3. CONCEPTUAL MODELLING

In modeling tool MARKER concepts were applied in the process of software development known as DSDM [4] together with the universal modeling language called UML [12].

From the identification of functional requirements that define the sequence of interaction with external agents, we model the use case diagram showing the overview of the features of the tool MARKER (Figure 2).

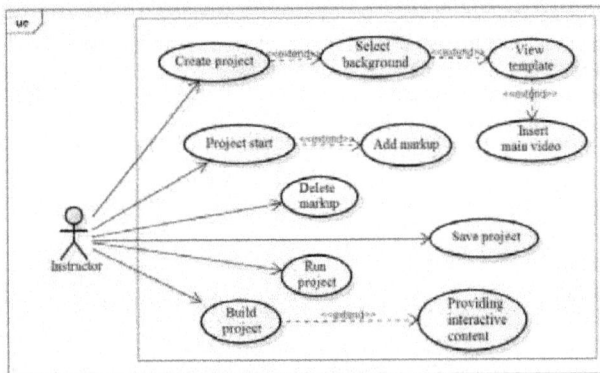

Figure 2 Use case diagram

The process of creating a project starts from your request. First the teacher selects a background for your application. Then he goes on to display the template that contains metrics to provisions of the content on the screen, such as the position of a button, viewing a video and keys triggering events. Finally, he makes the insertion of the main video that will be worked to insert interactions.

From the start of the project, the teacher can add markings making use of the insertion of various contents such as video, images, text, audio and applications gingaNCL Anytime, an inserted content can be removed from the project in progress.

The implementation consists of viewing content built by Ginga4Windows [4]. Thus, we can observe the actual state of the application at the time of its implementation. The construction of the project consists in deleting configuration files and temporary files used during the implementation. At the end of the process, the content can be made available and accessed by the remote user.

Building an application for iDTV requires three aspects: the profile of teachers, choosing a video source, and the choice of other media and other technological resources [17].

To choose the profile of teachers, we consider the goals of your educational content, and identify the particular aspects with regard to IM to be awakened.

The choice of the source video is in accordance with the identification of the application content to the needs raised by the teacher.

The choice of other media and other technological resources (other videos, links to the Internet, animation, audio, text and games) must be in accordance with the identified potential in the source video. It will be added to the application as a way to increase content and interaction.

The generated content is an application (on NCL) for the middleware Ginga. The main file of the application execution (*main.ncl*) is generated from a template.

In designing the templates were initially identified based elements to form an NCL document. They are needed to assemble a document NCL 3.0 compliant middleware Ginga. Thus, we can build an early model common to all applications.

From this initial model, the standardization of the provisions of the elements on the screen was held. The arrangement of the elements corresponds to the region where each element must occupy.

In building the application, the tool will populate this template with the code of the content produced by the teacher.

4. MARKER PROTOTYPE

The prototype was implemented in Java programming language. The computing environment of execution was previously configured with the installation package ffmpeg libraries [7]. So we can run multiple video formats. Another tool used was Ginga4Windows [4] which provided the execution of applications generated at the time of its development. In Figure 3 we have the home screen MARKER.

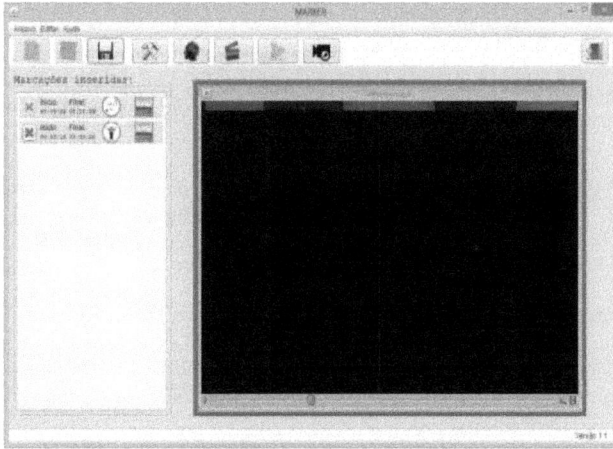
Figure 3 Home screen MARKER

The home screen contains a player (dark part of the screen) where will be displayed the source video. At the top are buttons regarding the following features: create a new project, open an existing project, save project, build the project, TIM (access to a local page with educational content), run (view contents of the application in Ginga4windows), start project, insert marking and out of the tool. On the left side of the player we have an area reserved for displaying the content inserted where you can delete it, view the start and end time that content is available for access, the icon used to represent the content and type of inserted media (audio, video, image, text or application gingaNCL).

At the end of creation, it will be provided a folder containing all the files needed to run this application. This folder will contain a file *main.ncl* (main file to run the application), a file containing the connector base ConnectorBase.ncl, and other files that are generated depending on the inclusion of interactions, and another folder called "media" containing all media application (audio, video, HTML pages and files NCL).

5. PRELIMINARY PROOF OF CONCEPT

The application used as source video one video lesson on ecology of Distance Education Course at the Federal University of Paraíba. From the selection of the source video, the possible moments of interactions are identified by the teacher and inserted through the button "Insert Marking". The icon "Compass Rose ", displayed at the top right of the screen shown in Figure 4, represents the complementary content entered by the teacher.

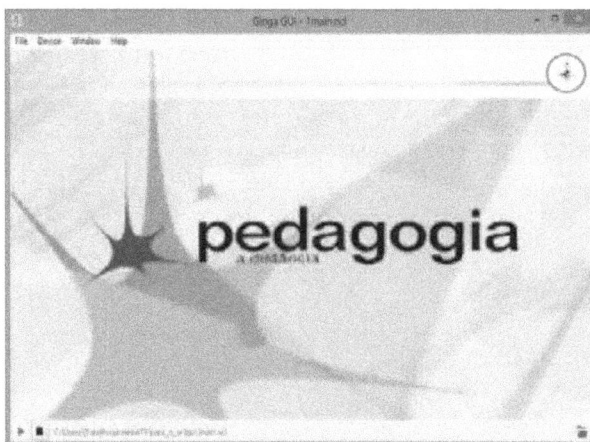
Figure 4 Using the "Compass Rose" icon

The interaction is performed using the green key on the remote control to display the corresponding content (Figure 5).

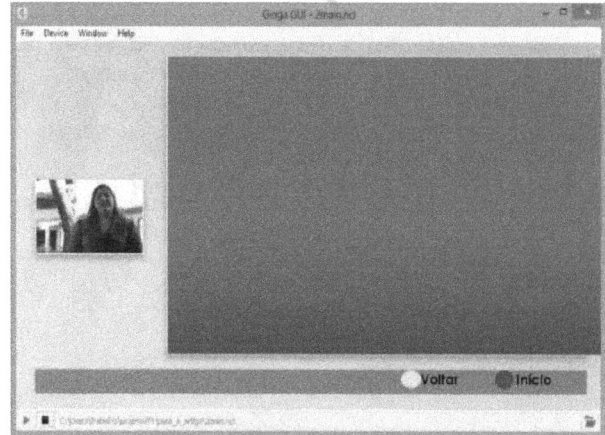
Figure 5 Musical content inserted

The source video was resized and positioned to the left of the alternate video (larger screen) and kept in a paused state. If you click on the blue button on the remote, the additional video will play. If you click on the yellow button, it closes and the video source remains displayed.

6. RELATED WORK

Celes [2] proposes an approach to creating content for the teaching area. This proposal consists of the design concepts of architectural styles to aid the construction of learning objects resulting in NCL template that will be filled using a language called Xtyle. Unlike MARKER, this approach requires specific knowledge of technology or customization of templates. Saade and Smith [16] proposed the XTemplate language for creating template describing hypermedia elements. The content authoring resembles in creating an application using the NCL language, ie, it is not friendly to a content creator.

7. FINAL CONSIDERATION

Building applications for T-Learning usually requires the formation of a multidisciplinary team. This has high costs. The adoption of these tools to create applications for iDTV by a teacher with basic computer solution is economically and technologically feasible.

The design of interactive content for TV, from the tool MARKER, is a pragmatic option, although still contains limitations, such as the need for greater customization of the display of the content and its characteristics. In the validation stage of the tool, we found that teachers with basic computer skills (opening a file, move on screens, run a video etc.) were able to create their applications. This seems to differentiate MARKER other studies analyzed in this article.

The tool also allows access via mobile, tablet and / or smartphone. However, more tests with students and teachers are needed.

8. ACKNOWLEDGMENT
The second author (Bezerra E. P.) is Coordinator of the project funded by CAPES - Proc. Number BEX 1487/12-4.

9. REFERENCES
[1] Carvalho, D.F., Chies, R., Freire, A. P., Martimiano, L. A. F., Goularte, R. *Video Steganography for Confidential*

Documents: Integrity, Privacy and Version Control. ACM – 2008

[2]   Celes, C. S. F. S. and Souza, C. T. *Estilos Arquiteturais de Software na Construção de Objetos de Aprendizagem para a TV Digital Interativa.* XVIII Simpósio Brasileiro de Informática na Educação - SBIE - Mackenzie – 2007

[3]   Cruz, R. *TV digital no Brasil: tecnologia versus política* – São Paulo: Editora Senac São Paulo, 2008.

[4]   Composer Telemidia, *Ginga4Windows.* (Junho, 2013), DOI=http://composer.telemidia.puc-rio.br/start?id=pt-br%2Fnews%2Fginga4windows_0.13.1_released.

[5]   DSDM Consortiun. (Fevereiro, 2012) DOI=http://www.dsdm.org/.

[6]   Fernades, J. L. and Silveira, G. – *Introdução à Televisão Digital Interativa: Arquitetura, Protocolos, Padrões e Práticas.* (Dezembro, 2013), DOI= http://www.cic.unb.br/docentes/jhcf/MyBooks/itvdi/texto/itvdi.pdf.

[7]   FFMPEG. (Junho, 2013), DOI=http://www.ffmpeg.org/.

[8]   IEL/NC Instituto Euvaldo Lodi/Núcleo Central. *TV digital: qualidade e interatividade.* Brasília, 2007.

[9]   ISO/IEC 18004-6, 2000. *Information technology - Automatic identification and data capture techniques - Bar code symbology* - QR Code. 2000.

[10] Lockhorn, J. *Video Tagging - An Introduction & Vendor Overview. Insight – avenue a razorfish.* (Dezembro, 2013), DOI=http://slant.avenuea-razorfish.com/0407_slant/Lockhorn_Video_Tagging.pdf.

[11] Neto, F. A. S., Bezerra, E.P., Dias, D. S. F. *ITV-Learning: a Prototype for Construction of Learning Objects for Interactive Digital Television. International Conference The Future of Education* – Ed. 2ª, 2012.

[12] OMG, *Unified Modeling Language – UML.* (Julho, 2013), DOI=http://www.uml.org/.

[13] Petitcolas, F. A. P., Ross, J., Kuhn, M. G. *Information Hiding: A Survey.* Proceedings of the IEEE, 87: 0018-9219, 1999.

[14] Proulx, M., and Shepatin, S., *Social TV, how marketers can reach and engage audiences by connecting television to the web, social media, and mobile.* Editora Wiley, ISBN 978-1-118-16746-5, Canadá, 2012.

[15] Costa, R., Maritan, T., Neto, G. B., Nobre, D. A., Kulesza, R., Lemos, G. Relatório Técnico LAVID.- *Um Estudo sobre o Uso de Marcações Autocontidas em Vídeo para Promoção de Interação Sensível ao Conteúdo em Múltiplos Contextos.* (Novembro, 2012), DOI= http://www.lavid.ufpb.br/files/1/RTLavid01-12.pdf.

[16]   Saade, D. C. M. and Soares, L. F. G. *XConnector & XTemplate: Improving the Expressiveness and Reuse in Web Authoring Languages.* The New Review of Hypermedia and Multimedia Journal. 2002.

[17] Soares, I. M., Bezerra, E. P., Brennand, E. G. G., Washington. S. *Uma ferramenta para a construção de conteúdos digitais a partir da Teoria das Inteligências Múltiplas de Gardner.* Revista Temática, Ano VII, n.11, 2012.

[18] Zandomeneghi, A. L. A. *Ícones representativos das inteligências múltiplas.*2005. 207f. Tese. Universidade Federal de Santa Catarina-UFSC. Programa de Pós-Graduação em Engenharia de Produção. Florianópolis, 2005.

An Alternative to Align Interactive Interfaces Construction and Return Channel Usage

Giuseppe Lima, Claudiana Batista, Felipe Oliveira, Ighor Barros, Marcelo Fernandes

Ideen Soluções em Informática LTDA

Av. João Câncio da Silva, 1676, Manaíra. Edifício Advance Center, sala 301

CEP 58037-050 – João Pessoa – Paraíba – Brasil

[giuseppe, claudiana, felipe, ighor, marcelo]@ideen.net.br

ABSTRACT

It is recommendable that Interactive Digital TV application development should be oriented by user interface structure and interaction design. Better interactivity experiences can be obtained with the return channel usage, contributing to the offering of more convergent applications and addressing their integration to remote businesses logics and services. Many solutions enable construction of interactive applications with textual/visual programming support, but a few of them considers the disposal between the services operated over a return channel, the underlying data and the application widgets. Usually, these solutions require the direct manipulation of intermediary models whose their structures and notations demand an additional learning effort and, in some cases, they only focus on the achievement of a specific domain application template, instead of the final application instance itself. An alternative for application authoring will be presented aiming to abstract both the visual programming interface structure domain and its behavior/responsiveness when it requires the usage of the return channel based on services over IP and meeting the expectances for agility and quality in digital interactive television conception.

Categories and Subject Descriptors

D.2.2 [**Software Engineering**]: Design Tools and Techniques – User interfaces; H.5.1 [**Information Interfaces and Presentation**]: Multimedia Information Systems; D.3.3 [**Programming Languages**]: Language Constructs and Features – Frameworks;

General Terms

Design, Languages

Keywords

Authoring Tool; Digital Interactive Television; Return Channel; Rapid Application Development.

1. INTRODUÇÃO

Tecnologicamente a convergência digital é o fenômeno resultante da migração de diversas funções para um único dispositivo, em que os protagonistas do cenário atual da convergência são os *smartphones*, os *tablets*, os videogames e as *smart* TVs (ou TVs conectadas). Seria a TV Digital Interativa (TVDI) também uma

protagonista? São muitos os desafios que as aplicações interativas enfrentam no Brasil e até agora elas não são assumiram o seu devido destaque, como outrora anunciavam o governo e a indústria de TV. As perspectivas de inclusão digital, serviços de *t-gov*, *t-commerce*, *t-banking*, dentre outros ainda não passam de protótipos em que geralmente são encontradas poucas aplicações capazes de reter a atenção, talvez por serem pouco usáveis e funcionais, mas principalmente por serem pouco massificadas junto aos seus públicos. Isso prejudica a real percepção de valor da TVDI, fator relevante para o fomento da indústria de TV interativa, que apesar dos avanços ainda é bastante incipiente. Ainda, a presença de conectividade é um fator determinante na aplicação da convergência, podendo contribuir para a melhoria do panorama atual de oferta e de procura de aplicações interativas, que na TVDI está intrinsecamente ligada ao canal de retorno.

Ainda, há que se ponderar as demandas por agilidade e qualidade da indústria televisiva. Comumente, as soluções para a produção de aplicações interativas não acompanham ferramentas capazes de reforçarem o *design* centrado no usuário e a efetiva abstração de detalhes de programação de plataformas específicas, como as do SBTVD. O foco no usuário é sempre sugestionado como promotor de uma compreensão integrada da usabilidade e do funcional de um software [1][2], principalmente nas aplicações de TVDI, em que a interface e a interação são requisitos fundamentais [3][4][5]. O alcance desses princípios pode demandar a obtenção de métodos mais abstrativos ao domínio de programação (agilidade) e mais centrados no domínio de interface e de sua interação (qualidade), afinal não existe TVDI sem o respeito à satisfação do usuário telespectador.

No cenário atual de TVDI se constata que os poucos exemplos de aplicativos distribuídos em larga escala possuem apenas interatividade do tipo local [6], em parte motivada pela indisponibilidade do canal de retorno e de acesso nos dispositivos terminais. Outro fator a ser considerado seria a necessidade de um maior alcance na redução dos esforços de programação na autoria de aplicações, em que o uso do canal de retorno também deve se incluir. Isso pode ocorrer na medida em que a elaboração da interface e da lógica das aplicações sejam modeláveis por ferramentas RAD (*Rapid Application Development*), baseadas em CBD (*Component Based Development*) ou similares, cuja adoção tem se ampliado no desenvolvimento dos sistemas atuais [7].

Em virtude do crescente uso de lógicas de negócio remotas e de mecanismos de componentização de interfaces se acenou com a possibilidade de adotar SOA (*Service Oriented Architecture*) na TVDI, justificada pelo uso já consolidado em aplicações Web e de dispositivos móveis. Esforços similares também são encontrados na TV interativa [5][8][9]. O emprego de SOA proporciona que a elaboração e execução da lógica de negócios de uma aplicação ocorram remota e simultaneamente com a separação da interface com o usuário. Então, por que não sugestioná-la no contexto de aplicações de TVDI com canal de retorno? Tais aplicações tendem a ter um tempo de interação mais curto devido à dependência do controle remoto e à concorrência com o conteúdo televisivo. Sendo assim, espera-se que elas se utilizem de conjuntos menores de serviços e de dados subjacentes, em que o canal de retorno possa ser adotado exclusivamente como meio de acesso a esses serviços.

Um suporte RAD que abstraia o desenvolvimento com canal de retorno em TVDI poderia explorar a diminuição do esforço e do conhecimento necessários para acessar serviços e manipular seus dados, integrando-os aos meios de elaboração da interface e de seus comportamentos. O desacoplamento entre a lógica e a interface, no desenvolvimento RAD para a TVDI, pode contribuir para uma maior abstração da lógica de negócio e para um maior foco na concepção da interface, desde que essa sirva de gatilho para associação de serviços e de seus dados. Nesse sentido, a elaboração da lógica de negócio poderia já existir, sendo inclusive delegada a terceiros; ou, ser adaptada; ou, ainda, ser desenvolvida a partir das demandas de serviços originados de uma construção antecipada da interface. Esse suporte RAD para a TVDI com canal de retorno necessita de um arcabouço que defina como os itens de interface, os seus comportamentos, os serviços e os dados se coligam, possibilitando a posterior geração de código para uma plataforma de execução predefinida. Ele pode ser instanciado através de um *framework*, que uma vez tendo suas etapas e modelos definidos, deve ser de fácil entendimento e manipulação, podendo a sua construção e operacionalização ser assistida por uma ferramenta de software de autoria.

O presente artigo objetiva propor uma solução no suporte RAD para a TVDI, considerando um uso do canal de retorno baseado em serviços, no seguinte formato: na seção 2, apresenta-se a estrutura e funcionamento de um *framework* baseado na manipulação de um meta-modelo de aplicação modificado para usar serviços sob o canal de retorno; na seção 3, realizar-se-á um resumo das principais soluções de TVDI que fornecem algum auxílio na autoria de aplicações interativas, em especial, as capazes de lidar com o canal de retorno; por fim, serão dispostas as considerações finais na seção 4 e os agradecimentos na seção 5.

2. O CANAL DE RETORNO EM UM FRAMEWORK DE AUTORIA DE INTERFACES INTERATIVAS

O caráter ágil, interdisciplinar e a demanda por um *design* centrado no usuário presente na TV interativa [10][5] pode se apropriar de métodos RAD, que permitam uma manipulação de modelos de desenvolvimento via ferramentas. Nem sempre os profissionais envolvidos em níveis mais conceituais de elaboração de aplicações dominam as tecnologias das plataformas necessárias para concretização de suas idéias, como conhecimentos em domínios de programação. Minimamente, um suporte RAD centrado na interface com o usuário teria que reforçar o projeto gráfico e de interação, a partir de componentes reusáveis com amplas possibilidades de configuração de apresentação e de comportamento.

Nessa perspectiva, foi concebido o AppITV, que busca oferecer um *framework* abstrativo à manipulação direta de código, sugerindo um processo de desenvolvimento baseado na montagem da interface sobre um meta-modelo de aplicação interativa. No AppITV a preparação da estrutura e da interação da interface são as referências fundamentais para construção de uma aplicação. A estrutura básica de seu meta-modelo (Figura 1) é inspirada em

metodologias de concepção de interfaces de referência [2], em que uma interface gráfica é composta por telas, que agrupam objetos de interação ou *widgets* de interface. Tais metodologias sugerem que a interface final pode ser obtida pela geração de código, a partir da conversão do modelo para a plataforma concreta. Para refletir o projeto de interação foram agregados aos *widgets* o conceito de objeto comportamental, que basicamente são capazes de avaliar qualquer aspecto do estado da aplicação interativa e executar um comportamento. Tais avaliações (asserções) também podem ser oriundas do estado de execução de outros comportamentos, da alteração de valores de dados da aplicação e de atributos de *widgets*. Dentre os comportamentos (*behaviour*) possíveis são oferecidos a execução de um conjunto de efeitos visuais (*effect*), de alterações nas propriedades de *widgets* e de navegação entre *widgets* e telas (*navigation*). O *behaviour execute-code* é uma extensão futura, capaz de executar um código diretamente na plataforma alvo.

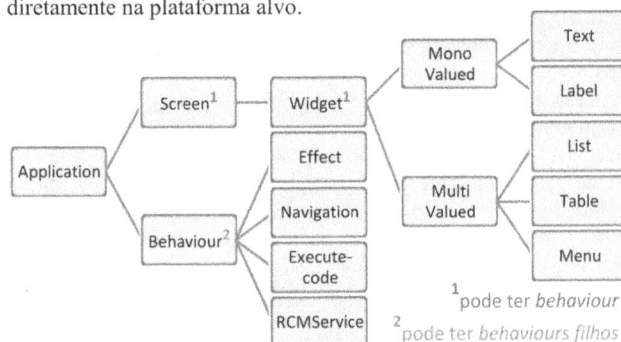

Figura 1. Hierarquia do meta-modelo de aplicação AppITV

O AppITV até o momento não considerava o suporte RAD no uso do canal de retorno, de fundamental importância para obtenção da interatividade plena e da convergência. Para obter esse suporte se assumiu que o canal de retorno atua de fato como uma fonte de mídias, incluindo-se os serviços web e os dados subjacentes. As aplicações de TV podem convergir lógicas remotas de negócio, em que o uso do canal de retorno condiciona a obtenção e envio de estruturas de dados pela rede, a partir da chamada de um serviço sempre processado na fonte.

Os dados envolvidos no uso de lógicas de negócios nas aplicações multimídias interativas podem ser considerados mídias quando os seus ciclos de obtenção e alteração estão relacionados com a interação direta do usuário via controle remoto, ou, por seus eventos derivados. Desta forma, o meta-modelo do AppITV se normalizou de maneira que essas operações são definidas como um comportamento da aplicação, ou seja, a execução dos serviços são especializações dos objetos comportamentais existentes, denominados objetos comportamentais de serviço (*RCMService*). Isso possibilitou o reuso de lógicas de negócios de diferentes fontes, protocolos e formatos de dados. Entretanto, sozinhos, os *RCMServices* não definem totalmente a especificação comportamental de uma aplicação. Há que se definir como a sua execução deve impactar na apresentação e na interação com a interface: como descrever e armazenar com facilidade os produtos provenientes das execuções de serviços (dados) para que o estado da interface possa se atualizar via objetos comportamentais? Portanto, tais dados passaram a ser compartilhados com os demais tipos de objetos comportamentais que dependem dos seus valores para serem ativados e com os *widgets* da interface que os apresentarão (*binding*).

Os dados passaram a ser guardados em estruturas de registro locais à aplicação, possibilitando apresentá-los (*binding* com *widgets*) e também reusá-los nos serviços (na parametrização de novas chamadas de serviços). Os registros de dados intermediam e notificam a alteração dos valores tanto oriundas do término da execução de um *RCMService*, quanto das modificações ocasionadas pelo usuário em *widgets* que possuam *binding* com o respectivo dado. Essa coordenação se inspirou em algumas soluções consolidadas de *databinding* que ligam objetos de modelo e de interface no que tange às etapas de notificação de alterações de valores de interesse e de conversão. Os dados provenientes do canal de retorno numa aplicação interativa com serviços, quase sempre, viajam de forma semi-estruturada, em que, as conversões são equivalentes a extrações de suas partes relevantes (derivações), que podem ser realizadas em dois níveis:

(i) de RAW para MODEL, em que, o dado RAW é obtido e atualizado como retorno de um *RCMService,* mantendo-se o mesmo formato de sua fonte. Os dados RAW podem se derivar em um ou mais dados MODEL dependendo da necessidade de reuso local (código local) ou na chamada de outros serviços, como parâmetro de entrada, pois o dado MODEL poderá manter os meta-dados de formato da sua fonte, se aplicável;

(ii) de MODEL para PRESENTATION, os dados MODEL podem se derivar em um ou mais dados PRESENTATION, úteis para apresentação do dado em um ou mais *widgets* da aplicação. Os *widgets* são classificados quanto ao *binding* de dados como mono e multivalorados (Figura 1), devendo receber dados PRESENTATION cuja extração deve corresponder a essas valorações.

O valor das versões derivadas de um dado RAW é sempre obtido dinamicamente, a partir da execução das regras de extração dispostas nas derivações MODEL e PRESENTATION. Ainda, os mecanismos de atualização podem atuar em dois sentidos: (i) quando um dado RAW é atualizado, notificando *widgets* que se ligam à dados PRESENTATION que dependem desse RAW para se derivar; e, (ii) quando um dado PRESENTATION é alterado na interação com o *widget* de interface, em que se atualiza o trecho equivalente no dado RAW de referência. Esse último sentido de atualização acaba por gerar o primeiro sentido, que propaga nos dados MODEL, que derivam daquele dado RAW, e que por fim propaga nos dados PRESENTATION que dependem daquele MODEL.

Os dois sentidos de atualização (Figura 2) possibilitam que os valores mantidos como dados RAW sejam equivalentes a uma sessão local dos dados oriundos dos retornos dos *RCMServices*. Ainda, esses sentidos mantêm a consistência por derivação com a garantia de que as atualizações vindouras da interface irão se propagar transparentemente no dado MODEL e vice-versa.

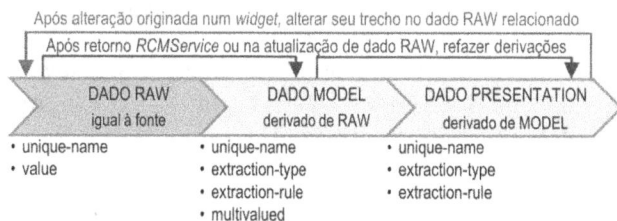

Figura 2. Sentidos de atualização de dados

O protocolo e o formato de dados usados nos serviços deliberarão a presença, o tipo e a estratégia de extração na derivação de dados MODEL e PRESENTATION, definidos ao longo da aplicação. Por exemplo, se o formato for XML se utiliza XQuery; se string plana, Regex; se JSON, seleciona-se um nó; se CSV, seleciona-se as colunas participantes da extração. O processo de extração pode

ser assistido por RAD com a utilização de descritores do serviço. Por exemplo, quando usado SOAP ou REST, os respectivos descritores WSDL e WADL contêm o que está disponível para ser extraído e pelo seu formato é possível sugerir uma estratégia. Caso o protocolo do serviço não disponha de descrição existe a possibilidade de descrever um serviço HTTP plano, que define o método HTTP e seus parâmetros de entrada e de saída para que a assistência nas extrações ainda seja possível. Para uma melhor compreensão, será disposto um esquema resumido de construção de uma aplicação de *t-commerce,* denominada *PizzaGo* (Figura 3), alinhada com a proposta de uso de objetos comportamentais de serviço apresentada. Assumir-se-á que a lógica está acessível via SOAP, utilizando-se XML como formato de dados e que a fonte disponibiliza os seguintes serviços:

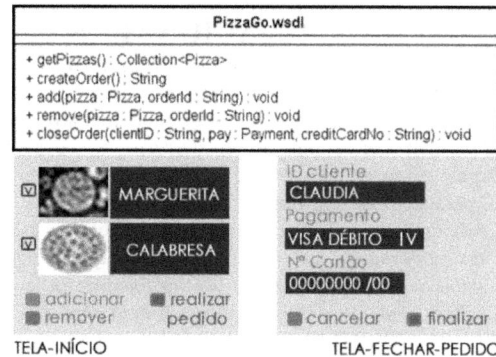

Figura 3. Exemplo simplificado da aplicação *PizzaGo*

Para definir comportamentos de serviço o desenvolvedor descreve primeiro a condição de sua execução. Por exemplo, um comportamento pode ser adicionado à TELA-INICIO quando a mesma entrar em exibição. Em seguida, se seleciona o serviço `getPizzas()`, dentre os disponibilizados na estrutura de descrição, atribuindo qual dado RAW será equivalente ao seu retorno. Nesse ponto, caso o serviço exija parâmetros de entrada, como em `closeOrder()` se deve informar quais os respectivos dados MODEL ou valores literais deverão ser utilizados na chamada. Uma vez definido um dado RAW já se pode realizar derivações para obtenção de um dado MODEL, como no caso do dado RAW, *pizzas-raw*, que é derivado para *pizzas-model* via consulta XQuery, que extrai apenas as 5 primeiras pizzas. Pelo resultado da consulta sabemos que o mesmo é multivalorado.

Para apresentar *pizzas-model* se seleciona um *widget* capaz de apresentar dados MODEL multivalorados, nesse exemplo foi escolhido o *widget Table*. Para definir o *binding* de dados de *Table* presente em TELA-INÍCIO se exige a associação de valores em suas colunas. Para cada coluna realizamos uma extração sob o dado *pizzas-model*, para cada item solicitado. Por exemplo, na primeira coluna se atribuiria um dado PRESENTATION cuja derivação retorna a URL da imagem e, na segunda, um dado PRESENTATION com o nome + descrição + preço, em que podemos utilizar XQuery e ainda formatar uma concatenação. Cada *widget* possui propriedades que indicam a correspondência de seu estado (de seleções do usuário, de preenchimento de valores, etc.) para eventual uso na definição de regras de disparo de outros objetos comportamentais ou no caso de não possuírem *binding* com dados PRESENTATION, o que ocorre nos *widgets* presentes na TELA-FECHAR-PEDIDO (exceto no componente de seleção de pagamento, que possui *binding* com o dado *Payment*). Por fim, um comportamento é adicionado ao botão `finalizar`, nessa mesma tela, quando o botão azul for pressionado. A essa interação se associa um novo *RCMService,* que usa `closeOrder()` e que requisitará a informação de parâmetros de entrada, atribuindo-se os valores dos *widgets* `ID cliente` e `N° Cartão` e do dado MODEL equivalente a seleção do item no *widget* de *binding* multivalorado `Pagamento`. Desta forma é possível montar a interface de uma aplicação integrada a uma lógica de negócios existente, a partir da especificação de comportamentos capazes de se executarem de acordo com uma asserção. Ressalta-se, que qualquer tipo de comportamento também pode ser disposto em hierarquia, em que cada um permite a inclusão de filhos, que são executados ao término do pai e podem realizar mais asserções para se executarem. Portanto, os comportamentos são o dínamo da máquina de estados estabelecida em conjunto com a obtenção dos dados RAW e de suas derivações MODEL e PRESENTATION.

3. TRABALHOS RELACIONADOS

Dentre os trabalhos relacionados que objetivam facilitar o uso do canal de retorno e que usam serviços é possível verificar alguns esforços em [5][8][9][11]. Em [8], se propõe uma arquitetura de *t-commerce* que sugere uma implementação do consumo dos serviços pelo reuso do acesso HTTP e pela conversão dos dados de XML para LUATables, ficando restrita ao domínio NCL/Lua. Em [5], se propõe o uso de um modelo de referência baseado na técnica de *storyboard*, em que a associação de serviços fica condicionada a pré-implementação de um domínio de aplicação num arquétipo (*template*). [9][11] se consideram uma evolução de [5] e propõem que a elaboração de *templates* abstratos e concretos é capaz de coligar estrutura, interação e representações de objetos, se valendo de notações UML e de estratégias de MDD / GSD, tornando possível reusar domínios específicos de aplicação, inclusive que usam serviços. Os modelos dessas últimas abordagens, apesar de sugerirem um apoio ferramental, culminam na obtenção de um *wizard* que então gerará o código final da aplicação, em que posteriores alterações ainda devem ser feitas diretamente no código ou se refazendo os modelos predecessores. Diferentemente disso, a adequação do meta-modelo do AppITV considera que serviços, dados e *widgets* podem ser associados diretamente sobre um único modelo, cujos comportamentos são definidos ao passo que os itens de interface vão sendo dispostos.

4. CONSIDERAÇÕES FINAIS

A abordagem proposta sugere que as aplicações interativas que usam serviços poderiam ser desenvolvidas tendo como referencial o desenvolvimento da própria interface, a partir do seguinte *workflow*: (i) disposição de telas; (ii) disposição de *widgets* de interface nas telas; (iii) enumeração de serviços a partir de descritores; (iv) definição de comportamentos de serviço, dispondo sua regra de execução com uma notação simples; (v) atribuição dos parâmetros de entrada do serviço a partir de sua associação com dados MODEL extraídos de dados RAW correspondentes; (vi) atribuição dos parâmetros de saída como dados RAW, que acabam por servir de sessão local de dados; (vii) realização do *binding* de dados PRESENTATION, com *widgets* de interface, mono ou multivalorados, obtidos pela derivação de dados MODEL.

A aderência dos *RCMServices* aos objetos comportamentais do *framework* objetivou um reuso mais natural de serviços e de dados remotos, sendo observada pelo seu alinhamento com o *workflow* de elaboração da interface. Ainda, a abordagem elimina a necessidade de operar modelos intermediários de aplicações, que eventualmente podem ter notação e atualização complexa, serem aplicáveis a um só domínio ou agregarem etapas adicionais para obtenção da aplicação final.

As notações usadas nas asserções de disparo de objetos comportamentais e na extração de dados para derivação estão sendo projetadas para exigirem o mínimo de esforço. Espera-se que a manutenção do meta-modelo do AppITV elimine a intervenção direta de código. Para isso, a definição de *RCMServices* e de dados consumidos por eles será assistida por uma ferramenta RAD/IDE, consolidando os níveis esperados de abstração na ligação interface/serviços/dados. Espera-se que esse ferramental agilize e abstraia o uso por profissionais não especializados em software. Estudos de caso preliminares constataram a aplicabilidade do modelo numa aplicação de enquete e de *t-commerce*. Contudo, avaliações em outros contextos e domínios de aplicações interativas estão em andamento, para aprimorar o grau de facilidade de uso e a abrangência na configuração da solução.

5. AGRADECIMENTOS

Ao CNPq, através do programa RHAE Pesquisador na Empresa.

6. REFERÊNCIAS

[1] Constantine, L. L. (2008) "Process Agility and Software Usability: Toward Lightweight Usage-Centered Design". Em: http://www.foruse.com/articles/agiledesign.htm

[2] Oliveira, K. M. A.; Aguiar, Y. P. C.; B. L. Jr *et al.* (2007). *O uso de Modelos e Múltiplos Protótipos na Concepção de Interface do Usuário*. Revista Princípia, Ano 11, Nº 15, pp. 15-29.

[3] Kunert, T. (2009). *User-Centered Interaction Design Patterns for Interactive Digital Television Applications*. Human–Computer Interaction Series. Springer-Verlag, London.

[4] Médola, A. S. L. D. and Teixeira, L. H. P. (2007). *Televisão Digital Interativa e o Desafio da Usabilidade para a Comunicação*. Revista Intexto, v. 2, n. 17, p. 1-15, julho/dezembro 2007. Porto Alegre, Universidade Federal do Rio Grande do Sul (UFRGS).

[5] Neto, M. C. M. (2011) *Contribuições para a Modelagem de Aplicações Multimídia para TV Digital Interativa*. Tese (Doutorado), Universidade Federal da Bahia.

[6] Sousa, M. F. (2010). *iTVnews: Uma Ferramenta para Construção de Aplicações Telejornalísticas em TVDI*, Dissertação (Mestrado), Universidade Federal da Paraíba.

[7] Qureshi, M. R. , Hayat S. A. (2007). *The Artifacts of Component-Based Development*. Journal Science International-Lahore, Vol. 19/3, pp. 187-192.

[8] Filho, M. C. S. (2011). *Arquitetura Orientada à Serviços para Comércio Eletrônico no Sistema Brasileiro de TV Digital*, Dissertação (Mestrado), Universidade de Brasília.

[9] Ferreira, T., Kulesza, R., Filho, G. L. S. (2012). *Uma Ferramenta de Autoria para Aplicações NCL e NCLua: uma Abordagem Orientada a Templates e com Suporte a Serviços Web*. In *WebMedia'12*, pp. 9-12.

[10] Veiga, E. G., Tavares, T. A. (2007). *Um Modelo de Processo para o Desenvolvimento de Programas para TV Digital e Interativa baseado em Metodologias Ágeis*. In Simpósio Brasileiro de Qualidade de Software (SBQS 2007), Porto de Galinhas – PE.

[11] Kulesza, R., Meira, S. R. L, Ferreira, T. P., Neto, V. R. S., Alexandre E. F. S., Filho, G. L. S. (2012). *Towards a generative software development approach for rapid prototyping iDTV applications*. In *WebMedia'12*, pp. 91-98.

Interactive Digital TV as Revealed through Words
Focuses and Research Sources

Samuel B. Buchdid
Institute of Computing - UNICAMP
Av. Albert Einstein N1251
Campinas-SP, Brazil
+55 19 3788-5870
buchdid@ic.unicamp.br

M. Cecília C. Baranauskas
Institute of Computing - UNICAMP
Av. Albert Einstein N1251
Campinas-SP, Brazil
+55 19 3788-5870
cecilia@ic.unicamp.br

ABSTRACT

Interactive Digital TV (iDTV) exists within a digital ecosystem that interconnects a variety of media, viewers and electronic devices, and it reaches new proportions as computers and hyper-connectivity are being incorporated into objects and also into everyday environments, in both public and private spheres. Every emergent technology suffers from a lack of references, processes and artifacts for developers and as they assess and design new solutions. In light of this context, this study sought to map out the main research focuses that have been addressed in the iDTV field in recent years. Data was collected and an analysis was conducted on research sources based on the frequency of words from paper titles and their abstracts; results reveal individual characteristics of one of the most relevant conferences in the field (EuroITV) and other publications found in the ACM-DL. Similarities and differences on these vehicles, allow an overview of contributions and gaps in the field. Moreover, this study presents detailed information about conferences, journals, affiliations and countries where work in the field is registered.

Categories and Subject Descriptors

H.m [**Information Systems**]: MISCELLANEOUS

General Terms

Measurement, Documentation, Verification, Human Factors

Keywords

Interactive Digital TV; Analysis; Conferences; Publications; Tag Clouds

1. INTRODUCTION

Digital TV convergence has been marked by major changes in content production, broadcasting and reception, as well as new possibilities for market issues. For end users, some examples of improvement include: quality in audio and video, electronic program guides (EPGs), mobility, and interactivity [11]. In parallel to the Digital TV convergence, the diversity of devices in

people's homes has also increased in recent years. A typical TV scenario presents a set of devices connected to the TV (e.g., a set-top box, DVD players, home theater, etc.), and each one has specific features that include different layouts, ways of interaction, remote controls, etc. [5]. Moreover, according to Rice et. al. [18], with technological progress and the convergence of information and communication technologies (ICTs), the Interactive Digital TV (iDTV) has become part of a digital ecosystem that interconnects a variety of consumer and electronic devices inside and outside people's homes (e.g., mobiles, cars, etc.). This ecosystem reaches new proportions as computers and hyper-connectivity are being incorporated into objects (e.g., toys, appliances, books, clothes and furniture) and also into everyday environments (e.g., airports, garages, malls, houses and offices), in both public and private spheres [7]. Furthermore, according to Sellen et.al. [20], this ecosystem has brought people together as citizens or members of global communities – changing the way we live with continually increasing digital presence in our lives.

This new scenario opens up a variety of possibilities for emerging services for digital television [18]. Some lines of research in iDTV are focused on technical, social and infrastructure-related issues involved in this medium, its context and its uses. Some authors consider the use of a second screen (e.g., smartphones and tablets) in the interaction with TV applications [12, 16] or a social sharing mode where the screen connects the viewer to the wider co-viewing audience [9]. Others suggest gestures [6] or voice [4] as new mechanisms of interaction with the TV that may replace the remote control. Viana et. al. [21], for example, suggest an extension of the set-top boxes functionality for service management of electronic devices in home networks.

Bannon [2] argues that instead of augmenting our choices and capabilities, the new devices may confuse and sometimes disable us. Thus, it is necessary to rethink the structure of our values; it is necessary to rethink the place of technology in our values frame, as well as how we live with and through technology, and also to give priority to human beings, their values, and their activities, tools and environments. For Sellen et. al. [20], it is necessary to incorporate truly human elements, and to conceptualize users as embodied individuals who have desires and concerns, and who belong to a social, economic and political ecology. Furthermore, there must be flexibility, since people's engagement with technology and the nature of their interactions with it change continuously. Some authors suggest bringing the end users and their viewpoints into the discussions on the projects in order to incorporate system features that go beyond technical issues, to identify conflicts, to understand impacts, and to shape the system to satisfy the audience [8, 18].

As for this scenario, this study sought to map out the main research sources that have been hosting the iDTV field in recent years in order to identify which emerging issues are being recognized in the field. This paper presents an analysis of words in the field, based on the content of the European Interactive TV Conference (EuroITV) and other publications on iDTV, which were found in the ACM Digital Library (ACM-DL). The discussion is based on the creation and analysis of tag clouds generated from titles of papers and their abstracts. The study sought to identify the main issues methods, devices, interactive features, etc. related to iDTV. Moreover, it explores information about conferences, journals, affiliations and countries where these papers were published. As a contribution, the paper reveals the individual characteristics of EuroITV and other publications found in the ACM-DL, the main focuses of research on iDTV, similarities and differences between sources. Finally, this analysis allows the identification of the main research focuses, especially regarding user experience issues, and offers ways of thinking that may help to promote future studies on the field.

The paper is organized as follows: the second section briefly presents the EuroITV conference and the ACM-DL; we also introduce related concepts and rationale for the use of tag clouds as data representation. The third section describes the method used for the data extraction. This data was, in turn, used to create the tag clouds and to conduct the analysis. The fourth section presents and discusses the findings. The last section presents the final considerations about the study and offers directions for future research.

2. STUDY CONTEXT

The ACM-DL represents the main repository of papers and proceedings of the EuroITV and other conferences in the area of iDTV, and it was the main source for this study. The proposed roadmap in the field of iDTV and related issues was drawn on with data from the EuroITV Conference series and the ACM-DL including conferences (e.g., Brazilian Symposium on Multimedia and the Web) and journals (e.g. Multimedia Tools and Applications and Computers in Entertainment) with tradition in the iDTV field, briefly described as follows:

The EuroITV began in 2003 in the city of Brighton in the UK, where it took place for another year. Since then, it has been held in many countries in Europe. It is held annually in countries such as Austria (2008), the Netherlands (2007), Greece (2006) and Denmark (2005). This study analyzes the conferences held in Belgium, Finland, Portugal and Germany between 2009 and 2012, respectively [7]. The conference is addressed to people who work "on different aspects of interactive television, e.g., IPTV, mobile TV, digital content production, entertainment computing, usability and user experience evaluation, changes in technical requirements and infrastructure, and future technologies." It aims to gather researchers and professionals from all over the world to "discuss the latest advances in media technology, human-computer interaction (HCI) systems and technology, media studies, personalization and recommender systems, intelligent user interfaces (IUI) and the content creation community" [10].

The ACM-DL is a comprehensive collection of full-text articles and bibliographic records that cover the fields of computing and information technology. The full-text database, with more than 2 million items, including journals, conference proceedings, magazines, newsletters, and multimedia titles. For each publication recorded there, one can search for abstracts, titles,

authors, conference proceedings, the article's number of accesses and citations, the article's year of publication, references, index terms, reviews, comments etc. One can also perform a refined search using keywords (e.g., defining the terms of the search), people (e.g., by name, institution, author, or reviewer), publications (e.g., year of publication, publication name) and conferences (e.g., by sponsor, event) [1].

2.1 Tag Cloud Representations and Tool

For an overview of the themes appearing in the analyzed conferences, we used tag cloud representation. A tag cloud is a visual representation of a set of words, typically tag words (labels). This term gained notoriety when it was used on social software websites such as "Del.icio.us®" or "Flickr®". Each word is highlighted within the cloud according to its frequency within the word set, and it is enhanced through the manipulation of visual features, such as font size, color, weight, etc. [3].

For Rivadeneira et. al. [19], this format is useful for quickly revealing the most prominent terms and relative importance of a specific word within the analyzed set. Depending on the context in which they are used, Rivadeneira et. al. [19] suggest four different tasks that can be supported by tag clouds: i) **Search:** to locate a specific term in a set. Often this term is a link for detailed information on the subject; ii) **Browsing:** as a means to browse. In this case, the user may not have a specific target, but s/he can access details if interested; iii) **Impression Formation or Gisting:** as a way of providing a basic idea about a subject. For this, it is important to highlight the dominant themes, but without omitting the terms of lowest frequency; and iv) **Recognition/Matching:** to recognize information through visual characteristics linked to each tag cloud generated, which creates a visual identity (e.g., one tag cloud for each different subject and with unique features that can easily be recognized).

In some specific cases, the tag clouds are less accurate and less efficient if compared to other visualization forms such as tables (e.g., to determine the presence or absence of a specific word) [15] or wordlists (e.g., to identify relationships among concepts) [13]. However, they are advantageous when capturing the essence, and they present a succinctly large amount of descriptive information, which improves user satisfaction [13]. The need for a summarized presentation of a large amount of data are some of the reasons we chose tag clouds as one of the resources in the analysis conducted in this study. For more accurate analyses, other representations were used as complements.

The tool used to create tag clouds in this study was Wordle [22]. The occurrence of each word in the source text is grouped together and the most recurrent words stand out more. The word proportionally reflects the number of times it appears in the input text, in the visualization. Some parameters defined for tag clouds creation are: i) **language:** to remove stop words (e.g., the, to, for, with) of the input text; ii) **maximum words:** maximum number of words to be shown in the tag cloud; iii) layout: defines rounder or straighter edges, word orientation (e.g., horizontal or vertical), font, color palette; and iv) **alphabetical order:** uses alphabetical order to show the words in the tag cloud.

The tool does not group ("stem") words. "Stemming" means understanding different words as variations of some root or stem (e.g., the words "walking", "walked" and "walks" are combined into a single representation of the word). Thus, if the user is not careful with stemming, similar words will be displayed separately, each one with one weight. As a final result, the word loses expressiveness within the group of words. One way to prevent similar words from appearing separately is to apply the Porter Stemming Algorithm [17] in the source text, which groups similar words by recurrence in a wordlist. The wordlist, with the weight (frequency) of words (as defined in advanced options), is used in advanced options to create tag clouds.

3. THE STUDY METHOD

Considering the fact that that the title of a text "indicates the general subject," and that the abstract "summarizes the essence of a publication" [14], we decided to perform an analysis based on information from titles and abstracts of papers. As additional analysis, we gathered information of which conferences, journals, magazines and newsletters host the papers, and which affiliations support them.

This method involved data collection and refinement, tag cloud generation, word quantification and comparison of sets. For this, the process was divided into four large blocks, as shown in Figure 1. In "Data Refinement", the goal was to gather information about existing publications from the data present in the ACM-DL. During the "Tag Clouds Analysis", the idea was to create tag clouds from the refined data and identifying differences and similarities between EuroITV and other research sources. The "Research Focus Mapping" stage was important for revealing the relationship among the wordlists created from the tag clouds. The "Overview Analysis" was important for finding out which research institutions are the most frequent, as well as which countries, journals and conferences were most frequent for a given area of study.

The initial step involved to use the Data Source (item 2 in Figure 1) of the ACM-DL portal (item 1 in Figure 1) to find out specific EuroITV publications and other publications related to iDTV. To find the EuroITV publications (item 3 in Figure 1), it was necessary to refine the search by "Events" in the "Refine your search by Conferences" field, and also to use "EuroITV" as a search term. We searched for proceedings of each year, and the conference papers collection was found from the "Table of Contents". In this study, publications between 2009 and 2012 were collected. To find other iDTV publications (item 4 in Figure 1), the search involved the publication period between 2009 and 2012, and it was refined by the "Interactive" and "Digital TV" keywords. The search was expanded to include "The ACM Guide to Computing Literature", where there are more than 2 million records of bibliographic citations from major publishers in the computing field. It includes the complete collection of ACM publications and an index for publications of other organizations affiliated with ACM (e.g., Evolutionary Computation, Journal of Usability Studies, Personal and Ubiquitous Computing and The International Journal on Very Large Data Bases). As a result, 434 items were found. They included the most important conferences, magazines and scientific journals, such as EuroITV, WebMedia, CHI, Computers & Education, and the Multimedia Tools and Applications, among others. For the sake of simplicity, in this paper, the other iDTV publications also are called just ACM-DL (e.g. tables and captions).

The searches resulted in two publication lists (item 5 in Figure 1) from which the relevant information (for this study) was manually extracted (item 6 in Figure 1). For the EuroITV publications (item 7 in Figure 1), it was possible to group the titles, abstracts, affiliations and affiliation location of the papers published in

conferences between 2009 and 2012. For the other iDTV publications (item 8 in Figure 1), in addition to the information grouped to EuroITV, the location and conference names related to the publications were identified. In the second case, an extra refinement of the results was necessary (item 9 in Figure 1) in order to remove EuroITV publications (64 items) and irrelevant information (e.g., proceedings names). The final data represents 347 papers used in this study. The removed data (87 items) was separated into another file for further analysis.

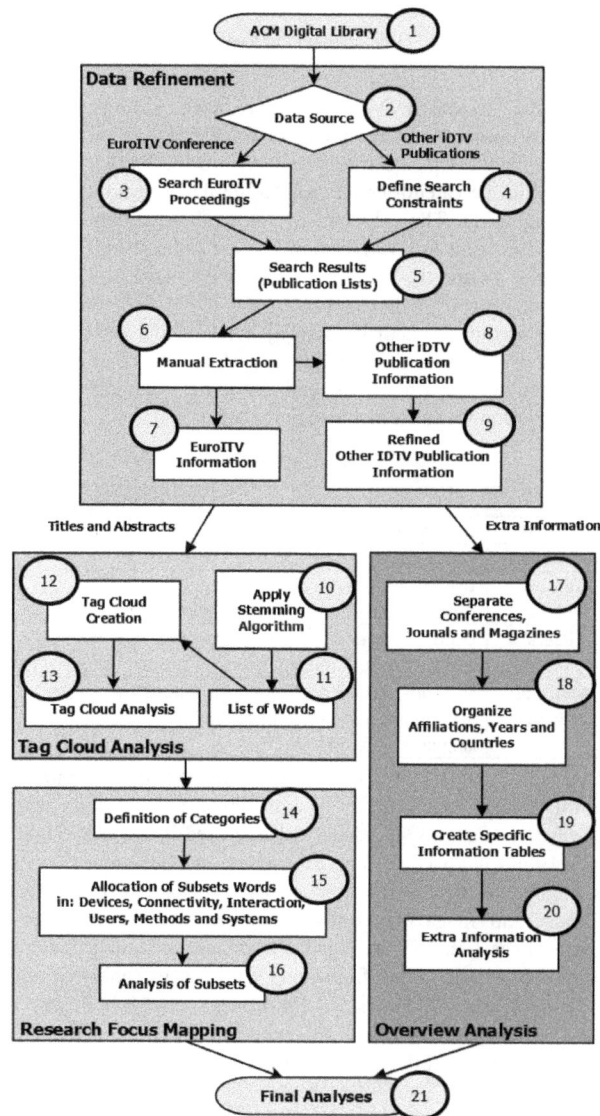

Figure 1. Steps in the Method.

The "Data Refinement" resulted in: i) the data ready for tag cloud generation, containing all titles and abstracts assigned to 2 files, one for EuroITV and the other for other iDTV publications; ii) a large table with extra information (e.g., affiliations, affiliation countries and publication year) for EuroITV publications; and iii) a large table with extra information for other iDTV publications (e.g., affiliations, published in, publication year and conference location).

The Porter Stemming Algorithm [17] (item 10 in Figure 1) was applied in order to generate wordlists with the weight of each word (item 11 in Figure 1). With the wordlists ready, tag clouds were created with Wordle [22] (item 12 in Figure 1), for each group of data (EuroITV and ACM-DL), from the titles and abstracts of publications. The advanced features were used for each data set: parameters such as language of text (defined as "English"), layout (defined as rounder edges and horizontal orientations), color (defined as black), alphabetical order (checked as true) and maximum words (defined as 100) were used in order to generate tag clouds suitable for further analysis. Different images created from EuroITV and other iDTV publications were then compared (item 13 in Figure 1). It was also possible to extract the list of the top 100 most recurring words in each tag cloud (item 11 in Figure 1).

During the "Research Focus Mapping" stage, to emphasize the highlights observed in the tag clouds, we seek for specific groups of words in the top 100 most recurring words. The words were allocated in the categories relevant to the iDTV ecosystem (item 15 in Figure 1). The initial categories and the criteria used to classify the words are described in Table 1 (item 14 in Figure 1). The categories and their definitions were extracted from relevant papers which reflect the focuses of the iDTV field on devices (such as second screens) [9, 12, 16], types of interaction [4, 6], connectivity [21], and users [8, 18]. After the first stage of classification, the "Methods and Systems" category seemed necessary, and was also included in the table.

Table 1. Classification Categories

Category	Definition
Devices	Devices for interaction.
Connectivity	Types of connection and data transmission.
Interaction	User interface and features, types of interaction, concepts and other man-machine relationships.
Users	Users, experiences, activities and behaviors, cultural, social, and work-related issues.
Methods and Systems	Methods, studies and other formal issues related to technology. Systems, applications protocols and languages related to iDTV.

"Overview Analysis" was performed using the two large data sets (EuroITV and other iDTV publications) created with extra information. For this, the data was organized into specific tables (item 19 in Figure 1), such as: **Journals and Magazines** (item 17 in Figure 1): which and how many publications come from journals and magazines (only for other iDTV publications); **Conferences** (item 17 in Figure 1): represents which and how many publications come from other conferences (only for other iDTV publications); **Years** and **Countries** (item 18 in Figure 1): how many papers were published per year and country (EuroITV and other iDTV publications); **Affiliations** (item 18 in Figure 1): which institutions most often host iDTV studies (EuroITV and other iDTV publications); and **Affiliations per Country** (item 18 in Figure 1): how many different institutions (determined by the papers' authors) and which countries these institutions are located in (EuroITV and other iDTV publications);

The extra information analysis (item 20 in Figure 1), along with the tag clouds created (item 12 in Figure 1) and the analysis of words classification in categories (item 16 in Figure 1) all support the discussions (item 21 in Figure 1) in the following sections.

4. SYNTHESIS OF RESULTS AND DISCUSSION

Based on the material produced during the "Data Refinement" stage and the information provided in the ACM-DL, it was possible to count the number of publications, the total number of words contained in all titles and abstracts for each group of papers. For EuroITV 161 papers with 23919 titles' and abstracts' words were analyzed. For ACM-DL 347 papers with 54555 words were analyzed. Altogether, more than 500 papers and more than 78,000 words were gathered. The tag clouds created and shown in Figures 2 and 3, were generated from valid words of the data collection. To emphasize the differences between the word sets, the more recurrent words, common to both sets, were omitted from the tag clouds shown in this paper. The omitted terms are "Interactive", "Digital", "Television" and "TV" (both the terms and their variants used in the search), and the word "paper" (which appears in most abstracts).

In a comparative analysis between the two images (Figures 2 and 3) it's possible to observe that:

- "User", "Content" and "Media" are the most frequent words in the EuroITV set, followed by "Services" and "Study".
- "System" and "Applications" are the most prominent words in the ACM-DL set, followed by "Services", "Video" and "User".
- "Content" and "User" appear frequently in ACM-DL, but with less emphasis than EuroITV. Inversely, the words "System" and "Application," appear with less emphasis in EuroITV than in ACM-DL.
- "Services" and "Technologies" appear at the same salient level in the two tag clouds, but "Services" appears with more frequency than "Technologies".
- "Video" appears at the same salient level in both sets of words. "Media" appears with more emphasis in the EuroITV set.
- "Study", "Results" and "Research" appear more frequently in the EuroITV set, while "Information" appears in ACM-DL more saliently.
- "Social" and "Experience" appear in EuroITV conferences more frequently than in the ACM-DL set.
- "Design" appears with more emphasis in the EuroITV set.
- Both conferences use the word "Mobile" with similar emphasis.
- "Network", "Model" and "Environment" are more salient in the ACM-DL set. The same result occurs with the words "Architecture", "Framework" and "Development".

In summary, Figures 2 and 3 suggest that the EuroITV set seems to put more emphasis in the user experience (e.g., "User" and "Experience"), as well on the applications design (e.g., "Design"), social issues (e.g., "Social"), media (e.g., "Media") and research (e.g., words "Study" and "Research"), while the ACM-DL set reveals more technological issues (represented by the words "System", "Application", "Technologies", "Network", "Architecture", "Framework" and "Development").

As for the results of the "Research Focus Mapping", Tables 2, 3 and 4 present the subsets of words created from the words found in tag clouds and classified in the categories defined in Table 1. The first set (Table 2) gathers the common words that appear in EuroITV and ACM-DL. The second and third sets refer to the words appearing exclusively in ACM-DL (Table 3) or EuroITV (Table 4), respectively. The last column of tables shows the number of words associated with each category, and the last row shows the unclassified words. The percentage was computed from the total number of words classified in the set.

Figure 2. EuroITV Tag cloud

Figure 3. ACM-DL Tag cloud

Table 2. Classification of Common Words

Category	Common Words	53 words
Devices	mobile, devices, control	5.66% (3)
Connectivity	network, web, iptv, internet, broadcasting	9.43% (5)
Interaction	interface, communication	3.77% (2)
Users	user, environment, people, experience, social, home, context, services, learning	16.98% (9)
Methods and Systems	development, standard, research, design, study, approach, architecture, model, analysis, system, applications, video, technologies, media, data, evaluation, platform	32.07% (17)
17 Unclassified words: present, based, used, proposed, different, results, concept, case, needs, important, allows, content, provide, order, support, information, work		

Table 3. Classification of ACM-DL Words

Category	ACM-DL Words	47 words
Devices	dtv, idtv	4.25% (2)
Connectivity	---	0.0% (0)
Interaction	selection, collaborative, personalized	6.38% (3)
Users	live, brazilian, knowledge	6.38% (3)
Methods and Systems	framework, method, techniques, computing, semantic, scheme, multimedia, program, ncl, 3d, image, declarative, performance, efficient, coding, language, processing	36.17% (17)
22 unclassified words: offer, become, create, possible, including, marketing, several, recommendation, specific, increasing, considered, generation, quality, solution, features, access, objects, management, integrated, multiple, resources, structure		

Table 2 shows that most of the 53 words in common are associated with "Methods and Systems" (17 words) followed by "User" (9 words). Table 3 refers to the words appearing exclusively in ACM-DL, and its shows that most of the words are also associated with "Methods and Systems". Table 4 refers to the words appearing exclusively in EuroITV publications. We observe that most of the words are distributed in similar proportion across the "Interaction", "Users", and "Methods and Systems" categories, followed by the "Devices" category. Words associated with "Connectivity" category appears only in Table 2.

Table 4. Classification of EuroITV Words

Category	EuroITV Words	47 words
Devices	screen, itv, 3dtv, remote	8.51% (4)
Connectivity	---	0.0% (0)
Interaction	feedback, watching, viewing, usage, share, living	12.76% (6)
Users	viewers, participants, role, audience, consumer	10.63% (5)
Methods and Systems	process, methods, production, integration, project, practices	12.76% (6)
26 unclassified words: related, creating, future, adoption, describe, factors, enables, number, potential, explore, changes, conducted, current, main, shows, insights, towards, advertising, consumption, interest, market, convergence, field, problems, issues, discuss		

A comparison of Tables 2, 3 and 4, with 50% of the top 100 most recurring words in common suggests that the research corpora of EuroITV and ACM-DL are aligned, and most of them involve technical issues (see Table 2). However, EuroITV has slightly more words related to "Interaction", "Users", and "Devices" individually (see Table 4), while ACM-DL has more "Methods and Systems" words (see Table 3). In addition, there is a low frequency of words regarding concepts related to "Devices". "Mobile" and "Screen" are the main words related to this category. Words such as "Tablet" and "Smartphones", which are important mobile devices used as second screens, do not appear among the most frequent words. The same results occurred when concepts related to "Interaction" were analyzed. Among the 100 most frequent words, there were no words such as "Gestures" or "Voice", and only a few references to passive types of interaction were found (e.g., "Watching" and "Viewing"). In the "Connectivity" category, few words were found (e.g., "Network" and "Internet") overlap between the two groups of data. Words

293

Table 6. Publications per Conference

Abbreviation	Conference Name	Percentage
WebMedia	Brazilian Symposium on Multimedia and the Web	14.14% (27)
SAC	ACM symposium on Applied Computing	5.76% (11)
DocEng	ACM symposium on Document engineering	4.19% (8)
IHC	Symposium on Human Factors in Computing Systems	2.62% (5)
MoMM	7th International Conference on Advances in Mobile Computing and Multimedia	2.62% (5)
CCNC	IEEE Conference on Consumer Communications and Networking Conference	2.09% (4)
UAHCI	International Conference on Universal Access in Human-Computer Interaction	2.09% (4)
	Other 107 Conferences	66.49% (127)
* 114 Different Conferences ****91 (over 79%) with only one publication**		Total: 191 publications

related to "Users" are a bit more frequent in the set of words (e.g., "Experience" and "Social"). Most of the words that appeared in the tag clouds are related to "Methods and Systems". These include "Design", "Architecture", "Applications", and "Data".

All categories were analyzed, and the findings show that most words are directly related to technical issues ("System and Methods"). "User" is the second most frequently considered category, but its emphasis is much less significant. Words related to the "Interaction" category are few in number, especially those related to new ways for users to interact more actively. The "Connectivity" category also is only slightly emphasized. The same scenario happens in the case of the "Devices" category, in which the word "Mobile" is the most frequently used in research from the iDTV field.

As a result of the "Overview Analyses", tables (5, 6, 7, 8, 9, 10 and 11) were created to organize the information. In the tables whenever the relative frequency is displayed, the number of occurrences of this information appears next in parentheses.

Table 5. Publication Frequency per Journals

Publication	Percentage
Multimedia Tools and Applications	19.48% (30)
Computers in Entertainment (CIE) (Magazine)	7.14% (11)
Expert Systems with Applications: An International Journal	5.19% (8)
Pattern Recognition	3.90% (6)
Telecommunications Policy	3.90% (6)
Telematics and Informatics	3.25% (5)
Computer Standards & Interfaces	2.60% (4)
International Journal of Advanced Media and Communication	2. 60% (4)
Other 62 Journals, Magazines and Newsletters	51.95% (80)
* 70 different Journals, Magazines and Newsletters ****47 (over 67%) with only one publication**	Total :154 Publications

Table 5 shows the frequency of other iDTV papers published in journals, magazines and newsletters. Here, we also found 2 books, which were not included in Table 5. Most publications were found in the "Multimedia Tools and Applications" journal (over 19%), followed by the "Computers in Entertainment" magazine (over 7%). We found less of 10 papers in each one of other journals. Altogether 70 different journals, magazines and

newsletters were found that addressed the issue of iDTV. Most of them (over 67%) have only one publication. The total number of publications (154) was used to calculate the frequency of the publications for each journal.

Table 6 shows the list of papers per conference that were published between the years 2009 and 2012. Most articles (27 papers, resulting in over 14%) were found on "Brazilian Symposium on Multimedia and the Web" (Webmedia) followed by the "ACM symposium on Applied Computing" (over 5%) and the "ACM symposium on Document engineering" (over 4%). In many of the conferences (over 79%), only one publication regarding iDTV was found. This shows that, apart from EuroITV, there are no conferences with exclusive focus on the subject.

Table 7 shows which institutions are more present in EuroITV or in other iDTV publications. In EuroITV, the "Ghent University (Belgium)" participated of 13 articles (over 8%) among 161 articles published between 2009 and 2012, followed by "University of Salzburg (Austria)" (9 papers) and "Vrije Universiteit Brussel (Belgium)" (8). For other iDTV publications, the "University of São Paulo (Brazil)" (21) published more papers, followed by the "Pontifical Catholic University of Rio de Janeiro (Brazil)" (16) and "University of Vigo (Spain)" (15).

Table 8. Number of iDTV Research Institutions per Country

EuroITV		ACM-DL	
Country	Percentage	Country	Percentage
Germany	9.66% (14)	Brazil	13.74% (47)
The Netherlands	9.66% (14)	Spain	8.19% (28)
United Kingdom	8.97% (13)	China	8.19% (28)
Belgium	6.21% (9)	USA	7.89% (27)
USA	6.21% (9)	United Kingdom	6.14% (21)
*29 Different Countries	Total: 145 Institutions	* 44 Different Countries	Total: 342 Institutions

Table 8 shows the number of research institutes per country that are hosting EuroITV and other iDTV publications. These research institutes were mapped out within the home country. In the case of EuroITV (at left in the table), the countries with the majority of research institutes are Germany and the Netherlands (14 that represent over 9% of 145 institutions that published in EuroITV), followed by United Kingdom (13), and then Belgium and USA

Table 7. Publication Frequency per Institution

EuroITV		ACM-DL	
Affiliation Name / Country	Percentage	Affiliation Name / Country	Percentage
Ghent University (Belgium)	8.07% (13)	University of São Paulo (Brazil)	6.05% (21)
University of Salzburg (Austria)	5.59% (9)	Pontifical Catholic University of Rio de Janeiro (Brazil)	4.61% (16)
Vrije Universiteit Brussel (Belgium)	4.97% (8)	University of Vigo(Spain)	4.32% (15)
University of Siegen (Germany)	4.35% (7)	Federal University of São Carlos(Brazil)	4.03% (14)
Federal University of Amazonas (Brazil)	3.11% (5)	Ghent University(Belgium)	2.88% (10)
*145 Different Institutions	Total: 161 publications	* 342 Different Institutions	Total: 347 publications

(9). For other iDTV publications, the country with more research institutes is Brazil (47 in 342), followed by Spain and China (28), and then USA (27).

Table 9 shows the frequency of publications per year of EuroITV conferences and other iDTV publications. The number of publications has not increased in recent years. This includes data from EuroITV, which is the main conference in the iDTV field.

Table 9. Frequency of Publication per Year

	EuroITV	ACM-DL
2009	22.4% (36)	35.5% (123)
2010	32.3% (52)	23.05% (80)
2011	24.8% (40)	21.6% (75)
2012	20.5% (33)	19.9% (69)
	Total: 161	Total: 347

Table 10 shows the number of EuroITV (left) and ACM-DL (right) for each country which publications genuinely are located in, respectively. It is important to note that in the ACM-DL portal, not all publications have affiliations or affiliation countries. For some of them, this information was found through additional searches (e.g., looking for other publications by same author in the ACM-DL, university websites, etc.). However, not all of them could be found and computed. In the case of EuroITV, all of them were found. The total number of publications was used to calculate the frequency of the publications for each country.

Table 10. Frequency of EuroITV and ACM-DL per Country

EuroITV		ACM-DL	
Country	Percentage	Country	Percentage
Belgium	15.53% (25)	Brazil	26.30% (91)
Brazil	8.70% (14)	Spain	10.98% (38)
Germany	8.07% (13)	USA	5.49% (19)
USA	8.07% (13)	China	4.34% (15)
Portugal / The Netherlands	5.59% (9)	Taiwan	4.05 % (14)
Other 19 Countries	33.54% (54)	Other 33 Countries	37.17% (129)
Joint	14.91% (24)	Joint	9.54% (33)
Info Not Found	0.00% (0)	Info Not Found	2.02% (7)
* 29 Different Countries	Total: 161 publications	* 44 Different Countries	Total: 347 publications

As shown in Table 10, the country that most published in EuroITV conferences between 2009 and 2012 was Belgium (over 15% of publications). With more than 8% are Brazil, Germany and USA, and with more than 5% are the Netherlands and also Portugal. The other countries (that published alone) represent more than 33% of the publications. Joint publications (with more than one country involved) represent over 14%. For other iDTV publications, Brazil has over 26% of the publications. Spain is in second with more than 10%. Between 4% and 6% are USA (over 5%), China (over 4%) and Taiwan (over 4%).

Analyzing Tables 7, 8 and 10, Brazil stands out for its number of researcher institutions and publications. This can be explained by the fact that, since the beginning of iDTV implantation in Brazil in 2007, researchers and normatization institutions, private companies and government alike are in an intense definition process for the Brazilian standard to attend the economic, social and geographic characteristics of a country as large and unequal as Brazil [11].

All countries found in the analysis are marked with flags in Figure 4. The blue flags represent the countries that published in EuroITV in recent years. Red flags represent the countries that

published in other conferences or journals in the area. The countries involved in iDTV research is mainly concentrated in Europe, as Figure 4 illustrates. All together, 48 different countries were identified in the both groups of publications.

Figure 4. Affiliation Countries that Published on iDTV

Finally, Table 11 shows the frequency of publications for each continent. Europe has more publications in the iDTV area in both EuroITV (over 65%) and other iDTV publications (over 38%). America is the second largest source of research publications in both groups. In this case, Brazil has most of the publications. In third place, Asia publishes more in both groups. In Australia and Africa, the number of publications is very small. The scenario represented by Table 11 can also be seen in Figure 4, where most of the countries that publish on iDTV are located in the European region.

Table 11. Frequency of Publication per Continent

Continent	EuroITV	ACM-DL
Europe	65.22% (105)	38.9% (135)
America	16.77%(27)	32.56% (113)
Asia	2.48% (4)	15.56% (54)
Oceania	0.62% (1)	0.86% (3)
Africa	0.00% (0)	0.29% (1)
Joint	14.91% (24)	9.80% (34)
Info Not found	0.00% (0)	2.02% (7)
	Total: 161 publications	Total: 347 publications

5. CONCLUSION

The new devices incorporated into the modern world are changing the way we interact and communicate. iDTV can be considered an emerging technology into an ecosystem of media which has not yet been explored to its full potential. Getting an overview of the main issues that have been addressed in recent years in the field is a way to identify lacking issues and research opportunities. Thus, this paper sheds light on the main focuses of research addressed by EuroITV and other iDTV publications from the ACM-DL, and these focuses are reflected in words from the contribution titles and abstracts.

Among the highlights, the results suggest that EuroITV and other vehicles addressing iDTV issues have over 50% of their most recurrent words in common, and this result suggests similarity in research focus; nevertheless, EuroITV reveals a unique focus on human issues, and addresses words such as design, user experience and social more than the other vehicles taken together.

ACM-DL reveals more about application development, systems, network, framework and architecture. The analysis also suggest that research categories more related to the user experience and new interaction modes, quoted by authors such as [4, 6, 8, 9, 12, 16, 18, 21], are still being modestly discussed in iDTV publications. It was still possible to identify that most of the terms in the data involve systems and methodological issues.

To illustrate some gaps identified in this study, future studies could consider the TV within a digital and social ecosystem. For instance, research could look into new devices that can be used collaboratively with the TV (second screens), connectivity services (connecting the TV with several media remotely), users (who may be in a wider context than that of the TV room), types of interaction (natural, intuitive, and for all). This research suggests opportunities for studies bringing more studies on the human- and device-related issues to the iDTV field.

Additional analyses reveal that many iDTV studies that were affiliated with Brazilian institutions have appeared in recent years. This scenario may be a result of the TV digitalization processes that started in 2007, and the social demands of the Brazilian context [11].

In a further study, we intend to explore the "interaction" aspects of iDTV concepts to bring subjects such as user motivation and affective aspects to the design of situated iDTV applications.

6. ACKNOWLEDGMENTS

This research is partially funded by CNPq (#142113/2013-1).

7. REFERENCES

[1] ACM-DL, 2013. ACM Digital Library. Retrieved on Jan 5, 2013, from http://dl.acm.org.

[2] Bannon, L. 2011. Reimagining HCI: Toward a More Human-Centered Perspective. *Interactions*, Vol. 18, Issue 4, 50-57.

[3] Bateman, S., Gutwin, C., Nacenta, M. 2008. Seeing things in the clouds: the effect of visual features on tag cloud selections. In *Proceedings of the 19th ACM Conference on Hypertext and Hypermedia* (Pittsburgh, USA, June 19-21, 2008). HT'08. ACM Press, New York, NY, 193-202.

[4] Berglund, A. and Johansson, P. 2004. Using speech and dialogue for interactive TV navigation. *Universal Access in Information Society* 3 (3-4), 224–238

[5] Bernhaupt, R., Weiss, A., Pirker, M. Wilfinger, D., Tscheligi, T. 2010. Ethnographic Insights on Security, Privacy, and Personalization Aspects of User Interaction in Interactive TV. In: *Proceedings of the 8th international interactive conference on Interactive TV and Video* (Tampere, Finland, June 9-11, 2010). EuroiTV'10. ACM Press, New York, NY, 187-196.

[6] Bobeth, J., Schmehl, S., Kruijff, E., Deutsch, S., Tscheligi, M. Evaluating performance and acceptance of older adults using freehand gestures for TV menu control. In: *Proceedings of the 10th European conference on Interactive tv and video* (Berlin, Germany, July 4-6, 2012). EuroiTV'12. ACM Press, New York, NY, 35-44

[7] Bødker, S. 2006. When second wave HCI meets third wave challenges. In *Proceedings of the 4th Nordic Conference on Human-computer Interaction: Changing Roles* (Oslo, Norway, October 14-18, 2006). NordiCHI'06. ACM Press, New York, NY, 1-8.

[8] Cesar, P., Chorianopoulos, K., Jensen, J. F. 2008. Social Television and User Interaction, *Computers in Entertainment (CIE) - Social television and user interaction*, Vol.6, No.1, 1-10.

[9] Doughty, M., Rowland, D., Lawson, S. 2012. Who is on your sofa?: TV audience communities and second screening social networks. In: *Proceedings of the 10th European conference on Interactive tv and video* (Berlin, Germany, July 4-6, 2012). EuroiTV'12. ACM Press, New York, NY, 79-86.

[10] EuroITV, 2013. European Interactive TV Conference. Retrieved on Jan 10, 2013, http://www.euro-itv.org.

[11] Fernandes, J., Lemos, G., Elias, G. Introdução à Televisão Digital Interativa: Arquitetura, Protocolos, Padrões e Práticas. In: *Jornada de Atualização em Informática do Congresso da Sociedade Brasileira de Computação* (Salvador, BA, August 2004), JAI-SBC'04. 1-56,

[12] Fonseca, J., Ferraz, C. 2012. Shared-TV: a framework to develop converged TV-centric applications. In: *Proceedings of the 18th Brazilian symposium on Multimedia and the web* (São Paulo, Brazil, October 15-18, 2012). WebMedia'12. ACM Press, New York, NY, 111-114.

[13] Kuo, B. Y.-L., Hentrich., T., Good., B. M., Wilkinson., M. D. 2007. Tag clouds for summarizing web search results. In *Proceedings of the 16th International Conference on World Wide Web* (Banff, Alberta, Canada, May 8-12, 2007). WWW'07. ACM Press, New York, NY, 1203-1204.

[14] Merriam-Webster, 2013. Retrieved on Jan 20, 2013, from http://www.merriam-webster.com.

[15] Oosterman, J., Cockburn, A. 2010. An Empirical Comparison of Tag Clouds and Tables. In *Proceedings of the 22nd Conference of the Computer-Human Interaction Special Interest Group of Australia on Computer-Human Interaction* (Brisbane, Australia, November 22-26, 2010). OZCHI'10. ACM Press, New York, NY, 288-295.

[16] Pedrosa, C., Martins, J. A. C. Jr, Melo E. L., Teixeira, C. A. C. 2012. A multimodal interaction component for digital television. In Proceedings of the 2011 ACM Symposium on Applied Computing (Taichung, Taiwan, March 21-24, 2011), SAC '11. ACM Press, New York, NY, 1253-1258.

[17] Porter, M.F. 1980. An algorithm for suffix stripping. *Program*, Vol. 14, No. 3, 130-137.

[18] Rice, M., Alm, N. 2008. Designing new interfaces for digital interactive television usable by older adults. In *Computers in Entertainment (CIE) - Social television and user interaction*, Vol. 6, No. 1, Article 6, 1-20.

[19] Rivadeneira, A. W., Gruen D. M., Muller, M. J., Millen D. R. 2007. Getting our head in the clouds: toward evaluation studies of tagclouds, In *Proceeding of the SIGCHI Conference on Human Factors in Computing Systems* (San Jose, California, USA, April 28-May 3, 2007). CHI'07. ACM Press, New York, NY, 995-998.

[20] Sellen, A., Rogers, Y., Harper, R., Rodden, T. 2009. Reflecting Human Values in the Digital Age, *Communications*, ACM 52, Issue 3, 58-66.

[21] Viana, N. S., Maia, O. B., Lucena V. F. Jr. 2009. Convergence model between the IDTV Brazilian middleware and home networking software platforms. In *Proceedings of the XV Brazilian Symposium on Multimedia and the Web.* (Fortaleza, Ceará, Brazil, October 5-7, 2009). WebMedia'09. ACM Press, New York, NY, Article No. 7

[22] Wordle, 2013. Wordle tool. Retrieved on Jan 5, 2013, from http://www.wordle.net.

Reducing the Complexity of NCL Player Implementations

Guilherme A. F. Lima   Luiz Fernando G. Soares   Roberto G. A. Azevedo   Marcio F. Moreno

Department of Informatics
PUC-Rio, Rio de Janeiro, Brazil
{glima,lfgs,razevedo,mfmoreno}@inf.puc-rio.br

ABSTRACT

In this paper, we present an approach for reducing the complexity of NCL player implementations. This approach consists, basically, in introducing in the player's architecture an initial conversion step that removes all syntactic sugar and reuse features from the source language. The output of this step, a redundancy-free version of the original input, is then fed to the player that interprets it and creates a corresponding multimedia presentation. In particular, we propose the use of the NCL Raw profile as this intermediate language. The Raw profile is an (almost) redundancy-free profile that is compatible with the NCL 3.0 EDTV (Enhanced Digital TV) profile, a property that guarantees a seamless integration with current EDTV profile implementations. The main targets of the proposed approach are NCL players running on HTML browsers. We discuss how the solutions presented by NCL4Web, WebNCL, and Ginga Plug-in can be tuned to overcome some problems pointed their authors. The same problems arise in similar contexts for other declarative languages, e.g., SMIL, and the solutions presented here can also be extended to those systems.

Categories and Subject Descriptors: I.7.2 [Document Preparation]: Hypertext/hypermedia, Language and systems, Standards

General Terms: Algorithms, Languages, Standardization

Keywords: NCL Raw profile; NCL players; web-based players

1. INTRODUCTION

Authoring hypermedia applications using imperative languages like Java, C, and C++, or scripting languages like JavaScript is usually more complex and error-prone than using declarative, domain-specific languages such as NCL [2, 8] or SMIL [4]. Declarative descriptions are generally easier to be devised and understood than imperative ones, which usually require programming expertise. The declarative approach also has advantages from an engineering point of view: It makes easier to maintain and reuse content, as opposed to the purely imperative approach. So is the case of NCL (Nested Context Language).

NCL is a declarative language for the specification of interactive multimedia presentations. NCL has a strict separation between application content and application structure. The language does not define any media itself; instead, it defines the glue that relates media objects in time and space, during multimedia presentations. The language flexibility, its reuse facility, multi-device support, presentation adaptability, API for building and modifying applications on-the-fly, and mainly, its ability for easily defining the spatial and temporal synchronization of media objects (including viewer interactions) make it an adequate solution for different multimedia application domains. For particular procedural needs, e.g., when complex, dynamic content generation is needed, NCL provides support for the use of imperative scripts written in Lua [7], a fast and lightweight scripting language.

NCL has been primarily used for developing interactive multimedia applications in digital TV (DTV) domain. Indeed, NCL is the ITU-T declarative language recommendation for IPTV services [8] and the declarative language of the Brazilian ISDB-T terrestrial DTV standard [2]. Since other DTV standards use HTML-based languages as their declarative support, in 2011, the ITU-T started a liaison process to harmonize the NCL and HTML-based approaches. On the one hand, NCL is a glue language that does not restrict nor prescribe media-object type, so it can embed HTML applications naturally as one of its media objects. (This feature is natively supported in both the ISDB-T standard and the ITU-T H.761 recommendation.) On the other hand, embedding NCL into an HTML-based DTV middleware is also possible and has been done, e.g., in the HbbTV [12] proprietary platforms. However, a platform independent solution is still missing.

NCL has also been available for publishing multimedia applications on the Web, but the lack of widely deployed tools has limited its impact. Trying to fill this gap, our group developed a browser plug-in, the Ginga Plug-in [13], for the Firefox and Chrome Web browsers, which contains the player of the reference implementation of Ginga-NCL. More recently, with the advance of HTML5 [3] and, in particular, of its graphic, audio, and video support, it became possible to develop standard-based applications that run natively in Web browsers. NCL4Web [14] and WebNCL [11] follow this approach.

However, the aforementioned solutions for embedding NCL into HTML pages (Ginga Plug-in, NCL4Web, and WebNCL) have persisted in the same shortcoming: They try to embed a player for the EDTV (Enhanced DTV) profile of NCL. The NCL EDTV profile has redundant constructs, which can be removed, giving rise to a simplified profile, called the NCL Raw profile. A player for the NCL Raw profile is easier to be designed and implemented than a player for the NCL EDTV profile. Moreover, such a player might implement a well-defined API for media objects, including media objects with HTML code and media objects with embedded NCL code (i.e., nested NCL applications), which allows for embedding more than one NCL into an HTML page, as NCL4Web and WebNCL do, and also makes possible to relate both the HTML host application and the embedded NCL application—similar to the solution adopted by Ginga Plug-in.

In this paper, we discuss how the solutions presented by NCL4-Web, WebNCL, and Ginga Plug-in can be tuned to overcome some problems pointed their authors. The same problems arise in similar contexts for other declarative languages, e.g., SMIL, and the solutions presented here can also be extended to those systems.

The rest of the paper is organized as follows. Section 2 discusses how a foreign language player can be embedded into an HTML browser, since this is the target engine we discuss in this paper. Section 3 presents some related work. Section 4 introduces the NCL Raw profile. Section 5 discusses the conversion of EDTV profile constructs into equivalent Raw profile constructs, and presents the approach we propose for embedding NCL players into HTML browsers. Finally, Section 6 concludes the paper.

2. RUNNING FOREIGN LANGUAGE APPLICATIONS IN HTML BROWSERS

There are at least three usual approaches to run a foreign language application in an HTML browser.

1. Use a browser plug-in containing the foreign language player.
2. Implement the foreign language player in JavaScript.
3. Use XSLT[1] to translate the foreign language application into an equivalent application in HTML+CSS+JavaScript.

The main disadvantage of approach (1) is that it is platform dependent. Nevertheless, plug-ins usually have a better performance and this can make a difference, especially when the presentation of several media objects must be synchronized in time and space. Ginga Plug-in [13] and SMIL State [9] together with the Ambulant SMIL Player[2] are examples of this approach, as discussed in Section 3.

In approach (2), there are, basically, two possibilities: (i) use the HTML browser media players to exhibit the media content of the foreign language application; or (ii) implement custom media players in JavaScript using its Canvas API. At least with the current state of HTML5 canvas API, the first variant seems to be more feasible. In this variant, the foreign language application entities are converted into HTML entities and a JavaScript library controls the multimedia presentation. The conversion to HTML can be done in its entirety before the starting of the application, or it can be done incrementally, during the presentation of the application. This is the approach followed by SmilingWeb [6] and WebNCL [11].

In approach (3), the foreign language application is converted into an equivalent HTML+CSS+JavaScript application. Since most HTML browsers support XSLT, this solution may be considered platform independent, like approach (2). Furthermore, in this variant we can explore the possibility of having the conversion done in server side, and not only in the client side. Indeed, if the conversion is done in the server side there is no need to be attained to an XSLT converter to be platform independent; one could use any language, which then is converted to HTML+JavaScript+CSS. NCL4Web [14] follows this approach, realizing the conversion at the client side, i.e., by the HTML browser via XSLT.

3. RELATED WORK

SMIL State [9] combines the SMIL [4] language with an external data model, specified in the XForms[3] declarative language, allowing for this data model to be shared with other components and, effectively, enabling its use as an API between components of an application. In particular, the data model is proposed as the way SMIL can communicate with its plug-ins and how SMIL can be embedded in another host player as a plug-in. The use of the shared data model as the communication paradigm between components decouples dependencies between these components: they only depend on a common understanding of the data model. The external data model allows for communication through setting values to variables by one side that can cause some action on the other communication side. This language bridge works fine from the SMIL side. The problem is on the other side of the bridge: As only SMIL State and XForms currently share the proposed data model, the integration into other languages requires some glue code. Following this direction, SMIL State [9] was implemented in the open-source Ambulant SMIL player plug-in for WebKit browsers. In the prototype, the glue is implemented with JavaScript code, which is triggered by DOM events when the data model changes.

A slightly different approach is used by Ginga Plug-in [13]. It defines an API that enables the host system (the HTML browser) to execute a series of actions, including those for controlling the plug-in life-cycle, e.g., `pause`, `resume`, or `abort` actions. The same API is used to answer to commands coming from the host system and to internal events, that occur during the plug-in execution. Unlike SMIL State, the reported events are not limited to those resulting from the attribution of variables. The NCL player API, part of the general API defined by the Ginga Plug-in, is inherited by the approach proposed in Section 5.

Timesheet.js [5] is an open-source library that supports the common subset of the SMIL Timing[4] and SMIL Timesheets [15] styling specifications. The approach uses HTML5+CSS3 for structuring and styling the multimedia content. Inline SMIL Timing elements can be inserted in the HTML document to handle timing, media synchronization, and user interaction. SMIL time constructs can also be inserted via an external timesheet. Timesheet.js, however, does not translate the entire SMIL language; it translates only its timing functionality, so it can be used on the Web. Moreover, in Timesheet.js, the SMIL time containers expose a significant part of the *HTMLMediaElement* API, which enables JavaScript code to control the SMIL time containers via the usual `play` and `pause` methods, check the current time via `currentTime` property, and receive `timeupdate` DOM events. As a consequence, a SMIL time container can be related to any other HTML5 element or other embedded SMIL time containers. This feature is also supported by Ginga Plug-in.

SimilingWeb [6] is a SMIL player that runs on any Web browser that supports HTML5. It uses a JavaScript library to control the presentation of the application. The current version of the player does not support all SMIL tags.

WebNCL [11] takes the same direction of SmilingWeb, in this case, however, to embed an NCL player into HTML5 browsers. In WebNCL, the NCL parser component translates the NCL document into the *NCL Representation Model*, an internal data structure that represents the NCL elements, e.g., link, media, connector, etc. The *NCL Player Manager* component controls the creation and destruction of HTML elements corresponding to the NCL specification and keeps track of the active media players, i.e., the media players

---

[1]http://www.w3.org/TR/xslt
[2]http://www.ambulantplayer.org/

[3]http://www.w3.org/MarkUp/Forms/
[4]http://www.w3.org/TR/SMIL3/smil-timing.html

Table 1. Characteristics of the embedment approaches.

	SMIL State	Ginga Plug-in	Timesheet.js	SmilingWeb	WebNCL	NCL4Web
Source language	SMIL	NCL	SMIL (Timing)	SMIL	NCL	NCL
Embedment approach	plug-in	plug-in	inline	JavaScript compilation	JavaScript incremental compilation	XSLT compilation
Supports all features of the language	Yes	Yes	No	No	No	No
Can embed more than one player	Yes	Yes	Yes	?	Yes	No
Defines a control/notification API	Yes	Yes	Yes	No	Partially	Partially
Uses the media players of the browser	No	No	Yes	Yes	Yes	Yes

controlled by the browser. The HTML5 elements corresponding to the NCL elements in the representation model are created incrementally (on demand) by the WebNCL player.

Melo et al. [11] argue that, in an NCL presentation, computer power is required more to media presentation than to media orchestration. Since the HTML browser is responsible for media presentation, and since browsers are usually implemented in native language, the performance difference between WebNCL and a native-code NCL player plugin would be irrelevant. This argument must be pondered considering synchronization issues in low-end platforms, like those found in DTV receivers. Nevertheless, WebNCL is certainly an adequate solution for high-end receivers.

NCL4Web [14], unlike WebNCL, transforms all NCL code into HTML+CSS+JavaScript before the whole presentation starts. A JavaScript file, called "ncl-complements.js," is inserted in the translated document; this file contains common function used by every translated NCL document, and manages user interactions. Instead of using JavaScript, the translation is done using an XSLT stylesheet. NCL4Web supports more NCL tags than WebNCL, e.g., switches and rules. Although NCL4Web proponents only explore client side conversion, the translation could also be realized in server side. This would allow for using the approach in Web browsers that do not support XSLT, e.g., some Android browsers.

More than one WebNCL presentation machine can be embedded in the same HTML page. NCL4Web was designed for presenting a standalone NCL application, but it can embedded in a Web page through using the HTML <iframe> element. However, in both solutions, an API for relating the embedded NCL applications was only partially defined. Both solutions rely on DOM events to report events coming from NCL presentations, although WebNCL also provides an API to post events to NCL entities.

The related works presented in this section rely on a language player engine embedded in HTML browsers that can be either implemented in some platform dependent language, which is the case of the plug-in approaches, or implemented in JavaScript. With the exception of Timesheet.js, which is intended for incorporating into HTML5 only the timing functionality of SMIL, all works aim at playing its source hypermedia language embedded in HTML. Moreover, these works try to convert a language profile that was conceived to help application authors, and thus is full of syntactic sugar and reuse features. This is one of the reasons why, except in the case of plug-ins, none of the players was able to contemplate the full expressiveness of its source language. Table 1 goes over the main points of these approaches.

In this paper, we argue that even in the case of plug-ins, the syntactic sugar and reuse features of the target language should be removed in an initial conversion step, before any of the solutions take place. Moreover, we also advocate the use of the Ginga Plug-in API by presentation engines targeting NCL. The next sections discuss the advantages of the proposed approach.

4. NCL RAW PROFILE

The authoring and presentation of hypermedia documents can be considered as the answer to four general questions: what to present, where, how, and when. To help authors in answering these four questions, several hypermedia specification languages have been proposed, like HTML, NCL, SMIL, etc. All these languages define much more than the needed entities to answer the questions, trying to help authors to logically structure the document specification, to choose between content alternatives, etc. All these languages also have reuse features and syntactic sugar add-ons to easy even more the authoring process.

However, language players should use data models as close as possible to the presentation engine's execution platform, to make a better use of the platform resources and to achieve an efficient and reliable implementation.

The different goals of the specification language data model and the player data model make them semantically distant. As a consequence, the process of converting one into another, during document presentation, can be complex and error-prone.

The solution usually adopted by language players, including all related work discussed in Section 3, is to sacrifice the presentation engine conception, obliging it to perform using a high-level data model. This alternative, although possible, especially in high performance platforms can lead to implementations that are more prone to efficiency and reliability problems due to code with redundant logic in the interpreter program.

An alternative for this approach come from identifying and defining procedures for redundancy removal in hypermedia specification languages. In doing this, we are, at the same time, giving a precise semantics for redundant elements and identifying which parts of our interpreter's code are likely to contain duplicated logic.

On the semantics side, we gain by trimming our specification. Each redundancy removal procedure functions as a precise definition for the removed element. Thus, given these procedures, we get a complete specification by just defining the behavior of the primitive elements. This approach also helps in formalizing, debugging, and maintaining the specification, because it keeps primitive behavior clearly separated from derived behavior. Here we consider primitive those concepts that are kept (they should be as minimum as possible) in the original conceptual model; and we consider derived the redundant concepts, identified by the removal procedures.

On the presentation engine side, the separation between what is primitive form what is derived induces, in terms of program logic, a similar separation between what should be compiled, or converted, from what should be interpreted.

In other words, the solution can come from introducing an intermediate conceptual data model. The problem is then moved to correctly choose this new data model to have both a translation process from the authoring data model to this intermediate data model, and another translation process, as a second step, towards a presentation data model simple enough that makes the implementation of converters and presentation engines simpler.

This intermediate conceptual data model can define an abstract syntax notation to which an authoring language can be compiled and from which the engine presentation model can be extracted. The intermediate syntax notation must have at least the same expressiveness of the authoring language. Ideally, it could have the expressiveness of different target authoring languages, allowing for application written in these different languages to share the common intermediate abstract syntax notation and thus share the same application player.

The first step in this direction was the definition of the NCL Raw profile [10]. The NCL Raw profile has been designed to allow simple converters for the NCL 3.0 EDTV profile and to allow a simpler Ginga-NCL implementation. It should be stressed that the profile goal is not the authoring process but to act as an intermediate language withing the conversion process.

The definition of the NCL Raw profile allows for its use not only in the client side, but also as the basis of a new transfer syntax. In this case, the conversion process could be done in the server side. This approach has some advantages. First, it allows for a simpler interpretation procedure at the client side. Since the client (receiver device) is usually a platform with limited resources, this can be an advantage. Second, as the Raw profile is not tailored for authoring, since it is less structured and has few reuse features, applications written in this profile are usually more difficult to be understood and thus, to be reverse engineered. Third, and the main one, the Raw profile can act as an intermediate notation for converters of other declarative languages. Thus the authoring phase can use languages other than NCL, without imposing any additional load on the receiver. Therefore, the NCL Raw profile can act as a liaison transfer syntax among several declarative hypermedia languages. This is an interesting point to be worked in the future.

The NCL Raw profile is backwards compatible; thus a Raw profile application should be able to run in any EDTV compatible player. In fact, this compatibility principle guided the profile design. Therefore, Ginga Plug-in, WebNCL, and NCL4Web are already able to run applications developed in the NCL Raw profile. In doing this, some of the limitations of the current implementations would vanish. For example, WebNCL would support, indirectly, the `<switch>` element. However, in Section 5 we go further: we propose the incorporation of the NCL Raw profile converter in the architecture of any NCL EDTV player, including those mentioned in this paper.

4.1 NCL Raw Profile Schema

Most redundant elements and attributes of NCL 3.0 EDTV profile were removed in defining the NCL Raw profile. Table 2 presents the elements of the NCL 3.0 Raw profile. In the table, parenthesis are used for grouping, the symbol (|) read as "or," (?) read as "zero or one," (*) read as "zero or more," and (+) read as "one or more." Child element order is not specified. Moreover, for simplicity, only the `<link>` and `<causalConnector>` elements of the *Linking* and *Extended CausalConnectorFunctionality* modules of NCL 3.0 are presented.

The schemas of the NCL Raw profile can be downloaded from

http://www.ncl.org.br/NCL3.0/RawProfile

In short, the 45 elements of NCL 3.0 EDTV profile were reduced to 22 in the Raw profile. Section 5.1 details the conversion process of NCL 3.0 EDTV profile documents into equivalent NCL 3.0 Raw profile documents.

Table 2. The NCL 3.0 Raw Profile.

Element	Content
`<ncl>`	(`<head>`?, `<body>`?)
`<head>`	(`<causalConnector>`)*
`<body>`	(`<port>`|`<property>`|`<media>`|`<context>`|`<link>`)*
`<media>`	(`<area>`|`<property>`)*
`<context>`	(`<port>`|`<property>`|`<media>`|`<context>`|`<link>`)*
`<area>`	-
`<port>`	-
`<property>`	-
`<link>`	(`<bind>`)+
`<causal-Connector>`	((`<simpleCondition>`|`<compoundCondition>`),(`<simpleAction>`|`<compoundAction>`))

5. EMBEDDING NCL APPLICATIONS

We propose a new approach for the architecture of NCL players with, at least, two translation phases: from NCL EDTV profile to NCL Raw profile, and then to the data model of the NCL Raw player. This process is illustrated in Figure 1, in which the *Raw Converter* module is in charge of the first step, and the *Data Model Converter* is in charge of the second step.

Figure 1. The conversion flow.

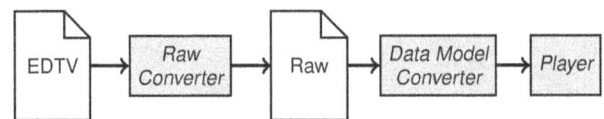

Note that if the NCL Raw player is embedded into another language player, like an HTML browser, the *Data Model Converter*, in Figure 1, should be divided into two further steps: (i) translating (usually, compiling) from NCL Raw profile to the language of the host environment, and then (ii) translating (interpreting) the result of the previous step into the execution data model of the host environment. Note also that the *Raw Converter* module can be implemented in the server side, as discussed in Section 4.

5.1 NCL Raw Profile Converters

In the NCL Raw profile, `<media>` and `<context>` properties must be defined using only `<property>` elements. Moreover, the *Layout*, *Descriptor*, and *DescriptorControl* modules of NCL 3.0 were removed. Since all properties must be defined in `<property>` elements, the *externable* attribute is used to determine if the given property may be referenced by links and ports.

As an example conversion, consider the conversion of `<region>` elements. The `<region>` element defines the position and size parameters of `<descriptor>` elements, which can be associated to `<media>` elements. Regions are declared within `<regionBase>` elements and may be nested to any level, so that a child region may define its attributes in relation to it's parent's attributes. We eliminate a region by converting its attributes (except *id*) into parameters of the associated descriptors, which later are converted into media properties. (Note that descriptors may also be referenced by `<bind>` elements; thus the need for the two conversion steps.) The transformation of `<region>` attributes into `<descriptorParam>`

300

elements is straightforward if (i) the attribute belongs to a root region, i.e., a region that is an immediate child of a `<regionBase>` element; (ii) the attribute is *zIndex*; or (iii) the attribute is *width* or *height* and its value is given in pixels. In these cases, all we have to do is to insert a corresponding `<descriptorParam>` element into the associated descriptors.[5] Thus, e.g., the excerpt

```
<region id='r' width='10px' zIndex='1'/>
...
<descriptor id='d0' region='r'/>
<descriptor id='d1' region='r'/>
```

reduces to

```
<descriptor id='d0'>
  <descriptorParam name='width' value='10px'/>
  <descriptorParam name='zIndex' value='1'/>
</descriptor>
<descriptor id='d1'>
  <descriptorParam name='width' value='10px'/>
  <descriptorParam name='zIndex' value='1'/>
</descriptor>
```

If, however, conditions (i)–(iii) are false, we must calculate the value of the region attribute in relation to its parent's attribute, which is either obtained by rules (i)–(iii) or must be calculated from its parent's parent's attribute, and so on. Let $P(r)$ denote the parent region of a child region r, and let $r[a]$ denote the value of attribute a of r. Then the value of $r[a]$ in relation to $P(r)$ is given by the "unnest" function U such that

$$U(r,a) =$$

$$\begin{cases} r[a] & \text{if (i), (ii), or (iii) hold for } r \text{ or } a \\ r[a] \cdot U(P(r),a) & \text{if } a = A_{wh} \\ r[a] + U(P(r),a) & \text{if } a = A_{tblr} \text{ and } r[a], U(P(r),a) \text{ are in pixels} \\ r[a] \cdot U(P(r),A_h) & \text{if } a = A_{tb} \text{ and } r[a] \text{ is in \% and both} \\ \quad + U(P(r),a) & U(P(r),A_h), U(P(r),a) \text{ are in pixels or \%} \\ r[a] \cdot U(P(r),A_w) & \text{if } a = A_{lr} \text{ and } r[a] \text{ is in \% and both} \\ \quad + U(P(r),a) & U(P(r),A_w), U(P(r),a) \text{ are in pixels or \%} \\ \uparrow \text{ (undefined)} & \text{otherwise,} \end{cases}$$

where $A_{x_1 x_2 \ldots x_n}$ stands for *width*, *height*, *top*, *bottom*, *left*, or *right* whenever $x_i = w, h, t, b, l, r$, for $1 \le i \le n$. The cases where $U(r,a)$ is undefined are those where we end up adding a pixel value to a percentage of screen's width or height, which cannot be done in conversion time because screen dimension is unknown.

The *TransitionBase* and *BasicTransition* modules were also removed from the EDTV profile in defining the Raw profile. Transitions are assumed to be media object's exhibition properties to be defined in `<property>` elements.

The Raw profile does not support any importing facility. Thus elements can only refer to elements defined in the same NCL document. This means that the *refer* attribute can only have an *id* value defined in the same document. Moreover, syntactic reuse is not allowed. Reuse is only allowed for presentation objects. Thus the *instance* attribute of `<media>` elements can only contain the values "instSame" or "gradSame."

We could have removed the `<context>` element, since it does not have a relevant role in presentation scheduling. But we have

---

[5]Note that a region may be referred by multiple descriptors, but each descriptor may refer to at most one region.

decided to keep it because it is required for document structuring, which can be helpful in the client side if live-editing is allowed and if link actions may be applied to a set of objects. The `<body>` element was kept in the Raw profile only for compatibility with the EDTV profile.

In the NCL Raw profile, content alternatives are not chosen from a `<switch>` element, instead, they are selected by links that test the global *settings* node of NCL. Thus the *TestRule*, *TestRuleUse*, *ContentControl*, and *SwitchInterface* were removed.

As another example conversion, we present the conversion of `<switch>` elements. The `<switch>` element defines a mutually exclusive set of `<media>`, `<context>`, or other `<switch>` components whose presentation depends on the evaluation of associated rules. A rule is a Boolean expression defined in the header section of the document, by `<rule>` or `<compositeRule>` elements; these are associated with the switch components via `<bindRule>` elements.

When we start a switch, its rules are evaluated in order of declaration. If a valid rule is found, the component associated with this rule is presented and no other rule is evaluated. If, however, no valid rule is found, either the default component, defined by the `<defaultComponent>` element, is presented, or no component is presented, in case there is no default.

We eliminate a switch by converting it into a specially crafted context that use links to implement the switch's logic. Before presenting the conversion algorithm, we define the semantics of the switch element. We deal first with the simplified case of switches that do not contain `<switchPort>` elements. The semantics and conversion algorithm for switches containing `<switchPort>` elements builds on the simplified case and will be given later.

Let S be a switch containing a list x_1, x_2, ..., x_m of `<media>`, `<context>`, or other `<switch>` elements, and a list b_1, b_2, ..., b_n of `<bindRule>` elements. Without loss of generality, assume that $m = n$ and that, for all $1 \le i \le n$, component x_i is associated with bind-rule b_i, i.e., $b_i[constituent] = x_i[id]$. (We may safely assume this because the switch semantics ignores dangling `<bindRule>` elements or components that are not referenced by any `<bindRule>` or `<defaultComponent>` elements.) Assume further that b_i is declared immediately before b_{i+1} in S. Then the algorithm for selecting which component of S is started when S is started is given by function G such that

$$G(S) =$$

$$\begin{cases} x_1 & \text{if } V(R(b_1)) \\ x_2 & \text{if } \neg V(R(b_1)) \wedge V(R(b_2)) \\ \vdots & \vdots \\ x_n & \text{if } \neg V(R(b_1)) \wedge \cdots \wedge \neg V(R(b_{n-1})) \wedge V(R(b_n)) \\ x_d & \text{if } \neg V(R(b_1)) \wedge \cdots \wedge \neg V(R(b_{n-1})) \wedge \neg V(R(b_n)) \\ & \text{and } x_d \text{ is the default component of } S \\ \varepsilon \text{ (none)} & \text{otherwise,} \end{cases}$$

where R is a function that returns the `<rule>` or `<compositeRule>` element referenced by a given `<bindRule>` element, and V is a unary predicate on the set of rules such that $V(r)$ holds iff (if, and only if) at the moment S started, rule r evaluates to true.

Let S be a switch containing no `<switchPort>` element. Then the algorithm for removing S from an arbitrary NCL document consists of the following six steps.

STEP 1. Create an empty context C such that $C[id] = S[id]$.

STEP 2. Insert into C a `<media>` element, with unique identifier w, of the form

```
<media id=w refer=w' instance='instSame'/>
```

where w' is the identifier of the document settings node, i.e., the media object that contains the global properties to be tested.

STEP 3. Insert into C an empty `<media>` element, with unique identifier t of the form

```
<media id=t/>
```

and a `<port>` element, with unique identifier t', pointing to t, of the form

```
<port id=t' component=t/>
```

Media t is used to trigger the links inserted in the next step.

STEP 4. For each `<bindRule>` element b_i, such that b_i is the i-th element in the ordered list of `<bindRule>` elements of S, insert into context C a new link of the form

```
<link xconnector=K>
  <bind role='onBegin' component=t/>
  <bind role=b_i[rule]1 component=w
      interface=R_1(R(b_i))[var]/>
  <bind role=b_i[rule]2 component=w
      interface=R_2(R(b_i))[var]/>
  ...
  <bind role=b_i[rule]k component=w
      interface=R_k(R(b_i))[var]/>
  <bind role='start' component=b_i[constituent]/>
  <bind role='stop' component=t[id]/>
</link>
```

where R_j is a function that returns the j-th `<rule>` element in the tree defined by a given `<rule>` or `<compositeRule>` element. In addition, insert into the document's connector base a new causal connector, with unique identifier K, of the form

```
<causalConnector id=K>
  <compoundCondition operator='and'>
    <simpleCondition role='onBegin'/>
    <compoundStatement operator='and'>
      Ā(R(b_1)) Ā(R(b_2)) ... Ā(R(b_{b_i-1})) A(R(b_{b_i}))
    </compoundStatement>
  </compoundCondition>
  <compoundAction operator='seq'>
    <simpleAction role='start'/>
    <simpleAction role='stop'/>
  </compoundAction>
</causalConnector>
```

where A is a function that converts a given rule into an equivalent `<assessmentStatement>` block and $\bar{A}$ denotes the negation of A; these functions are precisely defined below.

STEP 5. If S contains a `<defaultComponent>` element x_d, then insert into C a new link-connector pair, similar to those inserted in the previous step, which starts x_d and whose main assessment statement is a conjunction of

$$\bar{A}(R(b_1)) \ \bar{A}(R(b_2)) \ \cdots \ \bar{A}(R(b_{i-1})) \ \bar{A}(R(b_i)).$$

STEP 6. Finally, replace the switch S by context C.

The aforementioned function A, which converts a rule r into an equivalent `<assessmentStatement>` block, is defined as follows. If r is the j-th `<rule>` element encountered so far (starting at 1), then $A(r)$ is equal to

```
<assessmentStatement comparator=r[comparator]>
  <attributeAssessment role=r[id]j
    eventType='attribution'/>
  <valueAssessment value=r[value]/>
</assessmentStatement>
```

Otherwise, if r is a `<compositeRule>` element containing a list r_1, r_2, ..., r_n of member rules, then $A(r)$ is equal to

```
<compoundStatement operator=r[comparator]>
  A(r_1) A(r_2) ... A(r_n)
</compoundStatement>
```

The function $\bar{A}$, which converts a rule r into an `<assessmentStatement>` element that is equivalent to the negation of r, is defined by adding the attribute-value pair $isNegated$="true" to the root element of the tree returned by $A(r)$.

We proceed to prove (informally) the correctness of the previous switch removal algorithm. Let S be a switch containing no `<switchPort>` element, and let C be the context generated by the preceding algorithm. We want to show that

1. $G(S) = x$ iff x is the only component of C that gets started after C is started; and
2. $G(S) = \varepsilon$ iff no component gets started after C is started.

We shall prove the if-part of statement (1); the proof of the only-if-part of (1) and of both parts of (2) proceed in a similar fashion. Suppose $G(S) = x$, for some x in S. There are two possibilities: Either (i) there is a `<bindRule>` b_i such that b_i refers to x and

$$(\dagger) \qquad \neg V(R(b_1)) \wedge \neg V(R(b_2)) \wedge \cdots \wedge \neg V(R(b_{i-1})) \wedge V(R(b_i)),$$

or (ii) x is the `<defaultComponent>` of S and, for all i, $\neg V(R(b_i))$. We proceed to prove case (i); again, the proof of case (ii) is similar. Suppose that case (i) holds. Then, by the fourth step of the preceding algorithm, there is a link ℓ in context C that starts x immediately after C only if the conjunction of the series of statements

$$(\ddagger) \qquad \bar{A}(R(b_1)) \ \bar{A}(R(b_2)) \ \cdots \ \bar{A}(R(b_{i-1})) \ A(R(b_i))$$

evaluates to true. By construction, for all r, $A(r)$ evaluates to true iff $V(r)$; and $\bar{A}(r)$ evaluates to true iff $\neg V(r)$. Thus $(\dagger)$ implies $(\ddagger)$. Therefore, if we start C the condition of link ℓ is satisfied and x is started; moreover, no other link of C is satisfied, since they contain either an assessment statement of the form $A(R(b_j))$, for some $1 \le j < i$, which evaluates to false since $\neg V(R(b_j))$, or an assessment statement of the form $\bar{A}(R(b_i))$, which also evaluates to false since $V(R(b_i))$. Q. E. D.

We can easily extend the previous algorithm to deal with switches containing `<switchPort>` elements. This general version consists of the following five steps. STEP 1. Create a context C to represent S. STEP 2. For each `<switchPort>` element p in S, apply steps 1–5 of the previous algorithm to obtain a context C_p that represents the sub-switch defined by the switch-port p, i.e., that containing only the `<media>` elements referenced by the `<mapping>` elements of p and the corresponding `<bindRule>` elements, and insert C_p into C. Furthermore, insert into C a `<port>` element p' such that $p'[id] = p[id]$. STEP 3. Use steps 1–5 of the previous algorithm to obtain a context C_S, which will represent S, but this time considering all its components and `<bindRule>` elements, and insert C_S into C. Moreover, insert into C a `<port>` element, with unique identifier q, pointing to C_S. STEP 4. Update the links that reference S directly, i.e., without specifying a switch-port, to point to port q of C. STEP 5. Finally, replace S by C.

5.2 NCL Player API

In implementing a player for the Raw profile of NCL it is important to use the *Player API* defined by Ginga Plug-in, which is recommended for embedded NCL applications in the ITU-T reference implementation of Ginga-NCL. In obeying this API, it will be possible to relate more than one NCL embedded application to each other, and to relate an NCL application to host language elements, e.g., HTML elements. It is also important to implement the *input-ControlNotification API* to allow the NCL player to pass an gain control of the input devices. Reference [13] presents these APIs and discusses their use by the Ginga Plug-in implementation, together with some application use cases.

6. CONCLUSIONS

This paper recognizes the potential of HTML5 browsers in turning JavaScript into a target language for compilers (or converters) of other high-level languages. The wide distribution of HTML browsers can make JavaScript an important tool for bursting other language applications in the Web. Taking this into account, this paper also recognizes the importance of works like Ginga Plug-in, WebNCL, and NCL4Web in helping disseminate NCL applications. Contributing to those works, this paper encourages the use of NCL Raw profile as the target profile for NCL players, to allow for a simplified but complete implementation of the presentation engine.

Even if the developers of Ginga Plug-in, WebNCL, and NCL4-Web do not follow our suggestions, the conversion of NCL EDTV applications to NCL Raw profile application in the server side could use those players with advantages. For example, some features not supported today would become available.

However, the re-factoring of the current NCL players to support the "conversion flow" depicted in Figure 1 would allow for a simpler interpretation procedure in the client side, and therefore, probably smaller and less prone to bugs. Moreover, the NCL Raw profile can act as an intermediate syntax notation for converters of other declarative languages. Hence, in the authoring phase, languages other than NCL, more tailored to user's flavor, could be used without imposing any additional load on receivers. We are currently working on this issue in the definition of CASyNo, a common abstract syntax notation for hypermedia languages. For now, NCL Raw profile does not introduce features particular to other languages neither features to support the new NCL 4.0, e.g., those features coming from 3D object support.

We have a partial implementation of an EDTV to Raw profile converter tool, called DietNCL.[6] We are also working on an new NCL player for the Raw profile. These implementations are helping us to fine tune the semantics of NCL EDTV profile, since each redundancy removal procedure functions as a precise definition of the removed element. This approach also helps in formalizing, debugging, and maintaining the specification, because it keeps the primitive behavior clearly separated from the derived behavior.

In another direction, we are also planning to use a non-XML syntax for Raw profile by translating it, e.g., into MPEG-4 BIFS [1].

ACKNOWLEDGMENTS

This work was partially supported by the Brazilian CNPq, CAPES, and FAPERJ funding agencies, and by the Brazilian Ministry of Science, Research, and Innovation.

---

[6]Available at http://www.telemidia.puc-rio.br/~gflima

REFERENCES

[1] 14496-11:2005, I. Information technology – Coding of audio-visual objects – Part 11: Scene description and application engine. 2005.

[2] ABNT NBR 15606-2. Digital Terrestrial TV – Data coding and transmission specification for digital broadcasting – Part 2: Ginga-NCL for fixed and mobile receivers: XML application language for application coding. ABNT, São Paulo, SP, Brazil, November 2007.

[3] BERJON, R., FAULKNER, S., LEITHEAD, T., NAVARA, E. D., O'CONNOR, E., PFEIFFER, S., AND HICKSON, I. HTML5: A vocabulary and associated APIs, for HTML and XHTML. Candidate recommendation, W3C, August 2012.

[4] BULTERMAN, D. C., AND RUTLEDGE, L. W. *SMIL 3.0: Flexible Multimedia for Web, Mobile Devices and Daisy Talking Books*, 2nd ed. Springer, 2008.

[5] CAZENAVE, F., QUINT, V., AND ROISIN, C. Timesheets.js: when SMIL meets HTML5 and CSS3. In *Proceedings of the 11th ACM Symposium on Document Engineering - DocEng'11* (2011), ACM, New York, NY, USA, pp. 43–52.

[6] GAGGI, O., AND DANESE, L. A SMIL player for any web browser. In *Proceedings of the 17th International Conference on Distributed Multimedia Systems - DMS 2011* (Forence, Italy, August 2011), ACM, New York, NY, USA, pp. 114–119.

[7] IERUSALIMSCHY, R. *Programming in Lua*, 2nd ed. Lua.Org, 2006.

[8] ITU-T RECOMMENDATION H.761. Nested Context Language (NCL) and Ginga-NCL for IPTV Services. ITU-T, Geneva, Switzerland, April 2009.

[9] JANSEN, J., AND BULTERMAN, D. C. A. SMIL State: An architecture and implementation for adaptive time-based web applications. *Multimedia Tools and Applications 43*, 3 (2009), 203–224.

[10] LIMA, G. A. F., SOARES, L. F. G., NETO, C. S. S., MORENO, M. F., COSTA, R. R., AND MORENO, M. F. Towards the NCL Raw Profile. In *II Workshop de TV Digital Interativa (WTVDI) - Colocated with ACM WebMedia'10* (Belo Horizonte, MG, Brazil, October 2010).

[11] MELO, E. L., VIEL, C. C., TEIXEIRA, C. A. C., RONDON, A. C., SILVA, D. D. P., RODRIGUES, D. G., AND SILVA, E. C. WebNCL: A Web-based presentation machine for multimedia documents. In *Proceedings of the 18th Brazilian Symposium on Multimedia and the Web - WebMedia'12* (São Paulo, SP, Brazil, October 2012), ACM, New York, NY, USA, pp. 403–410.

[12] MERKEL, K. HbbTV: A hybrid broadcast-broadband system for the living room. In *Proceedings of the European Broadcasting Union* (Geneva, Switzerland, 2010).

[13] MORENO, M. F., MARINHO, R. S., AND SOARES, L. F. G. Ginga-NCL architecture for plug-ins. In *Proceedings of the 1st Workshop on Developing Tools as Plug-ins - TOPI'11* (Waikiki, Honolulu, HI, USA, 2011), ACM, New York, NY, USA, pp. 12–15.

[14] SILVA, E., SAADE, D. C. M., AND SANTOS, J. D. NCL4WEB - Translating NCL applications to HTML5 Web pages. In *Proceedings of the 13th ACM Symposium on Document Engineering - DocEng 2013* (Florence, Italy, September 2013), ACM, New York, NY, USA.

[15] VUORIMAA, P., BULTERMAN, D., AND CESAR, P. SMIL Timesheets 1.0. Working draft, W3C, January 2008.

GingaSpace: A Solution to Execute Multidevice Applications on BroadBand TV Systems

Álan L.V. Guedes, Luís F.S. Costa, Ana P.N. Guimarães, José I. Vilarouca Filho,
Fernando S. M. Brito, Carlos E.C.F. Batista, Guido L. Souza Filho

Centro de Informática - UFPB
Campus I - Cidade Universitária
João Pessoa/PB - 58059-900
{alan, luisf, anapaula, joseivan, fernando, bidu, guido}@lavid.ufpb.br

ABSTRACT

Advances in interactive digital TV have enabled the introduction of application scenarios that explore Internet content and multiple device interaction. However, the authorship and interoperability for such scenarios is hampered by the diversity of technologies and devices involved. This paper presents a software architecture for a portable application store based on the H.761 ITU recommendation for IPTV services. The application store concept is implemented as a Ginga-NCL application, which retrieves and executes other Ginga-NCL applications. The description of the proposed software architecture, the execution of systems and usability tests on a software prototype are presented as results.

Categories and Subject Descriptors

H.5.4 [**Information Interfaces and Presentation**]:
Hypertext/Hypermedia - Multimedia Information Systems

Keywords

TV Digital, second screen, multi devices, HAN, Broadband TV, NCL and Ginga,

1. INTRODUCTION

The concept of digital convergence can be understood as the integration of different technologies and devices. In the digital TV domain, one can recognize this integration in interactive digital TV in two recent usage scenarios: BroadBand TV receivers and applications that use multiple exhibition devices.

Broadband TV receivers [1], also known as Smart TV and Connected TV receivers, allow their users to retrieve conventional TV audiovisual content and interactive multimedia applications from the Internet through broadband connectivity. This kind of receiver usually provides some application store solution for distributing multimedia applications similar to the "TV Portal" in old cable TV services [2]. Over the last few years, the BroadBand TV has become increasingly important especially due to the popularization of broadband providers and Video On Demand (VOD) applications, such as YouTube, Hulu, and Netflix.

Multidevice applications [3], most known by the specific usage of a second screen, are applications that act as distributed multimedia presentations, between fixed and mobile devices interconnected by the same local network. In the digital TV domain, the

WebMedia'13, November 5–8, 2013, Salvador, Brazil.
Copyright 2013 ACM 978-1-4503-2559-2/13/11...$15.00.
http://dx.doi.org/10.1145/2526188.2526239

application is distributed between the TV receiver and personal computing devices, such as mobile phones or tablets. Recently, multidevice applications have become popular due to the massive presence of mobile devices and the emergence of technologies that interconnect them, such as UPnP[1] and Bluetooth[2].

Some TV platforms [4, 5, 6] are able to integrate both broadband connectivity and multidevice applications. However, each receiver has its own application store, which is embedded in the receiver and is able to execute only applications developed for that particular store, since these applications use the proprietary manufacture's APIs. Therefore, the integration of the mentioned scenarios is characterized by the lack of portability of the applications and the application store itself.

An effort to increase the interoperability of IPTV services is the H.761 ITU recommendation [7]. This recommendation proposes an interoperable ecosystem of receivers for IPTV services through the use of the Ginga-NCL presentation engine and its NCL language. With the aim of contributing to the interoperability aspects of this ecosystem, this paper presents an application store architecture based solely on the resources provided by the H.761 recommendation. In addition, the proposed architecture is capable of retrieve other H.761 applications from Internet, define a semantics that expresses the connectivity state [8] between the required devices.

The proposed architecture contributes to both authors and users of multidevice applications. For the authors, the solution offers a distribution service for different receivers based on H.761 recommendation. For users, it supports the execution of application and aims the configuration of required devices in Ginga-NCL applications [14]. The proposal is evaluated through the execution of system and usability tests over a prototype implementation.

The paper is organized as follows. Section 2 describes the architecture of the proposed solution and its main functional entities. Section 3 presents the implementation details of the software prototype. Section 4 presents the results of the execution of systems and usability tests over the prototype implementation. Finally, Section 5 presents the final remarks and possible future developments.

2. THE PROPOSED ARCHITECTURE

The architecture of the application store proposal consists of two subsystems. The first subsystem is the repository of applications, which provides a Web service to store and retrieve applications. The second subsystem is an H.761 application, called GingaSpace

---

[1]http://www.dlna.org/
[2]http://www.bluetooth.com/

that works as an application store. This application is able to retrieve and execute other H.761 applications, if the required devices are connected.

The Web service offered by GingaSpace repository was designed using the REST architectural model [10] and the OAuth authentication model, which works over the HTTP protocol. This configuration increases the interoperability and optimizes the network traffic [11] of GingaSpace. This strategy also avoids the use of libraries with system dependence not supported by the H.761 recommendation.

The GingaSpace is an H.761 application with essentially three media objects: a NCLua script [16] that implements the application store logic; a NCL settings node with the properties "system.devNumber(1)" and "system.devNumber(2)", which store the size of the passive and active devices class [14], respectively; and a nested NCL context, which contains the applications retrieved from the repository. This description is illustrated in Figure 1-B. In the figure, the NCLua script interacts with the other two media objects to identify the connectivity status of secondary devices and to execute other H.761 applications.

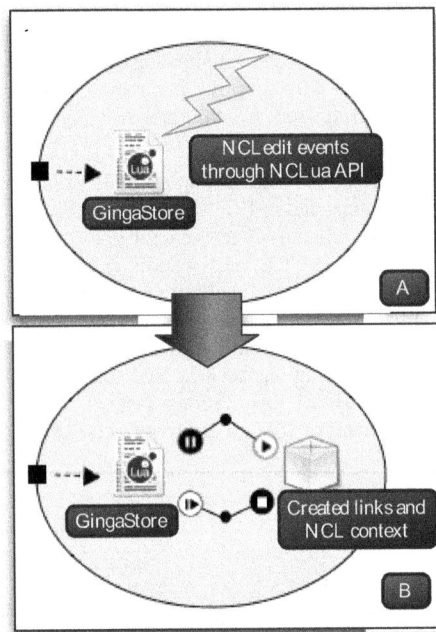

Figure 1: NCL structural view of GigaSpace before and after execution of NCLEdit commands

The identification of the device connectivity state assumes that TV applications with multiple devices are performed in a Smart Home environment. As pointed out by [8], these devices have a dynamic state of connectivity and it is important to present to the user some representation of the connectivity state between them. In [8] the authors illustrate the use of this concept with a "tile interaction", which tells the connectivity between a smartphone, a speaker, and a computer. In the case of GingaSpace, the repository stores the minimum amount of devices in "NCL Passive Class" and "Active NCL Class" that a multidevice application requests. Moreover, before running a retrieved application, the GingaSpace checks if this minimum amount is satisfied by using the variables "system.devNumber(1)" and "system.devNumber(2)", respectively, for "NCL Class Passive" and "Active NCL Class".

The execution of other H.761 applications by the GingaSpace is possible by extending the concept of dynamically reconfigurable Ginga-NCL applications [9]. Applications of this kind are composed of pre-existing media, but new media may be added dynamically via NCL editing commands (or NCLEdit) [7]. Such commands change the structure and content of an NCL document at runtime. These commands may be generated by NCLua scripts, invoked by the application itself, or by DSM-CC events, sent by broadcaster. In [9] is presented the use of this concept in an application, which uses NCLua scripts to present a dynamic list of videos (media objects). In the case of GingaSpace, the media objects added at runtime are other H.761 applications, which are executed according to user's choice.

Figure 1 also illustrates the structural view of the GingaSpace application before (Figure 1-A) and after (Figure 1-B) the execution of editing commands to run the requested application. The editing commands add an NCL context and related links. The NCL context has a *refer* attribute with NCL document requested by the user. This nested NCL document is related with the NCLua by the *onPauseStart* and *onEndResume* links. The links return the control to NCLua after the presentation end of the nested NCL document.

3. PROTOTYPE IMPLEMENTATION

The repository web service was developed using the framework RackOauth[3], which offers management services with REST OAuth[4] authentication. The GingaSpace prototype was tested on the reference implementation of Ginga-NCL[5] with the goal of being compatible only with the Ginga-NCL. The package diagram in Figure 2 presents the software organization of the GingaSpace application. This diagram shows that GingaSpace depends only on three NCLua modules of H.761 specification: (1) the canvas module, which is used to create the GingaSpace view; (2) the lua.io module, which enables the persistence of retrieved applications; and (3) the event module, which allows the use of TCP connections to establish repository connection and NCLEdit calls to execute applications.

The GingaSpace prototype uses three Lua libraries which are not present in the H.761 specification, but which have been developed only in Lua: (1) the JSON4Lua[6], which is used to parse applications metadata from repository; (2) a modified version of LuaOAuth[7], which allows access to the REST web service; and (3) the LuaDeflate[8] library, which allows the decompression of applications stored in the Deflate format from repository.

[3] https://github.com/nov/rack-oauth2
[4] http://oauth.net/
[5] http://www.softwarepublico.gov.br/ver-comunidade?community_id=1101545
[6] http://json.luaforge.net/
[7] https://github.com/ignacio/LuaOAuth
[8] https://github.com/davidm/lua-compress-deflatelua

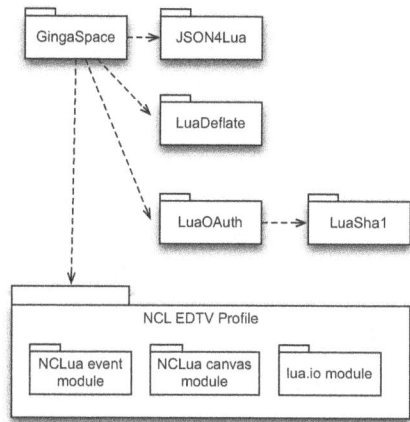

Figure 2: Package diagram of GingaSpace

The changes made in LuaOAuth and the choice for LuaDeflate instead LuaZip[9] were done to remove system dependencies non-compatible with H.761 recommendation. The original version of LuaOAuth uses the LuaSocket[10] and LibCrypto[11], which are wrappers to system libraries. These were replaced, respectively, by the event module of NCLua, for TCP connections, and the lua only LuaSha1[12] library, for encryption in OAuth protocol. By the same reasons, we exchange LuaZip to LuaDeflate, to realize decompression entirely in lua.

The user interface of GingaSpace application was designed with the following set of screens. The "main menu" screen presents actions to the screens "acquire app" and "my app". The "acquire apps" screen lists the compatible applications that are available in the repository. The "app description" screen displays details about an application to be acquired. The "installing app" screen indicates the recovery and persistence status of the application. And the "my apps" screen lists the installed applications and shows the connectivity status of required secondary devices.

4. EVALUATION

We evaluated the proposed software architecture in terms of receiver portability and user usability. The GingaSpace portability was evaluated by systems tests performed in a Toshiba LE5552I LED TV. This receiver is compatible with the middleware Ginga-NCL and supports both NCLEdit commands and lua.io features. Figure 3 presents the "main menu" (left) and "acquire app" (right) screens of the prototype.

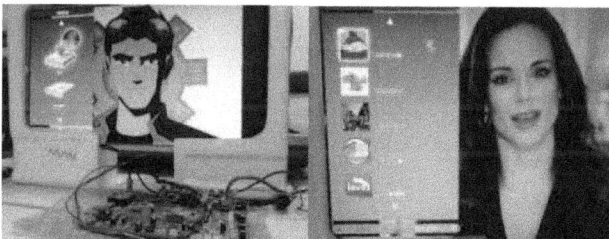

Figure 3 - GingaSpace prototype running on a Toshiba LE5552I TV

To evaluate the GingaSpace usage, a usability study of GingaSpace software prototype was realized. The methodology

---

[9] http://luaforge.net/projects/luazip/

[10] http://luaforge.net/projects/luasocket/

[11] http://luacrypto.luaforge.net/

[12] http://regex.info/blog/lua/sha1

and the results of the study are reported in [12]. The study aimed to evaluate the usability and user experience in multidevice applications with and without GingaSpace. The test case was applied to a group of 22 users arranged in 11 pairs. Figure 4 presents the location where the tests were applied. The location was assembled to simulate a real environment for TV content consumption. An AOpen mini PC with the Ginga-NCL reference implementation was used as TV receiver. Each pair of users had a remote control and two mobile devices running GingaMobile [13] with the "NCL AticveClass" service enabled.

Figure 4: Identification of device connectivity of the "World Cup" application in GingaSpace

The multidevice application, called "World Cup" [16], was selected for execution in GingaSpace. This application requests two "NCL Active Class" devices. At one point, the GingaSpace identifies that only one "NCL Active Class" device is connected (in the figure, the device highlighted in green). After activating the "NCL Active Class" services on the secondary device, GingaSpace can execute the application.

Among the considerations raised in [12], one in particular is relevant to our work. A question was made to users about the use of secondary devices with and without GingaSpace, and approximately 77% of users found it easier to understand when you need to use multiple devices with the aid of GingaSpace.

5. FINAL REMARKS

The GingaSpace architecture uses the dynamically reconfiguration [9] and multidevice [15] features of Ginga-NCL to integrate the multidevice applications and BroadbandTV scenarios. The tests applied to the GingaSpace prototype indicate that it is able to properly retrieve and execute H.761 applications on BroadBand receivers. Moreover, they suggest that GingaSpace can help users in identifying which secondary devices are needed in order to run a particular multidevice application.

Different from the application stores of other BroadbandTV platforms [4, 5, 6], GingaStore is compatible with H.761. The effort to achieve this compatibility may help in improving the market potential of the Ginga technology, which is a royalty-free ITU recommendation. This market potential is evidenced by the current success of application stores in the mobile phone domain, e.g., for Android and iOS devices.

We list as future works realize of more tests with the prototype in other Ginga-NCL implementations. In addition, we want to increase the repository support to the different settings of Ginga-NCL. For example, the repository may filter the available list of applications according to the user's profile, hardware, supported media players, multidevice services, etc.

ACKNOWLEDGMENTS

We thank CAPES and RNP/CTIC for the financial support given to research projects related to this paper.

REFERENCES

[1] FRID, A., 2011. The Connected TV Opportunity. Master Theses. Stockholm, Sweden: School of Media Technology Royal Institute of Technology.

[2] QUICO, C., 2003. Are communication services the killer applications for Interactive TV? or I left my wife because I am in love with the TV set. In Proceedings of 1st European Conference on Interactive Television: from Viewers to Actors.

[3] CRUICKSHANK, L, 2007.et al. Making Interactive TV Easier to Use: Interface Design for a Second Screen Approach. In The Design Journal, v. 10, n. 3, p. 41–53.

[4] YAHOOTV, 2013. Yahoo ConnectedTV developer guide. Available in http://developer.yahoo.com/connectedtv/kontxapiref/index.html.

[5] GOOGLETV, 2013. Google TV developer guide. Available in https://developers.google.com/tv.

[6] TOTVS 2010. Sticker Center: Workshop de Aplicações Interativas. In Proceedings of SET Congress 2010. Available in http://astrodevnet.com/AstroDevNet.

[7] ITU, 2009. ITU-T Rec. H.761, 2013. Overview of Multimedia Application Frameworks for IPTV. Available in http://www.itu.int/rec/T-REC-H.761.

[8] VAN DER VLIST, B. et al., 2010. Design Semantics of Connections in a Smart Home Environment. DeSForM2010: Design and Semantics of Form and Movement, p. 48-56.

[9] DE SOUSA JUNIOR, J. 2012. Uma Arquitetura para Aplicações Dinâmicas NCL Baseadas em Famílias de Documentos. Master Theses. Pontifícia Universidade Católica do Rio de Janeiro.

[10] FIELDING, R., 2000. Architectural Styles and the Design of Network-based Software Architectures. University of California.

[11] PAUTASSO, C. et al., 2008. RESTful Web Services vs. 'Big' Web Services: Making the Right Architectural Decision. In Proceedings of WWW '08: 17th international conference on World Wide Web.

[12] GUIMARÃES, A.P.N., 2012. Experiência de uso de Dispositivos Convergentes na TV Digital Brasileira: Um Estudo de caso baseado no Ginga. Master Theses. Universidade Federal da Paraíba.

[13] Daher, G. et al., 2010. Ginga-NCL em Dispositivos Portáteis: Uma Implementação para a Plataforma Android. In Proceedings of WebMedia '10: 16th Brazilian Symposium on Multimedia and the *Web*

[14] BATISTA, C.E.C.F. et al, 2010. Estendendo o uso das classes de dispositivos Ginga-NCL. In Proceedings of WebMedia '10: 16th Brazilian Symposium on Multimedia and the *Web*.

[15] BATISTA, C.E.C.F, 2013. GINGA-MD: Uma Plataforma para Suporte à execução de Aplicações Hipermídia Multi-Dispositivo Baseada em NCL. Phd Theses. Pontifícia Universidade Católica do Rio de Janeiro

[16] Santanna, F., Cerqueira, R. e Soares, L.F.G. NCLua – Objetos Imperativos Lua na Linguagem Declarativa NCL. In Proceedings of WebMedia '08: 14th Brazilian Symposium on Multimedia and the *Web*.

Modeling Digital Interactive TV Users Behavior

Samuel da Costa Alves Basílio   Marcelo Ferreira Moreno   Eduardo Barrére
{samuelbasilio,moreno,eduardo.barrere}@ice.ufjf.br
Universidade Federal de Juiz de Fora

ABSTRACT

System performance appraisal needed at the development of new large scale distributed systems are faced with the challenge of correct estimated load that is imposed on them. When dealing with Digital Tv, including terrestrial, cable, satellite and IPTV obtaining such load characterization from real deployment scenarios has proved very difficult, due to the impediment of experimental access to these operational broadcast networks. Thus, the researcher usually uses simulations that impose grossly approximate workloads, oversized or fictitious to his system, bringing uncertainty to potential service providers as to optimized design of the necessary equipment. We present at this paper a mathematical model of simple implementation, able to represent the behavior of users of Digital TV. The model can be parameterized to represent different behavior states of the simulated system and thus adapt to various interest scenarios.

Categories and Subject Descriptors

H.4.5 [**Hypertext**]: Hypermedia

General Terms

Algorithms, Management, Standardization

Keywords

TV Digital, Modelagem, Comportamento do usuário, Medição de Audiência, Interatividade, Simulação

1. INTRODUÇÃO

Pesquisadores na área de TV Digital (TVD) usualmente possuem a demanda de validar suas proposições de sistemas de software. Uma vez que o ambiente de TVD envolve milhões de usuários, os novos sistemas devem levar em conta requisitos não-funcionais como escalabilidade e disponibilidade, forçando o emprego de métodos de avaliação de desempenho para uma correta validação. A avaliação de desempenho necessária na proposição de qualquer novo sistema

distribuído de larga escala usualmente se depara com o desafio da correta estimativa da carga que a eles será imposta.

Sem dúvida, a melhor forma de aprimorar, corrigir erros e verificar os requisitos de um software é aplicá-lo a um ambiente real. No caso do ambiente de TV Digital este feito tem se mostrado difícil, pois o ambiente real não aceita testes experimentais com seus usuários finais de fato, os telespectadores. Um recurso que pode ser usado de forma eficiente, barata e confiável, neste caso, são simulações. No entanto, sem acesso ao real dimensionamento e comportamento dos telespectadores, normalmente o pesquisador em TVD recorre a simulações que impõem cargas de trabalho grosseiramente aproximadas, superdimensionadas ou mesmo fictícias ao seu sistema. Tal abordagem, apesar de ser útil para estimativas de pior caso, acaba levando os potenciais provedores daqueles novos serviços a incertezas quanto ao dimensionamento otimizado dos equipamentos necessários àquela proposta.

Atualmente, recursos computacionais são relativamente baratos e podem ser usados para simular ambientes com um vasto número de usuários. Contudo, para utilizarmos este recurso, precisamos de um modelo confiável, que represente de forma mais fiel possível o comportamento de peças-chave do ambiente real. Uma das maiores dificuldades em utilizarmos a simulação está no desenvolvimento e implementação do modelo a ser tomado como base para a geração de carga sintética. É necessário que o projetista observe atentamente o comportamento dos elementos principais do ambiente e consiga abstraí-los de forma simples no modelo.

Modelos voltados à simulação do comportamento de um sistema devem ter um balanceamento entre fidelidade ao ambiente real e simplicidade de implementação. De fato, não seria útil um modelo 100% fiel ao ambiente real que, no entanto, tenha complexidade tal que impeça sua implementação. Além disso, é desejável que modelos possam trazer ganhos não somente à simulação de carga em si, mas também a outros contextos. Por exemplo, no caso de um modelo capaz de representar o comportamento de usuários de TV interativa, ele poderia ser usado tanto para a sintetização de dados em simulações, quanto em estudos sobre propaganda direcionada, análise de contextos sociais, medição de audiência, entre outros.

Apresentamos neste trabalho um modelo matemático de fácil implementação que, ainda assim, é suficientemente fiel à realidade para ser usado em futuras simulações de diversos tipos de serviços ligados a TV.

Este artigo está estruturado da seguinte forma. A Seção 2 discute alguns trabalhos relacionados. A Seção 3 descreve o modelo matemático proposto para o comportamento de usuários de TV Interativa. A Seção 4 exemplifica uma instanciação deste modelo. Por fim, a Seção 5 mostra os objetivos alcançados e discute os trabalhos futuros.

2. TRABALHOS RELACIONADOS

A tentativa de modelar o comportamento dos usuários de sistemas de consumo de mídia não é um trabalho novo como vemos em [5], onde os autores caracterizam e modelam o comportamento dos usuários de seu sistema de vídeo sob demanda. Porém a medida que novas formas de interação aparecem, assim como novas tecnologias e novos sistemas de consumo de mídias, os modelos existentes muitas vezes não são adequados. O trabalho [2], mais recente, mostra além de uma arquitetura para medição de audiência um modelo de consumo de dados e algumas métricas para quantificação do impacto deste consumo. Esta mesma métrica é calculada de forma similar em [1].

Juntamente com o modelo do comportamento do usuário, alguns trabalhos mostram uma caracterização deste comportamento em um ambiente real. Este é o caso do trabalho [7] que caracteriza o comportamento com dados de um sistema com milhões de usuários. Uma métrica interessante apresentada neste trabalho é o tempo de sessão que é fundamental para simularmos o comportamento de vários usuários em períodos maiores de tempo.

Um ponto importante é citado em [6], onde um gerador de carga sintética é apresentado. Neste trabalho os autores citam a necessidade de heterogeneidade nos geradores de carga, pois muitos são apresentados na literatura, mas a grande maioria trabalha apenas de um grupo específico de dados, como dados educacionais. O trabalho apresentado em [9] também apresenta um gerador de carga sintética focando porém apenas no ambiente de IPTV, mas tem como vantagem a utilização dos dados de um sistema real com milhões de usuários.

3. MODELO MATEMÁTICO PARA O COMPORTAMENTO DE USUÁRIOS DE TVDI

Com objetivo de fundamentar possíveis simulações futuras, apresentamos neste capítulo um modelo Markoviano discreto das interações dos usuários de TV Digital Interativa. O trabalho apresentado em [5] apresenta uma modelagem similar, porém não compatível com as nossas necessidades. Além disso esse modelo apresentado é dependente dos dados observados pelos autores. Porém podemos aproveitar algumas métricas interessantes como o tempo esperado de permanência em cada estado e o tempo esperado até que o sistema seja desligado.

Mesmo que nem sempre estes modelos sejam os mais fiéis, eles são de fácil entendimento e implementação. Por isso escolhemos usá-los. Para definirmos o comportamento de usuários de TV Digital Interativa devemos considerar todas as possibilidade de interação do telespectador. Definimos abaixo os possíveis estados que o telespectador pode alcançar e suas transições. A Figura 1 ilustra os estados e as possíveis transições entre estes estados. A saber:

- E_i, quando uma aplicação interativa está sendo executada;

- E_n, quando apenas o vídeo da programação está em execução;

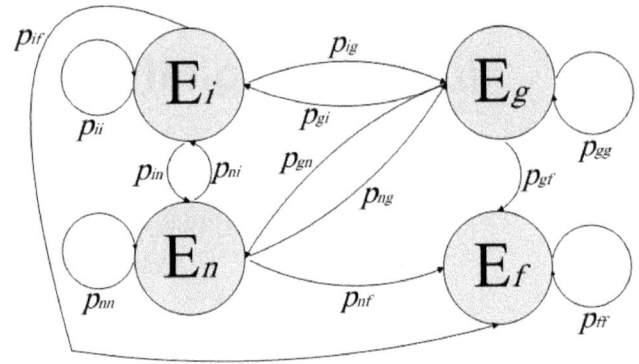

Figure 1: Modelo Markoviano das interações dos usuários.

- E_f, quando o telespectador desliga o receptor digital;

- E_g, quando uma aplicação nativa está sendo executada.

- p_{if}, probabilidade de uma aplicação interativa estar em execução e o receptor ser desligado;

- p_{ii}, probabilidade do telespectador executar uma interação com uma aplicação já em execução;

- p_{ig}, probabilidade de uma aplicação interativa estar em execução e o telespectador iniciar uma aplicação nativa(pausando a execução da aplicação);

- p_{in}, probabilidade de uma aplicação interativa em execução ser finalizada ou o telespectador mudar de canal (terminando a execução da aplicação);

- p_{ni}, probabilidade de uma aplicação interativa ser iniciada;

- p_{nn}, probabilidade do telespectador mudar de canal sem que nenhuma aplicação esteja em execução;

- p_{nf}, probabilidade do receptor ser desligado sem que nenhuma aplicação esteja em execução;

- p_{ng}, probabilidade do telespectador iniciar uma aplicação nativa;

- p_{gn}, probabilidade do telespectador selecionar um canal através de uma aplicação nativa (como o guia de programação);

- p_{gg}, probabilidade do telespectador interagir com uma aplicação nativa;

- p_{gf}, probabilidade de uma aplicação nativa estar em execução e o receptor ser desligado;

- p_{gi}, probabilidade de uma aplicação nativa ser encerrada depois de ser iniciada quando uma aplicação interativa estava em execução(recuperando o estado da aplicação interativa que estava então pausada);

- p_{ff}, probabilidade do receptor está desligado.

Diferenciamos o estado onde aplicações nativas[1] estão sendo executadas do estado onde aplicações interativas em geral estão sendo executadas pois, dependendo do modelo de captura de dados utilizado pode não ser possível capturar as interações de aplicações nativas[4][3]. Como estas aplicações nativas são um recurso disponibilizado pelo receptor digital, se o modelo de captura de dados por aplicações interativas for o usado, as interações do usuário com estas aplicações não poderão ser obtidas. Contudo, se o modelo de captura de dados por extensão do middleware for utilizado, todas as interações poderão ser obtidas, tanto as com as aplicações interativas como as com aplicações nativas. Em ambos os modelos as interações de mudança de canal podem ser obtidas.

Notemos que é simples estendermos o modelo apresentado para algum caso específico. Por exemplo, se quiséssemos adicionar ao modelo inicial uma aplicação interativa arbitrária qualquer, seria necessário apenas adicionar a cada estado E_x da aplicação as probabilidades p_{xy} e p_{yx}, onde m é o número de estados da cadeia, $E_x = \{E_{a1}, E_{a2}, ..., E_{am}\}$, $p_{xy} = \{p_{xn}, p_{xg}, p_{xi}, p_{xf}\}$ e $p_{yx} = \{p_{nx}, p_{gx}, p_{ix}, p_{fx}\}$. Neste caso devemos também remover o estado E_f, que representa o estado final da cadeia da aplicação, pois este estado será alcançado em algum momento quando alguma das probabilidades p_{xy} acontecerem.

Para exemplificar a extensão do modelo, mostramos na Figura 2(a) o modelo de uma aplicação interativa qualquer que possui dois estados ativos, E_{a1} e E_{a2}, e um estado final E_f. Para estender o modelo original removemos o estado E_f do modelo da aplicação e adicionamos os estados E_{a1} e E_{a2} ao modelo original, mantendo as probabilidades que relacionam os estados E_{a1} e E_{a2} e adicionando as probabilidades que relacionam E_{a1} e E_{a2} com E_i', E_g, E_n e E_f. Notemos que o estado E_i, que representava todas as aplicações interativas do modelo original, agora é chamado de E_i' e representa todas as outras aplicações interativas não especificadas. Se todas as aplicações forem representadas individualmente, o estado E_i' pode ser removido do modelo. O mesmo raciocínio pode ser aplicado ao estado E_g. A Figura 2(b) mostra o resultado final.

Uma métrica interessante que podemos obter deste modelo é o tempo esperado de uma sessão. O tempo de sessão de um telespectador pode ser estimado calculando a quantidade de passos necessários para alcançarmos o estado E_f. Apresentamos abaixo o formalismo para calcularmos este tempo retirado de[8].

Seja $(X_n)_{n \geq 0}$ uma cadeia de Markov com matriz de transição P. O tempo necessário para alcançarmos um subconjunto de A de I é chamado de *hitting time* e é definido pela variável aleatória $H^A : \Omega \to \{0, 1, 2, ...\} \cup \{\infty\}$ dada por:

$$H^A(\omega) = inf\{n \geq 0 : X_n(\omega) \in A\}$$

onde o tempo ínfimo para alcançarmos o conjunto vazio $\emptyset$ é ∞. A probabilidade que começando em i, $(X_n)_{n \geq 0}$ alcançará A é:

$$h_i^A = P_i(H^A < \infty).$$

Quando A é um conjunto absorvente, h_i^A é chamado de probabilidade de absorção. O tempo médio necessário para que

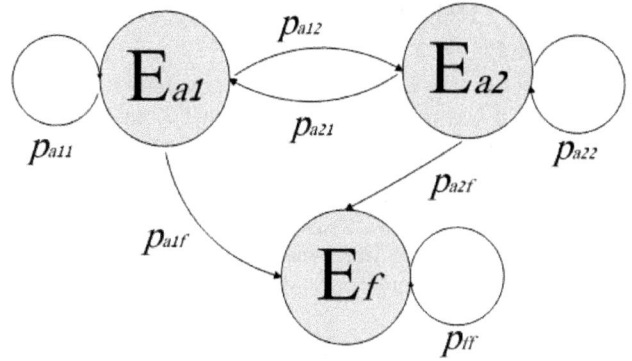

(a) Modelo markoviano de uma aplicação arbitrária

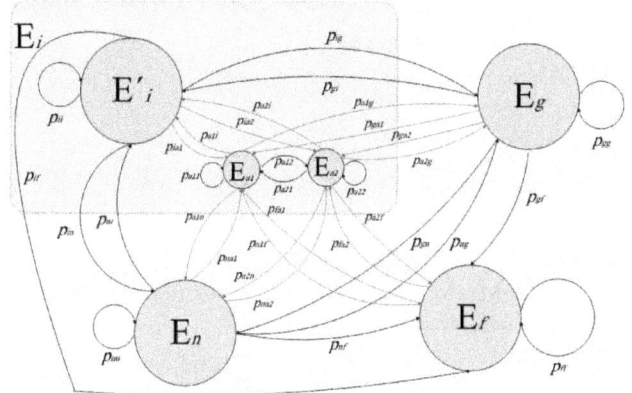

(b) Modelo markoviano extendido

Figure 2: Extensão do modelo.

$(X_n)_{n \geq 0}$ alcance A é dado por:

$$k_i^A = E_i(H^A) = \sum_{n < \infty} nP(H^A = n) + \infty P(H^A = \infty).$$

Para o nosso caso temos que $i = \{E_n\}$ e $A = \{E_f\}$. Fica claro que $k_{E_f} = 0$. Agora saindo de E_n e realizando um passo, com probabilidade p_{ni} vamos para E_i, com probabilidade p_{ng}, vamos para E_g, com probabilidade p_{nf} vamos para E_f, e com probabilidade p_{nn} continuamos em E_n. Então:

$$k_{E_n} = 1 + p_{ni}k_{E_i} + p_{ng}k_{E_g} + p_{nf}k_{E_f} + p_{nn}k_{E_n}$$

$$k_{E_n} = \frac{1 + p_{ni}k_{E_i} + p_{ng}k_{E_g}}{(1 - p_{nn})}$$

O 1 aparece pois contamos o tempo para o primeiro passo. Similarmente fazendo para k_{E_g} e k_{E_i} temos o seguinte sistema:

$$\begin{cases} k_{E_n} = \dfrac{1 + p_{ni}k_{E_i} + p_{ng}k_{E_g}}{(1 - p_{nn})} & (1a) \\[2ex] k_{E_g} = \dfrac{1 + p_{gi}k_{E_i} + p_{gn}k_{E_n}}{(1 - p_{gg})} & (1b) \\[2ex] k_{E_i} = \dfrac{1 + p_{ig}k_{E_g} + p_{in}k_{E_n}}{(1 - p_{ii})} & (1c) \end{cases}$$

---

[1]Consideramos aplicações nativas aquelas que são específicas do receptor digital, vindo de fábrica ou instaladas posteriormente, como guia de programação.

4. CASO DE USO:INSTANCIAÇÃO DO MODELO

Como parte dos trabalhos apresentados em [4] e [3] realizamos um experimento simples, no qual 27 telespectadores de uma certa região do país, escolhidos sem fundamento estatístico, tiveram suas interações com a TV capturadas. Utilizando os dados obtidos neste experimento, mostramos abaixou um modelo para o nosso caso específico. A Figura 3 nos mostra o modelo Markoviano específico para os nossos dados com um truncamento de quatro casas decimais.

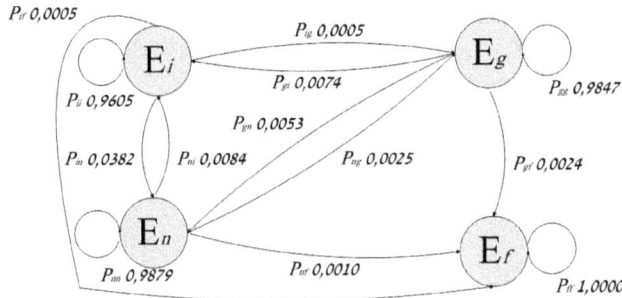

Figure 3: Modelo Markoviano específico das interações dos usuários.

Para definição destes dados o tempo do experimento foi discretizado em segundos. A partir disto foi calculado a quantidade de segundos em que um telespectador estava em cada estado E_i, E_g e E_n. Sabendo quanto tempo cada telespectador passou em cada estado e as transições entre os estados foi possível obter os dados da tabela acima.

Com o modelo apresentado em mãos é possível calcularmos o tempo esperado da sessão dos telespectadores do experimento substituindo os valores obtidos nas equações (1a), (1b) e (1c).

Resolvendo o sistema encontramos:

$$k_{E_n} = \frac{19903979}{22128} \approx 899.49290 \qquad (2)$$

Observando o resultado (2), concluímos a exatidão do nosso cálculo e das nossas probabilidades, pois como o experimento durou 15 minutos (900 segundos), este foi o tempo médio e logo, o esperado para o tamanho da sessão.

5. CONCLUSÃO E TRABALHOS FUTUROS

Neste trabalho apresentamos um modelo matemático de fácil implementação das interações dos usuários de TV Digital Interativa. Apesar de simples, este modelo é suficientemente fiel à realidade e pode ser utilizado para simulações das mais diversas finalidades. Mostramos também como é possível estender o modelo apresentado a modelos mais específicos e detalhados.

Como trabalhos futuros propomos extensões ao modelo proposto, aumentando sua especialização e complexidade. A utilização de dados obtidos em capturas com representatividade estatística também seria muito interessante, pois com isto poderíamos ter um modelo numérico muito mais confiável. Entretanto a captura destes dados atualmente é impossível dados os modelos de medição de audiência e interatividade dos telespectadores em vigência no Brasil.

6. REFERENCES

[1] F. Alvarez, D. Alliez, C. Martin, J. Menendez, and G. Cisneros. Audience measurement technologies for user centric media. In *Consumer Electronics, 2008. ISCE 2008. IEEE International Symposium on*, pages 1–4, 2008.

[2] F. Alvarez, C. Martin, D. Alliez, P. Roc, P. Steckel, J. Menendez, G. Cisneros, and S. Jones. Audience measurement modeling for convergent broadcasting and iptv networks. *Broadcasting, IEEE Transactions on*, 55(2):502–515, 2009.

[3] S. d. C. A. Basilio, M. F. Moreno, and E. Barrére. Interaction and audience analysis in interactive digital tv systems. In *Proceedings of the 18th Brazilian symposium on Multimedia and the web*, WebMedia '12, pages 359–366, New York, NY, USA, 2012. ACM.

[4] S. d. C. A. Basilio, M. F. Moreno, and E. Barrére. Supporting interaction and audience analysis in interactive tv systems. In *Proceedings of the 11th european conference on Interactive TV and video*, EuroITV '13, pages 23–30, New York, NY, USA, 2013. ACM.

[5] P. Branch, G. Egan, and B. Tonkin. Modeling interactive behaviour of a video based multimedia system. In *Communications, 1999. ICC '99. 1999 IEEE International Conference on*, volume 2, pages 978–982 vol.2, 1999.

[6] C. Costa, C. Ramos, I. Cunha, and J. Almeida. Genius: a generator of interactive user media sessions. In *Workload Characterization, 2004. WWC-7. 2004 IEEE International Workshop on*, pages 29–36, 2004.

[7] V. Gopalakrishnan, R. Jana, R. Knag, K. Ramakrishnan, D. Swayne, and V. Vaishampayan. Characterizing interactive behavior in a large-scale operational iptv environment. In *INFOCOM, 2010 Proceedings IEEE*, pages 1–5, 2010.

[8] J. Norris. *Markov Chains*. Number N° 2008 in Cambridge Series in Statistical and Probabilistic Mathematics. Cambridge University Press, 1998.

[9] T. Qiu, Z. Ge, S. Lee, J. Wang, J. Xu, and Q. Zhao. Modeling user activities in a large iptv system. In *Proceedings of the 9th ACM SIGCOMM conference on Internet measurement conference*, IMC '09, pages 430–441, New York, NY, USA, 2009. ACM.

XDTv: Agile Development of Applications for Digital TV

Mario Godoy Neto
Universidade Federal do Vale do São Francisco
(UNIVASF). Av. Antônio Carlos Magalhães, 510,
Country Club - 48.902-300 - Juazeiro - BA - Brazil
mgn@cin.ufpe.br

Carlos André Guimarães Ferraz
Centro de Informática – Universidade Federal de
Pernambuco (CIn/UFPE). Cidade Universitária - 50.740-
560 - Recife - PE - Brazil
cagf@cin.ufpe.br

ABSTRACT

Nowadays, more and more computing devices arise with different applicabilities. Software applications peculiarities for Digital TV (DTV), for example, require special attention in its development process, such as multimedia content gathering requirements (size, display time, location and timing) and development time (limited by the production time of the TV program). This work presents an agile and hybrid development method, instantiated for DTV environment and named eXtreme Digital Television (XDTv). The goal is to contribute with the handling of such peculiarities. Experimental results provide outcomes that XDTv contributes to improve the performance of software applications development for DTV.

Categories and Subject Descriptors

D.2.9 [**Management**]: Software Process Models, Life Cycle.

General Terms

Experimentation, Measurement.

Keywords

Digital TV, Software Engineering, Agile Methodologies.

1. INTRODUCTION

Digital TV (DTV) offers, besides high definition audio and video, a new computational platform able to execute interactive applications. The DTV standard, adopted to perform the experiments in this research, is the Japanese-Brazilian Integrated Services Digital Broadcasting-Terrestrial Brazil (ISDB-Tb) [1], which uses the Ginga middleware, recognized as an International Telecommunication Union (ITU) standard, for IPTV services (ITU-T H.761), improving its applicability. This middleware performs applications developed through the declarative language Nested Context Language (NCL) and Lua script. However, the contributions of this research are not restricted to ISDB-Tb. Independently of the adopted middleware, applications for DTV have peculiarities that demand special attention in their development process [2], [3].

Different types of software demand different approaches, because there are no universal development methods [4]. The report [5] revealed that, Agile projects were better than Cascade projects, having: **a)** 3% less failures; **b)** 14% less changes in budget or

WebMedia '13, November 05 - 08 2013, Salvador, Brazil
Copyright 2013 ACM 978-1-4503-2559-2/13/11 $15.00.
http://dx.doi.org/10.1145/2526188.2526240

functionalities; **c)** 17% more successes. Among Agile methods, the more used ones are Scrum and XP. However, those still do not predict the DTV peculiarities, demanding adaptations [6], [3].

For this research, an adequate method for development of applications for DTV must help the activities of Planning, Specification, Development and Tests, focusing in the treatment of their peculiarities, such as: **a)** coadjutant – the application is not the focus of users, it might add value to the audiovisual content; **b)** short lifecycle – the application is synchronized with the audiovisual, that may last a few minutes and be broadcasted during a few days [2]; **c)** user context – several for the same platform; informal environment; limited means of interaction; **d)** broadcast – sent unilaterally for all users; **e)** instantaneous impact – one city, region or the country receive the information simultaneously; **f)** multimedia objects – text, Lua code, images, audio and video files create a flow, with the need to gather their requirements: dimension, beginning, duration, stack, order, etc.; **g)** development speed – they must follow the fast audiovisual production: tv news, breaking news, among others [6], [2]; **h)** agility – adaptation to changing requirements; **i)** multidisciplinary team – art and audio directors, screenwriters, programmers and others, must communicate clearly [6], [2].

The specific objectives of this research are: **1)** to investigate the adequacy of Agile methods in the development of DTV applications; **2)** to present the hybrid and agile development method, called eXtreme Digital Television (XDTv), whose objective is to help the treatment of the peculiarities of such applications. The main contributions are: **a)** survey of applications peculiarities, improvement points and metrics about the adoption of Scrum, XP, Hybrid (Scrum/XP) and XDTv methods; **b)** the XDTv method and its artifacts. The research techniques adopted were: bibliographic, exploratory, qualitative, quantitative and experimental [7]. The control variables of the experiments were operationalized by orientation, supervision and standardization of materials and methods. The experiments were based in [8] and the development teams formed by students from the discipline called Advanced Topics in Software Engineering from the 10th period of Computing Engineering (UNIVASF). For data collection were adopted: objective questionnaire (Likert scale), descriptive questionnaire, synthesized by key-words, individual and group semi structured individual interview. The forms are available in: www.univasf.edu.br/~mario.godoy/xdtv.

The limitations of this research are: **a)** the controlled experiments might not reflect the industry; **b)** conclusions are restricted to the investigated methods; **c)** XDTv method must be evaluated by professionals; **d)** the quality of developed applications was not considered. The risks for the validity of the experiments are: **a)** despite the different non-functional requirements and the inspection of code not having evidence of its sharing, there is a small possibility of its partial sharing; **b)** despite the balancing of teams by an interview and curriculum analysis, it is possible that there is a member with more affinity or dedication.

2. RELATED WORK

The related works discussed below are focused in Ginga. Other works were not highlighted, because they are focused in the European MHP or American ATSC environments, having a smaller relationship with this paper.

In [2] is presented and agile process for requirement specification focused in the integration of literary and technical TV scripts, with the applications using exclusively textual descriptions to specify, creating the stories and storyboards. The conclusions highlight that the software team must adapt to requirements changes promptly in order to adequate itself with the TV professionals. The greater difficulty faced was the textual description as a way to gather the requirements. However, the author proposal is focused in the integration of different professionals, not having an approach focused in the development of applications and their peculiarities.

The work [3] presents the StoryToCode oriented for the conception of interactive components and code reuse for different platforms (DTV, Mobile, Web, etc), using storyboards as the source for requirement gathering. Among its limitations is the extraction of requirements in a non automated way and the rework needed to complete the code. According to the author, the specialized literature does not have a formal solution for the gathering of multimedia requirements, reuse and models of process development, which are the main problems in the development of applications for DTV. It also highlights the difficulty to perform testing in DTV context. However, it says that the Agile methods are potential candidates for this platform.

Differently from this research, the related works don't have a method for development of DTV applications and do not specify a way to collect multimedia requirements, which may cause the increase of development time [3]. This research presents the details of the performed experiments, allowing their replication. The proposed method (XDTv) does not use textual data for requirement gathering, its artifacts are developed to fulfill its peculiarities, specially, the collection of multimedia requirements.

3. EXPERIMENT 1

Experiment 1 evaluated the Scrum, XP, and Hybrid (Scrum/XP) methods. The dependent variables were: Adequacy and Time regarding Planning and Implementation. The research questions were: **Q1)** Which methods satisfy the peculiarities of DTV applications? **Q2)** Which method makes the implementation faster?

About the adequacy of methods to application peculiarities the following Null Hypotheses were defined: **H0** – the methods are equally adequate; **H1** – the development time is equivalent. As Alternative Hypothesis there are: **H2** – the methods may be improved; **H3** –Scrum method is more adequate; **H4** – XP method is more adequate; **H5** – Hybrid method is more adequate. The independent variables were: **a)** three members of each team, distributed in a balanced way according to curriculum analysis; **b)** inexperienced about DTV, 30 hours of training were dedicated; **c)** investigated methods: Scrum, XP and Hybrid (Scrum/XP); **d)** method adopted by raffling; **e)** identical application and requirements; **f)** dead-line: 3 weeks; **g)** client: the author of this research; **h)** meetings with the client: 6 of 30 minutes; **i)** three interactions; **j)** tools: Eclipse, VMware, Ginga Fedora and plug-ins RSE, Lua and NCL.

In brief, the developed application corresponded to the a virtual soccer grandstand, offering additional information about the championship and the teams, ranking, game visualization in four different angles, screen resizing, pause and video restart, advertising and product sales. The three teams implemented all required functionalities. The hours dedicated to the meetings were: Scrum = 16:00; XP = 15:30; Hybrid = 17:30 hours. The hours regarding implementation were: Scrum = 59:00; XP = 46:09; Hybrid = 38:29 hours. The methods (XP and Hybrid) reduced, in average, 21% (17 hours) of the workload to finish the projects.

The objective questions are: **P1)** the degree of developer wearing; **P2)** how much did the methodology helped; **P3)** the degree of application complexity; **P4)** the complexity to code its functionalities. The changes ranged from 0 to 4. The result of question P1 was equal (3) for all teams. The remaining points were: **a)** Scrum team – P2 = 3; P3 = 3; P4 = 2; **b)** XP team – P2 = 3; P3 = 2; P4 = 3; **c)** Hybrid team – P2 = 2; P3 = 2; P4 = 2. The descriptive questions raised the following strong points: **a)** the fast delivery makes the feedback efficient; **b)** the changing of requirements does not implies in refactoring; **c)** pair programming and stand-up meetings are productive. The weak points are: **a)** synchronous meetings; **b)** version integration; **c)** tiresome implementation. All teams judged the adopted methods to be appropriate with changes. The individual interview found: **a)** there is repetitive effort in NCL coding; **b)** the bigger the code is, the worse its comprehension is.

Seeking an analysis closer to the real market, a survey was performed, where 17 participants were considered to be valid, with formation in Computer Science and average time of experience in development of DTV applications of 2 years and 8 months, being: **a)** professional only = 2; **b)** academic only = 6; **c)** professional and academic = 9 participants. The level of education: **a)** undergraduate students = 3; **b)** master students = 3; **c)** specialist = 1); **d)** master = 2; **e)** PhD students = 5; **f)** PhD = 3. The average of the knowledge self-evaluation of DTV was 7.94, in a scale of: "0" (no knowledge), until "10" (specialist).

Regarding the adopted methods: don't use = 7 (41%); customized Scrum = 5; pure Scrum = 2. The others were mentioned once: Iconix, CMM, MPS, CMMi, XP and Story to Code, all of them customized. About software engineering practices essential to DTV: **a)** all = 6; **b)** specification = 8; **c)** testing = 5; **d)** planning = 4; **e)** reuse = 2; **e)** Story to Code = 1; **f)** TDD = 1; **g)** pair programming = 1. Documentation adopted: **a)** requirements document = 7; **b)** don't use = 4; **c)** low fidelity prototypes = 3; **d)** UML = 2; **e)** other (project planning, use cases, class diagram, IHC tools, conceptual maps, test documentation) were mentioned once. The average of XP to DTV adaptation = 6, variance = 4 and standard deviation = 2. The improvement point of XP is in the gathering of multimedia requirements. The average of Scrum adaptation = 7.18, variance = 1.56 and standard deviation = 1.25. The improvement points of Scrum are: **a)** sprints; **b)** documentation; **c)** tests; **d)** validation. The difference between the averages of XP and Scrum is 1.18 points and the standard deviation was 0.75 points. Both methods are a bit over the average (5) indicating the need of adaptations. The large amount of methods and documents used indicate the demand for standardization. Those results were used in the specification of the XDTv method.

4. THE XDTV METHOD

The eXtreme Digital Television (XDTv) method may be characterized as an Agile, Hybrid and customized method, because it aggregates techniques from several methods and is adapted to the inherent needs and peculiarities of DTV applications, hoping to help in: **a)** planning, specification and implementation; **b)** multimedia requirements and media flow; **c)** fail identification; **d)** requirements change. The activities of Evolution and Validation are outside the scope, but are considered to be future works.

The XDTv has two new artifacts, the model of Prototype for TV Applications (PTvA) and the Media Flow and Synchronism Model (MFSM). The PTvA, presented in Figure 1, is a prototype of low fidelity level [9], aimed to the media requirements gathering, an evolution of Storyboard, due to the logical sequence of user interaction, suggested in [6], [3].

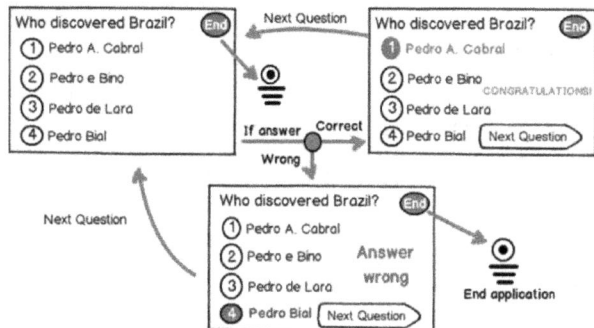

Figure 1. Artifact Prototype for TV Applications (PTvA)

The MFSM, presented in Figure 2, is an evolution of the structural view [10], helping in: communication, requirements gathering, media flow management, implementation and documentation, difficulties found in Experiment 1 and related works [3].

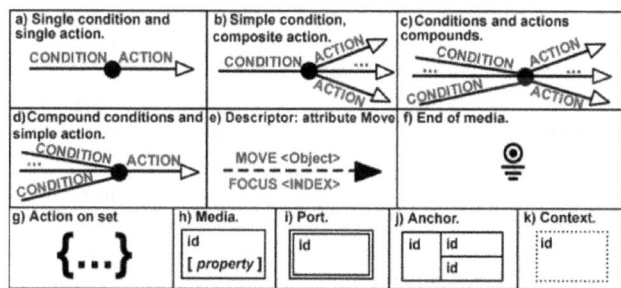

Figure 2. Media Flow and Synchronism Model (MFSM)

The MFSM improves the requirements gathering of PTvA model and specifies the characteristics of any application, performing the mapping of events (condition / actions). Items (**a, b, c, d, e f, g, h, i, j** and **k**) of Figure 2, represent the NCL elements. Figure 3 presents an example of a quiz application.

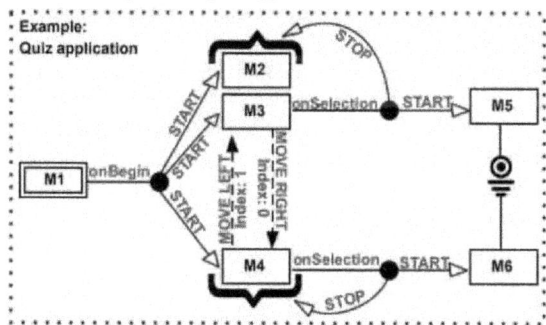

Figure 3. Example of quiz application modeled by MFSM

The process model (a) of XDTv method adopts characteristics of the iterative and incremental method, allowing: fast delivery of software, requirements change and constant failure identification, as presented in the process model of Figure 4.

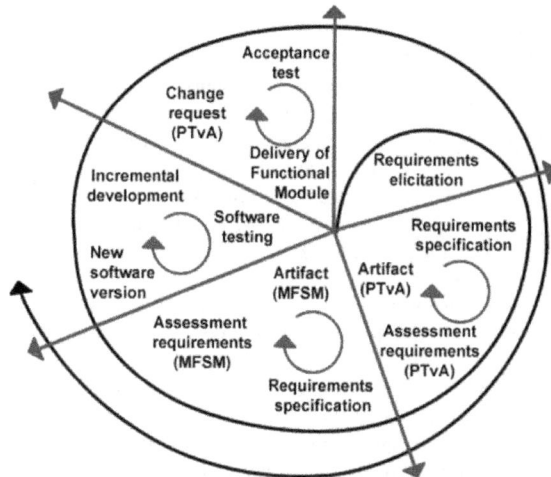

Figure 4. Process model of XDTv method

The lifecycle, presented in Figure 5, begins in the requirements gathering until the delivery of the functional module. For this, there are the roles of: Programmers (for all), Scrum Master and Prototyper. The Scrum Master accrues the function of Tracker, originally from XP. The Programmer accrues the function of tester. The Prototyper is responsible by the requirement engineering, by the use of PTvA and MFSM artifacts.

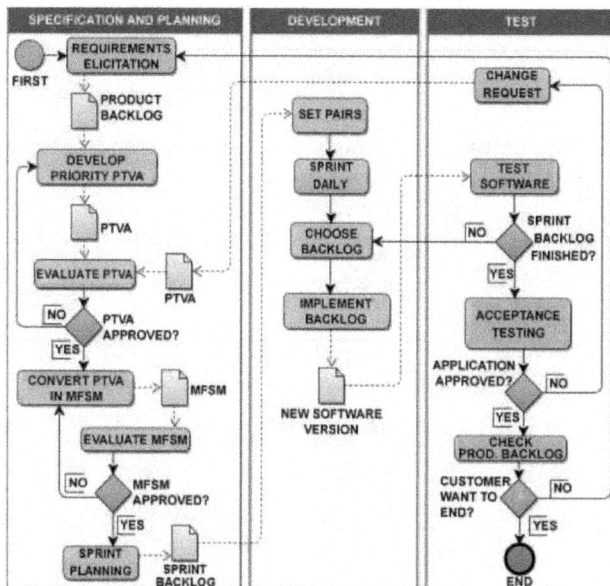

Figure 5. Lifecycle of XDTv method

The XDTv adopts: *Product Backlog, Sprint Planning, Sprint Backlog, Sprint Daily*, originally from Scrum, incorporated to the practices: pair programming, code standardization and constant version integration, originally from XP.

5. EXPERIMENT 2

In Experiment 2 the hybrid methods (Scrum/XP) and XDTv methods are investigated, their dependent variables were Adaptation and Time. The research questions were: **Q1)** Which is the better method for requirement gathering, planning and implementation of DTV applications? **Q2)** Which method makes the development faster? The Null Hypothesis were: **H0** – the development time is equal. **H1** – the Specification, Planning and Implementation are equally adapted. The Alternative Hypothesis points that HDTv is faster: **H2** – generally; **H3** – in Planning; **H4**

– in Specification; **H5** – in Implementation; **H6** – XDTv is generally more adequate.

The independent variables were: **a)** developers: 12 which did not take part in Experiment 1; **b)** four teams raffling: **A, B, C** and **D**; **c)** members by team: 3; **d)** members and applications raffling; **e)** functional requirements: identical; **f)** different non-functional requirements; **g)** serial implementation; **h)** activities performed in team; **i)** delivery time of 3 weeks; **j)** client is the author; **k)** six meetings with the client, 30 minutes, total: 3h by team; **l)** three interactions; **m)** one week per interaction; **n)** tools: Eclipse Helios; VMware virtual machine; Ginga Fedora; ManicTime in the gathering of implementation hours; **o)** multimedia content previously provided. The comparison relation between the teams was made by two Latin Squares (2x2) [11], each team developed integrally two applications with similar difficulty. In short, Application A corresponds to a vehicle shop, having information about its brands, models, test drive scheduling. Application B corresponds to a homebuilder having information about its buildings, several apartments and the storage of sales offers. Resources used are anchor, resize, properties, color buttons, directional arrows, NCL commands `start`, `stop`, `abort`, `resume`, scripts Lua, among others. Figure 6 presents the four teams results (A, B, C and D), considering the time dedicated to Planning (P), Specification (S) and Implementation (I).

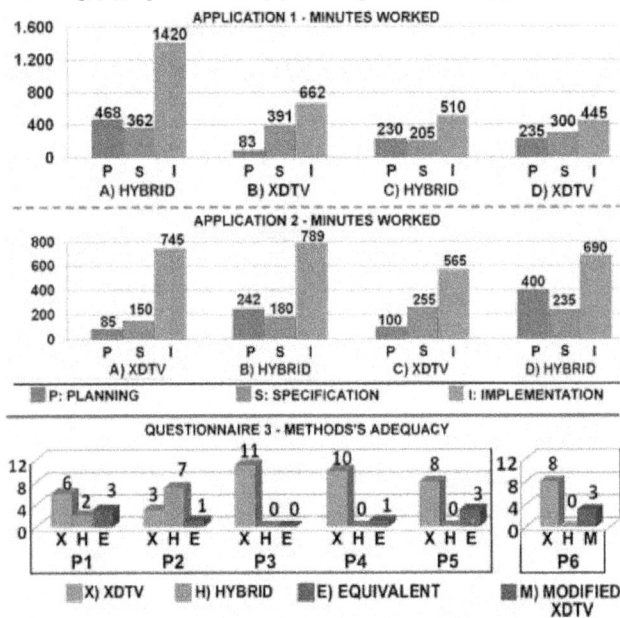

Figure 6. Experiment 2 – working hours and questionnaire

At the end of each application an objective questionnaire was applied – scale: 1 (inadequate) until 5 (adequate). The averages obtained by the Application 1 are: Hybrid = 47 and XDTv = 47.5, this small variation is due to the absence of benchmark. At the end of Application 2: Hybrid = 39 and XDTv = 47 points in average, the Hybrid method had a score 17% lower and the XDTv stayed constant. Figure 6 shows the answers of 11 from the 12 developers about Questionnaire 3 (descriptive). The objective was to find the method that better contributed to: **P1)** requirements? **P2)** planning? **P3)** implementation? **P4)** more adequate artifacts? **P5)** in a general way, which method contributed more? **P6)** which

method would the participant adopt? The adaptation of the Hybrid method (Scrum/XP) ranged between 4 and 7, with average = 6.36. The score of XDTv ranged between 8 and 10, with average = 9.18 – scale from 0 (inadequate) until 10 (totally adequate).

6. FINAL CONSIDERATIONS

Aiming to help the development of DTV applications, this research did the survey of specialist literature, the first experiment, followed by a survey with professionals, to define a synthesis of peculiarities of such applications. Based in the results gathered, the eXtreme Digital Television (XDTv) and its artifacts PTvA and MFSM were specified, whose objective is to help the development process of applications for DTV focused in the speed of Planning, Specification and Implementation activities.

The second experiment showed that the XDTv method had better performance and adaptation in all dependent variables, except in the Planning activity. The results gathered allowed the evaluation of the raised hypothesis, refuting the Null Hypotheses H0 and H1 and the Alternative Hypothesis H3, showing that the XDTv method has promising contributions. For the conclusion of this research it is intended to present improvements for the Planning activity and to perform a revaluation of the XDTv method and its artifacts through a new survey with experimented developers of DTV applications.

7. REFERENCES

[1] Soares, L. F. G., Moreno, M. F., Soares Neto, C. S., Moreno, M. F. "Ginga-Ncl: declarative middleware for multimedia IPTV services". In: Communications Magazine, IEEE, 2010.

[2] Lula, M. M. M., Guimarães, A. P., Tavares, T. A., "Um processo ágil para especificação de requisitos em programas interativos com foco em roteiros de tv". In: SBQS, 2011.

[3] Marques Neto, M. C., Santos, C. A. S.: "StoryToCode: a new model for specification of convergent interactive digital TV applications". J. Braz. Comp. Soc. 215-227, 2010.

[4] Sommerville, I. "Engenharia de software". Pearson, 9ª ed., 2011.

[5] CHAOS. "Summary for 2010", [online]. www.standishgroup.com, 2010.

[6] Tavares, T. A.; Veiga, E. G. "Um modelo de processo para o desenvolvimento de programas paraTv digital e interativa baseado em metodologias ágeis". In: Workshop de Desenvolvimento Rápido de Aplicações/SBQS, 2007.

[7] Marconi, M.A, Lakatos, E. "Fundamentos de metodologia científica". Ed.Atlas,SP,2003.

[8] Travassos, G.H. "Introdução à engenharia de software experimental". RT-ES-590/02, COPPE/UFRJ, 2002.

[9] Snyder, C. "paper prototyping: the fast and easy way to design and refine user interfaces", Morgan Kaufmann, 2003.

[10] Soares Neto, A. S., Soares, L. F. G., Rodrigues, R. F., Barbosa, S. D. J. "Construindo programas audiovisuais interativos utilizando a NCL 3.0 e a ferramenta Composer". Telemídia / PUC – Rio, 2ª ed., 2007.

[11] Sánchez, I. F. H. "Quadrados Latinos com aplicações em engenharia de software". Dissertação (Mestrado) – UFPE, Recife, 2011.

Hybrid Recommenders: Incorporating Metadata Awareness into Latent Factor Models

Edson B. Santos Junior, Marcelo G. Manzato, Rudinei Goularte
Mathematics and Computing Institute, São Paulo University
400 Trabalhador Sancarlense Ave., PO Box 668 – 13560-970
São Carlos, SP – Brazil
{ditusp,mmanzato,rudinei}@icmc.usp.br

ABSTRACT

This paper proposes a hybrid recommender algorithm which integrates a set of different user's inputs into a unified and generic latent factor model to improve prediction accuracy. The technique can exploit users' demographics, such as age, gender and occupation, along with implicit feedback and items' metadata. Depending on the personal information from users, the recommender selects content whose subject is semantically related to their interests. The method was evaluated in the MovieLens dataset and compared against other approaches reported in the literature. The results show the effectiveness of incorporating metadata awareness into a latent factor model.

Categories and Subject Descriptors

H.3.1 [**Information Storage and Retrieval**]: Content Analysis and Indexing—*Indexing methods*

General Terms

Design, Algorithms

Keywords

collaborative filtering, matrix factorization, implicit feedback, metadata awareness, demographic data.

1. INTRODUCTION

Due to the growth of available content on the Web, efforts to develop and enhance recommender systems have been required. To assist users in dealing with the information overload, the branch of Personalization researches aims to help them to find content in large data sources meeting individual needs [1, 2], generating personalized recommendations according to the user's preferences.

Two traditional mechanisms reported in the literature [3] can generate such recommendations: content-based and collaborative. In the content-based approach, the data are se-lected by attribute associations, in which each item is structured of its own characteristics [4]. However, if only metadata are considered, there may occur over-specialization, not allowing users to receive new and/or diverse content, in particular when their profile is restricted to descriptions of similar items that were visited [3]. Consequently, it has led companies, such as Google[1], Yahoo[2] and NetFlix[3] to make significant investments in the creation and deployment of collaborative systems.

In the collaborative filtering (CF) approach, two topics are studied: neighborhood models and latent factors. In the first case, clusters of items are formed to recommend items which are similar to the ones preferred by the user in the past. Alternatively, clusters of users can be formed to recommend items to a specific user, i.e. items appreciated by other users of similar preferences. In the second topic, the recommendation can be computed by uncovering latent associations among users or items. Thereby, an alternative path is comprised to transform both items and users into the same latent factor space, allowing them to be directly comparable [5, 6]. It is also possible to reduce the dimensionality of the matrices by gathering only the most relevant information associated with the users and items.

When comparing neighborhood and latent factor models, Bell & Koren [5] reported some lessons to guide researchers in the study of CF models. Among them, one particular lesson shows that latent factor models are generally effective at estimating an overall structure that relates simultaneously to most or all items, but they fail to detect strong associations among a small set of closely related items [7]. It is possible to address this issue by considering neighborhood models, but at the cost of having to compute many user-user or item-item pair distances according to the available ratings [8].

Another lesson reported by Bell & Koren is the importance of integrating different forms of user input data into the models. In fact, in addition to the explicit information provided by users, nowadays, the most studies in this direction deal with implicit feedback, which are indirect cues of users provided when interacting with the system [9]. Examples of explicit and implicit information are, respectively, the ratings manually assigned to visited items and the user's purchase history.

Considering the different forms of user's input to construct an accurate profile, hybrid recommenders are a good alter-

[1]http://www.google.com
[2]http://www.yahoo.com
[3]http://www.netflix.com

native for recommender systems, because they group the benefits of content-based and collaborative filtering. With such systems, problems associated with both approaches (e.g. cold-start, over-specialization, limited content analysis, etc.) can be reduced by combining the two strategies into a unified model [3]. However, most recent systems which exploit latent factor models consider neither metadata associated with the content nor demographic data. In fact, semantic and known descriptions of users and items could be added into the recommendation process, in contrast to the obscure and incomprehensive relations of latent factors. In face of the given scenario, we argue that additional information should be considered so that a latent factor-based filtering algorithm can be developed.

This paper proposes a technique that groups personal information from users, items metadata and implicit feedback into a unified and generic model to capture the user's preferences according to the semantics associated with the content. Our approach is based on latent factors, because it involves less computational cost than neighborhood models. At the same time, users and items metadata are incorporated into a hybrid approach to improve the prediction accuracy by detecting such small and semantic associations among the involved entities.

The paper is structured as follows: Section 2 addresses the related work; Section 3 describes the past models explored in this study; Section 4 presents our proposal in details; Section 5 describes the system's evaluation; finally, Section 6 addresses the final remarks and future works.

2. RELATED WORK

This section summarizes three features combined into a unified model to improve the recommendation accuracy. The first is implicit feedback, which provides additional mechanisms to characterize the users' interests; the second is the incorporation of metadata and their factorization to adjust their relative importance in face of the preferences of the users; and the third is demographic information from users, which involves cues used to infer their interests according to personal information.

Implicit feedback is an important mechanism to acquire user's preferences mainly when explicit feedback is either unavailable or incomplete [10, 11]. Oard & Kim [9] identified different types of implicit feedback and how they could be exploited in some recommendation strategies. More recent studies include the proposal of Hu et al. [12], which is a tool that allows transforming users' implicit feedback into a training data. A relevant model was also proposed by Koren [7, 6], who integrated indirect information into a neighborhood latent factor model to improve recommendation accuracy. The author also proposed the SVD++ algorithm, which is a latent factor model supported by implicit feedback.

Still concerning implicit feedback, Yang et al. [13] proposed a simple and effective local implicit feedback model that mines users' local preferences to achieve better results. Their work consisted in extending Koren's SVD++ by incorporating the notion of rating time interval to gather local and momentary interests. It differs from ours because we do not consider local implicit feedback, but incoporate item's metadata to improve accuracy.

Regarding metadata incorporation, a variety of content-based methods can be found in the literature [3]. Such meth-ods design matching mechanisms between the item metadata and the user's profile, so that the act of recommending becomes similar to information retrieval systems. However, content-based filtering algorithms usually have associated problems, such as occurrence of cold start and overspecialization, which can decay the recommendation results.

In order to reduce the aforementioned problems and acquire relevant information, collaborative filtering, whose main idea is to compute similarities of users/items to predict new items to users, is used. An efficient method to compute such similarities is by using matrix factorization models to reduce the dimensionality of the user-item matrix [7, 6]. However, as this matrix is very sparse, imputation methods are used, at the cost of distorting and/or overfitting the training data.

An alternative way to compute users' similarities by means of factorization techniques was proposed by [14]. The author created a user-category matrix factorization model to extract user's preferences about movies. The preferred categories are computed according to the users' similarities, supporting the collaborative filtering. However, such an approach is not accurate because it uses Singular Value Decomposition to factorize the matrix. A more recent study [8] conducted by the same author incorporates implicit feedback into a latent factors model with metadata awareness; however, it does not support user's personal information, such as demographic data.

The idea of a matrix factorization associated with metadata (e.g. movies' genres) was also considered by Gantner et al. [15]. The authors described a method that maps user's or items attributes to the latent features model. With such mappings, the factor-model is trained by standard techniques, which can be applied to the solve new user / item problems, while keeping its advantages, in particular, speed and predictive accuracy.

The third topic related to the proposed approach is the incorporation of demographic information. Demographic filtering is explored as a way of recommendation, assuming that users with common personal characteristics (e.g. country, gender, age, occupation) will also have similar preferences. Consequently, a simple and effective way to explore this fact is by using a CF model, boosted by demographic information. Chen and He [16] proposed a CF algorithm that computes users' similarities based on three demographic attributes and ratings of items separately. A new similarity is generated by combining the results. Lee and Woo [17] first segment all users by demographic characteristics and then apply a user clustering procedure to each segment according to the preference of items. Yapriady and Uitdenbogerd [18] proposed a simple measure of combining demographic data with traditional collaborative filtering techniques to improve recommendation precision.

The aforementioned techniques are related to the proposed aspects: first, there are methods which exploit implicit feedback, but consider neither the available metadata nor the demographic information; second, there is a set of models which exploit items' metadata and their factorization, but do not support implicit feedback; and third, demographic information is commonly used to support the computation of users' similarities in collaborative filtering, differently from our approach, which is used as additional parameter of a latent factor model to capture the user's interests, according to personal information.

3. PAST MODELS

This section describes the models reported in the literature which are related to the one proposed in this paper.

3.1 Notation

Following the same notation of [6], we use special indexing letters to distinguish users, items and metadata: users are indicated as u; items are referred to as i and j; and descriptions of users and items as d and g, respectively. As these descriptions may be of different types, we also use index letters z_u and z_i to refer, respectively, to different types of users and items' metadata. A summary of these indexes and the sets used in this paper are provided in Table 1.

A rating r_{ui} refers to the explicit feedback a user u has assigned to an item i, being distinguished from the predicted one $\hat{r}_{ui}$, which is a value guessed by the recommender algorithm. The (u,i) pairs for which r_{ui} is known are represented by set $K = \{(u,i)|r_{ui}$ is known$\}$.

Because the rating data is sparse, the models are prone to overfitting. To solve this issue, regularization is applied so that estimates are shrunk towards baseline defaults. Similarly to [6], we denote $\lambda_1, \lambda_2, ...$ the constants used for regularization. The values of these constants are defined in Section 5, which describes the experiments with the dataset adopted to evaluate the algorithm proposed.

Table 1: Notation for the different sets used in this paper.

Notation	Indexes	Definition
K	(u,i)	Set of known ratings
$R(u)$	i,j	Set of items rated by user u
$R(i)$	u,v	Set of users who rated item i
$N(u)$	j	Set of items for which user u provided an implicit feedback
$Z(u)$	z_u	Set of different demographic information considered in the system
$Z(i)$	z_i	Set of different items metadata considered in the system
$G(u;z_u)$	d	Set of descriptions of type x associated with user u
$G(i;z_i)$	g	Set of descriptions of type y associated with item i

3.2 Baseline Estimates

Baseline estimates are used to encapsulate systematic tendencies from the data according to users' and items' intrinsic characteristics. For example, a user may rate as 4 a great movie, whereas another user may adopt value 5 to indicate the same degree of interest. Similarly, an item may be rated differently by users, though some of these ratings may refer to the same likeness.

In order to overcome such differences, baseline estimates are used to adjust the data by accounting for these effects [6]. A baseline estimate for an unknown rating r_{ui} is denoted by b_{ui} and defined as:

$$b_{ui} = \mu + b_u + b_i \quad , \qquad (1)$$

where μ refers to the overall average rating and parameters b_u and b_i indicate the observed deviations of user u and item i, respectively, from the average. To estimate these

parameters, two methods can be adopted. The first consists in decoupling the calculation of the item biases from the user biases [19, 7, 6]. For each item i, the bias is computed as:

$$b_i = \frac{\sum_{u:(u,i)\in K}(r_{ui} - \mu)}{\lambda + |\{u|(u,i) \in K\}|} \quad . \qquad (2)$$

Then, b_i is used to calculate the user bias:

$$b_u = \frac{\sum_{i:(u,i)\in K}(r_{ui} - \mu - b_i)}{\lambda + |\{i|(u,i) \in K\}|} \quad . \qquad (3)$$

In the second and more accurate method, b_u and b_i are estimated by solving the least squares problem:

$$\min_{b_*} \sum_{(u,i)\in K} (r_{ui} - \mu - b_u - b_i)^2 + \lambda \left(\sum_u b_u^2 + \sum_i b_i^2 \right) \quad , \quad (4)$$

where the first term before regularization finds the user and item biases that fit the given ratings. The second term avoids overfitting by penalizing the magnitudes of the parameters.

3.3 Implicit Feedback

In recommender systems, an important issue is how to integrate different forms of user input into the models to precisely reflect the user's preferences [5]. The algorithms usually rely only on explicit feedback, which includes ratings assigned by users to items they have visited in the past. A good example is Netflix[4], which allows users to choose and assign an amount of stars for movies they have watched. The system constructs and controls the user's profile by considering each rating into their personal interests.

On the other hand, one can argue that explicit feedback is not always available due to cold start, or simply because users may not assign any ratings to their preferences. Consequently, the implicit feedback could be explored, since it is an abundant source of information and indirectly reflects the user's opinion by observing his/her behavior [9]. Examples of implicit feedback are purchase or rental history, browsing activity, search patterns, etc.

Koren [7, 6] proposed a set of models which faces implicit feedback when explicit feedback is also available. The proposed algorithms integrate both types of feedback by considering ratings assigned by users to visited items and also the set of movies rented in the past. The adopted dataset (Netflix) lacks this second type of implicit feedback, therefore the author simulated such information by considering the movies rated by the users, regardless of how they were rated.

The most accurate model reported by Koren is the SVD++ algorithm[5], which integrates explicit and implicit feedback into a factorization model representing the user's preferences. Each user u is associated with a user-factors vector $p_u \in \mathbb{R}^f$ and each item i with an item-factors vector $q_i \in \mathbb{R}^f$. A popular prediction rule would be:

---

[4]http://www.netflix.com

[5]In fact, Koren proposed a more accurate algorithm than SVD++, which integrates implicit feedback with a neighborhood model. However, this method is not in the scope of this paper, as it also incorporates similarities of users and items.

$$\hat{r}_{ui} = b_{ui} + p_u^T q_i \quad . \tag{5}$$

Based on Equation 5, Koren extended this basic model in order to consider implicit information. In fact, he used an additional factors vector $y_i \in \mathbb{R}^f$ and also considered set $N(u)$, which contains all items for which u provided an implicit preference. Thus, the SVD++ model is defined as:

$$\hat{r}_{ui} = b_{ui} + q_i^T \left(p_u + |N(u)|^{-\frac{1}{2}} \sum_{j \in N(u)} y_j \right) \quad . \tag{6}$$

The preferences of a user u are represented by a combination of explicit and implicit information. The user-factors vector p_u is learnt from the given explicit ratings, and complemented by the sum of y_j, which represents the implicit feedback. Again, the parameters are learnt by minimizing the associated squared error function through gradient descent [7, 6, 20, 21].

Still concerning implicit feedback, [8] proposed an extension of the SVD++ model taking into account the items' metadata, when available. This extension was denominated "gSVD++" and considers set $G(i; z_i)$, which contains the descriptions of type z_i associated with item i. It also defines a metadata factors vector $x_g \in \mathbb{R}^f$ containing the factors for each possible description. Equation 6 was rewritten in order to complement the items factor q_i with the available metadata, as follows:

$$\hat{r}_{ui} = b_{ui} + \left(q_i + \sum_{z_i \in Z(i)} |G(i; z_i)|^{-\alpha} \sum_{g \in G(i; z_i)} x_g \right)^T$$
$$\left(p_u + |N(u)|^{-\frac{1}{2}} \sum_{j \in N(u)} y_j \right) \quad . \tag{7}$$

The original Koren's solution considered the y_j factor vector to represent the indirect user's information (e.g. rental history). As an extension to this model, another factor vector x_g was added to represent the items metadata (e.g. genres), incorporating the feature of metadata awareness. The regularization constant α from Equation 7 is set to 1 when there are metadata associated with item i, and 0 otherwise. Similarly to previous approaches [7, 6, 21], the parameters are learnt by minimizing a squared error function through gradient descent.

4. PROPOSED METHOD

Differently from the previous approaches, the method proposed in this paper consists of a latent factor approach which integrates users' and items' metadata and implicit feedback into a unified model. Depending on the semantics associated with the user's profile and demographic information, the recommender selects those items whose subject is meaningfully related to the individual's tastes. The next subsections describes the proposed model in details, by gradually incorporating the various components which constitute the final schema.

4.1 Baseline Revisited

Subsection 3.2 described the baseline estimates, which model systematic tendencies according to users' and items'

intrinsic characteristics. Such a technique can be slightly improved by also incorporating the global effects of how users rate items depending on the contextual environment or demographic data. Considering the age group, for instance, children may rate an item differently from adults; similarly, if the user is interacting with their church friends, they may rate an item differently than when cycling.

In order to model such possibilities, we have extended the baseline estimates in Equation 1 by also considering the contextual environment or demographic information:

$$b_{ui}^{demo} = \mu + b_u + b_i + \sum_{z_u \in Z(u)} |G(u; z_u)|^{-1} \sum_{d \in G(u; z_u)} b_d \quad . \tag{8}$$

In this case, $Z(u)$ is the set of different types of user's information considered in the system and $G(u; z_u)$ represents all data of type z_u associated with user u. An example is when using the demographic information from the Movie-Lens dataset[6]. We denote $Z(u) = \{$occupation, age group, gender, zip code$\}$ and $z_u =$ occupation of a user u as $G(u;$ occupation$) = \{$programmer$\}$, for instance. It is worth mentioning that in most cases $|G(u; z_u)| = 1$, but we preferred to keep generality by using more than one piece of information associated with z_u.

The contextual biases b_d can be estimated by solving a least squares problem, as in Equation 4. In the experiments reported in Section 5, we employ a simple gradient descent scheme using the observed data to change the parameters in the opposite direction of the gradient [6, 21].

4.2 Incorporation of Item's Metadata

In addition to the global effects modeled in our extended estimated baseline, we aimed to create associations between the demographic data and the content metadata available for each item. Such an approach is important because depending on the actual contextual environment, demographic data or personal interests, users may prefer to visit items related to specific subjects. For instance, a 7-year-old user certainly prefers children's films, female users will probably like romantic and drama films, and a group of cyclists will enjoy sports and adventure content.

In order to capture such associations between users' and items' metadata, we incorporated another set of parameters h_{dg} to Equation 8 as follows:

$$\hat{r}_{ui}^{meta} = b_{ui}^{demo} + \sum_{z_i \in Z(i)} |G(i; z_i)|^{-1} \sum_{z_u \in Z(u)} |G(u; z_u)|^{-1}$$
$$\sum_{d \in G(u; z_u)} \sum_{g \in G(i; z_i)} h_{dg} \quad . \tag{9}$$

Here set $Z(i)$ denotes all different types of items' metadata, such as genres, list of actors and keywords. Set $G(i; z_i)$ represents all pieces of information of the same type z_i associated with item i. For instance, we could instantiate $Z(i) = \{$genre$\}$ and then an item i entitled "Star Wars" that would have a set of $G(i;$ genres$)$ composed of "Science Fiction", "Action" and "Adventure". The parameters represented by h_{dg} capture the weights of a user's demographic information d associated with an item description g. Again, such weights are learned from the observed data through gradient descent.

---

[6]http://www.grouplens.org/node/73

4.3 Factorization and Implicit Feedback

The last refinement of our model refers to the incorporation of latent factors and implicit feedback regarding users. By using latent factors, it is possible to capture a user's preference to different features, which characterize the whole item to be recommended. On the other hand, by using implicit feedback, it is possible to capture the user's preferences even if they have few ratings.

Such an enhancement in our algorithm is dictated by the combination between our approach (Equation 9) and Koren's SVD++ model [7, 6] described in Equation 6. Concretely, our unified model is defined by the following equation:

$$\hat{r}_{ui} = \hat{r}_{ui}^{meta} + q_i^T \left(p_u + |N(u)|^{-\frac{1}{2}} \sum_{j \in N(u)} y_j \right) \quad . \quad (10)$$

Instead of summing the items' metadata features with the factors vector q_i, as accomplished by the gSVD++ algorithm, the information is added as global effects into the baselines. Concomitantly, we combine users' demographics and items' metadata in order to capture the relationship between users' personal information and items' descriptions.

Similarly to the previous formulations, the parameters are learnt by minimizing the regularized squared error function associated with Equation 10 as follows:

$$
\begin{aligned}
\min_{b_*, h_*, q_*, p_*, y_*} \sum_{(u,i) \in K} & \Bigg(r_{ui} - \mu - b_u - b_i \\
& - \sum_{z_u \in Z(u)} |G(u; z_u)|^{-1} \sum_{d \in G(u; z_u)} b_d \\
& - \sum_{z_i \in Z(i)} |G(i; z_i)|^{-1} \sum_{g \in G(i; z_i)} b_g \\
- \sum_{z_i \in Z(i)} |G(i; z_i)|^{-1} & \sum_{z_u \in Z(u)} |G(u; z_u)|^{-1} \sum_{d \in G(u; z_u)} \sum_{g \in G(i; z_i)} h_{dg} \\
& - q_i^T \left(p_u + |N(u)|^{-\frac{1}{2}} \sum_{j \in N(u)} y_j \right) \Bigg)^2 \\
& + \lambda \Bigg(b_u^2 + b_i^2 + ||p_u||^2 + ||q_i||^2 \\
& + \sum_{z_u \in Z(u)} \sum_{d \in G(u; z_u)} b_d^2 + \sum_{z_i \in Z(i)} \sum_{g \in G(i; z_i)} b_g^2 \\
& + \sum_{z_u \in Z(u)} \sum_{z_i \in Z(i)} \sum_{d \in G(u; z_u)} \sum_{g \in G(i; z_i)} h_{dg}^2 + \sum_{j \in N(u)} y_j^2 \Bigg) ,
\end{aligned}
$$
(11)

Using the same strategy adopted by other authors [7, 6, 21], we employ a simple gradient descent scheme to solve the system indicated in Equation 11. Let us consider $e_{ui} \overset{def}{=} r_{ui} - \hat{r}_{ui}$. Using the training dataset, we loop over all known ratings in K. For a given training example r_{ui}, we change and move the parameters in the opposite direction of the gradient, as illustrated in Algorithm 1.

5. EVALUATION

The evaluation presented in this paper consists in comparing our model with other methods available in the literature. We also evaluate the different modules of the algorithm to

---

Input: Set of known ratings $(u, i) \in K$
Output: Learnt parameters $b_u, b_i, b_d, b_g, h_{dg}, p_u, q_i, y_j$
for $count = 1,...,\#Iter.$ do
  foreach $(u,i) \in K$ do
    $\hat{r}_{ui} \leftarrow$ Prediction according to Equation 10;
    $e_{ui} \leftarrow r_{ui} - \hat{r}_{ui}$;
    $b_u \leftarrow b_u + \gamma(e_{ui} - \lambda_1 b_u)$;
    $b_i \leftarrow b_i + \gamma(e_{ui} - \lambda_2 b_i)$;
    foreach $z_u \in Z(u)$ do
      foreach $d \in G(u; z_u)$ do
        $b_d \leftarrow b_d + \gamma(e_{ui} - \lambda_3 b_d)$;
      end
    end
    foreach $z_i \in Z(i)$ do
      foreach $g \in G(i; z_i)$ do
        $b_g \leftarrow b_g + \gamma(e_{ui} - \lambda_3 b_g)$;
      end
    end
    foreach $z_u \in Z(u)$ do
      foreach $z_i \in Z(i)$ do
        foreach $d \in G(u; z_u)$ do
          foreach $g \in G(i; z_i)$ do
            $h_{dg} \leftarrow h_{dg} + \gamma(e_{ui}|G(u; z_u)|^{-1}|G(i; z_i)|^{-1} - \lambda_3 h_{dg})$;
         end
        end
      end
    end
    $p_u \leftarrow p_u + \gamma_2(e_{ui}q_i - \lambda_4.p_u)$;
    $q_i \leftarrow q_i + \gamma_2(e_{ui}(p_u + |N(u)|^{-\frac{1}{2}} \sum_{j \in N(u)} y_j) - \lambda_4.q_i)$;
    foreach $j \in N(u)$ do
      $y_j \leftarrow y_j + \gamma_2(e_{ui}|N(u)|^{-\frac{1}{2}}q_i - \lambda_4.y_j)$;
    end
  end
  $\gamma \leftarrow \gamma * 0.9$;
  $\gamma_2 \leftarrow \gamma_2 * 0.9$;
end

Algorithm 1: Learning the factorized model through gradient descent.

---

check the contribution of each aspect to the final recommendation improvement.

The experiments were conducted with the well-known MovieLens 100k dataset[7]. It consists of 943 users, who assigned 100k ratings to 1682 movies. The dataset provides metadata regarding those users and items. Demographic data are also provided, such as age, occupation, gender and Zip code. In this evaluation, we consider all types of demographic data, except Zip code.

Regarding the users' age, we pre-processed such information in order to cluster those users in the same age group. Table 2 was configured experimentally in order to associate the same information with all users that belong to that group.

As a result, our set $Z(u)$ is composed of {age group, occupation, gender} and sets $|G(u, \text{age group})|$, $|G(u, \text{occupation})|$ and $|G(u, \text{gender})|$ have all size 1.

---

[7] http://www.grouplens.org/node/73

Table 2: Configuration of age group.

Age	Group
0 – 12	infant
12 – 18	teenager
18 – 25	young adult
25 – 35	adult
35 – 55	mature
55 – 60	aged
Over 60	elder

Table 3: Constants used in the evaluation.

Constant	Value
#Iter.	50
γ	0.03
γ_2	0.021
λ_1	$0.025 * |R(u)|^{-\frac{1}{2}}$
λ_2	$0.025 * |R(i)|^{-\frac{1}{2}}$
λ_3	0.025
λ_4	0.5

Regarding items' metadata, the MovieLens dataset provides the movie title, date of release, IMDB URL and the set of associated genres. In our experiments, we considered only the genres items' metadata; consequently, $|Z(i)| = 1$, and $|G(i, \text{genre})| \geq 1$, because one or more genres can be assigned to each movie i. In this version of the dataset, there are 19 different genres, all considered in this evaluation. The combination of two or more types of items' metadata is left to future work.

We chose three previous methods to be compared against our model in this evaluation:

- **Biased MF**: algorithm proposed by Rendle & Schmidt-Thie [22] and equivalent to Equation 5. According to the authors, this approach reduces the cold start by deriving an online-update algorithm for regularized kernel matrix factorization models. The algorithm is also flexible for nonlinear interactions between feature vectors.

- **SVD++**: algorithm proposed by Koren [7, 6] and represented by Equation 6. It was chosen in this evaluation because it is an accurate model which exploits implicit feedback from users and latent factors.

- **gSVD++**: an extension of Koren's model, proposed by Manzato [8] and represented by Equation 7. It incorporates items' metadata into the previous model to improve the prediction accuracy.

All methods were implemented using MyMediaLite library [23] and the results were measured as follows:

1. The prediction accuracy of all techniques in terms of RMSE (root mean squared error) and MAE (mean average error) was compared according to a varying number of factors.

2. For each technique, the best number of factors was selected, i.e., the value of f for which the RMSE and MAE computed in the previous step was minimal.

3. Using these specific values of f for each technique, all methods were compared in terms of precision accuracy and AUC (area under curve) at top 5 and top 10 recommendations.

For all experiments the 5-fold cross-validation was used to improve the results with more confidence.

The constants involved in this evaluation were defined experimentally and are summarized in Table 3. The details of their utilization can be found in Algorithm 1, as previously explained.

We started our evaluation by comparing the baseline estimates with and without demographic data and items' metadata. Table 4 shows the results. The traditional baseline represented by Equation 1 achieved 0.9437 of RMSE, as it considered only the user and item's biases. When demographic data in terms of global effects were added, the RMSE decreased to 0.9402. Furthermore, additional improvement was achieved when the items' metadata associated with the users' personal information were incorporated into the model. Such an approach decreased the RMSE to 0.9385, which is an improvement of approximately 0.52% over the traditional baseline. It is worth mentioning that in this first experiment, we considered all types of user's demographic information: age group, occupation and gender, which were combined with the items' metadata, e.g. genres.

Table 4: Comparison of baselines.

Algorithm	RMSE	MAE
Baseline (Equation 1)	0.9437	0.7480
Baseline Revisited (Equation 8)	0.9402	0.7432
Item's Metadata (Equation 9)	0.9385	0.7418

Next, we compared our unified model (Equation 10) with the three other latent factor-based approaches considered. Figure 1 shows the results according to variable factors. The related techniques tend to achieve better results when more factors are incorporated into the model, unlike the proposed algorithm, which gets worse when more factors are considered. This occurs because the first layer of our model (i.e. the value of $\hat{r}_{ui}^{meta}$) is not based on latent factors, although its significance is high when the final prediction is computed. An advantage of such an approach is that we can provide good recommendations for low values of f. Thereby, the computational cost becomes significantly lower in comparison with the related approaches. Tables 5 and 6 show the RMSE and MAE results for specific values of f. We can note that the proposed model achieved the best accuracy when $f = 40$, whereas all other techniques yielded the best results when $f = 350$. However, our algorithm outperformed SVD++ (0.9123 against 0.9144) and Biased MF (0.9123 against 0.9167). It could not outperform gSVD++ (0.9123 against 0.9085) because, besides considering metadata, it also uses latent factors to characterize such pieces of information. Thus, the accuracy curve tends to fall when more factors are added. On the other hand, when f was low ($f \leq 150$), our algorithm provided the best results from all techniques considered as shown in Figure 1.

Finally, our evaluation measured the quality of top-N recommendations for all techniques considered. This study was important because, as argued in the literature [24], the rec-

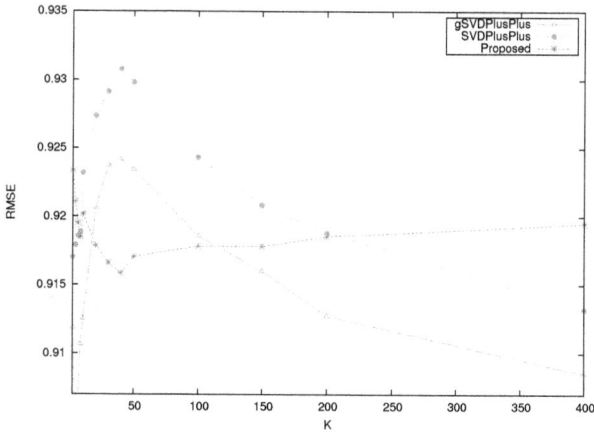

Figure 1: Comparison of the proposed method with other approaches

Table 5: RMSE comparison for different f values

Method	$f'40$	$f'100$	$f'150$	...	$f'300$	$f'350$
Biased MF	0.9352	0.9269	0.9227	...	0.9181	**0.9167**
SVD++	0.9307	0.9243	0.9208	...	0.9155	**0.9144**
gSVD++	0.9241	0.9185	0.9160	...	0.9090	**0.9085**
Proposed	**0.9123**	0.9147	0.9148	...	0.9157	0.9167

Table 6: MAE comparison for different f values

Method	$f'40$	$f'100$	$f'150$	...	$f'300$	$f'350$
Biased MF	0.7347	0.7310	0.7276	...	0.7253	**0.7245**
SVD++	0.7280	0.7244	0.7223	...	0.7194	**0.7190**
gSVD++	0.7213	0.7189	0.7175	...	0.7135	**0.7132**
Proposed	**0.7172**	0.7199	0.7206	...	0.7226	0.7237

Table 7: Comparison of strategies according to top-N and training and testing time.

Evaluation	Algorithm			
	BiasedMF	SVD++	gSVD++	Proposed
factors	350	350	350	40
AUC	0.6424	0.6402	0.6412	0.7859
prec@5	0.1256	0.1211	0.1165	0.1342
prec@10	0.1080	0.1046	0.0983	0.1183
training	0:00:49.09	1:07:27.51	1:12:54.59	0:08:44.63
testing	0:00:02.86	0:00:01.92	0:00:01.92	0:00:03.01

ommender systems aim to find few specific items which are supposed to be most appealing to the user, and common strategies, such as computing prediction accuracy in terms of RMSE and MAE are not a natural fit for evaluation.

Table 7 shows the AUC, precision@5 and precision@10 for the algorithms. It also shows the training and testing time captured on an Intel Core™ i5-2310 CPU @ 2.90GHz x 4 and 4GB RAM machine equipped with Ubuntu 13.04 operating system.

The proposed algorithm could recommend better items, which were more significant to the users' interests. It is worth mentioning that such results were obtained with only 40 factors, while Biased MF, SVD++ and gSVD++ required 350 factors (Table 7). Our method needed almost 9 minutes to train the model, whereas other techniques (except Biased MF) required over 1 hour. Regarding the Biased MF, because it processes fewer data, it could achieve the fastest training time even with 350 factors, but computed the worst predictions among all.

6. FINAL REMARKS

This paper has proposed a hybrid recommender based on latent factors which integrates users' demographics, items' metadata and implicit feedback into a unified model. The objective is to capture the user's preferences according to personal information and the semantics associated with the content. For instance, a 7-year-old child will probably like items specific for children (e.g. cartoons), whereas adult users will have different preferences, which are captured by latent factors. The technique involves less computational cost than neighborhood models, but at the same time, users and items metadata are incorporated into a hybrid approach to improve the prediction accuracy by detecting small and semantic associations among the entities involved.

Our technique is generic enough to deal with additional contextual constraints and/or other items/users metadata. For instance, given a scenario in which the system would have to recommend items to a group of friends from the church, one could label all individuals as belonging to that group and then incorporate such information as an additional attribute type into set $Z(u)$. Later, this attribute would be combined with the content's metadata to highlight those items whose subject is church-related, such as gospel, saints, etc.

We have provided a system's evaluation in terms of prediciton accuracy and precision at top-N recommendations. The study has shown that, differently from the related latent factors models, our system provides better results when low values of f are used.

As future work, we aim to incorporate additional types of items' and users' metadata and actual contextual information from users and their groups. A more robust evaluation is also necessary to measure the model's scalability, the importance of each metadata type, and the computation cost in comparison to other approaches.

7. ACKNOWLEDGEMENTS

The authors would like to thank São Paulo Research Foundation (FAPESP) for the financial support provided to this research (grant #2011/17366-2; grant #2011/00422-7).

8. REFERENCES

[1] M. Gartrell, X. Xing, Q. Lv, A. Beach, R. Han, S. Mishra, and K. Seada, "Enhancing group recommendation by incorporating social relationship interactions," 2010.

[2] F. Ricci, L. Rokach, B. Shapira, and P. B. Kantor, eds., *Recommender Systems Handbook*. Springer, 2011.

[3] G. Adomavicius and A. Tuzhilin, "Toward the Next Generation of Recommender Systems: A Survey of the State-of-the-Art and Possible Extensions," *IEEE Transactions on Knowledge and Data Engineering*, vol. 17, no. 6, pp. 734–749, 2005.

[4] R. Burke, "Hybrid Recommender Systems: Survey and Experiments," *User Modeling and User-Adapted Interaction*, vol. 12, no. 4, pp. 331–370, 2002.

[5] R. M. Bell and Y. Koren, "Lessons from the netflix prize challenge," *SIGKDD Explor. Newsl.*, vol. 9, pp. 75–79, Dec. 2007.

[6] Y. Koren, "Factor in the neighbors: Scalable and accurate collaborative filtering," *ACM Trans. Knowl. Discov. Data*, vol. 4, pp. 1:1–1:24, Jan. 2010.

[7] Y. Koren, "Factorization meets the neighborhood: a multifaceted collaborative filtering model," in *Proceedings of the 14th ACM SIGKDD international conference on Knowledge discovery and data mining*, KDD '08, (New York, NY, USA), pp. 426–434, ACM, 2008.

[8] M. G. Manzato, "gSVD++: supporting implicit feedback on recommender systems with metadata awareness," in *28th Symposium On Applied Computing*, (Coimbra), ACM - Association for Computing Machinery, 2013.

[9] D. Oard and J. Kim, "Implicit feedback for recommender systems," in *Proceedings of the AAAI Workshop on Recommender Systems*, pp. 81–83, 1998.

[10] E. Agichtein, E. Brill, and S. Dumais, "Improving web search ranking by incorporating user behavior information," in *Proceedings of the 29th annual international ACM SIGIR conference on Research and development in information retrieval*, SIGIR '06, (New York, NY, USA), pp. 19–26, ACM, 2006.

[11] T. Joachims, L. Granka, B. Pan, H. Hembrooke, and G. Gay, "Accurately interpreting clickthrough data as implicit feedback," in *Proceedings of the 28th annual international ACM SIGIR conference on Research and development in information retrieval*, SIGIR '05, (New York, NY, USA), pp. 154–161, ACM, 2005.

[12] Y. Hu, Y. Koren, and C. Volinsky, "Collaborative filtering for implicit feedback datasets," in *Proceedings of the 2008 Eighth IEEE International Conference on Data Mining*, ICDM '08, (Washington, DC, USA), pp. 263–272, IEEE Computer Society, 2008.

[13] D. Yang, T. Chen, W. Zhang, Q. Lu, and Y. Yu, "Local implicit feedback mining for music recommendation," in *Proceedings of the 6th ACM Conference on Recommender Systems*, RecSys '12, (New York, NY, USA), pp. 91–98, ACM, 2012.

[14] M. G. Manzato, "Discovering Latent Factors from Movies Genres for Enhanced Recommendation," in *Proceedings of the 6th ACM Conferece on Recommender Systems*, RecSys '12, (New York, NY, USA), pp. 249–252, 2012.

[15] Z. Gantner, L. Drumond, C. Freudenthaler, S. Rendle, and L. Schmidt-Thieme, "Learning attribute-to-feature mappings for cold-start recommendations," in *2010 IEEE 10th International Conference on Data Mining (ICDM)*, pp. 176–185, dec. 2010.

[16] T. Chen and L. He, "Collaborative filtering based on demographic attribute vector," in *Future Computer and Communication, 2009. FCC '09. International Conference on*, pp. 225–229, 2009.

[17] M. Lee, P. Choi, and Y. Woo, "A hybrid recommender system combining collaborative filtering with neural network," *Lecture Notes in Computer Science (including subseries Lecture Notes in Artificial Intelligence and Lecture Notes in Bioinformatics)*, vol. 2347 LNCS, pp. 531–534, 2002.

[18] B. Yapriady and A. L. Uitdenbogerd, "Combining demographic data with collaborative filtering for automatic music recommendation," in *Proceedings of the 9th international conference on Knowledge-Based Intelligent Information and Engineering Systems - Volume Part IV*, KES'05, (Berlin, Heidelberg), pp. 201–207, Springer-Verlag, 2005.

[19] J. Herlocker, J. A. Konstan, and J. Riedl, "An empirical analysis of design choices in neighborhood-based collaborative filtering algorithms," *Inf. Retr.*, vol. 5, pp. 287–310, Oct. 2002.

[20] S. Funk, "Netflix Update: Try This At Home." http://sifter.org/~simon/journal/20061211.html, 2006. [Online; accessed 26-September-2012].

[21] A. Paterek, "Improving regularized singular value decomposition for collaborative filtering," in *Proc. KDD Cup Workshop at SIGKDD'07, 13th ACM Int. Conf. on Knowledge Discovery and Data Mining*, pp. 39–42, 2007.

[22] S. Rendle and S.-T. Lars, "Online-updating regularized kernel matrix factorization models for large-scale recommender systems," in *Proceedings of the 2008 ACM conference on Recommender systems*, RecSys '08, (New York, NY, USA), pp. 251–258, ACM, 2008.

[23] Z. Gantner, S. Rendle, C. Freudenthaler, and L. Schmidt-Thieme, "MyMediaLite: A free recommender system library," in *Proceedings of the 5th ACM Conference on Recommender Systems*, RecSys '11, (New York, NY, USA), pp. 305–308, 2011.

[24] P. Cremonesi, Y. Koren, and R. Turrin, "Performance of recommender algorithms on top-n recommendation tasks," in *Proceedings of the fourth ACM conference on Recommender systems*, RecSys '10, (New York, NY, USA), pp. 39–46, ACM, 2010.

Measuring and Addressing the Impact of Cold Start on Associative Tag Recommenders

Eder Martins, Fabiano Belém, Jussara Almeida, Marcos Gonçalves

Departamento de Ciência da Computação
Universidade Federal de Minas Gerais, Brazil

{ederfm, fmuniz, jussara, mgoncalv}@dcc.ufmg.br

ABSTRACT

Tag recommendation methods that exploit co-occurrence patterns of tags have consistently produced state of the art results. However, tags are not present in significant portions of Web 2.0 objects, which may impact the effectiveness of such methods. This problem, known as cold start, is the focus of this paper. We here evaluate the impact of the cold start on a family of methods for recommending tags. Our results show that the effectiveness of these methods suffer greatly when they cannot rely on previously assigned tags in the target object and that the use of automatic filtering strategies to alleviate the problem yields limited gains. We then propose a new strategy that exploits both positive and negative relevance feedback (RF) from the users to iteratively select input tags to these methods. The results show that the proposed strategy generates significant gains (up to 45%) over the best considered baseline. It is also shown that the proposed method is robust to the lack of user cooperation.

Categories and Subject Descriptors

H.3.1 [**Information Storage and Retrieval**]: Content Analysis and Indexing; H.3.5 [**Information Storage and Retrieval**]: Online Information Services

Keywords

Tag Recommendation, Cold Start, Relevance Feedback

1. INTRODUÇÃO

O aumento da popularidade das aplicações da Web 2.0 propiciou a criação de ricas coleções de dados. A grande presença de mídias ricas (e.g., vídeos e imagens) em tais coleções cria desafios para as técnicas de recuperação de informação (RI) baseada em conteúdo atuais devido ao grande tamanho das mesmas e às altas taxas de *upload* [4]. Assim, muitos dos serviços de RI existentes exploram apenas o conteúdo textual, notadamente tags, comumente associado ao conteúdo multimídia. De fato, estudos recentes mostram que tags são um dos melhores atributos para dar suporte a serviços de classificação automática [6], busca [11], e recomendação de conteúdo [9].

Nesse contexto, serviços de recomendação de tags ajudam a melhorar a qualidade tanto das tags disponíveis quanto dos sistemas de RI que as exploram como fontes de dados. A literatura contém uma grande variedade de estratégias de recomendação de tags, sendo que as que exploram padrões de cooxorrência com tags previamente associadas aos objetos do sistema (incluindo tags disponíveis no próprio objeto alvo da recomendação), chamados de métodos associativos, têm produzido consistentemente resultados estado-da-arte. Tais métodos expandem um conjunto inicial de tags $\mathcal{I}_o$ do objeto alvo o com outras tags que frequentemente coocorrem com os termos em $\mathcal{I}_o$ [10, 18, 13, 2]. Em Belém *et al.* [2], por exemplo, foram explorados como fonte de informação para os métodos tanto os padrões de cooxorrência quanto métricas de relevância e termos extraídos de outros atributos textuais para recomendar tags mais relevantes para o objeto.

Entretanto, a maioria dos métodos associativos de recomendação de tags [10, 18, 13, 2] não foram avaliados em cenários onde o objeto alvo da recomendação não tem nenhuma tag (i.e., $\mathcal{I}_o = \emptyset$). Nesse cenário, a eficácia desses métodos pode ser muito prejudicada já que não podem utilizar os padrões de cooxorrência. Tal cenário, que aparece em uma parcela não desprezível (cerca de 18%) dos objetos em várias aplicações populares da Web 2.0 [6], é uma variação de um problema bem conhecido em sistemas de recomendação chamado *cold start* [17] e é o foco desse trabalho. Mais especificamente, aqui consideramos o problema de recomendar tags para objetos que não possuem tags. Isto é, nós consideramos um cenário em que o usuário está adicionando um novo objeto ao sistema, já preencheu alguns dos atributos textuais desse objeto e precisa de sugestões de termos relevantes para usar como tags. Aqui focamos em métodos baseados em cooxorrência, uma vez que eles alcançam notória eficácia (em cenários sem *cold start*) [2].

Começamos nosso trabalho avaliando dois métodos associativos, chamados Sum^+wTS e $LATRE^+wTS$ [2], em um cenário de *cold start*. Nós escolhemos esses dois métodos uma vez que eles superaram várias alternativas em cenários sem *cold start* [2]. Nós mostramos que a eficácia desses métodos é muito prejudicada em *cold start*, com uma redução média em precisão de até 84% em comparação com cenários onde o *cold start* não ocorre. Nós também mostramos que em um cenário de *cold start* tais métodos são superados por um método chamado Co-occurrence and Text-based

Tag Recommender (CTTR) [12], que não é baseado em tags previamente associadas ao objeto alvo da recomendação.

Nós então testamos várias estratégias automáticas para melhorar a eficácia dos métodos associativos de recomendação em *cold start*. Tais estratégias são baseadas na construção de um conjunto inicial de tags $\mathcal{I}_o'$ a partir do qual os padrões de coocorrência são obtidos. Nós avaliamos várias estratégias de filtragem para construir $\mathcal{I}_o'$ que utilizam métricas heurísticas para filtrar termos tanto de outros atributos textuais do objeto alvo quanto de outros objetos similares ao objeto alvo. Entretanto, verificamos que essas estratégias produziram ganhos marginais sobre o CTTR.

Nesse contexto, nossa principal contribuição nesse artigo é uma nova estratégia de recomendação bastante flexível que incorpora as preferências por tags específicas manifestadas pelo usuário durante o processo de recomendação (*relevance feedback - RF*). A ideia geral da estratégia proposta pode ser descrita em 3 passos: (i) um conjunto inicial de tags é apresentado para o usuário; (ii) o usuário seleciona tags relevantes nesse conjunto; (iii) as tags selecionadas como relevantes são usadas como entrada para o método de recomendação enquanto que as tags não relevantes (não selecionadas) são inseridas em uma lista negra para prevenir que elas sejam recomendadas novamente nas próximas iterações. Tal processo é repetido até que um resultado satisfatório seja obtido, ou seja, até que o usuário decida parar de adicionar tags ao objeto. Observe que a estratégia proposta leva em conta tanto as tags que foram selecionadas pelo usuário (*feedback* positivo), quanto as que não foram (*feedback* negativo) e requer apenas um pequeno esforço extra por parte do usuário[1] que é recompensado pela melhoria da qualidade das tags recomendadas. Isso corresponde a um cenário em que o usuário deseja atribuir tags com o máximo de qualidade (i.e., relevância) para promover seu objeto no sistema, mas realizando o menor esforço possível.

Nós avaliamos algumas variações do processo de RF descrito acima. Nossos resultados mostram que nossa estratégia aumenta significativamente a eficácia dos métodos associativos de recomendação e diminui o impacto do *cold start*. Nossa melhor estratégia é baseada no uso combinado de dois métodos de referência - CTTR e Sum^+wTS - juntamente com o processo de RF. Tal estratégia híbrida supera o melhor método de referência em até 45% na maioria dos cenários considerados. Também mostramos que nossa estratégia melhora significativamente a eficácia dos métodos associativos de recomendação mesmo em cenários nos quais o *cold start* não ocorre, com ganhos de até 39% em precisão.

A eficácia de estratégias baseadas em RF depende da colaboração do usuário. Logo, investigamos também a robustez da estratégia proposta à falta de cooperação do usuário, avaliando o impacto na eficácia das recomendações do não assinalamento de termos relevantes por parte do usuário. Os resultados mostram que nosso método híbrido supera outros métodos previamente propostos, mesmo que 50% das tags relevantes mostradas ao usuário não sejam selecionadas.

O restante desse artigo está organizado da seguinte forma: A Seção 2 discute os principais trabalhos relacionados, já a Seção 3 define mais formalmente o problema. A Seção 4 apresenta algumas métricas de relevância de tags. Os métodos de referência bem como nossas novas propostas são

apresentados na seção 5. Nossos principais resultados são discutidos na Seção 6. A Seção 7 sumariza o artigo.

2. TRABALHOS RELACIONADOS

Cold start, i.e., a ausência de informação sobre novos usuários ou itens que evita que eles sejam recomendados, é um problema bem conhecido em sistemas de recomendação de itens [15, 14, 17, 16, 7, 3, 21, 19]. Muitas das abordagens existentes para lidar com tal problema se baseiam em algoritmos de aprendizado de máquina para melhorar filtros colaborativos [3, 21]. Alguns trabalhos exploram atributos textuais (e.g., tags) associados ao objeto alvo da recomendação como uma fonte alternativa de informação [7, 16], enquanto outros combinam o uso de atributos textuais e filtros colaborativos para minimizar o problema do *cold start* [19].

Em contraste, existem poucos trabalhos que tratam do problema do *cold start* no contexto específico de recomendação de tags. Ness *et al.* [14] descrevem uma técnica baseada na análise do conteúdo de áudio que ajuda a melhorar a eficácia de um sistema de recomendação de tags para conteúdo musical frente ao *cold start*. Este tipo de método, entretanto, requer algoritmos especializados para cada tipo de mídia (e.g., imagens, vídeos), o que tipicamente tem uma alta complexidade computacional. Preisach *et al.* [15] propõem um algoritmo semi-supervisionado puramente baseado em grafos para realizar recomendações personalizadas. Esta abordagem visa personalização, que não é o nosso objetivo neste artigo, e não utiliza padrões de coocorrência. Logo, ela não pode ser diretamente comparada à nossa solução.

Muitos trabalhos tratam do problema de recomendação de tags sem considerar explicitamente restrições sobre as tags previamente associadas aos objetos. Dentre esses métodos, aqueles que exploram padrões de coocorrência, chamados métodos associativos, têm alcançado consistentemente resultados muito competitivos [18, 10, 13, 2]. Sigurbjornsson e Zwol [18], por exemplo, propõem a aplicação de métricas globais de coocorrência de termos (e.g., confiança) para produzir uma ordenação das tags por relevância. Belém *et al.* [2] estende o trabalho de [18] por meio da aplicação de métricas de relevância de tags a termos extraídos de múltiplos atributos textuais do objeto alvo da recomendação. Esses, assim como outros métodos anteriores [10, 13], foram avaliados apenas para objetos contendo algumas tags iniciais. Duas contribuições do presente artigo são a avaliação de tais métodos em cenários de *cold start* e novos métodos mais robustos em tal cenário.

Em outra direção, alguns trabalhos não exploram tags previamente associadas ao objeto alvo [12, 8]. Por exemplo, Lipczak *et al.* [12] propõem CTTR que extrai termos de outros atributos textuais do objeto alvo da recomendação, expande esses termos e os ordena pelo seu uso como tags em um conjunto de treino. Já Graham e Caverlee [8] propõem Plurality, um método que combina um modelo vetorial com *relevance feedback* (RF) provido por usuários e que, diferentemente de nossa estratégia, não explora o *feedback* negativo. Como esses métodos não exploram as tags previamente associadas, eles podem ser mais robustos ao *cold start*. Assim, eles são tratados aqui como métodos de referência para comparação com nossas estratégias.

De acordo com nossos conhecimentos, Plurality é o único método anteriormente proposto que explora RF para recomendação de tags. Entretanto, tanto o *feedback* positivo quanto o negativo têm sido largamente usados em vários

---

[1]Tipicamente tal esforço envolve apenas clicar em 2 ou 3 tags de uma lista de tags apresentadas ao usuário (geralmente 5 tags).

326

outros contextos de RI [5, 20]. Assim, o uso conjunto dos *feedbacks* positivo e negativo para lidar com o *cold start* em sistemas de recomendação de tags (principalmente aqueles baseados em métodos de coocorrência) é uma contribuição original de nosso trabalho. Mais ainda, a análise da robustez dos métodos de recomendação à falta de cooperação do usuário é inexistente na literatura.

3. RECOMENDAÇÃO ASSOCIATIVA

A tarefa de recomendar tags para um objeto alvo o pode ser definida como: *Dado um conjunto $\mathcal{I}_o$ de tags que já foram assinaladas a um objeto alvo o e um conjunto $\mathcal{F}_o = \{\mathcal{F}_o^1, \mathcal{F}_o^2, ..., \mathcal{F}_o^n\}$ dos outros atributos textuais associados a o, onde $\mathcal{F}_o^i$ é o conjunto de termos no atributo i, gere um conjunto de termos candidatos $\mathcal{C}_o$ e recomende os k termos de $\mathcal{C}_o$ de maior relevância* [2].

Muitos métodos de recomendação de tags existentes exploram padrões de coocorrência minerados sobre tags previamente associadas ao objeto alvo o (e.g., tags em $\mathcal{I}_o$) e outros termos de uma coleção de objetos [2, 13, 18]. Essas técnicas são comumente referidas na literatura como técnicas de recomendação associativa de tags, já que elas aprendem padrões de coocorrência explorando regras de associação sobre um conjunto de treino $\mathcal{D} = \{\langle \mathcal{I}_d, \mathcal{F}_d \rangle\}$, onde $\mathcal{I}_d$ ($\mathcal{I}_d \neq \emptyset$) é o conjunto de todas as tags e $\mathcal{F}_d$ são os outros atributos textuais associados ao objeto $d \in \mathcal{D}$. Os padrões aprendidos são então usados para recomendar tags para objetos em um conjunto de teste $\mathcal{O} = \{\langle \mathcal{I}_o, \mathcal{F}_o \rangle\}$.

Uma regra de associação é uma implicação do tipo $X \rightarrow y$, onde o *antecedente* X é um conjunto de tags e o *consequente* y é um termo candidato à recomendação. A importância de uma regra de associação é estimada com base no **suporte** (σ), que é o número de coocorrências de X e y no conjunto de treino $\mathcal{D}$, e na **confiança** (θ), a probabilidade de que y seja associado como tag a um objeto $d \in \mathcal{D}$ dado que todas as tags em X são também associadas a d. Como o número de regras mineradas a partir de $\mathcal{D}$ pode ser muito grande, limiares de suporte e confiança (σ_{min} e θ_{min}, respectivamente) são usados para selecionar apenas as regras mais confiáveis.

Dado um objeto de teste o, o recomendador seleciona as regras em que o antecedente X está em $\mathcal{I}_o$. Cada termo c que aparece como consequente de qualquer uma destas regras é tomado como um candidato à recomendação e inserido em $\mathcal{C}_o$. Mais ainda, cada termo $c \in \mathcal{F}_o$ é inserido em $\mathcal{C}_o$. Depois, a relevância de cada elemento em $\mathcal{C}_o$ é estimada (utilizando diferentes métricas, como será discutido na Seção 4), e os k termos mais relevantes são recomendados.

Cold start é usualmente definido como a falta de informação sobre novos usuários ou itens [17]. Do ponto de vista dos métodos associativos de recomendação de tags, uma variação deste problema ocorre quando o objeto o não possui tags previamente associadas (i.e., $\mathcal{I}_o = \emptyset$) mas pode conter termos em seus outros atributos ($\mathcal{F}_o^i$). Isso corresponde a um cenário em que um novo objeto está sendo adicionado ao sistema e queremos ajudar o usuário recomendando as primeiras tags que serão atribuídas a o. O problema do *cold start*, como definido aqui, impõe grandes desafios aos métodos associativos, já que eles não podem usar $\mathcal{I}_o$, que está vazio. Antes de apresentar nossas estratégias para combater o problema, faremos uma revisão de algumas métricas de relevância de tags que são usadas tanto pelos métodos de referência quanto por nossos métodos de recomendação.

4. MÉTRICAS DE RELEVÂNCIA DE TAGS

Várias heurísticas foram propostas para avaliar a relevância de um termo como candidato à recomendação [2, 18, 12]. Por exemplo, a métrica *Sum* estima a relevância de um candidato c como tag para o como a soma das confianças de todas as regras de associação contendo c como consequente:

$$Sum(c, o, \ell) = \sum_{X \subseteq \mathcal{I}_o} \theta(X \rightarrow c), \quad (X \rightarrow c) \in \mathcal{R}, |X| \leq \ell \quad (1)$$

onde $\mathcal{R}$ é um conjunto de regras de associação computadas *offline* sobre um conjunto de treino $\mathcal{D}$, dados limiares σ_{min} e θ_{min}, e ℓ é o tamanho limite para o número de elementos no antecedente de uma regra de associação.

Termos que são muito comuns e gerais ou muito raros e logo potencialmente muito específicos, não são bons candidatos para a recomendação. A métrica *estabilidade* (*Stab*) [18] tenta capturar este aspecto, dando mais importância a termos que ocorrem com frequências intermediárias, ou seja:

$$Stab(c, k_s) = \frac{k_s}{k_s + |k_s - \log(f_c^{tag})|} \quad (2)$$

onde f_c^{tag} é o número de objetos em $\mathcal{D}$ que contêm c como *tag*, e k_s representa a "frequência ideal" de um termo e deve ser ajustada de acordo com a coleção.

Um bom poder descritivo do conteúdo do objeto também é desejável para uma tag [2]. Tal característica é capturada pelo Espalhamento (*term spread* ou *TS*) de um termo candidato c em um objeto o. $TS(c, o)$ é dado pelo número de atributos textuais (exceto tags) associado a o que contêm c [6]. Uma variação do *TS* chamada *wTS* leva em conta diferenças no poder descritivo dos atributos textuais. *wTS* pondera a ocorrência de c em um atributo $\mathcal{F}_o^i$ de o pela capacidade descritiva média desse atributo em todos os objetos do treino $\mathcal{D}$. Tal capacidade é estimada usando uma métrica chamada *Average Feature Spread (AFS)* [6]. Seja *Feature Instance Spread* de um atributo $\mathcal{F}_d^i$ associado ao objeto $d \in \mathcal{D}$, $FIS(\mathcal{F}_d^i)$, a média dos *TS* sobre todos os termos em $\mathcal{F}_d^i$. $AFS(\mathcal{F}^i)$ é então definida como a média dos $FIS(\mathcal{F}_d^i)$ sobre todas as instâncias de $\mathcal{F}^i$ associadas com objetos em $\mathcal{D}$. Assim, o *wTS* de um candidato c em um objeto o é [2]:

$$wTS(c, o) = \sum_{\mathcal{F}_o^i \in \mathcal{F}_o} j, \text{ onde } j = \begin{cases} AFS(\mathcal{F}^i) & \text{se } c \in \mathcal{F}_o^i \\ 0 & \text{caso contrário} \end{cases}$$

$$(3)$$

5. MÉTODOS DE RECOMENDAÇÃO

Nessa seção apresentamos as estratégias de recomendação analisadas. A Seção 5.1 descreve os métodos de referência adotados, e a Seção 5.2 discute nossas estratégias.

5.1 Métodos de Referência

Nós consideramos quatro métodos estado da arte de recomendação de tags como referência. Dois deles foram propostos recentemente e se mostraram superiores a vários outros métodos em cenários sem *cold start* [2]. Os outros dois não exploram tags previamente associadas a o, e, portanto não sofrem degradação de sua acurácia em *cold start*. Mais ainda, um desses métodos explora o *feedback* positivo provido pelo usuário. Assim, esses métodos são referências naturais para comparação com nossas estratégias.

Os dois primeiros métodos de referência são Sum^+wTS e $LATRE^+wTS$, os dois melhores métodos associativos propostos em [2]. Ambos exploram conjuntamente tags previamente associadas ao objeto alvo, múltiplos atributos textuais e algumas métricas de relevância de tags. Tais métodos estendem dois métodos de recomendação anteriores, chamado Sum^+ [18] e $LATRE$ [13], pela introdução da métrica wTS (Eq. 3). Sum^+ estima a relevância de cada termo candidato c para um objeto o em função dos padrões de coocorrência de tags previamente associadas a o e da estabilidade do termo candidato c (Eq. 2), sendo definida como:

$$Sum^+(c, o, k_x, k_c, k_r) = \sum_{x \in \mathcal{I}_o} \theta(x \to c) \times Stab(x, k_x) \\ \times Stab(c, k_c) \times Rank(c, o, k_r) \qquad (4)$$

onde k_x, k_c e k_r são parâmetros de configuração. $Rank(c, o, k_r)$ é um fator de suavização definido como $k_r/(k_r + p(c, o))$, onde $p(c, o)$ é a posição de c quando se consideram os candidatos ordenados de acordo com a confiança das regras de associação. Já $LATRE$ ordena cada termo candidato c pela soma das confianças de todas as regras contendo c, isto é, ele usa a métrica Sum (Eq. 1) com $\ell \geq 1$, explorando assim apenas padrões de coocorrência.

Assim nossos dois primeiros métodos de comparação, Sum^+wTS e $LATRE^+wTS$, são definidos como:

$$Sum^+wTS(c, o, k_x, k_c, k_r, \alpha) = \\ \alpha Sum^+(c, o, k_x, k_c, k_r) + (1 - \alpha)wTS(c, o) \qquad (5)$$

$$LATRE^+wTS(c, o, \ell, \alpha) = \alpha Sum(c, o, \ell) + (1 - \alpha)wTS(c, o) \qquad (6)$$

O parâmetro α ($0 \leq \alpha \leq 1$) é usado como fator de ponderação. Assim como a métrica Sum (Eq. 1) em que são baseados, Sum^+ e $LATRE$ são computados sobre todos os candidatos gerados a partir das regras de associação com tags previamente associadas ao objeto o. Em contraste, wTS é computado também para os termos extraídos dos outros atributos textuais de o.

O terceiro método de referência é o *Co-occurrence and Text based Tag Recommender* (CTTR), que explora termos extraídos de outros atributos textuais do objeto alvo e uma métrica de relevância de tags, mas não considera tags previamente associadas ao objeto, e assim não sofre os efeitos de *cold start*. CTTR é uma adaptação do vencedor do ECML Discovery Challenge 2009 [12], que em adição aos dois aspectos anteriores mencionados leva em conta também o histórico de atribuição de tags para prover recomendações personalizadas. Nós deixamos o tratamento de recomendações personalizadas para trabalhos futuros.

De modo sucinto, CTTR extrai termos candidatos do título e descrição do objeto alvo. Para cada termo c, ele atribui um peso igual à fração de objetos na base de treino contendo c tanto no atributo textual considerado (título ou descrição) quanto como tag. Os autores então usam um *leading precision re-scorer* para reponderar os termos candidatos extraídos das diversas fontes de dados, produzindo assim um novo peso para cada termo c. Os novos pesos são então agregados em uma soma probabilística. Termos extraídos do título (primeiro passo) bem como da agregação do título e descrição são então expandidos através de regras de associação[2]. Maiores detalhes estão disponíveis em [12].

O último método estado-da-arte usado como referência é o *Plurality* [8], que explora *relevance feedback* obtido do usuário e, como o CTTR, não utiliza tags previamente associadas ao objeto alvo da recomendação. As sugestões iniciais de tags para um objeto alvo o são produzidas a partir de uma busca pelos objetos mais similares a o contidos na base de treino $\mathcal{D}$. Cada objeto $d \in \mathcal{D}$ é modelado como um *bag*

of terms extraídos de todos os seus atributos textuais (incluindo suas tags). A similaridade entre cada objeto $d \in \mathcal{D}$ e o é então computada usando a métrica do cosseno [1]:

$$Sim(d, o) = \frac{\vec{d} \bullet \vec{o}}{|d| \times |o|} = \frac{\sum_{i=1}^{|\mathcal{V}|} w_{i,d} \times w_{i,o}}{\sqrt{\sum_{i=1}^{|\mathcal{V}|} w_{i,d}^2} \times \sqrt{\sum_{i=1}^{|\mathcal{V}|} w_{i,o}^2}} \qquad (7)$$

onde $|\mathcal{V}|$ é o tamanho do vocabulário em $\mathcal{D}$, e o peso $w_{i,d}$ é uma variação do $TF \times IDF$, e.g., $w_{i,d} = \sqrt{freq(t_i, d)} \times (1 + log(\frac{|\mathcal{D}|}{df(t_i)+1}))$, onde $freq(t_i, d)$ é a frequência do termo t_i no objeto d e $df(t_i)$ é o número de objetos em $\mathcal{D}$ contendo t_i.

Para cada termo t contido em um dos top-n_{obj} objetos com maior similaridade com o, Plurality atribui o peso:

$$termScore(t, o) = \sum_{i=1}^{n_{obj}} Sim(o, d_i)^4 \times freq_{tag}(t, d_i) \qquad (8)$$

onde $freq_{tag}(t, d_i)$ é o número de vezes que t foi aplicado como tag ao objeto $d_i \in \mathcal{D}$[3]. As top-n_{tags} tags com os maiores pesos são então selecionadas como sugestões iniciais e mostradas ao usuário, que fornece *feedback* sobre a relevância dos mesmos com relação ao objeto ao qual se pretende fazer a recomendação. Tags julgadas relevantes são então expandidas com base em sua similaridade com outras tags de $\mathcal{D}$. As novas tags retornadas para o usuário são aquelas mais similares com as tags julgadas relevantes na iteração anterior. Este processo é repetido até que um resultado satisfatório ou um número máximo de iterações M seja atingido. Maiores detalhes sobre como Plurality computa a similaridade entre duas tags estão descritos em [8].

5.2 Estratégias Robustas ao Cold Start

Em cold start, métodos associativos não podem usar os padrões de coocorrências uma vez que $\mathcal{I}_o = \emptyset$. Uma abordagem para permitir o uso desses padrões é construir um conjunto alternativo $\mathcal{I}_o'$ e usá-lo como entrada para o recomendador no lugar de $\mathcal{I}_o$. Diferentes estratégias podem ser adotadas para se construir $\mathcal{I}_o'$. Por exemplo, podemos usar um outro método de recomendação que não utiliza tags previamente associadas a o e tem um desempenho razoável em cold start para produzir o conjunto inicial $\mathcal{I}_o'$, e, em seguida, usá-lo como entrada para o recomendador associativo. Alternativamente, poderíamos filtrar termos de outras fontes, como outros atributos do objeto alvo ou de outros objetos no conjunto de treinamento, e usá-los para construir $\mathcal{I}_o'$. Nós aqui consideramos ambas as abordagens. Primeiramente, filtramos termos de outros atributos textuais do objeto alvo o usando como critério de filtragem uma métrica de relevância de tags. Isto é, para cada termo $t \in \mathcal{F}_o$, nós atribuímos um peso dado pela métrica escolhida, e então selecionamos os k_{filter} termos de maior peso para construir $\mathcal{I}_o'$. Experimentamos com várias métricas, mas aqui reportamos resultados do uso de wTS como critério de filtragem. Segundo, nós extraímos tags de objetos similares no conjunto de treino usando para isso um filtro colaborativo inspirado no Plurality [8]. Isto é, os top-n_{obj} objetos mais similares a o em $\mathcal{D}$ são selecionados, usando a Equação 7. Então, de todas as tags desses objetos, nós selecionamos as k_{filter} com o maior peso, dado pela Equação 8.

Em comum, estas estratégias são baseadas em métodos automáticos para gerar $\mathcal{I}_o'$. Entretanto, como será visto na Seção 6, elas produzem apenas ganhos marginais sobre o melhor método de referência. Assim, a principal contribuição

---

[2]Aqui aplicamos o algoritmo *Apriori*.

---

[3]Note que em muitas aplicações uma mesma tag pode ser atribuída multiplas vezes a um mesmo objeto por usuários diferentes.

Algoritmo 1 Recomendação de Tags Baseadas em Relevance Feedback do Usuário.

Entrada: Objeto alvo o, número k_{rf} de tags mostradas ao usuário em cada iteração, máximo número de iterações M, and recomendador associativo rec

Saída: Lista de tags recomendadas R_o para o

Sejam R_o^i as tags recomendadas na i^{esima} iteração.

1: $R_o = \emptyset$
2: $BlackList_o = \emptyset$
3: $i = 0$
4: R_o^i = gere um conjunto inicial de tags
5: **while** $i \leq M$ **do**
6:     $R_o^i = R_o^i$ - $BlackList_o$
7:     Mostre as k_{rf} tags mais relevantes em R_o^i para o usuário
8:     Seja $\mathcal{I}_o'$ as tags selecionadas como relevantes pelo usuário
9:     Seja $\mathcal{N}_o$ as tags que não foram selecionadas como relevantes
10:     $R_o = R_o \cup \mathcal{I}_o'$
11:     $BlackList_o = BlackList_o \cup \mathcal{N}_o$
12:     **if** $(i \geq 1)$ **and** $(R_o^i = R_o^{i-1})$ **then break**
13:     $\mathcal{I}_o' = R_o$
14:     $i + +$
15:     **if** $i \leq M$ **then** $R_o^i = rec(o, \mathcal{I}_o')$
16: **end while**
17: **return** R_o

Table 1: Descrição geral das bases de dados.

Base de dados	# tags/objeto	# medio de tags/objeto	# objetos
Bibsonomy	2-120	4.9	483,932
Last.FM	2-507	7.8	235,492
YahooVideo	2-52	10.7	146,868
YouTube	2-77	8.9	5.5 milhões

deste artigo é propor e avaliar uma nova estratégia baseada em *relevance feedback* (RF) para construir e refinar $\mathcal{I}_o'$.

A estratégia proposta, apresentada no Algoritmo 1, consiste nos seguintes passos. Primeiro, é gerado um conjunto inicial de tags usando algum método de recomendação, em conjunto ou não com as estratégias automáticas de filtragem propostas (linha 4). A seguir, as k_{rf} tags mais relevantes (onde a relevância é medida pelo método usado na linha 4) são mostradas para o usuário (linha 7), que seleciona aquelas que ele considera relevantes. As tags selecionadas são então usadas para construir $\mathcal{I}_o'$ (linha 8). Tal conjunto é dado como entrada para um método de recomendação associativa que por sua vez, gera novas recomendações (linha 15). Diferentemente de outros métodos de recomendação como o Plurality [8], a estratégia proposta explora o feedback negativo implícito dado pelo usuário, isto é, tags que não foram selecionadas pelo usuário como relevantes são mantidas em uma lista negra (linha 11). Tags nessa lista não são consideradas como candidatas para a recomendação (linha 6) e, assim, não são mostradas para o usuário novamente. O processo é repetido até que as recomendações convirjam para o mesmo conjunto em iterações consecutivas ou um número máximo de iterações M seja alcançado[4].

Abordagens alternativas podem ser aplicadas tanto para gerar o primeiro conjunto de recomendações mostrados para o usuário (linha 4) quanto para gerar as recomendações subsequentes (linha 15). Por exemplo, é possível aplicar simplesmente o mesmo método associativo de recomendação (rec) com o conjunto $\mathcal{I}_o$ vazio ou com $\mathcal{I}_o'$ gerado a partir de alguma estratégia automática de filtragem. Em última instância, qualquer método de recomendação que funcione bem em cold start pode ser usado. O ponto dessa estratégia é tentar melhorar a acurácia dos métodos associativos de recomendação em cold start fornecendo a eles um bom conjunto inicial $\mathcal{I}_o'$ de tags, do qual eles podem obter boas tags candidatas a partir da geração de padrões de coocorrência. Assim, é importante que algumas das tags mostradas para o usuário sejam realmente relevantes. De outro modo, não haverá feedback positivo e o método associativo de recomendação não poderá se beneficiar dele. Note que, depois do primeiro feedback dado pelo usuário, o conjunto $\mathcal{I}_o'$ passa

a ser composto por todas as tags marcadas como relevantes pelo usuário em todas as iterações (linha 13). De modo similar, o conjunto final de recomendações consiste em todas as tags marcadas como relevantes pelo usuário em todas as iterações (R_o no algoritmo).

O processo de RF diminui o impacto do cold start pois ele introduz uma nova fonte de informação (i.e., o usuário), presumivelmente mais segura, aos métodos associativos de recomendação. Comparado ao Plurality [8], que também explora o RF, a nossa estratégia é utilizada conjuntamente com métodos estado-da-arte associativos de recomendação que, diferentemente do Plurality, distinguem entre diferentes atributos textuais e levam em conta a diferença de qualidade dos termos extraídos desses atributos para estimar a qualidade de uma tag candidata. Mais ainda, explorando apenas as tags marcadas como relevantes pelo usuário, Plurality leva em conta apenas o feedback positivo, ignorando o feedback negativo implícito que um usuário necessariamente fornece quando ele não seleciona uma tag como relevante.

Note ainda que, a estratégia proposta requer pouco esforço extra do usuário, já que tanto o feedback positivo quanto o negativo são obtidos de forma implícita a partir das tags recomendadas que são ou não selecionadas pelo usuário. A única ação que o usuário precisa tomar é clicar nas tags que ele considera relevante, um esforço que ele normalmente tem que fazer para usar qualquer sistema de recomendação. Mais ainda, como será mostrado na Seção 6.4, a convergência do processo é bem rápida. Assim, o esforço extra do usuário é recompensado pela melhoria da qualidade das tags recomendadas. Isso corresponde a um cenário em que o usuário deseja atribuir tags com o máximo de qualidade mesmo ao custo de um pequeno esforço equivalente à seleção das tags relevantes em 1 ou 2 iterações do processo RF, o que teria que ser feito de qualquer forma para usar o recomendador.

6. AVALIAÇÃO EXPERIMENTAL

Nessa seção, primeiramente apresentamos nossas bases de dados (Seção 6.1) e nossa metodologia de avaliação (Seção 6.2). Nós então discutimos o impacto do cold start sobre os métodos associativos de referência e os benefícios do uso de nossas estratégias automáticas para diminuir esse impacto (Seção 6.3). Nós também avaliamos nossas estratégias baseadas em RF para lidar com o problema (Seção 6.4).

6.1 Coleções de Dados

Os métodos de recomendação de tags foram avaliados em quatro bases de dados, cada uma contendo *título*, *tags* e *descrição* associados a objetos coletados das aplicações Bibsonomy, LastFM, YouTube e YahooVideo. Todas bases estão disponíveis publicamente[5]. Consideramos apenas objetos com atributos textuais em língua inglesa e utilizamos o algoritmo de Porter[6] para remoção de afixos em cada termo coletado, evitando assim recomendações triviais como plurais. Também foram removidas *stopwords* e termos que são

---

[4]Na prática, o processo pode ser interrompido pelo usuário quando um resultado satisfatório for obtido e ele parar de fornecer *feedback*.

[5]Bibsonomy: http://www.kde.cs.uni-kassel.de/bibsonomy/dumps; outras 3 bases: http://www.vod.dcc.ufmg.br/recc/

[6]http://tartarus.org/ martin/PorterStemmer/

Table 2: Parametrização dos Métodos de Recomendação de tags.

Parametros	Bibsonomy	Last.FM	YahooVideo	YouTube
σ_{min}	1	2	2	1
θ_{min}	0.1	0.2	0.2	0.1
$\alpha(Sum^+wTS)$	0.9	0.95	0.8	0.8
$\alpha(LATRE^+wTS)$	0.9	0.99	0.9	0.9
$\ell\ (LATRE^+wTS)$	3	3	3	3
$k_r/k_x/k_C/k_s$	5	5	5	5
k_{filter}	1	10	5	3
n_{obj}	10	10	10	10

Table 3: Impacto do Cold Start sobre os métodos associativos de recomendação de tags: P@5 médio e intervalos de confiança de 95%.

Método	Bibsonomy	Last.FM	YahooVideo	YouTube
CTTR	0.275±.002	0.260±.001	0.465±.004	0.376±.002
Sum$^+$wTS	0.436±.002	0.417±.002	0.707±.002	0.502±.003
LATRE$^+$wTS	0.420 ±.001	0.411±.001	0.733±.003	0.489±.003
Sum/LATRE$^+$wTS	0.207±.002	0.065±.001	0.419±.004	0.359±.002

muito frequentes (com mais de 100,000 ocorrências na coleção de dados) ou muito raros (com menos de 30 ocorrências), visto que tais termos raramente constituem boas recomendações [18]. A Tabela 1 resume as bases de dados.

6.2 Metodologia de Avaliação

De forma similar a [2, 13], foi adotada uma metodologia de avaliação automática: um subconjunto das tags associadas a cada objeto de teste foi usado como gabarito para a recomendação, ou seja, como tags relevantes para aquele objeto, sendo pois desconsideradas para o cálculo de métricas de relevância. Esta metodologia foi adotada porque o processo de avaliação manual é caro e pode ser afetado pela subjetividade dos julgamentos humanos. Note que os resultados obtidos representam limites inferiores, já que algumas das tags recomendadas podem não aparecer no gabarito mas serem de fato relevantes para o objeto.

Nossa avaliação foi feita sobre amostras de 150,000 objetos do YouTube, Last.FM e Bibsonomy e 120,000 objetos do YahooVideo. Cada amostra foi dividida em 5 partes iguais utilizadas em um procedimento experimental de validação cruzada. Ou seja, três partes são usadas como conjunto de treinamento $\mathcal{D}$, que por sua vez é usado para a extração das regras de associação e computação das outras métricas, uma parte é usada para a validação e ajuste de parâmetros, e a última parte é usada como o conjunto teste $\mathcal{O}$. Este processo é repetido cinco vezes, utilizando-se como conjunto de teste uma parte diferente a cada vez. Os resultados apresentados são médias dos cinco conjuntos de testes, juntamente com os intervalos de confiança de 95% correspondentes.

Seguindo a metodologia proposta, metade das tags de cada objeto o dos conjuntos de validação e teste são selecionadas aleatoriamente e incluídas em $\mathcal{I}_o$. A outra metade é incluída em $\mathcal{Y}_o$, o gabarito de o. Para avaliação dos métodos em cold start, tags em $\mathcal{I}_o$ foram ignoradas. Isso foi feito, ao invés de utilizá-las como parte da resposta esperada, de modo a manter o mesmo gabarito para os cenários com e sem cold start, possibilitando assim a comparação dos mesmos. Além disso foram utilizados título e descrição como atributos textuais em $\mathcal{F}_o$, para cada objeto o.

Como em [5], o gabarito $\mathcal{Y}_o$ foi usado para simular o *feedback* do usuário, usado tanto pelas estratégias baseadas em RF propostas quanto pelo Plurality. Em cada iteração do processo de RF, as tags recomendadas consideradas como relevantes (e.g., linha 8 no Algoritmo 1) são aquelas que estão em $\mathcal{Y}_o$. Inicialmente é simulado um usuário ideal que seleciona todas as tags relevantes mostradas a ele em cada iteração (tags que estão em $\mathcal{Y}_o$). Posteriormente esta premissa é relaxada, de modo a avaliar a sensibilidade das estratégias baseadas em RF ao nível de cooperação do usuário. Ressaltamos que as tags em $\mathcal{Y}_o$ que não foram "selecionadas pelo usuário" não são usadas no cálculo de métricas de relevância nem exploradas, de forma alguma, pelo recomendador.

Esta metodologia simula o *feedback* real dado pelos usuários e não afeta ou distorce nossa avaliação automática.

Avaliamos os métodos de recomendação usando a métrica $P@k$, com $k=5$. Ela é dada por $P@k(\mathcal{R}_o, \mathcal{Y}_o) = \frac{|\mathcal{R}_{k,o} \cap \mathcal{Y}_o|}{min(k,|\mathcal{Y}_o|)}$, onde $\mathcal{R}_{k,o}$ são as top-k tags recomendadas para o objeto o.

A Tabela 2 mostra os valores escolhidos para a parametrização dos métodos, que foram obtidos a partir da validação cruzada no conjunto de validação, como em [2]. Foi atribuído o valor 5 tanto para n_{tags} quanto k_{rf} por consitência com a métrica de avaliação $P@5$.

6.3 Impacto do Cold Start

Começamos avaliando o impacto do cold start sobre os métodos associativos Sum^+wTS e o $LATRE^+wTS$, comparando-os com o CTTR, que explora apenas os atributos textuais do objeto alvo. A Tabela 3 mostra os valores médios de $P@5$ juntamente com intervalos de confiança de 95% para cada base de dados. Conforme mencionado, em cold start, o Sum^+wTS e o $LATRE^+wTS$ convergem para a aplicação do wTS sobre termos extraídos de outros atributos textuais de o. Esse cenário é mostrado na Tabela 3 como $Sum/LATRE^+wTS$, que é simulado ignorando as tags em $\mathcal{I}_o$ (i.e., $\mathcal{I}_o=\emptyset$). O $CTTR$ não explora $\mathcal{I}_o$, logo seus resultados são os mesmos na presença e ausência de cold start.

Observamos que, consistentemente com as conclusões em [2], tanto o Sum^+wTS quanto o $LATRE^+wTS$ superam o CTTR em todas as bases na ausência de cold start. Porém, a precisão dos dois métodos em cold start ($Sum/LATRE^+wTS$) é bastante prejudicada. Neste cenário, as perdas do Sum^+wTS em $P@5$ médio são de 47% no Bibsonomy, 41% no Yahoo-Video e 28% no YouTube. Perdas similares são observadas para o $LATRE^+wTS$ nas três bases. O cold start é ainda mais danoso a ambos os métodos no Last.FM, causando uma perda em $P@5$ médio de 84%. Tal perda é primariamente explicada pelo concentração da métrica wTS em pequenos valores nessa base [6], o que dificulta distinguir termos "bons" de "ruins" com base apenas nessa métrica. Assim, a despeito da eficácia superior em objetos contendo algumas tags, tanto o Sum^+wTS quanto o $LATRE^+wTS$ têm grandes perdas de performance no cenário de cold start.

Continuando nossa avaliação, a Tabela 4 mostra os resultados da aplicação das estratégias automáticas de filtragem, discutidas na Seção 5.2, aos métodos Sum^+wTS e $LATRE^+wTS$ em cold start. Tais estratégias são baseadas na geração do conjunto $\mathcal{I}'_o$ a partir: (1) da filtragem de termos de $\mathcal{F}^i_o$ (wTS); (2) do uso de um filtro colaborativo (CF) (3) do uso das tags sugeridas por outro recomendador ($CTTR$). Os melhores resultados para cada base de dados (incluindo empates estatísticos de acordo com um teste-t pareado com 95% de confiança) são mostrados em negrito.

Comparando os resultados das Tabelas 3 e 4, é possível observar que, a despeito da melhoria na eficácia do Sum^+wTS em cold start, qualquer uma das abordagens consideradas apenas produziram uma melhora marginal (3-4%) sobre o $CTTR$. Já os resultados produzidos pelo $LATRE^+wTS$

Table 4: Estratégias automáticas para gerar $\mathcal{I}'_o$: P@5 médio e intervalos de confiança de 95%.

Estratégias de filtragem aplicadas ao Sum^+wTS			
Método	Bibsonomy	Last.FM	Yahoo Video	YouTube
$CTTR$	0.222 ± 0.002	0.211 ± 0.002	0.454 ± 0.002	0.379 ± 0.003
wTS	0.220 ± 0.002	0.151 ± 0.002	0.452 ± 0.003	0.373 ± 0.002
CF	**0.241 ± 0.002**	**0.240 ± 0.002**	**0.486 ± 0.003**	**0.386 ± 0.002**

Estratégias de filtragem aplicadas ao $LATRE^+wTS$			
Método	Bibsonomy	Last.FM	Yahoo Video	YouTube
$CTTR$	0.172 ± 0.002	0.064 ± 0.001	0.388 ± 0.003	0.334 ± 0.001
wTS	0.135 ± 0.002	0.132 ± 0.001	0.426 ± 0.002	0.331 ± 0.001
CF	0.193 ± 0.002	0.079 ± 0.001	0.389 ± 0.001	0.319 ± 0.002

Table 5: Métodos propostos baseadas em RF ($\mathcal{I}_o = \emptyset$): P@5 médio e intervalos de confiança de 95%.

Métodos de Referência			
Método	Bibsonomy	Last.FM	YahooVideo	YouTube
$CTTR$	0.275 ± 0.002	0.260 ± 0.001	0.465 ± 0.004	0.376 ± 0.002
$Sum/LATRE^+wTS$	0.207 ± 0.002	0.065 ± 0.001	0.419 ± 0.004	0.359 ± 0.002
Plurality	0.315 ± 0.002	0.300 ± 0.001	0.597 ± 0.001	0.331 ± 0.002

Estratégias propostas baseadas em RF			
Método	Bibsonomy	Last.FM	YahooVideo	YouTube
Sum^+wTS	0.285 ± 0.002	0.224 ± 0.002	0.751 ± 0.004	0.514 ± 0.002
$LATRE^+wTS$	0.289 ± 0.002	0.230 ± 0.002	0.778 ± 0.004	0.518 ± 0.002
$CTTR+Sum^+wTS$	**0.357 ± 0.002**	**0.362 ± 0.002**	0.781 ± 0.004	**0.545 ± 0.003**
$CTTR+LATRE^+wTS$	**0.360 ± 0.002**	**0.360 ± 0.002**	**0.787 ± 0.004**	0.537 ± 0.002

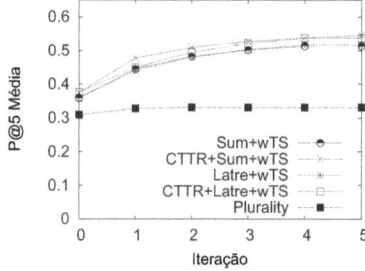

Figure 1: Métodos baseados em RF (YouTube).

combinado com as estratégias propostas são claramente piores que os do $CTTR$. Isso ocorre pois $\mathcal{I}'_o$ pode conter muitos termos ruins (ou irrelevantes) que fazem com que mais ruído seja considerado como candidato à recomendação. Assim é importante construir um conjunto $\mathcal{I}'_o$ sem esses termos ruins.

Como as estratégias automáticas não conseguiram ganhos significativos, na próxima seção nós investigamos o uso de RF para melhorar o processo de recomendação.

6.4 Métodos Baseados em Relevance Feedback

Essa seção discute os resultados da estratégias baseadas em RF propostas. São consideradas duas opções para gerar o primeiro conjunto de tags apresentado ao usuário (linha 4 do Alg. 1): (1) aplicar o método associativo original com um conjunto $\mathcal{I}'_o$ vazio e (2) usar o $CTTR$ para gerar o primeiro conjunto de recomendações[7] e então aplicar o método associativo nas iterações seguintes. Para distinguir entre essas abordagens, a segunda é chamada de $CTTR+método$, onde *método* pode ser Sum^+wTS ou $LATRE^+wTS$.

6.4.1 RF em Cenários de Cold Start

Focando em um cenário de cold start ($\mathcal{I}_o=\emptyset$), nós começamos pela avaliação da convergência do processo de RF para as nossas estratégias e para o Plurality. A Figura 1 mostra os valores médios de $P@5$ para as recomendações dadas por cada método em cada iteração do processo de RF para o YouTube. A iteração 0 corresponde às primeiras tags mostradas ao usuário. Note que todos os métodos convergem bem rapidamente, alcançando seus melhores resultados, ou próximo a isso, com apenas 1 *feedback* fornecido pelo usuário (1 iteração). De fato, os ganhos obtidos com os *feedbacks* subsequentes, que existem apenas para as estratégias propostas pois resultam do uso do *feedback* negativo, são bem pequenos. Assim pouco esforço é requerido do usuário para que a qualidade das recomendações melhore. Resultados para as outras bases são similares (omitidos).

A Tabela 5 mostra resultados para cada método após convergência. Os melhores resultados são mostrados em negrito. Comparando cada estratégia baseada em RF com

[7]O uso do $CTTR$ é motivado pela sua boa performance em cold start e para mostrar a flexibilidade do arcabouço proposto.

o método original sobre o qual ela foi construída (linha $Sum/LATRE^+wTS$) os ganhos médios em $P@5$ obtidos com as novas estratégias atingem 73%, 51% e 87% para o Bibsonomy, YouTube e YahooVideo, e 457% para o Last.FM. Os ganhos médios da melhor estratégia proposta (vide discussão abaixo) sobre o melhor método de referência em cada base de dados são 57%, 58%, 35% e 40%, para o Bibsonomy, Last.FM, YahooVideo e YouTube, respectivamente.

No geral, $CTTR+Sum^+wTS$ é o melhor método de recomendação analisado, atingindo resultados similares aos do $CTTR+LATRE^+wTS$, mas com um custo computacional menor. $CTTR+Sum^+wTS$ também supera o Plurality em até 64%. Tais ganhos se devem ao uso do *feedback* negativo e à combinação de métodos baseados em coocorrência com métricas que exploram a diferença de qualidade entre os vários atributos textuais dos objetos, o que, como mostrado na Tabela 5, supera métodos mais simples de filtragem colaborativa sobre os quais o Plurality é construído.

6.4.2 RF em Presença de Tags Iniciais

Nesta seção são avaliadas as estratégias baseadas em RF em um cenário no qual os objetos possuem tags previamente associadas ($\mathcal{I}_o \neq \emptyset$). Como mostrado na Tabela 6, o processo de RF melhora a precisão dos dois métodos associativos de recomendação em todas as bases de dados. Novamente, o uso do $CTTR$ para gerar o primeiro conjunto de tags recomendadas, ao invés de um método associativo, melhora os resultados, exceto no YahooVideo onde o $LATRE^+wTS$ teve um desempenho semelhante ao do $CTTR+LATRE^+wTS$.

$CTTR+Sum^+wTS$ é novamente nossa melhor estratégia baseada em RF, alcançado ganhos sobre o melhor método de referência (que pode ser Sum^+wTS ou o $LATRE^+wTS$ sem o uso de RF) que variam de 17% a 39%. Note que, no YahooVideo, $CTTR+LATRE^+wTS$ (e $LATRE^+wTS$ com RF) obtém ganhos marginais (2%) sobre o $CTTR+Sum^+wTS$ que não compensam o custo computacional extra do seu uso. Note novamente a grande superioridade de nossa estratégia tanto sobre o $CTTR$ quanto sobre o Plurality

6.4.3 Robustez à Falta de Cooperação do Usuário

Finalmente, foi analisada a sensibilidade do melhor método baseado em RF, o $CTTR+Sum^+wTS$, à falta de cooperação do usuário, considerando um cenário em que a cada iteração do processo de RF o usuário clica em somente $r\%$ ($r \leq 100\%$) das tags relevantes mostradas a ele. A Figura 2(a-b) mostra os resultados para vários valores de r, tanto na presença (a) quanto na ausência (b) de cold start, para o YouTube. Resultados similares foram obtidos para as outras bases. Como pode ser visto, a eficácia do método diminui quando r diminui, já que, como a estratégia explora *feedback* negativo, *tags* que não são marcadas como relevantes pelo usuário são consideradas irrelevantes e deixam de ser

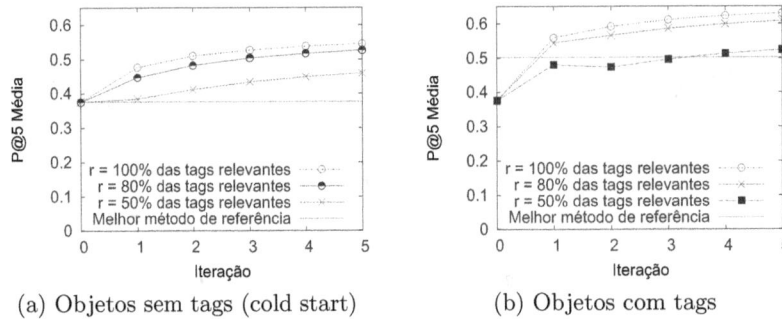

(a) Objetos sem tags (cold start) (b) Objetos com tags

Figure 2: Sensibilidade da estratégia $CTTR+Sum^+wTS$, baseada em RF, à cooperação do usuário (YouTube).

Table 6: Métodos propostos baseadas em RF ($\mathcal{I}_o \neq \emptyset$): P@5 média e intervalos de confiança de 95%.

Métodos de Referência				
Método	Bibsonomy	Last.FM	YahooVideo	YouTube
CTTR	0.275±0.002	0.260±0.001	0.465±0.004	0.376±0.002
Sum$^+$wTS	0.436±0.002	0.417±0.002	0.707±0.002	0.502±0.003
LATRE$^+$wTS	0.420±0.002	0.411±0.001	0.733±0.003	0.489±0.003
Plurality	0.315±0.002	0.315±0.001	0.595±0.001	0.332±0.002

Estratégias propostas baseadas em RF				
Método	Bibsonomy	Last.FM	YahooVideo	YouTube
Sum$^+$wTS	0.501±0.002	0.523±0.001	0.833±0.003	0.609±0.002
LATRE$^+$wTS	0.541±0.002	0.525±0.002	**0.872±0.003**	0.620±0.002
CTTR+Sum^+wTS	0.549±0.002	**0.579±0.002**	0.854±0.003	**0.633±0.002**
CTTR+$LATRE^+wTS$	**0.558**±0.002	0.557±0.002	**0.872±0.007**	0.623±0.003

recomendadas em iterações futuras. Entretanto, note que o $CTTR+Sum^+wTS$ produz resultados, se não superiores, tão bons quanto os resultados do melhor método de referência, tanto na presença quanto na ausência de cold start, mesmo que até 20% das tags relevantes mostradas para o usuário (ou 50%, se em cold start) não sejam selecionadas.

7. CONCLUSÕES E TRABALHOS FUTUROS

Neste artigo avaliamos métodos associativos de recomendação de tags considerados estado-da-arte em objetos sem tags previamente associadas, uma variação do problema do cold start, e mostramos que a acurácia de tais métodos é muito prejudicada em tal cenário. Mostramos também que o uso várias estratégias automáticas de filtragem para gerar um conjunto inicial de tags leva a um ganho marginal. Nós então propusemos uma nova estratégia de recomendação de tags baseada em *relevance feedback* mais robusta a tal cenário. Nossos resultados mostraram que nossa melhor estratégia baseada em RF conseguiu alcançar ganhos de até 45% em precisão em cenários de cold start e 39% em cenários onde o objeto alvo possui tags. Mostramos também que nossa estratégia é robusta à falta de cooperação do usuário. Trabalhos futuros incluem estratégias mais flexíveis para lidar com o feedback negativo bem como adaptações para realizar recomendações personalizadas.

8. AGRADECIMENTOS

Esta pesquisa é parcialmente financiada pelo Instituto Nacional de Ciência e Tecnologia para a Web - INCTWeb (MCT/CNPq 573871/2008-6), CNPq, CAPES e FAPEMIG.

9. REFERENCES

[1] R. Baeza-Yate and B. Ribeiro-Neto. *Modern Information Retrieval*. Addison-Wesley, 1999.

[2] F. Belém, E. Martins, T. Pontes, J. Almeida, and M. Gonçalves. Associative Tag Recommendation Exploiting Multiple Textual Features. In *SIGIR*, 2011.

[3] J. Bobadilla, F. Ortega, A. Hernando, and J. Bernal. A collaborative filtering approach to mitigate the new user cold start problem. *Knowl.-Based Syst.*, 2012.

[4] S. Boll. MultiTube–Where Web 2.0 And Multimedia Could Meet. *IEEE MultiMedia*, 2007.

[5] C. Ferreira, J. Santos, R. Torres, M. Gonçalves, R. Rezende, and W. Fan. Relevance feedback based on genetic programming for image retrieval. *Pattern Recognition Letters*, 2011.

[6] F. Figueiredo, F. Belém, H. Pinto, J. Almeida, M. Gonçalves, D. Fernandes, and E. Moura. Assessing the Quality Of Textual Features in Social Media. *Information Processing & Management*, 49(1), 2013.

[7] S. Givon and V. Lavrenko. Predicting social-tags for cold start book recommendations. In *RecSys*, 2009.

[8] R. Graham and J. Caverlee. Exploring Feedback Models in Interactive Tagging. In *WI 08*, 2008.

[9] I. Guy, N. Zwerdling, I. Ronen, D. Carmel, and E. Uziel. Social media recommendation based on people and tags. In *SIGIR*, 2010.

[10] P. Heymann, D. Ramage, and H. Garcia-Molina. Social Tag Prediction. In *SIGIR*, 2008.

[11] X. Li, L. Guo, and Y. E. Zhao. Tag-based Social Interest Discovery. In *WWW*. ACM, 2008.

[12] M. Lipczak, Y. Hu, Y. Kollet, and E. Milios. Tag Sources For Recommendation In Collaborative Tagging Systems. In *PKDD*, volume 497, 2009.

[13] G. Menezes, J. Almeida, F. Belém, M. Gonçalves, A. Lacerda, E. Moura, G. Pappa, A. Veloso, and N. Ziviani. Demand-Driven Tag Recommendation. In *PKDD*, 2010.

[14] S. Ness, A. Theocharis, G. Tzanetakis, and L. Martins. Improving automatic music tag annotation using stacked generalization of probabilistic svm outputs. In *ACM Multimedia*, 2009.

[15] C. Preisach, L. Marinho, and L. S.-Thieme. Semi-supervised Tag Recommendation - Using Untagged Resources to Mitigate Cold-Start Problems. In *PAKDD(1)*, 2010.

[16] A. Said, R. Wetzker, W. Umbrath, and L. Hennig. A hybrid plsa approach for warmer cold start in folksonomy recommendation. In *RecSys*, 2009.

[17] A. Schein, A. Popescul, L. Ungar, and D. Pennock. Methods and metrics for cold-start recommendations. In *SIGIR*, 2002.

[18] B. Sigurbjornsson and R. van Zwol. Flickr Tag Recommendation Based On Collective Knowledge. In *WWW*, 2008.

[19] D. Sun, Z. Luo, and F. Zhang. A novel approach for collaborative filtering to alleviate the new item cold-start problem. In *ISCIT*, 2011.

[20] B. Yang, T. Mei, X. Hua, L. Yang, S. Yang, and M. Li. Online video recommendation based on multimodal fusion and relevance feedback. In *CIVR*, 2007.

[21] Ke Zhou, Shuang-Hong Yang, and Hongyuan Zha. Functional matrix factorizations for cold-start recommendation. In *SIGIR*, 2011.

An Investigation of the Relationship between the Amount of Extra-textual Data and the Quality of Wikipedia Articles

Marcelo Yuji Himoro,
Raiza Tamae Sarkis Hanada,
Maria da Graça Campos Pimentel
São Paulo University
Institute of Mathematics and Computer Sciences
São Carlos, SP, Brazil
himoro@usp.br
{rhanada, mgp}@icmc.usp.br

Marco Cristo
Federal University of Amazonas
Computer Institute
Manaus, AM, Brazil
marco.cristo@icomp.ufam.edu.br

ABSTRACT

Wikipedia, a web-based collaboratively maintained free encyclopedia, is emerging as one of the most important websites on the internet. However, its openness raises many concerns about the quality of the articles and how to assess it automatically. In the Portuguese-speaking Wikipedia, articles can be rated by bots and by the community. In this paper, we investigate the correlation between these ratings and the count of media items (namely images and sounds) through a series of experiments. Our results show that article ratings and the count of media items are correlated.

Categories and Subject Descriptors

H. Information Systems [**H.3 INFORMATION STORAGE AND RETRIEVAL**]: H.3.m Miscellaneous

Keywords

Extra-textual data, Correlations, Wikipedia, Content Quality.

1. INTRODUCTION

The rapid popularization of the Internet and the falling costs of broadband access, along with the development of new technologies, paved the way for new possibilities, but more importantly, changed habits and created new trends over the last years. The so-called Web 2.0 technologies, which include social networks, blogs, video sharing sites, wikis and collaborative work systems, podcasts, hosted services, web applications, mashups and folksomy share a common characteristic: a deep need for social interaction. It is all about a new way of thinking which breaks with the static web paradigm; dynamics that have been driving the industry to a new way of doing business [12]. The user now plays an active role in the content creation.

In this context, wikis emerge. The most well-known wiki is Wikipedia[1], a collaborative, multilingual, free Internet encyclopedia. Available in 286 languages and totaling over 26 million articles [22], it ranks at 6th as the most accessed website in the world [2]. Portuguese-speaking Wikipedia currently contains 780,893 articles and a very active community.

Wikipedia owes its current size largely to the voluntary work of many people around the world. On the other hand, the very same reason for Wikipedia's success is also the cause of many of its problems. Besides the information inaccuracy - more often than not, caused by vandalism - there are many less obvious factors that negatively affect the quality of the articles: lack of coherence, cohesion and clarity in the texts. This is because most contributors usually rewrite only small portions of the texts, causing them to contain intermingled high- and low-quality places. In order to solve such problems, besides editors who watch the latest edits or specific articles they are interested in keeping track of, Wikipedia's community created different ways of assessing the quality of the articles - both manually and automatically -, and thus identifying and better coordinating the community's efforts. Despite many earlier works suggesting using the count of existing images in the articles as an additional evidence to estimate the quality of the articles, none of them actually focuses on the direct relationship between quality and the existence/amount of extra-textual information.

Therefore, in this work, we sought to check whether the rating of Portuguese-speaking Wikipedia articles assigned by the community and the amount of extra-textual elements. As a result of this work, we observed a correlation between the count of images and the ratings, which it is a little bit higher when the quality is estimated by robots.

In the section 2 some of the works containing related studies on the quality of Wikipedia's articles present in the literature are briefly presented. In the section 3 we discuss how the ratings of the articles are obtained. In the section 4 we describe the collection used in the course of the experiments. In the section 5 we report the experiments and its main results. Finally, conclusions and future research perspectives are presented in the section 6.

---

[1]http://wikipedia.org/

2. RELATED WORK

In the literature, there are many works dealing with the issue of quality of Wikipedia articles. Stvilia et al. (2005) [15] explore ways of assessing the quality of Wikipedia articles by using different IQ metrics. Blumenstock (2008) [4] propose using the word count as a measure of quality for the articles. Lim et al. (2006) [11] suggest considering the authority of the editors and the quality of the articles which they contributed with to infer quality, while Hu et al. (2007) [9] and Adler et al. (2008) [1] suggest also that well-reputed contributors make good quality edits, and that quality may be associated with these edits lifespan. In the other hand, Suzuki and Yoshikawa (2012) [14] make use of the authority of the editors instead of considering the edits lifespan, so that texts attacked by vandalism do not have their ratings decreased.

Moturu and Liu (2009) [13] propose a model in terms of quality and credibility to assess the trustworthiness of Wikipedia content. Wöhner and Peters (2009) [23] propose metrics by studying the lifecycle of high and low quality articles. Dondio and Barrett (2007) [7] conducted experiments to try to infer quality in Wikipedia articles. Calzada and Dekhtyar (2010) [6] present quality models for the articles and validate the results with humans, showing that different kinds of articles should have their quality assessed differently. Anderka et al. (2012) [3] investigate frequent quality flaws in Wikipedia articles and how to predict them. Dalip et al. (2012) [5] explore quality indicators and their capability to assess the quality of the articles. Wang and Iwaihara (2011) [16] propose a network structural model and calculate an indicator combining different metrics for evaluating the quality of the articles, and compare it to existing metrics. In the context of Portuguese-speaking Wikipedia, Hanada (2013) [8] studies link analysis metrics and their relationship with quality and popularity, in order to underlie investigations to propose new metrics for Wikipedia.

Although some authors (Dalip et al. (2012) [5], Dondio and Barrett (2007) [7] and Stvilia et al. (2005) [15]) take into account the count of images existing in the articles as one of the criteria of their quality assessment metrics, we were unable to find in the literature any works dealing directly with the relationship between the quality of the articles and the existence/amount of extra-textual elements. This is the question this work addresses.

3. BACKGROUND

In this section, we will describe basic concepts for the understanding of this work. Particularly, we are going to provide details on how ratings are assigned and how Wikipedia uses media, as well as Kendall-τ metric, which was used to assess the correlations between the rankings.

3.1 Wikipedia

Wikipedia is a digital multilingual encyclopedia. Unlike the traditional printed encyclopedias or even other digital encyclopedias, it is a free encyclopedia, that is, written collaboratively and free in the internet. Everyone can edit an existing article or create a new one and contribute with the project.

3.1.1 Quality of the articles

Wikipedia's community has a constant concern about the quality of the articles. Editorial control is made by the edi-

tors themselves, who watch articles or the latest edits, and can quickly detect vandalism and revert edits that compromise the integrity of the articles [8]. It is also possible to question uncited or unsourced claims. Besides, each article has a "Talk" page where editors from the community can discuss its content, adding, improving or even removing parts of the article, achieving a consensual content.

In order to assess the quality of an article, Portuguese-speaking Wikipedia currently adopts a rating taxonomy composed of 6 classes. The classes in this scale are: featured (6 - *destacados*), good (5 - *bons*), well-developed (4 - *desenvolvidos*), poorly developed (3 - *pouco desenvolvidos*), stub (2 - *esboços*), minimum/very limited stubs (1 - *mínimos/esboços muito limitados*), unrated (0 or ?) [21].

The main way to assess the quality of the articles is the ratings assigned by the community. Editors can nominate any articles as good or featured. They are reviewed, and either promoted or rejected. As for the remaining classes, any editor can assign or change a rating, according to the scale and the criteria established by the community [20]. There are other two assessment approaches: an automatic one (done by robots, and currently temporarily suspended) [17] and one assigned by the readers (limited to articles in a special consensus category) [18].

3.1.2 Media files

Wikipedia articles can be further enriched with image and sound files [19]. We considered in this work both types of media as extra-textual elements. Many limitations apply to what materials can be uploaded due to copyright restrictions.

3.2 Kendall rank correlation coefficient-τ

Kendall rank correlation coefficient-τ [10] measures the similarity degree between two given sets of ranks. It is given by:

$$\tau = \frac{C - D}{\sqrt{(C + D - T_x)(C + D - T_y)}}$$

where C is the number of concordant pairs, D is the number of discordant pairs, T_x and T_y correspond respectively to ties in the variables x and y. A pair is concordant if, for any given pairs (x_i, y_i) and (x_j, y_j), $x_i > x_j$ and $y_i > y_j$ or $x_i < x_j$ and $y_i < y_j$, in other words, if values in both coordinates of a variable are greater (or lesser) than those from the other one. This coefficient is calculated by directly measuring an ordered pair. Coefficient τ varies in the interval of [-1, 1], 1 being the perfect positive correlation, -1 the perfect negative correlation (inversely proportional), and 0 indicates no relationship. A possible interpretation of the values of τ is:

- High correlation: 0.5 to 1.0 or -0.5 to 1.0
- Moderate correlation: 0.3 to 0.5 or -0.3 to .5
- Low correlation: 0.1 to 0.3 or -0.1 to -0.3

4. COLLECTIONS

In this work, a database dump of Portuguese-speaking Wikipedia (ptwiki) was obtained from the Wikimedia[2] website, dated March 23, 2013. 1,679,655 pages were imported,

---

[2]http://dumps.wikimedia.org/

out of which 773,959 are articles, and the remaining ones are templates, media/file descriptions and primary meta-pages. Among all articles, 62,296 (8.1%) were rated by the community and 76,963 (9.9%) were rated by robots, totaling 97,918 (12.6%) rated articles.

	Images	Sounds
Rated	95,648	279
Total	717,234	866

Table 1: Amount of rated articles containing media.

In this work, we used only articles containing some kind of media and quality ratings. In the extracted dataset, the following data from these articles were grouped: id, title, ratings (assigned by the community and by the robots), count of images and sounds, total of media (sum of the amount of images and the amount of sounds). Table 2 presents the amount of articles containing images and sounds rated by the community and the robots.

		Images		Sounds		Total (I + S)	
		C	C+R	C	C+R	C	C+R
	1	53,736	78,743	26	55	53,736	78,743
	2	4,810	11,569	20	37	4,810	11,569
Qua	3	1,687	3,412	39	48	1,687	3,412
	4	493	1,002	44	60	495	1,002
	5	399	399	58	58	399	399
	6	523	523	21	21	523	525
Total		61,648	95,648	208	279	61,650	95,648

Table 2: Amount of articles containing images, sounds and total of media, according to the ratings assigned by the community (C) and by the community and by the robots at same time (C+R). It is important to point out that there is an intersection between the articles containing images and sounds

Looking at the Table 2, one observes that only a few articles contain sounds. Most sound files in the dataset are part of articles related to music, such as articles about music styles, singers or bands. It is important to keep in mind that ratings assigned by the robots vary from 1 to 4, since articles can only be assigned a rating 5 or 6 after going through a careful nomination and voting process.

5. EXPERIMENTS

In order to check the correlation between the quality ratings of Wikipedia articles and the amount of extra-textual contents, we will use rank correlation measures. The idea is to establish a ranking of Wikipedia articles according to the count of media items (images, sounds and the sum of both) and the article ratings. We will use Kendall Tau-b coefficient [10] to infer if these rankings are correlated. Since we had unbalanced distributions, we chose to use smaller, randomly selected samples, containing the same quantity of articles for each of the 6-level rating groups.

We assessed the correlation between the ratings assigned by the community and the count of images and sounds. For the count of images, a sample containing 2,394 articles was used. Since the group with the smallest amount of articles (rating 5) contained 399 articles, we decided to conduct the experiment using all 399 articles from this group. For the remaining groups, we used 399 randomly selected articles. In order to compare the results obtained, we created 10

sub-samples containing 600 articles (100 randomly selected articles for each rating group). We assessed the correlation between the ratings and the random count of images to use as a random baseline. As for the sounds, we selected only articles containing this kind of media. Since group 2 had the smallest amount of articles (20), we used all 20 articles from that group and 20 randomly selected articles for each of the remaining groups. We assessed the correlation between the ratings and any randomly assigned count of images for 10 samples containing 60 articles (10 randomly selected articles of each rating) as a random baseline.

The obtained results are presented in the Table 3. As expected, the results for correlations using the real ranking were quite higher than those from the random ranking. Moderated correlation was found between the ratings and the count of images, which proves the evidence of correlation. However, given the small amount of articles containing sounds in the dataset, we cannot claim the same about the correlation between the ratings and the number of sounds.

	R X I	R X S
Random ranking	-0.0087	0.0044
Real ranking	0.4351	0.1241

Table 3: Kendall τ values obtained by testing the correlations between ratings (R) and the count of existing media in an article (images - I, sounds - S) using a random ranking as a baseline and a real ranking.

In order to discover which kind of rating is more correlated to the media, we conducted another experiment, now using only articles rated by the community and by the robots at same time. Since only ratings 1 to 4 can be assigned by robots, articles whose ratings were 5 or 6 were ignored. In the case of the count of images, since the group with the smallest amount of articles (rating 4) contained 179 articles, we used all the 179 articles from that group, plus 179 randomly selected articles from each of the remaining groups, totaling 716 articles. As for the ratings by the robots, since the group with the smallest amount of articles (also rating 4) contained 170 articles, we used all 170 articles from that group, plus 170 randomly selected articles from the remaining groups, totaling 680 articles. In the case of the count of sounds, we used a sample of 32 articles (in other words, all articles rated by both the community and robots at same time containing sounds). We then assessed the correlations between the count of images and sounds and the ratings by the community and the robots.

Table 4 presents the obtained correlations for articles rated by the community and the robots.

	R X I	R X S
Community	0.4416	0.1130
Robots	0.4663	0.1361

Table 4: Kendall τ values obtained by testing the correlations between ratings (R) assigned by the community and the robots and the count of existing media in an article (images - I, sounds - S).

The results show that, for both images and sounds, ratings assigned by the robots tend to me slightly more correlated to the media than those assigned by the community.

6. CONCLUSIONS

The purpose of this work was to investigate if the amount of extra-textual elements (in this case, images and sounds) is an evidence of quality of Wikipedia articles. our experiments show moderate correlation between the ratings assigned by the community and the count of images, and low correlation between the same ratings and the count of sounds. Despite being inconclusive, the first result may have been influenced or affected by a relatively considerable amount of images of little or no relevance to the contents of the articles.

As for the sounds, the fact that there are few articles in the Portuguese-speaking Wikipedia containing that type of media prevent us from drawing more solid conclusions. This limitation could perhaps be avoided by using a bigger dataset, such as English Wikipedia, which may contain more articles with sounds. We also observed that the correlation between the total of media and the ratings were slightly higher for ratings assigned by the robots. That may indicate that the robots take into account the number of images when assessing the quality of an article.

Future research directions would be studying the behavior of the media. Other possible works are investigating what determines if an article has many sound files, the relationship between this fact and the category to which an article belongs, or what kind of articles have images unrelated to its contents.

7. ACKNOWLEDGMENT

The authors would like to thank CNPq (grants 307.861/ 2010-4 and 484.816/2011-0) and FAPEAM by financial support for this research. M.G. Pimentel would like to thank FAPESP, CAPES and CNPq by financial support, and FAPESP by financial support to present this work.

8. REFERENCES

[1] B. T. Adler, K. Chatterjee, L. de Alfaro, M. Faella, I. Pye, and V. Raman. Assigning trust to wikipedia content. In *Proceedings of the 4th International Symposium on Wikis*, WikiSym '08, pages 26:1–26:12, New York, NY, USA, 2008. ACM.

[2] Alexa. Wikipedia site info, 2013. Acesso em: 22 maio 2013.

[3] M. Anderka and B. Stein. A breakdown of quality flaws in wikipedia. In *Proceedings of the 2nd Joint WICOW/AIRWeb Workshop on Web Quality*, WebQuality '12, pages 11–18, New York, NY, USA, 2012. ACM.

[4] J. E. Blumenstock. Size matters: word count as a measure of quality on wikipedia. In *Proceedings of the 17th international conference on World Wide Web*, WWW '08, pages 1095–1096, New York, NY, USA, 2008. ACM.

[5] D. H. Dalip, M. A. Gonçalves, M. Cristo, and P. Calado. Automatic assessment of document quality in web collaborative digital libraries. *J. Data and Information Quality*, 2(3):14:1–14:30, Dec. 2011.

[6] G. De la Calzada and A. Dekhtyar. On measuring the quality of wikipedia articles. In *Proceedings of the 4th workshop on Information credibility*, WICOW '10, pages 11–18, New York, NY, USA, 2010. ACM.

[7] P. Dondio and S. Barrett. Computational trust in web content quality: A comparative evalutation on the wikipedia project. *Informatica*, 31(2):151–160, 2007.

[8] R. T. S. Hanada, M. da Graça Campos Pimentel, and M. Cristo. Relação entre métricas de análise de ligações e qualidade, importância e popularidade na wikipédia. In G. Bressan, R. M. Silveira, E. V. Munson, A. Santanchà, and M. da Graça Campos Pimentel, editors, *Brazilian Symposium on Multimedia and the Web, WebMedia'13, Salvador, Brazil, Novembro, 2013 (to appear)*. ACM, 2013.

[9] M. Hu, E.-P. Lim, A. Sun, H. W. Lauw, and B.-Q. Vuong. Measuring article quality in wikipedia: models and evaluation. In *Proceedings of the sixteenth ACM conference on Conference on information and knowledge management*, CIKM '07, pages 243–252, New York, NY, USA, 2007. ACM.

[10] M. Kendall. *Rank correlation methods*. Griffin, London, 1948.

[11] E.-P. Lim, B.-Q. Vuong, H. W. Lauw, and A. Sun. Measuring qualities of articles contributed by online communities. In *Proceedings of the 2006 IEEE/WIC/ACM International Conference on Web Intelligence*, WI '06, pages 81–87, Washington, DC, USA, 2006. IEEE Computer Society.

[12] M. Mortazavi. Why web 2.0 has come to exist?. on the margins, 2006. Acesso em: 22 maio 2013.

[13] S. T. Moturu and H. Liu. Evaluating the trustworthiness of wikipedia articles through quality and credibility. In *Proceedings of the 5th International Symposium on Wikis and Open Collaboration*, WikiSym '09, pages 28:1–28:2, New York, NY, USA, 2009. ACM.

[14] Y. Suzuki and M. Yoshikawa. Mutual evaluation of editors and texts for assessing quality of wikipedia articles. In *Proceedings of the Eighth Annual International Symposium on Wikis and Open Collaboration*, WikiSym '12, pages 18:1–18:10, New York, NY, USA, 2012. ACM.

[15] B. S. M. B. Twidale. Assessing information quality of a community-based encyclopedia. In *In Proceedings of the International Conference on Information Quality*, pages 442–454, 2005.

[16] S. Wang and M. Iwaihara. Quality evaluation of wikipedia articles through edit history and editor groups. In *Proceedings of the 13th Asia-Pacific web conference on Web technologies and applications*, APWeb'11, pages 188–199, Berlin, Heidelberg, 2011. Springer-Verlag.

[17] Wikipedia. Wikipédia:avaliação automática, 2013. Acesso em: 22 maio 2013.

[18] Wikipedia. Wikipédia:avaliação de artigos, 2013. Acesso em: 22 maio 2013.

[19] Wikipedia. Wikipédia:conteúdo restrito, 2013. Acesso em: 29 maio 2013.

[20] Wikipedia. Wikipédia:escolha do artigo em destaque, 2013. Acesso em: 22 maio 2013.

[21] Wikipedia. Wikipédia:versão 1.0/avaliação, 2013. Acesso em: 22 maio 2013.

[22] Wikipedia. Wikipedia, 2013. Acesso em: 22 maio 2013.

[23] T. Wöhner and R. Peters. Assessing the quality of wikipedia articles with lifecycle based metrics. In *Proceedings of the 5th International Symposium on Wikis and Open Collaboration*, WikiSym '09, pages 16:1–16:10, New York, NY, USA, 2009. ACM.

Using Genetic Programming to Detect Fraud in Electronic Transactions

Carlos A. S. de Assis
CEFET-MG
carlos.assis.79@gmail.com

Adriano C. M. Pereira
UFMG
adrianoc@dcc.ufmg.br

Marconi de A. Pereira
UFSJ
marconi.arruda@gmail.com

Eduardo G. Carrano
UFMG
egcarrano@ufmg.br

ABSTRACT

The volume of online transactions has raised a lot in last years, mainly due to the popularization of e-commerce, such as Web retailers. We also observe a significant increase in the number of fraud cases, resulting in billions of dollars losses each year worldwide. Therefore it is important and necessary to developed and apply techniques that can assist in fraud detection, which motivates our research. This work proposes the use of Genetic Programming (GP), an Evolutionary Computation approach, to model and detect fraud (charge back) in electronic transactions, more specifically in credit card operations. In order to evaluate the technique, we perform a case study using an actual dataset of the most popular Brazilian electronic payment service, called *UOL PagSeguro*. Our results show good performance in fraud detection, presenting gains up to 17.72% percent compared to the baseline, which is the actual scenario of the corporation.

Categories and Subject Descriptors

K.4 [**Computers and society**]: Electronic Commerce

Keywords

Genetic Programming, Web Transactions, Fraud

1. INTRODUÇÃO

Em 2012, o comércio eletrônico brasileiro faturou R$ 22,5 bilhões e apresentou um crescimento de 20% em relação ao ano anterior, conforme dados da 27ª edição do relatório Webshoppers[1]. O estudo foi realizado pela e-bit[2]. O aumento no volume de transações é acompanhado do crescimento das fraudes neste setor; assim, o aperfeiçoamento das técnicas de prevenção é fundamental para as empresas da área.

---

[1] http://www.webshoppers.com.br/
[2] http://www.ebit.com.br/

Este artigo propõe o uso de Programação Genética (PG) para avaliação de transações eletrônicas online - em especial pagamentos com cartão de crédito - e identificação de fraudes. As principais contribuições deste trabalho são: (a) aplicação de PG como ferramenta de apoio a detecção de fraudes em transações eletrônicas em cenários reais; (b) disponibilização desta ferramenta como um *framework open-source*[3].

O restante deste artigo está organizado da seguinte forma: a Seção 2 descreve alguns trabalhos correlatos; a Seção 3 apresenta uma descrição sobre a técnica de PG implementada; a Seção 4 descreve a metodologia que será aplicada na Seção 5 e finalmente, a Seção 6 apresenta a conclusão.

2. TRABALHOS RELACIONADOS

Para uma pesquisa sobre os desenvolvimentos relativos à detecção de fraudes com cartão de crédito, de forma mais geral, podem ser consultados os trabalhos de [6], [4], [1], [2].

Guo [6] apresenta uma forma de modelar uma sequência de operações no processamento de transações em cartão de crédito usando uma rede neural combinada com nível de confiança. Isto é, se uma transação de cartão de crédito não for aceita pelo modelo de rede neural, inicialmente treinado, com um mínimo de confiança, ela é considerada fraudulenta.

Ghosh [4] apresenta um detector de fraudes baseado em redes neurais. Esta rede foi treinada com um grande número de amostras de transações pré-classificadas. O estudo de viabilidade demonstrou que este método reduziu de 20% a 40% nas perdas em fraudes.

Bolton e Hand [1] propõem uma técnica de detecção não supervisionada utilizando análise de *breakpoint* para identificar mudanças em comportamentos de gastos. *Breakpoint* é uma observação ou um instante onde um comportamento anormal é detectado. Um exemplo é o aumento repentino no número de transações que pode indicar comportamento fraudulento.

Para Duman e Ozcelik [2], soluções de detecção de fraude têm o objetivo típico de minimizar o número de transações mal classificadas. A classificação errada de cada operação não tem o mesmo efeito de um cartão na mão de fraudadores. Assim, o custo de má classificação deve ser tomado como o limite disponível no cartão. Isso é o que visam minimizar neste estudo. Quanto ao método de solução, é feito uma combinação de duas metaheurísticas: os algoritmos ge-

---

[3] http://data-mining-genetic-programming.googlecode.com/

néticos e *scatter search*. O método foi aplicado em dados reais e os resultados obtidos foram bem sucedidos.

Percebe-se, com essa análise dos estudos, que diversos trabalhos na literatura abordam o tema das fraudes eletrônicas, porém poucos utilizando a PG.

3. FUNDAMENTOS CONCEITUAIS

A Programação Genética (PG) foi desenvolvida por [8] na década de 90 com base nos trabalhos de [7] e pode ser visto como uma extensão do Algoritmo Genético (AG).

Segundo Pereira [11], a PG possui grande semelhança com o AG. A principal diferença está na representação dos indivíduos: enquanto no AG codifica-se os indivíduos em código binário, real ou outro, a PG codifica os indivíduos na forma de uma árvore. Essa codificação apresentada na PG, gera alterações significativas nos operadores genéticos, além de possibilitar benefícios, tais como conter não somente valores de variáveis, mas também funções. Detalhes da técnica proposta serão apresentados na Seção 3.1.

3.1 O Algoritmo - NGPA

Foi proposto um algoritmo de PG - *NGPA (Niched Genetic Programming Algorithm)*, o mesmo se baseia no trabalho de Pereira [11] e traz aperfeiçoamentos em termos de implementação com uma nova arquitetura de software e extensões.

Nas próximas Seções iremos apresentar mais detalhes.

3.1.1 Indivíduo

O indivíduo é modelado para representar uma regra de classificação e é utilizado como um filtro para a seleção de padrões no banco de dados. Duas partes compõem o indivíduo: (a) a árvore que codifica o filtro dos atributos; e (b) o rótulo da classe que indica a qual classe as amostras selecionadas pela regra pertencerão.

Os nós da árvore podem ser dos seguintes tipos: (a) nós funções são formados por funções que nesta implementação possuem exatamente dois parâmetros e formam o conjunto possível de nós internos; (b) nós terminais: o conjunto de nós terminais é formado por valores gerados aleatoriamente ou por atributos do banco de dados.

O conjunto de nós funções é composto por funções ou operadores, tais como =, <, >, >=, <=, AND e OR,

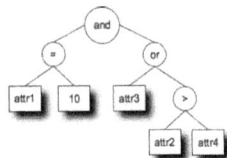

Figura 1: Representação do indivíduo

3.1.2 Mutação

O operador de mutação consiste na troca de um nó (terminal ou não) por outro nó (terminal ou uma sub-árvore) gerado.

Para Pereira [11], diferentemente do que acontece no AG, o operador de mutação da PG não é simples de ser implementado. Primeiramente, é necessário ter certeza de que a árvore do indivíduo se mantém válida após a mutação, isto é, o operador de mutação não pode substituir um nó (ou sub-árvore) por um nó de tipo de dado diferente.

3.1.3 Cruzamento

O operador de cruzamento consiste na troca de material genético entre os indivíduos pais. A operação de cruzamento em relação ao conceito biológico corresponde ao processo de reprodução sexuada [10]. Dois indivíduos são selecionados e recombinados para gerar outros dois indivíduos a partir de seus valores de *fitness*. Um ponto aleatório de cruzamento é escolhido em cada indivíduo-pai e os nós abaixo destes pontos são trocados.

3.1.4 Nichos

A utilização de técnica de nicho consiste em dividir-se a população em subpopulações a fim de proporcionar que as subpopulações sejam capazes de encontrar outros ótimos locais. A utilização da técnica de nicho visa a evitar a obtenção de um único ponto ótimo. Existem problemas que podem apresentar mais de um ponto ótimo. Assim, pode-se desejar conhecer uma maior variedade de pontos que minimizam a função objetivo em um problema de otimização.

Goldberg [5] propôs a utilização da técnica de nicho, a fim de se obter as melhores regras de classificação para as n classes do problema a cada execução do algoritmo. Com utilização de técnicas de nicho permite-se um maior compartilhamento dos indivíduos no espaço de busca.

3.1.5 Matriz de Confusão

A matriz de confusão é aquela cuja dimensão é dada pelo número de classes que sumariza os resultados de dado classificador. A diagonal principal da matriz exibe o número de acertos para as classes analisadas, enquanto os elementos fora desta diagonal, o número de erros.

O valor referente a verdadeiros positivos (TP) é o número de tuplas cobertas pela regra representada no indivíduo em questão. O falso positivo (FP) é calculado contando-se o número total de tuplas obtidas pela regra codificada pelo indivíduo e que não pertençam à classe predita por essa regra. O valor de verdadeiros negativos (TN) é calculado a partir da contagem do número de tuplas que não pertençam à classe em questão, subtraído pelo número de FP. A quantidade de falsos negativos (FN) é calculada contando-se a quantidade de tuplas que pertençam à classe em questão, subtraído do número de TP [11].

3.1.6 Função Fitness

O cálculo da função *fitness*[4] utiliza os valores de acurácia, sensibilidade e especificidade medidos para cada indivíduo. A Equação utilizada neste trabalho é:

$$f(I, X) = Acur(I, X) * Sens(I, X) * Espec(I, X) \quad (1)$$

Onde *f(I, X)* é o valor de *fitness* e *I* é o indivíduo que identifica padrões pertencentes à classe *X*. As expressões relacionadas são descritas a seguir:

- Acurácia: $\frac{(TP+TN)}{(TP+TN+FP+FN)}$;

- Sensibilidade: $\frac{(TP)}{(TP+FN)}$;

- Especificidade: $\frac{(TN)}{(TN+FP)}$.

---

[4]Medida do desempenho do indivíduo com relação ao modelo matemático do problema de otimização.

Os coeficientes da matriz são calculados considerando cada uma das classes do problema. O cálculo da *fitness* é realizado através de consultas *SQL*, realizadas no banco de dados.

3.1.7 Cálculo da Eficiência Econômica

No contexto da fraude existem perdas financeiras associadas a erros de classificação. Assim, não só a cobertura da fraude deve ser levada em consideração, mas também a eficiência econômica do resultado. O conceito de Eficiência Econômica trata-se da avaliação financeira dos resultados obtidos. Esta Equação é baseada na contabilização dos ganhos e das perdas financeiros, de acordo com os estados definidos na matriz de confusão. O cálculo de Eficiência Econômica *(EE)* é apresentado na Equação 2 [9].

$$EE = \sum_{j=1}^{n} G * k - L * (1 - k) \qquad (2)$$

Onde n representa o número de transações existente; k é o percentual que o mercado eletrônico fatura em cada transação; G representa o valor financeiro das transações classificadas como não fraude corretamente, L é o valor financeiro das transações classificadas como não fraude incorretamente. Aplicando a Equação 2 para a classificação fornecida pelas técnicas, é possível verificar o lucro ou prejuízo obtido.

4. METODOLOGIA

Esta Seção apresenta a metodologia adotada neste trabalho, sintetizada na Figura 2.

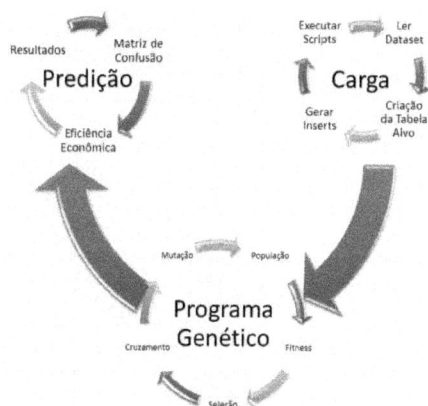

Figura 2: Metodologia proposta

4.1 Carga

Uma fonte de dados é recebida previamente tratada. Isso quer dizer que foram feito alguns tratamentos nos dados, ou seja, limpeza, seleção de atributos e caracterização.

Utiliza-se um software utilitário criado para a carga do *dataset*, assim é feita uma leitura da fonte de dados em formato *.csv*, onde a primeira linha do arquivo são os nomes das colunas: essa informação será base para a criação da tabela alvo e as demais linhas são utilizadas para a inserção dos registros.

4.2 Programação Genética

Para geração dos modelos é usado um algoritmo proposto de PG, que produz como resultado os modelos mais aptos,

ou seja, aqueles que classificaram melhor as informações na etapa de treinamento. Após a geração dos modelos de PG, os mesmos são organizados para que na próxima etapa o algoritmo de predição seja executado em uma base de testes.

4.3 Predição

De posse dos modelos, é possível realizar a predição da classe da transação, de acordo com uma probabilidade de pertencer a uma determinada classe (p. ex, fraude), que pode ser representada como um ranking. Foram propostas oito abordagens a fim de avaliar o desempenho das regras obtidas, conforme apresentado na Tabela 1. Ao final, através da Equação 2, é possível avaliar o resultado da predição, comparando-o com o resultado real da empresa, que serve como linha de base.

Tabela 1: Técnicas de predição baseadas em regras.

1	Melhores regras que casam com a classe de fraude: a probabilidade de fraude é gerada de acordo com a quantidade de regras que casam com a classe de fraude, e o ranking é ordenado de acordo com essa probabilidade, que será um número entre 0 e 1.
2	Melhores regras que casam com a classe de fraude com ordenação decrescente por valor de transação: parecido com a abordagem anterior, a probabilidade de fraude é gerada de acordo com a quantidade de regras que casam com a classe de fraude, e o ranking é ordenado de acordo com essa probabilidade e posteriormente é ordenado de forma decrescente pelo valor da transação.
3	Melhor regra que casa com a classe de fraude: cada regra de gerada é avaliada individualmente e o ranking é gerado de acordo com a probabilidade; nesse caso o retorno será 0 ou 1.
4	Melhor regra que casa com a classe de fraude com ordenação decrescente por valor de transação: parecido com a abordagem anterior, agora o ranking leva em consideração também o valor da transação; nesse caso o retorno será 0 ou 1.
5	Melhores regras que casam com a classe de fraude e não fraude: a probabilidade de fraude é gerada de acordo com a quantidade de regras que casam com a classe de fraude e não fraude, o ranking é ordenado com a probabilidade; que será um número entre −1 e 1.
6	Melhores regras que casam com a classe de fraude e não fraude com ordenação decrescente por valor de transação: parecido com a abordagem anterior, porém o ranking é ordenado levando em consideração também o valor da transação.
7	Melhor regra que casa com a classe de fraude e não fraude: nessa abordagem todas as regras de fraude confrontam com a não fraude, assim o ranking leva em consideração a melhor combinação de regras das duas classes; nesse caso o retorno será 0 ou 1.
8	Melhor regra que casa com a classe de fraude e não fraude com ordenação decrescente por valor de transação: parecido com a abordagem anterior, porém o ranking leva em consideração o valor da transação também.

5. ESTUDO DE CASO

Este artigo utiliza o cenário do UOL PagSeguro para avaliação da abordagem proposta.

5.1 Visão geral

Para o estudo de caso em questão utilizamos uma base de dados real obtida em cooperação com o UOL PagSeguro. Fizemos uma seleção inicial de treze atributos, dentre os quais temos informações da transação (p. ex., valor, número de parcelas do pagamento, hora), do comprador (p. ex., idade, localidade), do cartão de crédito (p. ex., operadora) e do vendedor (p. ex., categoria do produto que vende).

Durante os experimentos descritos nesta Seção, o algoritmo proposto foi configurado com os parâmetros descrito na Tabela 2.

O método *houldout* foi utilizado em todos os experimentos a fim de treinar e testar as regras geradas. Não foi permitida a existência de padrões repetidos nas partições, isto é, os conjuntos de dados são avaliados a fim de eliminar conteúdo duplicado. As informações de cada partição são selecionadas considerando os dias do mês, ou seja, para treinamento

Tabela 2: Configurações do NGPA

ID	Nicho	Tx. Mut.	Tx. Cruz.	Ger.	Pop.
1	0	2,50%	75%	100	200
2	0	2,50%	75%	200	500
3	1	2,50%	75%	100	200
4	1	2,50%	75%	200	500

foram considerados do dia 1 até o dia 22, para testes do dia 23 em diante.

O experimento completo foi executado 15 vezes para cada configuração da Tabela 2, com o objetivo de gerar 60 resultados. O desempenho obtido é apresentado na Seção 5.2.

5.2 Resultados

Nesta Seção é feita uma comparação entre os oito classificadores propostos na Tabela 1 *versus* as configurações do PG propostas na Tabela 2, o que gerou 32 combinações.

Tabela 3: Resultados

Config.	Classif.	Ef. Ec. Rel.	Pos. Rel. Rank
1	1	0,71%	2,66%
2	1	3,42%	2,36%
3	1	1,62%	1,94%
4	1	5,28%	3,53%
1	2	1,46%	2,61%
2	2	4,55%	2,17%
3	2	2,30%	1,58%
4	2	7,46%	2,05%
1	3	6,83%	1,57%
2	3	7,80%	0,62%
3	3	10,92%	1,81%
4	3	8,41%	14,02%
1	4	14,17%	1,04%
2	4	14,82%	0,96%
3	4	14,84%	1,00%
4	4	15,37%	0,91%
1	5	1,83%	3,58%
2	5	9,12%	2,84%
3	5	4,73%	1,27%
4	5	7,85%	2,58%
1	6	1,71%	3,57%
2	6	9,12%	2,84%
3	6	4,76%	1,26%
4	6	7,85%	2,58%
1	7	11,57%	1,67%
2	7	16,33%	1,24%
3	7	14,69%	1,46%
4	7	14,20%	3,41%
1	8	14,70%	0,69%
2	8	**17,72%**	1,01%
3	8	16,71%	2,84%
4	8	16,54%	2,93%

Para efeito de comparação, entende-se que o percentual apresentado na Tabela 3 parte de uma linha de base do UOL PagSeguro, ou seja, resultado atual obtido pela empresa.

Todos os classificadores apresentados tiveram ganhos superiores a linha de base: o maior percentual foi de 17,72%.

Os resultados apresentam informações interessantes sobre nichos. Em quase todos os cenários, o uso desta técnica apresentou ganhos.

Quanto maior o numero de gerações demostraram maior eficiência. Segundo Koza [8], uma população de tamanho maior aumenta a probabilidade cumulativa de se satisfazer o predicado de sucesso de um problema de PG.

Assim também se faz com a quantidade de indivíduos, para Koza [8], a probabilidade cumulativa de satisfazer o predicado de sucesso de um problema inevitavelmente cresce ou pelo menos não decresce.

6. CONCLUSÃO

O algoritmo implementado demonstrou ser eficaz para a geração de regras. Também conclui-se que o uso de nichos é eficaz para geração de modelos de melhor qualidade.

O uso da função de eficiência econômica também se demostrou muito eficaz para a predição de fraudes.

É possível perceber que valores expressivos podem ser economizados com a metodologia aplicada.

Como trabalhos futuros, objetiva-se uma nova execução dessa metodologia para a seleção de mais atributos que sejam significativos para o processo. Além da aplicação da eficiência econômica como parte do processo de avaliação dos indivíduos dentro do PG.

7. REFERÊNCIAS

[1] R. J. Bolton and D. J. Hand. Unsupervised profiling methods for fraud detection. *Conference on Credit Scoring and Credit Control*, September 2001.

[2] E. Duman and M. H. Ozcelik. Detecting credit card fraud by genetic algorithm and scatter search. *Expert Syst. Appl.*, 38(10):13057–13063, Sept. 2011.

[3] S. Ghosh. Credit card fraud detection with a neural-network. In *System Sciences, 1994. Proc. of the 27th Hawaii International Conference on*, volume 3, pages 621–630, Jan 1994.

[4] D. E. Goldberg. *Genetic Algorithms in Search, Optimization and Machine Learning*. Addison-Wesley Longman Pub. Co., Inc., Boston, MA, USA, 1st edition, 1989.

[5] T. Guo. Neural data mining for credit card fraud detection. In *International Conf. on Machine Learning and Cybernetics*, volume 7, July 2008.

[6] J. H. Holland. *Adaptation in Natural and Artificial Systems*. University of Michigan Press, Ann Arbor, MI, USA, 1975.

[7] J. R. Koza. *Genetic Programming: On the Programming of Computers by Means of Natural Selection*. MIT Press, Cambridge, MA, USA, 1992.

[8] R. A. F. Lima and A. C. M. Pereira. Fraud detection in web transactions. In *Proceedings of the 18th Brazilian symposium on Multimedia and the web*, WebMedia '12, pages 273–280, New York, NY, USA, 2012. ACM.

[9] R. Linden. *Algoritmos Genéticos (2a edição)*. BRASPORT, 2008.

[10] M. d. A. Pereira. *Classificação de Dados Híbridos Através de Algoritmos Evolucionários*. PhD thesis, Universidade Federal de Minas Gerais, 2012.

Risk Analysis of Electronic Transactions in Tourism Web Applications

Ruhan Bidart, Lucas Silveira, Adriano C. M. Pereira, Adriano Veloso
Departamento de Ciência da Computação (DCC)
Universidade Federal de Minas Gerais (UFMG)
{ruhanbidart, lucasmaia, adrianoc, adrianov}@dcc.ufmg.br

ABSTRACT

Recently it has been observed a world wide increase of online sales, mainly due to agility to buy and attractive prices that are offered on the Web. However, fraud has also been increased on the same rate or more. In order to address this problem it is very important to understand the characteristics of fraudsters and their typical behavior. On the tourism e-market it is not different, thus millions of frauds occur each year. In this work we analyze a representative amount (thousands) of online transactions of a tourism Web system. We try to understand the characteristics of fraudsters with the main goal to support decision of e-payment evaluation of transactions. Our results are promising, achieving up to 64% of increase in accuracy in comparison to the baseline.

Categories and Subject Descriptors

I.5.2 [**Design Methodology**]: Classifier design and evaluation

Keywords

Web Transactions, e-Payment, Tourism Site, Risk analysis, Fraud

1. INTRODUÇÃO

Na última década tem-se observado um aumento significativo no volume de transações eletrônicas, principalmente devido à popularização do comércio eletrônico (*e-commerce*). Tal popularização, associada ao grande volume financeiro envolvido e ao tráfego de informações sigilosas como, por exemplo, CPF e número do cartão de crédito, tem atraído a atenção de criminosos, que visam obter ganhos com atividades ilícitas. Segundo Bhatla et al.(2003) [4], a taxa em que fraudes ocorrem na Internet é 12 a 15 vezes maior do que no "mundo físico", de tal forma que vendas pela *Web* podem representar uma maior ameaça para os comerciantes. De acordo com o Mindware Research Group(2011)[11], nas vendas *online* da América do Norte estima-se que a perda

de receita total em 2011 foi de aproximadamente US\$ 3,4 bilhões, um aumento de US\$ 700 milhões em relação a 2010.

Neste contexto, nos últimos anos o mercado de vendas online de produtos de turismo também tem crescido muito no Brasil [2]. Isso se deve ao fato de que as vendas de produtos online terem um custo menor, tanto para o cliente final quanto para o fornecedor, uma vez que a Internet possibilita a redução de custo operacional para as empresas.

No entanto, o crescimento de transações fraudulentas têm sido diretamente proporcional ao crescimento do mercado. Por conta disso, torna-se necessário que se desenvolvam ferramentas para auxiliar no crescimento sólido deste mercado, minimizando os problemas com fraude. Essas ferramentas precisam tornar o processo de análise e aprovação de compras mais robusto e confiável.

Este trabalho propõe a utilização de métodos de classificação supervisionados [8] para avaliação de transações eletrônicas de turismo, mais especificamente de passagens aéreas. Tais métodos adotam conceitos de aprendizado de máquina no intuito de automatizar o processo de aprovação de uma compra para que este se torne de mais baixo custo, uma vez que na maioria dos casos ou o processo é executado manualmente ou possui um custo de, em média, 6% utilizando ferramentas de avaliação de risco. Os resultados são promissores, com ganhos de até 64% em relação a um *baseline* aleatório.

O artigo se organiza da seguinte forma: na Seção 2 apresenta-se uma breve visão de trabalhos relacionados e sua contribuição para este artigo. Na Seção 3 são demonstrados os dados que foram utilizados para caracterização e os atributos que foram selecionados para serem utilizados pelo algoritmo de classificação. Na Seção 4 apresentamos a metodologia que foi utilizada para se desenvolver o trabalho. Por último, a Seção 5 apresenta as conclusões desse trabalho, suas contribuições e os trabalhos futuros.

2. TRABALHOS RELACIONADOS

Existem muitas pesquisas que desenvolvem métodos para detecção de fraudes [10], [7] e [3]. Nota-se que essas metodologias podem diferir significativamente por conta de suas peculiaridades. O trabalho Phua et al. [12] faz um estudo de outros trabalhos relacionados à detecção de fraude usando mineração de dados e apresentando esses métodos e técnicas, bem como suas limitações. De acordo com os autores, existem três abordagens em que esses algoritmos são baseados: estratégias supervisionada, não supervisionada e híbrida. Na estratégia supervisionada [9], algoritmos de aprendizado de máquina examinam todas as transações previamente demarcadas para determinar matematicamente a classificação de uma fraude e estimar seu risco. Em estratégias não supervisionadas [6] os métodos não requerem conhecimento da classificação das transações, esses métodos são menos assertivos mas detectam mudanças no comportamento de transações incomuns. A estratégia híbrida consistem em utilizar as duas abordagens para compor um único mecanismo de classificação.

Entre todos os trabalhos relacionados, não encontramos nenhum que avaliasse compras de passagens aéreas, utilizando-se dos atributos específicos para este problema. Além disso, os trabalhos encontrados relacionam-se exclusivamente à análise de fraudes (*charge back*), enquanto o foco desse trabalho é automatizar o processo de reprovação de compras feito por seres humanos, considerando para essa análise apenas o comportamento do analisador humano em relação à compra, ou seja, não se consideram os atributos de *charge back* mas apenas os atributos do comprador e da compra para automatizar o processo humano.

Os trabalhos relacionados nos motivaram a estudar e escolher técnicas para aplicar em nosso cenário de classificação de compras e avaliar o desempenho delas usando dados reais.

3. DADOS

Os dados utilizados neste trabalho compreenderm 4.928 transações de compra de passagens aéreas que ocorreram em um portal de turismo, no período de setembro de 2012 a junho de 2013. Os dados que temos disponíveis para cada transação estão separados em 6 grupos numerados de 1 a 6, que são listados a seguir: dados relacionados à compra, dados do cartão de crédito, dados da viagem, dados do passageiro, a forma de pagamento e, por fim, a classificação que foi dada ao pedido por um avaliador humano, onde se determina se o pedido foi aceito ou negado. Na Tabela 1 é possível ver um maior detalhamento dos dados disponíveis.

Agrupamento	Dados do Grupo
1:Dados da compra	Data de efetivação da compra
2:Dados do cartão	Bandeira, CPF, nome, identificador, endereço da fatura
3:Dados do passageiro	Idade, nome, sexo, sobrenome
4:Dados da viagem	Cia aérea, classe, data chegada, data partida, origem, destino, ida e volta
5:Forma de pagamento	Valor total, número de parcelas
6:Classificação	Pedido negado ou aceito

Table 1: Tipos de Requisições

A partir dessas informações, iniciou-se um processo de categorização para compreender essas informações e a relação entre elas. A primeira distribuição que decidiu-se verificar estava relacionada ao uso de um mesmo cartão para mais de uma compra. Descobriu-se então que nessa distribuição haviam cartões que foram utilizados mais do que 7 vezes, os quais representavam *outliers* no gráfico de quantidade de usos por cartão. Esses cartões tinham praticamente todos os pedidos classificados como negados. Ao verificar com maior profundidade descobriu-se que tais cartões eram utilizados para testes do sistema. Desse modo, suas transações foram removidas da base de dados, para que não avaliássemos transações de teste como transações reais. Ao remover essas transações, que eram um total de 6,43% do total, passamos

agora à análise de 4.611 transações ao invés de 4.928 que existiam antes.

3.1 Seleção de Atributos

A escolha correta das características que devem ser utilizadas por um classificador é um ponto crucial para qualquer algoritmo de classificação, uma vez que é por meio delas que serão avaliadas e classificadas as instâncias.

Também é importante conhecer detalhadamente o problema que está sendo tratado para se poder adaptar os dados disponíveis de forma a facilitar o trabalho do algoritmo classificador. O conhecimento que tínhamos do problema nos levou a gerar outras duas características a partir dos dados que possuíamos, que são importantes atributos para auxiliar na diferenciação do risco das transações. São elas o *tempo de estadia*, calculado a partir da subtração entre a *data da partida* e a *data da chegada*, e o *tempo de distância da viagem*, calculado a partir da subtração entre a *data da partida* e a *data de efetivação da compra*.

Para decidir quais atributos seriam importantes para o classificador, iniciamos um processo de categorização. O principal aspecto que procuramos foi da relação de cada atributo com a classificação do pedido. Para isto, fizemos vários testes visuais. Entre eles, destacamos o teste de reprovação da transação por idade e o teste de reprovação da transação por bandeira ou operadora do cartão de crédito. Nosso objetivo com cada um desses testes era verificar se havia alguma distribuição perceptível das transações reprovadas para determinada segmentação de valores de cada um dos atributos que analisávamos. No caso da distribuição por idades (Figura 1) pode-se perceber que as transações feitas por pessoas com idade entre 12 e 40 anos possuem um grau de negação de pedido muito elevado. Já no caso da Figura 2 nota-se que, neste sistema, transações com a bandeira *Diners* possuem um forte grau de reprovação enquanto transações utilizando a bandeira *American Express* possuem um grau muito baixo de reprovação. Esse tipo de tendência em cada atributo é o que buscávamos pois o algoritmo de classificação procura encontrá-las para decidir a classe do pedido analisado. Assim, escolhemos os atributos na etapa de caracterização dos dados considerando o grau de tendência que apresentavam na inspeção visual.

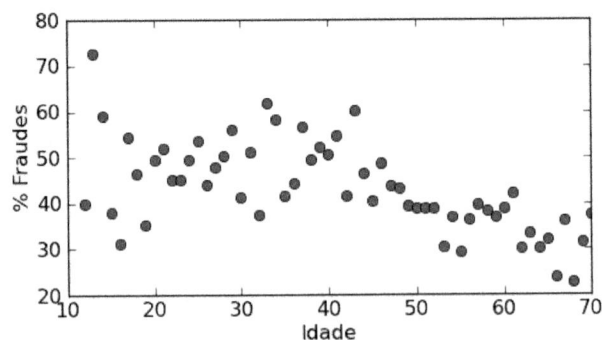

Figure 1: Número de fraudes de acordo com a idade do comprador

Os atributos escolhidos estão apresentados na Tabela 2. É possível notar que foram removidos 11 atributos e adicionados dois, os quais foram gerados a partir dos dados que

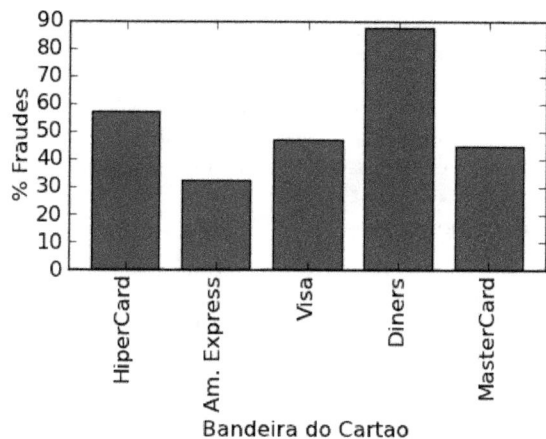

Figure 2: Número de fraudes considerando a bandeira do cartão de crédito

possuíamos. Foram adicionados aos (*dados da viagem*) as seguintes informações: *tempo de estadia* e *tempo de distância da viagem*. Os atributos que foram removidos têm como justificativa para sua remoção a razão de que eles não apresentavam ganho de informação e portanto dificultavam obter melhor resultado com os modelos gerados pelos algoritmos de classificação.

Agrupamento	Dados do Grupo
1:Dados da compra	Data de efetivação da compra
2:Dados do cartão	Bandeira
3:Dados do passageiro	Idade, sexo
4:Dados da viagem	Cia aérea, data de ída e volta, tempo de estadia, tempo de distância da viagem
5:Forma de pagamento	Valor total, número de parcelas
6:Classificação	Pedido negado ou aceito

Table 2: Tipos de Requisições

4. ANÁLISE DE RISCO - RESULTADOS

A análise de risco desenvolvida por este trabalho visa verificar, por meio de uma transação de compra e seus atributos, se o pedido deve ser aceito ou não pelo vendedor do produto. Em um cenário real, essa análise se baseia em mais informações do que as que utilizamos nesse trabalho. Um analista utiliza, por exemplo, informações do Serviço de Proteção ao Crédito (SPC) e Receita Federal do Brasil acerca do CPF do cliente, além de outras que podem não estar previstas no processo de avaliação que a empresa utiliza. Este trabalho não pretende automatizar a análise por meio da discriminação computacional de um processo humano, mas sim encontrar outras características não identificáveis facilmente por um humano que possam ser capazes de direcionar a classificação do pedido em negado ou aceito.

Como não visamos comparar nosso acerto com o da análise humana mas sim aproximar-se à ela, consideramos como *baseline* a classificação do pedido em aceito ou negado seguindo a distribuição real das classes ou o modelo aleatório, que possui 50% de pedidos aceitos na base real. Portanto como linha-de-base (*baseline*) temos 50% de acerto no modelo aleatório de classificação.

Primeiramente é importante ressaltar que foram experi-

mentadas diversas categorizações dos dados até encontrarmos a que citamos na Seção 3. Para cada uma delas aplicou-se a classificação estudando-se os resufltados. Entre essas categorizações destacaremos três. A primeira delas foi intuitiva e considerou os seguintes atributos para a classificação:

- Pedido negado ou aceito
- Bandeira do cartão
- Idade
- Sexo
- Cia aérea
- Origem
- Destino
- Ida e volta
- Tempo de estadia
- Tempo da distância da viagem
- Parcelamento
- Valor da compra

Essa categorização intuitiva não levou a resultados satisfatórios. A taxa de acerto praticamente não superou o *baseline*, estando muito próxima a 50%. Na Tabela 3 podem ser vistos os quatro algoritmos que obtiveram o melhor resultado. Nota-se também que todos eles não superaram o *baseline* aleatório de maneira satisfatória, o que nos fez concluir que havia um erro em nossa modelagem.

Table 3: Resultados da classificação - Primeira modelagem

Algoritmo	Taxa de Acerto %	Taxa de Erro %
J48	50,45	49,55
Bagging	51,7	48,3
Boosting	52,81	47,19
MultiBoosting	52,93	47,07

Partiu-se então para outra modelagem. Ao verificarmos graficamente a relação reprovação da transação/origem e reprovação da transação/destino, percebemos que as cidades de origem e destino poderiam não interferir na classificação, algo que na visão intuitiva demonstrava-se o reverso. Deste modo, resolvemos remover esses dois atributos da classificação e executar os classificadores novamente.

Table 4: Resultados da classificação - Segunda modelagem

Algoritmo	Taxa de Acerto %	Taxa de Erro %
J48	55,67	44,33
Bagging	57,22	42,78
Boosting	58,37	41,63
MultiBoosting	60,21	39,79

Como pode ser visto na Tabela 4, obtivemos melhores resultados do que na primeira modelagem. No entanto, os resultados ainda apresentavam uma baixa precisão. Analisando os dados novamente, identificou-se que o valor da compra variava muito então decidimos aplicar uma técnica de agrupamento [5] visando relacionar compras com valores similares. O algoritmo que escolhemos foi o X-Means e o agrupamento gerado por ele obteve como resultado dois grupos. Um grupo (com 30% das instâncias) possuindo valores acima de R\$ 1.500,00 e o outro grupo (com 70% das instâncias) possuindo valores abaixo de R\$ 1.500,00. Com esse agrupamento obteve-se uma melhora de 36% em relação a última modelagem. Esses resultados podem ser vistos na Tabela 5, a qual apresenta como melhor algoritmo classificador o MultiBoosting [1], que obteve 82,03% de acerto. Este resultado supera em 64% o *baseline* que utilizamos.

Table 5: Resultados da classificação - Terceira modelagem

Algoritmo	Taxa de Acerto %	Taxa de Erro %
J48	78,13	21,87
Bagging	79,95	20,05
Boosting	80,21	19,79
MultiBoosting	82,03	17,97

É importante ressaltar que este estudo de caracterização e modelagem e análise de risco de transações eletrônicos de serviços Web de turismo, mais especificamente, aquisição online de passagens aéreas, foi uma primeira investigação, que alcançou resultados satisfatórios, mas preliminares sobre o problema em questão. Pretendemos estudar mais detalhadamente esse cenário e criar modelos que permitam aperfeiçoar o resultado, que será base de um importante arcabouço de suporte à decisão para avaliação de transações online de pacotes turísticos. Dentre as contribuições que sua aplicação prevê está uma melhor agilidade na avaliação e aprovação das transações, diminuição dos altos custos que uma análise manual de risco possui, bem como melhor otimização da margem de lucro deste concorrido segmento de turimo.

5. CONCLUSÃO

Com esse trabalho percebeu-se que a automatização de processos humanos, especialmente quando se trata de transações eletrônicas de compra, possui elevada dificuldade de resolução. Isso ocorre porque, para classificar uma compra por meio das informações do comprador, é necessário avaliar diversos atributos e encontrar padrões que auxiliam nessa classificação é uma tarefa minusciosa, onde erros em pequenos detalhes podem causar grandes diferenças nos resultados. Em muitos casos uma análise humana por meio de um processo manual e intuitivo pode resultar em um melhor aproveitamento do que os resultados de um computador, mesmo que sejam utilizadas técnicas avançadas de aprendizado de máquina. Isso ocorre porque um ser humano pode adicionar elementos e informações no processo de maneira imprevisível, algo que um computador não consegue desenvolver.

O problema de classificação pode ser minimizado a partir de uma boa caracterização para escolha dos atributos e técnicas a ser utilizadas. Para isso deve-se realizar uma análise mais detalhada no intuito de escolher os atributos que são realmente importantes para realizar a avaliação.

A principal contribuição deste trabalho está na caracterização desenvolvida especificamente para transações de passagens aéreas, bem como na escolha e avaliação do melhor método de classificação, embasados em sua aplicação em uma carga de trabalho real e com milhares de transações sendo analisadas. Como trabalhos futuros pretende-se:

- Trabalhar melhor a modelagem dos dados, por meio da geração de novas características a partir das que já possuímos;
- Aplicar outras técnicas de classificação especialmente utilizando algoritmos genéticos;

- Fazer uma análise mais apurada das compras relacionando o problema de classificação de compras com o *charge back*, para isso procuraremos formas de inserir nos algoritmos a informação de *charge back*, ampliando assim o problema de classificação de compras ao adicionar à ele a possibilidade de análise de risco.

Agradecimentos

Este trabalho foi parcialmente patrocinado pelo Instituto Nacional de Ciência e Tecnologia para a Web (CNPq no. 573871/2008-6), CAPES, CNPq, Finep, e Fapemig.

Referências

[1] *Machine Learning*, 40(2), 2000. ISSN 0885-6125.
[2] World travel and tourism council 2011. http://www.wttc.org/site_media/uploads/downloads/traveltourism2011.pdf, 2011. [Online; acessado em 10-Julho-2013].
[3] Emilie Lundin Barse, Håkan Kvarnström, and Erland Jonsson. Synthesizing test data for fraud detection systems. In *Proceedings of the 19th Annual Computer Security Applications Conference*, ACSAC '03, pages 384–, 2003. ISBN 0-7695-2041-3.
[4] Tej Paul Bhatla, Vikram Prabhu, and Amit Dua. *Understanding Credit Card Frauds*. USA, 2003.
[5] Hans-Hermann Bock. Handbook of data mining and knowledge discovery. chapter Data mining tasks and methods: Classification: the goal of classification, pages 254–258. 2002. ISBN 0-19-511831-6.
[6] Richard J. Bolton, David J. Hand, and David J. H. Unsupervised profiling methods for fraud detection. In *Proc. Credit Scoring and Credit Control VII*, pages 5–7, 2001.
[7] Tom Fawcett and Foster Provost. Adaptive fraud detection. *Data Min. Knowl. Discov.*, 1(3), January 1997.
[8] S. B. Kotsiantis. Supervised machine learning: A review of classification techniques. In *Proceedings of the 2007 conference on Emerging Artificial Intelligence Applications in Computer Engineering: Real Word AI Systems with Applications in eHealth, HCI, Information Retrieval and Pervasive Technologies*, pages 3–24, 2007. ISBN 978-1-58603-780-2.
[9] Sam Maes, Karl Tuyls, Bram Vanschoenwinkel, and Bernard Manderick. Credit card fraud detection using bayesian and neural networks. In *In: Maciunas RJ, editor. Interactive image-guided neurosurgery. American Association Neurological Surgeons*, pages 261–270, 1993.
[10] Rafael Maranzato, Adriano Pereira, Marden Neubert, and Alair Pereira do Lago. Fraud detection in reputation systems in e-markets using logistic regression and stepwise optimization. *SIGAPP Appl. Comput. Rev.*, 11(1), June 2010.
[11] CyberSource Mindware Research Group. *2011 Online Fraud Report*. California, USA, 12th annual edition, 2011.
[12] Clifton Phua, Vincent C. S. Lee, Kate Smith-Miles, and Ross W. Gayler. A comprehensive survey of data mining-based fraud detection research. *CoRR*, abs/1009.6119, 2010.

Author Index

9 781450 326834